Footballer of the Year
Maurice Fitzgerald of Kerry
in action in the 1997
All-Ireland Football Final.
(See Sports Chapter)

Lori Gabriel Knapp

IRISH
ALMANAC
AND
YEARBOOK OF FACTS
—1998—

**ARTCAM
PUBLISHING LTD.**

THE **ULTIMATE** ANNUAL IRISH ALMANAC
AND BOOK OF FACTS

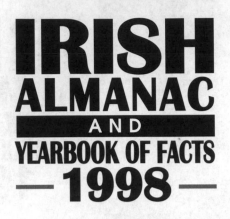

IRISH ALMANAC
AND
YEARBOOK OF FACTS
— 1998 —

ARTCAM PUBLISHING LTD, SPEENOGE, BURT, CO. DONEGAL
Telephone & Fax: 077 68186

N.I. Reg. Office: 16 High Street, Derry, Northern Ireland.
Telephone: 01504 - 308041   Fax: 01504 308363
Code from R.O.I.: 0801504 308041   Code from U.S.: 011 44 1504 308041
e mail address: editor@almanac.iol.ie

Editor *Pat McArt*
Associate Editor's *Colm McKenna and Dónal Campbell*
Sub-Editor *Helen Curley*
Researchers *Anita Gallagher, Damian Dowds, Jenni Doherty*
Financial Director *Philip O'Dwyer A.C.A.*
Design/Layout *Dónal Campbell*
Printed by *Techman Ireland Ltd.*

ISBN *0 9529596 2 3*

Published October 1997 by *ArtCam Publishing Ltd.*
© ArtCam Publishing Ltd.

EDITOR'S FOREWORD

By **Pat McArt**,
Editor Irish Almanac & Yearbook of Facts

Current Taoiseach, Bertie Ahern pictured with SDLP leader John Hume when they launched the first edition of the Irish Almanac and Yearbook of Facts in November 1996. Included are Artcam directors, Pat McArt, Colm McKenna and Dónal Campbell.

In America almanacs first made their appearance more than 130 years ago, and sales there are now in excess of 30 million annually. Indeed, most of the countries on mainland Europe have similar publications. Yet until Artcam launched the "Irish Almanac and Yearbook of Facts" last year there was no outlet or publication where one could turn for an authoritative source which would give a comprehensive overview on what was happening on this island, North and South. Therefore, it was gratifying for all of us engaged in this project that the response to that book was universally positive with a number of reviewers, on both sides of the Border, unequivocally stating that our publication was the "ultimate guide to Ireland."

This year we have built on that solid foundation. This book is comprehensive in every respect. The planning and research have been both exhaustive and, at times, exhausting, but the final result is a book that contains the complete record of what is happening on the island of Ireland.

The 1998 Irish Almanac and Yearbook of Fact has more information, more facts, more statistics about what is happening here than any book ever published. It is a one stop archive which covers every aspect of life on the island of Ireland, from politics to profiles of Irish writers, from population figures to football.

Included also this year are major articles from some of Ireland's leading academics, commentators, and public figures. Their insightful, sometimes controversial, but always thought-provoking pieces have added considerably not only to the authority but also to the comprehension of the subjects they are writing on.

This year's publication has been the result of magnificent team effort by a dedicated staff, aided and abetted by, quite literally, thousands of people all across the country. We thank them all for their quite exceptional generosity.

Pat Mc Art

PAT McART
EDITOR

ACKNOWLEDGEMENTS

IN the course of compiling the Irish Almanac & Yearbook of Facts 1998 the production team have made many demands on people's time, resources and patience. We wish to express our sincere thanks all those who responded, many above the call of duty. Without their whole-hearted cooperation it would not be possible to produce the ultimate Irish reference book.

The Directors would also like to record their sincere appreciation of the work carried out by the editorial staff, research team and the many contributors who have cooperated admirably in producing this publication. Their collaborative spirit made involvement in the production a privilege.

Finally, gratitude is long overdue to our families and friends who have been a constant source of support and encouragement in the last few years as we strived to first establish and then perfect the Irish Almanac. A special mention, as always, to Fr. Kevin O'Doherty who has remained mentor and friend to the editorial team.

The Editors and Researchers would like to thank the following people and organisations for their much valued assistance in compiling information for this publication: Tom O'Sullivan, Research Assistant; Bill Breslin, Wholesale Newspaper Services, Derry; Patrick Bradley, Chief Electoral Officer, Northern Ireland; Ray Basset, Department of Foreign Affairs; Sally O'Neill, Tyrone Productions; Frances Gill, Fruit of the Loom, Buncrana, Donegal; Deirdre O'Sullivan, University College Cork; All at Pacemaker, Photocall and Inpho; Victor Ryan, Association of Irish Festival Events; Seán Donnelly, Political Analyst, Dublin; Tony Heffernan, Democratic Left; Rita Sexton, Orlagh Scott, House of the Oireachtas; Patricia Farnan, Áras an Uachtaráin; Pauline Martin, Sinn Féin; Bobby Dobbins, Derry City Council; Hazel Legge, Ulster Unionist Council; Sheila, Don McAleer, Northern Ireland Information Service; Raymond Keane, European Commission; Ann Smith, EU Information Unit; Progressive Unionist Party; Ulster Democratic Party; Marie Duffy, Department of the Marine and Natural Resources; Patricia McAuley, Stormont Castle; Louise Kenny, Department of Health & Children; John Harney, Department of Defence; Department of Enterprise, Trade and Employment; Mary O'Rourke, Department of Education; Seosamh Ó hAghmaill, Department of Arts, Heritage, Gaeltacht & the Islands; Mary Donohoe, Department of the Environment; Department of the Environment for Northern Ireland; Jill Heron, Department of Economic Development; George Martin, Department of Finance & Personnel; Liam Kenny, Susan Boardman, General Council of County Councils; Michael R. J. Wilson, Northern Ireland Information Service; Conor Long, Irish Embassy in Switzerland; Brian Earls, Irish Embassy in Russia; Joanna Betson, Irish Embassy in Germany; A. M. Zurn, Luxembourg Embassy in London; Monica O'Connor, Department of Foreign Affairs; K. Slattery, Irish Embassy in Washington D.C.; Aurora Díaz-Rato, Spanish Embassy in Ireland; Akiko Watanabe, Irish Embassy in Japan; Michael Roche, Australian Embassy in Dublin; Philip Pinnington, Canadian Embassy in Dublin; Francis O'Donoghue, Irish Embassy in Peoples Republic of China; Aidan O'Hara, Irish Embassy in Czechoslovakia; Brian McElduff, Embassy of Sweden; Síle Maguire, Embassy of Spain; Nicholas Twist, Irish Embassy in Austria; Dermot McGauran, Irish Embassy in Greece; Pascual O'Dogherty, Ramon O'Dogherty, Spain; Dermot McLaughlin, Wildlife Officer, Buncrana; Eamon Murphy, Niall Brooks, Met Éireann; M. McDermott, Ordnance Survey; North Down Borough Council; Laois County Council; Galway County Council; Brian Connolly, Cavan County Council; Carrickfergus Borough Council; Westmeath County Council; Donegal County Council; Tipperary North Council; Gerry McGivern, Banbridge District Council; Sandra Pollock, Strabane District Council; Magherafelt District Council; Limerick County Council; Pat Quigley, Fingal County Council; M. Crankin, Chief Executive, Ballymena Borough Council; Ards Borough Council; Armagh City and District Council; Dun Laoghaire / Rathdown County Council; Mayo County Council; Clare County Council; Kathleen Nevin, Meath County Council; Martin O'Donoghue, Kerry County Council; Lisburn Borough Council; Leitrim County Council; Monaghan County Council; Alan Rodgers, Omagh District Council; Waterford County Borough Council; Ledu; Forbairt; Forfas; Brian Walsh, The Institute of Chartered Accountants in Ireland; Hugh O'Donnell, Central Bank of Ireland; Timothy Quinn, Deloitte & Touche; Marie Porter, Carlin McLaughlin & Company, Buncrana, Donegal; Business and Finance; Ulster Business; Nigel Higgins, Coopers & Lybrand; Gerard Cahillane, National Treasury Management Agency; Paddy O'Keeffe, Department of Finance; Irish Bankers Federation; Irish Banks Information Service; PA Consulting Group, Belfast; Chapman Flood Chartered Accountants; Irish Auctioneers and Valuers Institute; Sean Molloy, Irish Dairy Board; Norma O'Connell, Labour Market, Central Statistics Office; Paula Carey, Irish Congress of Trade Unions; John McLoughlin, Coillte; Irish Trade Board; Anna McHugh, An Post; Sharon McGrath, Department of Agriculture, Food and Forestry; Teresa O'Reilly, Kathleen Regan, Ena Howley, Department of the Marine and Natural Resources; National Council for Forest Research and Development; John Keating, Teagasc; Livestock & Meat Commission for Northern Ireland; Chris Forde, Colm Donlan, Industrial Development Agency; Industrial Development Board, Northern Ireland; Geraldine Morrison, George McFarland, Department of Agriculture for Northern Ireland; Donal Clarke, Bord na Móna; Siobhan Browne, Nadine Duffy, Electricity Supply Board; Troy Armour, Donegal; Susan Loughnan, Water Service Northern Ireland; Chris Boyd, Northern Ireland Electricity; Bord Gáis Éireann; Met Office, Hillsborough; Janet Hoy, Energy Division, Department of the Environment for Northern Ireland; Fr. Brown, St. Marys Presbytery, Sligo; John Connolly, The Church of Jesus Christ, Latter Day Saints, Dublin; Caroline Smith, National Spiritual Assembly of the Bahai, Dublin; Dublin Meditation Centre; Gerard Ryan, Dianetics and Scientology, Dublin; Rev. Edmund T. I. Mawhinney, Methodist Church, Belfast; Miriam Crozier, Claire Forsyth, Presbyterian Church in Ireland, Belfast; June Howard, Church of Ireland, Belfast; Jim Cantwell, Catholic Press and Information Office, Dublin; Seamus Smith, Golfing Union of Ireland; Marie Fitzpatrick, Rónán Whelan, Department of Arts, Heritage, Gaeltacht & the Islands; Deirdre O'Halloran, Carmel Healy, Bord Fáilte; Elaine Gowen, Tourism and Travel Section, CSO; National Trust; Kristine Gillespie, Northern Ireland Tourist Board; Cork / Kerry Tourism; Dublin Tourism; Ireland West Tourism; Midlands-East Tourism; North West Tourism; South East Tourism; Shannon Development; John G. McKinley, Sean Willis, Gordon Thompson, Roads Service; Neil McLaren, Automobile Association, Belfast; Paul Dale, Automobile Association, Derry; Conor Faughnan, Daragh Owens, David Skelly, Automobile Association, Dublin; Paul King, Transportation Unit; C. M. Caughey, J. G. Mullan, Trevor Evans, Driver & Vehicle Licensing Northern Ireland; Gary Lynch, National Roads Authority; Cyril McIntyre, Bus Éireann; Dympna Kelledy, Córas Iompair Éireann; Translink; Iarnrod Éireann; Stena Line Ferries; P & O European Ferries; Irish Ferries; Society of Irish Motor Industry; Fred Campbell, Staff Officer, RUC; Phil O'Flaherty, Ann Walsh, Orla O'Gorman, Department of the Environment; Adrienne Downes, Department of Public Enterprise; Tax Office, Donegal County Council; Christine McMahon, The Revenue Commissioners; Daragh Green, Customs & Excise; Martin Thompson, Kathryn Jamison, Bill Stewart, Wendy Montgomery, Department of Education Northern Ireland; South Eastern Education and Library Board; Lisburn College of Further Education; Alun Bevan, An Chomhairle Leabharlanna; Cork University; Nora Murphy, Louise O'Dwyer, Susan M. Hedigan, Colm Tobin, A. Scannell, University College Dublin; Mary Browne, Mary O'Rourke, Department of Education; Jonathan King, Department of Enterprise, Trade and Employment; Diane Wilson, North Eastern Education and Library Board; Orla Christle, Susan Butler, Higher Education Authority; Máire Bean Uí Bhruadair, Ultach Trust, Belfast; Belfast Institute of Further & Higher Education; J. A. Hunter, University of Ulster; Belfast Education and Library Board; Lynn Boyd, Queen's University; Southern Education and Library Board; Northern Ireland Hotel & Catering College; Tadgh O'Leary, Department of Health and Children; Russell McLornon, Southern Health and Social Services Board, Armagh; Tony Whelan, South Eastern Health Board, Kilkenny; Emer Lalor, Western Health Board, Galway; Mena Cunningham, Sharon Rea, Department of Health and Social Services; D. O'Dwyer, Midland Health Board, Offaly; Gillian Seeds, RUC HQ, Belfast; Mary Burke, Department of Justice, Equality and Law Reform; Linda Telford, Northern Ireland Court System; Captain Rodger McGrath, Defence Forces Headquarters, Dublin; Colonel Hodges, Northern Ireland Armed Forces; Helen Moore, Solicitor, Galway; Gael Linn; Méabh Ní Chatháin, Bord na Gaeilge; Máire Seo Breathnach, Údarás na Gaeltachta, Galway; Adelaide Nic Chárthaigh, Comhdháil Náisiúnta na Gaeilge; An Coimisiun Le Rinci Gaelacha; Gerry Lundberg Promotions, Riverdance; Damian Smyth, Northern Ireland Arts Council; Peter Harland, Bookwatch, London; Sinéad Glynn, Pat Egan Sound Ltd.; Hugh Harley, Claire Lundy, Derry City Council; David McLaughlin, Rialto, Derry; Aidan H. O'Flanagan, The Friends of National Collections in Ireland; Ulster Museum; Tom Kennedy, Albertine Kennedy Publishing; Kristina Fallenius, Nobel Foundation (Sweden); Appletree Press, Belfast; Karen Carleton, Drama League of Ireland; Irish Traditional Music Archive; Michelle Hoctor, Music Network, Dublin; Tim Godfray, Booksellers Association of Great Britain and Ireland; Mena Ward, Eurovision Song Contest, RTE; Ciarán Walsh, Dublin Theatre Festival; Maeve Whooley, Gill & Macmillan Publishers; ITV, London; Bernadette O'Leary, Aosdána; Jane Collins, Irish Association of Art Historians; Brian Coyle, James Adam & Sons; Valerie Keogh, National Gallery of Ireland; Sara Cochran, Media Desk; The Arts Council; Catriona Hailes, Harrison Cowley PR, Belfast; Denis Kirwan, The National Lottery, Dublin; Luke Dodd, Film Institute of Ireland; Tommy McCabe, Audio Visual Federation, IBEC; Carrie Wilson, BBC Northern Ireland; Alacoque Kealy, Audience Research Department, RTÉ; Jacqui Barkley, UTV; Jane O'Keeffe, Radio Ireland; Sinéad Owens, Independent Radio and Television Commission; Charlie Collins, Highland Radio; Ann-Marie Lenihan, National Newspapers of Ireland, Dublin; Neil Russell, Audit Bureau of Circulations; Karen McManus, Provincial Newspapers of Ireland; The Irish Family Paper, Westmeath; The Roscommon Herald; Kerry's Eye; Radio Kilkenny; The Nationalist and Leinster Times, Carlow; The Herald & Post Newspapers, Belfast; The Western People, Mayo; Armagh - Down Observer; The Kildare Nationalist; The Sunday Business Post, Dublin; The Irish News, Belfast; The Mayo News; The Limerick Leader Ltd.; Examiner Publications, Cork; Century Newspapers, Belfast; Shannonside / Northern Sound, Longford; Vivienne Clarke, Radio 3, Tullamore; Sinéad O'Connell, FM104, Dublin; Kelly, Downtown Radio & Cool FM; Ronnie & Paul, More than Music, Derry; Sounds Around, Derry; Brendan McKenna, Football Association of Ireland; Ronnie Long, Bord Lúthchleas na hÉireann; Danny Lynch, Gaelic Athletic Association; Peadar Casey, Irish Amateur Rowing Union; Peg Smith, The Pitch and Putt Union of Ireland; M. P. Turvey, Irish Ladies Golf Union; Patrick Murray, Northern Ireland Sports Council; The Irish Sports Council; Liam Ó Malomhichil, Gaelic Games; Patrick Boyd, Irish Sailing Association; Barry Holohan, Olympic Council of Ireland; Derek Scott, Irish Cricket Union, Dublin; Veronica Byrne, Irish Amateur Swimming Association; J. McQuay, Irish Bowling Association, Down; Jim Graves, Castlereagh Knights; Mary FitzGerald, Irish Horce Racing Authority; Alex Sinclair, Royal Irish Automobile Club, Dublin; Pauline Murray, Royal Yachting Association, Belfast; Harry Havelin, Motor Cycle Union of Ireland, Dublin; Pam Robinson, Irish Amateur Boxing Association; Cora Harris, Golfing Union of Ireland, Dublin; Eavan Lyons, Irish Rugby Football Union, Dublin; Sheila Wallace, Cumann Camógháochta na nGael; Irish Women's Cricket Union, Dublin; Special Olympics Ireland, Dublin; L. Royal, Northern Ireland Blind Sports; Ulster Gliding Club; Ruth Irvine, Ulster Squash, Belfast; Irene Johnston, Irish Ladies Hockey Union, Dublin; Sam Jones, Joan Morgan, Irish Hockey Union; Tony Allen, Federation of Irish Cyclists; Equestrian Sport of Ireland; C. Walsh, Northern Ireland Kung Fu Association, Belfast; Moira Scully, Irish Basketball Association, Dublin; Jan Singleton, Tennis Ireland; Jack Burke, North McQuay, Bowling League of Ireland; Rosemary McWhinney, Northern Ireland Netball Association; Shay McDonald, Irish Amateur Gymnastics Association; Zoe Lally, Irish Surfing Association; Hugh Bancroft, Chamber of Commerce Ireland; Valerie, Northern Ireland Chamber of Commerce & Industry; Sally Farren, Sally Campbell, Citizens Advice Bureau; Gareth Ferguson, Jennifer Maguire, Department of Health and Social Security; Department of Social, Community and Family Affairs; Passport Office; Pearse Callaghan, Killea, Donegal; Kelly McDevitt, Kathleen Conrad, Belfast; Feargal MacGiolla, Leitrim; Michael McCarron, Derry; Sharon McQuaid, Dundalk; Seán Ralph, Carlow; Central Library Staff, Derry and Letterkenny; Tom Lawlor, Fine Arts Ltd.; Brian McManus, Portmarnock Community School; Jenny Witt, Derry; Eddie Cox, F.A.I.; John McCafferty, Rathfarnham, Dublin; Eunan McElwaine, Social Welfare Office, Buncrana.

QUICK CONTENTS

FREQUENTLY USED ABBREVIATIONS

A.T.M. Automated Teller Machine
Approx. Approximately
Avg. Average
B.B.C. British Broadcasting Corporation
B.I.K. Benefit(s) in Kind
B.I.M. Bord Iascaigh Mhara
E.S.B. Electricity Supply Board.
G.D.P. Gross Domestic Product
G.N.P. Gross National Product
I.D.A. Industrial Development Agency
I.D.B. Industrial Development Board
I.M.M.A. Irish Museum of Modern Art, Dublin.
IR£ Irish punt (pound)
L.S.D. Lysergic acid diethylamide
N.A.T.O. North Atlantic Treaty Organisation
N.C.A.D. National College of Art and Design, Dublin.
N.I. Northern Ireland
N.I.E. Northern Ireland Electricity.
N.I.O. Northern Ireland Office

N.I.T.B. Northern Ireland Tourist Board
R.H.A. Royal Hibernian Academy of Arts.
R.I.R. Royal Irish Regiment
R.O.I. Republic of Ireland
R.U.C. Royal Ulster Constabulary
S.E.A. Single European Act
T.B.A. To be announced
T.E.U. Treaty on European Union
V.A.T. Value Added Tax
£STG: Pound sterling

COUNTRIES/CONTINENTS
IRE. Ireland
BEL. Belgium
DEN. Denmark
GER. Germany
FRA. France
NETH. Netherlands
BRIT Britain
POR. Portugal
SWE. Sweden
FIN. Finland
U.S. United States of America

E.U. European Union

POLITICAL PARTIES: See Politics Chapter

SI UNITS: See Useful Information Chapter. Metric units are used in most cases throughout this book. See Useful Information chapter for units and formulae.

OTHER MEASUREMENTS:
dwt: Deadweight
lwt: Liveweight
ha: Hectares
dcw: Dressed carcass weight
kV: Kilo volts
kW: Kilo watts
Mt: Million tonnes
MW: Mega Watts
tpa: Tonnes per annum

READING THE TABLES:
- : Information less than 0.5 of a unit
n/a: Information not available

INTRODUCTION

Ireland:
A Changed and Changing Place

By *Moya Doherty*, *Riverdance Producer*

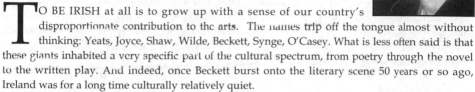

T O BE IRISH at all is to grow up with a sense of our country's disproportionate contribution to the arts. The names trip off the tongue almost without thinking: Yeats, Joyce, Shaw, Wilde, Beckett, Synge, O'Casey. What is less often said is that these giants inhabited a very specific part of the cultural spectrum, from poetry through the novel to the written play. And indeed, once Beckett burst onto the literary scene 50 years or so ago, Ireland was for a long time culturally relatively quiet.

Today Ireland is a changed and changing place. The Celtic Twilight of Yeats and company has given way to the Celtic Tiger, a young European country of growing prosperity. And yet once again Irish ideas and creative energies are numerous and high-profile, making a national and international impact. But there's a difference. This time it isn't individual towering figures in an exclusively literary landscape. Now it's a broad energy, networked and exciting, bursting out across the entire cultural spectrum.

In literature the impact ranges from the Nobel prize-winning poetry of Seamus Heaney through the novels of McGahern and Banville, Dermot Bolger and Colm Toibin and Anne Enright. On the stage the dramatic tradition revitalised by the Druid Theatre and director Garry Hynes is manifest in the mature work of Brian Friel and the youthful command of the new generation represented by Vincent Woods, Sebastian Barry and Martin McDonagh. And straddling two worlds with originality and vibrant humour are the internationally best-selling books and TV and cinema scripts of Roddy Doyle.

In film itself, where Ireland until recently had little presence, the crop of bright new native film-makers is topped off by the stature in Hollywood of Neil Jordan and Jim Sheridan, of Liam Neeson and Gabriel Byrne. In rock music U2 have been followed and echoed by the huge international success of the Cranberries and the Corrs and by performers as mutually distinct as Enya and Ash.

Self-congratulation is dangerously easy. But for those of us fortunate enough to be working in the arts in Ireland and bringing Irish work abroad, it is a heady - if sometimes exhausting - time. But why is it happening? Is it a freak phenomenon or something natural, sustainable?

Yeats, the great theoretician, claimed that great art was the product of great imperial societies translating their mastery into exquisite artifacts. He found the Ireland of his day grey and philistine. What he would have made of Temple Bar, or Pop Mart or a Macnas parade is anybody's guess.

Even those unconvinced of Yeats's grand theories may have concluded that guilt, separation, loss, were the authentic Irish experience and the natural essence of our creativity. *Success is troublesome*, one writer remarked in the 1960s; *failure we can always offer up*. The dark humour of Beckett and bleak visions of Flann O'Brien seemed to sum up a society and situation to which, Joyce concluded, the only proper responses were silence, cunning and exile.

Neither view sits easily with the present time, when unprecedented economic regeneration and modernisation go hand in hand with a cultural flowering on a broad scale. More comfortable and secure than at any former time, we are more widely and successfully creative too. It might be thought that comfort and modern consumer convenience would be antithetical to a vibrant arts sector.

But painful though aspects of change will always be, modernity appears to have offered Ireland more solutions than problems. And it may be that the changes that have made Ireland a small economic miracle connect directly with the energy and imagination so very evident in the arts.

Both spring from the same root. Arguably Ireland is a community whose potential, artificially depressed for many generations, is now being realised. Economically we are for the first time in hundreds of years providing for ourselves and our people. In an open, risky, competitive economic world we are now showing the commercial, business aptitudes long remarked on in the Irish abroad. We are finding our way.

The cultural argument is parallel. The immediate tensions of independence and nationhood have, in the present generation, settled down. Our history, so long bitter, divisive and problematic, may be moving toward healing and resolution. The population is young, inquiring, ambitious in all kinds of ways. The society has moved out of the pains of childhood and adolescence and is in its early adulthood - an exciting, optimistic outgoing state of mind.

The electricity driving the Celtic Tiger arguably is the same that is powering the cultural phenomenon - a people using its energies, finding its level, acquiring a sense of its own space. And behind it all is a broad confidence that has quietly become part of the Irish experience: confidence in what we can do, and above all in what we are and can be.

There was a time when important cultural resources like language, music, dance were cultural/political icons first and foremost, albeit in a society unsure of what it wanted to be. They were often regarded suspiciously, uncomfortably. Now they are embraced.

Film likewise belonged to others, but not to us: a one-way gateway to a fantastic, unattainable outside world. Now we are telling our own stories on film. In the process - as in *Michael Collins* - history and culture meet in a communal effort to revisit and understand our past, an effort unimaginable a short time ago.

It is remarkable enough that rock music, with no roots in Ireland, now bears the indelible stamp worldwide of the talent of U2. Remarkable too how talents like Bill Whelan or Donal Lunny both express the distinct character of Irish music and yet connect with strands and influences outside. And Irish dance, once marginalised even in our own culture, has shown itself able to embrace modern forms and rhythms and emerge revitalised, transformed and yet true to itself and its tradition.

As schoolchildren we learned of how the old Gaelic culture absorbed and reprocessed invaders and their ways: Viking, Norman. Like many clichés it has a core of truth and there is a continuity. As a small anglophone island, we are open to being swamped by the huge Anglo-American commercial culture that washes over much of the world. The actuality is more positive. We appear to be holding our own - taking aspects of music, film, dance, reworking them through our own eyes, feet, voices and feeding them back into the world culture with the success once known only in literature.

Can it be sustained? The particular clustering of talent now apparent may be unusual. But confidence goes deep. It is hard-gained but not easily forgotten. If the flowering of creativity of recent years says anything, it is that Ireland is getting to know itself and the world around it. It is expressing that knowledge and self-knowledge through every medium available: poem, novel, drama, film, dance, song.

We like the experience. We're good at it. Why stop now?

The author is the producer of the acclaimed "Riverdance - The Show" and is a widely respected figure in the television and radio broadcasting sectors in Ireland.

DEATH OF A SOLDIER: The last British soldier to die in the current phase of the "The Troubles" was Lance Bombardier Stephen Restorick (23) who was shot dead, on February 12th, by an IRA sniper while manning a checkpoint at Bessbrook, Co. Armagh. Lorraine McElroy, whose vehicle Bombardier Restorick was checking when hit, was also grazed by the sniper's bullet. Despite their son's death, the soldier's parents, in a public statement, appealed for the Republican movement to be allowed into the all-party talks.

ROCCA RYAN RUMPUS: In one of the most high profile media cases in Ireland in recent years former Miss Ireland, Michelle Rocca, current partner of the international singing star, Van Morrisson, was awarded £7,500 damages in her action against Mr. Cathal Ryan, a member of the "Ryanair" family, for assault. In a case which brought to the front pages the lifestyles of the country's rich and famous, Ms. Rocca had alleged that Mr. Ryan, with whom she had a relationship for a number of years, had assaulted her by slapping her across the face, a charge Mr. Ryan denied.

COSTLY B.S.E SCARE: While the final figure has yet to be ascertained, the BSE beef scare has proved very costly for Irish farmers. As early as February, 1997, the Department of Agriculture had confirmed that the scare had cost the Irish beef industry £500 million. Just a month earlier the country's £180 million live export trade with Egypt was suspended after a tabloid newspaper there alleged that "mad cows" were being imported from Ireland. Unofficial estimates suggest that the final cost to the Irish Exchequer could be in the region of £1 billion.

THE HEPATITIS C / ANTI-D SCANDAL: The Macken report, published on August 1st, into the handling by the State agencies of the hepatitis C/Anti-D issue was unequivocal, Mr. Justice Macken stating: "The hepatitis C /Anti-D issue is the biggest health scandal in the history of the state . . . The approach adopted [by the Government] was bereft of compassion or sensitivity to Mrs. [Brigid] McCole or to the interests of others who were infected through the negligence of a State institution." Following the publication of the report the family of the late Mrs. McCole, a Donegal woman who died after she had received contaminated blood products, indicated they would be taking legal action against the State. Earlier in the year, Mr. Justice Finlay had chaired a tribunal which heard evidence in regard to the whole contamination issue, and his subsequent report (published in March) was sent by the Government to the Director of Public Prosecutions to decide whether legal action should be taken against named individuals. In April, in a surprise development, the Blood Transfusion Services Board admitted legal liability and this was followed, on May 6th, by an announcement from the Government that it had raised its offer for aggravated damages by an estimated £40 million. This decision, which represents a 20 per cent "top-up" on general awards, is expected to push the overall compensation package to around £240 million.

NORTHERN KILLINGS: Despite the insistence of both the Combined Loyalist Military Command and the Northern Ireland Office that loyalist paramilitaries were maintaining their ceasefire, it was conceded by the security forces that loyalists were responsible for a number of particularly brutal sectarian murders. The cycle of killing began on May 8th when the death took place of 25-year-old Catholic, Robert Hamill, who died eleven days after being kicked unconscious by a Loyalist gang in Portadown. The following day, May 9th, an off-duty RUC man, Darren Bradshaw (24) was shot dead by the INLA in a Belfast bar. Late on May 12th, Loyalists abducted a 61-year-old Catholic, Sean Browne, a prominent GAA official from Bellaghy, in Co. Derry, and his body was found an hour later beside his burned-out car near Randalstown, in Co. Antrim. On June 1st, an RUC Constable, Greg Taylor was kicked to death by loyalists who attacked him as he left a pub in Ballymoney. Two more policemen were to die just over a fortnight later when, on June 16th, the IRA shot dead Constable John Graham (34) and Reserve Constable David Andrew Johnston (30) in Lurgan - they were the 300th and 301st RUC officers killed in the line of duty since the Troubles began. A Catholic girl, 18-year-old Bernadette Martin died on July 15th when she was shot four times in the face by a gun man as she slept in the home of her Protestant boyfriend in the village of Aghalee, near Lurgan. A particularly horrific murder was that of 16-year-old Catholic boy, James Morgan from Castlewellan, in Co. Down. His battered body was found, not far from his home, in a water-logged pit where animals were usually dumped.

HAUGHEY IN TROUBLE: Former Taoiseach, Charles Haughey, could face a jail sentence and/or a heavy fine in the wake of the findings of Mr. Justice McCracken. In his report (published August 25th) on the Tribunal of Inquiry into Payments to Politicians (Dunnes Stores Tribunal), Justice McCracken stated that Mr. Haughey's attitude to the Tribunal "might amount" to an offence, adding that he was sending all relevant papers to the Director of Public Prosecutions for his consideration and decision as to whether the former Fianna Fáil leader should face prosecution. The publication of the report was the climax of an unprecedented chapter in Irish political life which began in November, 1996, when, following revelations in the *Irish Independent*, the Minister for Transport, Energy and Communications, Mr. Michael Lowry resigned after it was alleged that former supermarket tycoon, Ben Dunne had paid £208,000 for an extension to the Minister's home. Shortly after this, rumours began circulating that Mr. Dunne had also made substantial donations to a senior Fianna Fáil figure. At first Mr. Haughey denied being the recipient of any monies but on July 9th, almost four months after the Tribunal had begun its investigations, he stated, through his legal team, that as a result of "reviewing the excellent work of the tribunal and considering the very helpful documentation recently received from Mr. Ben Dunne's solicitors" that he "now accepted" that he had received £1.3million from Mr. Dunne. He also accepted, in addition, that Mr. Dunne had personally handed him £210,000 at his (Mr. Haughey's) home at Kinsealy. Current Taoiseach, Bertie Ahern, described himself as "deeply shocked" by Mr. Haughey's admissions stating that there were no parallels "in the annals of our democracy". Fine Gael leader, John Bruton, said if Mr. Haughey received £1.3 million from one donor, he wanted to know if payments were made privately to him from any other sector, particularly the beef industry.

ELECTIONS - NORTH AND SOUTH: It was a year of big change on the political front on the island of Ireland with elections on both sides of the Border. In the North, the main talking point at the election count centres on May 2nd was Sinn Féin's performance in taking two seats - Gerry Adams re-taking West Belfast from the SDLP's Joe Hendron and Martin McGuinness ousting the DUP's William McCrea in Mid-Ulster. In addition, party Vice-President, Pat Doherty, received a very impressive 14,000 plus votes in the newly created seat of West Tyrone. It was also good news for the Ulster Unionist Party which increased its representation at Westminster from nine to ten; its candidate, William Thompson, taking the new West Tyrone seat. Both the SDLP and DUP lost a seat. In the Republic, Bertie Ahern's Fianna Fáil party emerged victorious from the General Election of June 6th. Twenty days later Mr. Ahern led his party into Government with the support of his Coalition partner, the Progressive Democrats, who had four members elected. The new Government has a majority of eight seats, four independents having also agreed to support it. Mr. Ahern, at 45 years of age, is the youngest Taoiseach in the history of the state. Another fact of note was that Caoimhghín O'Caoláin became Sinn Féin's first T.D. to accept his seat in Dail Éireann following the party's decision, in the mid-eighties, to drop its abstentionist policy.

DRUMCREE AND ITS AFTERMATH: More than one hundred people were injured and damage to property was estimated in the region of £20 million within forty-eight hours of an Orange Order march being forced down the Garvaghy Road as it made its way from Drumcree church. The reaction to the decision in nationalist areas was intense - 550 attacks on security force personnel, 700 petrol bombings, 500 fire service call outs, 150 ambulance calls, 41 arrests. The reaction came in the wake of a huge security operation at Garvaghy Road when the RUC and British army, in the early hours of Sunday, July 6th, sealed off the strongly nationalist-Catholic area to allow the Orange men to march along what they claim is a traditional route. It was the second year such a widescale operation was put in place to force the march through, and RUC Chief Constable, Ronnie Flanagan, who apologised for the decision, said he had made the choice to allow the march to go ahead as he considered it the lesser of two evils. The Taoiseach, Bertie Ahern, described himself as "deeply disappointed" with the decision. Northern Ireland Secretary of State, Mo Mowlam, who had consistently told residents groups that she would personally inform them of any decision made, rejected claims that she had "betrayed" the nationalist community. However, this was publicly rejected by nationalist leaders across the board, particularly so when a leaked document suggested that Dr. Mowlam and security chiefs had accepted as early as June 21st that Orange feet marching on Drumcree was the "least worst option" in the absence of any agreement between residents and the loyal institutions. By July 10th the statistics had risen to 128 injured, 2,500 plastic bullets fired, 835 attacks on security forces, 1,520 petrol bombings, 476 hijackings and 133 arrests. In a rapidly worsening political climate, the heat was taken out of the situation when the Orange Order announced that it would re-route its contentious parades in Armagh, Belfast, Derry and Newry.

PAEDOPHILE PRIEST CONTROVERSY: The death, on August 21st, of Fr. Brendan Smyth, brought to a close a most embarrassing episode for the Catholic church in Ireland. Smyth, a member of the Norbertine Order, was buried in secrecy at his Order's grounds in Kilnacrott Abbey, Co. Cavan. A month before his death he had been jailed for 12 years by Dublin's Circuit Criminal Court after admitting 74 charges of sexual abuse against young children. Prior to these convictions, he had served two sentences in the North of Ireland for similar offences. During his Dublin trial, the court was told that Smyth had shown no remorse for his victims, some of whom had attempted suicide, while others had suffered broken marriages and mental illness. Three days after his death, a journalist, Helen Lucy Burke, interrupted a Mass in Dublin to tell the priest that his sermon amounted to "an apologia for Brendan Smyth". It is now believed that several of Smyth's victims are actively pursuing legal claims against both the Catholic church and the Norbertine Order.

SECOND IRA CEASEFIRE: With tension in the North still running high in the wake of events at Drumcree, the announcement of a restoration of the IRA's ceasefire of August 1994 came unexpectedly. Making its announcement, in a statement released to RTE reporter, Charlie Bird, the leadership of the IRA said that having assessed the current political situation, it had ordered the restoration of the "unequivocal" ceasefire which it had "reluctantly abandoned" on February 9th, 1996. During that period the IRA alleged the British Government and the unionists blocked any possibility of real or inclusive negotiations. Reacting to the IRA statement Ulster Unionist party leader, David Trimble, claimed "the Provos pulled a fast one" with the ceasefire expecting there would be the "usual knee jerk reaction of unionists losing their temper." The IRA could then claim to the world, said Mr. Trimble, that the problem was not with republicanism but with unionism. David Ervine of the the Loyalist PUP welcomed the IRA's move.

October 1996 - September 1997

OCTOBER

01: Tributes were paid to retiring Archbishop of Armagh and Primate of All-Ireland, Cardinal Cahal Daly, by political and church leaders. The Cardinal spoke to the media with his successor, Dr. Sean Brady, and appealed to the IRA to reinstate their ceasefire.

02: Ms. Brigid McCole, a Donegal mother of 12, died from liver failure in St. Vincent's Hospital, Dublin. She had contracted the hepatitis C virus through infection from contaminated blood products, and had reached a settlement with the Blood Transfusion Service Board shortly before her death. She had brought the first test case to the High Court seeking compensation for the infection.

02: For the first time since the mid-1960's Government revenue from taxes exceeded its spending. Borrowing for 1996 is now likely to be £400 million lower than forecast in last January's budget.

02: Following a Gardaí search of farmland on the Louth border with Armagh, 21 mortars, frames and mortar tubes were located.

02: As part of an official visit to the Republic of Ireland, the German Chancellor, Dr Helmut Kohl, addressed a full sitting of the Dáil and later held talks with the Taoiseach, Mr. Bruton, at Government Buildings.

03: The funeral of Diarmuid O'Neill, the suspected IRA man, took place in the Cork village of Timoleague amid tight Garda security. O'Neill was shot dead during a police raid in London on September 23rd.

06: Mr. John Gilligan, (44) who has stated publicly that gardaí suspect him of involvement in the murder of journalist Veronica Guerin, was arrested at Heathrow Airport, London. Police arrested Gilligan, who lives in Kildare, as he prepared to board an aircraft for Amsterdam carrying £300,000 in cash.

06: Around 5,000 Irish pilgrims travelled to Rome for the beatification of Edmund Ignatius Rice, founder of the Christian Brothers and the Presentation Brothers. The ceremony was presided over by Pope John Paul II, who delayed his admission to hospital in order to be present.

07: More than 30 people were injured and one person killed following a double bomb attack on the British Army Headquarters at Thiepval Barracks in Lisburn, Co. Antrim. The first explosion occurred some 100 yards from the main administration block while the second blast occurred near the medical centre, apparently in an attempt to catch military personnel attending to those injured from the first explosion. The attack, which claimed the life of Warrant Officer James Bradwell, was immediately blamed on the IRA.

07: John Gilligan, being held by English police since his arrest in London on 6th October, was charged with concealing money in order to avoid drug-trafficking offences.

08: The IRA admitted responsibility for the double bomb attack on the British army headquarters in Lisburn.

Sinn Féin president, Mr. Gerry Adams, warned that the 'political vacuum' must be filled in order to avoid further incidents, while PUP spokesman, Mr. David Ervine, asked loyalist paramilitaries to maintain their ceasefire.

09: Over 1,200 new jobs in the computer and pharmaceutical fields are to be created in Dublin and Cork respectively.

10: 94-year-old novelist Mr. Francis Stuart was honoured by being elected as a Saoí of Aosdána. Due to an administration mix-up, the President, Mrs. Robinson, who was expected to hand over the award to Mr. Stuart, was not in attendance.

14: In London the former Taoiseach, Mr. Albert Reynolds, began a High Court libel action against the *Sunday Times*. The article in question, titled "Goodbye Gombeen Man", claimed, among other things, that Mr. Reynolds had misled the cabinet over the Father Brendan Smyth case.

14: The Blood Transfusion Service Board revealed that up to 30 blood donors who tested positive for hepatitis C in 1991 following routine screening were not informed until 1993.

15: The signing of a beef export protocol with Russia which excludes animals from counties Tipperary, Cork and Monaghan was met with anger by Irish farmers. The exclusion was blamed on the incidence of BSE in those counties. Mr Ivan Yates, the Minister for Agriculture, said he was opposed to the Russian measures, but in the interest of maintaining links with the £300 million Russian beef market, he had to sign the deal.

16: The Minister for Health, Mr Michael Noonan, unreservedly apologised for comments made in the Dáil during a debate on the hepatitis C affair. Minister Noonan's comments, relating to Mrs Brigid McCole, who suffered from hepatitis C, was directed at the deceased woman's solicitors, asking could they not have selected a test case "in a better condition to sustain the stress of a High Court case?"

20: A 32 year-old Dubliner, Mr Paul Ward, was charged at Dublin District Court with conspiracy to murder *Sunday Independent* journalist Veronica Guerin. Ms Guerin was shot dead in Dublin in June.

21: Mr Pat Byrne, the Garda Commissioner, denied suggestions that there was "widespread corruption" among gardaí. He confirmed, however, that investigations were being carried out in Cork and Dublin.

21: Despite criticism from Irish farming representatives, Russia said it would only lift its ban on imported beef from counties Cork, Monaghan and Tipperary when BSE levels in those counties fell.

26: Gardai confirm that a primed mortar found in the Inishowen peninsula of Co. Donegal was ready to be used, most probably in an attack on security forces in Northern Ireland.

28: An inquest at Belfast Coroner's Court found that Mr. Maurice Callaghan, who died from CJD, had probably contracted the disease from exposure to BSE infected meat. The court also heard that fourteen cases of the new strain had been identified, and more were expected.

30: A meeting of EU agriculture ministers agreed a £400m. BSE compensation package for beef farmers. Ireland's share of package is worth £45m. Irish Minister, Ivan Yates, described it as "exceptional".

31: A new Irish language television service, Teilifís na Gaeilge, was launched by RTE.

02: The record Lotto jackpot - £7,486,024 - was shared between two winners, one in Cavan the other in Meath.

03: Dr. Sean Brady was installed as Catholic Primate of All-Ireland and Archbishop of Armagh.

07: The Minister for Justice, Nora Owens, found herself at the centre of a political storm after the sudden release, and re-arrest, of sixteen prisoners who, it was found, were being held in unlawful custody. The problems arose when it was discovered that while the Government had acceded to Judge Dominic Lynch's request to be removed from the Special Criminal Court on August 1st., the judge had not been informed. The Government's acceptance of the request meant his involvement in the court had been invalid.

08: In a landmark legal ruling, the High Court in Belfast decided that citizens of the Republic would be eligible for jobs in the Northern Ireland Civil Service.

14: On the first anniversary of the deaths of seven fishermen, the Minister for the Marine, Mr. Sean Barrett announced a £19m. review of air and sea search and rescue operations.

18: The Cathaoirleach of the Seanad, Liam Naughten, died in a road accident.

19: Former Taoiseach, Albert Reynolds won his libel case against the Sunday Times but the jury in the case awarded him "zero" damages. Mr. Reynolds is liable for the cost of the case, believed to be around of £800,000.

20: Former Taoiseach, Albert Reynolds, was awarded "one penny" by the judge in his libel action against the Sunday Times. Mr. Reynolds described the result as "unjust and immoral".

21: Bomb experts defused a 600lb car bomb planted outside the RUC headquarters in Derry city. The bomb was planted by a grouping calling itself "The IRA Continuity Army Council".

23: Ireland's most renowned sports commentator, Michael O'Hehir, died in Dublin. He was 76. From 1938 until he suffered a stroke in 1985, he had covered almost all the All-Ireland hurling and football finals for RTE.

27: Roisin McAliskey (25), daughter of former Mid-Ulster M.P., Bernadette McAliskey appeared in court in London on an extradition warrant which accused her of being involved in an IRA bombing in Germany earlier this year.

27: Senator Liam Cosgrave, Fine Gael, was elected Cathaoirleach of the Seanad. He succeeds Liam Naughten who was killed in a road accident.

28: The Irish Government refused to endorse the British Government's stance on the admission of Sinn Féin to the All-party talks. Earlier, in the Westminster Parliament, British Prime Minister, John Major had made a unilateral statement to the House of Commons setting our his Government's terms for a new IRA ceasefire and Sinn Féin's entry into the talks. Mr. Major rejected proposals drawn up by SDLP leader, John Hume, and Sinn Féin President, Gerry Adams, backed by Dublin, which, they argued, would secure an IRA ceasefire if the British Government would acceded to them.

28: Just a little over a third of the people eligible to vote turned out to exercise their franchise in the Bail referendum.

29: A newspaper report has alleged that the Minister for Transport, Energy and Communication, Mr. Michael Lowry, had an £208,000 extension to his home in Tipperary paid for by Dunnes Stores. The Taoiseach, Mr Bruton, came in for criticism from opposition leaders for stating that the payments occurred before Mr Lowry became a minister.

30: Minister Lowry initially refused to resign stating he was confident that when all the details were presented everyone would be satisfied. However, by late evening he offered his resignation to the Taoiseach, John Bruton. Mr Lowry was later replaced by Mr Alan Dukes, former leader of the Fine Gael party.

30: Protests outside Harryville Catholic Church, in Ballymena, ended in violence when mass-goers were attacked by loyalists.

30: Despite initial estimates of a 35% turnout, it was confirmed that only 29.2% voted in the Bail referendum. Of those 74.8% voted in favour.

03: A prominent unnamed member of Fianna Fáil was reported to have received more than £1m. from Dunnes Stores, paid into different bank accounts in London. Fianna Fail leader, Bertie Ahern, said he was confident none of his front bench team was involved.

04: Though the Minister for Arts, Culture and the Gaeltacht, Michael D. Higgins had earlier indicated that up to 95% nationwide would be able to receive Teilifís na Gaeilge it was confirmed that almost one in four would be unable to receive the station unless they acquired another aerial.

05: The Taoiseach, Mr Bruton, stated that he personally approached former Dunnes Stores boss, Mr Ben Dunne, for financial donations to the Fine Gael party after he became leader of the party in 1990. Mr Bruton said that up to 100 business people had been approached.

05: Health authorities have contacted patients who were treated by a doctor at Letterkenny and Limerick hospitals who has since tested HIV positive. Although authorities have stated that there is very little danger of the disease being passed from the doctor, who has since left the country, to the patients he treated, they are being offered testing.

07: A man, believed to be a leading Dublin drug dealer, was shot dead in Dublin. Peter Judge was well known to Gardaí in North Dublin in the illicit drugs trade.

08: Rev Martin Smyth, the Ulster Unionist MP for South Belfast, announced his resignation as Grand Master of the Orange Order. Rev Smyth had been at the head of the Orange Order since 1972.

09: The London Anglo-Irish summit concluded with unresolved differences between the two sides. No timeframe was agreed for Sinn Féin involvement in talks. Mr Bruton appealed for a new IRA ceasefire.

09: Judge Gerard Buchanan began the task of examining the controversial Price Waterhouse report which contains the names of politicians who might have benefited from financial contributions from the then boss of Dunnes Stores, Mr Ben Dunne.

10: 4,000 new jobs are to be created in north Dublin. IBM, the American computer giant, is expected to provide almost 3,000 of the jobs.

11: At a Press Conference, the newly elected Grand Master of the Orange Order, Mr Robert Saulters, found himself in trouble over remarks on July 12, when he controversially stated that the leader of the British Labour Party, Mr Tony Blair, was "disloyal" because of his marriage to a Catholic.

14: Agreement was reached at the EU summit in Dublin with steady progress being made on monetary union and joint anti-crime measures. Ireland's handling of the presidency was praised by member-states. The new Euro banknotes were displayed for the first time.

14: Police seized a Loyalist banner after six men in paramilitary style uniforms carried the insignia of the outlawed UFF (a Loyalist terror group) through Derry city centre during an Apprentice Boys march. This caused outrage among the mainly nationalist population and prompted fears of resentment towards future marches in the city.

17: Minister for Health, Mr Michael Noonan, announced to the Dáil that optional HIV testing would be provided for people who received blood products between 1981 and 1985.

17: President Bill Clinton stated that Sinn Féin should be admitted to talks once the IRA restored their ceasefire. President Clinton's views reflected those of the Taoiseach's earlier statement.

18: British Prime Minister, Mr John Major, on a visit to Northern Ireland, acknowledged that the talks process was at a standstill.

19: Former minister, Mr Michael Lowry, admitted to the Dáil that he had made an incomplete declaration of his tax affairs to the Taoiseach on being appointed a minister in 1994. In the course of a forty-five minute statement, he dealt with speculation surrounding payments made by Dunnes Stores to build an extension to his home. He maintained that the work to his Tipperary home was income for professional services and not a loan.

19: Mr John Hume, the leader of the SDLP, announced that he was prepared to act as guarantor for the credibility of a future IRA ceasefire. Mr Hume met with loyalist and IRA prisoners to discuss the problems in the peace process.

20: An RUC officer was slightly wounded in an IRA attack in Belfast Children's Hospital. The target of the gunman was DUP secretary, Mr Nigel Dodds, who was visiting his sick child at the time.

21: A car bomb in Ardoyne, in north Belfast injured leading republican, Mr Eddie Copeland, and plunged the peace process into further crisis. It is thought that the attack was carried out by the Loyalist UVF. Mr Copeland suffered severe leg injuries in the attack.

23: Leader of the Ulster Unionist Party, Mr David Trimble, stated that with local and Westminster elections scheduled for 1997, it was unlikely that any progress would be made in the talks process. The statement was criticised by SDLP leader, Mr John Hume.

23: A full-scale murder investigation was under way in Dunmanus West, in Cork, following the discovery of the body of 38-year-old Ms Sophie Toscan Du Plantier on a laneway near her holiday home near Schull.

26: Popular Irish horse, Danoli, won the Denny Gold Medal Chase at the St. Stephens Day meeting at Leopardstown.

28: SDLP leader, Mr John Hume, accused the Conservative government of being afraid of taking decisions on the Northern Ireland peace process. Calling for an immediate renewal of the IRA ceasefire, Mr Hume stated that Mr Major should call an early British general election.

29: Ms Belinda Pereira, a native of Sri Lanka, was found in an apartment in the city centre of Dublin. The dead woman had suffered extensive head injuries.

30: Talks are taking place to solve the difficulties over the policies of BUPA, the British health insurer, who were due to begin operating on New Years Day. The problems arose between the British company and VHI.

31: Broadcaster Terry Wogan and BBC broadcasting journalist Fergal Keane were awarded OBEs in the British New Year honours list. Keane had worked with the *Irish Press* and RTE before joining the BBC.

31: A 1000lb bomb was discovered in a hijacked van in the grounds of Belfast Castle on New Years Eve night. Loyalist politicians described the find as a further blow to the ailing peace process

JANUARY

01: Madison Doyle became the first baby born in the New Year when she was born four minutes after midnight at the Rotunda Hospital in Dublin, weighing in at 5lb 13oz.

02: The Irish Times confirmed Sinn Féin had written to the SDLP inviting it to discuss electoral strategy for the forthcoming Westminster Elections. The offer was rejected by the SDLP.

03: Minister for Finance, Ruairí Quinn disclosed that the Government recorded a surplus of close to £300m. on its current budget last year, the strongest Exchequer performance for many years.

04: Ireland's rugby team lost 37-29 to Italy at Lansdowne Road.

06: An RUC constable was treated in hospital for minor injuries after an improvised IRA rocket struck, but failed to penetrate, his security hut near the Law Courts in Belfast.

06: Four prison officers held hostage by inmates in Mountjoy Prison's high security Separation Unit were released unharmed.

07: Ireland's £180m. per annum live meat export trade with Egypt was suspended after an Egyptian tabloid newspaper claimed that "mad cows were being imported from Ireland."

07: The Education Bill, one of the most comprehensive pieces of legislation in the history of the Dáil, was published today. The Bill provides for the setting up of 10 regional education boards and for compulsory school management boards which should be designed in such a way as to reflect all of those involved in education.

07: Former Minister, Mr. Michael Lowry, who resigned in the wake of claims that the £208,000 extension to his home had been paid for by supermarket tycoon, Ben Dunne, received the unanimous support of his North Tipperary constituency executive after announcing his intention to seek the party nomination at the next election.

07: Unemployment figures showed a drop of 15,300 in the live register to 267,000 at end of 1996.

07: The cabinet confirmed the appointment of Mr. Bob Collins as the next RTE director general.

08: Shannon Airport had its best year ever for traffic in 1996, 1.74 million passengers using the facility

08: The Government nominated the former Democratic Left T.D., Mr. Pat McCartan and Mr. Joseph G. Mathews SC for appointment by the President, Mrs. Robinson, as judges of the Circuit Court. nnn

09: According to a survey carried out for the Aer Lingus Young Scientist Exhibition almost 70 per cent of teenagers have begun drinking alcohol by the age of 15.

13: Following controversy first raised in Donegal about the holding of District Courts on premises which did not have planning permission for that purpose, the Attorney General, Dermot Gleason, advised the Government that it was his opinion that premises which housed court sittings should have specific planning permission to cover the holding of legal proceedings therein. The opinion raises questions about the validity of thousands of court decisions over the past two and half years.

15: Three people, Cavan Co. Sheriff, Mr. Tommy Owens and two assistants, were shot near Bawnboy, Co. Cavan when they attempted to enforce an eviction order against a German national who was living in a cottage in the area. None was seriously injured.

15: According to a report by the child-care agency, Barnardos, cases of confirmed child abuse almost trebled in eight years while cases of confirmed child sexual abuse more than trebled between 1985 and 1995.

21: A Francisan Brother, Larry Timmons, from Devlin, Co. Westmeath, was shot dead by a policeman in Kenya. He died after calling the police to deal with a gang of fifteen men who had broken into his home in the Rift Valley Province.

21: Irish poet, Seamus Heaney, has won the Whitbread Book of the Year with his collection, "The Spirit Level".

22: Allied Irish Banks is in the process of concluding the biggest ever deal by an Irish company, paying £840m. for the American bank, Dauphin Deposit Corporation.

24: It has been confirmed that four Irish universities have between them received £30m. from the philanthropic foundations established by a reclusive Irish-America, Mr. Charles "Chuck" Feeney, of New Jersey. The biggest donation was £15 m. to the University of Limerick.

27: One of Fianna Fail's most highly rated political figures, Maire Geoghegan-Quinn (46), sent shock waves through the Irish political establishment with her announcement that she is to quit politics at the next general election. The former minister cited the media's "invasion of privacy" as the prime reason for her decision.

FEBRUARY

02: The Ulster Unionist party leader, David Trimble, and East Londonderry M.P., William Ross complained to the British Foreign Office about visits by the President, Mary Robinson, to Northern Ireland. Mr. Ross asked how "someone who claims jurisdiction over part of the UK can come in and unveil plaques as President of all-Ireland.

02: In the biggest demonstration seen in Derry for years, an estimated 40,000 people marched in the city to commemorate the thirteen people shot dead by British troops in the city on "Bloody Sunday", January 30th, 1972

03: In an unprecedented move the Belfast's unionist newspaper, the News Letter, called for an unambiguous apology from the British Government to the relatives of the thirteen men shot dead by British troops on "Bloody Sunday". The News Letter described the events of that day as "unforgivable".

04: The hepatitis C tribunal ended its deliberations after 27 days with its chairman, Mr. Justice Finlay, expressing "a deep feeling of sympathy and, indeed, sorrow," for the victims.

04: A Dublin man, Mr. Paul Ward (32), of Windmill Rd., Walkinstown, appeared in court today charged with the murder of investigative journalist, Veronica Guerin, at Clondalkin, on June 26th, last year.

04: The Irish Exchequer took in £1.19 billion in tax revenue in January, almost 30% more than for the same period last year. The figure was boosted by VAT increases of £120m., carried over from last year, but despite this tax revenue still grew by 16 per cent.

05: Mr. Wim Duisenberg, the head of the Dutch Central bank, has named Ireland as likely to be in the first wave of states moving to the single currency in 1999. Mr. Duisenberg is being tipped as "the man most likely" to be president of the new European Central BanK.

10: The White House denied reports in the London media that there was to be a major shift in policy on Northern Ireland towards a more pro-British stance. It also denied claims that moves were afoot to ensure that the American Ambassador to Ireland, Jean Kennedy-Smith would not serve a second term.

11: The Dublin Government approved the drafting of legislation which will make it an offence to have child pornography for personal use, punishable by up to three years in prison. Trafficking in children for the purposes of sexual exploitation will also be severely punished.

11: Compaq, the US multi-national electronics company, announced the setting up of its telecommunications centre in Dublin. It is expected to create 550 jobs.

12: Lance Bombardier Stephen Restorick, a 23-years-old British soldier, was killed by an IRA sniper at a checkpoint at Bessbrook, Co. Armagh.

13: In one of the most publicised court actions in recent years Michelle Rocca, a former Miss Ireland and current partner of international singing star, Van Morrison, was awarded £7,500 damages in her action for assault against Mr. Cathal Ryan, a member of the "Ryanair"

family.

18: Five people were arrested and more than 100 lengths of Semtex-filled plastic tubing were found when Gardai uncovered what is believed to be a major IRA bomb making factory near Portlaw, Co. Waterford.

19: A mesolithic or middle-Stone Age wooden canoe has been found in the Shannon Estuary. According to a report in the "Irish Times" it has been radio carbon dated at 4800 B.C., indicating the presence of a hunter-gatherers community in the region 7,000 years ago. It is one of the oldest signs of human settlement discovered in Ireland.

19: The House of Lords at Westminster was told by former West Belfast M.P., Lord Fitt that statistics he had received from the RUC revealed that in 1995 twenty boys and fifty girls under the age of 14 were raped; in 1996, 45 girls under 14 were raped. Of the 692 females sexually abused in 1995,157 were between ages of six and ten. In 1996, 199 of the 764 cases of abuse of females involved girls in the same age group. Such is the extent of the problem 55 detectives, six inspectors and 11 sergeants are employed full-time in a special unit which deals with sex abuse crimes.

19: The Minister for Equality and Law Reform, Mervyn Taylor has announced that he will be leaving politics at the next general election.

20: SDLP leader, John Hume, launched a fierce attack on Sinn Féin claiming that to make an electoral pact with that party without an IRA ceasefire would be the equivalent of asking his party's voters to support the killing of innocent human beings by the IRA.

20: Hong Kong group, Hanny, announced the setting up a hi-tech £16m. plant in Belfast. It is expected to create 150 jobs over the next three years.

20: Irish Republicans reacted angrily to the news that pregnant IRA suspect, Roisin McAliskey, has been stripped searched more than eighty times in Holloway jail in London. The Director of Britain's Prison Service, Mr. Richard Tilt, revealed the figures in a letter to Labour's former spokesman on Northern Ireland, Kevin McNamara.

24: The first sitting of the tribunal to investigate payments by former supermarket tycoon, Mr. Ben Dunne, to politicians and public servants got underway today in Dublin.

26: Divorce became law in the Republic. It has been confirmed by the Legal Aid Board that 900 people have sought to commence divorce proceedings.

27: The Tribunal investigating payments to politicians was told today that Mr. Ben Dunne will hand over all documents relating to matters under investigation, including the affidavit in which it is believed he will state that he gave £1.1m. to a senior Fianna Fail politician

28: The Department of Agriculture confirmed that since the start of the year 19 cases of BSE have been detected. Agriculture experts state that the disease has cost the Irish economy nearly £500m. since the British government first announced, last March, that there might be a link between eating BSE infected meat and a new form of CJD in young people.

MARCH

03: Irish Army bomb disposal personnel found two and half kilos of the commercial explosive, Powergel, behind the Sinn Féin offices in Monaghan. While no loyalist grouping claimed responsibility for the attempted bombing, Powergel has been used in a number of attacks by loyalist paramilitaries, particularly the UVF.

04: The Taxi Advisory Committee of the four Dublin local authorities have agreed that 200 new taxi plates, at a cost of £15,000, will be available in the Greater Dublin area.

05: Members of the Orange Order travelled to Dublin for a meeting with Minister for State, Avril Doyle to discuss a role for the Order in next year's commemoration of the 1798 Rebellion.

05: The report of the Review Body on Higher Remuneration in the Public Sector, which the government has accepted, will mean that Taoiseach, John Bruton and Chief Justice Liam Hamilton will now receive an annual salary of £103,500, a rise of 2.7%. The Tánaiste will get a raise of 2.9% to bring his salary to £89,000 while Ministers, the Attorney General and the Ceann Comhairle will now get £82,600, an increase of 3%. T.D.'s got one-tenth of the 30% pay rise they had sought bringing them from £34,362 to £35,400 while Senators' salary rose from £21,763 to £22,400. The Garda Commissioner's salary will increase by 12.5% to £77,316 and the Army Chief of Staff's pay will increase by 2.9% to £70, 750. The overall cost of the increases in pay for the "top people" will add £4m. on to the current £130m. bill.

06: Former Minister, Michael Lowry, announced his resignation from the Fine Gael party, almost four months after it was revealed that businessman, Ben Dunne, had paid for the £208,000 extension to his home. He indicated, however, that he would be standing as an independent candidate in the forthcoming election.

07: Gardai in Dublin have described as "pure calculated evil" the murder of two women, Sylvia Shields (57), from Dublin, and Mary Callinan (61), from Cork, whose bodies were found in separate bedrooms in the Eastern Health Board house at Orchard View, Grangegorman. Both bodies were badly mutilated by the murderer who, according to the Gardai, had displayed signs of being cool and calculating.

07: According to the Central Statistics Office the downward drift in the number signing on the dole saved the Exchequer £75m. in the last year.

10: Cannabis with a street value of £4m. was seized from a truck which disembarked from the Cherbourg-Rosslare ferry.

11: The Irish Government has referred the report into the Hepatitis C scandal, written by Mr. Justice Thomas Finlay, to the Director of Public Prosecutions. The report was strongly critical of named officials with the Blood Transfusion Service Board.

16: More than 1,000 guests attended the launch of Radio Ireland which began broadcasting at midnight from its headquarters in Dublin's Jervis Centre.

17: An estimated 400,000 people turned out in Dublin to watch the annual St. Patrick's Day parade. Many of the most senior political figures, from North and South, were special guests at a reception at the White House in Washington.

20: The High Court discharged the jury in the libel case brought by Minister for Social Welfare, Proinsias De

Rossa against Independent Newspapers for an article written by columnist Eamon Dunphy. After nine hours of deliberations they failed to produce a majority verdict.

23: A planned mass breakout by IRA prisoners from the Maze Prison, near Belfast, was foiled after a prison officer, on a random search, uncovered an elaborately constructed tunnel leading to the perimeter fence at H-Block 7. The officer became suspicious when he noted soft ground near the security fence.

24: Waterford-Wedgewood, the Irish led crystal and china manufacturing company, which was on the verge of collapse five years ago, today reported a 29% rise in pre-tax profits of almost £35m. Sales were at an all time high of £376.3m.

24: Rev. David Templeton (42) died of a heart attack six weeks after receiving, what the RUC described as, a "vicious beating" from Loyalist paramilitaries. It was believed the attack was the result of the publication of a newspaper article in which it was claimed that Mr. Templeton had been questioned by Custom officials about being in possession of gay videos.

26: Michael McMorrow who, unable to find any transport to get him home, took a bike from outside a Garda Station in Kinnegad, Co. Mayo and cycled through the night to his home in Co. Cavan, more than eighty miles away. He was ordered to pay £50 compensation to the bike's owner by Judge Oliver McGuinness at a sitting of Dowra District Court.

27: A meeting in Ballymena which was attempting to find a compromise on the Dunloy and Harryville crises, had to be abandoned when an estimated 300 dissident Orangemen gathered outside Carnlea Orange Hall. Faced with the situation outside, the organisers decided to suspend the meeting. Minutes later hundreds of the Orangemen entered the hall where they were addressed by the Spirit of Drumcree leader, Joel Patton, who told reporters the message his grouping was sending out was "No surrender to republicans on parades".

30: The Bishop of Derry and Raphoe, Rt. Rev. Dr. James Mehaffey has described last year's events surrounding Drumcree as "a defining moment" in our history. Speaking in Derry's St. Columb's Cathedral, Dr. Mehaffey said short term gains for some turned out to be long term losses for us all.

30: The former Minister for Justice, Jim Mitchell, has admitted that he authorised phone taps on about forty people. Mr. Mitchell told the "Irish Times" that it was sometimes necessary to monitor the phone of someone who was in no way suspected of wrongdoing.

31: There was a controversial finish to the Irish Grand National, in front of record 25,000 spectators, at Fairyhouse, when Amble Speedy, which had been led to the winner's enclosure, was found to have been pipped by Mudahim. The outcome of the race also resulted in history being made, Mudahim's trainer, Jenny Pitman, completing a clean sweep of Grand National victories in Ireland, England Scotland and Wales

31: It was the warmest March for 40 years in some places, and, according to the Met Office, the warmest for at least seven years everywhere. The Valentia Observatory recorded a temperature of 19.1.C., on March 11th, the warmest March day in 32 years.

31: What is believed to be the world's biggest currach was launched today in west Kerry. The 37ft. boat was built to commemorate the death of St. Colmcille in 597AD, and will be rowed from Derry to Iona in June.

APRIL

02: 1,250 new jobs will be created by 17 IDA-backed projects, it was announced today. The biggest single development in the £36m investment package is the expansion by Berlitz in Dun Laoghaire, Co. Dublin, where 240 jobs will come on stream in its multimedia/software division.

03: An agreement was signed today which will ensure that the 1998 Tour de France will start in Dublin. The world's biggest cycling event, and Europe's top sporting event, it involves in addition to the 198 riders, nearly 2,000 team and race officials plus a press corps of around 1,000. More than 1,500 trucks are needed to move the vast amount of equipment involved. It will be the 13th time the race has been started outside France.

05: Former Police Authority chairman, David Cook, stated that he did not believe Orangemen had the right to march down the Garvaghy Road. Speaking at a meeting on policing at Drumcree Mr. Cook remarked that many people in positions of power in Northern Ireland found it difficult to acknowledge how deeply society was divided.

07: The Government in Dublin has put a temporary ban on live poultry imports from Northern Ireland, following confirmation that there had been an outbreak of Newcastle disease.

10: An RUC full time reservist, Alice Collins (46), a mother of three, was seriously wounded in a gun attack outside the courthouse in Derry city centre. The IRA claimed responsibility for the attack.

11: Two standing committees of the North Western Health Board recommended to the Board that the vasectomy services at Letterkenny General Hospital be continued "in line with the guidelines laid down by the Minister for Health." There service had ceased last month after a number of protests.

12: At the Labour Party's annual conference in Limerick, party leader Dick Spring ruled out any coalition deal with Fianna Fail after the election. He also ruled out any alliance with the Progressive Democrats. Mr. Spring told delegates that they made a choice to come out of a Fianna Fail led Coalition Government in 1994 and they should stick by that decision in the forthcoming election.

12: The Royal Ulster Constabulary has confirmed that it has seized the IRA's "supergun" which has been used in the assassination of eleven policemen and soldiers over the past five years. The Barrett Light .50 rifle, captured near Crossmaglen, in South Armagh, can fire a bullet half an inch in diameter at 2,000 miles an hour. It can kill up to a mile away.

14: The makeup of the Republic's population is, according to Economic and Social Research Institute, at its most favourable for 200 years. Prof. John FitzGerald and Dr. Tony Fahey said the Republic has entered an era of unprecedented opportunity. Included in their findings is that the number of people at work will continue to rise and the unemployment rate will be halved by the year 2010.

15: People found guilty of attacks in which contaminated blood filled syringes pierce the skin face life imprisonment. In the Non-Fatal Offences against the Person bill Justice Minister, Nora Owen, also proposes that stalking should carry a maximum five year jail penalty; syringe attack, maximum ten years jail; possession or abandonment of a blood filled syringe, seven years maximum; poisoning, three year maximum sentence but greater if the person is seriously harmed or dies; tug-of-love child abduction outside the country, up to seven years..

15: The rate of new house-building in the Republic is the highest in Europe. Minister for State at the Department of the Environment, Liz McManus claimed the Republic's rate, of 9.5 units per 1,000 of the population, was three times higher than that of the U.K.

15: The Minister for Transport, Energy and Communications, Mr. Alan Dukes, in an attempt to defuse the television deflector controversy in rural constituencies, issued proposals for a new short term licensing scheme to provide multi-channel TV on the UHF band.

16: Gardai took to the streets of Dublin today in the first public protest by members of the force since it was established 76 years ago.

17: In a surprise development the Republic's Blood Transfusion Services Board admitted legal liability in all cases of hepatitis C caused by the use of contaminated blood products.

18: The Minister for State at the Department of Justice, Ms. Joan Burton told the "Irish Times" that she was "very worried" that foreign agents were targeting Ireland as an easy country to smuggle people into. Up to the week ending April 11th a total of 843 had officially sought asylum, compared to 1,179 for the whole of 1996.

18: Former Ulster Unionist leader, Sir James Molyneaux, has been elevated to the House of Lords in the Honours List announced by British Prime Minister, John Major.

18: Two million stolen and contraband cigarettes, worth around £300,000, have been seized by gardai and Customs officials in a warehouse at Coolock, in north Dublin.

19: The Redemptorist magazine, Reality, has found that just 61% of Catholic teenagers questioned attend Mass weekly. Thirty-six per cent of those say they only do so because of parental pressure.

21: Approximately 100 headstones in Glasnevin Cemetery, in Dublin, were desecrated in a rampage by a gang of youths.

22: Mr. Noel Fox, an accountant, has supported claims by former supermarket tycoon, Ben Dunne that he paid former Taoiseach, Mr. Charles J. Haughey almost £1.3m. to help him out of his financial difficulties. Mr. Fox was giving evidence to the Tribunal of Inquiry (Dunnes Payments)

22: Mr. Ben Dunne told the Tribunal of Inquiry (Dunnes Payments) that the question of political influence never arose in relation to his dealings with either former Minister, Michael Lowry or former Taoiseach, Charles J. Haughey. He said he had no explanation for the unusual manner of some of the payments to Mr. Lowry.

22: Fr. Brendan Smyth, a Catholic priest, was remanded in custody after he affirmed guilty pleas at Dublin Circuit Court to 74 charges of indecent and sexual assaults on twenty victims over a thirty five year period to 1993.

24: Fine Gael's general secretary, Jim Miley, confirmed to the Tribunal of Inquiry (Dunnes Payments) that Mr. Ben Dunne had given £185,000 to the party over a four year period. This made Mr. Dunne the party's largest single donor in recent times.

25: Joel Patton, leader of the hardline Orange grouping, the Spirit of Drumcree, has urged Orangemen throughout the North to follow the lead of the Co. Antrim lodge in refusing to negotiate with community groups for the right to march.

27: The leader of Fianna Fail, Bertie Ahern, launched an attack on Taoiseach, John Bruton, claiming he had allowed "a fatal prevarication", on the decommissioning issue, after the IRA had called their unequivocal ceasefire.

29: Six more cases of BSE were reported this month, bringing the 1997 total to 30. According to the Department of Agriculture the number of cases identified here since 1989 stands at 219.

MAY

01: An aircraft bound for Manchester was forced to land at Shannon airport after a brawl broke out at 35,000 feet. The fight, involving two men from Liverpool, forced the pilot to take action eight hours into a nine hour flight from Cancun, Mexico.

02: Sinn Féin has claimed two seats in the Westminster elections, Party President Gerry Adams regaining West Belfast from the SDLP's Joe Hendron, and Martin McGuinness gaining Mid-Ulster at the expense of the DUP's William McCrea. Sinn Féin were the main beneficiaries on the day increasing their vote from the 1992 general election by 6 per cent to 16%, which is a half a per cent increase on their 15.5% showing in last year's Forum Elections. The largest nationalist party, the SDLP, also increased its share on 1992, from 23.5 per cent to 24 per cent. However, the loss of Dr. Hendron's seat means they now have only three M.P.s at Westminster. On the Unionist side, William Thompson's victory in the new seat of West Tyrone increases the UUP's representation to ten, while the loss of Mr. McCrea's seat reduces the DUP's representation at Parliament to two.

02: Unemployment hit a six year low last month after a fall of almost 7,000 on the "live register".

02: The DUP leader, Ian Paisley, has described the election of Sinn Féin's Martin McGuinness as a catastrophe for Northern Ireland. "It is a very dark day for Ulster," remarked Dr. Paisley. In contrast, Mr. McGuinness thanked the "intelligent electorate" for returning someone who, he said, was in favour of peace talks and a peaceful settlement.

03: Newly elected British Prime Minister, Mr. Tony Blair M.P., has confirmed that his new Secretary of State for Northern Ireland will be Dr. Mo Mowlam. In accepting the appointment Dr. Mowlam said she was committed to the reform of the RUC and to promoting equality of employment. She also expressed a desire to see Sinn Féin in the Stormont talks if there was an unequivocal

IRA ceasefire, and promised to implement the North report on marches and parades.

05: Gardai have confirmed that seven people died in weekend accidents, making it one of the worst in recent times.

05: Dubliner Ken Doherty was crowned snooker's world champion tonight after defeating Scotsman, Stephen Hendry by 18 frames to 12. He also received a cheque for £210,000. It is believed that he will be earn in the region of £1m. in the coming twelve months

06: The Government has raised its offer for aggravated damages to people infected with hepatitis C, through the state 's use of contaminated blood products, by an estimated £40m. The new offer, a top-up of 20 per cent on general awards, is expected to push the overall compensation costs to an estimated £240 million.

06: In an unprecedented statement by a Catholic bishop, Dr. Willie Walsh, the Bishop of Killaloe, said his church's *Ne Temere* ruling on mixed marriages was contrary to the spirit of christian generosity and love. The ruling had demanded that the children of mixed marriages had to be brought up as Catholics.

07: Four people died near the village of Croagh, on the main Limerick-Tralee road, when a twelve wheel truck and five oncoming cars collided.

07: The Church of Ireland Archbishop of Dublin, Dr. Walton Empey, has warmly welcomed the apology from the Catholic Bishop of Killaloe, Dr. Willie Walsh, for the pain caused to "our non Roman brethren" by the *Ne Temere* mixed-marriages decree. The Archbishop described Dr. Walsh's comments as "another remarkable statement from a remarkable man, and a very wonderful person."

08: A 25-year-old Catholic, Robert Hamill, died eleven days after being attacked and beaten by a loyalist gang in Portadown, Co. Armagh. Political and religious leaders appealed to nationalists to remain calm.

09: A wind farm project, capable of generating enough electricity to meet the needs of 100,00 people, was formally switched on by Energy Minister, Emmet Stagg at Barnesmore Gap, in Co. Donegal.

09: Darren Bradshaw (24), an RUC constable, was shot dead in a bar in Belfast. The INLA has admitted responsibility for the shooting. It was the second tragedy for the Bradshaw family, another brother, Simon, having been killed last year in car crash while serving with the British army.

10: Some 2,000 mourners attended the funeral of Robert Hamill, beaten to death by loyalists in Portadown in late April. A nearby RUC patrol was accused of not intervening, and by September 18,000 people had signed a petition calling for the suspension of the officers allegedly involved.

12: The RUC believe that a dissident loyalist grouping, the Loyalist Volunteer Force (LVF) was responsible for the murder of 61-years-old Sean Brown, chairman of the Bellaghy GAA club, in Co. Derry. Mr. Brown was abducted while locking up the club and an hour later he was found dead beside his burning car near Randalstown, Co. Antrim, ten miles away.

13: An Irish Marketing Survey has revealed that more than 70 per cent of the electorate in the Republic is opposed to the legalisation of abortion in any circumstances and 62 per cent want a referendum on the issue.

13: Bord Fáilte chiefs have predicted that Ireland is on course to become the first country in the world to triple its earnings from tourism in a twelve year period. International marketing director, Noel Toolan, said he was confident that visitor numbers by the end of this year would be up 7 per cent on last year's 4.7m figure. Last year's £1.8bn. in tourist earnings is expected to rise by 9 per cent.

13: An E.C. report has revealed that Ireland accounts for 22 per cent of all EU grants to the beef sector-- despite having just 6 per cent. The report points out that Ireland has received almost £750m. in export subsidies, cattle headage grants and intervention buying to support the market.

14: Unemployment in Northern Ireland have gone down last month over March by more than 2,000. The total number of unemployed is 64, 800, which is 8.4 per cent of the population.

14: The Dáil was told that Irish troops will, for the first time, operate under a NATO-led command in Bosnia where 50 soldiers will take part in a United Nations operation.

15: Taoiseach John Bruton dissolved the Dáil and called a General Election for June 6.

16: In a major speech at Balmoral, near Belfast, Prime Minister, Tony Blair, signalled that British officials will recommence dialogue with Sinn Féin, provided that "events on the ground" did not make this impossible. While the SDLP leader, John Hume and the Irish government welcomed Mr. Blair's speech, as opening the door to peace, republicans publicly stated that the tone and content of the speech was "firmly pro-unionist."

16: One man died and eight people were injured in a family fight in Clondalkin, Co. Dublin last night. More than 20 gardaí separated the two groups during another stand-off later in the day.

16: Former Minister for Agriculture and Waterford Fine Gael candidate Austin Deasy claimed that he had left the party front bench in 1992 because he was expected to collect money from big business.

16: French police in Roscoff and Cherbourg intercept a total of 34 Romanians attempting to enter Ireland with false papers.

17: A fifth of prisoners in Dublin's Mountjoy jail use heroin every day or several times a week, a new study revealed.

19: Sinn Féin MPs Martin McGuinness and Gerry Adams went to the British Parliament in London to request members' passes. They had been banned from the parliament for refusing to swear the oath of allegiance to the British Queen but were permitted to enter the building in the days prior to the ban coming into force.

21: A report by the World Economic Forum ranked Ireland 16th amongst the world's 20 most competitive economies.

21: Sinn Féin negotiators met British officials at Stormont, the first such meeting in 15 months. Martin McGuinness said a start had been made in overcoming the difficulties of the peace process and another meeting was due in the near future.

22: Seán Ó'hUiginn, former consul general in New York, was named as the new Irish ambassador to the United

States.

23: For the first time ever Unionists lost control over Belfast City Council. They also lost control of Fermanagh, Strabane and Cookstown in the local government elections. Sinn Féin increased its vote winning 70 seats in total and removing the SDLP's overall control of Derry City Council.

23: Dublin's Lord Mayor Brendan Lynch and his driver Tony Salmon sustained minor injuries while beating off two muggers.

25: A crude bomb was discovered in Dundalk, fuelling fears of loyalist attacks in the Republic.

26: Some 100 new asylum seekers arrive in Ireland each week, according to the Department of Justice. It had received 1,266 new applications for asylum by May 1997 compared to 1,179 for the whole of 1996.

26: Some Dublin shop-owners have banned Romanian families from entering their premises amidst accusations of shoplifting. Fine Gael TD Jim Mitchell said refugees were becoming an issue on the election trail, raised "in almost racialist terms" which he found "very distasteful".

26: On the election campaign trail Tánaiste Dick Spring said a vote for Sinn Féin was a vote for peace, contradicting coalition partner Taoiseach John Bruton who said it was tantamount to voting for the IRA. Meanwhile Minister for Justice Nora Owen urged voters in Cavan-Monaghan to vote for any candidate bar to Sinn Féin.

26: Róisín McAliskey, imprisoned in Britain awaiting extradition proceedings in connection with an IRA bombing in Germany gave birth to a 5lb 13oz baby girl, Loinnir, at London's Whittington Hospital yesterday. She had been granted bail 4 days earlier subject to her remaining at the hospital.

27: Radio Ireland controversially re-broadcast Taoiseach John Bruton's faux pas of 1995 when he told a reporter he was "sick of answering questions about the f.....g peace process".

27: The surge in Dublin house prices continued when a four bedroom home in Killiney was sold for £1,055,000, or £400,000 more than its pre-auction guide price.

28: A report by civil liberties group Human Rights Watch/Helsinki claimed a series of RUC actions had exacerbated last year's Drumcree crisis. It listed excessive use of force, the indiscriminate use of plastic bullets and a failure to remove illegal roadblocks while the RUC abandoned its "traditional policing function in some areas".

28: A "grave injustice" was done to the families of the Bloody Sunday dead, Taoiseach John Bruton said after briefing relatives of the victims on a new report into the killings being prepared by the Irish government.

29: The Ryanair flotation on the Dublin and New York stockmarkets yielded more than £50m in cash for the airline. It was valued at £498m after the share price soared from 195p to 315p, with the Ryan family's holding amounting to £166m.

29: Jason Ryan (11) died in a swimming accident in Dublin's Grand Canal after becoming trapped in a submerged shopping trolley. His friend, 13-year old Keith Mahon was critical after trying to rescue him.

31: Loyalist protesters again blocked the road outside Harryville's Catholic church prior to Saturday evening mass, one man was arrested for disorderly behaviour.

31: The UUP and the DUP have demanded separate conference facilities at the peace conference in South Africa to avoid any contact with Sinn Féin but the PUP and the UDP attended a shared workshop.

31: A pedestrian, 17-year old Priscilla Kinsella and motorist Desmond Hyland are killed in two separate traffic accidents.

JUNE

01: Tensions rose as off-duty RUC Constable Greg Taylor (41) was kicked to death by a dozen loyalists in Ballymoney.

01: A 1000lb bomb was discovered in West Belfast.

01: Tony Blair implicitly apologised for Britain's failure to tackle the Irish potato famine in a letter to Cork's Famine commemoration organisers. Some 12,000 people attended a commemorative concert with Van Morrison, Shane McGowan and other artists.

01: Gerry Adams accused Taoiseach John Bruton of abdicating his responsibility to the Irish people in the North and damaging the peace process.

01: A pilot was killed in a crash during an air display at Carrick-on-Shannon.

02: Belfast City Council elected its first nationalist Lord Mayor, SDLP councillor Alban Maginness. Ulster Unionist councillor Jim Rodgers became deputy Lord Mayor.

02: A heroin shortage in Dublin has led to a quadrupling of its price.

03: Fianna Fáil leader Bertie Ahern and the Progressive Democrats' Leader Mary Harney dropped the Progressive Democrats controversial plans to cut 25,000 public sector jobs.

04: An RUC man's son and three others were charged with the murder of RUC Constable Greg Taylor three days ago.

04: The Irish government set up the Irish Film Commission to sell Ireland abroad as a movie location.

05: An armed robber shot by gardaí in Dublin died in hospital. The INLA claimed 26-year old John Morris as one of its members.

05: Radioactivity in Irish Sea lobsters off the west Cumbrian coast has risen to unprecedented levels, according to British Nuclear Fuels' own figures. **06:** In a general election in the Irish Republic only two thirds of voters turned out, 2% less than in 1992 and almost 10% less than in 1981. A significant 55% said they were floating voters.

06: UUP leader David Trimble relaxed his insistence on decommissioning prior to the multi-party talks but maintained that Sinn Féin could only enter substantive talks in the event of an IRA cease-fire and the handover of some weapons.

06: The DUP denounced the Women's Coalition (a party elected to the NI talks process) as being made up of "feckless women" with "limited intellect".

06: Minister for Agriculture Ivan Yates announced the lifting of Egypt's six-month ban on live cattle exports from the Republic.

06: A questionnaire completed and signed by Oscar Wilde fetched £23,000 when auctioned by Christie's. Wilde had said his aim in life was "Success, fame or even notoriety."

07: Barristers in Northern Ireland dropped a declaration promising to serve the Queen of England, one year after the oath of allegiance to the Queen was considered unlawful and scrapped.

08: President Robinson was welcomed to the Scottish island of Iona where she took part in celebrations for the 1,400th anniversary of the death of St. Colmcille.

08: Sean McNally, a 24-year old victim of a punishment shooting in Belfast's Markets area, had his leg amputated.

08: A further recount was ordered in the Dublin South East constituency to determine whether Green Party candidate John Gormley had ousted the PDs' Michael McDowell from his post. Green Party members accused the PDs of delaying tactics.

09: Fianna Fáil emerged from the Republics general election as the leading party with 77 seats, followed by Fine Gael with 54, Labour with 17, and the Progressive Democrats and Democratic Left with four seats each. The Greens won two seats, Sinn Féin won their first seat since 1957 and independent candidates shared seven seats between them.

09: The average price for a new house rose 14% to £73,523. In Dublin the increase was even greater at 17.3% and an average price of £84,000. Second-hand houses were up 21% at £89,067.

09: President Mary Robinson said Protestants in Scotland and Ireland should celebrate the two nations' Celtic heritage which should not be mistaken for Catholicism or nationalism.

09: Armed thieves hijacked a 24-foot truck carrying £1m worth of computer parts in Dublin, left the driver tied to a wall in Roundwood, Co. Wicklow, and made off with the truck.

10: The vast majority of plastic bullets used in last year's Drumcree stand-off were faulty, it emerged. The issue of compensation would "clearly arise", said Mo Mowlam.

10: Duty-free facilities will definitely be abolished in 1999, the European Commission confirmed in response to a question from MEP Mary Banotti.

10: Former civil service chief Sir Kenneth Bloomfield criticised ex-economy minister Baroness Denton, saying her complaints against the civil service were ill-informed and little short of irresponsible.

11: Police and customs officers smashed a cannabis gang, seized £6m of property, £2m of illicit alcohol and £500,000 in cash in a series of raids in Britain and Ireland. The gang had links to the UDA and its leader was being interviewed by the RUC in Belfast.

11: Computer giant Seagate announced 1,000 new jobs and a £150m investment for Cork.

11: The Queen paid a one-day visit to the North and dropped in on the Speedwell project to chat to children from Protestant and Catholic backgrounds. She held a garden party in Hillsborough for 300 couples celebrating their golden wedding anniversary.

12: Irish workers are the happiest, healthiest and hardest-working in Europe, according to a new study published in Dublin today.

14: A young Catholic Belfast man, 21-year old Martin Gavin, was left for dead in a Shankill Butcher-style attack, only three days after former Butcher member Robert Bates was shot dead on nearby Woodvale Road. Around five men stopped Mr. Gavin on his way

home, called him a "Fenian bastard" and then cut his throat, his head and hand and fractured his skill. He received 41 stitches in total.

14: The Green Party candidate for Dublin South East, John Gormley, was finally confirmed as the area's TD after eight days of vote checking. He ousted the PD candidate and lawyer Michael McDowell. Mr. McDowell later announced his retirement from politics.

15: Tyrone GAA player Paul McGirr (18) died after an accidental collision with the Armagh goalkeeper when he scored the winning goal in the Ulster Minors match. McGirr sustained a ruptured liver.

16: The IRA shot dead at close range RUC officers Constable John Graham (34) and reserve Constable David Andrew Johnston (30) in Lurgan, sparking fears of a full return to republican and loyalist violence.

16: The British government suspended contact with Sinn Féin following the Lurgan killings.

17: The UN General Assembly approved President Mary Robinson as UN High Commissioner for Human Rights but left open her starting date.

17: Northern Secretary Dr Mo Mowlam said she would announce her decision on the Garvaghy Road march at least six days before the parade was scheduled to go ahead. She later met nationalist residents who told her they needed a breathing space from parades this year after the events of previous.

17: Two Scots Guards serving life sentences for the murder of unarmed Belfast teenager Peter McBride in 1992 did not deserve early release, Lord Mayhew - formerly Sir Patrick Mayhew - told the High Court in Belfast.

18: The Irish government has paid a total of £740,057 sterling towards the multi-party talks at Stormont between June 1996 and February 1997, according to Northern Secretary Dr Mo Mowlam. Both governments share the running costs, she said.

19: Former Security Minister Sir John Wheeler clashed with the Police Authority when he refused to make the RUC's oath of office more acceptable to nationalists, it emerged today. The PANI has written to Mo Mowlam with a call for action and hopes for a new oath similar to that of the Scottish police who do not swear allegiance to the queen.

19: Retail giant Sainsbury's announced plans to open 20 stores in the Republic of Ireland in a joint venture with Fitzwilton, Dr. Tony O'Reilly's investment company.

19: Telecom Éireann announced a 76% rise in pre-tax profits, reaching £204m in the 12 months to March 1997.

19: The new Fianna Fáil/Progressive Democrats government published its 'Action Programme' with plans to cut income tax rates to 42% and 20%, increase the old-age pension to £100 a week, and boost private sector involvement in the prison sector. It also imposed 4% and 5% caps respectively on current and capital spending growth.

19: Central Statistics Office figures confirmed a record 8% rate of growth in the Irish economy last year, five times the EU average.

19: The British Army defused a 1.5 lb bomb left under the car of Sinn Féin Co. Antrim councillor James McCarry, the attempted bombing was presumed to be the work of Loyalists.

20: A Co. Meath man, 47-year old Brendan Doherty, appeared before Ennis District Court over allegations of an attempted £3m Revenue fraud. He was charged with trying to obtain a £3,823,716 cheque with the aid of a false VAT return.

20: James Hendrick jnr who admitted shooting dead his father after years of sexual abuse walked from the Central Criminal Court with a suspended five-year sentence.

20: RUC Chief Constable Ronnie Flanagan said he expected trouble at Drumcree because an agreement between residents and the Orange Order was now unlikely. But he wanted to avoid a 1996-style scenario when nationalists felt betrayed by the RUC.

21: The longest day of the year saw more rain on top of recent torrential downpours which caused flooding in many parts of the country. Rosslare recorded twice its average June rainfall.

21: Canon Seán Connolly suspended Saturday evening Mass in the beleaguered Harryville chapel in Ballymena until September 6. The church's Saturday evening mass had been picketed by loyalists for 41 weeks. The RUC had said it would be unable to guarantee the safety of Harryville parishioners on July 12, Canon Seán Connolly confirmed.

22: Orange parades passed off relatively peacefully in the nationalist areas of Bellaghy, Co.Derry, in Mountfield, Co. Tyrone, and in Keady, Co. Armagh although re-routed marchers in Mountfield said the RUC had capitulated to nationalists. The deputy grand master of the Orange Order, Robert Overend, also warned that today's peaceful parades did not mean there would not be another stand-off at Drumcree again this year.

23: Garda figures showed a sharp increase in road deaths over the past year. In May 1996 34 people died in road accident, but by May 1997 the figure had rocketed to 53 deaths.

24: Derry suffered a major job loss blow when United Technology Automotive announced it would close its Creggan plant and lay off all 525 workers.

24: Taoiseach John Bruton told the British government that the disputed British Governments Widgery Inquiry into Derry's Bloody Sunday was a second injustice to the victims.

25: The British government imposed a five-week deadline on the IRA to call a cease-fire. Substantive talks on the future of Northern Ireland would start on September 15 and conclude in May 1998, it said.

26: Minister for Justice Nora Owen gave new powers to immigration officers, allowing them to refuse entry to people who do not meet the "normal criteria" when passing entry points from Britain or the North.

26: The new government was elected by an eight-vote majority in the Dáil with 84 in favour and 76 against. Fianna Fáil leader Bertie Ahern sought the support of three independent TDs and was elected as the country's youngest ever Taoiseach at 45 years with 85 votes to 78.

26: Sinn Féin TD Caoimhghín Ó'Caoláin was one of four independent TDs voting for Bertie Ahern. The others were Jackie Healy-Rae, Mildred Fox and Harry Blaney. He also gained 77 Fianna Fáil votes and four from the PDs. He was opposed by 54 Fine Gael deputies, 16 Labour, four Democratic Left, two Greens,

and two independents: Tony Gregory and Joe Higgins. A third independent TD, Tom Gildea, abstained.

26: Newly-elected Taoiseach Bertie Ahern appointed virtually his entire front bench to the new cabinet, with Michael Smith being the only non-runner. David Andrews, Ray Burke, Brian Cowan, Charlie McCreevy, Joe Walsh and Michael Woods all had previous ministerial experience. Mary Harney, the PD leader, became the first female Tánaiste.

27: Hotel chain Jury's complained that it could not fill vacancies at £260 a week because young people were over-educated.

27: The RUC confirmed that a Russian-made RPG7 rocket was used in an attack on a police patrol in north Belfast the previous day.

28: Farmers living near the Aughinish Alumina plant in Askeaton, Co. Limerick asked the Environmental Protection Agency to delay its ruling on a new pollution control licence until the deaths of 62 horses on one farm had been explained.

28: The UUP and the DUP boycotted the installation dinner for Belfast's first ever nationalist mayor, the SDLP's Alban Maginness, blaming the presence of Sinn Féin president Gerry Adams.

28: County Clare received a new lifeboat station, the first such station in the Shannon estuary and the first RNLI station opened in Munster in 100 years.

30: Charles Haughey's late accountant, Des Traynor, had managed up to £40m belonging to Mr Haughey and other Irish residents in a secret off-shore account, the Dunnes payments to politicians tribunal heard

30: Charles Haughey's counsel Eoin MacGonigal said the former Taoiseach had not been aware that Ben Dunne had lodged £1.3m to his then accountant Des Traynor.

30: The tribunal heard that Westmeath Fine Gael TD Paul McGrath was told not to oppose a Dunnes Stores development in 1994 and that Haughey's bankers put up the securities for loans to Celtic Helicopters, the company owned by Charles Haughey's son Ciaran.

30: UUP deputy leader John Taylor came under fire for saying that any violence in Portadown next weekend would arise from "intolerance and bigotry by extremist republicans" and that the British government should use force against any nationalists blocking the Garvaghy Road. SDLP councillor Brid Rodgers said his comments were "less than helpful" and "quite provocative".

30: The leaders of Fianna Fáil and the Progressive Democrats, Bertie Ahern and Mary Harney, reached an agreement over the Seanad elections, giving the PDs four of the Taoiseach's nominees. In exchange the PDs would not contest the elections and ask their 37 councillors to vote for Fianna Fáil candidates.

JULY

01: The Northern Ireland Office and the RUC said they would only announce their decision on the Drumcree parade two or three days in advance, despite Mo Mowlam's earlier promise to reveal it at least six days ahead of the contentious march.

01: Taoiseach Bertie Ahern and Foreign Affairs Minister Ray Burke said it would be a mistake to force through Sunday's Drumcree parade. Bertie Ahern said in Belfast he did not want residents screened off or hemmed in and Ray Burke said a repeat of last year would be "too horrendous" to contemplate.

01: Bertie Ahern nominated Liz O'Donnell and Michael Smith as the first two of 17 junior ministers

01: June was the wettest since records began, said Met Eireann. But in an aberration from the norm Malin Head in Donegal only got three quarters of its normal rainfall and 3% more sunshine while Rosslare in the sunny south east notched up two and a half times its normal rainfall.

02: The Dunnes tribunal heard that Fine Gael TD Paul McGrath, who opposed a Mullingar Dunnes Stores development, told Tipperary TD Michael Lowry to "f... off" when Lowry approached him on it. Lowry insisted that he had never made representations on behalf of Dunnes Stores, despite evidence that a Dunnes manager had earlier phoned him over a summons from the Department of Agriculture. The manager's call was not designed to influence the case, the tribunal was told.

02: Tension rose further in the run-up to the Drumcree parade today when the Loyalist Volunteer Force (LVF) issued a death threat to "civilians in the Republic", warning of killings if this years Orange Order Garvaghy Road parade was stopped.

02: Angry Garvaghy Road residents representatives revealed that the RUC had banned their planned community festival. It was to coincide with an Orange parade on July 6. Some residents began holding overnight vigils and a women's roadside peace camp was set up.

02: The Sunday Independent, fighting a libel action brought by former social welfare minister Proinsias de Rossa, won its application to send a judge to Moscow to take witness statements on Russian archive documents and their signatures. Mr de Rossa was fighting claims that he had signed a letter to Moscow requesting donations for the Workers Party.

03: The families of the Bloody Sunday presented Northern Secretary Mo Mowlam with a 40,000-signature petition for a new inquiry

03: Hopes for a resolution of the Drumcree conflict faded as Mo Mowlam met security chiefs. 500 Garvaghy Road residents held an overnight vigil and installed an alarm system to alert their neighbours of any attempts to seal off their area. Their representative, Breandán Mac Cionnaith, doubted the Orange parade would be re-routed away from the nationalist area since the British government had already banned a street festival organised by the residents for the same day.

03: Taoiseach Bertie Ahern had his first prime ministerial meeting with British PM Tony Blair and reiterated that he did not want to see Orange marchers forced down the Garvaghy Road.

03: For the third time, a jury was sworn in for the Proinsias de Rossa/Sunday Independent libel case.

03: TV and radio host Gerry Ryan signed a contract worth £1m over five years with RTÉ

04: The Dunnes tribunal took another bizarre twist when former transport minister Michael Lowry admitted that he had used "weasel words" in the Dáil. He did have money in offshore accounts when he resigned over an extension paid for by Ben Dunne but he had given TDs the impression that he had no offshore deposits.

04: Dunnes Stores had paid Tipperary TD Michael Lowry at least £710,000, the Dunnes tribunal ascertained. About £395,000 was paid in connection with his house.

04: Bell Lines, Ireland's biggest carriers of on/off cargo, and four related companies went into liquidation owing millions of pounds in debts after a rescue package collapsed.

04: Mass anxiety gripped many areas the North as thousands of people fled the region to avoid getting caught up in a repeat of last year's Drumcree stand-off.

04: As tension continued to rise throughout Northern Ireland 60 families were evacuated from the Garvaghy Road Area following a Loyalist bomb scare. Craigavon Area Hospital prepared emergency contingency plans for a possible stand-off and cancelled next week's out-patient clinics.

04: Kerry rape victim Caroline Carey had left Ireland with her family following threats including that she and her children would be "cut into little pieces", it emerged today.

04: Local authorities will lose their powers to raise the level of motor tax in their areas in the November budget,

05: The risk of getting cancer is rising by 10% every decade and one in four deaths is due to cancer, according to the National Cancer Registry's first report.

06: The RUC in a massive pre-dawn operation entered the Garvaghy Road area in order to secure it and enable an Orange march through Garvaghy Road later in the day. RUC officers with their faces covered by fire-proof balaclavas sealed off both sides of the street in an operation beginning at 3am.

06: In what was reported to have been the biggest security operation ever in Northern Ireland the RUC and British Army used thousands of officers and soldiers in full riot gear in an operation lasting until 8am to clear the road and clear a route for the annual Orange Order parade .

06: Five priests celebrated an open-air mass in front of a row of army saracens for Catholic Garvaghy Road residents who could not reach their place of worship due to army and police cordons. This was reported as the first time in hundreds of years that Catholics in Ireland had been prevented going to mass by British troops. The priests shook the hands of the soldiers as a sign of peace.

06: At noon in almost total silence 1200 Orangemen proceeded from Drumcree Church to march six abreast, with their traditional Orange Sashes and Bowler hats to and along the Garvaghy Road.

06: RUC Chief Constable Ronnie Flanagan apologised to the Garvaghy Road residents for his eleventh-hour decision to allow the parade to go ahead. He said he had been faced with a choice between two evils.

06: In gloomy reactions, Taoiseach Bertie Ahern voiced "deep disappointment" about the Drumcree decision and SDLP councillor Mark Durkan said Mo Mowlam was now a "dead duck" but she retorted that no one had been betrayed. Sinn Féin's Martin McGuinness urged nationalists to demand justice on the streets. However, UUP leader David Trimble said the Orange Order was merely doing what it had done for the past 190 years.

06: Health minister Brian Cowen came under pressure to open a new inquiry into evidence that mentally handicapped children were used for drugs trials in orphanages in the 1960s and 1970s.

07: Retired pediatrician Dr Victoria Coffey admitted to the Irish Independent that she had co-operated in carrying out trials of the controversial 3-in-1 vaccine and the polio vaccine on children in orphanages in 1961. A total of 58 children were used in the trials conducted by Professors Patrick Meenan and Irene Hillary of UCD with four medical scientists from US pharmaceutical company Wellcome.

07: Damage worth £20m had been caused in the North since Sunday's Drumcree parade. The AA has advised people to avoid certain 'no-go' areas, particularly Newry which was "completely impassable". Rioting and hijackings also continued in Derry and Belfast.

07: In overnight violence over 100 people were injured with six in a serious condition. One man died when handling an explosive device. A 14-year old Catholic boy was in a coma after being hit in the head by a plastic bullet and a 14-year old Protestant boy was struck on the shoulder by a rifle bullet in Belfast.

07: Over the past two days, the RUC and British army had fired 1,600 plastic bullets. Some 550 attacks on security forces and 700 separate bombings were logged and hundreds of vehicles hijacked and burned, 41 people were arrested. The fire service had received 500 call-outs, the ambulance service 150.

07: A South African MP and independent observer, Gora Ebrahim, said the scenes on the Garvaghy Road had reminded him of police brutality in Sharpeville. He believed the decision to force through the parade had not come from the chief constable but from "much higher".

07: A leaked document suggested that Mo Mowlam and the security chiefs had accepted as early as 21 June that an Orange parade would go through Drumcree and that this was the "least worst option" in the absence of agreement between residents and the loyal institutions.

07: Two former executives of Larry Goodman's Anglo-Irish Beef Processors received suspended six-year sentences for their roles in a £900,000 intervention beef fraud.

07: Fungie the Dingle dolphin (26) was revealed to be courting a female bottlenose dolphin. Locals and tourism operators voiced fears that she might lure him away from Dingle Bay.

08: Mo Mowlam announced an inquiry into the leaking of a secret NIO document which implied an early consensus between the government and security chiefs that "Orange feet" would have to march on the Garvaghy road this year. This consensus had been reached prior to Mo Mowlam engaging in discussions with nationalist residents groups on the basis that no decisions had been arrived at.

08: Ahead of annual Orange Order parades across Northern Ireland on July 12th nationalists angered by the events at Garvaghy announce plans to block planned Orange parades through nationalist areas including Armagh, Belfast's Ormeau Rd, Derry , Newry, Strabane and Bellaghy. Appeals were made for support from nationalists from outside these areas to prevent by weight of numbers peacefully protesting any further Orange parades through nationalist areas.

08: The INLA issued a death threat to those Orange Order members it sees as "responsible" for forcing any more parades through nationalist areas.

08: US Congressman Joseph Kennedy proposed a motion in the Congress calling for a halt to all Orange marches, the motion was backed by over 100 Congressmen.

09: In yet another spectacular admission to the Dunnes Payments to Politicians tribunal, Charles Haughey said that he had after all received over £1.3m from Ben Dunne. He revealed this fact after Ben Dunnes' solicitor delivered records of communication with Charles Haughey. The former Taoiseach said it was "a very helpful document".

09: Ben Dunne had offered Charles Haughey a further £1m earlier this year to help the former Taoiseach cover his potential tax repayments.

09: The British government promised Sinn Féin an immediate meeting with ministers once a cease-fire had been announced.

09: Four members of a Co. Antrim family died in a ferocious house fire near Lisburn. Mr Maurice McKinstry, the sole survivor, was unable to rescue his parents, his sister and her 5-year old daughter.

09: The 474 Irish doctors with more than 1,000 medical card patients on their books were paid an average of £93,591 by the State in 1996.

09: The Republic has a smaller share of its population in prison than many of its European neighbours. At 60 per 100,000 of the population it is on a par with Norway, Finland and Greece. Only Switzerland was lower with 58 per 100,000. Britain topped the league: Scotland jailed 110 per 100,000 compared to Wales' and England's 99. In Northern Ireland, the figure came to 106.

10: With the possibility of a civil war situation being opening discussed in a dramatic about-turn less than 48 hours before this weekend's Orange parades, the Orange Order announced that it would re-route its contentious parades in Armagh, Belfast, Derry and Newry. The Order's late-night decision followed a day of intense negotiations with RUC chief Ronnie Flanagan and former UUP leader Lord Molyneaux and Orange Order leaders. It was reported that Mr Flanagan had informed the Order that he would be unable to guarantee the safety of its members if the parades went ahead

10: While news of the re-routing decision was greeted with intense relief in nationalist quarters, a split immediately emerged in the Orange Order. An angry crowd gathered outside the Ballynafeigh Lodge in anticipation of its decision to divert its parade from the Lower Ormeau Road. Re-routing supporters had argued that Protestants living in majority Catholic areas could be under threat if the situation continued to deteriorate.

10: More than 100 illegal refugees had been turned back in the two weeks since the government introduced new immigration controls between Britain and Ireland, said Justice Minister John O'Donoghue.

10: Management at the Asahi textiles plant in Killala, Co. Mayo, announced that it would close the loss-making operation with 320 employees. SIPTU rejected claims that a rejected cost-cutting package had led to the closure.

11: Orangemen voluntarily agreed to reroute a parade in Newtownbutler, Co. Fermanagh, after talking to residents of the 80% nationalist village. Meanwhile, Derry's Orange deputy grand master Dougie Caldwell expressed the Order's leadership's relief, saying he was happy not to have someone's possible death on his conscience.

11: UUP leader David Trimble said he had mixed feelings about the rerouting decision. It had been taken "in order to deny Sinn Féin/IRA the opportunity to cause mayhem" and the Order did not want the decision to be seen as permanent.

11: Charles Haughey had received £24,000 a month for almost three years towards his bills and lifestyle, the Dunnes tribunal heard. Meanwhile, Dunnes Stores facilitated a £275,000 soft loan to Celtic Helicopters, the company part-owned by Charles Haughey's son Ciaran.

11: The Republic's biggest dairy merger was completed when 83% of Waterford members and 98% of Avonmore members at the shareholders' meeting voted to create the world's fourth biggest dairy group.l.

11: An anti-drugs activist from Dublin's inner city was jailed for nine months for painting the slogan "Garda stop harassing anti-drug activists" on a gable wall.

12: Orange Order Grand Master Robert Saulters told the main Belfast parade that the decision to avoid the Lower Ormeau Road had saved the North from "downright mayhem". Rev Edward Smyth also praised the Ballynafeigh Lodge for putting others' lives before their civil rights.

12: An RUC landrover policing the Dunloy parade featured a handpainted rat with a crown and the words KING RAT, the nickname of a Portadown loyalist believed to have been responsible for the killings of dozens of Mid-Ulster nationalists. A relative of one of King Rat's victims said the RUC should take immediate action.

12: Mayo brothers Peter and John McMenamon had an amazing escape from flash floods which swept through their house. John was washed to a neighbour's house and hauled inside through a window while Peter managed to cling on to a wall and hold out there for two hours until the storm let up. The floods left 15 people homeless and caused £1m in damage at Glencullen, Co. Mayo.

13: The RUC found 500 pounds of explosives and three booster charges on Derry's Creggan estate.

14: Dublin City Council gave the go-ahead to the route of the controversial Dublin Port Tunnel despite six years of challenges to the original route from residents' groups.

14: An Bord Pleanála added a twist to the Planning Act when it ruled that a Co. Donegal hotel room could be used as a courtroom, reversing an earlier decision.

14: There were renewed hopes that 162 clothing jobs could be saved at the Farah plant in Kiltimagh, Co. Mayo, when workers accepted a proposed management buyout they had rejected in a previous ballot.

14: The punt threatened to break through its permitted ceiling in the European monetary system when it came within a penny of its ceiling against the French franc. It fell to 89p sterling.

15: Catholic teenager Bernadette Martin was killed with four shots to the head as she lay asleep in her Protestant boyfriend's home in Aghalee near Lurgan.

16: Government leaders Bertie Ahern and Mary Harney condemned Charles Haughey's behaviour as "unacceptable" and indicated the need for a new tribunal.

16: The DUP and the UK Unionists walked out of the Stormont talks, complaining that the British government would not clarify its position on paramilitary disarmament

16: The Apprentice Boys of Derry governor Alistair Simpson confirmed that he would not talk to Derry's Bogside Residents Group about the organisations planned parade around the city's walls because the residents group contained republicans.

16: Proinsias de Rossa, Democratic Left leader, told the High Court that he had burnt Workers' Party material in a Christmas bonfire in 1992. The court also heard that a printing company, Repsol, was connected to the Workers' Party and that one of its staff had disappeared without a trace.

17: Charles Haughey had £15,000 worth of outstanding loans with Patrick Gallagher's Merchant Banking Ltd. when it collapsed in 1982. Labour Party leader Dick Spring had raised the issue in a letter to Haughey in 1990. The former taoiseach replied that he "categorically" rejected any such "outrageous" suggestions.

17: Drug abusers are responsible for more than 80% of burglaries, muggings and thefts from cars in Dublin which lead to charges, a new study revealed.

17: Forbes business magazine listed Irish Independent owner Dr Tony O'Reilly as a billionaire and one of the world's 200 richest people.

18: Hopes for a new IRA cease-fire rose after Sinn Féin's Gerry Adams and Martin McGuinness called on the organisation to restore the 1994 cessation. In an earlier statement, Gerry Adams and John Hume had said the remaining obstacles to a new cease-fire could be removed.

18: Unionists treated signs of a new IRA cease-fire with suspicion. The UUP said it would be a tactical cessation, the DUP said the IRA would resort to violence whenever it wished to do so, and the UDP's Gary McMichael said he was sceptical but hoped that it would mean an absolute end to all military operations.

18: Proinsias de Rossa admitted in the High Court that the Workers' Party general secretary Seán Garland had probably signed a letter asking the Soviet Communist Party for £1 million. De Rossa also said he was in Moscow when the letter was sent but he did not know of its existence.

18: Ireland's black economy was worth £3.6m, according to a Revenue spokeswoman.

18: Fingal County Council asked the Circuit Court to strike out cases against householders who had not paid their water charges. It would no longer seek their disconnection but pursue them through the small debts court instead.

18: Youths attacked five German tourists who had refused demands for money in Dun Laoghaire, Co. Dublin.

19: The IRA today announced that it would restore its 1994 cease-fire at 12 O Clock noon on the 20th July 1997, the announcement was generally welcomed but unionists were sceptical as to whether the cease-fire was tactical or permanent

20: US President Bill Clinton welcomed the new IRA ceasefire and assured Sinn Féin of US support for future negotiations. These, however, would "not fulfil all the desires of any one party or community," he cautioned.

20: Taoiseach Bertie Ahern said he was "satisfied" that there was nothing untoward about a £30,000 donation to Foreign Affairs minister Ray Burke from a building firm in the 1989 general election campaign.

20: A pig slurry leak on the rivers Martin and Shournagh, Co. Cork killed around 100,000 fish. Cork Corporation said an estimated 140,000 people nearly lost their water supply.

20: President Mary Robinson unveiled a national Famine monument, a 26 ft by 20 ft bronze coffin ship, at the foot of Croagh Patrick, County Mayo in front of 2,000 people.

21: Paedophile priest Brendan Smyth had shown no remorse for his victims, Dublin Circuit Criminal Court heard. One of the victims, giving evidence, said he hated Smyth so much he could kill him. Others had attempted suicide and suffered broken marriages or mental illness.

21: The Fianna Fáil/PD government announced plans for an ethics commission with a status similar to that of the High Court, as suggested in a Fianna Fáil submission to the Dunnes tribunal. It would scrutinise he tax affairs of members of the Oireachtas and local authorities.

21: Sinn Féin entered Stormont for preliminary talks. Representatives said if admitted to the all-party talks they would pursue a united, independent Ireland.

21: Irish Steel was valued at £100m, just 14 months after the government sold it for a nominal £1. Its new owners, Ispat International, announced plans for a £2.8m flotation in early August.

21: Dublin emerged as a favourite city break destination with British tourists in a new survey. It reached the top 10 for the first time, trailing Paris, Amsterdam, Bruges, Brussels, Barcelona, Rome, Prague, Venice and Madrid.

21: A national strike at Bus Éireann was avoided after an 11th-hour intervention by the Minister for Public Enterprise, Mary O'Rourke. She called on the company to defer introducing the new urban minibus routes and asked the unions to cancel their strike action.

21: Six people died in a collision between a car and a lorry on the Dublin to Belfast road near Drogheda. The truck driver and the car's five passengers, including two 16-year old girls, all died in the accident.

22: Relatives of five of the 33 people killed in the Dublin and Monaghan bombings in 1974 said they would bring their case to Europe, based on the RUC's failure to establish a murder inquiry.

22: The 14-year old plastic bullet victim who had spent three days in a coma after being shot in the wake of the Drumcree parade was released from hospital today.

22: The Department of Foreign Affairs stopped all funding for new projects to Goal, the relief agency. The Department said Goal's accounts had shown irregularities, a claim hotly disputed by the agency.

22: The Special Criminal Court set 12 January 1998 as the trial date for the case against Paul Ward, the man accused of killing journalist Veronica Guerin last year.

22: The paedophile Brendan Smyth, charged with 74 sex abuse offences, offered a public apology to his 20 victims in a statement read out in court where the priest had never spoken.

23: MEPs from various EU member states backed calls for the release of files relating to the 1974 Dublin and Monaghan bombings. The UVF claimed responsibility, but the victims' families claim the RUC hampered Garda investigations and say British intelligence was involved.

23: The VHI announced a 9% premium increase, bringing their total increase to 33% over the past four years.

23: The Limerick 2000 Broadcasting Group gained the Limerick local radio franchise after the IRTC's won a long legal battle with the former franchisees, Radio Limerick, over a breach of contract.

23: Three Christian Brothers and a former member of the order, all in their 50s and 60s, appeared on a total of 51 indecent and common assault charges at Galway District Court.

23: The GAA shelved plans to honour former Kilkenny hurling star Martin Coogan because of his convictions for the sexual abuse of two young girls in the 1980s.

23: Sunday Independent counsel Michael McDowell stressed that the paper had never intended to portray Mr de Rossa as a criminal. However, the Workers' Party had been born out of the republican movement and IRA training camps were as lethal in the 1060's as in the 1990s.

23: The Anglo-Irish decommissioning document was rejected by the unionist parties at the Stormont talks. Both governments said this would not derail the start of substantive negotiations on 15 September.

24: Unionists must stay in the talks to win the propaganda war, said UUP leader David Trimble. It was possible to make the process work and Sinn Féin would sooner or later sign up to a partitionist settlement. The Belfast Newsletter advised unionists to pay close attention to his words.

24: Triple murderer Brendan O'Donnell died at Dublin's Central Mental Hospital. There were no obvious signs of suicide but he had attempted to take his life a few days ago.

24: The Revenue Commissioners announced a crackdown on those whose lifestyle does not match their declared income. This followed the discovery of £38m in bank deposits during the Dunnes tribunal. Jail sentences would now be imposed in blatant tax evasion cases, a spokesman said.

24: The Birmingham Six announced that they would seek compensation in the European Court after British Home Secretary Jack Straw told them he would not meet them or re-evaluate their case. The Six were wrongly imprisoned for 16 years and received £200,000 each in compensation plus interim payments. But Jack Straw did apologise for the miscarriage of justice.

25: Bertie Ahern met SDLP leader John Hume and Sinn Féin president Gerry Adams in Dublin. In a joint statement, the three reiterated their commitment to a peaceful solution to the Northern question. Bertie Ahern also invited David Trimble, the UUP leader, to meet him in Dublin.

25: Nationalists in Castlewellan cancelled a planned protest against a loyalist band parade after residents and band representatives hammered out a deal in direct discussions.

25: Cayman banker John Furze, a key source of information on Charles Haughey's financial affairs, died four days after undergoing heart surgery in the US.

26: Mother of four and former UDR member Janet O'Donaghue was found strangled in her Armagh home. A 23-year old man was charged for her murder later in the week.

27: The battered body of 16-year old James Morgan from Castlewellan, Co. Down, was found in a water-logged pit full of animal parts where his killers had dumped him. He had disappeared after hitching on Thursday. The RUC said it did not suspect a sectarian motive.

27: A west Belfast man beaten for joyriding hung himself on the railings of a Belfast motorway. He had appealed for more youth facilities at an anti-joyriding meeting only hours before he took his life.

28: Co. Down man Norman James Coopey (26) was charged with the murder of Castlewellan teenager James Morgan. The RUC now said it could not rule out a sectarian motive for the killing in an about-turn on its previous statements.

28: A 23-year old was arrested in connection with the murder of Janet O'Donaghue in Armagh two days ago. A second man was also charged with the murder of teenager James Morgan.

29: The government set Thursday, 30 October, as the date for the presidential election.

29: Aid agency Goal agreed to co-operate with a departmental audit of its accounts and reversed its claims that the Department of Foreign Affairs was conducting a vendetta against it.

29: The de Rossa libel trial took another twist when a garda said he found wastepaper bags full of experimental prints of £5 notes in a Workers' Party building in 1983.

30: The Blood Transfusion Service Board asked 500 women to come forward for testing amidst fears that they may have received contaminated anti-D in the 1970s. Statistically, the BTSB expected 50 of them to have hepatitis C.

30: The British government admitted two further instances of radioactive material being dumped in the Irish Sea, one in 1957 and the other in 1976. Earlier this month, it had admitted that up to two tonnes of radioactive waste were dumped in Beaufort's Dyke.

30: The number of farm accidents had halved over the past five years, according to a Teagasc study.

31: The Rainbow government knew of BTSB negligence in the manufacture of anti-D, yet it still contested the case brought by the late Brigid McCole. The Government denied BTSB liability for 17 months and admitted it two weeks before Ms McCole's death, it emerged today.

31: Independent Newspapers faced one of the largest libel bills in the history of the state after the High Court awarded £300,000 in damages to Proinsias de Rossa over an article written by columnist Eamon Dunphy. The costs for this and previous hearings will total £1.5m.

31: There were four new BSE cases reported in Irish cattle in July, bringing the total for 1997 to 41 so far. In 1996, 74 BSE cases were recorded.

AUGUST

01: Relatives of hepatitis C victim Brigid McCole said they would consider legal action against the state following today's publication of the report on the Rainbow government's legal strategy. The BTSB admitted ordinary liability but had threatened to fight her in court over aggravated damages.

01: The Supreme Court ruled that two U2 concerts could go ahead in Lansdowne Road, overturning last month's High Court judgement.

01: A 24-year old Protestant building worker was found dead near his home in Larne. Two men were arrested five days later in connection with his murder.

02: The Garda announced 2,000 new road checkpoints to curb speeding over the holiday weekend. **03:** Munster's bank holiday weekend was a wash-out with a month's rain falling in just over 12 hours.

03: Hundreds of people commemorated the nine Claudy people killed by three car bombs in 1972. An inter-denominational service was held in the village. No paramilitary organisation ever claimed responsibility for the explosion on the day the British army entered no-go areas in Derry.

04: Positive Action, the group representing women infected by anti-D, said it would establish a public forum where politicians from this and the previous government could explain their actions. Around 4,000 women who received potentially contaminated anti-D in 1990 had remained untested.

04: The IRA had stopped all action in the first two weeks of its cease-fire, said the RUC.

04: Garda riot squads broke up an eight-hour clash between 200 members of two Traveller families in Navan, Co. Meath.

05: Elderly people had claimed £7.5m in assistance for security measures such as window locks, door chains and alarm systems over the past 18 months, said the Department for Social, Community and Family Affairs.

05: Derry's Bogside Residents Group gave a cautious agreement to the 9 August Apprentice Boys parade in the city after the RUC announced that it would reroute feeder parades in Bellaghy, Dunloy and on Belfast's Lower Ormeau Road. The BRG cancelled its planned protests.

05: Northern Secretary Mo Mowlam and Sinn Féin's Gerry Adams held their first face-to-face talks since the IRA announced its new cease-fire.

06: A helicopter crash in the Lebanon claimed the life of one Irish soldier, Sgt John Lynch, and four Italian soldiers on UN duty. The crash was blamed on a mechanical fault or pilot error.

06: The breakaway Loyalist Volunteer Force admitted it tried to kill a Catholic taxi driver in Co. Armagh.

06: The Church of Ireland Gazette's editorial urged the unionist parties to "hasten to the table" as long as the IRA cease-fire continued, even though they would talk to "the agents of IRA murderers." Decommissioning should not become "a ploy" to prevent negotiations.

06: A 67-year old Co. Clare farmer was found drowned in a flooded field near Ballyvaughan as rainfall let up in Munster and South Leinster and the River Suir in Clonmel began to fall.

07: Foreign Affairs minister Ray Burke denounced newspaper reports that he had received £30,000 in political contributions as "a vicious campaign of rumour". He had received £30,000 from Joseph Murphy Structural Engineers as long-standing Fianna Fáil supporters, he said.

07: The cost of living increased by 1.2% over the past 11 months, latest figures showed.

08: An Irish woman was jailed for four months in Cyprus

for falsely accusing three Irish soldiers of raping her.

09: The government won a working majority in the Seanad elections with 23 seats for Fianna Fáil, 16 for Fine Gael, four for Labour and six for independents. The PDs did not stand. Ten outgoing senators (four FG, three FF, one each DL, Labour and Independent) lost their seats.

09: The Apprentice Boys' march in Derry, the first in three years to be unopposed by nationalists, saw scuffles after loyalist bandsmen attacked nationalist onlookers in the city centre. Earlier in the day, Craigavon Bridge had been blocked off following a bomb warning.

09: The Royal Black Preceptory cancelled its planned march through the nationalist village of Newtownbutler, Co. Fermanagh.

11: A split emerged in Fianna Fáil with some TDs and senators backing John Hume as a potential presidential candidate and others supporting Albert Reynolds.

11: Lightning and more torrential rain triggered 10,000 business alarms, blacked out 10,000 homes and businesses, and put Aer Lingus' reservation system out of action.

12: Ireland's economy should grow by 7% and create 89,000 new jobs in the next two years, said the latest report by the Economic and Social Research Institute.

12: Total investment in the construction sector would surge by 15% in 1997, the ESRI said. Irish exports were forecast to rise by 11% and the gross domestic product should also notch up 11% growth. But the Institute predicted a £49m, or 20%, fall in agricultural output due to the bad weather.

12: Sinn Féin MP Martin McGuinness began a court challenge to the rule demanding the oath of allegiance to the Queen of Westminster members.

12: The UUP's Ken Maginnis and Sinn Féin's Martin McGuinness met head-on in a televised debate on the BBC's 'Newsnight' programme.

12: Limerick barman Noel Pyper (48) was beaten to death in a frenzied attack. The Gardaí later said he may have been killed because he opposed drug dealing on his premises.

12: A mere 1% of radio listeners were tuning in to Radio Ireland, listenership figures revealed,

13: There were fears about the future of over 3,000 Fruit of the Loom jobs in Derry and Donegal when the US headquarters served redundancy notices on Irish directors Willie and John McCarter and finance director Seamus McEleney.

13: Tourism Minister Dr Jim McDaid ordered Bord Fáilte to return the shamrock to Ireland's tourism logo

14: Sinn Féin president Gerry Adams received a US visa from Secretary of State Madeleine Albright.

14: John Gilligan, the self-confessed "prime suspect" for the murder of Veronica Guerin, had smuggled 17 tonnes of cannabis into Ireland over three years and owned £20m in "dirty money", a prosecutor told London's Woolwich Crown Court where Gilligan was standing trial.

14: Fruit of the Loom said jobs in its Irish operations were safe. It appointed Andy McCarter to take over the seven plants.

15: An acute skills shortage in the computer sector prompted the announcement of 2,000 new college places by Education Minister Michael Martin at a cost of £5m.

16: Gardaí found an IRA bomb factory in a Co. Cavan farmhouse, the biggest such operation discovered in recent years. It contained remote-control technology for driverless car bombs but was not thought to have been operational in recent weeks.

16: Catherine and Carl Doyle, the parents of four children, were found stabbed to death in Carane, Co. Roscommon, where they had moved under the Rural Resettlement Scheme. Two days later, a Dublin man was charged with their murder.

18: The British government downgraded the security status of 13 republican prisoners in Britain, promising to move them out of Special Secure Units and into main prison accommodation.

19: In a controversial move, Belfast's Queens University students union took down English-Irish signs after a consultants' report said they created a "chill factor" for Protestant students. The union has a policy to promote bilingualism in its day-to-day running.

21: Brendan Smyth, the convicted child-abusing priest, died of a heart attack in the Curragh prison, Co. Kildare, one month into his 12-year sentence for 74 sexual offences.

24: Author and journalist Helen Lucy Burke interrupted a Dublin mass to tell the priest that his sermon amounted to "an apologia for Brendan Smyth" and did not show compassion for the victims.

25: The McCracken tribunal report said former Taoiseach Charles Haughey had obstructed or hindered the tribunal for which he could face two years in jail or a £10,000 fine. Former transport minister Michael Lowry could also face prosecution for evading tax and exchange control rules.

25: The Revenue Commissioners said they would take immediate action against Charles Haughey and Michael Lowry who used offshore accounts for serious tax evasion. There were also no records of Ben Dunne's £400,000 payments for the extension to Mr Lowry's house.

25: Double European swimming champion Michelle Smith de Bruin arrived to a triumphant reception in Dublin, including Sports Minister Jim McDaid who had said he would not be there.

25: Under a new programme by the Irish Society for the Prevention of Cruelty to Children, Leanbh, begging children will be pointed out to the gardaí who will then track down the parents.

26: Former Taoiseach Charles Haughey may face not only a £10,000 fine or imprisonment for obstructing the tribunal, but also up to £1m in legal costs and tribunal expenses, it emerged.

26: Foreign Affairs Minister Ray Burke and Northern Secretary Mo Mowlam signed an agreement establishing an independent international commission on decommissioning.

26: Eight delegates to an international social work conference were refused visas under Ireland's stringent new immigration laws. Six were from Ghana and two from Pakistan. The Irish Association of Social Workers was "embarrassed" about the Department's decision.

27: Freak weather claimed two more lives as two men were found dead in their cars after a night of floods in west Cork, west Limerick and Co. Waterford.

27: The Rose of Tralee contest was buffeted by such strong winds that the organisers were forced to postpone the event, normally held in a canvas dome, by a day.

27: A man who lost three family members in the 1974 Dublin bombings was refused permission to inspect Garda files detailing the investigation by the High Court.

27: Magill magazine, the current affairs periodical published between 1975 and 1991, re-appeared on the shelves with a title picture of Charles Haughey captioned "Grotesque".

28: The cabinet met and approved in principle the establishment of a new payments to politicians tribunal.

28: The Department of Justice received 244 divorce applications since the legislation became operational on June 27. Of these, 64 were granted.

28: Northern Secretary Mo Mowlam worried unionists when she told the Belfast Telegraph she did not define consent in numerical terms. She later reassured them that only the majority of people in Northern Ireland could change its status.

29: Sinn Féin received the green light to enter the Stormont talks when Mo Mowlam assessed the IRA cease-fire as being genuine.

29: Taoiseach Bertie Ahern and British Prime Minister Tony Blair joined forces and appealed to unionists to join the talks on 15 September. The UUP had one week left to decide whether or not to take its seats.

30: Two Dublin teenage girls burned to death in a derelict building where they had slept rough for the night. Caoimhe Wall and Sarah-Jane Lawrence, both 16, could only be identified by their dental records. They were believed to have built a fire to keep themselves warm.

31: British Prime Minister Tony Blair said a devolved Northern assembly within the United Kingdom and increased north-south co-operation were "the twin foundations" for the North's future.

SEPTEMBER

02: Flags on all government buildings should be flown at half-mast during Princess Diana's funeral next Saturday, the Republics government decided. Books of condolences have been opened throughout the island and in Northern Ireland both unionists and nationalists queued up to sign.

03: An unnamed senior Ulster GAA personality was to be charged with over 70 sexual offences, the Garda confirmed.

04: Accidents at work soared by 21% from 13,400 to 16,900 last year, the Health and Safety Authority revealed. Twice as many people were off work with occupational illnesses as in 1995 but fatal accidents at work decreased from 78 in 1995 to 59 in 1996.

04: More than 600 guests paid $500 a head to hear Sinn Féin MPs Gerry Adams and Martin McGuinness and TD Caoimhghín Ó'Caoláin speak at a Sinn Féin fund-raising dinner at New York's prestigious Waldorf Astoria Hotel.

04: Shops,libraries and businesses in both nationalist and unionist areas of Northern Ireland said they would close on the morning of the Princess's funeral.

05: Taoiseach Bertie Ahern backed up his Foreign Affairs Minister Ray Burke, saying that the £30,000 donation to Burke had "nothing to do with corruption and dishonesty."

05: Drug addicts caused two out of three Dublin crimes in a bid to pay for the £29m worth of heroin consumed per year. But they rarely committed violent offences, new Garda figures showed.

05: The Garda said it would seek the extradition of John Gilligan, the self-confessed prime suspect in the Veronica Guerin murder, to face charges of importing cannabis and possessing firearms.

05: Annette Mangan, the woman who had wrongly accused three Irish soldiers of raping her in Cyprus, was released from Nicosia central prison and returned to Ireland.

05: Some 200 women now fed their drugs habit through prostitution in Dublin, a conference heard.

08: Mary Robinson paid her last visit as Irish president to the North. Previous trips had angered unionists, particularly her handshake with Gerry Adams in 1993.

08: SDLP leader John Hume turned down the chance to stand as a candidate for the Irish presidency, ending weeks of speculation. It would have been "a great honour", he said, but he felt a duty to stay with the SDLP at this "crucial stage" of the peace process.

09: Foreign Affairs Minister Ray Burke said a united Ireland would best facilitate economic progress but insisted that only the majority of Northern Irish people could end partition.

09: Sinn Féin signed up to the Mitchell Principles, binding the party to exclusively peaceful means in pursuing its goals and paving the way for its entry to the Stormont talks.

09: One of the last Catholic families on the loyalist Bellykeel estate in Ballymena finally left its home of 33 years after a petrol bomb attack.

10: Foreign Minister Ray Burke told the Dáil that he had not exchanged any favours for the £30,000 donation from building firm JMSE which he had received during the 1989 general election. He said the book was now closed on this issue.

10: Drogheda multi-millionaire and cannabis smuggler Paddy Farrell (49) and his 29-year old girlfriend, Lorraine Farrell were found dead with gunshot wounds in her mother's home. Later, her family claimed that the couple had made a suicide pact.

10: Twenty Irish lung cancer sufferers and relatives announced that they would sue tobacco companies in the High Court, following recent successful cases in the US.

10: Taoiseach Bertie Ahern paid tributes to Mother Theresa, the Albanian-born leader of the Sisters of Charity, who had died of a heart attack on 5 September in Calcutta, she was given a full Indian State funeral.

11: The government mooted plans to bill financial institutions for the costs of jailing debtors they were prosecuting for outstanding debts.

11: In an interview with An Phoblacht, the republican newspaper, an IRA spokesman said he did not agree with all of the Mitchell principles to which Sinn Féin had signed up this week. The statement caused major concern amongst unionists and led to calls for Sinn Féin's expulsion from the Stormont talks.

12: President Mary Robinson signed her official resignation and boarded a Geneva-bound jet to take up her new job as UN Commissioner for Human rights.

12: A bomb exploded in Drogheda city centre, close to a hackney business run by the partner and mother of Lorraine Farrell who had been found shot dead with her boyfriend two days ago. Gardaí ruled out any paramilitary involvement

13: A witness who was said to have agreed to testify against self-confessed drug dealer and murder suspect John Gilligan was placed under police protection. Another witness was already in protective custody. Gilligan remained in London where gardaí were applying for his extradition.

15: The UUP delegation stayed away from Stormont's Castle Buildings where the Alliance Party, Labour, the SDLP, Sinn Féin and the Women's Coalition attended the first day of talks.

15: Donegal County Council became the first council to nominate Dana (Rosemary Scallon) for the presidential candidacy. It was followed the same day by Kerry, Longford, Tipperary and Wicklow, making Dana the first officially selected candidate.

16: A large bomb exploded in Markethill, Co. Armagh. There were no injuries. The hardline Continuity Army Council, linked to Republican Sinn Féin, later claimed responsibility.

16: The Labour Party nominated anti-nuclear campaigner Adi Roche for the presidential elections. Fine Gael put forward MEP Mary Banotti. She was endorsed by the Greens and Democratic Left.

17: Belfast law lecturer Prof. Mary McAleese ousted former Taoiseach Albert Reynolds in a surprise victory as Fianna Fáil's presidential candidate. She gained 62 votes compared to the former Taoiseach's 48 at the end of what was labelled the "anyone but Albert" campaign.

17: The UUP returned to the Stormont talks and said it would demand Sinn Féin's exclusion on the grounds that the IRA had publicised "difficulties" with the Mitchell principles.

17: Ireland's embattled tourism logo emerged in a redesigned version, replacing the previous logo, launched only last November, which featured two embracing figures. A sole, stylised shamrock was chosen to represent Ireland abroad.

18: The government announced an unprecedented inquiry into the reasons for a 25% house price increase in Dublin and by substantial amounts in other areas.

18: Russia relaxed its ban on Irish beef imports from eight counties and re-admitted beef from Co. Wexford. It had only one BSE case this year compared to eight in 1996.

19: The Northern Ireland Office said Economy Minister Adam Ingrain had not been consulted over the new all-Ireland tourism logo. The Northern Ireland Tourist Board would continue to use the previous logo of two embracing figures with a small shamrock, the NIO said.

20: Around 170 hardline loyalists returned to picket Harryville's Catholic church. They had interrupted their 41-week picket when mass was cancelled over the summer but vowed to resume and continue the pickets.

21: Presidential candidate Adi Roche faced allegations of bullying from 13 former employees and members of the Chernobyl Children's Project. Two employees resigned in protest at a policy document penned by Ms

Roche which said employees should be taken "by the scruff of the neck" and taken through procedures "in baby steps." The group of employees, calling itself The Concerned Group Not Supporting Adi Roche for President, held a press conference in Cork.

21: The British government had met the IRA for 25 years, according to a former MI6 man, Frank Steele, who set up the first meetings in 1972.

23: The UUP failed to oust Sinn Féin from the Stormont talks over allegations that it was inextricably linked with the IRA which disagreed with some of the Mitchell principles. The BBC screened a programme alleging that Sinn Féin president Gerry Adams had been a senior IRA figure.

23: The government appointed High Court judge Michael Moriarty to head up the new payments to politicians tribunal.

24: In a major breakthrough in the Northern talks, the unionist parties dropped their demand for upfront decommissioning of republican arms and all parties agreed to move on to substantive negotiations next week. Canadian General John de Chastelain who appeared to be the unionists preferred candidate was appointed as chair of the independent commission on illegal arms decommissioning. This was the first time in 70 years that unionists and republicans sat at the same talks table.

24: The leader of the UK Unionist Party, Robert McCartney, received the second letter bomb in two months. It was defused by the army.

24: Ennis was named as Ireland's Information Age Town in a competition and stood to receive £15m in hi-tech IT investment from Telecom Éireann and private companies to transform it into a showcase for the future.

24: Irish workers gained an extra day's statutory leave when the Minister of State for Labour, Tom Kitt, signed the Working Time Act into force. There are now 16 official holidays a year.

24: A former soldier turned state witness against self-proclaimed murder suspect John Gilligan, was told he would not be charged in connection with journalist Veronica Guerin's murder. But Charles Bowden (32) pleaded guilty to drugs and firearms charges at Dublin's Circuit Criminal Court. The Irish authorities were still fighting for Gilligan's extradition from Britain.

26: Clare county council nominated former garda Derek Nally as the fifth candidate for the presidency. Mr Nally is the founder and president of Victim Support, a group dedicated to helping the victims of crime.

28: Loyalists who resumed their picket outside Harryville chapel eight days ago vowed to extend their protest to Catholic churches in Lisburn, Ballycastle and Dervcock. They insisted that they would picket until the Orange Order received permission to parade through the village of Dunloy.

29: The first man entered the race for the presidency when Derek Nally gained nominations from Wexford, Carlow, Kildare and South Dublin county councils in addition to that of Clare which he had obtained last week.

29: Some 1,000 unionists and supporters of the DUP and UKUP gathered in Belfast's Ulster Hall for a rally entitled "Ulster's Crisis - Where Now?". DUP leader Ian Paisley claimed the peace talks were a sell-out and demanded an immediate referendum on the union with Britain.

29: The garda said a former TD and senator, who cannot be named for legal reasons, would be charged with 70 sexual abuse offences this week. Ex-pupils of the former teacher had complained of abuse dating back up to 30 years.

30: Tory Leader William Hague paid his first official visit to Northern Ireland. He did not meet any political leaders.

30: Gardaí detained five Romanian stowaways who had jumped from a container lorry near Youghal, Co. Cork.

30: Unionist and republican delegates at the Stormont peace talks agreed the format for substantive negotiations on Northern Ireland's future. Discussions on the three strands, dealing with the North's internal government, with North-South relations and with Anglo-Irish relations, were all due to begin on Tuesday, 7 October.

Stormont All-Party Talks
Proposed Seating Arrangements

"Not only was there not a gunfight, not only did he not fire any shots, but it now appears that he didn't even have a weapon. We have to start asking questions about his involvement or his alleged involvement."

Gerry Adams speaking about the death of Irish youth, Diarmuid O'Neill at the hands of British police during raids on alleged IRA suspects in London.

"I am fearful that there may have been a policy of shoot-to-kill in this instance."

John O'Donoghue (Fianna Fáil spokesperson on Justice), following the revelation that Mr. O'Neill was unarmed when he was shot.

"Mr. O'Neill may be dead but there would be many other people dead if the IRA's objectives were achieved in London."

John Bruton (Taoiseach), after the explosives find in London.

"He came, he saw, he did a runner. To use the word chicken would be unfair to chickens."

Lord Williams, counsel for Albert Reynolds in his action against *The Sunday Times*, on Fergus Finlay's failure to take the witness stand.

"I haven't eaten for days. I'll never do the Lotto again."

Mary Kelly, from Co. Cavan, who won half of the £7.4 million jackpot.

"Don't mess about with the Irish. We are a proud people and we won't take it."

Albert Reynolds (Former Taoiseach), talking about the British at a Fianna Fáil fund-raiser in New York.

"Zero Costs."

Foreman of the jury in the Albert Reynolds's libel trial stating the amount of damages that should be awarded to the former Taoiseach.

"It is unjust and immoral to win on the substantial issue of the case and then for somebody to ask you to pay the costs of the person you defeated."

Albert Reynolds after his victory

in the Sunday Times libel case.

"We handed a letter to the Minister of Justice a short time ago with seven questions. The reason we handed it to her is to make sure she received it."

Mary Harney (Leader of the Progressive Democrats) on the ongoing row in Dublin over the Judge Lynch affair.

"It was a DUP Councillor who started the recent disgraceful protests outside Roman Catholic chapels in north Antrim without any thought for the basic unionist tenet which upholds civil and religious liberty for all."

Ken Maginnis (Ulster Unionist security spokesman), blaming Ian Paisley's DUP party for igniting the trouble at Harryville.

"Their right to worship is an inalienable one and should be defended."

Ian Paisley (DUP leader), condemning the Harryville protests.

"It was disloyal of Mr. Blair to have married a Roman Catholic. I think if he can turn one way, he can turn in the management of the country."

Robert Saulters (the new Grand Master of the Orange Order) on Tony Blair (the British Prime Minister and leader of the Labour Party). The comment was made previous to his election as Grand Master.

"Nick Faldo would like to lease our two courses, underwrite any debt and build us a new clubhouse and I suppose he wants to upgrade both courses."

A Ballyliffin golf club member commenting on Nick Faldo's proposal to develop the Donegal club.

"Heaney is not only a Nobel prize-winner but he represents some of the most powerful, original and energetic work in the language. Other poets admire him to the level of idolatry. He is the poet of poets."

Malcolm Bradbury (writer) on Seamus Heaney.

"I didn't intend to maim, disable or disfigure anybody. My Mother died

last Wednesday. That was the reason I frightened them off. She asked me to (let her) die with dignity, that's why I frightened them."

Gerrit Isenboerger (German national) who shot three bailiffs who arrived at his Cavan home, to evict him.

"We know there are two roads before us. One is the road to further conflict and the other is the road to the negotiating table. We have declared ourselves in favour of travelling to the negotiating table. There is nowhere else for us to go."

Martin McGuinness (Sinn Féin's chief negotiator), speaking at the 25th Bloody Sunday commemoration.

"Politics demands - and rightly demands - energy, commitment, idealism and resilience. When politics demands - and wrongly demands - that a T.D.'s family members serve as expendable extensions of the elected member, I will not serve."

Maire Geoghan-Quinn (Fianna Fáil TD), in her statement of resignation from Irish politics in the June elections.

"He was smiling at me when it happened. He was just there and so nice and somebody killed him."

Lorraine McElroy, the woman grazed by a sniper's bullet which killed British soldier Lance Bombardier Stephen Restorick in Armagh.

"This has been going on for a long time and has taken its toll on the family. The majority of people in this country believe in Michelle. They know that Michelle won these medals fair and square and its unfortunate that certain people, for their own agenda, have written these articles discrediting her achievements."

Brian Smith (Michelle Smith's father), on ongoing innuendo that the triple Olympic gold medallist swimmer had improved her performance by taking banned substances.

"There was a crisis in Tiananmen Square after a month in which the civil authority was being defied, and they took action about it. Very well. We can criticise it in exactly the same way as people criticise Bloody Sunday in Northern Ireland, but that isn't by any means the whole story. Why can't we look at the rest of his achievement?"

Sir Edward Heath (former British Prime Minister), speaking on a BBC television programme.

"To make an electoral pact with Sinn Féin without an IRA ceasefire would be the equivalent of asking our voters to support the killing of innocent human beings by the IRA."

John Hume (leader of the SDLP), commenting on the lack of an electoral pact with Sinn Féin.

"Keep your rosaries off our ovaries."

Words on a placard of a student campaigner calling for the right of choice on matters relating to abortion.

"It has been a difficult decision for me and I have, with great reluctance, decided not to seek a second term in office."

Mary Robinson (President of Ireland) announcing she would not put herself forward for a second term.

"She was the best President we ever had."

John Bruton (Taoiseach) on Mary Robinson.

"I truly believe that no words of mine can ever adequately apologise to the 1,600 women and men for the damage done to them by a system in which they had previously placed their fullest trust and confidence."

Michael Noonan (Minister for Health), on the hepatitis C scandal.

"Human error is the simple and only explanation for what occurred."

Liam Dunbar (the Chief Executive of the Blood Transfusion Service Board), on the fact that women infected with hepatitis C through contaminated anti-D, were asked to donate blood last year.

"For those who did have hurtful experiences, I apologise and ask forgiveness."

Brother Edmund Garvey (Congressional Leader of the Irish Christian Brothers).

"Have we reached a stage that we are now no more than units of traffic going home from A to B with total disregard to what is going on around us?"

Judge Cyril Kelly who expressed dismay that the only civilian to help a young woman being attacked in a Dublin street was an English tourist.

"The Taoiseach boasted in 1994 that he was the best person to make peace with unionists. Two and a half years on he made no progress. Fianna Fáil as a party that represents nationalist Ireland, is better placed to reach an historic compromise with unionism, if anyone can."

Bertie Ahern (Fianna Fáil leader) on the handling on the peace process by the then Taoiseach John Bruton.

"They have gone away, you know."

Gerry Adams (Sinn Féin President), in a subtly-amended reference to a comment he once made about the IRA - 'They haven't gone away, you know' - about John Major and Margaret Thatcher.

"When I'd hear of someone's financial problems I'd say *yes, sure.*"

Ben Dunne on his alleged payments of £1.3 million to former Taoiseach Charlie Haughey.

"Look there's something for yourself."

Ben Dunne's alleged words to Charles Haughey, when, according to Mr. Dunne, he gave Mr. Haughey three bank drafts worth £210,000.

"Thank you big fella."

Charlie Haughey's response, according to Ben Dunne.

" I think my mum set about five or six churches back home ablaze, she was lighting so many candles."

Ken Doherty (Dublin snooker player) after winning the Embassy World Snooker Championship in Scotland.

"The Church was in a ferociously vulnerable position and, as a result of cover-ups in the past, may have over compensated by allowing the pendulum to swing to the other extreme. My case may restore the balance and I think the church authorities must begin to conceive of a situation when an allegation is made and the person is innocent."

Fr. Edward Kilpatrick (Donegal Parish Priest), speaking after he was cleared of sexually abusing two young altar boys.

"I am ready to make one further effort to proceed with the inclusive talks process. My message to Sinn Féin is clear. The settlement train is leaving. I want you on that train. But it is leaving anyway, and I will not allow it to wait for you. You cannot hold the process to ransom any longer. So end the violence and end it now."

Tony Blair (British Prime Minister) announcing that his government will meet with Sinn Féin representatives without a ceasefire being in place.

"The train Mr. Blair is referring to is the Dublin train and we will not be on it."

Rev. Ian Paisley (DUP leader) gives his reaction to Mr. Blair's speech.

"We should be very happy today. The sun was out this morning and the rainbow will be out in a few weeks."

Mary Harney (Leader of the Progressive Democrats) speaking as the 27th Dáil was dissolved.

"The rainbow always prevails over the shower."

John Bruton (Taoiseach and Leader of Fine Gael) reacting to Mary Harney's comments.

"I think the sad epitaph of this rainbow government will be: Here lies the rainbow, red, white and blue, which worked for itself but never for you."

Bertie Ahern (Leader of Fianna Fáil) adds to the rainbow platitudes.

"I'm being cagey in what I say and quite consciously so. But I am saying - because it's a matter of record - that it was a Fianna Fáil government which helped initiate the peace process and a Fine Gael led government that squandered it."

Gerry Adams (Sinn Féin President), when asked if he wanted to see Mr. Ahern as Taoiseach.

"As John Bruton himself said, a vote for Sinn Féin is a vote for murder. Two out of three of the nationalist community in Mid Ulster voted for murder and they will live to regret it. It's not the power of the ballot box, it's the bullet."

William McCrea (former Mid-Ulster MP), reacting to Sinn Féin's success in the local government elections.

"The club would like to express its disgust. This could lead to what happened to Sean Brown. It was a very ominous statement, very provocative. People in the area are very angry. He's making them sound as if they're legitimate targets. We call on him to withdraw the statement."

A spokesperson for Sean O'Leary's GAA club in Newbridge commenting on Rev. McCrea's claims.

"It has been an unsatisfactory election campaign. Most of the important questions have gone unanswered."

Vincent Browne (broadcaster and columnist) on the Irish elections of June 6th.

"One point that has occurred to us is: is it possible for it to be worse than Dick Spring? It might be."

David Trimble (Leader of Ulster Unionist Party) on the Republic's new government.

"Too often, in an Irish context, Celtic or Gaelic culture has been identified with Catholicism and nationalism, which has had the effect of inhibiting those of the Protestant and unionist tradition from claiming part of their inheritance."

Mary Robinson delivering a lecture in Scotland's only gaeltacht on St. Columba's Day.

"If you look at the motivation behind that gesture, it's a really genuine, sincere effort to reduce tension and therefore it has to be welcomed. I would like to see that sort of generosity of spirit, that regard for others, reciprocated."

Ronnie Flanagan (RUC Chief Constable), on the suspension of Mass at Harryville church.

"Those who governed in London at the time failed their people through standing by while a crop failure turned into a massive human tragedy."

Tony Blair (British Prime Minister), apologising for the failure of British authorities to tackle the famine which claimed one million Irish lives and led to mass emigration 150 years ago.

"That's the one thing that I've done in my life, apart from having children, that I'm really proud of doing."

Sinead O'Connor (Dublin pop singer) on tearing up the picture of the Pope.

"It signifies a bold step towards the creation of a partnership amongst the political traditions in this divided city; a partnership in which there is neither victory nor defeat but the triumph of tolerance."

Alban Maginnis, of the SDLP, on his election as Lord Mayor of Belfast, ending a century of unionist control at City Hall, Belfast.

"Can the PD's live with Fianna Fáil's cosy relationship with Sinn Féin?"

Prionsias De Rossa (Democratic Left leader).

"[The words of] a desperate man trying to save a drowning government."

Albert Reynolds (former Taoiseach), in reply to Mr. De Rossa.

"I was really angry and I can find no pity for him now. This brings back terrible memories. I've a photo of my brother on the wall. He was a wonderful man, and when I think of the way they left him, like a piece of meat that a butcher would put on a block."

Charlie Neeson, brother of one of the victims of the Shankill Butchers, speaking after Bate's death.

"One thing about Bertie is that he is trustworthy. If you have a private meeting with him it stays private. He keeps his word."

David Trimble (leader of the Ulster Unionist Party), on the Fianna Fáil leader Bertie Ahern.

"A terrible shame."

A local Garda in Monaghan commenting on the election of Caoimhghin O'Caolain in the Cavan / Monaghan constituency on the first anniversary of the death of Garda Jerry McCabe.

"If I had the authority to do it, I'd order you to be flogged."

Judge Keiran O'Connor to a teenager who kidnapped and sexually assaulted a five-year-old boy.

"A simple stark choice in terms of balancing two evils. I had to take a course of action that would result in less violence, and I'm talking about serious violence, and I am talking about serious violence. I'm talking about the risk of loss of life."

Ronnie Flanagan (RUC Chief Constable) on why he made the decision to allow Orangemen to march down the Garvaghy Road.

"Anyone being faced down or anyone being pushed through is a bad decision. I was aware last weekend what was likely to happen. Now we are in a position where it has happened. I certainly am disappointed with that. I regret it."

Bertie Ahern (Taoiseach) expresses open criticism at the decision to allow the parade.

"The security forces behaved in a way that was deliberately provocative. I witnessed plastic bullets being fired at eye level and people being beaten with batons. Such use of plastic bullets was a flagrant breach of the RUC's own guidelines."

Patricia McKenna (Green MEP), an independent observer at the Garvaghy Road.

"Your voice is not ignored. I understand your feelings and will address them in legislating on this issue. I am only sorry that option was not open to me this summer."

Mo Mowlam addressing nationalists.

"I don't intend to speak to that woman again."

Breandán Mac Cionnaith (Garvaghy Road residents representative), on Mo Mowlam.

"I have seen this kind of thing in Sharpeville in 1960 with the Saracens moving in. I was shocked to see the anxiety of mothers over their children and the brutality of the police. It reminded me of South Africa where the police would remove people by dragging and beating them."

Gora Ebrahim (South African independent observer and MP) on events at the Garvaghy Road.

"I wish to thank the chairman for yesterday's adjournment. As a result of reviewing the excellent work of the tribunal and considering the very helpful documentation recently received from Mr Ben Dunne's solicitor, I now accept that I received the £1.3m from Mr Ben Dunne."

Charles Haughey's statement to the Dunne's Payment Tribunal.

"The leadership of the IRA are announcing a complete cessation of military operations from 12 o'clock midday on Sunday, July 20, 1997. We have ordered the unequivocal restoration of the ceasefire of August 1994."

The announcement from the IRA which raised hopes of a negotiated and political settlement in the North of Ireland.

"I don't see the word permanent. I don't see anything that indicates this is long term or something that is based on a new strategy. We can all engage in wishful thinking but we have got to come back to reality."

Ken Maginnis (UUP security spokesman) giving his reaction to the ceasefire.

"Who ever done that, I have no feelings for them. I can forgive them ... but God might never forgive them. But if it was [sectarian] we do not want any repercussions or people claiming reprisals ... and if her death means it is the last death in this country, then maybe it is worth something and we can live in peace."

Laurence Martin, father of 18-year old Bernadette Martin shot dead by loyalists as she slept in the home of her Protestant boyfriend in Aghalee, Co. Down.

"Any good deed I have done I've left it without any strings attached."

Ben Dunne, denying that he expected anything in return for the £1.3 million he gave to the former Taoiseach, Charles Haughey.

"I said it had come to my knowledge that my brother had given him £1.1m. He was totally relaxed about

it, and he said: 'I can't be responsible for what your brother says' ... He said he felt my brother was unstable. That was the line of the conversation ... He neither confirmed nor denied it to me."

Margaret Heffernan, Ben Dunnes' sister, who asked Haughey to return the money.

"Certainly there would be no place in our party today for that kind of past behaviour, no matter how eminent the person involved or the extent of their prior services to the country."

Bertie Ahern, April 1997.

"I had tremendous respect for him and I continue in my own way to respect him. It would have crossed my mind ... [that] it would not have been nice to see our Prime Minister in huge financial difficulties."

Ben Dunne on why he gave money to Charles Haughey.

"If a serving Taoiseach received £1.3m from one donor, he was obviously open to receive donations from others ... I want to know, for instance, if payments were made privately to Mr Haughey from the beef industry."

John Bruton (former Taoiseach and Fine Gael leader).

"The Provos pulled a fast one with their ceasefire, expecting there would be the usual knee-jerk reaction of unionists losing their temper, shouting their heads off, and that the world consequently would say: 'Oh look, there's those republicans making a positive move and there are the unionists behaving like that - the real problem is unionism."

David Trimble (UUP leader), on the IRA ceasefire.

"While the great majority of these cases occurred 20 to 30 years ago I recognise them all for what they were: sins against God, offences against individual persons and offences against the laws of the state. I take this opportunity to renew sincerely and wholeheartedly my deep sorrow and regret for any psychological hurt or trauma any of the these young people may have experienced as a result of their association with me in the Republic of Ireland ... Whatever sentence the court decrees I will be happy to

serve in full, should the Lord spare me, knowing it is God's holy will for me, at this time and in this place."

Brendan Smyth's statement to the court. He was jailed for 12 years.

"I hate Smyth so much I could kill him. All my life I have feared that man. From this day forward I do not fear him anymore."

Victim of paedophile priest Fr. Brendan Smyth in the High Court in Dublin.

"The Hepatitis C/Anti-D issue is the biggest health scandal in the history of the State ... The approach adopted [by the government] was bereft of compassion or sensitivity to Mrs McCole or to the interests of others who were infected through the negligence of a State institution."

The Macken report on the hepatitis C scandal.

"The IRA have wound it down completely. It's completely dead. I have never seen it as quiet. There is no targeting, no surveillance. Everything has gone silent."

RUC officer commenting on the IRA ceasefire.

"All pints at £1.50 during the flood - goldfish races at 4.30pm."

Sign outside Kitty Keily's flooded bar in Clonmel, Co. Tipperary.

"The attitude of Charles Haughey in relation to the Tribunal has been such as might amount to an offence ... All relevant papers will be sent to the Director of Public Prosecutions for his consideration and decision as to whether Charles Haughey should be prosecuted ..."

Report of the Dunnes payments to politicians tribunal.

"Michelle, we love you, don't mind the begrudgers!"

Fan of the swimming champion welcoming her home amidst continued unsubstantiated allegations of drug use by the swimmer.

"I was determined that justice and rightness was on my side."

Prionsias de Rossa (Democratic Left leader), after being awarded £300,000 after a jury found the article written by Eamon Dunphy to be libellous.

"All we can hope is that the first hammer blows to his head killed our son."

Philomena Morgan, mother of 16 year-old James, who was murdered by Loyalists in Co. Down.

"What the heck has the man got?"

Editorial in the Sun newspaper reacting to the news that more than 8,000 people flocked to Daniel O'Donnell's tea party in Donegal.

"I don't blame people for thinking it's a joke. I thought it was a joke, too, at first."

Sheila Brown (Dana's mother), commenting on her daughter's campaign to replace Mary Robinson as President of the Republic of Ireland.

"Criticising Dana is like clubbing a baby seal - there may be good reasons for the cull, but with those big eyes looking up at you, you'd have to be an awful swine to do it."

Fintan O'Toole (Irish Times columnist), replying to charges of anti-Catholicism.

"These people are complete hypocrites. Their argument was that even if the loyalist paramilitaries did not do anything, they should not officially call a ceasefire."

David Ervine, (Progressive Unionist Party spokesperson), claiming DUP members agitated against the loyalist ceasefire of 1994.

"They know me for 20 years. They know the experience I have, that I am very suitable for the job and that I'm going out there to win."

Albert Reynolds (former Taoiseach), 90 minutes before his party, Fianna Fáil, voted to nominate Professor Mary McAleese as its presidential candidate instead.

"With Ulster Unionists at the table, there will be no united Ireland; there will be no joint sovereignty; no joint authority, actual or disguised; the Anglo-Irish diktat and the illegal territorial claim will under constant attack."

David Trimble (UUP leader), after re-entering the Stormont talks.

Unacceptable and untrue ... quite unbelievable ... equally unbelievable ... not believable ... most unlikely ... incomprehensible, factually incorrect ... quite incredible."

Mr. Justice McCracken, commenting on former Taoiseach Charles Haughey's testimony at the tribunal.

Charles J. Haughey -
Then and Now!

OBITUARIES

Ahern, Dr. John J. Born 1911. Former Bishop of Cloyne. Last surviving Irish Bishop to have attended all sessions of the Second Vatican Council. Died Cork September.

Baird, Bill Leading architect, specialising in georgian buildings. Admitted to the Fellowship of the Royal Institute of the Architects in Ireland. Assisted in the foundation of Kilbarrack Sailing Club. Died May.

Blume, Herbert (Nicky) Worked in the motor industry - car assembly. Director of Fiat Auto Ireland. Agent for German fish-processing equipment in Ireland.

Bourke, Kevin Musician. Died March.

Brady, Charles Born America 1926. Served in US Navy. Enrolled in the Arts Students League in 1948. Came to Ireland in 1956. Appointed Guard at the Metropolitan Museum. Avid painter, specialising in landscapes. Lecturer of Painting at the National College of Art and Design during the 1970's. Member of Aosdána. Died Dublin August.

Browne, Dr. Noel Born Waterford 1915. Elected T.D. in Dublin for Clan na Poblachta in 1948. Appointed Minister for Health in 1948. Co-ordinated a campaign to eradicate T.B., Introduced the 'Mother and Child Scheme' in 1951. Resigned from government in 1951. Co-founder of the National Progressive Democratic Party (1958-1963). Died Galway May.

Brown, Nigel Joined the Irish Times in the early 1960's as a journalist, responsible for the formation of the Irishman's / Irishwoman's Diary. Died June.

Butler, Susan Born 1905/1906. Promoter and enthusiast of Kilkenny Arts.

Byrne, Eamon President of the St. Vincent de Paul Society, representing the Society abroad. Governed the Dublin Branch of the Multiple Sclerosis Society.

Cameron, Dick Born America 1929. Spent 15 years as a folk singer, psycho-analyst.

Channing, Austin Managing Director of the People Newspapers. Editor of Ireland's Own magazine.

Wrote and published Motoring Life, Motoring Correspondent with Independent Newspapers.

Childers, Lt.-Col. Bobby Born London 1911. Son of Erskine. Staff Officer to the Chief-of-Staff (1941-1945), Lt.-Col. (1945-1956).

Clonmore, Elennor Born Dublin 1914. Architect. Senator of the Labour Party. First Woman Fellow of the Royal Institute of Architects in Ireland. Countess of Wicklow. Died Dublin February.

Collins, Liam Born 1923. Nephew of Michael Collins. Graduated as Solicitor in 1943. Died March.

Collins, Tom Born Clare 1949. Basketball official - helped to develop and promote the game throughout Irish schools. Died March.

Connolly, James C. Involved in Peace Keeping Forces for over 35 years. Joined Garda Síochána in 1952. Joined United Nations Field Service in 1956. Died Dublin January.

Cowan, Dr. Adrian W. D. Qualified as a dentist 1941. First vice-dean of Faculty of Dentistry at Royal College of Surgeons in Ireland (1963-1966) and Dean (1966-1969), President of the Irish Dental Association (1977-1978).

Crowley, Flor Born Cork 1934. Elected to Fianna Fáil in 1965, lost his seat in 1981 and elected to Seanad. Died Cork May.

Dand, David Born Dublin 1932. Businessman, responsible for the success of Baileys Irish Cream. Died January.

Delany, Cathleen An actress, made theatrical debut in the Gate Theatre in 1933 at the production of Agamemnon of Aeschylus before touring London and Egypt. Starred in a number of film productions such as 'December Bride' and 'The Dead'. Last appeared on stage at the Gate Theatre in May.

Dillon, Eoin General Manager of Aer Lingus London Tara Hotel, Shelbourne Hotel and Gresham Hotel, Catering Manager at the Shelbourne Hotel. Assisted in the foundation of Irish Hotels and Catering Institute. Named 'Hotelier of the Year' in 1987. Died August.

Dillon-Mahon, Luke Managing director and Chairman of Arks advertising agency in Dublin. Awarded honourary life fellowship of the Institute of Advertising Practitioners of Ireland. Founder and Director of the Samaritans in Galway (1976). Died July.

Donohue, Fred Born Roscommon. Civil servant, elected to Roscommon County Council in 1947, moving to Dublin County Council in 1954. Joined the Health Authority in 1960. Involved in the formation of Eastern Health Board in 1971. Community Care Programme Manager since 1971.

Doolan, Dr. Bridget Born Waterford. Joined the Cork School of Music (1956), progressing to Director (1973-1992). Member of the Music Faculty at Waterford RTC, Member of the European Piano Teachers' Association. Member of the Arts Council.

Doran, Eamon Born Meath 1938. Vintner and restaurateur. Died March.

Doyle, Ursula Born 1931. Entertainer. Producer and director.

Finnegan, John Theatre Critic.

Friess, Dean Herbert Friedrich Born Germany 1909. Rector of Crossmolina in 1964. Dean of Killala (1968-1973). Died Mayo March.

Furlong, Declan Born 1967. Rugby player with Barnhall rugby club. Died February.

Gibb, Rosy Born Dublin 1942. One of the first females to join the magic circle, entertained as a clown and toured England with the British Council. Awarded the Craig Trophy from the International Brotherhood of Magicians in 1996. Died July.

Gilligan, Edward Born Westmeath 1907. Land Agitator during the 1930's. General secretary of the Land League. Died Mullingar February.

Hand, Michael Born Louth 1937. Journalist with the Sunday Press (1963-75), The Sunday Independent (1975-76), The Sunday Tribune. Editor of the Sunday Independent (1984), Died Dublin July.

Hanna, Vincent Born Belfast 1939. Industrial Correspondent with the

Sunday Times in 1969. Joined the BBC in 1969. Co-presented 'A Week in Politics' on television and guest-presented 'Talkback' on BBC Radio Ulster. Died July.

Healy, Dr. Kevin G. Born Louth 1920. Lecturer in dental surgery, pathology and pharmacology at Trinity. Honourary treasurer of the faculty of dentistry at the Royal College of Surgeons in Ireland in 1976. Dean of faculty (1981-84). Died January.

Healy, Martin Born 1957. Writer. Editor of Force 10 magazine. Died Sligo March.

Hennebry, Tom Born Waterford. Surgeon in English hospitals, Fellow of the Royal College of Medicine, Fellow of the British Orthopaedic Association. Died February.

Herzog, Chaim Born Belfast, 1928. Studied law and called to the Bar in 1942. Ambassador to the United Nations (1975-1978). President of Israel from 1983. Died April.

Judge, Joseph Senior associate editor of the National Geographic magazine.

Kemmy, Jim Born Limerick 1936. Editor of Limerick Socialist (1972-81) and Limerick Journal since 1979. Founder member of the Democratic Socialist Party (1982) and President. Elected to Dáil as Independent (1981). Joined the Labour Party (1991), Vice-Chairperson of Labour Party (1991-92), Chairperson (1993-1997), Member of British-Irish Parliamentary Body since 1993, Member of Limerick City Council (1974-1997), Mayor (1991-92), Died September.

Kerney-Walsh, Dr. Micheline Born France 1919. Historian, lectured Spanish in Salamanca University highlighting the bonds between Spain and Ireland. Assistant Director of the Overseas Archives. Developed an account of Hugh O'Neill's life - 'Destruction by Peace'. Made a Dame of the Order of Isabel la Catolica, by the King of Spain. Died May.

Lappin, Mary Born Sligo 1929. Public Relations Officer of Yeats Summer School. Promoted the works of young poets. Radio Correspondent for the Irish Press (1972-78). Died July.

Lever, Professor Nora Teacher of Speech and Drama. Founder of the 37 Theatre Club, Professor from the Royal Academy of Music, Concerned about animal welfare - founded the Cats' Protection League. Died January.

Lewis, Cecil Born 1898. Airman with the Royal Flying Corps from 1915. Scriptwriter for BBC in the 1920's, won an Oscar for his screenplay of 'Pygmalion' in 1938. Died January.

Lewis-Crosby, J.E.C. Born Dublin 1919. Founder member of Radio Eireann Singers. Manager of the Radio Eireann Symphony & Light Orchestra. Secretary General of CEMA (Arts Council for Northern Ireland). Director of the National Trust of Northern Ireland (1960-1979). Founded the Ulster Coastline Appeal in 1962. Fine Arts Consultant with Christies of London (1979-1990).

Lloyd-Blood, Nevil Born Dublin 1921. Studied law, called to the Bar in 1950. Editor of the Irish Law Reports. Died January.

McAuliffe Curtin, John Born 1917. President of the Royal College of Surgeons in Ireland (1974-76). Founder and Past President of the Irish Otolaryngological Society. Assisted in the development of the School of Speech Therapy. Died April.

McCollum, Stanley T. Born 1918. Consulting Surgeon in various Dublin hospitals. Regius Professor of Surgery at Trinity College from 1973, Vice-President (1974) and President (1976) of Royal College of Surgeons in Ireland. Died Dublin March.

McDonagh, Maire General secretary of the Association of Secondary Teachers, Ireland (1958-83). Elected to the Executive committee of FIPESO, the secondary teachers' international association in 1973.

McGirr, Paul Born Tyrone 1980. Played gaelic football for the Tyrone Minor football team, died as a result of an accidental collision while scoring the winning goal during an Ulster football minor championship match with Armagh. Died June.

McHugh, Kevin Born Zambia 1970. Grew up in Ireland (Donegal), Contributed regular US stories of Irish interest to Irish newspapers. Arts and entertainments editor of the New York paper, Irish Echo. Died America September.

McMenamin, Liam Donegal State solicitor (1957-1982). District Judge in 1982, working in Dublin, Galway and Limerick, returning to Donegal in 1986.

Mason, Ronald Born Ballymena 1926. Head of Programmes for BBC Northern Ireland (1970-1976). Founded Radio Ulster in 1975. Head of Radio Drama at BBC London from 1977. Died London January.

Moore, Henry William Served with the British Army during the Second World War, Founder and Chairman of the Irish Parachute Club.

Moriarty, Dr. Paddy Born Kerry 1926. Chairman of the RTE Authority (1979-81). Chief Executive (1981-91) and Chairman (1991-96) of the Electricity Supply Board. Board member of Siamsa Tiro, Kerry Airport and Leopardstown Racecourse. Awarded 'Kerry Person of the Year' in 1991. Died June.

Mulhare, Edward Born Cork 1923. Appeared in film, theatre and television. Leading man of the Liverpool Repertory Company. Replaced Rex Harrison in the Broadway production of My Fair Lady. Died America May.

Murphy, Professor Thomas Born Wexford 1915. Medical officer with Bord na Mona (1943-48). Assistant Medical Officer of Health (1948-51), advancing to the Department of Health in 1951. Appointed to the new Chair of Social and Preventative Medicine in UCD in 1955. Appointed Dean of the Faculty of Medicine (1962). Appointed Registrar of UCD (1964). Appointed President of UCD (1972). Member of the Higher Education Authority (1968-72), Deputy Chairman of the Board of Management of the Mater Misericordiae Hospital (1986-88). Appointed Chairman of the Primary Education Review Body in 1988. Chairman of the National Council for Curriculum and Assessment (1990-95). Chairman of the Philatelic Advisory Committee (1984-96). Died June.

Naughten, Senator Liam Born Westmeath 1944. Senator and Seanad Leas-Chathaoirleach (1989-1996).

Nolan, Jim Born 1929. Director of the Institute of Advertising Practitioners in Ireland (1958-1995). Died January.

O'Donnell, Matthew Rev. President of Maynooth College. Professor of Philosophy in Maynooth for more than 30 years. Dean of Faculty of Philosophy.

O'Hehir, Michael Born Dublin 1920. Started commenting on gaelic sports - football and hurling in 1938. First RTE Head of Sport (1960-72). Worked with Irish Independent until 1960 and later produced a weekly column with the Irish Press. Published his autobiography 'My Life and Times' in November 1996. Died November.

O hEocha, Colm Born Waterford 1926. President of University College Galway. Chairman of the New Ireland Forum. UCG's First Professor of Biochemistry in 1962. Chairman of the National Science Council in 1967. Pro-vice Chancellor of the National University of Ireland. Chairman of the Arts Council. Chairman of the Interim Local Radio Commission. Died Galway May.

O'Neill, Chris Producer, dramatist, writer, actor and director. Died America, April.

O Síocháin, Seán Born Cork 1914. General Secretary/ Director General of the GAA (1964-1979). Starred in various Drama productions on Radio Éireann. Founder Member of the Alert Movement Against Drink and Drug Abuse. Died Dublin, February.

Patterson, George G. Managing director (1970-1976) and Chairman (1970-1982) of Lyons Irish Holdings. Died December 1996.

Pyle, Fergus Born Dublin 1935. Journalist, covering Europe and Northern Ireland. First European Correspondent for the Irish Times, Editor of the Irish Times in 1977.

Died Dublin, April.

Reilly, Dr. Noel Born 1916. Secretary General of the Irish Medical Association from (1958-1983). Died March.

Rosen, Albert Born Austria 1924. Principal Conductor of the RTE Symphony Orchestra (1968-1981). Resident Conductor of the Prague National Opera. Director of the Smetana Opera in Prague. Died Dublin, May.

Siegmund-Schultze, Dorothea Head of English Literature at the University of Halle, Wittenberg, Germany. Founded the biennial Halle conferences on Ireland: Culture and Society in Ireland (1976-1988).

Slevin, Gerard Born Cork 1919. Entered Civil Service in 1944, worked in Genealogical Office. Assistant to the Chief Herald. Appointed Chief Herald (1954-1981). Died January.

Smyth, Fr. Brendan A member of the Norbertine Order. Convicted of numerous charges of child abuse on both sides of the border. Died August.

Smith, Paul Born Dublin 1920. Novelist. Died January.

Sweeney, Clair L. Born 1923. Worked in the engineering department of Dublin Corporation. Interested in waterways and published his work - 'Rivers of Dublin' in 1991. Presented with the Lord Mayor's Award in 1988 for his work. Died June.

Twomey, Eileen Born Cork.

Appointed Naturalist in the Fisheries Branch of the Department of Agriculture (1953). Progressed to Inspector of Fisheries in 1966, focusing on salmon conservation. Member of the International Council for the Exploration of the Sea, progressing to Chairman. Died Dublin June.

Twomey, Michael Born 1930 Cork. Hotel worker with the Ritz Hotel in London, progressing to Head Waiter in the exclusive 'Palm Court' serving royalty, film stars, musicians and politicians. Died July.

Wall, Mervyn Born Dublin 1908. Novel writer. Civil Servant. Programme Assistant of Radio Eireann in 1948. Secretary of the Arts Council. Died Dublin May.

Walsh, Sean Secretary of the National Union of Tailor and Garment Workers. Member of the Executive Council of Irish Congress of Trade Unions (1972-75). Member of the Employment Appeals Tribunal (1974-80). Died May.

Woodcock, Joseph A. Born 1919. Consultant Anaesthetist and First Director of the Artificial Kidney Unit at Jervis Street Hospital. Founded and directed the Pensions Information Service. Dean of the Faculty of Anaesthetists of the Royal College of Surgeons. Founded the Credit Union in Rathgar, Represented Ireland (Shooting) at the 1968 Olympics in Mexico. Died August.

POLITICS

The Peace Process

*By **Ken Reid**, Ulster Television.*

ELECTIONS, Elections and then more elections - that seemed to be the weary path for politicians, voters and journalists in 1997. Irish and British General Elections, local government and finally the Irish presidential campaign.

Just for good measure the Stormont talks are finally appearing to find some sort of shape, although don't hold your breath waiting for the outbreak of sweetness and light outside the Castle buildings.

As far as political progress is concerned, the Labour victory at Westminster is probably the most significant event. It is already clear Tony Blair recognises he has a limited amount of time to get things moving and he's not waiting about.

Within two weeks of entering Downing Street, he was in Belfast telling Sinn Féin the train was leaving and a new IRA ceasefire was needed if they were to get their ticket.

Lo and behold, by the end of July, the ceasefire was in place and Gerry Adams was on his way to the talks table. All this has been hard for the unionists to take. David Trimble and his party decided to go to Stormont, but predictably, the D.U.P. and the U.K. Unionists have opted out. So where does this leave the process?

What is clear is that the governments are using the framework documents as the basis for negotiation. This, it is envisaged, will lead to some form of devolution for Northern Ireland, following Scotland and Wales.

There will also be North-South bodies, possibly co-ordinated by some sort of council. There will also be the potential for the powers in this area to be expanded in coming years. A referendum is due to be held north and south of the border to underscore any agreement.

Nonetheless, things are moving. Significantly, the United States is playing the honest broker and expect Bill Clinton to make occasional helpful interventions.

Peace . . . time will tell.

The author is the political editor for U.T.V.

POLITICS R.O.I.

INTRODUCTION TO THE REPUBLIC OF IRELAND

Explanatory Notes on the President, Parliament and Government

The Republic of Ireland is a parliamentary democracy. The Oireachtas (parliament) consists of the President and the Legislature, which has two houses - Dáil Éireann, which is a house of representatives, and Seanad Éireann, which is a senate. The basis of the political system was set out in the 1937 Constitution of Ireland, enacted by referendum. As such, the power of the Oireachtas remains vested in the people.

Presidential elections are held every seven years, and the President is elected by the direct vote of the people.

The 166 Teachta Dála (members of the Dáil) in Dáil Éireann are also elected directly by the people by a system of proportional representation and a single transferable vote. General Elections must be held at least once every five years. Seanad Éireann has 60 Seanadoirí (members of the Senate); 11 are nominated by the Taoiseach, 6 are elected by the graduates of Trinity College Dublin and the National University of Ireland, and the remaining 43 are elected by five panels. The electoral constituency of the Seanad comprises the incoming T.D.s, the outgoing members of the Seanad, and the members of county councils and county borough councils.

Eighteen is the age at which a person becomes eligible to vote, and candidates for the Dáil or Seanad must be aged 21 or older.

THE OFFICE OF PRESIDENT OF IRELAND.

The office and function of the President of Ireland is dealt with in Articles 12 and 13 of the Constitution. The President is Head of State only, and although she/he does not have any executive powers and acts only on the advice and authority of the government, she/he does hold a limited number of functions. All Bills passed by the Oireachtas are promulgated by him/her and she/he may, after consultation with the Council of State*, refer any Bill (excluding money Bills) to the Supreme Court to attest its constitutionality.

The President appoints the Taoiseach on the nomination of Dáil Éireann and appoints government ministers on the advice of the Taoiseach. The Taoiseach also advises him/her on accepting the resignations of ministers, and on the summoning and dismissing of the Dáil (she/he reserves the right of refusing to dissolve the Dáil but this right has, as yet, never been exercised).

The supreme command of the defence forces is vested in the President (subject to the 1954 Defence Act), and she/he receives and accredits ambassadors. The President is elected by the direct vote of the people, anyone entitled to vote in general elections can vote in a Presidential election. A Presidential candidate must be an Irish citizen over the age of thirty-five. The duration of a term of office is seven years and a President may serve no more than two terms.

*The members of the Council of State are the incumbent Taoiseach, Tánaiste, Ceann Comhairle, Cathaoirleach of the Seanad, Attorney General, President of the High Court and the Chief Justice. Other members are any previous Taoisigh, President, or Chief Justice willing to serve and up to seven nominees of the President him/herself.

STATE EMBLEMS OF THE REPUBLIC OF IRELAND

Name of State, National Flag, Emblem, and National Anthem

NAME OF STATE: Article 4 of the 1937 Constitution states 'The name of the State is Éire, or in the English language, *Ireland* '. From independence in 1922 until the enactment of the constitution the state was known as Saorstat Éireann or the Irish Free State. The Republic of Ireland Act 1948 allowed for the state to be described as the the Republic of Ireland, but Article 4 naming the state as Éire has not been altered.

The name Éire is derived from the name Ériu, a goddess in Irish mythology. Julius Caesar gave Ireland its Latin name when he referred to it as *Hibernia* in the first century B.C., while the second century Greek cartographer Ptolemy referred to Ireland as *iouernia*.

THE NATIONAL FLAG: Article 7 of the Constitution states 'The national flag is the tricolour of green, white and orange'. The tricolour is rectangular, the width being twice the depth. The colours are of equal size, vertically disposed with the green closest to, and the orange furthest from, the staff. It was the official flag from independence and its position was formally enshrined in the Constitution. In 1848 Thomas Francis Meagher - a member of Daniel O'Connell's Repeal Association - received the tricolour as a gift from the citizens of France (on whose flag the Irish tricolour is no doubt based). Initially a flag of the 'Young Ireland' movement it came to be identified as the national flag in the aftermath of the 1916 Rising when it was flown from the G.P.O.

The colours signify the union between older Gaelic and Anglo-Norman Ireland (green) and the newer Protestant Planter Ireland (orange), while the white, in Meagher's words 'signifies a lasting truce between the Orange and the Green'.

THE ARMS OF STATE: The Arms of State have no official statute or regulation, but the President's seal of office has an heraldic harp engraved on it. It is also emblazoned on the President's standard as a gold harp with silver strings on a sky blue background. The harp - modelled on the 14th century Brian Boru harp - is depicted on the coinage and banknotes of the state and is used by all government departments.

THE NATIONAL ANTHEM: The national anthem is Amhrán na bhFiann (The Soldier's Song). Peadar Kearney (1883-1942) wrote the lyrics, while Patrick Heeney (1881-1911) helped him compose the music. The anthem was composed in 1907 and first published in 1912 in the newspaper *Irish Freedom*. It was immediately adopted by the Irish Volunteers and was formally adopted as the national anthem in 1926 replacing 'God Save Ireland'.

REPUBLIC OF IRELAND POLITICAL PARTIES
Main political parties in the Republic of Ireland

FIANNA FÁIL
13 Upper Mount Street, Dublin 2. Tel. (01) 6761551
http://ireland.iol.ie/fiannafail/

Founded by Éamon de Valera in 1926 Fianna Fáil (Soldiers of Destiny) comprised anti-treaty Sinn Féin members. The party did not take its seats in the Dáil until 1927. De Valera was the first leader of the party, a position he held until 1959.

Fianna Fáil has had six Taoisigh, Éamon de Valera (re-elected six times), Seán Lemass (re-elected twice), Jack Lynch (re-elected twice), Charles Haughey (re-elected three times), Albert Reynolds and the current Taoiseach, Bertie Ahern. In government, Fianna Fáil was responsible for the drafting of the Constitution in 1937, maintaining Irish neutrality during World War II and the accession of Ireland into the European Economic Community in 1973. The party introduced major housing developments in the 1960s and established the Industrial Development Authority in 1950.

The aims of the party as set out in 1926, and still broadly holding today, are to establish an agreed Ireland through inclusive political talks with structures based on partnership and equality throughout the island; to restore and promote the Irish language as a living language of the people; to develop a distinctive national life within the European context, incorporating the diverse traditions of the Irish people; to guarantee the diverse religious and civil liberties and eradicate all forms of discrimination; to develop the resources and wealth of Ireland to their full potential through a spirit of enterprise, self-reliance and social partnership; to protect the natural environment and heritage of Ireland; to maintain a balance between town and country and between the regions; to promote the family and a wider sense of social responsibility; and to reform the laws and institutions of state, making them more humane and caring.

On Europe the party aims to maintain Ireland's status as a sovereign nation within the European Union and pledges to retain neutrality but to take part in genuine peace-keeping missions. The party is allied to the Union for Europe bloc in the European parliament.

At the last election, Fianna Fáil won 77 seats and remains the largest political party in the state, a position it has held since the 1930s. The current party leader and Taoiseach is Bertie Ahern T.D., the party chairman is Dr. Rory O'Hanlon T.D., and the general secretary is Pat Farrell.

FINE GAEL
51 Upper Mount Street, Dublin 2. Tel. (01) 6761573
www.finegael.com

Fine Gael (Tribes of the Irish People) was formed in 1933 by the amalgamation of Cumann na nGaodheal, the Centre Party and the Army Comrades Association (the Blueshirts), its first leader was General Éoin O'Duffy.

The party has been in government six times, each time as the major party in a coalition. It has had four Taoisigh namely John A. Costello (twice), Liam Cosgrave, Garret FitzGerald (twice) and John Bruton. In government, the party was instrumental in the Declaration of the Republic of Ireland in 1949, the signing of the Sunningdale Agreement in 1973, the convening of the New Ireland Forum in 1983 and the signing of the Anglo-Irish Agreement in 1985. The party is committed to constitutional change and has introduced referenda which legalised divorce (1995) and approved the denial of bail to likely re-offenders (1996).

Fine Gael has a policy of facilitating enterprise through a mixture of state encouragement for private enterprise and direct state involvement. It wants to see decision making devolved to the appropriate level, particularly involving women and young people, and it promotes fairer opportunities in education, an improvement in social welfare provisions and greater tax equity. On Northern Ireland, the party recognises and respects both the nationalist and unionist traditions and believes inclusive all-party negotiations are the best way to achieve reconciliation.

In the European Parliament, the party is a member of the European People's Party grouping of Christian democrats. Fine Gael believes that Ireland's future lies within a safe and prosperous Europe.

At the last election, 54 Fine Gael T.D.s were elected and the party remains the second biggest in the Dáil. The current party leader is John Bruton T.D., the party chairman is Phil Hogan T.D., and the general secretary is Jim Miley.

THE LABOUR PARTY
17 Ely Place, Dublin 2. Tel. (01) 6612615
www.labour.ie/

The Labour Party was founded in 1912 by James Connolly, Jim Larkin and William O'Brien as the political wing of the Irish Trade Union Congress. In the interests of unity, the party did not contest the general elections of 1918 and 1921 and as a consequence lost a generation of supporters.

The party has been in government seven times, each time as a coalition partner, and its leader has held the position of Tánaiste on each occasion. In government the party's achievements reflect those of their coalition partners, and in recent times the leader, Dick Spring, has been the Irish government's main negotiator in Anglo-Irish matters. In this position he was an influential figure in the drafting of the Downing Street Declaration in 1993 and the Framework Document in 1995. In government, from 1993 until June 1997, Labour T.D.s held the important ministerial portfolios of Finance, Foreign Affairs and Education among others.

A socialist party, it hopes to use the four main tenets of socialism, namely, freedom, equality, community and democracy, to build a just society. Twelve trade unions are affiliated to the party, representing 50% of all trade union members in the state.

The party's successful campaign on behalf of its nominated candidate, Mary Robinson, in the 1990 presidential campaign remains one of their finest achievements.

In Europe, the party is a member of the Party of European Socialists.

At the last election, the Labour party saw their vote decrease and their representation in the Dáil drop to 17 T.D.s; nevertheless, it remains the third largest party in the Dáil. The current party leader is Dick Spring T.D., the party chairman was Jim Kemmy T.D. who died recently, and the general secretary is Ray Kavanagh.

DEMOCRATIC LEFT
69 Middle Abbey Street Dublin 1. Tel. (01) 8729550
www.connect/users/dl

Democratic Left was formed in March 1992, following a split in the Workers' Party. The party is organised in both Northern Ireland and the Republic.

It has been in government once, as part of a 'rainbow' coalition with Fine Gael and the Labour Party. Its leader, Proinsias de Rossa, was Minister for Social Welfare in that government.

The party is a modern, democratic and socialist organisation whose main policy document is 'Strategy 2000', published in 1993. It welcomes moves towards European union along democratic and non-military lines, wants to underline the clear separation of Church and State and is opposed to discrimination on any grounds. The party believes that the Republic's territorial claim on Northern Ireland should be removed and replaced by an aspiration for the unity of the people of the island and that the future of Northern Ireland must be decided by those who live there.

At the last election the party won four Dáil seats. The current party leader is Proinsias de Rossa

T.D., the party chairperson is Councillor Pat Brady, and the general secretary is John Gallagher.

THE PROGRESSIVE DEMOCRATS
25 South Frederick Street, Dublin 2.
Tel. (01) 6794399
http://ireland.iol.ie/pd/

Founded in 1985 by Des O'Malley, Mary Harney and other former members of Fianna Fáil following a split within that party.

The party is currently in government and was in government once before, a coalition with Fianna Fáil (1989-92). As junior coalition partners, they played an important part in Ireland's presidency of the E.C. (July-December 1990) and in securing the ratification of the Maastricht Treaty in 1992.

The Progressive Democrats are a modern, liberal party of Europe, striving to create an enterprising society, favouring further integration with Europe and believing in the devolution of some decision making to local level.

The party advocates the lowering of tax rates, the abolition of employees' P.R.S.I., the tightening of bail laws, a new constitution and Bill of Rights for Northern Ireland, increased access to adult education and the creation of more prison places.

At the last election, the Progressive Democrats won four seats and entered into a coalition with Fianna Fáil. The current party leader is Mary Harney T.D., the party chairman is Alderman Declan McDonnell and the national organiser is Garvan McGinley.

THE GREEN PARTY
5A Upper Fownes Street, Dublin 2.
http://ireland.iol.ie/resource/green/index.htm

Founded in 1981 at a public meeting in Dublin as the Ecology Party of Ireland, the party was renamed The Green Party in 1986.

It supports open government, locally based decision making, the use of renewable energy sources, recycling, neutral peace keeping in Northern Ireland, workers co-operatives and small businesses, and the wider use of public transport. The party is opposed to the depopulation of rural areas and consequent overcrowding in cities, pollution, the exploitation of animals, the control of industry by large national and multinational companies, nuclear power and weapons, land and property speculation, the exploitation of the Third World, and both state and paramilitary violence in Northern Ireland.

The party won two Dáil seats at the last General election and had two M.E.P.s elected in 1994. The party is allied to Greens in 28 other countries and is part of the Green group in the European Parliament.

The party does not have a leader per se;

instead, it elects a coordinator and a co-coordinating annually. The 1996-97 coordinator was Mary Bowers.

THE WORKERS' PARTY
28 Gardiner Place, Dublin 1. Tel. (01) 8740716
www.workers-party.org/

The Workers' Party adopted its current name in 1982, having its roots in the Sinn Féin split of 1969. The party membership was drawn from the ranks of Official Sinn Féin, and from 1977-1982, it was known as Sinn Féin The Workers' Party.

The party is organised throughout the 32 counties and has as its aim the creation, through democratic means, of a single, secular and socialist, unitary Republic on the island of Ireland.

Following a national convention in 1992, six of the seven T.D.s seceded from the party after failing to change the party's constitution and established *Democratic Left*. The Workers' Party suffered both organisationally and financially but has since recovered somewhat. The party has no representation in Dáil Éireann but does have councillors on Dublin, Waterford and Cork Corporations. The current president is Tom French and the general secretary is Pat Quearney.

MINOR POLITICAL PARTIES IN THE REPUBLIC OF IRELAND

THE COMMUNIST PARTY OF IRELAND
James Connolly House, 43 East Essex Street, Temple Bar, Dublin 2. Tel. (01) 6711943.

COMHAR CRÍOSTAÍ / THE CHRISTIAN SOLIDARITY PARTY
54a Booterstown Avenue, Blackrock, Co. Dublin. Tel. (01) 2880273.

THE NATIONAL PARTY
16 Revington Park, North Circular Road, Limerick. Tel. (061) 326599.

THE NATURAL LAW PARTY
39 Pembroke Lane, Ballsbridge, Dublin 4. Tel. (01) 6689773.

MUÍNTÍR na hÉIREANN
87 Griffith Avenue, Dublin 9. Tel. (01) 2831484.

SOCIALIST PARTY
141 Thomas Street, Dublin 8. Tel. (01) 6772592.

SOCIALIST WORKERS' PARTY
P.O. Box 1648, Dublin 9.

REPUBLIC OF IRELAND POLITICAL PARTY LEADERS
Leaders of major Irish political parties, 1922-1997

FIANNA FÁIL	
Eamon de Valera	(1926-59)
Seán Lemass	(1959-66)
Jack Lynch	(1966-79)
Charles J. Haughey	(1979-92)
Albert Reynolds	(1992-94)
Bertie Ahern	(1994-)

CUMANN NA nGAEDHEAL	
William T. Cosgrave	(1922-33)

FINE GAEL	
Eoin O'Duffy	(1933-34)
William T. Cosgrave	(1935-44)
Richard Mulcahy	(1944-59)
James Dillon	(1959-65)
Liam Cosgrave	(1965-77)
Garret FitzGerald	(1977-87)
Alan Dukes	(1987-90)
John Bruton	(1990-)

CLANN NA POBLACHTA	
Seán MacBride	(1946-65)

THE LABOUR PARTY	
Tom Johnson	(1922-27)
T.J. O'Connell	(1927-32)
William Norton	(1932-60)
Brendan Corish	(1960-77)
Frank Cluskey	(1977-81)
Michael O'Leary	(1981-82)
Dick Spring	(1982-)

PROGRESSIVE DEMOCRATS	
Desmond O'Malley	(1985-93)
Mary Harney	(1993-)

DEMOCRATIC LEFT	
Proinsias De Rossa	(1992-)

KEY TO POLITICAL PARTIES IN DÁIL ÉIREANN

D.L.	Democratic Left	Lab.	Labour
F.F.	Fianna Fáil	P.D.	Progressive Democrats
F.G.	Fine Gael	S.F.	Sinn Féin
G.P.	Green Party	S.P.	Socialist Party
Ind.	Independents		

R.O.I. POLITICS - "THE FAMILY TREE"
Origins of the main Irish Political Parties

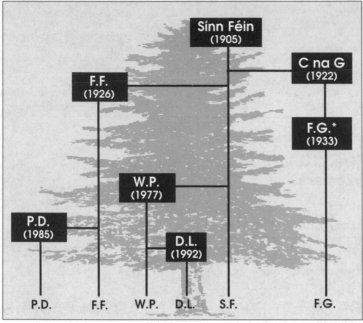
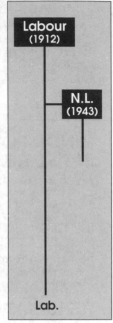

Abbreviations: **(S.F.)** Sinn Féin; **(F.F.)** Fianna Fáil; **(P.D.)** Progressive Democrats; **(W.P.)** Workers Party; **(D.L.)** Democratic Left; **(C.nG.)** Cumann na nGaedheal; **(F.G.)** Fine Gael; **(N.L.)** New Labour.
** Fine Gael: Amalgamation of **Cumann na nGaedheal, National Centre Party, Army Comrades Association.***

GENERAL ELECTION RESULTS 1997
Republic of Ireland General Election Results, June 6 1997.

CARLOW-KILKENNY
Seats: 5; **Candidates:** 11; **Electorate:** 85,097; **Turnout:** 67.15%; **Quota:** 9,409; **Elected:** Liam Alyward (F.F.) 11,849 - 1st Ct; Phil Hogan (F.G.) 9,642 - 1st Ct; John Browne (F.G.) 9,378 - 8th Ct; John Mc Guinness (F.F.) 9,310 - 8th Ct.; Seamus Pattison (Lab.) 9,026 - 8th Ct.

CAVAN-MONAGHAN
Seats: 5; **Candidates:** 12; **Electorate:** 82,129; **Turnout:** 73.23%; **Quota:** 9,925; **Elected:** Caoimhghín O'Caoláin (S.F.) 11,531 - 1st Ct; Brendan Smith (F.F.) 10,434 - 6th Ct; Seymour Crawford (F.G.) 10,288 - 7th Ct.; Andrew Boylan (F.G.) 9,706 - 7th Ct; Rory O'Hanlon (F.F.) 9,551 - 7th Ct.

CLARE
Seats: 4; **Candidates:** 12; **Electorate:** 71,505; **Turnout:** 66.24%; **Quota:** 9,378; **Elected:** Donal Carey (F.G.) 10,078 - 6th Ct; Tony Killeen (F.F.) 9,937 - 7th Ct: Síle de Valera (F.F.) 9,709 - 7th Ct; Brendan Daly (F.F.) 9,042 - 9th Ct.

CORK EAST
Seats: 4; **Candidates:** 10; **Electorate:** 63,234; **Turnout:** 68.65%; **Quota:** 8,616; **Elected:** Ned O'Keefe (F.F.) 9,295 - 6th Ct; Michael Ahern (F.F.) 9,295 - 6th Ct; Paul Bradford (F.G.) 8,733 - 7th Ct; David Stanton (F.G.) 7,735 - 8th Ct.

CORK NORTH CENTRAL
Seats: 5; **Candidates:** 14; **Electorate:** 71,873; **Turnout:** 61.8%; **Quota:** 7,335; **Elected:** Bernard Allen (F.G.) 7,746 - 1st Ct; Liam Burke (F.G.) 7,544 - 9th Ct; Dan Wallace (F.F.) 7,583 - 10th Ct; Billy Kelleher (F.F.) 7,317 - 11th Ct; Noel O'Flynn (F.F.) 6,475 - 11th Ct.

CORK NORTH WEST
Seats: 3; **Candidates:** 6; **Electorate:** 47,119; **Turnout:** 74.63%; **Quota:** 8,691; **Elected:** Michael Creed (F.G.) 9,367 - 2nd Ct; Michael Moynihan (F.F.) 9,249 - 2nd Ct; Donal Moynihan (F.F.) 8,541 - 3rd Ct.

CORK SOUTH CENTRAL
Seats: 5; **Candidates:** 15; **Electorate:** 84,288; **Turnout:** 65.73%; **Quota:** 9,174; **Elected:** Micheál Martin (F.F.) 9,652 - 1st Ct; Hugh Coveney (F.G.) 9,524 - 1st Ct; Batt O'Keefe (F.F.) 9,194 - 7th Ct; John Dennehy (F.F.) 8,975 - 9th Ct; Deirdre Clune (F.G.) 8,469 - 9th Ct.

CORK SOUTH WEST
Seats: 3; **Candidates:** 9; **Electorate:** 49,382; **Turnout:** 71.51%; **Quota:** 8,749; **Elected:** P.J. Sheehan (F.G.) 9,545 - 3rd Ct; Jim O'Keefe (F.G.) 8,841 - 3rd Ct; Joe Walsh (F.F.) 8,516 - 3rd Ct.

DONEGAL NORTH EAST
Seats: 3; **Candidates:** 8; **Electorate:** 52,459; **Turnout:** 68.53%; **Quota:** 8,883; **Elected:** Cecelia Keaveney (F.F.) 9,712 - 4th

Ct; Harry Blaney (Ind.) 9,387 - 4th Ct; Jim McDaid (F.F.) 8,244 - 5th Ct.

DONEGAL SOUTH WEST
Seats: 3; Candidates: 9; Electorate: 51,463; Turnout: 63.92%; Quota: 8,111; Elected: Mary Coughlan (F.F.) 8,203 - 6th Ct; Dinny McGinley (F.G.) 8,165 - 6th Ct; Thomas Gildea (Ind.) 7,983 - 6th Ct.

DUBLIN CENTRAL
Seats: 4; Candidates: 14; Electorate: 63,657; Turnout: 57%; Quota: 7,149; Elected: Bertie Ahern (F.F.) 12,175 - 1st Ct; Tony Gregory (Ind.) 7,546 - 7th Ct; Marian McGennis (F.F.) 7,594 - 10th Ct; Jim Mitchell (F.G.) 6,650 - 10th Ct.

DUBLIN NORTH
Seats: 4; Candidates: 13; Electorate: 64,032; Turnout: 64.85%; Quota: 8,232; Elected: Ray Burke (F.F.) 8,901 - 1st Ct; G.V. Wright (F.F.) 8,622 - 5th Ct; Nora Owen (F.G.) 8,302 - 7th Ct; Trevor Sargent (G.P.) 8,165 - 7th Ct.

DUBLIN NORTH CENTRAL
Seats: 4; Candidates: 14; Electorate: 66,345; Turnout: 65.75%; Quota: 8,634; Elected: Ivor Callely (F.F.) 11,190 - 1st Ct; Seán Haughey (F.F.) 8,901 - 2nd Ct; Richard Bruton (F.G.) 8,639 - 5th Ct; Derek McDowell (Lab.) 6,992 - 11th Ct.

DUBLIN NORTH EAST
Seats: 4; Candidates: 14; Electorate: 59,338; Turnout: 63.48%; Quota: 7,461; Elected: Michael Woods (F.F.) 7,566 - 7th Ct; Michael J. Cosgrave (F.G.) 7,748 - 8th Ct; Tommy Broughan (Lab.) 7,738 - 8th Ct; Martin Brady (F.F.) 6,745 - 10th Ct.

DUBLIN NORTH WEST
Seats: 4; Candidates: 15; Electorate: 60,169; Turnout: 61.83%; Quota: 7,340; Elected: Noel Ahern (F.F.) 11,075 - 1st Ct; Pat Carey (F.F.) 9,041 - 2nd Ct; Róisín Shortall (Lab.) 6,970 - 10th Ct; Proinsias de Rossa (D.L.) 5,933 - 10th Ct.

DUBLIN SOUTH
Seats: 5; Candidates: 14; Electorate: 90,270; Turnout: 64.61%; Quota: 9,665; Elected: Tom Kitt (F.F.) 9,904 - 1st Ct; Séamus Brennan (F.F.) 12,058 - 6th Ct; Olivia Mitchell (F.G.) 10,136 - 8th Ct; Alan Shatter (F.G.) 9,364 - 8th Ct; Liz O'Donnell (P.D.) 9,070 - 8th Ct.

DUBLIN SOUTH CENTRAL
Seats: 4; Candidates: 21; Electorate: 67,687; Turnout: 60.76%; Quota: 8,116; Elected: Gay Mitchell (F.G.) 8,910 - 1st Ct; Seán Ardagh (F.F.) 8,222 - 15th Ct; Ben Briscoe (F.F.) 8,005 - 15th Ct; Pat Upton (Lab.) 7,085 - 15th Ct.

DUBLIN SOUTH EAST
Seats: 4; Candidates: 14; Electorate: 63,619; Turnout: 58.21%; Quota: 7,335; Elected: Eoin Ryan (F.F.) 9,377 - 7th Ct; Frances Fitzgerald (F.G.) 9,567 - 9th Ct; Ruairi Quinn (Lab.) 9,043 - 10th Ct; John Gormley (G.P.) 6,801 - 11th Ct.

DUBLIN SOUTH WEST
Seats: 5; Candidates: 15; Electorate: 75,646; Turnout: 55.91%; Quota: 6,976; Elected: Brian Hayes (F.G.) 7,048 - 5th Ct; Chris Flood (F.F.) 7,346 - 7th Ct; Pat Rabbitte (D.L.) 7,037 - 7th Ct; Mary Harney (P.D.) 6,687 - 7th Ct; Conor Lenihan (F.F.) 6,485 - 7th Ct.

DUBLIN WEST
Seats: 4; Candidates: 14; Electorate: 66,421; Turnout: 60.67%; Quota: 8,015; Elected: Joe Higgins (S.P.) 8,094 - 6th Ct; Brian Lenihan (F.F.) 8,544 - 7th Ct; Liam Lawlor (F.F.) 7,797 - 9th Ct; Austin Currie (F.G.) 7,698 - 9th Ct.

DÚN LAOGHAIRE
Seats: 5; Candidates: 14; Electorate: 87,994; Turnout: 62.1%; Quota: 9,043; Elected: Seán Barrett (F.G.) 9,223 - 1st Ct; David Andrews (F.F.) 9,195 - 3rd Ct; Monica Barnes (F.G.) 9,857 - 7th Ct; Mary Hanafin (F.F.) 9,584 - 7th Ct; Eamon Gilmore (D.L.) 9,381 - 8th Ct.

GALWAY EAST
Seats: 4; Candidates: 11; Electorate: 61,078; Turnout: 71%; Quota: 8,584; Elected: Paul Connaughton (F.G.) 8,826 - 5th Ct; Ulick Burke (F.G.) 8,569 - 5th Ct; Michael Kitt (F.F.) 8,455 - 5th Ct; Noel Treacy (F.F.) 7,970 - 5th Ct.

GALWAY WEST
Seats: 5; Candidates: 14; Electorate: 76,684; Turnout: 63.5%; Quota: 8,036; Elected: Frank Fahey (F.F.) 9,321 - 1st Ct; Eamon Ó Cuiv (F.F.) 8,250 - 1st Ct; Pádraic McCormack (F.G.) 8,495 - 7th Ct; Michael D. Higgins (Lab.) 8,456 - 11th Ct; Bobby Molloy (P.D.) 8,217 - 11th Ct.

KERRY NORTH
Seats: 3; Candidates: 6;

(KERRY NORTH continued, col 3)
Electorate: 51,348; Turnout: 70.23%; Quota: 8,945; Elected: Dick Spring (Lab.) 10,699 - 1st Ct; Jimmy Deenihan (F.G.) 9,711 - 2nd Ct; Denis Foley (F.F.) 9,719 - 4th Ct.

KERRY SOUTH
Seats: 3; Candidates: 9; Electorate: 47,908; Turnout: 74.72%; Quota: 8,875; Elected: John O'Donoghue (F.F.) 10,346 - 5th Ct; Jackie Healy-Rae (Ind.) 9,163 - 5th Ct; Breeda Moynihan-Cronin (Lab.) 9,960 - 7th Ct.

KILDARE NORTH
Seats: 3; Candidates: 8; Electorate: 52,388; Turnout: 60.49%; Quota: 7,850; Elected: Bernard Durkan (F.G.) 7,932 - 3rd Ct, Charlie McCreevy (F.F.) 8,156 - 4th Ct; Emmet Stag (Lab.) 8,952 - 5th Ct.

KILDARE SOUTH
Seats: 3; Candidates: 8; Electorate: 47,030; Turnout: 62.03%; Quota: 7,203; Elected: Alan Dukes (F.G.) 7,419 - 3rd Ct; Seán Power (F.F.) 8,066 - 4th Ct; Jack Wall (Lab.) 6,870 - 5th Ct.

LAOIS-OFFALY
Seats: 5; Candidates: 12; Electorate: 83,232; Turnout: 70.42%; Quota: 9,679; Elected: Brian Cowen (F.F.) 10,865 - 1st Ct; John Moloney (F.F.) 9,800 - 4th Ct; Seán Flemming (F.F.) 10,367 - 5th Ct; Tom Enright (F.G.) 9,558 - 5th Ct; Charles Flanagan (F.G.) 9,266 - 5th Ct.

LIMERICK EAST
Seats: 5; Candidates: 14; Electorate: 76,717; Turnout: 65.24%; Quota: 8,284; Elected: Willie O'Dea (F.F.) 12,581 - 1st Ct; Michael Noonan (F.G.) 10,092 - 1st Ct; Eddie Wade (F.F.) 9,632 - 8th Ct; Desmond O'Malley (P.D.) 8,419 - 9th Ct; Jim Kemmy (Lab.) 7,173 - 11th Ct.

LIMERICK WEST
Seats: 3; Candidates: 9; Electorate: 46,763; Turnout: 72.66%; Quota: 8,407; Elected: Michael Collins (F.F.) 11,692 - 6th Ct; Dan Neville (F.G.) 8,601 - 6th Ct; Michael Finucane (F.G.) 7,330 - 7th Ct.

LONGFORD-ROSCOMMON
Seats: 4; Candidates: 11; Electorate: 63,942; Turnout: 74.82%; Quota: 9,457; Elected: Albert Reynolds (F.F.) 9,847 - 3rd Ct; Denis Naughten (F.G.) 12,868 - 7th Ct; Seán Doherty (F.F.) 9,693 - 7th Ct; Louis Belton (F.G.) 9,632 -

8th Ct.
LOUTH
Seats: 4; **Candidates:** 15; **Electorate:** 71,806; **Turnout:** 64.16%; **Quota:** 9,002; **Elected:** Dermot Ahern (F.F.) 10,192 - 1st Ct; Seamus Kirk (F.F.) 9,399 - 9th Ct; Brendan McGahon (F.G.) 8,262 - 12th Ct; Michael Bell (Lab.) 7,430 - 12th Ct.

MAYO
Seats: 5; **Candidates:** 13; **Electorate:** 87,719; **Turnout:** 71.22%; **Quota:** 10,310; **Elected:** Michael Ring (F.G.) 10,350 - 3rd Ct; Jim Higgins (F.G.) 11,163 - 7th Ct; Beverly Cooper-Flynn (F.F.) 11,087 - 7th Ct; Enda Kenny (F.G.) 10,428 - 7th Ct; Tom Moffat (F.F.) 9,676 - 8th Ct.

MEATH
Seats: 5; **Candidates:** 16; **Electorate:** 90,125; **Turnout:** 63.54%; **Quota:** 9,449; **Elected:** John Bruton (F.G.) 13,037 - 1st Ct; Noel Dempsey (F.F.) 9,518 - 7th Ct; Mary Wallace (F.G.) 9,452 - 8th Ct; John Farrelly (F.G.) 10,892 - 10th Ct; Johnny Brady (F.F.) - 10th Ct.

SLIGO-LEITRIM

Seats: 4; **Candidates:** 11; **Electorate:** 63,522; **Turnout:** 71.81%; **Quota:** 9,034; **Elected:** Matt Brennan (F.F.) 10,513 - 5th Ct; John Ellis (F.F.) 9,071 - 5th C.; John Perry (F.G.) 8,874 - 6th Ct; Gerry Reynolds (F.G.) 8,688 - 6th Ct.

TIPPERARY NORTH
Seats: 3; **Candidates:** 8; **Electorate:** 54,180; **Turnout:** 74.36%; **Quota:** 9,989; **Elected:** Michael Lowry (Ind.) 11,638 - 1st Ct; Michael O'Kennedy (F.F.) 10,196 - 2nd Ct; Michael Smith (F.F.) 9,754 - 7th Ct.

TIPPERARY SOUTH
Seats: 3; **Candidates:** 6; **Electorate:** 51,327; **Turnout:** 69.43%; **Quota:** 8,816; **Elected:** Noel Davern (F.F.) 8,995 - 1st Ct; Theresa Ahearn (F.G.) 9,117 - 3rd Ct; Michael Ferris (Lab.) 8,409 - 5th Ct.

WATERFORD
Seats: 4; **Candidates:** 13; **Electorate:** 69,662; **Turnout:** 65.26%; **Quota:** 8,960; **Elected:** Austin Deasy (F.G.) 11,277 - 7th Ct; Brendan Kenneally (F.F.) 10,080 - 9th Ct; Brian O'Shea (Lab.) 9,273 -

9th Ct; Martin Cullen (F.F.) 8,729 - 9th Ct.
WESTMEATH
Seats: 3; **Candidates:** 8; **Electorate:** 49,002; **Turnout:** 67.52%; **Quota:** 8,197; **Elected:** Willie Penrose (Lab.) 8,271 - 2nd Ct; Mary O'Rourke (F.F.) 8,233 - 3rd Ct; Paul McGrath (F.G.) 8,449 - 4th Ct.

WEXFORD
Seats: 5; **Candidates:** 10; **Electorate:** 83,776; **Turnout:** 67.28%; **Quota:** 9,282; **Elected:** Ivan Yates (F.G.) 10,024 - 1st C.; Brendan Howlin (Lab.) 9,510 - 1st Ct; Michael D'Arcy (F.G.) 11,046 - 7th Ct; John Browne (F.F.) 9,570 - 7th Ct; Hugh Byrne (F.F.) 8,416 - 8th Ct.

WICKLOW
Seats: 5; **Candidates:** 14; **Electorate:** 80,500; **Turnout:** 65.5%; **Quota:** 8,717; **Elected:** Joe Jacob (F.F.) 8,997 - 8th Ct; Dick Roche (F.F.) - 8th Ct; Liz McManus (D.L.) 8,568 - 9th Ct; William Timmins (F.G.) 8,526 - 9th Ct; Mildred Fox (Ind.) 8,348 - 9th Ct.

CURRENT POSITION OF PARTIES

PARTY	SEATS
Fianna Fáil	77
Fine Gael	54
Labour	17
Progressive Democrats	4
Democratic Left	4
Green Party	2
Sinn Féin	1
Socialist Party	1
Others	6
TOTAL	**166**

REPUBLIC OF IRELAND GOVERNMENT SYSTEM

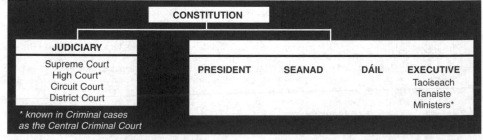

• President appoints the Taoiseach on the nomination of the Dáil. The Taoiseach is head of the executive, and the Tánaiste is his/her deputy.

• Taoiseach nominates Ministers, seeks the approval of the Dáil, and the President appoints them.

• All 166 members of the Dáil are elected by proportional representation in either a general or by-election.

• The Seanad has 60 members of which 11 are appointees of the Taoiseach, 6 are elected by graduates of Trinity College Dublin and the National

University of Ireland, and 43 are elected from five panels (representing Culture & Education, Agriculture, Labour, Industry & Commerce and Public Administration). The electorate consists of county council members, corporations of county boroughs, members of the outgoing Seanad and members of the incoming Dáil.

• Judges are appointed by the President on the advice of the Government.

• The Executive acts collectively and is responsible to the Dáil.

• Each government department has at least one Minister of State (i.e. a junior minister) attached to it.

MEMBERS OF THE EXECUTIVE ARE MINISTERS:
* Enterprise, Employment and Trade
* Finance
* Foreign Affairs
* Justice, Equality and Law Reform
* Education, Science and Technology
* Health and Children
* Environment and Rural Development
* Social, Community and Family Affairs
* Public Enterprise
* Agriculture, Food and Forestry
* Defence
* Marine
* Arts, Heritage, Gaeltacht and the Islands
* Tourism, Sport and Recreation

GOVERNMENT OF THE REPUBLIC OF IRELAND

The Government (appointed Thursday, June 26, 1997)

DEPARTMENT	MINISTER
Taoiseach	Bertie Ahern
Tánaiste	Mary Harney
Enterprise, Employment and Trade	Mary Harney
Finance	Charlie McCreevy
Foreign Affairs	Ray Burke
Justice, Equality and Law Reform	John O'Donoghue
Education, Science and Technology	Michael Martin
Health and Children	Brian Cowen
Environment and Rural Development	Noel Dempsey
Social, Community and Family Affairs	Dermot Ahern
Public Enterprise	Mary O'Rourke
Agriculture, Food and Forestry	Joe Walsh
Defence	David Andrews
Marine	Michael Woods
Arts, Heritage, Gaeltacht and the Islands	Síle de Valera
Tourism, Sport and Recreation	Jim McDaid
Government Chief Whip	*Seamus Brennan*
Attorney General	*David Byrne S.C.*

Ministers of State (appointed Tuesday, July 8, 1997)

RESPONSIBILITY	MINISTER
Department of the Taoiseach	Seamus Brennan
Defence	Seamus Brennan
To the Government	Bobby Molloy
Environment	Bobby Molloy
Education	Michael Smith
Enterprise and Employment	Michael Smith
Agriculture, Food and Forestry	Noel Davern
Transport, Energy and Communications	Joe Jacob
Health and Children	Frank Fahey
Education	Willie O'Dea
Enterprise and Employment	Tom Kitt
Tourism and Trade	Chris Flood
Environment	Danny Wallace
Agriculture, Food and Forestry	Ned O'Keefe
Marine	Hugh Byrne
Justice, Equality and Law Reform	Mary Wallace
Finance	Martin Cullen
Arts, Culture and the Gaeltacht	Eamon Ó Cuiv
Foreign Affairs	Liz O'Donnell
Health	Tom Moffat

THE TWENTY-EIGHTH DÁIL
Members of the Twenty-Eighth Dáil *(constituency in italics)*

Ahearn, Theresa: (F.G.) Ballindoney, Grange, Clonmel, Co. Tipperary; (052) 38142; *(Tipperary South)*.

Ahern, Bertie: (F.F.) 'St. Lukes', 161 Lower Drumcondra Road, Dublin 9; (01) 8374129; *(Dublin Central)*.

Ahern, Dermot: (F.F.) Hill Cottage, The Crescent, Blackrock, Dundalk, Co. Louth; (042) 39609; *(Louth)*.

Ahern, Michael: (F.F.) 'Libermann', Barryscourt, Carrigtwohill, Co. Cork; (021) 883592; *(Cork East)*.

Ahern, Noel: (F.F.) 25 Church Avenue, Drumcondra, Dublin 9; (01) 8325911; *(Dublin North-West)*.

Allen, Bernard: (F.G.) 7 Mount Prospect, Shanakiel, Cork; (021) 303068; *(Cork North-Central)*.

Andrews, David: (F.F.) 102 Avoca Park, Blackrock, Co. Dublin; Tel.2835755; *(Dún Laoghaire)*.

§Ardagh, Seán: (F.F.) 168 Walkinstown Road, Dublin 12; (01) 4566390; *(Dublin South-Central)*.

Aylward, Liam: (F.F.) Aghaviller, Hugginstown, Co. Kilkenny; (056) 68703; *(Carlow-Kilkenny)*.

†Barnes, Monica: (F.G.) 5 Arnold Park, Glenageary, Co. Dublin; (01) 2853751; *(Dún Laoighaire)*.

Barrett, Seán: (F.G.) 'Avondale', 3 Ballinclea Road, Killiney, Co. Dublin; (01) 2852077; *(Dún Laoghaire)*.

Bell, Michael: (Lab.) 122 Newfield Estate, Drogheda, Co. Louth; (041) 38573; *(Louth)*.

†Belton, Louis J: (F.G.) Kenagh, Co. Longford; (043) 22245; *(Longford Roscommon)*.

§Blaney, Harry: (Ind.) Rossnakill, Co. Donegal; (074) 59014; *(Donegal North-East)*.

Boylan, Andrew: (F.G.) Derrygarra, Butlersbridge, Co. Cavan; (049) 31747 *(Cavan-Monaghan)*.

Bradford, Paul: (F.G.) Mourneabbey, Mallow, Co. Cork; (022) 29375; *(Cork-East)*.

§Brady, Johnny: (F.F.) Springville, Kilskyre, Kells, Co. Meath; (046) 40852; *(Meath)*.

§Brady, Martin: (F.F.) 37 Grangemore Drive, Dublin 13; (01) 8484509; *(Dublin North-East)*.

Brennan, Matt: (F.F.) Ragoora, Cloonacool, Tubbercurry, Co. Sligo; (071) 85136; *(Sligo-Leitrim)*.

Brennan, Séamus: (F.F.) 31 Finsbury Park, Churchtown, Dublin 14; (01) 2957171; *(Dublin South)*.

Briscoe, Ben: (F.F.) Newtown, Celbridge, Co. Kildare; (01) 6288426; *(Dublin South-Central)*.

Broughan, Tommy: (Lab.) 23 Riverside Road, Coolock, Dublin 17; (01) 8477634; *(Dublin North-East)*.

Browne, John: (F.G.) Ballinacarrig, Carlow; (0503) 333033; *(Carlow-Kilkenny)*.

Browne, John: (F.F.) Kilcannon, Enniscorthy, Co. Wexford; (054) 35046; *(Wexford)*.

Bruton, John: (F.G.) Cornelstown, Dunboyne, Co.Meath; (01) 6620138; *(Meath)*.

Bruton, Richard: (F.G.) 210 Griffith Avenue, Drumcondra, Dublin 9; (01) 8368185; *(Dublin North-Central)*.

Burke, Liam: (F.G.) 9 Lavets Quay, Cork; (092) 892707; *(Cork North-Central)*.

Burke, Ray: (F.F.) 'Briargate', Malahide Road, Swords, Co. Dublin; (01) 8401734; *(Dublin North)*.

§Burke, Ulick: (F.G.) Eagle Hill, Abbey, Loughrea, Co. Galway; (01)6789911; *(Galway East)*.

Byrne, Hugh: (F.F.) Air Hill, Fethard-on-Sea, Co. Wexford; (051) 397125; *(Wexford)*.

Callely, Ivor: (F.F.) 'Landsdale House', 7 St. Lawrence Road, Clontarf, Dublin 3; (01) 8330350; *(Dublin North-Central)*.

Carey, Donal: (F.G.) 3 Thomond Villas, Clarecastle, Ennis, Co. Clare; (065) 29191; *(Clare)*.

§Carey, Pat: (F.F.) 69 Bourne View, Ashbourne, Co. Meath; (01) 8350544; *(Dublin North-West)*.

§Clune, Deirdre: (F.G.) Adare, Rochestown Road, Cork; (01) 6789911; *(Cork South-Central)*.

§Collins, Michael: (F.F.) White Oaks, Red House Hill, Patrickswell, Co. Limerick; (061) 355182; *(Limerick West)*.

Connaughton, Paul: (F.G.) Mountbellew, Ballinasloe, Co. Galway; (0905) 79249; *(Galway East)*.

§Cooper-Flynn, Beverly: (F.F.) 2 Manor Village, Westport Road, Castlebar, Co. Mayo, (01) 6789911; *(Mayo)*.

†Cosgrave, Michael Joe: (F.G. 22 College Street, Baldoyle, Dublin 13; (01) 8322554; *(Dublin North-East)*.

Coughlan, Mary: (F.F.) The Lodge Cranny, Inver, Co. Donegal; (073) 36002; *(Donegal South-West)*.

Coveney, Hugh: (F.G.) Laharn, Minane Bridge, Co. Cork; (021) 274474; *(Cork South-Central)*.

Cowen, Brian: (F.F.) Ballard, Tullamore, Co. Offaly; (0506) 52047; *(Laois-Offaly)*.

Crawford, Seymour: (F.G.)

Drumkeen, Aghabog, Monaghan; (047) 54038; *(Cavan-Monaghan)*.

Creed, Michael: (F.G.) Codrum, Macroom, Co. Cork; (026) 41177; *(Cork North-West)*.

Cullen, Martin: (F.F.) Abbey House, Abbey Road, Ferrybank, Waterford; (051) 51112; *(Waterford)*.

Currie, Austin: (F.G.) 'Tullydraw', Ballyowen Lane, Lucan, Co. Dublin; (01) 6265047; *(Dublin West)*.

†D'Arcy, Michael: (F.G.) 7 Annie Court, Gorey, Co. Wexford; (055) 28177; *(Wexford)*.

†Daly, Brendan: (F.F.) Cooraclare, Kilrush, Co. Clare; (065) 59040; *(Clare)*.

Davern, Noel: (F.F.) Tannersrath, Fethard Road, Clonmel, Co. Tipperary; (052) 22991; *(Tipperary South)*.

Deasy, Austin: (F.G.) Kilrush, 'Marquis', Dungarvan, Co. Waterford; (058) 43003; *(Waterford)*.

Deenihan, Jimmy: (F.G.) Finuge, Lixnaw, Co. Kerry; (068) 40154; *(Kerry North)*.

Dempsey, Noel: (F.F.) Newtown, Trim, Co. Meath; (046) 31146; *(Meath)*.

§Dennehy, John: (F.F.) Avondale, Westside Estate, Togher, Cork; (021) 962908; *(Cork South-Central)*.

De Rossa, Proinsias: (D.L.) 5 Main Street, Finglas, Dublin 11; Tel. (01) 8742513; *(Dublin North-West)*.

De Valera, Síle: (F.F.) 9 Chapel Lane, Ennis, Co.Clare; Tel. (065) 21100*(Clare)*.

Doherty, Seán: (F.F.) Coothall, Boyle, Co. Roscommon; (079) 67005; *(Longford-Roscommon)*.

Dukes, Alan M.: (F.G.) Tullywest, Kildare Co. Kildare; (045) 521912; *(Kildare South)*.

Durkan, Bernard J.: (F.G.) Timard, Maynooth, Co. Kildare; (01) 6286063; *(Kildare North)*.

Ellis, John: (F.F.) Fenagh, Ballinamore, Co. Leitrim; (078) 44252; *(Sligo-Leitrim)*.

†Enright, Tom: (FG) 3 John's Mall, Birr, Co. Offaly; (0509) 20293; *(Laois-Offaly)*.

†Fahey, Frank: (F.F.) 4 Carrig Bán, Menlo, Galway; *(Galway West)*.

†Farrelly, John V: (F.G.) Hurdlestown, Kells, Co. Meath; (046) 41290; *(Meath)*.

Ferris, Michael: (Lab.) Rosanna, Tipperary; (062) 52265; *(Tipperary South)*.

Finucane, Michael: (F.G.)

Ardnacrohy, Newcastle West, Co. Limerick; (069) 62742; *(Limerick West)*.

Fitzgerald, Frances: (F.G.) 116 Georgian Village, Castleknock, Dublin 15; (01) 8211796; *(Dublin South-East)*.

Flanagan, Charles: (F.G.) Glenlahen, Stradbally Road, Portlaoise, Co. Laois; (0502) 60707; *(Laois-Offaly)*.

§**Fleming, Seán**: (F.F.) 'Silveracre', Castletown, Portlaoise, Co. Laois; (01) 6789911; *(Laois-Offaly)*.

Flood, Chris: (F.F.) 22 Birchview Lawn, Kilnamanagh, Tallaght, Dublin 24; (01) 4518574; *(Dublin South-West)*.

Foley, Denis: (F.F.) 2 Staughton's Row, Tralee, Co. Kerry; (066) 21174; *(Kerry North)*.

Fox, Mildred: (Ind.) Lower Calary, Kilmacanogue, Co. Wicklow; (01) 2876386; *(Wicklow)*.

§**Gildea, Thomas**: (Ind.) Stranaglough, Glenties, Co. Donegal, (01) 6789911; *(Donegal South-West)*.

Gilmore, Eamon: (D.L.) 1 Corbawn Close, Shankill, Co. Dublin; (01) 2821363 *(Dún Laoghaire)*.

§**Gormley, John**: (G.P.) 71 Stella Gardens, Irishtown, Dublin 4; (01) 6609418; *(Dublin South-East)*.

Gregory, Tony: (Ind.) 5 Sackville Gardens, Ballybough, Dublin 3; (01) 8729910; *(Dublin Central)*.

§**Hanafin, Mary**: (F.F.) 7 Oaklands Drive, Rathgar, Dublin 6; (01) 4964300; *(Dún Laoghaire)*.

Harney, Mary: (P.D.) 11 Serpentine Terrace, Ballsbridge, Dublin 4; (01) 6793882; *(Dublin South-West)*.

Haughey, Seán: (F.F.) Chapelfield Lodge, Baskin Lane, Kinsealy, Dublin 17; (01) 8450111; *(Dublin North-Central)*.

§**Hayes, Brian**: (F.G.) 27 The Dale, Kingswood Heights, Tallaght, Dublin 24, (01) 6789911; *(Dublin South-West)*.

§**Healy-Rae, Jackie**: (Ind.) Main Street, Kilgarvan, Co. Kerry, (01) 6789911; *(Kerry South)*.

Higgins, Jim: (F.G.) Devlis, Ballyhaunis, Co. Mayo; (0907) 30052; *(Mayo)*.

§**Higgins, Joe**: (S.P.) 155 Briarwood Close, Mulhuddart, Dublin 15; (01) 6789911; *(Dublin West)*.

Higgins, Michael D.: (Lab.) Letteragh, Rahoon, Circular Road, Galway; (091) 24513; *(Galway West)*.

Hogan, Philip: (F.G.) 25 The Sycamores, Kilkenny; (056) 61572; *(Carlow-Kilkenny)*.

Howlin, Brendan: (Lab.) Whiterock Hill, Wexford; (053) 24036; *(Wexford)*.

Jacob, Joe: (F.F.) Main Street, Rathdrum, Co. Wicklow; (0404) 46528; *(Wicklow)*.

Keaveney, Cecilia: (F.F.) 'Loreto', Moville, Co. Donegal; Tel. (077) 82177; *(Donegal North-East)*.

§**Kelleher, Billy**: (F.F.) Ballyphilip, White's Cross, Glanmire, Cork; (021) 883846; *(Cork North-Central)*.

Kemmy, Jim: (Lab.) Died on September 25, 1997.

Kenneally, Brendan: (F.F.) 38 Viewmount Park; Waterford; (051) 55964; *(Waterford)*.

Kenny, Enda: (F.G.) Tucker Street, Castlebar, Co. Mayo; (094) 22299; *(Mayo)*.

Killeen, Tony: (F.F.) Kilnaboy, Corofin, Co. Clare; (065) 41500; *(Clare)*.

Kirk, Séamus: (F.F.) Rathiddy, Knockbridge, Dundalk, Co. Louth; (042) 31032; *(Louth)*.

Kitt, Michael P.: (F.F.) Castleblakeney, Ballinasloe, Co. Galway; (0905) 78147; *(Galway East)*.

Kitt, Tom: (F.F.) 3 Pine Valley Drive, Rathfarnham, Dublin 16; (01) 2982304; *(Dublin South)*.

Lawlor, Liam: (F.F.) Somerton, Lucan, Co. Dublin; (01) 6280507; *(Dublin West)*.

Lenihan, Brian: (F.F.) 'Longwood', Somerton Road, Strawberry Beds, Dublin 20; Tel. (01) 8214058; *(Dublin West)*.

§**Lenihan, Conor**: (F.F.) 6 Aylmer Road, Newcastle, Co. Dublin, (01) 6789911; *(Dublin South-West)*.

Lowry, Michael: (Ind.) Glenreigh, Holycross, Thurles, Co. Tipperary; (0504) 43182; *(Tipperary North)*.

Martin, Micheál: (F.F.) 'Lios Laoi', 16 Silver Manor, Ballinlough, Cork; (021) 295388; *(Cork South-Central)*.

McCormack, Pádraic: (F.G.) 3 Renmore Park, Galway; (091) 753992; *(Galway West)*.

McCreevy, Charlie: (F.F.) Hillview House, Kilcullen Road, Naas, Co. Kildare; (045) 876816; *(Kildare North)*.

McDaid, James: (F.F.) 2 Sylvan Park, Letterkenny, Co. Donegal; (074) 21652; *(Donegal North-East)*.

McDowell, Derek: (Lab.) 3 Dunluce Road, Clontarf, Dublin 3; (01) 8336138; *(Dublin North-Central)*.

McGahon, Brendan: (F.G.) Annaverna, Ravensdale, Dundalk, Co. Louth; (042) 32620; *(Louth)*.

§**McGennis, Marian**: (F.F.) 44

Bramley Walk, Castleknock, Dublin 15; (01) 8212340; *(Dublin Central)*.

McGinley, Dinny: (F.G.) Bunbeg, Letterkenny, Co. Donegal; (075) 31025; *(Donegal South-West)*.

McGrath, Paul: (F.G.) Carna, Irishtown, Mullingar, Co. Westmeath; (044) 40746; *(Westmeath)*.

§**McGuinness, John**: (F.F.) Windsmoor, Brooklawn, Ballyfoyle Road, Kilkenny, (01) 6789911; *(Carlow-Kilkenny)*.

McManus, Liz: (D.L.) 1 Martello Terrace, Bray, Co. Wicklow; (01) 2868407; *(Wicklow)*.

Mitchell, Gay: (F.G.) 192 Upper Rathmines Road; Dublin 6; (01) 4903744; *(Dublin South-Central)*.

Mitchell, Jim: (F.G.) 4 Rathdown Crescent, Terenure, Dublin 6, (01) 6789911; *(Dublin Central)*.

§**Mitchell, Olivia**: (F.G.) 18 Ballawley Court, Dundrum, Dublin 16; (01) 2953033); *(Dublin South)*.

Moffatt, Tom: (F.F.) Ballina House, Castle Road, Ballina, Co. Mayo; (096) 71588; *(Mayo)*.

Molloy, Robert: (P.D.) 'St. Mary's', Rockbarton, Salthill, Galway; (091) 21765; *(Galway West)*.

§**Moloney, John**: (F.F.) 27 Patrick Street, Mountmellick, Co. Laois; (0502) 24391; *(Laois-Offaly)*.

Moynihan-Cronin, Breeda: (Lab.) 10 Muckross Grove, Killarney, Co. Kerry; (064) 34993; *(Kerry South)*.

Moynihan, Donal: (F.F.) Gortnascarty, Ballymakeera, Macroom, Co. Cork; (026) 45019; *(Cork North-West)*.

§**Moynihan, Michael**: (F.F.) Meens, Kiskeam, Mallow, Co. Cork, (01) 6789911; *(Cork North-West)*.

§**Naughten, Denis**: (F.G.) Ardkennan, Drum, Athlone, Co. Roscommon, (01) 6789911; *(Longford Roscommon)*.

§**Neville, Dan**: (F.G.) Kiltannan, Croagh, Co. Limerick, (01) 6789911; *(Limerick West)*.

Noonan, Michael: (F.G.) 18 Gouldavoher Estate, Fr. Russell Road, Limerick; (061) 229350; *(Limerick East)*.

O'Dea, Willie: (F.F.) 2 Glenview Gardens, Farranshore, Co. Limerick; (061) 454488; *(Limerick East)*.

O'Donnell, Liz: (P.D.) 23 Temple Gardens, Rathmines, Dublin 6; (01) 4960993; *(Dublin South)*.

O'Donoghue, John: (F.F.) Garranearagh, Caherciveen, Co. Kerry; (066) 72413; *(Kerry South)*.

§**O'Flynn, Noel**: (F.F.) 'Melvindale House', Coolowen, Blarney, Co. Cork; (021) 505840; *(Cork North-*

Central).

O'Hanlon, Rory: (F.F.) Carrickmacross, Co. Monaghan; (042) 61530; *(Cavan-Monaghan).*

O'Keeffe, Batt: (F.F.) 8 Westcliffe, Ballincollig, Co. Cork; (021) 871393; *(Cork South-Central).*

O'Keeffe, Jim: (F.G.) Old Chapel, Bandon, Co. Cork; (023) 41399; *(Cork South-West).*

O'Keeffe, Ned: (F.F.) Ballylough, Michelstown, Co. Cork; (022) 25285; *(Cork East)*

O'Kennedy, Michael: (F.F.) Gortlandroe, Nenagh, Co. Tipperary; (01) 6789911; *(Tipperary North).*

O'Malley, Desmond J.: (P.D.) 11 Cecil Street, Limerick; (01) 6789911; *(Limerick East).*

O'Rourke, Mary: (F.F.) 'Aisling', Arcadia, Athlone, Co. Westmeath; (0902) 75065; *(Westmeath).*

O'Shea, Brian: (Lab.) 61 Sweetbriar Lawn, Tramore, Co. Waterford; (051) 381913; *(Waterford).*

§Ó Caoláin, Caoimhghín: (S.F.) 21 Dublin Street, Monaghan; (047) 82917; *(Cavan-Monaghan).*

Ó Cuív, Eamon: (F.F.) Corr na Móna, Co. na Gaillimhe; (092) 562846; *(Galway West).*

Owen, Nora: (F.G.) 17 Ard na Mara, Malahide, Co. Dublin; (01) 8451041; *(Dublin North).*

Pattison, Seamus: (Lab.) 6 Upper New Street, Kilkenny; (056) 21295; *(Carlow-Kilkenny).*

Penrose, William: (Lab.) Ballintue, Ballynacargy, Mullingar, Co. Westmeath; (044) 73264; *(Westmeath).*

§Perry, John: (F.G.) Main Street, Ballymote, Co. Sligo; (071) 83372; *(Sligo-Leitrim).*

Power, Seán: (F.F.) Castlekealy, Caragh, Naas, Co. Kildare; (045) 6285754; *(Kildare South).*

Quinn, Ruairí: (Lab.) 23 Strand Road, Sandymount, Dublin 4; (01) 6789911; *(Dublin South-East).*

Rabbitte, Pat: (D.L.) 56 Monastery Drive, Clondalkin, Dublin 22; (01) 4593191; *(Dublin South-West).*

Reynolds, Albert: (F.F.) Mount Carmel House, Dublin Road, Longford; (043) 45070; *(Longford-Roscommon).*

†Reynolds, Gerry: (F.G.) Tully, Ballinamore, Co. Leitrim; (078) 44444; *(Sligo-Leitrim).*

Ring, Michael: (F.G.) The Paddock, Westport, Co. Mayo; Tel. (098) 25734; *(Mayo).*

Roche, Dick: (F.F.) 2 Herbert Terrace, Herbert Road, Bray, Co. Wicklow; *(Wicklow).*

Ryan, Eoin: (F.F.) 19 Vavasour Square, Sandymount, Dublin 4; (01) 6600082; *(Dublin South-East).*

Sargent, Trevor: (G.P.) 37 Tara Cove, Baile Brigín, Co. Atha Cliath; (01) 8412371; *(Dublin North).*

Shatter, Alan: (F.G.) 57 Delbrook Manor, Dundrum, Dublin 16; (01) 6610317; *(Dublin South).*

Sheehan, P.J.: (F.G.) Main Street, Goleen, Co. Cork; (028) 35236; *(Cork South-West).*

Shorthall, Róisín: (Lab.) 12 Iveragh Road, Gaeltacht Park, Whitehall, Dublin 9; Tel. (01) 8370563; *(Dublin North-West).*

Smith, Brendan: (F.F.) 3 Carrickfern, Cavan, Co. Cavan; (049) 62366; *(Cavan-Monaghan).*

Smith, Michael: (F.F.) Lismackin, Roscrea, Co. Tipperary; (0505) 43157; *(Tipperary North).*

Spring, Dick: (Lab.) Cloonanorig, Tralee, Co. Kerry; (066) 25337; *(Kerry North).*

Stagg, Emmet: (Lab.) 736 Lodge Park, Straffan, Co. Kildare; (01) 6272149; *(Kildare North).*

§Stanton, David: (F.G.) Geragh Cross, Coppingerstown, Midleton, Co. Cork, (01) 6789911; *(Cork East).*

Timmins, Billy: (F.G.) Shrughaun, Baltinglass, Co. Wicklow; (0508) 81016; *(Wicklow).*

Treacy, Noel: (F.F.) Gurteen, Ballinasloe, Co. Galway; (0905) 77094; *(Galway East).*

Upton, Pat: (Lab.) 1 College Drive, Terenure, Dublin 6W; (01) 4909653; *(Dublin South-Central).*

§Wade, Eddie: (F.F.) Cahernorry, Drombanna, Co. Limerick; (061) 351467; *(Limerick East).*

Wallace, Dan: (F.F.) 13 Killeen's Place, Farranree, Cork; (021) 307465; *(Cork North-Central).*

Wallace, Mary: (F.F.) Ennistown, Fairyhouse Road, Ratoath, Co. Meath; (01) 8256259; *(Meath).*

§Wall, Jack: (Lab.) Castlemitchell, Athy, Co. Kildare; (01) 6789911; *(Kildare South).*

Walsh, Joe: (F.F.) 5 Emmet Square, Clonakilty, Co. Cork; (023) 33575; *(Cork South-West).*

Woods, Michael J.: (F.F.) 13 Kilbarrack Grove, Dublin 5; (01) 323357; *(Dublin North-East).*

†Wright, G.V.: (F.F.) 58 The Moorings, Malahide, Co. Dublin; (01) 8452642; *(Dublin North).*

Yates, Ivan: (F.G.) Blackstoops, Enniscorthy, Co. Wexford; (054) 33793; *(Wexford)*

KEY:
§= New T.D.
†= Previous member of the Dáil, but not the 27th Dáil.

SALARIES OF MEMBERS OF THE OIREACHTAS

T.D.'s salary	£34,967
Senator's salary	£22,242
Ceann Comhairle	£81,502
Minister of State's salary	£54,380
Minister's salary	£70,978
Tánaiste's salary	£76,086
Taoiseach's salary	£88,854

CURRENT BREAKDOWN OF SEANAD ÉIREANN

PARTY	SEATS
Fianna Fáil	28
Fine Gael	16
Labour	4
Progressive Democrats	4
Independents	8
TOTAL	60

MEMBERS OF SEANAD ÉIREANN

CULTURAL AND EDUCATIONAL

Paschal Mooney (F.F.)
Labhrás Ó Murchú (F.F.)
Ann Ormonde (F.F.)
Maurice Manning (F.G.)
Madeline Taylor-Quinn (F.G.)

AGRICULTURAL PANEL

Paddy Burke (F.G.)
Peter Callanan (F.F.)
John Connor (F.G.)
Avril Doyle (F.G.)
Tom Hayes (F.G.)
Rory Kiely (F.F.)
Paddy McGowan (F.F.)
Pat Moylan (F.F.)
Francis O'Brien (F.F.)
Kathleen O'Meara (Lab.)
Jim Walsh (F.F.)

LABOUR PANEL

Donie Cassidy (F.F.)
Denis (Dino) Cregan (F.G.)
Liam Fitzgerald (F.F.)
Des Hanafin (F.F.)

Mary Jackman (F.G.)
Daniel Kiely (F.F.)
Don Lydon (F.F.)
Jarlath McDonagh (F.G.)
Brian Mullooly (F.F.)
Therese Ridge (F.G.)
Sean Ryan (Lab.)

INDUSTRIAL AND COMMERCIAL

Eddie Bohan (F.F.)
Ernie Caffrey (F.G.)
Paul Coghlan (F.G.)
Liam T. Cosgrave (F.G.)
Margaret Cox (F.F.)
Willie Farrell (F.F.)
Pat Gallagher (Lab.)
Mick Lanigan (F.F.)
Denis O'Donovan (F.F.)

ADMINISTRATIVE PANEL

Fintan Coogan (F.G.)
Joe Costello (Lab.)
Joe Doyle (F.G.)
Michael Finneran (F.F.)
Camillus Glynn (F.F.)

Tony Kett (F.F.)
Fergus O'Dowd (F.G.)

NATIONAL UNIVERSITY OF IRELAND

Joe O'Toole (Ind.)
Feargal Quinn (Ind.)
Brendan Ryan (Ind.)

UNIVERSITY OF DUBLIN

Mary Henry (Ind.)
David Norris (Ind.)
Shane Ross (Ind.)

TAOISEACH'S NOMINEES

Dr. Edward Haughey (Ind.)
Dr. Maurice Hayes (Ind.)
Helen Keogh (P.D.)
Mairín Quill (P.D.)
Jim Gibbons (P.D.)
John Dardis (P.D.)
Tom Fitzgerald (F.F.)
Dr. Dermot Fitzgerald (F.F.)
Enda Bonner (F.F.)
Anne Leonard (F.F.)
Frank Chambers (F.F.)

PRESIDENTS OF IRELAND FACT FILE

Name	Politics	Born	in	Inaug.	Age	Died	Age	Terms
Douglas Hyde	non-party	17.01.1860	Roscommon	25.06.1938	78	12.07.1949	89	1
Seán T. Ó Ceallaigh	Fianna Fáil	25.08.1882	Dublin	25.06.1945	63	23.11.1966	84	2
Éamon de Valera	Fianna Fáil	14.10.1882	New York	25.06.1959	76	29.08.1975	92	2
Erskine Childers	Fianna Fáil	11.12.1905	London	25.06.1973	67	17.11.1974	68	1
Cearbhall Ó Dálaigh*	non-party	12.02.1911	Wicklow	19.12.1974	63	21.03.1978	67	1
Patrick Hillery	Fianna Fáil	02.05.1923	Clare	03.12.1976	53	-		2
Mary Robinson†	non-party	21.05.1944	Mayo	03.12.1990	46	-		1

Ó Dálaigh resigned as President on October 22, 1976. † Robinson resigned as President on Sept. 12, 1997.

BIOGRAPHIES OF THE PRESIDENTS OF IRELAND

DOUGLAS HYDE (1938-45)

Born Frenchpark, Co. Roscommon, January 17, 1860. Nominated without opposition and inaugurated as first President of Ireland on June 25, 1938, aged 78. Served a full term in office and retired June 24, 1945.

The son of a Church of Ireland minister, Dr. Hyde was to the forefront of the turn-of-the-century cultural revival, co-founding Conradh na Gaeilige (The Gaelic League) and serving as its first President from 1893 to 1915. Remembered for his play *Casadh an tSúgáin* and his collection of translated poetry *Lovesongs of Connacht*. Was first Professor of Modern Irish at University College Dublin where he taught from 1909 until 1932; was also a member of Seanad Éireann from 1925 to 1938.

Died, July 12, 1949, aged 89.

SEÁN T. Ó CEALLAIGH (1945-59)

Born Dublin, August 25, 1882. Elected to the Presidency on June 16, 1945 and inaugurated on June 25. Re-elected unopposed in 1952 and served the max-

imum two terms, retiring on June 24, 1959.

A veteran of the 1916 Easter Rising, he was a founding member of Sinn Féin in 1907 and, subsequently, Fianna Fáil in 1926. Elected to the first Dáil in 1918, became its Ceann Comhairle (speaker) and Minister for Irish. Retained his Dáil seat until 1945, serving in a number of ministries including Local Government and Public Health (1932-39) and Finance (1939-45). Also served as Vice President of the Executive Council (1932-37) and Tánaiste (1937-45).

Died, November 23, 1966, aged 84.

ÉAMON de VALERA (1959-73)

Born New York, October 14, 1882 - the son of an Irish immigrant mother and a Spanish immigrant father - and moved to Ireland in 1885. Elected to the Presidency on June 17, 1959, and inaugurated on June 25 at the age of 76, was re-elected on June 1, 1966 - the only incumbent President to be opposed. Remained in office until 1973.

A commandant at Boland's Mills during the 1916

Rising, the British authorities commuted his death sentence because they were unsure of his nationality and wished to avoid alienating the United States by executing one of its citizens. Elected as a Sinn Féin M.P. for East Clare in 1917 - a seat he held until he became President. Was also elected M.P. for East Mayo (1918-21); Down (1921-29); and South Down (1933-37), although he never took his seat at Stormont.

Was President of Sinn Féin (1917-26); President of the Irish Volunteers (1917-22); President of the Irish Republic (1919-20); founder of Flanna Fáil in 1926 and that party's President until 1959; President of the Council of the League of Nations at its 68th and Special Sessions (September and October 1932); and President of the Assembly of the League of Nations in 1938. Founded *The Irish Press* in 1931. In government he was President of the Executive Council (1932-37); Minister for External Affairs (1932-48); Taoiseach (1937-48, 1951-54, and 1957-59) Minister for Local Government (1940); and Minister for Education (1939-40). He also had a significant input in the drafting of the 1937 Constitution of Ireland.

Died, August 29, 1975, aged 92.

ERSKINE CHILDERS (1973-74)
Born London, December 11, 1905. Elected as the fourth President of Ireland on May 30, 1973 and inaugurated on June 25, 1973 at the age of 67. .His father, Erskine, signatory of the 1921 Anglo-Irish Treaty, was executed by Free State soldiers in 1922 .

First elected to Dáil Éireann in 1938 and held a number of ministerial portfolios, including Posts and Telegraphs (1951-54 and 1966-69); Lands (1957-59); Transport and Power (1959-69); and Tánaiste (1969-73).

Died in office on November 17, 1974, aged 68.

CEARBHALL Ó DÁLAIGH (1974-76)
Born Bray, Co. Wicklow, February 12, 1911. Nominated unopposed for the Presidency following the death of Erskine Childers and formally inaugurated on December 19, 1974, aged 63. His tenure was brief, he resigned on October 22 1976 "to protect the dignity and independence" of the office of President, following comments made by the then Minister for Defence, Patrick Donegan, about his referral of the Criminal Law (Jurisdiction) Bill to the Supreme Court to attest its constitutionality (the bill was found to be constitutional).

Mr. Ó Dálaigh was a barrister by profession and had a distinguished legal career both in Ireland and Europe. He was the Attorney General on two occasions, 1946-48 and 1951-53; Chief Justice and President of the Supreme Court 1961-73, having been a Supreme Court Judge from 1953; in 1973 he became a Judge of the Court of Justice of the European Communities and in 1974 became President of the First Chamber of that court.

Died on March 21, 1978, aged 67.

DR PATRICK HILLERY (1976-1990)
Born Milltown Malbay, Co. Clare, May 2, 1923. Returned unopposed to the Presidency, following the resignation of Cearbhall Ó Dálaigh, and inaugurated on December 3, 1976, aged 53. Returned unopposed again in 1983, he went on to serve two full terms and retired from the position on December 2, 1990.

A Fianna Fáil T.D. for Clare (1951-73), he held the following ministerial portfolios: Education (1959-65); Industry and Commerce (1965-66); Labour (1966-69); and Foreign Affairs (1969-73). As Minister for Foreign Affairs, he negotiated Ireland's accession to the European Economic Community in 1973 and became Ireland's first Commissioner to the E.E.C. serving as Vice President of the Commission with special responsibilities for Social Affairs from 1973 until his elevation to the Irish Presidency in 1976.

MARY ROBINSON (1990-97)
Born Ballina, Co. Mayo, May 21, 1944. Elected President on November 7, 1990, and inaugurated on December 3, 1990, aged 46. She was the first woman and the youngest person ever to hold the office.

A qualified barrister prior to her election, she was the Professor of Constitutional and Criminal Law (1969-75) and lecturer on European Community Law (1975-90) at Trinity College Dublin. A Senator from 1969 to 89 and initially a member of the Labour Party, she resigned from the party in protest at the signing of the Anglo-Irish Agreement in 1985. A series of visits, both domestic and overseas, has resulted in a dramatic increase in the profile of the office.

Appointed United Nations commissioner for Human Rights in June 1997, Mrs. Robinson resigned from the presidency on September 12, 1997, and took up her U.N. posting on the same day.

PRESIDENTIAL ELECTION RESULTS, 1945-90

Year	Candidates	Turnout %	1st Count	Transfers	Result	Elected
1945	McCartan, Patrick	63.0	212,834	-212,834	-	
	MacEoin, Seán	-	335,539	+117,886	453,425	
	Ó Ceallaigh, Seán T.	-	537,965	+27,200	565,165	Seán T.Ó Ceallaigh
1959	de Valera, Éamon	58.4	538,003	-	-	Éamon de Valera
	MacEoin, Seán	-	417,536	-	-	
1966	de Valera, Éamon	65.4	558,861	-	-	Éamon de Valera
	O'Higgins, Thomas F.	-	548,144	-	-	
1973	Childers, Erskine	62.2	635,867	-	-	Erskine Childers
	O'Higgins, Thomas F.	-	587,771	-	-	

continued from previous page

Year	Candidates	Turnout %	1st Count	Transfers	Result	Elected
1990	Currie, Austin	64.1	267,902	-267,902	-	
	Lenihan, Brian	-	694,484	+36,789	731,273	
	Robinson, Mary	-	612,265	+205,565	817,830	Mary Robinson

TAOISIGH AND TÁNAISTÍ OF IRELAND, 1922-97

Date appointed	Head of Government	Deputy Head of Government	Date appointed
	President of the Executive Council	*Vice President of Executive Council*	
Dec. 6, 1922	William T. Cosgrave	Kevin O'Higgins	Dec. 26, 1922
		Ernest Blythe	July 10, 1927
March 9, 1932	Eamon de Valera	Seán T. Ó Ceallaigh	March 9, 1932

	Taoiseach	Tánaiste	
Dec. 29, 1937	Eamon de Valera	Seán T. Ó Ceallaigh	Dec. 29, 1937
		Seán Lemass	June 14, 1945
Feb. 18, 1948	John A. Costello	William Norton	Feb. 18, 1948
June 13, 1951	Eamon de Valera	Seán Lemass	June 13, 1951
June 2, 1954	John A. Costello	William Norton	June 2, 1954
March 20, 1957	Eamon de Valera	Seán Lemass	March 20, 1957
June 23 1959	Seán Lemass	Seán MacEntee	June 23, 1959
		Frank Aiken	April 21, 1965
Nov. 10, 1966	Jack Lynch	Frank Aiken	Nov. 10, 1966
		Erskine Childers	July 2, 1969
March 14, 1973	Liam Cosgrave	Brendan Corish	March 14, 1973
July 5, 1977	Jack Lynch	George Colley	July 5, 1977
Dec. 11, 1979	Charles Haughey	George Colley	Dec. 11, 1979
June 20, 1981	Garret FitzGerald	Michael O'Leary	June 20, 1981
March 9, 1982	Charles Haughey	Ray McSharry	March 9, 1982
Dec. 14, 1982	Garret FitzGerald	Dick Spring	Dec. 14, 1982
		Peter Barry	Jan. 20, 1987
March 10, 1987	Charles Haughey	Brian Lenihan	March 10, 1987
		John Wilson	Nov. 13, 1990
Feb. 11, 1992	Albert Reynolds	John Wilson	Feb. 11, 1992
		Dick Spring	Jan. 12, 1993
		Bertie Ahern	Nov. 19, 1994
Dec. 15, 1994	John Bruton	Dick Spring	Dec. 15, 1994
June 26, 1997	Bertie Ahern	Mary Harney	June 26, 1996

BIOGRAPHIES OF IRISH TAOISIGH

WILLIAM T. COSGRAVE (1922-32)

Born Dublin, June 6, 1880. Chairman of the Provisional Government (August 25-December 6 1922), and President of the Executive Council of the Irish Free State (1922-1932). Founding member of Cumann na nGaedheal in March 1923 and its only leader. A founding member of Fine Gael in September 1933, he was its leader from September 21, 1934, until his retirement on January 18, 1944.

He was a veteran of the 1916 Rising and was first elected as a Sinn Féin M.P. in 1917 and became Minister for Local Government in the first Dáil, a position he retained in the Provisional Government until the death of Michael Collins. During his premiership he also served as Minister for Finance (1922-23), Minister for Defence (1924) and Minister for Justice (1927).

His government dealt severely with the anti-treaty I.R.A. during a bloody civil war with atrocities on both sides, ordering the executions of 77 prisoners and retaining a series of Emergency Powers to maintain law and order after the war ended in April 1923. The government also established the Garda Síochana (1923), gained the admittance of the Irish Free State to the League of Nations (1923), initiated the Shannon hydro-electric scheme(1925) and was instrumental in the 1926 Imperial Conference in defining the 'autonomous communities' of the British Empire as 'equal in status' and in no way subordinate to one another.

Died on November 16, 1965, aged 85.

ÉAMON de VALERA* (1932-48, 1951-54 & 1957-59)

Born New York, October 14, 1882. President of the Executive Council (1932-37) and Taoiseach on three occasions (1937-48, 1951-54, and 1957-59). In addition, he held the ministerial portfolios of External Affairs (1932-48), Education (1939-40), and Local Government (1941). He was a founding member of Fianna Fáil in May 1926 and remained that party's leader until June

1959.

A commandant in the 1916 Rising, he was the only high ranking male to escape execution. He was elected as a Sinn Féin M.P. in 1917 and became President of the Dáil (1919-22). He withdrew from the Dáil over the signing of the Anglo-Irish Treaty, but abstentionism did not suit him, and in 1927, he led Fianna Fáil into the Oireachtas.

In government, he set about deleting all trappings of the Crown from public life, abolishing the Oath of Allegiance in 1933, limiting the powers of the Governor General and eventually abolishing the office, and he took advantage of the 1936 abdication crisis to remove all reference to the King from the constitution. The culmination of this policy was the drafting of the Constitution in 1937. The constitution, although it acknowledged other religions, recognised a special position for the Roman Catholic church. He also engaged in a prolonged and damaging economic war with Britain in the 1930s over the withholding of land annuities. Despite heavy international pressure, especially from Britain and the U.S., de Valera steered Ireland on a neutral course during World War II. In 1953 his government passed a Health Act providing free mother-and-child benefits. Elected as President of Ireland on June 17, 1959, he served two full terms. He is the only person to have been both President and Taoiseach.

Died on August 29, 1975, aged 92.
See also Presidential biographies.

JOHN A. COSTELLO (1948-51 & 1954-57)

Born Dublin, June 20, 1891. Although never a leader of the Fine Gael party, he was Taoiseach (1948-51 and 1954-57) and Minister for Health briefly in 1951, following Dr. Noel Browne's enforced resignation. Both of the administrations he headed were multi-party coalitions and it is testament to his skills that governments of such disparate parts were cohesive and constructive.

As Attorney General (1926-32), he played an important role in achieving the freedoms implicit in the Anglo-Irish Treaty culminating in the Statute of Westminster (1931). Elected to Dáil Éireann in 1933, he retained his seat until 1969. In 1948 his government passed the Republic of Ireland Act, and Ireland formally left the Commonwealth the following year. It was also during his premiership that the Industrial Development Authority was established (1950), Ireland was admitted to the United Nations Organisation (1955) and tuberculosis was successfully eradicated.

Died on January 5, 1976, aged 84.

SEÁN LEMASS (1959-66)

Born Dublin, July 15, 1899. Taoiseach (1959-66). In government he served as Minister for Industry and Commerce (1932-39, 1941-48, 1951-54, and 1957-59), Minister for Supplies (1939-45) and Tánaiste (1945-48, 1951-54, and 1957-59). A founding member of Fianna Fáil in 1926, he was the party leader from 1959 to 1966.

A veteran of the 1916 Rising, the War of Independence and the Civil War, where he fought on the republican side, he was elected to Dáil Éireann in 1924. As Minister for Industry and Commerce, he established the national airline, Aer Lingus (1936); Irish Shipping (1941) and the Irish Tourist Board, Bord Fáilte (1952). As Taoiseach he espoused free trade and competitiveness as the way forward for Ireland economically. A free trade agreement with Britain was signed (1966), free secondary school education (announced 1966) and Radio Telefís Éireann made its first broadcast (Dec 31, 1961). Lemass also held two groundbreaking meetings with the Prime Minister of Northern Ireland, Terence O'Neill, in 1965

Died on May 11, 1971, aged 71.

JACK LYNCH (1966-73 & 1977-79)

Born Cork, August 15, 1917. Taoiseach (1966-73 and 1977-79). Elected to the Dáil in 1948, he held the ministerial portfolios of Education (1957-59 and 1968), Gaeltacht (1957), Industry and Commerce (1959-65) and Finance (1965-66). He was leader of Fianna Fáil from 1966 until 1979. In his youth, he won a record six consecutive All-Ireland medals (five hurling and one football) with his native Cork.

Lynch's time as Taoiseach was marked by the breakdown of law and order in Northern Ireland. He dismissed ministers Neil Blaney and Charles Haughey for their out spoken statements on the situation; both were later charged and acquitted of supplying arms to republicans in the north. He recalled the Irish ambassador to London in protest at Bloody Sunday in 1972. Lynch presided over Ireland's entry into the European Economic Community in 1973 and, in 1979, negotiated Ireland's entry to the European Monetary System thus ending the one-for-one parity with sterling.

Retired from politics in 1981.

LIAM COSGRAVE (1973-77)

Born Dublin, April 13, 1920. Son of W.T. Cosgrave, first President of the Executive Council. First elected to Dáil Éireann in 1943, Mr. Cosgrave was leader of Fine Gael (1965-77) and Taoiseach (1973--77) of a Fine Gael/Labour coalition. In government, he served as Minister for External Affairs 1954-57 and Minister for Defence (1976).

His administration struggled with the recession caused by the international oil crisis of the mid-1970s; inflation soared and unemployment rose, but this was a global, and not simply, an Irish phenomenon. He led the Republic's delegation to the tripartite Sunningdale talks in 1973, which established the short lived Northern Ireland Executive. His government also introduced selective broadcasting censorship in the form of Section 31 of the Broadcasting Act.

Retired from politics in 1981.

CHARLES J. HAUGHEY (1979-81, 1982 & 1987-92)

Born Mayo, September 16, 1925. Taoiseach on three occasions. First elected to the Dáil in 1957, he held the Ministerial portfolios of Justice (1961-64), Agriculture and Fisheries (1964-66), Finance (1966-70), Health and Social Welfare (1977-79) and Gaeltacht (1987-92).

Elected leader of Fianna Fáil in 1979.

His early administrations struggled through a difficult economic climate. On returning to power in 1987, he saw the referendum on the Single European Act approved, the first Balance of Payments surplus since the 1930s and inflation and interest rates plummet. In 1989, he became the first Fianna Fáil leader to enter into a coalition when he aligned his party with the Progressive Democrats. Bedevilled by controversy throughout his career (he was charged and acquitted of supplying arms to northern republicans in 1970), he resigned as Taoiseach and leader of Fianna Fáil in February 1992 when allegations about a 1982 phone-tapping scandal re-surfaced. The spectre of scandal returned to haunt Mr. Haughey again in July 1997 when he admitted receiving £1.3million in donations from Ben Dunne of Dunnes Stores at the payment to politicans tribunal.

DR. GARRET FITZGERALD (1981-82 & 1982-87)

Born Dublin, February 9, 1926. Taoiseach on two occasions, both administrations being Fine Gael/ Labour coalitions. First elected to the Dáil in 1969, he had served as a Senator (1965-69). He was Minister for Foreign Affairs (1973-77) and leader of the Fine Gael party from 1977 until 1987.

As Taoiseach, his most notable achievements were on Northern Ireland. In 1983 he convened the New Ireland Forum which gave impetus to Anglo-Irish negotiations resulting in the Anglo-Irish Agreement in 1985. The agreement, fiercely opposed by unionists, gave the Irish government a limited input into the government of Northern Ireland via a joint ministerial conference of British and Irish ministers and a permanent secretariat. While in office, Ireland's economic situation improved considerably. Social legislation put to referendum such as prohibiting the legalisation of abortion was passed while the legalisation of divorce was defeated.

Since retiring from Dáil Éireann in 1992, he has maintained a high profile through lecturing and writing on Irish politics.

ALBERT REYNOLDS (1992-94)

Born Roscommon, November 3, 1932. Taoiseach February-November 1992 of a Fianna Fáil/Progressive Democrats coalition and November 92-December 1994 of a Fianna Fáil/Labour coalition. First elected to the Dáil in 1977, he held the following ministerial posts: Posts and Telegraphs (1979-81),Transport (1979-81), Industry and Energy (1982) and Finance (1988-91). He became leader of Fianna Fáil in February 1992.

In government, his main concern was Northern Ireland. He was instrumental in the drafting of the Downing Street Declaration in 1993. In it, the Irish government agreed to promote changes in the constitution to reflect the principle of the need for the consent of the majority in Northern Ireland, and the British government stated it had 'no selfish strategic or economic interest in Northern Ireland' and would uphold the democratic wishes of the majority. He held ground-breaking talks with Gerry Adams and John Hume, and broadcasting

bans were lifted north and south. It was in this climate that the I.R.A. declared a ceasefire in August 1994 followed two months later by a loyalist paramilitary ceasefire.

A referendum was held on the question of abortion (November 1992), where the right to travel and receive information regarding abortion was approved but the wider availability of abortion was restricted; the Maastricht Treaty was ratified by referendum (June 1992) and over £7 billion in E.C. structural and cohesion funds were secured during the lifetime of his government.

Mr. Reynolds resigned in November 1994 when the appointment of Harry Whelehan, Attorney General, as President of the High Court proved unacceptable to his coalition partners in Labour.

JOHN BRUTON (1994-97)

Born Dublin, May 18, 1947. Taoiseach of the three-party 'rainbow' coalition of Fine Gael, Labour and Democratic Left. His was the first government in the history of the state to take office without a general election being held. First elected to the Dáil in 1969, he held the ministerial posts of Finance (1981-82 and 1986-87); Industry and Energy (1982-83); Industry, Trade, Commerce and Tourism (1983-86) and the Public Service (1987).

The Irish economy has grown continuously during his premiership, leaving Ireland well-prepared for European Monetary Union. Referenda have been held dealing with the legislation of divorce (1995) and the denial of bail to likely re-offenders (1996). The 'Framework Document' signed by him and former British Prime Minister John Major in February 1995 helped establish multi-party talks on the future of Northern Ireland; yet the I.R.A. ceasefire broke down just over a year later. This resumption of violence and widespread unrest during the marching season placed the peace process under great strain.

Mr Bruton,who has been leader of Fine Gael since 1990, stood down as Taoiseach on June 26, 1997.

BERTIE AHERN (1997-)

Born Dublin, September 1951. On June 26, 1997, he became Taoiseach of a Fianna Fáil-Progressive Democrat coalition government. First elected to the Dail in 1977, he held the ministerial posts of Finance (1991-), Industry and Commerce (January-February 1993) and Labour (1987-91).

He formally distanced himself from his erstwhile mentor Charles J. Haughey, when rumours of Ben Dunne's payments to the former Taoiseach emerged, and he has pledged to make the government and its members more accountable. Since the government has come to power, he has been instrumental in facilitating an IRA ceasefire. He is seen as more favourably disposed towards nationalists in Northern Ireland than his predecessor, John Bruton, having openly avowed his interest in protecting their rights.

GOVERNMENTS OF IRELAND, 1919 - 1997

NOTES

Following the General Election of 1918, elected Sinn Féin representatives met for the first time on January 21, 1919, as the first Dáil Éireann. The new assembly elected a cabinet. The second Dáil met for the first time on August 26, 1921, and again elected a cabinet. The cabinet was superseded by the Provisional Government in January 1922 which was, in turn, superseded by the Executive Council in December 1922.

(1) Cathal Brugha was acting President of the First Dáil, January - April 1919.

(2) Upon his release from prison, Éamon de Valera became President of the first Dáil, April 1919 - August 1921, and President of the second Dáil from August 1921 - January 1922. De Valera and others who opposed the Anglo-Irish Treaty withdrew from the Dáil in January 1922.

(3) Michael Collins was Chairman of the Provisional Government which came into being after the Dáil ratified the Anglo-Irish Treaty in January 1922.

(4) W.T. Cosgrave became Chairman of the Provisional Government following the assasination of Michael Collins in August 1922.

From December 1922 until December 1937, the office of Prime Minister was known as President of the Executive Council. From December 1937, that position became known as Taoiseach.

MINISTERS FOR FINANCE

Taoiseach	Minister	App.
Brugha (1)	Eoin MacNeil (S.F.)	1919
De Valera (2)	Michael Collins (S.F.)	1919
Collins (3)	Michael Collins (S.F.)	1922
Cosgrave (4)	W.T. Cosgrave (C.G.)	1922
Cosgrave	Ernest Blythe (C.G.)	1923
De Valera	Seán MacEntee (F.F.)	1932
De Valera	Seán T. O'Kelly (F.F.)	1939
De Valera	Frank Aiken (F.F.)	1945
Costello	P.J. McGilligan (F.G.)	1948
De Valera	Seán MacEntee (F.F.)	1951
Costello	Gerard Sweetman (F.G.)	1954
De Valera	James Ryan (F.F.)	1957
Lemass	James Ryan (F.F.)	1959
Lemass	Jack Lynch (F.F.)	1965
Lynch	Charles Haughey (F.F.)	1966
Lynch	George Colley (F.F.)	1970
Cosgrave	Richie Ryan (F.G.)	1973
Lynch	George Colley (F.F.)	1977
Haughey	Michael O'Kennedy (F.F.)	1979
Haughey	Gene Fitzgerald (F.F.)	1981
FitzGerald	John Bruton (F.G.)	1981
Haughey	Ray McSharry (F.F.)	1982
FitzGerald	Alan Dukes (F.G.)	1982
FitzGerald	John Bruton (F.G.)	1986
Haughey	Ray McSharry (F.F.)	1987
Haughey	Albert Reynolds (F.F.)	1988
Reynolds	Bertie Ahern (F.F.)	1991
Bruton	Ruairí Quinn (Lab.)	1994
Ahern	Charlie McCreevy (F.F.)	1997

MINISTERS FOR JUSTICE

Taoiseach	Minister	App.
Brugha (1)	Michael Collins (S.F.)	1919
De Valera (2)	Arthur Griffith (S.F.)	1919
De Valera (2)	Austin Stack (S.F.)	1921
Collins (3)	Edmond Duggan (S.F.)	1922
Cosgrave (4)	Kevin O'Higgins (C.G.)	1922
Cosgrave	W.T. Cosgrave (C.G.)	1927
Cosgrave	J. Fitzgerald Kenny (C.G.)	1927
De Valera	James Geoghegan (F.F.)	1932
De Valera	P.J. Ruttledge (F.F.)	1933
De Valera	Gerald Boland (F.F.)	1939
Costello	Seán MacEoin (F.G.)	1948
Costello	Daniel Morrissey (F.G.)	1951
De Valera	Gerald Boland (F.F.)	1951
Costello	James Everitt (Lab..)	1954
De Valera	Oscar Traynor (F.F.)	1957
Lemass	Oscar Traynor (F.F.)	1959
Lemass	Charles Haughey (F.F.)	1961
Lemass	Seán Lemass (F.F.)	1964
Lemass	Brian Lenihan (F.F.)	1964
Lynch	Brian Lenihan (F.F.)	1966
Lynch	Mícheál O'Moráin (F.F.)	1968
Lynch	Desmond O'Malley (F.F.)	1970
Cosgrave	Patrick Cooney (F.G.)	1973
Lynch	Gerry Collins (F.F.)	1977
Haughey	Gerry Collins (F.F.)	1979
FitzGerald	Jim Mitchell (F.G.)	1981
Haughey	Sean Doherty (F.F.)	1982
FitzGerald	Michael Noonan (F.G.)	1982
FitzGerald	Alan Dukes (F.G.)	1986
Haughey	Gerry Collins (F.F.)	1987
Haughey	Ray Burke (F.F.)	1989
Reynolds	Pádraig Flynn (F.F.)	1992
Reynolds	Máire Geoghegan-Quinn (F.F.)	1993
Bruton	Nora Owen (F.G.)	1994
Ahern	John O'Donoghue (F.F.)	1997

In 1924, the Office of Minister of Home Affairs became known as the Department of Justice. In June 1997, it became known as the Department of Justice, Equality and Law Reform.

MINISTERS FOR DEFENCE

Taoiseach	Minister	App.
Brugha (1)	Richard Mulcahy (S.F.)	1919
De Valera (2)	Cathal Brugha (S.F.)	1919
Cosgrave	Richard Mulcahy (C.G.)	1922
Cosgrave	W. T. Cosgrave (C.G.)	1924
Cosgrave	Peter Hughes (C.G.)	1924
Cosgrave	Desmond Fitzgerald (C.G.)	1927
De Valera	Frank Aiken (F.F.)	1932
De Valera	Oscar Traynor (F.F.)	1939
Costello	Thomas F. O'Higgins (F.G.)	1948

Costello	Seán MacEoin (F.G.)	1951
De Valera	Oscar Traynor (F.F.)	1951
Costello	Seán MacEoin (F.G.)	1954
De Valera	Kevin Boland (F.F.)	1957
Lemass	Kevin Boland (F.F.)	1959
Lemass	Gerald Bartely (F.F.)	1961
Lemass	Michael Hilliard (F.F.)	1965
Lynch	Michael Hilliard (F.F.)	1966
Lynch	James Gibbons (F.F.)	1969
Lynch	Jerry Cronin (F.F.)	1970
Cosgrave	Patrick Donegan (F.G.)	1973
Cosgrave	Liam Cosgrave (F.G.)	1976
Cosgrave	Oliver J. Flanagan (F.G.)	1976
Lynch	Bobby Molloy (F.F.)	1977
Haughey	Pádraig Faulkner (F.F.)	1979
Haughey	Sylvester Barrett (F.F.)	1981
Fitzgerald	James Tully (Lab.)	1981
Haughey	Patrick Power (F.F.)	1982
FitzGerald	Patrick Cooney (F.G.)	1982
FitzGerald	Patrick O'Toole (F.G.)	1986
Haughey	Michael J. Noonan (F.F.)	1987
Haughey	Brian Lenihan (F.F.)	1989
Haughey	Brendan Daly (F.F.)	1991
Reynolds	John Wilson (F.F.)	1992
Reynolds	David Andrews (F.F.)	1993
Bruton	Sean Barrett (F.G.)	1994
Ahern	David Andrews (F.F.)	1997

MINISTERS FOR FOREIGN AFFAIRS

Taoiseach	Minister	App.
Brugha (1)	Count Plunkett (S.F.)	1919
De Valera (2)	Count Plunkett (S.F.)	1919
De Valera (2)	Arthur Griffiths (S.F.)	1921
Cosgrave (4)	Desmond Fitzgerald (C.G.)	1922
Cosgrave	Kevin O'Higgins (C.G.)	1927
Cosgrave	W.T. Cosgrave (C.G.)	1927
Cosgrave	Patrick McGilligan (C.G.)	1927
De Valera	Eamon de Valera (F.F.)	1932
Costello	Seán MacBride (C.P.)	1948
De Valera	Frank Aiken (F.F.)	1951
Costello	Liam Cosgrave (F.G.)	1954
De Valera	Frank Aiken (F.F.)	1957
Lemass	Frank Aiken (F.F.)	1959
Lynch	Frank Aiken (F.F.)	1966
Lynch	Patrick Hillery (F.F.)	1969
Lynch	Brian Lenihan (F.F.)	1973
Cosgrave	Garret FitzGerald (F.G.)	1973
Lynch	Michael O'Kennedy (F.F.)	1977
Haughey	Brian Lenihan (F.F.)	1979
Fitzgerald	John Kelly (F.G.)	1981
Haughey	Gerry Collins (F.F.)	1982
FitzGerald	Peter Barry (F.G.)	1982
Haughey	Brian Lenihan (F.F.)	1987
Haughey	Gerry Collins (F.F.)	1989
Reynolds	David Andrews (F.F.)	1992
Reynolds	Dick Spring (Lab.)	1993
Bruton	Dick Spring (Lab.)	1994
Ahern	Ray Burke (F.F.)	1997

Until 1973, the Department of Foreign Affairs was known as the Department of External Affairs.

MINISTERS FOR LOCAL GOVERNMENT

Taoiseach	Minister	App.
De Valera (2)	W.T. Cosgrave (S.F.)	1919
Collins (3)	W.T. Cosgrave (S.F.)	1922
Cosgrave (4)	Ernest Blythe* (C.G.)	1922
Cosgrave	James Burke* (C.G.)	1923
Cosgrave	Richard Mulcahy (C.G.)	1927
De Valera	Seán T. O'Kelly (F.F.)	1932
De Valera	P.J. Ruttledge (F.F.)	1939
De Valera	Eamon de Valera (F.F.)	1941
De Valera	Seán MacEntee (F.F.)	1941
Costello	Timothy J. Murphy (Lab.)	1948
Costello	Michael J. Keyes (Lab.)	1949
De Valera	Patrick Smith (F.F.)	1951
Costello	Patrick O'Donnell (F.G.)	1954
De Valera	Patrick Smith (F.F.)	1957
De Valera	Neil Blaney (H.F.)	1957
Lemass	Neil Blaney (F.F.)	1959
Lynch	Kevin Boland (F.F)	1966
Lynch	Bobby Molloy (F.F.)	1970
Cosgrave	James Tully (Lab.)	1973-77

* Not a member of the Executive Council.

The Minister for Local Government was not a member of the Executive Council until 1927. In 1924 the office of Local Government became Local Government and Public Health. In 1947 Local Government and Public Health was divided into two ministerial briefs, the Department of Local Government and the Department of Health (see below). The Department of Local Government ceased to exist in 1977, replaced by the new Department of the Environment.

MINISTERS FOR ENVIRONMENT

Taoiseach	Minister	App.
Lynch	Sylvester Barrett (F.F.)	1977
Haughey	Sylvester Barrett (F.F.)	1979
Haughey	Ray Burke (F.F.)	1981
FitzGerald	Peter Barry (F.G.)	1981
Haughey	Ray Burke (F.F.)	1982
FitzGerald	Dick Spring (Lab.)	1982
FitzGerald	Liam Kavanagh (Lab.)	1983
FitzGerald	John Boland (F.G.)	1986
Haughey	Pádraig Flynn (F.F.)	1987
Reynolds	Michael Smith (F.F.)	1992
Bruton	Brendan Howlin (Lab.)	1994
Ahern	Noel Dempsey (F.F.)	1997

In June 1997, the Department was renamed the Department of the Environment and Rural Development.

MINISTERS FOR ECONOMIC AFFAIRS

Taoiseach	Minister	App.
De Valera (2)	Robert C. Barton (S.F.)	1921
Collins (3)	Kevin O'Higgins (S.F.)	1922
Cosgrave (4)	Joseph McGrath (C.G.)	1922

The Department of Economic Affairs merged with the

Department of Industry and Commerce on 6th December 1922.

MINISTERS FOR INDUSTRY AND COMMERCE

Taoiseach	Minister	App.
De Valera (2)	Eoin MacNeill (S.F.)	1919
Cosgrave (4)	Joseph McGrath (C.G.)	1922
Cosgrave	Patrick McGilligan (C.G.)	1924
De Valera	Seán Lemass (F.F.)	1932
De Valera	Seán MacEntee (F.F.)	1939
De Valera	Seán Lemass (F.F.)	1941
Costello	Daniel Morrissey (F.G.)	1948
Costello	Thomas F. O'Higgins (F.G.)	1951
De Valera	Seán Lemass (F.F.)	1951
Costello	William Norton (Lab.)	1954
De Valera	Seán Lemass (F.F.)	1957
Lemass	Jack Lynch (F.F.)	1959
Lemass	Patrick Hillery (F.F.)	1965
Lemass	George Colley (F.F.)	1966
Lynch	P.J. Lalor (F.F.)	1970
Cosgrave	Justin Keating (F.G.)	1973-77

In 1977, Industry and Commerce became Industry, Commerce and Energy.

MINISTERS FOR INDUSTRY, COMMERCE & ENERGY

Taoiseach	Minister	App.
Lynch	Des O'Malley (F.F.)	1977-79

In 1979, Industry, Commerce and Energy was split into two briefs - The Department of Energy, and the Department of Industry, Commerce and Tourism.

MINISTERS FOR ENERGY

Taoiseach	Minister	App.
Haughey	George Colley (F.F.)	1979
FitzGerald	Michael O'Leary (Lab.)	1981
Haughey	Albert Reynolds (F.F.)	1982
FitzGerald	John Bruton (F.G.)	1982
FitzGerald	Dick Spring (Lab.)	1983
FitzGerald	Gemma Hussey (F.G.)	1987
Haughey	Ray Burke (F.F.)	1987
Haughey	Robert Molloy (P.D.)	1989
Reynolds	Robert Molloy (P.D.)	1992
Reynolds	Albert Reynolds (F.F.)	1992

Between 1982 and 1983 the Department of Energy was known as the Department of Industry and Energy. From 1993 its functions were carried out by the Department of Transport, Energy and Communications, now the Department of Public Enterprise.

MINISTER FOR INDUSTRY, COMMERCE & TOURISM

Taoiseach	Minister	App.
Haughey	Des O'Malley (F.F.)	1979
FitzGerald	John Kelly (F.G.)	1981

In 1982 the Department of Industry, Commerce and Tourism was split into two briefs - Industry became part of the Energy portfolio, and a new Department of Trade, Commerce and Tourism was established.

MINISTERS FOR TRADE, COMMERCE & TOURISM

Taoiseach	Minister	App.
Haughey	Des O'Malley (F.F.)	1982
Haughey	Albert Reynolds (F.F.)	1982
Haughey	Pádraig Flynn (F.F.)	1982
FitzGerald	Frank Cluskey (Lab.)	1982-83

In 1983, the department's functions were taken over by the Department of Industry, Trade, Commerce & Tourism.

MINISTER FOR INDUSTRY, TRADE, COMMERCE & TOURISM

Taoiseach	Minister	App.
FitzGerald	John Bruton (F.G.)	1984-86

In December 1983 the Department of Industry, Trade, Commerce & Tourism was established. In 1986 the Department of Industry, Trade, Commerce and Tourism was divided into two briefs - the Department of Industry and Commerce, and the Department of Tourism Fisheries and Forestry.

MINISTERS FOR INDUSTRY & COMMERCE

Taoiseach	Minister	App.
FitzGerald	Michael Noonan (F.G.)	1986
Haughey	Albert Reynolds (F.F.)	1987
Haughey	Des O'Malley (P.D.)	1989
Reynolds	Des O'Malley (P.D.)	1992
Reynolds	Pádraig Flynn (F.F.)	1992
Reynolds	Bertie Ahern (F.F.)	1993

In 1993, this department was abolished and the Department of Enterprise and Employment was established.

MINISTERS FOR ENTERPRISE & EMPLOYMENT

Taoiseach	Minister	App.
Reynolds	Ruairí Quinn (Lab.)	1993
Bruton	Richard Bruton (F.G.)	1994
Ahern	Mary Harney (P.D.)	1997

In June 1997, this department became the Department of Enterprise, Employment and Trade.

MINISTERS FOR LABOUR

Taoiseach	Minister	App.
De Valera (2)	Countess Markievicz (S.F.)	1919
De Valera (2)	Countess Markievicz (S.F.)	1921
Collins (3)	Joseph McGrath (C.G.)	1922
Cosgrave (4)	Joseph McGrath (C.G.)	1922
Lemass	Patrick Hillery (F.F.)	1966
Lynch	Patrick Hillery (F.F.)	1966
Lynch	Joseph Brennan (F.F.)	1969

Cosgrave	Michael O'Leary (Lab.)	1973
Lynch	Gene Fitzgerald (F.F.)	1977
Haughey	Gene Fitzgerald (F.F.)	1979
Haughey	Thomas Nolan (F.F.)	1981
Fitzgerald	Liam Kavanagh (Lab.)	1981
Haughey	Gene Fitzgerald (F.F.)	1982
FitzGerald	Liam Kavanagh (Lab.)	1982
FitzGerald	Ruairí Quinn (Lab.)	1983
FitzGerald	Michael Noonan (F.G.)	1987
Haughey	Bertie Ahern (F.F.)	1987
Reynolds	Brian Cowen (F.F.)	1992-93

The Department of Labour was re-established in 1966, following a lapse of 34 years. The Department of Equality and Law Reform replaced the Department of Labour in 1993.

MINISTERS FOR AGRICULTURE

Taoiseach	Minister	App.
De Valera (?)	Robert C. Barton (S.F.)	1919
De Valera (2)	Art O'Connor (S.F.)	1921
Collins (3)	Patrick Hogan (S.F.)	1922
Cosgrave (4)	Patrick Hogan* (C.G.)	1922
De Valera	James Ryan (F.F.)	1932
De Valera	Patrick Smith (F.F.)	1947
Costello	James Dillon (Ind.)	1948
De Valera	Thomas Walsh (F.F.)	1951
Costello	James Dillon (F.G.)	1954
De Valera	Frank Aiken (F.F.)	1957
De Valera	Senator Seán Moylan (F.F.)	1957
De Valera	Patrick Smith (F.F.)	1957
Lemass	Patrick Smith (F.F.)	1959
Lemass	Charles J. Haughey (F.F.)	1964
Lynch	Neil Blaney (F.F.)	1966
Lynch	James Gibbons (F.F.)	1970
Cosgrave	Mark Clinton (F.G.)	1973
Lynch	James Gibbons (F.F.)	1977
Haughey	Ray MacSharry (F.F.)	1979
FitzGerald	Alan Dukes (F.G.)	1981
Haughey	Brian Lenihan (F.F.)	1982
FitzGerald	Austin Deasy (F.G.)	1982
Haughey	Michael O'Kennedy (F.F.)	1987
Reynolds	Joe Walsh (F.F.)	1992
Bruton	Ivan Yates (F.G.)	1994
Ahern	Joe Walsh (F.F.)	1997

* Not a member of the Executive Council.

The Minister for Agriculture was not a member of the Executive Council until 1927. In 1924 Agriculture became Lands and Agriculture. In 1928 Land and Agriculture reverted to the Department of Agriculture. In July 1965, Fisheries was added to the Agricultural brief, and became known as the Department of Agriculture and Fisheries. In February 1977 Fisheries became a separate department. In January 1993 the Department of Agriculture and Food became known as the Department of Agriculture, Food and Forestry.

MINISTERS FOR THE MARINE

Taoiseach	Minister	App.
De Valera (2)	Seán Etchingham* (S.F.)	1920

Cosgrave	Fionán Lynch* (C.G.)	1922
De Valera	P.J. Ruttledge (F.F.)	1932
De Valera	Joseph Connolly (F.F.)	1933
Cosgrave	Patrick Donegan (F.G.)	1977
Lynch	Brian Lenihan (F.F.)	1977
Haughey	Patrick Power (F.F.)	1979
FitzGerald	Tom Fitzpatrick (F.G.)	1981
Haughey	Brendan Daly (F.F.)	1982
FitzGerald	Patrick O'Toole (F.G.)	1982
FitzGerald	Liam Kavanagh (Lab.)	1986
Haughey	Brendan Daly (F.F.)	1987
Haughey	John Wilson (F.F.)	1989
Reynolds	Michael Woods (F.F.)	1992
Reynolds	David Andrews (F.F.)	1993
Bruton	Sean Barrett (F.G.)	1994
Ahern	Michael Woods (F.F.)	1997

* Not a member of the Executive Council.

The Minister for Fisheries was not a member of the Executive Council until 1927. In 1928 the Department of Fisheries became the Department of Land and Fisheries. In 1934 it became the Department of Lands (see below). In July 1965 Fisheries was attached onto the brief of Agriculture. In February 1977 Fisheries became a separate department. Forestry was incorporated into the brief in 1979. In 1987 the Department of Fisheries adopted its current title as Department of the Marine.

MINISTERS FOR LANDS

Taoiseach	Minister	App.
De Valera	Frank Aiken (F.F.)	1936
De Valera	Gerald Boland (F.F.)	1936
De Valera	Thomas Derrig (F.F.)	1939
De Valera	Séan Moylan (F.F.)	1943
Costello	Joseph Blowick (C.T.)	1948
De Valera	Thomas Derrig (F.F.)	1951
Costello	Joseph Blowick (C.T.)	1954
De Valera	Erskine Childers (F.F.)	1957
Lemass	Erskine Childers (F.F.)	1959
Lemass	Mícheál O'Móráin (F.F.)	1959
Lynch	Mícheál O'Móráin (F.F.)	1966
Lynch	Pádraig Faulkner (F.F.)	1968
Lynch	Sean Flanagan (F.F.)	1969
Cosgrave	Thomas J. Fitzpatrick (F.G.)	1973
Cosgrave	Patrick Donegan (F.G.)	1977

This department was discontinued in 1997.

MINISTERS FOR EDUCATION

Taoiseach	Minister	App.
De Valera (2)	J.J. O'Kelly* (S.F.)	1921
Collins (3)	Fionán Lynch (S.F.)	1922
Cosgrave (4)	Eoin MacNeill (C.G.)	1922-25
Cosgrave	John M. O'Sullivan (C.G.)	1926
De Valera	Thomas Derrig (F.F.)	1932
De Valera	Seán T. O'Kelly (F.F.)	1939
De Valera	Eamon de Valera (F.F.)	1939
De Valera	Thomas Derrig (F.F.)	1940
Costello	Richard Mulcahy (F.G.)	1948
De Valera	Seán Moylan (F.F.)	1951

Taoiseach	Minister	App.
Costello	Richard Mulcahy (F.G.)	1954
De Valera	Jack Lynch (F.F.)	1957
Lemass	Patrick Hillery (F.F.)	1959
Lemass	George Colley (F.F.)	1965
Lemass	Donogh O'Malley (F.F.)	1966
Lynch	Donogh O'Malley (F.F.)	1966
Lynch	Jack Lynch (F.F.)	1968
Lynch	Brian Lenihan (F.F.)	1968
Lynch	Pádraig Faulkner (F.F.)	1969
Cosgrave	Dick Burke (F.G.)	1973
Cosgrave	Peter Barry (F.G.)	1976
Lynch	John Wilson (F.F.)	1977
Haughey	John Wilson (F.F.)	1979
FitzGerald	John Boland (F.G.)	1981
Haughey	Martin O'Donohue (F.F.)	1982
Haughey	Charles J Haughey (F.F.)	1982
Haughey	Gerard Brady (F.F.)	1982
FitzGerald	Gemma Hussey (F.G.)	1982
FitzGerald	Patrick Cooney (F.G.)	1986
Haughey	Mary O'Rourke (F.F.)	1987
Reynolds	Seamus Brennan (F.F.)	1992
Reynolds	Niamh Bhreathnach (Lab.)	1993
Bruton	Niamh Bhreathnach (Lab.)	1994
Ahern	Micheál Martin (F.F.)	1997

* Not a member of the Executive Council.
The department is now entitled the Department of Education, Science and Technology.

MINISTERS FOR THE GAELTACHT

Taoiseach	Minister	App.
De Valera (2)	Séan T. O'Kelly (S.F.)	1919
Costello	Richard Mulcahy (F.G.)	1956
Costello	P.J. Lindsay (F.G.)	1956
De Valera	Jack Lynch (F.F.)	1957
De Valera	Mícheál O'Moráin (F.F.)	1957
Lemass	Mícheál O'Moráin (F.F.)	1959
Lemass	Gerald Bartley (F.F.)	1959
Lemass	Mícheál O'Moráin (F.F.)	1961
Lynch	Mícheál O'Moráin (F.F.)	1966
Lynch	Pádraig Faulkner (F.F.)	1968
Lynch	George Colley (F.F.)	1969
Cosgrave	Thomas O'Donnell (F.G.)	1973
Lynch	Dennis Gallagher (F.F.)	1977
Haughey	M. Geoghegan-Quinn (F.F.)	1979
FitzGerald	Paddy O'Toole (F.G.)	1981
Haughey	Pádraig Flynn (F.F.)	1982
Haughey	Denis Gallagher (F.F.)	1982
FitzGerald	Patrick O'Toole (F.G.)	1982
Haughey	Charles J. Haughey (F.F.)	1987
Reynolds	John Wilson (F.F.)	1992
Reynolds	Michael D. Higgins (Lab.)	1993
Bruton	Michael D. Higgins (Lab.)	1994
Ahern	Síle de Valera (F.F.)	1997

De Valera's cabinet of 1919-1921 had a Minister for 'Irish', Sean O'Kelly. In July of 1956 the Department of the Gaeltacht was created. In 1993 the Department of the Gaeltacht was reconstituted as the Department of Arts, Culture and the Gaeltacht. In 1997 it was renamed the Department of Arts, Heritage, Gaeltacht and the Islands.

MINISTERS FOR POSTS AND TELEGRAPHS

Taoiseach	Minister	App.
Collins	J.J. Walsh (S.F.)	1922
Cosgrave	J.J. Walsh (C.G.)	1922
Cosgrave	Ernest Blythe (C.G.)	1927
De Valera	Senator Joseph Connolly (F.F.)	1932
De Valera	Gerald Boland (F.F.)	1933
De Valera	Oscar Traynor (F.F.)	1936
De Valera	Oscar Traynor (F.F.)	1938
De Valera	Thomas Derrig (F.F.)	1939
De Valera	P.J. Little (F.F.)	1939
Costello	James Everett (Lab.)	1948
De Valera	Erskine Childers (F.F.)	1951
Costello	Michael J. Keyes (Lab.)	1954
De Valera	Neil Blaney (F.F.)	1957
De Valera	John Ormonde (F.F.)	1957
Lemass	Michael Hilliard (F.F.)	1959
Lemass	Joseph Brennan (F.F.)	1965
Lynch	Erskine Childers (F.F.)	1966
Lynch	P.J. Lalor (F.F.)	1969
Lynch	Gerry Collins (F.F.)	1970
Cosgrave	Conor Cruise O'Brien (Lab.)	1973
Lynch	Pádraig Faulkner (F.F.)	1977
Haughey	Albert Reynolds (F.F.)	1979
FitzGerald	Patrick Cooney (F.G.)	1981
Haughey	John Wilson (F.F.)	1982
FitzGerald	Jim Mitchell (F.G.)	1982-84

Until 1924 the Minister for Posts and Telegraphs was known as the Postmaster General. The position did not have a place at cabinet until 1927. In 1984 under the coalition government the department was renamed the Department of Communications.

MINISTERS FOR COMMUNICATIONS

Taoiseach	Minister	App.
FitzGerald	Jim Mitchell (F.G.)	1984
Haughey	John Wilson (F.F.)	1987
Haughey	Ray Burke (F.F.)	1987
Haughey	Seamus Brennan (F.F.)	1991-92

This department was abolished in 1992, when the Departmnet of Tourism, Transport & Communications was created.

MINISTERS FOR TOURISM, TRANSPORT AND COMMUNICATIONS

Taoiseach	Minister	App.
Reynolds	M. Geoghegan-Quinn (F.F.)	1992-3

In 1993 the Department of Transport, Energy and Communications was created.

MINISTERS FOR TRANSPORT, ENERGY & COMMUNICATIONS

Taoiseach	Minister	App.
Reynolds	Brian Cowen (F.F.)	1993
Bruton	Michael Lowry (F.G.)	1994
Bruton	Alan Dukes (F.G.)	1996

The Department was renamed the Department of Public Enterprise in June 1997.

MINISTERS FOR PUBLIC ENTERPRISE

Taoiseach	Minister	App.
Ahern	Mary O'Rourke (F.F.)	1997

MINISTERS FOR HEALTH

Taoiseach	Minister	App.
Costello	Noel Browne (Ind.)	1948
Costello	John A. Costello (F.G.)	1951
De Valera	James Ryan (F.F.)	1951
Costello	Thomas F. O'Higgins (F.G.)	1954
De Valera	Seán MacEntee (F.F.)	1957
Lemass	Seán MacEntee (F.F.)	1959
Lemass	Donogh O'Malley (F.F.)	1965
Lemass	Séan Flanagan (F.F.)	1966
Lynch	Séan Flanagan (F.F.)	1966
Lynch	Erskine Childers (F.F.)	1969
Cosgrave	Brendan Corish (Lab.)	1973
Lynch	Charles J. Haughey (F.F.)	1977
Haughey	Michael Woods (F.F.)	1979
FitzGerald	Eileen Desmond (Lab.)	1981
Haughey	Michael Woods (F.F.)	1982
FitzGerald	Barry Desmond (Lab.)	1982
FitzGerald	John Boland (F.G.)	1987
Haughey	Rory O'Hanlon (F.F.)	1987
Reynolds	John O'Connell (F.F.)	1992
Reynolds	Brendan Howlin (Lab.)	1993
Bruton	Michael Noonan (F.G.)	1994
Ahern	Brian Cowen (F.F.)	1997

From 1924 Health was included under the brief of Local Government and Public Health. In 1947 the Department of Health was established. It is now known as the Department of Health and Children.

MINISTERS FOR SOCIAL WELFARE

Taoiseach	Minister	App.
De Valera	James Ryan (F.F.)	1947
Costello	William Norton (Lab.)	1948
De Valera	James Ryan (F.F.)	1951
Costello	Brendan Corish (Lab.)	1954
De Valera	Patrick Smith (F.F.)	1957
Lemass	Seán MacEntee (F.F.)	1959
Lemass	Kevin Boland (F.F.)	1961
Lynch	Joseph Brennan (F.F.)	1966
Lynch	Kevin Boland (F.F.)	1969
Lynch	Joseph Brennan (F.F.)	1970
Cosgrave	Brendan Corish (Lab.)	1973
Lynch	Charles J. Haughey (F.F.)	1977
Haughey	Michael Woods (F.F.)	1979
FitzGerald	Eileen Desmond (Lab.)	1981
Haughey	Michael Woods (F.F.)	1982
FitzGerald	Barry Desmond (Lab.)	1982
FitzGerald	Gemma Hussey (F.G.)	1986
Haughey	Michael Woods (F.F.)	1987
Reynolds	Charlie McCreevy (F.F.)	1992
Reynolds	Michael Woods (F.F.)	1993
Bruton	Proinsias de Rossa (D.L.)	1994
Ahern	Dermot Ahern (F.F.)	1997

The Dept. of Social Welfare was established in 1947. In June 1997, it was renamed the Department of Social, Community and Family Affairs.

MINISTERS FOR TRANSPORT AND POWER

Taoiseach	Minister	App.
Lemass	Erskine Childers (F.F.)	1959
Lynch	Brian Lenihan (F.F.)	1969
Lynch	Michael O'Kennedy (F.F.)	1973
Cosgrave	Peter Barry (F.G.)	1973
Cosgrave	Thomas Fitzpatrick (F.G.)	1976
Lynch	Pádraig Faulkner (F.F.)	1977

The brief of Transport and Power was established in July 1959. In 1977 this was renamed the Department of Tourism and Transport.

MINISTERS FOR TOURISM & TRANSPORT

Taoiseach	Minister	App.
Lynch	Pádraig Faulkner (F.F.)	1977-79
Haughey	John Wilson (F.F.)	1987
Haughey	Seamus Brennan (F.F.)	1989-92

The department was discontinued between 1979 and 1987 and abolished in 1992.

MINISTERS FOR TRANSPORT

Taoiseach	Minister	App.
Haughey	Albert Reynolds (F.F.)	1979
FitzGerald	Patrick Cooney (F.G.)	1981
Haughey	John Wilson (F.F.)	1982
FitzGerald	Jim Mitchell (F.G.)	1982-84

MINISTERS FOR TOURISM, FISHERIES AND FORESTRY

Taoiseach	Minister	App.
FitzGerald	Liam Kavanagh (Lab.)	1986
FitzGerald	Paddy O'Toole (F.G.)	1987

The department was briefly established in 1986 but was incorporated into Tourism and Transport in 1987.

MINISTERS FOR TOURISM & TRADE

Taoiseach	Minister	App.
Reynolds	Charlie McCreevy (F.F.)	1993
Bruton	Enda Kenny (F.G.)	1994
Ahern	Jim McDaid (F.F.)	1997

The Department of Tourism and Trade was established in 1993. In 1997, it was reconstituted as the Department of Tourism, Sport and Recreation, with the brief of Trade going to Department of Enterprise and Employment.

MINISTERS FOR PUBLIC SERVICES

Taoiseach	Minister	App.
Cosgrave	Richie Ryan (F.G.)	1973
Lynch	George Colley (F.F.)	1977
Haughey	Gene Fitzgerald (F.F.)	1979

FitzGerald	Liam Kavanagh (Lab.)	1981
Haughey	Gene Fitzgerald (F.F.)	1982
FitzGerald	John Boland (F.G.)	1982
FitzGerald	Ruairí Quinn (Lab.)	1986
FitzGerald	John Bruton (F.G.)	1987
Haughey	Ray MacSharry (F.F.)	1987

In November 1973, the Department of the Public Service was created. It was discontinued in 1987.

MINISTERS FOR ECONOMIC PLANNING AND DEVELOPMENT

Taoiseach	Minister	App.
Lynch	Martin O'Donoghue (F.F.)	1977

The brief of Economic Planning and Development was established in 1977, and abolished in 1979.

MINISTERS FOR EQUALITY AND LAW REFORM

Taoiseach	Minister	App.
Reynolds	Ruairí Quinn (Lab.)	1993
Bruton	Mervyn Taylor (Lab.)	1994

The Department of Equality and Law Reform was abolished in 1997 and its functions transferred to the Department of Justice.

ATTORNEYS-GENERAL

Taoiseach	Minister	App.
Collins (3)	H. Kennedy*	1922
Cosgrave (4)	H. Kennedy*	1922
Cosgrave	J. O'Byrne	1924
Cosgrave	J.A. Costello	1926
de Valera	C.A. Maguire	1932

de Valera	J. Geoghegan	1936
de Valera	P. Lynch	1936
de Valera	K. Haugh	1940
de Valera	K. Dixon	1942
De Valera	C. O'Dalaigh	1946
Costello	C. Lavery	1948
Costello	C.F. Casey	1951
De Valera	C. O'Dalaigh	1951
De Valera	T. Teevan	1953
Costello	P. McGilligan	1954
De Valera	A. O'Caoimh	1957
Lemass	A. O'Caoimh	1959
Lemass	C. Condon	1965
Lynch	C. Condon	1966
Cosgrave	D. Costello	1973
Lynch	A.J. Hederman	1977
Haughey	A.J. Hederman	1979
Haughey	P. Connolly	1982
FitzGerald	P. Sutherland	1982
FitzGerald	J. Rogers	1986
Haughey	J. L. Murray	1987
Reynolds	H. Whelehan	1992
Bruton	D. Gleeson	1994
Ahern	D. Byrne	1997

* In 1922 the post of Attorney-General was known as 'Law Officer'.

Frank Aiken was Minister for Co-ordination of Defensive Measures from September 1939 until June 1945. Sean Lemass was Minister for Supplies from September 1939 until July 1945.

Key to defunct political parties:
C.G. Cumann na nGaedhael
C.P. Clann na Poblachta
C.T. Clann na Talmhan

VOTES RECORDED AT DÁIL ELECTIONS, 1948-1997

Date of Election	Registered Electors	Votes Cast	Valid Votes	Spoiled Votes	% Turnout
04.02.1948	1,800,210	1,336,628	1,323,443	13,185	74.2
30.05.1951	1,785,144	1,343,616	1,331,724	11,892	75.3
18.05.1954	1,763,828	1,347,932	1,335,202	12,730	76.4
05.03.1957	1,738,278	1,238,559	1,227,019	11,540	71.3
04.10.1961	1,670,860	1,179,738	1,168,404	11,334	70.6
07.04.1965	1,683,019	1,246,415	1,253,122	11,293	75.1
18.06.1969	1,753,388	1,334,963	1,318,953	16,010	76.9
28.02.1973	1,783,604	1,366,474	1,350,537	15,937	76.6
16.06.1977	2,118,606	1,616,770	1,603,027	13,743	76.3
11.06.1981	2,275,450	1,734,379	1,718,211	16,168	76.2
18.02.1982	2,275,450	1,679,500	1,665,133	14,367	73.8
24.11.1982	2,335,153	1,701,385	1,688,720	12,665	72.9
17.02.1987	2,445,515	1,793,506	1,777,165	16,341	73.3
15.06.1989	2,448,813	1,677,592	1,656,813	20,779	68.5
25.11.1992	2,557,036	1,751,351	1,724,853	26,498	68.5
06.06.1997	2,731,652	1,807,015	1,789,006	18,009	66.2

ALL-IRELAND GENERAL ELECTION, 14TH DECEMBER, 1918.

105-seat election. Unionists: 22 seats; Nationalists: 6 seats; Sinn Féin: 73 seats, Labour Unionist: 3 seats; Independent Unionist: 1 seat. Sinn Féin form Dáil Éireann on 21st January 1919.

GENERAL ELECTION TO PARLIAMENT OF SOUTHERN IRELAND, 24TH MAY, 1921

128-seat election. Sinn Féin: 124 seats; Independents: 4 seats (Trinity College). No seats contested. The Sinn Féin members abstained from the southern Ireland House of Commons and constituted themselves as the Second Dáil on 16th August 1921. They were joined by the Sinn Féin member of the Northern Ireland House of Commons, John O'Mahony of Fermanagh South.

Date of Election	Fianna Fáil	Fine Gael	Labour Party	Farmers' Parties	Republican parties	Others	Turnout %	Total seats
16.06.1922	36	58	17	7	-	10	45.5	128
27.08.1923	44	63	14	15	-	17	61.2	153
09.06.1927	44	47	22	11	5	24	68.1	153
15.09.1927	57	62	13	6	-	15	69.0	153
16.02.1932	72	57	7	3	-	14	76.5	153
24.01.1933	77	48	8	11	-	9	81.3	153
01.07.1937	69	48	13	-	-	8	76.2	138
17.06.1938	77	45	9	-	-	7	76.7	138
22.06.1943	67	32	17	15	-	7	74.2	138
30.05.1944	76	30	8	13	-	11	67.7	138
04.02.1948	68	31	14	7	10	17	74.2	147
30.05.1951	69	40	16	6	2	14	75.3	147
18.05.1954	65	50	19	5	3	5	76.4	147
05.03.1957	78	40	12	3	5	9	71.3	147
04.10.1961	70	47	16	2	1	8	70.6	144
07.04.1965	72	47	22	-	1	2	75.1	144
18.06.1969	75	50	18	-	-	1	76.9	144
28.02.1973	69	54	19	-	-	2	76.6	144
16.06.1977	84	43	17	-	-	4	76.3	148
11.06.1981	78	65	15	-	2	6	76.2	166
18.02.1982	81	63	15	-	-	7	73.8	166
24.11.1982	75	70	16	-	-	5	72.9	166
17.02.1987	81	51	12	-	-	22	73.3	166
15.06.1989	77	55	15	-	-	19	68.5	166
25.11.1992	68	45	33	-	-	20	67.5	166
06.06.1997	77	54	17	-	1	17	66.2	166

Fianna Fáil includes Anti-Treaty Sinn Féin (1922-23).
Fine Gael takes in Pro-Treaty Sinn Féin (1922) and Cumann na nGaedheal (1923-32).
Farmers' Parties takes in the Farmers' Union (1922-44), the National Centre Party (1933) and Clann na Talmhan (1943-61).
Republican parties takes in Clann na Poblachta (1948-65); Sinn Féin (June 1927 - 5 T.D.s; 1957 - 4 T.D.s; 1997 - 1 T.D.); and the National H-Block Committee (1981 - 2 T.D.s).
Others includes smaller groups and independents, as well as the following:

National League: June 1927 (8 T.D.s); Aug. 1927 (2 T.D.s).
National Labour: 1944 (4 T.D.s); 1948 (5 T.D.s).
National Progressive Democrats: 1961 (2 T.D.s).
Sinn Féin Workers' Party and **Workers' Party**: 1981 (1 T.D.); Feb. 1982 (3 T.D.s); Nov. 1982 (2 T.D.s); 1987 (4 T.D.s); 1989 (7 T.D.s).
Progressive Democrats: 1987 (14 T.D.s); 1989 (6 T.D.s); 1992 (10 T.D.s); 1997 (4 T.D.s).
Green Party: 1989, 1992 (1 T.D.); 1997 (2 T.D.s).
Democratic Left: 1992 (4 T.D.s); 1997, (4 T.D.s).

CONSTITUTIONAL REFERENDA, 1937-96

Date	Issue	Turnout (%)	For (%)	Against (%)	Spoiled (%)
July 1, 1937	**Endorse new constitution**	75.8	56.5	43.5	10.0
June 17, 1959	**Introduction of plurality system** *(replacing proportional representation)*	58.4	48.2	51.8	4.0
October 16, 1968	**T.D.-population ratio**	65.8	39.2	60.8	4.3
October 16, 1968	**Introduction of plurality system** *(replacing proportional representation)*	65.8	39.2	60.8	4.3
May 10, 1972	**Allow E.E.C. membership**	70.9	83.1	16.9	0.8
December 7, 1972	**Lower voting age to 18**	50.7	84.6	15.4	5.2
December 7, 1972	**Abolish 'special position' of the Catholic church**	50.7	84.4	15.6	5.5
July 5, 1979	**Protect adoption system**	28.6	99.0	1.0	2.5
July 5, 1979	**Allow alteration of university representation in Seanad Éireann**	28.6	92.4	7.6	3.9
September 7, 1983	**Prohibit legalisation of abortion**	53.7	66.9	33.1	0.7
June 14, 1984	**Extend voting rights to non-citizens**	47.5	75.4	24.6	3.5
June 26, 1986	**Allow legalisation of divorce**	60.8	36.5	63.5	0.6
May 26, 1987	**Allow signing of Single European Act**	43.9	69.9	30.1	0.5
June 18, 1992	**Allow ratification of the Maastricht Treaty on European Union**	57.3	69.1	30.9	0.5
November 25, 1992	**Restrict availability of abortion**	68.2	34.6	65.4	4.7
November 25, 1992	**Right to travel guarantee**	68.2	62.4	37.6	4.3
November 25, 1992	**Right to information guarantee**	68.2	59.9	40.1	4.3
November 24, 1995	**Right to divorce**	61.9	50.3	49.7	0.3
November 28, 1996	**Restrictions on right to bail**	29.2	74.8	25.2	-

SELECTED BIOGRAPHIES OF POLITICAL FIGURES IN THE REPUBLIC OF IRELAND

Bertie Ahern, born Dublin 1951; elected Taoiseach June 1997; leader of Fianna Fáil since 1994. *See biographies of Taoisigh.*

Dermot Ahern, born Louth 1955; Fianna Fáil T.D. since 1987; appointed Minister for Social, Community and Family Affairs, June 1997; previously Government Chief Whip (1991-92).

David Andrews, born Dublin 1935; Fianna Fáil T.D. since 1965; appointed Minister for Defence June 1997; has held various ministerial portfolios including Foreign Affairs (1992-93) and Defence (1993-94).

Séamus Brennan, born Galway 1948; Fianna Fáil T.D. since 1981; Senator (1977-81); appointed Minister of State at Departments of the Taoiseach and Defence and Government Chief Whip June 1997.

John Bruton, born Dublin 1947; former Taoiseach; leader of Fine Gael since 1990. *See biographies of Taoisigh.*

Ray Burke, born Dublin 1943; Fianna Fáil T.D. since 1973; appointed Minister for Foreign Affairs June 1997; has held a number of ministerial portfolios including Justice (1989-92) and Energy and Communications (1987-88).

Hugh Byrne, born Wexford 1943; Fianna Fáil T.D. (1981-89 and since 1992); Senator (1989-92); appointed Minister of State at the Department of the Marine, July 1997.

Liam Cosgrave, born Dublin 1920; former Taoiseach and leader of Fine Gael. *See biographies of Taoisigh.*

Brian Cowen, born Offaly 1960; Fianna Fáil T.D. since 1984; appointed Minister for Health and Children, June 1997; formerly Minister for Labour (1992-93) and

Transport, Energy and Communications (1993-94).

Martin Cullen, born Waterford 1954; Progressive Democrat T.D. (1987-89 and from 1992); appointed Minister of State at the Department of Finance, July 1997.

Noel Davern, born Tipperary 1945; Fianna Fáil T.D. (1969-81 and since 1987); appointed Minister of State at Department of Agriculture, Food and Forestry, July 1997.

Noel Dempsey, born Meath 1953; Fianna Fáil T.D. since 1987; appointed Minister for Environment and Rural Development, June 1997; previously a Minister of State.

Proinsias De Rossa, born Dublin 1940; founding member of Democratic Left (1992) and party leader; T.D. since 1982; M.E.P. (1989-92); Minister for Social Welfare (1994-97); leader of The Workers' Party (1988-92).

Alan Dukes, born Dublin 1945; Fine Gael T.D. since 1981; leader of Fine Gael (1987-90); has held various ministerial portfolios including Finance (1982-86) and Justice (1986-87).

Frank Fahey, born Dublin 1951; Fianna Fáil T.D. (1982-92 and since 1997); Senator (1993-97); appointed Minister of State at the Department of Health and Children, July 1997.

Garret FitzGerald, born Dublin 1926; former Taoiseach and leader of Fine Gael. See biographies of Taoisigh.

Chris Flood, born Westmeath 1947; Fianna Fáil T.D. since 1987; appointed Minister of State at the Department of Tourism, Sport and Recreation, July 1997. Responsible for National Drugs Strategy team.

Pádraig Flynn, born Mayo 1939; Commissioner to the E.U. since 1993 with responsibility for Social Affairs; Fianna Fáil T.D. (1977-93) holding various ministries.

Tony Gregory, born Dublin 1947; independent T.D. since 1982; prominent on local issues for his Dublin constituency.

Mary Harney, born Galway 1953; Tánaiste and Minister for Enterprise, Employment and Trade; T.D. since 1981; Senator (1977-81); formerly a member of Fianna Fáil; founding member of the Progressive Democrats in 1985 and the party's leader since 1993.

Charles Haughey, born Mayo 1925; former Taoiseach and leader of Fianna Fáil. See biographies of taoisigh.

Michael D. Higgins, born Limerick 1941; Labour Party T.D. (1981-82 and since 1987); Minister for Arts, Culture and the Gaeltacht (1993-97); author of poetry collections Betrayal (1990) and The Season of Fire (1993).

Patrick Hillery, born Clare 1923; former government minister and President. See biographies of Irish Presidents.

Brendan Howlin, born Wexford 1956; Labour Party T.D. since 1987; Minister for Health (1993-94) and Minister for the Environment (1994-97).

Joe Jacob, born Clare 1939; Fianna Fáil T.D. since 1987; appointed Minister of State at the Department of Public Enterprise, July 1997.

Tom Kitt, born Galway 1952; Fianna Fáil T.D. since 1987; appointed Minister of State at the Department of Enterprise, Employment and Trade, July 1997.

Michael Lowry, born Tipperary 1954; T.D. since 1987; Minister for Transport, Energy and Communications (1994-96); resigned following revelations of irregular payments to him from Dunnes Stores. Failing to secure an election nomination from Fine Gael, he left the party in early 1997, ran as an independent and topped the poll.

Jack Lynch, born Cork 1917; former Taoiseach and leader of Fianna Fáil. See Biographies of Taoisigh.

Charlie McCreevy, born Kildare 1949; Fianna Fáil T.D. since 1977; appointed Minister for Finance, June 1997; has previously been Minister for Social Welfare (1992-1993) and Tourism and Trade (1993-94).

Dr. Jim McDaid, born Donegal 1949; Fianna Fáil T.D. since 1989; appointed Minister for Tourism, Sport and Recreation, June 1997.

Ray MacSharry, born Sligo 1938: Fianna Fáil T.D. (1969-89); held ministerial portfolios of Agriculture (1979-81) and Finance (1982 & 1987-88) and was Tánaiste (1982); M.E.P. (1984-87); E.U. Commissioner for Agriculture (1989-93).

Martin Manseragh, born England 1947; influential adviser to Albert Reynolds and Bertie Ahern on matters relating to Northern Ireland.

Micheál Martin, born Cork 1960; Fianna Fáil T.D. since 1989; appointed Minister for Education, Science and Technology, June 1997.

Tom Moffat, born Mayo 1940; Fianna Fáil T.D. since 1992; appointed Minister of State at the Department of Health and Children, July 1997.

Bobby Molloy, born Galway 1936; T.D. since 1965; appointed as Minister of State to the Government and at the Department of the Environment and Rural Development, July 1997; left Fianna Fáil in 1986 to join the Progressive Democrats.

Michael Noonan, born Limerick 1943; Fine Gael T.D. since 1981, holding various ministerial portfolios including Justice (1982-86) and Health (1994-97).

Conor Cruise O'Brien, born Dublin 1917, Labour T.D. (1969-77); minister for Posts and Telegraphs (1973-77); has converted to unionism on his personal road to Damascus and is a United Kingdom Unionist delegate to the multi-party talks.

Caoimhghín Ó Caoláin, born Monaghan 1953, elected to Dáil Éireann in 1997, becoming the first Sinn Féin T.D. to take his seat in Leinster House since 1922.

Éamon Ó Cuiv, born Dublin 1950; Fianna Fáil T.D. since 1992; Senator (1989-92); appointed Minister of State at the Department of Arts, Culture, Gaeltacht and the Islands, July 1997; grandson of Éamon de Valera.

Willie O'Dea, born Limerick 1952; Fianna Fáil T.D. since 1982; appointed Minister of State at the Department of Education, Science and Technology, July 1997.

Liz O'Donnell, born Dublin 1956; Progressive Democrats T.D. since 1992; appointed Minister of State at the Department of Foreign Affairs, July 1997.

John O'Donoghue, born Kerry 1956; Fianna Fáil T.D. since 1987; appointed Minister for Justice, Equality and Law Reform, June 1997.

Ned O'Keefe, born Cork 1942; Fianna Fáil T.D. since 1982; Senator 1982; appointed Minister of State at the Department of Agriculture, Food and Forestry, July 1997.

Des O'Malley, born Limerick 1939; T.D. since 1968, holding a number of ministerial portfolios; expelled from

Fianna Fáil 1985; founder of the Progressive Democrats 1985 and former leader of that party (1985-93).

Mary O'Rourke, born Westmeath 1937; T.D. since 1982; Senator (1981-82); Minister for Public Enterprise since 1997; has held several portfolios including Education (1987-91); deputy leader of Fianna Fáil since 1994.

Nora Owen, born Dublin 1945; T.D. (1981-87 and since 1989); Minister for Justice (1994-97); deputy leader of Fine Gael since 1993.

Séamus Pattison, born Kilkenny 1936; Labour Party T.D. since 1961 and father of the Dáil; elected Ceann Comhairle, June 1997.

Ruairí Quinn, born Dublin 1946; T.D. (1977-81 and since 1982); Senator (1981-82); has held various ministerial portfolios including Labour (1983-87) and Finance (1994-97); deputy leader of the Labour Party since 1989.

Albert Reynolds, born Roscommon 1932; former Taoiseach and leader of Fianna Fáil. *See Biographies of Taoisigh.*

Mary Robinson, born Mayo 1944. President of Ireland (1990-97). *See Biographies of Presidents.*

Michael Smith, born Tipperary 1940; Fianna Fáil T.D. (1969-73, 1977-82 and since 1987); appointed as Minister of State at the Departments of Education, Science & Technology and Enterprise, Employment & Trade, July 1997.

Dick Spring, born Kerry 1950; former Tánaiste; leader of the Labour Party since 1982; T.D. since 1981 has held various ministerial portfolios including Foreign Affairs (1993-97) and Tánaiste (1982-87 & 1993-97); was chief negotiator for the Irish government on Northern Ireland matters.

Seán Treacy, born Tipperary 1923; T.D. (1961-97); expelled from Labour Party 1985; Ceann Comhairle (1973-77 & 1987-97).

Síle de Valera, born Dublin 1954; Fianna Fáil T.D. (1977-81 and since 1987); appointed Minister for Arts, Heritage, Gaeltacht and the Islands, June 1997; granddaughter of Éamon de Valera.

Danny Wallace, born Cork 1942; Fianna Fáil T.D. since 1982; appointed Minister of State at the Department of the Environment and Rural Development, July 1997.

Mary Wallace, born Dublin 1959; Fianna Fáil T.D. since 1989; Senator (1987-89); appointed Minister of State at the Department of Justice, Equality and Law Reform, July 1997.

Joe Walsh, born Cork 1943; Fianna Fáil T.D. (1977-81 and since 1982); Senator (1981-82); appointed Minister for Agriculture, Food and Forestry June 1997; Minister for Agriculture (1992-94).

Michael Woods, born Wicklow 1935; Fianna Fáil T.D. since 1977; appointed Minister for the Marine, June 1997; has held various ministerial portfolios including Social Welfare (1979-81, 1982, 1987-91 and 1993-94) and Agriculture and Food (1991-92).

Ivan Yates, born Dublin 1959; Fine Gael T.D. since 1981; Minister for Agriculture, Food and Forestry (1994-97).

HOW WE VOTED, THEN AND NOW

WESTMINSTER PARLIAMENTARY ELECTION, DECEMBER 1918

(Last election on an all island basis)

	Total	Sinn Féin	Nationalist	Unionist	Lab. Unionist
Seats	105	73	6	23	3

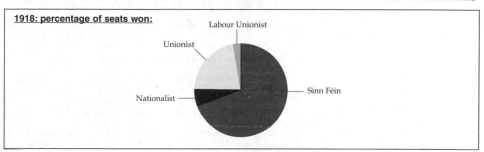

1918: percentage of seats won:

REPUBLIC OF IRELAND DÁIL ELECTION, JUNE 1997

	Total	F.F.	F.G.	Lab.	P.D.	D.L.	S.F.	Green	Others
Votes Cast	1,789006	706,576	499,942	186,045	83,765	44,901	42,733	47,573	177,471
%		39.5	27.9	10.4	4.7	2.5	2.4	2.7	9.9
Seats	166	77	54	17	4	4	1	2	7

NORTHERN IRELAND WESTMINSTER ELECTION, MAY 1997

	Total	U.U.P.	S.D.L.P.	S.F.	D.U.P.	All.	Other U.	Con.	Others
Votes Cast	790,884	258,439	190,844	126,921	107,348	62,972	23,745	9,858	10,757
%		32.7	24.1	16.0	13.6	8.0	3.0	1.2	1.3
Seats	18	10	3	2	2	0	1	0	0

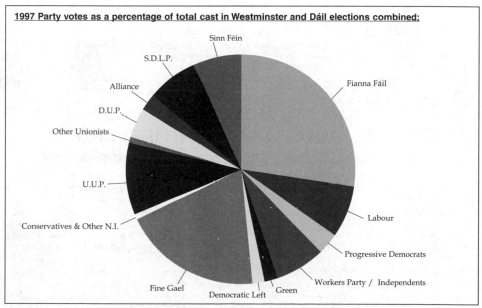

1997 Party votes as a percentage of total cast in Westminster and Dáil elections combined:

Multi party talks are currently in progress involving the British and Irish Governments and the Northern Ireland political parties. "Both governments intend that the outcome of these negotiations will be submitted for democratic ratification through referendums, North and South." - Framework Document 1995. It is currently the intention of the governments that referenda will be held jointly in May 1998.

POLITICS N.I.

INTRODUCTION TO NORTHERN IRELAND

Explanatory notes on Northern Ireland

Northern Ireland contains the counties of Antrim, Armagh, Derry, Down, Fermanagh and Tyrone. Part of the United Kingdom of Great Britain and Northern Ireland it was established by the Government of Ireland Act 1920 until its parliament voted to opt out of the Irish Free State in December 1922. From 1921 until 1972 Northern Ireland had its own parliament which dealt with local matters while the Imperial parliament at Westminster dealt with wider matters such as the Crown, taxation and defence.

From March 1972 until January 1974 Northern Ireland was under direct rule from Westminster embodied in the powers vested in the Secretary of State. The Northern Ireland Constitution Act 1973 provided for devolved government in the form of a power sharing executive. The executive took office in January with ministers from the U.U.P.,the S.D.L.P. and Alliance. It was brought down in May of that year by the Ulster Workers' Council strike. The collapse was followed by the reintroduction of direct rule.

Since May 1974 Northern Ireland has been ruled directly from Westminster under the terms of the Northern Ireland Act 1974 by the Secretary of State for Northern Ireland who is a member of the cabinet. He/she is responsible for the departments in the Northern Ireland Office and has a team of four junior ministers who head these departments. The departments are: Finance and Personnel; Economic Development; Education, Health and Social Services; Environment and Agriculture.

Subsequent constitutional initiatives such as the 'rolling devolution' of the 1982 Northern Ireland Assembly, the Anglo-Irish Agreement (1985), the Downing Street Declaration (1993) and the Frameworks documents (1995) have done little to change the constitutional status of Northern Ireland.

The legislature consists of the monarch, as head of state, and two houses: the House of Commons (a house of representatives) and the House of Lords (consisting of members of the Peerage). All bills passed by the houses of parliament must be promulgated by the monarch.

The House of Commons has 659 members of which Northern Ireland returns 18. All M.P.s are elected by the 'first past the post' system. Northern Ireland also returns three members to the European Parliament.

The House of Lords (as of June 23 1997) consists of 1,222 hereditary peers, law lords, life peers and Anglican bishops.

Northern Ireland has 26 district and borough councils which have limited powers of local government.

HEAD OF STATE

The Head of State is Elizabeth II Alexandra Mary of Windsor. Born London April 21 1926, she ascended to the throne on February 6, 1952 and was crowned at Westminster Abbey on June 2, 1953. Married Philip Mountbatten November 20, 1947. They have four children: Charles, Prince of Wales; Anne, the Princess Royal; Andrew, the Duke of York; and Prince Edward. The Queen is represented in Northern Ireland by a Lord Lieutenant in each county or city; they are The Lord O'Neill (Antrim), Colonel J.E. Wilson (Belfast), The Earl of Caledon (Armagh), W.J. Hall (Down), The Earl of Erne (Fermanagh), Sir Michael McCorkell (Derry), J.T. Eaton (Derry City) and the Duke of Abercorn (Tyrone).

STATE EMBLEMS OF NORTHERN IRELAND

Name of State, National Flag, Emblem, and National Anthem

NAME OF STATE: The name of state is Northern Ireland which is part of the United Kingdom of Great Britain and Northern Ireland. Established by the Government of Ireland Act 1920. It consists of six of the nine counties in the province of Ulster.

THE NATIONAL FLAG: The national flag is the union flag. It is a combination of the cross of St. George (a red cross on a white background), the cross of St. Andrew (a diagonal white cross on a blue background) and the cross of St. Patrick (a diagonal red cross on a white background). From partition in 1922 until the imposition of direct rule in 1972 the flag was a six pointed star enclosing a red hand surmounted by a crown at the centre of a red cross on a white background.

THE NATIONAL ANTHEM: The national anthem is 'God Save the Queen'.

NATIONALIST NON-ALLEGIANCE: It is a widely recognised fact that a majority of nationalists do not give their allegiance to the Northern Ireland state. This historical and political reality has been evident in the intermittent civil unrest since the foundation of the Northern state. Since 1969 there has been a serious escalation in this unrest which has resulted in more than 3,000 deaths. There is also statutory recognition of nationalist derogation from the Northern state in official documents on both sides of the border, including Articles 2 and 3 of the Republic of Ireland's Constitution, Article 5 of the Anglo-Irish Agreement and Articles 18 and 21 of the Framework for Agreement document.

NORTHERN IRELAND POLITICAL PARTIES
Main political parties in Northern Ireland

ULSTER UNIONIST PARTY
3 Glengall Street, Belfast BT12 5AE
Tel. (01232) 324601. www.uup.org

The U.U.P. was founded as the Ulster Unionist Council in 1905. Initially opposed to partition, it went on to govern Northern Ireland from 1921 until 1972. Since the introduction of direct rule from Westminster, the party has consistently been the single largest party in Northern Ireland in terms of M.P.s and councillors.

The U.U.P. was divided over the power-sharing arrangement in 1974. The participation of leader Brian Faulkner brought about his resignation and saw the majority of the party enter into a loose pan-unionist coalition with the D.U.P. and the Ulster Vanguard. When this arrangement collapsed in the late 1970s, the U.U.P. plotted a more independent course, refusing to enter into electoral pacts in marginal constituencies. It opposed the 'rolling devolution', suggested by Secretary of State James Prior in 1982, and the Anglo-Irish Agreement in 1985. The opposition to the Agreement saw the revival of tactical cooperation with the D.U.P. in marginal constituencies, and this has remained the case in each subsequent Westminster election. The party curently commands around 33% of the poll in Northern Ireland.

The party has as its aims the maintenance of Northern Ireland under the Crown as an integral part of the United Kingdom; the safeguarding of British citizenship for the people of Northern Ireland; the promotion of a democratic system of local government; and that any change in the constitutional status must be brought about by the consent of a majority within Northern Ireland. The party supports a Bill of Rights and the establishment of a Council of the British Isles to promote and formalise relationships within these islands.

At the last Westminster election, the party secured ten seats and won 186 seats in the local government elections. The party president is Josias Cunningham, general secretary is Jim Wilson and party leader is David Trimble M.P. The party has three delegates to the multi-party talks.

SOCIAL DEMOCRATIC AND LABOUR PARTY
Cranmore House, 611C Lisburn Road,
Belfast BT9 7GT Tel. (01232) 247700
www.indigo.ie/sdlp

The Social Democratic and Labour Party was founded in 1970 by the amalgamation of the Northern Ireland Labour Party, Republican Labour, the Nationalist Party and leading figures from the civil rights movement. The party had representatives on the short-lived Power Sharing exec-utive in 1974 and contributed to the New Ireland Forum in 1983. The party opposed 'rolling devolution' in 1982 but strongly supported the Anglo-Irish Agreement in 1985.

The party has performed well in all Northern Ireland elections since its inception and has consistently been represented at Westminster and on local councils, and since 1979 John Hume, the current party leader, has been a member of the European Parliament. It currently commands around 24% of the poll in Northern Ireland.

A moderate left-of-centre nationalist party, it promotes a united Ireland, freely negotiated and agreed by people both north and south, and contests elections on the following points: the abolition of all forms of discrimination and the promotion of equality among all citizens; the promotion of culture and the arts and the recognition and cherishing of their diversity; the public ownership of all essential services and industries; and the protection of the environment.

The S.D.L.P., through John Hume, was instrumental in brokering both the 1994 and 1997 I.R.A. ceasefires, although he came in for criticism for engaging in negotiations with Sinn Féin President Gerry Adams.

The party has consistently been the major party within nationalism and at the last elections had three M.P.s and 119 councillors elected. The party leader is John Hume M.P., M.E.P., the party chairperson is Johnathon Stephenson and the general secretary is Gerry Cosgrave.

SINN FÉIN
51-55 Falls Road, Belfast BT12 4PD
Tel. (01232) 230261
www.irlnet.com/sinnfein

Sinn Féin (from the Gaelic meaning "We Ourselves") was founded in 1905 as an umbrella group for small nationalist organisations. It won an overwhelming majority in the 1918 general election, and its members constituted themselves as Dáil Éireann. The party was to split in 1922 over the signing of the Anglo-Irish treaty and its republican rump withdrew from the Dáil. Small, abstentionist and ineffective, the party suffered a further split in 1970 when two factions emerged - 'Official' Sinn Féin (later to become the Workers' Party) and 'Provisional' Sinn Féin'.

The party revived its electoral fortunes in the period after the 1981 Hunger Strike, contesting each election in Northern Ireland from 1982 onwards. The party has had members elected to Westminster and to most local councils in Northern Ireland and currently commands around 17% of poll in Northern Ireland.

Sinn Féin is a republican party committed to ending the union with Britain and as part of the 'republican movement' has consistently been described, despite vehement denials, as the political wing of the I.R.A. The party is committed to the establishment of an agreed, inclusive Ireland and believes that a non-sectarian and pluralist society is the way forward. The party was instrumental in brokering the I.R.A. ceasefire of August 1994. Sinn Féin was admitted to the multi-party talks following the restoration of the I.R.A. ceasefire in July 1997.

The party is organised throughout Ireland, and at the last elections in Northern Ireland Sinn Féin had two M.P.s and 74 councillors elected. In the Republic the party has one T.D. and 31 councillors. The party president is Gerry Adams M.P., the chairperson is Councillor Mitchel McLaughlin and the general secretary is Lucilita Bhreatnach.

DEMOCRATIC UNIONIST PARTY
91 Dundela Avenue, Belfast BT4 3BU
Tel. (01232) 471155
www.dup.org.uk

The D.U.P. was founded in 1971 by the leader of the Protestant Unionist Party, Rev. Ian Paisley, and former Ulster Unionist M.P., Desmond Boal. Opposed to the 1974 Power Sharing arrangement, it initially secured a vote of around 10%. Its major breakthroughs came in 1979 when it won three Westminster seats and its leader, Rev. Paisley, topped the poll in the European Parliament election. Staunch in its opposition to the Anglo-Irish Agreement in 1985, it at last found common ground with the U.U.P. and all subsequent elections have seen cooperation in a number of marginal constituencies where only one unionist candidate has been nominated. The party currently commands around 14% of the poll in Northern Ireland.

The party stands for the union with Britain and opposes the Anglo-Irish agreement on the grounds that it gives the foreign government of the Republic of Ireland a role in the day-to-day affairs of Northern Ireland. It seeks a legislative and administrative devolved government for Northern Ireland where no one party has the right of veto. Such an administration, drawn from elected Northern Ireland representatives, would be underpinned by a bill of rights. The party calls for the removal of the "immoral, illegal and criminal claim over the territory" of Northern Ireland by Articles two and three of the Irish Constitution as a prerequisite to friendly relations between Northern Ireland and the Republic. Despite being in talks with loyalists, the party will not speak with republicans until all republican weapons are decommissioned.

At the last general election, the D.U.P. had its representation at Westminster reduced to two. It is the first time since 1979 that it has had less than three M.P.s. At the 1997 local elections it won 92 seats. The party leader is the Rev. Ian Paisley M.P., M.E.P., the chairperson is James McClure and the general secretary is Alan Ewart.

ALLIANCE PARTY OF NORTHERN IRELAND
88 University Street, Belfast BT7 1HE
Tel. (01232) 324274
www.unite.net/customers/alliance

The Alliance party was founded in 1970. Attracting support from disaffected unionists following the O'Neill split and from supporters of the Northern Ireland Labour Party, its members took part in the 1973 Sunningdale conference and went on to take up ministries in the Power Sharing executive in 1974. Strongly in favour of 'rolling devolution' in the 1982 Convention, it lost support when it gave qualified support to the Anglo-Irish Agreement in 1985. The party currently commands around 8% of the poll in Northern Ireland.

The party is a moderate unionist party and believes a regional power-sharing government for Northern Ireland is the best method of governance and the best chance for achieving a sustainable and lasting peace. It also advocates a Bill of Rights and a constructive and co-operative North/South relationship. It believes the future of Northern Ireland must be decided by the people of Northern Ireland and through the principle of consent. It believes in the viability of decommissioning illegal weapons in parallel with negotiations.

The party has never had representation in the House of Commons, but at the recent local elections, it secured 41 seats. The party leader is Lord Alderdice, the party chairperson is Councillor Eileen Bell and the general secretary is Councillor David Ford.

ULSTER DEMOCRATIC PARTY
36 Castle Street, Lisburn, Co. Antrim
Tel. (01846) 667056 www.udp.org

The Ulster Democratic Party was founded in 1981 by John McMichael. It emerged from and, although now autonomous, retains strong links with the Ulster Defence Association. It played a major role in bringing about the Combined Loyalist Military Command cease-fire of October 1994.

The party is committed to the continuance of the Union and opposes the consultative role the Republic of Ireland has in the governing of Northern Ireland. It believes that the best means to govern Northern Ireland is a devolved legislative government elected by proportional representation, a written constitution and a bill of rights. The party also proposes a Council of the British Isles to promote co-operation between all parts of these islands.

On the issue of decommissioning, the U.D.P. believes disarmament before negotiations is not feasible and that it will most likely be part of an overall settlement.

The current party leader is Councillor Gary McMichael, party chairman is Joe English and the general secretary is Philip Dean. The party has four councillors on the Lisburn, Belfast and Newtownabbey councils and two delegates to the multi-party talks.

PROGRESSIVE UNIONIST PARTY
182 Shankill Road, Belfast BT13 2BL.
Tel. (01232) 326233 www.pup.org

The Progressive Unionist Party was formed in 1977. It has close links with the Ulster Volunteer Force and played a major part in the negotiating of the Combined Loyalist Military Command ceasefire of October 1994.

The party is committed to maintaining the Union with Great Britain and believes that the principle of power sharing with nationalists is the best method for the governance of Northern Ireland. Dedicated to a non-sectarian, pluralist and equitable society, it believes that a written constitution and bill of rights should be implemented to safeguard human rights, minorities and institutions.

The current party leader is Hugh Smyth O.B.E., the chairman is William Smyth and the general secretary is William Mitchell. The party has councillors on the Belfast, Newtownabbey and North Down councils and has two delegates to the multi-party talks.

MINOR POLITICAL PARTIES IN NORTHERN IRELAND

GREEN PARTY
537 Antrim Road, Belfast 15; Tel. (01232) 776731.

ULSTER INDEPENDENCE MOVEMENT
316 Shankill Road, Belfast BT13 1AB;
Tel. (01232) 236815.

NORTHERN IRELAND WOMEN'S COALITION
30 Donegall Street, Belfast; Tel. (01232) 330051.

WORKERS' PARTY
6 Springfield Road, Belfast 12; Tel. (01232) 328663.

NATURAL LAW PARTY
103 University Street, Belfast 7; Tel. (01232) 311466.

UNITED KINGDOM UNIONIST PARTY
10 Hamiton Road, Bangor, Co. Down BT20 4LE;
Tel. (01247) 272994.

CONSERVATIVE PARTY
2 May Ave, Bangor, Co Down. Tel. (01247) 469210.

NORTHERN IRELAND POLITICAL PARTY LEADERS
Leaders of major Northern Ireland political parties

ULSTER UNIONIST PARTY

Edward James Saunderson	(1905-06)
Walter H. Long	(1906-10)
Sir Edward Carson	(1910-21)
Sir James Craig	(1921-40)
John Miller Andrews	(1940-43)
Sir Basil Brooke	(1943-63)
Capt. Terence O'Neill	(1963-69)
Maj. James Chichester-Clark	(1969-71)
Brian Faulkner	(1971-74)
Harry West	(1974-79)
James Molyneaux	(1979-95)
David Trimble	(1995-)

DEMOCRATIC UNIONIST PARTY

Rev. Ian Paisley	(1971-)

SOCIAL DEMOCRATIC AND LABOUR PARTY

Gerry Fitt	(1970-79)
John Hume	(1979-)

PROVISIONAL SINN FÉIN

Ruairí Ó Brádaigh	(1970-83)
Gerry Adams	(1983-)

ALLIANCE PARTY

Phelim O'Neill	(1972-73)
Oliver Napier	(1973-84)
John Cushnahan	(1984-87)
John Alderdice	(1987-)

ULSTER DEMOCRATIC PARTY

John McMichael	(1981-1987)
Raymond Smallwoods	(1987-1994)
Gary McMichael	(1994-)

PROGRESSIVE UNIONIST PARTY

Hugh Smyth	(1977-)

GENERAL ELECTION RESULTS 1997
Northern Ireland General Election Results, 1 May 1997

ANTRIM EAST
Candidates: 9; Electorate: 58,963; Turnout: 58.26%; Elected: Roy Beggs (U.U.P.) 13,318; Other Candidates: Sean Neeson (All) 6,929; Jack McKee (D.U.P.) 6,682; Terence Dick (Con.) 2,334; Billy Donaldson (P.U.P.) 1,757; Danny O'Connor (S.D.L.P.) 1,576; Robert Mason (Ind.) 1,145; Chrissie McAuley (S.F.) 543; Maura McCann (N.L.P.) 69.

ANTRIM NORTH
Candidates: 7; Electorate: 72,411; Turnout: 63.78%; Elected: Ian Paisley (D.U.P.) 21,495; Other Candidates: James Leslie (U.U.P.) 10,921; Sean Farren (S.D.L.P.) 7,333; James McCarry (S.F.) 2,896; David Alderdice (All.) 2,845; Bronagh Hinds (N.I.W.C.) 580; John Wright (N.L.P.) 116.

ANTRIM SOUTH
Candidates: 6; Electorate: 69,414; Turnout: 57.91%; Elected: Clifford Forsythe (U.U.P.) 23,108; Other Candidates: Donovan McClelland (S.D.L.P.) 6,497; David Ford (All.) 4,668; Hugh Smyth (P.U.P.) 3,490; Henry Cushinan (S.F.) 2,229; Barbara Briggs (N.L.P.) 203.

BELFAST EAST
Candidates: 9; Electorate: 61,744; Turnout: 63.21%; Elected: Peter Robinson (D.U.P) 16,640; Other Candidates: Reg Empey (U.U.P.) 9,886; Jim Hendron (All.) 9,288; Sarah Dines (Con.) 928; Dominic Corr (S.F.) 810; Patricia Lewsley (S.D.L.P.) 629; Derek Dougan (N.I.F.T.) 541; Joseph Bell (W.P.) 237; David Collins (N.L.P.) 70.

BELFAST NORTH
Candidates: 7; Electorate: 64,577; Turnout: 64.19%; Elected: Cecil Walker (U.U.P.) 21,478; Other Candidates: Alban Maginness (S.D.L.P.) 8,454; Gerry Kelly (S.F.) 8,375; Tom Campbell (All.) 2,221; Peter Emerson (Green) 539; Paul Treanor (W.P.) 297; Andrea Gribben (N.L.P.) 88.

BELFAST SOUTH
Candidates: 10; Electorate: 63,439; Turnout: 62.24%; Elected: Martin Smyth (U.U.P.) 14,201; Other Candidates: Alasdair McDonnell (S.D.L.P.) 9,601; David Ervine (P.U.P.) 5,687; Steve McBride (All.) 5,112; Sean Hayes (S.F.) 2,019; Annie Campbell (N.I.W.C.) 1,204; Myrtle Boal (Con.) 962; Niall Cusack (Ind. Lab.) 292; Patrick Lynn (W.P.) 286; James Anderson (N.L.P.) 120.

BELFAST WEST
Candidates: 6; Electorate: 61,785; Turnout: 74.27%; Elected: Gerry Adams (S.F.) 25,662; Other Candidates: Joe Hendron (S.D.L.P.) 17,753; Frederick Parkinson (U.U.P.) 1,556; John Lowry (W.P.) 721; Liam Kennedy (H.R.) 102; Mary Daly (N.L.P.) 91.

FERMANAGH & SOUTH TYRONE
Candidates: 5; Electorate: 64,600; Turnout: 74.75%; Elected: Ken Maginnis (U.U.P.) 24,862; Other Candidates: Gerry McHugh (S.F.) 11,174; Tommy Gallagher (S.D.L.P.) 11,060; Stephen Farry (All.) 977; Simeon Gillan (N.L.P.) 217.

FOYLE
Candidates: 5; Electorate: 67,620; Turnout: 70.71%; Elected: John Hume (S.D.L.P.) 25,109; Other Candidates: Mitchel McLaughlin (S.F.) 11,445; William Hay (D.U.P.) 10,290; Helen-Marie Bell (All.) 817; Donn Brennan (N.L.P.) 154.

LAGAN VALLEY
Candidates: 8; Electorate: 71,225; Turnout: 62.21%; Elected: Jeffrey Donaldson (U.U.P.) 24,560; Other Candidates: Seamus Close (All.) 7,635; Edwin Poots (D.U.P.) 6,005; Dolores Kelly (S.D.L.P.) 3,436; Stuart Sexton (Con.) 1,212; Sue Ramsey (S.F.) 1,110; Frances McCarthy (W.P.) 203; Hugh Finlay (N.L.P.) 149.

LONDONDERRY EAST
Candidates: 8; Electorate: 58,831; Turnout: 64.77%; Elected: William Ross (U.U.P.) 13,558; Other Candidates: Gregory Campbell (D.U.P.) 9,764; Arthur Doherty (S.D.L.P.) 8,273; Malachy O'Kane (S.F.) 3,463; Yvonne Boyle (All.) 2,427; James Holmes (Con.) 436; Clare Gallen (N.L.P.) 100; Ian Anderson (Nat. Dem.) 81.

MID ULSTER
Candidates: 6; Electorate: 58,836; Turnout: 86.12%; Elected: Martin McGuinness (S.F.) 20,294; Other Candidates: William McCrea (D.U.P.) 18,411; Denis Haughey (S.D.L.P.) 11,205; Ephren Bogues (All.) 460; Marian Donnelly (W.P.) 238; Maureen Murray (N.L.P.) 61.

NEWRY & ARMAGH
Candidates: 5; Electorate: 70,652; Turnout: 75.40%; Elected: Seamus Mallon (S.D.L.P.) 22,904; Other Candidates: Danny Kennedy (U.U.P.) 18,015; Patrick McNamee (S.F.) 11,218; Peter Whitcroft (All.) 1,015; David Evans (N.L.P.) 123.

NORTH DOWN
Candidates: 8; Electorate: 63,010; Turnout: 58.03%; Elected: Robert McCartney (U.K.U.P.) 12,817; Other Candidates: Alan McFarland (U.U.P.) 11,368; Oliver Napier (All.) 7,554; Leonard Fee (Con.) 1,810; Marietta Farrell (S.D.L.P.) 1,602; Jane Morrice (N.I.W.C.) 1,240; Tom Mullins (N.L.P.) 108; Robert Mooney (N.I.P.) 67.

SOUTH DOWN
Candidates: 5; Electorate: 69,855; Turnout: 70.84%; Elected: Eddie McGrady (S.D.L.P.) 26,181; Other Candidates: Dermot Nesbitt (U.U.P.) 16,248; Mick Murphy (S.F.) 5,127; Julian Crozier (All.) 1,711; Rosaleen McKeon (N.L.P.) 219.

STRANGFORD
Candidates: 7; Electorate: 69,980; Turnout: 59.47%; Elected: John Taylor (U.U.P.) 18,431; Other Candidates: Iris Robinson (D.U.P.) 12,579; Kieran McCarthy (All.) 5,467; Peter O'Reilly (S.D.L.P.) 2,775; Gilbert Chalk (Con.) 1,743; Garret O Fachtna (S.F.) 503; Sarah Mullins (N.L.P.) 121.

continued on next page

UPPER BANN
Candidates: 8; **Electorate:** 70,398; **Turnout:** 67.88%; **Elected:** David Trimble (U.U.P.) 20,836; **Other Candidates:** Brid Rodgers (S.D.L.P.) 11,584; Bernadette O'Hagan (S.F.) 5,773; Mervyn Carrick (DUP) 5,482; William Ramsey (All.) 3,017; Tom French (W.P.) 554; Brian Price (Con.) 433; Jack Lyons (N.L.P.) 108.

WEST TYRONE
Candidates: 6; **Electorate:** 58,168; **Turnout:** 79.55%; **Elected:** William Thompson (U.U.P.) 16,003; **Other Candidates:** Joe Byrne (S.D.L.P.) 14,842; Pat Doherty (S.F.) 14,280; Ann Gormley (All.) 829; Tommy Owens (W.P.) 230; Robert Johnstone (N.L.P.) 91.

GOVERNMENT & LEGAL SYSTEM

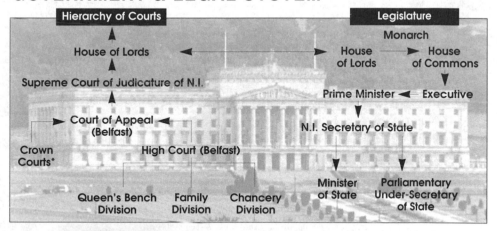

Hierarchy of Courts

House of Lords

Supreme Court of Judicature of N.I.

Court of Appeal (Belfast)

Crown Courts*

High Court (Belfast)

Queen's Bench Division — Family Division — Chancery Division

Legislature

Monarch

House of Lords — House of Commons

Prime Minister ◄ Executive

N.I. Secretary of State

Minister of State — Parliamentary Under-Secretary of State

Inferior Courts**
County Courts
(incl. small claims court)

Magistrates Courts
(incl. juvenile court)

* Deals with criminal cases.
** Deals largely with civil matters and misdemeanours.

GOVERNMENT OF NORTHERN IRELAND
Northern Ireland Government System

*The Queen is head of state and head of the Anglican Church.
*The House of Commons has 659 members elected on a 'first past the post' basis. Northern Ireland returns 18 members to the House of Commons.
* The Queen appoints the leader of the party who can command a majority in the House of Commons and appoints him/her as Prime Minister. The Prime Minister in turn appoints the members of the cabinet.
*The cabinet acts collectively.
*All acts passed by the Houses of Parliament must be promulgated by the Queen, i.e. given a royal assent.
*As head of the Judiciary, the Lord Chancellor is responsible for the appointment of judges and magistrates. The Lord Chancellor also has a seat in cabinet.
*Britain does not have a written constitution rather a series of documents and legislation which govern the functions of state. These are: common law, legislation (from the Houses of Parliament), conventions, the law and custom of parliament, European Union law and works of authority.

NORTHERN IRELAND EXECUTIVE 1974
(It is important to note that this was the last indigenous Government of Northern Ireland)

Executive	
Chief Minister	Brian Faulkner (O.U.P.)
Deputy Chief Minister	Gerry Fitt (S.D.L.P.)
Minister of Agriculture	Leslie Morrell (O.U.P.)
Minister of Commerce	John Hume (S.D.L.P.)
Minister of Education	Basil McIvor (O.U.P.)

Minister of Environment ....Roy Bradford (O.U.P.)
Minister of Finance...Herbert V Kirk (O.U.P.)
Minister of Health and Social Service ....Paddy Devlin (S.D.L.P.)
Minister of Housing and Local Government ....Austin Currie (S.D.L.P.)
Minister of Information..John Lawson Baxter (O.U.P.)
Minister of Legal Minister & Head of Office of Law Reform ....Oliver Napier (All)

Administration*

Chief Whip ....Major Lloyd Hall-Thompson (O.U.P.)
Minister of Community Relations..Ivan Cooper (S.D.L.P.)
Minister of Manpower Services..Robert Cooper (O.U.P.)
Minister of Planning and Coordination ....Eddie McGrady (S.D.L.P.)

The Administration also included all members of the Executive.

The Northern Ireland 'power sharing' Executive took office on January 1 1974. Its ministers were drawn from
S.D.L.P., Alliance and Official Unionist Party members elected to the Northern Ireland Assembly in June of 1973.
The executive and the N.I. Assembly were brought down by the Ulster Workers Council (See History chronology)
general strike of May 1974 and direct rule re-imposed.

BRITISH GOVERNMENT MINISTERS IN NORTHERN IRELAND

Secretary of State

Northern Ireland Office and the Northern Ireland departments ....Dr. Mo Mowlam M.P.

Ministers of State

Political Development, Finance and Personnel, Information and the E.U......................................Paul Murphy M.P.
Security, Economic Development and North/South Co-operation ....Adam Ingram M.P.

Parliamentary Under Secretaries of State

Education, Health and Social Services, Community Relations and Employment Equality ....Tony Worthington M.P.
Environment and Agriculture..Lord Dubs

KEY TO THE MAIN POLITICAL PARTIES

All...Alliance
D.U.P....Democraric Unionist Party
Ind...Independent
N.I.W.C....Northern Ireland Women's Coalition
P.U.P...Progressive Unionist Party
S.D.L.P....Social Democratic and Labour Party
S.F...Sinn Féin
U.K.U.P...United Kingdom Unionist Party
U.U.P....Ulster Unionist Party

CURRENT POSITION OF THE PARTIES *(at Westminster)*

PARTY	SEATS
U.U.P.	10
S.D.L.P.	3
S.F.	2
D.U.P.	2
U.K.U.P.	1
TOTAL	18

NORTHERN IRELAND MEMBERS OF PARLIAMENT

(Parliamentary constituency in italics)

Gerry Adams: (S.F.) 51-55 Falls Road, Belfast 12; Tel. (01232) 230261; *(Belfast West)*.

Roy Beggs: (U.U.P.) 41 Station Road, Larne, Co. Antrim BT40 3AA; Tel. (01574) 273258; *(Antrim East)*.

Jeffrey Donaldson: (U.U.P.) 38 Railway Street, Lisburn, Co. Antrim BT28 1XP; Tel. (01846) 668001; *(Lagan Valley)*.

Clifford Forsythe: (U.U.P.) 19 Fountain Street, Antrim BT 41 4BG. Tel. (01849) 460776; *(Antrim South)*.

John Hume: (S.D.L.P.) 5 Bayview Terrace, Derry BT48 7EE; Tel. (01504) 265340; *(Foyle)*.

Robert McCartney: (U.K.U.P.) *(Down North)*.

Eddie McGrady: (S.D.L.P.) 32 Saul Street, Downpatrick, Co. Down BT30 6NQ; Tel. (01396) 61288; *(Down South).*

Martin McGuinness: (S.F.) 15 Cable Street, Derry BT48; Tel. (01504) 361949; *(Mid Ulster).*

Ken Maginnis: (U.U.P.) 20 Brooke Street, Dungannon, Co. Tyrone BT71 7AN; Tel. (01868) 723265; *(Fermanagh and South Tyrone).*

Seamus Mallon: (S.D.L.P.) 15 Cornmarket, Newry, Co. Down BT35 8BG; Tel. (01693) 67933; *(Newry and Armagh).*

Rev. Ian Paisley: (D.U.P.) 17 Cyprus Avenue, Belfast BT5 5NT; Tel. (01232) 454255; *(Antrim North).*

Peter Robinson: (D.U.P.) 51 Gransha Road, Dundonald, Belfast BT16 0HB; Tel. (01232) 473111; *(Belfast East).*

William Ross: (U.U.P.) 89 Teevan Road, Turmeel, Dungiven, Co. Derry BT47 4SL; Tel. (015047) 41428; *(Londonderry East).*

Rev. Martin Smyth: (U.U.P.) 117 Cregagh Road, Belfast BT 6 0LA; Tel. (01232) 457009; *(Belfast South).*

John Taylor: (U.U.P.) 6 William Street, Newtownards, Co. Down BT23 4AE; Tel. (01247) 814123; *(Strangford).*

William Thompson: (U.U.P.) 156 Donaghanie Road, Beragh, Omagh, Co. Tyrone BT79 0XE; Tel. (01662) 758214; *(West Tyrone).*

David Trimble: (U.U.P.) 2 Queen Street, Lurgan, Co. Armagh BT66 8BQ; Tel. (01762) 328088; *(Upper Bann).*

Cecil Walker: (U.U.P.) 20 Oldpark Road, Belfast BT 14 6FR; Tel. (01232) 755996; *(Belfast North).*

SALARIES OF M.P.S AND N.I. MINISTERS

M.P.'s salary	£43,860
*Parliamentary Under Secretary of State's salary	£67,483
Minister of State's salary	£74,985
Secretary of State's salary	£103,860
Prime Minister's salary	£143,860

Lord Dubs, does not draw an M.P.'s salary.

THE NORTHERN IRELAND FORUM AND MULTI- PARTY TALKS

Background to the Forum election

The election to the Northern Ireland Forum was first proposed by the then British Prime Minister, John Major, on January 24, 1996. Speaking in response to the report of the International Body on Decommissioning (the Mitchell Report) in the House of Commons, he accepted Mitchell's suggestion that an election would be an appropriate confidence-building measure en route to all-party negotiations

On March 21, 1996, the British government published a paper on its "framework for a broadly acceptable elective process leading to all-party negotiations." It provided for elections to be held in Northern Ireland on May 30, 1996, and for all-party talks to commence on June 10, 1996. Five representatives, to be chosen from a list of party members published prior to the election, were to be elected from each of the 18 Westminster constituencies. Voters would cast a single vote for their party of choice. The total vote for each party across Northern Ireland was to be aggregated, and the ten most successful parties would gain an extra two seats in the 110-member Forum.

The representatives to the all-party talks were drawn from those elected to the Forum.

N. IRELAND FORUM ELECTION, MAY 30, 1996

PARTY	VOTES	% OF TOTAL VALID VOTE	SEATS WON	PARTY REPRESENTATIVES*
U.U.P.	181,829	24.17	30	John Gorman, Anthony Alcock
S.D.L.P.	160,786	21.37	21	Donita Field, Johnathon Stephenson
D.U.P.	141,413	18.80	24	Gregory Campbell, Eric Smyth
S.F.	116,377	15.47	17	Luciletta Bhreatnach, Pat Doherty
All.	49,176	6.54	7	Seamus Close, Eileen Bell
U.K.U.P.	27,774	3.69	3	Cedric Wilson, Conor Cruise O'Brien
P.U.P.	26,082	3.47	2	Hugh Smyth, David Ervine
U.D.P.	16,715	2.22	2	Gary McMichael, John Whyte
N.I.W.C.	7,731	1.03	2	Monica McWilliams, Pearl Sagar
Lab.	6,425	0.85	2	Malachi Curran, Hugh Casey
Others	17,988	2.39		
TOTAL:	752,388		110	

Total Electorate: 1,166,104. Total Poll: 754,296. Turnout: 64.69%.
Spoiled Votes: 1,908. Total Valid Poll: 752,388.

The above party representatives were nominated to the Forum by each of the ten parties receiving the most votes in the election.

DELEGATES TO THE MULTI-PARTY TALKS

Progressive Unionist Party:
David Ervine and Hugh Smyth.
Ulster Democratic Party:
Gary McMichael and John Whyte.
Northern Ireland Women's Coalition:
Monica McWilliams and Pearl Sagar.
Labour:
Malachi Curran and Hugh Casey.

Social Democratic and Labour Party:
John Hume, Seamus Mallon and Eddie McGrady.
Democratic Unionist Party:
Rev. Ian Paisley, Peter Robinson and Rev. William McCrea.
Ulster Unionist Party:
David Trimble, John Taylor and Reg Empey.

United Kingdom Unionist Party:
Robert McCartney, Cedric Wilson and Conor Cruise O'Brien.
Alliance:
Lord Alderdice, Seamus Close and Sean Neeson.
*Sinn Féin:
Gerry Adams, Gerry Kelly and Martin McGuinness.
*Not admitted until September 1997.

STATUS OF THE MULTI-PARTY TALKS

A SHORT CHRONOLOGY OF THE MULTI-PARTY TALKS

1996

May 30: Elections to Northern Ireland Forum *(see results above)*.

June 6: British and Irish governments publish proposals for the Opening Plenary session, draft rules of procedure and a draft talks agenda.

June 10: Talks opened by an Taoiseach John Bruton and British Prime Minister John Major. In the absence of an I.R.A. cease-fire, Sinn Féin are refused entry.

June 12: Senator George Mitchell assumes Chair of Opening Plenary session after acrimonious discussion. General John de Chastelain agreed as Chairman of Strand Two* and Harri Holkeri agreed as an alternate Chairman. All delegations commit themselves to the six Mitchell principles of democracy and non-violence.

July 29: New Rules of Procedure agreed by the parties. Business Committee established.

Talks break for the summer.

September 9: Resumption of Opening Plenary session after the summer recess. Discussion focuses on decommissioning.

October 10: Statement to Dáil Éireann on the progress of the talks by An Taoiseach John Bruton.

November 20: Anglo-Irish governmental conference discusses progress of the talks.

December 18: Talks break for Christmas. Statement by the chairmen acknowledging the slow progress but stressing that progress could be made on the issue of decommissioning.

1997

January 13: Statement by chairmen calling for renewed effort on the part of all participants. Bilateral meetings between participants.

January 27: Resumption of Opening Plenary session following Christmas break.

March 5: Talks adjourned until after the Westminster and local council elections in May.

May 2: Mo Mowlam appointed as the new Northern Ireland Secretary of State following Labour's victory in the British general election.

June 3: Resumption of the Opening Plenary session

following elections.

June 26: Bertie Ahern elected as Taoiseach, Ray Burke appointed as Minister for Foreign Affairs.

June 25: British Prime Minister Tony Blair announces September 15 as the date for the beginning of substantive talks with May 1998 set as the target for their completion. The British government also set a five week deadline for the I.R.A. to call a ceasefire.

July 14: British and Irish governments publish a joint paper on Decommissioning.

July 19: I.R.A. announces a new cease-fire.

July 21: Sinn Féin officials take up offices at Stormont. Robert McCartney's United Kingdom Unionist Party withdraws from the talks.

July 23: British/Irish Decommissioning paper rejected by unionist parties. Democratic Unionist Party announce their intention to withdraw from the talks.

August 28: Mo Mowlam accepts that the I.R.A. ceasefire is unequivocal and announces that Sinn Féin will be admitted to multi-party talks on September 9.

September 9: Sinn Féin delegates admitted to Stormont in advance of plenary session on September 15.

September 15: Plenary session reopens with the British and Irish governments, the Women's Coalition, Alliance, the Labour Party, Sinn Féin and the S.D.L.P. present. None of the unionist parties were present.

September 24: The Ulster Unionist Party drop their demand that the Decommissioning issue must be settled before the commencement of substantive negotiations. An Independent Commission on Illegal Arms decommissioning was set up under the chairmanship of General John de Chastelain.

September 30: The business committee at Stormont agreed that substantive negotiations on the future of Northern Ireland, i.e. all three strands of the talks, will begin on Tuesday, October 6, 1997.

* Strand One of the talks deals with internal settlement within Northern Ireland; Strand Two deals with North-South relations; and Strand Three deals with Anglo-Irish relations.

GOVERNORS OF NORTHERN IRELAND (1922-73)

Governors of Northern Ireland Statistics

Name	Born	Appointed	Aged	No. of Terms
Duke of Abercorn	1869	06.12.1922	53	4
Vice-Admiral Earl Granville*	1880	07.09.1945	65	2
Lord Wakehurst*	1895	01.12.1952	57	2
Lord Erskine of Rerrick*	1893	01.12.1964	71	1
Lord Grey of Naunton	1910	03.12.1968	58	1

*the annotated governors resigned from the office.

The governor was the monarch's representative in Northern Ireland and was appointed by the monarch for a six year term. He summoned, prorogued and dissolved the Northern Ireland parliament in the monarch's name, read the monarch's speech at the beginning of a new parliamentary session and gave or withheld the Royal Assent to bills passed by both Houses. The post was abolished on July 18, 1973, by the Northern Ireland Constitution Act.

NORTHERN IRELAND PRIME MINISTERS FACT FILE

No.	Name	Politics	Born	In	Appoint.	at age	Died	aged
1	Sir James Craig	UUP	1871	Belfast	June1921	50	1940	69
2	John M. Andrews	UUP	1871	Co. Down	Nov. 1940	69	1956	85
3	Sir Basil Brooke	UUP	1888	Co. Fermanagh	April 1943	54	1973	85
4	Capt. Terence O'Neill	UUP	1914	London	March 1963	48	1990	75
5	James Chichester-Clark	UUP	1923	Co. Derry	May 1969	46		
6	Brian Faulkner	UUP	1921	Co. Down	March 1971	50	1977	56

BIOGRAPHIES OF NORTHERN IRELAND PRIME MINISTERS (1921-72)

SIR JAMES CRAIG (1921-40)

Born January 8, 1871, in Belfast. Appointed as the first Prime Minister of Northern Ireland on June 7, 1921, a position he held until his death. His tenure as P.M. was contemporaneous with his leadership of the Ulster Unionists.

A veteran of the Boer War, he was elected to Westminster in 1906 and was vociferous in his opposition to Home Rule. He was an influential member of the Ulster Volunteer Force and was Quarter-Master General of the force (1914-16) - renamed the 36th (Ulster) Division during World War I. Craig used his influence at Westminster to present the unionist case when the Government of Ireland Act 1920 was drafted. The act provided for the partition of Ireland and the creation of the Northern Ireland state.

As P.M. he introduced a Special Powers Act in 1922 (made permanent in 1933), which gave the authorities virtually unlimited powers of arrest and detention. His government abolished proportional representation for local elections in 1922 and for Stormont elections in 1929, and it implemented an extensive system of gerrymandering in nationalist areas, famously commenting in 1934: "We have a Protestant parliament and a Protestant state." He was made Viscount Craigavon on January 20, 1927.

Died on November 24, 1940.

JOHN MILLER ANDREWS (1940-43)

Born July 17, 1871, at Cumber, Co. Down. Appointed Prime Minister on November 25, 1940, he resigned as P.M. and leader of the Ulster Unionists on April 28, 1943.

Elected to the House of Commons at Stormont in 1921, he held two ministerial posts prior to his premiership, namely, Minister for Labour (1921-37) and Minister for Finance (1937-40). He resigned from Stormont in 1953. His prominence in the Orange Order was reflected in his holding the position of Grand Master of the Imperial Grand Council of the World (1949-54) and Grand Master in Ireland (1948-54).

Died on August 6, 1956.

SIR BASIL BROOKE (1943-63)

Born June 9, 1888 at Colebrook, Co. Fermanagh. Appointed Prime Minister on April 28, 1943, he remained in office until his resignation on March 25, 1963. He was also leader of the Ulster Unionists during this period and remained an M.P. until he resigned in 1967.

He was a prominent figure in the Ulster Volunteer Force. He saw front line action during World War I and was decorated for his bravery. A unionist M.P. from 1929, he was Minister for Agriculture (1933-41) and Minister for Commerce and Production (1941-45). As P.M. he introduced social welfare legislation to harmonise Northern Ireland standards with those in Britain, and the important Education Act of 1947, which provided free secondary schooling for all. His government dealt ruthlessly with the I.R.A. border campaign of 1956-62, enacting tough security legislation. He refused to have any official contacts with Roman Catholics or trade unionists during his time in office. He was elevated to the peerage as Viscount Brookeborough on July 4, 1952.

Died on August 18, 1973.

TERENCE O'NEILL (1963-69)

Born September 10, 1914, in London. He was appointed Prime Minister on March 25, 1963, but resigned on April 28, 1969, when tensions within his party made his position untenable.

He saw action throughout World War II as a captain in the Irish Guards. Elected to Stormont in 1946, he was Minister for Finance (1956-63). As P.M. he advocated closer ties with the Republic, and in 1965 met with Taoiseach Seán Lemass in Belfast, the first meeting of its kind, followed by a meeting in Dublin. O'Neill also attempted to introduce measures granting civil rights to the minority Catholic population, and his premiership was marked by the rise of the civil rights movement. Such concessions resulted in fierce opposition from both within his party and the unionist community at large. The resignation of senior ministers from his government precipitated his resignation, but ultimately, his failing was that he had raised the expectations of the Catholic community and was unable to deliver the necessary reforms. He was elevated to the peerage as Lord O'Neill of the Maine in January 1970.

Died on June 13, 1990, aged 75.

JAMES CHICHESTER-CLARK (1969-71)

Born February 12, 1923, at Castledawson, Co. Derry. Appointed Prime Minister May 1, 1969, he resigned from the post March 20, 1971. Leader of the Ulster Unionist Party during that period.

Elected to the Northern Ireland House of Commons in 1960, he was the Minister for Agriculture from 1967 until April of 1969 when he resigned over O'Neill's reforms. In August 1969 he requested that Whitehall send British troops to help quell the civil unrest endemic from July 1969. His request was granted, and British troops duly arrived on August 15. The B-Specials were disbanded in April of 1970, and this, coupled with the transferral of the control of security matters to the army, led to his resignation in March 1971.

He was made a life peer taking the title Lord Moyola in June 1971.

BRIAN FAULKNER (1971-72)

Born February 18, 1921, at Helen's Bay, Co. Down. He was appointed Prime Minister of Northern Ireland on March 23, 1971, and was the last man to hold the post. His tenure ended with the introduction of Direct Rule from London on March 24, 1972. He was leader of the Ulster Unionist Party from March 1971 until January 1974.

First elected to the Northern Ireland House of Commons in 1949, he held a number of ministerial portfolios, including Home Affairs (1959-63), Commerce (1963-69) and Development (1969-71). In 1969 he resigned from government on the grounds that Terence O'Neill, the then Prime Minister, was introducing too many reforms at too great a pace.

As P.M., Faulkner presided over two events which signalled the end of the Northern Ireland Parliament, namely, the the introduction of internment without trial on August 9, 1971, which was directed almost exclusively at nationalists and 'Bloody Sunday' on January 30, 1972, where 13 civilians on a civil rights march were shot dead by British paratroopers in Derry (one man later died from his injuries). These events changed both world and British government opinion and precipitated Direct Rule.

In January 1974, he became the Chief Minister in the short lived 'Power Sharing' Executive, which was brought down less than five months later by the Ulster Workers' Council strike. He retired from politics in August 1976 and was elevated to the peerage in January 1977.

Killed in a riding accident on March 3, 1977.

GOVERNMENTS OF NORTHERN IRELAND

Northern Ireland Governments, 1921- 1972

MINISTERS FOR AGRICULTURE

Prime Minister	Minister	Appointed
Craig	E.M. Archdale	1921
Craig	Sir B. Brooke	1933
Andrews	Lord Glentoran	1941
Brooke	R. Moore	1943
Brooke	H.W. West	1960
O'Neill	J. Chichester-Clark	1967
Chichester-Clark	P.R.H. O'Neill	1969
Faulkner	H.W. West	1971

MINISTERS FOR COMMERCE

Prime Minister	Minister	Appointed
Craig	E.M. Archdale	1921
Craig	J.M. Barbour	1925
Andrews	Sir B. Brooke	1941
Brooke	Sir R. T. Nugent	1945
Brooke	W.B. Maginness	1949
Brooke	W.V. McCleerey	1949
Brooke	Lord Glentoran	1953
Brooke	J.L.O. Andrews	1961
O'Neill	A.B.D. Faulkner	1963
Chichester-Clark	R.H. Bradford	1969
Faulkner	R.J. Bailie	1971

MINISTERS FOR DEVELOPMENT

Prime Minister	Minister	Appointed
O'Neill	W. Craig	1965
O'Neill	W.K. Fitzsimmons	1966
O'Neill	I. Neill	1968
Chichester-Clark	W.J. Long	1969
Chichester-Clark	A.B.D. Faulkner	1969
Faulkner	R.H. Bradford	1971

The Department of Development was established in 1965 to take on the functions of local government, following the reorganisation of the Department of Health and Local Government.

MINISTERS FOR COMMUNITY RELATIONS

Prime Minister	Minister	Appointed
Faulkner	D. Bleakley	1971
Faulkner	W.B. McIvor	1971

MINISTERS FOR EDUCATION

Prime Minister	Minister	Appointed
Craig	Lord Londonderry	1921
Craig	Lord Charlemont	1926
Craig	J.H. Robb	1937
Brooke	Rev. R. Corkey	1943
Brooke	S.H. Hall-Thompson	1944
Brooke	H. Midgley	1950
Brooke	W.M. May	1957
Brooke	I. Neill	1962
O'Neill	H.V. Kirk	1964
O'Neill	W.K. Fitzsimmons	1965
O'Neill	W.J. Long	1966
O'Neill	W.K. Fitzsimmons	1968
Chichester-Clark	P.R.H. O'Neill	1969
Chichester-Clark	W.J. Long	1969
Faulkner	W.J. Long	1971

MINISTERS FOR FINANCE

Prime Minister	Minister	Appointed
Craig	H.M. Pollock	1921
Craig	J.M. Andrews	1937
Andrews	J.M. Barbour	1941
Brooke	J.M. Sinclair	1943
Brooke	W.B. Maginess	1953
Brooke	G.B. Hanna	1956
Brooke	T. O'Neill	1956
O'Neill	J.L.O. Andrews	1963
O'Neill	I. Neill	1964
O'Neill	H.V. Kirk	1965
Chichester-Clark	H.V. Kirk	1969
Faulkner	H.V. Kirk	1971

MINISTERS FOR HEALTH

Prime Minister	Minister	Appointed
Brooke	W. Grant	1944
Brooke	Dame Dehra Parker	1949
Brooke	J.L.O. Andrews	1957
Brooke	W.J. Morgan	1961
O'Neill	W. Craig	1964
O'Neill	W.J. Morgan	1965
Chichester-Clark	R.W. Porter	1969
Chichester-Clark	W.K. Fitzsimmons	1969
Faulkner	W.K. Fitzsimmons	1971

The Department of Health was known as Health and Local Government from its inception in 1944 until 1965. From 1965 it was known as Health and Social Services.

MINISTERS FOR HOME AFFAIRS

Prime Minister	Minister	Appointed
Craig	R. D. Bates	1921
Brooke	W. Lowry	1943
Brooke	J.E. Warnock	1944
Brooke	W.B. Maginess	1949
Brooke	G.B. Hanna	1953
Brooke	T. O'Neill	1956
Brooke	W.W.B. Topping	1956
Brooke	A.B.D. Faulkner	1959
O'Neill	W. Craig	1963
O'Neill	R.W. McConnell	1964
O'Neill	W. Craig	1966
O'Neill	W.J. Long	1968
Chichester-Clark	R.W. Porter	1969
Chichester-Clark	J. Chichester-Clark	1970
Faulkner	B. Faulkner	1971

MINISTERS FOR LABOUR

Prime Minister	Minister	Appointed
Craig	J.M. Andrews	1921
Craig	D.G. Shillington	1937
Craig	I.F. Gordan	1939
Brooke	W. Grant	1943
Brooke	W.B. Maginess	1945
Brooke	H. Midgley	1949
Brooke	I. Neill	1951
Brooke	H.V. Kirk	1962
O'Neill	W.J. Morgan	1964

From 1946 until 1965 the department was known as Labour and National Insurance. In 1965 it was incorporated into the new Department of Health and Social Services.

MINISTERS FOR PUBLIC SECURITY

Prime Minister	Minister	Appointed
Andrews	W. Grant	1941
Andrews	H. Midgley	1942

The Parliament of Northern Ireland first met on June 7, 1921. It was prorogued March 30, 1972, and Direct Rule from Westminster introduced. The Parliament was formally abolished July 18, 1973.
All members of government (1921-72) were members of the Ulster Unionist Party.

NORTHERN IRELAND SECRETARIES OF STATE

1972-1973	William Whitelaw
1973-1974	Francis Pym
1974-1976	Merlyn Rees
1976-1979	Roy Mason
1979-1981	Humphrey Atkins
1981-1984	Jim Prior
1984-1985	Douglas Hurd
1985-1989	Tom King
1989-1992	Peter Brooke
1992-1997	Patrick Mayhew
1997-	Dr. Mo Mowlam

NORTHERN IRELAND EXECUTIVE, 1974

Northern Ireland's last form of government, the Northern Ireland 'power sharing' Executive took office on January 1 1974. Its ministers were drawn from S.D.L.P., Alliance and Official Unionist Party members elected to the Northern Ireland Assembly in June of 1973. The executive and the N.I. Assembly was brought down by the Ulster Workers Council General strike of May 1974 and direct rule re-imposed.

NORTHERN IRELAND ELECTIONS TO WESTMINSTER, 1922-1997

DATE	NO. OF SEATS	U.U.P.	N.	D.U.P.	S.D.L.P.	S.F.	OTHER U.	OTHER N.	OTHER LAB.	V.U.P.P.
15.11.1922	13	11	2	-	-	-	-	-	-	-
06.12.1923	13	11	2	-	-	-	-	-	-	-
29.10.1924	13	13	-	-	-	-	-	-	-	-
30.05.1929	13	11	-	-	-	-	-	2*	-	-
27.10.1931	13	11	2	-	-	-	-	-	-	-
14.11.1935	13	11	-	-	-	-	-	2*	-	-
05.07.1945	13	9	2	-	-	-	1	-	1	-
23.02.1950	12	10	-	-	-	-	-	2*	-	-
25.10.1951	12	9	-	-	-	-	-	2*	1	-
26.05.1955	12	10	-	-	-	2	-	-	-	-
08.10.1959	12	12	-	-	-	-	-	-	-	-
15.10.1964	12	12	-	-	-	-	-	-	-	-
31.03.1966	12	11	-	-	-	-	-	-	1	-
18.06.1970	12	8	-	-	-	-	1	2*	1	-
28.02.1974	12	7	-	1	1	-	-	-	-	3
10.10.1974	12	6	-	1	1	-	-	1*	-	3
03.05.1979	12	5	-	3	1	-	2	1	-	
09.06.1983	17	11	-	3	1	1	1	-	-	
11.06.1987	17	9	-	3	3	1	1	-	-	
09.04.1992	17	9	-	3	4	-	1	-	-	
01.05.1997	18	10	-	2	3	2	1	-	-	

* 1929 ....Other N = National League
* 1950/51..............Other N = Anti-Partition League
* 1974 ....Other N = Independent

* 1935........Other N = Nationalist Abstentionists
* 1970.........Other N = Unity Candidates

KEY
U. = Unionist/Ulster Unionist Party
N. = Nationalist
D.U.P. = Democratic Unionist Party
S.D.L.P. = Social and Democratic Labour Party

S.F. = Sinn Féin
Other U. = Other Unionist groupings
Other N. = Other Nationalist groupings
Other Lab. = Various Labour Groupings
V.U.P.P. = Vanguard Unionist Progressive Party.

PARLIAMENT OF NORTHERN IRELAND, 1921-73

DATE	NO. OF SEATS	U.U.P.	N	N.I.L.P.	OTHER N.	OTHER U.	OTHER Lab.	IND.
24.05.1921	52	40	6	-	6	-	-	-
03.04.1925	52	32	10	3	2	4	-	1
22.05.1929	52	37	11	1	-	3	-	-
30.11.1933	52	36	9	2	2	3	-	-
09.02.1938	52	39	8	1	-	3	1	-
14.06.1945	52	33	10	2	-	2	3	2
10.02.1949	52	37	9	-	-	2	2	2
22.10.1953	52	38	7	-	2	1	3	1
20.03.1958	52	37	7	4	1	-	2	1
31.05.1962	52	34	9	4	-	-	3	2
25.11.1965	52	36	9	2	1	-	2	2
24.02.1969	52	36	6	2	-	3	2	3

KEY
U.U.P. ....Ulster Unionist Party
N. ....Nationalist Party
N.I.L.P. ....Northern Ireland Labour Party
Other N. ....Other nationalist
Other U. ....Other unionist
Other Lab. ....Other Labour
Ind. ....Independent

CHANGING STATE OF THE PARTIES, 1977-97 (%)

ELECTION	U.U.P.	S.D.L.P.	D.U.P.	S.F.	All.	Others
1977 Local	29.6	20.6	12.7	-	14.4	22.7
1979 Gen.	36.6	18.3	10.2	-	11.8	23.1
1979 Euro.	21.9	24.6	29.8	-	6.8	16.9
1981 Local	26.5	17.5	26.6	-	8.9	20.5
1982 Asm.	29.7	18.8	23.0	10.1	9.3	9.1
1983 Gen.	34.0	17.9	20.0	13.4	8.0	6.7
1984 Euro.	21.5	22.1	33.6	13.3	5.0	4.5
1985 Local	29.5	17.8	24.3	11.8	7.1	9.5
1987 Gen.	37.8	21.1	11.7	11.4	10.0	8.0
1989 Local	31.3	21.0	17.7	11.2	6.9	11.9
1989 Euro.	22.2	25.5	29.9	9.1	5.2	8.1
1992 Gen.	34.5	23.5	13.1	10.0	8.7	10.2
1993 Local	29.4	22.0	17.3	12.4	7.6	11.3
1994 Euro.	23.8	28.9	29.2	9.9	4.1	4.1
1996 Forum	24.2	21.4	18.8	15.5	6.5	13.6
1997 Gen.	32.7	24.1	13.6	16.1	8.0	5.5
1997 Local	27.8	20.7	15.6	16.9	6.6	12.4

KEY:

Asm.	Northern Ireland Assembly Election
Euro.	European Parliament Election
Forum	Northern Ireland Forum Election
Gen.	General Election
Local	District Council Election

CONSTITUTIONAL REFERENDA

Date	Issue	Turnout %	For %	Against %
March 8, 1973	Northern Ireland remaining within the United Kingdom	59	98.9	1.1
June 5, 1975	United Kingdom remaining within the E.E.C.	47	52.1	47.9

SELECTED BIOGRAPHIES OF POLITICAL FIGURES IN NORTHERN IRELAND

Gerry Adams, born Belfast 1949, President of Sinn Féin since 1983; M.P. (1983-92 & since 1997); interned (1971-72 and 1973-77); a noted writer, his works include *Falls Memories, The Politics of Irish Freedom* and the autobiographical *Before the Dawn.*

John Alderdice, born Antrim 1955, leader of the Alliance Party of Northern Ireland since 1987; former Belfast City councillor; created a life peer in 1996.

Roy Beggs, born 1936; Ulster Unionist Party M.P. since 1983.

James Chichester-Clark, born Derry 1923, former Prime Minister of Northern Ireland. *see Biographies of Northern Ireland Prime Ministers.*

Jeffrey Donaldson: born 1963, deputy Grand Master of the Orange Lodge of Ireland.

Lord Dubs, born Czechoslovakia 1932; Labour M.P. (1979-87); created life peer in 1994; junior minister at the Northern Ireland Office, responsible for Departments of Environment and Agriculture; answers on Northern Ireland matters in the House of Lords.

David Ervine, spokesperson for the Progressive Unionist Party; elected Belfast city councillor since 1997.

Clifford Forsythe, born 1929; Ulster Unionist Party M.P. since 1983.

John Hume, born Derry 1937, leader of Social Democratic and Labour Party since 1979; M.P. since 1983; M.E.P. since 1979; founding member of S.D.L.P. (1970); prominent in civil rights movement; enjoys high international profile.

Billy Hutchinson, elected Belfast city councillor in 1997; press officer of the Progressive Unionist Party.

Adam Ingram, born Scotland 1947; Labour M.P. since 1987; Minister of State at the Northern Ireland office responsible for security and the Department of Economic Development.

Bernadette McAliskey, born Tyrone 1947, prominent in civil rights campaign in Northern Ireland; M.P. (1969-74); founding member of Irish Republican Socialist Party (1974); survived loyalist gun attack in 1981.

Bob McCartney, born Belfast 1936, leader of the United Kingdom Unionist Party; M.P. since 1995; expelled from U.U.P. in 1987; delegate to the multi-party talks.

Eddie McGrady, born Co. Down 1935; S.D.L.P. M.P. since 1987.

Martin McGuinness, born Derry 1950, M.P. since May 1997; Sinn Féin's chief negotiator in talks with representatives of the British government; senior Sinn Féin strategist.

Gary McMichael, born Antrim 1971, leader of the Ulster Democratic Party since 1994; member of Lisburn

Borough Council since 1993; delegate to the multi-party talks.

Alban Maginness, born Belfast 1950; S.D.L.P. councillor since 1985; elected as Belfast's first ever nationalist Lord Mayor in June 1997.

Ken Maginness, born 1938; Ulster Unionist Party M.P. since 1983.

Seamus Mallon, born Co. Armagh 1942; deputy leader of the S.DL.P. since 1978; M.P. since 1986; Senator (1981-82).

James Molyneaux, born Antrim 1920, M.P. (1970-97); leader of Ulster Unionist Party (1979-95); elevated to the peerage as Lord Molyneaux of Killead in 1997.

Mo Mowlam, born Coventry 1949, Secretary of State for Northern Ireland since May 3, 1997; Labour M.P. since 1987.

Paul Murphy, born Wales 1948; Labour M.P. since 1987; Minister of State at the Northern Ireland Office reponsible for political development and the Department of Finance and Personnel.

Rev. Dr. Ian Paisley, born Armagh 1926, founder and leader of the Democratic Unionist Party (1971); M.P. since 1971; M.E.P. since 1979; established Free Presbyterian Church (1951).

Peter Robinson, born Belfast 1948, M.P. since 1979; deputy leader of the Democratic Unionist Party; delegate to the multi-party talks.

William Ross, born 1936; Ulster Unionist Party M.P. since 1974.

Hugh Smyth, founding member and leader of the Progressive Unionist Party; Belfast City Councillor; Lord Mayor of Belfast (1994-95); delegate to the multi-party talks.

Rev. Martin Smyth, born 1931; Ulster Unionist Party M.P. since 1982; Grand Master of the Orange Lodge of Ireland (1972-96).

Gusty Spence, born Belfast 1933; former member of the U.V.F. currently co-ordinator of the Progressive Unionist Party.

John Taylor, born Armagh 1937, M.P. since 1983; M.E.P. (1979-89); deputy leader of the Ulster Unionist Party since 1995; survived republican gun attack in 1972.

Thompson, William (born Tyrone, 1939) An Ulster Unionist, in 1997 he became the first M.P. elected by the new constituency of West Tyrone.

David Trimble, born Co. Down 1944, leader of the Ulster Unionist Party since 1995; M.P. since 1990; former deputy leader of the Vanguard Ulster Progressive Party (1975-77); has played a prominent role in Orange Order parades at Drumcree, Portadown.

Tony Worthington, born 1941; Labour M.P. since 1987; Junior minister at the Northern Ireland Office responsible for Education and Health and Social Services.

Cecil Walker, born 1924; Ulster Unionist Party M.P. since 1983.

EUROPEAN UNION

Europe: The *Irish* Solution

*By **Tommie Gorman**, RTÉ European Correspondent*

IRELAND joined the Common Market on January 1st, 1973. The 25 years of EU membership since have been a hugely positive experience. The next quarter century will be different and more complex.

The farmers were the first people to appreciate the benefits of belonging to the Brussels club. The smallest of small holders quickly grasped the merits of understanding the intricacies of green pounds, subsidies and quotas.

Bank managers in rural towns who had relied on the merchant classes suddenly appreciated the new affluence of the farming sector. Finance was offered for new sheds and farmhouse renovations: farmers dared to buy new tractors and new cars. Farmers sons and daughters were encouraged to go to university. It was revolution from the bottom up or the outside in. Long before urban Ireland got a sniff of the tangible benefits of EU membership, the love affair had taken root in the farming community.

Structural Funds, beginning with the major share-outs supervised by Jacques Delors, spread the largesse. Once in 1990 I said to Charlie Haughey, the then Taoiseach, that Ireland was receiving six pounds for every one it contributed to the Brussels kitty. Without even thinking he instantly replied, "it's not enough."

EU membership brought other changes. Seventy per cent of our exports went to the UK markets in the early '70's. Nowadays the figure is under 30 per cent because of a growth in trade with the likes of France and Germany. The multinational companies at the heart of our economic development are in Ireland partly because they are guaranteed access to EU markets, the most important market-place in the world.

The nature of our relationship with Britain has been altered. Membership of a powerful bloc has ended the isolation of being a small island behind a bigger island on the edge of Europe.

The European Union is on the threshold of change. Within a decade it will have several new member states from the former communist bloc. Monetary union, its most ambitious project, will begin on January 1st, 1999. Can the EU grow deeper as well as wider? Is the development of a common defence policy inevitable? Will the multi-nationals stay as Ireland becomes more affluent as labour costs increase and EU funds dry up? Will, as seems to be happening, the price of houses become the same in Dublin as in Hamburg as the logic of the single market penetrates? What will happen to the first converts to the EU gospel, the farmers, as the Common Agricultural Policy's influence and resources dwindle?

Once, in the early '90's, after he had received a delegation comprised of Ian Paisley, John Hume and Jim Nicholson on a farming issue, the then Agriculture Commissioner, Ray McSharry, made an interesting prediction. Economics rather than politics would play an important role in resolving the Northern Ireland problem, he said. Borders and the nation state would become less important. Communities and countries would come to recognise the mutual benefits of coexistence.

The intriguing question is . . . can a Union, set up to ensure Europe would never tear itself asunder in war, play a part in ending the last remaining war within its borders?

The author is a noted expert on the European Union and is the RTÉ European Correspondent.

ORIGINS OF THE EUROPEAN UNION

The E.U. originated in the period immediately after World War II largely as a result of one man's vision of how to reconcile the inevitable revival of the then ravaged German economy and nation with the fears of her neighbours of future attempts at domination. Jean Monnet, a French economic expert, who, in 1950, was the originator of what became known as the Schuman Plan (a scheme to pool French and German coal and steel production - the two essential elements for war at that time). He was the visionary who sought to unify Europe politically, socially and economically.

Since neither France nor Germany felt secure unless they controlled all the coal and steel resources available, and consequently all territory containing them, Monnet's proposal was to place the whole of German and French production under an international authority. Membership of this authority was to be open to other European countries, and this authority was to have as its purpose the unification of the conditions of production, leading to a gradual extension of effective co-operation in other areas.

Monnet's solution contained sufficient political symbolism to attract political and popular support and had a technical content sufficiently detailed to address the the difficulties of translating a complex scheme into a practical reality. Thus, after an international conference, the Treaty on the European Coal and Steel Community (E.C.S.C.) was signed in Paris in April, 1951, between France, Germany, the Benelux countries and Italy.

The E.C.S.C. Treaty provided for the creation of four institutions:

• **The High Authority**: A body which was politically independent of any member country and given the role of interpreting the treaty and ensuring its implementation. (It is comparable to the current E.U. commission.)
• **The Council of Ministers:** An institution comprised of ministers from member countries whose role as elected representatives was to control the powers of the Higher Authority. (The council's control is comparable to that of the current Council of Ministers in today's E.U. commission.)
• **The Common Assembly:** A parliamentary-type body created to provide democratic input into the community's actions. (It is comparable to the current E.U. parliament.)
• **The Court of Justice:** A court designed to settle conflicts or arguments between member states. (It is comparable to the current European Court of Justice.)

The aim of the E.C.S.C. was not, according to Monnet, to replace the responsibilities of the existing steel companies with that of the Higher Authority, but rather to create the conditions of true competition in a vast market where producers, workers and consumers would all gain. The continuation of these aims can be seen in later E.E.C. (European Economic Community) and E.U. policies and treaties.

Winston Churchill, in a speech in Zurich in 1946, called for "a kind of United States of Europe," and Monnet stated frequently that he had no doubt that the process of the E.E.C. development would lead eventually to a United States of Europe. He also argued that it

was impossible to say if such a Europe would be a federation or confederation or a combination of the two, as the entire project was without precedent.

Ireland and Britain did not join the E.U. at its initial stages but for very different reasons. Ireland had an agriculturally based economy at the time (no coal or steel) and was so economically integrated with Britain that it was not feasible for it to consider joining any European grouping without Britain.

Britain was in a different position from that of the rest of Europe after World War II. Its economic infrastructure, although damaged, was still largely intact (the decline of this infrastructure made Britain structurally uncompetitive in future years). It was still politically committed to its empire, it had not been invaded and British political debate in post-war era focused more on the future balance of public and private industry than on economic reconstruction or on the country's strategic political future.

Mr. Churchill stated in his Zurich speech that the first step towards European union must be a partnership between France and Germany. He later added that if France and Germany could be woven "so closely together economically, socially and morally as to prevent the occasion of new quarrels, and make old antagonisms die in the realisation of mutual prosperity and interdependence, Europe would rise again." Mr. Churchill also believed that the integration of Europe would best be achieved without British involvement at this time.

Critically, in the then prevailing atmosphere of uncertainty, there was a consensus in Britain that it should not commit itself to Europe to such an extent that it lost its independent viability. If Europe collapsed economically or militarily, Britain must retain the ability to survive and continue to develop its American and Commonwealth connections.

Britain has maintained this policy and, until recent times, the Republic of Ireland had little or no option but to follow a similar path. The break with punt-pound parity was one of Ireland's first real signs of economic independence, and Ireland's commitment to join a single European currency regardless of British intentions has been its most recent show of autonomy.

Monnet went on to become the architect of the European Economic Community. His aim was to substitute the arbitration of differences by force with rules of conduct between nations and to substitute attempts to negotiate individual reciprocal advantages with the pursuit of a common objective in the common interest.

In seeking to build a Europe-wide democratic union, one of Monnet's guiding principles was that at birth all men are the same, but as they grow they do so within a system of rules, which determines their later behaviour and under which they seek to maintain the privileges they have gained, often by a policy of domination.

On the basis of Monnet's principles and taking the view that the benefits of integration, as opposed to just co-operation, would outweigh what appeared to some to be some loss of sovereignty, the six members of the E.C.S.C. signed the Treaties of Rome in 1957 to found the E.E.C. and Euratom. These treaties were Monnet's basis for a framework for the people of Europe's future. On January 1, 1973, the Republic of Ireland, Northern Ireland (via Britain's accession) and Denmark joined these founding six members.

EUROPEAN COMMUNITY DEVELOPMENTS - A CHRONOLOGY

1951 Treaty of Paris to found the E.C.S.C. (the European Coal and Steel Community). The signatories were France, Germany, Belgium, Luxembourg, Italy and the Netherlands.

1957 Treaty of Rome to found the E.E.C. (the European Economic Community) and Euroatom. Once again the signatories were France, Germany, Belgium, Luxembourg, Italy and the Netherlands.

1961 The first accession application by Ireland, Britain and Denmark. Vetoed by France.

1965 A merger of European institutions is created by the treaties of Paris and Rome.

1967 The second accession application by Ireland, Britain and Denmark. Vetoed by France.

1968 The phased abolition of tariffs between existing members is completed, and a customs union is finalised.

1970 The opening of negotiations on accession with Ireland, Britain, Denmark and Norway.

1973 Ireland, Britain and Denmark become the first post-foundation members of the E.E.C.

1979 First direct elections to the European Parliament.

1979 The European Monetary system is established.

1981 Greece joins the E.E.C.

1986 Spain and Portugal join the E.E.C.

1986 An intergovernmental conference closes with a revised treaty, resulting in the Single European Act. The act increases majority voting, provides direction for creating a single market and lays the legal basis for the practice of political co-operation.

1987 The Single European Act (S.E.A.) is ratified by referenda by the Republic of Ireland and by the British parliament.

1989 A political declaration of the Social Chapter by 11 of the 12 E.C. states. Britain opts out of the declaration, and its provisions do not apply in Northern Ireland.

1989 The Committee of E.C. Central Banks proposes a three-stage path towards a single European currency.

1990 Two parallel conferences open to consider the questions of both European Monetary Union (E.M.U.) and political union.

1991 The above conferences result in completion of the Maastricht Treaty (the T.E.U. creates a legal framework for the creation of a single currency - the E.M.U. - with a British opt-out provision). Members commit themselves to an even closer union, increased powers for the European Parliament and the European Court, and a Common Foreign and Security Policy is established.

1993 The Single Internal Market, brought about by Single European Act is almost complete, abolishing most border controls. Maastricht comes into effect after referendum difficulties in Denmark The E.C. subsequently becomes the E.U.

1995 Austria, Finland and Sweden join the E.U.

1996 The Dublin E.U. Summit finalises plans for E.M.U. by confirming the starting date for the new currency and by displaying for the first time the new European Bank Notes.

1997 The Amsterdam Summit. Resulted in the E.U.'s latest treaty.

EUROPEAN UNION INSTITUTIONS

The four major institutional pillars of the E.U. are the European Commission, the European Council Of Ministers, the European Parliament and the European Court of Justice

The European Commission is the executive organ of the community which ensures that the community's rules and the provisions of treaties are implemented and observed correctly. It puts forward policy proposals and executes the decisions taken by the Council of Ministers. The Republic of Ireland has one commissioner, while Northern Ireland is included in the allocation of two commissioners to Britain. Commissioners are each allocated an individual portfolio and are required to act in the general interests of the community, not as national representatives.

The European Council of Ministers is the executive or decision-making body of the E.U.. It is the principal meeting place of the members' national governments and is the only institution in which members represent each country in direct negotiations between member states. The council is normally convened in the country that holds the presidency of the E.U., which rotates between the member countries every six months.

The E.U. Parliament provides for the democratic input of the people of Europe in the E.U. Its members are elected from member states every five years and sit in the parliament according to political affiliations rather than nationalities - for example, the European Peoples group, the Socialist Group, the Rainbow Group, etc. The parliament has acquired increased powers in recent years and can propose its own legislation. Its opinion must now be sought on important legislative proposals or else they will be rendered invalid.

Prior to 1987, any legislation coming before the parliament was subject to a consultative procedure. The Single European Act created two new procedures - the co-operation procedure and the assent procedure - while the Treaty on European Union introduced the co-decision procedure.

Each of the above procedures applies to different types of legislation. The co-operation procedure requires the co-operation of the European Parliament to avoid delaying legislation. The European Parliament can veto legislation put before it only under the co-decision procedure.

The European Court of Justice interprets E.U. law and ensures its application throughout the E.U. It has a wide-ranging role, being required by various treaty articles to act as an international court, an administrative court, a civil court, an industrial tribunal and a transnational constitutional court. Where there is conflict between European law and the domestic laws of member countries, European law prevails and domestic parliaments must amend their laws to take into account the opinions of the European court.

EUROPEAN ACTS

THE SINGLE EUROPEAN ACT 1987
The four main aims of the act are:
A Common External Tariff;
Free Movement of Goods, Services, Persons and Capital;
Competition rather than co-operation between companies within the E.U. and
Approximation of regulations, rather than common or new regulations.

THE EUROPEAN SOCIAL CHAPTER
This is a political declaration by most members of the E.U., including Ireland, but was opted out of by Britain (and therefore Northern Ireland). It provides workers with the right to improved living and working conditions;
Freedom of movement (the right to work anywhere in the E.U.) and equal tax treatment;
The right to exercise an occupation or trade anywhere in the E.U.;
Social protection by host states of E.U. citizens in gainful employment;
Basic daily and weekly rest periods;
A maximum 48 working-hour week;
Maximum night work of 8 hours in 24;
Four weeks' holidays per annum;
Rest periods at work (minimum standards);
Fair wages;
Freedom of association (the right to join or not to join a trade union);
The right to vocational training throughout a person's working life;
Equal pay for work of equal value;
Workers' rights to information at their place of work, as well as participation in the decision-making process, and protection at the workplace from any dangers; and
Rights for pregnant women (time off, protection in the workplace etc.).

THE AMSTERDAM SUMMIT OF JUNE 1997
Key Treaty Changes arising from the summit are as follows:
New powers to co-ordinate member states' drive for jobs;
The enshrining of sustainable development as a core environmental value;
Enhanced E.U. powers in public health, consumer rights and social exclusion;
Enhanced equality provisions;
The end of the British opt-out on social policy;
The right to correspond with E.U. institutions in Irish;
A treaty right of access to official documents;
A commitment by the 13 continental members to open their internal borders by 2004;
Opt-outs for Ireland and Britain allowing them to retain control of their borders;
Enhanced co-operation in the fight against crime and new powers for Europol;
The potential involvement of the E.U. in peace-keeping and humanitarian military missions;
No merger with the Western European Union and a dilution of the Maastricht aspiration to an eventual common defence;
A new foreign and security analysis and planning unit for Brussels;
A new foreign policy supremo and reorganisation of the E.U.'s diplomatic troika;
Postponement of much institutional reform;
No change in the entitlement of member states to a commissioner;
A pledge that large states will get a re-weighting of votes in their favour;
Marginal extension of majority voting;
Extra powers for the Commission President to share in picking his team and then reshuffling it;
Extension of M.E.P.s' powers to approve legislation; and
'Flexibility' provisions to allow groups of states to collaborate on projects that do not have unanimous support.

The treaty, now unalterable, was signed by E.U. Foreign Ministers in October, 1997 prior to ratification by each of the member states.

R.O.I. EUROPEAN PARLIAMENT ELECTION RESULTS 1979-94

YEAR	TOTAL No. of seats	TURNOUT %	F.F. seats	F.G. seats	LAB. seats	W.P. seats	P.D. seats	GREEN seats	OTHERS seats
1979	15	63.6	5	4	4	-	-	-	2
1984	15	47.6	8	6	-	-	-	-	1
1989	15	68.3	6	4	1	1	1	-	2
1994	15	44.0	7	4	1	-	-	2	1

NORTHERN IRELAND EUROPEAN PARLIAMENT ELECTION RESULTS 1979-94

YEAR	TOTAL SEATS	S.D.L.P.	U.U.P.	D.U.P.
1979	3	1	1	1
1984	3	1	1	1
1989	3	1	1	1
1994	3	1	1	1

REPUBLIC OF IRELAND M.E.P.S *(by political allegiance)*

The European Parliament has 626 members. The Republic of Ireland Members of the European Parliament are as follows:

FIANNA FÁIL/ UNION FOR EUROPE
Niall Andrews (Dublin), 43 Molesworth St., Dublin 2. Tel: (01) 6794368.
Gerard Collins (Munster), The Hill, Abbeyfeale, Co. Limerick. Tel: (01) 6620068.
Brian Crowley (Munster), 39 Sunday's Road, Cork. Tel: (021) 394598.
Jim Fitzsimmons (Leinster), 43 Molesworth St., Dublin 2. Tel: (01) 6719189.
Pat the Cope Gallagher (Connacht-Ulster), Dungloe, Co.Donegal. Tel: (075) 21276.
Liam Hyland (Leinster), Fearagh, Ballacolla, Portlaoise, Co. Laois. Tel: (0502) 34051.
Mark Killilea (Connacht-Ulster), Caherhugh House, Belclare, Tuam, Co. Galway. Tel: (093) 55414.

FINE GAEL/ EUROPEAN PEOPLE'S PARTY
Mary Banotti (Dublin), 43 Molesworth St., Dublin 2. Tel: (01) 6625100.
Alan Gillis (Leinster), Ballyhook House, Grangew Con, Co. Wicklow. Tel: (0508) 81229.
Joe McCartan (Connacht-Ulster), Mullyaster, Newtowngore, Carrick-on-Shannon, Co. Leitrim. Tel: (049) 33395.

GREEN PARTY/ GREENS
Nuala Ahern (Leinster), 5 Oaklands, Greystones, Co. Wicklow. Tel: (01) 2876574.
Patricia McKenna (Dublin), 43 Molesworth St., Dublin 2. Tel: (01) 6616833.

LABOUR PARTY/ PARTY OF EUROPEAN SOCIALISTS
Bernie Malone (Dublin), 43 Molesworth St., Dublin 2. Tel: (01) 6765988.

INDEPENDENT/ GROUP OF THE EUROPEAN LIBERAL AND REFORMIST PARTY
Pat Cox (Munster), 21 Cook Street, Cork. Tel: (021) 278488.

NORTHERN IRELAND M.E.P.S *(by political allegiance)*

Ian Paisley M.P. (D.U.P./ Independent) 17 Cyprus Avenue, Belfast BT5 5NT. Tel. (01232) 454255.
John Hume M.P. (S.D.L.P./Party of European Socialists) 5 Bayview Terrace, Derry. Tel. (01504) 265340.
Jim Nicholson (U.U.P./European's People Party) 3 Glengall Street, Belfast BT12 5AE. Tel. (01232) 439431.

EUROPEAN REFERENDA RESULTS IN IRELAND

Due to the Republic of Ireland's Constitution, most European treaties are required to be ratified by a referendum. In Northern Ireland, because Britain does not have a written constitution, treaties such as the Maastricht Treaty need only to be ratified by a parliamentary majority, although some have been put to a referendum in Britain as a whole.

NORTHERN IRELAND RESULTS

DATE	ISSUE	TURNOUT (%)	FOR (%)	AGAINST (%)
June 5, 1975	United Kingdom remaining within the E.E.C.	47	52.1	47.9

REPUBLIC OF IRELAND RESULTS

DATE	ISSUE	TURNOUT (%)	FOR (%)	AGAINST (%)	SPOILED (%)
May 10, 1972	Allow E.E.C. membership	70.9	83.1	16.9	0.8
May 26, 1987	Allow signing of Single European Act	43.9	69.9	30.1	0.5
June 18, 1992	Allow ratification of the Maastricht Treaty on European Union	57.3	69.1	30.9	0.5

SALARIES OF MEMBERS OF THE EUROPEAN PARLIAMENT AND EUROPEAN COMMISSIONERS

M.E.P.s are paid a salary equivalent to that of their locally elected representatives.
European Commissioners are paid in Belgian Francs. Their salaries are adjusted annually in line with inflation.

	BFr	IR£	STG£
M.E.P.	-	34,706	43,860
Commissioner*	7,253,496	131,404	116,335

Calculated using the exchange rate as of July 9, 1997. IR£ = 55.2 BFr, STG£ = 61.35 BFr.

THE EUROPEAN UNION AND HOW IT MAY EFFECT THE REPUBLIC OF IRELAND'S NEUTRALITY

Northern Ireland is part of Britain and, as such, is part of NATO; the Republic of Ireland is not and has traditionally been neutral. However, developments within the EU may be seen as a watering down of this neutrality, as they include a commitment by all members to a common security policy.

Article J1 of the TEU states the following: The union and its members shall define and implement a common foreign and security policy, governed by the provisions of this title and covering all areas of foreign and security policy.

As can be seen from above, there is no doubt that Ireland's future lies within the EU, and current Republic of Ireland and British governments' political and commercial planning is based on this premise.

PUBLIC ADMINISTRATION

REPUBLIC OF IRELAND: GOVERNMENT DEPARTMENTS

Department of Agriculture, Food and Forestry

Kildare Street, Dublin 2. Tel. (01) 6072000.
Minister: Joe Walsh, T.D.
Secretary: John Malone.
Description: The department is responsible for administering E.U. schemes, providing farm improvement grants, carrying out measures of improving livestock production, controlling and terminating animal disease and, in general, promoting the agriculture and food industries.
State Bodies / Agencies: Teagasc, An Bord Glas, An Bord Bia, the Irish Horseracing Authority, the Irish National Stud Company Limited, the National Milk Agency, Bord na gCon.

Department of Arts, Heritage, Gaeltacht & the Islands

'Dun Aimhirgin', 43-49 Mespil Road, Dublin 4. Tel. (01) 6670788.
Minister: Síle de Valera, T.D.
Secretary: Tadhg Ó hEaláithe.
Description: The department is responsible for the welfare of the Gaeltacht - socially, culturally and economically; promoting the Irish language; formulating national policy relating to arts and culture; promoting cultural institutions in the state; encouraging the living arts; formulating national policy on broadcasting and the audiovisual industry; and formulating and implementing national policy on heritage.
State Bodies / Agencies: the National Gallery of Ireland, the National Library of Ireland, the National Museum of Ireland, the National Archives, an Chomhairle Ealaíon (The Arts Council), the National Theatre Society, the Irish Museum of Modern Art, the National Concert Hall, the Chester Beatty Library, an Chomhairle Oidhreachta (the Heritage Council), Bord Scannán na hÉireann (the Irish Film Board), the Irish Manuscripts Commission, Radio Telefís Éireann, the Independent Radio and Television Commission, the Broadcasting Complaints Commission, Údarás na Gaeltachta, Bord na Gaeilge, Bord na Leabhar Gaeilge.

Department of Defence

Colaiste Caoimhin, Mobhi Road, Glasnevin, Dublin 9. Tel. (01) 8042000.
Minister: David Andrews, T.D.
Secretary: David O'Callaghan.
Description: The department is responsible for the administration, training, organisation, maintenance, equipment, management, discipline, regulation and control of the military defence forces. The department must ensure that it provides value for money military services which meet the needs of the government and the public and encompass an effective civil defence capability.
State Bodies / Agencies: Coiste an Asgard, the Irish Red Cross Society, the Army Pensions Board.

Department of Education

Marlborough Street, Dublin 1. Tel. (01) 8734700.
Minister: Michael Martin, T.D.
Secretary: Dr. Don Thornhill.
Description: The department manages public, private, post-primary, and special education and subsidises third level institutions in the Republic of Ireland. It is responsible for formulating and implementing national policies in relation to education. It is also responsible for other national youth and sporting agencies.
State Bodies / Agencies: Advisory Council for English Language Schools, Dublin Institute for Advanced Studies - Council, Dublin Institute for Advanced Studies - School of Celtic Studies, Dublin Institute for Advanced Studies - School of Cosmic Physics, Dublin Institute for Advanced Studies - School of Theoretical Physics, Gaisce, the Higher Education Authority (HEA), the Irish Sports Council, Institiúid Teangeolaíochta Éireann, Léargas, the National Centre for Guidance in Education, National Coaching and Training Centre, National Council for Curriculum and Assessment, National Council for Educational Awards, National Council for Vocational Awards, Secondary Teachers Registration Council, Teastas - the Irish National Certification Authority.

Department of Enterprise, Trade and Employment

Kildare Street, Dublin 2. Tel. (01) 6614444.
Minister: Mary Harney, T.D.
Secretary: Paul Haran.
Description: The department aims to promote employment by encouraging enterprise, ensuring competitiveness, securing an educated workforce, tackling exclusion from the labour market, promoting a fair employment environment and implementing an effective business system.
State Bodies / Agencies: Forfás, Forbairt, IDA Ireland, Shannon Free Airport Development Company Ltd., FÁS, the Health and Safety Authority, an Bord Trachtala, Nítrigin Éireann Teo, the Labour Court, the Labour Relations Commission, the Rights Commissioner, the Employer-Labour Conference, the Employment Appeals Tribunal, the Competition Authority, the County Enterprise Boards.

Department of Environment

Custom House, Dublin 1. Tel. (01) 6793377.
Minister: Noel Dempsey, T.D.
Secretary: Jimmy Farrelly.
Description: The department is responsible for environmental programmes and other services associated with the local government system. It aims to ensure, in partnership with local authorities and its own agencies, that Ireland has a high quality environment where infrastructure and amenities meet economic, social and

environmental needs and where development is properly planned and sustainable.

State Bodies / Agencies: An Bord Pleanála, an Comhairle Leabharlanna (The Library Council), Dublin Docklands Development Authority, the Environmental Information Service (ENFO), the Environmental Protection Agency (EPA), the Fire Services Council, the Housing Finance Agency PLC., the Local Government Computer Services Board, the Local Government Management Services Board, the National Building Agency Ltd., the National Roads Authority, the National Safety Council, the Rent Tribunal, Temple Bar Properties Ltd., Temple Bar Renewal Ltd., the Medical Bureau of Road Safety, Dublin Transportation Office.

Department of Finance

Government Buildings, Upper Merrion Street, Dublin 2. Tel. (01) 6767571.
Minister: Charlie McCreevy, T.D.
Secretary: Patrick H. Mullarkey.
Description: The department is responsible for public expenditure, taxation, the budget, economic policy and managing the public service.
State Bodies / Agencies: A.C.C. Bank, the Central Bank of Ireland, the Civil Service Commission, the Economic and Social Research Institute, I.C.C. Bank, the Institute of Public Administration, the National Lottery, the National Treasury Management Agency, the Office of Public Works, the Office of the Ombudsman *(see below)*, the Office of the Revenue Commissioners, the Ordnance Survey, the State Laboratory, the Trustee Savings Bank, the Valuation Office.

Department of Foreign Affairs

80 St. Stephen's Green, Dublin 2. Tel. (01) 4780822.
Minister: Ray Burke, T.D.
Secretary: Pádraig MacKernan.
Description: The department is responsible for advising the government on the country's external affairs and provides a link between foreign governments and international organisations. The department's internal units handle Anglo-Irish and Northern Irish affairs, administration, protocol and cultural matters, political and economic matters relating to the E.U. and other international organisations, development and cooperation programmes and legal affairs.
State Bodies / Agencies: None.

Department of Health & Children

Hawkins House, Dublin 2. Tel. (01) 6714711.
Minister: Brian Cowen, T.D.
Secretary: Jerry O'Dwyer.
Description: The department is responsible for the administration and controlling of health services throughout the country. It also formulates and implements policy on the provision of these services.
State Bodies / Agencies: an Bord Altranais, an Bord Uchtala, Beaumont Hospital Board, the Blood Transfusion Service Board, the Board for the Employment of the Blind, the Board of the Adelaide and Meath Hospitals, Bord na Radharcmhastóirí, Comhairle na nOspideal, Comhairle na Nimheanna, the Dental Council, Drug Treatment Centre Board, Dublin Dental Hospital Board, the Eastern Health Board, the Food Safety Advisory Board, the Food Safety Board of Ireland, General Medical Services (Payments) Board, the Health Research Board, the Health Service Employers' Agency, the Hospital Bodies Administrative Bureau, the Irish Medicines Board, Leopardstown Park Hospital Board, the Medical Council, the Midland Health Board, the Mid-Western Health Board, the National Cancer Registry Board, the National Council on Ageing and Older People, the National Rehabilitation Board, the North Eastern Health Board, the North Western Health Board, the Postgraduate Medical and Dental Board, St. James Hospital Board, St. Luke's and St. Anne's Hospital Board, the South Eastern Health Board, the Southern Health Board, Tallaght Hospital Board, the Voluntary Health Insurance Board, the Western Health Board, the Women's Health Council.

Department of Justice, Equality & Law Reform

72-76 St. Stephen's Green, Dublin 2. Tel. (01) 6028202.
Minister: John O'Donoghue, T.D.
Secretary: Tim Dalton.
Description: The department manages the courts, prisons and police force in keeping with law and order. It is also responsible for terminating inequality for all social groups that face discrimination in any form. It oversees citizenship matters, E.U. matters, the courts, the Garda Síochána, immigration, prisons and the probation and welfare service.
State Bodies / Agencies: The Charitable Donations & Bequests for Ireland, the Criminal Injuries Compensation Tribunal, Censorship of Publications, the Data Protection Commissioner, the Forensic Science Laboratory, the Garda Síochána Complaints Board, the Irish Film Censor's Office, the Land Registry, the Probation and Welfare Service, the Registry of Deeds and the State Pathologist.

Department of the Marine & Natural Resources

Leeson Lane, Dublin 2. Tel. (01) 6785444.
Minister: Michael Woods, T.D..
Secretary: Thomas A. Carroll.
Description: The department oversees the general development and protection of the marine. Under this remit, it is responsible for saving lives at sea, developing fishing sectors, developing marine transport and promoting the growth of coastal areas for economic and leisure purposes.
State Bodies / Agencies: Bord Iascaigh Mhara, the Central Fisheries Board, Coillte, the Regional Fisheries Boards, the Marine Institute, Arramra Teo, the Salmon Research Agency, the Foyle Fisheries Commission, the Port Companies, the Harbour Authorities,

Department of Social, Community & Family Affairs

Aras Mhic Dhiarmada, Store Street, Dublin 1. Tel. (01) 8748444.
Minister: Dermot Ahern, T.D.
Secretary: Edmond Sullivan.
Description: The department formulates policies relating to the social security system within the country and is responsible for the administration of this system. It deals with the provision of social welfare services, pensions, child benefits, social welfare appeals, disability and injury benefits, unemployment schemes and employment support services
State Bodies / Agencies: The Social Welfare Appeals

Office.

Department of the Taoiseach

Government Buildings, Upper Merrion Street, Dublin 2. Tel. (01) 6624888.
Taoiseach: Bertie Ahern, T.D.
Secretary: Patrick Teahon.
Description: The department is responsible for communication between government departments and the President, for the National Economic and Social Council and for Government Information Services. The Taoiseach carries out functions under the Constitution and under statute, including the administration of public services, the co-ordination of local policies and the administration of the collection, compilation, abstraction and publication of statistics. The department also takes fundamental responsibility for a number of programmes, including the co-ordination of local development policy, support at central government level for development of the West and the Strategic Management Initiative in the public service.
State Bodies / Agencies: The National Economic and Social Council, the Government Information Services, the Central Statistics Office, the Law Reform Commission.

Department of Tourism, Sport & Recreation

Kildare Street, Dublin 2. Tel. (01) 6621444.
Minister: Jim McDaid, T.D.

Secretary: Margaret Hayes.
Description: The department is responsible for the promotion and development of the tourism industry and the encouragement of sports within Ireland. The day-to-day implementation of these policies has been devolved to the four bodies listed below.
State Bodies / Agencies: Bord Fáilte Éireann (the Irish Tourist Board), Shannon Development, CERT (the State Tourism Training Agency), An Bord Trachtala (the Irish Trade Bord).

Department of Public Enterprise

44 Kildare Street, Dublin 2. Tel. (01) 6707444.
Minister: Mary O'Rourke, T.D..
Secretary: John Loughrey.
Description: The department develops and implements national policies in relation to aviation and airports; rail and road transport; telecommunications; postal, radio and meteorological services; the supply and use of energy; and the exploration and extraction of minerals and petroleum. It is also responsible for investigating hazards to health from ionising radiation and radioactive contamination of the environment.
State Bodies / Agencies: Aer Lingus, Aer Rianta, an Post, Bord Gais Éireann, Bord na Mona, Córas Iompair Éireann, the Electricity Supply Board, the Irish National Petroleum Corporation, the Irish Aviation Authority, Met Éireann, the Radiological Protection Institute of Ireland, Telecom Éireann.

OFFICE OF THE OMBUDSMAN, R.O.I.

52 St. Stephen's Green, Dublin 2. Tel. (01) 678 5222.

The purpose of the Office of the Ombudsman: to ensure that public bodies within the Republic of Ireland adhere to the principles of good administration by dealing with citizens in a proper, fair and impartial manner. The Ombudsman receives and handles complaints regarding maladministration, where public bodies fail to observe the principles of good administration.

COMPLAINTS HANDLED IN 1996

Complaints received in 1996............................3,181
Complaints outside jurisdiction 645

Complaints within jurisdiction.........................2,536
Complaints carried forward from 1995 878
Breakdown of Complaints:

Civil Service	1,601
Social Welfare	807
Agriculture, Food & Forestry	310
Revenue Commissioners	176
Education	151
Environment	40
Other Civil Service Dept.'s	117
Local Authorities	792
Health Boards	577
Telecom Éireann	370
An Post	74

Total **3,414**

ACTION TAKEN

Complaints Resolved	444
Assistance Provided	547
Not Upheld	943
Discontinued	482
Withdrawn	50
Carried Forward to 1997	948

Total **3,414**

COMPLAINTS OUTSIDE JURISDICTION

Private Companies/persons	197
Public Bodies outside Jurisdiction	143
Banking/Insurance Matters	142
Legal Matters/Professions	64
Planning Permissions/Pensions/Recruitment etc.	37
Pay and Conditions	22
Miscellaneous	40

Total **645**

NORTHERN IRELAND: GOVERNMENT DEPARTMENTS

Department of Agriculture for Northern Ireland

(DANI) *Dundonald House, Upper Newtownards Road, Belfast, Co. Antrim, BT4 3SB. Tel. (01232) 520100.*
Minister: Lord Dubs (Parliamentary Under Secretary of State)
Secretary: Peter Small.
Description: The D.A.N.I. is responsible for encouraging sustainable economic growth and the development of the countryside in Northern Ireland by promoting the competitive development of the agri-food, fishing and forestry sectors of the economy; by being both proactive and responsive to the needs of consumers with regard to food; and by being responsible for the welfare of animals and the conservation of the environment. In addition, it aims to strengthen the economy and social infrastructure of disadvantaged rural areas.
State Bodies / Agencies: the Agricultural Research Institute of Northern Ireland; the Agricultural Wages Board for Northern Ireland; the Fisheries Conservancy Board for Northern Ireland; the Foyle Fisheries Commission; the Livestock and Meat Commission for Northern Ireland; the Northern Ireland Fishery Harbour Authority; the Pig Production Development Committee.

Department of Economic Development (D.E.D.)

Netherleigh, Massey Avenue, Belfast, Co. Antrim, BT4 2JP. Tel. (01232) 529900.
Minister: Adam Ingram (Minister of State)
Secretary: Gerry Loughran.
Description: The D.E.D. is responsible for providing an optimum framework for strengthening economic development in Northern Ireland. Its aims are the promotion of economic growth, leading to increased employment in Northern Ireland; the achievement of a fair and flexible labour market; the targeting of programmes at regions of social and economic deprivation and at the needs of the long-term unemployed; and the administration of the D.E.D.'s financial and human resources. The D.E.D is organised on a model that is similar to a holding company with specific operation subsidiary businesses or bodies:
State Bodies / Agencies: The Industrial Development Board (IDB), the Training and Employment Agency (T&EA), the Industrial Research and Technology Unit (IRTU). *DED-sponsored non-departmental bodies:* the Local Enterprise Development Unit, the Northern Ireland Tourist Board, the Labour Relations Agency, the Fair Employment Commission, the Equal Opportunities Commission, the General Consumer Council, the Health & Safety Agency.

Department of Education for Northern Ireland (D.E.N.I.)

Rathgael House, Balloo Road, Bangor, Co. Down, BT19 7PR. Tel. (01247) 279279.
Minister: Tony Worthington (Parliamentary Under Secretary of State).
Secretary: Pat Carvill.
Description: The Department of Education for Northern Ireland (D.E.N.I.) caters for the whole range of education, sport and recreation and youth services in Northern Ireland; for the arts and culture; for libraries and for community relations with and between schools. It plays an important role in developing and implementing education policies, from nursery level through to further and higher education. D.E.N.I. administers teachers' salaries and their superannuation scheme on behalf of the Education and Library boards, the Council for Catholic Maintained Schools (see local administration) and specific voluntary grammar and grant-maintained schools. Under the new regime, it is to be joined with the Training & Employment Agency - currently the responsibility of the Department of Economic Development - and brought under the control of one minister.
State Bodies / Agencies: the Arts Council of Northern Ireland; the Council for Catholic Maintained Schools; the Northern Ireland Schools Examinations and Assessment Council; the Sports Council for Northern Ireland; the Ulster Folk and Transport Museum; the Ulster Museum; the Youth Council for Northern Ireland; the Staff Commission for Education and Library Boards.

Department of Environment for Northern Ireland

Clarence Court, 10-18 Adelaide Street, Belfast, Co. Antrim, BT2 8GB. Tel. (01232) 540540.
Minister: Lord Dubs (Parliamentary Under Secretary of State)
Secretary: Ronnie Spence.
Description: The Department of the Environment is responsible for a wide range of services which affect the daily lives of everyone in Northern Ireland, including planning, roads, water and works services, housing and transport policies and fire services. It also administers specific controls over local government and manages certain lands and properties, urban regeneration, country parks, nature reserves, areas of outstanding natural beauty, environmental protection, the registration of titles of land and deeds and the listing and preservation of historic buildings, ancient monuments and archaeological surveys.
State Bodies / Agencies: the Central Policy and Management Unit; the Construction Service; Driver and Vehicle Testing Agency; the Driver and Vehicle Licensing Agency; the Environment and Heritage Service; the Land Registers of Northern Ireland; the Urban Regeneration Division; the Ordinance Survey Agency; the Planning Service; the Public Record Office for Northern Ireland; the Rate Collection Agency; the Roads Service; the Water Services.

Department of Finance and Personnel

Parliament Buildings, Belfast, Co. Antrim, BT4 3SW. Tel. (01232) 520400.
Minister: Paul Murphy (Minister of State).
Secretary: John Semple.
Description: The department supervises and controls the expenditure of the Northern Ireland departments and liaises with Her Majesty's Treasury and the Northern Ireland Office with regard to a number of financial and socio-economic areas. It also develops,

and administers the equal opportunities policy for the civil service in Northern Ireland and is responsible for personnel, pay, pensions, conditions of service and the coordination of pay policies in the civil service. Its other functions include providing personnel for the Civil Service Commission, an independent organisation responsible for recruiting non-industrial staff for the civil service in Northern Ireland.

State Bodies / Agencies: the Law Reform Advisory Committee for Northern Ireland; the Northern Ireland Economic Council; the Statute Law Committee for Northern Ireland.

Department of Health and Social Services (D.H.S.S.)

Dundonald House, Upper Newtownards Road, Belfast, Co. Antrim, BT4 3SF. Tel. (01232) 520500.
Minister: Tony Worthington (Parliamentary Under Secretary of State)
Secretary: Clive Gowdy.
Description: The function of the D.H.S.S. is to maintain and improve the health and social well-being of the peo-

ple of Northern Ireland by formulating policies and strategies, providing health and personal social services and securing the planning and delivery of these services through the Health and Social Services Boards, the Health Trusts and general practitioners. The department is also responsible for child support, social security and a wide range of social legislation, in addition to providing financial support for those who are retired sick, disabled, unemployed or in need through the Social Security Agency.

State Bodies / Agencies: the Child Support Agency; Central Services Agency; Northern Ireland Blood Transfusion Service Agency; Health Promotion Agency; N.I. Regional Medical Physics Agency; N.I. Guardian Ad litem Service Agency; the Mental Health Commission for Northern Ireland; the National Board for Nursing, Midwifery and Health Visiting for Northern Ireland; the Northern Ireland Council for Post-Graduate Medical and Dental Education; the Social Security Agency.

LOCAL ADMINISTRATION IN IRELAND

City and County/District and Borough Councils

REPUBLIC OF IRELAND
General Council of County Councils, 3 Greenmount House, Harold's Cross Road, Dublin 6W.
Tel: (01) 4548700
(see also County Profiles)

Carlow - County Offices, Carlow. Tel: (0503) 31126.
Cavan - Courthouse, Cavan. Tel: (049) 61565.
Clare - New Road, Ennis, Co. Clare. Tel: (065) 21616.
Cork - County Hall, Carrigrohane Road, Cork. Tel: (021) 276891.
Cork - City Hall, Cork. Tel: (021) 966222.
Donegal - County House, Lifford, Co. Donegal. Tel: (074) 72222.
Dublin City - Wood Quay, Dublin 8. Tel: (01) 6796111.
Dún Laoghaire-Rathdown - County Hall, Dún Laoghaire, Co. Dublin. Tel: (01) 2806961.
Fingal - P.O. Box 174, 46-49 Upper O'Connell Street, Dublin 1. Tel: (01) 8727777.
Galway - County Buildings, Prospect Hill, Galway. Tel: (091) 563151.
Galway - City Hall, College Road, Galway. Tel: (091) 568151.
Kerry - Áras an Chontae, Tralee, Co. Kerry. Tel: (066) 21111.
Kildare - St. Mary's, Naas, Co. Kildare. Tel: (045) 876875.
Kilkenny - County Hall, John Street, Kilkenny. Tel: (056) 52699.

Laois - County Hall, Portlaoise, Co. Laois. Tel: (0502) 22044.
Leitrim - Governor House, Carrick-on-Shannon, Co. Leitrim. Tel: (078) 20005.
Limerick - P.O. Box 53, County Buildings, 79-84 O'Connell Steet, Limerick. Tel: (061) 318477.
Limerick - City Hall, Limerick. Tel: (061) 415799.
Longford - Longford. Tel: (043) 46231.
Louth - County Offices, Dundalk, Co. Louth. Tel: (042) 35457.
Mayo - Áras an Chontae, Castlebar, Co. Mayo. Tel: (094) 24444.
Meath - County Hall, Navan, Co. Meath. Tel: (046) 21581.
Monaghan - County Offices, Monaghan. Tel: (047) 82211.
Offaly - Courthouse, Tullamore, Co. Offaly. Tel: (0506) 21419.
Roscommon - Courthouse, Roscommon. Tel: (0903) 26100.
Sligo - Riverside, Sligo. Tel: (071) 43221.
South Dublin - P.O. Box 4122, Town Centre, Tallaght, Dublin 24. Tel: (01) 4620111.
Tipperary (North Riding) - Courthouse, Nenagh, Co. Tipperary. Tel: (067) 31771.
Tipperary (South Riding) - Áras an Chontae, Emmet Street, Clonmel, Co. Tipperary. Tel: (067) 31711.
Waterford - Davitt's Quay, Dungarvan, Co. Waterford. Tel: (058) 42822.

Waterford City - City Hall, Waterford. Tel: (051) 873501.
Westmeath - Mullingar, Co. Westmeath. Tel: (044) 40861.
Wexford - County Hall, Spawell Road, Wexford. Tel: (053) 42211.
Wicklow - County Buildings, Wicklow. Tel: (0404) 67324.

NORTHERN IRELAND
(see also County Profiles)

Antrim Borough - The Steeple, Antrim BT41 1BJ. Tel: (01849) 463113.
Ards Borough - 2 Church Street, Newtownards, Co. Down BT23 4AP. Tel: (01247) 824000.
Armagh City and District - Council Offices, The Palace Demesne, Armagh BT60 4EL. Tel: (01861) 529600.
Ballymena Borough - Ardeevin, 80 Galgorm Road, Ballymena, Co. Antrim BT42 1AA. Tel: (01266) 44111.
Ballymoney Borough - Riada House, 14 Charles Street, Ballymoney, Co. Antrim BT53 6DZ. Tel: (012656) 62280.
Banbridge District - Civic Building, Downshire Road, Banbridge, Co. Down BT32 3JY. Tel: (018206) 62991.
Belfast City - City Hall, Belfast, Co. Antrim BT1 5GS. Tel: (01232) 320202.
Carrickfergus Borough - Town Hall, Carrickfergus, Co. Antrim

BT38 7DL. Tel: (01960) 351604.
Castlereagh Borough - 368 Cregagh Road, Belfast, Co. Antrim BT6 9EZ. Tel: (01232) 799021.
Coleraine Borough - Cloonavain, 41 Portstewart Road, Coleraine, Co. Derry BT52 1EY. Tel: (01265) 52181.
Cookstown District - Burn Road, Cookstown, Co. Tyrone BT80 8DT. Tel: (016487) 62205.
Craigavon Borough - Civic Centre, P.O. Box 66, Lakeview Road, Craigavon, Co. Armagh BT64 1AL. Tel: (01762) 341199.
Derry City - 98 Strand Road, Derry BT48 7NN. Tel: (01504) 365151.
Down District - 24 Strangford Road, Downpatrick, Co. Down BT30 6SR. Tel: (01396) 610800.

Dungannon District - Council Offices, Circular Road, Dungannon, Co. Tyrone BT71 6DT. Tel: (01868) 725311.
Fermanagh District - Town Hall, Enniskillen, Co. Fermanagh BT74 4BA. Tel: (01365) 325050.
Larne Borough - Smiley Buildings, Victoria Road, Larne, Co. Antrim BT40 1RU. Tel: (01574) 272313.
Limavady Borough - 7 Connell Street, Limavady, Co. Derry BT49 0HA. Tel: (015047) 22226.
Lisburn Borough - The Square, Hillsborough, Co. Down BT26 6AH. Tel: (01846) 682477.
Magherafelt District - 50 Ballyronan Road, Magherafelt, Co. Derry BT45 6EN. (01648) 32151.
Moyle District - Sheskburn House,

7 Mary Street, Ballycastle, Co. Antrim BT54 6QH. Tel: (012657) 62225.
Newry and Mourne District - Monaghan Row, Newry, Co. Down BT35 8DL. Tel (01693) 65411.
Newtownabbey Borough - 1 The Square, Ballyclare, Co. Antrim BT39 9BA. Tel: (01960) 352681.
North Down Borough - Town Hall, The Castle, Bangor, Co. Down BT20 4BT. Tel: (01247) 270371.
Omagh District - The Grange, Mountjoy Road, Omagh, Co. Tyrone BT79 7BL. Tel: (01662) 245321.
Strabane District - 47 Derry Road, Strabane, Co. Tyrone BT82 8DY. Tel: (01504) 382204.

HISTORY

Ireland since Seán Lemass

By **Professor Joe Lee**, *University College Cork.*

IRELAND has changed with dramatic speed in the 30 years since the resignation of Seán Lemass as Taoiseach in November 1966. Lemass himself is often credited with initiating the transformation, insofar as a single politician could, which transformed Ireland from the staid, inward looking, 'traditional' age of de Valera to the dynamic, bustling, outward looking, Ireland of today. There is a great deal of caricature in this image, particularly in the profile of de Valera, who has become a fashionable hate figure for many later *ignoranti.* Lemass did indeed inject vitality into public affairs. But he was also a patriot of the old school, a nationalist prepared to die for his country, a believer in social solidarity, of a type as alien in its way to the fashionable individualism of the 1990s as the more austere pieties of de Valera.

The changes that marked post-Lemass Ireland derived from a cluster of developments that coincided with, or arose from, his own succession to de Valera as Taoiseach in 1959. The wager on multinationals as the engine of economic growth that had eluded native enterprise, the image of President John F. Kennedy, the Second Vatican Council, and above all, the coming of television and later the growing dominance of that television by the values of the Anglo-American Australian media classes, all contributed to the rapidly changing social mores.

Those mores have certainly changed rapidly. It is not so much change, but the speed of change, that has been so dramatic in the past 30 years. This has been most striking of all in the area of sexual morality and of family relationships. Where the initial response to the economic growth of the 1960s was a fall in the age of marriage, and a sharp rise in the marriage rate, a new generation adopted different values. Marriage rate has since fallen sharply again, and completed family size, although somewhat above the western European average, has nearly halved in the past generation - a dramatic rate of decline. Births outside marriage, once among the lowest in western Europe, at less than 5 per cent, are now among the highest at about 25 percent. The proportion of unmarried mothers, also once the lowest in western Europe, is also now among the highest. Whether these changes are for better or for worse is a matter of opinion. But that dramatic changes occurred is self-evident.

The change has derived partly from economic factors, and partly from the triumph of media values over 'traditional', particularly Catholic, values. Scandals in the Catholic Church, perhaps even more the manner in which the Church has responded to scandals, has reinforced the loss of confidence in what seemed only a generation ago an impregnable bastion of loyalty and continuity.

At least two other factors have contributed to the pace of change. One was joining the European Community in 1973. Although many of the changes deriving from membership have been more cosmetic than substantial, nevertheless the realisation that London was not necessarily the centre of the globe has arguably injected a badly needed self-confidence into Irish self-images, a self-confidence brilliantly harnessed by the symbolically and supremely successful presidency of Mary Robinson, a presidency which itself symbolised the rapidly changing self-image, and objective role, of women in the society. The other is the increased access to second and third level education for a sharply rising proportion of young people. Whether Ireland is now better educated than ever before, as often claimed, may be a matter for debate. But it is certainly longer educated than ever before, and with that also comes enhanced self-confidence.

The growth in self-confidence from the later 1980s, as recovery from the largely self-inflicted economic depression of the first half of the 1980s gathered pace, has been consolidated by the remarkable economic growth rates of the last five years, growth rates so spectacular by European standards that they have led many to dub Ireland the Celtic Tiger.

What the future trajectory of the tiger may be remains to be seen. But the tiger is certainly a more satisfying tag than the tortoise. If only economic growth could now be paralleled by an enduring settlement of the Northern Ireland tragedy, the late 20th century could turn out to have been a good time to have been Irish.

The author is Professor of Modern History at University College Cork and a columnist with The Sunday Tribune.

HIGH KINGS OF IRELAND

Succession to kingship in Ireland was not based on primogeniture (i.e. the eldest son automatically becomes king). Any member of the *derbhfine* (i.e. the family group extending to cousins whose direct ancestor was king within the past five generations) was eligible. Usually the man with the most supporters (*clients*) became king.

....Niall Noígiallach	734-43...Áed Allán
....Nath Í mac Fiachrach	743-63...Domnall Midi
....Lóeguire mac Néill	763-70..Niall Frossach
463-482...............................Ailill Molt mac Nath Í	770-97...Donnchad Midi
482-507.................................Lugaid mac Lóeguiri	797-819 ....Áed Oirdnide mac Néill
507-36 ....Muirchertach Mac Ercae	819-33 ....Conchobar mac Donnchado
536-44 ....Tuathal Máelgarb mac Cormaic Caích	833-846...Niall Caille
544-65 ....Diarmait mac Cerbaill	846-62 ....Máel Sechnaill I
565-66 ....Forggus mac Muirchertaig	862-79 ....Áed Findlaith
566-69 ....Ainmuire mac Sétnai	879-916...Flann Sinna
569-72 ....Báetán mac Muirchertaig	916-19..Niall Glúndub
572-86..Báetán mac Ninnedo	919-44...Donnchad Donn
586-98 ....Áed mac Ainmuirech	944-56...Congalach Cnogba
598-604.............................Áed Sláine mac Diarmato	956-80 ....Domnall ua Néill
604-12............................. Áed Allán mac Domnaill	980-1002 ....Máel Sechnaill II
612-14...Máel Cobo	1002-14 ....Brian Bóruma
614-28 ....Suibne Menn mac Fiachnai	1014-22 ....Máel Sechnaill II
628-42.......................................Domnall mac Áedo	1022-72 ...the kingship was suspended or contested in
642-58 ....Cellach mac Máele Cobo	this period
658-65 ....Diarmait mac Áedo Sláine	1072-86..............................Toirrdelbach ua Briain
665-71 ....Sechnussach mac Blathmaic	1086-14............................Muirchertach Ua Briain
671-74 ....Cenn Fáelad	1114-22 ....Domnall Ua Lochlainn
674-95 ....Fínsnechta Fledach	1122-56...................Toirrdelbach Ua Conchobair
695-704 ....Loingsech mac Óengusso	1156-66.......................Muirchertach Mac Lochlainn
704-10 ....Congal Cennmagair	1166-86 ....Ruaidrí Ua Conchobair
710-22 ....Fergal mac Máele Dúin	
722-24...Fogartach mac Néill	
724-28 ....Cináed mac Írgalaig	*These dates, particularly the earlier ones,*
728-34 ....Flaithbertach mac Loingsig	*are approximate.*

CHRONOLOGY OF IRISH HISTORY 2500 B.C. - 1996

1 = SEE HISTORICAL MOVEMENTS/ORGANISATIONS CHAPTER
3 = SEE RECENT DOCUMENTS CHAPTER
5 = SEE HISTORICAL PROCLAMATIONS CHAPTER
7 = SEE WHO WAS WHO CHAPTER

2 = SEE HISTORICAL DOCUMENTS CHAPTER
4 = SEE HISTORICAL FIGURES CHAPTER
6 = SEE POLITICS CHAPTER
8 = SEE IRISH WRITERS CHAPTER

B.C.

2500 B.C. Radiocarbon dating for the building of Newgrange (Co. Meath).
680 B.C. Radiocarbon dating for first inhabited enclosure at Navan Fort (Co. Armagh).
51 B.C. Julius Caesar refers to Ireland as 'Hibernia' in written text.

1-1000 A.D.

130-80 Detailed map of Ireland appears in Ptolemy's 'Geography'.
297 Irish raids on Roman Britain begin, continue until middle of fifth century.
367 Irish, Picts and Saxons stage major raid on Britain.
431 Arrival of the first bishop in Ireland, Palladius[4], sent by Pope Celestine.
432 St. Patrick's[4] mission begins.
493 Traditional date of Patrick's death (March 17).
546 Derry founded by St. Column Cille[4]
563 Monastery at Iona founded by St. Columcille.
575 Convention at Druim Cett (Co.Derry). Poets threatened with exile by kings, and alliances between kings forged.
670-90 Hagiographical writings on St. Patrick[4], combining the lives of several missionaries especially Palladius, into one legend. Part of an attempt to establish Armagh's primacy in the Irish Church.
740 Compilation of the law text 'Senchas Már'.
750-800 Book of Kells illuminated.
795 First Viking raids on Ireland.
841 Vikings establish settlements at Dublin and Louth.
876 Beginning of 'Forty Years Peace', a respite in Viking attacks.
914 Viking fleet arrives in Waterford, marking the beginning of a second wave of Viking attacks.
922 Foundation of Viking settlement at Limerick.
995 First mint established by the Vikings in Dublin.

1001-1299 A.D.

1005 Brian Boru[4] (high-king 1002-1014) visits Armagh and confirms its primacy in the Church.
1014 Battle of Clontarf. Brian Boru defeats the Vikings decisively but is killed himself.
1028-36 Christchurch Cathedral, Dublin, built.
1095 First Crusade proclaimed by Pope Urban II. Irish join in great numbers.
1124 Round tower at Clonmacnoise completed.
1142 First Cistercian monastery in Ireland founded at Mellifont.
1152 Synod of Kells-Mellifont establishes diocesan organisation of Church, with four dioceses - Armagh, Dublin, Cashel and Tuam. Armagh enjoys the primacy.

1169 Normans arrive in Ireland at invitation of exiled Leinster king, Diarmait Mac Murchada[4] (Dormot MacMurrough).
1169-c.1300 Normans conquer much of Leinster, north and east Ulster, Munster and parts of Connacht.
1171 (May) Richard de Clare (Strongbow[4]) succeeds Diarmait Mac Murchada as king of Leinster.
1171 (October) Henry II, king of England, lands at Waterford.
1175 Treaty of Windsor: Ruairdhí Ua Conchobair (high-king) recognises Henry II as his overlord, while Henry recognises Ua Conchobair as high-king of unconquored parts of Ireland.
1177 Prince John (son of Henry II) appointed lord of Ireland. Becomes king of England 1199.
1204 Normans start building Dublin Castle.
1216 (October) John, king of England, dies. Succeeded by Henry III as king and lord of Ireland.
1216 (November) Magna Carta issued for Ireland.
1254 Henry's son Edward is styled 'Lord of Ireland'.
1272 Henry III dies, succeeded by Edward I.

THE 1300s

1301- 5 Irish soldiers fight with Edward I in Scotland. Scots, led by William Wallace, defeated 1305.
1307 Edward I dies succeeded by Edward II.
1315 Edward Bruce (crowned king of Scotland 1306) arrives in Ulster. Crowned king of Ireland in 1316 (but never reigned). Killed 1318 at Battle of Faughart.
1327 Edward II abdicates, his queen rules until their son Edward III comes of age in 1330.
1348 First record of Black Death in Ireland. Occurrences at Howth and Drogheda.
1366 Parliament at Kilkenny. Statute of Kilkenny[2] enacted, designed to prohibit assimilation of Anglo-Irish and Gaelic Irish.
1377 Edward III dies, succeeded by Richard II.
1395 Richard II defeats Leinster Irish in battle. Most Irish kings and rebel Normans submit to him.
1399 Richard II deposed, Henry IV crowned king of England, also Lord of Ireland.

THE 1400s

1413 Henry IV succeeded by Henry V.
1422 Henry V succeeded by Henry VI.
1446 The term 'Pale' - used to denote area of Norman influence around Dublin - appears for the first time in a written text.
1460 Irish parliament declares that only acts passed by it are binding on the country.
1461 Edward IV assumes English Crown and with it the lordship of Ireland.
1470 Henry VI reinstalled to the English Crown.
1471 Edward IV restored to the throne.

1479 Gearóid Mór Fitzgerald, the eighth earl of Kildare, appointed Lord Deputy (king's representative in Ireland).

1483 (April) Edward V, son of Edward IV succeeds to throne on his father's death.

1483 (June) Edward V deposed, replaced by Richard III.

1485 Henry Tudor kills Richard III at Battle of Bosworth and becomes king as Henry VII.

1494 Edward Poynings appointed Lord Deputy. 'Poynings' Law'[2] enacted by parliament at Drogheda. All legislation passed by subsequent Irish parliaments to be approved by the king. Act not amended until 1782.

1496 Earl of Kildare reappointed Lord Deputy.

THE 1500s

1504 Battle of Knockdoe - Clanricard and O'Brien defeated by forces of the Pale, the Lord Deputy and O'Donnell, king of Tír Conaill.

1509 Death of Henry VII. Accession of his son Henry VIII.

1513 Gearóid Óg Fitzgerald, ninth earl of Kildare, appointed Lord Deputy following the death of his father.

1534 (June) Thomas Fitzgerald (Silken Thomas[4]) son of Gearóid Óg rebels against English rule. Surrenders August 1535 and is imprisoned. Executed February 1537.

1534 Gearóid Óg dies in Tower of London.

1536 Reformation parliament held in Dublin recognising Henry VIII as the temporal head of the Church in Ireland.

1537 Act of Irish parliament provides for suppression of monasteries throughout the country.

1541 Act of Irish parliament recognises Henry VIII as king of Ireland. The English king had hitherto been styled 'lord of Ireland'.

1541 First instance of the system of 'surrender and regrant' where Irish lords revoke their Gaelic title, assume an English one and gain a royal grant of their lands.

1547 Accession of Edward VI following death of his father, Henry VIII.

1549 Act of Uniformity orders the use of the Book of Common Prayer in England and Ireland.

1553 Mary I accedes to the throne on the death of Edward VI. Pace of Reformation halted.

1557 Plantation of Laois and Offaly begins.

1558 Death of Mary I. Accession of the virgin queen, Elizabeth I. Reformation gains a new vigour.

1562 Shane O'Neill, earl of Tyrone in rebellion. Submits to Lord Deputy in 1563 but continues warring with local lords until his death in 1567.

1570 Elizabeth I excommunicated by the Pope.

1568-74 Desmond Rebellion in Munster.

1579-83 Further rebellion in Munster. Earl of Desmond killed in 1583.

1582 Pope Gregory XIII reforms calendar - 4/10/1582 to be followed by 15/10/1582 - and year to commence on January 1.

1583 Hugh O'Neill[4] takes the Gaelic title of The O'Neill. Conferred with title of earl of Tyrone in 1587.

1587 First grant of land in the plantation of Munster.

1588 Spanish Armada founders off Irish coast, 25 ships wrecked, survivors aided in Connacht and Ulster but put to death elsewhere.

1592 Trinity College Dublin established.

1595-1603 Nine Years' War - Rebellion of Hugh O'Neill, earl of Tyrone, and Red Hugh O'Donnell who enlist Spanish support (troops land at Kinsale in 1601).

THE 1600s

1601 Battle of Kinsale - Forces of O'Neill and O'Donnell heavily defeated by Lord Mountjoy (Lord Deputy).

1603 (March) Accession of James I (James VI of Scotland), first of Stuart line, following the death of Elizabeth I.

1603 (March) Treaty of Mellifont. O'Neill submits to Mountjoy and pledges loyalty to the Crown.

1607 'Flight of Earls'. Earls of Tyrone and Tír Connail leave Ireland sailing from Lough Swilly. Their lands are forfeited to the Crown.

1608 Cahir O'Doherty, the last Irish chieftain, in rebellion. Sacks Derry. Killed in Donegal, the rebellion collapses and O'Doherty's lands are forfeited to the Crown.

1609 Beginning of the plantation of Ulster in Counties Donegal, Derry, Tyrone, Armagh, Cavan and Fermanagh.

1625 Death of James I, accession of Charles I.

1632 Compilation of the Annals of the Four Masters[2], a significant historical work, begins and is completed 1636.

1641 A rising, ostensibly in support of Charles I, begins in Ulster and spreads southwards. Thousands of Protestants reported massacred.

1649 (January) Execution of Charles I. England a republic until 1660.

1649 (August) Oliver Cromwell lands in Ireland. Massacre of Catholics in Drogheda and Wexford.

1653 Acts providing for the transplanting of Catholic Irish to Connacht and Ulster Presbyterians to Munster. Their lands are subsequently taken by Cromwellian soldiers and English settlers.

1660 Charles II proclaimed king in Dublin following restoration of the monarchy.

1673 Non-Anglicans excluded from public office by Test Act.

1685 Accession of James II on the death of Charles II.

1689 (February) William and Mary crowned as joint monarchs.

1688 James II flees to France from England.

1689 (April) Siege of Derry. Jacobites (followers of James II) lay siege to the city until July when sea-borne supplies arrive.

1690 William defeats James at river Boyne (July 1); James departs for France (July 4); unsuccessful siege at Limerick by Williamite forces (August 9 - 30).

1691 Jacobites defeated at Battle of Aughrim (July 12).

1691 Siege of Limerick (August 25 - September 24) followed by a truce allowing the signing of the Treaty of Limerick[2] (October 3), which guaranteed Catholic rights of worship and free passage of Jacobite soldiers to France.

1691 (December) First of the penal laws[2] passed, Catholics excluded from parliament and public office by means of oath of supremacy.
1692-1703 Williamites begin confiscation of land from those who support James.
1694 Death of Mary II.

THE 1700's

1702 William III dies and is succeeded by Queen Anne.
1714 Queen Anne dies without an heir, succeeded by George I, first of the Hanoverian line.
1718 Significant numbers of Ulster Scots (largely Presbyterian) begin emigration to North America.
1719 Toleration Act passed for dissenting protestants. Legal toleration of their religion.
1720 Declatory Act - British parliament affirms its right to legislate for Ireland.
1727 George I succeeded by George II.
1737 First edition of The Belfast Newsletter.
1740-1 Severe famine in Ireland; several hundred thousand die.
1745 The Rotunda Maternity Hospital is founded in Dublin.
1752 George II reforms the calendar - 2/9/1752 followed by 14/9/1752.
1756 Work begins on construction of Grand Canal.
1760 (March) Catholic Committee[1] founded in Dublin to lobby for removal of penal laws.
1760 (October) George III becomes king on death of his grandfather George II.
1778 Volunteer Movement[1] founded in Belfast.
1782 Ireland attains legislative independence. Declaratory Act 1720 repealed, and Poynings' Law 1494 amended.
1783 Bank of Ireland begins trading.
1791 Society of United Irishmen[1] founded in Belfast.
1793 Catholic Relief Act[2] - Catholics given rights to vote, to third level education and to hold all but the highest offices of state.
1795 (September) Orange Order[1] founded in Armagh.
1795 (October) Roman Catholic seminary opens at Maynooth.
1797 (July) Fourteen are killed in violence at an Orange parade in Stewartstown, Co. Tyrone.
1798 (May) United Irishmen rebellion begins. Fighting confined to Leinster and Ulster. Government forces defeat the rebels.
1798 (August) French troops land in Mayo in support of the rebellion. Surrender on September 8.
1798 (November) Theobald Wolfe Tone[4], leader of United Irishmen, arrested at Buncrana. Convicted of treason by court martial and sentenced to death. Commits suicide before sentence can be carried out.

THE 1800's

1800 Act of Union[2] passed to provide for legislative and political union between Great Britain and Ireland.
1801 Union of Great Britain and Ireland commences.
1803 Rebellion in Dublin led by Robert Emmet[4]. Emmet hanged for treason September 20.
1813 Four men are killed following violence at an Orange parade in Belfast.
1814 Apprentice Boys of Derry formed.
1820 Death of George III, accession of George IV.
1822 Act of parliament provides for an all-Ireland police force.
1823 Catholic Association[1] founded in Dublin to lobby for Catholic Emancipation.
1825 Unlawful Societies (Ireland) Act passed, Catholic Association dissolves, as does the Grand Lodge of the Orange Order (not reconstituted until 1828). The law is ignored by Orange lodges who continue to parade.
1828 Daniel O'Connell[4] elected to House of Commons but unable to take his seat because he is Roman Catholic.
1829 (April) Catholic Emancipation[2] granted. Roman Catholics permitted to enter parliament and hold the high offices of state.
1829 Sixteen die in violence accompanying Orange marches during the summer.
1830 Death of George IV, accession of William IV.
1831 (June) 'Tithe war' begins. Recurring outbreaks of violence at the collection of Anglican tithes from members of all religious denominations.
1831 (November) Scheme for nationwide primary schooling initiated - the first in the world.
1832 Party Procession Act passed curtailing marches.
1834 First railway line in Ireland comes into operation.
1836 (April) Grand Lodge of the Orange Order dissolves itself to avoid suppression.
1836 (May) Irish Constabulary[1] formed (earns prefix 'Royal' in 1867).
1837 Queen Victoria accedes to the throne on death of William IV.
1838 Total Abstinence Movement[1] founded in Cork by Fr. Arnold Matthew and William Martin.
1839 (January 6) Night of the Big Wind, storms cause widespread damage.
1840 Daniel O'Connell forms the Loyal National Repeal Association[1] to lobby for the repeal of the union between Ireland and Great Britain.
1841 Census. Population of Ireland - 8,175,124.
1841 First edition of The Cork Examiner.
1843 Daniel O'Connell organises 'Monster meetings' in support of Repeal throughout the country; the biggest is at Tara (an estimated 750,000 attend).
1845 (June) Party Processions Act lapses, Orange Order reforms itself.
1845 (July) Queen's Colleges Act provide for the establishment of new third level colleges.
1845 (September) First report of potato blight. Beginning of the Famine. Crop decimated in 1846. 1847 (Black '47) is worst year. Blight and famine continue until 1850. In excess of 1 million die and more than 1 million emigrate.
1848 'Young Ireland'[1] rebellion in Munster easily put down. Leaders transported.
1849 Opening of Queen's Colleges at Belfast, Cork and Galway.
1850 (March) Party Processions Act renewed, police empowered to seize weapons and emblems.

1850 (August) Irish Tenant League[1] formed to lobby for rights of tenant farmers.
1851 Census. Population of Ireland 6,552,385.
1854 Catholic University of Ireland (now University College Dublin) opens.
1855 First edition of *The Irish News*.
1858 Irish Republican Brotherhood[1] founded in Dublin. A sister movement, the Fenian Brotherhood[1] founded in New York 1859.
1859 First edition of *The Irish Times*.
1861 Census. Population of Ireland - 5,798,967.
1867 (February/March) Fenian rising in Munster easily suppressed.
1867 (July) Orange procession against Party Processions Act leads to a reduction in its powers. Marches now permitted in non-contentious areas. Party Processions Act formally repealed 1872.
1869 Irish Church Act[2] provides for disestablishment of Church of Ireland.
1870 (August) Gladstone's first Land Act[2].
1871 Census. Population of Ireland - 5,412,377.
1872 Ballot Act. Secret voting introduced.
1873 (May) Isaac Butt[4] forms the Home Rule League[1], precursor of Irish Parliamentary Party.
1877 Charles Stewart Parnell[4] becomes leader of Home Rule Confederation of Great Britain (elected chairman of Irish Parliamentary Party[1] 1880).
1879 Irish National Land League[1] formed in Dublin to agitate for land reform. Proscribed 1882.
1879-82 'The Land War'. Huge increase in rural crime. Directed almost exclusively at landlords and their agents.
1880 'Boycotting' of land agent Charles Cunningham Boycott[7] in Mayo.
1881 (April) Census. Population of Ireland 5,174,836.
1881 (August) Gladstone's second Land Act[2].
1882 Murders of the Chief Secretary and his Under Secretary (the principal government officials in Ireland) in the Phoenix Park by the Invincibles[1].
1884 Gaelic Athletic Association[1] founded in Thurles.
1885 (May) Irish Loyal and Patriotic Union[1] formed to oppose Home Rule and maintain the union.
1885 (August) Ashbourne Act[2] provides government loans to tenant farmers for land purchase.
1886 First Home Rule Bill[2] defeated in House of Commons. Fifty people lose their lives in sectarian rioting in Belfast.
1888 (November) Borough of Belfast created a city by charter.
1888 Pioneer and Total Abstinence Association founded by James Cullen S.J.
1890 Parnell ousted from leadership of Irish Parliamentary Party. He is cited as co-respondent in the William O'Shea[7] divorce petition. Unacceptable to Liberal Party and Catholic hierarchy. The party split.
1891 (March) Irish National Federation, an anti-Parnellite party, is founded.
1891 (April) Census. Population of Ireland - 4,704,750.
1891 (August) Balfour Act[2]. Extends tenant purchase scheme and establishes Congested Districts Board.
1891 First edition of the *Evening Herald*.
1892 (June) Ulster Convention at Belfast. Delegates vote to oppose workings of a Home Rule parliament.
1892 (June) Primary school education made compulsory.
1893 (July) Conradh na Gaeilige[1] (the Gaelic League) formed.
1893 (September) Home Rule Bill[2] passed in the House of Commons but defeated in House of Lords.
1894 (April) Irish Agricultural Organisation Society[1] founded.
1894 (April) Trade Union Congress held for first time.
1898 Local Government (Ireland) Act. Establishes county and district councils.
1899 (May) Irish Literary Theatre[1] founded in Dublin.
1899 (October) Beginning of the Boer War.

1900 - 1909

1900 Irish Parliamentary Party reunites with John Redmond[4] as leader.
1901 (January) Queen Victoria dies. Accession of Edward VII.
1901 (March) Census. Population of Ireland - 4,458,775.
1903 (March) St. Patrick's Day, March 17, declared a bank holiday.
1903 (June) Independent Orange Order founded in Belfast.
1903 (August) Wyndham Act[2]. Culmination of the series of land acts dating back to 1870.
1905 (March) Ulster Unionist Council[1] formed to oppose Home Rule.
1905 First edition of the *Irish Independent*.
1907 (April) Sinn Féin League[1] founded (adopts name Sinn Féin 1908).
1907 (July) Irish Crown jewels stolen. They have never been recovered.
1908 (August) Irish Universities Act[2], instituting the National University of Ireland (N.U.I.).
1908 (December) Irish Transport and General Workers' Union[1] (I.T.G.W.U.) founded in Dublin.

1910 - 1919

1913 Irish becomes a compulsory subject for matriculation in N.U.I.
1910 Death of Edward VII, accession of George V.
1911 (April) *Titanic* launched in Belfast.
1911 (April) Census. Population of Ireland - 4,390,219.
1911 (August) Parliament Act abolishes veto powers of House of Lords.
1912 (April) *Titanic* sinks on her maiden voyage.
1912 (June) Labour Party founded at Clonmel, Co. Tipperary.
1912 (September) Ulster Solemn League and Covenant[2] signed by 218,000 men pledging to use all necessary means to oppose Home Rule.
1913 (January) Ulster Volunteer Force[1] founded in Belfast.

1913 (August) Beginning of the Dublin 'Lock-Out', where Dublin Employers' Federation shuts out members of I.T.G.W.U. from their places of employment. Continues until January 1914.

1913 (November) Irish Citizens Army founded[1] in Dublin to protect the locked-out workers.

1913 (November) Irish Volunteers[1] founded in Dublin in response to U.V.F.

1914 (March) Curragh Incident - British officers serving at the Curragh indicate that they will not aid the imposition of Home Rule in Ulster.

1914 (April) Gunrunning by Ulster Volunteers at Larne passes off without incident.

1914 (July) Four civilians killed by troops when Irish Volunteers engage in gunrunning at Howth.

1914 (August 4) Britain declares war on Germany. Thirty-sixth Ulster Division is established, drawing on U.V.F. membership.

1914 (September) Home Rule Bill[1] passed but suspended because of World War I.

1914 (September) Split in Irish Volunteers. Majority answer John Redmond's call to join the war. Remainder become National Volunteers under leadership of Éoin Mac Neill[4].

1915 I.R.B. reorganised and Military Council formed. Plans for an Irish rebellion at advanced stage.

1916 (April) Easter Rising in Dublin. Independent Irish Republic proclaimed[2]. Rebellion suppressed within five days; over 3,000 injured and 450 killed.

1916 (May) Fifteen of the leaders of the Rising executed, including the seven signatories[4] of the proclamation - Thomas J. Clarke, Seán MacDiarmada, Thomas MacDonagh, Padraig Pearse, Eamonn Ceannt, James Connolly and Joseph Plunkett.

1916 (July) Battle of the Somme begins (continues until November). Ulster Division decimated.

1916 (August) Sir Roger Casement[4] hanged for his part in the Easter Rising.

1918 (November 11) Armistice day. End of World War I.

1918 (November) Universal Suffrage granted. Women win right to vote and right to sit in parliament.

1918 (December) Final all-Ireland general election, to Westminster parliament, takes place. Seats: S.F. 73, O.U.P. 25, Nat 6, Ind. 1.

1919 (January 21) Sinn Féin M.P.s, in keeping with their declared policy of abstention, do not take their seats at Westminster and meet as Dáil Éireann at the Mansion House in Dublin.

1919 (January 21) First engagement of War of Independence; two policemen killed in Tipperary.

1919 (June) First non-stop transatlantic flight completed when Alcock and Brown land in Galway.

1919 (October) Irish Volunteers swear allegiance to the Irish Republic becoming the Irish Republican Army[1].

THE 1920's

1920 (January) First British soldiers are recruited by R.I.C., commonly termed the Black and Tans[1]. Auxiliaries[1] recruited from July onwards.

1920 (November) 'Bloody Sunday'. Fourteen British secret agents assassinated by I.R.A. in Dublin. Black and Tans retaliate by shooting into a crowd watching a Gaelic football match at Croke Park, killing 12.

1920 (December) Black and Tans and Auxiliaries destroy centre of Cork city.

1920 (December) Government of Ireland Act[2] - Provides for the partition of Ireland and two Home Rule parliaments, one in Dublin, one in Belfast.

1921 (May) General election to Northern Ireland parliament. Seats: O.U.P. 40, Nat. 6, S.F. 6.

1921 (May) A total of 124 Sinn Féin and 4 independent M.P.s are returned unopposed to southern Irish parliament.

1921 (May) Custom House in Dublin is destroyed by I.R.A.

1921 (June) Northern Ireland parliament opened by George V.

1921 (June) Parliament of southern Ireland meets in Dublin. Only the four independent M.P.s turn up; the 124 Sinn Féin M.P.s refuse to accept its legitimacy and do not take their seats.

1921 (July) Truce agreed between I.R.A. and British army.

1921 (July) Fifteen Catholics killed and 68 seriously injured in one day when members of Orange Order aided by police officers attack Catholic areas in Belfast.

1921 (August) Sinn Féin M.P.s elected to the parliament of southern Ireland meet in the Mansion House as the second Dáil.

1921 (December) Anglo-Irish Treaty[2] signed in London establishing the Irish Free State.

1922 (January) Anglo-Irish Treaty approved by Dáil Éireann by 64 votes to 57. Split in Sinn Féin; those in opposition to the Treaty walk out. Michael Collins[4] becomes the Provisional Government Chairman.

1922 (May) Royal Ulster Constabulary established.

1922 (May) I.R.A. declared an illegal organisation in Northern Ireland.

1922 (June) General election in Irish Free State. Seats: Pro-treaty S.F. 58, anti-treaty S.F. 36, Lab. 17, Farmers' Party 7, others 10. Pro-treaty Sinn Féin form the government.

1922 (June) Civil War breaks out in Irish Free State.

1922 (August) Chairman of Provisional Government and Commander in Chief of the Free State forces, Michael Collins, is assassinated in Cork.

1922 (October) Dáil Éireann ratifies the Constitution of the Irish Free State[2] (approved by British parliament in December).

1922 (November) Provisional Government orders the first of 77 executions of anti-treaty prisoners.

1922 (November) Northern Ireland elections to Westminster. Seats: O.U.P. 11, Nat. 2.

1922 (December) Executive Council of the Irish Free State takes office with W.T. Cosgrave[4] as President.

1922 (December) Northern Ireland parliament opts out of the Irish Free State.

1923 (March) Cumann na nGaedheal[1] founded from pro-treaty Sinn Féin.

1923 (May) Civil war ends.

1923 (August) Garda Síochána established by act of Free State Dáil.

1923 (August) General election in Free State. Seats: Cumann na nGaedheal 63, S.F. 44, Lab. 14, Farmers' Party 15, others 17. Cumann na nGaedheal form the government.

1923 (September) Irish Free State becomes member of the League of Nations.

1923 (November) W.B. Yeats[8] receives Nobel Prize for literature.

1923 (December) Northern Ireland elections to Westminster. Seats: O.U.P. 11, Nat. 2.

1924 (March) Mutiny in Irish Free State army.

1924 (September) B.B.C. starts radio broadcasts from Belfast as 2BE.

1924 (October) Northern Ireland elections to Westminster. O.U.P. win all 13 seats.

1925 (April) General election to Northern Ireland parliament. Seats: O.U.P. 32, Nat. 10, other U. 4, other Lab. 3, other Nat. 2, Ind. 1.

1925 (July) Shannon hydro-electric scheme approved by Dáil.

1925 (December) Governments of Britain, Northern Ireland and Irish Free State agree to rescind powers of the Boundary Commission.

1926 (January) 2RN, the forerunner of R.T.E. commences radio broadcasts.

1926 (April) Census. Population of Northern Ireland - 1,256,561. Population of Irish Free State - 2,971,992.

1926 (May) Fianna Fáil[6] founded by Éamon de Valera[4].

1926 (November) George Bernard Shaw[8] receives Nobel Prize for literature.

1927 (June) General election in Free State. Seats: Cumann na nGaedheal 47, F.F. 44, Lab. 22, Farmers' Party 11, National League 8, S.F. 5, others 16. Cumann na nGaedheal remain in office.

1927 (July) Kevin O'Higgins[4], Minister for Justice in the Irish Free State, assassinated.

1927 (August) Éamon de Valera takes Oath of Allegiance and leads Fianna Fáil into Dáil Éireann.

1927 (September) Cumann na nGaedheal 62, F.F. 57, Lab 13, Farmers' Party 6, others 15. Cumann na nGaedheal retain office.

1929 (April) Proportional Representation abolished in Northern Ireland parliamentary elections.

1929 (May) General election to Northern Ireland parliament. Seats: O.U.P. 38, Nat.11, other U. 3.

1929 (May) Northern Ireland elections to Westminster. Seats: O.U.P. 11, Nat. 2.

1929 (July) Censorship of Publications Act[2] in Irish Free State establishes a board with wide-ranging powers of censorship.

1929 (October) Shannon hydro-electric scheme comes into operation.

THE 1930's

1931 (September) First edition of the *Irish Press*.

1931 (October) I.R.A. declared an illegal organisation in Irish Free State.

1931 (October) Northern Ireland elections to Westminster. Seats: O.U.P. 11, Nat. 2.

1931 (December) Statute of Westminster[2] passed by British parliament. Gives Dominion parliaments equal status with Imperial parliament at Westminster.

1932 (February) Quasi-fascist Army Comrades Association - Blueshirts[1] - founded.

1932 (February) General election in Free State. Seats: F.F. 72, Cumann na nGaedheal 57, Lab. 7, Farmers' Party 4, others 13. Fianna Fáil form the new government.

1932 (June) Payment of land annuities to Britain withheld. Beginning of economic war between Ireland and Britain.

1933 (January) General election in Free State. Seats: F.F. 77, Cumann na nGaedheal 48, Lab. 8, National Centre Party 11, others 9. Fianna Fáil remain in office.

1933 (May) Oath of Allegiance removed from constitution of Irish Free State.

1933 (September) Fine Gael[6] formed by amalgamation of Cumann na nGaedheal, Centre Party and National Guard (Blueshirts). Éoin O'Duffy[4] first leader.

1933 (November) General election to Northern Ireland parliament. Seats: O.U.P. 36, Nat. 9, other U. 3, other Nat. 2, other Lab. 2.

1935 (July) Nine are killed and 2,241 Catholics are intimidated out of their homes in riots accompanying the 'Twelfth'.

1935 (November) Northern Ireland elections to Westminster. Seats O.U.P. 11, Nat. 2.

1936 (January) Death of George V, accession of Edward VIII.

1936 (April) Census in Irish Free State. Population - 2,968,420.

1936 (May) Senate of Irish Free State abolished by Dáil.

1936 (June) I.R.A. declared an illegal organisation in Irish Free State.

1936 (August) Aer Lingus established as national airline of the Irish Free State.

1936 (November) Irish brigade, under leadership of Éoin O'Duffy, join General Franco's fascists in Spanish Civil War.

1936 (December) External Relations Act[2] passed by Dáil during abdication crisis in Britain. It removes all reference to the Crown from the constitution.

1936 (December) Connolly Column[1], under leadership of Frank Ryan[7], join socialists in Spanish Civil War.

1937 (February) Spanish Civil War (Non-intervention) Act forbids involvement of Free State citizens in the war.

1937 (February) Census in Northern Ireland. Population - 1,279,745.

1937 (July 1) Constitution of Éire is ratified by referendum and comes into effect December 29 *(see Law and Defence Chapter).* General election in Free State. Seats: F.F. 69, F.G. 48, Lab. 13, others 8. Fianna Fáil retain office.

1938 (February) General election to Northern Ireland parliament. Seats: O.U.P. 39, Nat. 8, other U. 3, other Lab. 2.

1938 (April) Economic War with Britain ends, and Britain transfers the 'treaty ports' to Éire.

1938 (June) General election in Éire. Seats: F.F. 77, F.G. 45, Lab. 9, others 7. Fianna Fáil remain in government.

1938 (June) Douglas Hyde[4] inaugurated as the first

President of Ireland.
1939 (September 2) De Valera announces Éire will remain neutral during World War II. Britain declares war on Germany (September 3).

THE 1940's

1941 (April/ May) German air-raids on Belfast kill almost 1,000.
1941 (May) Germans bomb North Strand in Dublin, killing 34.
1942 American troops arrive in Northern Ireland.
1943 General election in Éire. Seats: F.F. 67, F.G. 32, Lab 17, Clann na Talmhan[1] 14, others 8. Fianna Fáil form the government.
1944 (May) General election in Éire. Seats: F.F. 76, F.G. 30, Clann na Talmhan 11, Lab. 8, others 10. Fianna Fáil remain in office.
1944 (December) Coras Iompair Éireann established as national transport company.
1945 (May 8) War ends in Europe (Ends in Pacific on August 14).
1945 (June) General election to Northern Ireland parliament. Seats: O.U.P. 33, Nat.10, other Lab. 4, other U. 2, Ind. 2, other Nat. 1.
1945 (June) Seán T. Ó Ceallaigh[4] inaugurated as President.
1945 (July) Northern Ireland elections to Westminster. Seats: O.U.P. 9, Nat. 2, others 2.
1946 (May) Census in Éire. Population - 2,955,107.
1946 (June) Bórd na Móna established.
1947 Education Act[2] in Northern Ireland provides free secondary school education for all.
1948 (February) General Election in Éire. Seats: F.F. 68, F.G. 31, Lab. 14, Clann na Poblachta[1] 10, Clann na Talmhan 7, others 17. Inter-party government formed by Fine Gael, Labour, Clann na Poblachta, Clann na Talmhan and independents.
1948 (December) Republic of Ireland Act[2] passed by Dáil. Republic declared on April 18, 1949 accompanied by a formal withdrawal from the British Commonwealth.
1949 (February) General election to Northern Ireland parliament. Seats: O.U.P. 37, Nat. 9, other U. 2, Ind. 2, other Nat.1, other Lab. 1.
1949 (February) Government announces it cannot join North Atlantic Treaty Organisation because of Britain's sovereignty in Northern Ireland.
1949 (May) Council of Europe established. Ireland and Britain are amongst founding members.
1949 (June) Ireland Act[2] passed at Westminster recognising Ireland's withdrawal from the Commonwealth and reaffirming the constitutional position of Northern Ireland.

THE 1950's

1950 Northern Ireland elections to Westminster. Seats: O.U.P. 10, Nat. 2.
1951 (April) Census. Republic of Ireland population - 2,960,593. Northern Ireland population - 1,370,921.
1951 (April) Opposition to the Mother-and-Child Scheme from the Roman Catholic hierarchy results in resignation of Minister for Health and collapse of the government.
1951 (May) General election in Republic. Seats: F.F. 69, F.G. 40, Lab. 16, Clann na Talmhan 6, Clann na Poblachta 2, others 14. Fianna Fáil form a minority government.
1951 (October) Northern Ireland elections to Westminster. Seats: O.U.P. 9, Nat. 2, others 1.
1951 (November) E.T.S. Walton[7] awarded Nobel Prize for Physics.
1952 (February) Death of George VI, accession of Elizabeth II.
1952 (July) Bord Fáilte, Irish tourist board, established by Act of Dáil Éireann.
1953 (January) Car ferry between Stranraer and Larne sinks with loss of 130 lives.
1953 (May) B.B.C. begins television transmissions from Belfast.
1953 (October) General election to Northern Ireland parliament. Seats: O.U.P. 38, Nat. 7, other Lab. 3, other Nat. 2, other U. 1, Ind. 1.
1954 (April) Flags and Emblems (Display) Act in Northern Ireland makes it an offence to interfere with the Union Jack and empowers police to remove flags or emblems likely to incite trouble.
1954 (May) General election in Republic. Seats: F.F. 65, F.G. 50, Lab. 19, Clann na Talmhan 5, Clann na Poblachta 3, others 5. Inter-party government formed by Fine Gael, Labour, Clann na Talmhan and Clann na Poblachta.
1955 (May) Northern Ireland elections to Westminster. Seats: O.U.P. 10, S.F. 2.
1955 (July) Led by Brian Faulkner[4], M.P., and protected by 300 R.U.C. officers, 12,000 Orangemen march along a contentious route at Annalong, Co. Down.
1955 (December) Republic of Ireland admitted to United Nations Organisation.
1956 (April) Census in Republic of Ireland. Population - 2,898,264.
1956 (December) Beginning of I.R.A. border campaign (ends February 1962).
1957 General election in Republic. Seats: F.F. 78, F.G. 40, Lab. 12, Clann na Poblachta 5, Clann na Talmhan 3, others 9. Fianna Fáil form the government.
1958 General election to Northern Ireland parliament. Seats: O.U.P. 37, Nat. 7, other Lab. 6, other Nat. 1, Ind. 1.
1959 (June) Éamon de Valera elected President; proposal to abolish proportional representation in Republic defeated by referendum.
1959 (October) Northern Ireland elections to Westminster. Seats: O.U.P. 12.
1959 (October) First broadcast by Ulster Television.

THE 1960's

1960 (November) Nine Irish soldiers killed while serving as U.N. peacekeepers in Belgian Congo.
1961 (April) Census. Republic of Ireland population - 2,818,341. Northern Ireland population - 1,425,042.
1961 (October) General election in Republic. Seats: F.F. 70, F.G. 47, Lab. 16, Clann na Talmhan 2, Clann na Poblachta 1, others 8. Fianna Fáil remain in office.
1961 (December 31) Inaugural television broadcast of Radio Telefís Éireann.

1962 (May) General election to Northern Ireland parliament. Seats: O.U.P. 35, Nat. 9, other Lab. 7,others 1.

1962 (July) M1 between Belfast and Lisburn - the first motorway in Northern Ireland - opens.

1963 President of the United States, John Fitzgerald Kennedy, pays official visit to Ireland.

1964 Northern Ireland elections to Westminster. Seats: O.U.P. 12.

1965 (January) Taoiseach Seán Lemass[4] and Prime Minister Terence O'Neill[4] meet in Belfast followed by a meeting in Dublin in February.

1965 (April) General election in Republic. Seats: F.F. 72, F.G. 47, Lab. 22, Clann na Poblachta 1, others 2. Fianna Fáil form government.

1965 (June) New Towns Act in Northern Ireland provides for establishment of Craigavon.

1965 (November) General election in Northern Ireland. Seats: O.U.P. 36, Nat. 9, other Lab. 4, others 3.

1966 (March) Nelson's pillar in Dublin is blown up.

1966 (March) Northern Ireland elections to Westminster. Seats: O.U.P. 11, Republican Lab. 1.

1966 (April) Census. Republic of Ireland population - 2,884,002.

1966 (June) Éamon de Valera re-elected President.

1966 (October) Census in Northern Ireland. Population - 1,484,775.

1967 (January) Northern Ireland Civil Rights Association[1] (N.I.C.R.A.) formed.

1968 (August) Higher Education Authority established in Republic.

1968 (August) N.I.C.R.A. holds its first demonstration.

1968 (October) Proposal to abolish proportional representation defeated by referendum in Republic.

1969 (January) Civil rights march attacked by loyalists at Burntollet, Co. Derry.

1969 (February) General election in Northern Ireland. Seats: O.U.P. 39, Nat. 6, other Lab. 4, others 3.

1969 (June) General election in Republic. Seats: F.F. 75, F.G. 50, Lab. 18, others 1. Fianna Fáil remain in government.

1969 (August) British troops move into Northern Ireland, following sustained clashes between Bogside residents and the 'B' Specials[1] in Derry sparked off by the annual Apprentice Boys march.

1969 (October) Samuel Beckett[8] awarded Nobel Prize for literature.

1969 (December) Act of Northern Ireland parliament establishes Ulster Defence Regiment (U.D.R.).

THE 1970's

1970 (January) Split in Sinn Féin between abstentionists (Provisional Sinn Féin[1]) and non-abstentionists (Official Sinn Féin[1]). I.R.A. splits along same lines.

1970 (April) 'B' Specials disbanded.

1970 (April) Alliance[6] party of Northern Ireland founded.

1970 (May) Irish Government ministers Charles Haughey[6] and Neil Blaney[7] charged with procuring arms for the I.R.A., Blaney's charges are dropped; Haughey is acquitted.

1970 (June) Northern Ireland elections to Westminster. Seats: O.U.P. 8, others 4.

1970 (August) Social Democratic and Labour Party[6] founded.

1971 (February) Decimal currency introduced in both Northern Ireland and the Republic.

1971 (April) Census. Republic of Ireland population - 2,978,248. Northern Ireland population - 1,536,065.

1971 (August) Internment without trial reintroduced in Northern Ireland. Measures aimed at nationalist community in particular. Continues until December 1975. All parades and marches are banned for six months.

1971 (September) Democratic Unionist Party[6] founded by Ian Paisley.

1971 (September) Protestant paramilitary organisation, the Ulster Defence Association[1] (U.D.A.) formed.

1972 (January) 'Bloody Sunday' - 13 civilians on civil rights march in Derry shot dead by British army paratroopers. One man later dies from his injuries.

1972 (February) British embassy in Dublin is attacked and burned following 'Bloody Sunday'.

1972 (March) Northern Ireland parliament prorogued and direct rule from Westminster introduced.

1972 (May) Entry of the Republic to European Economic Community (E.E.C.) approved by referendum.

1972 (December) Referendum in the Republic lowers the voting age to 18 and removes the special position of the Roman Catholic church from the constitution.

1973 (January) Republic of Ireland joins E.E.C. along with Britain and Denmark.

1973 (February) General election in Republic. Seats: F.F. 69, F.G. 54, Lab. 19, others 2. Fine Gael and Labour form coalition government.

1973 (March) Referendum in Northern Ireland on remaining within United Kingdom. 98.9% in favour, 1.1% against (nationalists boycott poll).

1973 (May) Erskine Childers[4] elected as President; inaugurated June 25.

1973 (June) Elections to Northern Ireland Assembly. Seats: O.U.P. 23, S.D.L.P. 19, Alliance 8, D.U.P. 8, V.U.P.P[1]. 7, others 13.

1973 (July) Northern Ireland Constitution Act[2]. Northern Ireland parliament abolished and provision made for a 12-member executive.

1973 (December) Tripartite Conference results in Sunningdale Agreement[2]. Power-sharing executive for Northern Ireland agreed upon.

1974 (January) Power-sharing executive takes office.

1974 (February) Northern Ireland elections to Westminster. Seats: O.U.P. 7, D.U.P. 1, S.D.L.P. 1, V.U.P.P. 1.

1974 (May) Ulster Workers' Council[1] declares general strike in opposition to power-sharing executive. Executive falls after two weeks of widespread disruption.

1974 (October) Seán MacBride[4] shares Nobel Peace Prize.

1974 (October) Northern Ireland elections to Westminster. Seats: O.U.P. 6, D.U.P. 1, S.D.L.P. 1, V.U.P.P. 1, others 1.

1974 (December) Cearbhall Ó Dálaigh[4] inaugurated as

President following death of Erskine Childers.

1975 (May) Election to Northern Ireland Convention. Seats: O.U.P. 19, S.D.L.P. 17, V.U.P.P. 14, D.U.P. 12, Alliance 8, others 8.

1976 (March) Special category status for persons convicted of paramilitary offences phased out, followed by Republican protests in Long Kesh.

1976 (July) British ambassador to the Republic killed in I.R.A. bomb attack in Dublin.

1976 (August) Peace People founded.

1976 (November) Betty Williams and Mairead Corrigan, founding members of the Peace People awarded Nobel Peace Prize.

1976 (December) Dr. Patrick Hillery[6] inaugurated as President following the resignation of Cearbhall Ó Dálaigh.

1977 (June) General election in Republic. Seats: F.F. 84, F.G. 43, Lab. 17, others 4. Fianna Fáil return to government.

1978 (November) Second national television channel established by R.T.E.

1979 (January) Oil tanker explodes at Whiddy Island oil terminal Cork, killing 50.

1979 (March) Ireland joins European Monetary System, ending parity between Punt and Sterling.

1979 (April) Census in Republic. Population - 3,368,405.

1979 (May) General election in Northern Ireland. Seats: U.U.P. 5, D.U.P. 3, S.D.L.P. 1, others 3.

1979 (June) Elections to European parliament. Seats in Republic: F.F. 5, F.G. 4, Lab. 4, others 2. Seats in Northern Ireland: S.D.L.P. 1, U.U.P. 1, D.U.P. 1.

1979 (August) Earl Mountbatten is killed by I.R.A. bomb explosion on his boat off the Co. Sligo coast. Three others including two teenagers also die. Eighteen British soldiers are killed in an explosion in Co. Down on same day.

1979 (September/ October) Pope John Paul II visits Ireland, celebrating public mass at Knock, Drogheda and Dublin and a private mass at Maynooth.

THE 1980's

1980 (April) Two Irish soldiers serving as U.N. peacekeepers shot dead in Lebanon.

1981 (February) 48 die as fire sweeps through Stardust Ballroom at Artane, Dublin. Over 160 injured.

1981 (March) Republican hunger strike to regain special category status, led by Bobby Sands[7], begins in Long Kesh.

1981 (April) Imprisoned hunger striker Bobby Sands elected to House of Commons in Fermanagh & South Tyrone by-election. He and nine other prisoners die during the hunger strike before it is called off in October. Sixty-four die in accompanying disturbances throughout Northern Ireland.

1981 (April) Census. Republic of Ireland population - 3,443,405. Northern Ireland population - 1,481,959.

1981 (June) General Election in Republic. Seats: F.F. 78, F.G. 65, Lab. 15, W.P.[6] 1, others 7 (including two hunger strikers). Fine Gael and Labour form coalition government.

1981 (August) Death of hunger striker Kieran Doherty

T.D.

1982 (February) General election in Republic. Seats: F.F. 81, F.G. 63, Lab. 15, W.P. 3, others 3. Fianna Fáil form minority government.

1982 (October) General election to Northern Ireland Assembly. Seats: U.U.P. 26, D.U.P. 21, S.D.L.P. 14, Alliance 10, S.F. 5. Assembly dissolved July 1986.

1982 (November) General election in Republic. Seats: F.F. 75, F.G. 70, Lab. 16, W.P. 2, others 3. Fine Gael and Labour form coalition government.

1982 (December) Seventeen killed in I.N.L.A. bombing of a disco in Co. Derry.

1983 (May) New Ireland Forum meets for first time.

1983 (June) Northern Ireland elections to Westminster. Seats: U.U.P. 11, D.U.P. 3, S.D.L.P. 1, S.F. 1, others 1.

1983 (August) Twenty-two republicans convicted on the word of supergrass Christopher Black (18 have their convictions quashed within three years).

1983 (September) Thirty-nine I.R.A. inmates escape from Long Kesh - 20 are almost immediately recaptured.

1984 (May) Report of the New Ireland Forum published.

1984 (June) Ronald Regan, President of the United States, pays official visit to Ireland.

1984 (June) Elections to European parliament. Seats in Republic: F.F. 8, F.G. 6, others 1. Seats in Northern Ireland: S.D.L.P. 1, U.U.P. 1, D.U.P. 1.

1984 (October) I.R.A. bomb the Brighton hotel where the Conservative Party conference is being held. Five are killed and many members of the British cabinet narrowly escape serious injury or death.

1985 (June) Air India jet crashes off Co. Kerry coast with loss of 329 lives.

1985 (October) First commercial flight from Knock airport.

1985 (November) Anglo-Irish Agreement[3] signed by British and Irish governments. Setting up British/Irish governmental conference.

1985 (December) Progressive Democrats[6] founded.

1986 (January) 15 by-elections in N.I. caused by simultaneous resignation of all unionist M.P.s in protest at the Anglo-Irish Agreement. Seats:O.U.P. 10, D.U.P. 3, S.D.L.P. 1, others 1.

1986 (June) Referendum in Republic rejects legalisation of divorce.

1986 (April) Census in Republic. Population 3,540,643.

1987 (January) Government reveals that one-third of the country's haemophiliacs contracted H.I.V. through the transfusion of contaminated blood.

1987 (February) General election in Republic. Seats: F.F. 81, F.G. 51, P.D. 14, Lab. 12, W.P. 4, others 4. Fianna Fáil form minority government.

1987 (March) National Lottery launched in the Republic.

1987 (May) Eight members of the I.R.A. and one passer-by killed in a British army ambush at Loughgall, Co. Armagh.

1987 (May) Referendum in Republic ratifies Single European Act[6].

1987 (June) Northern Ireland elections to Westminster. Seats: U.U.P. 9, D.U.P. 3, S.D.L.P. 3, S.F. 1, others 1.

1987 (November) I.R.A. bomb kills eleven at Remembrance Day service in Enniskillen.

1988 Dublin celebrates its Millennium Year.

1988 (March) Week of unrest in Northern Ireland following killing of three I.R.A. members in Gibraltar by S.A.S. Three mourners killed at their funerals by loyalist gunman. Two soldiers killed at subsequent funerals.

1988 (August) Eight British soldiers killed in an I.R.A. explosion near Ballygawley, Co. Tyrone.

1988 (October) British government introduces a broadcasting ban, based on the Republic's Section 31, on direct statements by paramilitary organisations.

1989 (January) Forty-five die in British Midland air crash on London-Belfast route.

1989 (February) Belfast lawyer Pat Finucane shot dead by the U.F.F.

1989 (March) Three Irish soldiers serving with the U.N. in Lebanon killed by a landmine.

1989 (May) Church of Ireland General Synod votes in favour of the ordination of women.

1989 (June) General election in Republic. Seats: F.F. 77, F.G. 55, Lab. 15, W.P. 7, P.D.[6] 6, others 6. Government formed by Fianna Fáil/Progressive Democrat coalition.

1989 (June) Elections to European Parliament. Seats in Republic: F.F. 6, F.G. 4, Lab. 1, W.P. 1, P.D. 1, others 2. Seats in Northern Ireland: U.U.P. 1, S.D.L.P. 1, D.U.P. 1.

1989 (September) Ten British army bandsmen are killed by an I.R.A. bomb explosion at their headquarters in Deal.

1989 (October)'Guildford Four', imprisoned in October 1975, have their convictions quashed and are released.

THE 1990's

1990 (January) Beginning of the six-month Irish presidency of the European Community.

1990 (April) Minor earthquake (5.2 on the Richter scale) felt along the east coast of Ireland.

1990 (May) Report of the Stevens inquiry finds evidence of collusion between the U.D.R. and loyalist paramilitaries.

1990 (August) Brian Keenan, Irish hostage in the Lebanon, released after four-and-a-half years in captivity.

1990 (November) Mary Robinson becomes the first woman to be elected President.

1991 Dublin is the European City of Culture for the year.

1991 (January) Fourteen are killed by violent storms in the first weekend of the new year.

1991 (March) The 'Birmingham Six', convicted of the 1974 Birmingham pub bombings which killed 18, have their convictions quashed and are released having spent more than 16 years in prison.

1991 (April) Census. Republic of Ireland population - 3,525,719. Northern Ireland population - 1,577,836.

1991 (April) Talks begin in Northern Ireland under the chairmanship of Sir Ninian Stephens (they break down in July).

1991 (October) Tribunal of Inquiry into the Irish beef industry begins.

1992 (January) Eight workmen die when their van is blown up by an I.R.A. bomb at Teebane crossroads, Co. Tyrone.

1992 (February) Five men are shot dead in a betting shop on Belfast's Ormeau Road by the U.D.A. Four I.R.A. members are killed by the British army following an attack on Cookstown R.U.C. station.

1992 (February) The Supreme Court overturns the Attorney General's injunction against a 14 year-old girl, preventing her travelling to Britain to procure an abortion in what came to be known as the 'X-Case'.

1992 (April) Northern Ireland elections to Westminster. Seats: U.U.P. 9, S.D.L.P. 4, D.U.P. 3, others 1.

1992 (May) Bishop Eamon Casey resigns as Bishop of Galway following revelations that he had an 18-year-old son in the United States and had used diocesan funds to pay maintenance.

1992 (July) Three of the 'U.D.R. Four' are released when the Northern Ireland Court of Appeal finds their convictions unsafe.

1992 (June) Maastricht treaty on European Union[6] ratified by referendum in the Republic.

1992 (October) President Robinson becomes the first head of state to visit hunger stricken Somalia.

1992 (November) General election in Republic. Seats: F.F. 68, F.G. 45, Lab. 33, P.D. 10, D.L.[6] 4, others 6. Coalition government formed by Fianna Fáil and Labour.

1992 (November) Referendum on abortion. Right to travel and right to information passed. Availability of abortion in the Republic of Ireland (the 'substantive issue') rejected.

1993 (January) Single European market comes into effect.

1993 (March) I.R.A. bomb in Warrington kills two children and provokes widespread and sustained public outcry.

1993 (July) Tribunal of Inquiry into the beef industry comes to an end after 226 days.

1993 (October) I.R.A. bomb explodes prematurely on Belfast's Shankill road killing ten including the bomber; loyalist gunmen retaliate one week later by killing seven at a pub in Greysteel, Co. Derry.

1994 (January) Irish government revokes the Section 31 broadcasting ban.

1994 (June) Elections to European Parliament. Seats in Republic: F.F. 7, F.G. 4, G.P. 2, Lab. 1, Ind. 1. Seats in Northern Ireland: U.U.P. 1, S.D.L.P. 1, D.U.P. 1.

1994 (June) Six Catholics killed by the U.V.F. in a Co. Down pub while watching the Republic of Ireland v. Italy World Cup soccer match.

1994 (August) I.R.A. ceasefire begins. Loyalist paramilitary ceasefire begins in October. British government lifts broadcasting ban.

1994 (November) Fianna Fáil/Labour coalition collapses, replaced by Fine Gael/Labour/Democratic Left 'rainbow' coalition.

1995 (February) Taoiseach John Bruton and British Prime Minister John Major launch the Framework Document[3].

1995 (May) *The Irish Press* newspaper goes out of business with the loss of 600 jobs.

1995 (October) Derry poet Seamus Heaney[8] awarded the Nobel Prize for Literature.

1995 (November) Referendum on legalisation of divorce in the Republic - 50.3% in favour, 49.7% against.

1995 (November) President Clinton visits Ireland

receiving a rapturous welcome in Belfast, Derry and Dublin. Addresses a full sitting of both houses of the Oireachtas.

1996 (February) I.R.A. ceasefire ends with bombing of London's Docklands.

1996 (April) Census in Republic. Population 3,621,035.

1996 (May) Elections to Northern Ireland Forum. Seats: U.U.P. 30, D.U.P. 24, S.D.L.P. 21, S.F. 17, Alliance 7, other U. 7, other Lab. 2, others 2.

1996 (June) Multi-party talks under the chairmanship of George Mitchell get under way at Stormont. Sinn Féin refused entry because of the absence of an I.R.A. ceasefire.

1996 (June) Investigative journalist Veronica Guerin shot dead outside Dublin in an apparent 'contract killing'.

1996 (July) Ireland assumes a six-month presidency of the European Union.

1996 (July) Northern Ireland experiences its worst rioting in 15 years following the decision of the R.U.C. to ban an Orange Order march along the nationalist Garvaghy Road and the subsequent reversal of that decision.

1996 (November) Referendum on the denial of bail to likely reoffenders - 74.8% in favour, 25.2% against.

1997 - see Chronology of 1997

HISTORICAL MOVEMENTS AND ORGANISATIONS

ANCIENT ORDER OF HIBERNIANS: Founded 1641 and reformed in 1838. Has been traditionally associated with nationalism and the defence of the Catholic faith. Marches are held annually on the Feast of the Assumption, 15th August.

WILD GEESE: 14,000 Irish Jacobite soldiers, largely under the command of Patrick Sarsfield, who left Ireland after the Treaty of Limerick (October 1691) and distinguished themselves on European battlefields in the 18th century.

CATHOLIC COMMITTEE: Founded in March 1760 by Dr. John Curry, Charles O'Connor and Thomas Wyse. It organised the small urban Catholic middle-class and lobbied government for a relaxation of the Penal Laws. Met with considerable success in early 1790's, culminating in a Catholic Relief Act in 1793, which repealed many of the Penal Laws.

WHITEBOYS: First emerged October 1761 in Munster. Generic term for different Catholic secret societies. Violent disturbances were connected with resentment to taxes and changes in farming from arable to dairy as much as to sectarianism.

DEFENDERS: Nationalist secret society founded after a sectarian skirmish in Armagh, July 1784. Absorbed by the United Irishmen in the 1790's.

PEEP O' DAY BOYS: Founded in July 1784 in Armagh. A Protestant Secret Society founded after the above sectarian clash. A further engagement with the Defenders at Loughgall, Co. Armagh, led to the formation of the Orange Order.

THE VOLUNTEER MOVEMENT: Founded in March 1778. An armed corps established to help defend Ireland against French or Spanish invasion. Lobbied for free trade, legislative independence and relaxation of the Penal Laws. Banned in March 1793.

UNITED IRISHMEN: Founded in October 1791 in Belfast by middle-class radical Presbyterians and led by Theobald Wolfe Tone. An oath-bound secret society that aimed to secure an Irish republic, it procured French aid for its rising in 1798, which tragically turned into a sectarian massacre in Wexford and which the government put down with great force. The rising's leaders were executed and the movement crushed.

ORANGE ORDER: Founded in Armagh in September 1795, following serious disturbances between Catholics and Protestants. The Order came into existence as a Protestant response to the relaxation of the anti-Catholic penal laws at the end of the 18th century. It was comprised of protestant males who pledged their allegiance to the Crown (as long as it remained Protestant) and their Protestant faith. The Order commemorates the Battle of the Boyne (1690) and, in later years, the Battle of the Somme (1916) with marches each summer. The main marches are held at different county centres throughout Northern Ireland on July 12.

The Order has played a significant role in Irish politics; it was prominent in the formation of the Ulster Unionist Council in 1905, it organised the Solemn League and Covenant in 1912 and harnessed Protestant opposition to Home Rule. With its membership concentrated in Northern Ireland, it played a central role in the formation of the Northern Ireland state - each of Northern Ireland's six Prime Ministers were Orangemen.

CATHOLIC ASSOCIATION: Founded May 1823 by Daniel O'Connell and Richard Lalor Shiel to agitate for Catholic Emancipation. It collected a 'Catholic Rent', allowing all ranks of Catholic society to play its part. In 1826 it succeeded in having four pro-emancipation M.P.s elected. O'Connell's victory in the 1828 Clare by-election forced the British government to grant Catholic Emancipation on April 13, 1829, but the Act disenfranchised many Catholic voters. The association was dissolved on February 12, 1829.

APPRENTICE BOYS: Founded in Derry in 1814 to commemorate the Siege of Derry (which began with the closing of the city gates by apprentice boys in April 1689) and its relief (July of 1689). The organisation was affiliated to the Ulster Unionist Council from 1911 until the mid 1970s and holds marches throughout Northern Ireland in the summer months.

ROYAL IRISH CONSTABULARY (R.I.C.): The Irish Constabulary was formed in 1836 as a national police force, it was awarded the prefix 'Royal' for its part in putting down the 1867 Fenian Rising. A hugely unpopular force due to its role in enforcing evictions and quelling the agrarian violence endemic in the late 19th century, it was, in practice, a police force doing work more suited to an army. Its members suffered terribly during the War of Independence; many resigned out of fear or disapproval of the tactics of the Black and Tans,and many more were dismissed because of their nationalist sympathies. It was disbanded in 1922 following the Anglo-Irish Treaty, but its northern members were absorbed into the Royal Ulster Constabulary by an Act of the Northern Ireland Parliament in May 1922.

TOTAL ABSTINENCE MOVEMENT: A temperance movement founded in 1838 by Fr. Theobald Matthew and William Martin. It reputedly recorded 5 million pledges in Ireland and revenue from alcohol dropped from £1.4 million in 1839 to £350,000 in 1844.

LOYAL NATIONAL REPEAL ASSOCIATION: Founded by Daniel O'Connell in April 1840 to secure the Repeal of the Act of Union and create an Irish legislature (to be subservient to Westminster). It was organised along the same lines as the Catholic Association, using mass agitation and organised 'monster meetings'. Its finest year was 1843 with over 750,000 attending a monster meeting at Tara. The onset of famine in 1845, tensions between O'Connell and the 'Young Irelanders', which came to a head in 1846, and O'Connell's death in 1847 lead to the movement petering out with its objective no closer to realisation.

YOUNG IRELANDERS: The name given to the adherents of the nationalism expounded by Thomas Davis, Charles Gavan Duffy and John Blake Dillon in their newspaper - *The Nation* (first published in October 1842). Not content with Repeal, they wanted to achieve an independent Ireland and were prepared to use physical force. This propensity towards physical force lead to their break from the Repeal movement in 1846 when O'Connell sought a pledge stipulating that force could never be justified.

In July 1848 a short-lived and poorly organised rebellion staged by of the Irish Confederation broke out in Munster. It was put down, its leaders were either transported or fled the country and the movement disappeared.

IRISH CONFEDERATION: Founded in Dublin in 1847 by Young Irelanders who had split from the Loyal National Repeal Association. It promoted the idea of an independent, self-sufficient Ireland and linked self-determination to the land question.

1848 saw revolutions throughout Europe, and inspired by this, the Confederation drafted plans for an Irish rebellion, but by July the government had suspended *habeas corpus* and made membership of the Confederation illegal. In July they staged a poorly planned and ill-timed rebellion which was easily defeated. The movement, having lost its leaders through arrest and transportation, collapsed.

IRISH TENANT LEAGUE: Founded in Dublin in August 1850 by Charles Gavan Duffy and Frederick Lucas. It aimed to secure the 'three Fs' - fair rent, fixity of tenure and free sale for tenant farmers. Its membership was drawn from larger tenant farmers. Following the 1852

general election, it combined with the Irish Brigade to form the Independent Irish Parliamentary Party which had the allegiance of about 40 M.P.s. The league collapsed in 1855 when Lucas died and Duffy emigrated.

INDEPENDENT IRISH PARTY: Founded in September 1852 in Dublin at the Irish Tenant League conference. It was an amalgamation of the League, the Irish Brigade and 41 liberal M.P.s who were sympathetic to the plight of the tenant farmers. It demanded land reform, the repeal of the Ecclesiastical Titles Act and the disestablishment of the Church of Ireland. Beset by splits and defections, it fizzled out by the mid 1850s.

PHOENIX SOCIETY: Founded at Skibbereen, Co. Cork in 1856 by Jeremiah O'Donovan (later known as O'Donovan Rossa). Outwardly, it had the appearance of a debating society but it was, in reality, a revolutionary society and precursor to the Irish Republican Brotherhood into which it was subsumed in 1859.

IRISH REPUBLICAN BROTHERHOOD (I.R.B.): Founded in Dublin by James Stephens on St. Patrick's Day, 1858. A secret oath-bound organisation, it aimed to overthrow British rule and create an independent Irish republic by means of force. Its 1867 rebellion was easily put down.

It survived this suppression and went on to infiltrate nationalist movements such as the Gaelic Athletic Association, the Gaelic League and the Land League. Reorganised in 1904, it infiltrated the Irish Volunteers and with the outbreak of World War One, its military council began planning the Easter 1916 rebellion, which was defeated after five days. It was again reorganised (all of its leaders had been executed) and exerted much influence between 1916 and 1919. Its influence declined during the War of Independence, and a split occured during the Civil War. The movement dissolved itself in 1924.

FENIAN BROTHERHOOD: Founded in New York in April 1859 by John O'Mahony as an American auxiliary of the I.R.B., its name came to be used when describing both groups. Chiefly concerned with the procurement of weapons for the I.R.B., it did, however, stage an abortive attack at New Brunswick in Canada in 1866. It formally merged with the I.R.B. in 1916.

CLAN NA GAEL: Founded in New York in June 1867 by Jerome Collins, it was a secret organisation which recognised the Supreme Council of the Irish Republican Brotherhood as the legitimate government of Ireland. The Clan supported Parnell and Davitt's 'New Departure' in the 1880s.

The Clan played an active role in plans for the 1916 Rising, especially in procuring German aid. The Clan survived the aftermath of the Rising but became embroiled in bitter personal disputes between its leading members. Factions backed different sides in the Civil War, and the organisation petered out in the early 1940s.

AMNESTY ASSOCIATION: Founded in 1868 by John Nolan to campaign for the release of Fenians imprisoned after the 1867 rebellion, who were being held under harsh conditions in British jails. Prominent figures for whom amnesties were secured were O'Donovan Rossa and John O'Leary. The organisation lapsed in the 1870s and 1880s but was reformed in the early 1890s to campaign for the releases of remaining Fenian prisoners. Dynamite expert Thomas J. Clarke was the last of the Fenian prisoners to be released in September 1898, and the association was wound up.

HOME RULE LEAGUE: Founded in Dublin in November 1873 by Issac Butt. A precursor to the Irish Parliamentary Party, its aim was to achieve self-government for Ireland. It won 60 seats in the 1874 general election.

IRISH PARLIAMENTARY PARTY (I.P.P.): Evolved from the Home Rule League. The securing of Home Rule was its primary objective, but it was also concerned with the plight of the tenant farmer (this gave it widespread appeal as land reform was the biggest single political issue of the day). Ineffective under the leadership of Issac Butt, save for its filibustering obstruction of business at Westminster, it met with huge success especially with regard to the land question under the leadership of Charles Stewart Parnell (elected chairman May 1880).

The party became the model for modern political parties in that it developed an extensive grass roots constituency organisation, established a party whip and had its members take a party pledge to vote en bloc. These innovations and the skill of its leadership helped achieve significant land reform and brought Home Rule to the top of political agenda at Westminster. Despite its success, the party, under pressure from Gladstone's Liberal Party and the Catholic hierarchy in Ireland, split in 1890 following revelations about Parnell's adulterous affair with Katharine O'Shea.

Reunited under the leadership of John Redmond in 1900, it went on to secure the passage of the third Home Rule Bill in 1914, the implementation of which was suspended until after the World War I. The 1916 Rising and subsequent executions and British government attempts to introduce conscription in 1918 precipitated a huge swell in support for Sinn Féin at the expense of the I.P.P. Their representation at Westminster fell from 70 M.P.s in 1910 to 6 in 1918. Sinn Féin replaced the party as the major party within nationalism. The Northern rump of the party reconstituted itself as the Nationalist Party of Northern Ireland in 1921, but its southern counterpart disappeared with its members taking refuge in Cumann na nGaedheal after 1923.

LAND LEAGUE OF MAYO: Founded in Westport, Co. Mayo, in August 1879 by Michael Davitt. It had the securing of the 'three Fs' *(see Irish Tenant League)* and was the organisation on which the Irish National Land League modelled itself.

IRISH NATIONAL LAND LEAGUE: Founded in Dublin, October 1879, by Charles Stewart Parnell and Michael Davitt, its aims were the protection of tenant rights through the securing of the 'three Fs' and the complete

abolition of landlordism. Ostensibly a moral force organisation which developed and utilised the tactic of 'boycotting', it enjoyed the support of the Fenians, Clann na Gael and the I.R.B.

The appeal of the League was wide and all classes of society, encompassing all religions, were members. The Land Act of August 1881 was a major success, but it was accompanied by a Coercion Act which banned the League. The League was reformed by Parnell in October 1882 under the name of the National League where the emphasis was on Home Rule rather than land reform.

LADIES LAND LEAGUE: Founded in New York in October 1880 by Fanny Parnell, it was established in Ireland in January 1881 by her sister Anna. Both women were sisters of Charles Stewart Parnell. The league stepped into the breach when the Land League was banned in 1881 and was vociferous in the campaign against landlordism,.

The first Irish political movement organised by women, it met with opposition from elements within the Catholic Church and the Irish Parliamentary Party who found their radicalism unacceptable. When Charles Stewart Parnell was released from prison in May 1882, he cut their funding and in August of that year suppressed the movement entirely.

INVINCIBLES: Founded 1881, extremist group which broke away from the Irish Republican Brotherhood. In May 1882, it assassinated the Chief Secretary and the Under Secretary (the top government officials in Ireland) in what became known as the Phoenix Park Murders. The leaders of the group were tried in May 1883, convicted of the murders and hanged.

NATIONAL LEAGUE: Founded in Dublin on October 17, 1882, by Charles Stewart Parnell to replace the Land League which had been proscribed in 1881. It was the 'grass roots' organisation of the Irish Parliamentary Party and, unlike the Land League, had the securing of Home Rule as its primary objective with land reform of secondary importance. The movement provided finance and delegates for the I.P.P. and had the support of the majority of the Catholic clergy. The League split along the same lines as the I.P.P. in 1890 and soon petered out to be replaced by the United Irish League in 1900, when the I.P.P. was reunited.

GAELIC ATHLETIC ASSOCIATION (G.A.A.): Founded Thurles, Co. Tipperary, on November 1, 1884, by Michael Cusack and Maurice Davin under the patronage of the Archbishop of Cashel, Dr. T.W. Croke. The G.A.A.'s primary aim was the preservation and cultivation of Irish pastimes, such as gaelic football and hurling, which had been slipping into decline because of disorganisation and apathy; it also organised athletic meetings. Unashamedly nationalist in outlook, it prohibited its members from playing foreign games (such as rugby, hockey and soccer) and excluded members of the Crown forces from its membership.

The association spread gradually until it established itself in every parish in the country providing Gaelic pastimes to vast numbers of people and becoming the largest organisation (sporting or otherwise) in the country, a distinction it retains.

IRISH LOYAL AND PATRIOTIC UNION: Founded May 1885. It was a political association of unionist landlords, businessmen and scholars who opposed Home Rule. It contested the 1885 general election but won little support. It was superseded in 1891 by the Irish Unionist Alliance.

CONGESTED DISTRICTS BOARD: Established by the 'Balfour' Land Act in August 1891. It was a government appointed board of commissioners whose function was to give aid to designated congested areas (in the province of Connacht and in the counties of Clare, Cork, Donegal, Limerick and Kerry). Funded by income from the sale of church land provided for by the 1869 Irish Church Act it made grants available to improve the infrastructure, to modernise methods of farming and to aid indigenous industries, such as fishing and the blossoming cottage industries.

The Board was empowered to purchase estates and distribute the land to small farmers, often involving re-location. It was dissolved in 1923 by the Free State government and its functions transferred to the Land Commission.

IRISH UNIONIST ALLIANCE: The successor to the Irish Loyal and Patriotic Union, it was founded in 1891 with the aim of opposing Home Rule. The membership of the Alliance comprised mainly southern unionists. Despite a rather small membership, the alliance exerted considerable influence in the Westminster parliament and in the House of Lords, in particular. It was rendered obsolete by the passing of the Home Rule Bill in 1914.

THE GAELIC LEAGUE (CONRADH NA GAEILIGE): Founded in July 1893 by Dr. Douglas Hyde, Eoin MacNeill and Fr. Eugene O'Growney. The League's aims were the preservation of the Irish language as a spoken language and the de-Anglicisation of Ireland. The league lobbied for the recognition of the Irish language and culture and met with considerable success, including the recognition of St. Patrick's Day as a national holiday (1903) and the inclusion of Irish as a matriculation subject in the N.U.I. (1908).

The League sent teachers (or *timirí*) around the country to set up classes and had up to 600 branches around the country by 1908. The movement was infiltrated by the I.R.B. and in 1915 Douglas Hyde resigned as President because of the increasingly political role it was fulfiling. Following the formation of the Free State in 1922, it lobbied successfully for Irish to be made a compulsory subject in both primary and secondary schools. The League remains one of the largest Irish language organisations in the country.

IRISH AGRICULTURAL ORGANISATION SOCIETY: Founded in April 1894 by Sir Horace Plunkett and Fr. Thomas Finlay to co-ordinate the activities of the nationwide Co-operative Movement. The Co-operative Movement was established in 1890 to allow dairy producing farmers to collectively sell their produce.

IRISH SOCIALIST REPUBLICAN PARTY: Founded in a Dublin pub in May 1896 by James Connolly. A small socialist nationalist party, it was reorganised and renamed the Socialist Party of Ireland in 1903. In 1921 the Socialist Party was reorganised as the Communist Party of Ireland.

IRISH LITERARY THEATRE: Founded in Dublin in May 1899 by William Butler Yeats. A literary society dedicated to the promotion of Irish culture and customs through the production of Irish plays written and set in Ireland. It was the first society to stage a play in the Irish language (Douglas Hyde's *Casadh an tSúgáin)*. It was dissolved in 1904 and was absorbed into the Abbey Theatre.

CUMANN NA nGAEDHEAL: Formed in September 1900 by Arthur Griffith and William Rooney as an umbrella group for small organisations whose objective was the de-Anglicisation of Ireland. The organisation called on the I.P.P. to abstain from Westminster in 1902 and organised protests against the visit of Edward III in July 1903. It became part of Sinn Féin in 1907. It had no link to the political party of the same name founded by W.T. Cosgrave in 1923.

NATIONAL COUNCIL: Formed in June 1903 by Arthur Griffith to oppose the impending visit of Edward III. Its members included senior figures from Cumann na nGaedheal. It became part of Sinn Féin in 1908.

ULSTER UNIONIST COUNCIL: Founded in Belfast in March 1905 following a conference of Ulster unionist M.P.s. It was a political organisation the members of which were drawn from the Orange Order, the Apprentice Boys of Derry, unionist associations and M.P.s and peers. The Solemn League and Covenant in 1912, the formation of the Ulster Volunteer Force in 1913 and the Larne gun-running in 1914 were all organised under its auspices. In 1913 it appointed a Provisional Government for Ulster to take effect should Home Rule become law. The Council initially opposed partition but went on to play a significant role in the formation of Northern Ireland. Its political arm, the Ulster Unionist Party went on to govern Northern Ireland from 1921 until 1972. The council remains in place today as an executive for the Ulster Unionist Party.

SINN FÉIN LEAGUE: Founded at Dundalk, Co. Louth in April 1907 by the amalgamation of the Dungannon Clubs with Cumman na nGaedheal. It was absorbed into Sinn Féin in September 1908 *(See Politics Chapter).*

IRISH TRANSPORT AND GENERAL WORKERS' UNION: Founded in Dublin in December 1908 by James Larkin. Action by the union resulted in the 'Lock-Out' (September 1913-February 1914) when employers refused to accede to union demands and closed their factories down. Internal bickering, power struggles and splits tore at the union from 1923 until 1959 when it reunited with the Workers Union of Ireland (an offshoot which had broken away in 1924) to form the Irish Congress of Trade Unions.

ULSTER VOLUNTEER FORCE (U.V.F.): Founded January 1913 by the Ulster Unionist Council to oppose the implementation of Home Rule by military force if necessary. James Craig and Sir Edward Carson were prominent members of its leadership. Guns were procured through landings at Larne in April 1914. The outbreak of World War I and the suspension of Home Rule resulted in the U.V.F. becoming the 36th (Ulster) Division of the British Army. The division was all but wiped out in the Battle of the Somme (July-November 1916). Following partition the force was disbanded and its members recruited by the R.U.C.

The U.V.F. was re-established in 1966 by Gusty Spence, amongst others, and it immediately declared war on the I.R.A. but was banned by Prime Minister Terence O'Neill in June of that year. It called a cease-fire in October 1994 under the auspices of the Combined Loyalist Military Command.

IRISH CITIZEN ARMY: Founded in Dublin in November 1913 by James Connolly and James Larkin with the purpose of protecting workers during the 1913 Lock-Out. With the end of the Lock-Out Connolly turned his attention to the creation of a workers' republic.

Connolly's intention to stage a Citizen Army rebellion caused alarm within the I.R.B., and their leaders informed him of plans for the Easter 1916 rebellion. Connolly pledged his army's support for the Rising and when it came, the Citizen's Army fought with distinction. It fought in the War of Independence and on the anti-treaty side in the Civil War. It was disbanded after the Civil War ended in 1923.

IRISH VOLUNTEERS: Founded Dublin in November 1913 by Éoin MacNeill and Bulmer Hobson in response to the formation of the Ulster Volunteer Force. They secured arms in a gun-running episode at Howth in July 26. Membership had reached around 180,000 at the outbreak of World War I when in September 1914 leader of the Irish Parliamentary Party John Redmond called on the Volunteers to join "in defence of right, of freedom and religion in this war" Over 170,000 did, renaming themselves the National Volunteers. Approximately 11,000 remained with the Irish Volunteers.

Many of the senior posts of the Volunteers were now filled by members of the I.R.B.'s Supreme Council, and the Volunteers fought in the 1916 Rising. Despite their defeat and due to the massive wave of sympathy following the executions of the Rising's leaders and the abortive attempt to introduce conscription, the Volunteers reorganised and became a powerful force. When the first Dáil met in 1919, the Volunteers took an oath to the Republic and fought in the War of Independence as the Irish Republican Army.

IRISH REPUBLICAN ARMY (I.R.A.): The oath to the Republic taken by the Volunteers in January 1919 can be seen as the starting point of the I.R.A. It successfully adopted and developed guerrilla warfare during the War of Independence and created such a state of disorder that the British government sued for a truce. The Anglo-Irish Treaty that followed was not accepted by the I.R.A. as a whole, and it split along pro- and anti-Treaty lines. There followed a bloody and bitter civil war where erstwhile comrades fought one another; those who supported the Treaty became the army of the Free State, whereas the republicans became known as the 'Irregulars'. Defeat for the Irregulars followed and a truce was called in May 1923. The I.R.A. formally withdrew from Sinn Féin in November 1925. The organisation was proscribed in Northern Ireland in 1922 and in the Free State in 1931

The I.R.A. staged an offensive in England (January 1939-March 1940) which resulted in further anti-republican legislation being passed in both jurisdictions in Ireland. It was relatively inactive from then until the period 1956-62 when it engaged in a 'Border Campaign'. The advent of the Civil Rights movements in the late 1960s saw an increasingly political and non-militaristic I.R.A. emerge particularly in the south. The arrival of British troops in Northern Ireland in August 1969 precipitated a decisive split between the Marxist, southern-based leadership, whose commitment to physical force was on the wane, and northern members, who were less concerned with ideology now that British troops were once again in Ireland. The movement split in December 1968 into 'Provisional' (largely northern-based) and 'Official' (largely southern-based) wings.

BLACK AND TANS: The name given to demobilised British soldiers who were recruited by the Royal Irish Constabulary from January 1920 to compensate for the widespread resignations and dismissals from the force caused by the War of Independence. The name derived from the force's uniform which consisted of both army and police issue.

The Black and Tans were given a free hand in their fight against the I.R.A. and acted with extreme lawlessness. The fierceness of their reputation was based on their attacks on innocent civilians and major atrocities such as the burning of Cork City and Balbriggan, Co. Dublin, and Bloody Sunday at Croke Park in November 1921, when they shot into the crowd and killed eleven spectators and one player. Their demise accompanied that of the R.I.C.

THE AUXILIARIES: A force similar to the Black and Tans, but its members were drawn from demobilised officers of the British army, recruitment began in July 1920. The force was even less under the control of the R.I.C. than the Black and Tans. The Auxiliaries demise accompanied that of the R.I.C.

ULSTER SPECIAL CONSTABULARY: An auxiliary part-time police force established in 1922 to supplement the Royal Ulster Constabulary and defend the newly founded Northern Ireland from I.R.A. attack. There were three grades - 'A', 'B' and 'C' - of which the 'A' and 'C' specials were only used in the 1920s. Membership of the force was exclusively Protestant. The 'B' Specials went on to gain notoriety, especially in the late 1960s when they attacked civil rights marches. The force was disbanded in April 1970, and many of its members joined the newly established Ulster Defence Regiment.

IRREGULARS: The name given to the anti-Treaty I.R.A. which fought the Free State army during the Civil War (June 1922-April 1923). Their leader was Liam Lynch, and his death in April 1923 was swiftly followed by a truce.

FARMERS' PARTY: It contested Dáil Éireann elections between 1922 and 1932, winning eleven seats in its first election in 1922. Its best return came in 1923 when it secured 15 seats, drawing its support from more affluent farmers. Following a disastrous election in 1932 when it won only four seats, its members went on to found the National Centre Party.

CUMANN NA nGAEDHEAL: Formed in March 1923 from the elements within Sinn Féin who supported the Treaty. W.T. Cosgrave was the party's first and only leader. Due to the republican policy of abstentionism, Cumann na nGaedheal formed every government from the Provisional Government in 1922 until 1932.

The party played an important role in the formation and consolidation of the fledgling Free State, ruthlessly pursuing the anti-treaty I.R.A., executing 77 republicans during the Civil War and crushing the very real threat that the I.R.A. posed. The party also provided for the establishment of the Garda Síochána, the Electricity Supply Board, the Shannon hydro-electric scheme and the Agricultural Credit Corporation. In the field of foreign affairs, the party set about attaining the full benefit of the freedoms implicit in the Treaty. Its members were prominent at Commonwealth Conferences in exploring these freedoms. Their greatest success came in 1931 with the Statute of Westminster which put the parliaments of the Dominions (including Ireland) on an equal footing with the Imperial Parliament at Westminster.

The party lost power in 1932, and less than a year later it merged with the Blueshirts and the National Centre Party to form Fine Gael.

BLUESHIRTS: Founded in February 1932 with Edmund Cronin as its first leader. Consisting mainly of veterans from the Free State army, the organisation adopted a distinctive uniform of a blue shirt and black beret (hence the name). Elected as leader in July 1933, Eoin O'Duffy, the former Garda Commissioner, changed the name of the movement to the National Guard. It was an anti-communist, quasi-fascist organisation and drew inspiration from Mussolini and his Blackshirt movement.

In October 1933 it merged with Cumann na nGaedheal and the National Centre Party to form Fine Gael with O'Duffy as its first president. It declined in the years 1934-36, but in November 1936 O'Duffy with the blessing of members of the Catholic hierarchy, raised an 'Irish Brigade' to fight with Franco in the Spanish Civil War. They returned in June 1937.

BROY HARRIERS: An armed auxiliary police force whose members were mostly former members of the anti-Treaty I.R.A. The group was formed by Garda Commissioner Eamon Broy in 1933 when the formation of the Blueshirts caused alarm in government and throughout the state. It was disbanded in 1935 when the Blueshirt threat had dissipated.

CONNOLLY COLUMN: Formed in December 1936 by Frank Ryan, the column was a group of republican volunteers who joined the Abraham Lincoln Battalion in the 15th International Brigade and fought with the socialists against Franco in the Spanish Civil War (1936-39).

CLANN NA TALMHAN: Founded Galway in 1938 by Michael Donnellan it was a political party concerned with the plight of the small western farmer. It contested the general election of 1943 when it secured 14 seats but it won a decreasing number of seats at each subsequent election until its representation was reduced to two T.D.s. In 1948-51 and 1954-57, it was part of the Inter-Party coalition and its leader, Joseph Blowick, was Minister for Lands. The party did not contest the 1965 general election.

COMDHÁIL NÁISIÚNTA NA GAEILIGE (THE NATIONAL CONGRESS OF THE IRISH LANGUAGE): Founded in October 1943 as a co-ordinating body for Irish language organisations, including Conradh na Gaeilige.

CONGRESS OF IRISH UNIONS: Formed in April 1945 by William O'Brien who broke away from the Irish Trades Union Congress and the Labour Party, because of "communist tendencies within the I.T.U.C." In February 1959 it reunited with the I.T.U.C. to form Irish Congress of Trade Unions.

CLANN NA POBLACHTA: The political party founded in July 1946 by Sean MacBride, former Chief-of-Staff of the I.R.A. A republican party, it was part of the Inter-Party coalition of 1948-51 and held two central ministerial portfolios, MacBride at Foreign Affairs and Dr. Noel Browne at the Department of Health. The controversy engendered by Dr. Browne's 'Mother and Child' scheme brought about the fall of the government in May 1951 and split the party. It was never again to be a political force and did not fulfil its promise of providing a viable republican alternative to Fianna Fáil. Winning only one seat in both the 1961 and 1965 general elections, it formally dissolved in 1965.

FIANNA ULADH: A republican political party founded in Tyrone in 1953. Its leader, Liam Kelly, was elected to the Seanad in 1954, thus breaking the traditional republican policy of not recognising the legitimacy of the Oireachtas. The party was banned in 1956, and it ceased to operate.

SAOR ULADH: Republican group which split from the I.R.A. in 1954 and carried out attacks on police barracks without I.R.A. approval. The group, allied to Fianna Uladh, was proscribed in 1956 but carried out attacks until 1959.

NORTHERN IRELAND CIVIL RIGHTS ASSOCIATION: Founded in Belfast in February 1967 and organised along the same lines as the British National Council for Civil Liberties. The Association called for an end to gerrymandering; the introduction of one man-one vote in local elections; the disbanding of the 'B' Specials; the repeal of the Special Powers Act; and the fair allocation of public housing. The main weapon of the association was protest marches, the first of which was held in Dungannon in August 1968. Marches were organised throughout the late 1960s and early 1970s and often led to clashes with the R.U.C. The association's influence declined from the mid 1970s.

PEOPLE'S DEMOCRACY: Founded at Queen's University, Belfast, in October 1968 by Michael Farrell and Bernadette Devlin. A socialist organisation, it demanded an end to discrimination against Catholics in Northern Ireland, one man-one vote and the revoking of the Special Powers Act. The group was involved in one of the bloodiest encounters of the Civil Rights era when unarmed marchers were attacked by baton-wielding loyalists at Burntollet on January 4th, 1969. Some of its leaders were interned in August 1971, and with the increasing violence of the 'troubles', it became less significant.

'OFFICIAL' IRISH REPUBLICAN ARMY: Formed following the split in the I.R.A. in late 1969. It was allied to 'Official' Sinn Féin and was more Marxist than its 'provisional' counterpart. A feud ensued between the two wings of the I.R.A. with casualties on both sides. The Official I.R.A. has ceased to operate since it called a ceasefire on May 29, 1972, but strongly contested allegations have persisted that the group continued to exist and carried out robberies and assassinations well into the 1980s.

'PROVISIONAL' IRISH REPUBLICAN ARMY: Formed from the split in the I.R.A. in late 1969. The split was led by the I.R.A.'s northern command who felt that the ideological swing to the left by the southern-based leadership was detrimental to the movement as a whole. With the traditional enemy in the form of the British army on the streets of Northern Ireland, the 'Provisionals' felt that it was time to leave politics behind and respond in a military fashion.

'OFFICIAL' SINN FÉIN: Formed in January 1970 following a split with what became known as 'Provisional' Sinn Féin at the Ard-Fheis in Dublin. The new party was led by Tomás MacGiolla and applied a socialist analysis to the conflict in the North. The party was organised throughout the 32 counties and, in 1977, changed its name to Sinn Féin The Workers Party. It underwent a further name change, becoming simply The Workers Party.

ULSTER DEFENCE REGIMENT (U.D.R.): Founded by an act of parliament in December 1969. It was largely a part-time force under the command of the British Army. Many of its members were drawn from the disbanded 'B' Specials, and its original aim of recruiting from both communities was never realised with only 3% of the force being Catholic. The U.D.R. was used as a back up for R.U.C. patrols. Its members were targeted both on and off duty by the I.R.A. and I.N.L.A., and 197 members were killed from its inception until it was disbanded in 1992. The Regiment was amalgamated with the

Royal Irish Rangers in 1992 to form the Royal Irish Regiment.

VANGUARD UNIONIST PROGRESSIVE PARTY: Founded by William Craig in March 1973 it was a unionist political party whose roots were in the Ulster Vanguard, the majority of its members were drawn from the ranks of the U.U.P. The party contested the 1973 Northern Ireland Assembly election, winning seven seats, and it won three Westminster seats in both general elections in 1974. Opposed to Direct Rule, the Sunningdale Agreement and the power sharing executive, it became part of the United Ulster Unionist Council and was prominent in the Ulster Workers' Council strike in 1974. It split in 1977 when its leader suggested some form of voluntary coalition with the S.D.L.P. and in 1978 ceased to function as a party. Current Ulster Unionist Party leader David Trimble was a prominent member and was deputy leader of the party (1977-78).

UNITED ULSTER UNIONIST COUNCIL: Formed in January 1974 to oppose the Sunningdale Agreement. It consisted of the Ulster Unionist Party, the Democratic Unionist Party and the Vanguard Unionist Progressive Party. The Council opposed all aspects of the Sunningdale Agreement, and the Council of Ireland proposals in particular. It called for the removal of the power-sharing executive and co-operated fully with, and gave support to, the Ulster Workers' Council (U.W.C.) strike in May 1974 which paralysed Northern Ireland and brought down the power-sharing executive.

It suffered a split in 1975 when the V.U.P.P. suggested some form of coalition that would include the S.D.L.P. The Council collapsed when paramilitary groups were admitted and when prominent M.P.s John Dunlop and Rev. Ian Paisley supported the abortive 1977 loyalist strike which the U.U.P. opposed.

ULSTER WORKERS' COUNCIL: Formed in 1974, to oppose the workings of the Sunningdale Agreement and the imposition of Direct Rule. It organised the loyalist strike of May 14-29, 1974, which was enforced by loyalist paramilitaries. The cutting off of electricity supplies ensured the strike's success, and the executive fell on May 28. Prominent members of the U.W.C. co-ordinating committee were the leaders of the main unionist parties, including Harry West (U.U.P.), Rev. Ian Paisley (D.U.P.) and William Craig (V.U.P.P.). The U.D.A., the U.V.F and other loyalist paramilitary groups also had members on the co-ordinating committee.

The committee organised an abortive loyalist strike in May 1977 which was ineffective, failing to get unanimous unionist support. The council was reorganised in 1981.

IRISH NATIONAL LIBERATION ARMY: Formed in Dublin in 1975, it is a splinter republican group responsible for some of the most ruthless attacks in Northern Ireland during the 'troubles'. Initially, it drew members mainly from those disenchanted with the 'Official' I.R.A. It later attracted members from the fringes of the 'Provisionals'. The I.N.L.A. has been plagued by feuds since the late 1980s, resulting in the deaths of many of its members. The organisation, unlike the I.R.A. and the Combined Loyalist Military Command, has not called a ceasefire.

SIGNIFICANT DOCUMENTS IN IRISH HISTORY

STATUTE OF KILKENNY - Enacted in 1366 by the Irish Parliament meeting at Kilkenny. The statute was a series of apartheid-type laws forbidding English settlers to assimilate with native Gaelic Irish and to adopt their culture. Gaelic laws, customs and language were banned among the settlers, as was marriage between the 'races'. The laws were ultimately ineffective and were revoked in 1537.

POYNINGS' LAW - Enacted December 1, 1494, and named after the Lord Deputy Sir Edward Poynings. It forbade the Irish parliament to convene without the King's prior permission, and all intended legislation had to be approved by him. The law was almost completely repealed in 1782; the only part of it which remained was the Crown's right to veto a bill.

THE ANNALS OF THE FOUR MASTERS (1632-36) - A history of Ireland compiled in book form by religious scribes in Donegal Town. The annals were completed by Michael O'Clery and others on August 10, 1636.

TREATY OF LIMERICK - Signed on October 3, 1691, by the Irish leader Patrick Sarsfield and the Dutch General Ginkel. The Treaty allowed Irish soldiers their liberty and the freedom to go to France to join other Jacobites. Roman Catholics were to be allowed rights to worship, to retain their property and to practice their professions. The articles dealing with religious freedoms for Catholics were not honoured by the British parliament which within two months had put in place an anti-Catholic Oath of Supremacy and, in the years 1695-1709, enacted a comprehensive series of penal laws.

PENAL LAWS (1695-1709) - The collective name for a series of primarily anti-Catholic but also anti-Dissenter laws designed to secure the privileged position of members of the Church of Ireland and the established Church. The laws were aimed at eradicating the Roman Catholic religion in the country and showed little tolerance towards Presbyterianism. The laws included restrictions on rights of education, the bearing of arms, the purchase of land, taking a seat in parliament and holding any government office. The Roman Catholic clergy, including virtually all of the hierarchy, was banished in 1697 (although some priests were permitted to stay) and the ordination of new priests was forbidden. A Toleration Act for Protestant Dissenters was passed in 1719, while Catholics had to wait until late in the century for many of their restrictions to be formally repealed and until 1829 before they could sit in parliament or hold high public office.

CATHOLIC RELIEF ACT - Enacted April 9, 1793, it was one of a series of acts which repealed the penal laws. It enabled Catholics to hold selected public and military positions, extended the parliamentary franchise to Catholics and removed the official bar on Catholics receiving university degrees.

ACT OF UNION - Enacted July 2, 1800, and came into effect on January 1, 1801. It provided for the union of the legislatures of Great Britain and Ireland. The Irish Parliament was abolished and henceforth Irish M.P.s and Lords sat in the Houses of Parliament at Westminster. The act also provided for the amalgamation of the Church of Ireland with the Church of England. The act was superseded by the Government of Ireland Act, 1920, and the Anglo-Irish Treaty of 1921.

ROMAN CATHOLIC RELIEF ACT - April 13, 1829. The act enabled Roman Catholics to sit in the Houses of Parliament; belong to any corporation; and hold the higher offices of State by replacing the oaths of allegiance, supremacy and abjuration with a new oath, which Roman Catholics could take.

IRISH CHURCH ACT - Enacted July 26, 1869, and came into effect 1st January 1871. The act provided for the separation of the Churches of England and Ireland, but it dealt in the main with the disestablishment of the Church of Ireland (i.e. the dissolution of the legal union of Church and State); confiscated property of the Church of Ireland; discontinued grants to Maynooth College and the Presbyterian Church (although compensation was paid); disbanded Ecclesiastical Courts; abolished the tithe paid by Irish people of all denominations to the Church of Ireland; and finally, made provision for tenants on Church of Ireland lands to purchase their holdings.

LAND ACTS

Landlord and Tenant (Ireland) Act - (Gladstone) August 1, 1870. The act attempted but failed to legalise the 'Ulster Custom' of not evicting tenants who had paid their rent in full and allowing tenants to sub-let their holdings. Landlords would in future have to pay compensation for any improvements made by a tenant to his holding. The most significant clause was the 'Bright Clause' which provided tenants with a government loan of 66% of the cost of their holdings to enable them to buy their own farm.

Land Law (Ireland) Act - (Gladstone) August 22, 1881. The act gave tenants the 'Three F's': Fair rents (to be decided by arbitration); Fixity of tenure (tenants who had their rent fully paid could not be evicted); and Free sale (which ensured payment for any improvements paid). A Land Commission was established to determine the 'fair rents' and a Land Court to arbitrate in tenant-landlord disputes. A land purchase scheme providing a 75% loan to tenants wishing to purchase their holdings.

Purchase of Land (Ireland) Act - (Ashbourne) August 14, 1885. The act provided £5 million to tenants in the form of a 100% loan to buy out their holdings, the repayments of which were frequently less than rents. The money available was subsequently increased to £10 million (1888).

Purchase of Land (Ireland) Act - (Balfour) August 5, 1891. The Act made £33 million available to tenants to purchase their holdings. It also provided for the establishment of a Congested Districts Board to administer aid to designated congested areas.

Irish Land Act - (Wyndham) August 14, 1903. Funds of £83 million were provided to tenants to buy out their lands, and landlords got a bonus if they sold their entire estate.

HOME RULE BILLS

1886 - Defeated in the House of Commons by 341 votes to 311 on June 8, 1886. It proposed the establishment of a two-tier Irish legislature which would have limited powers. No Irish representatives would sit at Westminster. The Lord Lieutenant would remain the Crown's representative in Ireland and would give the royal assent to Bills of the Irish parliament. Revenue would come from taxes collected within Ireland, excluding customs and excise, and from a portion of the imperial taxes. Control of the R.I.C. would remain with the Imperial parliament.

1893 - Defeated in the House of Lords by 419 votes to 41 on September 9, 1893. Similar to the 1886 Bill in that it proposed the establishment of a two-tier parliament, but Ireland would continue to send representatives to Westminster. The same restrictions were to apply to the powers of the parliament, and revenue would be raised in the same way. Control of the police would remain with the Imperial parliament.

1914 - Introduced in the House of Commons in 1912, it was defeated in the House of Lords but the veto of the Lords had been restricted to two years by the 1911 Parliament Act. Signed into law by the King on September 18, 1914, its implementation was suspended (with agreement of the Ulster Unionists and the Irish Parliamentary Party) for the duration of World War I.

It again provided for a two-tier elected assembly and gave Ireland 42 seats in the Imperial parliament. The legislature would be subject to the same restrictions as before, but the articles providing for the raising of revenue allowed the Irish government more independence in the imposition and collection of tax, including customs and excise. Control of the R.I.C. was to revert to the Irish parliament after six years had elapsed.

IRISH UNIVERSITIES ACT - August 1, 1908. Provided for the abolishing of the Royal University and the establishing of two new universities namely the National University of Ireland (consisting of University Colleges Cork, Dublin and Galway and other smaller constituent colleges) and the Queen's University of Belfast. The National University of Ireland, although officially nondenominational, had a significant number of Roman Catholic bishops on its governing body.

ULSTER'S SOLEMN LEAGUE AND COVENANT - 28 September 1912. This was a promise signed by 218,000 men to oppose the Home Rule conspiracy by 'using all means which may be found necessary' and, in the event of a Home Rule parliament being foisted on Ireland, to refuse to recognise its authority.

PROCLAMATION OF THE IRISH REPUBLIC - Issued on April 24, 1916, it declared the intention of the Irish

Volunteers to strike for freedom, and asserts the right of the Irish people to the ownership of a sovereign, independent Irish Republic. The Proclamation guaranteed religious and civil liberties, equal rights and opportunities to all and promised to cherish all the nation's children equally. It was signed by Thomas J. Clarke, Sean MacDiarmada, Thomas McDonagh, P.H. Pearse, Eamonn Ceannt, James Connolly and Joseph Plunkett on behalf of the provisional government. Each one of these signatories was executed within three weeks.

GOVERNMENT OF IRELAND ACT - December 23, 1920. It repealed the Home Rule Act of 1914 and proposed to establish two Home Rule parliaments - one in Belfast to legislate for the counties of Antrim, Armagh, Derry, Down, Fermanagh and Tyrone and one in Dublin. Control of finance and defence would be retained by Westminster. A Council of Ireland, comprising M.P.s from both Irish parliaments, was also proposed to deal with matters of mutual interest. The council would have limited powers and would pave the way for an end to partition when both parliaments would assent to it. The act was superseded in the Free State by the Anglo-Irish Treaty of 1921 and in Northern Ireland by the Northern Ireland Constitution Act and the Northern Ireland Assembly Act, both of which were passed by the British parliament in 1973.

ARTICLES OF AGREEMENT FOR A TREATY BETWEEN GREAT BRITAIN AND IRELAND - signed on December 6, 1921 by the Irish delegation to the treaty negotiations - Arthur Griffith, Michael Collins, Robert Barton, Charles Gavan Duffy, and Eamon Duggan - and representatives of the British government, including Prime Minister David Lloyd George and Winston Churchill. Ratified by Dáil Éireann on January 7, 1922, by 64 votes to 57, and by the British parliament on December 5, 1922.

It provided for the creation of the Irish Free State, a nation of the British Empire with dominion status (article 1). The Crown was to be represented by a Governor (article 3), and all members of the the Free State parliament would be obliged to take an oath of allegiance to the King (article 4). Ireland was to assume a portion of the United Kingdom's war debt (article 5). Britain retained control of a number of 'treaty ports' and of Ireland's coastal defence (article 7) while a limit was set on the size of the Irish army (article 8). Articles 11 and 12 made provision for Northern Ireland to opt out of the jurisdiction of the parliament and government of the Free State and to set up a Boundary Commission to determine the boundaries between the two entities, compatible with economic and geographic conditions, should it choose to do so. Religious discrimination in any form was expressly forbidden in either jurisdiction by article 16.

CIVIL AUTHORITIES (SPECIAL POWERS) ACT (NORTHERN IRELAND) - Passed by the Northern Ireland parliament on April 7, 1922, it gave wide-ranging powers to the Minister for Home Affairs to take any steps necessary to preserve the peace. Arrest without warrant, internment without trial, flogging, execution, banning of organisations or publications were just some of the powers it contained. Initially, it was renewed every year, but in 1928 it was renewed for five years and was made permanent in 1933. It was rescinded in 1972.

CONSTITUTION OF THE IRISH FREE STATE - (Saorstát Éireann) approved by Dáil Éireann October 25, 1922, and ratified by the British parliament, along with the Anglo-Irish Treaty, on December 5, 1922. It declared the Irish Free State place as a co-equal member of the British Commonwealth of Nations. It established the legislature of the new state (the King, the Senate and the Dáil), the Irish language was recognised as the national language with official recognition of status of the English language, *habeas corpus* was ensured, freedom to practice religion and the free expression of opinion was assured as was the right to free elementary education. The Oath of Allegiance, as agreed in the Treaty, was included. Articles relating to eligibility to vote and run for public office were also included. The Constitution was superseded by the Constitution of 1937.

CENSORSHIP OF PUBLICATIONS ACT - Passed by the Dáil in July 1929. The act provided for a censorship board of five members who were empowered to censor or ban publications, the main targets being obscenity and information about birth control. Yet such was the nature of the act that thousands of books, including many by Ireland's most eminent authors, were banned. No adequate avenue for appeal was provided until the act was amended in 1967.

STATUTE OF WESTMINSTER - Enacted by the British parliament on December 11, 1931. It gave the parliaments of the British Dominions equal status to the Imperial parliament at Westminster in that they were free to pass any law and amend or repeal any existing or future law enacted by Westminster. Additionally, they would not have to implement any act with which they did not agree.

EXTERNAL RELATIONS ACT - passed on December 12, 1936, during the abdication crisis of Edward VIII. The Crown was now recognised only for purposes of external association (i.e. accreditation of diplomats and international agreements). The Constitution Amendment (No. 27) Bill passed on December 11 deleted all reference to the crown from the Irish Free State Constitution and abolished the office of Governor General, making the Free State a republic in all but name.

CONSTITUTION OF IRELAND - Ratified by referendum on July 1, 1937. *see Law and Defence chapter.*

EDUCATION ACT - (Northern Ireland), passed on 27 November 1947. As well as grants towards the building and extension of schools, it provided financial assistance to any student, irrespective of denomination or economic background, to go to university on the basis that they attained the required educational standards. It also established universal secondary schooling.

REPUBLIC OF IRELAND ACT - passed on December 21, 1948, but not implemented until April 18, 1949. It repealed the 1936 External Relations Act and declared the 26 counties of Éire a Republic, taking the Republic of Ireland out of the British Commonwealth of Nations.

IRELAND ACT - Enacted by the British parliament on June 2, 1949, recognising the Republic of Ireland's withdrawal from the British Commonwealth. It affirmed the position of Northern Ireland within the United Kingdom and stated that no change could be effected on its status without the consent of the Northern Ireland parliament. The act also stated that Irish citizens would not be considered as aliens in Britain and enshrined a free travel area between the two countries.

EUROPEAN MONETARY SYSTEM - established on March 13, 1979. The Republic of Ireland joined, Britain did not, ending the one-for-one parity that existed between the Irish and British currencies since independence.

RECENT DOCUMENTS

Significant Documents in Recent Times

ANGLO-IRISH AGREEMENT - Signed November 15, 1985, by an Taoiseach Garret FitzGerald and British Prime Minister Margaret Thatcher. Its main points are as follows:

Article One: The two governments affirm that the change in status of Northern Ireland could only come about with the consent of the majority in Northern Ireland. They recognise that there is no wish on the part of the majority for a change, but should a change come about, the respective parliaments would put in place the necessary legislation to effect such change.

Articles Two and Three: These deal with establishing an intergovernmental conference concerned with relations within Northern Ireland and between both parts of the island and the establishment of a permanent secretariat. Political, security and legal matters would be within the remit of the conference, as would

the promotion of cross-border cooperation (the specific terms of reference of which were set out in **Articles Five to Ten**). It is explicitly stated that there is "no derogation from sovereignty" of either government.

Article Twelve: provides for the establishment of an Anglo-Irish parliamentary body.

DOWNING STREET DECLARATION - Signed December 15, 1993, by An Taoiseach Albert Reynolds and British Prime Minister John Major. Its main points are as follows:

Article Four: The British government reiterates that it has no "selfish strategic or economic interest in Northern Ireland" and affirms that it will uphold the democratic wish of the people of Northern Ireland should they "prefer to support the Union or a sovereign united Ireland." It also agrees that it is for the people of

Ireland alone and the two parts, respectively, to exercise their right of self-determination.

Article Five: The Irish government accepts that the "right of self-determination by the people of Ireland as a whole must be achieved and exercised with, and subject to, the agreement and consent of a majority of the people in Northern Ireland".

Article Seven: The Taoiseach accepts that there are elements in the Constitution which are deeply resented by unionists and confirms that in the event of an overall settlement, the Irish government would put forward proposals to change the Constitution to reflect the principle of consent in Northern Ireland.

Article Ten: Both governments confirm that parties with a democratic mandate, who demonstrate a commitment to exclusively peaceful methods, can participate fully in democratic politics and dialogue.

Article Eleven: The Irish government announces its intention to convene a Forum for Peace and Reconciliation to explore ways to establish agreement and trust between the opposing traditions.

FRAMEWORK DOCUMENT (A New Framework for Agreement) -Signed by An Taoiseach John Bruton and British Prime Minister John Major on February 22, 1995. It sets out the shared understanding of both governments on the parameters of a possible outcome to the talks process. Its guiding principles, as set out in paragraph ten, are the principle of self-determination in keeping with the principle of consent; agreement to be pursued, and achieved through, exclusively democratic and peaceful methods; and new political arrangements that must afford parity of esteem to both traditions.

The governments aim to establish interlocking and mutually supportive institutions on three levels:

(a) Structures within Northern Ireland where locally elected representatives will "exercise shared administrative and legislative control over agreed matters" (paragraph 13). It is considered that these structures "will be most effectively negotiated, as part of a comprehensive three-stranded [talks] process."

(b) North/South institutions where the functions would fall into three categories, namely, consultative, harmonising and executive. Paragraph 36 provides for a parliamentary forum composed of members of the Oireachtas and agreed institutions in Northern Ireland.

(c) East/West structures in the form of a new Agreement "reflecting the totality of relationships between the two islands" (paragraph 39) where an intergovernmental conference supported by a permanent secretariat would be maintained, providing "a continued institutional expression for the Irish government's recognised concern and role in relation to Northern Ireland" (paragraph 42).

Issues of self-determination and consent from the Joint Declaration reiterate that Northern Ireland's status will not be changed without the consent of its majority and that the British government will not stand in the way of a united Ireland. Paragraph 21 reaffirms the "existing birthright of everyone born in either jurisdiction in Ireland to be part, as of right, of the Irish nation".

The governments encourage the adoption of a charter or covenant encapsulating the fundamental rights of everyone living in both parts of Ireland (paragraph 51).

In conclusion, the governments agree that the document and the issues raised by it should be examined in negotiations between democratically mandated parties committed to peaceful means (paragraph 54) and that the outcome of those negotiations will be submitted for ratification through referenda, north and south (paragraph 55).

PREVENTION OF TERRORISM (TEMPORARY PROVISIONS) ACT - Passed by the Westminster parliament on November 29, 1974, it has two main powers: (a) exclusion orders can be placed on those suspected of terrorism excluding them from Britain, Northern Ireland or the entire jurisdiction; (b) police have the power to detain terrorist suspects for 48 hours without charge and to extend the detention by a further five days, subject to authorisation from the Home Secretary or the Secretary of State for Northern Ireland. Powers were also granted to proscribe organisations, and in 1988 remission in prison sentences for those convicted of terrorist offences was reduced from 50 to 33 per cent.

SUNNINGDALE AGREEMENT - Signed on December 9, 1973, following tripartite talks between the Irish and British governments and the incoming Northern Ireland executive (containing members from Alliance, the S.D.L.P. and the U.U.P.). In it the Irish government accepted that there could be no change in the status of Northern Ireland without the consent of the majority there, and the British government affirmed Northern Ireland's position within the United Kingdom but stated in the event of a majority in Northern Ireland demonstrating a wish for a united Ireland, they would support that wish.

The most controversial proposal, however, was the revival of the Council of Ireland (see the 1920 Government of Ireland Act) which would have limited consultative and legislative powers. Issues regarding policing and the administration of justice were also discussed.

REPORT OF THE NEW IRELAND FORUM - Published May 2, 1984. The parties that attended the Forum were Fianna Fáil, the Labour Party, Fine Gael and the S.D.L.P. The report made clear the parties' desire to realise a united Ireland but made proposals on joint authority in Northern Ireland to be exercised by both the Irish and British governments and a federal arrangement. The report also indicated that the participating parties were willing to discuss any other suggestions which could help realise a political settlement. The report was dismissed by unionists, Sinn Féin and the British government.

NORTHERN IRELAND CONSTITUTION ACT - Passed by Westminster July 18, 1973, it superseded the Government of Ireland Act 1920 and formally abolished the parliament of Northern Ireland and the office of Governor.

It provides the fundamental legislation for a system of devolved government in the form of a 12-member executive (expanded to 15 by amendment in December 1973) which, along with the 78-member assembly (provided for by the Northern Ireland Assembly Act), would have lawmaking powers. Control of national matters, such as the Crown and parliament, defence, taxation, etc., would remain within the jurisdiction of the Westminster parliament.

The act contains a 'constitutional guarantee' that the position of Northern Ireland will not change, save for a change in the wishes of the people who live there, as demonstrated in a border poll. It also renders all discriminatory legislation void and makes discrimination by public authorities illegal. Provision is made for the Secretary of State and a team of junior ministers to carry out the functions of the Northern Ireland departments in the absence of devolution (as has been the case since May 1974).

NORTHERN IRELAND ASSEMBLY ACT - Passed by the British parliament on May 3, 1973. It provided for a 78-member assembly, elected by proportional representation from the 12 existing Westminster constituencies. The Assembly had law-making powers under devolution, and it was the body to which the power-sharing executive were ultimately responsible.

THE 'MITCHELL' REPORT - Published on January 22, 1996, it is the report of the International Body on the Decommissioning of Illegal Arms under the chairmanship of former U.S. Senator George Mitchell. The body included Canadian General John de Chastelain and former Finnish Prime Minister Harri Holkeri. The Body's report is divided into broad sections dealing with principles of democracy and non-violence, commitment to decommissioning, decommissioning during all-party negotiations, guidelines on the modalities of decommissioning and confidence-building measures.

The six "Mitchell principles" of democracy and non-violence to which the report recommends that all parties "affirm their total and absolute commitment" are as follows: the use of democratic and exclusively peaceful means to resolve political issues; the total disarmament of paramilitary weapons; the agreement that disarmament must be independently verifiable; the renouncing of the use of force by themselves or by other organisations; the acceptance of the outcome of negotiations, no matter how repugnant it may be; the use of democratic methods only to alter that outcome; and the cessation of 'punishment' killings and beatings.

The report suggests that 'some decommissioning would take place *during* the process of all-party negotiations rather than before or after' and believes that the parties should use this as a tangible confidence-building measure. The report insists that decommissioning 'should take place to the satisfaction of an independent commission, acceptable to all parties'. The commission would be able to use the technical expertise of the British and Irish armies but organisations 'should also have the option of destroying their weapons themselves', subject to the commission's verification. The report also insists that those involved in handing weapons over must not be prosecuted, that forensic examinations of decommissioned weapons must not be conducted and that information gleaned from the process should be inadmissible in courts of law north and south.

The report concludes by suggesting confidence-building measures, such as movement by the governments on prisoners, a review of the situation on legally registered weapons and the use of plastic bullets, and more progress towards a more balanced representation on the police force. The suggestion of an elected body was focused on by British Prime Minister John Major whose government initiated legislation for elections to what became the Northern Ireland Forum.

THE 'NORTH' REPORT - Published in 1997, it is the report of the *Independent Review of Parades and Marches* which was chaired by Dr. Peter North and had two other members - Fr. Oliver Crilly and the Rev. John Dunlop. The report considers the challenges posed for society in Northern Ireland, the nature of the parades issue, the parading organisations and the legal and human rights framework. It also details what they were told in the form of submissions and details the main events of 1996. It concludes by making a 43 recommendations on the contentious parades issue.

The recommendations open by proposing a number of fundamental principles, including the protection of the right to peaceful free assembly, subject to certain qualifications; that those exercising that right should take account of the impact it is likely to have on other parts of the community; that difficulties should be resolved locally by those involved; and that adjudication over disputed parades should be applied as openly and consistently as possible.

The report recommends the creation of an independent Parades Commission, consisting of five members appointed by the Secretary of State, and notes that the responsibility for decisions on contentious parades should lie with the commission, rather than the R.U.C. The report also recommends that Public Order legislation with regard to parades be amended to consider 'the impact of the parade on relationships within the community' and that the Secretary of State's powers over parades should also be amended accordingly. The Commission's decisions should be applied for all disputed parades in the area and should, where appropriate, be enforced for more than 12 months. The Secretary of State shall retain the right to reconsider the Commission's decision subject to the same criteria that the body itself used. It is also recommended that individuals who use the 'force of numbers or the threat of disorder' to contravene the commission's findings should be charged by the police.

The commission will adjudicate on contentious parades on grounds of the parade's physical location and route, its impact on the community, its purpose, its particular features and the approach to local accommodation adopted by interested parties. The commission also recommends the drafting of a *code of conduct* which would have a statutory basis and which would cover the behaviour of those involved in the parade and those opposing it. A similar code should also be drawn up for open air public meetings.

Other recommendations include a registration scheme for bands, more detailed information on parades to be collected by the R.U.C. and the application of controls on the consumption of alcohol on those travelling to parades.

HISTORICAL ANNIVERSARIES

200 years ago

1798: United Irishmen rebellion in Leinster and Ulster. French troops land in Mayo. Government quickly quells the rebellion. United Irishmen leader, Theobald Wolfe Tone, is sentenced to death for treason but commits suicide in prison. Other leaders executed.

150 years ago

1848: Potato crop fails again as Ireland endures its third year of famine. Short-lived 'Young Ireland' rebellion in Tipperary easily put down. Leaders transported.

100 years ago

1898: Creation of county and district councils legislated for in Local Government (Ireland) Act.

75 years ago

1923: The Civil War comes to an end with a cease-fire on May 24, Garda Síochana established by act of the Free State parliament, W.B. Yeats awarded Nobel Prize for literature.

50 years ago

1948: First inter-party government takes office in Éire with John Costello as the new Taoiseach. Republic of Ireland Act provides for declaration of a republic and secession from the Commonwealth.

25 years ago

1973: Ireland and Britain join the European Economic Community on January 1. Fine Gael/ Labour coalition take office and replace the outgoing Fianna Fáil government, following a February General Election in the Republic. Northern Ireland Assembly created, and members elected by proportional representation. Northern Ireland parliament abolished. Foundations laid for a power-sharing executive. Sunningdale Agreement sees Irish and British governments agreeing to cooperate on security measures and agreeing that the status of Northern Ireland must be in line with the wishes of the majority there.

BURIAL PLACES OF FAMOUS IRISH PEOPLE

Name	Description	Died	Burial place
St Patrick	Irish Patron Saint	490	Downpatrick
St. Brigid	Irish Saint	525	Downpatrick
St. Colmcille	Irish Saint	597	Iona, Scotland
Brian Boru	High King of Ireland	23.04.1014	Armagh
Strongbow	Norman invader	1176	Christchurch Cathedral, Dublin
Red Hugh O'Donnell	Chieftain and Military Strategist	10.09.1602	Valladolid, Spain
Grace O'Malley	Pirate Queen	c.1603	Clare Island, Co. Mayo
Jonathan Swift	Political satirist	19.10.1745	St. Patrick's Cathedral, Dublin
Edmund Burke	Politician	09.07.1797	Beaconsfield, Bucks., England
Theobald Wolfe Tone	Revolutionary leader	19.11.1798	Bodenstown, Co. Kildare
Lord Edward Fitzgerald	Revolutionary leader	19.05.1798	St Werburgh's Church, Dublin
Daniel O'Connell	'The Great Liberator'	15.05.1847	Glasnevin Cemetery, Dublin
Maria Edgeworth	Novelist	22.05.1849	Edgeworthstown, Longford
Duke of Wellington	British Prime Minister and Soldier	14.09.1852	St. Paul's Cathedral London
Charles Stewart Parnell	Irish Parliamentary leader	06.10.1891	Glasnevin Cemetery, Dublin
Oscar Wilde	Playwright and Wit	30.11.1900	Père-Lachaise Cemetery, Paris
O'Donovan Rossa	Fenian	30.06.1915	Glasnevin Cemetery, Dublin
Padraig Pearse	Leader of 1916 Rebellion	03.05.1916	Arbour Hill
James Connolly	Leader of 1916 Rebellion	12.05.1916	Arbour Hill
John Redmond	Irish Parliamentarian	06.03.1918	Wexford
Michael Collins	Militant revolutionary leader	22.08.1922	Glasnevin Cemetery, Dublin
Matthew Talbot	Religious Devotee	07.06.1925	Glasnevin Cemetery, Dublin
Countess Constance Markievicz	Revolutionary	15.07.1927	Glasnevin Cemetery, Dublin
Kevin O'Higgins	Minister of the Irish Free State	10.12.1927	Glasnevin Cemetery, Dublin
Lady Augusta Gregory	Playwright	22.05.1932	Coole Park, Galway
Sir Edward Carson	Unionist leader	22.10.1935	St Anne's Cathedral, Belfast
William Butler Yeats	Poet and Nobel laureate	28.01.1939	Drumcliffe, Co. Sligo
Sir James Craig	Northern Ireland Prime Minister.	24.11.1940	Stormont, Belfast
James Joyce	Novelist	13.01.1941	Zurich, Switzerland
Douglas Hyde	First President of Ireland	12.07.1949	Portahard
Maud Gonne	Revolutionary	27.04.1953	Glasnevin Cemetery, Dublin
Éamon de Valera	Former Taoiseach and President	29.08.1975	Glasnevin Cemetery, Dublin
Christy Ring	Legendary Hurler	02.03.1979	Cloyne, Co. Cork
Bobby Sands	Leader of Republican hunger strike	05.05.1981	Milltown Cemetery, Belfast
Samuel Beckett	Author and Nobel laureate	22.12.1989	Montparnasse Cemetery, Paris

FAMOUS SPEECHES

ROBERT EMMET'S SPEECH FROM THE DOCK - Robert Emmet was tried and convicted of treason on September 19, 1803. In chains, he gave an speech to the court refuting the charge that he was an emissary of France and stating plainly that his aim was 'the total separation between Great Britain and Ireland - to make Ireland totally independent of Britain'. The speech concluded thus:"Let no man write my epitaph; for as no man who knows my motives dares now vindicate them, let not prejudice or ignorance asperse them. Let them rest in obscurity and peace: my memory be left in oblivion, and my tomb remain uninscribed, until other times and other men can do justice to my character. When my country takes her part among the nations of the earth, then, and not till then, let my epitaph be written." Emmet was hanged and beheaded the following day.

DANIEL O'CONNELL'S ELECTION SPEECH IN CLARE - On July 5, 1828, Daniel O'Connell became the first Roman Catholic to be elected to the House of Commons since the Williamite revolution in the late 17th century. His election finally forced the government to grant Roman Catholic Emancipation. The following is an extract from his election speech: "Electors of county Clare! Choose between me and Mr. Vesey Fitzgerald [the opposing Protestant candidate] ... choose between the sworn libeller of the Catholic faith, and one who has devoted his early life to your cause; who has consumed his manhood in a struggle for your liberties, and who has ever-lived, and is ready to die for the integrity, the honour, the purity of the Catholic faith, and the promotion of Irish freedom and happiness." O'Connell was re-elected unopposed in July 1829 and took his seat in the House of Commons on February 4, 1830.

CHARLES STEWART PARNELL'S '*NE PLUS ULTRA*' SPEECH - Given by Charles Stewart Parnell at Cork on January 21, 1885. It came in the early days of the Home Rule campaign, and its most famous lines are: "... no man has the right to fix the boundary to the march of a nation. No man has a right to say to his country: 'Thus far shalt thou go and no further'; and we have never attempted to fix *'Ne plus ultra'* to the progress of Ireland's nationhood, and we never shall'.

LORD RANDOLPH CHURCHILL'S 'ULSTER WILL FIGHT' SPEECH - Conservative M.P. Randolph Churchill was invited to Belfast for the culmination of a series of anti-Home Rule rallies. Addressing a crowd at the Ulster Hall at Belfast he coined the maxim 'Ulster will fight and Ulster will be right.' A believer in playing the orange card to oppose the imposition of Home Rule he told his listeners "there will not be wanting to you those of position and influence in England who are willing to cast in their lot with you - whatever it may be - and who will share your fortune."

PADRAIG PEARSE'S ORATION AT THE GRAVESIDE OF O'DONOVAN ROSSA - Jerimiah O'Donovan Rossa, a veteran of the Fenian rising of 1867 died on June 30, 1915. At his funeral in Glasnevin Cemetery, Dublin Padraig Pearse lamented the death of this old fenian thus "Life springs from death: and from the graves of patriot men and women spring living nations. The Defenders of this Realm have worked well in secret and in the open. They think that they have pacified Ireland. They think they have purchased half of us and intimidated the other half. They think they have foreseen everything; but the fools, the fools, the fools! They have left us our Fenian dead, and while Ireland holds these graves, Ireland unfree shall never be at peace."

WINSTON CHURCHILL'S VICTORY SPEECH - Delivered in a radio broadcast on May 13, 1945, it criticised Éire's neutrality during World War II and thanked Northern Ireland for its help in Britain's hour of need: 'Owing to the action of Mr. de Valera, so much at variance with the temper and instinct of thousands of southern Irishmen who hastened to the battle-front to prove their ancient valour, the approaches which the southern Irish ports and airfields could so easily have guarded were closed by the hostile aircraft and U-boats. This was indeed a deadly moment in our life, and if it had not been for the loyalty and friendship of Northern Ireland, we should have been forced to come to close quarters with Mr. de Valera or perish forever from the earth. However, with a restraint and poise to which, I say, history will find few parallels, His Majesty's government never laid a violent hand upon them, though at times it would have been quite easy and quite natural, and left the de Valera government to frolic with the Germans and later with the Japanese representatives to their hearts content.'

DE VALERA'S RIPOSTE TO CHURCHILL - De Valera replied to Winston Churchill's attack with a radio broadcast on May 16: "... Mr. Churchill is proud of Britain's stand alone after France had fallen and before America entered the war. Could he not find it in his heart the generosity to acknowledge that there is a small nation that stood alone not for one year or two, but for several hundred years against aggression; that endured spoliations, famine, massacres, in endless succession; that was clubbed many times into insensibility, but each time on returning consciousness took up the fight anew; a small nation that could never be got to accept defeat and has never surrendered her soul ... it is indeed difficult for the strong to be just to the weak but acting justly has its rewards. By resisting his temptation [to violate Éire's neutrality] in this instance, Mr. Churchill, instead of adding another horrid chapter to the already blood-stained record of the relations between England and this country, has advanced the cause of international morality an important step."

JAMES CRAIG'S ORANGEISM - Speaking to the Northern Ireland House of Commons on April 24, Prime Minister James Craig stated "I have always said that I am an Orangeman first and a politician and a member of this parliament afterwards ... they still boast of southern Ireland being a Catholic state. All I boast is that we have a Protestant parliament and a Protestant state."

HISTORICAL FIGURES

1= See Biographies of Taoisigh
2= See Biographies of Irish Presidents
3= See Biographies of Northern Ireland Prime Ministers

Andrews, John Miller[3] born Co. Down, 1871; Prime Minister of Northern Ireland (1940-43). Died 1956.

Boru, Brian born 926, High King of Ireland (1002-14); his forces were victorious in the decisive defeat of the Vikings in Ireland at the Battle of Clontarf, but he himself was killed. Died 1014.

Brooke, Sir Basil[3] born Fermanagh, 1888; Prime Minister of Northern Ireland (1943-63). Died 1973.

Butt, Isaac born Donegal, 1813; founded Home Rule Movement in 1870 and was leader until 1877; leader of Irish Parliamentary Party in the House of Commons (1871-79). Died 1879.

Carson, Sir Edward born Dublin, 1854; a barrister, he prosecuted the homosexual writer Oscar Wilde; M.P. (1892-1921); leader of Irish Unionists at Westminster (1910-21), minister in the British war cabinet; supported the formation of the Ulster Volunteer Force; led 218,000 Ulster unionists in the signing of the Solemn League and Covenant in 1913. Knighted in 1900, he was elevated to the peerage in 1921 as Lord Carson of Duncairn. Died 1935.

Casement, Roger born Dublin, 1864; knighted in 1911 for his work with the British colonial service. A member of the Irish Volunteers, he secured German weapons for the 1916 Rising but was captured at Banna Strand, Co. Kerry. Tried for treason and hanged on August 3, 1916. His remains were re-interred in Dublin in 1965.

Childers, Erskine[2] born London, 1905; President of Ireland from 1973 until his death in 1974.

Saint Column Cille born Donegal, 521; patron saint; founded monastic settlements at Derry and Kells; founded monastery at Iona in 563 from which missionaries brought Christianity to Scotland and northern England. Died 597.

de Clare, Richard Fitz Gilbert (Strongbow) born Wales; Norman adventurer who arrived in 1170 at the request of Diarmait MacMurchada. MacMurchada promised him his daughter in marriage and succession to the kingship of Leinster; king of Leinster from 1171. Died 1176.

Collins, Michael born Cork, 1890; veteran of the 1916 Rising; leader of the Irish Republican Brotherhood during War of Independence. Elected to the first Dáil; Minister of Finance in the Republican government; signatory of the Anglo-Irish Treaty 1921. Chairman of the Provisional government (January-August 1922); Commander-in-Chief of the Free State army during the civil war. Killed in an ambush on August 22, 1922.

Connolly, James born Edinburgh, 1868; revolutionary socialist; founded Independent Labour Party of Ireland in 1912; founded Citizen's Army in 1913 to protect workers from police attacks during the Dublin Lockout; joined Irish Republican Brotherhood 1915; a signatory of the Proclamation of the Republic, he served as commanding officer in the General Post Office during the 1916 Rising. Executed while in a chair May 12, 1916.

Cosgrave, William Thomas[1] born Dublin, 1880; President of Executive Council (1922-32). Died 1965.

Costello, John A.[1] born Dublin, 1891; Taoiseach (1948-51 and 1954-57). Died 1976.

Craig, Sir James[3] born Belfast, 1871; Prime Minister of Northern Ireland (1921-40). Died 1940.

de Valera, Éamon[1+2] born New York 1882, Taoiseach and President of Ireland. Died 1975.

Emmet, Robert born Dublin 1778, leader of a rebellion in Dublin in 1803; remembered for his speech from the dock; hanged and beheaded on September 20, 1803.

Faulkner, Brian[3] born Co. Down, 1921; Prime Minister of Northern Ireland (1971-72). Died 1977.

Fitzgerald, Lord Edward born Kildare, 1763; veteran of the American War of Independence; leading member of the United Irishmen; captured May 1798, he died from his wounds before he could be tried.

Fitzgerald, Thomas Lord Offaly (Silken Thomas), born Kildare, 1513; appointed Lord Deputy in 1534; instigated a rebellion almost immediately; surrendered in 1535, assured of a pardon. Hanged, drawn and quartered in February 1537.

Grattan, Henry born Dublin, 1746; M.P. who lobbied successfully for the repeal of Poyning's Law in 1782; opposed the Act of Union (1800); advocate of Catholic Emancipation at Westminster; died 1820.

Griffith, Arthur born Dublin, 1871; founded Sinn Féin 1905; proposed Irish abstentionism from Westminster and establishment of indigenous assembly; M.P. (1917-22); served as Minister for Justice and Minister for Foreign Affairs; signatory of 1921 Anglo-Irish Treaty; President of Dáil Éireann (January-August 1922). Died 1922.

Hyde, Douglas[2] born Roscommon, 1860; President of Ireland (1938-45). Died 1949.

Lemass, Seán[1] born Dublin, 1899; Taoiseach (1959-66). Died 1971.

MacBride, Seán born Dublin, 1904; fought with republicans during the civil war; chief-of-staff of the I.R.A. (1936-37); founder and leader of the republican party Clann na Poblachta (1946-65); T.D. (1947-1957), Minister for Foreign Affairs (1948-51); U.N. commissioner for Namibia (1973-75); chairman of Amnesty International 1973-76; awarded Nobel Prize for Peace (1974) and Lenin Peace Prize (1978). Died 1988.

McCracken, Henry Joy born Belfast, 1767; Presbyterian and founding member of the United Irishmen. Led the United Irishmen rebellion in Antrim in 1798, captured and hanged on July 17, 1798.

MacMurchada, Diarmait born Wicklow, 1110; king of Leinster; banished by high king Ruaidrí Ua Conchobair in 1166; solicited help from Henry II of England; succeeded in attracting Richard de Clare to Ireland by offering him his daughter in marriage and succession to the kingship of Leinster. Died 1171.

MacNeill, Eoin born Antrim, 1867; co-founder of the Gaelic League (1893) and Irish Volunteers (1913); T.D. (1918-27); Minister for Education (1922-25). Irish representative to the Boundary Commission (1924-25) but resigned. Noted Gaelic scholar. Died 1945.

Markevicz, Countess Constance born London, 1868;

founded Na Fianna,1909; member of the Citizen's Army; sentenced to death but pardoned for her role in the 1916 Rising; T.D. (1918-22 & 1923-27); first female elected to House of Commons (1918); Minister for Labour in Dáil Éireann (1919-22); founding member of Fianna Fáil. Died 1927.

Ó Ceallaigh, Seán T.[2] born Dublin, 1882; President of Ireland (1945-59). Died 1966.

O'Connell, Daniel *'The Liberator'* born Kerry, 1775; founded Catholic Association in 1823 to lobby for Catholic Emancipation which was achieved in 1829. In 1828, became first Roman Catholic elected to the House of Commons. Lobbied for the repeal of the Act of Union but was unsuccessful. Died 1847.

Ó Dalaigh, Cearbhall[2] born Wicklow, 1911; President of Ireland (1974-76). Died 1978.

O'Donnell, Red Hugh born Donegal, circa 1571; inaugurated Chief of O'Donnell Clan in 1592. Allied with Hugh O'Neill, he engaged in the 'Nine Years' War'. Left Ireland after the Battle of Kinsale in 1602 to obtain further Spanish aid, but was poisoned at the Spanish court, died 1602.

O'Duffy, Eoin Born Monaghan, 1892; Garda Commissioner (1922-33); previously Chief-of-Staff of the Free State Army. Founded the Army Comrades Association (Blueshirts) in 1932; founding member and first leader of Fine Gael (1933-34). Leader of an Irish Brigade (1936-38) which fought in the Spanish civil war on the side of General Franco's fascists. Died 1944.

O'Higgins, Kevin born Laois, 1892; T.D. (1918-27); supported Anglo-Irish Treaty; Minister for Justice in first Free State government, 77 anti-treaty I.R.A. members were executed in reprisals by this government during the civil war. Influential in establishing the Garda Síochana, he was assassinated on July 10, 1927.

O'Malley, Grace born Mayo, circa 1530; legendary pirate queen along the Mayo coast. Died 1603.

O'Neill, Hugh born Tyrone, 1550; Earl of Tyrone and chief of the O'Neill Clan from 1583; his forces and the forces of Red Hugh O'Donnell engaged the English in the nine-years war culminating in his surrender and the Treaty of Mellifont in 1603. Unable to adapt to these new circumstances, he and other Gaelic chieftains fled Ireland in the 'Flight of Earls' in 1607.

O'Neill, Owen Roe born Tyrone, circa 1590; nephew of Hugh. Served with distinction in Spanish army; arrived in Ulster in 1642 and became military leader of the rebellion; recorded notable victory over Monro at Battle of Benburb; died 1649.

O'Neill, Terence[3] born London, 1914; Prime Minister of Northern Ireland (1963-69). Died 1990.

Parnell, Anna born Wicklow 1852; sister of Charles Stewart Parnell; established Ladies Land League in Ireland, January 1881; first radical female agitator in Irish history.

Parnell, Charles Stewart (the uncrowned king of Ireland) born Wicklow, 1846; leader of Home Rule Movement from 1877; leader of Irish Parliamentary Party (1880-90). Lobbied successfully in the House of Commons for land reform and successfully manoeuvred Irish public opinion in favour of Home Rule. Ousted from leadership of the I.P.P. in 1890 when cited as co-respondent in a divorce petition. Married divorcee Katharine O'Shea in 1891. Died October 1891.

St. Patrick, born Wales, foremost of Ireland's three patron saints. A missionary bishop, he arrived in 432 bringing Christianity to Ireland. Established See at Armagh. Died circa 460.

Pearse, Pádraig born Dublin, 1879; poet and veteran of 1916 Rising; founded the all-Irish Scoil Éanna, 1908; founding member of Irish Volunteers, 1913; member of the Irish Republican Brotherhood; Commander-in-Chief of the Volunteers during the Rising; President of the Provisional Government and signatory of Proclamation of the Republic; executed May 3, 1916.

Plunkett, Joseph Mary born Dublin, 1887; poet and veteran of 1916 Rising; member of Irish Republican Brotherhood and the Irish Volunteers; chief military strategist for the Volunteers during the Rising; signatory of Proclamation of the Republic; executed May 4, 1916.

Redmond, John born Wexford, 1856; M.P. (1881-1918); leader of Irish Parliamentary Party (1900-18). A major figure in the passage of the 1912 Home Rule Bill; he called in 1914 on the Irish Volunteers to join British Army - almost 200,000 did. Died 1918.

Sarsfield, Patrick born Dublin. Jacobite, Brigadier General in army of James II. Signed the Treaty of Limerick which allowed him and his men safe passage to join James in France. Killed at Battle of Landen 1693.

Tandy, James Napper born Dublin 1740; founding member of United Irishmen; leader of French expeditionary force in 1798 which landed in Donegal but retreated; captured and sentenced to death; Napoleon demanded and obtained his extradition in 1802; died Bordeaux, 1803.

Wolfe Tone, Theobald born Dublin, 1763; founding member of the Society of United Irishmen in 1791; solicited French aid for the 1798 rebellion. Captured at Buncrana, he was found guilty of treason and sentenced to be hanged. Committed suicide while awaiting execution.

GOVERNORS GENERAL OF THE IRISH FREE STATE

Timothy Healy	1922-28
James MacNeill	1928-32
Domhnall Ua Buachalla*	1932-37

The office of Governor General was provided for by Article 3 of the 1921 Anglo Irish Treaty. Its function was to represent the Crown in the Free State. It was formally abolished in 1936 by the External Relations Act.

*Ua Buachalla was merely a figurehead, his only function being to sign bills presented by the government. He did not reside in the official residence, and he was referred to as 'Seanascal' - translation: high steward - rather than Governor General.

LORD LIEUTENANTS AND CHIEF SECRETARIES, 1800-1922

LORD LIEUTENANTS

The Lord Lieutenant was the monarch's representative in Ireland and was, in theory, responsible for the administration of civilian government, as well as the control of military forces. In practice, however, the real power was vested in the office of the Chief Secretary.

1800-1801	Lord Cornwallis
1801-1806	3rd Earl of Hardwicke
1806-1807	6th Earl of Bedford
1807-1813	4th Duke of Richmond
1813-1817	Viscount Whitworth
1817-1821	1st Earl Talbot of Hensol
1821-1828	Richard Colley Wellesley
1828-1829	1st Marquess of Anglesey
1829-1830	3rd Duke of Northumberland
1830-1833	1st Marquess of Anglesey
1833-1834	Richard Colley Wellesley
1834-1835	9th Earl of Haddington
1835-1839	2nd Earl of Mulgrave
1839-1841	Chichester Fortescue-Parkinson
1841-1844	Thomas Philip de Gray, 1st Earl
1844-1846	2nd Baron Heytesbury
1846-1847	4th Earl of Bessborough
1847-1852	4th Earl of Clarendon
1852-1853	13th Earl of Eglinton
1853-1855	3rd Earl of St. Germans
1855-1858	7th Earl of Carlisle
1858-1859	13th Earl of Eglinton
1859-1864	7th Earl of Carlisle
1864-1866	John Wodehouse, 1st Earl of Kimberley
1866-1868	1st Duke of Abercorn
1868-1874	John Poyntz Spencer, 5th Earl
1874-1876	1st Duke of Abercorn
1876-1880	7th Duke of Marlborough
1880-1882	7th Earl of Cowper
1882-1885	John Poyntz Spencer, 5th Earl
1885-1886	4th Earl of Carnarvon
1886-1886	1st Marquess of Aberdeen
1886-1889	6th Marquess of Londonderry
1889-1892	3rd Earl of Zetland
1892-1895	1st Marquess of Crewe
1895-1902	5th Earl of Cadogan
1902-1905	2nd Earl of Dudley
1905-1915	1st Marquess of Aberdeen
1915-1918	2nd Baron Wimborne
1918-1921	1st Earl French of Ypres
1921-1922	1st Viscount FitzAlan of Derwent

In December 1922, the powers of the Lord Lieutenant were transferred to the Governor General of the Irish Free State, Timothy Healy, who was sworn in on December 6, 1922. The Duke of Abercorn was sworn in as the first Governor of Northern Ireland on December 12, 1922.

CHIEF SECRETARIES

The Chief Secretary was the de facto head of the Irish Executive after the Act of Union 1800. Usually an M.P., the functions of his office were carried out from Westminster. He was responsible for the implementation United Kingdom government policy and controlled the Irish Civil Service and the Royal Irish Constabulary.

1800-1801	Lord Castlereagh
1801-1802	Charles Abbot
1802-1804	William Wickham
1804-1805	Sir Evan Nepean
1805-1805	Sir Nicholas Vansittart
1805-1806	Charles Lang
1806-1807	William Elliot
1807-1809	Arthur Wellesley
1809-1812	William Wellesley-Pole
1812-1818	Sir Robert Peel
1818-1821	Charles Grant
1821-1827	Henry Goulbourn
1827-1828	William Lamb
1828-1830	Francis Levenson Gower
1830-1830	Sir Henry Hardinge
1830-1833	Lord Stanley
1833-1833	Sir John Cam Hobhouse
1833-1834	Edward John Littleton
1834-1835	Sir Henry Hardinge
1835-1841	Viscount Morpeth
1841-1845	Lord Eliot
1845-1846	Baron Cottosloe
1846-1846	Earl of Lincoln
1846-1847	Henry Labouchere
1847-1852	Sir William Somerville
1852-1853	Lord Naas
1853-1855	Sir John Young
1855-1857	Edward Horsman
1857-1858	Henry A. Herbert
1858-1859	Lord Naas
1859-1861	Edward Cardwell
1861-1865	Sir Robert Peel
1865-1866	Chichester Fortescue-Parkinson
1866-1868	Lord Naas
1868-1868	Lord Winmarleigh
1868-1870	Lord Carlingford
1870-1874	Marquis of Hartington
1874-1878	Sir Michael E. Hicks-Beach
1878-1880	James Lowther
1880-1882	W. E. Forster
1882-1882	Lord Freederick Cavendish
1882-1884	Sir G. O. Trevelyan
1884-1885	Henry Campbell-Bannerman
1885-1886	Sir W. Hart Dyke
1886-1886	W. H. Smith
1886-1886	John Morley
1886-1887	Sir M. E. Hicks-Beach
1887-1891	Arthur J. Balfour
1891-1892	William Lawless Jackson
1892-1895	John Morley
1895-1900	Gerald W. Balfour
1900-1905	George Wyndham
1905-1905	Walter Hume Long
1905-1907	James Bryce
1907-1916	Augustine Birrell
1916-1918	H. E. Duke
1918-1919	Edward Shortt
1919-1920	Ian McPherson
1920	Sir Hamar Greenwood

The powers of the Chief Secretary were superseded by those of the Chairman of the Provisional Government, Michael Collins, on January 16, 1922, and by those of the Prime Minister of Northern Ireland, James Craig, on June 7, 1921.

WHO WAS WHO

Alexander, Cecil Frances (born Dublin, 1818) hymn composer; most famous hymns are *All Things Bright and Beautiful* and *Once in Royal David's City*. Died 1895.

Alexander, Harold R. (born Tyrone, 1891) British army officer during both World Wars, promoted to Field Marshal in 1944. Governor-General of Canada (1946-52); elevated to the peerage 1959. Died 1969.

Andrews, Eamon (born Dublin, 1922) broadcaster; best known for presenting *This is Your Life* and *The Eamon Andrews Show*. Died 1987.

Andrews, Thomas (born 1813) established the composition of ozone. Died 1885.

Ashe, Thomas (born Kerry, 1885) veteran of 1916 Rising; force fed, he died on hunger strike 1917.

Auchinleck, Claude (born Tyrone, 1884) served as a British army officer in World War I; a general during World War II; promoted to field-marshal 1946. Died 1981.

Bacon, Sir Francis (born Dublin, 1909) famous painter. Died 1992

Balfe, Michael (born Dublin 1808) opera composer and violinist. Wrote many operas including *The Bohemian Girl*, (1843) and the music to La Scala's ballet, *La Perouse*. Died 1870.

Ballance, John (born Antrim, 1839) Prime Minister of New Zealand (1891-93). Died 1893.

Barnardo, Thomas (born Dublin, 1845) established Dr. Barnardo's homes for homeless children in 1867. Died 1905.

Barry, Kevin (born Dublin, 1902) member of I.R.A.; captured and hanged November 1920.

Barry, Tom (born Cork, 1897) I.R.A. 'flying column' leader during War of Independence. Died 1980.

Barton, Robert (born Wicklow, 1881) signatory of the Anglo-Irish Treaty. Died 1975.

Beckett, Samuel - *See Famous Irish Writers*

Behan, Brendan - *See Famous Irish Writers*

Beresford, John G. (born Dublin, 1773) Church of Ireland Archbishop of Armagh and Primate of All Ireland (1822-62). Died 1862.

Bergin, Osborn (born Cork, 1873) gaelic scholar and professor of Early and Medieval Irish at U.C.D. Died 1950.

Bernard, John Henry (born Wicklow, 1860) Church of Ireland Archbishop of Dublin (1915-27) and Provost of Trinity College (1919-27). Died 1927.

Beaufort, Francis (born Meath, 1774) devised the *Beaufort Scale* of wind measurement. Died 1857.

Berkeley, George (born Kilkenny, 1685) Church of Ireland Bishop of Cloyne (1734-52); established the philosophical theory of 'immaterialism': things exist only in the mind and knowledge is restricted to what can be perceived. Died 1753.

Biggar, Joseph (born Belfast, 1828) member of Irish Parliamentary Party (1874-90) and noted obstructionist. Died 1890.

Black, Joseph (born Bordeaux (of Belfast parents) 1728) established many of the basic principles of modern chemistry. Died 1799.

Blackburn, Helen (born Kerry, 1842) influential figure in the Women's Suffrage movement in Victorian England. Died London, 1903.

Blackham, Dorothy (born Dublin, 1896) noted artist. Died 1975.

Blaney, Neil T. (born Donegal, 1922) T.D. (1948-95); M.E.P. (1979-84 & 1989-94); held various ministries in Fianna Fáil governments. Charged with gunrunning in 1970 but had charges dismissed; independent T.D. from 1971. Died 1995.

Blythe, Ernest (born Antrim, 1889) M.P. and T.D. (1918-33); held various ministries in Cumann na nGaedheal governments; life long supporter of the restoration of the Irish language. Died 1975.

Boycott, Captain Charles Cunningham (born 1832) gave the verb 'boycott' to the English Language. In 1873, tenants of the Mayo estate, where he was a land agent, protested at his refusal to reduce rents by refusing to work the land, leaving crops to rot in the soil. Died 1897.

Boyle, Robert (born Waterford, 1627) pioneer of modern chemistry; Boyle's Law is: the volume of gas is inversely proportional to its pressure at a constant temperature. Died 1691.

Bracken, Thomas Irish born poet who wrote the National Anthem of New Zealand - *God Save New Zealand*.

Brendan, St. (born in Kerry, c.484) 'Brendan the Navigator'. Believed to have discovered America between 535 and 553. Died 578.

Brennan, Robert (born Wexford, 1881) leader of 1916 Rising in Wexford. Irish Ambassador to the United States during World War Two. Died 1964.

Brigid, St. (born Louth, mid 5th century). Patron saint who founded religious house in Kildare. Her feast day is February 1st, marked throughout Ireland, by the construction of crosses made from rushes. Died c. 525.

Brontë, Patrick (born Co. Down, 1777) his daughters were the famous writers Charlotte, Emily and Anne. Died 1861.

Brown, William (born Mayo, 1777) veteran of the Royal Navy; founder of the Argentine navy in 1813. Died 1857.

Browne, Noël (born Waterford, 1915) T.D. (1948-82); Minister at centre of controversial 'mother and child scheme' in 1951. Died 1997.

Browning, Miciaih (born Derry) his vessel ended the Siege of Derry (1689) by breaking the boom across the Foyle. Died 1689.

Broy, Eamonn (born Kildare, 1887) Garda Commissioner (1932-38); enlisted former I.R.A. members (the Broy Harriers) to counter the Blueshirts. Died 1972.

Brugha, Cathal (born Dublin, 1874) veteran of 1916 Rising; T.D. (1918-22); Minister for Defence(1919-22); fought with anti-treaty forces during the civil war. Killed 1922.

Bull, Lucien (born Dublin, 1876) invented electrocardiograph (1908). Died 1972.

Burke, Edmund (born Dublin, 1729) M.P. (1765-97); author of *Reflections on the Revolution in France* (1790) which condemned the revolution; advocated reform of the penal laws and Irish self government. Died 1797.

Callan, Fr. Nicholas (born in Dundalk 1799) Invented the induction coil (fore-runner of modern transformer). Died 1864.

Ceannt, Eamonn (born Galway, 1881) veteran of 1916 Rising and signatory of the Proclamation of the Republic. Executed by firing squad May 8, 1916.

Childers, Robert Erskine (born London, 1870) veteran of Boer war; involved in Howth gun-running in 1914; served in the British navy during World War I; secretary to the Irish delegation at Anglo-Irish treaty negotiations; executed by Free State authorities November 1922.

Clarke, Austin - See famous Irish writers.

Clarke, Thomas (born Isle of Wight, 1857) veteran of 1916 Rising and signatory of the Proclamation of the Republic. Executed May 3, 1916.

Connell, Jim (born Meath c.1850) Wrote the famous socialist song 'The Red Flag'. Died 1929

Conway, William (born Belfast, 1913) Roman Catholic Archbishop of Armagh and Primate of All Ireland from 1963, created Cardinal 1965. Died 1977.

Cooke, Henry (born Derry, 1788) moderator of Presbyterian General Assembly (1841 & 1862); vociferous opponent of Repeal and the disestablishment of the Church of Ireland. Died 1868.

Cousins, Margaret (born Roscommon, 1878) major figure in Irish suffragette movement; emigrated to India 1915 where she became that country's first female magistrate. Died 1954.

Croke, Thomas W. (born Cork, 1824) Roman Catholic Archbishop of Cashel from 1875 and Patron of the Gaelic Athletic Association who named their Jones' Road headquarters after him. Died Cashel,1902.

Crozier, Francis (born Co. Down, 1796) naval explorer; died while searching for the North-West Passage in 1848.

Cullen, Paul (born Kildare 1803) Ireland's first Cardinal. Archbishop of Armagh (1850-52), Archbishop of Dublin from 1852. Founded Catholic University (1854) and Clonliffe College (1859). Primate of All-Ireland from June 1866 until his death. Died 1878.

Cusack, Cyril (born Keyna, 1910) famous stage and screen actor; gained an Oscar nomination in 1952; famous movies include 'The Blue Veil' and 'Day of the Jackal'. Also remembered for his television roles in 'Strumpet City' and 'Glenroe'. Died 1993.

Cusack, Michael (born Clare, 1847) Founding member of the GAA in 1884, a stand is named after him in Croke Park. Died Dublin, 1906.

D'Alton, John (born Mayo, 1883) Roman Catholic Archbishop of Armagh and Primate of All Ireland from 1946, created Cardinal 1953. Died 1963.

D'Arcy, Charles F. (born Dublin, 1859) Church of Ireland Archbishop of Armagh and Primate of All Ireland (1920-38). Died 1938.

Davis, Thomas (born Cork, 1814) Young Irelander and founding member of its newspaper 'The Nation'. A noted poet, he wrote 'A Nation Once Again' and 'The West's Awake'. Died 1845.

Davitt, Michael (born Mayo, 1846) Founding member of the Irish National Land League in 1879. Imprisoned in England as a Fenian in 1870, released in 1877. Died Dublin, 1906.

Dease, William (born Cavan, 1750) founded Royal College of Surgeons in Dublin 1784. Died 1798.

Devoy, John (born Kildare, 1842) member of Irish Republican Brotherhood; later an influential figure in the republican American group Clan na Gael; raised finance for republican groups in Ireland including the Irish Volunteers and Sinn Féin. Died 1928.

Dill, Sir John (born Armagh, 1881) veteran of the Boer War and World War I; Field Marshal and Chief of Staff of the British army 1940. Died 1944.

Dillon, James (born Wexford,1902) T.D. (1932-69); Minister for Agriculture (1948-51 & 1954-57); leader of Fine Gael (1959-65). Died 1986.

Dempsey, Jack - See Sports Who Was Who

Devlin, Joe (born Belfast, 1871) M.P. (1902-34) at Westminster and Stormont; Member of Irish Parliamentary Party; president of Ancient Order of Hibernians (1905-34). Died 1934.

Dillon, John (born Dublin, 1851) M.P. (1885-1918); exponent of Home Rule and leading figure in Irish Parliamentary Party. Died 1927.

Donnelly, Charles (born Tyrone, 1910) poet who fought and died with the 15th International Brigade in the Spanish Civil War. Died 1937.

Dowland, John (born Dublin, 1562) Composer and lutenist to Royal Courts at Copenhagen and London. Wrote three volumes of 'Books of Songs or Ayres'. Died 1626.

Doyle, Jack - See Sports Who Was Who

Duffy, Charles Gavan (born Monaghan, 1816) member of Young Ireland movement; co-founded The Nation in 1842; Prime Minister of Victoria, Australia (1871-72); knighted 1873. Died 1903.

Duggan, Eamonn (born Meath, 1874) T.D. (1918-33); signatory of Anglo-Irish Treaty. Died 1936.

Dunlap, John (born Tyrone, 1747) founded the first daily newspaper in North America, the Pennsylvania Packet; was first to print the Declaration of Independence. Died 1812.

Dunlop, John (born Scotland, 1840) moved to Belfast in 1860s, produced the first pneumatic tyre. Died 1921.

Elliot, Shay - See Sports Who Was Who

Fair, James G. (born Tyrone, 1831) gold prospector in California; founded Bank of Nevada; American Senator (1881-87). Died 1894.

Farley, John (born Armagh, 1842) Archbishop of New York (1902-18), created Cardinal 1911. Died 1918.

Farquhar, George (born Derry, 1678) playwright; most famous plays are The Recruiting Officer and The Beaux Stratagem. Died 1707.

Ferguson, Harry (born Co. Down, 1884) invented the hydraulically controlled plough (1939); set up the Ferguson company to produce tractors in 1947. Died 1960.

Field, John (born Dublin, 1782) Composer of seven concerts and four sonatas and pioneer of the nocturne in 1814 which influenced composers in later years. Spent most of his life in Russia where he died in 1837.

Fitzmaurice, James C. (born Dublin, 1898) veteran of World War I; subsequently officer in the Irish Air Corps; accompanied by two Germans he completed the first east-west crossing of the atlantic by air in 1928. Died 1965.

Flanagan, John J - See Sports Who Was Who

Flood, Henry (born Kilkenny, 1732) M.P. in Irish House of Commons, leader of Patriot Party which agitated for legislative independence. Died 1791.

Fowke, Francis (born Antrim 1823) Designed the Royal Albert Hall in London and the National Gallery of Ireland in Dublin. Died 1865.

French, Percy (born Roscommon, 1854) singer/songwriter; most famous compositions are '*The Mountains of Mourne*' and '*Are ye Right there Michael*' Died 1920.

Gallaher, David (born Donegal, 1873) first captain of the New Zealand All-Blacks. A soldier during World War I he was killed in 1917.

Gallagher, Pat 'the Cope' (born Donegal, 1873) set up an extremely successful co-operative society in Dungloe; senior figure in the Irish Agricultural Organisation Society. Died 1964.

Gandon, James (born London, 1743) Architect who designed some of the finest buildings in nineteenth century Dublin, including the Custom House, the Four Courts and Kings Inn. Died Dublin, 1823.

Glendy, John (born Derry, 1778) Presbyterian minister and member of United Irishmen; emigrated to the U.S. and became a Commodore in the U.S. navy. Died 1832.

Gough, Sir Hubert de la Poer (born Waterford, 1870) veteran of the Boer war; served as Lieutenant-General during World War One. Died 1963.

Graves, Thomas (born Derry 1747) Admiral in the British navy (1812-14). Died 1814.

Gregg, John (born Monaghan 1867) stenographer, his method of shorthand is widely used. Died 1948.

Guinness, Arthur (born Kildare, 1725) founded Guinness brewery at St James' Gate in 1759. Died 1803.

Halpin, Captain Robert Charles (born Wicklow, 1836) laid first transatlantic cable (completed 1866) Valentia to Newfoundland. Died 1894.

Hamilton, Gustavus (born Fermanagh, 1639) founded the 'Enniskilleners'- a Williamite regiment; fought at the Battle of the Boyne; elevated to the peerage by George I. Died 1723.

Harland, Edward (born Yorkshire, 1831) established Harland and Wolff shipyard in Belfast in 1862. M.P. (1889-95). Died 1895.

Harrison, Celia (born Co. Down, 1863) painter and advocate for women's rights. Died 1941.

Healy, Cahir (born Donegal, 1877) nationalist representative at Stormont from 1925-65 for Fermanagh South and MP for Fermanagh and South Tyrone 1950-55 at Westminster. Died 1970

Healy, Timothy (born Cork, 1855) M.P. (1880-1918). Governor-General of Irish Free State (1922-28). Died 1931.

Hennessy, Richard (born Cork, 1720) fought with Irish regiments on continental Europe. Founded the Hennessy Brandy distillery in 1763. Died 1800

Henry, Paul (born Belfast,1877) landscape artist. Died 1958.

Hill, Wills (born Co. Down, 1718) minister in various British governments; became Marquis of Downshire in 1789; rebuilt Hillsborough castle. Died 1793.

Hincks, Francis (born Belfast, 1807) Prime Minister of Canada (1851-54); subsequently Governor of Barbados. Died 1885.

Hobart, Henry (born Co. Down, 1858) noted Ulster architect. Died 1938.

Hobson, Bulmer (born Co. Down 1883) founded the Dungannon Clubs (1905); founding member of Fianna Éireann (1909); member of the Irish Republican Brotherhood but opposed the 1916 Rising. Died 1969.

Hobson, Florence (born Kildare, 1881) Ireland's first female architect (qualified 1893).

Hone, Evie (born Dublin, 1894) overcame poor health to become one of the foremost stained glass artists of the twentieth century. Died 1955.

Horan, James (born Mayo, 1912) parish priest at Knock, Co. Mayo (1967-86); built a new 10,000 capacity basilica; hosted Pope John Paul II on his trip to Ireland in 1979; driving force behind the building of Knock airport (completed 1986). Died 1986.

Hughes, Desmond (born Belfast, 1919) fighter pilot; veteran of World War Two; deputy commander of British forces in Cyprus (1972-74). Died 1992.

Hughes, John (born Tyrone, 1797) first Roman Catholic Archbishop of New York (1850-64). Died 1864.

Hussey, Thomas (born Meath, 1741) noted for his diplomatic skills in the service of George III in continental Europe. First president of Maynooth College and later Bishop of Waterford and Lismore. Died 1803.

Ingram, Rex (born Dublin, 1893) film director whose credits include '*The Four Horsemen of the Apocalypse*' and '*Under Crimson Skies*'. Died 1950.

Jervas, Charles (born Offaly, c.1675) Member of the Courts of George I and II of England. He was the official portrait artist. Died 1739.

Jones, Les manager of the British Olympic team at the 1992 Barcelona Olympics. Died 1992.

Joyce, James - *see Famous Irish Writers*

Kane, Richard (born Antrim, 1666) Governor of Gibraltar and Minorca (1720-25). Died 1736.

Kavanagh, Patrick - *see Famous Irish Writers*

Kearney, Peadar (born Dublin, 1883) wrote the words to the Irish national anthem, '*Amhrán na bhFiann*'; veteran of 1916 Rising. Died 1942.

Kennedy, Arthur (born Co. Down, 1810) Governor of Hong Kong (1872-77) and Queensland (1877-83). Died 1883.

Kennedy, Jimmy (born Tyrone, 1902) wrote the songs '*The Hokey Cokey*', '*Red Sails in the Sunset*', '*South of the Border, Down Mexico Way*' and '*The Teddy Bear's Picnic*'. Died 1984.

Kernohan, Joseph (born Derry, 1869) founded Presbyterian Historical Society (1906). Died 1923.

Killen, William (born Antrim 1806) ordained 1829, President of the Presbyterian College Belfast in 1870s. Died 1902.

King, William (born Antrim, 1850) Church of Ireland Archbishop of Derry (1690-1703); Archbishop of Dublin (1703-1729). Died 1729.

Lamb, Charles (born Armagh, 1893) landscape painter and member of the Royal Hibernian Academy. Died 1964.

Lane, Hugh (born Cork, 1875) art dealer whose spurned offer of paintings to the Dublin Municipal gallery is recalled in Yeats's poem '*September 1913*'. Died when the Lusitania was torpedoed on May 7, 1915.

Larkin, Jim (born Liverpool, 1876) founding member of Irish Transport and General Workers Union (1908);

charismatic workers' leader during the Dublin Lock-out (1913-14); founded Workers' Union of Ireland (1924); T.D. (1928-32, 1937-38 & 1943-44). Died 1947.

Lavery, Sir John (born Belfast, 1856) noted artist. Famous works include portrait of his wife, Hazel (used on Irish banknotes for half a century) and Michael Collins lying in state. Knighted in 1918. Died 1941.

Le Mesurier McClure, Robert John (born Wexford,1807) Discovered the North-west Passage (i.e. the link between the Pacific and Atlantic via the Arctic Ocean). Died 1873.

Lenihan, Brian (born Louth, 1930) T.D. (1961-73 & 1977-95); M.E.P. (1973-79); held various ministries in Fianna Fáil governments. Defeated candidate in 1990 Presidential election. Died 1995.

Lester, Seán (born Antrim, 1888) Irish Free State representative to League of Nations; appointed Acting Secretary General of the League in 1040. Died 1959.

Logan, James (born Armagh, 1674) appointed Governor of Pennsylvania 1736. Died 1751.

Logue, Michael (born Donegal, 1840) Archbishop of Armagh (1887-1924), created Cardinal 1893. Died 1924.

Lundy, Robert Governor of Derry when King James and his army lay siege to the city in 1689. Was removed from office by the citizens of Derry when he suggested surrender to the besiegers. Lundy escaped but was later imprisoned in the Tower of London. His effigy is burned annually at celebrations commemorating the relief of the siege.

Lyons, F.S.L. (born Derry, 1923) Provost of Trinity College (1974-81); historian and author of *Ireland Since the Famine* and *John Dillon*, a biography. Died 1983.

McAuley, Catherine (born Dublin, 1778) nun who founded the Sisters of Mercy in 1831. The Sisters of Mercy have been responsible for educating hundreds of thousands of Irish students. Her portrait is on the current five pound note. Died 1841.

MacBride, John (born Mayo 1865) he fought in the Boer War against the British. He fought in the 1916 Rising and was executed on May 5 1916.

MacBride, Maud Gonne (born Aldershot, 1865) renowned beauty with whom W.B. Yeats was besotted. A fervent nationalist she married John MacBride, 1903. Died 1953.

McCormack, John (born Athlone, 1884) world famous tenor. Created a papal Count in 1928. Died 1945.

McCormick, Liam (born Derry, 1916) internationally acclaimed church architect. Died 1996.

McCracken, Henry Joy (born Belfast, 1767) founding member of the Society of United Irishmen (1791); Leader of United Irishmen uprising in Antrim in 1798. Hanged 1798.

MacDiarmada, Seán (born Leitrim, 1884) veteran of 1916 Rising; member of Irish Republican Brotherhood and Irish Volunteers; re-organised the I.R.B. in the years before the Rising; signatory of the Proclamation of the Republic; executed May 12, 1916.

MacDonagh, Thomas (born Tipperary, 1878) poet and veteran of 1916 Rising; senior figure in the Irish Volunteers, member of Irish Republican Brotherhood; signatory of the Proclamation of the Republic; executed May 3, 1916.

MacEoin, Seán (born Longford, 1893) the most successful guerrilla leader in the War of Independence he supported the Treaty and became Chief of Staff of the Free State army. He was later a Government Minister in two Coalition Governments. Died 1973.

MacHale, John (born Mayo, 1791) Archbishop of Tuam from 1834 until his death. An outspoken nationalist he enthusiastically backed Catholic Emancipation, Repeal of the Union and Land Reform. Died 1881.

McKenzie, John (born Tyrone, 1648) Presbyterian minister who survived the Siege of Derry and published his account of it in 1690, *'Narrative of the Siege of Londonderry'*. Died 1696.

McManus, Seamus (1869-1960) - *see Famous Irish Writers*

McNally, Ray (born Donegal, 1925) stage and screen actor; starred in films such as *'Cal'*, *'The Mission'*, and *'My Left Foot'*. Died 1989.

MacNeill, James (born Antrim, 1869) Governor-General of Irish Free State (1928-32). Died 1938.

McNamara, Kevin (born Clare, 1926) Roman Catholic Archbishop of Dublin (1985-87).

McQuaid, John Charles (born Cavan, 1895) Roman Catholic Archbishop of Dublin (1940-72); despite his good record on social issues he was perceived as the most influential and conservative member of the Catholic hierarchy. Died 1973.

MacRory, Joseph (born Tyrone, 1861) Roman Catholic Archbishop of Armagh and Primate of All Ireland (1928-45), created Cardinal 1929. Died 1945.

MacSwiney, Terence (born Cork, 1879) prominent member of the Irish Volunteers; elected Lord Mayor of Cork in 1920; imprisoned in August 1920 he commenced a hunger strike and died after 74 days.

Mackey, Mick - *See Sports Who Was Who*

Mallet, Robert (born Dublin, 1810) Pioneer of Seismology (the study and measurement of earthquakes). Died 1881.

Matthew, Fr Theobald (born Tipperary, 1790) formed a temperance society in 1838, a forerunner of the current Pioneer Total Abstinence Association. Died 1856.

Meagher, Thomas Francis (born Waterford, 1823) deported to Van Diemen's land for his part in the abortive Rising of 1848 he escaped and went to the United States where he became a General in the Union Army in the American Civil War and later Governor of Montana. Died 1867.

Moore, Thomas (born Dublin, 1779) Poet and socialite, most notably in London. Published many works, including his *Irish Melodies* between 1807 and 1834. Died 1852.

Moran, D.P. (born Waterford, 1871) founder and editor of the *Leader* renowned for its fierce nationalist tone. Died 1936.

Mulcahy, Richard (born Waterford, 1886) veteran of 1916 Rising; Chief-of-Staff of I.R.A.; fought with the Free State forces during the civil war becoming Commander-in-Chief following the death of Michael Collins; T.D. (1918-37, 1938-43 & 1944-61); member of Cumann na nGaedheal and Fine Gael he served in various government ministries. Died 1971.

Murphy, Fr. John (born Wexford, 1753) Leader of Rising of 1798. Led the rebellion against British, taking the towns of Enniscorthy, Wexford and Ferns. Captured by the British following defeats at Arklow and Vinegar

Hill, and hanged. Died 1798.

Murphy, William Martin (born Cork 1844) M.P. (1885-92); founded *Irish Independent* (1905); led the employers' federation during the 1913 Dublin Lock-out. Died 1919.

Newman, Alec (born Waterford, 1905) editor of *The Irish Times* 1954-61. Died 1972.

Ó Buachalla, Domhnall (born Kildare, 1866) veteran of 1916 Rising; Governor-General of the Irish Free State (1932-37). Died 1963.

O'Callaghan, Dr. Pat - *See Sports Who Was Who*

O'Casey, Sean - *see Famous Irish Writers*

Ó Cléirigh, Mícheál - *see Famous Irish Writers*

O'Dea, Jimmy (born Dublin 1899) comedian and actor, starred in the film '*Darby O'Gill and the Little People*'. Died 1965.

O'Doherty, Cahir (born Donegal, 1587) the last Irish Chieftain. He was killed in 1608 after attacking both Derry and Strabane.

O'Donnell, Peadar - *see Famous Irish Writers*

Ó Fiaich, Tomás (born Armagh, 1923) President of Maynooth College (1974-77); Roman Catholic Archbishop of Armagh and Primate of All Ireland (1977-90), created Cardinal 1979. Died 1990.

O'Growney, Fr Eugene (born Meath, 1863) a key figure in the revival of the Irish language in the last century he was vice-president of the Gaelic League from 1893 and Professor of Irish at Maynooth College 1891-96. Died 1899.

O'Hehir, Mícheál (born Dublin, 1920) legendary R.T.É. commentator on Gaelic games and horse-racing; commentated on 99 All Ireland finals between 1939 and 1984. Died 1996.

O'Malley, Donogh (born Limerick, 1921) T.D. (1954-68); as minister for education he introduced free post primary education in 1966. Died 1968.

O'Neill, Phelim (born 1604) leader of the 1641 Rising, he was executed for that role in 1653.

O'Nolan, Brian (born Tyrone, 1911) journalist, humourist, and novelist who used the pseudonyms Flann O'Brien and Myles na gCopaleen. Died 1966.

Ó Riada, Seán (born Cork, 1931) traditional music composer; remembered for the music score in the 1959 documentary *Mise Éire*. Died 1971.

O'Shea, Katharine (born Essex, 1845) the mistress of Charles Stewart Parnell she married him in 1891 after he had been ousted from the leadership of the Irish Parliamentary Party. Died 1921.

O'Shea, Captain William (born Dublin 1840) the first husband of Katharine O'Shea he cited Parnell as co-respondent in his divorce papers, precipitating Parnell's political fall. Home Rule MP for Clare 1880-5 and Galway 1885-6. Died 1905.

Ó hUiginn, Tadhg Dall (born Sligo, 1550) Bardic poet who dedicated his poems to the Gaelic lords in his surrounding area. Died 1591.

Parker, Dehra (born Derry, 1882) M.P. (1921-29 & 1933-60); Minister of Health (1949-57), the only woman to hold ministerial office in the Northern Ireland government. Died 1963.

Parsons, Charles (born Offaly, 1884) Invented turbine for use in ships. Died 1931.

Plunkett, Saint Oliver (born Meath, 1625) Archbishop of Armagh from 1669. Hanged, drawn and quartered in 1681 following spurious charges of involvement in a 'Popish Plot'. Canonised in 1975.

Reid, Nano (born Louth, 1905) noted landscape artist. Died 1981.

Rice, Edmund (born Kilkenny, 1762) founded his first school in 1803 in what was to be the beginning of the Christian Brothers. Pope Pius VII officially recognised the Christian Brothers in 1820 and Brother Ignatius as he was then known became Superior-General. Died 1844. Beatified in 1996.

Ring, Christy - *see Who Was Who Irish Sport*

Ryan, Frank (born Limerick, 1902) fought with anti-treaty I.R.A. during civil war; founded Saor Éire; led 200 Irish volunteers to fight with the socialists in the Spanish civil war (1936-37). Died 1944.

Sands, Bobby (born Belfast, 1954) I.R.A. man imprisoned in 1977; commenced hunger strike March 1, 1981 to regain political status; elected M.P. for Fermanagh & South Tyrone on April 9; died May 5, 1981 after 66 days without food.

Shanahan, Joseph (born Tipperary, 1871) Roman Catholic missionary priest to Nigeria from 1902; bishop in Nigeria (1920-31). Died 1943.

Shaw, George Bernard - *See Famous Irish Writers*

Sheridan, Marty - *See Sports Who Was Who*

Stack, Austin (born Kerry, 1879) captained Kerry's All-Ireland football winning team of 1904. Sinn Féin M.P. for Kerry from 1917, opposed Treaty and was imprisoned during the Civil War. Died 1929.

Stoker, Bram - *See Famous Irish Writers*

Synge, John Millington - *See Famous Irish Writers*

Talbot, Matthew (born Dublin, 1856) Took a pledge of total abstinence in 1884 following an early life of heavy drinking. Devoted himself to religion and good deeds. Died 1925 and conferred with the title Venerable by the Catholic Church in 1976.

Taylor, George (born 1716) member of American Continental Congress, he was a signatory of the American Declaration of Independence.

Thompson, William/Lord Kelvin (born Belfast 1824) Professor of Natural History at University of Glasgow. A leading scientist of Nineteenth Century. Main achievement was discovery of 2nd Law of Thermodynamics (Kelvin's absolute scale of temperature). Died 1907.

Yeats, Jack Butler (born London, 1871) noted artist. Famous works include *At the Galway Races, On Drumcliffe Strand* and *Memory Harbour*. Died 1957.

Yeats, William Butler - *see Famous Irish Writers*

Walker, Rev George (born Tyrone, 1618) Protestant minister who was joint governor of Derry during the siege (April - July 1689). Appointed bishop of Derry following the siege he was killed in battle in 1690.

Walton, Ernest T.S. (born Waterford, 1903) jointly awarded the Nobel Prize for Physics in 1951 with John Cockcroft for their work in splitting the atom. Invented the Cockcroft-Walton accelerator used in this procedure. Died 1995.

Wilde, Oscar - *See Famous Irish Writers*.

Listed below, in alphabetical order, are persons who are major decision makers or of serious influence in their particular sphere in society on the island of Ireland.

Adams, Gerry (born Belfast, 1949) President of Sinn Féin since 1983, Current M.P. for West Belfast.

Ahern, Bertie (born Dublin, 1951) Elected Taoiseach June 1997, Leader of Fianna Fáil since 1994, T. D. since 1977.

Alderdice, Lord John (born Antrim, 1955) Leader of the Alliance Party of Northern Ireland since 1987.

Allen, Rev. Dr. David Henry (born Down, 1933) Former Moderator of Presbyterian Church in Ireland (1996-97).

Anderson, Gerry (born Buncrana) Television and radio presenter with BBC, former showband musician with *The Chessman*.

Banotti, Mary (born Dublin, 1939) T.D. since 1982, and M.E.P. since 1984. Nominated Candidate for 1997 Presidential Elections.

Best, George (born Belfast, 1946) Midfielder. European Player of the Year (1968). Capped 37 times by Northern Ireland, Scored nine international goals.

Best, Rev. Kenneth Former President of Methodist Church in Ireland (1996-97), influential in negotiating Loyalist ceasefire in 1994.

Bhreatnach, Lucilita General Secretary of Sinn Féin and member of the Northern Ireland Forum.

Bird, Charlie RTÉ Special Correspondent, popular television reporter specialising in dramatic live reporting of current affairs as the story breaks.

Bono (Hewson, Paul) (born Dublin, 1960) Lead vocalist and lyricist with supergroup U2.

Boothman, Jack (born Wicklow) Former President of the Gaelic Athletic Association (1994-97).

Brady, Conor (born Offaly, 1949) Editor of *The Irish Times* since 1986, previously editor of the Sunday Tribune (1981-82).

Brady, Archbishop Sean (born Cavan, 1939) Roman Catholic Archbishop of Armagh and Primate of All Ireland since November 1996.

Branagh, Kenneth (born Belfast, 1960) Actor and film director noted for his film versions of Shakespeare.

Brosnan, Pierce (born Meath, 1952) Film and television actor, appearing in productions such as *Remington Steele* (1982), and films such as *Mrs. Doubtfire* (1993). Current James Bond.

Bruton, John (born Dublin, 1947) Former Taoiseach (1994-1997). Leader of Fine Gael since 1990.

Buckley, Michael (born 1945) Businessman, Managing Director of AIB Capital Markets, director on board of AIB and Chairman of the Remuneration Review Group for the Public sector.

Burke, Ray (born Dublin, 1943) Fianna Fáil T.D. since 1973. Appointed Minister for Foreign Affairs June 1997.

Byrne, Gabriel (born Dublin, 1950) Film and television actor, appearing in productions such as *The Riordans* and *Bracken*, and films such as *Into the West* (1991) and *The Usual Suspects* (1995.)

Byrne, Gay (born Dublin, 1934) Broadcaster, presenter and executive producer of *The Late Late Show* since 1962. Radio presenter of *The Gay Byrne Show* since 1972.

Byrne, Patrick (born Cork, 1945) Garda Commissioner since July 1996. Joined the Garda Siochána in 1965. Deputy Commissioner (1994-96).

Carey, D. J., (born Kilkenny, 1971) Hurling player. Captained the Kilkenny team in 1997. Won two All-Ireland Hurling medals and four All-Star Awards.

Casey, Bishop Eamon (born Kerry, 1927) Former Roman Catholic Bishop. Resigned in 1992 following the revelation that he had a son by American, Annie Murphy.

Cassells, Peter General Secretary of the Irish Congress of Trade Unions.

Cassidy, Angela (born Roscommon, 1955) Current President of the Civil and Public Service Union.

Clifford, Archbishop Dermot (born Kerry, 1939) Roman Catholic Archbishop of Cashel since 1986.

Collins, Tom Editor of *The Irish News.*

Connell, Archbishop Desmond (born 1926) Roman Catholic Archbishop of Dublin and Primate of Ireland since 1988.

Cooper, Matt Editor of *the Sunday Tribune.*

Cosgrave, Liam (born Dublin, 1920) Former Taoiseach (1973-77) and Leader of Fine Gael (1965-77).

Cosgrove, Dr. Art President of University College Dublin.

Costelloe, Paul (born Dublin, 1945) Fashion designer. Worked in Milan, Paris and New York, now working in Ireland and recognised worldwide as an successful designer.

Coulter, Phil (born Derry, 1942) Songwriter, composer and pianist. Wrote *The Town I Loved So Well,* and *Puppet on a String,* the 1968 winning Eurovision song for Sandie Shaw.

Curran, Edmund (born Tyrone, 1944) Editor of *The Belfast Telegraph* since 1993.

Daly, Cardinal Cahal (born Antrim, 1917) Former Cardinal and Archbishop of Armagh (1990-96).

Dana (Brown, Rosemary) (born Derry, 1951) first Irish winner of Eurovision Song Contest in 1970. Nominated Candidate for 1997 Presidential Elections.

Davis, Derek (born Down, 1949) R.T.É. presenter of shows such as *Live at Three and Davis.* Previously worked with the B.B.C. and A.B.C. as a news journalist.

Doherty, Moya (born Donegal, 1958) Former television producer. Promoter of *Riverdance,* Co-founder and on the board of directors of Radio Ireland.

Donaldson, Jeffrey (born 1963) Ulster Unionist M.P., Assistant Grand Master of the Orange Lodge of Ireland since 1994.

Downes, Margaret (born Mayo, 1934) Chairwoman of health insurance company BUPA (Ireland). Former Director of the Bank of Ireland.

Dunne, Ben (born Cork, 1949) Former Chief Executive at Dunnes Stores.

Dunphy, Eamon (born Dublin, 1945) Journalist and former footballer. Capped 23 times for the Republic of

Ireland. Currently working for the *Sunday Independent.*

Dunseith, David B.B.C. Northern Ireland presenter.

Eames, Archbishop Robert (born Belfast, 1937) Church of Ireland Archbishop of Armagh and Primate of All Ireland since 1986.

Empey, Reg (born Armagh, 1947) Current member of the Ulster Unionist Party and member of Belfast city council since 1985.

Empey, Archbishop Walton (born 1934) Church of Ireland Archbishop of Dublin and Primate of Ireland since 1996.

Ervine, David (born Belfast, 1953) Joined Progressive Unionist Party (1981), current spokesperson. Involved in the Loyalist Ceasefire of 1994.

Fanning, Aengus (born Kerry, 1943) Joined *Independent Newspapers* 1969. Editor of the *Sunday Independent* since 1984.

Fanning, Dave (born Dublin, 1955) Television and radio broadcaster. Presenter of 2TV and The Movie Show on television and a nightly show on 2FM.

Faul, Mgr. Denis (born Louth, 1932) Catholic priest. Prison chaplain at Long Kesh during the 1981 hunger strike. President of St. Patrick's Academy.

Finucane, Marian (born Dublin, 1950) R.T.É. radio and television presenter since 1974, presenter of *The Marian Finucane Show* on radio, and Co-presenter of *Crimeline* on television.

FitzGerald, Dr. Garrett (born Dublin,1926) Former Taoiseach (1981-82, 1982-87) and leader of Fine Gael (1977-87).

Fitzgerald, Maurice (born Kerry, 1970) Kerry Gaelic footballer. Winner of one All-Ireland Medal (1997), two All-Star Awards, Man of the Match in the 1997 All-Ireland Final.

Flanagan, Ronnie Appointed RUC Chief Constable in November 1996, joined RUC in 1970. Former positions have included Detective Superintendent (1987-90), Chief Superintendent (1990-92) and Assistant Chief Constable (1992-94).

Flannery O.P., Austin (born Tipperary, 1925) Religious editor and writer, entered Dominican Order (1943), Ordained Priest (1950), editor of the Dominican journal *Doctrine and Life* (1957-88).

Fricker, Brenda (born Dublin, 1944) Academy Award winning actress for *My Left Foot* (1988), she also had parts in *The Field* (1989) and television's *Casualty.*

Friel, Brian (born Tyrone, 1929) Dramatist, renowned for plays such as *Philadelphia, Here I Come!* (1964) and *Dancing at Lughnasa* (1990).

Gageby, Douglas (born Dublin, 1918) Editor of the *Evening Press* (1954), editor of *The Irish Times* (1963-74 and 1977-86).

Geldof, Bob (born Dublin, 1954) Founded rock group *The Boomtown Rats* in 1975, organised the 1984 recording *Do They Know it's Christmas* and the 1985 concert *Live Aid.*

Giles, Johnny (born Dublin, 1940) Midfielder. Capped 59 times (with a record 30 as captain) by the Republic. Player-manager from 1973-80.

Goan, Cathal (born Antrim, 1954) Ceannasaí (Head) of Teilifís na Gaeilge since 1996. Former radio producer for R.T.É.

Goodman, Larry (born Louth, 1939) Businessman. Involved in the meat processing industry. Chief Executive of Irish Food Processors

Greevy, Bernadette (born Dublin, 1940) Noted operatic singer. Sung at Pope's mass in Phoenix Park (1979).

Hamilton, The Hon. Mr. Liam (born Cork, 1928) High Court Judge since 1974. Current Chief Justice of the Supreme Court since 1994.

Hanifin, Des (born Tipperary, 1930) Senator (1969-92). Leading figure in Anti-Divorce and Pro-Life organisations.

Hanlon, Noel (born Longford, 1940) Former factory owner and car dealer. Current Chairman of VHI and Aer Rianta since 1992 and Great Southern Hotels since 1995.

Harney, Mary (born Galway, 1953) Tánaiste and Minister for Enterprise, Trade and Employment since June 1997. Leader of Progressive Democrats since 1993.

Haughey, Charles (born Mayo, 1925) former Taoiseach (1979-81, 1982, 1987-92) and Leader of Fianna Fáil (1979-92).

Hayes, Liam (born Meath, 1962) Former Meath inter-County Gaelic footballer (1981-92), and winner of two All-Ireland Football medals (1987, 1988). Current Editor of *Ireland on Sunday.*

Heaney, Seamus (born Derry, 1939) Poet, renowned for poems such as *Wintering Out* (1972) *Station Island* (1985). Won the Nobel Prize for Literature in 1995.

Heffernan, Margaret (born Cork,1944) Chief Executive of Dunnes stores.

Hume, M.P., M.E.P., John (born Derry, 1937) Founding member (1970) and Leader of Social Democratic and Labour Party since 1979.

Hurley, S.J., Rev Michael Jesuit priest, founder of Irish School of Ecumenics and Columbanus Ecumenical Society.

Hutchinson, Rt. Rev. Dr. Samuel (born Belfast, 1937) Current Moderator of the Presbyterian Church in Ireland.

Jennings, Pat (born Newry, 1945) Goalkeeper. Northern Ireland's most capped player. Made his debut in 1964, won his 119th cap in the 1986 World Cup finals.

Jordan, Eddie (born Dublin, 1948) Owner of the Jordan Peugeot Formula One motor racing team.

Jordan, Neil (born Sligo, 1950) Film director and writer. Academy Award winning director of *The Crying Game* (1992).

Keane, Fergal (born London, 1961) Foreign correspondent for B.B.C. television, former *Irish Press* and R.T.É. journalist. Author of *Letter to Daniel.*

Keane, Roy (born Cork, 1971) Midfielder. Current Manchester United captain. Won 38 caps with the Republic and scored three goals.

Keenan, Brian (born Belfast, 1950) Former Beruit hostage (1986-90). Writer, Won the Irish Times Prize for non-fiction (1993), among other accolades, for his book *An Evil Cradling* (1992).

Kelly, Gerry (born Co. Antrim, 1948) Broadcaster with Ulster Television and presenter of the popular *Kelly Show.*

Kelly, Sean (born Tipperary, 1956) Number one ranked cyclist in the world (1984-88). Won five stages in the Tour de France.

Kenny, Pat (born 1949) Popular R.T.É. presenter of

Kenny Live on television and The Pat Kenny Show on radio.

Lee, Professor Joseph (born Kerry, 1942) Professor of Modern History at University College Cork, Senator (1992-97).

Lord Moyola (Clarke, James Chichester) (born Derry, 1923) Former Prime Minister of Northern Ireland (1969-71).

Loughnane, Ger (born Clare, 1954) Hurling All-Star. Railway Cup and National League winner in 1970s. Managed Clare hurlers to two All-Ireland victories (1995, 1997).

Loughrey, Patrick Controller of B.B.C. Northern Ireland.

Lowry, Michael (born Tipperary, 1954) Former Minister for Transport, Energy and Communications (1994-96). T.D. since 1987. Resigned as Minister, following revelations of irregular payments to him by Dunnes Stores.

Lynch, Jack (born Cork, 1917) Former Taoiseach (1966-73, 1977-79) and Leader of Fianna Fáil (1966-79).

McAleese, Mary (born Belfast, 1951) Academic and lawyer. Currently pro-vice-chancellor at Queen's University. Nominated Candidate for 1997 Presidential Elections.

McAliskey, Bernadette Devlin (born Tyrone, 1947) founder of I.R.S.P. (1974). Civil rights activist. M.P. (1969-74).

McBride, Willie John (born Antrim, 1940). Won 63 caps for Ireland between 1962 and 1975 (including a record 52 consecutively).

McCarter, Willie (born Derry, 1947) Former Managing Director at Fruit of the Loom (1987-1997). Current chairman of International Fund for Ireland since 1989.

McCarthy, Mick (born England, 1959) Current Republic of Ireland Soccer manager, since January 1996. Captain of the Republic of Ireland team during the Italia '90 campaign.

McCartney, Bob (born Belfast, 1936) Leader of the United Kingdom Unionist Party. M.P. since 1995, delegate to the multi-party talks.

McCracken, Mr. Justice Judge responsible for the Tribunal of Inquiry into Payments to Politicians.

McCreevy, Charlie (born Kildare, 1949) Fianna Fáil T.D. since 1977. Appointed Minister for Finance June 1997.

McCurtain, O.P., Sr. Margaret (born 1929) Historian and religious writer. Professor of History at UCD until 1994.

McDonagh, Rev. Enda (born Mayo, 1930) Writer and current President of the National Council of Priests of Ireland.

McDonagh, Joe (born Galway, 1954) President of the Gaelic Athletic Association since April 1997. Hurling All Star (1976) and All-Ireland Championship (1980) winner.

McGrath, Paul (born Ealing, 1959) Defender. Capped 82 times by the Republic, scoring six international goals. Awarded the F.A.I. Player of the Year in 1990 and 1991. Currently with Sheffield United.

McGuinness, Martin (born Derry, 1950) M.P. since May 1997. Sinn Féin's chief negotiator in talks with representatives of the British government.

McGuinness, Paul (born Germany, 1951) Manager of rock-group U2 and director of Principle Management Ltd.

McKenna, Sr. Breige Spiritual healer and writer.

McKeown, Shay (born Tyrone, 1952) Chartered Accountant. Joined Powerscreen International on a short-term basis in 1979. Current Chief Executive.

McMahon, Lt. Gen. Gerry (born Limerick) Current Chief-of-Staff of Defence Forces since 1995. Former Brigadier General (1992-93), Major General and Quartermaster General (1993-95). Current President of the Defence Forces Rugby Team.

McMichael, Gary (born Antrim,1971) Leader of the Ulster Democratic Party since 1994. Delegate to the multi-party talks.

McSharry, Ray (born Sligo, 1938) Fianna Fáil T.D. (1969-89). Held ministerial portfolios of Agriculture (1979-81), Finance (1982, 1987-88) and Tánaiste (1982). M.E.P. (1984-87). E.U. Commissioner for Agriculture (1989-93).

Macken, Justice Judge responsible for the Hepatitis C / Anti D case.

Magahy, Laura (born Dublin, 1961) Managing director of Temple Bar Properties. Influential in the regeneration of Dublin's Temple Bar.

Magee, Rev. Roy (born Antrim, 1930) Presbyterian Minister. Negotiator in Loyalist Ceasefire (1994).

Maginnis, Ken (born 1938) Ulster Unionist Party M.P. since 1983.

Maguire, Seán (born Belfast, 1924) Traditional fiddle player. Renowned for his rendition of The Mason's Apron.

Mallon, M.P., Seamus (born Armagh, 1942), Deputy Leader of the S.D.L.P. since 1978. M.P. since 1986, Senator (1981-82).

Marcus, David (born 1929) Journalist, editor and writer. Former editor of Irish Writing (1946-54) and Poetry Ireland (1948-54). Literary editor of Irish Press (1968-85)

Marcus, Louis Chairperson of the Irish Film Board.

Martin, Geoff Editor of the Belfast and Ulster Newsletter.

Mason, Patrick (born 1951) Theatre director. Former resident director of Abbey Theatre (1977-80) and current Artistic Director.

Mhac a' tSaoi, Máire (born Dublin, 1922) Irish language poet, publications include Margadh na Saoire (1956) and An Cion go dtí Seo (1987).

Moloney, Paddy (born Dublin, 1938) Founding member of The Chieftans (1961). Uilleann pipes and tin whistle player with the band.

Molyneaux, Sir James (born Antrim, 1920) M.P. (1970-97). Leader of Ulster Unionist Party (1979-95). Elevated to the peerage as Lord Molyneaux of Killead in 1997.

Moore, Christy (born Kildare, 1945) Singer and songwriter. Renowned for works such as Ordinary Man (1985) and The Christy Moore Collection (1991).

Morrisson, Van (born Belfast, 1945) Musician, founder of Them (1963), went solo in 1966 to enjoy a successful career with albums such as Moondance (1970) and No Guru, No Method, No Teacher (1986).

Mowlam, Mo (born Coventry, 1949) Secretary of State for Northern Ireland since May 1997. Labour M.P. since 1987.

Mulholland, Joe (born Donegal, 1940) Current

Managing Director of television at R.T.É. since April 1997.

Murphy, Mike (born Dublin, 1941) Television and radio presenter. Currently hosting the weekly National Lottery game show *Winning Streak*.

Murray, Mgr. Raymond Human rights activist in Northern Ireland. Publications include *The S.A.S. in Ireland*.

Nally, Derek (born Tipperary, 1936) Founder and Honourary President of the Irish Association of Victim Support. Former General Secretary of the Association of Garda Sergeants and Inspectors.

Neary, Archbishop Michael (born 1946) Roman Catholic Archbishop of Tuam since 1995.

Neeson, Liam (born Antrim, 1953) Actor. Notable films include *A Prayer for the Dying* (1987), *Schindler's List* (1993) and *Michael Collins* (1996).

Ní Dhomhnaill, Nuala (born England, 1952) Irish language poet whose work includes *An Dealg Droighin* (1981) and *Féar Suaithinseach* (1984).

O'Brien, Edna (born Clare, 1932) Writer whose novels include *The Country Girls* (1960) and short stories such as *A Frantic Heart* (1985).

O'Brien, Vincent (born Cork, 1917) Retired horse trainer, his charges won Grand Nationals and Gold Cups and Champion Hurdles at Cheltenham. Winner of 16 English and 27 Irish Classics.

O'Callaghan, Miriam (born Dublin, 1961) Qualified solicitor and television presenter. Current presenter of R.T.É.'s current affairs programme *Primetime*.

O'Caolain, Caoimhghin (born Monaghan, 1953) Elected to Dáil Éireann in June 1997 becoming the first Sinn Féin T.D. to take his seat in Leinster House since 1922.

Ó Cearúlláin, Gearóid (born Belfast, 1957) Uachtarán (President) of Conradh na Gaeilge.

O'Connor, James (born Clare, 1972) Hurling player, Won two All-Ireland hurling medals with Clare (1995, 1997).

O'Connor, John (born Dublin, 1947) Irish pianist. Professor of Piano at the Royal Irish Academy of Music. Appointed director in 1994.

O'Connor, Sinéad (born Dublin, 1966) Controversial rock singer, whose albums include *The Lion and the Cobra* (1987) and *Universal Mother* (1994).

O'Donnell, Daniel (born Donegal, 1961) Ireland's leading country performer, also widely popular in Britain. Major hits include *I Just Want to Dance With You* and *Donegal Shore*.

Ó Gallchóir, Pól Ceannaire (Head) of Raidío na Gaeilge.

O'Leary, Olivia (born Carlow, 1949) Freelance broadcast journalist with R.T.É. and formerly with the B.B.C. and Yorkshire T.V. in Britain, political commentator with the *Sunday Tribune*.

O'Móráin, Donall (born Kerry, 1923) Founder and Chief Executive of Gael Linn (1963), former Chairman of R.T.É. Authority (1970-72).

Ó Muircheartaigh, Mícheál Gaelic games broadcaster, Cathaoirleach (Chairman) of Bord na Gaeilge.

Ó Muirchú, Labhras (born Tipperary, 1939) Ardstiúrthóir (director) of Comhaltas Ceoltóirí Éireann.

O'Reilly, Dr. Tony (born Dublin, 1936) Current President of H.J. Heinz and Chairman of Independent

Newspapers. Former rugby player. Winner of 29 international caps in his record breaking 16 year career (1955-70).

O'Se, Paidi (born Kerry, 1955) Former Kerry Gaelic football. Winner of eight All-Ireland medals, and five All-Star Awards. Current football manager of Kerry, the 1997 football champions.

Ó Sé, Séan (born Cork, 1936) Irish traditional musician.

Ó Searcaigh, Cathal (born Donegal, 1956) Former R.T.É. broadcaster and Irish language poet whose works include *Súile Shuibhne* (1983) and *Suibhne* (1987).

Ó Súilleabháin, Mícheál (born Tipperary, 1950) Noted traditional composer and musician. Professor of Music at the University of Limerick since 1994.

O'Sullivan, Sonia (born Cork, 1969) Ireland's top female athlete, holds all Irish records from 800m to 5,000m, representing Ireland at World Championship and Olympic Games level.

Owen, Nora (born Dublin, 1945) Deputy leader of Fine Gael since 1993. T.D. (1981-87 and since 1989). Former Minister for Justice (1994-97).

Paisley, M.P., M.E.P., Rev. Dr. Ian (born Armagh, 1926) Founder and Leader of the Democratic Unionist Party (1971). M.P. since 1971. M.E.P. since 1979. Established Free Presbyterian Church (1951).

Pattison, Séamus (born Kilkenny, 1936) Elected Ceann Comhairle June 1997. Labour Party T.D. since 1961.

Potter, Maureen (born Dublin, 1925) Stage actress and comedienne. Began career in Olympia Theatre with Jimmy O'Dea (1953).

Quinn, Feargal (born Dublin, 1936) Independent Senator since 1993. Chief Executive of Superquinn supermarket chain.

Quinn, Patricia (born Dublin, 1959) Current Director of the Arts Council. Former radio critic for *In Dublin* magazine.

Quinn, Peter (born Fermanagh) Former President of the G.A.A. (1991-94).

Quinn, Ruairí (born Dublin, 1946) T.D. (1977-81 and since 1982). Senator (1981-82). Former Minister of Finance (1994-97). Deputy Leader of the Labour Party since 1989.

Rafferty, Sean Former presenter with B.B.C. Northern Ireland, now with B.B.C. Radio Three.

Reid, Rev. Alex Catholic priest. Negotiator in 1994 ceasefire.

Reynolds, Albert (born Roscommon, 1932) Former Taoiseach (1992-94) and Leader of Fianna Fáil (1992-94).

Robinson, Mary (born Mayo, 1944) Former President of Ireland (1990-97). Took up post of United Nations Commissioner for Human Rights in September 1997.

Robinson, M.P., Peter (born Belfast, 1948) M.P. since 1979. Deputy Leader of the Democratic Unionist Party. Delegate to the multi-party talks.

Roche, Adi (born Tipperary, 1955) Aid worker and anti-nuclear campaigner. Founder of the Cork based Chernobyl Children's Project (1990). Nominated Candidate for 1997 Presidential Elections.

Roche, Stephen (born Dublin, 1959) Cyclist. Won the Giro d'Italia, the World Championship and the Tour de France in 1987. The winner of 57 races, he retired in

1993.

Rodgers, Bríd (born Donegal) Former General Secretary of SDLP (1981-83). Chairperson (1978-80). Current spokesperson on Women's Issues and Irish Language.

Rodgers, Patsy Dan (born Donegal) King of Tory Island, (Rí Thoraí). Member of the Naive Painting School.

Ryan, Gerry (born 1956) Popular R.T.É. television and radio personality. Presenter of the *Gerry Ryan Show* on 2FM since 1988.

Ryan, Dr. Tony (born Tipperary, 1936) Businessman. Founder of Guinness Peat Aviation (now General Electric Capital Aviation Services) in 1975. Chairman of Ryanair. Governor of the National Gallery of Ireland.

Shaw, Helen (born 1960, Dublin) R.T.É.'s Director of radio. Formerly B.B.C. Northern Ireland Editor of radio current affairs.

Sheridan, Jim (born Dublin, 1949) Film director whose movies include *My Left Foot* (1988), *The Field* (1989) and *In the Name of the Father* (1993).

Smith, Michelle (born Dublin, 1969) Swimmer. Won three gold medals and one bronze at the 1996 Olympic Games in Atlanta.

Smurfit, Michael (born Dublin, 1936) Businessman. Chief Executive of Jefferson Smurfit Ltd. Honourary consul of Ireland to Monaco. Chairman of Irish Racing Board (1985-90).

Smyth, Desmond (born Co. Derry, 1950) Managing Director of Ulster Television since 1983. Joined U.T.V. in 1975. Director of Northern Ireland Electricity.

Smyth, Hugh (born Belfast, 1941) Founding member and leader of the Progressive Unionist Party. Belfast City Councillor, Lord Mayor of Belfast (1994/95). Delegate to the multi-party talks.

Spence, Gusty (born Belfast, 1933) Former member of the U.V.F. Currently involved with the Progressive Unionist Party.

Spring, T.D., Dick (born Kerry, 1950) Former Tánaiste (1994-97). Leader of the Labour Party since 1982. T.D. since 1981.

Stephenson, Sam (born Dublin, 1939) Architect, whose buildings include the Central Bank, E.S.B. Offices and Bord na Móna Offices in Dublin.

Stokes, Niall (born Dublin, 1951) Founder, editor and publisher of *Hot Press*. Chairman of the Independent Radio and Television Commission since 1993.

Sutherland, Peter (born 1946) Former Attorney General (1982-86), E.C. Commissioner (1985-89), Appointed Director General of G.A.T.T. in 1993.

Taggart, Rev. Norman (born Belfast, 1935) Current President of the Methodist Church.

Taylor, M.P., John (born Armagh,1937) M.P. since 1983. M.E.P. (1979-89). Deputy Leader of the Ulster Unionist Party since 1995.

Treacy, Philip (born Galway, 1967) Milliner. Most famous hat designer in Europe, possibly the world. Worked with prominent couture houses in Europe, particularly Chanel.

Treacy, Seán (born Tipperary, 1923) T.D. (1961-97). Former Ceann Comhairle (1973-77) and (1987-97).

Trimble, David (born Down, 1944) Leader of the Ulster Unionist Party since 1995. M.P. since 1990.

Wallace, Dr. Patrick (born Limerick) Archaeologist and current Director of the National Museum of Ireland since 1988.

Whelehan, Harry (born Westmeath, 1944) Former Attorney General (1991-94). At the centre of the collapse of the Fianna Fáil / Labour Party coalition in 1994.

Whitaker, Ken (born Down, 1916) Author of the 1958 *Programme for Economic Expansion*. Governor of the Central Bank (1969-76). President of E.S.R.I. (1974-87). Chairman of the Committee of Enquiry into the Penal System (1983-85).

GEOGRAPHICAL & ENVIRONMENT

"Man's impact on the Environment"

*By **Oscar J. Merne**.*

THE last Ice Age effectively wiped the slate clean and when the ice retreated it left behind a landscape totally different from that which existed before. Much of the solid geology remained the same, apart from mountains and outcropping rock which had been ground down by the moving ice sheet, but eskers, moraines, drumlins, and an overburden of glacial till were major relics of the Ice Age. Sea level rise, due to the release of waters from the melting ice, dramatically changed Ireland's coastline and separated us from Britain and the Continent.

In time the bleak post-glacial landscape was colonised by plants and animals moving back from warmer areas as the ice sheet retreated. This phase climaxed in much of the country being cloaked in deciduous and coniferous forest.

Then came Man, with his tools, his livestock, his agriculture. Forests were felled, to clear land for farming, to provide timber for houses and boats, and to make charcoal for smelting. As the human population increased and the methods for manipulating the landscape grew more sophisticated, the impact on the vegetation and fauna became more and more severe. By the 17th century almost all the forests had been cleared. Most of the Irish woodland today originates from replanting which has been carried out over the last two hundred years or so.

Nowadays we are increasingly concerned, and rightly so, about our impact on the environment -- through agricultural intensification, urbanisation and industrialisation, pollution, the large-scale planting of exotic conifers, the massive exploitation of our bogs, and so on. But it is appropriate to view these in the context of the enormous changes which Man has wrought over the millennia since his first arrival here. But what is particularly worrying about the way we are degrading the environment nowadays (especially over the last half century) is the speed at which things are changing. This is largely due to recent advances in technology and science which have led to increased mechanisation and the production of a vast array of chemicals. It is very difficult for natural habitats, and plant and animal communities to withstand and adjust to the rapid changes which we have brought about in recent times.

Ireland is an agricultural country and our soils and climate are suitable for the production of a wide range of products -- meat and dairy products, cereals, vegetables, and so on. All necessary to feed our population of about five-and-half million people, and to generate economic prosperity through exports. But modern farming with powerful and sophisticated machinery, heavy use of artificial fertilisers and chemicals to control and eradicate pests and weeds is relentlessly efficient and overly productive. The environmental costs are high. Waters are polluted by silage effluent, slurry run-off and fertiliser leachate. Herb-rich meadows with their attendant diversity of animal life are gone from many parts of the countryside. Hedge rows have been grubbed up to make more land for crops and allow more space for farm machinery. Hillsides have been cleared by burning and machines to provide more sheep grazing, and in some areas mountains have been overgrazed to such an extent that serious soil erosion is occurring.

These problems are being increasingly recognised both here and at European Union level, and various schemes (such as set-aside and REPS - the Rural Environment Protection Scheme) are being put in place to curb overproduction and environmental degradation, while at the same time ensuring that farmers do not lose out financially. The most important areas for wildlife and natural habitats are being given direct protection through designation as Special Areas of Conservation or Special Protection Areas under E.U. Directives on habitats, flora, fauna and birds.

As mentioned earlier, most of our natural climax forest was cleared long ago and what woodland we have now has been recently planted. During most of this century nearly all the planting has been carried out by the State, and nearly all of this has been done with exotic conifers from North America. In recent years this planting has accelerated, with E.U. financial support. In spite of premium payments favouring planting of hardwoods, fast-growing exotic conifers are still favoured by both the State and private sectors. Such forests do benefit certain species of birds (for example Woodcock, Coal Tits, Goldcrests, Chaffinches), but unfortunately much of the planting has been done on blanket peats and this important habitat is under severe pressure. In addition to the conifer plantations the bogs are under threat from mechanical peat harvesting and overgrazing by sheep.

Agriculture and forestry occupy over 90% of the land surface of Ireland. The rest is made up of freshwater lakes and rivers, terrestrial natural habitats, urban/industrial areas and man-made infrastructures such as roads. In densely populated, urbanised and industrialised parts of Europe there are serious concerns about the loss of countryside to concrete, brick and tarmac. In Ireland this is a relatively minor problem in general and is localised to our major urban centres such as Dublin, Belfast, Cork, Derry, Limerick, Galway and other large towns. From a nature conservation viewpoint the direct loss of green space to urban sprawl may be significant only at a local level, and may be at least partially compensated for by the mosaic of developing suburban gardens which provide new and perhaps more diverse habitats for a wide variety of wildlife.

In Ireland we have seen serious loss and degradation of the landscape, natural and semi-natural habitats and wildlife in recent times due to Man's activities. Indeed, some habitats, plants and animals have been brought close to extinction here -- for example the Corn Cockle and the Corncrake. A better-informed public and an increasing concern for environmental matters, both here and internationally, are bringing about a welcome change in attitude favouring the maintenance and restoration of a healthy environment. No longer is it acceptable to pursue economic goals with scant regard for the countryside, the impacts of water and air pollution, and the well-being of wild fauna and flora. This changing attitude is reflected in new legislation and regulations at national and E.U. level. But in spite of these positive moves safeguarding the environment requires eternal vigilance.

The author is a noted expert on wildlife and forestry in the Republic of Ireland.

'THE FACT FILE'
IRISH GEOGRAPHICAL AND PHYSICAL STATISTICS

Ireland	Total Area	32,593 sq. miles
Republic of Ireland	Total Area	27,137 sq. miles
Republic of Ireland	Land	26,401 sq. miles
Republic of Ireland	Water	736 sq. miles
Northern Ireland	Total Area	5,456 sq. miles
Northern Ireland	Land	5,156 sq. miles
Northern Ireland	Water	300 sq. miles
Greatest Length	North to South	302 miles (486 km)
Greatest Width	East to West	171 miles (275 km)
Total Coastline	Ireland	1970.5 miles (3,152 km)
Total Coastline	Republic of Ireland	1,737 miles
Total Coastline	Northern Ireland	232 miles
Highest Point	Carrantuohill, Co. Kerry	3,414ft (1024.2m)
Lowest Point		No point in Ireland is below sea-level
Largest Island		Achill Island, Mayo (36,248 acres)
Longest River	The Shannon (rises - Cavan, meets Atlantic - Limerick)	224 miles (358km)
Largest Lake	Lough Neagh, N. Ireland	149.61 sq. miles (95,748 acres)
Highest Waterfall	Powerscourt, Co. Wicklow	350ft (106m)
Highest Cliff	Croaghan, Achill Island, Co. Mayo	2192ft (668m)
Longest Stalactite	Pollan Ionain, Co. Clare	20ft 4" (6.2m)
Deepest Cave	Carrowmore Cavern, Co. Sligo	459ft (140m)
Highest Temperature Recorded*	Kilkenny Castle (26 June 1887)	920F/33.3°C
Lowest Temperature Recorded	Omagh, (Edenfel) Co. Tyrone (23 January 1881)	2.920F/-19.4°C
Heaviest Rainfall	Orra Beg, North Antrim (1 August 1980)	3.82in (97mm) in 45 min
Driest Year Recorded		1887
Longest Drought Recorded	Co. Limerick	3 April to 10 May 1938 (37 days)
Heaviest Snowfall		January 1917
Highest Windspeed	Kilkeel, Co. Down (January 1974)	108 knots
Northernmost Point		Malin Head, Co. Donegal
Northernmost Town / Village	(Town) Carndonagh, Co. Donegal	(Village) Malin, Co. Donegal
Southernmost Point		Mizen Head, Co. Cork
Southernmost Town / Village	(Town) Skibbereen, Co. Cork	(Village) Baltimore, Co. Cork
Easternmost Point		Wicklow Head, Co. Wicklow
Easternmost Town		Wicklow Town, Co. Wicklow
Westernmost Point		Dunmore Head, (Slea Head) Co. Kerry
Westernmost Town / Village	(Town) Dingle, Co. Kerry	(Village) Ballyferriter, Co. Kerry
Largest County	Cork	2,878 sq. miles
Smallest County	Louth	318 sq. miles
Biggest Dam		Poulaphuca Reservoir, Co. Wicklow
Tallest Building		County Hall, Cork (Cork Corporation)
Tallest Structure	E.S.B. Chimneys, Moneypoint, Co. Clare	738 ft (225 m)
Longest Bridge Span		Barrow Railway Bridge

* A slightly higher temperature - 33.4°C - was recorded on July 16, 1876, in the Phoenix Park, just before official records were started in 1881.

THE ISLAND OF IRELAND - PHYSICAL FEATURES

The island of Ireland, located in the Atlantic Ocean to the west of Great Britain and the extreme north-west of the continent of Europe, lies between a latitude 51.5 and 55.5 degrees north and a longitude 5.5 and 10.5 degrees west.

The island consists of a large central plateau, the elevation of which is generally less than 150 m above sea level, ringed almost entirely by coastal highlands which vary considerably in geological structure. To the south, the mountain ridges consist of old red sandstone separated by deep limestone river valleys. The mountains of Donegal, Mayo and Galway are geologically dominated

by granite, as are those in counties Down and Wicklow. Almost 5 per cent of the island's total area is between 300 and 600 m above sea level, ensuring sparse plant life. The north-east of the island is predominantly covered by a basalt plateau, while the central plain is largely covered with glacial deposits of sand and clay. The central plain also contains numerous areas of bog, the most notable of these being the Bog of Allen, and is interspersed with lakes.

Geologists state that the Irish terrain, marked by "ice-smoothed rock, mountain lakes, glacial valleys and deposits of sand, gravel and clay," points to at least two great glaciations of the island. They also state that Ireland was separated from mainland Europe following the last Ice Age.

Ireland is also separated from the island of Britain by the Irish Sea, the distances between the two islands ranging from 11 to 120 miles apart at its closest and farthest points, respectively.

Climate: Ireland's climate is influenced by the warm waters of the Gulf Stream, with the result that the climate is temperate. The relatively small size of the island and the prevailing south-west winds ensure a uniform temperature over the whole country.

Irish winters are generally mild while the summers are generally cool. The coldest months of the year are usually January and February, with temperatures averaging between 4°C and 7°C. During the winter months snow does fall from time to time but is normally not severe and is short-lived, generally lasting for only a few days at a time. May and June are the sunniest months, averaging 5 - 7 hours of sunshine per day. July and August are the warmest summer months, averaging between 14°C and 16°C. The minimum length of day occurs in late December, around 7 to 7.5 hours, and the longest occurs in late June and ranges between 16.5 and 17.5 hours between sunrise and sunset. Rainfall, carried in from the Atlantic by prevailing westerly winds, is well-distributed all over the island; however, the west has generally a greater annual rainfall than the east due to its proximity to the Atlantic Ocean and its being much more mountainous. In low lying areas the average annual rainfall is between 800 and 1,200mm (31" to 47"), and in mountainous areas as much as 2,000mm (79") per annum is not unusual.

IRELAND AREA COMPARISON TABLE

The total land area of the island of Ireland is 32,595 sq. miles while, for example, Australia has 2,966,200 sq. miles. Consequently, Ireland would fit into Australia more than 91 times. The comparison table below indicates the country's size in relation to the land area of selected countries throughout the world.

(+ = Number of times greater; - Number of times smaller.)

Argentina	1,073,518 sq. miles	+ 33	Monaco	0.75 sq. miles	- 32,594
Australia	2,966,200 sq. miles	+ 91	Netherlands	16,033 sq. miles	- 2
Austria	32,378 sq. miles	1	New Zealand	104,454 sq. miles	+ 3
Brazil	3,286,500 sq. miles	+ 101	Norway	125,050 sq. miles	+ 4
Canada	3,849,674 sq. miles	+ 118	Pakistan	339,697 sq. miles	+10
China	3,696,100 sq. miles	+ 113	Peru	496,225 sq. miles	+ 15
Greenland	840,000 sq. miles	+ 26	Philippines	115,860 sq. miles	+ 4
Egypt	385,229 sq. miles	+ 12	Poland	120,728 sq. miles	+ 4
Ethiopia	437,794 sq. miles	+ 13	Portugal	35,574 sq. miles	1
France	210,026 sq. miles	+ 6	Russia*	6,592,800 sq. miles	+ 202
Germany	137,823 sq. miles	+ 4	Saudi Arabia	865,000 sq. miles	+ 27
India	1,222,243 sq. miles	+ 37	South Africa	472,281 sq. miles	+ 14
Iraq	167,975 sq. miles	+ 5	Spain	194,898 sq. miles	+ 6
Indonesia	741,052 sq. miles	+ 23	Sweden	173,732 sq. miles	+ 5
Iran	632,457 sq. miles	+ 19	Switzerland	15,940 sq. miles	- 2
Israel	7,992 sq. miles	- 4	Syria	71,498 sq. miles	+ 2
Italy	116,334 sq. miles	+ 4	Thailand	198,115 sq. miles	+ 6
Japan	145,850 sq. miles	+ 4	U.K.	94,251 sq. miles	+ 3
Kenya	224,961 sq. miles	+ 7	U.S.A.	3,679,192 sq. miles	+ 113
Libya	678,400 sq. miles	+ 21	Venezuela	352,144 sq. miles	+ 11
Luxembourg	999 sq. miles	- 33	Vietnam	127,246 sq. miles	+ 4
Mexico	756,066 sq. miles	+ 23	Zimbabwe	150,872 sq. miles	+ 5

* [Prior to 1992]

(All figures are approximations).

REPUBLIC OF IRELAND: AREA BY PROVINCE AND PERSONS PER SQUARE KILOMETRE

Province	Total area (hectares)	Selected lakes, rivers and tideways (hectares)	Land and other waters (hectares)	Persons per square kilometre
Republic of Ireland	7,028,510	139,054	6,889,456	51
Leinster	1,979,432	16,097	1,963,335	97
Munster	2,468,874	56,136	2,412,738	42
Connacht	1,771,342	59,170	1,712,172	24
Ulster*	808,862	7,651	801,211	29

* Cavan, Donegal and Monaghan

IRELAND: WORLD TIME DIFFERENCES

Hours Plus or Minus GMT

The 0 degree meridian has been established as the reference line for setting time. This line runs through Greenwich in London and is known as Greenwich Mean Time (or GMT). Because of Ireland's proximity to London, it shares the same time zone as Britain. The times listed below should be added to standard time in Ireland to ascertain various world time differences in relation to Ireland.

Accra (Ghana)	00.00	**Lisbon** (Portugal)	00.00
Adelaide (Australia)	+09.30	**Liverpool** (England)	00.00
Amsterdam (Netherlands)	+01.00	**London** (England)	00.00
Athens (Greece)	+02.00	**Los Angeles** (United States)	-08.00
Baghdad (Iraq)	+03.00	**Madrid** (Spain)	+01.00
Bangkok (Thailand)	+07.00	**Manchester** (England)	00.00
Beijing (China)	+08.00	**Melbourne** (Australia)	+10.00
Berlin (Germany)	+01.00	**Mexico City** (Mexico)	-06.00
Brussels (Belgium)	+01.00	**Montevideo** (Uruguay)	-03.00
Buenos Aires (Argentina)	-03.00	**Montreal** (Canada)	-05.00
Cairo (Egypt)	+02.00	**Moscow** (Russia)	+03.00
Calgary (Canada)	-07.00	**Nairobi** (Kenya)	+03.00
Cape Town (South Africa)	+02.00	**New Delhi** (India)	+05.30
Cardiff (Wales)	00.00	**New York** (United States)	-05.00
Chicago (United States)	-06.00	**Oslo** (Norway)	+01.00
Christchurch (New Zealand)	+12.00	**Paris** (France)	+01.00
Colombo (Sri Lanka)	+05.30	**Perth** (Western Australia)	+08.00
Copenhagen (Denmark)	+01.00	**Rio de Janeiro** (Brazil)	-03.00
Detroit (United States)	-05.00	**Rome** (Italy)	+01.00
Durban (South Africa)	+02.00	**San Francisco** (United States)	-08.00
Glasgow (Scotland)	00.00	**Seoul** (Korea)	+09.00
Gibraltar (Spain)	+01.00	**Singapore** (Malaysia)	+08.00
Halifax (Canada)	-04.00	**Stockholm** (Sweden)	+01.00
Helsinki (Finland)	+02.00	**Sydney** (Australia)	+10.00
Hong Kong (China)	+08.00	**Tehran** (Iran)	+03.30
Honolulu (Hawaii)	-10.00	**Tokyo** (Japan)	+09.00
Houston (United States)	-06.00	**Toronto** (Canada)	-05.00
Istanbul (Turkey)	+02.00	**Valletta** (Malta)	+01.00
Jakarta (Indonesia)	+07.00	**Vancouver** (Canada)	-08.00
Johannesburg (South Africa)	+02.00	**Warsaw** (Poland)	+01.00
Karachi (Pakistan)	+05.00	**Wellington** (New Zealand)	+12.00
Lagos (Nigeria)	+01.00	**Winnipeg** (Canada)	-06.00
Lima (Peru)	-05.00	**Zurich** (Switzerland)	+01.00

METEOROLOGICAL STATIONS

Met Éireann Stations
(Met Éireann, Glasnevin Hill, Dublin 9. Tel: 01 8064200)

The Irish Meteorological Service has 13 synoptic stations throughout the Republic of Ireland, manned on a 24-hour basis, the main function of which is to maintain a continuous watch on the weather and to make detailed reports every hour on the hour. These reports provide the basis for all advice and information supplied to the general public regarding the 'weather forecast' and to the various specialised sectors.

Meteorological Office Stations
(Belfast Climate Office, 32 College Street, Belfast, BT1 1BQ. Tel: 01232 328457)

Two synoptic stations are maintained under the auspices of the Meteorological Office in Northern Ireland:
The Principle Meteorological Office, Belfast International Airport, Belfast, BT29 4AB. *Tel: (01849) 422804.*
The Meteorological Office, Hillsborough, Maze, Lisburn, Co. Antrim, BT27 5RF. *Tel: (01846) 682416.*

Station	Established	County
Valentia Observatory	1866	Kerry
Birr	1872	Offaly
Malin Head	1885	Donegal
Shannon Airport	1938	Clare
Dublin Airport	1939	Dublin
Mullingar	1943	Westmeath
Casement Aerodrome	1943	Dublin

Station	Established	County
Clones	1950	Monaghan
Belmullet	1956	Mayo
Rosslare	1956	Wexford
Kilkenny	1957	Kilkenny
Cork Airport	1961	Cork
Knock Airport	1996	Mayo

REPUBLIC OF IRELAND: METEOROLOGY
MEAN DAILY TEMPERATURES, 1994-1996

Synoptic Station	Temperatures (°C)		
	1994	1995	1996
Cahirciveen	11.0	11.5	10.5
Claremorris	9.3	10.6	8.7
Cork Airport	9.8	10.6	9.6
Dublin Airport	9.6	10.1	9.1
Kilkenny	9.9	10.6	9.5
Malin Head	9.6	10.1	9.5
Mullingar	9.2	9.9	9.0
Shannon Airport	10.7	11.4	10.5

REPUBLIC OF IRELAND: METEOROLOGY
TOTAL PRECIPITATION, 1994-1996

Synoptic Station	Millimetres		
	1994	1995	1996
Cahirciveen	1,804.4	1,540.3	1,567.7
Claremorris	1,358.4	1,109.1	995.7
Cork Airport	1,450.2	1,254.8	1,432.3
Dublin Airport	791.6	707.7	783.9
Kilkenny	1,002.8	822.7	943.8
Malin Head	1,188.6	1,754.4	924.9
Mullingar	1,016.8	895.4	869.0
Shannon Airport	1,194.3	1,032.8	878.7

IRISH MAMMALS

Mammal	Irish Name	Family	Latin Name
American Mink	Minc Mheiriceánach	Mustelidae	Mustela vison
Badger	Broc	Mustelidae	Meles meles
Bank Vole	Vól Bruaigh	Muridae	Clethrionomys glareolus
Bats:			
Daubenton's Bat	Ialtóg Dhaubenton	Vespertilionidae	Myotis daubentoni
Whiskered Bat	Ialtóg Ghiobach	Vespertilionidae	Myotis mystaciuus
Natterer's Bat	Ialtog Natterer	Vespertilionidae	Myotis nattereri
Leisler's Bat	Ialtóg Leisler	Vespertilionidae	
Pipistrelle	Ialtóg Fheaserach	Vespertilionidae	Pipistrellus pipistrellus
Long-Eared Bat	Ialtóg Chluasach	Vespertilionidae	Plecotus auritus
Lesser Horseshoe Bat	Ialtóg	Rhinolophidae	Rhinolophus hipposideros
Deer (Red)	Fia Rua	Cervidae	Cervus elaphus
Deer (Fallow)	Fia Buí	Cervidae	Dama dama
Deer (Japanese Sika)	Fia Seapánach	Cervidae	Cervus nippon
Feral Goat	Gabhar Fia	Bovidae	Capra hircus
Field Mouse	Luch Fhéir	Muridae	Apodemus sylvaticus
Fox	Sionnach / Madra Rua	Canidea	Vulpes vulpes
Hare (Irish or Blue)	Giorria Éireannach	Lagomorpha	Lepus timidus hibernicus
Hare (Brown)	Giorria	Lagomorpha	Lepus capensis
Hedgehog	Gráinneog	Erinaceidae	Erinaceus europaeus
Irish Stoat	Easóg	Mustelidae	Mustela erminea hibernica
Otter	Dobharchú	Mustelidae	Lutra lutra
Pine Marten	Cat Crainn	Mustelidae	Martes martes
Pygmy Shrew	Dallóg Fhraoigh	Soricidae	Sorex minutus
Rabbit	Coinín	Lagomorpha	Oryctolagus cuniculus
Rat (Brown)	an Francach Donn	Muridae	Rattus norvegicus
Rat (Black)	an Francach Dubh	Muridae	Rattus rattus
Squirrel (Grey)	Iora Glas	Sciuridae	Sciurus carolinensis
Squirrel (Red)	Iora Rua	Sciuridae	Sciurus vulgaris

Most of the above mammals are protected under the Wildlife Act, 1976.
However, regulated hunting of certain species is permitted.

BIRDS OF IRELAND

(includes resident species, winter and summer visitors, partial migrants and passing migrants)

Arctic Skua	Firecrest	Little Stint	Sanderling
Arctic Tern	Fulmar	Little Tern	Sand Martin
Avocet	Gadwall	Long-Eared Owl	Sandwich Tern
Barnacle Goose	Gannet	Long-Tailed Duck	Scaup
Barn Owl	Garden Warbler	Long-Tailed Tit	Sedge Warbler
Bar-Tailed Godwit	Glaucous Gull	Magpie	Shag
Bean Goose	Goldcrest	Mallard	Shelduck
Bewick's Swan	Goldeneye	Mandarin	Shore Lark
Bittern	Golden Pheasant	Manx Shearwater	Short-Eared Owl
Blackbird	Golden Plover	Meadow Pipit	Shoveler
Blackcap	Goldfinch	Mediterranean Gull	Siskin
Black Guillemot	Goosander	Merlin	Skylark
Black-Headed Gull	Goshawk	Mistle Thrush	Slavonian Grebe
Black-Necked Grebe	Grasshopper Warbler	Moorhen	Smew
Black-Tailed Godwit	Great Black-Backed Gull	Mute Swan	Snipe
Black-Throated Diver	Great Crested Grebe	Nightjar	Snow Bunting
Blue Tit	Great Northern Diver	Oystercatcher	Song Thrush
Brambling	Great Skua	Partridge	Sparrowhawk
Brent Goose	Great Tit	Peregrine Falcon	Spotted Flycatcher
Bullfinch	Greenfinch	Pheasant	Spotted Redshank
Buzzard	Green Sandpiper	Pied Wagtail	Starling
Canada Goose	Greenshank	Pink-footed Goose	Stock Dove
Carrion Crow	Grey Heron	Pintail	Stonechat
Chaffinch	Greylag Goose	Pochard	Storm Petrel
Chiffchaff	Grey Phalarope	Pomarine Skua	Swallow
Chough	Grey Plover	Puffin	Swift
Cirl Bunting	Grey Wagtail	Purple Sandpiper	Teal
Coal Tit	Guillemot	Raven	Treecreeper
Collared Dove	Hen Harrier	Razorbill	Tree Sparrow
Common Gull	Herring Gull	Red-Breasted Merganser	Tufted Duck
Common Sandpiper	Hooded Crow	Red Grouse	Turnstone
Common Scoter	House Martin	Red-Leg Partridge	Turtle Dove
Common Tern	House Sparrow	Red-Necked Grebe	Twite
Coot	Hybrid Carr / Hood	Red-Necked Phalarope	Velvet Scoter
Cormorant	Iceland Gull	Redpoll	Water Rail
Corn Bunting	Jackdaw	Redshank	Waxwing
Corncrake	Jack Snipe	Red-Throated Diver	Wheatear
Crossbill	Jay	Redwing	Whimbrel
Cuckoo	Kestrel	Reed Bunting	Whinchat
Curlew	Kingfisher	Ringed Plover	White-Fronted Goose
Curlew Sandpiper	Kittiwake	Ringneck Parakeet	Whitethroat
Dipper	Knot	Ring Ouzel	Whooper Swan
Dunlin	Lapwing	Robin	Wigeon
Dunnock	Lesser Black-Backed Gull	Rock Dove	Willow Warbler
Egyptian Goose	Linnet	Rock Pipit	Woodcock
Eider	Little Auk	Rook	Wood Pigeon
Feral Pigeon	Little Grebe	Roseate Tern	Wren
Fieldfare	Little Gull	Ruff	Yellowhammer

EXTINCT AND ENDANGERED IRISH BIRDS

INDETERMINATE

Barn Owl	*(Tyto alba)*
Tree Sparrow	*(Passer montanus)*
Twite	*(Carduelis flavirostris)*

RARE

Bearded Tit	*(Panurus biarmicus)*
Black-necked Grebe	*(Podiceps nigricollis)*
Black-tailed Godwit	*(Limosa limosa)*
Gadwall	*(Anas strepera)*
Garganey	*(Anas querquedula)*

Goosander	*(Mergus merganser)*
Greenshank	*(Tringa nebularia)*
Merlin	*(Falco columbarius)*
Pintail	*(Anas acuta)*
Pochard	*(Aythya ferina)*
Red-throated Diver	*(Gavia stellata)*
Ring Ouzel	*(Turdus torquatus)*
Short-eared Owl	*(Asio flammeus)*
Shoveler	*(Anas clypeata)*
Wood Warbler	*(Phylloscopus sibilatrix)*

VULNERABLE	
Dunlin	(Calidris alpina)
Golden Plover	(Pluvialis apricaria)
Little Tern	(Sterna albifrons)

ENDANGERED	
Common Scoter	(Melanitta nigra)
Corn Bunting	(Miliaria calandra)
Corncrake	(Crex crex)
Grey Partridge	(Perdix perdix)
Hen Harrier	(Circus cyaneus)
Nightjar	(Caprimulgus europaeus)
Red-necked Phalarope	(Phalaropus lobatus)
Roseate Tern	(Sterna dougallii)

EXTINCT	
Bittern	(Botaurus stellaris)
Capercaillie	(Tetrao urogallus)

Golden Eagle	(Aquila chrysaetos)
Marsh Harrier	(Circus aeruginosus)
White-tailed Eagle	(Haliaeetus albicilla)
Woodlark	(Lullula arborea)

INTERNATIONALLY IMPORTANT	
Chough	(Pyrrhocorax pyrrhocorax)
Peregrine	(Falco peregrinus)
Storm Petrel	(Hydrobates pelagicus)
Whooper Swan	(Cygnus cygnus)
Geese:	
Barnacle	(Branta leucopsis)
Greenland White-fronted	(Anser albifrons flavirostris)
Light-bellied Brent	(Branta bernicla hrota)

COUNTIES OF IRELAND, LARGEST TO SMALLEST
Ranked by size, 1-32

Size No.	County
1	Cork
2	Galway
3	Mayo
4	Donegal
5	Kerry
6	Tipperary
7	Clare
8	Tyrone
9	Antrim
10	Limerick
11	Roscommon
12	Down
13	Wexford
14	Meath
15	Derry
16	Kilkenny
17	Wicklow
18	Offaly
19	Cavan
20	Waterford
21	Sligo
22	Westmeath
23	Laois
24	Kildare
25	Fermanagh
26	Leitrim
27	Dublin
28	Monaghan
29	Armagh
30	Longford
31	Carlow
32	Louth

─── FACT FILE ───

Cork is the largest county on the island of Ireland with a total land area of 2,878 sq. miles, followed in succession by: Galway 2,349 sq. miles, Mayo 2,159 sq. miles and Donegal 1,876 sq. miles. Louth is the smallest county on the island with a total land area of just 318 sq. miles. Tyrone is the largest county in Northern Ireland and also ranks eighth largest in an all-island context, while Armagh is the smallest county in Northern Ireland. Lough Neagh, which is bordered by four counties in Northern Ireland has a total area of 149.61 sq meters, almost half the size of County Louth.

POPULATION

Through the Eyes of the Census

How the Island of Ireland is Changing - What the Figures tell Us

IF WE could look a few decades into the future, the chances are that we would find an island of Ireland that looks very different to that of today. While exact predictions are impossible, the data contained in various censuses and surveys give us a reasonable idea of what the future may hold, if current trends continue. Here is what the Irish Almanac uncovered:

POPULATION: Combining figures from the Northern Ireland (1991) and Republic of Ireland (1996) Censuses, the island of Ireland has a population 5,198,800, with 30.5 per cent living in Northern Ireland and the remainder living in the Republic. Leinster has the largest population - 1,921,835 - and the ancient province of Ulster (nine counties) currently has the second highest population - 1,811711. In 1991, 24.4 per cent of Northern Ireland's population was under 15 years compared with 26.67 per cent of the Republic's, but by 1996 the Republic's under 15 population had fallen to 23.86 per cent. In 1991, 12.6 per cent of Northern Ireland's population was over 65 compared with 11.43 per cent in the Republic.

LANGUAGE: The most common language used on the island of Ireland is English; however, there are some Gaeltacht areas, mainly in the west of the Island, where Gaelic is the predominant language. Interest in the Gaelic language is increasing throughout the island especially as a medium of education, with an increasing number of Gaelic speaking schools being opened on both sides of the border. According to the 1991 Census, 32.5 per cent of the Republic's population claimed to be able to speak Gaelic (their level of competence is not clearly defined). A total of 79,000 people in Northern Ireland claim to be able to read, write and speak Gaelic fluently, while a further 63,000 claim to have some knowledge of the language. The resurgence in interest in Celtic culture and languages in Ireland is mirrored in Scotland, Wales, Brittany, Cornwall, the Isle of Man and across America, and this trend is likely to continue.

LIFE EXPECTANCY: Life expectancy at birth in the Republic is approximately 72 years for men and 78 years for women. This is below the average for the E.U. and may be due to the very high death rates from heart disease and various cancers, especially lung, colo-rectal and breast cancers. Our increasingly sedentary lifestyles, bad eating habits and high rates of smoking and drinking suggest that this trend will continue. Although we may live longer than our predecessors, our quality of life, with regard to health in the later stages of life, will be relatively poor.

HOW WE LIVE: Between 1992 and 1995, birth rates per 1,000 of the estimated population have fallen from 14.4 to 13.5 and 15.8 to 14.5 in Northern Ireland and the Republic, respectively. The trend in falling birth-rates is likely to continue, especially in the Republic, as the country becomes increasingly prosperous. Births outside marriage have increased in the Republic from 18 to 22.2 percent, and a similar trend exists in Northern Ireland. Over the same period, marriages declined from 4.7 to 4.4 per 1,000 of the population in the Republic and from 5.8 to 5.2 per 1,000 in Northern Ireland. It appears likely that these trends are likely to continue with a convergence of social attitudes across the island. Less people are getting married, more are deciding to live together and increasing numbers are being born outside of marriage.

FURTHER SHORES: The trend in net migration outwards from the Republic (134,170) between 1986 and 1991 was reversed between 1991 and 1996 with a net inflow of people into the Republic of 3,185. This has largely been achieved by the return of emigrants from countries experiencing recessions (i.e. England / Germany) to a booming economy in the Republic. Emigration from Northern Ireland of 69,420 between 1981-91 is thought to have been reduced in recent years as the North's economy improved. It is thought that the trends in both parts of the island will continue, especially as the prospect of a political settlement in the North and an economic boom in the South combined with reduced numbers leaving school will reduce the economic necessity to emigrate.

IN GOD WE TRUST: The 1991 census tells us that on the island as a whole, 2.5 per cent of us profess to have no religion while 7.1 per cent of us are Church of Ireland, 6.9 per cent are Presbyterians, 75.1 per cent are Catholic and 3.9 per cent preferred not to state religious affiliations.

In the Republic, 2.4 per cent is Church of Ireland while 91.6 per cent of the population is Catholic and less than 0.7 per cent are members of other Protestant denominations. In Northern Ireland, Catholics are the largest denomination, having risen from 477,919 in 1971 to 605,639 in 1991, while Presbyterians are the second most numerous denomination with 336,891, and the Church of Ireland has 279,280 or 17.7 per cent of the population.

The trend between 1971 and 1991 shows rising numbers of Catholics in the Republic, in line with the general population rise. Significantly, there is a rise in Catholic numbers in Northern Ireland that if continued, would see a Catholic majority in Northern Ireland some time in the first half of the next century. Statisticians argue over whether or not this pace of increase is likely to continue, but it does seem a trend that is likely to continue at least in the medium term. While Protestant numbers show small falls in both parts of Ireland, followers of "Other" religions seem to be on the rise as are persons with no religion.

WHAT WE EARN: The average hourly labour cost in Northern Ireland is $12.79 compared with $14.12 in the Republic. These figures compare favourably with most E.U. countries and the U.S. (i.e. France - $19.34; the U.S. - $17.74) and is no doubt a factor in international companies locating on the island. With inflation in the Republic now very low - 2.5 per cent - and national wage agreements in place, the country is likely to remain competitive for the foreseeable future. Northern Ireland's inflation rate is also quite low, and with unemployment relatively high, wage rates are also likely to remain competitive.

WHERE WE LIVE: Rural depopulation, particularly from the Atlantic seaboard and midland counties, continues as Irish people move to one of our five major cities - Dublin, Belfast, Cork, Derry and Limerick - to live. Dublin is the island's most populous city, followed by Belfast. The counties surrounding these cities - Kildare, Meath, and Wicklow and Antrim and Down, respectively - have consequently experienced surges in population. One happy exception to the shift in population from the West coast is the increase in population in Galway city and county. The county has experienced a 4 per cent increase in population since the beginning of the 1990s, which is associated with the economic boom in the area. Leitrim has the smallest county population with only 25,032 inhabitants, and its population, along with that of Counties Longford and Monaghan, has been in decline since 1991.

───────────◯───────────

DEMOGRAPHIC STATISTICS
Republic of Ireland and Northern Ireland

Description (000's)	Northern Ireland 1991	Republic of Ireland 1996	Republic of Ireland 1991
Population:	1,577.8	3,621.0	3,525.7
Aged 0 - 14	385.1	864.2	940.6
Aged 15 - 24	253.7	635.3	601.6
Aged 25 - 44	433.0	1,001.8	959.0
Aged 45 - 64	306.8	704.9	621.7
Aged 65+	199.1	414.9	402.9
Births:	31.6	249.4	277.5
Deaths:	15.1	157.3	158.3
Marriages:	9.2	81.6	91.1
Marital Status:			
Single	773.7	-	1,953.4
Married	661.1	-	1,384.6
Widowed	96.7	-	187.7
Distribution of Population:	52%	29.2%	29%
Numbers receiving full-time education: (1994/5)	453.1	952.2	-
Primary School Pupils:	196.5	491.3	-
Secondary School Pupils:	153.6	371.2	-
Third Level Pupils: (including F.E. Colleges)	102.9	89.7	-
Unemployment:	99.1	190.0	209.0

REPUBLIC OF IRELAND CENSUS STATISTICS
Overview Irish Census Information (1891-1996)

Total Population

Year	Persons	Births registered	Deaths registered	Marriages registered	Natural increase	Change in population	Estimated net migration*	Intercensal period
1891§	3,468,694	835,072	639,073	145,976	195,999	-401,326	-597,325	1881-91
1901§	3,221,823	737,934	588,391	148,134	149,543	-246,871	-396,414	1891-01
1911§	3,139,688	713,709	534,305	153,674	179,404	-82,135	-261,539	1901-11
1926	2,971,992	968,742	731,409	230,525	237,333	-167,696	-405,029	1911-26
1936	2,968,420	583,502	420,323	136,699	163,179	-3,572	-166,751	1926-36
1946	2,955,107	602,095	428,297	159,426	173,798	-13,313	-187,111	1936-46
1951	2,960,593	329,270	201,295	80,868	127,975	+5,486	-122,489	1946-51
1956	2,898,264	312,517	178,083	79,541	134,434	-62,329	-196,763	1951-56
1961	2,818,341	302,816	170,736	76,669	132,080	-79,923	-212,003	1956-61
1966	2,884,002	312,709	166,443	80,754	146,266	+65,661	-80,605	1961-66
1971	2,978,248	312,796	164,644	95,662	148,152	+94,246	-53,906	1966-71
1979	3,368,217	548,413	267,378	171,705	281,035	+389,969	+108,934	1971-79
1981	3,443,405	146,224	65,991	42,728	80,233	+75,188	-5,045	1979-81
1986	3,540,643	333,457	164,336	95,648	169,121	+97,238	-71,883	1981-86
1991	3,525,719	277,546	158,300	91,141	119,246	-14,924	-134,170	1986-91
1996	3,621,035	249,428	157,297	81,607	92,131	+95,316	+3,185	1991-96

* incoming less outgoing   § includes Northern Ireland Counties

NORTHERN IRELAND CENSUS STATISTICS
Overview Northern Ireland Census Information (1891-1991)

Total Population

Year	Persons	Births registered	Deaths registered	Natural increase	Change in population	Estimated net migration	Intercensal period
1891	1,236,056	312,249	240,339	71,910	68,760	140,670	1881-91
1901	1,236,952	314,795	246,161	68,634	+896	67,738	1891-01
1911	1,250,531	309,502	230,506	78,996	+13,579	65,417	1901-11
1926	1,256,561	431,148	317,545	113,603	+6,030	107,573	1911-26
1937	1,279,745	280,641	199,806	80,835	+23,184	57,651	1926-37
1951	1,370,921	402,187	243,744	158,443	+91,176	67,267	1937-51
1961	1,425,042	298,808	152,459	146,349	+54,121	92,228	1951-61
1966	1,484,775	182,489	85,055	97,434	+59,733	37,701	1961-66
1971	1,536,065	148,706	72,578	76,128	+51,290	24,838	1966-71
1981*	1,532,196	274,786	167,232	107,554	-3,869	111,423	1971-81
1991	1,577,836	273,227	158,167	115,060	+45,640	69,420	1981-91

During the Republican Hunger Strikes of 1981, a substantial number of households were not enumerated. These were subsequently estimated on a 'usually resident' basis, the population effect being approx. 44,500.

MARRIAGES, BIRTHS AND DEATHS IN THE REPUBLIC OF IRELAND

	1992	1993	1994	1995
Marriages	16,636	15,728	16,297	15,623
Births:				
Male	26,567	25,449	24,744	25,032
Female	24,990	24,007	23,184	23,498
Births within Marriage	42,258	39,634	38,024	37,742
Births outside Marriage	9,299	9,827	9,904	10,788
% of births outside Marriage	18.0	19.9	20.7	22.2
Total	51,089	49,461	47,928	48,530
Deaths:				
Male	16,518	16,928	16,274	16,680
Females	14,417	14,996	14,572	14,814
Total	30,935	31,924	30,846	31,494
Natural increase	20,154	17,537	17,082	17,036
Rates per 1,000 of estimated population:				
Marriages	4.7	4.4	4.6	4.4
Births	14.4	13.9	13.4	13.5
Deaths	8.7	9.0	8.6	8.8

MARRIAGES, BIRTHS AND DEATHS IN NORTHERN IRELAND

	1992	1993	1994	1995
Live Births	25,572	24,909	24,289	23,860
Males	13,033	12,620	12,465	12,385
Females	12,539	12,289	11,824	11,475
Still Births	127	130	154	147
Perinatal Deaths	212	220	236	250
Infant Deaths	153	176	147	169
Males	83	99	81	93
Females	70	77	66	76
All Deaths	14,988	15,633	15,114	15,310
Males	7,469	7,731	7,362	7,482
Females	7,519	7,902	7,752	7,828
Marriages	9,392	9,060	8,683	8,576

Rates per 1,000 of estimated population:

Live Births	15.8	15.3	14.8	14.5
Still Births	.5	.5	.6	.6
Perinatal Deaths	.8	.9	.10	.10
Infant Deaths	.6	.7	.6	.7
All Deaths	9.3	9.6	9.2	9.3
Marriages	5.8	5.6	5.3	5.2

REPUBLIC OF IRELAND POPULATION: PROVINCE AND COUNTY, 1991-1996

Province and County	1991			1996			Change 91-96	
	Persons	Males	Females	Persons	Males	Females	Actual	%
TOTAL	5,103,826	2,515,452*	2,588,374*	3,621,035	1,797,596	1,823,439	95,316	2.7
CONNACHT	423,031	214,131	208,900	432,551	218,013	214,538	9,520	2.3
Galway	180,364	91,005	89,359	188,598	94,424	94,174	8,234	4.6
Leitrim	25,301	13,203	12,098	25,032	13,015	12,017	-269	-1.1
Mayo	110,713	55,981	54,732	111,395	56,297	55,098	682	0.6
Roscommon	51,897	26,694	25,203	51,881	26,639	25,242	-16	0.0
Sligo	54,756	27,248	27,508	55,645	27,638	28,007	889	1.6
LEINSTER	1,860,949	913,849	947,100	1,921,835	943,212	978,623	60,886	3.3
Carlow	40,942	20,785	20,157	41,616	21,090	20,526	674	1.6
Dublin	1,025,304	492,432	532,872	1,056,666	508,145	548,521	31,362	3.1
Kildare	122,656	62,207	60,449	134,881	67,958	66,923	12,225	10.0
Kilkenny	73,635	37,447	36,188	75,155	38,059	37,096	1,520	2.1
Laois	52,314	26,904	25,410	52,798	27,122	25,676	484	0.9
Longford	30,296	15,542	14,754	30,138	15,478	14,660	-158	-0.5
Louth	90,724	44,823	45,901	92,163	45,660	46,503	1,439	1.6
Meath	105,370	53,291	52,079	109,371	55,119	54,252	4,001	3.8
Offaly	58,494	29,892	28,602	59,080	29,962	29,118	586	1.0
Westmeath	61,880	31,006	30,874	63,236	31,536	31,700	1,356	2.2
Wexford	102,069	51,444	50,625	104,314	52,413	51,901	2,245	2.2
Wicklow	97,265	48,076	49,189	102,417	50,670	51,747	5,152	5.3
MUNSTER	1,009,533	507,095	502,438	1,033,045	517,752	515,293	23,512	2.3
Clare	90,918	46,367	44,551	93,914	47,730	46,184	2,996	3.3
Cork	410,369	204,542	205,827	420,346	209,159	211,187	9,977	2.4
Kerry	121,894	61,932	59,962	125,863	63,655	62,208	3,969	3.3
Limerick	161,956	81,094	80,862	165,017	82,528	82,489	3,061	1.9
Tipperary	132,772	67,422	65,350	133,308	67,447	65,861	536	0.4
Waterford	91,624	45,738	45,886	94,597	47,233	47,364	2,973	3.2
ULSTER†	1,810,313	880,377	929,936	233,604	118,619	114,985	1,398	0.6
Antrim	562,216	264,242	297,974	-	-	-	-	-
Armagh	141,585	70,184	71,401	-	-	-	-	-
Cavan	52,796	27,314	25,482	52,903	27,263	25,640	107	0.2
Derry	213,035	100,766	112,269	-	-	-	-	-
Donegal	128,117	64,817	63,300	129,435	65,233	64,202	1,318	1.0
Down	454,411	222,662	231,749	-	-	-	-	-
Fermanagh	54,033	27,232	26,801	-	-	-	-	-
Monaghan	51,293	26,212	25,081	51,266	26,123	25,143	-27	-0.1
Tyrone	152,827	76,948	75,879	-	-	-	-	-

* The overall totals for males and females include estimates for Northern Ireland.

† Figures for Counties Antrim, Armagh, Derry, Down, Fermanagh and Tyrone are estimates; (figures for 1996 are not available).

REPUBLIC OF IRELAND:BY AGE GROUP

Persons (000's)	1971	1979	1981	1986	1991	1996
0 - 14 years	931.2	1,029.9	1,043.7	1,024.7	940.6	864.2
15 - 24 years	483.0	583.6	602.6	617.5	601.6	635.3
25 - 44 years	626.2	797.4	837.8	922.6	959.0	1,001.8
45 - 64 years	608.1	595.9	590.4	591.4	621.7	704.9
65+ years	329.8	361.4	369.0	384.4	402.9	414.9
TOTAL	2,978.3	3,368.2	3,443.5	3,540.6	3,525.8	3,621.1

NORTHERN IRELAND POPULATION: COUNCIL AREA, 1981-1991

District Council Area	1981 Persons	1981 Males	1981 Females	1991 Persons	1991 Males	1991 Females	Change 81-91 Actual	Change 81-91 %
Antrim	44,384	22,226	22,158	44,516	22,135	22,381	132	0.3
Ards	57,626	28,127	29,499	64,764	31,527	33,237	7,138	11.7
Armagh	47,618	23,658	23,960	51,817	25,741	26,076	4,199	8.5
Ballymena	54,426	26,743	27,683	56,641	27,830	28,811	2,215	4.0
Ballymoney	22,873	11,439	11,434	24,198	12,022	12,176	1,325	5.6
Banbridge	29,885	14,855	15,030	33,482	16,568	16,914	3,597	11.4
Belfast	295,223	138,889	156,334	279,237	130,820	148,417	-15,986	-5.6
Carrickfergus	28,458	13,762	14,696	32,750	15,871	16,879	4,292	14.0
Castlereagh	60,757	29,234	31,523	60,799	28,946	31,853	42	0.1
Coleraine	46,272	22,438	23,834	50,438	24,369	26,069	4,166	8.6
Cookstown	26,624	13,288	13,336	31,082	15,503	15,579	4,458	15.5
Craigavon	71,202	34,755	36,447	74,986	36,511	38,475	3,784	5.2
Derry	83,384	41,183	42,201	95,371	46,708	48,663	11,987	13.4
Down	52,869	26,459	26,410	58,008	28,835	29,173	5,139	9.3
Dungannon	41,073	20,682	20,391	45,428	22,556	22,872	4,355	10.1
Fermanagh	51,008	25,969	25,039	54,033	27,095	26,938	3,025	5.8
Larne	28,929	14,129	14,800	29,419	14,318	15,101	490	1.7
Limavady	26,270	13,418	12,852	29,567	15,042	14,525	3,297	11.8
Lisburn	82,091	40,535	41,556	99,458	48,653	50,805	17,367	19.1
Magherafelt	30,825	15,501	15,324	36,293	18,177	18,116	5,468	16.3
Moyle	14,252	7,183	7,069	14,789	7,355	7,434	537	3.7
Newry & Mourne	72,243	35,857	36,386	82,943	41,307	41,636	10,700	13.8
Newtownabbey	71,631	34,881	36,750	74,035	35,760	38,275	2,404	3.3
North Down	65,849	31,404	34,445	71,832	34,284	37,548	5,983	8.7
Omagh	41,159	20,866	20,293	45,809	23,022	22,787	4,650	10.7
Strabane	35,028	17,736	17,292	36,141	18,116	18,025	1,113	3.1
TOTAL:	1,481,959	725,217	756,742	1,577,836	769,071	808,765	95,877	6.3

NORTHERN IRELAND: BY AGE GROUP

Persons (000's)	1971	1981	1991	Persons (000's)	1971	1981	1991
0 - 4 years	156.2	130.8	128.3	40 - 44 years	84.3	81.2	97.9
5 - 9 years	157.1	134.3	129.2	45 - 49 years	86.1	76.1	89.9
10 - 14 years	143.6	148.8	127.9	50 - 54 years	80.1	76.0	76.6
15 - 19 years	126.3	144.5	127.6	55 - 59 years	78.5	75.1	71.1
20 - 24 years	114.9	122.3	126.1	60 - 64 years	72.0	68.0	69.3
25 - 29 years	101.9	100.0	122.2	65 - 69 years	60.2	63.4	65.0
30 - 34 years	86.7	98.7	113.5	70 plus years	105.8	120.5	134.1
35 - 39 years	82.4	92.5	99.3				

1971 Census of Population Total: 1,536.1   1981 Census of Population Total: 1,532.2
1991 Census of Population Total: 1,578.0

REPUBLIC OF IRELAND: BY GENDER

Total Number of Males (000's)		Total Number of Females (000's)	
1971	1,495.8	1971	1,482.5
1979	1,693.3	1979	1,674.9
1981	1,729.4	1981	1,714.1
1986	1,769.7	1986	1,771.0
1991	1,753.4	1991	1,772.3
1996	1,797.6	1996	1,823.5

NORTHERN IRELAND: BY GENDER

Total Number of Males (000's)		Total Number of Females (000's)	
1971	754.7	1971	781.4
1981	749.4	1981	782.7
1991	769.1	1991	808.6

REPUBLIC OF IRELAND:
OVERVIEW RELIGIOUS DENOMINATIONS (1881-1991)

Year	Total Persons	R.C.	C.O.I.	Presb.	Meth.	Jewish	Other	No Religion	Not Stated
1881	3,870,020	3,465,332	317,576	56,498	17,660	394	-	12,560	-
1891	3,468,694	3,099,003	286,804	51,469	18,513	1,506	-	11,399	-
1901	3,221,823	2,878,271	264,264	46,714	17,872	3,006	-	11,696	-
1911	3,139,688	2,812,509	249,535	45,486	16,440	3,805	-	11,913	-
1926	2,971,992	2,751,269	164,215	32,429	10,663	3,686	-	9,730	-
1936	2,968,420	2,773,920	145,030	28,067	9,649	3,749	-	8,005	-
1946	2,955,107	2,786,033	124,829	23,870	8,355	3,907	-	8,113	-
1961	2,818,341	2,673,473	104,016	18,953	6,676	3,255	5,236	1,107	5,625
1971	2,978,248	2,795,666	97,739	16,052	5,646	2,633	6,248	7,616	46,648
1981	3,443,405	3,204,476	95,366	14,255	5,790	2,127	10,843	39,572	70,976
1991	3,525,719	3,228,327	89,187	13,199	5,037	1,581	38,743	66,270	83,375

NORTHERN IRELAND:
OVERVIEW OF RELIGIOUS DENOMINATIONS

Year	Total Persons	R.C.	Presb.	C.O.I.	Meth.	Breth.	Bapt.	Cong.	Unitn.	Other	None	Not Stated
1961	1,425,042	497,547	413,113	344,800	71,865	16,847	13,765	9,838	5,613	23,236	-	28,418
1971	1,519,640	477,919	405,719	334,318	71,235	16,480	16,563	10,072	3,975	40,848	-	142,511
1981	1,481,959	414,532	339,818	281,472	58,731	12,158	16,375	8,265	3,373	72,651	-	274,584
1991	1,577,836	605,639	336,891	279,280	59,517	12,446	19,484	8,176	3,213	79,129	59,234	114,827

REPUBLIC OF IRELAND PERSONS BY RELIGIOUS DENOMINATION, BY PROVINCE AND COUNTY, 1991

Province & County	Total Persons	R.C.	C.O.I.	Prot.	Presb.	Meth.	Jewish	Other	No Religion	Not Stated
TOTAL	3,525,719	3,228,327	82,840	6,347	13,199	5,037	1,581	38,743	66,270	83,375
CONNACHT	423,031	397,848	5,321	516	333	286	21	3,208	5,392	10,106
Galway	180,364	168,640	1,358	228	81	76	16	1,772	3,191	5,002
Leitrim	25,301	23,682	721	41	17	61	-	80	217	482
Mayo	110,713	105,839	817	116	101	27	2	601	929	2,281
Roscommon	51,897	50,204	358	28	13	21	2	221	333	717
Sligo	54,756	49,483	2,067	103	121	101	1	534	722	1,624
LEINSTER	1,860,949	1,685,334	50,912	3,391	3,799	2,815	1,439	24,829	48,843	44,587
Carlow	40,942	37,767	1,747	42	15	25	5	262	343	736
Dublin	1,025,304	911,454	26,169	2,157	2,716	1,895	1,383	17,571	33,269	28,690
Kildare	122,656	113,828	2,923	147	153	102	9	1,212	1,859	2,423
Kilkenny	73,635	68,699	1,586	74	143	56	2	559	822	1,694
Laois	52,314	48,461	2,417	41	38	94	1	312	256	694
Longford	30,296	28,645	705	24	46	37	-	161	163	515
Louth	90,724	85,770	939	49	137	20	5	907	974	1,923
Meath	105,370	98,766	1,926	133	142	42	2	797	1,236	2,326
Offaly	58,494	55,172	1,604	52	39	142	1	279	323	882
Westmeath	61,880	58,508	1,059	80	32	38	-	401	528	1,234
Wexford	102,069	94,832	3,287	169	81	77	8	554	1,052	2,009
Wicklow	97,265	83,432	6,550	423	257	287	23	1,814	3,018	1,461
MUNSTER	1,009,533	941,675	15,758	1,385	548	1,185	111	9,192	15,402	24,277
Clare	90,918	84,847	699	72	55	43	12	861	1,778	2,551
Cork	410,369	379,011	8,864	792	240	690	57	4,291	7,567	8,857
Kerry	121,894	114,253	1,415	173	46	34	17	920	1,696	3,340
Limerick	161,956	152,364	1,409	158	86	210	15	1,365	2,084	4,265
Tipperary	132,772	125,607	2,132	101	52	147	1	885	1,074	2,773
Waterford	91,624	85,593	1,239	89	69	61	9	870	1,203	2,491

Province & County	Total Persons	R.C.	C.O.I.	Prot.	Presb.	Meth.	Jewish	Other	No Religion	Not Stated
ULSTER (part of)	232,206	203,470	10,849	1,055	8,519	751	10	1,514	1,633	4,405
Cavan	52,796	46,703	3,622	160	710	94	1	240	291	975
Donegal	128,117	111,427	5,602	555	5,412	603	8	866	1,029	2,615
Monaghan	51,293	45,340	1,625	340	2,397	54	1	408	313	815

N. IRE. PERSONS BY RELIGIOUS DENOMINATIONS, BY DISTRICT COUNCIL AREA, 1991

District Council Area	Total	Male	Female	R.C.	Presb.	C.O.I.	Meth.	Other	None	Not Stated
Total	1,577,836	769,071	808,765	605,639	336,891	279,280	59,517	122,448	59,234	114,827
Antrim	44,516	22,135	22,381	14,117	13,614	6,384	786	3,600	2,025	3,990
Ards	64,764	31,527	33,237	7,341	25,219	12,137	3,386	7,069	3,904	5,708
Armagh	51,817	25,741	26,076	23,518	8,627	10,604	1,236	3,964	825	3,043
Ballymena	56,641	27,830	28,811	10,392	26,067	6,869	1,442	6,115	1,845	3,911
Ballymoney	24,198	12,022	12,176	7,311	9,411	3,151	123	2,184	524	1,494
Banbridge	33,482	16,568	16,914	9,256	9,608	6,362	624	3,977	929	2,726
Belfast	279,237	130,820	148,417	108,954	47,743	50,242	14,667	20,113	14,756	22,762
Carrickfergus	32,750	15,871	16,879	2,269	10,166	7,698	3,162	4,390	2,476	2,589
Castlereagh	60,799	28,946	31,853	5,743	17,445	14,638	5,323	8,481	3,797	5,372
Coleraine	50,438	24,369	26,069	11,323	15,946	12,550	784	4,214	2,104	3,517
Cookstown	31,082	15,503	15,579	16,522	4,779	5,288	331	2,131	382	1,649
Craigavon	74,986	36,511	38,475	30,060	7,718	18,666	3,904	7,190	1,955	5,493
Derry	95,371	46,708	48,663	66,260	10,539	8,503	853	2,629	1,353	5,234
Down	58,008	28,835	29,173	32,507	9,025	6,183	559	3,454	1,658	4,622
Dungannon	45,428	22,556	22,872	25,299	5,822	8,245	912	2,416	384	2,350
Fermanagh	54,033	27,095	26,938	29,657	1,549	14,283	2,724	2,534	745	2,541
Larne	29,419	14,318	15,101	6,510	11,136	4,083	1,107	2,771	1,291	2,521
Limavady	29,567	15,042	14,525	15,281	5,683	4,699	203	1,035	512	2,154
Lisburn	99,458	48,653	50,805	26,786	20,980	26,286	4,095	9,154	4,780	7,377
Magherafelt	36,293	18,177	18,116	21,377	5,466	4,372	165	2,632	313	1,968
Moyle	14,789	7,355	7,434	7,723	2,766	2,587	29	452	254	978
Newry & Mourne	82,943	41,307	41,636	59,555	8,890	3,861	314	3,376	947	6,000
Newtown-abbey	74,035	35,760	38,275	9,635	23,610	14,976	6,437	8,125	4,476	6,776
North Down	71,832	34,284	37,548	6,435	23,658	16,591	5,077	7,500	6,140	6,431
Omagh	45,809	23,022	22,787	29,469	5,141	5,766	785	1,910	570	2,168
Strabane	36,141	18,116	18,025	22,339	6,283	4,256	489	1,032	289	1,453

NORTHERN IRELAND: OVERVIEW OF RELIGIOUS DENOMINATIONS BY PERCENTAGE

Year	Total Persons	R.C.	Presb.	C.O.I.	Meth.	Breth.	Bapt.	Cong.	Unitn.	Other	None	Not Stated
1961	1,425,042	34.9%	29.0%	24.2%	5.0%	1.2%	1.0%	0.7%	0.4%	1.6%	-	2.0%
1971	1,519,640	31.4%	26.7%	22.0%	4.7%	1.1%	1.1%	0.7%	0.3%	2.7%	-	9.3%
1981	1,481,959	28.0%	22.9%	19.0%	4.0%	0.8%	1.1%	0.6%	0.2%	4.9%	-	18.5%
1991	1,577,836	38.4%	21.4%	17.7%	3.8%	0.8%	1.2%	0.5%	0.2%	5.0%	3.7%	7.3%

N. IRELAND PERSONS BY DISTRICT COUNCIL AREA, BY RELIGIOUS DENOMINATIONS, 1991 (%)

District Council Area	Total	Male	Female	R.C.	Presb.	C.O.I.	Meth.	Other	None	Not Stated
Antrim	44,516	22,135	22,381	31.7%	30.6%	14.3%	1.8%	8.1%	4.5%	9.0%
Ards	64,764	31,527	33,237	11.4%	38.9%	18.8%	5.2%	10.9%	6.0%	8.8%
Armagh	51,817	25,741	26,076	45.4%	16.6%	20.5%	2.4%	7.6%	1.6%	5.9%
Ballymena	56,641	27,830	28,811	18.4%	46.0%	12.1%	2.5%	10.8%	3.3%	6.9%
Ballymoney	24,198	12,022	12,176	30.2%	38.9%	13.0%	0.5%	9.0%	2.2%	6.2%
Banbridge	33,482	16,568	16,914	27.6%	28.7%	19.0%	1.9%	11.9%	2.8%	8.1%
Belfast	279,237	130,820	148,417	39.0%	17.1%	18.0%	5.3%	7.2%	5.3%	8.1%
Carrickfergus	32,750	15,871	16,879	6.9%	31.0%	23.5%	9.7%	13.4%	7.6%	7.9%
Castlereagh	60,799	28,946	31,853	9.4%	28.7%	24.1%	8.8%	14.0%	6.2%	8.8%
Coleraine	50,438	24,369	26,069	22.4%	31.6%	24.9%	1.5%	8.4%	4.2%	7.0%
Cookstown	31,082	15,503	15,579	53.1%	15.4%	17.0%	1.1%	6.9%	1.2%	5.3%
Craigavon	74,986	36,511	38,475	40.1%	10.3%	24.9%	5.2%	9.6%	2.6%	7.3%
Derry	95,371	46,708	48,663	69.5%	11.0%	8.9%	0.9%	2.8%	1.4%	5.5%
Down	58,008	28,835	29,173	56.0%	15.5%	10.7%	1.0%	5.9%	2.9%	8.0%
Dungannon	45,428	22,556	22,872	55.7%	12.8%	18.1%	2.0%	5.3%	0.9%	5.2%
Fermanagh	54,033	27,095	26,938	54.9%	2.9%	26.4%	5.0%	4.7%	1.4%	4.7%
Larne	29,419	14,318	15,101	22.1%	37.8%	13.9%	3.8%	9.4%	4.4%	8.6%
Limavady	29,567	15,042	14,525	51.7%	19.2%	15.9%	0.7%	3.5%	1.7%	7.3%
Lisburn	99,458	48,653	50,805	27.0%	21.1%	26.4%	4.1%	9.2%	4.8%	7.4%
Magherafelt	36,293	18,177	18,116	58.9%	15.1%	12.0%	0.4%	7.3%	0.9%	5.4%
Moyle	14,789	7,355	7,434	52.2%	18.7%	17.5%	0.2%	3.1%	1.7%	6.6%
Newry & Mourne	82,943	41,307	41,636	71.8%	10.7%	4.7%	0.4%	4.1%	1.1%	7.2%
Newtownabbey	74,035	35,760	38,275	13.0%	31.9%	20.2%	8.7%	11.0%	6.0%	9.2%
North Down	71,832	34,284	37,548	9.0%	32.9%	23.1%	7.1%	10.4%	8.5%	9.0%
Omagh	45,809	23,022	22,787	64.3%	11.2%	12.6%	1.7%	4.2%	1.3%	4.7%
Strabane	36,141	18,116	18,025	61.8%	17.4%	11.8%	1.3%	2.9%	0.8%	4.0%

REPUBLIC OF IRELAND: OCCUPATIONS BY INDUSTRIAL GROUP, 1996

Industrial Group (000's)	Persons	Males	Females
Agriculture, forestry, fishing	136.5	121.8	14.7
Mining, quarrying and turf production	4.8	4.5	0.4
Manufacturing industries	246.5	172.4	74.1
Electricity, gas and water supply	13.6	11.7	2.0
Building and construction	86.0	81.7	4.3
Commerce	193.0	114.1	78.9
Wholesale distribution	48.3	35.3	13.0
Retail distribution	144.6	78.8	65.9
Insurance, finance and business services	79.7	39.7	40.0
Transport, communication and storage	80.1	62.3	17.8
Public administration and defence	76.4	48.1	28.3
Professional services	238.6	84.1	154.5
Personal services	99.0	37.7	61.3
Other industries	31.0	19.2	11.8
TOTAL:	1285.2	797.3	488.1

NORTHERN IRELAND: OCCUPATIONS BY INDUSTRIAL GROUP, 1991

Industrial Group	Persons	Males	Females
Agriculture, forestry, fishing	23,962	22,274	1,688
Mining & ores	9,147	7,566	1,581

Industrial Group	Persons	Males	Females
Manufacturing industries	60,174	33,992	26,182
Food, drink & tobacco	18,142	12,201	5,941
Textiles, clothing, footwear and leather	24,035	7,877	16,158
Wood and wood products	6,819	6,102	717
Paper, paper products, printing and publishing	6,198	4,026	2,172
Rubber and plastic products	4,344	3,417	927
Other manufacturing	636	369	267
Energy and water industries	7,180	6,120	1,060
Building and construction	41,079	38,489	2,590
Banking, insurance, finance, business services and leasing	40,075	21,200	18,875
Transport and communications	24,484	19,604	4,880
Distribution, hotels and catering	103,228	55,273	47,955
Metal, engineering and vehicle industries	32,929	26,451	6,478
Government employment / training scheme	13,245	8,649	4,596
Others	219,447	89,782	129,665
TOTAL:	**574,950**	**329,400**	**245,550**

R.O.I. SELECTED OCCUPATIONS STATISTICS (1991)

Description	Persons	Males	Females
Religion	8,484	5,053	3,431
Primary Education	24,795	5,968	18,827
Secondary Education	21,490	8,267	13,223
Vocational Education	9,077	4,100	4,977
University Education	11,203	6,349	4,854
Health Board Hospitals etc	30,209	6,415	23,794
Dentistry	2,060	879	1,181
Veterinary Surgery	1,481	958	523
Accountancy	11,634	6,842	4,792
Legal Services	10,350	3,703	6,647
Banking and Finance	28,747	12,517	16,230
Garda Síochána	10,851	10,146	705
Defence	11,902	11,605	297
Forestry	2,298	2,222	76
Fishing	2,895	2,669	226
Plumbing and Domestic Heating	4,557	4,414	143
Painting and Decorating	5,623	5,233	390
Hotels	15,569	6,324	9,245
Hairdressing, Beauty Parlours and Saunas	9,946	1,387	8,559
Turf Production	2,756	2,586	170
Beverages	6,190	4,945	1,245
Tobacco	1,240	755	485
Air Transport	8,580	5,795	2,785
Railway Transport	5,625	5,036	589
Road Passenger Transport	10,670	9,753	917
Road Freight Transport	10,759	10,015	744
Postal, Telegraph and Radio communications	21,438	16,401	5,037
Theatres and Broadcasting	5,219	3,450	1,769
Bookmaking	2,101	957	1,144

N.I. SELECTED OCCUPATIONS STATISTICS (1991)

Description	Persons	Males	Females
Sales Personnel	42,119	16,381	25,738
Managers and Administrators (private and public industry)	82,270	62,372	19,898
Teaching Professionals	26,843	10,266	16,577
Legal Professionals	1,788	1,334	454
Architects, Townplanners and Surveyors	1,536	1,402	134
Computer Analysts and Programmers	1,736	1,307	429
Health Professionals	11,792	1,489	10,303
Literary, Artistic and Sports Professionals	4,082	2,817	1,265
Armed Forces	9,388	8,546	842
Security and Protective Services	16,061	14,647	1,414

IRELAND'S EUROPEAN RANKING IN HOME OWNERSHIP LEVELS (1996)

Country	% Home Ownership
Finland	78
Spain	78
Ireland	76
Britain	66
Sweden	62
France	62
Netherlands	40
Germany	38

MAIN IRISH TOWNS
Irish Cities and Towns with a population of 3,000 or over, 1991

Town (County)	Population	Town (County)	Population
Greater Dublin	915,516	Mullingar (Westmeath)	11,867
Belfast City	279,237	Navan (Meath)	11,706
Cork County Borough	174,400	Enniskillen (Fermanagh)	11,436
Derry City	101,200	Naas (Kildare)	11,141
Limerick County Borough	75,436	Greystones (Wicklow)	10,778
Galway County Borough	50,853	Limavady (Derry)	10,764
Waterford County Borough	41,853	Letterkenny (Donegal)	10,726
		Cookstown (Tyrone)	10,472
Newtownabbey (Antrim)	57,103	Downpatrick (Down)	10,257
Bangor (Down)	52,437	Killarney (Kerry)	9,950
Lisburn (Antrim)	42,110	Celbridge (Kildare)	9,629
Dundalk (Louth)	30,061	Tullamore (Offaly)	9,430
Ballymena (Antrim)	28,717	Dungannon (Tyrone)	9,420
Bray (Wicklow)	26,953	Holywood (Down)	9,252
Drogheda (Louth)	24,656	Craigavon (Armagh)	9,201
Newtownards (Down)	24,301	Portmarnock (Dublin)	9,173
Newry (Down)	22,975	Comber (Down)	8,516
Carrickfergus (Antrim)	22,885	Portlaoise (Laois)	8,360
Lurgan (Armagh)	21,905	Ballymoney (Antrim)	8,242
Portadown (Armagh)	21,299	Cobh (Cork)	8,219
Antrim	20,878	Ballina (Mayo)	8,167
Coleraine (Derry)	20,721	Arklow (Wicklow)	7,987
Sligo	17,964	Shannon (Clare)	7,920
Tralee (Kerry)	17,862	Ballyclare (Antrim)	7,761
Swords (Dublin)	17,705	Balbriggan (Dublin)	7,724
Kilkenny	17,669	Enniscorthy (Wexford)	7,655
Larne (Antrim)	17,575	Castlebar (Mayo)	7,648
Omagh (Tyrone)	17,280	Mallow (Cork)	7,521
Ennis (Clare)	16,058	Newcastle (Down)	7,214
Clonmel (Tipperary)	15,562	Magherafelt (Derry)	7,143
Wexford	15,393	Skerries (Dublin)	7,032
Athlone (Westmeath)	15,358	Thurles (Tipperary)	6,955
Armagh	14,640	Dungarvan (Waterford)	6,920
Carlow	14,027	Longford	6,824
Lucan (Dublin)	13,574	Carrigaline (Cork)	6,482
Leixlip (Kildare)	13,194	Portstewart (Derry)	6,459
Dundonald (Down)	12,943	Wicklow	6,215
Dunmurry (Antrim)	12,771	Kilkeel (Down)	6,123
Banbridge (Down)	12,529	New Ross (Wexford)	6,079
Malahide (Dublin)	12,088	Tramore (Waterford)	6,064
Newbridge (Kildare)	12,069	Maynooth (Kildare)	6,027
Strabane (Tyrone)	11,981	Midleton (Cork)	5,951

Continued from previous page

Irish Cities and Towns with a population of 3,000 or over, 1991

Town (County)	Population	Town (County)	Population
Monaghan	5,946	Trim (Meath)	4,185
Ballinasloe (Galway)	5,892	Birr (Offaly)	4,056
Youghal (Cork)	5,828	Ballycastle (Antrim)	4,005
Nenagh (Tipperary)	5,825	Gorey (Wexford)	3,840
Portrush (Antrim)	5,703	Coalisland (Tyrone)	3,802
Warrenpoint (Down)	5,637	Whitehead (Antrim)	3,761
Tuam (Galway)	5,540	Edenderry (Offaly)	3,742
Cavan	5,254	Dromore (Down)	3,708
Athy (Kildare)	5,204	Westport (Mayo)	3,688
Ballynahinch (Down)	5,196	Maghera (Derry)	3,631
Carrick-on-Suir (Tipperary)	5,143	Newcastle (Limerick)	3,612
Greenisland (Antrim)	4,967	Passage West (Cork)	3,606
Tipperary	4,963	Ardee (Louth)	3,604
Rush (Dublin)	4,839	Listowel (Kerry)	3,597
Donaghadee (Down)	4,799	Kells (Meath)	3,539
Bandon (Cork)	4,741	Roscommon	3,427
Fermoy (Cork)	4,462	Laytown-Bettystown-Mornington (Meath)	3,360
Ashbourne (Meath)	4,411	Carrickmacross (Monaghan)	3,341
Buncrana (Donegal)	4,388	Loughrea (Galway)	3,271
Randalstown (Antrim)	4,290	Portarlington (Laois)	3,211
Carryduff (Down)	4,270	Bessbrook (Armagh)	3,147
Roscrea (Tipperary)	4,231	Michelstown (Cork)	3,090
Kildare	4,196	Mountmellick (Laois)	3,003

REPUBLIC OF IRELAND CENSUS
How the system works / statistics

The census figures in the Republic relate to the de facto population - that is, the numbers of persons actually in the state on the night the census is taken. Visitors to the state are included in the census as are those visitors in residence, while usual residents who are absent from the state are excluded. The intercensal change in population reflects vital events (e.g. births and deaths) and all movement into and out of the state.

Vital Statistics: In the 1986-1991 intercensal period, the excess of births over deaths was 119,246 while statistics abstracted from the census indicated a population decrease of 14,924 which implied a net outward migration of 134,170 people. In the 1991-1996 intercensal period the excess of births was 92,131 and the census indicated a population increase of 95,316, implying a net inward migration of 3,185. Since 1980 there has been a noticeable decline in the birth rate. In that year there were 74,388 births registered and the natural increase was 41,400. Despite this, 1996 saw a slight increase in the number of births registered - 50,390 - compared with 48,530 in 1995. The death rate in 1996 was 8.7 per 1,000 population - the actual number of deaths registered for the year being 31,514. The marriage rate is also in decline; 21,792 in 1980 decreasing to 16,255 in 1996.

The most recent census carried out in the Republic of Ireland was on April 28, 1996.

NORTHERN IRELAND CENSUS
How the system works / statistics

The Northern Ireland census is enumerated somewhat differently than that of the Republic. The actual population is calculated as being the number of people usually resident in Northern Ireland, excluding visitors but including those who were stated as being usually resident there, irrespective of whether or not they were at their usual address on census night. This resulted in a population of 1,577,836. However, the actual population enumerated on the census night was 1,569,971.

Vital Statistics: The 1985/86-1989/90 period saw a net inward migration of 28,400 people, while the 1990/91-1994/95 period saw a net outward migration of 10,075. Since 1986, there has been a decline in the birth rate - in that year there were 28,152 births registered. In 1995, the number of births registered was 23,860 (compared with 24,289 in 1994). The death rate in 1995 was 9.3 per 1,000 population - the actual number of deaths registered for the year being 15,310. The marriage rate is also in decline, with 10,225 in 1986 decreasing to 8,576 in 1995.

The most recent census carried out in Northern Ireland was on April 21, 1991.

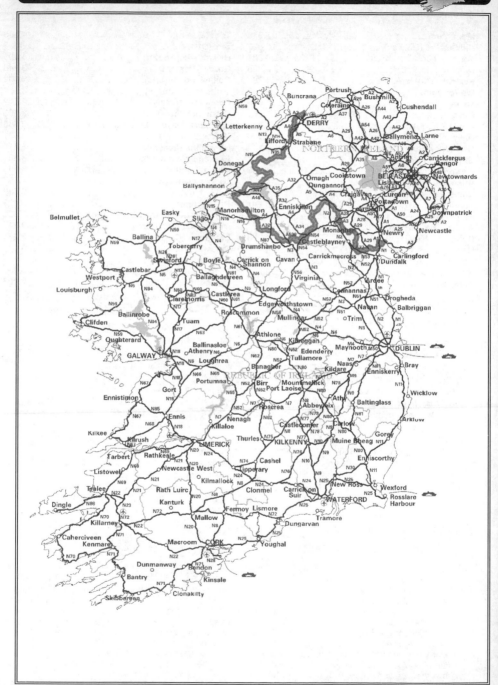

COUNTY ANTRIM
(Province: Ulster)

County Antrim is set in the north-east corner of Ireland. The county could be described as a basaltic tableland. Its most remarkable feature is the Giant's Causeway, found on the north-western part of the county and designated a world heritage site. The causeway is made up of around 40,000, mostly hexagonal, basaltic columns that are packed tightly together. The columns were formed from the cooling of lava from volcanic eruptions, and solidified lava can be seen in the cliffs, 90 feet thick in places. The ancient Irish legends attributed the geological phenomenon to the giant Finn MacCool, who fell in love with a lady giant in Scotland and built the causeway for her, so that she could cross the sea to visit him. Further east along the coast can be found the Glens of Antrim; nine green river valleys that are bisected by rivers and waterfalls and full of wild flowers and birds. Their occupants are mostly descended from old Irish and Hebridean Scots, and the Glens were one of the last places in Northern Ireland where Gaelic was spoken.

The Antrim coast is where Ireland's first inhabitants - nomadic boatmen from Scotland - landed circa 7000 B.C. The early Christians and the Vikings were also drawn to Antrim's coast. The Normans conquered the county and began building castles; John de Courcy built a huge castle in 1180 at Carrickfergus, and Richard de Burgh, the Earl of Ulster, first built Dunluce Castle, a fortification that clings on to the sea cliffs on the north. Edward Bruce, King of Scotland, landed in Larne in 1315 and besieged Carrickfergus Castle for more than a year. This established a pattern for the castle and town of Carrickfergus for the next several centuries, owing to the site's strategic importance at the entrance of Belfast Lough. The MacDonnells had possession of Dunluce Castle and its surrounding environs in the late 15th century, while the rest of the Armagh region was ruled over by the MacQuillans, the O'Neills and the Hebridean Scots of the Glens, indicating that Antrim was unofficially planted by the Scots long before the formal plantation of the other counties in Ulster in 1610. The Bushmill Whiskey Distillery, which is still in operation, was established at Bushmills in 1608, making it the world's oldest legal distillery. Antrim was one of the few counties in Ireland to be directly affected by the Industrial Revolution. It, along with Armagh and Monaghan, was a county of domestic linen production and consequently, was heavily populated, particularly in southern Antrim. This led to tension over occupation of land, dislocation and ultimately, the growth of Belfast as a major industrial centre with a large Protestant working class.

ORIGIN OF COUNTY NAME: Derived from the Irish 'Aontroim', meaning solitary farm.

LAND AREA: 1,093 sq. miles

LARGEST TOWN: Belfast.

MAIN TOWNS: Antrim, Ballymena, Ballycastle, Belfast, Carrickfergus, Larne, Lisburn, Newtownabbey.

MAIN INDUSTRIES: Agriculture, airport services, chemicals production, clothing manufacturing, construction, electricity suppliers, electrical engineering, electronic products manufacturing, ferryport services, food wholesalers, forestry, fishing, glass-fibre manufacturing, meat processing, mechanical engineering, packaging manufacturing, poultry processing, recreation services, retailing, service industries, soft drinks manufacturing, supermarket retailers, telecommunications sales and services, tobacco manufacturing, tyre production, ventilation engineering, video recording manufacturing, whiskey distilling, wine and spirit wholesalers.

CENSUS DETAILS: 562,216 *(estimated)*.

NUMBER OF SCHOOLS: 198 primary schools, 43 secondary schools, 5 institutes of further and higher education, 1 university.

NAMES OF COUNCILS: Antrim Borough Council, Ballymena Borough Council, Ballymoney Borough Council, Belfast City Council,

KEY TO MAP
* ✳ **Giant's Causeway**
* ▲ **Trostan Mountain (551m)**
* ■ **Belfast City**
* ● **Main towns**
* ■ **Lakes / Rivers**

Carrickfergus Borough Council, Castlereagh Borough Council, Larne Borough Council, Moyle District Council, Newtownabbey Borough Council.

CHIEF EXECUTIVES: Antrim: S.J. Magee; Ballymena: Mervyn Rankin; Ballymoney: J.C. Alderdice; Carrickfergus: Raymond Boyd; Castlereagh: C.B. Sneddon *(acting)*; Larne: Trevor Clarke; Moyle: Richard Lewis; Newtownabbey: Norman Dunn.

CHAIRMEN / MAYORS: Antrim: F.R.H. Marks; Ballymena: James Currie; Ballymoney: Frank Campbell; Carrickfergus: D.W. Hilditch; Castlereagh: John Norris; Larne: Joan Drummond; Moyle: Richard Kerr; Newtownabbey: E.J. Crilly.

COUNCIL MEETING DATES: Antrim: second Tuesday of each month; Ballymena: first Monday of each month; Ballymoney: first Monday of each month; Carrickfergus: first Monday of each month; Castlereagh: last Thursday in each month; Larne: first Monday of each month; Moyle: second and fourth Monday of each month; Newtownabbey: last Monday of each month.

RADIO STATIONS: B.B.C. Radio Ulster.

NEWSPAPERS: Antrim Guardian, (Editor: Liam Heffron). Ballymena Guardian, (Editor: M. O'Neill). Ballymena/Antrim Times and Ballymena Observer, (Morton Newspapers). Carrick Times, (Editor: Terrence Ferry). Carrickfergus Advertiser, (Editor: Ian Greer). Lisburn Echo, (Editor: Joe Fitzpatrick).

MAJOR TOURIST ATTRACTIONS: Andrew Jackson Centre, the site of the ancestral home of the seventh U.S. president; angling; Antrim Castle Gardens, Massereene Demesne; Arthur Ancestral Home, the site of the 21st U.S. president; Ballintoy; Ballycastle Museum; Ballypatrick Forest; the Ballance House, the birthplace of John Ballance, New Zealand's prime minister 1891-93; the beach at White Rocks; Benvarden Garden, Dervock; Carrick-a-rede Rope Bridge, a famous landmark linking the mainland to a rocky outcrop; Carrickfergus Gas Works; Carrickfergus Marina; Carrickfergus Town Walls, built circa 1610; Causeway School Museum; Cushendun, a village admired for its Cornish architecture; Dunluce Centre, Portrush; Ford Farm Park & Museum, Islandmagee; the Giant's Causeway; Glenariff Forest Park; Irish Linen Centre & Lisburn Museum; Knight Ride & Heritage Plaza, Carrickfergus; Langford Lodge Wartime Centre, Crumlin; Larne & District Historical Centre; Larne Interpretive Centre; Loughareema, a vanishing lake; Slemish Mountain, where St. Patrick tended pigs; St. Gobbans, Ireland's smallest church; the Ulster Way; the U.S. Rangers Centre, Boneybefore; Whitehead Beach.

FAMOUS NATIVES OF THE PAST: James Brown Armour (Presbyterian Minister; died 1928), John Ballance (New Zealand Prime Minister 1891-1893; died 1893), Sam Hanna Bell (writer/radio producer, born Scotland; died 1990), Sir. John Biggart (pathologist/ created Northern Ireland blood transfusion service; died 1973), Ernest Blythe (revolutionary/politician/theatre promoter; died 1975), Patrick Boyle (novelist; died 1982), Alexander Brown (founder of oldest investment bank in U.S. - died 1834), Fred Daly (golfer; died 1990), Sir. Richard Dawson (politician; died 1949), Arthur Dobbs (Governor of North Carolina 1753/ Surveyor General of Ireland; born 1689), Francis Fowke (designed Belfast's Royal Albert Hall/Dublin's National Gallery; died 1865), Sir Joseph Larmour (mathematician/physicist; died 1941), Michael A. MacConnaill (anatomist; died 1987), Samuel McCaughey (Australian sheep magnate; died 1919), Samuel S. McClure (pioneer of reform journalism/launched first U.S. syndicate 1884; died 1949), Sir Ivan Whiteside Magill (anaesthetist; died 1986), Captain Terence O'Neill (politician, born London; died 1990), Archibald Hamilton Rowan (United Irishman/revolutionary; died 1834), Elisha Scott (soccer goalkeeper; born 1894), Alexander Turney Stewart (conceived/built first department store in U.S. 1850; died 1876).

COUNTY ARMAGH
(Province: Ulster)

Set in the north-east of Ireland, Armagh is an inland county, although it is almost surrounded by water - with the River Blackwater in the west, the River Bann in the east and Lough Neagh, Ireland's largest lake, in the north. Armagh's rolling hilly terrain is due to its being part of Ireland's drumlin belt. South Armagh is home to the Ring of Gullion, with its varied mountainous topography. The gentle landscape of the north-east of the county is ideal for fruit growing, which has led Armagh to be called the Orchard County. Records reveal that apples have been grown in Armagh for more than 3,000 years. St. Patrick himself reputedly planted an apple tree at Ceangoba, an ancient settlement east of Armagh city. The Bramley apple has proven to be the easiest species to grow in the northern climate, and an orchard trust has been established by local growers to keep alive traditional orchards and old apple varieties that are currently under threat from the cheaper, more standard varieties.

Armagh, particularly the city of Armagh, holds an important place in Irish history. Navan Fort or 'Emain Macha', two miles west of the city, was home to the kings of Ulster. Although traces of man at the site date back to 5500 B.C., it is thought that Navan Fort was at its height from 700 B.C. It is the focal point of the Ulster cycle in early Irish literature. This literature recounts Celtic rituals and the history of CúChulainn and the Táin. Although tradition has it that Armagh became the centre of Irish Christianity during the fifth century with the arrival of St. Patrick, in reality a collection of hagiographic writings on St. Patrick, compiled between A.D. 670 and 690, attempted to bring the primacy of the Irish church to Armagh. This attempt proved successful, and Armagh's primacy within the Irish Church was officially confirmed in 1005 by Brian Boru, the high king at that time. Armagh still retains its place as ecclesiastical capital of Ireland. During medieval times, Armagh was ruled over by the O'Neills, but was planted in 1610 along

KEY TO MAP
* ✳ *Navan Fort*
* ▲ *Slieve Gullion (575m)*
* ■ *Armagh City*
* ● Main towns
* ■ Lakes / Rivers

with other counties in Ulster. In 1646, Owen Roe O'Neill rose up against the settlers at the Battle of Benburb. In the centuries that followed, bloody conflicts continued between the native Irish and the Protestant settlers. The Orange

Order was founded in Armagh in 1795 and united disparate Protestant groups. During the 18th century, Richard Robinson, the Church of Ireland Primate, used a large portion of his personal wealth to convert Armagh into a city of Georgian splendour, rivalling that of Dublin, and many of the city of Armagh's public buildings date to this time.

ORIGIN OF COUNTY NAME: Derived from the Irish 'Ard Macha', meaning Macha's Height and referring to the legendary queen Macha who reputedly built a fortress on top of a hill around the mid-first millennium B.C.

LAND AREA: 484 sq. miles. **LARGEST TOWN:** Armagh.

MAIN TOWNS: Portadown, Lurgan and Keady.

MAIN INDUSTRIES: Agriculture, apple growing, construction, craft and design, farming, food wholesalers, fork lift manufacturing, light engineering, milk and dairy production, poultry breeding, refrigeration, retailing, service industries, tourism.

CENSUS DETAILS: 141,585 *(estimated)*.

NUMBER OF SCHOOLS: 89 primary schools, 22 secondary schools, 2 institutes of further and higher education, 1 university.

NAMES OF COUNCILS: Armagh City and District Council, Craigavon Borough Council.

CHIEF EXECUTIVES: Armagh: Desmond Mitchell; Craigavon: Trevor Reaney.

CHAIRMEN / MAYORS: Armagh: Pat Brannigan; Craigavon: Kenneth Twyble.

COUNCIL MEETING DATES: Armagh: fourth Monday in the month; Craigavon: first and third Monday of each month.

RADIO STATIONS: B.B.C. Radio Ulster.

NEWSPAPERS: Armagh-Down Observer, (Editor: Desmond Mallon). Craigavon Echo, (Editor: David Armstrong). Ulster Gazette, (Editor: Richard Stewart). Armagh Standard, (Editor: Karen Bushby).

MAJOR TOURIST ATTRACTIONS: angling; Ardress House, Annaghmore; the Argory, Moy; Armagh County Museum; Armagh Friary; Armagh Observatory; Armagh Planetarium; Armagh Public Library; Benburb Valley Park; Cardinal O'Fiaich Heritage Centre; Dan Winter's Cottage, Loughgall; Derrymore House, Bessbrook; Eamhain Macha or 'Navan Fort', Ulster's most important historical site; Folly Glen, a natural wooded glen; Gosford Forest Park; Keady Heritage Centre; Killevy Churches; Lough Neagh Discovery Centre; Maghery Country Park; Mullaghbawn Folk Museum; the Palace Demesne; Palace Stables Heritage Centre, which recreates Georgian Armagh; Peatlands Park; road bowls, a game that is only played in Cork and Armagh; the Royal Irish Fusiliers Museum; Shambles Market; Slieve Gullion Forest Park; St. Patrick's Roman Catholic Cathedral and St. Patrick's Church of Ireland Cathedral; St. Patrick's Trian, an exciting interpretive centre that depicts 'The Armagh Story' from prehistoric times to the present day;

FAMOUS NATIVES OF THE PAST: Frank Aiken (politician/revolutionary; died 1983), Brian Boru (High King of Ireland, buried Armagh 1014), Edward Bunting (musician; died 1843), Donn Byrne (novelist, born New York, reared in Armagh; died 1928), Thomas Cooley (architect; died 1784), Greer Garson (best actress Oscar winner 1942; born 1908), St. Malachy (church reformer/scholar; died 1148), Sir Robert McCarrison (medical scientist; died 1960), Tomás Ó Fiaich (Archbishop of Armagh/Primate of All Ireland; died 1990), E.J. Opik (astronomer, born Estonia; died 1985), St. Patrick (Ireland's patron saint; died 490), George Farquhar Patterson (historian/antiquarian/curator/creator of Armagh County Museum, born Canada; died 1971), George Russell (author/co-op movement promoter/economist/mystic; died 1935).

COUNTY CAVAN

(Province: Ulster)

Cavan, the most southerly of the nine Ulster Counties, is divided into the eastern highlands, the Erne valley and the mountainous region of west Cavan. An inland county, it is bounded by six other counties. Cavan plays host to two great river systems: the Shannon, the longest river in Ireland, which rises from the Shannon Pot on the southern slopes of the Cuilcagh Mountain near Glangevlin, and the River Erne, which rises east of Lough Gowna and contains Ireland's largest heronry, based in Upper Lough Erne.

In the tenth century, the county formed the greater part of the ancient kingdom of Breifne (together with west Leitrim) ruled over by the Clan Uí Raghallaigh, with the O'Reillys in East Breifne and the O'Rourkes in West Breifne. In 1584, East Breifne was formed into the present county of Cavan and added to Ulster. A favourite legend is that the ancient town of Cavan lies beneath the waters of the Green Lake. Cavan was assimilated into the province of Ulster in the 17th century and subsequently settled by the English and Scottish. It was one of the three Ulster counties to be incorporated into the Irish Free State in 1921.

ORIGIN OF COUNTY NAME:
From the Irish 'Cabhánn', a hollow.

LAND AREA: 730 sq. miles. **COUNTY CAPITAL:** Cavan Town.

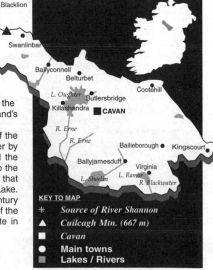

KEY TO MAP

✱	*Source of River Shannon*
▲	*Cuilcagh Mtn. (667 m)*
■	*Cavan*
●	**Main towns**
■	**Lakes / Rivers**

MAIN TOWNS: Cavan, Cootehill, Bailieboro, Kingscourt, Belturbet.

MAIN INDUSTRIES: Agriculture, bacon and pork processing, building and civil engineering, building products manufacturing, crystal glass making, dairy processing, footwear production, livestock auctioneering, meat processing, mining and construction equipment, paints production, plastics manufacturing, shower enclosures manufacturing, telecommunications, tourism, transformer manufacturing.

CENSUS DETAILS: Total population - 52,903 - a 0.2% increase since 1991.

NUMBER OF SCHOOLS: 81 primary schools, 10 secondary schools, 1 third-level institute.

COUNTY MANAGER: Brian Johnson.

CHAIRMAN OF COUNTY COUNCIL: Paddy O'Reilly.

NAMES OF ALL COUNCILLORS: Daniel Brady (F.F.), Patrick J. Conaty Jnr. (F.F.), Eddie Feeley (F.F.), Francie Fitzsimons (F.F.), Michael Giles (F.F.), Clifford Kelly (F.F.), Gerry Murray (F.F.), Michael Smith (F.F.), Sean Smith (F.F.), T.P. Smith (F.F.), Anthony P. Vesey (F.F.), Andrew Boylan (F.G.), Dessie Boylan (F.G.), Aidan Boyle (F.G.), Mary Maguire (F.G.), Philip Miney (F.G.), Joe O'Reilly (F.G.), Andy O'Brien (F.G.), Paddy O'Reilly (F.G.), Paddy O'Reilly (F.G.), May Coleman (Ind.), Matthew Fitzpatrick (Ind.), Seamus Harten (Ind.), Dolores Smith (Ind.), Winston Turner (Ind.).

COUNCIL MEETING DATES: Second Monday of each month.

RATEABLE VALUE TOTALS: £389,077,10.

RADIO STATIONS: Shannonside/Northern Sound.

NEWSPAPERS: The Anglo-Celt, (Editor: Johnny O'Hanlon).

MAJOR TOURIST ATTRACTIONS: Áras Cilian - St. Kilian Interpretative Centre; Bawnboy, one of Ireland's two Buddhist Centres; The Black Pig's Dyke, an ancient frontier fortification at Dowra; the Burren, Blacklion; Carraig Craft Visitors' Centre, Mountnugent; Cavan County Museum; Cavan Crystal Factory, Ireland's second oldest glass making factory; Church of Ireland Cathedral, Kilmore; Clough Oughter Castle; Crover Folk Museum; the Cuilcagh Mountains; Drumlane Church and Round Tower; Dún a Rí Forest Park; 'Finn McCool's Fingers', bronze age stones, Shantemon; the G.A.A. Gallery; the Genealogical Research Centre; Killykeen Forest Park; Lifeforce Corn Mill; Lough Navar Forest Park; The 'Pighouse' Folk Museum; Redhills

Equestrian Centre; the Shannon Pot; the Spa Wells, Swanlinbar; St. Mary's Franciscan Abbey.

FAMOUS NATIVES OF THE PAST: Dr. William Bedell (first translator of Bible into Irish; died 1642), Sir Eyre Coote (Commander-in-Chief British Regiment India; died 1783), Richard Coote (Governor of New York, Massachusettes and New Hampshire; died 1701), Marcus Daly 'The Copper King' (owned mines in U.S., died 1900), Patrick Donohoe (published first U.S.A. Catholic newspaper; died 1901), Matthew Gibney (Bishop of Perth, Australia; died 1925), Bunda Hunt (writer; circa 1880), St. Kilian of Wurtzburg (c.640-689), Sheridan Le Fanu (gothic novelist/newspaper proprietor; died 1873), John C. McQuaid (Roman Catholic Archbishop of Dublin; died 1973), St. Mogue (circa 555-632), Alexander O'Reilly (Field Marshall of Spanish Army; died 1792), Francis O'Reilly (Brother Potamian, made first medical test of the X-ray in Ireland; died 1917), John K. O'Reilly (nationalist; died 1926), Phil Sheridan (U.S. Civil War General; died 1888), Richard Brinsley Sheridan (writer; died 1816), Rev. Thomas Sheridan Jr. (lexicographer/theatrical manager/writer; died 1788), Francis Sheehy-Skeffington (socialist/writer; died 1916), General Eric Dorman-Smith/O'Gowan (Commander in North Africa, World War II; died 1969), Baron Thomas Von Brady (Field Marshal Austrian Army; died 1827).

COUNTY DERRY
(Province: Ulster)

County Derry is situated on the north-west coast of Northern Ireland. It has a hilly terrain particularly in the south-west where the Sperrin Mountains are found. It is bordered on the west by the River Foyle, which flows into Lough Foyle, on the north by the Atlantic Ocean, on the east by County Antrim and on the south by County Tyrone and Lough Neagh.

The county's early Christian history is dominated by St. Columba, who died in 597 and who successfully advanced Christianity in both his native land and Scotland. He established a monastery in Derry 546, out of which Derry city grew, and went on to establish a large family of churches around Scotland's Atlantic seaboard. The O'Neills held sway over much of the county around the middle ages, although Richard de Burgh the 'Red Earl' of Ulster took control of the little port of Derry with a view to developing it as a stronghold.at the beginning of the 14th century. However, he was defeated in battle by Edward Bruce in 1315 and lost control of Ulster for a time. The O'Neills assumed power during the 14th century and shared this power in Derry county with the O'Donnells and the O'Cahans in the 15th century. After the defeat of the native Irish at the Battle of Kinsale, Derry was selected, along with the rest of Ulster to be planted in 1610. Most of the area included in the current County Derry was known as Coleraine prior to the plantation. Following the plantation, the area was

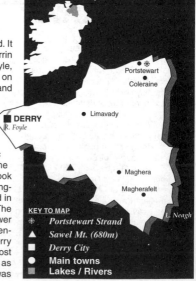

KEY TO MAP
* **Portstewart Strand**
▲ **Sawel Mt. (680m)**
■ **Derry City**
● **Main towns**
■ **Lakes / Rivers**

formally assigned county status in 1613 and, along with the city, was renamed Londonderry after the intervention of the London-based society, which rebuilt the city after it was sacked. In 1641, the old Catholic landowners rose against the new Protestant planters in Ulster, but the rising was crushed by Cromwell when he arrived in 1649. During the Jacobite/Williamite war, many of the county's planter population sought refuge in Derry, which came under siege in 1689. The Williamites broke the siege, and the planters retained control of the county.

ORIGIN OF COUNTY NAME: The name Derry is derived from the Irish 'Doire', meaning Oak Grove.

LAND AREA: 798 sq. miles

LARGEST TOWN: Derry.

MAIN TOWNS: Coleraine, Derry, Dungiven, Limavady, Maghera, Magherafelt, Portstewart.

MAIN INDUSTRIES: These include agriculture, computer services, dairy food processing, garment manufacturing, meat processing, oil distribution, retailing, service industries, tourism.

CENSUS DETAILS: 213,035 *(estimated)*.

NUMBER OF SCHOOLS: 72 primary schools, 23 secondary schools, 3 institutes of further and higher education.

NAMES OF COUNCILS: Coleraine Borough Council, Derry City Council, Limavady Borough Council, Magherafelt District Council.

CHIEF EXECUTIVES: Coleraine: H.W.T. Moore; Limavaday: John Stevenson; Magherafelt: John McLaughlin.

CHAIRMEN / MAYORS: Coleraine: James McClure; Limavady: Gerard Lynch; Magherafelt: P.E. Grogan;

COUNCIL MEETING DATES: Coleraine: last Tuesday in the month. Limavady: first Thursday in each month; Magherafelt: second Tuesday of each month.

RADIO STATIONS: BBC Radio Foyle, Q102FM.

NEWSPAPERS: Coleraine Chronicle, (Editor: Grant Cameron). Derry Journal, (Editor: Pat McArt). Londonderry/Limavady Sentinel, Editor: James Cadden. Mid-Ulster Mail, Morton Newspapers. Northern Constitution, Editor: Grant Cameron.

MAJOR TOURIST ATTRACTIONS: Banagher Old Church, Dungiven; Bellaghy Bawn; Benone Strand, near Limavady; Downhill Castle, Castlerock; Dungiven Priory and O'Cahan's Tomb; Earhart Centre & Wildlife Sanctuary, Ballyarnett; Garvagh Museum & Heritage Centre, Garvagh; Hezlett House, Coleraine; Hilltop Open Farm, Ballyarnet; Knockcloghrim Windmill, Maghera; Maghera Old Church; Magilligan Strand; the Martello Tower, Magilligan Point; Mountsandel Fort, Coleraine; Mussenden Temple, Downhill; Ness Wood Country Park, near Derry; Portstewart Strand; Roe Valley Country Park, Limavady; Sampson Tower, Limavady; Springhill, a 17th-century manor house, Moneymore; William Clark & Sons, a old linen factory with a museum and artifacts; the Wilson Daffodil Garden, Coleraine, (a rare collection of Irish-bred daffodils and other narcissi).

FAMOUS NATIVES OF THE PAST: Arthur Joyce Lunel Cary (writer/British Race Relations officer/; died 1957), Henry Cooke (Presbyterian leader; died 1868), Peter Doherty (international footballer; died 1990), Thomas Graves (British Admiral; died 1814), Sam Henry (folksong collector/public servant; died 1952), Jimmy Kelly (boxer; born 1912), Henry Knox (first Commander-in-Chief of American Army; died 1806), William Ferguson Massey (led New Zealand through World War I; died 1925), Edward McAteer (politician, born Scotland, moved to Derry, aged two years; died 1986), John Alexander McCelland (academic; died 1920), John Mitchel (Young Irelander;died 1875), Francis Stuart (novelist, born Australia of Ulster parents/reared in Derry; born 1902), Charles Williams (journalist/founded The Press Club 1896; died 1904).

COUNTY DONEGAL
(Province: Ulster)

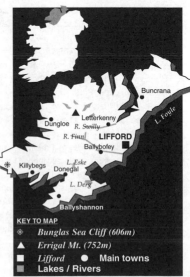

Donegal, Ireland's fourth-largest county, can be found on the northwest seaboard of the country. Containing more beaches than any other county, Donegal's dramatic coastline includes the highest sea cliffs in Europe at Slieve League, with the cliff face at Bunglas towering more than 606 m above the ocean. Inland, the county's mountains and secluded glens are cast in an ever changing light, resulting from the sudden weather changes swept in by the Atlantic Ocean.

The inaccessibility of Donegal's highlands assisted in preserving its ancient Celtic culture and language and in remaining the last county to be taken over by the English - Cahir O'Donnell was the last chieftain in Ireland to be defeated in 1608. Donegal has numerous historical sites, including dolmens, souterrains, and 40 Bronze Age cairns. The most famous of these sites is the Grianan of Aileach, an ancient fortress and sun temple. Donegal's rich early Christian history centres around St. Column Cille (Columba of Iona) who gave his name to Glencolumbkille and founded Derry.

KEY TO MAP
* *Bunglas Sea Cliff (606m)*
▲ *Errigal Mt. (752m)*
■ *Lifford*   ● **Main towns**
■ **Lakes / Rivers**

ORIGIN OF COUNTY NAME: Derived from the Irish 'Dún na nGall', meaning the fort of the foreigners.

LAND AREA: 1,876 sq. miles. **COUNTY CAPITAL:** Lifford.

MAIN TOWNS: Ballybofey, Ballyshannon, Buncrana, Bundoran, Carndonagh, Dungloe, Letterkenny, Lifford, Moville.

MAIN INDUSTRIES: Agriculture, automotive components manufacturing, cattle auctions; china manufacturing, cloth and clothing manufacturing, dairy production and processing, fish processing and exports, , fish sales, general merchants, healthcare product manufacturing, ladieswear, leisurewear production, medical instrument manufacturing, polyester yarns production, sugar and chocolate confectionery production, tweed and hand-woven garment manufacturing.

CENSUS DETAILS: Total population - 129,435 - a 1% increase since 1991.

NUMBER OF SCHOOLS: 180 primary schools, 24 secondary schools, 1 R.T.C., 1 college.

COUNTY MANAGER: Michael McLoone.

CHAIRMAN OF COUNTY COUNCIL: Maureen Doohan.

NAMES OF ALL COUNCILLORS: Francis Brennan (F.F), Hugh Conaghan (F.F.), Mary Coughlan (F.F.), Cecilia Keaveney (F.F.), Peter Kennedy (F.F.), James McBrearty (F.F.), Seán McEniff (F.F.), Noel McGinley (F.F.), Bernard McGlinchey (F.F.), Denis McGonagle (F.F.), Patrick McGowan (F.F.), Maureen Doohan (F.G.), Colm Gallagher (F.G.), Seamus Gill (F.G.), Paddy Harte (F.G.), Joachim Loughrey (F.G.), Bernard McGuinness (F.G.), Frank O'Kelly (F.G.), J.J. Reid (F.G.), Harry Blaney (Ind.), Fred Coll (Ind.), Danny Harkin (Ind.), Padraig Kelly (Ind.), Anne O'Donnell (Ind.), Jim Devenney (D.P.P.), Jim Ferry (S.F.), Seán Maloney (Lab.), Seamus Rodgers (D.L.).

COUNCIL MEETING DATES: Last Monday of each month (except August).

RATEABLE VALUE TOTALS: £581,886.25.

RADIO STATIONS: Donegal Highland Radio, North West Radio, Raidió na Gaeltachta.

NEWSPAPERS: The Derry Journal, Editor: (Pat McArt). Derry People and Donegal News, (Editor: Columba Gill). Donegal Democrat, (Editor: John Bromley). Donegal People's Press, (Editor: Paddy Walsh).

MAJOR TOURIST ATTRACTIONS: Abbey Assaroe Mills and Waterwheels; Ards Forest Park, Cresslough; Arranmore Island; Buncrana Castle and the O'Doherty Keep; Bocan Stone Circle, Culdaff; Cavancor House Pottery and Art Gallery, Ballindrait; the High Cross (believed to be the oldest in Ireland), Carndonagh; The Colmcille Heritage Centre and Glebe House, Churchill; Cooley Cross, Moville; Corn and Flax Mill, Newmills; The County Museum, Letterkenny; Donegal Castle; Donegal Parian China Factory; Donegal Historical Society's Museum, Rossnowlagh; Dunree Fort; Donegal Town Craft Village; Flight of the Earls Centre, Rathmullan; Fintown-Glenties Railway; The Folk Village and Museum, the Ulster Cultural Centre, Glencolumbkille; Glenveagh National Park, Grianan of Aileach, ancient fortress and sun temple, Burt; Inishkeel Island, Inis Eoghain Peninsula; Killybegs, Ireland's premier commercial fishing port; Kinnagoe Bay; Lakeside Centre, Dunlewy; Letterkenny Library and Arts Centre; Lifford Old Courthouse Visitor Centre; Lough Derg, known as St. Patrick's Purgatory where only pilgrims are allowed access; Lurgyvale Thatched Cottage, Kilmacrennan; Malin Head, Ireland's most northerly point, and Banba's Crown; Marine Art Gallery, Straid; Maritime Museum, Norman Castle and Martello tower, Greencastle; Mura cross slab, Fahan; The Rosses, (with its wild Atlantic seaboard); Slieve League, Europe's highest marine cliffs; Teelin; Tory Island; Tullyarvan Mill and Vintage Car Museum, Buncrana.

FAMOUS NATIVES OF THE PAST: William Allingham (poet; died 1889), Neil Blaney (politician; died 1995), Stopford Augustus Brooke (author/chaplain-in-ordinary to Queen Victoria; died 1916), Isaac Butt (leader of Irish parliamentary Party/founded Home Rule Movement, son of Donegal father; died 1879), St. Columba (patron saint/Scottish missionary; died 597), John Doherty (British trade union organiser; died 1854), Dave Gallagher (first ever All-Blacks Captain; died 1917), Patrick 'The Cope' Gallagher (promoter of the rural co-op; died 1964), Patsy Gallagher (international footballer; born 1894), Rory Gallagher (rock musician; 1970s), John Pitt Kennedy (engineer/agriculturalist, constructed Great Himalayan Highway; died 1879), Michael Logue (Roman Catholic Cardinal; died 1924), Ray McAnally (actor; died 1989), Charles Macklin (alias Cathal McLaughlin, actor/writer; died 1797), Patrick MacGill (author/poet; died 1963), Seosamh MacGrianna (novelist/short story writer; died 1990), Muiredach MacRobartaigh (St. Marianus Scotus of Ratisbon; founded St.Peter's Abbey, Rome; died 1088), Thomas Nesbitt (invented the harpoon gun; died 1759), Michael O'Cleary (chief scribe of historic Annals of the Four Masters; born 1575), Sir. Cahir O'Doherty (the last Irish Chieftain; died 1608), Red Hugh O'Donnell (led Irish in Nine Years War; died 1602), Peadar O'Donnell (writer/socialist; died 1986), Séamus Ó'Grianna (short story writer/novelist; died 1969), Patrick J. Whitney (founded St. Patrick's Foreign Missionary Society; died 1942).

COUNTY DOWN
(Province: Ulster)

Down is situated on the north-east coast of Ireland and is bounded on three sides by water with more than 200 miles of coastline; the Irish Sea lies in the east, Belfast Lough in the north and Carlingford Lough in the south. The Mourne Mountains cover the southern part of the county. In the north-west lies the city of Belfast, with its industry and commerce, while in the east, the Ards Peninsula curves around to protect the waters of Strangford Lough, designated Northern Ireland's premier marine nature reserve, due to its marine wildlife, which is among the richest in Europe.

Humans have lived around the county's coast for around 9,000 years, and many ancient tales from the Ulster cycle are set in this region. St. Comgall founded a monastery in Bangor in A.D. 558, and monks from the monastery set sail to spread Christianity throughout Europe. The importance of this site in the Dark Ages was such that Bangor features on the famous Mappa Mundi, while London does not. John de Courcy, the Norman who gained control of east Ulster in the 12th century, pledged to bring the remains of Saints Patrick, Brigid and Columbanus to Bangor. Some believe that this pledge was based on the debt the Normans owed the Irish for keeping the Christian faith alive during the Dark Ages. The monastery was revived by St. Malachy in the 12th century but by 1469 was once more in ruins due to the dissolution of the Irish monasteries in the 1540s. The monastic lands were taken over by the O'Neills of Clandeboye and remained in their domain until they were divided by King James I between Hugh Montgomery and James Hamilton. As this shows, the lands in parts of Down were already in Scottish or English hands before the plantation of the rest of Ulster in 1610. During the 18th century, the coast from Newcastle to Greencastle became notorious for smuggling, and merchandise disappeared via smugglers' trails through the mountains such as the Brandy Pad.

ORIGIN OF COUNTY NAME: Derived from the Irish 'an Dún', meaning Fort.

LAND AREA: 945 sq. miles

LARGEST TOWN: Newtownards.

MAIN TOWNS: Ballynahinch, Bangor, Banbridge, Castlewellan, Donaghadee, Downpatrick, Dromore, Hillsborough, Holywood, Kilkeel, Newcastle, Newry, Newtownards, Portaferry.

MAIN INDUSTRIES: These include agriculture, business services, chemist retailing, clothing manufacturing, construction, dairy production, distribution, domestic heating appliance manufacturing, engineering, footwear manufacturing, plastic injection moulding, plastic tube extrusion, quarrying, recreation services, retailing, services, textile production, tourism, transport.

CENSUS DETAILS: 454,411 *(estimated)*.

NUMBER OF SCHOOLS: 191 primary schools, 46 secondary schools, 3 institutes of further and higher education.

NAMES OF COUNCILS: Ards Borough Council, Banbridge District Council, Down District Council, Lisburn Borough Council, Newry & Mourne District Council, North Down Borough Council.

CHIEF EXECUTIVES: Ards: David Fallows; Banbridge: R.A. Gilmore; Down: Owen O'Connor; Lisburn: M.S. Fielding; Newry & Mourne: Kevin O'Neill; North Down: Adrian McDowell.

CHAIRMEN / MAYORS: Ards: Ronnie Ferguson; Banbridge: Joan Baird; Down: Pat Tonan; Lisburn: George Morrison; Newry & Mourne: Charlie Smith; North Down: Mrs. I.R. Cree.

COUNCIL MEETING DATES: Ards: second Tuesday of each month; Banbridge: first Monday of each month; Down: third Monday of each month; Lisburn: fourth Tuesday of each month; Newry & Mourne: first Monday of each month; North Down: fourth Tuesday of each month.

RADIO STATIONS: Down Town Radio.

KEY TO MAP
✳ **Strangford Lough (Marine Reserve)**
▲ **Slieve Donard (852m)**
■ **Bangor**
● **Main towns**
■ **Lakes / Rivers**

NEWSPAPERS: Banbridge Chronicle Press, (Editor: Brian Hooks). Banbridge Leader Press, (Editor: Richard Stewart). County Down Spectator, (Editor: Paul Flowers). Down Recorder, (Editor: Paul Symington). Dromore Star. Mourne Observer, (Editor: Terence Bowman). Newry Reporter, (Editor: D. O'Donnell). Newtownards Chronicle, (Editor: John Savage). Newtownards Spectator, (Editor: Paul Flowers). North Down Herald & Post, (Editor: Caroline Cooper). North Down news, (Editor: Julie McClay). The Outlook, (Editor: Ken Purdy).

MAJOR TOURIST ATTRACTIONS: Angling; Annalong Corn Mill, (dating back to 1830); Ards Arts Centre, Newtownards; the Ark 'Rare Breeds' Open Farm; Ballycopeland Windmill, Millisle (a late 18th century tower mill still in working order); Brontë Homeland Interpretive Centre, (where Patrick Brontë, father of the Brontë sisters taught ad preached in Rathfriland); Burren Heritage Centre, Warrenpoint; Castle Espie, (Ireland's largest collection of ducks, geese and swans); Castle Ward, Strangford; Castlewellan Forest Park; Cloghskelt early Bronze Age cemetry; Clough Castle, Clough; Copeland Islands, (noted for their diverse bird population); Crawfordsburn Country Park; Delamont Country Park; Down County Museum, Downpatrick;

Dundrum Castle, Dundrum, (built by John de Courcy circa 1177); Exploris, an aquarium with thousands of species, Portaferry; Greencastle, Kilbroney Park; Kilkeel, (dating back to medieval times); Grey Abbey, (a ruined Cistercian abbey); Hillsborough Fort, built in 1650; Inch Abbey, Downpatrick; Jordan's Castle, (one of a group of castles built to protect the port of Ardglass in medieval times); the Mountains of Mourne; Mount Stewart House and Gardens, Newtownards; Murlough National Nature Reserve; the Museum of Childhood, Bangor, (contains toys, books, prams and clothes from Victorian times to the 1960s); Nendrum Monastic Site, Comber; Newry Museum; North Down Heritage Centre, Bangor; Quoile Countryside Centre, Downpatrick; Raholp Church, Strangford; Redburn Country Park; Rowallane Gardens, Saintfield; Scarva Visitor Centre, gives the history of canals in Ireland; Scrabo Tower and Country Park; Seaforde Gardens, with its butterfly house, Seaforde; the Silent Valley; Somme Heritage Centre, Newtownards, (a history of the Battle of the Somme); Struell Wells, healing wells and bath houses near Downpatrick; Tollymore Forest Park; Ulster Folk & Transport Museum, Holywood; Ulster Wildlife Centre.

FAMOUS NATIVES OF THE PAST: Thomas Andrews (chief designer of Titanic; died 1912), John Millar Andrews (Prime Minister for Northern Ireland 1940-43; died 1956), John Barbour (Scottish settler, established major linen-thread works 1823), Geoffrey Henry Cecil Bing (Attorney-General of Ghana 1957-61; died 1977), Patrick Brontë (father of novelists Anne, Charlotte and Emily Brontë; born 1777), Francis Rawdon Chesney ('father of Suez Canal', died 1872), St. Columbanus of Luxeuil (established missions in France/Switzerland; died 615), William Coulson (first Irish damask producer 1764), Captain Francis Crozier (arctic explorer/discovered North West Passage; died 1848), Lord Faulkner (Prime Minister of N. Ireland 1971-72; died 1977), Harry Ferguson (engineer/inventor/built first Irish aeroplane 1909/invented tractors; died 1960), Hamilton Harty (composer/pianist/ organist; died 1941), Bulmer Hobson (founded Ulster Literary Theatre/revolutionary; died 1969), James Martin (invented aircraft ejector seat; died 1981), Jimmy McLarnin (boxer; born 1906), William Pirrie (head of Harland & Wolffe; died 1924), Robert Lloyd Praeger (natural historian; died 1953), Sir Joshua Reynolds (portrait artist; died 1792), John J. Rooney (chemist; born 1935), Michael Henry Rooney (journalist; died 1990), Amanda McKittrick Ros (novelist/poet; died 1939), George Russell (penname A.E., poet/painter; died 1935), Joseph Scriven (wrote 'What a friend we have in Jesus'; died 1886), John Simpson (surgeon on the H.M.S. Plover's Arctic expedition; died in 1855), Sir Hans Sloane (naturalist/physician/founded British Museum in 1759; died 1753), Helen Waddell (literary scholar/medievalist, born Tokyo; died 1965), Kenneth Whitaker (economist; born 1916), John Butler Yeats (artist/essayist; died 1922).

COUNTY FERMANAGH
(Province: Ulster)

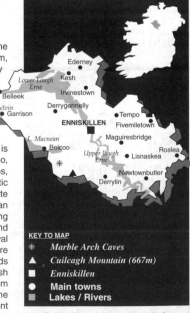

Fermanagh is an inland county in the north-west of the island. The length of the county is spanned by the Erne River and Lake system, which stretches southwards for 50 miles. The system has recently been joined to the River Shannon via the Shannon-Erne Waterway. Both systems were previously linked by a canal, constructed in 1860. However, it closed to commercial traffic after nine years with the arrival of steam and railways. The county is also home to the extensive Marble Arch cave system, which be navigated by boat during the drier months.

Fermanagh's ancient Celtic and early Christian heritage is revealed on the islands of its lakes and the Burren area near Belcoo, an area rich in archaeological monuments, such as portal tombs, wedge tombs and a court tomb. On Boa Island, there are two Celtic Janus (two-faced) statues, possibly dating from the first century; White Island is home to seven enigmatic statues, housed in an early Christian church; while Devenish Island contains a large monastic ruin, dating back to the sixth century. The monastery holds a 12th-century round tower, which monks used to spot possible attackers. During medieval times, the Maguires held sway over the Fermanagh region and were said to police the Erne with a private navy of 1,500 boats. Their lands were confiscated after the 17th century wars and settled by English and Scottish planters. The many stately homes in the county date from this time onwards. These include the superb Castle Coole, home to the Earls of Belmore, which dates back to the 18th century, and the elegant Florence Court, with its graceful Rococo plasterwork, dating to the mid-18th century. Another location of historic note is Belleek Pottery - Ireland's oldest and most famous manufacturer of fine glazed porce-

KEY TO MAP

❋ *Marble Arch Caves*

▲ *Cuilcagh Mountain (667m)*

◼ *Enniskillen*

● Main towns

◼ Lakes / Rivers

lain. Enniskillen, the county capital, contains a wealth of historic sites, including the medieval Maguire Castle, the

Museum of the Royal Inniskilling Fusiliers, the Watergate and Arcaded Barracks.

ORIGIN OF COUNTY NAME: Derived from the Irish 'Fear Manach', the men of Manach.

LAND AREA: 647 sq. miles.

LARGEST TOWN: Enniskillen.

MAIN TOWNS: Enniskillen, Irvinestown, Lisnaskea and Roslea.

MAIN INDUSTRIES: Agriculture, craft & design, pottery making, quarrying, retailing, service industries, tourism.

CENSUS DETAILS: 54,033 *(estimated)*.

NUMBER OF SCHOOLS: 47 primary schools, 15 secondary schools, 1 college.

NAME OF COUNCIL: Fermanagh District Council

CHIEF EXECUTIVE: Mrs. Aideen McGinley.

CHAIRMAN: Patrick McCaffrey.

COUNCIL MEETING DATES: First Monday of each month.

RADIO STATIONS: Shannonside/Northern Sound.

NEWSPAPERS: Fermanagh Herald, (Editor: Dominic McClements). Fermanagh News, (Editor: R. Mallon).

MAJOR TOURIST ATTRACTIONS: Angling; Ardess Craft Centre; Ardhowen Theatre, Enniskillen; Belleek Pottery; Carrothers Family Heritage Museum, Tamlaght; Carrotheers Family Heritage Museum; Castle Archdale, (a location containing a marina and jetty with a nature reserve and tourist amenities); Castle Balfour, Lisnaskea; Castle Caldwell Nature Reserve; Castle Coole, Enniskillen; Crom Estate, Newtownbutler, one of Northern Ireland's most important nature conservation reserves; cruising on the Erne; Devenish Island; Drumskinny Stone Circle; Ely Lodge Forest Park; Enniskillen Castle; Enniskillen Craft & Design Centre, the Buttermarket; Explore Erne Exhibition, Belleek; Fermanagh Crystal Factory, Belleek; Fermanagh Lakeland Forum Leisure Centre, Enniskillen; Florence Court House and Forest Park, Enniskillen; Folklife Display, Lisnaskea Library; Forthill Park & Cole Monument, Enniskillen; Garrison, a popular angling centre; Loughs Erne, MacNean and Melvin; Lough Navar, a scenic drive that provides a lovely view of Lower Lough Erne; Marble Arch Caves; Marlbank Scenic Loop, a scenic walk; Monea Castle, a 17th century Plantation Castle, near Enniskillen; the Pettigoe Plateau, with its blanket bogland; Roslea Heritage Centre, Roslea; the Ulster Way, (a designated walk that runs between Loughs MacNean and Erne); watersports at Fermanagh's many activity centres, including canoeing, water skiing and wind surfing; White Island, accessible by ferry from Castle Archdale.

FAMOUS NATIVES OF THE PAST: Robert Barton (wrote music for Australia's 'Waltzing Matilda'), Thomas Barton ('French Tom', set up the Barton wine business; born 1695), Alan Francis Brooke Alanbrook (first viscount British Field Marshal, ninth child of Victor Brooke of Colebrook; died 1963), Sir Basil Brook (Lord Brookeborough, Northern Ireland Prime Minister 1943-1963/helped train U.V.F., died 1973), Denis Parsons Burkitt (African surgeon/discovered form of children's cancer 'Burkitt's Lymphoma'; died 1993), Gustavus Hamilton (founded 'The Enniskilleners', Williamite regiment; died 1723), Bobbie Kerr (athletic/represented Ireland/Canada Olympics 1908-1928; born 1882).

COUNTY MONAGHAN
(Province: Ulster)

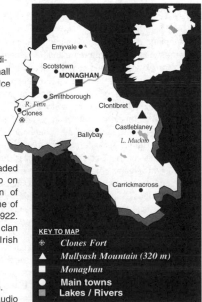

An inland county, its rolling hilly landscape and myriad of lakes indicate that it is part of the drumlin belt in Ireland, a swath of small steep-sided hills that were formed by the melting glaciers of the Ice Age.

Monaghan was occupied before the bronze age, and its many low hills were natural sites for the tombs, forts and cairns of the county's early settlers. The county was part of the ancient Kingdom of Uladh or 'Ulster'. As the power of this kingdom declined, the Monaghan area was subsumed into the Oriel Kingdom and was ruled by the O'Carrolls. After the Normans invaded in 1169, the MacMahons rose to power, but they lost their grip on Monaghan to the English in the 17th century, and the town of Monaghan became a Scottish Calvinist town. The county was one of the three Ulster counties to be included in the Irish Free State in 1922.

ORIGIN OF COUNTY NAME: Derived from the name of a ruling clan in Monaghan - the MacMahons - or derived from the Irish 'Muineachán', the place of the shrubs.

LAND AREA: 500 sq miles.

COUNTY CAPITAL: Monaghan Town.

MAIN TOWNS: Castleblaney, Carrickmacross, Clones, Monaghan.

MAIN INDUSTRIES: Agriculture, animal feed manufacturing, audio

KEY TO MAP

* ✱   *Clones Fort*
* ▲   *Mullyash Mountain (320 m)*
* ■   *Monaghan*
* ●   **Main towns**
* ■   **Lakes / Rivers**

speaker manufacturing, beer/spirit/wine importing and wholesaling, chicken processing, cold storage distribution, dairy produce manufacturing, duck processing, egg production, food production, frozen ready meals manufacturing, furniture manufacturing, meat deboning and vacuum packing, mushroom processing and marketing, poultry processing, provender milling, PVC tiles and floor covering, retailing, tank container manufacturing, timber frame house manufacturing, tourism, towel manufacturing, truck mounted fork lift manufacturing.

CENSUS DETAILS:
Total population - 51,266 - a 0.1% decrease since 1991.

NUMBER OF SCHOOLS: 69 primary schools, 11 secondary schools.

COUNTY MANAGER: J.O. Gavin.

CHAIRMAN OF COUNTY COUNCIL: John F. Conlan.

NAMES OF ALL COUNCILLORS: Brendan Hughes (F.F.), Olivia Keenan (F.F.), Jimmy Leonard (F.F.), Willie McKenna (F.F.), Pádraig McNally (F.F.), Francis O'Brien (F.F.), Rosaleen O'Hanlon (F.F.), Patsy Treanor (F.F.), Arthur Carville (F.G.), John F. Conlan (F.G.), Bill Cotter (F.G.), Seymour Crawford (F.G.), Patrick Jones (F.G.), Stephen McAree (F.G.), Hugh McElvaney (F.G.), Noel Maxwell (N.P.), Peter Murphy (N.P.), Walter Pringle (N.P.), Brian McKenna (S.F.), Caoimhghin Ó Caoláin (S.F.).

COUNCIL MEETING DATES: First Monday of each month.

RATEABLE VALUE TOTALS: £337, 665.96.

NEWSPAPERS: The Northern Standard, (Editor: Martin Smyth).

MAJOR TOURIST ATTRACTIONS: Angling; the antique lace exhibition at Clones; Bellamont House; Castle Leslie, Glaslough; Clones Fort and Clones Medieval Abbey; the early Christian ruins at Donagh Graveyard; Fane River Park and River Walk; Hilton Park, Clones; Hope Castle; Lough Muckno Leisure Park; Monaghan County Museum, (a centre that features archaeology, folk life, crafts, transport, coinage, industry and the arts); Newbliss; Patrick Kavanagh Rural and Literary Resource Centre at Iniskeen; St. Patrick's Church of Ireland; Tyrone Guthrie Centre (Annamakerrig House); the towns of Monaghan, Clones, Carrickmacross, Castleblayney and Ballybay.

FAMOUS NATIVES OF THE PAST: Lord Blayney (gave name to Castleblayney), Sir Charles Gavin Duffy (co-founded 'The Nation' newspaper/Australian statesman; died 1903), Thomas Lipton (founder of Liptons Teas; died 1931), John Joseph Lynch (first Archbishop of Toronto; died 1888), John R. Gregg (inventor of shorthand; died 1948), Tyrone Guthrie (theatre producer/benefactor, born Tunbridge Wells, left house to the state for writers/artists residence; died 1971), Patrick Kavanagh (poet; died 1967), Charles David Lucas (first recipient of Victoria Cross; died 1914), Canon Patrick Moynagh (organised mass emigration to Prince Edward Island, Canada, just before 1845), Eoin O'Duffy (Garda commissioner/General; died 1944), Sir William Whitla (physician; died 1933).

COUNTY TYRONE
(Province: Ulster)

An inland county, Tyrone is set in the centre of the province and is the largest county in Northern Ireland. The Sperrin mountains dominate the Tyrone skyline, and the county is bounded by Armagh, Derry, Donegal, Fermanagh, Monaghan and Lough Neagh.

Evidence of human settlement in the area dates back 6,000 years. The Beaghmore Stone Circles, near Cookstown, attest to this ancient inhabitation, as do other burial chambers, monuments and cairns found throughout the county. The hilltop enclosure of Tullyhogue Fort served for a time as the inauguration site for the Celtic kings of Ulster. Tyrone is rich in early Christian remains; Ardstraw was the seat of the Bishopric in the region from the sixth century. Other examples of such remains include the Ardboe High Cross, which depicts biblical scenes, and Donaghmore High Cross. Tyrone is renowned for its connection with the O'Neills, the clan from which it takes its name. Their domain at one stage incorporated parts of Tyrone, Armagh, Derry and Donegal. They ruled over Ulster for more than four centuries and hindered the English in their attempts to colonise the region. After the defeat of the chieftains at the Battle of Kinsale in 1601, however, their power waned and they eventually left Ireland, an event that has been termed the 'Flight of Earls'. Their lands were forfeit to the crown, and in 1610, Tyrone, along

KEY TO MAP
* **Ulster American Folk Park**
▲ **Mullaghclogha (634m)**
■ **Omagh**
● **Main towns**
■ **Lakes / Rivers**

with most of the counties in Ulster was planted by Scottish and English settlers. Many inhabitants of the area, particularly those of Presbyterian Scottish Stock, suffered religious persecution during the 18th century along with the native Irish and emigrated from Tyrone to America in the early 1700s. There is a strong connection culturally between Tyrone and the Appalachian mountain region in Virginia. In particular, the musical culture of the emigrants has had a formative influence on American folk music.

ORIGIN OF COUNTY NAME: Derived from the Irish 'Tír Eoghain', meaning the territory of Eoghan who was one of the sons of Niall of the Nine Hostages, St. Patrick's abductor.

LAND AREA: 1,211 sq. miles

LARGEST TOWN: Omagh.

MAIN TOWNS: Augher, Castlederg, Clogher, Cookstown, Coalisland, Dungannon, Omagh, Strabane.

MAIN INDUSTRIES: Agriculture, dried milk processing, ham and bacon curing, hosiery manufacturing, meat processing, meat wholesalers, poultry processing, retailing, service industries, tourism.

CENSUS DETAILS: 152,827 *(estimated)*.

NUMBER OF SCHOOLS: 169 primary schools, 30 secondary schools, 3 colleges.

NAMES OF COUNCILS: Cookstown, Dungannon, Omagh, Strabane.

CHIEF EXECUTIVES: M. McGuckian (Cookstown), W. Beattie (Dungannon), J.P. McKinney (Omagh), V. Eakin (Strabane).

CHAIRMEN / MAYORS: Cookstown: Sean Begley; Dungannon: Derek Irwin; Omagh: Joe Byrne; Strabane: Eugene Mullen.

COUNCIL MEETING DATES: Cookstown: Second Tuesday of each month; Dungannon: Second Monday of each month; Omagh: First Tuesday of each month; Strabane: Second and fourth Tuesday of each month.

RADIO STATIONS: Highland Radio, Q102FM, Radio Foyle.

NEWSPAPERS: Democrat, (Editor: Desmond Mallon). Dungannon News and Tyrone Courier, (Editor: R. Montgomery). Dungannon Observer, (Editor: Desmond Mallon). Mid-Ulster Observer, (Editor: Desmond Mallon). Mid-Ulster Mail, (Ediotr: Gary McDonald). Strabane Weekly News, (Editor: Wesley Atchison). Strabane Chronicle, (Editor: Paddy Cullen). Tyrone Constitution, (Editor: Wesley Atchison). Tyrone Times (Editor: Paul McCreary). Ulster Herald, (Editor: Paddy Cullen).

MAJOR TOURIST ATTRACTIONS: Altmore Open Farm; angling; Ardboe High Cross; Ardstraw monastic ruins; Artigarvan Waterwheel; Beaghmore Stone Circles; Benburb Valley Park and Heritage Centre; Castlederg Visitor Centre, Castlederg; the Coach & Carriage Museum, Fivemiletown; the Corn Mill Heritage Centre, (tells the story of Coalisland's industrial history); Corrick Abbey; an Creagán Visitor Centre, Creggan; Derg Valley Leisure Centre; Donaghmore Heritage Centre, Donaghmore; the druids' alter at Castlederg; Drum Manor Forest Park, Cookstown; Fivemiletown Display Centre; Gortin Glen Forest Park, near Omagh; Grant Ancestral Home, Ballygawley, (the ancestral home of the 18th U.S. president); Grey's Printing Press, (associated with famous Ulster men, including John Dunlap, the printer of the U.S. Declaration of Independence); Newtownstewart Gateway Centre; Ogilby's Castle, Donemana; Parkanaur Forest Park, near Dungannon; Riversdale Leisure Centre; Sperrin Heritage Centre, (containing natural history and gold mining exhibits); Silverbrook Mill, Donemana; Tullaghoge Fort, where the great Hugh O'Neill was crowned in 1593; Ulster-American Folk Park, Omagh, (tells the story of 200 years of emigration to America); Ulster History Park, Cullion, (narrates the history of human settlement in Ulster); Wellbrook Beetlin Mill, (an 18th-century linen hammer mill), Cookstown; Wilson Ancestral Home, (the ancestral site of Woodrow Wilson, 28th U.S. president).

FAMOUS NATIVES OF THE PAST: Harold R. Alexander (British Field Marshal/Governer General of Canada 1946-52; died 1969), Mrs. Cecil Frances Alexander (celebrated poetess/hyme writer, 'There is a Green Hill Faraway'/'All Things Bright and Beautiful'), Sir Guy Carleton (first Baron Dorchester/Military Governor of Quebec during War of Independence; born 1724), William Carleton (writer; died 1869), John Crockett (Davy Crockett's father; legendary 'King of the Wild Frontier'; emigrated to U.S. 1782), John Dunlap (printer/journalist/founded first U.S. daily newspaper/printed 'The Declaration of Independence'; died 1812), Rev. John Hughes (first Catholic Archbishop of New York City 1850; died 1864), Jimmy Kennedy (lyricist, 'Teddy Bear's Picnic'/'Hokey, Cokey'/'Red Sails in the Sunset'; died 1984), John McKenzie (Presbyterian minister/published narrative of Siege of Derry; died 1696), Joseph MacRory (Roman Catholic Bishop of Down and Connor/Archbishop of Armagh/Primate of All Ireland 1928-1945; died 1945), Sir William McArthur (first Irish Lord Mayor of London; born 1809), Thomas McKeen and Thomas Nelson (signatories to Declaration of Independence 1776), John James Nolan (academic; died 1952), Owen Roe O'Neill (led Ulster forces who rebelled supporting Charles I/nephew of Hugh; died 1649), Hugh O'Neill (Clan Chieftain/second Earl of Tyrone/gaelic leader; died 1616), Brian O'Nolan (writer under the pseudonyms Flann O'Brien and Myles naGopaleen; died 1966), Dr. George Sigerson (zoologist/social reformer/poet/writer; born 1836), Rev. George Walker (Protestant Minister/joint Governer of Derry during siege; died 1690), James Wilson (emigrated to U.S. 1807, printer/grandfather of Woodrow Wilson - President of U.S. 1913-21).

COUNTY CARLOW
(Province: Leinster)

KEY TO MAP
*   *Castlecomer Plateau*
▲   *Mt. Leinster (793 m)*
■   *Carlow*
●   **Main towns**
■   **Lakes / Rivers**

An inland county in the south-east of the country, Carlow is the second smallest county in Ireland and is one of the few inland counties that does not constitute part of the central plain. Carlow is bounded in the east by the granite walls of the Blackstairs Mountains and is split in three by the great rivers of the Barrow and the Slaney as they travel southwards. The Castlecomer Plateau, which Carlow shares with County Kilkenny, contains coal shale, is a geological feature that has given Carlow an industrial tradition, unusual in Ireland.

    The county's fertile land has been prized for centuries, and this factor, along with Carlow's strategic position between Kilkenny and the east coast, has contributed to the county's violent history. During early Christian times, Carlow's rich river valleys were the sites for many monastic settlements, most of which were destroyed by the Vikings. In the 14th century, Art MacMurrough Kavanagh of Borris became king of Leinster and a thorn in the side of the English armies. His attacks on the Pale were so frequent that Richard II was himself compelled to confront the chieftain with an estimated 10,000 strong expeditionary force. However, Art Oge, as he was known, inflicted defeat upon defeat on the king, giving Richard's enemies the chance to usurp the English throne. Carlow remained a stronghold of Gaelic power until after the Cromwellian plantation of the 1650s. County Carlow and County Wexford were the sites of most of the fiercest fighting in the 1798 rebellion, and more than 600 rebels were slaughtered in the county. A monument now commemorates them at Graiguecullen.

ORIGIN OF COUNTY NAME: Derived from the Irish 'Ceatharlach', meaning quadruple lake.
LAND AREA: 346 sq. miles.
COUNTY CAPITAL: Carlow.
MAIN TOWNS: Carlow, Tullow.
MAIN INDUSTRIES: Agriculture, diet feeder machine manufacturing, hair dryer manufacturing, hydraulic cylinders manufacturing, livestock auctioneering, personal care appliances production, press tool and dye manufacturing, sugar distribution, veterinary products manufacturing.
CENSUS DETAILS: Total population - 41,616 - a 1.6% increase since 1991.
NUMBER OF SCHOOLS: 43 primary schools, 11 secondary schools, 1 R.T.C.
COUNTY MANAGER: Brian Johnson.
CHAIRMAN OF COUNTY COUNCIL: Michael Doyle.
NAMES OF ALL COUNCILLORS: Mary Kinsella (F.F.), Nicholas Carpenter (F.F.), Arthur Kennedy (F.F.), Arthur McDonald (F.F.), Jimmy Murnane (F.F.), Enda Nolan (F.F.), Deputy M.J. Nolan (F.F.), John Pender (F.F.), Brendan Walsh (F.F.), Declan Alcock (F.G.), John Browne (F.G.), Michael Deering (F.G.), Michael Doyle (F.G.), Fred Hunter (F.G.), Mary McDonald (F.G.), Pat O'Toole (F.G.), Des Hurley (Lab.), John McNally (Lab.), Michael Meaney (Lab.), Jim Townsend (Lab.), Walter Lacey (P.D.).
COUNCIL MEETING DATES: First Monday in each month (except August).
RATEABLE VALUE TOTALS: £229,981.95.
RADIO STATIONS: Carlow Kildare Radio.
NEWSPAPERS: The Carlow People, Editor: Gerard Walsh. The Nationalist and Leinster Times, Editor: Thomas Money.
MAJOR TOURIST ATTRACTIONS: Altamount Gardens, Tullow; Ballymoon Castle; the Barrow River, one of the most beautiful cruising areas of Ireland; the Barrow Way, a tow path walk; Black Castle, one of the Ireland's earliest Norman Castles; Leighlinbridge; Borris Castle, residence of the ancient rulers of Leinster; Brownshill Dolmen, believed to be the largest in Europe; the Celtic Cross, a memorial of 1798 massacre in Carlow Town; the Catholic Cathedral of the Assumption, Carlow Town; Carlow Museum; Castletown Castle; Dunlckney Manor, Bagnalstown; Eagle Hill, where views take in most of the county, Hacketstown; Haroldstown Dolmen, Tullow; St. Lazerian's Cathedral, one of Leinster's foremost monastic houses, Old Leighlin; MacMurrough's Castle; St. Moling's Mill, a blessed well and bath house, and St. Mullin's Abbey; Myshall House; 'Old Derry' House and the site of the first monastery founded by St. Diarmuid, Killeshin; the Red River, coloured by iron from the mining area of Crettyard; Royal Oak village and the Stone Fort of Rathgall, where ancient kings are believed to be buried.
FAMOUS NATIVES OF THE PAST: Peter Fenlon Collier (founded first subscription publishing enterprise, emigrated to U.S. 1866; died 1909), William Dargan (constructed the first Irish railway; died 1867), Michael Farrell (physician/marathon novelist; died 1962), Samuel Haughton (scientist/mathematician/doctor, calculated drop needed for instant death by hanging; died 1897), Art Mac Murrough Kavanagh (Art Oge, King of Leinster; 14th century), Patrick Francis Moran (Australia's first Cardinal; died 1911), John Tyndall (scientist, discovered why sky is blue 1859; died 1893).

COUNTY DUBLIN
(Province: Leinster)

County Dublin is located on the east coast of Ireland at the edge of the Irish Sea. It could be described, in geological terms, as the seaward extension of the central limestone plain lying to the west. The Liffey, the Dodder and the Tolka are its main rivers, and the county is bounded by granite mountains in the south and rich pastureland, bordered by river estuaries and a long sandy coast, in the north. The city dominates the county, having gradually subsumed many of the county's villages within its parameters. Roughly one-third of the Republic of Ireland's population now lives in the Dublin region.

Dublin county had a strong early Christian presence; there are well-preserved round towers in Clondalkin and Swords, and monastic ruins can be found at Lusk, Tallaght, Newcastle and Saggart. The Vikings established a major settlement in Dublin, as reflected in town names such as Howth, but were finally defeated by Brian Boru at the Battle of Clontarf in Dublin on Good Friday, 1014. The county was part of the English Pale from the 12th to the 16th century. Its English past is reflected in the many stately homes and gardens and the model villages found throughout the county. However, Dublin has always been a hotbed of Irish political activity - the Easter 1916 Rising occurred here and paved the way for Irish Independence - and it was in Dublin that most Irish literary and artistic movements began and flourished. Today, Dublin's villages are for the most part picturesque fishing ports with interesting shops and restaurants.

ORIGIN OF COUNTY NAME: Derived from the Irish 'Dubh Linn', meaning black pool. The Irish for Dublin - Baile Átha Cliath - is translated as the town of the hurdle ford, which refers to barriers placed to prevent the Liffey flooding.

LAND AREA: 49 sq. miles *(Dun Laoghaire/Rathdown),* 173 sq. miles *(Fingal),* 223 sq. miles *(South Dublin).*

COUNTY CAPITAL: *Dun Laoghaire/Rathdown* - Dun Laoghaire; *Fingal* - Dublin; *South Dublin* - Tallaght.

MAIN TOWNS: *Dun Laoghaire/Rathdown* - Dun Laoghaire, Monkstown and Sandyford; *Fingal* - Balbriggan, Malahide, Skerries and Swords; *South Dublin* - Brittas, Clondalkin, Greenhills, Killakee, Lucan, Rathcoole, Rathfarnham, Saggart, Tallaght, Terenure.

MAIN INDUSTRIES: Agriculture, air transportation, brewing distillery, building materials suppliers, clothing manufacturing, computer networking software, computer software manufacture and distribution, dairy export production, electricity supply, electronics production, fishing, food processing, fruit and vegetables imports and distribution, industrial holding companies, market gardening, metals processing and engineering, non-metallic minerals processing, petrol distributors, pharmaceutical manufacture, print and packaging, publishing communications, retailing, service industries to Ireland's largest international airport, telecommunications, textiles production, tourism, transportation, wholesaling.

CENSUS DETAILS: 189,836 - a 2.4% increase since 1991*(Dun Laoghaire/Rathdown);* 167,433 - *a* 9.6% increase since 1991 *(Fingal);* 218,401 - a 4.6% increase since 1991 *(South Dublin).*

NUMBER OF SCHOOLS: 62 primary schools, 38 secondary schools, 1 college of art & design, 1 college of education *(Dun Laoghaire/Rathdown).* 70 primary schools, 23 secondary schools *(Fingal).* 91 primary schools, 30 secondary schools, 1 R.T.C. *(South Dublin).*

COUNTY MANAGERS: Kevin O'Sullivan *(Dun Laoghaire/Rathdown County Council),* William Soffe *(Fingal County Council),* Frank Kavanagh *(South Dublin County Council).*

CHAIRMEN OF COUNTY COUNCILS: Donal Marren *(Dun Laoghaire/Rathdown County Council),* Cyril Gallagher *(Fingal County*

Council), Eamonn Walsh *(South Dublin County Council).*

NAMES OF ALL COUNCILLORS: *Dun Laoghaire/Rathdown County Council* - David Boylan (F.F.), Larry Butler (F.F.), Betty Coffey (F.F.), Richard Conroy (F.F.), Don Lydon (F.F.), Tony Fox (F.F.), Paddy Madigan (F.F.), Trevor Matthews (F.F.), Liam T. Cosgrave (F.G.), William Dockrell (F.G.), Mary Elliott (F.G.), Patrick Hand (F.G.), Donal Lowry (F.G.), Donal Marren (F.G.), Olivia Mitchell (F.G.), Frank Buckley (Lab.), Jane Dillon-Byrne (Lab.), Mairead Doohan (Lab.), Sean Mistéil (Lab.), Frank Smyth (Lab.), Helen Keogh (P.D.), Larry Lohan (P.D.), Colm Breathnach (Ind.), Bernadette Connolly (G.P.), Larry Gordon (G.P.), Patrick Fitzgerald (D.L.), Denis O'Callaghan (D.L.), Richard Greene (MnÉ); *Fingal County Council* - Liam Creavan (F.F.), Christopher C. Gallagher (F.F.), Sean Gilbride (F.F.), Joe Higgins (F.F.), Michael Kennedy (F.F.), Jack Larkin (F.F.), Marian McGennis (F.F.), G.V. Wright (F.F.), Ned Ryan (F.F.), Cathal Boland (F.G.), Michael J. Cosgrave (F.G.), Anne Devitt

(F.G.), Philip Jenkinson (F.G.), Joan Maher (F.G.), Tom Morrissey (F.G.), Peter Coyle (Lab.), Ken Farrell (Lab.), Tom Kelleher (Lab.), Michael O'Donovan (Lab.), Sean Ryan (Lab.), Thea Allen (G.P.), David Healy (G.P.), Sean Lyons (N.P.), Sheila Terry (P.D.); *South Dublin County Council* - Sean Ardagh (F.F.), Finbarr Hanrahan (F.F.), Margaret Farrell (F.F.), John Hannon (F.F.), Colm McGrath (F.F.), Charles O'Connor (F.F.), Ann Ormonde (F.F.), Peter Brady (F.G.), Stanley Laing (F.G.), Mary Muldoon (F.G.), Therese Ridge (F.G.), Alan Shatter (F.G.), Ned Gibbons (Lab.), Máire Hennessy (Ind.), Pat Upton (Lab.), Eamon Walsh (Lab.), Breda Cass (Ind.), Gus O'Connell (Ind.), John O'Halloran (Ind.), Cait Keane (P.D.), Catherine Quinn (P.D.), Colm Tyndall (P.D.), Mick Billane (D.L), Don Tipping (D.L.), Máire Mullarney (G.P.), Brian Hayes.

COUNCIL MEETING DATES: Second Monday of each month *(Dun Laoghaire/Rathdown)*, second Monday of each month *(Fingal)*, the second Monday of each month, except August, (*South Dublin)*
RATEABLE VALUE TOTALS: £2,035,837.20 *(Dun Laoghaire/Rathdown)*, £1,450,175 *(Fingal)*, £1,759,037.05 (*South Dublin)*.
RADIO STATIONS: Anna Livia FM; Atlantic 252; Classic Hits; 98FM; FM104; Radió na Life 102 FM; Radio Ireland, RTÉ1; 2FM, FM3 Music; RTÉ Radió na Gaeltachta,
NEWSPAPERS: 46A Magazine. Fingal Independent. Life Times Newspaper. Liffey Champion, (Editor: Vincent Sutton). Southside Edition and Westside Edition, Local News Publications. Southside People, (Editor: Ken Finlay).
MAJOR TOURIST ATTRACTIONS: Ardgillan Castle; Ayesha Castle, Killiney; Bushy Park, Rathfarnham; Corkagh Regional Park, Clondalkin; Dalkey Island and Village; Dodder Valley Linear Park, Firhouse; Drimnagh Castle, Longmile Road; the Dublin Mountains; Dun Laoghaire, (the site of Ireland's first railway in 1831 and now a major ferry port); the Grand Canal; Griffeen Valley Linear Park, Lucan; Howth Head and Peninsula, (provides a panoramic view of Dublin Bay; Howth Castle Gardens, (boasts over 2,000 rhododendron varieties); the James Joyce Museum at Sandycove Martello Tower; Killiney Hill; Lambay Island, (a noted bird sanctuary); Lusk Heritage Centre; Lambert Puppet Theatre & Museum, Monkstown; Malahide Castle and the Fry Model Railway Museum; Marino Casino, (a small folly house built in the 18th century); Marino Crescent, birthplace of Bram Stoker, the author of *Dracula*; Marlay Park; the Martello towers along the coast of the county; Montpelier Hill, (the location of the Hell Fire Club, where the first Earl of Rosse conducted Satanic rites with his friends in the 18th century); the National Maritime Museum of Ireland, Dun Laoghaire; Newbridge House, (an important 18th century Georgian mansion in Donabate); the Pearse Museum, Rathfarnham; Portrane House, (once the home of Esther Johnson, Jonathan Swift's lover); Rathfarnham Castle Park, Rathfarnham; Rush seaside resort; Sean Walsh Memorial Park, Tallaght; Skerries; the Strawberry Beds along the Liffey Valley; Tymon Regional Park, Greenhills.
FAMOUS NATIVES OF THE PAST: C.S. Andrews (revolutionary; died 1985), Eamonn Andrews (broadcaster; died 1987), Sir Francis Bacon (painter; died 1992), Michael Balfe (opera composer; died 1870), Lucien Ball (inventor/pioneer of early cinematography; died 1972), Dr. Thomas John Barnardo (philanthropist; died 1905), Kevin Barry (revolutionary; hanged 1920), Piaras Béaslaí (gaelic scholar/revolutionary/writer, moved to Dublin aged 23; died 1965), Samuel Beckett (playwright; died 1989), Brendan Behan (author/poet/playwright; died 1964), Louis Bennett and Helen Chevenix (trade unionists/founded Irish Women's Suffrage Federation in 1911), Christy Brown (poet/novelist, *My Left Foot*; died 1981), Edmund Bourke (parliamentarian/writer; died 1797), Alfie Byrne (Lord Mayor for nine years; died 1956), Edward Byrne (archbishop of Dublin; died 1940), Patrick Campbell (journalist/author/broadcaster; died 1980), George Canning (British Prime Minister in 1827), Jackie Carey (international footballer; died 1996), Edward Carson (lawyer/politician; died 1935), Austin Clarke (poet/playwright/novelist; died 1974), Frank Cluskey (politician; died 1988), George Colley (politician/solicitor; died 1983), James Connolly (socialist/labour leader/revolutionary, born Edinburgh; died 1916), Patrick Reardon Connor (novelist; died 1991), John Dowland (composer; died 1626), Tom Dreaper (horse trainer; died 1975), Frank Duff (founded Legion of Mary 1921; died 1980), Robbin Edwards (historian; died 1988), Shay Eliott (cyclist; born 1934), Seamus Ellis (uilleann pipes player; died 1982), Robert Emmet (United Irishman; died 1803), Barry Fitzgerald (Oscar-winning actor; died 1961), James C. Fitzmaurice (aviator; died 1965), William 'Monk' Gibbon (poet/critic/scholar; died 1987), James Gill (cricketer; born 1911), Oliver St. John Gogarty (surgeon/poet/writer; died 1957), Veronica Guerin (investigative journalist; murdered 1996), Bert Healion (athlete; born 1919), Seán Lemass (politician/revolutionary; died 1971), Sr. Catherine McAuley (founded Sisters of Mercy 1831; died 1841), Thomas Moore (poet/socialist; died 1852), Pádraic Ó Conaire (novelist; died 1928), Micheál O'Hehir (broadcaster/sports commentator; died 1996), Seán O'Kelly (President of Ireland 1945-59; died 1966), William Orpen (artist; died 1931), Captain William O'Shea (first husband of Kitty O'Shea; died 1905), Sir William Petty (British Prime Minister 1782-83; died 1805), Joseph Mary Plunkett (republican/poet; died 1916), Noel Purcell (actor; died 1985), Patrick Sarsfield (leader of Irish Forces at Siege of Limerick 1691; died 1693), George Bernard Shaw (playwright/polemicist; died 1950), Bram Stoker (author of 'Dracula'; died 1912), Jonathan Swift (political pamphleteer; died 1745), John Millington Synge (playwright/director of Abbey Theatre; died 1909), Matt Talbot (labourer/mystic; died 1925), James Napper Tandy (co-founder of United Irishman 1791; died 1803), Katherine Tynan (poet/novelist/essayist; died 1931), Oscar Wilde (playwright/writer; died 1900).

COUNTY KILDARE
(Province: Leinster)

An inland county in the east of the country, Kildare is bounded by the Wicklow mountain range to the east, the foothills of which extend westwards to meet the unique plain known as the Curragh of Kildare, an area renowned for horse racing, training and breeding. The great Bog of Allen touches the west of Kildare, and Ireland's two canal systems, the Grand and the Royal canals, both flow through the county, as do the three major rivers of the Liffey, the Barrow and the Boyne. Kildare's river valleys, bogs, woodlands and canals are the preserve of wild fowl, birds and animals, with nature reserves at Pollardstown and Ballinafagh.

Kildare's history can be traced back to ancient times, with evidence of raths, earthworks and standing stones to be found around the Curragh. The early Christian era in the county is marked by Kildare's ties to St. Brigid, the sixth century saint who is one of the three patrons of Ireland. However, the legend of St. Brigid could originate from the fact that a pagan sanctuary commemorating the pagan goddess Brigda was located on the same site. The county has been associated with armies since the Anglo-Normans came to Ireland in the 12th century, and military garrisons have been sited here since the 18th century. The Curragh has been the main training base for the Irish army since Ireland gained its Independence.

KEY TO MAP
- *   *The Curragh*
- ▲   *Dunmurry (234m)*
- ■   *Naas*
- ●   Main towns
- ■   Lakes / Rivers

ORIGIN OF COUNTY NAME: Derived from the Irish 'Cill Dara', meaning Church of the Oak Tree, which alludes to St. Brigid's monastery beneath an oak tree.

LAND AREA: 654 sq. miles.

COUNTY CAPITAL: Naas.

MAIN TOWNS: Athy, Celbridge, Kildare, Leixlip, Maynooth, Naas, Newbridge (Droichead Nua).

MAIN INDUSTRIES: Agriculture; building construction; bloodstock auctioneering; grocery, wine and spirit distribution; civil engineering; a European site computer systems manufacturer; semiconductor manufacturing; a manufacturing and distribution centre for oral care, retailing, service industries, and tourism.

CENSUS DETAILS: Total population - 134,881 - a 10% increase since 1991.

NUMBER OF SCHOOLS: 93 primary schools, 27 secondary schools, 1 university.

COUNTY MANAGER: Niall Bradley.

CHAIRMAN OF COUNTY COUNCIL: Liam Doyle.

NAMES OF ALL COUNCILLORS: Gerry Brady (F.F.), Liam Doyle (F.F.), Martin Miley (F.F.), Seán Ó'Fearghail (F.F.), Jimmy O'Loughlin (F.F.), John O'Neill (F.F.), Paddy Power (F.F.), P.J. Sheridan (F.F.), Mary French (F.G.), Senan Griffin (F.G.), Rainsford Hendy (F.G.), Michael McWey (F.G.), Michael Nolan (F.G.), Jim Reilly (F.G.), Seán Reilly (F.G.), Jim Keane (Lab.), John McGinley (Lab.), Colm Purcell (Lab.), Timmy Conway (P.D.), John Dardis (P.D.), Sean English (G.P.), Patsy Lawlor (Ind.), Catherine Murphy (D.L.), Paddy Wright (S.F.), Francis Browne.

COUNCIL MEETING DATES: Last Monday of each month.

RATEABLE VALUE TOTALS: £775,386.63.

RADIO STATIONS: Carlow Kildare Radio Ltd.

NEWSPAPERS: Kildare Nationalist, (Editor: Eddie Coffey). Leinster Leader, (Editor: Vicky Weller). Liffey Champion, (Editor: Vincent Sutton).

MAJOR TOURIST ATTRACTIONS: Angling; Ardenode Deer Farm, Ballymore Eustace; Athy, (a designated heritage town); the Barrow Valley; the Butterfly farm, Straffan; the canals; Castletown House, Celbridge, (Ireland's largest and finest Palladian House); Celbridge Abbey Grounds; Coolcarrigan House and Gardens, Naas; Crookstown Mill, Athy; Cross of Moone, Timolin; cruising; Fontstown Fruit Farm; Furness, Naas; Grange Castle, west of Carbury; horse racing; Irish Pewtermill and Moone High Cross Centre; Japanese Gardens, Tully; the Kildare Way, (a walking route); Killdraught House, Celbridge; Leixlip Castle; Lodge Park Walled Garden, Straffan; Martinstown House, the Curragh; Maynooth Castle; Maynooth Ecclesiastical Museum; Mondello Park car racing circuit; National Irish Stud and Horse Museum, Tully; Newbridge Silverware, Newbridge; Peatland World Visitor Centre, Lullymore; Pollardstown Fen, near Newbridge; Punchestown horse racing course; the Quaker Village of Ballitore and the Quaker Museum located there; the round tower, crosses and church at Castledermot; the Spa area in Leixlip; St. Brigid's Cathedral, Kildare town; Straffan Steam Museum; St. James's ruined medieval church at Coghlanstown; St. Patrick's College, Maynooth; Wonderful Barn Leixlip, (an 18th century conical granary).

FAMOUS NATIVES OF THE PAST: Paul Cullen (Ireland's first Cardinal/founder of U.C.D. 1854), Christian Cavanagh Davies (woman soldier, posed as a male; died 1739), Jack Dempsey (boxer; died 1895), Sir John Michael de Robeck (Naval Commander; died 1928), John Devoy (founded *Irish Nation* and *Gaelic American* newspapers; died 1928), Sir Thomas Dongan (first Catholic Governor in American colonies; died 1715), Lord Edward Fitzgerald (United Irishman; died 1798), Lord Thomas Fitzgerald ('Silken Thomas', instigated a rising 1534), Henry Grattan (the 18th century orator, lived for a time at Celbridge), Arthur Guinness (founded Guinness brewery in 1759), John de Courcy Ireland (maritime historian/linguist/teacher/author, born India/son of British Army Major from County; born 1911), Gerard Manly Hopkins (major English romantic poet, lectured in Maynooth for a time), Molly Keane (novelist/playwright; died 1996), Earl of Kildare ('The Kildare Geraldines', most powerful Irish family over three generations; 15-16th century), Dame Kathleen Yardley Lonsdale (eminent crystallographer; born 1903), William Norton (politician; died 1963), Domhnall Ó'Buachalla (Governor General Irish Free State 1932; died 1963), Lawrence O'Toole (Abbot of Glendalough/first Irish saint to be canonised, 1130-1180), Ernest Henry Shackleton (antarctic explorer; died 1922), Esther Van Homrigh (immortalised as Vanessa by Jonathan Swift), Sir Charles Wogan (Governor of L.A./Spanish Army General; died 1754), Theobald Wolfe Tone (United Irishman; died 1798).

COUNTY KILKENNY
(Province: Leinster)

Kilkenny is an inland county in the south-east of the country. The great Barrow, Nore and Suir rivers drain its low lying hills and plains as they wend their way southwards. To the northeast of the county is the Castlecomer Plateau with its adjoining uplands of damp pasture layered on shale, sandstones and seams of anthracite coal. The county is also noted for its marble, a dark black stone, prized in Georgian and Victorian times, that led to Kilkenny being named the Marble City.

Kilkenny county is steeped in history, as evidenced by the ruined settlements left by the Celts, Vikings, Normans and the English. Kilkenny city itself was the medieval capital of Ireland and still retains much of its Norman origins and medieval structure. Dominating the city is Kilkenny Castle, which was built between 1192 and 1207 for Strongbow's son, William. The county's strong early Christian ties can still be seen in the abbeys at Jerpoint, Kilkenny and in Kells Priory. As Kilkenny was the country's medieval capital, many sessions of the Irish Parliament were held there, including the infamous one in 1366 that led to the unsuccessful Statute of Kilkenny, forbidding the Anglo-Irish to integrate with the Gaelic Irish, and the Confederation of Kilkenny in 1642, where Irish Catholics sided with Charles I. Kilkenny has long been a national centre for crafts and design.

ORIGIN OF COUNTY NAME: Derived from the Irish 'Cill Chainnigh', the Church of Cainneach, which was founded in Kilkenny City by St. Canice in the sixth century.

LAND AREA: 796 sq. miles.

COUNTY CAPITAL: Kilkenny

MAIN TOWNS: Callan, Castletown, Graiguenamanagh, Kilkenny, Thomastown.

MAIN INDUSTRIES: Agriculture, brewing, dairy and meat processing, design and crafts, pork and bacon processing, tourism.

CENSUS DETAILS: Total population - 75,155 - a 2.1% increase since 1991.

NUMBER OF SCHOOLS: 79 primary schools, 16 secondary schools.

COUNTY MANAGER: P. J. Donnelly.

CHAIRMAN OF COUNTY COUNCIL: Dick Dowling.

NAMES OF ALL COUNCILLORS: Robert Aylward (F.F.), Ann Blackmore (F.F.), James J. Brett (F.F.), Dick Dunphy (F.F.), Michael Fenlon (F.F.), Kevin Fennelly (F.F.), Martin Fitzpatrick (F.F.), Michael Lanigan (F.F.), John J. McGuinness (F.F.), Michael J. McGuinness (F.F.), Patrick Millea (F.F.), Brigid Murphy (F.F.), John Brennan (F.G.), Andy Cotterell (F.G.), Kieran Crotty (F.G.), Dick Dowling (F.G.), Philip Hogan (F.G.), William Ireland (F.G.), Mary Hilda Kavanagh (F.G.), John Maher (F.G.), Tom Maher (F.G.), Margaret Tynan (F.G.), Dick Brennan (Lab.), Michael O'Brien (Lab.), Seamus Pattison (Lab.), Joe Walsh (Lab.).

COUNCIL MEETING DATES: Third Monday of each month (except August).

RATEABLE VALUE TOTALS: £258,704.05.

RADIO STATIONS: Radio Kilkenny.

NEWSPAPERS: Kilkenny People, (Editor: John Kerry Keane).

MAJOR TOURIST ATTRACTIONS: Ballyragget Castle; Bennettsbridge Exhibition of Pottery; the Black Abbey, Kilkenny; Bród Tullaroan and the Lory Meagher Heritage Centre; the Butler Gallery, Kilkenny Castle; Callan Augustinian Friary; Castlecomer Demesne Estate; the Cityscope Exhibition, Kilkenny; Clara Castle; Duiske Abbey and Abbey Centre; Dunmore Cave, (containing some of the best calcite formations found in any Irish cave); Graiguenamanagh; Grannagh Castle; the high crosses at Kilree,

Killamery and Kilkieran; Jenkinstown Park; Jerpoint Abbey, Thomastown; Jerpoint Glass Studio, Thomastown; Kells Priory; Kilfane Glen and Waterfall, Thomastown; Kilkenny Castle; Kilkenny Design Centre; Kilkenny City's streets and monuments; Nore Valley Folk Museum; Nore Valley Park Open Farm; the portal dolmen near Knocktopher; Rice House, (the birthplace of Brother Edmund Rice), Callan; Rothe House, Kilkenny; Shee Alms House; the South Leinster Way, (a designated walking route); St. Canice's Cathedral; the stone circle at Killmacoliver Hill, Tullaghought; the Watergate Theatre; Woodstock Estate Forest Park, Inistioge.

FAMOUS NATIVES OF THE PAST: George Berkeley (bishop/philosopher; died 1753), Daniel Bryan (colonel/founder of Military History Association of Ireland; died 1985), Hubert Marshall Butler (translator/essayist/obtained visas for Nazi-fleeing Austrian Jews; died 1991), Abraham Colles (surgeon, diagnosed 'Colles Fracture'; died 1843), Michael Cudahy (made first commercial use of refrigeration; died 1910), Richard Joseph Downey (youngest-ever Catholic Archbishop aged 47 years 1928; died 1953), Thomas Grubb (engineer, manufacturer of telescopes; died 1878), James Hoban (designed the White House, Washington; died 1831), Francis MacManus (novelist; died 1965), Edmund Rice (Brother Ignatius, founded Christian Brothers 1803; died 1844), James Stephens (founded Irish Republican Brotherhood, son of auctioneer's clerk from county; died 1901).

COUNTY LAOIS
(Province: Leinster)

An inland county in the east of Ireland, Laois is the only county that does not border on another county touching the sea. It is largely bounded by raised bog, highlands and rivers - namely, the Barrow and Nore Rivers and the Slieve Bloom mountains. To the south-east of the county is the Castlecomer Plateau and its adjoining uplands, which are layered on Upper Carboniferous shales and sandstones, with some coal seams.

There are more than 1,000 historical sites and monuments in the county, some telling the story of the Mesolithic times of 8,500 years ago, others tracing the history of the Neolithic farmers. The county had a strong Christian establishment by the sixth century, but many of its monasteries fell prey to the Viking hordes, as evidenced by a re-discovered Viking longphort at Dunrally. The Normans gained control of the best land in the county by around 1325, but a gaelic revival occurred during the 14th century. This revival was summarily ended when the O'Mores had their lands confiscated by the English in the 16th century. Laois was established out of a number of unrelated Gaelic territories and earlier chiefdoms and referred to as the Queen's County by a parliamentary act in 1556, during the reign of Queen Mary. It, along with Offaly, became the first area to be planted in Ireland.

ORIGIN OF COUNTY NAME: Initially called 'Queen's County, it was renamed Laois after the War of Independence, in honour of the Loigis/Loigsi, late Iron Age Pict mercenaries who helped Welsh invaders (the Laigin) conquer Leinster.

LAND AREA: 664 sq. miles.

COUNTY CAPITAL: Portlaoise (9,814)

MAIN TOWNS: Abbeyleix, Montrath, Mountmellick, Portarlington.

MAIN INDUSTRIES: Agriculture, jewellery making, labelstock manufacturing and distribution, soap manufacturing, structural steel engineering and fabrication, tennis ball manufacturing, tourism.

CENSUS DETAILS: Total population - 52,798 - a 0.9% increase since 1991.

NUMBER OF SCHOOLS: 79 primary schools, 13 secondary schools.

COUNTY MANAGER: Niall Bradley.

CHAIRMAN OF COUNTY COUNCIL: Mary Wheatley.

NAMES OF ALL COUNCILLORS: Raymond Cribbin (F.F.), Joseph Digan (F.F.), Joseph Dunne (F.F.), Thomas Jacob (F.F.), Jeremiah Lodge (F.F.), Seamus McDonald (F.F.), John Moloney (F.F.), Teresa Mulhare (F.F.), Fintan Phelan (F.F.), Kieran Phelan (F.F.), Eamonn Rafter (F.F.), Mary Wheatley (F.F.), William Aird (F.G.), James Daly (F.G.), James Deegan (F.G.), Charles Flanagan (F.G.), Thomas Keenan (F.G.), Michael Lalor (F.G.), John Moran (F.G.), Martin Phelan (F.G.), Larry Kavanagh (Lab.), Cathy Honan (P.D.), James Kelly (N.P.).

COUNCIL MEETING DATES: Last Monday of each month.

RATEABLE VALUE TOTALS: £384,086,05.

NEWSPAPERS: Laois Nationalist, (Editor: Tom Mooney). Leinster Express, (Editor: Teddy Fennelly).

MAJOR TOURIST ATTRACTIONS: Abbeyleix House and Gardens; Ballaghmore Castle; Ballyfin House; St. Canice's Monastery; Coolbanagher

KEY TO MAP
* *Slieve Bloom*
▲ *Arderin Mountain (528m)*
■ *Portlaoise*
● **Main towns**
■ **Lakes / Rivers**

Church and Tower House; Cullahill Tower House; Donaghmore Museum and Open Farm; Dysart's 'Merry Fair' and Dysart Castle; Emo Court and Gardens; The Great Heath of Maryborough, (one of the most important archeological sites in Ireland); Heywood Gardens, Ballinakill; Killeshin Church, (contains some of Ireland's finest medieval stonework); Kinnity Castle; Lea Castle; Mountmellick Quaker Museum; Portlaoise Equestrian Centre; Piggott's Castle; Rock of Dunamase; Slieve Bloom Environmental Park; Srahan Castle and Moat; the 'Stony Man', (a cairn on the highest point of Slieve Bloom); Stradbally Steam Museum; Timahoe Church and Round Tower.

FAMOUS NATIVES OF THE PAST: Jacob Arthur (discovered eye membrane; died 1874),1834), Patrick Cahill (prominent tenant-leader/first editor of Leinster Leader), Oliver J. Flanagan (politician; died 1987), Liam Miller (publisher; died 1987), Kevin O'Higgins (politician; died 1927), Owny MacRory O'More (chieftain; died 1600), Roger O'More (rebel; 17th century), Frank Power (acting British Consul in French Foreign Legion; died 1884).

COUNTY LONGFORD
(Province: Leinster)

An inland county set in the River Shannon basin and the upper catchment of the River Erne, Longford contains lakeland, bogland, pastureland and wetland. It is bordered to the west by the River Shannon and Lough Ree, while its largest lakes, Loughs Gowna and Kinale, both form the boundary between Longford and Cavan.

Longford's bogland contributes to its history. A trackway of large oak planks was recently discovered in a bog at Corlea. This trackway is very important in archaeological terms, as it's the only find from Ireland that can be dated back to the early Iron Age. An exhibition centre, focusing on the Corlea Trackway, has now been built in the area. Longford figures in many Irish myths; the Black Pig's Dyke can be found near Granard, and the route of the Táin crosses through the county. Longford was ruled in the eleventh century by O'Farrell, a hero at the Battle of Clontarf (1014 A.D.), who marched westwards and took control of the region by force. The present county was established in 1547 by the Tudors. Some of the fiercest fighting of the 1798 rebellion occurred in the county, mainly around Ballinamuck. The Great Famine in 1847 took a heavy toll on the county's population, and during this time, a Longford-Argentine connection was established, resulting from the many families in the county emigrated to Argentina.

ORIGIN OF COUNTY NAME: Derived from the Irish 'Longford Ui Fearraill' - the stronghold of the O'Farrell family.

LAND AREA: 403 sq. miles.

COUNTY CAPITAL: Longford.

MAIN TOWNS: Ballymahon, Edgeworthstown, Granard, Longford.

MAIN INDUSTRIES: Agriculture, bread and confectionery making, mill feed production, oil and gas valves manufacturing, pet food manufacturing, textiles manufacturing, timber processing, tourism.

CENSUS DETAILS: Total population - 30,138, - a 0.5% decrease since 1991.

NUMBER OF SCHOOLS: 43 primary schools, 10 secondary schools.

COUNTY MANAGER: Michael Killeen.

CHAIRMAN OF COUNTY COUNCIL: Seamus Finnan.

NAMES OF ALL COUNCILLORS: Jimmy Coyle (F.F.), Mickey Doherty (F.F.), Paddy Farrell (F.F.), Fintan Flood (F.F.), Peter Kelly (F.F.), Brian Lynch (F.F.), Luie McEntire (F.F.), Michael Nevin (F.F.), Barney Steele (F.F.), James Bannon (F.G.), Louis J. Belton (F.G.), Gerry Brady (F.G.), Seamus Finnan (F.G.), Adrian Farrell (F.G.), Philo Kelly (F.G.),Victor Kiernan (F.G.), Maura Kilbride-Harkin (F.G.), Seán Lynch (N.P.), Peter Murphy (N.P.), John Nolan (N.P.), Mae Sexton (N.P.).

COUNCIL MEETING DATES: Third Monday of each month (except August).

RATEABLE VALUE TOTAL: £204,124.55.

RADIO STATIONS: Shannonside/Northern sound.

NEWSPAPERS: The Longford Leader, (Editor: Eugene Magee). The Longford News, (Editor: Paul Healy).

MAJOR TOURIST ATTRACTIONS: Angling; Ardagh Heritage Village, (built in the 1860's following a Swiss design); the Backstage Theatre, Longford; the Black Pig's Dyke, (one of the most dominant ancient boundary formations in the country); Carrigglas Manor, Longford; Cashel Museum, Newtowncashel; Castleforbes Demesne; the Cistercian Abbeys at Abbeylara and Abbeyshrule; Clondra's Teach Cheoil; Corlea Trackway Exhibition Centre; Edgeworthstown, (the home of the Edgeworth family); Goldsmith Country; Lilac Activity Centre, Lanesboro; Longford County Museum; Lough Ree; Michael Casey's Bog Oak sculptures at Barley Harbour; the Royal Canal; Ringdong Pet Farm; the Shannon; St. Mel's Cathedral; St. John's Church, near Lanesboro; the Táin Trail.

FAMOUS NATIVES OF THE PAST: John Keegan Casey (ballad poet,'The Rising of the Moon'), Pádraic Colum (poet/playwright, wrote the song 'She moves through the fair'; died 1972), Maria Edgeworth (author, born Oxfordshire, father from Longford; died 1849), Abbé Henry Edgeworth (confessor to King Louis XVI at his execution; died 1807), Oliver Goldsmith (writer/essayist/novelist; died 1774), Thomas Lefroy (Chief Justice of Ireland, said to be the person on whom Jane Austen's character D'Arcy is based), Seán MacEoin (Blacksmith of Ballinalee, Guerrilla leader in the War of Independence; died 1973), Augustin Magaidrin (wrote important 14th century hagiography, now in Oxford's Bodleian Library), Edward Pakenham (Earl of Longford, playwright/theatre producer; died 1961), James Bonterre O'Brien (chartist leader/journalist; died 1864), Edel Miro O'Farrell (former President of Argentina), Fr. Joseph Mullooly (19th century archaeologist, discovered ancient temple of Mithras, Rome).

COUNTY LOUTH
(Province: Leinster)

Louth, situated on the eastern seaboard, is the smallest county in Ireland. Despite this, it contains more than 30 miles of coastline. The underlying rock in the county, except the Cooley Peninsula, is limestone. The pressure of the Ice Age caused the surface to crumble and form rich and often deep soil with well-wooded areas and sandy beaches. Louth is in a prime location situated half-way between Belfast and Dublin.

The ancient and historic town of Drogheda straddles the River Boyne, Ireland's most historic river. In the 1970's, a 'flint', shaped in palaeolithic times, was found near the town and is believed to be the oldest of objects ever discovered in Ireland. According to the Táin, one of Ireland's great folk tales, it was in Ardee that the legendary folk hero Cuchulainn single-handedly defeated the armies of Ulster. In early Christian times, Monasterboice in south Louth was an important Christian centre. The Normans took power in the late 13th century and built the two main towns of Drogheda and Dundalk. The remnants of Dundalk's old walls still exist, despite Oliver Cromwell's attack on the city in 1649, when he murdered around 2,600 of the town's inhabitants. With the arrival of the Protestant ascendancy in the 17th century, the native Irish were dispossessed. However, the 19th century saw the demise of this landlord class and gave rise to the relatively small farms and fields that are evident in Louth today.

ORIGIN OF COUNTY NAME: Derived from the Irish 'Lú', referring to the River Lud or a hollow.

LAND AREA: 318 sq. miles.

COUNTY CAPITAL: Dundalk.

MAIN TOWNS: Ardee, Drogheda, Dundalk.

MAIN INDUSTRIES: Cigarette and tobacco manufacturing, lager brewing, cement making, disc-drive manufacturing, domestic appliances manufacturing, food production and distribution, margarine making, soft drink concentrates and beverage bases production.

CENSUS DETAILS: Total population - 92,163 - a 1.6% increase since 1991.

NUMBER OF SCHOOLS: 73 primary schools, 17 secondary schools, 1 R.T.C.

COUNTY MANAGER: John Quinlivan.

CHAIRMAN OF COUNTY COUNCIL: Martin Bellew.

NAMES OF ALL COUNCILLORS: Declan Breathnach (F.F.), Frank Godfrey (F.F.), Seamus Keelan (F.F.), Noel Lennon (F.F.), Nicholas McCabe (F.F.), John McConville (F.F.), Jimmy Mulroy (F.F.), Tommy Murphy (F.F.), Maria O'Brien-Campbell (F.F.), Mícheál O'Donnell (F.F.), Tommy Reilly (F.F.), Peter Savage (F.F.), Terry Brennan (F.G.), Jim Lennon (F.G.), Bernard Markey (F.G.), Conor McGahon (F.G.), Fergus

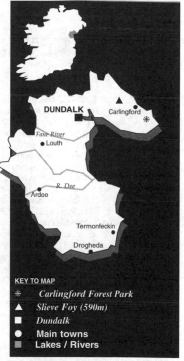

KEY TO MAP

✳	*Carlingford Forest Park*
▲	*Slieve Foy (590m)*
■	*Dundalk*
●	Main towns
■	Lakes / Rivers

O'Dowd (F.G.), Oliver Tully (F.G.), Betty Bell (Lab.), Michael Bell (Lab.), Helen Bellew (N.P.), Martin Bellew (N.P.), Hugh Conlon (N.P.), Jim Cousins (P.D.), Seán Kenna (S.F.), Finian McCoy.

COUNCIL MEETING DATES: Third Monday of every month.

RATEABLE VALUE TOTALS: £309,818.25.

RADIO STATIONS: LM FM Radio.

NEWSPAPERS: The Argus, (Editor: Kevin Mulligan). Drogheda Independent, (Editor: Paul Murphy). Dundalk Democrat, (Editor: T.P. Roe).

MAJOR TOURIST ATTRACTIONS:

Carlingford Adventure Centre; Carlingford Forest Park; Carlingford Village, (a designated heritage town); the Cooley Peninsula; the Darcy Magee Centre, Carlingford; the Droichead gallery, Stockwell Street; Drogheda town's gates and walls; Drogheda Museum; Dromiskin Cross; Dundalk Arts Centre; Dundalk Bird Sanctuary, (one of the biggest in Ireland); Dundalk Courthouse, (a greek revival building from the 1820s); Dundalk Motte and Bailey; Dun Dealgan; Dundalk Museum; King John's Castle, Carlingford; the Jumping Wall, Ardee; Mansfieldstown 17th-century church; the Medieval Churches, Drogheda; The Millmount, Drogheda; Mill Street Bell Tower; 'The Mint' (15th-century tower), Carlingford; St. Mochta's 12th century church; O'Grady's Garden, Monasterboice; Old Mellifont Abbey, Collon; Monasterboice's inscribed crosses and round tower; Proleek dolmen; Riverstown Mill, Cooley; Roodstown Castle, Ardee; Seatown Windmill (the largest surviving windmill in Ireland); St. Bridget's Pillar, Faughart; St. Patrick's Church, Dundalk; Termonfeckin high cross and tombstones; White River Mill, (a working watermill in Dunleer).

FAMOUS NATIVES OF THE PAST: Fr. Nicholas J. Callan (invented the induction coil; died 1864), Brian Lenihan (politician; died 1995), Dorothy MacArdle (historian; died 1958), Sir Francis Leopold McClintock (arctic explorer; died 1907), Tom McCormack (professional boxer; born 1890), Sean MacEoin (Lieutenant-General; born 1910), Thomas D'Arcy McGee (Irish-Canadian politician/journalist; died 1868), Frank O'Reilly (Catholic Truth Society of Ireland; died 1957), Nano Reid (artist; died 1981), Tom Sharkey (world champion boxer; born 1873).

COUNTY MEATH
(Province: Leinster)

Situated in the eastern part of the country, Meath comprises a rich limestone plain that is the basis of the county's fertile farmlands. Meath is bordered by the Irish sea in the east and by County Dublin in the south. The two major rivers flowing through the county are the Blackwater and the history-steeped Boyne.

Once part of the fifth ancient province of Ireland, Meath has been inhabited for more than 8,000 years. The county is referred to as Royal Meath, as it was once home to the kings of pagan and early Christian Ireland at Tara and the place from which the ancient roads of Ireland radiated. In the Boyne Valley lie the celebrated megalithic burial grounds at Newgrange, Knowth and Dowth, the oldest Neolithic structures in Europe, predating the pyramids and Stonehenge. Newgrange could lay claim to being possibly the oldest astronomically aligned Stone Age structure in the world. The Boyne Valley has been significant in most eras in Irish history from prehistory to the Battle of the Boyne in 1690, when King James II was vanquished by King William III for the crown of England. Arguably the most important early Christian artifact - The Book of Kells - came from Kells in Meath. Other important archaeological finds include the Tara Brooch, found on the beach at Bettystown. The hill at Tara continued to play an important role in Irish history - it is said that St. Patrick was first given permission to convert Ireland to Christianity. The British army defeated Irish rebels during the 1798 rebellion at Tara, and Daniel O'Connell held a 'monster' rally here in 1843, leading an estimated one million people to protest against the Act of Union.

ORIGIN OF COUNTY NAME: Derived from the Irish 'An Mhí', meaning the middle.

LAND AREA: 905 sq. miles.

COUNTY CAPITAL: Navan.

MAIN TOWNS: Athboy, Dunshaughlin, Kells, Navan, Slane, Trim.

MAIN INDUSTRIES: Agriculture, aluminium and metal manufacturing, bloodstock sales, carpet manufacturing, concrete production, construction materials packaging and production, corrugated case manufacturing, envelope manufacturing, excavator attachments production, integrated circuits manufacturing, mineral exploration and mining, polyester and nylon fibres manufacturing, snackfoods manufacturing, tourism.

CENSUS DETAILS: Total population - 109,371 - a 3.8% increase since 1991.

NUMBER OF SCHOOLS: 105 primary schools, 19 secondary

KEY TO MAP
* ✳   *Newgrange Megaliths*
* ▲   *Sliabh na Galligh (279m)*
* ■   *Navan*
* ●   **Main towns**
* ■   **Lakes / Rivers**

schools.

COUNTY MANAGER: Joe Horan.

CHAIRMAN OF COUNTY COUNCIL: Gabriel Cribben.

NAMES OF ALL COUNCILLORS: John Brady (F.F.), Garbriel Cribbin (F.F.), Patrick Fitzsimons (F.F.), Hugh Gough (F.F.), Owen Heaney (F.F.), Patricia Hegarty (F.F.), Colm Hilliard (F.F.), Michael Lynch (F.F.), Seamus Murray (F.F.), Sebastian Rooney (F.F.), Conor Tormey (F.F.), Mary Wallace (F.F), Jimmy Weldon (F.F.), William Carey (F.G.), John Fanning (F.G.), John V. Farrelly (F.G.), Noel Foley (F.G.), Gerry Gibney (F.G.),

Tom Kelly (F.G.), Shaun Lynch (F.G.), Patsy O'Neill (F.G.), Mary Sylver (F.G.), Brendan Clusker (Lab.), Jimmy Cudden (Lab.), Brian Fitzgerald (Lab.), Philip Lowe (Lab.), Jack Fitzsimons (N.P.), Gerry Marry (N.P.), Christy Gorman (D.L.).

COUNCIL MEETING DATES: First Monday of each month.

RATEABLE VALUE TOTALS: £854,346.

RADIO/T.V. STATIONS: Atlantic 252; Radio Tara Ltd. Province 5 Television (Ireland's only community station on air, 12 hours daily to Meath and North Dublin).

NEWSPAPERS: The Meath Chronicle, (Editor: Ken Davis).The Meath Topic, (Editor: Dick Hogan).

MAJOR TOURIST ATTRACTIONS: Angling; Beau Park House, Navan; Bective Abbey, Navan; Bettystown and Laytown; Brú na Bóinne Visitor Centre, Donore; Butterstream Gardens, Trim; Children's House, Kilpatrick, Navan; Dardistown Castle, Julianstown; Dunsany Castle; Grove Gardens, Fordstown, Navan; the Hill of Tailte, (where the Tailtean Games and Fair were held in ancient times); the Hill of Tara, Navan; Hamwood House and Gardens, Dunboyne; Francis Ledwidge Cottage Museum, Slane; Lloyd Park and Tower, Kells; Lough Crew, (a series of hills with passage graves); the Mary McDonnell Craft Studio, Slane; the megaliths at Knowth, Dowth and Newgrange; Mountainstown House, Navan; Newgrange Open Farm, Slane; Oldcastle, (a village dating from the 18th century); Sommerville House, Balrath; St. John's Castle, Trim, (contains has the largest castle fortifications in Ireland and the location of the film *Braveheart*); St. Mary's Abbey, Trim, (where the Duke of Wellington was educated); the town of Trim, (a designated heritage town).

FAMOUS NATIVES OF THE PAST: Francis Beaufort (devisor of the Beaufort Scale; died 1857), Thekla Beere (founder member and president of An Óige/Irish Youth Hostel 1931; died 1991), Jim Connell (wrote the famous socialist song 'The Red Flag', died 1929), Kate Kennedy (formed America's first schoolteachers' union; died 1890), Francis Ledwidge (poet; died 1917 in the Great War), John McHale (Archbishop of Tuam/nationalist; early 19th century), Turlough O'Carolan (harpist; died 1738), Charles Y. O'Connor (noted marine engineer in Australia; died 1881), Ambrosio and Bernardo O'Higgins (Chilean heroes; died 1801 and 1842, respectively), Edward Lovett Pearce (architect/canal builder; died 1733), Horace Plunkett (founded Irish Co-op movement 1889, born Gloucestershire/related to Lord Dunsany; died 1932), St. Oliver Plunkett (Archbishop of Armagh; died 1681).

COUNTY OFFALY
(Province: Leinster)

Offaly, an inland county, is located at the heart of Ireland and is bordered by Slieve Bloom mountain range in the south-east and the River Shannon in the west. The county's Clara bog is one of the largest remaining relatively intact raised bogs in Western Europe and is now recognised as being of international importance. Offaly's bogs and wetlands are home to several species of native and migrant birds; a total of 87 species have been recorded to date.

In the past, the Shannon acted as the main route for the county. The Danes sailed up it to Clonmacnoise, one of the largest monastic sites in Ireland, and raided it. Clonmacnoise was a major early Christian site, and its ruins include a cathedral, three high crosses, two round towers and eight churches. In addition, Ireland's earliest Irish language manuscript was produced here and Ireland's last high king - Rory O'Connor - is buried here. After the English conquered the area, Offaly was known as King's County from 1556 and was, along with Laois, the first region in Ireland to be planted by the English. Other structures of historical note in the county include castles, the Martello Tower in Banagher and the Napoleonic fortifications at Lusmagh and Shannonbridge. One of the more spectacular castles in Ireland - Birr Castle Demesne - is situated in Offaly. Within its confines can be found a fabulous array of rare and exotic plants, as well as a giant telescope dating from 1845, once the largest in the world. A new telescope and observatory have recently been installed, and the demesne is to be the home of Ireland's proposed science museum.

ORIGIN OF COUNTY NAME: From the Irish 'Uíbh Fhailí', meaning Failghe's People.

LAND AREA: 771 sq. miles. **COUNTY CAPITAL:** Tullamore.

MAIN TOWNS: Banagher, Birr, Edenderry, Ferbane, Tullamore.

MAIN INDUSTRIES: Agriculture, animal feeds production, clothing manufacturing, convenience foods manufacturing, desktop publishing,

KEY TO MAP
* Clara Bog
▲ Arderin Mtn. (528m)
■ Tullamore
● Main towns
■ Lakes / Rivers

field bean processing, food and beverage packaging, liquor and whiskey distilling, machinery packaging, pharmaceutical companies, service industries, software package companies, turf cutting and distribution, wrought iron production.

CENSUS DETAILS: Total population - 59,080 - a 1% increase since 1991.
NUMBER OF SCHOOLS: 68 primary schools, 13 secondary schools.
COUNTY MANAGER: Niall Sweeney.
CHAIRMAN OF COUNTY COUNCIL: Noel Bourke.
NAMES OF ALL COUNCILLORS: Noel Bourke (F.F.), Barry Cowen (F.F.), Eamon Dooley (F.F.), Joseph Dooley (F.F.), Thomas Feighery (F.F.), James Flanagan (F.F), Séamus Loughnane (F.F.), Patrick J. Moylan (F.F.), Miriam O'Callaghan (F.F.), Francis Weir (F.F.), Percy Clendennen (F.G.), Bernard Corcoran (F.G.), Thomas Enright (F.G.), Michael Fox (F.G.), Constance Hanniffy (F.G.), Thomas McKeigue (F.G.), John Butterfield (N.P.), Thomas C. Dolan (N.P.), John Flanagan (N.P.), Patrick Gallagher (Lab.), Brigid Emerson (P.D.).
COUNCIL MEETING DATES: Third Monday of each month, except August.
RATEABLE VALUE TOTALS: £357,711.30.
RADIO STATIONS: Radio 3.
NEWSPAPERS: The Leinster Express, (Editor: Teddy Fennelly). The Tullamore Tribune, (Editor: Ger Scully). The Offaly Topic, (Editor: Dick Hogan). Offaly Independent, (Editor: Margaret Grennan). The Westmeath Examiner, (Editor: Nicholas Nally).
MAJOR TOURIST ATTRACTIONS: Angling; artillery fortifications at Shannonbridge and Lusmagh, (from Napoleonic times); Ashbrook Open Farm, Shannonbridge; Birr, (a designated heritage town); Birr Castle and Demesne; the Blackwater Bog, (a raised bog of major significance near Clonmacnoise); Bloomhill's ancient road of flagged sandstone, (discovered under a 5,000 year old bog); Charleville Castle and Demesne, Tullamore; Clara Bog; Cloghan Castle, Banagher; Clonmacnoise monastic ruins; Clonmacnoise and West Offaly Railway; Clonony Castle; cruising on the River Shannon and the Grand Canal; Durrow Abbey and High Cross; the Geological Nature Trail; Killeen River; Killeigh, (with its seven holy wells and two medieval abbeys); Kinnitty Cross and Castle; Leap Castle, Clareen; Lough Ennel; the Martello Tower, Banagher; Multyfarnahm Castle; the Old Mill, Cadamstown; the Rock of Dunamaise; the Silver River; the Slieve Bloom mountain range; St. Finbar's Abbey; Tullamore, (the county capital and a designated heritage town).
FAMOUS NATIVES OF THE PAST: Charles Jervas (portrait artist in the courts of George I and II; died 1739), George Johnstone Stoney (first to propose existence of electrons; died 1911), John Joly (developed first practical colour photography system and radioactivity treatment for cancer; died 1933), Charles Parsons (invented the turbine; died 1931), Lawrence Parsons (brother of Charles, determined temperature of moon surface; died 1908), William Parsons (Earl of Rosse, astronomer, born New York/educated Offaly/Dublin; died 1867).

COUNTY WESTMEATH
(Province: Leinster)

An inland county at the heart of Ireland, Westmeath's northern regions are dotted with drumlins - small steep-sided hills that were formed by the melting glaciers of the Ice Age - while the central and southern regions of the county are flatter, with bogs and lakes. The southern part also contains a long line of low hills, or eskers, another feature dating from the Ice Age, formed from sand and rounded stones.

Westmeath has played a prominent role in Ireland's history. As one of its principal towns, Athlone is a major crossing point on the River Shannon. Two centuries prior to St. Patrick's arrival, the county was home to the seat of the High King of Ireland at Uisneach, near Mullingar, which was also the meeting point of the five ancient provinces of Ireland. St. Patrick brought Christianity to Westmeath in the fifth century, and there are a number of notable, early monastic sites in the county, particularly that of Fore, established by St. Fechin. The Normans arrived in the region circa 1170, and their numerous mottes-and-baileys can still be seen. The county was originally part of the ancient province of Meath, but in 1542, an act of law designated it as a separate county.

ORIGIN OF COUNTY NAME: Derived from the Irish 'an Lar Mhí', meaning the west of Meath.
LAND AREA: 710 sq. miles.
COUNTY CAPITAL: Mullingar.
MAIN TOWNS: Athlone, Moate.
MAIN INDUSTRIES: Agriculture, anaesthesiological tubes and catheter production, aluminium and stainless steel manufacturing, bathroom/ceramic tiles retailing, computer component manufacturing and

KEY TO MAP
❋ *Hill of Uisneach*
▲ *Mullaghmeen (260m)*
■ *Mullingar*
● **Main towns**
■ **Lakes / Rivers**

services, electric cable manufacturing, electronics manufacturing, heating and plumbing services, joinery and UPVC production, machinery manufacturing, pharmaceutical retail and distribution, precision plastics coating, tennis ball manufacturing, tobacco processing, vinyl floor manufacturing.

CENSUS DETAILS: Total population - 63,236 - a 2.2% increase since 1991.

NUMBER OF SCHOOLS: 78 primary schools, 15 secondary schools, 1 R.T.C., 2 Colleges.

COUNTY MANAGER: Jack A. Taaffe.

CHAIRMAN OF COUNTY COUNCIL: Tom Cowley.

NAMES OF ALL COUNCILLORS: Thomas Bourke (F.F), Donie Cassidy (F.F), P.J. Coghill (F.F), Tom Cowley (F.F), Camillus Glynn (F.F), Kieran Molloy (F.F), Egbert Moran (F.F), Patrick O'Shaughnessy (F.F), Michael Ryan (F.F), Ciaran Temple (F.F), Thomas Wright (F.F), Joseph Flanagan (F.G.), J.H. Keegan (F.G.), Frank McDermott (F.G.), Brendan McFadden (F.G.), Paul McGrath (F.G.), Joe Whelan (F.G.), Des Coleman (Lab.), Michael Dollard (Lab.), Mark Nugent (Lab.), Willie Penrose (Lab.), Stephen Price (Ind.).

COUNCIL MEETING DATES: Last Monday of each month.

RATEABLE VALUE TOTALS: £517,985.25.

RADIO STATIONS: Radio 3, Shannonside.

NEWSPAPERS: The Irish Family Newspaper, (Editor: R. Hogan). Westmeath Examiner, (Editor: Nicholas Nally). Westmeath Topic, (Editor: Dick Hogan). Westmeath Independent, (Editor: Margaret Grennan).

TOURIST ATTRACTIONS: Athlone Castle Interpretative Centre, Athlone; Belvedere Gardens; the Catstone on Uisneach Hill; the Dower House of the Pollard Family, Castlepollard; Dun na Sí Heritage Centre, Moate; An Dun Transport and Heritage Museum, Ballinahown, Athlone; Fore Abbey; St. Fechin's Church; Gigginstown House and Mearescourt House, Mullingar; Glendeer Pet Farm, Athlone; Knockdrin Castle; Locke's Distillery, (one of the world's oldest licensed whiskey distilleries); Loughs Owel, Ennell, Derravaragh and Lene; Lough Park House; the Military Museum, Columb Barracks; Mullingar Town; Mullingar Bronze and Pewter Visitor Centre; Tullynally Castle and Gardens, Castlepollard; Turbotstown House, Castlepollard; Tyrrellspass Castle and Museum.

FAMOUS NATIVES OF THE PAST: Thomas St. George Armstrong (founded Argentine stock exchange/Buenos Aires Bank, emigrated 1817), Colonel Charles Howard Bury (commanded first British Everest expedition 1921; died 1963), Mary Josephine Hannon (one of first Irish female doctors), Count John McCormack (famous tenor; died 1945), Brinsley McNamara (author/dramatist), Thomas Power O'Connor (publisher; died 1929), Myles 'Slasher' O'Reilly (defended Finea 1646), Captain Richard Tyrrell (defeated Elizabethan army during Nine Years War), James Woods (Annals of Westmeath author).

COUNTY WEXFORD
(Province: Leinster)

Known as the 'Model County', Wexford is set in the south-east coast of Ireland and enjoys the best of Irish weather. It is bounded by the sea on the east - St. George's Channel - and by hills and the River Barrow on the west. The River Slaney, a noted salmon river, flows through the county.

    The county's history has been shaped by the many invasions It has endured. The Vikings attacked and settled the main town of Wexford, from the 9th to the 12th centuries, to be followed by the Normans, who captured the town of Wexford after they landed in the country in 1169. The county then suffered Cromwell's attacks in 1649, when he attacked the town and murdered 200 people. The men of Wexford were among the main instigators in the 1798 Rebellion. Their opposition to the English came to a head at the Battle of Vinegar Hill in Enniscorthy.

ORIGIN OF COUNTY NAME: Wexford is Viking in origin; the Irish 'Loch Garman' means inlet by the sea-washed bank.

LAND AREA: 909 sq. miles. **COUNTY CAPITAL:** Wexford.

MAIN TOWNS: Bunclody, Enniscorthy, Gorey, New Ross, Wexford.

MAIN INDUSTRIES: Agriculture, boning manufacturing, baby food processing, beverage manufacturing, builders' merchants, cable harness production, car rental, concrete manufacturing, dairy processing, D.I.Y. manufacturing, fish and shellfish processing, freight forwarders, haulage and shipping, hygiene rental and laundry services, international transportation, livestock auctioneering, mushroom processing and production, ophthalmic lens manufacturing, pump manufacturing, retailing, textile manufacturing, tourism.

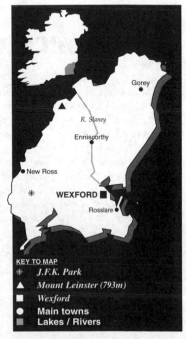

Gorey

R. Slaney

Enniscorthy

New Ross

WEXFORD ■

Rosslare

KEY TO MAP
*   *J.F.K. Park*
▲   *Mount Leinster (793m)*
■   *Wexford*
●   **Main towns**
■   **Lakes / Rivers**

CENSUS DETAILS: Total population - 104,314 - a 2.2% increase since 1991.
NUMBER OF SCHOOLS: 103 primary schools, 20 secondary schools.
COUNTY MANAGER: Seamus Dooley.
CHAIRMAN OF COUNTY COUNCIL: John A. Browne.
NAMES OF ALL COUNCILLORS: Lorcan Allen (F.F.), John T. Browne (F.F.), Gus Byrne (F.F.), Hugh Byrne (F.F.), John A. Browne (F.F.), Jimmy Curtis (F.F.), Michelle Sinnott (F.F.), Jim Walsh (F.F.), Deirdre Bolger (F.G.), Jack Bolger (F.G.), Pat Codd (F.G.), Michael D'Arcy (F.G.), James Gahan (F.G.), Rory Murphy (F.G.), Laurence O'Brien (F.G.), John Walsh (F.G.), Leo Carthy (N.P.), Helen Corish-Wylde (N.P.), Seán Doyle (N.P.), Padge Reck (N.P.), Thomas Carr (Lab.).
COUNCIL MEETING DATES: Second Monday of each month.
RATEABLE VALUE TOTALS: £558,074.00.
RADIO STATIONS: South-East Radio.
NEWSPAPERS: The Echo, The Wexford Echo, The Gorey Echo, New Ross Echo, (Editor: Tom Mooney). The Guardian, The New Ross Standard, The People, (Editor: Gerard Walsh).
MAJOR TOURIST ATTRACTIONS: Angling; art galleries in Ballyhack, Crossabeg, Gorey, New Ross and Wexford; Ballyhack Castle; Ballylane Open Farm; Ballymore Historic Features Exhibition, Camolin; Ballybrittas portal tomb; bird watching around Wexford's cliffs and at the Wexford Wildfowl Reserve; the Bull Ring, Wexford town; Craanford Mills; Curracloe Nature Trail; Duncannon Fort, an Iron Age structure; Dunbrody Abbey and Visitor Centre, Campile; Dunmain House, New Ross; the earthworks at Baginbun; Enniscorthy Castle; Ferns Castle; the high crosses at Arthurstown, Ballinaray, Carrick and Killesk; Hook Lighthouse, (one of the oldest lighthouses in Europe, dating from the 12th century); the House of Storytelling, Camolin; Johnstown Castle and Gardens, Wexford; John F. Kennedy Park, (marks the birthplace of the late president's father); the Irish National Heritage Park, Ferrycarrig; Kilmokea Gardens, Campile; Lady's Island, an important religious site, predating early Christian times; the Martello towers in Duncannon and elsewhere along the Wexford coast; the monastic site at Ferns; the motte at Ballymonty More; Pirates Cove, Courtown; Ram House Garden, Coolgreany; Rathmacknee Castle; Raven Point Nature Reserve; Selskar Abbey, Wexford; Shortalstown Gardens; Shrule Deer Farm; Slade Castle; St. Beoc's Stone, Carne; St. Iberius Church, Wexford; Tintern Abbey; Westgate Heritage Centre; Wexford County Museum, Enniscorthy; Wexford town, (a designated heritage town); the Windmill at Tacumshane; Whitechurch Standing Stones; Woodlands Honey Farm; Woodville Victorian Walled Garden, New Ross; Young McDonald's Animal Park, Askamore.
FAMOUS NATIVES OF THE PAST: James Annesley (title claimant, inspiration for Robert Louis Stevenson's *Kidnapped*; died 1760), Charles Blacker Vignoles (Ireland's first railway engineer-in-chief; died 1875), Brendan Corish (politician; died 1990), James A. Cullen (Jesuit priest, launched Pioneer Total A.A. 1898; died 1921), James Dillon (politician; died 1986), Robert John Le Mesurier McClure (discovered Northwest Passage for Arctic expeditions; died 1873), Fr. John Murphy (led Wexford 1798 rising), John Redmond (led Parnellite fraction of Home Rule Party; died 1890), William Redmond (politician; died 1917), Jem Roche (boxer 1900's), Michael James Whitty (founded first U.K. Penny Daily Newspaper 1855; died 1873).

COUNTY WICKLOW
(Province: Leinster)

A small maritime county on the east coast of Ireland, Wicklow is known as the 'Garden of Ireland'. A raised granite ridge runs through it, which contains two of the highest passes in the country - the Sally Gap and the Wicklow Gap - that are major routes to the east and west for the county. To the north of this ridge is Dublin city, to the west lie the Blessington lakes and to the east is the tranquil valley of Glendalough, which was a centre of early Christianity in Ireland. In addition to lakes at Blessington and Roundwood, the county is criss-crossed by rivers.

The county's history is directly related to its physical setting. Glendalough was established as a monastic city from a sixth century hermitage set up by St. Kevin in the peaceful setting of 'the Glen of Two Lakes'. Although the county's highlands assisted in protecting the county's Gaelic heritage, the lowlands of the west and the east coast were more susceptible to the successive raids launched by the Vikings, the Normans and the English. The county's Viking past is reflected in the town names. Dermot McMurrough, a Wicklow chieftain and King of Leinster, invited the Normans to help him repossess his lands, and it was this act that led to English taking power and that ultimately direct-

KEY TO MAP
* ✳ **Powerscourt Waterfall**
* ▲ **Lugnaquilla (927m)**
* ■ *Wicklow*   ● **Main towns**
* ■ **Lakes / Rivers**

ed the course of Irish history. Their sojourn in the county is marked by the many stately homes and gardens scattered around the county, the most notable of these being Powerscourt and Russborough House. Many of Wicklow's villages still reflect their English origins as estate villages. The Irish kept their hold on the highlands, providing refuge to rebels, and the people of Wicklow played a prominent role in the 1798 rebellion. However, after the rebellion, the British built the Military Road through the county to provide them with easier access to the rebel strongholds.

ORIGIN OF COUNTY NAME: Derived from 'Vykinglo' - the original Viking settlements founded in the county around the eighth century.

LAND AREA: 782 sq. miles.

COUNTY CAPITAL: Wicklow.

MAIN TOWNS: Arklow, Bray, Greystones, Wicklow.

MAIN INDUSTRIES: Agriculture, bathroom suite manufacturing and distribution, beef processing, building and civil engineering, clothing and weaving manufacturing, computer software manufacturing, crop production, dairy processing, electric motors for air conditioning and refrigeration, grain merchants, livestock production, pig meat processing, plastic injection moulders, pharmaceutical chemicals manufacturing, printing, sawmiller manufacturing, security printing, shipping, telecommunications transmission equipment manufacturing, veterinary product manufacturing.

CENSUS DETAILS: Total population - 102,417 - a 5.3% increase since 1991.

NUMBER OF SCHOOLS: 84 primary schools, 21 secondary schools.

COUNTY MANAGER: Blaise Treacy.

CHAIRMAN OF COUNTY COUNCIL: Pat Vance.

NAMES OF ALL COUNCILLORS: Joe Behan (F.F.), Pat Doyle (F.F.), Joe Jacob (F.F.), Tom Keenan (F.F.), Michael D. Lawlor (F.F.), James O'Connell (F.F.), Dick Roche (F.F.), Pat Vance (F.F.), Vincent Blake (F.G.), Thomas Honan (F.G.), Shane Ross (F.G.), Godfrey Timmins (F.G.), Mildred Fox (Ind.), George Jones (Ind.), Vincent McElheron (Ind.), James Ruttle (Ind.), John Byrne (Lab.), Thomas Cullen (Lab.), Susan Philips (N.P.), Liam Kavanagh (Lab.), James O'Shaughnessy (Lab.), Kevin Ryan (Lab.), Emer Singleton (G.P.), Colm Kirwan (D.L.).

COUNCIL MEETING DATES: First and second Mondays of each month.

RATEABLE VALUE TOTALS: £715,433.

RADIO STATIONS: East Coast Radio.

NEWSPAPERS: The Bray People, The Wicklow People, (Editor: Gerard Walsh). The Wicklow Times.

MAJOR TOURIST ATTRACTIONS: the abbey at Baltinglass; Altidore Castle; Arklow Pottery; Avoca Hand Weavers, Avoca; Avondale House, (the home of Charles Stewart Parnell); Ballyorney House, Enniskerry; Blessington lakes; Bray, (a Victorian seaside resort); Charleville House, Enniskerry; Clara, (said to be the smallest village in Ireland); coarse fishing; Dwyer McAllister Cottage, Dunlaving; the Devil's Punchbowl, (a waterfall in the Devil's Glen); Glenart forest, (provides a viewing point of the Vale of Avoca); Glencree Valley; Glendalough, (with its many monastic ruins); Greenane Farm Museum Maze, Rathdrum; hillwalking; horse drawn caravans, (available at Carrigmore); Killruddery House and Gardens, (one of the two venues for the annual Festival of Music in Great Irish Houses); Knockmore Gardens; the lakes at Roundwood; the Maritime Museum, Arklow; the Meeting of the Rivers, near Avoca; Mount Usher gardens; the National Aquarium at Bray; National Garden Exhibition Centre, Kilquade; Parnell Memorial Park, Rathdrum; Powerscourt Gardens, (containing the impressive ruins of Powerscourt House); Roundwood village, (the highest village in Ireland); Russborough House, (an 18th century Palladian mansion that houses the internationally renowned Sir Alfred Beit art collection); the Sally Gap; sea angling; seaside resorts - Brittas Bay, Arklow, Clogga, Sliver Strand, Bray and Greystones; the Sugar Loaf Mountain; Tiglin Adventure Centre, Ashford; Tinakilly House, Rathnew, (the home of Captain Halpin whose ship laid the first trans-Atlantic cable); the Wicklow Gap Drive; Wicklow Mountains National Park; the Wicklow Way, (a walking trail).

FAMOUS NATIVES OF THE PAST: Robert Barton (signatory of Anglo-Irish Treaty; died 1975), Harry 'The Brad' Bradshaw (golfer; died 1990), Robert Erskine Childers (writer/nationalist, born London/worked here, father of President Erskine Childers; died 1922), Dame Ninette de Valois (ballet dancer/choreographer; born 1898), Michael Dwyer (1798 rebellion leader), Captain Robert Charles Halpin (one of the greatest navigators of 19th century), Peter J. O'Connor (world record athlete 1901; born 1874), Cearbhall O'Dálaigh (President of Ireland; died 1978), Anna Parnell (sister of Charles, founded the Ladies Land League, 1881; died 1911), Charles Stewart Parnell (leader of the Home Rule Party; died 1891), Joshua Pim (only Irish Wimbledon Singles tennis champion 1893; born 1869).

COUNTY CLARE
(Province: Munster)

Clare is situated on the west coast of the country and could be referred to as a peninsula, joined on its north-east border to Galway and bounded by Lough Derg in the east, the biggest of the River Shannon's lakes; by the Shannon estuary in the south; by the Atlantic Ocean in the west and by Galway Bay in the north-west. The county has a diverse topography, which includes the bare karst landscape of the Burren National Park, the Cliffs of Moher and the beaches of the Atlantic Coast.

Evidence of human habitation in Clare dates back to the Stone Age. There are around 120 dolmens and wedge tombs in the Burren National Park, the most famous being Poulnabrone Dolmen. Brian Boru, the high king of Ireland, who defeated the Vikings, had over-lordship of Clare. The Normans failed to secure a permanent hold in the county, and the English did not appear in Clare until Murrough O'Brien was made Earl of Thomond in 1541. The earl leaned towards Charles I but reluctantly allowed Cromwell's forces to garrison at Bunratty Castle. The wars of this period ravaged the county, leaving it ruined by famine and depopulation. Although the native people were oppressed by the Penal Laws of the 18th century, they led the way towards civil and religious liberty. It was they who returned Daniel O'Connell as a Member of Parliament, which led to Catholic Emancipation in 1829, earning Clare the title of the Banner County. However, the county fared badly during the Great Famine, and its population fell from 286,000 in 1841 to half this number in 1871.

KEY TO MAP
- ✳ **Cliffs of Moher**
- ✳✳ **The Burren**
- ▲ **Slieve Glennagallaigh (533m)**
- ■ *Ennis* ● **Main towns**
- ■ **Lakes / Rivers**

ORIGIN OF COUNTY NAME: From the Irish 'An Clár', meaning plain.
LAND AREA: 1,262 sq. miles. **COUNTY CAPITAL:** Ennis.
MAIN TOWNS: Ennis, Kilkee, Killaloe, Kilrush, Shannon Town.
MAIN INDUSTRIES: Agriculture, aircraft maintenance and overhaul, dental alloy manufacturing, display and printed circuit boards, electrical components and supports, fine chemicals, food and food ingredients supplies, freight forwarding distribution, industrial diamond processing, industrial seal manufacturing, livestock auctioneering, medical instruments and supplies, mushroom growing, plastic products, precision tools manufacturing, softwood veneer and plywood processing, smoked fish manufacturing, tourism.
CENSUS DETAILS: Total population: 93,914, a 3.3% increase since '91
NUMBER OF SCHOOLS: 125 primary schools, 19 secondary schools.
COUNTY MANAGER: William Maloney.
CHAIRMAN OF COUNTY COUNCIL: P.J. Kelly.
NAMES OF ALL COUNCILLORS: Michael Begley (F.F.), James Breen (F.F.), Tom Burke (F.F.), Bill Chambers (F.F.), Peter Considine (F.F.), Flan Garvey (F.F.), Raymond Greene (F.F.), Bernard Hanrahan (F.F.), Michael Hillery (F.F.), Seán Hillery (F.F.), Patrick Keane (F.F.), P.J. Kelly (F.F.), Tony Killeen (F.F.), Pat McMahon (F.F.), Jimmy Nagle (F.F.), Joe O'Gorman (F.F.), Tom Prendeville (F.F.), Colm Wiley (F.F.), Cissie Keane (F.G.), Tony McMahon (F.G.), Anna Mulqueen (F.G.), Sonny Scanlan (F.G.), Madeline Taylor-Quinn (F.G.), Martin Lafferty (Lab.), Thomas Brennan (Ind.), P.J. Burke (Ind.), Christy Curtin (Ind.), Brigid Makowski (Ind.), Patricia McCarthy (Ind.), Mary Mannion (P.D.), Michael Kelly (?).
COUNCIL MEETING DATES: Second Monday of each month.
RATEABLE VALUE TOTALS: £492,088.70.
RADIO STATIONS: Clare FM.
NEWSPAPERS: The Clare Champion, (Editor: Gerry Collison).
MAJOR TOURIST ATTRACTIONS: Aillwee Caves; angling; Ballycasey Craft Design Centre;Bunratty Castle and Folk Park; the Burren National Park; the Burren Perfumery and Floral Centre; the Burren Smokehouse; Carnelly House, Clarecastle; the Cliffs of Moher; Corcomroe Abbey; Craggaunowen Bronze Age lake dwellings; Cratloe Woods House, Cratlow; Dolphin Watch, Carrigaholt (gives observers the chance to see Ireland's only resident group of bottlenose dolphins); Doolin; Dromoland Castle; Dromore Wood; Dunguaire Castle, Kinvara; Dysert O'Dea Castle, with its archaeology centre; Ennis Friary and Ennis Museum; Killaloe; Kilkee Bay, (rated as the best diving location in Europe and among the top five in the world); Kilrush Creek Marina; Knappogue Castle, Quin; Lahinch Seaworld and Leisure Centre; Lisdoonvarna, (with its matchmaking festival); Loop Head Scenic Drive; Lough Derg; Mooghaun Fort, (an Iron Age ring fort); Newtown Castle, Ballyvaughan; Poulnabrone Dolmen; Quin Abbey, (dating back to the 14th century); Scattery Island, (the island of battles); sea angling; the Shannon;

FAMOUS NATIVES OF THE PAST: Sir Frederick Burton (painter/director of National Gallery, London; died 1900), Willie Clancy (multi-instrumentalist; died 1975), Michael Cusack (founding member of G.A.A.; died 1906), Thomas Dermody (poet; died 1802), Biddy Early (wise woman/white witch; died 1874), John Philip Holland (created first commercially successful submarine; died 1914), Brian Merriman (wrote 'The Midnight Court', the most translated poem in gaelic; died 1805), Pat McDonald (U.S. Olympic medalist shot-put, 1920), Edward Anthony Edgeworth MacLysaght (genealogist/scholar; died 1986), Mike McTigue (boxer; died 1892), William Mulready (painter; died 1863), William Smith O'Brien (young Ireland leader/revolutionary; died 1864), Eugene O'Curry (celebrated Irish scholar; died 1862), Michael O'Gorman (founded first medical institution in Buenos Aires; died 1819), 1917), Harriet Smithson (actress/wife of the French composer Berlioz; died 1854).

COUNTY CORK
(Province: Munster)

Located on the south-west coast of Ireland, Cork is Ireland's largest county. Long ridges of sandstone traverse the county, and the Rivers Blackwater, Lee and Bandon flow west to east along the fertile valleys between these limestone ridges, each turning sharply to empty southwards into the sea. The Gulf Stream touches Ireland first at Cork, providing warm, mild weather that ensures lush growth in the county's fertile farmlands. Little bays and harbours are indented all along the county's Atlantic coastline, making Cork an ideal location for sailing. The oldest yacht club in the world is based in Cork at Crosshaven and dates back to 1720.

The heaviest concentration of stone circles in Ireland and Britain is to be found in the south-west region, with around 80 such monuments located in the Cork-Kerry area alone. The purpose of these ancient rings remains a mystery. It is certain they have some sort of ritualistic associations and could possibly have an astrological purpose. Cork's early Christian history centres around St. Finbarr who founded a church in the area of Cork city. Viking raiders attacked the region around A.D. 820 but later integrated with the local population. When the Anglo-Norman force attacked in 1172, the Danish overlords and the McCarthy clan had to submit. The Battle of Kinsale, the event that heralded the end of Gaelic Ireland, took place off the coast of Cork in 1601, when the Irish along with their Spanish allies were defeated. Cork was also prominent in two other major Irish historic disasters, when the French entered Bantry Bay in 1689 and again in 1798 to aid the Irish. Cork's attachment to its Irish culture is manifested in its Gaeltacht region, an Irish speaking area near the Derrynasaggart Mountains. The county played a prominent role in all struggles for Independence, and Michael Collins, Ireland's best known revolutionary, came from Cork.

ORIGIN OF COUNTY NAME: Derived from the Irish 'Corcaigh', meaning marsh and referring to the swampy estuary of the River Lee upon which the city of Cork was founded.

LAND AREA: 2,878 sq. miles.

COUNTY CAPITAL: Cork City.

MAIN TOWNS: Bantry, Clonakilty, Cobh, Cork, Fermoy, Kinsale, Mallow, Mitchelstown, Skibbereen, Youghal.

MAIN INDUSTRIES: These include agriculture, brewing, concentrates manufacturing, computer data storage, computer manufacturing, dairy production, fertilisers and chemical manufacturing, food production, livestock auctioneering, natural gas transmission and distribution, pharmaceutical intermediates and production, shipping, steel manufacturing, tourism, vehicle distribution, wholesale distribution.

CENSUS DETAILS: Total population - 420,346 (including Cork City) - a 3.5% increase since 1991.

NUMBER OF SCHOOLS: 313 primary schools, 63 secondary schools.

COUNTY MANAGER: Noel Dillon.

CHAIRMAN OF COUNTY COUNCIL: John Mulvihill.

NAMES OF ALL COUNCILLORS: Maurice Ahern (F.F.), Vivian Callaghan (F.F.), Peter Callanan (F.F.), Barry Cogan (F.F.), Alan Coleman (F.F.), Daniel Fleming (F.F.), Patrick Carey Joyce (F.F.), Laurence Kelly (F.F.), Annette McNamara (F.F.), Donal Moynihan (F.F.), John B. Murphy (F.F.), Denis O'Donovan (F.F.), Batt O'Keeffe (F.F.), Ned O'Keeffe (F.F.), Tom O'Neill (F.F.), Ted O'Riordan (F.F.), Jack Roche (F.F.), Donal F. O'Rourke (F.F.), Donnchadh O'Sullivan (F.F.), Matt Ahern (F.G.), Billy Biggane (F.G.), Paul Bradford (F.G.), Braham Brennan (F.G.), Sylvester Cotter (F.G.), Michael Creed (F.G.), Frank Crowley (F.G.), Michael Harrington (F.G.), Michael Hegarty (F.G.), Eddie Lucey (F.G.), John Cal McCarthy (F.G.), Frank Metcalfe (F.G.), Gerard Murphy (F.G.), Kevin Murphy (F.G.), Aileen D. Pyne (F.G.),

Conor O'Callaghan (F.G.), Tadg O'Donovan (F.G.), Jim O'Sullivan (F.G.), Thomas Ryan (F.G.), P.J. Sheehan (F.G.), Michael J. Calnan (Lab.), Paula Desmond (Lab.), John Mulvihill (Lab.), Sheila O'Sullivan (Lab.), Noel Collins (Ind.), Paddy Hegarty (Ind.), Michael Pat Murphy (Ind.), Derry Canty (P.D.), Joe Sherlock (D.L.).

COUNCIL MEETING DATES: Second and fourth Monday of each month.

RATEABLE VALUE TOTALS: £2,181,868.40.

RADIO STATIONS: Community Radio Youghal, Cork Campus Radio, 96 FM, 103 FM.

NEWSPAPERS: The Examiner, (Editor: Brian Looney). Southern Star, (Editor: Liam O'Regan).

MAJOR TOURIST ATTRACTIONS: Allihies, (the remains of a 19th-century copper mining centre); Anne's Grove Gardens; Bantry House; Barryscourt Castle; the Beara Peninsula; the Blackwater Vale; Blarney Castle and the Blarney stone; Buttevant, (where steeplechase horse racing originated); Castle Curious, (a folly tower); Castlefreke, (a gothic ruin near Rosscarbery); Charles Fort, Kinsale; Creagh Gardens, Skibbereen; Crosshaven; Desmond Castle, Kinsale; Doneraile Park; the Drombeg stone circle; Dunkathel, Glanmire; Dunmanus Castle; Dursey Island; Fastnet Rock Lighthouse; Fota Wildlife Park; Garinish

Island; Glandore Harbour; Goat's Pass, near Kilcrohane; Gougane Barra National Park; Healy Pass in the Caha Mountains; Kilcoe Castle; Kilnarune Pillarstone; Kinsale Town; Labbacallee, (a huge prehistoric monument); Midleton, (the home of Jameson Whiskey); Millstreet, (the staging location for international equestrian events and the 1993 Eurovision Song Contest); Mizen Head; Molana Abbey; the Queenstown Story, (an exhibition that tells how Cobh was the embarkation point from many thousands of Irish emigrants); Riverstown House, Glanmire; road bowls, (a game that is only played in Cork and Armagh); Roche Castle, Glanworth; the Royal Gunpowder Mills, Ballincollig; Schull Planetarium; Sherkin Island; West Cork, (with its many harbours and beaches); Timoleague Abbey and Timoleague Castle Gardens; the West Cork Museum, (contains many mementos of Michael Collins); Youghal, (formerly a busy textile centre and now a popular seaside resort and designated heritage town).

FAMOUS NATIVES OF THE PAST: Leonara Barry (U.S. labour leader; born 1849), Ann Bonny (Caribbean female pirate; born 1700), Richard Boyle (the Great Earl of Cork in 1610/20's), Robert Boyle (chemist/physicist; died 1691), Edward Bransfield (first European to sight Antarctica; died 1852), Francis Browne (Jesuit priest/photographer; died 1960), William Bourke (notorious murderer in Edinburgh; died 1829), Richard Croker (U.S. coroner/politician; died 1922), Thomas W. Croke (Roman Catholic Archbishop of Cashel/G.A.A. patron; died 1902), Thomas Davies (Young Irelander/poet; died 1845), Jack Doyle (boxer/vaudeville artist; died 1978), Ben Dunne (founder of Dunnes Stores), Aloys Fleischmann (composer/teacher/author, born Munich; died 1992), Henry Ford (car manufacturer, son of Cork Irish emigrant; died 1947), Edward Galvin (co-founded St. Columban's Foreign Mission/established Ireland's first mission in China; died 1956), Timothy Healy (Governor-General of Irish Free State 1922-28; died 1931), John Holland (inventor of submarines; died 1914), William R. Grace (first Catholic Mayor of New York/shipping magnate; died 1904), Mary Harris Jones (U.S. union activist; born 1830), Richard Hennessy (founded Hennessy Brandy Distillery in France in 1763; died 1800), Hugh Lane (art collector, died 1915), Con Leahy (athlete; died 1921), Tomás MacCurtain (nationalist; died 1920), John B. McDonald (built New York's first subway; died 1911), Micheál MacLiammóir (author/actor/artist/theatrical designer, born London; died 1978), Sam Maguire (fooballer, after whom the eponymous G.A.A. cup is named; died 1927), Terence McSwiney (Irish Volunteers member; died on hunger strike 1920), William Martin Murphy (businessman/newspaper proprietor; died 1919), Dr. Pat O'Callaghan (first Irish Olympic gold medalist; born 1905), Fergus E. O'Connor (British Chartist movement leader; died 1855), Jeremiah O'Donovan Rossa (Fenian; 1915), Standish O'Grady (historic novelist; died 1928), Con O'Kelly (Olympic gold medalist - wrestling; died 1947), Peadar Ó Laoghaire (priest/writer; died 1920), Francis O'Neill (author/collector/flute player; died 1936), Seán Ó Riada traditional music composer; died 1971), William Penn (founded Pennsylvania, family came from Shanagarry), Edel Quinn (Legion of Mary envoy to East Africa; died 1944), Christy Ring (hurler; died 1979), Francis Leslie Scott (chemist; born 1928), Canon Patrick A.Sheehan (playwright/scholar; died 1913), Edith Anna Somerville (writer/researcher, born Corfu, reared in Cork; died 1949), Edmund Spencer (late 16th century poet, 'The Faerie Queene'), Esmé Stuart Lennox Robinson (playwright; died 1958), James J. Wood (inventor; died 1928).

COUNTY KERRY
(Province: Munster)

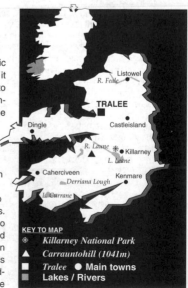

County Kerry is situated in the south-west of Ireland on the Atlantic seaboard. A great ridge of mountains dominates the county dividing it into the open countryside of the north and east, which extends into Ireland's Golden Vale, and the mountainous western region that consists of three jutting peninsulas. A county of superlatives, Kerry is home to Ireland's highest mountains, most westerly point and oldest tourist destination - Killarney - promoted by Lord Kenmare in the 18th century and still the most popular tourist centre in the country. The Gulf Stream washes the Kerry coast and brings with it several species of sub-tropical and marine mammals, many of which can be seen in the Dingle Sea Life Centre.

    Kerry's history can be traced back to prehistoric peoples, who travelled across the county's peninsulas, seeking mineral treasures. Copper was extracted here and sent to Spain some 4,000 years ago by these peoples. The great forts and castles of the Celtic races and later groups are still highly visible, along with many fine early Christian sites, including the early Christian monastery on the Skellig Islands and the Gallarus Oratory, which at more than 1,000 years old is the oldest church in Ireland and is still structurally intact. Although the

KEY TO MAP
❉ *Killarney National Park*
▲ *Carrauntohill (1041m)*
■ *Tralee* ● **Main towns**
■ **Lakes / Rivers**

Normans arrived in the county in the 13th century, it was not until the wars of the 16th and 17th centuries that the county's native Irish came under direct threat. The county was formally demarcated in 1606. Nonetheless, it continued to maintain its unique and rich Irish culture. The Irish language is still spoken here, no doubt helped by the relative isolation imposed by the county's inaccessible mountains.

ORIGIN OF COUNTY NAME: Derived from the Irish 'Ciarraí', meaning Ciar's People and referring to an early Celtic tribe who settled in the county.

COUNTY CAPITAL: Tralee.

LAND AREA: 1,815.16 sq. miles.

MAIN TOWNS: Ballybunion, Cahirceveen, Dingle, Kenmare, Killarney, Listowel, Tralee.

MAIN INDUSTRIES: Agriculture, animal feed manufacturing, automotive components/glowplugs/ sensors manufacturing, crane manufacturing,dairy products, electrical wholesalers, financial services, fishing and fish distribution, food processing, livestock auctioneers, pharmaceutical production, photo-finishing, small engine manufacturing, supermarket and leisure goods retail, textile production, vacuum cleaner manufacturing.

CENSUS DETAILS: Total population - 125,863, 3.3% increase since 1991.

NUMBER OF SCHOOLS: 682 primary schools, 32 secondary schools, 1 R.T.C.

COUNTY MANAGER: Martin Nolan.

CHAIRMAN OF COUNTY COUNCIL: P.J. Cronin.

NAMES OF ALL COUNCILLORS: Dan Barry (F.F.), Noel Brassil (F.F.), Michael Cahill (F.F.), Ted Fitzgerald (F.F.), Tom Fleming (F.F.), Denis Foley (F.F.), Jackie Healy-Rae (F.F.), Dan Kiely (F.F.), Breandán Mac Gearailt (F.F.), Tom McEllistrim (F.F.), John O'Donoghue (F.F.), Brian O'Leary (F.F.), Michael O'Shea (F.F.), Ned O'Sullivan (F.F.), Bernie Behan (F.G.), Tim Buckley (F.G.), Paul Coghlan (F.G.), Danny Kissane (F.G.), Michael Connor-Scarteen (F.G.), Bobby O'Connell (F.G.), John Commane (Lab.), Pat Leahy (Lab.), Breeda Moyhnihan-Cronin (Lab.), Maeve Spring (Lab.). James Courtney (N.P.), P. J. Cronin (N.P.), Tommy Foley (Ind.).

COUNCIL MEETING DATES: Third Monday in each month.

RATEABLE VALUE TOTALS: £594,441.25.

RADIO STATIONS: Radio Kerry.

NEWSPAPERS: The Kerryman/The Corkman, (Editor: Gerard Colleran). Kerry's Eye, (Editor: Padraig Kennelly).

MAJOR TOURIST ATTRACTIONS: the Aqua Dome, Tralee; Ardfert, (an early Christian centre and seat of the Fitzmaurices in Norman times); Ballybunion, (a busy seaside resort); the beehive huts, (dwellings of early Christian monks on the Dingle Peninsula); Beginish Island's Viking ruins; the Blasket Islands; Blennerville Windmill; Carrauntuohill - Ireland's highest mountain; Castlegregory Seaside Resort; Cill Rialaig Arts and Crafts Village; the Connor Pass, Dingle; Coomanaspig Pass, (one of the highest points in Ireland that is accessible by car); Crag Cave, Castleisland; Derrycunnihy Cascade; Derrynane National Park; Dingle, (home of Fungi the Dolphin and the film location for *Ryan's Daughter* and *Far and Away*; Dingle Sea Life Centre); Fenit Sea World; the Gap of Dunloe; Glanleam Subtropical Gardens; Glenbeigh; Inch Beach Anascaul; Kenmare, (a designated heritage town); Kenmare Heritage Centre; the Kerry Bog Village Museum; the Kerry Way, (a long distance walking route); Kilgarvan Motor Museum; Killarney National Park; Killorglin, (the venue of the annual Puck Fair); Knockreer House, Killarney; Listowel, (home of literary luminaries, such as Brian McMahon and John B. Keane); Lough Gill, (contains the only colony of Natterjack toads in Ireland); Muckross Friary, Muckross House and Gardens and Muckross traditional farms; the National Transport Museum, Killarney; Rattoo Round Tower, Ballyduff; the Ring of Kerry; Ross Castle, home to the Earls of Kenmare; Siamsa Tíre; Tralee; the Skellig Experience, (an exhibition that details the story of the Skellig Islands); the Skellig Islands' bird colonies; Slea Head; Sneem Sculpture Park; Staigue Fort, one of the largest stone forts in Ireland, dating from the early Christian era; Torc Waterfall, Killarney; the Tralee and Dingle Light Railway; Tralee's Geraldine Experience Exhibition; Uragh Wood, (a rare forest of sessile oak); Valentia Heritage Museum, Knightstown; Waterville.

FAMOUS NATIVES OF THE PAST: Thomas Ashe (poet/musician/revolutionary; died 1917), St. Brendan the Navigator (abbot/traveller, reputedly discovered America; died 577), Helen Blackburn (Women's Suffrage Movement pioneer; died 1903), Roger Casement (landed German submarine on Banna Strand 1916; died 1916), Bernard Connor (physician to Polish King; died 1698), Thomas Crean (Captain Scott's companion on Antarctic expedition; 1900's), Fr. Patrick Dinneen (priest/lexicographer/completed first Irish/English dictionary; died 1934), Jack Duggan (the wild colonial boy; born 1809), Desmond Fitzgerald (revolutionary / politician / philosopher; born London, settled here; died 1947), Lord Horatio Herbert Kitchener (British Field Marshal; died 1916), Fionán Lynch (revolutionary/judge/politician; died 1966), Eibhlín Dhubh Ní Chonaill (wrote lament 'Caoineadh Airt Uí Laoghaire', died 1800), Daniel O'Connell (politician/liberator; died 1847), Tomás Ó Criomhthainn (writer/fisherman/stonemason; died 1937), Aodhagán Ó Rahathaille (poet; died 1726), Pádraig Ó Siochfhradha (novelist/short story writer, pen name 'An Seabhac'; died 1964), Eoghan Rua Ó Súilleabháin (gaelic poet; died 1784), Muiris Ó Súilleabháin (writer; died 1950), Michael Quill (trade union organiser; died 1966), Peig Sayers (storyteller; died 1958), Daniel Spring (politician, father of Dick; died 1988), Austin Stack (revolutionary; died 1929).

COUNTY LIMERICK
(Province: Munster)

The county of Limerick is located on Ireland's south-west coast between Clare and Kerry. A fertile limestone plain constitutes the greater part of its north, central and east regions and is commonly referred to as the Golden Vale. The county is bounded by the wide mouth of the Shannon estuary to the north-west, the high peaks of the Galtee mountains to the south-east and heathery uplands to the west.

Human habitation of the region can be traced back to around 3500 B.C., with the megalithic remains at Duntryleague dating to this time. However, most of Limerick does not appear to have been settled until the fifth century, with the arrival of Christianity and the establishment of monasteries at Ardpatrick, Mungret and Killeedy. The Ardagh Chalice, which dates from this era, was found in a west Limerick ring fort. The Vikings launched attacks on the county, sailing up the Shannon Estuary in 922 and establishing a settlement on an island in the estuary, which was to form the origins of Limerick City. The Normans attacked in 1194, after Dónal Mór O'Brien, the King of Munster, died, and the county of Limerick was formally recognised in 1210. The Normans built hundreds of castles in the region - Limerick has more castles than any other county in Ireland. The Earls of Desmond, or the Geraldines as they were known, were at the centre of Norman power in Munster and led a revolt against the English in 1571. This rebellion was put down and the Geraldines' lands confiscated. The revolt was to be the start of centuries of wars and sieges centred around Limerick City. The native Irish suffered badly in the Great Famine, and Limerick endured waves of emigration. However, in the 1950s and 1960s, the region experienced an economic upturn as a result of the development of the Shannon Region and Shannon Airport.

ORIGIN OF COUNTY NAME: The origin of the name of Limerick, or the Irish 'Luimneach', is unclear. One explanation given is that the name is derived from 'Luamanach', meaning a place covered in cloaks, and could possibly refer to cloaks or mantles observed floating on the Shannon after some prehistoric battle.

LAND AREA: 1,030 sq. miles.

COUNTY CAPITAL: Newcastle West (3,287).

MAIN TOWNS: Abbeyfeale, Kilmallock, Limerick, Newcastle West, Rathkeale.

MAIN INDUSTRIES: Agriculture, automotive components manufacturing, baby food manufacturing, bottled soft drinks production, cable television suppliers, canned meat production, cement manufacturing, chicken processing, civil engineering, computer manufacture and sales, computer-related products manufacturing, costume jewellery making, data processing, electrical appliance production, infant nutritional products manufacturing, integrated circuits manufacturing, livestock and property auctioneering, magnetic media manufacturing, medical instrument production, metal door and frame production, metal products fabrication, mineral water bottling and distribution, nonferrous metals extraction and exporting, oil distribution, ophthalmic lens manufacturing, surgical implants manufacturing.

CENSUS DETAILS: Total population (including Limerick City) - 165,017 - a 2.7% increase since 1991.

NUMBER OF SCHOOLS: 118 primary schools, 24 secondary schools.

COUNTY MANAGER: Roibeard O'Ceallaigh.

CHAIRMAN OF COUNTY COUNCIL: John Finucane.

NAMES OF ALL COUNCILLORS: Maureen Barrett (F.F.), Michael Barry (F.F.), Michael Brennan (F.F.), John Clifford (F.F.), Michael J. Collins (F.F.), John Cregan (F.F.), Noel Gleeson (F.F.), John Griffin (F.F.), Michael Healy (F.F.), Mary Jackman (F.G.), Michael O'Kelly (F.F.), William Sampson (F.F.), Kevin Sheahan (F.F.), Eddie Wade (F.F.), Seán Broderick (F.G.), Matt Callaghan (F.G.), Michael Finucane (F.G.), James Houlihan (F.G.), Mary Jackman (F.G.), Jim McCarthy (F.G.),

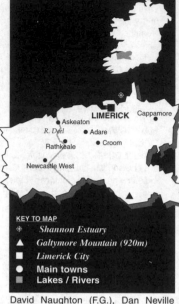

KEY TO MAP

✳   *Shannon Estuary*

▲   *Galtymore Mountain (920m)*

■   *Limerick City*

●   **Main towns**

■   **Lakes / Rivers**

David Naughton (F.G.), Dan Neville (F.G.), Michael Whelan (F.G.), Peader Clohessy (P.D.), Eddie Creighton (P.D.), John Finucane (P.D.), Tim O'Malley (P.D.), Mary Kelly (Lab.).

COUNCIL MEETING DATES: Fourth Friday of each month.

RATEABLE VALUE TOTALS: £954,709.40.

RADIO STATIONS: Radio Limerick 95 FM, Wired 103 FM.

NEWSPAPERS: Limerick Chronicle, Limerick Leader, (Editor: Brendan Halligan). Limerick Post.

MAJOR TOURIST ATTRACTIONS: the abbeys at Ardpatrick, Manister, Mungret and Killeedy; Adare village; angling; Askeaton Island Castle; Clare Glens; Croom, (the celebrated 18th century meeting place of the poets of the Maigue); Currahchase Forest Park; Castle Matrix, (said to be the place where Edmund Spenser met Sir Walter Raleigh and the first place where the potato was grown in Ireland); the Celtic Park and Gardens, Kilcornan; Croom Mills Waterwheel; Curraghchase Forest Park; the de Valera Museum, Bruree; Foynes Flying Boat Museum; the Galtee Mountains; Glenquin Castle; Glenstal Abbey; Glin Castle; Hospital, (a town that takes its name from the St. John's Knights Hospitallers); the Irish Dresden Factory, Dromcolliher; the Irish Palatine Exhibition, Rathkeale; Killaliathan Church; Limerick's other castles (numbering more than 400 in total);

Lislaughtin Abbey; Lough Gur Interpretative Centre; Mitchelstown Caves; Newcastle West castle ruins; the oratories at Killaloe; Portrinard Castle; Reerasta Fort, (where the Ardagh Chalice was found); Springfield Castle Deer Centre, Dromcolliher;

FAMOUS NATIVES OF THE PAST: Dan and Tim Ahearne (brothers, triple jump olympic winners; 1908-1910), Fr. William Casey (fought against landlordism; died 1907), Kathleen Clarke (first female Lord Mayor of Dublin; died 1972), Thomas James Clarke (revolutionary; died 1916), Tomás de Bhaldraithe (scholar/lexicographer; died 1966), Philip Embury (with Barbara Ruttle Heck, co-founded Methodism in U.S. 1768), John J. Flanagan (Olympic hammer thrower for U.S.A; born 1873), Jim Kemmy (politician; died 1997), Mick Mackey (hurler; died 1982), James Clarence Mangan (poet/writer; died 1849), Kate O'Brien (writer; died 1974), Terence Albert O'Brien (Bishop; died 1651), William Smith O'Brien (Irish freedom fighter; born 1848), Donogh O'Malley (politician; died 1968), Michael Maurice O'Shaughnessy (engineer, rebuilt much of San Francisco after 1906 earthquake; died 1934), Seán Ó Tuama (poet; late 18th century), Thomas Spring Rice (Chancellor of Exchequer; 1820's), Paddy Ryan (Olympic hammer thrower for U.S., died 1964).

COUNTY TIPPERARY
(Province: Munster)

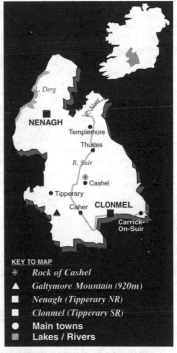

Located in the south of Ireland, Tipperary is Ireland's largest inland county. It is bordered by several mountain ranges - the Galtees and the Knockmealdowns in the south, the Silvermines and Arra Mountains in the west, Devilsbit mountain in the north and the Slieveardagh Hills and Slievenamon in the south-east. The River Suir cuts through the centre of the county and Lough Derg forms its boundary in the north-west. The great central-southern limestone plain in the county, which extends into County Limerick, is better known as the Golden Vale and is famed for its fertile farmlands. Tipperary's diverse geology has resulted in coal mines and slate quarries. It is the only county in Ireland that is divided into ridings - an old English land demarcation - and is still administered as the North Riding and the South Riding.

Tipperary contains a wealth of historical sites, most prominent being the Rock of Cashel, which was the centre of ecclesiastical and secular life in Munster from the end of the fourth century until well into medieval times. The Kings of Munster ruled from Cashel until Brian Boru came into power, and in 1101, Muircheartach O'Brien gave the Rock of Cashel to the church. Tipperary was spared most of the ravages of the Viking attacks, and when the Normans arrived, the county was placed in the hands of the Butlers, whose royal patronage protected the county from all plantations except that of Cromwell. The Cromwellian Plantation had disastrous consequences for most of the native Irish in the county; some remained on as tenant farmers, while others moved to the bogland areas. Those who stayed on had to pay exorbitant rents, pushing them into joining the Whiteboy movement in the 18th century and carrying out violent reprisals against the English overlords. This ran concurrently with faction fighting that led the county to be christened 'Turbulent Tipperary'. By the middle of the 19th century, the county had a strong Fenian following. It defiantly elected John Mitchel, a Young Ireland transportee on two occasions and played a full political role in the formation of Ireland's fledgling state.

ORIGIN OF COUNTY NAME: Derived from the Irish 'Tiobraid Arann', the well of Era, referring to the River Ara.
LAND AREA: 1,647 sq miles.
COUNTY CAPITAL: Nenagh (North Riding), Clonmel (South Riding).
MAIN TOWNS: Cahir, Carrick-on-Suir, Cashel, Clonmel, Nenagh, Rocrea, Templemore, Tipperary, Thurles.
MAIN INDUSTRIES: Agriculture, animal feeds, cider manufacturing, collapsible tube manufacturing, construction engineering, co-op creameries, dairy production and processing, drinks distribution, electronic and mechanical games, fibreboard manufacturing, food distribution and processing, health care products, icecream manufacturing, meat processing and packaging, narrow fabric production, oil distribution, pharmaceuticals, retailing, tourism.

CENSUS DETAILS: Total population - 133,308 - a 0.8% increase since 1991.
NUMBER OF SCHOOLS: 776 primary schools, 36 secondary schools.
COUNTY MANAGER: *Tipperary North:* John McGinley, *Tipperary South:* Edmund Gleeson.
CHAIRMAN OF COUNTY COUNCIL: *Tipperary North:* Harry Ryan;*Tipperary South:* Michael Anglim.
NAMES OF ALL COUNCILLORS: *Tipperary North:* Jim Casey (F.F.), John Egan (F.F.), Jane Hanafin (F.F.), Tom Harrington (F.F.), Michael Hough (F.F.), Tony McKenna (F.F.), Seán Mulrooney (F.F.), Harry Ryan (F.F.), Mattie Ryan (F.F.), John Sheehy (F.F.), Dan Smith

(F.F.), Noel Coonan (F.G.), Gerard Darcy (F.G.), Willie Kennedy (F.G.), Philip Lowry (F.G.), Mae Quinn (F.G.), Denis Ryan (F.G.),Tom Ryan (F.G.), Martin Kennedy (Lab.), John Ryan (Lab.), Joseph O'Connor (N.P.); *Tipperary South:* Tom Ambrose (F.F.), Michael Anglim (F.F.), Denis Bourke (F.F.), Seán Byrne (F.F.), Con Donovan (F.F.), Bridie Hammersley (F.F.), Michael Maguire (F.F.), Seán McCarthy (F.F.), Susan Meagher (F.F.), Pat Norris (F.F.), Deputy Theresa Ahearn (F.G.), Jack Crowe (F.G.), Tom Hayes (F.G.), Jimmy Hogan (F.G.), John Holohan ((F.G.), Michael Fitzgerald (F.G.), Brendan Griffin (F.G.), Seán Sampson (F.G.), Tom Wood (F.G.), Ted Boyle (Ind.), Seamus Healy (Ind.), Christy Kinahan (Ind.), Edmond Brennan (Lab.), Michael Ferris (Lab.), Denis Landy (Lab.), Seán Lyons (Lab.),

COUNCIL MEETING DATES: *North:* Third Monday in each month. *South:* First Monday in each month.

RATEABLE VALUE TOTALS: £1,420,85.93.

RADIO STATIONS: Tipp FM. Tipperary Mid-West Radio.

NEWSPAPERS: Nenagh Guardian, (Editor: Gerry Slevin). Nationalist Newspaper, (Editor: Tom Corr). Tipperary Star, (Editor: Michael Dundon).

MAJOR TOURIST ATTRACTIONS: art galleries in Clonmel and Tipperary; Athassel Abbey; Bansha Wood; the Bianconi Coach Road, Slieve na Muck; the bird sanctuary at Marlfield Lake; Cahir Abbey and Cahir Castle; Carrick-on-Suir, (with its riverside location, castle, heritage centre and showrooms for Tipperary Crystal); Cashel, (with its heritage tram, folk village, Cashel of Kings Heritage Centre and Bru Boru Heritage Centre); the Celtic Plantarum at Dundrum; Clare Glens; the early Norman Mottes at Ardmayle and Knockgraffon; Fethard Augustinian Friary and Folk Farm and Transport Museum; the field monuments around the Glen of Aherlow; Glenleigh Gardens at Clogheen; G.P.A. Bolton Library, (some of the collection of which dates from the beginning of the age of printing); Holycross Abbey, (one of the most picturesque monasteries in Ireland); Marle Bog Development, Dundrum; Mitchelstown Caves, (containing some of Europe's finest calcite formations); the parish church at Emly, (dating back to the sixth century); Parsons Green Park and Pet Farm, Clogheen; the Pilgrim Way, (an ancient trackway from Ardmore to Cashel); the Rock of Cashel; the slate quarries at Ahenny, (with their outdoor sculptural displays); St. Mary's Church, (dating from the 13th century); the Swiss Cottage at Cahir, (dating from 1810); Tipperary, (a designated history town, dating from 12th century); Tipperary County Museum; Toureen Peakaun ancient monastic site;

FAMOUS NATIVES OF THE PAST: John Joe Barry ('The Ballincurry Hare', world record holding athlete; born 1924), Charles Bianconi (operated car services throughout county 1815, born Italy; died 1875), Brendan Rendall Bracken (British politician/publisher; died 1958), Dan Breen (revolutionary; died 1969), Michael Browne (Cardinal; died 1971), Edward Conway (biochemist/physiologist; died 1968), the Davins brothers (Maurice, Pat, Tom, athletes; died 1927, 1949, 1894), Pádraig De Brún (academic/poet/priest/translator; died 1960), Sir Henry Kellett (explorer; died 1975), Sean Kenny (set designer; died 1973), Charles Kickham (Fenian/journalist/novelist; died 1882), Fr. Theobald Matthew (founded Temperance Society 1838; died 1856), Thomas McDonagh (revolutionary/poet; died 1916), James Mitchell (athlete; died 1921), Tom Semple (hurler/long puck exponent/G.A.A. stadium named after him; died 1943), Bob Tisdall (Olympic athlete, born Sri Lanka, raised Nenagh; born 1907).

COUNTY WATERFORD
(Province: Munster)

Waterford is situated on the south-eastern seaboard. Its coast stretches from Youghal Bay to Waterford Harbour. The Comeragh, Knockmealdown, and Monavullagh mountain ranges dominate the landscape and border the county to the north and north-west. The River Blackwater and its tributary, the River Bride, carve out the western boundary and the River Suir defines the eastern boundary. The diversity of the landscape found in Waterford is based on the three main rock types - the old red sandstone of the mountain ranges, the shale found in the north and the limestone belt found in the south-west.

Waterford's history gives testament to the fact that it has been one of the few counties to successfully assimilate the three diverse races of the Gaels, the Vikings and the Normans. Because of Waterford Harbour's wide sea route into the heart of the country, the county was the focus of Viking, Norman and English activity. The city of Waterford was designated a royal city circa 1171 and became one of Ireland's major ports and merchant centres. The county has a unique feature for the east coast in that it has a surviving Gaeltacht area - Ring - located near Dungarvan. This is despite the county's subjection to four centuries of an active Viking presence, as reflected in many of the town names, and subsequent waves of Norman invasion and settlement. The ability to endure these attacks carried on through the turbulent events of the 18th and 19th centuries. Waterford's population showed a talent

KEY TO MAP

✳ *Nire Valley*
▲ *Knocknaree Mtn. (679 m)*
■ *Waterford City*
● Main towns
■ Lakes / Rivers

for surviving and prospering; Thomas Francis Meagher, a fervent nationalist, was sentenced to death in 1848, but he escaped to the U.S. and went on to become Governor of Montana.

ORIGIN OF COUNTY NAME: Derived from the Viking 'Vethrafjorthr', meaning weather haven. The Irish 'Port Láirge' means the Port of Laraig, Laraig being a tenth century Viking.

LAND AREA: 713.08 sq. miles. **COUNTY CAPITAL:** Waterford City.

MAIN TOWNS: Dungarvan, Tramore, Waterford.

MAIN INDUSTRIES: Agriculture, alumina extraction, animal feeds production, business services, crystal and ceramic manufacturing, dairy processing, food manufacturing, meat processing, oatmilling, poultry processing, retailing, tourism.

CENSUS DETAILS: Total population - 94,597 (including Waterford city) - a 6.9% increase since 1991.

NUMBER OF SCHOOLS: 59 primary schools, 11 secondary schools.

COUNTY MANAGER: Donal Connolly.

CHAIRMAN OF COUNTY COUNCIL: Lar Hart.

NAMES OF ALL COUNCILLORS: Thomas Cunningham (F.F.), Dan Cowman (F.F.), Jackie Fahey (F.F.), Austin Flynn (F.F.), Patrick Kenneally (F.F.), Patrick Leahy (F.F.), Geoffrey Power (F.F.), Kieran O'Ryan (F.F.), James Quirke (F.F.), Ollie Wilkinson (F.F.), John Carey (F.G.), Con Casey (F.G.), Oliver Coffey (F.G.), Patrick Coffey (F.G.), Nora Flynn (F.G.), William McDonnell (F.G.), Garry O'Halloran (F.G.), Richard Power (F.G.), Michael Queally (F.G), Lar Hart (Lab.), Billy Kyne (Lab.), Patrick O'Callaghan (Lab.), Tony Wright (D.L.).

COUNCIL MEETING DATES: Second Monday each month.

RATEABLE VALUE TOTALS: £380,528.

RADIO STATIONS: WLR FM.

NEWSPAPERS: Dungarvan Leader and Southern Democrat, (Editor: Colm J. Nagle). Dungarvan Observer and Munster Industrial Advocate, (Editor: P. Lynch). The Munster Express, (Editor: Kieran Walsh). Waterford News and Star, (Editor: Peter Doyle). Waterford Today, (Editor: Patrick Gallagher).

MAJOR TOURIST ATTRACTIONS: angling; Ann Valley Walk; Ardmore Round Tower; the Augustinian Abbey, Dungarvan; Ballynamona Court Cairn, near Ring; Cappoquin House Gardens; Castle Open Farm, Cappagh; Clonea's 12th century church; Curraghmore Estate; deep sea fishing; Dromana, a Hindu-Gothic gate lodge; Dungarvan; Kialgreany Cave, Whitechurch; King John's Castle, Dungarvan; Dunhill Castle; Helvick Head; Knockmaun Castle; Laserworld; Lismore, (a designated heritage town and its castle); Mahon Falls; the Master McGrath Monument, (possibly the only public monument to a greyhound in Ireland); Mount Congreve Gardens, Kilmeadan; Mount Mellerey Abbey; the Munster Way, (a designated walk); the Pilgrim Way, (another walk); Portlaw; Passage East, (the area where Strongbow landed in 1170); the Nire Valley, (a scenic area, with glens and waterfalls); Portlaw, (a model village founded by a Quaker family); Strancally Castle; Touraneena Heritage Farm Centre, Ballynamult; Tourin House and Gardens; Tramore; the Vee, (a spectacular scenic route through the Knockmealdown mountains); Waterford City's monuments; Waterford Crystal Factory; West Waterford Vinyards, Cappoquin.

FAMOUS NATIVES OF THE PAST: Robert Boyle ('The Father of Chemistry', devised Boyle's law; died 1691), Sir Hubert de la Poer Gough (British General/Irish unionist; died 1963), John Hogan (sculptor/poet, 'the Bard of Dunclug'; died 1858), Master McGrath (greatest-ever racing greyhound), David Patrick Moran (author/journalist; died 1936), Tadhg Gaelach O'Suilleabháin (gaelic poet; died 1795), Tyrone Power (film actor, grandfather came from Kilmacthomas; born 1903), Ernest Thomas Sinton Walton (scientist, first achieved splitting of atoms/joint Nobel-laureate 1951; died 1995).

COUNTY GALWAY
(Province: Connacht)

The second largest county in Ireland, Galway is set in the west coast of Ireland. Its heavily indented Atlantic coastline provides a myriad of wide bays, sheltered harbours, deep fjords and island clusters. Lough Corrib, Ireland's second largest lake, divides the county in two - the fertile farmlands, with their traditional dry stone walls in the east, and mountainous Connemara, where the Irish culture and language thrives, in the west. At the mouth of Galway Bay lie the three Aran Islands - Inishmore, Inishmaan and Inisheer, whose inhabitants also maintain a distinctly Gaelic culture. Towering mountain ranges such as the Twelve Bens and the Maamturks fortify the west coast of the county. The land is bounded in the east by the Shannon and Suck Rivers.

Humans first inhabited the Galway Region over 5,000 years ago. Stone monuments on the Aran Islands date back as far as 2000 B.C. and include the famous Dun Aengusa, a stone fort situated at the edge of a sea cliff and dating back to around the time of Christ. With the arrival of Christianity, monasteries were built at Roscam, Inchagoill Island and Annaghdown. These monasteries attracted the attentions of the Vikings and Roscam was raided in 830. Around 1232, Richard de

KEY TO MAP
* *Connemara National Park*
▲ *Benbaun (727 m)*
■ *Galway City* ● Main towns

Burgo, a Norman Baron, attacked Connacht. Galway city expanded with the arrival of English, Welsh and Flemish settlers, but the native Irish regained their power as the Normans adopted the Irish language and tradition. Around this time, 14 prominent merchant families came to power and held this position until Cromwell's attack on the county. The Irish in Galway were finally routed at the Battle of Aughrim in 1691. Following this defeat, the native population lost most of their lands and suffered under the penal laws. They endured further suffering during the Great Famine and the population was decimated. Towards the close of the 19th century Galway, became the centre of the the Irish Literary Renaissance. Lady Gregory's home at Coole Park attracted many writers, and Lady Gregory herself, along with Yeats and Synge founded the Abbey Theatre in Dublin 1904.

ORIGIN OF COUNTY NAME: Derived from the Irish 'Abhainn na Gaillimhe' - the Galway River - which was named after Galvia, a mythological princess who supposedly drowned in the river.

LAND AREA: 2,349.79 sq. miles.

COUNTY CAPITAL: Galway.

MAIN TOWNS: Ballinasloe, Galway, Loughrea, Tuam.

MAIN INDUSTRIES: Agricultural manufacturing, builders providers, computer software, dairy processing, electric manufacturing, electrical components manufacturing, animal feed production, fertilisers, fresh meat wholesalers and exporters, hardwoods and steel stockists, health care products processing, livestock trading and marts, marine research, medical and laboratory supplies, poultry and frozen food distribution, salmon farming and processing, scientific instruments manufacturing, seaweed processing, telecommunications, transport refrigeration equipment manufacturing, writing instruments manufacturing.

CENSUS DETAILS: Total population - 188,896.7 - a 13.8% increase since 1991.

NUMBER OF SCHOOLS: 215 primary schools, 39 secondary schools.

COUNTY MANAGER: Dónal O'Donoghue.

CHAIRMAN OF COUNTY COUNCIL: Michael Finnerty.

NAMES OF ALL COUNCILLORS: Joe Callanan (F.F.), Michael Cunningham (F.F.), Michael Fahy (F.F.), Patrick J. Finnegan (F.F.), Tom Hussey (F.F.), Matt Loughnane (F.F.), Paddy T. McHugh (F.F.), Connie Ni Fhatharta (F.F.),
Eamon Ó'Cuiv (F.F.), Séan Ó'Neachtain (F.F.), Pat O'Sullivan (F.F), Michael Regan (F.F.), Kathleen Quinn (F.F.), Toddie Byrne (F.G.), Deputy Paul Connaughton (F.G.), Michael Finnerty (F.G.), John M. Mannion (F.G), Jimmy McClearn (F.G.), Pádraic McCormack (F.G.), Jarlath McDonagh (F.G.), Michael Mullins (F.G.), Michael Ryan (F.G.), Tiarnan Walsh (F.G.), Joe Brennan (N.P.), Seamus Gavin (N.P.), Peadar O'Tuathail (N.P.), Joe Burke (P.D.), Willie Burke (P.D.), Michael O'Neill (P.D.), Evelyn Varley (P.D.).

COUNCIL MEETING DATES: Fourth Monday and second Friday in each month.

RATEABLE VALUE TOTALS: £758,812.30.

RADIO STATIONS: Connemara Community Radio, Galway Bay FM, Flirt FM, Raidió na Gaeltacht.

NEWSPAPERS: The Connacht Herald, (Editor: John Cunningham). The Connacht Sentinel, (Editor: Brendan O'Carroll). The Connacht Tribune, (Editor: Michael Glynn). The Galway Advertiser, (Editor: Ronnie O'Gorman). Tuam Herald, (Editor: David Burke).

MAJOR TOURIST ATTRACTIONS: the Aran Islands; Athenry Castle; Aughnanure Castle, near Oughterard; Ballinasloe, (famed for its annual horse fair); the Battle of Aughrim Interpretative Centre, Ballinasloe; Bunowen Castle, (once the home of Grace O'Malley); Ceantar na nOilean, (a group of islands off south Connemara); Claregalway Abbey; Clarinbridge, (famed for its oyster festival); Clonfert Cathedral, (with its heavily ornate door); Connemara National Park; Coole Park, (the home of Lady Gregory and birthplace of the Irish Literary Renaissance); Dan O'Hara's Homestead in the Connemara Heritage & History Centre; Derrigimlagh Bog, (the location of Marconi's 1907 telegraph station and landing site for Alcock and Brown in 1919 after their transatlantic flight); Dún Aenghus, Inishmore; Dunguaire Castle; the Fields of Athenry Thatched Heritage Cottage; Heather Island; Ionad Árann, Aran's Heritage Centre; Inishbofin, an island off Connemara's coast; Joyce Country; Killary Harbour, Kylemore Abbey, (the home of the Benedictine Nuns); Kilmacduagh Round Tower; Knock Shrine; Lackagh Museum, Lackagh; Leenane, (the location for the film 'The Field') and its cultural centre, (a cultural centre displaying the history of wool/sheep); the Maamturk Mountains; the Little Mill, Tuam; Lough Corrib, (with its 365 islands); Loughrea, (contains Ireland's only working Medieval moat); the picturesque towns and villages of Connemara; Portumna Castle and Forest Park; Rathbaun Open Farm, Ardrahan; Rinville Park, Oranmore; Rosmuck, (with its memorial cottage in honour of Padraig Pearse); Spiddal Craft Village; Thoor Ballylee, (the home of W.B. Yeats and inspiration for his poems in 'The Tower'); the Tropical Butterfly Centre, Costelloe; Turoe Pet Farm and Leisure Park; Turoe Stone, circa 200 B.C. (highly decorated in the La Téne Celtic Style); the Twelve Bens; West Rail Steam Train, Tuam-Athenry.

FAMOUS NATIVES OF THE PAST: Robert O'Hara Burke (leader of the first European expedition to cross Australia; died 1861), Eamonn Ceannt (revolutionary; died 1916), Padraic Fallon (poet/playwright; died 1974), John Ford (Irish-American film director, born Maine, Galway parents; died 1973), Lady Gregory (dramatist, founder of Abbey Theatre; died 1932), William Brook Joyce - Lord Haw Haw - (propagandist/ broadcaster, born New York/educated Galway; died 1946), Charles Lamb (artist; died 1964), John Lynch (signatory of the American Declaration of Independence), Walter Macken (actor/novelist/playwright; died 1967), Máirtín Ó Cadhain (short story writer/novelist/teacher; died 1970), Liam O'Flaherty (novelist/short story writer; died 1984), Breandán Ó hEithir (journalist/writer/broadcaster; died 1991), Muiris Ó Súileabháin (writer; died 1950), Eoghan Ó Tuairisc (poet/novelist/playwright/soldier; died 1982), Oliver St. John Gogarty (surgeon/ writer).

COUNTY LEITRIM
(Province: Connacht)

Leitrim is situated in the north-west of the country. Although mostly an inland county, a tiny stretch of Leitrim touches on the Atlantic coastline near Bundoran in Co. Donegal. The parameters of Leitrim's northern border are defined by Loughs MacNean and Melvin and the River Erne, and the county is divided by the great river Shannon. The two major rivers have recently been joined by a canal to form the Shannon-Erne Waterway.

The O'Rourke clan ruled most of the county in Celtic times but were supplanted by the Normans and later by the English, who imposed a policy of land confiscation and plantation on Leitrim at the beginning of the 17th century. Towns such as Carrick-on-Shannon, Manorhamilton and Jamestown were established and fortified during this time. Emigration from famine times onwards caused the population to dramatically drop from a high of 155,000 in the early 19th century to around 25,000 today.

ORIGIN OF COUNTY NAME: Derived from the Irish 'Liathdroim' , meaning the grey hillridge.

LAND AREA: 614 sq. miles

COUNTY CAPITAL: Carrick-on-Shannon

MAIN TOWNS: Carrick-on-Shannon, Drumshanbo, Manorhamilton.

MAIN INDUSTRIES: Agriculture, butter manufacturing and cold storage, candle-making, car mirror manufacturing, ceramics, construction, furniture manufacturing, glass products, handcrafts, joinery, meat processing, mineral water production, precision and light engineering, river cruiser hiring, wholesale retailing, timber growing and processing, textiles, tourism.

CENSUS DETAILS: Total population - 25,032, - a 1.1% decrease since 1991.

NUMBER OF SCHOOLS: 43 primary schools, 9 secondary schools.

COUNTY MANAGER: Patrick Fahey.

CHAIRMAN OF COUNTY COUNCIL: Jim Joe Shortt.

NAMES OF ALL COUNCILLORS: Mary Bohan (F.F.), John Ellis (F.F.), Tony Ferguson (F.F.), Aodh Flynn (F.F.), Michael Guckian (F.F.), Farrell McElgunn (F.F.), Seán McGowan ((F.F.), Pascal C. Mooney (F.F.), Jim Joe Shortt (F.F.), Damian Brennan (F.G.), Charlie Cullen (F.G.), Thomas P. Faughnan (F.G.), Thomas F. McCartin (F.G.), Siobhán McGloin (F.G.), Jim McPadden (F.G.), John McTernan (F.G.), Thomas Mulligan (F.G.), Gerard Reynolds (F.G.), Gerry Dolan (N.P.), Pauline McKeon (N.P.), Liam McGirl (S.F.), Larry McGowan (Ind.).

COUNCIL MEETING DATES: Second Monday of each month.

RATEABLE VALUE TOTAL: £186,910.20

RADIO STATIONS: Shannonside/Northern Sound.

NEWSPAPERS: Leitrim Observer, Editor: (Anthony Hickey).

MAJOR TOURIST ATTRACTIONS: Angling; the Barr Scenic Route; Benbo Mountain; Corn Mill Theatre and Arts Centre, Carrigallen; Costello Chapel (the smallest chapel in Ireland); Creevylea Abbey ruin (set on the banks of the Bonet river, Dromahair); Cruising on the Shannon; Drumcoura City Western Riding Farm, Ballinamore; Glencar Waterfall; Hodson Bay, Lough Ree; Leitrim Heritage Centre; the Leitrim Way; Lough Rynn House and Gardens, Mohill; O'Rourke's Table Mountain; Parke's Castle, Dromahair; the riverside villages of Dromod, Roosky, Drumsna and Jamestown; the Shannon-Erne Waterway; Sliabh an Iarain Visitor Centre, Drumshanbo; the Wild Rose Country surrounding Manorhamilton.

FAMOUS NATIVES OF THE PAST: Charles Atlas (famous strong man), Rev. Peter Conefrey (did much to foster Irish culture in the 1930's), Anthony William Durnford (colonel/fought at Battle of Isandhlwana; died 1879), Seán Mac Diarmada (revolutionary; died 1916), Gus Martin (academic; died 1995), John McKenna (traditional musician; died 1947), Joe Mooney (established 'An Tostal' festival), Turlough O'Carolan (harpist), Thomas Parke (surgeon/first Irishman to traverse the African continent; died 1893), Robert Strawbridge (founded Methodist Church, U.S.), Anthony Trollope (English writer, lived in Drumsna for a time), Gordon Wilson (senator/peacemaker; died 1995).

KEY TO MAP
* **Glencar Waterfall**
▲ **Benbo Mountain (633m)**
■ **Carrick-on-Shannon**
● **Main towns**
■ **Lakes / Rivers**

COUNTY MAYO
(Province: Connacht)

KEY TO MAP
- ✳ **Céide Fields**
- ▲ **Mweelrea Mountain (819m)**
- ■ **Castlebar**
- ● **Main towns**
- ■ **Lakes / Rivers**

Mayo is a maritime county on the west coast of Ireland and is the third largest county in Ireland. Its topography varies from the relatively flat land in east Mayo through the island-dotted lakes of Loughs Conn, Mask, Cullin and Carra to the bare quartzite mountains along Mayo's indented Atlantic coastline. The county is bounded by Lough Corrib and the fjord of Killary Harbour in the south; Killala Bay and Erris in the north; Achill Island, Clew Bay and the Mullet Peninsula in the west; and the counties of Sligo and Roscommon in the east.

North Mayo holds extensive tracts of blanket bog, under which have been recently discovered a system of corralled fields, enclosures and tombs - the Céide Fields - dating from about 5,000 years ago. The county's early Christian history shows significant associations with St. Patrick. The Normans took over Mayo in 1235, providing the county with some of its now familiar surnames. During Cromwellian times, native Irish who had their lands confiscated in the east were settled in Mayo. The French, under the leadership of General Humbert, landed at north Mayo on August 22, 1798, and overpowered the British. However, the Franco-Irish force were routed at Ballinamuck in Co. Longford, and many of those suspected of helping the French were executed. There was wide-scale emigration from Mayo from the famine times onwards. In 1879, Michael Davitt set up the Mayo Land League, which eventually became a national organisation and led to tenant farmers becoming landowners.

ORIGIN OF COUNTY NAME: Derived from the Irish 'Maigh Eo', meaning the plain of yew trees.

LAND AREA: 2,159 sq. miles.

COUNTY CAPITAL: Castlebar.

MAIN TOWNS: Ballina, Ballinrobe, Ballyhaunis, Castlebar, Charlestown, Claremorris, Crossmolina, Swinford, Westport.

MAIN INDUSTRIES: Agriculture, automotive components manufacturing, electric cable manufacturing, fish feed manufacturing, health care products manufacturing, livestock auctioneering, medical products manufacturing and distribution, pharmaceuticals manufacturing, printing and publishing, tourism.

CENSUS DETAILS: Total population - 111,395 - a 0.6% increase since 1991.

NUMBER OF SCHOOLS: 191 primary schools, 29 secondary schools.

COUNTY MANAGER: D. Mahon.

CHAIRMAN OF COUNTY COUNCIL: Pat Kilbane.

NAMES OF ALL COUNCILLORS: Geraldine Bourke (F.F.), Frank Chambers (F.F.), Brian Golden (F.F.), Jack Heneghan (F.F.), Deputy Seamus Hughes (F.F.), Jimmy Maloney (F.F.), Al McDonnell (F.F.), Pat McHugh (F.F.), Stephen Molloy (F.F.), P.J. Morley (F.F.), Paddy Oliver (F.F.), Martin J. O'Toole (F.F.), Annie May Reape (F.F.), Tim Quinn (F.F.), Michael Burke (F.G.), Senator Patrick Burke (F.G.), Ernie Caffrey (F.G.), John Noel Carey (F.G.), John Devaney (F.G.), John Flannery (F.G.), Pat Higgins (F.G.), Henry Kenny (F.G.), Pat Kilbane (F.G.), Jim Mannion (F.G.), Seán McEvoy (F.G.), Michael Ring (F.G.), Eddie Staunton (F.G.), Paraic Cosgrove (N.P.), Richard Finn (N.P.), Johnny Mee (Lab.), Beverley Cooper-Flynn (F.G.).

COUNCIL MEETING DATES: Second Monday of each month (except August).

RATEABLE VALUE TOTAL: £554,818.60.

RADIO STATIONS: Mid and North West Radio.

NEWSPAPERS: Connacht Telegraph, (Editor: Tom Gillespie). Mayo News, (Editor: Seán Staunton). The Western People, Editor: Terry Reilly.

MAJOR TOURIST ATTRACTIONS: Adventure centres in Achill and Westport; angling; the Artisan Village, Kiltimagh; archaeological sites near Cong; Ashford Castle; Ballintubber Abbey, Ballintubber; bird sanctuaries on the islands of Inishkea; Carraig Abhain open farm; Céide Fields, near Ballycastle; Cong, (famous for its cross and as the location of the film *The Quiet Man*); Croagh Patrick; Downpatrick Head; Enniscoe House, Ballina; Foxford Woollen Mills Visitor Centre; Glenans Sailing Centre, Collanmore Island; Granuaile Centre; Hennigans Heritage, Killasser; Knock Marian Shrine and Folk Museum; the Linenhall Arts Centre, Castlebar; Michael Davitt Museum; Moore Hall; North Mayo Sculpture Trail; Old Coastguard Station, Westport; Partry House, Claremorris; Rosserk Abbey; the Salmon Research Agency Centre, Furnace; scenic areas of the Mullet Peninsula and Achill Island; St. Deirbhile's sixth century church; Straide Friary; Turlough; the 13th century Carmelite friary, Burriscarra; the deserted village on Achill Island; Clare Island; Westport House and Children's Zoo; Westport International Clay Pigeon Shooting Range.

FAMOUS NATIVES OF THE PAST: John D'Alton (Roman Catholic Archbishop of Armagh/Primate of All Ireland/Cardinal 1953; died 1963), Fr. John Blowick (co-founded St. Columban's Foreign Mission Society, China 1920; died 1972), Louis Brennan (inventor of first helicopter; died 1932),

William Brown (founded Argentine Navy; died 1857), Declan Costello (politician/lawyer/judge; born 1927), Captain Charles Cunningham Boycott (land agent; died 1897), Michael Davitt (founded Irish National Land League 1879; died 1906), John Healy (journalist/broadcaster/author; died 1991), James Horan (Catholic priest who established Knock international airport; died 1986), Cecil Day-Lewis (poet-laureate 1968; died 1972), Henry Blosse Lynch (explorer; died 1873), Thomas Kerr Lynch (brother of Henry, explorer; died 1891), John MacBride (revolutionary, father of Seán/husband of Maud Gonne; died 1916), George A. Moore (writer; died 1933), Delia Murphy (singer), William O'Dwyer (New York City Mayor/Mexican Ambassador), John O'Hart (genealogist), Ernest O'Malley (republican/writer; died 1957), Grace O'Malley (pirate queen; died 1603), Antaine Ó Reaftaraí (gaelic bard), Margaret Burke-Sheridan (opera singer; died 1958), Martin J. Sheridan (U.S. Olympic medal winner; died 1918).

COUNTY ROSCOMMON
(Province: Connacht)

KEY TO MAP
✳ *L. Key Forest Park*
▲ *Slieve Bawn (264m)*
■ *Roscommon*
● Main towns
■ Lakes / Rivers

Roscommon is an inland county in Connacht. Two-thirds of it is bounded by water, with the River Shannon and Lough Ree to the east, the River Suck to the west and Loughs Key, Gara and Boderg to the north. One-third of the county is under bog, mostly in the west.

Many traces of early colonisation are evident in Roscommon; the county has numerous burial mounds, megalithic tombs and ring forts. Rathcroghan, at the centre of the county, was home to the kings of Connacht from the earliest times and later became home to the high kings of Ireland. The O'Conors and the MacDermotts, two of Roscommon's great families, were among the leading Gaelic clans in medieval Ireland. Nearly all of the county's lands were confiscated during the various English plantations. These were subsequently reclaimed by the Irish Land Commission in the 1920s and 1930s.

ORIGIN OF COUNTY NAME: Derived from the Irish 'Ros', meaning a wooded or pleasant gentle height and 'Coman', the name of the county's famous Irish saint and the first bishop of the see.
LAND AREA: 984 sq. miles.
COUNTY CAPITAL: Roscommon.
MAIN TOWNS: Boyle, Castlerea, Elphin, Roscommon, Strokestown.
MAIN INDUSTRIES: Agriculture, bacon production, cannery production, dairy food export manufacturing and processing, livestock auctioneering, pork production, retailing, tourism, truck vehicle importation.
CENSUS DETAILS: Total population - 51,881 (unaltered since 1991).
NUMBER OF SCHOOLS: 95 primary schools, 13 secondary schools.
COUNTY MANAGER: Eddie Sheehy.
CHAIRMAN OF COUNTY COUNCIL: Tom Foxe.
NAMES OF ALL COUNCILLORS: Des Bruen (F.F.), Tom Crosby (F.F.), Patrick Dooney (F.F.), Michael Finneran (F.F.), Paul Lynch (F.F.), Seán McQuaid (F.F.), Jim Morris (F.F.), Brian Mullooly (F.F.), Eugene Murphy (F.F.), Colm O'Donnell (F.F.), Seán Beirne (F.G.), Thomas Callaghan (F.G.), Domnick Connolly (F.G.), John Connor (F.G.), Gerard Donnelly (F.G), Kitty Duignan (F.G.), Charlie Hopkins (F.G.), Patrick Moore (F.G.), Michael McGreal (F.G.), Denis Naughten (F.G.), Michael Scally (F.G.), Paul Beirne (N.P.), Danny Burke (N.P.), Deputy Tom Foxe (N.P.), Patrick Moylan (N.P.), Eithne Quinn (N.P.).
COUNCIL MEETING DATES: Fourth Monday of each month.
RATEABLE VALUE TOTAL: £440,689.
NEWSPAPERS: Roscommon Champion, (Editor: Paul Healy). Roscommon Herald, (Editor: Christina McHugh).
MAJOR TOURIST ATTRACTIONS: Arigna Scenic Drive; Boyle Cistercian Abbey; Clonalis House, Castlerea; Dr. Douglas Hyde Interpretive Centre, Frenchpark; Elphin Windmill; Frybrook House; Keadue Village, (national tidy towns winner); Glendeer Open Farm; King House, Boyle; Lough Key Forest Park; Rock of Doon near Boyle; Rathcroghan and Carnfree Ancient Celtic Sites; Roscommon Abbey and County Museum; Roscommon Castle; Strokestown Park House and Famine Museum; Tullyboy Animal Farm, Boyle; the Old Schoolhouse Museum, Ballintubber; Woodbrook House.
FAMOUS NATIVES OF THE PAST: James Dillon (politician; died 1986), George French (Lieutenant-Colonel/founded the Canadian Mounties 1873; born 1941), Percy French (painter/songwriter; died 1920), Douglas Hyde (academic/translator/former President of Ireland; died 1949), Sir Alferd Keogh (British Army Director-General, father county-born; died 1936), the King family (owned Rockingham demesne), the Mahons (notorious landlords of Strokestown), The O'Connors (high kings; the oldest family in Europe

who can trace their ancestry back to 75 A.D.), the MacDermotts (leading Gaelic family), Turlough O'Carolan (blind harpist), Fr. Michael O'Flanagan (priest/republican; died 1942), Maureen O'Sullivan (film actress/mother of Mia Farrow; born 1911), Patrick J. Whitney (founded St. Patrick's Foreign Missionary Society 1932; died 1942), Sir William Wilde (surgeon/inventor of the ophthalmoscope/father of Oscar Wilde).

COUNTY SLIGO
(Province: Connacht)

Sligo is a maritime county on the north-west coast of Ireland. Its Atlantic coast is dominated by the great bays of Killala, Sligo and Donegal. The county's topography is characterised by unusually shaped hills rising from steep valleys, including Benbulben at the prow of Kings Mountain; Knocknarea, the alleged burial site of Queen Maeve; and the ancient Ox Mountains, the oldest mountain range in Sligo at 600 million years old.

Evidence of human habitation in Sligo dates back nearly 6,000 years; one of the largest Stone Age cemeteries in Europe and one of the oldest in Ireland is situated to the west of Sligo town at Carrowmore. The remains of early Christian monasteries can be found on Inishmurray Island and at Drumcliffe. Near Drumcliffe, Saints Columcille and Finian fought a battle in the sixth century for the copy of a psalter that Columcille had secretly made. Columcille's self-imposed exile to Iona was a direct result of this battle, possibly the earliest battle over copyright. Most historical events in Sligo reflect the fact that the area was of strategic importance as one of the main conduits to the North. As a result, the region, but particularly Sligo town, suffered attacks from both the Northern chieftains and the English. The town of Sligo was established in Viking times, and an abbey and castle were founded by the Norman Maurice Fitzgerald during the 13th century. These were destroyed in 1641 by Sir Frederick Hamilton who burned the town and murdered its inhabitants. The town was subsequently rebuilt and became a prosperous port during the 19th century.
ORIGIN OF COUNTY NAME: Derived from the Irish 'Sligeach', meaning Shelly River.
LAND AREA: 709 sq. miles. **COUNTY CAPITAL:** Sligo.
MAIN TOWNS: Ballymote, Grange, Sligo, Tubbercurry.
MAIN INDUSTRIES: Agriculture, agricultural co-op, business services, clock and scales manufacturing, dairy processing, engineering products, food and drink production, healthcare and nutrition suppliers, pharmaceutical manufacturing, rubber appliance production, service industries, transport, telecommunications, veterinary product manufacturing, videotape manufacturing.
CENSUS DETAILS: Total population - 55,645 - a 1.6% increase since 1991.
NUMBER OF SCHOOLS: 75 primary schools,16 secondary schools, 1 R.T.C., 1 college.
COUNTY MANAGER: Hubert Kearns.
CHAIRMAN OF COUNTY COUNCIL: Michael 'Boxer' Conlon.
NAMES OF ALL COUNCILLORS: Matthew Brennan (F.F.), Aidan A. Colleary (F.F.), Leo Conlon (F.F.), Michael 'Boxer' Conlon (F.F.), Patrick Conway (F.F.), Jimmy Devins (F.F.), Willie Farrell (F.F.), Gerry Healy (F.F.), Seán McManus (F.F.), Syl Mulligan (F.F.), Eamon Scanlon (F.F.), John Sherlock (F.F.), Mary Barrett (F.G.), P. J. Cawley (F.G.), Paul Conmy (F.G.), Ita Fox (F.G.), Peter Henry (F.G.), Tommy Lavin (F.G.), Joe Leonard (F.G.), Jim McGarry (F.G.), Tony McLoughlin (F.G.), Gerry Murray (F.G.), Deputy Declan Bree (Lab.), Michael Carroll (Ind.), Margaret Gormley (Ind.).
COUNCIL MEETING DATES: First Monday of each month.
RATEABLE VALUE TOTAL: £280,015.95.
NEWSPAPERS: Sligo Champion, (Editor: Seamus Finn). Sligo Weekender, (Editor: Brian McHugh).

KEY TO MAP
✳ **Carrowmore Megaliths**
▲ **Truskmore (647m)**
■ **Sligo**
● **Main towns**
■ **Lakes / Rivers**

MAJOR TOURIST ATTRACTIONS: Aughris Head; Ballymote Castle; Carrowmore Megalithic cemetery; Carrowkeel passage tombs, near Castlebaldwin; Carrowmably martello tower, near Drumore West; Creevykeel Court Tomb; the Caves of Keshcorran, (where legend has it Diarmuid and Gráinne took refuge); Easkey, (popular for water sports); the Glen, (an area of botanical importance, near Strandhill); Gleniff Horseshoe; Heapstown Cairns, Riverstown; Innismurray Island, (with its early Christian remains); Knocknashee, near Cloonacool; the Lake Isle of Innisfree on Lough Gill; Lissadell House; Lough Gill and Lough Arrow; the metal man at Rosses Point, (one of four left in the world); the Model Arts Centre, Sligo; Mullaghmore, (a seaside resort); Enniscrone, (a seaside resort with its own hot sea water baths); Rathcarrick House; the scenic drive along the Ox Mountains; Sligo Abbey; St. John's Church, (dating back to the 13th century); the Seabog of Ballyconnell; Sligo Municipal Art Gallery, (containing paintings by Jack Yeats); Streedagh beach, (with the remains of three Spanish Armada galleons); Tobernalt, (a holy well outside Sligo town); Woodville working

farm; Yeats's grave at Drumcliffe.
FAMOUS NATIVES OF THE PAST: Michael Coleman (traditional fiddler; died 1945), Mary Colum (critic/essayist/teacher; died 1957), Eva Gore-Booth (poet/dramatist/feminist/artist; died 1926), William Higgins (proposed existence of atoms 1789; died 1825), Maurice Fitzgerald (Norman founder of Sligo town), Countess Constance Markievicz (revolutionary, sister of Eva Gore-Booth, born London/reared Sligo; died 1927), James Morrison (fiddler/teacher/bandleader; died 1947), Tadhg Dall Ó hUiginn (bardic poet; died 1591), Susan Pollexfen (daughter of a shipping merchant/mother of Jack and William Butler Yeats), Nicholas Taaffe (Lieutenant-general of Australian army 1752; died 1769), William Butler Yeats (poet; died 1939), Jack B. Yeats (artist/writer, born London/brother of William; died 1952).

DUBLIN CITY
(County Dublin)

Set in Dublin Bay at the confluence of the Liffey, Dodder, Poddle and Tolka Rivers, Dublin is the centre of Irish political, economic, social and cultural activity. The Liffey divides the city into two sides, the north side and the south side, a division that is as much social and economic as it is geographical. The city's architecture, although currently under threat from the many building developments that are taking place, reveals the wealth of Dublin's past, from its Viking underpinnings, its medieval lanes, its elegant Georgian Squares and the contemporary feel of the city's cultural quarter in the Temple Bar.

As with all of Ireland's major towns and cities, Dublin has had a tumultuous past. Evidence of human habitation appears to date back millennia. King Conor MacNessa gave the town a name - the town of the hurdle ford - when he built a ford to prevent flooding from the Liffey. The Vikings later sailed up the river, attacking monastic sites and establishing a settlement, the remains of which have been excavated at Wood Quay. The Vikings were defeated by Brian Boru at Clontarf in 1014 and subsequently integrated with the native Irish. By the time the Normans attacked, city walls had been built but were not strong enough to hold back Strongbow. The Normans took over Dublin, and an era of 700 years of foreign control began.

In the 18th century, the town was molded into a Georgian City, making it one of the most elegant and cosmopolitan cities of its day. Handel first performed the Messiah in Dublin in 1742. Dublin's reign as an English cosmopolitan centre ended in 1800 with the Act of Union, when Dublin ceased to be a political force. The 19th century saw increasing pressure to bring about Home Rule. This culminated in the 1916 Rising in Dublin, during which British gun boats sailed up the Liffey and bombed the city, and the War of Independence in 1921. These conflicts, along with the internecine turmoil that followed independence, left Dublin badly damaged. The city changed very little until the 1960s, when moves were made to address the conditions of the people who lived in Dublin's inner city tenements. The economic boom of the 1960s resulted in many changes for Dublin. Today it is the heart of Ireland's Celtic tiger, leading the way economically and culturally.

ORIGIN OF COUNTY NAME: Derived from the Irish 'Dubh Linn' - black pool - which is a reference to an area above the Liffey where Dublin Castle is now located. The Irish for Dublin - Baile Átha Cliath - is translated as the town of the hurdle ford, which refers to the barriers placed to prevent the Liffey flooding.
LAND AREA: 44.4 sq. miles.
MAIN INDUSTRIES: These include the centres for corporate administration, government administration, finance and business.
CENSUS DETAILS: Total population - 480,996 - 0.5% increase since 1991.
NUMBER OF SCHOOLS: 227 primary schools, 97 secondary schools, 3 universities, 1 college of art & design, 1 institute of technology, 1 college of industrial relations, 2 colleges of education.
CITY MANAGER: John Fitzgerald.
LORD MAYOR: John Stafford.
NAMES OF ALL COUNCILLORS: Noel Ahern (F.F.), Michael Barrett (F.F.), Olga Bennett (F.F.), Martin Brady (F.F.), Ben Briscoe (F.F.), Ivor Callely (F.F.), Pat Carey (F.F.), Michael Donnelly (F.F.), Patrick J. Farry (F.F.), Liam Fitzgerald (F.F.), Dermot Fitzpatrick (F.F.), Ita Green (F.F.), Sean Haughey (F.F.), Tony Kett (F.F.), Mary Mooney (F.F.), Michael Mulcahy (F.F.), Eoin Ryan (F.F.), John Stafford (F.F.), Thomas Stafford (F.F.), Tony Taaffe (F.F.), Paddy Bourke (Lab.), Tommy Broughan (Lab.), Joe Connolly (Lab.), Joe Costello (Lab.), Mary Freehill (Lab.), Sean Kenny (Lab.), Dermot Lacey (Lab), Derek McDowell (Lab.), Eamon O'Brien (Lab.), Roisin Shortall (Lab.), Brendan Brady (F.G.), Joe Doyle (F.G.), Cathy Fay (F.G.), Mary Flaherty (F.G.), John Kearney (F.G.), Ruairi McGinley (F.G.), Donna Cooney (G.P.), Ciaran Cuffe (G.P.), John Gormley (G.P.), Claire Wheeler (G.P.), Michael Conaghan (Ind.), Tony Gregory (Ind.), Vincent Jackson (Ind.), Carmencita Hederman (N.P.), Sean Dublin Bay Loftus (N.P.), Brendan Lynch (N.P.), Tomas Mac Giolla (W.P.), Lucia O'Neill (W.P.), Eric Byrne (D.L.), Christy Burke (S.F.), Alan Robinson (P.D.), Anthony Creevey.
COUNCIL MEETING DATES: First Monday of each month.
RATEABLE VALUE TOTALS: £5,845,614.
RADIO STATIONS: Anna Livia FM; Atlantic 252; Classic Hits; 98FM; FM104; Pulse 103; Radió na Life

102 FM; Radio Ireland, RTÉ1; 2FM, FM3 Music; RTÉ Radió na Gaeltachta.

NEWSPAPERS: Evening Herald, (Editor: P. Drury). Inner City News, (Editor: John Hedges). Irish Independent, (Editor: V. Doyle). Irish Times, (Editor: Conor Brady). The Star, (Editor: Gerard O'Reagan).

MAJOR TOURIST ATTRACTIONS: the Ark, (a cultural centre for children); Arthouse Multimedia Centre for the Arts, Temple Bar; the Bank of Ireland, College Green; the Brazen Head, (Ireland's oldest pub); Christ Church Cathedral, (originally built in 1038 by Sitric, the Danish King of Dublin); the Custom House Visitor Centre; Dublin Castle, (containing magnificent state apartments and the Chester Beatty Library and Gallery of Oriental Art); Dublinia, (a permanent multi-media exhibition on Dublin's past); Dublin's theatres, (including the Abbey, the Gate and the Olympia); Dublin's Viking Adventure and Feast, Essex Quay; Dublin Writers Museum, Parnell Square; Dublin Zoo, Phoenix Park; Fernhill Gardens, Sandyford; the Garden of Remembrance, Parnell Square; the General Post Office, (where bullet holes from the 1916 Rising can still be seen); the Guinness Brewery on James's Street; the Ha'penny Bridge; the Hugh Lane Municipal Gallery of Modern Art; the Irish Whiskey Corner, Bow Street; the Iveagh Gardens, Clonmel Street; Kilmainham Gaol, Inchicore Road; Leinster House; the Masonic Hall, Molesworth Street, (houses a collection of Masonic artifacts); Merrion Square, (whose residents in the past have included Oscar Wilde, W.B. Yeats and Daniel O'Connell); Moore Street fruit market; Mother Redcap's Market; the National Art Gallery, Merrion Square; the National Botanic Gardens, Glasnevin; the National Concert Hall, Earlsfort Terrace; the National Library and the National Museum of Ireland, Kildare Street; the National Wax Museum, off Parnell Square; the Natural History Museum, Merrion Row; Newman House, St. Stephen's Green; Number 29, (a recreated Georgian home in Lower Fitzwilliam Street); Phoenix Park Visitor Centre; Powerscourt Town House, South William Street; the Rotunda Hospital, (the first maternity hospital in Europe); the Royal Hibernian Academy's Gallagher Gallery; the Royal Hospital, Kilmainham, (the location of the Irish Museum of Modern Art); St. Audoen's Church, (one of Ireland's oldest surviving medieval parish churches); St. Mary's Abbey, off Capel Street; St. Michan's Church; St. Patrick's Cathedral, (the most famous dean of which was Jonathan Swift); St. Stephen's Green; the Temple Bar area, (with its wide variety of cafes, cultural centres, shops bars and restaurants); Trinity College, (Ireland's oldest university and home to the Book of Kells); War Memorial Gardens, Islandbridge; Waterways Visitor Centre, Grand Canal Quay; the Zoological Gardens, Phoenix Park.

FAMOUS NATIVES OF THE PAST: Thomas Barnardo (established homes for homeless children 1867; died 1905), Don Boucicault (actor/dramatist; died 1890), Elizabeth Bowen (novelist; died 1973), Brian Boydell (composer/conductor; born 1917), Cathal Brugha (revolutionary; killed 1922), Evie S. Hone (artist; died 1955), Brian St. John Inglis (author/broadcaster/journalist; died 1993), Brian Rex Ingram (film-maker/writer/sculptor; died 1950), George N. Jacob (biscuit manufacturer; died 1940), Denis Johnson (playwright; died 1984), Peadar Kearney (songwriter; died 1942), Phil Lynott (rock musician; died 1986), Seán MacBride (politician/founded Amnesty International, born Paris, only son of Maud Gonne/John Mac Bride; died 1988), Jack MacGowran (actor; died 1973), Mother Mary Martin (founded Medical Missionaries of Mary; died 1975), Charles Gerard Mitchel (actor/broadcaster/archaeologist; died 1996), Thomas Moore (balladeer/poet/writer; died 1852), Sean O'Casey (playwright/prose writer; died 1964), Jimmy O'Dea (film actor; died 1965), Dan O'Dowd (uillean piper/pipe maker; died 1989), Patrick Pearse (revolutionary/writer/educationalist; died 1916), William Pearse (revolutionary/sculptor; died 1916), James Stephens (writer; died 1950), Oscar Traynor (politician; died 1963), Arthur Wesley (Duke of Wellington, Prime Minister 1828-1830; died 1852), T. Desmond Wllliams (historian; died 1987), Theobald Wolfe Tone (United Irishman; died 1798).

BELFAST CITY
(County Antrim)

Belfast is located in County Antrim and is the capital of Northern Ireland. It is set on the River Lagan and ringed by high hills. Belfast has an industrial tradition that dates back to the beginning of the industrial revolution, with industries such as linen manufacturing, rope making and ship building directly affecting the city's growth. It now accommodates some of Northern Ireland's leading employers and is a major education and retailing centre for the region. One-third of Northern Ireland's population lives here. Buildings of note in the city include Queen's University, the Linen Hall Library, the Botanic Gardens, the Grand Opera House and the new Waterfront Hall.

The area was first settled circa 1177 around an ancient fort. Its growth as a city stems from the 17th century with the arrival of English settlers and Huguenot refugees who developed linen weaving in the area. It was one of the few areas in Ireland to be directly affected by the Industrial Revolution due to its linen producing capacity, and consequently, it grew as a major industrial centre with a large Protestant working class. In the 1790s, it was plunged into the throes of agitation for Irish Independence when the Society of United Irishmen was founded by a native son - Henry Joy

McCracken. However, by the end of the 19th century, the city was strongly unionist to the extent that the emerging Protestant proletariat gained economic and social ascendancy. In 1888, the borough was established as a city by charter. From this time onwards, the city became the centre of opposition to Home Rule in Ireland. After the partition of Ireland in 1920, Belfast was established as the capital of the self-governing British province of Northern Ireland, a form of governance that continued until the imposition of direct rule from London in 1972. The city was bombed during World War II and over 1,000 of its citizens lost their lives. The strife of the troubles from the 1960s onwards also served to badly scar the city, both physically and economically.

ORIGIN OF CITY NAME: Derived from the Irish 'Beal Feiriste', meaning the mouth of the Farset, a river flowing through Belfast.

LAND AREA: 25 sq. miles.

MAIN INDUSTRIES: Aircraft manufacturing, beer and spirits distribution, building suppliers, business services, car and vehicle distribution, civil engineering, computers, construction businesses, electricity suppliers, grocery wholesaling, milk and dairy production, petrol and oil distribution, pharmaceutical goods production, retailing, shipbuilding, soft drinks manufacturing, transport services and terminals, telecommunications, television and radio production, textile production.

CENSUS DETAILS: 279,237.

NUMBER OF SCHOOLS: 113 primary schools, 46 secondary schools, 2 institutes of further and higher education, 3 universities, 2 teacher training colleges.

CHIEF EXECUTIVE: Brian Hannah.

LORD MAYOR: Alban Maginess.

COUNCIL MEETING DATES: First day of the month (but not if it falls on Fridays, week-ends or bank holidays).

RADIO STATIONS: BBC Radio Ulster, Cool FM, Downtown Radio, United Christian Broadcasters.

NEWSPAPERS: Andersonstown News. Belfast Newsletter, (Editor: Geoff Martin). Belfast Telegraph, (Editor: Edmund Curran). Herald and Post Newspapers, (Editor: Nigel Tilson). Irish News, (Editor: Tom Collins). Ulster News Letter, (Editor: Geoff Martin).

MAJOR TOURIST ATTRACTIONS: Arts Council Sculpture Park; Belfast City Hall, Donegall Square; Belfast Zoo; Cave Hill Country Park, (with archaeological and natural features); Colin Glen Woodland Park; Crown Liquor Saloon, (a gas-lit Victorian pub); Dundonald Ice Bowl; the Giant's Ring; the Lagan Lookout Centre (explains the River Lagan's weir); Lagan Valley Regional Park, Lisburn; Malone House, (an early 19th-century house in parkland); Minnowburn Beeches, Shaw's Bridge; the Ormeau Baths Gallery, Ormeau Avenue; Palm House Botanic Gardens, Stranmillis Road; Royal Ulster Rifles Museum; Royal Ulster Constabulary Museum; Sir Thomas & Lady Dixon Park, Upper Malone Road; Streamvale Open Dairy Farm; Ulster Museum, Botanic Gardens.

FAMOUS NATIVES OF THE PAST: Joe Bambrick (record goal scoring international footballer; born 1905), George Birmingham (novelist; died 1950), Danny Blanchflower (international footballer/manager; died 1993), Jimmy Breun (professional golfer; died 1972), William Conway (Cardinal of Armagh; died 1977), Sir James Craig (Prime Minister of Northern Ireland 1921-40; died 1940), Joe Devlin (politician/journalist; died 1934), John Dunlop (produced first pneumatic tyre, born Scotland; died 1921), Benjamin Glazer (first Irish Oscar winner 1927-28; died 1956), Edward Harland (established Harland & Wolff shipyard 1862, born Yorkshire; died 1895), Paul Henry (oil painter; died 1958), John Hewitt (poet/art critic; died 1987), Chaim Herzog (President of Israel 1983-93; born 1918), Francis Hincks (Prime Minister of Canada 1851-54; died 1885), Denis Ireland (writer/broadcaster; died 1974), Sir John Lavery (artist; died 1941), C.S. Lewis (novelist/academic/theologian; died 1963), Henry Joy McCracken (founding member of United Irishmen; died 1798), Siobhán McKenna (actress, wife of Denis O'Dea who died 1978; died 1986), Louis MacNeice (poet/dramatist/broadcaster; died 1963), Colin Middleton (painter; died 1983), 'Rinty' John Joseph Monaghan (professional boxer; died 1984), Stewart Parker (playwright; died 1988), Francis McPeake and family (instrumentalists/singers; 1885-1960's), Forrest Reid (novelist; died 1947), Bobby Sands (republican hunger striker/M.P. who died in 1980), Betty Sinclair (trade unionist/communist; died 1981), Sam Thompson (playwright; died 1965).

DERRY CITY
(County Derry)

Derry city is Northern Ireland's second largest city and the capital of the north-west region. The River Foyle effectively divides the city in two - the Waterside and the Cityside - the latter, containing the walls of Derry, built in the 17th century.

The city's existence can be traced back to pagan times when Calgach, a warrior, made his camp on the 'island' of Derry. St. Columb founded his first monastery in 546 in the vicinity. In 1164, the first bishop of Derry built a cathedral in the city near the monastic site, and Derry came to be known as Doire Columcille, in honour of St. Columb. During Norman times, the city was ruled over by the de Burgos, the earls of Ulster. The first defensive fortifications around the city were built by the English in 1566. These were breached in 1608 when Derry was sacked by Cahir O'Doherty. He was subsequently killed in Donegal and the rebellion he incited died. The city of London sent master builders and money between 1614 and 1619 to rebuild the ruined medieval city and construct its famous walls.

During the 17th century, Derry endured a number of sieges - those of 1641, 1649 and the Great Siege of 1689, when the apprentice boys locked out the invading Jacobite forces. It was 105 days later that relief came when the Williamites broke the boom across the river. In the 18th century, Derry's reputation as a major port grew from the numbers embarking from its docks to emigrate from the county. Its industrial base in the 19th century as a centre for ship building and shirt manufacturing confirmed its status as an important trading port. During World War II, the city was one of the major naval bases for the Allied troops during the Battle of the Atlantic. Derry became a focal point for conflict during the troubles that started in 1969; it was the site of 'Bloody Sunday' in January 1972, when 13 civilians were shot dead by British army paratroopers during a civil rights march. One man died later from his injuries. Derry has been rejuvenated in recent years with major new building developments and community initiatives, but it still remains an unemployment black spot in Northern Ireland.

ORIGIN OF CITY NAME: Derived from the Irish 'Doire', meaning Oak Grove (the prefix London was added in 1613 when the city's second charter of incorporation changed its name to Londonderry).

LAND AREA: 3.4 sq. miles.

MAIN INDUSTRIES: These include computer services, dairy food processing, garment manufacturing, meat processing, oil distribution, retailing, service industries, tourism, wholesaling.

CENSUS DETAILS: 101,200.

NUMBER OF SCHOOLS: 8 nursery schools, 48 primary schools, 14 secondary schools, 1 college of further education, 1 university.

CHIEF EXECUTIVE: John Keanie.

CITY MAYOR: Martin Bradley.

COUNCIL MEETING DATES: Fouth Tuesday in every month.

RADIO STATIONS: BBC Radio Foyle, Q102FM.

NEWSPAPERS: Derry Journal, (Editor: Pat McArt). Londonderry/Limavady Sentinel, (Editor: James Cadden). North West Belfast Telegraph, (Editor: Suzanne Rodgers).

MAJOR TOURIST ATTRACTIONS: the Calgach Centre, Butcher Street; Carlisle Square Sculpture; the city walls and gates; the courthouse; the Context Gallery, Artillery Street; the craft village; Derry's murals and monuments; Derry Visitor and Convention Bureau; the Diamond, with its war memorial; Foyle Bridge; Foyle Arts Centre; Foyle Valley Railway Centre; the Gordon Galleries; the Guildhall; the Harbour Museum; the Heritage Library; Long Tower Church, built in 1786 on the site of Derry's first Cathedral; Magee College University; the masonic hall, formerly the dwelling of the Protestant Bishop of Derry; the memorial to Bloody Sunday, the Bogside; O'Doherty Tower; the old Derry Jail; Orchard Gallery; the Playhouse; St. Augustine's Church; St. Brecan's church ruins in St. Columb's Park; St. Columb's Cathedral, dating back to 1633; St. Columb's Hall; St. Eugene's Cathedral, dating back to 1873; the Tower Museum.

FAMOUS NATIVES OF THE PAST: Liam Ball (international swimmer), Miciaih Browning (responsible for breaking 'the Boom' that ended The Siege of Derry 1689; died 1689), Willie Carson (photographer; died 1996), Henry Cooke (Presbyterian General Assembly Moderator 1862; died 1868), Fay Coyle (international footballer), George Farquhar (playwright; died 1707), William Hare (notorious Scottish murderer; died 1860), John Glendy (United Irishman/Commodore in U.S. Navy; died 1832), Robert Lundy (Governor of Derry at time of Jacobite siege), James McCafferty (musician/choir master/musical director; died 1995), Liam McCormack (architect; died 1996), Norah McGuinness (painter; died 1980), Patsy O'Hara (hunger striker; died 1981), William Scott (founded Derry shirt Industry 1831; born 1755).

CORK CITY
(County Cork)

Cork City, Ireland's third city after Dublin and Belfast, was established on the River Lee and gradually ascended up the steep banks of the river. The city can claim a distinct heritage, which stems from its origins as an important seaport. Indeed some of the Cork's main streets are built over channels where ships docked centuries ago.

The city began as a monastic site, founded by St. Finbarr in the sixth century. The settlement was raided by the Vikings and the Normans, but survived and thrived. Cork, and Cork City in particular, maintained its reputation for resistance and autonomy and came to be called 'Rebel Cork'. The city's reputation for stubborn resistance to the English overlords resulted from the it being the base of the 19th-century Fenian movement and playing a pivotal role in the Irish struggle for independence.

CENSUS DETAILS: Total population - 127,092 - a 0.1% decrease since 1991.

NUMBER OF SCHOOLS: 63 primary schools, 31 secondary schools, 1 university, 1 R.T.C.

CITY MANAGER: Jack Higgins.

CHAIRMAN OF CITY COUNCIL: David McCarthy.

NAMES OF ALL COUNCILLORS: Tim Brosnan (F.F.), Donal Counihan (F.F.), John Dennehy (F.F.), Tim Falvey (F.F.), Michael Martin (F.F.), David McCarthy (F.F.), Tom O'Driscoll (F.F.), Noel O'Flynn (F.F), Damien Wallace (F.F.), Colm Burke (F.G.), Liam Burke (F.G.), Tom Considine (F.G.), James Corr (F.G.), Denis Cregan (F.G.), P.J. Hourican (F.G.), Michael Ahern (Lab.), John Murray (Lab.), Frank Nash (Lab.), Joe O'Callaghan (Lab.), Joe O'Flynn (Lab.), Frank Wallace (Lab.), Brian

Bermingham (P.D.), Maírín Quill (P.D.), Pearse Wyse (P.D.), Pat Murray (N.P.), Con O'Leary (N.P.), John Kelleher (D.L.), Kathleen Lynch (D.L.), Dan Boyle (G.P.), Jimmy Homan (W.P.), Ted McCarthy.

COUNCIL MEETING DATES: Second and fourth Monday of each month.

RATEABLE VALUE TOTALS: £1,230,908.80.

MAJOR TOURIST ATTRACTIONS: the Berwick Fountain, (a monument to Irish patriots); Bishop Lucey Park; the Coal Quay, (an open air market steeped in Cork's folk culture); the Cork Heritage Park, Blackrock; Cork Opera House; the Crawford Municipal Art Gallery, (houses a fine sculpture collection, including some Rodins); the monument to Fr. Theobald Matthew, (a 19th-century temperance advocate); the Old English Market in Grand Parade; the old gaol in Sunday's Well; Patrick's Hill; the riverside quadrangle at University College Cork; Shandon Church, (with its famous bells, clock and weathervane); St. Finbarr's Cathedral; St. Mary's Cathedral, (with its notable carvings);Triskel Arts Centre, Tobin Street.

FAMOUS NATIVES OF THE PAST: Edward Hallran Bennett (diagnosed 'Bennett's fracture' ; died 1907), George Boole (mathematician/professor, 'Boolean Algebra'; died 1864), Richard Church (Liberator of Greece, died 1873), Michael Collins (revolutionary/statesman; died 1922), Thomas Croker (folklorist/antiquary; died 1854), Daniel Corkery (writer/teacher; died 1964), Francis Fogarty (R.A.F. Chief Marshal; died 1973), Frank Gallagher (first editor of Irish Press newspaper; died 1962), Terence MacSwiney (revolutionary; died 1920), Havelock Nelson (conductor/composer; died 1996), Frank O'Connor (short story writer/novelist/translator; died 1966), Seán O'Faolain (short story writer/novelist; died 1991), Seán Ó Muirthuile (Lieutenant-General; died 1941); Seán Ó Riada (arranger/composer/musician; died 1971), George Salmon (mathematician/theologian; died 1904).

LIMERICK CITY
(County Limerick)

Limerick City is set in the north-east of the county on the River Shannon. Its charter is 800 years old, making it older than London. The origins of the city date back to when the Vikings sailed up the Shannon Estuary in 922 and founded a settlement on an island. With the arrival of the Normans in 1194, St. Mary's Cathedral and the great castle of King John were built. The Geraldines' rebellion against the English in 1571 was the first of many such wars and sieges centred around Limerick City, including the year-long siege against Oliver Cromwell in 1651 and the 1690 and 1691 sieges. The 1690 siege resulted in General Patrick Sarsfield leading the Jacobite cause, which was supported by the Catholic Irish. The end of this siege led to the signing of the Treaty of Limerick in 1691, the terms of which were dishonoured by the English parliament. The city's walls were taken down in the 18th century and the city developed westwards into an area known as Newtown Pery, famed for its elegant houses and wide streets.

Limerick City began to prosper in the 1950s and 1960s with the industrial development arising from Shannon Airport, the geographical location of which made it the first suitable landing site for long-distance air travel from and to America. Shannon Free Airport Development Company was established in 1959 to ensure that the region maintained its viability in air transport activity. The effects of this agency were quickly felt throughout the Shannon region, particularly in Limerick City. The success of the city today attests to the agency's initiatives. Among the many regional development organisations located in Limerick City is the National Technological Park, Plassey, a centre for high technology with facilities for research, development, applications and education. Shannon Development, the region's key coordinating body, is now internationally recognised by the O.E.C.D. for its success in forward planning and its ability to keep in touch with local conditions.

CENSUS DETAILS: Total population - 52,042 - a 0.1% decrease since 1991.

NUMBER OF SCHOOLS: 34 primary schools, 17 secondary schools, 1 R.T.C., 1 university.

CITY MANAGER: Maurice Maloney.

CITY MAYOR: Frank Leddin.

NAMES OF COUNCILLORS: Jack Bourke (F.F.), Bobby Byrne (F.G.), Tim Ledden (F.G.), Patrick Kennedy (F.G.), Gus O'Driscoll (F.G.), Seán Griffin (Lab), Frank Leddin (Lab.), Judy O'Donoghue (Lab), Frank Prendergast (Lab), Jan O'Sullivan (Lab), Kieran O'Hanlon (P.D.), John Quinn (P.D.), Dick Sadlier (P.D.), John Gilligan (Ind.), Joe Harrington (Ind.), John Ryan (D.L.).

COUNCIL MEETING DATES: Second Monday of each month.

RATEABLE VALUE TOTALS: £463,561.20.

MAJOR TOURIST ATTRACTIONS: the Belltable Arts Centre, O'Connell Street; the Dominican Church; the Exchange at Nicholas Street; the Granary, Michael Street; Hunt Museum, which includes a fine medieval collection; John's Square; Kilrush Church, dating back to 1201; King John's Castle; Limerick City Walls; Limerick Lace Making at the Good Shepherd Convent, Clare Street; Limerick Museum; the O'Connell Monument; the Rugby Heritage Centre, Thomond Park; Sarsfield Bridge; the Sarsfield Memorial; St. John's Cathedral; St. Mary's Cathedral; Tait Clock; the Treaty Stone, off Thomond Bridge;

FAMOUS NATIVES OF THE PAST: Andrew N. Bonaparte-Wyse (public servant; died 1940), John Hunt (scholar/antiquarian; died 1976), Séan Keating (artist; died 1977), Jim Kemmy (politician; died 1997), Mick Mackey (hurler; died 1982), Lola Montez (adventuress/dancer; died 1861), Michael J. O'Kelly (archaeologist; died 1982).

GALWAY CITY
(County Galway)

Galway City is one of the fastest growing cities in Europe and has a young population, two factors that contribute to it being regarded as Ireland's most vibrant city.

Galway as a city was already 500 years old when it was granted its charter in 1484 by Richard III. It had already assumed a commercial importance - Christopher Columbus visited the city while trading from Lisbon in 1477. Around this time 14 wealthy merchant families ruled the city, earning Galway the name of the 'City of the Tribes'. These families were proud of their status and created their own special coat of arms, often without heraldic authority, which they had carved on to the facades of their premises. The tribes held their position for the next 170 years, until 1651 when a Cromwellian force, under Sir Charles Coote, besieged the city. Galway surrendered, and the tribes lost all their power. Although Irish Catholics temporarily regained the city, they soon lost this control following the Battle of Aughrim. During the 18th century, Galway declined in status and in 1841, lost its classification as a city. Nonetheless, it still maintained strong trading links and many industries flourished. Queens College, Galway, was established in 1845. This was the time of the Great Famine, when many thousands died in the city and its environs. By 1899, the population of Galway had been halved. In 1916, a rising against the British was instigated by Liam Mellowes in the city but failed. It became an urban municipality once again in 1937. The fortunes of the city began to look up in the 1960s, with the expansion of industry and tourism in the country. It is now an industrial centre for the west, with a thriving arts scene.

CENSUS DETAILS: Total population - 57,095 - a 12.3% increase since 1991.
NUMBER OF SCHOOLS: 26 primary schools, 11 secondary schools, 1 R.T.C., 1 university.
CITY MANAGER: Joe Gavin.
CITY MAYOR: Michael Leahy.
NAMES OF ALL COUNCILLORS: Margaret Cox (F.F.), Michael Leahy (F.F.), Henry O'Connor (F.F.), Michael G. Ó h-Uiginn (F.F.), Fintan Coogan (F.G.), Angela Lupton (F.G.), Padraic McCormack (F.G.), John Mulholland (F.G.), Martin Connolly (P.D.), Donal Lyons (P.D.), Declan McDonnell (P.D.), Bridie O'Flaherty (P.D.), Tom Costello (Lab.), James Mullarkey (Lab.), Paddy Lally (Ind.).
COUNCIL MEETING DATES: First and third Monday of each month.
RATEABLE VALUE TOTALS: £501,800.65.
MAJOR TOURIST ATTRACTIONS: the 17th century Browne Dorway; the Black Box performance facility; the Claddagh district, which gave rise to the popular Claddagh Ring; the Corrib, a renowned salmon river; Eyre Square with statues of Padraic O'Conaire and Liam Mellowes and the Quincentennial fountain; Galway Irish Crystal Heritage Centre; Kirwan's Lane, one of Galway's last remaining medieval lanes; the leaping salmon statue at the Salmon Weir Bridge; Leisureland; the Lynch Memorial Window; the medieval walls and quays of the city, which have been unearthed through intensive archaeological excavation; Nora Barnacle House Museum; the restored Bridge Mills at O'Brien's Bridge; the restored Shoemaker and Penrice Towers; Royal Tara China Visitor Centre; Salthill, one of Ireland's busiest seaside resorts; Shop Street, a medieval street that contains the 15th century Lynch's Castle; Siamsa na Gaillimhe, the Spanish Arch; street furniture such as footscrapers, jostle stones, mermaid carvings, marriage stones and water troughs; St. Nicholas Collegiate Church, which Christopher Columbus supposedly visited; Tigh Neachtain pub, once the home of the Richard Martin - 'Humanity Dick'; the Town Hall Theatre.
FAMOUS NATIVES OF THE PAST: Ellis Dillion (author; died 1993), Frank Harris (writer/journalist; died 1931), Gerard Anthony Hayes-McCoy (historian; died 1975), Dónall MacAmhlaigh (novelist/short story writer; died 1989), Liam Mellowes (leader of failed Galway rising 1916), Pádraic Ó Conaire (short story writer/novelist; died 1928).

WATERFORD CITY
(County Waterford)

CENSUS DETAILS: Total population - 42,516 - a 5.4% increase since 1991.
NUMBER OF SCHOOLS: 19 primary schools, 11 secondary schools, 1 R.T.C.
CITY MAYOR: Thomas Cunningham.
CITY MANAGER: Edward J. Breen.
NO. OF COUNCILLORS: 4 F.F., 3 F.G., Liam 3 Lab., 2 Ind., 2 W.P., Patrick Gallagher D.L.
COUNCIL MEETING DATES/NUMBER: Second Monday each month.
RATEABLE VALUE TOTALS: £380, 528.00
WHO WAS WHO: Noel Browne (politician/medical doctor; died 1997), Alexis Fitzgerald (lawyer/economist/senator; died 1985), Thomas Francis Meagher (part of 1848 Rising/Governor of Montana; died 1867), Richard Mulcahy (revolutionary/soldier/politician; died 1971), William Vincent Wallace (composed the opera *Maritana*).

BUSINESS, FINANCE & TRADE

The Irish Economy, The Fallen Star and the Celtic Tiger

By Gerry Murray

THE last year has seen the subject of Home Rule emerge again in British politics, but this time in the context of Scotland. At the turn of the century, it was an Irish issue, and at that time, the economy of the north-east of Ireland was thriving through industry and commerce. The position has radically changed and 1996 may mark a significant watershed of that change. Ten years ago, according to O.E.C.D. statistics, incomes in the Republic of Ireland, measured by GDP per head, were just 63% of those in Britain, and the Republic was one of the poorest countries in Europe. On the same measure, ten years later, the Republic has surpassed Britain and now stands close to the average in the European Union. By contrast, the economy of Northern Ireland has languished, and become ever-dependent upon the British Exchequer.

Average annual growth in the Republic of Ireland has been around 7per cent double that in Britain, while government borrowing has fallen to almost nothing. Recently published forecasts by the Economic and Social Research Institute (E.S.R.I.) indicate that the Republic's economy could grow annually by 5.5 per cent on average to the year 2000, with an average growth of 5 per cent in the first five years of the new century. It is no wonder that the Republic has been dubbed 'The Celtic Tiger' of Europe, given the remarkable transformation in its economy. Ireland has been a major European beneficiary of inward investment especially in hi-tech, food processing, pharmaceuticals and tele-marketing industries. Nearly one-third of all personal computers sold in Europe are now made in the Republic of Ireland. The growth of the Irish economy has now demonstrated that a small country on the periphery of Europe can prosper, and that the global economy can be an opportunity as well as a threat. Considerable resources have been allocated to attracting inward investors, and ensuring that a highly educated and skilled workforce is ably equipped to meet the needs of employers. As a guide to priorities, Ireland pays its teachers more in relation to average earnings than in any other European country.

By contrast, annual economic growth in Northern Ireland is around 3 per cent, and the economy continues to rely heavily on subvention from the British Exchequer to the tune of £4 billion per annum. Public Expenditure figures have shown that there will be massive reductions in this subsidy, and £125 million was cut from the North's financial allocation for 1997/98. There are no indications that savings resulting from the renewal of the IRA ceasefire will be re-invested in the north. There is a high concentration on the traditional industries on which its 19th-century industrialisation was based. Almost 70,000 jobs were lost in the manufacturing sector in the two decades to 1993. The hi-tech inward investment by Seagate in the north-west has been the beginning of attempts to create a cluster of hi-tech industry.

The challenges for the North's economy are great, but there appear to be inadequate mechanisms to radically transform this situation. As the main emphasis seems to be on finding a formula on constitutional arrangements, the economy will continue to suffer.

The author is a senior partner in an accountancy firm and a regular columnist with the Derry Journal *newspaper.*

INTRODUCTION

REPUBLIC OF IRELAND: In 1997 the Republic of Ireland's description as "The Celtic Tiger", continued to be justified. The rate of inflation averaged 1.5% in 1997, unemployment ran at 11.7% and exchequer returns for the half year to 30/6/97 showed a current budget surplus of £721 million. The unemployment rate of 11.7% contrasts with a rate of 15.5% in 1993, while the current budget surplus position contrasts with a deficit for the four years 1990 - 1993. The Exchequer Borrowing Requirement is expected to be less than IR£300 million for 1997. This compares to a budget target of IR£637 million and would be the lowest borrowing requirement of any year in the nineties (IR£437 million in 1996, IR£713 million in 1992). Private car sales, the retail sector and the housing market all experienced broad-based growth.

The textbook performance of the economy - high economic growth, low inflation, fiscal stability and positive job creation leaves Ireland on course for participation in EMU in 1999. The Maastricht treaty criteria for entrance to the EMU have, to date, been adhered to and are likely to be watched ever closer in 1998. The creation of a single currency will undoubtedly be the most momentous event of the nineties. It will have an impact on all our lives, from the micro-level of learning to deal with day-to-day transactions using a different currency to the macro-level of affecting the relationship between countries.

Is there any danger that the bubble could burst? Is it possible for example that the EMU could mean member states converging at higher rather than lower interest rates? This would have grave implications for the Irish housing market with the possible development of negative equity situations, as happened in London in the mid-eighties. It also seems likely that in future years expanding labour opportunities will be met by increased labour market participation so that the unemployment rate will be slow to decline towards 10 per cent by the end of the decade. A weak Irish pound in relation to sterling could carry some inflationary dangers.

The only thing certain about economies is that they move in cycles. The length of either an upward or a downward cycle cannot be predicted, but it would be naive in the extreme to believe that an economy will continue to grow indefinitely. The Irish economy would currently appear to be in party mood. Now might be the best time to provide for the inevitable hangover.

NORTHERN IRELAND: As measured by all the available indicators, economic activity was extremely strong across all sectors in Northern Ireland in 1997, except agriculture, where the aftermath of the B.S.E. crisis continues to unfold. The economic growth of the province has been consistently better than that in Britain in the nineties. G.D.P. grew by an average of 2.6% per annum from 1992-95, compared to 1.8% per annum in Britain while manufacturing output has grown by 3% per annum , faster than every year since 1988. In 1997, of the eleven standard regions in the Britain, only East Anglia is projected to grow faster.

The unemployment rate in Northern Ireland in 1997 averaged out at 9.6%, the lowest rate since the mid-eighties. House prices continued to outpace inflation, while personal disposable income increased by 3.75%. The average hourly wage cost is the second lowest in Europe. Exports were up 21% in 94/95 - twice the growth rate of Britain. The strong economic growth has resulted in a decrease in the subvention from Westminster.

As ever in Northern Ireland, everything depends on politics. The future of the Northern economy depends to a large extent on two major factors. Firstly, a lasting settlement needs to be found to the troubles. In 1995 during the IRA ceasefire, for example, the number of holiday visitors to the province rose by 85% compared to the previous year. In 1996, the Canary Wharf bomb led to an immediate 30% decline in visitors compared to the same month in 1995.

The second factor is whether or not Britain will stay out of the single currency. This has implications for interest rates in the North and the rate of sterling against the Euro. No one can say for sure whether Euro interest rates will be lower than sterling interest rates and whether sterling will fall against the Euro. This does at least put the Northern Ireland economy in a familiar position: having to cope with uncertainty, something it has had plenty of practice at over the last 30 odd years!

COMPANIES
TOP 30 COMPANIES IN THE REPUBLIC OF IRELAND

Rank	Company	Nature of Business	Turnover (IR£m)	Profit (IR£m)	No. of employees
1	Smurfit Group	Paper / Packaging	3,033	420.1	25,000
2	Intel Ireland	Computer Manufacturing	2,400	n/a	3,000
3	Cement Roadstone Holdings	Building Materials	1,911	160.5	15,331
4	Dell	Computer Manufacturing	1,900	n/a	1,300
5	The Irish Dairy Board	Export Dairy produce	1,249	20.8	2,009
6	Avonmore Foods	Dairy/Food Products	1,225	32.1	6,464
7	Kerry Group	Food Processing	1,199	43.2	9,203
8	Fyffes plc	Fruit & Veg. Distribution	1,120	42.0	5,015
9	Dunnes Stores	Retailing	1,100	n/a	9,500
10	Telecom Eireann	Telecommunications	1,094	117.2	12,372
11	ESB	Electricity Supply	1,026	(284)	10,362
12	Power Supermarkets	Supermarket Retail	900	n/a	7,500
13	Aer Lingus	Air Transportation	795	17.8	10,102
14	Waterford Foods	Food Products	787	24.9	3,642
15	Musgrave	Wholesale Distribution	738	17.9	1,500
16	Apple Computer	Computer Manufacturing	720	n/a	1,500
17	Guinness Ireland	Brewing	703	148.0	2,400
18	Irish Food Processors	Meat Process & Export	700	n/a	2,600
19	Dairygold Co-op Society	Dairy Products	635	14.5	2,899
20	Irish Distillers Group	Distillers	567	43.7	2,100
21	Golden Vale	Dairy Products	564	16.5	2,090
22	IAWS Group	Agri Business	554	18.5	900
23	DCC	Industrial Holding Co.	529	28.9	2,081
24	Coca Cola Atlantic	Soft Drinks	520	n/a	332
25	Glen Dimplex	Domestic Appliances Mfg.	500	n/a	6,000
26	Microsoft EOC	Software Mfg. & Distrib.	500	n/a	500
27	Microsoft WPGI	Software Localisation	500	n/a	500
28	Oracle Corporation	Software Mfg. & Sales	488	n/a	250
29	Pepsi Cola Manufacturing	Soft Drinks	470	n/a	150
30	Swords Laboratories	Pharmaceutical Mfg.	470	0.3	274

TOP 20 FINANCIAL INSTITUTIONS IN THE R.O.I.

Rank	Company	Assets (IR£m)	Shareholder Funds (IR£m)	Profit (IR£m)	No. of employees
1	A.I.B.	23,873	1,157	373	15,214
2	Bank of Ireland	20,959	1,227	316	12,630
3	Ulster Bank	7,740	432	120	4,309
4	Irish Life	6,632	79	56	2,144
5	Central Bank of Ireland	5,828	1,370	198	578
6	Irish Permanent	4,075	226	42	1,454
7	Bank Nationale de Paris	3,869	n/a	n/a	73
8	Anglo Irish Bankcorp	2,396	116	24	233
9	First National Building Society	2,330	119	24	854
10	Woodchester Investments	2,156	202	36	1,051
11	Scotia Bank of Ireland	1,820	206	28	34
12	Educational Building Society	1,764	132	23	540
13	Irish Intercontinental Bank	1,724	69	16	170
14	Norwich Union Insurance	1,700	n/a	n/a	560
15	G.P.A.	1,531	105	34	44
16	T.S.B. Bank	1,370	86	18	1,093
17	National Irish Bank	1,302	68	21	868
18	A.C.C. Bank	1,300	61	13	556
19	I.C.C. Bank	1,226	74	12	320
20	New Ireland Holdings	1,193	34	10	847

TOP 10 SOFTWARE COMPANIES IN THE R.O.I.

Rank	Company	Turnover (IR£m)	No. of Employees	Turnover per Employee (IR£m)
1	Microsoft E.O.C.	500	500	1.00
2	Microsoft W.I.P.G.I.	500	500	1.00
3	Oracle	488	250	1.90
4	Novell Ireland	370	80	4.62
5	CapGemini	306	76	4.02
6	Digital B.V.	270	440	0.61
7	Corel	200	130	1.53
8	Infomix	178	130	1.37
9	Lotus Development	135	443	0.30
10	Stratus Computer	112	224	0.50

TOP 30 COMPANIES IN NORTHERN IRELAND

Rank	Company	Nature of Business	Estimated Turnover (£STGm)	Profit (£STGm)	Number of Employees
1	Northern Ireland Electricity	Electricity Service	560.9	59.8	2,689
2	Short Brothers	Aircraft Manufacturers	391.2	33.8	8,781
3	Glen Electric Ltd.	Domestic Heating	334.9	19.7	343
4	United Dairy Farmers	Dairy/Milk Products	318.3	0.85	759
5	Powerscreen Int.	Screening Equipment Mfg.	304.8	36.0	1,974
6	F.A. Wellworth	Supermarkets	274.1	19.1	4,850
7	Stewarts Supermarkets	Supermarkets	256.1	8.5	3,878
8	F.G. Wilson Eng.	Electricity Generators	218.7	34.9	1,217
9	Dunnes Stores (Bangor)	Supermarkets	194.2	8.7	1,615
10	Nacco Materials Hd.	Forklift Manufacturer	187.1	3.7	816
11	Charles Hurst Ltd.	Vehicle Distributors	186.4	3.0	741
12	Nortel (NI)	Telecommunications	170.9	24.3	998
13	Moy Park Ltd.	Poultry Products	169.4	0.6	2,739
14	J & J Haslett	Grocery Wholesale	166.6	4.6	1,063
15	John Henderson Ltd.	Grocery Wholesale	163.0	2.6	806
16	Nigen Ltd.	Electricity Supply	145.7	25.8	422
17	Crazy Prices (NI)	Supermarkets	123.4	3.4	1,658
18	Lamont Textiles	Textile Products	120.7	(-5.5)	1,525
19	Harland and Wolff	Ship Building	118.1	3.0	1,400
20	Maxol Oil Ltd.	Oil/Petroleum Distributors	110.5	(-0.9)	1918
21	Premier Power	Electricity Supply	109.8	5.5	428
22	NI Transport Holding	Transport	106.1	4.5	3,776
23	Andrews Holdings	Animal Feeds and Flour	101.9	4.4	1,032
24	Desmond & Sons Ltd.	Clothing Manufacturers	101.3	3.5	2,907
25	Alchem Plc.	Pharmaceuticals	100.9	2.1	229
26	Leckpatrick Dairies.	Dairy Products	97.4	(-0.7)	233
27	Boxmore Int.	Packaging	88.5	14.3	1,017
28	Bridgewater Country Foods	Pork Suppliers	88.5	(-4.1)	813
29	Fane Valley Co-op	Milk and Dairy Products	87.5	1.8	309
30	Irish Bonding Co. Ltd.	Wine/Spirits Wholesaler	85.1	8.7	230

TOP PUBLIC COMPANIES IN NORTHERN IRELAND

Rank	Company	Market Cap (£Stg million)	Share Price (pence)	P/E
1	N.I.E.	646	460.0	21.3
2	Powerscreen	620	701.5	19.4
3	Boxmore International	219	308.5	19.3
4	Ulster Television	120	229.0	21.9
5	Lamont Holdings	39	131.5	6.7
6	Ewart	16	54.5	8.5
7	Mackie International	2	23.5	1.1

TOP PUBLIC COMPANIES IN THE R.O.I.

Rank	Company	Market Cap (IR£m)	Share Price (pence)	P/E
1	Allied Irish Banks	4,737	560	14.7
2	Bank of Ireland	3,795	780	15.0
3	Elan Corporation	3,141	3,272	31.5
4	CRH	2,736	720	14.8
5	Jefferson Smurfit Group	2,421	230	27.1
6	Kerry	1,228	750	19.2
7	Irish Life	1,057	348	10.4
8	Independent Newspapers	945	390	20.2
9	Avonmore Waterford	815	280	13.6
10	Waterford Wedgwood	631	89	18.9

TOP TEN ACQUISITIONS INVOLVING IRISH COMPANIES 1996

Rank	Acquirer	Target Company	Country	IR£M
1	Bank of Ireland	Bristol & West	UK	600 (stg)
2	Elan Corporation	Athena Neurosciences	US	395
3	Independent Newspapers	Wilson & Horton	AUS	210
4	Unisource	Telecom Eireann	IRL	183
5	CRH	Tilcon Inc.	US	157
6	Rubicon (UK)	Higgins Engineering	IRL	103
7	Irish Life	Guaranteed Life Reserve	US	99
8	C.R.H.	Allied Buildings Products	US	76
9	Unilever Ireland	Lyons Irish Holdings (minority)	IRL	73
10	Clondalkin Group	Van Der Windt Groep	NETH	58

TOP TEN ACQUISITIONS INVOLVING IRISH COMPANIES 1997*

Rank	Acquirer	Target Company	Country	IR£M
1	Allied Irish Banks	Dauphin Deposit Corp.	US	840
2	Musgraves Ltd.	Wellworths Supermarkets	NI	67
3	Avonmore Foods Plc.	Beni Foods	UK	54
4	Dunloe Plc	Monarch Properties/Aviette	IRL	50
5	Allied Irish Banks	WBK Polish Bank	POL	43
6	Irish Wire Products	Constance Carroll Holdings	UK	39
7	Emergency Markets Data	eMisis Infocom	UK	17
8	IA.W.S. Plc	P B Kent Ltd.	UK	10
9	Smurfit Group Plc	Celulosa de Coronel Suarez	ARG	9
10	Smurfit Group Plc	Asindus	ARG	9

Table to June 30, 1997

TOP TEN SHARE SHOWINGS - IRISH COMPANIES 1996

Rank	Company	Share Price Performance %
1	Minmet	275
2	Kingspan	164
3	Impshire Thoroughbreds	106
4	Dunloe House	83
5	Dana Exploration	58
6	New Ireland	57
7	Grafton Group	57
8	Boxmore	56
9	Powerscreen	53
10	Norish	53

NUMBER OF OVERSEAS COMPANIES IN THE REPUBLIC OF IRELAND, 1995

Country	No. of Companies
U.S.A.	400
Germany	180
Britain	160
Northern Ireland	50
Sweden	40
Japan	38
France	35
Other	175
TOTAL	**1,078**

TAXATION
REPUBLIC OF IRELAND TAX TABLE (1997/98)

INCOME TAX

RATES

	Single	Married
26% on first	IR£9,900	£IR19,800
48% on balance		

MAIN ALLOWANCES

	IR£
Single Person	2,900
Married Couple	5,800
Widowed Person*	3,400
P.A.Y.E. Allowance	800
Child Allowance (Incapacitated)	700
Dependent Relative Allowance	110
Age 65 or over (single)	400
Age 65 or over (married)	800

Widow in year of bereavement - IR£5,400

RELIEFS

VHI & PHI Premiums

Relief for 1997-98 is available at 26% only for the premium paid in 1996-97.

Rented Accomodation

Relief is allowed at the standard rate of tax on the first £500 paid for private residential rented accommodation.

Pension Contributions

Relief is available for contributions to revenue approved schemes at the marginal rate. Contributions are limited to 15% of net relevant earnings.

Medical Expenses

Relief is available at the taxpayers marginal rate for expenses paid in excess of £200 (£100 single person).

Mortgage Interest

80% of interest paid less IR£100 for single & widowed, IR£200 for married. For 97/98 relief is at the standard rate of tax only (26%). The maximum relief is:

	Single	Married	Widow
Existing Mortgages	1,900	3,800	2,780
First Time Buyer	2,500	5,000	3,600

P.R.S.I. & Levies

The P.R.S.I. rates are:

	Rate %	Contribut. Ceiling IR£	Exempt Income IR£
Employee	4.5	23,200	80/week
Employer*	12.0	27,900	-
Self-Employed	5.0	23,200	20/week
Public Sector	0.9	23,200	20/week

* 8.5% if earning less than IR£13,520

The Income Levies are comprised of the **Health** levy and the **Employment** levy which are 1.25% and 1.0 % on all income (less benefits in kind), respectively. Both levies apply only where annual income is over £10,250.

CORPORATION TAX

RATES

Standard Rate*	36%
Manufacturing Rate	10%

* A rate of 28% applies to the first IR£50,000 of taxable income.

CAPITAL GAINS TAX

RATES

	Single	Married
Annual Exemption	IR£1,000	IR£2,000
Rate*	40%	

* A rate of 26% applies to disposals of shares in certain unquoted Irish companies.

CAPITAL ACQUISITIONS TAX

CLASS THRESHOLDS

Relationship to Disponer:	IR£
Child, minor child of deceased child	182,550
Other blood relatives	24,340
None of the above	12,170

NORTHERN IRELAND TAX TABLE (1997/98)

RATES (£STG)
20% on first 4,100
23% on next 22,000
40% on balance

MAIN ALLOWANCES

	£Stg.
Personal allowance	4,045
Married couple's allowance*	1,830
Additional widow's bereavement allowance*	1,830
Additional one-parent families' allowance*	1,830
Blind person's allowance	1,280
Age allowance 65 to 74 (single)†	5,220
Age allowance 65 to 74 (married)†	3,185
Age allowance 75 and over (single)†	5,400
Age allowance 75 and over (married)†	3,225

* Relief restricted to 15%
† Excess over basic allowances withdrawn by £1 for every £2
on income over £15,600.

RELIEFS

Personal Equity Plans (P.E.P.s)

Annual Maximum:	£STG
Standard P.E.P.	6,000
Single company P.E.P.	3,000

Tax Exempt Special Savings Accounts (TESSAs)

Annual Maximum:	£STG
First year	3,000
Subsequent years	1,800
Investment cannot succeed	9,000

Pension Contributions
Relief for private pension contributions is limited as follows:

	% of Net Relevant Earnings	
Age	**P.P.P.**	**R.A.P.**
35 or under	17.5	17.5
36 to 45	20.0	17.5
46 to 50	25.0	17.5
51 to 55	30.0	20.0
56 to 60	35.0	22.5
61 or over	40.0	27.5

The general earnings cap is £STG84,000.

Mortgage Interest
Mortgage Interest Relief at Source is 15%. (10% from April 1998 onwards.) The maximum mortgage amount on which this may be claimed is £30,000.

National Insurance
Earnings Limits are as follows :

	Lower Earnings Limit - Annual (£STG)	Upper Earnings Limit - Annual (£STG)
Class 1 employee	3,244	24,180
Class 2 employee	3,480	24,180
Class 4 employee	7,010	24,180
Employer	3,224	-

Class 1 employees not contracted out rates:

Annual Salary £STG	First £3,244 %	Employees Balance %	Employers %
Below 3,244	0	0	0
3,244 - 5,720	2	10	3
5,721 - 8,060	2	10	5
8,061 - 10,920	2	10	7
10,921 - 24,180	2	10	10
Over 24,180	0	0	10

Abatements apply to the above national insurance contribution rates for contracted-out employees with salaries between the upper and lower limits. For the employee the abatement rate is 1.6%, leading to a contribution rate of 8.4%. For employers the abatement rate is 3% for salary-related schemes and 1.5% for money-purchase schemes.

CORPORATION TAX

RATES

Standard rate	31%
Small companies rate	21%
Small companies rate limit	£300,000
Marginal relief limit	£1,500,000
Marginal rate	35.5%

CAPITAL GAINS TAX

RATES

Individual Annual Exemption	£6,500
Trusts	£3,250
Rates	20%; 23%; 40%

INHERITANCE TAX

THRESHOLDS

Transfer after 5/4/97	£215,000
Death Rate	40%

AFTER TAX EARNINGS COMPARISON
R.O.I. AND N.I. (1997/98)

STATUS: Single Person, **MORTGAGE:** None, **GROSS SALARY:** £20,000 p.a.

	R.O.I - IR£	N.I - £STG
Salary	20,000	20,000
Less Personal Allowances and Reliefs	(3,700)	(4,045)
Taxable Income	16,300	15,955
Total Income Tax Payable	5,646	3,547
P.R.S.I./N.I.C. and Levies	1,163	1,740
Net Annual Income	13,191	14,713
NET WEEKLY INCOME:	**253.67**	**282.94**

STATUS: Married Couple, **MORTGAGE:** £50,000, **MORTGAGE INTEREST:** £5,000, **GROSS SALARIES:** £30,000 each p.a.

	R.O.I - IR£	N.I - £STG
Salaries	60,000	60,000
Less Personal Allowances and Reliefs	(7,400)	(8,540)†
Taxable Income	52,600	51,460
Total Income Tax Payable	19,904*	11,315
PRSI / N.I.C and Levies	3,142	4,317
Net Annual Income	36,954	44,368
NET WEEKLY INCOME:	**710.65**	**853.24**

† Mortgage interest is limited to £30,000 of mortgage; therefore only three-fifths of interest is deemed to be allowable at 15%.
* Mortgage interest credit calculated as £3,800 at 26%.

STATUS: Married Couple, wife not working, **MORTGAGE:** £50,000, **MORTGAGE INTEREST:** £5,000, **GROSS SALARY:** £60,000 p.a.

	R.O.I. - IR£	N.I - £STG
Salary	60,000	60,000
Less Personal Allowances and Reliefs	(6,600)	(4,495)
Taxable Income	53,400	55,505
Total Income Tax Payable	20,288	17,367
PRSI / N.I.C and Levies	2,318	2,158
Net Annual Income	37,394	40,475
NET WEEKLY INCOME:	**719.12**	**778.36**

AFTER TAX EARNINGS EUROPEAN AVERAGE

STATUS: Married Couple, **CHILDREN:** Two, **MORTGAGE INTEREST:** £5,000, **PACKAGE:** Yes, **GROSS ANNUAL SALARIES:** £50,000 p.a. plus company car.

Country	Income Tax	Social Insurance	Total
Luxembourg	6,980	5,179	12,159
Spain	14,790	1,309	16,099
NORTHERN IRELAND	15,395	2,136	17,531
Germany	11,497	6,526	18,023
Greece	11,128	7,950	19,078
REPUBLIC OF IRELAND	17,744	1,751	19,495
Portugal	13,843	6,160	20,003
Belgium	13,737	6,794	20,531
Netherlands	19,005	1,925	20,930
Italy	15,912	5,149	21,061
Austria	17,164	4,363	21,527
France	13,667	9,914	23,581
Finland	19,308	4,471	23,779
Sweden	26,552	1,186	27,708
Denmark	26,284	3,808	30,092
AVERAGE	**16,198**	**4,575**	**20,773**

BUDGET HIGHLIGHTS N.I (JULY 97)

Changes in Rates	Old Rate %	New Rate%
Stamp duty for houses worth more than £250,000	1.0	1.5
Stamp duty for houses worth more than £500,000	1.0	2.0
Tax write off on production costs of films with budgets up to £15m.	0	100
Corporation tax	33	31
Small companies tax	23	21
V.A.T. rate on fuel	8	5
Mortgage Interest Relief at Source	15	10

Other Changes	Amount
Increase in petrol	4p per litre
Increase in packet of 20 cigarettes	19p
Money to be raised by introduction of windfall tax on privatised utilities	£5.5bn
Cost of abolishment of the gas levy	£400m
Savings through abolition of tax relief on private medical insurance	£140m
Savings through abolishment of tax credits paid to pension funds (three years)	£3.0bn
Introduction of employers' subsidy re: long term unemployed	£75 per week
New allowance for child-care costs for lone parents	£100 per week
Cost of Welfare to Work package	£3.5bn
Additional allocation to the N.H.S. 1998-99	£1.2bn
Additional allocation to the education sector	£1.0bn
Capital Investment Programme re: disrepair of schools	£1.3bn

BUDGET HIGHLIGHTS R.O.I. (JANUARY 97)

Changes in Rates	Old Rate %	New Rate%
Stamp duty for houses from £150,001 to £160,000	6	7
Stamp duty for houses from £160,001 to £170,000	6	8
Stamp duty for houses worth more than £170,001	6	9
Corporation tax	38	36
Corporation tax applicable to first £50,000 of profits	30	28
Standard rate of income tax	27	26
Relief for transfer of assets in family businesses under C.A.T.	75	90
P.R.S.I. for class A and class H contributors	5.5	4.5
Disposal of shares in certain unquoted Irish companies under C.G.T.	26	27

Other Changes	Amount
Increases in leaded petrol	2.5p per litre
Increases in packet of 20 cigarettes	7p
Cost of abolishment of Residential Property Tax	£16m
New employers' P.R.S.I. ceiling	£27,900
New employees' P.R.S.I. ceiling	£23,200
Cost of conversion of the Irish Statute Book to electronic format	£750,000
Increase in social welfare personal rates	£3 per week
Increase in child benefit - first and second children	£1 per week
Increase in child benefit - third and subsequent children	£5 per week
Increase in Family Income Supplement	£6 per week
New income exemption limit (single person)	£4,000
Provision to improve the security of the elderly	£2m

TAXATION YIELDS R.O.I 1996

Sector	1996 IR£m
P.A.Y.E.	3,894
Self-employed	527
Income Tax from non-PAYE sources	158
V.A.T.	3,109
Excise duty on tobacco	533
Excise duty on alcohol	552
Tax on motor vehicles	353

Excise duty on hydrocarbons	795
Other indirect taxes	71
Corporation tax	1,428
Stamp duty	332
Residential property tax	14
Other capital taxes	166
Revenue investigations and audits	133
Other	31
Total net tax receipts	**12,096**

EXPORTS AND IMPORTS

CROSS BORDER TRADE 1990 - 1995

Year	Imports by R.O.I from N.I (IR£m)	Exports by R.O.I to N.I (IR£m)
1990	500.1	816.1
1991	496.1	789.4
1992	468.2	825.1
1993	417.2	701.0
1994	536.8	721.9
1995	638.6	790.5

GEOGRAPHICAL DISTRIBUTION OF EXPORTS AND IMPORTS - R.O.I, 1995

Country	Imports (IR£m)	Imports %	Exports (IR£m)	Exports %
Britain	6,593.3	32.4	6,314.9	22.8
Germany	1,438.6	7.1	3,991.2	14.4
Other E.U. member states	3,506.8	17.2	9,777.6	35.3
Non-E.U. member states	486.4	2.4	873.8	3.2
U.S.	3,563.7	17.5	2,269.6	8.2
Japan	1,063.5	5.2	815.0	2.9
All other countries	3,695.0	18.2	3,638.8	13.2
TOTAL	**20,347.3**	**100.0**	**27,680.9**	**100.0**

COMPOSITION OF EXPORTS AND IMPORTS - REPUBLIC OF IRELAND, 1995

Sector	Imports (IR£m)	Imports %	Exports (IR£m)	Exports %
Food and live animals	1,460.9	7.2	4,855.6	17.5
Beverages and tobacco	193.7	1.0	477.2	1.7
Crude materials (inedible), except fuels	405.1	2.0	560.4	2.0
Mineral fuels and lubricants	666.9	3.3	119.1	0.4
Animal and vegetable oil, fats and waxes	79.9	0.4	23.6	0.1
Chemicals and related products	2,624.2	12.9	5,193.3	18.8
Manufactured goods	2,340.4	11.5	1,341.3	4.8
Machinery and transport equipment	8,626.3	42.3	9,568.2	34.6
Miscellaneous manufactured articles	2,294.7	11.3	4,005.6	14.5
Other	1,655.2	8.1	1,536.6	5.6
TOTAL TRADE:	**20,347.3**	**100.0**	**27,680.9**	**100.0**

REPUBLIC OF IRELAND VALUE OF EXPORTS AND IMPORTS, 1975-1997

Year*	Imports (IR£m)	Exports (IR£m)	Trade balance (IR£m)
1975	1,704	1,447	-257
1980	5,421	4,082	-1,339

1985	9,428	9,743	315
1990	12,469	14,337	1,868
1995	20,347	27,681	7,334
1996	22,346	30,084	7,738
1997†	23,727	32,617	8,890

Value at current prices   † Forecast

REP. OF IRE. VOLUME AND PRICE OF EXPORTS AND IMPORTS, 1990 -1995

Year	Volume Index Imports	Volume Index Exports	Price Index Imports	Price Index Exports
1990	100.0	100.0	100.0	100.0
1991	100.8	105.6	102.3	99.3
1992	105.6	121.1	100.2	96.6
1993	113.0	133.4	105.4	103.9
1994	127.9	153.2	108.1	103.0
1995	146.2	183.9	112.7	105.7

NORTHERN IRELAND MANUFACTURING COMPANIES EXPORT SALES, 92/93 - 95/96

	92-93 (£STGm)	93-94 (£STGm)	94-95 (£STGm)	95-96 (£STGm)
Total Sales	6,827	7,267	7,848	8,705
Northern Ireland	2,425	2,578	2,631	2,826
External Sales	4,402	4,689	5,217	5,879
Great Britain	2,422	2,514	2,614	2,806
Export Sales	1,980	2,175	2,603	3,073
Republic of Ireland	498	544	631	710
Rest of European Union	879	916	1,047	1,242
Rest of World	603	715	925	1,121

NORTHERN IRELAND MANUFACTURING COMPANIES EXPORT SALES BY SECTOR 95/96

Sector	Total Sales (£STGm)	External Sales (£STGm)	Exports (£STGm)
Food, drink and tobacco	2,796	1,548	663
Textiles, clothing and leather	1,098	955	271
Transport equipment	742	693	374
Electrical and optical equipment	714	648	421
Other machinery and equipment	687	597	407
Chemicals and man-made fibres	596	463	393
Rubber and plastics	505	375	227
Paper and printing	403	173	102
Other non-metallic mineral products	345	93	53
Basic metals and fabricated metal products	343	147	76
Wood and wood products	286	90	38
Other manufacturing	190	97	48
TOTAL:	8,705	5,879	3,073

TONNAGE: EXPORTS AND IMPORTS - N.I, 1992/96

Year	Imports by Tonnage	Exports by Tonnage
1992	12,937	4,392
1993	13,859	4,688
1994	14,830	4,958
1995	14,952	5,083
1996	14,918	4,981

FINANCE

EXCHANGE RATE OF REPUBLIC OF IRELAND IR£, 1980-1994

Year	US dollar	Sterling	DM	ECU
1980	2.06	0.89	3.73	1.48
1985	1.07	0.82	3.11	1.40
1990	1.66	0.93	2.67	1.30
1994	1.43	0.98	2.42	1.26
1995	1.60	1.01	2.30	1.23
1996	1.60	1.03	2.41	1.28
1997†	1.56	0.95	2.62	1.35

† Average for first and second quarter.

PURCHASING POWER OF THE IR£, 1922-1995

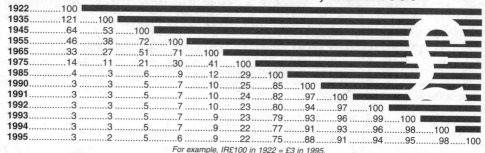

1922	100												
1935	121	100											
1945	64	53	100										
1955	46	38	72	100									
1965	33	27	51	71	100								
1975	14	11	21	30	41	100							
1985	4	3	6	9	12	29	100						
1990	3	3	5	7	10	25	85	100					
1991	3	3	5	7	10	24	82	97	100				
1992	3	3	5	7	10	23	80	94	97	100			
1993	3	3	5	7	9	23	79	93	96	99	100		
1994	3	3	5	7	9	22	77	91	93	96	98	100	
1995	3	2	5	6	9	22	75	88	91	94	95	98	100

For example, IR£100 in 1922 = £3 in 1995.

R.O.I. BALANCE OF INTERNATIONAL PAYMENTS 1990 -96

Year	Current A/C Balance IR£m	Capital A/C Balance IR£m	Net Residual IR£m
1990	-224	-1,290	1,514
1991	209	-1,169	960
1992	320	-589	269
1993	1,248	-2,016	768
1994	998	-2,217	1,219
1995	1,070	-934	-136
1996	862	-1,241	379

R.O.I. CURRENT ACCOUNT 1996 - 1999

	1996 (iR£m)	*1997 (IR£m)	†1998 (IR£m)	†1999 (IR£m)
Current Expenditure:				
Central Fund Services	3,161	3,260	3,354	3,435
Supply Services	9,501	10,131	10,585	10,965
Total	12,662	13,391	13,939	14,400
Current Revenue:				
Taxation	12,520	13,263	13,869	14,584
Non Tax	434	321	311	339
Total	12,954	13,584	13,584	14,923
Current Budget Surplus	292	193	241	523
% of GNP	0.8%	0.5%	0.6%	1.2%

* Post-Budget Estimate   † Projection

R.O.I. CURRENT EXPENDITURE 1996

Sector	% of Expenditure
Health	15.2
Security	7.2
Infrastructure	0.6
Service of public debt	15.2
Education	13.9
Social welfare	28.8
Other social services	1.1
Economic services *(industry, agriculture, tourism)*	7.5
Other	10.5
TOTAL	**100.0**

REPUBLIC OF IRELAND CURRENT REVENUE 1996

Sector	% of Expenditure
Income tax	35.1
Value Added Tax	24.9
Excise duties	17.8
Corporation tax	10.3
Stamp duties	2.2
Motor vehicle duties	2.1
Customs	1.6
Agricultural levies	0.1
Employment and training levy	1.3
Capital taxes	1.0
Non-tax revenue	3.6
TOTAL	**100.0**

R.O.I. CAPITAL ACCOUNT 1996 - 1999

	1996 (IR£m)	*1997 (IR£m)	†1998 (IR£m)	†1999 (IR£m)
Capital Expenditure:				
Exchequer Capital Programme	1,458	1,579	1,602	1,581
Other *(non programme)*	78	26	100	150
Total	1,536	1,605	1,702	1,731
Capital Resources:				
Exchequer Capital Resources	807	775	780	835
Exchequer Borrowing for Capital Purposes	(729)	(830)	(922)	(896)
Exchequer Borrowing Requirement (E.B.R.) before contingency	(437)	(637)	(681)	(373)
General Contingency Provision	-	-	175	325
E.B.R with contingency	(437)	(637)	(856)	(698)
E.B.R. as % of G.N.P.	1.2%	1.6%	1.6%	0.8%

* Post Budget Estimate † Projection

R.O.I. NATIONAL DEBT , 1977-96 (IR£M)

	1977	1987	1990	1996
Domestic Debt	3,190	14,001	16,235	21,194
Foreign Debt	1,039	9,693	8,848	8,718
Total national Debt	**4,229**	**23,694**	**25,083**	**29,911**
General Government Debt	-	24,636	26,600	32,000

INTEREST COST OF R.O.I. NATIONAL DEBT, 1990-96

Year	IR£m
1990	2,109
1991	2,132
1992	2,106
1993	2,076
1994	2,029
1995	1,963
1996	2,052

CURRENCY COMPOSITION OF FOREIGN DEBT (R.O.I.)

Currency	(IR£m)	%
Sterling	2,430	27.9
U.S. dollar	1,741	20.0
Deutschmark	1,326	15.2
French franc	1,208	13.9
Swiss franc	988	11.3
Yen	411	4.7
E.C.U.	244	2.8
Dutch guilder	122	1.4
Others	248	2.8
TOTAL	8,718	100.0

R.O.I. NATIONAL BORROWING TREND 1992 - 1997

Year	Current Budget Deficit/Surplus (IR£m)	% of G.N.P.	Exchequer Borrowing Requirement (E.B.R. - IR£m)	% of G.N.P.	Public Sector Borrowing Requirement (IR£m)	% of G.N.P.
1990	(152)	(0.6)	462	1.9	588	2.4
1991	(298)	(1.2)	499	2.0	762	3.0
1992	(446)	(1.7)	713	2.7	910	3.4
1993	(379)	(1.3)	690	2.5	862	3.1
1994	15	0.1	672	2.2	782	2.6
1995	(362)	(1.1)	627	1.9	826	2.5
1996	292	0.8	437	1.2	531	1.5
1997*	193	0.5	637	1.6	764	1.9

*1997 figures are the Budget Target predictions. However, exchequer returns for the half year to 30/6/97 showed a current budget surplus of £721m. Therefore, the E.B.R. is expected to be 'less than IR£300m' and not the budget target of IR£637m.

N.I. GROSS DOMESTIC PRODUCT 1993 - 1995

Industry	1993 £Stg. m	1994 £Stg. m	1995 £Stg. m	1995 %
Agriculture, fisheries and forestry	542	625	678	4.9
Mining and quarrying	59	72	82	0.6
Manufacturing	2,430	2,531	2,707	19.5
Electricity, gas and water	375	380	408	2.9
Construction	701	695	763	5.5
Distribution, hotels and catering	1,561	1,645	1,807	13.0
Transport and communication	632	676	700	5.0
Financial and business services	1,764	1,884	1,962	14.2
Public administration and H.M. Forces	1,824	1,831	1,860	13.4
Education and health services	2,070	2,317	2,310	16.7
Other services	503	560	591	4.3
GROSS DOMESTIC PRODUCT	12,463	13,216	13,868	100.0
GDP per head	£7,637	£8,050	£8,410	

N.I. PUBLIC EXPENDITURE: 94/95 - 97/98

Sector	94-95 £Stg. m	95-96 £Stg. m	96-97 £Stg. m	97-98 £Stg. m
Law, order and protective services	921	893	858	858
National agriculture and fisheries support	141	162	165	172
N.I. agriculture, forestry and fisheries support	160	142	149	149
Industry, energy, trade and employment	432	452	474	478
Transport	177	174	170	168
Housing	226	240	248	267
Envirnomental and Miscellanous services	206	237	222	231
Fire Service	40	41	43	44
Education, arts and libraries	1,295	1,350	1,395	1,423
Health and personal social services	1,418	1,529	1,577	1,622

Social security	2,253	2,434	2,549	2,639
Other public services	75	88	56	58
Euro-regional funded expenditure	62	79	108	100
Total	**7,407**	**7,823**	**8,015**	**8,210**

THE BRITISH SUBVENTION TO NORTHERN IRELAND

Year	Amount (£STGm)	% of Public Spending
1969-70	73	16
1978-79	945	43
1981-82	1,024	32
1984-85	1,413	35
1987-88	1,554	32
1990-91	1,975	34
1993-94	3,390	51

NORTHERN IRELAND: LOCAL AUTHORITY EXPENDITURE: 92/93 - 95/96

Sector	94/95 Current £STGm	95/96 Current £STGm	94/95 Capital £STGm	95/96 Capital £STGm
Agriculture, fisheries and forestry	0	0	1	2
Energy	6	7	7	7
Roads & transport	1	1	6	7
Environmental services	102	108	17	19
Education, arts and libraries	56	59	18	20
Total:	**165**	**175**	**49**	**54**

ECONOMIC STATISTICS 1995 - 1997

Year	Real Change 1995 %	Real Change 1996 %	Real Change 1997 %
NORTHERN IRELAND:			
Gross Domestic Product	+3.0	+3.0	+3.0
Consumer Spending	+2.5	+3.0	+3.5
Personal Disposal Income	+2.5	+3.0	+3.8
Industrial Output	+4.0	+2.0	+3.0
REPUBLIC OF IRELAND:			
Gross National Product	+7.7	+5.0	+4.0
Inflation	+2.5	+1.6	+1.8

BANKING AND POST OFFICES

REPUBLIC OF IRELAND BANKING STATISTICS*

* includes data compiled by the Irish clearing banks only.	1992	1993	1994	1995	1996
Current accounts (IR£m)	1.75	1.83	1.90	2.20	2.10
Deposit/savings accounts (IR£m)	5.24	5.24	4.71	4.72	4.4
No. of A.T.M. cards in circulation (m)	1.5	2.1	2.0	1.7	2.1
No. of A.T.M. transactions (m)	51	64	74	90	97
Value of A.T.M. transactions (IR£m)	2,400	2,500	3,200	3,700	4,200
No. of Credit cards in circulation (m)	0.84	1.0	1.1	1.3	1.4
No. of Credit card transactions (m)	19	26	30	37	39
Value of credit card transactions (IR£m)	800	1,100	1,300	1,800	1,800
No. of Cheques issued (m)	151	164	159	154	n/a
Value of cheques issued (IR£m)	264,000	323,000	342,000	351,000	n/a
No. of Direct debits (m)	33	31	32	42	n/a
Value of direct debits (IR£m)	11,000	34,000	36,000	40,000	n/a
No. of Credit transfers (m)	44	71	73	93	n/a
Value of credit transfers (IR£m)	50,000	290,000	302,000	237,000	n/a

R.O.I. BANKING INDUSTRY* PERFORMANCE, 1990- 96

Year	After Tax Profits IR£m	Total Assets IR£bn	No. of Branches	No. of Employees
1990	174	39.1	705	17,500
1991	194	40.0	705	17,900
1992	251	42.0	714	19,300
1993	414	46.1	705	19,800
1994	537	48.6	726	20,200
1995	575	55.0	729	20,500
1996	669	57.3	732	20,800

*Statistics for clearing banks only

IRISH BANKING EUROPEAN COMPARISONS 1996

Country	Population million	No. of Banks	No. of Employees	No. of Branches	Employees Per Branch	Population Per Branch
Austria	8,015	57	16,171	738	21.91	10,860
Belgium	10,155	145	76,133	7,668	9.93	1,324
Britain	58,375	483	307,900	11,678	26.37	4,999
Denmark	5,226	121	43,010	2,215	19.42	2,359
Finland	5,108	11	21,153	755	28.02	6,766
France	58,147	421	202,000	10,497	19.24	5,539
Germany	81,610	331	217,550	7,522	28.92	10,850
Greece	10,478	40	45,138	2,733	16.52	3,834
Iceland	270	3	2,070	128	16.17	2,109
IRELAND	3,582	55	21,000	964	21.78	3,716
Italy	57,284	351	335,426	21,061	15.93	2,720
Luxembourg	407	220	18,255	356	51.28	1,143
Netherlands	15,458	174	103,939	6,635	15.67	2,330
Norway	4,350	20	13,937	453	30.77	9,603
Portugal	9,846	47	58,892	3,729	15.79	2,640
Spain	39,234	170	147,452	17,841	8.26	2,199
Sweden	8,885	26	39,505	2,267	17.43	3,919
Switzerland	7,010	285	109,200	1,894	57.66	3,701
TOTAL	441,920	3,438	2,143,031	111,134	20.62	3,976

NORTHERN IRELAND BANKING STATISTICS

Bank	Head Office	No. of Branches, agencies and sub offices	Authorised Capital £STGm	Issued Capital £STGm	Paid Up Capital £STGm
Northern Bank Ltd	Belfast	119	100	88	88
Ulster Bank Ltd	Belfast	108	150	105	105
Bank of Ireland	Dublin	46	1,074	497	497
First Trust Bank (AIB Group)	Belfast	76	20	20	20

NORTHERN IRELAND FINANCE HOUSES, CREDIT EXTENDED, 1991 - 1995

	1991 £STGm	1992 £STGm	1993 £STGm	1994 £STGm	1995 £STGm
Private cars - new	85.3	88.5	110.0	124.9	121.2
Private cars - second-hand	116.4	115.3	124.3	131.9	149.2
Commercial motor vehicles - new	28.2	27.8	36.7	40.8	57.1
Commercial motor vehicles - second-hand	18.2	20.0	22.2	24.0	26.8
Farm Equipment - new	3.8	4.0	2.5	3.3	3.5
Farm Equipment - second-hand	1.0	1.1	2.2	2.8	3.4
Industrial Equipment - new	16.1	15.2	16.4	20.2	31.3
Industrial Equipment - second-hand	7.8	7.9	10.1	9.4	11.3
All other goods	45.7	38.2	51.5	55.4	58.2
Total new credit extended:	322.5	318.0	375.9	412.7	462.0

INVESTMENT RETURNS 10 YEAR PERIOD

IR£10,000 invested	10 Years IR£	7 Years IR£	5 Years IR£
Pension Funds:			
Average fixed interest fund	31,694	20,398	16,189
Average general equity fund	29,044	18,423	19,285
Average Irish equity fund	28,108	17,476	21,221
Average international fund	30,234	19,387	18,000
Average managed growth fund	29,053	19,363	18,252
Deposits:			
An Post 11th Saving Certs	n/a	15,683	14,002
E.B.S. Top Yield	16,099	13,726	12,140
F.N.B.S. Inv. Share	14,531	12,549	11,193
Ir. Permanent Supergro 60	16,213	13,809	12,146
National Ir. Demand Deposit	13,000	11,773	10,818
A.I.B. Demand	12,817	11,630	10,682
An Post Deposit Account	13,664	12,194	11,144
A.I.B. Cashsave	11,987	11,089	10,481

This table shows how IR£10,000 invested in deposit accounts performed against pension funds in the last 10 years.

REPUBLIC OF IRELAND: POST OFFICE NETWORK AND STATISTICS

	1992	1993	1994	1995	1996
MAIL:					
Letter Post: Items delivered *(million)*	483.5	518.1	551.7	559.8	578.0
Pieces of mail per capita	137.2	146.9	156.5	158.8	159.6
SYSTEM SIZE:					
No. of Delivery Points *(million)*	1.144	1.178	1.208	1.232	1,260
POST OFFICE NETWORK:					
Company Post Offices	95	95	95	96	96
Sub Post Offices	1,907	1,876	1,854	1,838	1,825
Total: Post Office Network	**2,002**	**1,971**	**1,949**	**1,934**	**1,921**
Other Company Premises	36	38	38	40	41
No. of Postal Motor Vehicles	2,020	2,147	2,208	2,214	2,239
PERSONNEL:					
Headquarters	477	487	481	484	541
Savings Services	215	211	204	190	184
Remittance Services	71	75	71	68	67
Inspection	35	35	38	45	40
Postmen/women	4,264	4,323	4,058	4,066	3,876
Postal Sorters	539	530	648	766	759
Post Office Clerks	1,210	1,165	1,125	1,154	1,244
Other Grades	771	827	765	737	718
Temporary	598	879	711	515	681
Total: Personnel	**8,180**	**8,532**	**8,101**	**8,025**	**8,110**
Postmasters: Engaged as Agents	1,907	1,876	1,854	1,838	1,825

NORTHERN IRELAND: PARCELFORCE STATISTICS

Operational Statistics	1994-95	1995-96
Traffic *(parcels)*	599,000	725,000
Revenue *(£Stg)*	2,789,000	3,323,000

HOUSING AND PROPERTY

REPUBLIC OF IRELAND HOUSE PRICES 1996

Location	New IR£	Secondhand IR£
Dublin	78,222	83,760
Cork	68,558	63,206
Galway	76,179	66,655
Limerick	53,777	55,315
Waterford	67,380	51,648
Other areas	69,222	61,957
NATIONAL AVERAGE	71,592	69,599

N. IRELAND PROPERTY PRICES, 1995 - 1997

Location	1995 £Stg.	1996 £Stg.	1997 £Stg.
Belfast	45,085	51,885	57,604
North Down	51,195	58,020	55,424
Lisburn	52,274	57,003	56,876
East Antrim	44,577	49,507	53,276
Derry/Strabane	47,260	52,993	56,554
Antrim/Ballymena	45,905	50,307	53,982
Coleraine/Limavady	48,237	54,798	56,382
Enniskillen/Fermanagh/S.Tyrone	51,531	55,087	58,398
Mid-Ulster	46,165	49,125	49,178
Mid & South Down	52,996	56,830	60,166
Craigavon/Armagh	43,208	51,013	47,025
NATIONAL AVERAGE	47,665	53,483	55,751

R.O.I. AVERAGE NEW HOMES PRICES, 1993 - 1996

Year	Dublin IR£	Whole Country IR£
1993	59,500	55,000
1994	65,000	57,300
1995	69,066	61,466
1996	78,222	71,592

N.I. AVERAGE HOUSE PRICES 1990 - 1997

Year	Average Price £STG	% Increase
1990	34,372	2.5
1991	38,105	10.9
1992	37,171	-2.5
1993	39,491	6.2
1994	42,263	7.0
1995	47,665	12.8
1996	53,483	12.2
1997	55,751	4.2

NORTHERN IRELAND HOUSE PRICES 1997

Type of Property	Price £Stg.
Detached House	89,696
Semi-Detached House	51,112
Terrace	35,171
Detached Bungalow	70,656
Semi-detached Bungalow	49,924
All Property	55,751

COST OF PROPERTY RETAIL RENTS

	Dublin IR£	Belfast IR£	Derry IR£	Provincial N.I IR£	Provincial R.O.I IR£
Zone A Retail Rents (IR£/Sq Ft/Annum)	180	140	70	35 - 55	25 - 40

CAPITAL GROWTH IN PROPERTY, 1990 - 1996

Year	Industrial Property % Growth	Office Property % Growth	Retail Property % Growth
1990	12.3	6.1	2.9
1991	-2.5	-7.5	-5.4
1992	-5.7	-10.2	-7.5
1993	1.6	-3.1	0.7
1994	10.1	5.5	7.6
1995	4.9	3.4	5.6
1996	9.0	7.1	7.4

INCOME RETURN FROM PROPERTY, 1990 - 1996

Year	Industrial Property % Return	Office Property % Return	Retail Property % Return
1990	9.9	6.2	6.2
1991	8.6	5.8	6.3
1992	9.0	6.4	7.1
1993	10.5	8.0	8.6
1994	11.2	8.8	8.7
1995	10.3	8.4	8.5
1996	10.4	8.6	8.5

% SHARE OF MORTGAGE MARKET, 1992 - 1996

	1992 %	1993 %	1994 %	1995 %	1996 %
Banks	70.8	62.9	54.4	32.9	33.8
Building Societies	27.6	36.0	45.0	66.6	65.9
Local Authorities	1.6	1.1	0.6	0.5	0.3

R.O.I. CONSUMER PRICE INDEX, 1994 - 1997

Year	Base: Nov. 1989 = 100	Increase (%)
1994	112.4	2.4
1995	115.2	2.5
1996	117.1	1.6
1997 *	118.0	0.1

* Average 4 months Jan - April 97

PROPERTY COSTS: INTERNATIONAL COMPARISONS

Location	Rent Prime Offices (IR£ / Sq Ft / Annum)	Rent Prime Industrial (IR£ / Sq Ft / Annum)
London	46.3	8.3
Frankfurt	33.9	5.3
Paris	31.3	9.5
Berlin	24.1	4.8
Milan	18.1	5.2
Lisbon	17.8	7.1
DUBLIN	18.0	6.0
Amsterdam	17.0	4.5
Brussels	16.1	4.5
Madrid	15.5	3.6

Barcelona ....12.0...4.3
BELFAST ....9.3...4.0

INTEREST RATES, 1990 - 1996

Year	* Mortgage Rate (%)	† Associated Banks Overdraft Rate (%)	Interbank Rate (%)
1990	11.00 - 11.70	10.50	11.10
1991	10.75 - 11.45	11.30	10.70
1992	13.75 - 14.45	19.00	18.00
1993	7.75 - 8.45	7.00 - 7.40	6.60
1994	6.85 - 7.25	6.21 - 6.25	5.75
1995	6.85 - 7.79	6.00 - 6.13	5.45
1996	6.50 - 6.75	5.73 - 5.75	5.20

Rates shown are for the end of periods 1990 - 1995. The rates shown for 1996 are those for quarter two.
* The mortgage rate refers to a building society annuity rate.
† The overdraft rate are percentages charged to large commercial borrowers for short-term borrowings

N.I. CONSUMERS' EXPENDITURE, 1990 - 1994

Industry	1990 £m	1991 £m	1992 £m	1993 £m	1994 £m
Food	1,085	1,143	1,208	1,245	1,248
Alcoholic Drink	414	457	479	525	584
Clothing and Footwear	607	753	776	690	720
Tobacco	251	296	327	342	353
Housing	899	1,011	1,143	1,310	1,456
Fuel and Power	390	429	426	426	424
Household & Services	570	601	644	647	668
Transport & Communications	1,607	1,596	1,573	1,625	1,785
Recreation, Entertainment, Education	634	632	668	770	870
Other Goods and Services	1,248	1,377	1,524	1,636	1,726
Household Expenditure Abroad	436	452	450	443	447
CONSUMERS' EXPENDITURE	8,141	8,745	9,219	9,660	10,283
Personal Disposable Income	9,158	10,243	11,091	11,800	12,372
Balance : Saving	1,017	1,498	1,872	2,140	2,089
SAVING RATIO (%)	11.1	14.6	16.9	18.1	16.9

WHO'S WHO IN IRISH BUSINESS

Brosnan, Dennis (born Tralee, 1944) Managing director Kerry Group plc. Principal founding partner of Kerry Co-operative. Helped develop Kerry into the largest food-processing company in Ireland. Also has interests in the leisure and bloodstock industries.

Desmond, Dermot Controls the International Investment and Underwriting (IIU) company. Investments include 13.1% of Unidare, 10% of Celtic football club, 20% of Esat Digifone, 100% of London City Airport and 7.5% of Radio Ireland. Recently sold two of his companies, NCB Stockbrokers and Quay Financial Software and a portion of the south block in the IFSC.

Downes, Margaret (born 1934) Chartered accountant and businesswoman. Partner in Coopers and Lybrand (1964-84). In 1984, she became the first woman to become a director of Bank of Ireland. Holds numerous directorships in the U.K and Ireland and is a trustee of the Chester Beatty Library and the Douglas Hyde Gallery.

Duggan, Noel C. (born Cork, 1933) Left school aged 13. Developed family hardware business into a lucrative structural steel trade. Built a major equestrian centre, Green Glens (1990-93), which hosts international showjumping and entertainment events. Succeeded in bringing the Eurovision Song Contest to Millstreet in 1993.

Dunne, Ben (born 1949) Dunne was the principal developer of the Dunnes Stores retail empire founded by his father, Ben. He sold his stake in the business three years ago under acrimonious circumstances to his brothers and sisters. He was said to have incurred a £40m. tax liability on the breaking up of the Dunnes Stores trust. Since leaving Dunnes Stores he has made a number of low profile investments and these with other assets make his estimated wealth around £80m.

Goodman, Larry (born Co. Louth, 1939) Chief executive of Irish Food Processors. In the mid-1980s, his company, Goodman International was the largest processor and exporter of beef in Europe. In 1992 the group went into examinership with debts of over £500 million and subsequently came under intense scrutiny from the beef tribunal. Goodman later regained control of the group through an agreement with its creditors

Haughey, Edward (born Co. Louth, 1944) Founded Norbrook Laboratories in 1969 with an initial capital of £1,200. The company now exports to over 100 countries and is the world's largest producer of veterinary ethical sterile injectibles. He is also the Irish Aviation Authority chairman and a director of Shorts.

Heffernan, Margaret (born 1943) Heffernan's fortune is based on the £600m. Dunnes Stores group of companies. Together with her brother Frank she has had a greater say in the running of the company since their brother Ben was sacked as chairman in 1994. Her ownership of the business came from being a beneficiary of the Dunnes Trust and an interest held via a company called Ringmahon.

Magnier, John (born 1952) Owns Coolmore Stud in partnership with Vincent O' Brien and Robert Sangster. Coolmore stud controls about 42% of British and Irish thoroughbred horse breeding. Its Irish Interests are worth £33m. alone due primarily to its tax free status and it also has assets in Kentucky and Australia. Magnier also operates in international finance markets together with JP McManus and Joe Lewis.

Mahony, Tim (born 1932) The first major distributor of Toyota motor vehicles in Ireland, Mahony saw the turnover of his company, Killeen Investments, reach £130m. in 1996. Other assets include the 1,400 acre Mount Juliet sporting estate and hotel in Co. Kilkenny.

McManus, JP (born 1951) Became a bookmaker at 20, but switched to the other side of the rails on finding gambling more rewarding. Nicknamed the Sundance Kid for his duels with British bookmakers in the 1970s. He now plays the international foreign exchange markets from a base in Geneva. Other assets include a stud farm, 90 horses and a share in the Sandy Lane hotel in Barbados.

McCann, Neil (born Louth, 1924) Chairman and chief executive of Fyffes plc. Fyffes is the largest fruit importing and distributing business in Ireland and Spain and a major operator in other markets.

McGuinness, Gerard (born Dublin, 1938) After an early career in advertising, he founded the *Sunday World* - Ireland's first tabloid newspaper - in 1972. The paper quickly established itself as one of the great success stories of modern Irish journalism.

O' Reilly, Tony (born Dublin, 1936) Chief executive of Heinz International. Has numerous other commercial activities, including Fitzwilton, Waterford, Independent Newspapers and global media interests. His combined wealth with wife Chryss Goulandris is estimated at £1,000 million.

Panoz, Don (born 1935) Founded Elan, the Athlone pharmaceuticals company, in 1969 with $50,000. He has since become rich through selling shares in the company. In four years he has raised more than £120m. and now holds less than 1% of the equity worth more than £15m. Other assets include a leisure complex in Georgia.

Quinn, Fergal (born 1936) Supermarket owner. Opened his first store in Dundalk in 1960 ('Superquinn') and went on to open a number of branches in the Dublin suburbs in the following decades. Served as chairman of An Post 1979-90. Senator since 1993.

Quinn, Lochlan (born 1942) Owns 26% of Glen Dimplex, the domestic appliance manufacturer. A brother of Ruairí Quinn, he is also the chairman of AIB. He has a 25% share of the £25m. Merrion hotel in Dublin with his partner in Glen Dimplex, Martin Naughton.

Quinn, Seán (born Fermanagh, 1946) Head of family company, the Seán Quinn Group Ltd. He left school at age 15 in 1973 to found company from shale reserves under family farm. Net worth is now estimated at £130 million. The company manufactures cement, concrete floor and quarry products. It has a hotel and leisure division, comprising 11 pubs and 7 hotels, and a direct insurance division.

Robinson, Gerard (born Donegal, 1948) Major figure in British television market and is chairman of LWT, ITN and BSkyB. Chief executive of the giant media and leisure group Granada. Successfully bid £3.9 billion for control of Forte hotel and catering group in 1995.

Ryan, Tony (born Co. Tipperary, 1936) Founded Guinness Peat Aviation in 1975. The business developed into a major international group leasing planes to some 100 airlines around the world. However, it collapsed in 1992 after a failed flotation. In 1996 he became the non-executive chairman of Ryanair, the independent Irish airline controlled by his sons.

Smurfit, Michael (born 1936) Director and chief executive of Jefferson Smurfit Corp. since 1977. Through his initiative and drive, Smurfits developed from a small family business to a major multinational in packaging, print and financial services. Has served as chairman of Telecom Éireann and the Racing Board and is currently honorary consul for Ireland in Monaco.

Sutherland, Peter (born 1946) Attorney-General (1981-2 and 1982-4) in Fine Gael-Labour coalition governments and E.C. Commissioner (1985-9) with responsibility for competition policy. Returned to Ireland at the end of his term to become chairman of A.I.B. and director of a number of other companies. In June 1993, he became director general of GATT. Recently appointed chairman of Goldman Sachs group.

INDUSTRY

Irish Businesses and America

*By **Willie McCarter**, Chairman International Fund for Ireland.*

W HEN people who want to start out in business for themselves or people who are running small and medium-sized businesses who want another product or service or indeed a new business to develop, one very good source of ideas is to look to the United States of America and Canada.

The reason for this is that in the United States and Canada there are large and vibrant economies which are continually producing new products and services. Frequently, in small and medium-sized business in North America the products and services never find their markets outside of a regional area of the United States or Canada. For this reason, in a lot of cases, there is tremendous opportunity for taking the products and services of U.S. and Canadian businesses and developing them for the European Union market. In the U.S. alone, there have been something like 4 million new jobs created over the last three to four years - a lot of them in new industries and new businesses.

People in this part of the world who are looking to start businesses or looking for new products or services for existing businesses could do well to turn to agencies such as Forbairt, Udaras na Gaeltachta or the IDA in the Republic or LEDU or the IDB in Northern Ireland. These Agencies have quite a number of contacts, and indeed programmes, to help people and companies in this part of the world to acquire products and services coming out of the U.S. and Canada to use Ireland as a bridge to the European Union.

The International Fund for Ireland has a number of programmes partnering the development agencies in helping to build partnerships with North America.

From 1985 to 1987 our family company W.P. McCarter & Co. Ltd. of Buncrana, Co. Donegal, decided to try seeking a joint venture in the U.S. and as a result, over the next ten years, turned 470 jobs into nearly 3,000 with the Fruit of the Loom company.

The same kind of thing can be done perhaps on a slightly lesser scale by a lot of people in this part of the world simply by determination in deciding what sort of product or service they want and what kind of partnership they want with the U.S. or Canadian company and then devoting time and effort in order to make it happen. In this process the developrnent agencies, both north and south, can be of considerable assistance, and there are also private companies which can be very helpful in this kind of process.

Certainly, for anybody who is looking for a new product or service, this is an avenue that too many people do not realise the full potential of and that where, provided time and effort is put into it, good results can be obtained.

The author is the Chairman of the International Fund for Ireland.

INTRODUCTION

REPUBLIC OF IRELAND: When the modern Irish state was founded in 1922 the industrial sector was made up of a small number of manufacturers largely in the traditional sectors - food, drink, textiles - producing almost exclusively for the home market. The 1930s saw the introduction of protectionist measures to encourage the expansion of indigenous industry, but by the 1950s, it was clear that these measures were causing economic stagnation rather than development. Ireland's industrial breakthrough had its roots in a change in direction towards export-based industrial development which emerged in the late 1950s.

In 1952, Coras Trachtála was established, and 1958 saw the first tax incentives introduced to encourage the expansion of industrial exports. The Anglo-Irish Free Trade Agreement in 1965 contributed to the opening-up of the Irish economy, and this was quickly followed by accession to the E.E.C. in 1973. In the early 1970s, the I.D.A. encouraged industry in export-orientated growth sectors such as electronics, pharmaceuticals and engineering to set up in Ireland. Exports of goods and services amounted to 37% of GNP in 1973, 56% in 1983 and 90% in 1995. The table below demonstrates best how Ireland changed from an economy heavily dependant on agriculture to one more reliant on services and industry.

SECTORAL SHARES IN EMPLOYMENT			
Sector	1949	1979	1995
Agriculture (%)	42.9	19.3	11.3
Industry (%)	21.5	31.9	27.7
Services (%)	35.6	48.8	61.0

In the mid -1980s, the economy faced a number of serious difficulties, the most important of which were rising unemployment, substantial emigration and a rapidly rising national debt. To deal with these problems, the Government, employers and trade unions agreed in 1987 on a three-year Programme for National Recovery. This emphasised fiscal and monetary stabilisation, tax reform and pay moderation. It was followed by two other initiatives: the Programme for Economic and Social Progress (1991-93) and the Programme for Competitiveness and Work (1994-97).

Over the period of these programmes, economic growth has been over twice the E.U. average, inflation has fallen to one of the lowest rates in the E.U., emigration has declined significantly and employment in the private non-agricultural sector has shown an annual average growth of about 2.5%. Improved fiscal management in budgetary matters has resulted in Ireland having one of the lowest government deficits in the E.U. The 1995 *World Competitiveness Report*, rating the competitive position of almost 50 countries, ranked Ireland 10th on the 'internationalisation' criteria which measured trade and inward investment strength.

NORTHERN IRELAND: The history of industry in Northern Ireland is much less clear. A number of factors have played a part in confusing the picture - inter-communal violence, a worldwide decline in the old traditional industries and the North's economic dependency on the British economy. In addition, as part of Britain, it has not received the same E.C. support as the Republic because of the different criteria applied to assess the economic needs of both countries. Further complications have arisen from the fact that the Troubles have actually created employment, particularly in the security and public sector areas.

During the period 1968 to 1986, manufacturing jobs in Northern Ireland declined from 172,000 to 105,000. In contrast, the Republic saw an increase during the same period from 196,000 to 224,000. The New Ireland Forum's Economic Report indicated that the total economic cost of violence up to 1982 was in excess of £1.63 billion, while an independent economic research study in 1987 estimated that violence had cost 40,000 jobs from 1971 to 1983. According to a British Government paper of 1993, Northern Ireland was by far the most economically disadvantaged area of the U.K. and was one of the least prosperous regions in the E.C.

In 1991, public sector employment reached almost 40 percent of the total workforce in Northern Ireland (175,000 people employed) compared with just over 20% in 1960. It is estimated that 35,000 of the new jobs have been created by the Troubles. Northern Ireland annually receives a subvention from the British Exchequer. For the year 1994/1995 this amounted to £7.6 billion which did not include a further £90 million allocated to the Department of Agriculture and Fisheries.

Recent years have seen a dramatic improvement in industry in Northern Ireland. A permanent end to violence and political stability are the keys to further growth in Northern Ireland's industries.

MANUFACTURING

REPUBLIC OF IRELAND EMPLOYMENT FIGURES CLASSIFIED BY ECONOMIC SECTOR

Economic Sector (1996)	Males (Thousand)	Females (Thousand)	Total
Agriculture, Forestry and Fishing	121.8	14.7	136.5
Other Production Industries	188.5	76.4	264.9
Building and Construction	81.7	4.3	86.0
Commerce, Insurance, Finance and Business Services	153.8	118.9	272.7
Transport, Communications and Storage	62.3	17.8	80.1
Public Administration and Defence	48.1	28.3	76.4
Professional Services	84.1	154.5	238.6
Other	56.9	73.1	130.0
Total: All Economic Sectors	797.2	488.0	1,285.2

NORTHERN IRELAND EMPLOYMENT FIGURES CLASSIFIED BY ECONOMIC SECTOR

Economic Sector (1996)	Males Thousand	Females Thousand	Total
Agriculture, Forestry and Fishing	16.4	2.3	18.7
Manufacturing	68.8	33.0	101.8
Construction	20.2	2.4	22.6
Transport, Communications and Storage	16.4	5.2	21.6
Public Administration and Defence	35.6	23.8	59.4
Wholesale and Retail Trade, Repairs	42.6	47.1	89.7
Hotels and Restaurants	10.4	16.9	27.3
Financial Intermediation	5.3	8.2	13.5
Real Estate Renting and Business Activities	14.9	18.0	32.9
Education	17.7	45.1	62.8
Health and Social Work	16.0	72.9	88.9
Self-Employed - Agriculture	18.5	1.3	19.8
Self-Employed - Production	22.1	1.0	23.1
Self-Employed - Services	25.5	9.2	34.7
Other	19.8	13.9	33.7
Total: All Sectors	350.2	300.3	650.5

LABOUR FORCE STATISTICS (1996)

	Republic of Ireland	Northern Ireland
Civil Employed & Trainees:		
Males	797,300	360,000
Females	488,000	306,300
Total	**1,285,300**	**666,300**
Unemployed :		
Males	137,700	65,500
Females	52,200	19,200
Total	**189,900**	**84,700**
Total In Labour Force :		
Males	935,000	425,500
Females	540,200	325,500
Total	**1,475,200**	**751,000**
Employment (1995) In :		
Agriculture	11.3%	6.1%
Industry	27.7%	24.6%
Services	61.0%	69.3%
Total	**100.0%**	**100.0%**

R.O.I. PUBLIC SECTOR EMPLOYMENT FIGURES

Sector	1993 Thousand	1994 Thousand	1995 Thousand	*1996 Thousand
Prison Officers	2.3	2.5	2.5	2.5
Non-Industrial - Civil Service	26.5	26.0	27.0	26.8
Industrial - Civil Service	1.8	2.0	2.0	2.2
Others - Civil Service	0.6	0.6	0.5	0.6
Defence	14.0	14.3	14.0	13.5
Garda Síochána	11.2	10.8	10.7	10.7
Education - Primary	21.5	21.4	21.5	21.4
Education - Secondary	16.8	17.4	17.7	17.6
Education - Third level	7.9	8.1	9.0	7.7
VEC (Incl RTCs)	16.9	16.7	17.7	14.2
Local Authorities	29.0	28.9	28.6	29.6
Other Regional Bodies	1.4	1.5	1.5	1.8
Commercial Semi State Companies	56.6	55.6	55.0	55.7
Non-Commercial Semi-State Companies	7.8	7.9	7.9	8.1
Health Boards	39.7	40.8	41.8	†41.8
Voluntary Hospitals	22.1	23.2	23.4	†23.4
TOTAL PUBLIC SECTOR:	276.1	277.7	280.8	277.6

Employment figures at Sept. 1996   † Employment figures at Dec. 1995

N.I. PUBLIC SECTOR EMPLOYMENT FIGURES

Department	1993 Thousand	1994 Thousand	1995 Thousand	1996 Thousand
Economic Development	2.8	2.6	2.5	2.6
Health and Social Services	8.1	7.9	7.8	8.0
Agriculture	4.2	4.0	3.8	3.8
Finance and Personnel	1.4	1.4	1.4	1.4
Education	0.7	0.6	0.6	0.6
Environment	9.5	9.0	8.5	8.4
Royal Ulster Constabulary	16.6	16.6	16.8	16.5
Prison Service	3.3	3.2	3.2	3.1
Fire Service	2.1	2.2	2.2	2.2
Northern Ireland Office	1.4	1.4	1.4	1.4
Other N.I. Central Government	0.1	0.1	0.1	0.1
Bodies under the aegis of NI Central Govt	85.6	84.0	71.8	72.4.
U.K. Central Government	6.2	6.3	6.2	6.2
Local Government	9.2	9.2	8.8	9.0
N.I.-based Public Corporations	11.9	8.0	7.7	7.5
U.K.-based Public Corporations	4.4	4.5	4.4	4.4
N.H.S. Trusts	30.5	33.6	48.2	48.0
TOTAL PUBLIC SECTOR:	198.0	194.8	195.3	195.6

REPUBLIC OF IRELAND MANUFACTURING INDUSTRIES EMPLOYMENT FIGURES

Annual Year	Average (000)	Annual Year	Average (000)
1990	191.8	1993	194.0
1991	193.9	1994	199.3
1992	193.9	1995	211.5

REPUBLIC OF IRELAND INDUSTRIAL WORKERS WEEKLY EARNINGS, 1990 -1995

Year	Avg weekly Earnings (IR£)	Increase on Previous Year (IR£)	Hours Worked (%)	Earnings Per Hour (IR£)
1990	225.16	4.0	41.4	5.43
1991	235.23	4.5	41.0	5.73
1992	244.27	3.8	40.6	6.01
1993	258.00	5.6	40.5	6.36
1994	265.13	2.8	41.0	6.47
1995	270.70	3.6	40.9	6.62

NORTHERN IRELAND ADULT EMPLOYEES GROSS WEEKLY EARNINGS, 1992 -1996

Year	Avg weekly Earnings - Male (£STG)	Increase on Previous Year (%)	Average weekly Earnings - Female (£STG)	Increase on Previous Year (%)
1992	298.20	9.5	224.20	11.2
1993	313.60	5.2	232.50	3.7
1994	319.20	1.8	236.70	1.8
1995	330.90	3.7	251.40	6.2
1996	337.40	2.0	256.90	2.2

INDUSTRIAL WORKERS' AVERAGE WEEKLY EARNINGS IN REPUBLIC OF IRELAND

Industry sector	1992 (ir£)	1993 (ir£)	1994 (ir£)	1995 (ir£)
Overall Average: All Industries	245.34	261.84	264.42	270.97
Clothing, Footwear and Leather	136.19	143.69	150.15	153.44
Chemicals	319.15	332.41	343.82	344.42
Drink and Tobacco	380.49	388.07	404.47	418.13
Electricity, Gas and Water	314.56	366.75	362.05	365.02
Food	224.61	242.95	243.26	253.83
Manufacturing Industries	238.86	252.51	255.96	264.25
Metals and Engineering	234.15	243.05	249.32	259.17
Mining, Quarrying and Turf	333.78	377.26	383.58	361.68
Miscellaneous Industries (rubber/plastic, etc.)	235.36	244.42	253.56	255.59
Non-Metallic Mineral Products	295.37	309.88	317.32	327.54
Paper and Printing	293.03	314.24	307.67	321.82
Textile Industry	195.14	210.89	207.96	210.29
Timber and Wooden Furniture	191.67	215.61	204.35	210.04
Transportable Goods Industries	241.17	255.75	259.12	266.36

N.I. AVERAGE GROSS WEEKLY EARNINGS

Industry sector	1995 (£STG) Male	1996 (£STG) Male	1995 (£STG) Female	1996(£STG) Female
Overall Average: All Industries	330.9	337.4	251.4	256.9
Agriculture, Hunting and Forestry	172.7	180.3	-	-
Mining and Quarrying	-	287.2	-	-
Manufacturing	289.4	300.1	189.9	195.2
Electricity, Gas and Water Supply	399.4	398.5	-	-

Construction	313.3	295.5	-	-
Wholesale and Retail Trade	268.5	287.0	194.2	191.1
Hotels and Restaurants	211.2	191.6	195.7	177.0
Transport, Storage and Communication	315.7	323.1	212.2	281.1
Financial Intermediation	513.9	531.9	324.5	297.3
Real Estate, Renting and Business Activities	288.6	301.1	199.9	212.7
Public Administration and Defence	421.9	423.0	258.2	264.2
Education	412.1	407.2	347.0	356.6
Health and Social Work	360.8	364.1	268.0	279.6
Other	262.6	292.8	182.4	221.3

Full-time adult employees including overtime

REPUBLIC OF IRELAND AVERAGE HOURLY EARNINGS COMPARISON TABLE, 1987-95*

Year	UK	Germany	France	Italy	USA	Japan	Ireland
1987	100.00	100.00	100.00	100.00	100.00	100.00	100.00
1988	114.80	103.10	102.70	104.90	102.60	113.70	104.20
1989	123.30	106.40	107.20	116.70	113.60	117.80	108.10
1990	127.70	111.90	114.40	125.60	103.30	102.30	114.30
1991	141.10	117.40	118.70	135.50	110.30	118.10	120.80
1992	140.30	131.10	125.20	138.30	111.10	120.80	127.50
1993	135.70	142.20	133.60	124.70	126.10	152.80	128.40
1994	140.00	148.10	136.70	124.50	127.50	166.50	131.70
1995	134.10	157.30	140.40	116.50	119.10	116.10	131.00

Indices are in common currency terms.

1997 AVERAGE HOURLY LABOUR COST COMPARISON TABLE

Country (Rate £1 = $1.56)	$	£	Country (Rate £1 = $1.56)	$	£
Germany	31.88	21.25	Finland	24.45	16.30
Switzerland	28.34	18.90	France	19.34	12.90
Belgium	26.07	17.38	Italy	18.08	12.05
Norway	24.95	16.64	Britain	14.19	9.45
Netherlands	23.33	15.55	REPUBLIC OF IRELAND	14.12	9.41
Japan	21.04	14.02	Spain	13.29	8.86
Denmark	24.38	16.25	NORTHERN IRELAND	12.79	8.52
Sweden	24.56	16.37	Portugal	5.37	3.58
U.S.	17.74	11.82			

ANNUAL PAY RATES IN REPUBLIC OF IRELAND AND NORTHERN IRELAND

Public Service: *	Republic of Ireland (IR£ - 1996)	Northern Ireland (£STG - 1995)
Lowest grade	8,191 - 12,167	6,928 - 9,826
Highest grade	76,173	82,415

* based on selected pay scales

INTERNATIONAL UNEMPLOYMENT 1997 (%)

Country	(1997) %	Country	(1997) %
Spain	22.2	European Union	10.8
NORTHERN IRELAND	9.6	Belgium	9.9
France	11.6	REPUBLIC OF IRELAND	11.7
Italy	12.4		

SEASONALLY ADJUSTED UNEMPLOYMENT STATISTICS

Year	Republic of Ireland (%)	Northern Ireland (%)	Republic of Ireland (Number)	Northern Ireland (Number)
1990	13.3	12.8	176,000	95,300
1991	14.7	12.9	209,000	99,100
1992	15.5	13.8	221,000	104,700
1993	15.6	13.7	230,000	103,700
1994	14.1	12.6	221,000	97,100
1995	12.2	11.4	190,000	88,100
1996	11.9	10.9	177,600	84,000

UNEMPLOYMENT IN IRELAND (1996)

Area	% Unemployed	Area	% Unemployed
NORTHERN IRELAND		**REPUBLIC OF IRELAND**	
Ballymena	6.0	Border	15.2
Belfast	8.2	Dublin	12.3
Coleraine	11.2	Mid-East	10.3
Cookstown	13.0	Midland	9.6
Craigavon	7.6	Mid-West	9.0
Dungannon	11.1	South-East	12.5
Enniskillen	11.1	South-West	11.7
Derry	13.3	West	11.7
Magherafelt	9.8		
Newry	13.1		
Omagh	10.9		
Strabane	15.3		

REPUBLIC OF IRELAND STRIKES: NUMBER AND DAYS LOST, 1986-1995

Year	Total No.	Total days lost	Official No.	Official days lost	Unofficial No.	Unofficial days lost	Public Sector No.	Public Sector days lost	Private Sector No.	Private Sector days lost
1986	100	315,500	62	295,500	38	20,500	35	246,000	65	69,500
1987	76	260,000	54	235,000	22	25,000	30	148,500	46	111,500
1988	72	130,000	46	123,500	26	6,500	24	69,000	48	61,000
1989	41	41,400	28	29,800	13	11,600	14	8,000	27	33,400
1990	51	203,700	35	196,900	16	6,800	19	6,500	32	197,200
1991	52	82,960	39	73,645	13	9,315	31	55,000	21	27,900
1992	41	189,623	30	186,819	11	2,804	15	52,100	26	137,600
1993	48	65,027	39	60,212	9	4,815	19	43,100	29	29,900
1994	32	24,000	27	20,203	5	3,797	11	6,000	21	18,000
1995	36	130,556	29	129,702	7	854	20	23,050	16	107,506

N.I. STRIKES: NUMBER AND DAYS LOST, 1986-1995

Year	Number	Days lost	Workers Affected
1986	49	35,135	16,976
1987	45	100,772	31,621
1988	32	53,577	35,500
1989	73	32,281	28,177
1990	24	18,322	12,479
1991	12	16,926	16,805
1992	5	7,734	3,905
1993	7	15,723	15,870
1994	14	4,949	3,849
1995	7	4,919	4,391

IDA-SUPPORTED JOBS IN THE REPUBLIC OF IRELAND, 1994 - 1996

Description	1994	1995	1996
Total New Jobs Filled	9,867	11,676	13,319
Job Losses	4,743	5,155	5,828
Net Change	5,124	6,521	7,491
First-time Jobs Filled	8,348	10,166	11,937
Total Full-time employment in IDA companies	83,453	89,974	97,465
Total Temporary Contract Employment	8,970	11,398	9,563
Corporation Tax paid by IDA Companies	£443m	£410m	£520m
Total Number of IDA Companies	906	961	1,047
Total IDA Grants Paid	£73 m	£95 m	£143m
Average Cost-per-job Sustained over 7 years	£13,263	£12,193	£11,920

SALES OF IDB COMPANIES IN NORTHERN IRELAND BY DESTINATION

Country	1994/95 £Stg M	% Change 1993/94 - 1994/95
Northern Ireland	1,733	4.6
Britain	2,466	3.1
Republic of Ireland	471	10.3
Rest of Europe	1,071	18.7
Rest of World	944	29.2
TOTAL SALES	6,665	9.4
Total External Sales	4,932	11.3
Total Exports	2,486	20.7

IDB-SUPPORTED JOBS IN NORTHERN IRELAND, 1993/94 - 1995/96

Description	1993-94	1994-95	1995-96
Total New Jobs filled	5,512	5,992	6,593
Job Losses	4,601	4,519	4,967
Net Change	911	1,473	1,626
New projects by externally owned companies	34	36	35
New projects by locally owned companies	43	40	28
Total projects with new companies	77	76	63
Investment by externally owned companies	£321m	£252m	£432m
Investment by locally owned companies	£184 m	£142m	£75m
Total Investment by new companies	£505m	£394m	£507m
IDB assistance given to externally owned companies	£78m	£66m	£133m
IDB assistance given to locally owned companies	£49m	£36m	£18m
Total IDB assistance	£127m	£102m	£151m
Total IDB Contribution (%) to new companies	25%	26%	30%

REPUBLIC OF IRELAND BREWING INDUSTRY STATISTICS

Description	Units
Value of Irish Beer Market	£1.6bn
Volume of Irish Beer Market	4.9m hectolitres
Public Houses in Republic of Ireland	10,500
No. of people employed in brewing industry	44,000
Stout share of beer market	47%
Lager share of beer market	42%

ORIGINS OF IDA-ASSISTED OVERSEAS COMPANIES IN REPUBLIC OF IRELAND

Country of origin	Number
U.S.A.	429
Germany	139
Britain	156
Rest of Europe	223
Asia - Pacific	57
Rest of World	43
TOTAL	1,047

REPUBLIC OF IRELAND FOOD INDUSTRY STATISTICS 1994 - 1996

Industry Sector	1994	1995	*1996
Dairy Sector:			
Output (gallons)	1.1bn	1.1bn	1.1bn
Output	£1.8bn	£2.0bn	£1.9bn
Exports	£1.4bn	£1.6bn	£1.5bn
Employment	7,988	7,792	8,168
Beef Sector			
No. Slaughtered	1.27bn	1.3bn	1.0bn
Exports	411,800 tonnes	420,312 tonnes	438,000 tonnes
Employment	4,876	4,737	4,796
Sheep meat Sector			
No. Slaughtered	3.6m	3.6m	3.7m
Exports	62,400 tonnes	64,500 tonnes	66,200 tonnes
Employment	1,000	1,000	1,050
Pig meat Sector			
No. Slaughtered	3.3m	3.2m	3.0m
Output	£283m	£350m	£403m
Exports	£170m	£210m	£230m
Employment	3,220	3,170	2,955
Prepared Consumer Foods Sector			
Output	£.95bn	£1.08bn	£1.2bn
Exports	£400m	£478m	£592m
Employment	8,900	10,375	11,227
Fish Processing Sector			
Output	£270m	£300m	£350m
Exports	£185m	£213m	£225m
Employment	2,363	2,460	2,013

* Estimate

R.O.I. INDUSTRIAL PRODUCTION 1991 - 1995 *

Industry	1991	1992	1993	1994	1995
Non-metallic Mineral Products	109.5	113.8	109.8	121.3	132.4
Chemicals	181.5	212.9	234.0	279.4	324.0
Metals & Engineering	184.3	205.7	218.4	252.7	337.1
Food	136.5	149.1	156.7	168.9	187.2
Drink & Tobacco	122.9	122.4	122.3	129.6	136.2
Textiles	119.0	125.5	128.4	131.8	132.9
Clothing, Footwear & Leather	77.2	73.6	68.8	65.8	63.5
Timber & Wooden Furniture	117.5	120.4	121.9	134.6	141.8
Paper & Printing	151.1	165.1	176.6	180.2	199.9
Miscellanous Industries	127.5	133.1	130.2	140.9	150.5
Total Manufacturing Industries	153.9	169.6	178.8	201.6	242.1
Percentage Change	3.2%	10.2%	5.4%	12.8	20.1

Mining & Quarrying	107.0	98.6	114.6	116.4	137.4
Total Transportable Goods Industries	152.4	167.3	176.7	198.8	238.7
Electricity, Gas & Water	116.0	120.4	127.1	133.5	137.9
All Industries	**148.4**	**162.2**	**171.3**	**191.7**	**227.9**
Percentage Change	**3.2%**	**9.3%**	**5.6%**	**11.9%**	**18.9%**

* Volume Index (1985 = 100)

TRADE UNIONS IN IRELAND

The Irish Congress of Trade Unions (I.C.T.U.) is the main body for the trade union movement in Ireland. The central function of the I.C.T.U. is to co-ordinate the work of trade unions operating in Ireland. In all, 66 unions are affiliated to the I.C.T.U., 50 of which are based in the Republic, and overall membership is estimated at 682,211. The membership of the Amalgamated Transport and General Workers' Union (A.T.G.W.U.) and Services Industrial Professional Technical Union (S.I.P.T.U.) accounts for 44% - 208,000 members - of the total membership of the I.C.T.U. in the Republic. Thirty-two of the unions affiliated to the I.C.T.U. have their headquarters in Northern Ireland and in Britain, with 17 unions organising in both the Republic and Northern Ireland. Unions not affiliated to the I.C.T.U. represent about 3% of total union membership in the Republic of Ireland and 8% in Northern Ireland.

Irish Congress of Trade Unions
19 Raglan Road, Ballsbridge, Dublin 4. Tel: (01) 668 0641
Northern Ireland Office:
3 Wellington Park, Belfast BT9 6DJ. Tel: (0801232) 681726

AFFILIATED UNIONS

Amalgamated Engineering and Electrical Union: Hayes Court, West Common Road,Bromley, Kent. Members: 27,010
Amalgamated Transport and General Workers' Union: Transport House, Smith Square, London. Members: 54,487
Association of First Division Civil Servants: 2 Caxton Street, London SW1H 0QH. Members: 332 (Northern Ireland).
Association of Higher Civil Servants: 4 Warner's Lane, Dartmouth Road, Dublin 6. Members: 1,880
Association of Irish Traditional Musicians: 32 Cearnóg Belgrave, Monkstown, Co. Dublin. Members: 120
Association of Secondary Teachers, Ireland: ASTI House, Winetavern Street, Dublin 8. Members: 14,900
Association of University Teachers: United House, 9 Pembridge Road, London. Members: 1,434 (Northern Ireland).
Automobile, General Engineering and Mechanical Operatives Union: 22 North Frederick Street, Dublin 1. Members: 2,063
Bakery and Food Workers'

Amalgamated Union: 37 Lower Gardiner Street, Dublin 1. Members: 886
British Actors' Equity Association: Guild House, Upper St. Martin's Lane, London. Members: 400
Broadcasting, Entertainment, Cinematograph and Theatre Union 111, Wardona Street, London Members: 592
Building and Allied Trades Union: Arus Hibernia, Blessington Sreet, Dublin 7. Members: 8,030
Chartered Society of Physiotherapy: Royal Victoria Hospital, Grosvenor Road, Belfast. Members: 905
Civil Service Alliance: Four Courts, Dublin 7. Members: 83
Civil and Public Services Association: 160 Falcon Road, London. Members: N.I 656
Civil and Public Service Union: 72 Lower Leeson Street, Dublin 2. Members: 12,003
Communications Managers' Association: Hughes House, Ruscombe Road, Twyford, Reading, Berkshire. Members: N.I 228
Communications Managers' Union: 577 North Circular Rd., Dublin 1. Members: 1,035
Communication Workers' Union: Aras Ghaibréil, 575 North Circular Road, Dublin 1. Members: 19,600
Communication Workers' Union: CWU House, Crescent Lane, London. No. of Members: 5,797
Cork Operative Butchers' Society: 55 North Main Street, Cork. Members: 95

ESB Officers' Association: 43 East James's Plc., Lower Baggot St., Dublin 2. Members : 2,375
Federated Union of Government Employees: 32 Parnell Sq., Dublin 1. Members : 1,300
Fire Brigades' Union: Bradley House, 68 Coombe Road, Kingston-upon-Thames, Surrey. Members: 1,500 (Northern Ireland)
General Municipal Boilermakers: 22-23 Worple Road, London. Members : 18,726
Graphical, Paper and Media Union: 63-67 Bronham Road, Bedford . Members : 6,530
Guinness Staff Association: St. James's Gate, Dublin 8. Members : 1,142
Irish Municipal, Public and Civil Trade Union: Nerney's Court, Dublin 1. Members: 30,000
Institution of Professionals, Managers and Specialists: 75-79 York Road, London. Members: 351
Irish Airline Pilots' Association: Corballis Park, Dublin Airport, Dublin. Members: 516
Irish Bank Officials' Association: 93 St. Stephen's Green, Dublin 2. Members: 15,640
Irish Federation of Musicians and Associated Professions: 63 Lower Gardiner Street, Dublin 1. Members: 562
Irish Federation of University Teachers: 11 Merrion Sq., Dublin 2. Members: 1,320
Irish Medical Organisation: 10 Fitzwilliam Place, Dublin 2.

Members: 3,000

Irish National Teachers' Organisation: 32 Parnell Square, Dublin 1. Members: 23,222

Irish Nurses' Organisation: 11 Fitzwilliam Place, Dublin 2. Members: 14,100

Irish Print Union: 35 Lower Gardiner Street, Dublin 1. Members: 2,587

Irish Veterinary Union: 32 Kenilworth Square, Dublin 6. Members: 639

MANDATE: 9 Cavendish Row, Dublin 1. Members: 29,136

Marine, Port and General Workers' Union: 14 Gardiner Place, Dublin 1. Members: 3,000

Manufacturing Science Finance: 64-66 Wandsworth Common, Northside, London . Members: 31,000

National Association of Probation Officers: 3-4 Chivalry Road, Battersea, London. Members: N.I 131

National Association of Teachers in Further and Higher Education: 27 Britannia Street, London. Members: N.I 1,921

National League of the Blind of Ireland: 21 Hill Street, Dublin 1. Members: 120

National Union of Insurance Workers: 27 Old Gloucester Street, London. Members: N.I 265

National Union of Journalists: Acorn House, 314-321 Gray's Inn Road, London. Members: 3,692

National Union of Knitwear, Footwear and Apparel Trades: 55 New Walk, Leicester. Members: 346 (Northern Ireland)

National Union of Rail, Maritime and Transport Workers: Unity House, Euston Road, London. Members: 356

National Union of Sheet Metal Workers of Ireland: 6 Gardiner Row, Dublin 1. Members: 730

Northern Ireland Musicians' Association: 3rd Floor, Unit 4, Fortwilliam Business Park, Dargan Rd., Belfast. Members: 1,003

North of Ireland Bakers, Confectioners and Allied Workers' Union: 80 High Street, Belfast. Members: N.I 1,002

Northern Ireland Public Service Alliance: 54 Wellington Park, Belfast. Members: 35,160

Operative Plasterers and Allied Trades Society of Ireland: Arus Hibernia, 13 Blessington Street, Dublin 7. Members: 2,001

Prison Officers' Association: Millmount Hse, Upper Drumcondra Road, Dublin 9. Members: 2,300

Public Service Executive Union: 30 Merrion Square, Dublin 2. Members: 6,500

Public Services, Tax and

Commerce Union: 5 Great Suffolk St., London. Members: 1,574

Sales, Marketing and Administrative Union of Ireland: 37 Lower Gardiner Street, Dublin 1. Members: 620

Seamen's Union of Ireland: 61 North Strand Road, Dublin 3. Members: 620

Services Industrial Professional Technical Union: Liberty Hall, Dublin 1. Members: 225,000

Teachers' Union of Ireland: 73 Orwell Road, Rathgar, Dublin 6. Members: 9,349

Technical, Engineering and Electrical Union: 5 Cavendish Row, Dublin 1. Members: 24,206

Transport Salaried Staffs' Association: Walken House, 10 Melton Street, Euston, London. Members: 2,134

Union of Construction, Allied Trades and Technicians: Abbeyville Rd., Clapham, London. Members: 12,020

Union of Shop, Distributive and Allied Workers: 188 Wilmslow Road, Fallowfield, Manchester. Members: N.I 6,099

UNISON: 1 Mabledon Place, London. Members: N.I 31,650

Veterinary Officers' Association: 4 Warner's Lane, Dartmouth Road, Dublin 6. Members: 320

SECTORAL ANALYSIS OF UNION MEMBERSHIP

Industry Sector	Union Membership
Buildings & Construction	43%
Production	54%
Retail & Finance	30%
Transport and Communications	71%
Professional Services	57%
Public Administration & Defence	76%
Part-time Workers	20%

FATAL ACCIDENTS IN THE WORKPLACE

Sector	1993	1994	1995	1996
Agriculture, Hunting & Forestry	21	22	28	13
Fishing	7	1	19	8
Construction	11	10	13	9
Manufacturing	7	4	4	4
Mining and Quarrying	3	1	0	1
Transport, Storage & Communication	7	6	9	8
Electricity, Gas & Water	3	1	0	0
Other	5	5	5	15
TOTAL	64	50	78	58
Non-fatal Accidents	3,986	4,823	4,880	n/a

AGRICULTURE

INTRODUCTION

The B.S.E. scare, which started in March 1996, continued to be the single most important issue in Irish agriculture in 1997. In February, the Department of Agriculture in Dublin confirmed the scare had cost the Irish beef industry £500 million. In Northern Ireland, things have scarcely improved since 1996. The plea that northern farmers be treated differently from British farmers, because the computerised registration of all cattle in Northern Ireland reduces the likelihood of infected meat entering the food chain, fell on deaf ears in Europe. The moratorium stands.

Agriculture's place at the centre of the Irish economy has changed. In the Republic in 1960, agriculture was a £2 billion industry, providing a quarter of the country's £8.3 billion Gross Domestic Product. By 1994, the GDP had risen to almost £31 billion, but by this time, agriculture had slipped from 25 per cent of GDP to 9 per cent. Farm sizes are growing; in 1980, there was almost 70,000 farms of ten hectares and less, but by the mid-nineties, there was less than 40,000 such farms. The number of people working on farms is also shrinking. Between 1987 and 1995 over 1.25 million hectares has been lost the by farming industry.

In Northern Ireland the impact was similar, though agriculture remains an important industry, giving employment to almost 60,000 people and worth in excess of £1 billion annually to the economy. The usage of land has changed significantly in this decade; between 1992 and 1996, there has been an eleven per cent drop in the amount of land producing crops. While it can be seen that more land is used for grazing than previously, the total amount of land used for agricultural production has dropped by 9,000 hectares in just four years.

REPUBLIC OF IRELAND & NORTHERN IRELAND: AGRICULTURAL BODIES/ORGANISATIONS

Bord Bia, An (Irish Food Board) *Clanwilliam Court, Lower Mount Street, Dublin 2. Tel. (01) 6685155.*

Bord Glas, An (Horticultural Development Board) *8-11 Lower Baggot Street, Dublin 2. Tel. (01) 6763567.*

Bord Iascaigh Mhara (Irish Sea Fisheries Board) *Crofton Road, Dun Laoghaire, Co. Dublin. Tel. (01) 2841544.*

Bord na Móna (Irish Peat Board) *Main Street, Newbridge, Co. Kildare. Tel. (045) 439000.*

British Wool Marketing Board *20 Tirgracey Road, Muckamore, Co. Antrim BT41 4PS. Tel. (01494) 64919.*

Central Fisheries Board *Balnagowan, Mobhi Boreen, Glasnevin, Dublin 9. Tel. (01) 8379206.*

Coilte (Irish Forestry Board) *Leeson Lane, Dublin 2. Tel. (01) 6615666.*

Food from Britain *109 Church Street, Portadown, Craigavon, Co. Armagh BT62 3DB. Tel. (01762) 333144.*

Foyle Fisheries Commission *8 Victoria Road, Derry BT47 2AB. Tel. (01504) 42100.*

Livestock and Meat Commission *57 Malone Road, Belfast, Co. Antrim BT9 6SA. Tel. (01232) 381022.*

Marine Institute *80 Harcourt Street, Dublin 2. Tel. (01) 4780333.*

National Milk Agency *19 Sandymount Avenue, Dublin 4. Tel. (01) 6603396.*

Nitrigin Éireann Teoranta *Wilton Park House, Wilton Place, Dublin 2. Tel. (01) 6681204.*

Northern Ireland Agricultural Producers' Association *15 Molesworth Street, Cookstown, Co. Tyrone BT80 8NX. Tel. (016487) 65700.*

Northern Ireland Food & Drink Association *Interpoint, 20 York Street, Belfast, Co. Antrim. Tel: (01232) 468360*

Northern Ireland Meat Exporters' Association *24 Balldown Road, Banbridge, Co. Down. Tel: (018206) 24657*

Pigs Marketing Board for Northern Ireland *Bridgewater House, Bridge Street, Lisburn, Co. Antrim. Tel. (01846) 677070.*

Royal Ulster Agricultural Society *Showgrounds, Balmoral, Belfast, Co. Antrim BT9 6GW. Tel. (01232) 665225.*

Seed Potato Promotions (NI) Ltd *Cathedral Buildings, 64 Donegall Street, Belfast, Co. Antrim BT1 2GT. Tel. (01232) 230490.*

Teagasc (Agriculture & Food Development Authority) *19 Sandymount Avenue, Ballsbridge, Dublin 4. Tel. (01) 6688188.*

Ulster Agricultural Organisation Society Ltd. *109 Church Street, Portadown, Co. Armagh. Tel: (01762) 333144*

Ulster Farmers' Union *475 Antrim Road, Belfast, Co. Antrim BT15 3BP. Tel. (01232) 370222.*

AGRICULTURAL LANDS MARKET IN THE R.O.I.

Year	Average Price (IR£) / ha. Agricultural land
1990	1,606
1991	1,508
1992	1,574
1993	1,582
1994	1,695
1995	1,771

PERSONS FARMING IN NORTHERN IRELAND

Persons (000's)	1993	1994	1995	1996
Farmers, Partners & Directors:				
Full-time	21.3	21.2	20.2	19.5
Part-time	13.1	14.2	14.1	14.9
Total: Farmers, Partners & Directors	34.4	35.4	34.3	34.4
Family Workers:				
All Spouses	5.8	5.5	6.0	6.0
Other Family (Full-time)	2.1	1.9	1.8	1.7
Other Family (Part-time)	4.7	4.3	4.4	4.2
Other Family (Casual / Seasonal)	3.4	3.4	3.7	3.6
Total: Family Workers	16.0	15.1	15.9	15.5
Hired Workers:				
Full-time	1.9	1.8	1.8	1.8
Part-time	1.3	1.3	1.3	1.3
Casual / Seasonal	6.1	6.0	6.4	6.1
Total: Hired Workers	9.3	9.1	9.5	9.2
GRAND TOTAL:	**59.7**	**59.6**	**59.7**	**59.1**

R.O.I. PERSONS IN FARMING, 1991

Category	Males	Females	Persons
Farmers (horse, pig or poultry)			
Under 10 acres	16	2	18
10 acres and under 15	3	3	6
15 acres and under 30	8	2	10
30 acres and under 40	3	1	4
40 acres and under 50	4	1	5
50 acres and under 70	9	-	9
70 acres and under 100	3	2	5
100 acres and under 150	13	2	15
150 acres and under 200	2	1	3
200 acres and more	41	6	47
area not stated	122	26	148
Total	**224**	**46**	**270**
Other Farmers:			
Under 10 acres	1,400	141	1,541
10 acres and under 15	2,604	243	2,847
15 acres and under 30	12,506	1,168	13,674
30 acres and under 40	12,017	920	12,937
40 acres and under 50	11,808	862	12,670
50 acres and under 70	19,755	1,128	20,883
70 acres and under 100	17,356	894	18,250
100 acres and under 150	13,610	687	14,297
150 acres and under 200	5,005	257	5,262
200 acres and more	4,180	235	4,415
area not stated	4,510	273	4,783
Total	**104,751**	**6,808**	**111,559**
Farmers' sons (in-law) and daughters (in-law) assisting	11,257	65	11,322
Farmers' other relatives assisting	3,527	6,116	9,643
Farm Managers	1,152	96	1,248
Agricultural Labourers	13,610	835	14,445
Other Agricultural Workers	3,037	579	3,616
GRAND TOTAL:	**137,558**	**14,545**	**152,103**

AGRICULTURE IN RELATION TO POPULATION AND LABOUR FORCE IN REPUBLIC OF IRELAND

Persons (000's)	1987	1992	1995
Total Population	3,546	3,549	3,582
Total Labour Force	1,323	1,360	1,423
Total at work:	1,090	1,139	1,231
Agriculture, Forestry & Fishing	164	153	139
Industry	300	318	342
Services	626	668	751
Agriculture	159	148	133
Agriculture as % of total at work	14.6%	13.0%	10.8%

R.O.I. AGRICULTURAL WAGES

Age	Minimum Weekly Rate from:				
	March '94	February '95	October '95	June '96	December '96
15 years and under 16	75.48	76.99	78.91	80.88	81.69
16 years and under 17	89.20	90.98	93.25	95.58	96.54
17 years and under 18	102.93	104.99	107.61	110.30	111.40
18 years and under 19	116.64	118.97	121.97	124.99	126.24
19 years and over	137.24	139.98	143.48	147.07	148.54

N.I. AGRICULTURAL WAGES

Earnings & Hours	1986	1990	1994	1995
Average Hourly Earnings	£2.45	£3.10	£3.93	£4.00
Average Weekly Hours	42.21	42.22	42.84	42.80
Average Weekly Earnings	£105.60	£130.86	£168.53	£171.20

R.O.I.: GROSS AGRICULTURAL OUTPUT

Produce (IR£m)	1987	1992	1994	1995
Livestock and Products:				
Cattle	1,057	1,267	1,282	1,324
Milk and Dairy Products	982	1,078	1,141	1,204
Pigs	144	221	200	233
Poultry and Eggs	111	134	135	137
Sheep and Lambs	128	153	169	155
Horses	68	49	62	58
Wool and Other Products	9	6	10	12
Total:	**2,499**	**2,908**	**2,999**	**3,123**
Crops and Turf:				
Barley	106	104	58	87
Wheat	32	72	36	46
Sugar Beet	59	57	60	61
Potatoes	59	56	76	75
Fresh Vegetables	62	93	108	107
Other Crops / Fruit	20	38	40	50
Turf	35	36	24	24
Total:	**373**	**456**	**402**	**450**
Gross Agricultural Output	2,872	3,364	3,401	3,573
Inputs of Materials & Services	1,179	1,380	1,563	1,653
Gross Agricultural Product at Market Prices	1,692	1,984	1,838	1,920
Subsidies less Levies	491	361	638	711
Gross Agricultural Product at Factor Cost	1,810	2,345	2,476	2,631
Depreciation	-292	-347	-359	-379
Wages & Land Annuities	-130	-181	-178	-182
Income from Self-Employment & Other Work	1,386	1,816	1,937	2,069

N.I.: GROSS AGRICULTURAL OUTPUT

Livestock / Product	Unit of Quantity	Quantity 1994	1995	Value (£m) 1994	1995
Livestock:					
Finished Cattle & Calves	000 head	501.0	493.0	414.6	414.4
Finished Sheep & Lambs	000 head	1,571.0	1,555.0	95.8	96.6
Finished Pigs	000 head	1,273.0	1,203.0	83.9	95.9
Poultry	000 tonnes (d.w.t.)	105.7	108.4	77.4	78.1
Total Livestock:		**345.07**	**3,359.4**	**671.7**	**685.0**
Products:					
Eggs	m. dozen	74.6	75.8	35.8	39.6
Milk	m. litres	1,375	1,380.0	288.9	338.4
Total Products:		**1,449.6**	**1,455.8**	**324.7**	**378.0**
Other Livestock / Products		0	0	12.1	12.6
TOTAL:		**1,794.67**	**4,815.2**	**1,008.5**	**1,075.6**

N.I.: GROSS AGRICULTURAL OUTPUT

Product	Tonnes (000) 1994	1995	Value (£m) 1994	1995
Crops:				
Potatoes	192.4	195.5	24.0	34.7
Barley	61.5	68.6	10.5	14.2
Wheat	30.9	32.4	4.5	5.3
Oats	4.2	5.3	0.8	1.0
Other Crops	0	0	2.1	2.0
Total Crops:	**289.0**	**301.8**	**41.9**	**57.2**
Products:				
Fruit	36.1	41.8	5.3	6.8
Vegetables	45.0	40.8	8.7	9.2
Mushrooms	22.9	23.2	27.2	30.4
Flowers	0	0	8.5	8.5
Total Products:	104.0	105.8	49.7	54.9
TOTAL:	**393.0**	**407.6**	**91.6**	**112.1**

REPUBLIC OF IRELAND: AGRICULTURAL PRODUCTION AND EXPORTS

Value of Exports (IR£m)*	1987	1992	1994	1995
Beef	590.1	615.4	773.4	770.5
Live Cattle	115.7	67.1	119.5	109.6
Dairy Products	725.1	1,242.5	1,009.9	1,246.2
Pigs, Pork and Bacon	61.3	144.5	126.5	141.8
Sheep, Mutton and Lamb	59.3	134.5	143.5	101.7
Horses and Horsemeat	48.3	39.9	56.6	39.0
Food Preparations	640.6	893.7	1,444.7	1,743.7
Other Agricultural Exports	453.6	615.9	706.4	777.1
Total Agricultural Exports	2,693.9	3,753.6	4,380.5	4,929.6
TOTAL EXPORTS:	10,723.5	16,628.8	22,753.4	27,296.7
Agriculture & Food as % of total	25.1%	22.6%	19.3%	18.1%

Export-related subsidies are not included.

R.O.I.: SELECTED PRICES FOR FARM PRODUCTS

Product (IR£/Unit)	unit	1987	1992	1994	1995
Wheat	tonne	121.7	111.7	94.1	117.9
Feed Barley	tonne	106.0	104.6	88.8	106.7
Malting Barley	tonne	115.2	121.4	95.9	126.8
Potatoes	tonne	69.0	86.0	184.0	155.0
Sugar Beet	tonne	36.7	42.0	44.4	40.2
Creamery Milk	litre	0.176	0.203	0.218	0.232
Bullocks (450-499 kg)	100 kg lwt	124.0	118.1	131.0	128.9
Heifers (350-399 kg)	100 kg lwt	108.0	108.7	122.3	118.6
Pigs (25-34 kg)	head	30.9	31.2	27.1	33.1
Sheep (40-49 kg)	head	51.5	38.0	46.3	44.4

N.I.: SELECTED PRICES FOR FARM PRODUCTS

Product (£Stg. / Unit)	unit	1992	1993	1994	1995
Finished steers, heifers & young bulls	head	600	672	698	717
Finished steers, heifers & young bulls	kg dwt	1.97	2.24	2.23	2.22
Calves slaughtered or exported	head	158	158	160	154
Culled cows & bulls	head	405	495	491	518
Culled cows & bulls	kg dwt	1.47	1.78	1.74	1.76
Store cattle exported	head	383	432	442	456
Finished sheep & lambs	head	32.60	39.57	43.85	42.96
Finished sheep & lambs	kg dwt	1.70	2.03	2.16	2.05
Culled ewes & rams	head	15.11	18.36	18.44	14.45
Finished clean pigs	head	71.07	65.75	65.51	79.09
Finished clean pigs	kg dwt	1.06	0.96	0.95	1.12
Culled sows & boars	head	116.58	87.47	97.03	119.71
Milk	litre	0.19	0.21	0.21	0.25
Eggs	dozen	0.36	0.43	0.40	0.40
Broilers	kg dwt	0.57	0.57	0.56	0.55
Potatoes: ware main crop*	tonne	77.92	62.46	118.37	170.58
Potatoes: seed	tonne	107.46	84.78	159.73	238.91
Barley	tonne	118.22	124.40	112.48	119.61
Wheat	tonne	124.75	125.27	114.35	123.22
Mushrooms	tonne	1,120	1,161	1,190	1,309
Apples	tonne	129.36	136.57	118.95	137.76

This does not include early potatoes or potatoes bought under the stockfeed scheme.

R.O.I.: USE OF LAND FOR AGRICULTURAL PURPOSES

Agricultural Activity (000 hectares)	1987	1992	1994	1995
Cereal:				
Wheat	56.1	90.6	74.1	70.7
Oats	22.9	20.1	20.9	19.9
Barley	255.3	184.4	169.7	178.6
Other Cereals	1.9	5.2	5.3	4.7
Total: Cereals	**336.2**	**300.3**	**270.0**	**273.9**
Crops:				
Beans & Peas	2.3	2.7	5.6	4.8
Oilseed Rape	-	5.9	6.4	4.1
Potatoes	29.2	22.1	21.4	22.4
Turnips	8.9	5.5	5.6	5.3
Sugar Beet	37.1	31.3	35.4	35.1
Fodder Beet	6.4	11.0	9.8	8.9
Kale & Field Cabbage	2.9	1.9	1.8	1.5
Vegetables	3.7	4.3	4.8	4.7
Fruit	1.5	1.7	1.7	1.6
Nurseries etc	1.1	1.1	1.3	1.2
Other crops	8.6*	5.3	36.6	36.0
Total Non-cereal Crops	**101.7**	**92.8**	**130.4**	**125.6**
Silage	676.6	813.7	917.4	933.6
Hay	612.4	415.1	410.1	357.2
Pasture	2,930.2	2,195.6	2,201.3	2,238.9
Total:	**4,219.2**	**3,424.4**	**3,528.8**	**3,529.7**
Crops & Pasture	4,657.1	3,817.5	3,929.2	3,929.2
Rough grazing	998.6	595.9	461.5	459.5
TOTAL: AREA FARMED	**5,655.7**	**4,413.4**	**4,390.7**	**4,388.7**

This figure includes Oilseed Rape.

NORTHERN IRELAND: USE OF LAND FOR AGRICULTURAL PURPOSES

Agricultural Activity (000 hectares)	1992	1993	1994	1995	1996
Agricultural Crops:					
Oats	2	2	2	3	2
Wheat	7	7	7	6	7
Winter Barley	5	6	6	7	7
Spring Barley	32	32	28	26	26
Potatoes	11	9	8	9	9
Other crops	6	7	8	6	5
Total	63	63	59	57	56
Horticultural Crops:					
Fruit	2	2	2	2	2
Vegetables	2	1	1	1	1
Total	4	3	3	3	3
Grass:					
Under 5 years old	179	192	189	188	184
Over 5 years old	582	584	585	591	597
Total	761	776	774	779	781
Total: Crops & Grass	828	842	836	839	840
Rough grazing	182	180	179	174	172
Woods & Plantations	13	12	12	12	12
Other land	29	22	21	19	19
TOTAL AREA:	1,052	1,056	1,048	1,044	1,043

DIRECT INCOME PAYMENTS (SUBSIDIES) 1990-1995

REPUBLIC OF IRELAND: Payments (IR£m)	1990	1992	1994	1995
Cattle headage	49.9	81.1	93.8	80.21
Beef cow	9.5	16.5	19.0	17.03
Suckler cow	54.5	65.7	89.9	106.12
Special beef premium	51.0	51.8	122.5	169.82
Deseasonalisation premium	-	-	15.6	15.02
Sheep headage	16.5	19.9	20.8	20.35
Ewe premium	140.3	114.4	117.3	107.97
Extensification premium	-	-	47.5	59.78
Total headage / aid	321.7	349.4	526.4	576.30
Arable Aid	-	-	66.0	82.40
Disease Eradication Schemes	19.9	22.2	17.2	20.94
Other milk payments	29.8	23.9	36.6	13.36
Forest premium scheme	-	-	1.0	3.50
Installation aid for farmers	-	2.2	2.3	4.18
REPS	-	-	1.2	30.85
Others	12.3	7.5	15.8	9.14
Total Payments:	383.7	405.2	666.5	740.67
Total Levies:	51.7	44.5	31.8	36.6
NET PAYMENTS:	332.0	360.7	634.7	704.07

NORTHERN IRELAND: Payments (IR£m)	1992	1994	1995	1996*
Beef special premium	7.6	35.5	36.0	44.7
Suckler cow	16.1	34.6	29.8	50.2
Extensification Supplement	-	15.0	15.1	16.4
Deseasonalisation premium	-	4.6	0.5	-
Hill Livestock compensatory Allowance	13.1	10.7	10.4	10.7
Beef Marketing Payment			-	4.5
Sheep premium	28.8	27.8	30.3	35.7
Hill Livestock Compensatory Allowance	6.2	4.0	3.6	3.8
Cereals	0.1	4.7	7.7	8.2
Other Crops	0.3	0.4	0.2	0.1
Other Subsidies	11.9	14.7	7.0	93.9

Total Payments:	84.2	152.0	140.6	268.2
Total Levies**:	5.1	2.5	9.9	4.4
NET PAYMENTS:	79.1	149.5	130.7	263.8

provisional figures. ** This does not include non-government levies.*

REPUBLIC OF IRELAND: LIVESTOCK FIGURES

Livestock (000's)	1992	1993	1994	1995
Cattle:				
Dairy cows	1,261.5	1,274.1	1,269.1	1,267.1
Other cows	911.8	928.3	956.7	988.7
Dairy heifers in calf	197.9	192.5	207.4	232.6
Other heifers in calf	112.4	113.2	97.3	114.2
Bulls	31.1	32.2	32.7	34.2
Cattle 2 years & over	890.0	827.7	866.0	857.4
Cattle 1-2 years	1,387.0	1,374.6	1,422.8	1,404.1
Cattle under 1 year	1,472.9	1,565.8	1,557.9	1,633.3
Total:	**6,264.6**	**6,308.4**	**6,409.9**	**6,531.6**
Sheep:				
Breeding ewes	4,806.4	4,676.4	4,545.0	4,372.3
Breeding rams	129.8	128.4	123.8	121.8
Other sheep	1,188.8	1,186.0	1,103.4	1,089.0
Total:	**6,125.0**	**5,990.8**	**5,772.2**	**5,583.1**
Pigs:				
Breeding pigs (gilts, sows & boars)	178.0	175.1	167.0	180.8
Other pigs	1,244.7	1,312.2	1,331.3	1,361.5
Total:	**1,422.7**	**1,487.3**	**1,498.3**	**1,542.3**
Poultry:				
Ordinary fowl	10,062.2	10,966.4	11,905.8	11,220 9
Other fowl	1,428.9	1,232.0	1,600.2	1,760.7
Total:	**11,491.1**	**12,198.4**	**13,506.0**	**12,981.6**
Horses & Ponies:	**65.1**	**66.2**	**67.0**	**68.0**
Deer:	**12.5**	**15.2**	**15.0**	**15.9**

NORTHERN IRELAND: LIVESTOCK FIGURES

Livestock (000 heads)	1992	1993	1994	1995	1996
Cattle:					
Dairy cows in milk	249	250	255	252	260
Dairy cows in calf	20	19	19	20	21
Dairy heifers in calf	46	49	50	56	62
Beef cows in milk	228	235	237	235	241
Beef cows in calf	39	43	42	43	44
Beef heifers in calf	30	33	29	29	32
Cattle over 2 years	159	148	147	141	162
Cattle 1-2 years	375	369	370	364	380
Cattle under 1 year	430	432	432	437	448
Total:	**1,576**	**1,578**	**1,581**	**1,577**	**1,650**
Sheep:					
Breeding ewes	1,238	1,245	1,218	1,185	1,235
Other sheep	1,419	1,366	1,312	1,285	1,235
Total:	**2,657**	**2,611**	**2,530**	**2,470**	**2,470**
Pigs:					
Sows & gilts	59	60	58	57	57
Other pigs	529	534	504	491	492
Total:	**588**	**594**	**562**	**548**	**549**
Poultry:					
Laying birds	3,132	3,121	3,195	3,096	3,028
Growing pullets	928	1,087	1,071	1,244	1,148
Breeding flock	922	1,205	1,353	1,532	1,724
Broilers	6,968	7,578	7,596	8,618	8,464
Other poultry	352	391	427	457	465
Total:	**12,302**	**13,382**	**13,672**	**14,947**	**14,829**
Goats	**7**	**6**	**5**	**5**	**4**
Horses & Ponies	**8**	**10**	**10**	**11**	**11**

REPUBLIC OF IRELAND: CHIEF CROPS

Crops	1994 Area 000 ha	1994 Yield tonnes / ha	1994 Production 000 tonnes	1995 Area 000 ha	1995 Yield tonnes / ha	1995 Production 000 tonnes
Wheat	74.1	7.7	572.0	70.7	8.2	583.0
Oats	20.9	6.1	128.0	19.9	6.5	129.0
Barley	169.7	5.4	910.0	178.6	6.1	1,084.0
Beans & peas	5.6	4.5	25.0	4.8	4.0	19.0
Oilseed rape	6.4	2.6	17.0	4.1	3.3	13.0
Potatoes	21.4	30.1	642.0	22.4	27.6	618.0
Sugar beet	35.4	39.3	1,390.0	35.1	44.1	1,547.0
Turnips	5.6	53.1	296.0	5.3	54.1	289.0
Fodder beet	9.8	59.0	579.0	8.9	66.8	596.0
Kale & field cabbage	1.8	44.5	81.0	1.5	39.0	57.0

NORTHERN IRELAND: CHIEF CROPS

Product	1994 Area 000 ha	1994 Yield tonnes / ha	1994 Production 000 tonnes	1995 Area 000 ha	1995 Yield tonnes / ha	1995 Production 000 tonnes
Potatoes	8.4	31.8	268.2	8.7	32.0	278.9
Barley	33.4	4.70	157.2	32.7	5.16	169.0
Wheat	7.0	7.05	49.6	6.4	7.78	49.9
Oats	2.4	4.63	11.3	2.5	4.84	12.3
Oilseed Rape	0.6	2.46	1.5	0.3	2.93	1.0
Hay	29.2	7.82	228.2	38.0	7.10	269.7
Grass Silage	268.1	29.95	8,031.8	255.5	29.87	7,631.0

REPUBLIC OF IRELAND
AREA UNDER CROPS AND PASTURE

CROPS / PASTURE (000 ha)	1992	1993	1994	1995
Cereals:				
Wheat	90.6	79.2	74.1	70.7
Oats	20.1	20.2	20.9	19.9
Barley	184.4	180.8	169.7	178.6
Other cereals	5.2	4.7	5.3	4.7
Total: Cereals	**300.3**	**284.9**	**270.0**	**273.9**
Crops, fruit & horticulture:				
Beans & peas	2.7	6.1	5.6	4.8
Oilseed rape	5.9	3.4	6.4	4.1
Potatoes	22.1	21.6	21.4	22.4
Turnips	5.5	5.2	5.6	5.3
Sugar beet	31.3	32.2	35.4	35.1
Fodder beet	11.0	10.9	9.8	8.9
Kale & field cabbage	1.9	1.8	1.8	1.5
Vegetables	4.3	4.6	4.8	4.7
Fruit	1.7	1.6	1.7	1.6
Nursery etc	1.1	1.0	1.3	1.2
Other crops	5.3	30.5	36.6	36.0
Total: Crops, fruit & horticulture	**92.8**	**118.9**	**130.4**	**125.6**
Pasture:				
Silage	813.7	872.3	917.4	933.6
Hay	415.1	425.9	410.1	357.2
Pasture	2,195.6	2,202.5	2,201.3	2,238.9
Total:	**3,424.4**	**3,500.7**	**3,528.8**	**3,529.7**
Rough grazing:	**595.9**	**499.7**	**461.5**	**459.5**
GRAND TOTAL:	**4,413.4**	**4,404.2**	**4,390.7**	**4,388.7**

N.I.: AREA UNDER CROPS AND PASTURE

CROPS / PASTURE (000 ha)	1992	1993	1994	1995
Agricultural Crops:				
Oats	2.3	2.2	2.4	2.5
Wheat	7.4	6.7	7.0	6.4
Winter barley	5.4	6.2	5.8	6.7
Spring barley	31.6	32.4	27.6	26.0
Mixed corn	0.1	0.1	0.1	0.1
Oilseed rape	1.1	0.8	0.6	0.5
Potatoes	10.8	9.0	8.4	8.7
Arable crop silage	3.6	3.7	4.2	4.6
Other field crops	1.1	1.7	1.6	1.2
Total:	**63.4**	**62.8**	**57.7**	**56.7**
Horticultural Crops:				
Fruit	1.9	1.8	1.8	1.7
Vegetables	1.5	1.5	1.4	1.4
Other horticultural crops	0.1	0.1	0.1	0.1
Total:	**3.5**	**3.4**	**3.3**	**3.2**
Grass:				
5 years & under	178.6	192.2	188.9	187.9
5 years & over	581.7	584.4	585.4	590.6
Total:	**760.3**	**776.6**	**774.3**	**778.5**
Rough grazing	182.0	179.8	179.0	173.6
Woods & plantations	13.4	11.7	11.6	11.5
Other land	29.2	21.5	21.5	19.3
GRAND TOTAL	**1,051.8**	**1,055.8**	**1,047.4**	**1,042.8**

R.O.I: DAIRY EXPORTS BY COUNTRY, 1996

Country / Area	%
Africa	7.9
Central & South America	9.9
North America	13.5
Middle & Far East	9.6
Britain	22.5
European Union Countries (excluding Britain)	35.0
Other European Countries	1.6
	100.0

REPUBLIC OF IRELAND: DAIRY EXPORTS BY PRODUCT, 1992 - 1995

Products	Quantity (Tonnes)				Value IR£ (000)			
	1992	1993	1994	1995	1992	1993	1994	1995
Animal Feed	6,319	2,258	4,724	7,521	6,000	3,000	5,545	9,771
Butter	172,364	98,923	96,206	120,874	415,000	254,000	247,439	328,425
Butter Oil	8,079	12,429	14,036	18,448	22,000	31,000	32,358	49,714
Casein & Caseinates	39,290	31,374	30,596	42,322	189,000	161,000	150,380	215,478
Cheese	97,910	73,945	88,719	77,561	231,000	200,000	225,379	199,711
Chocolate Crumb	62,578	57,642	34,055	11,146	74,000	65,000	46,861	16,393
Cream	1,701	1,151	2,117	3,858	3,000	2,000	1,665	3,793
Cream Liqueurs	45,836	58,818	42,330	61,872	183,000	241,000	186,664	272,165
Skimmed Milk Powder	248,881	122,419	79,689	145,892	365,000	207,000	130,666	256,476
Whole Milk Powder	33,189	27,656	45,609	41,223	68,000	84,000	93,992	88,043
Others					236,000	305,000	292,067	363,960
TOTAL:	**716,147**	**486,615**	**438,081**	**530,717**	**1,792,000**	**1,553,000**	**1,413,016**	**1,803,929**

R.O.I. FARMS BY SIZE AND NUMBER

Farm Size (Hectares)	1980 (Thousands)	1985	1991	1993
1 - 10	69.3	70.0	41.8	38.8
10 - 20	67.7	63.8	48.3	44.9
20 - 30	36.3	36.9	31.0	29.4
30 - 50	30.3	29.9	28.4	27.4
50 or more	19.7	19.6	19.6	18.9
TOTAL:	223.3	220.2	169.1	159.4

N.I. FARMS BY SIZE AND NUMBER, 1996

Hectares	Farms by Total Area		Farms by Area: Crops / Grass	
	Farms	Hectares	Farms	Hectares
Nil	-	-	540	-
0.1 - 9.9	4,934	30,725	5,944	36,614
10.0 - 19.9	6,591	96,488	6,968	101,221
20.0 - 29.0	4,668	114,835	4,543	111,268
30.0 - 49.9	5,378	207,686	4,922	189,137
50.0 - 99.9	4,466	303,335	3,717	249,781
100.0 - 199.9	1,253	164,587	832	106,722
200.0 or over	257	82,599	81	21,039
TOTAL	27,547	1,000,255	27,547	815,782

IMPORTS OF CATTLE TO NORTHERN IRELAND FROM THE REPUBLIC OF IRELAND

Year (000 heads)	Stores	Fin. Cattle	Others (incl. cows)	Total
1987/88	92.2	62.7	3.7	158.6
1988/89	77.9	75.8	1.3	155.0
1989/90	48.1	67.6	7.3	123.0
1990/91	39.7	50.9	1.2	91.8
1991/92	31.4	43.7	1.0	76.1
1992/93	22.0	29.0	1.4	52.4
1993/94	13.4	28.7	1.5	43.6
1994/95	7.3	8.4	1.8	17.5
1995/96	9.1	9.2	1.2	19.5

FISHERIES
INTRODUCTION

Bord Iascaigh Mhara (BIM) is the state agency primarily responsible for development of the seafish and aquaculture industry in the Republic of Ireland. BIM provides an extensive range of financial, educational, resource development, technical training and marketing services to the processing and marketing sectors of the fishing industry. The main species of sea fish landed in Irish ports are herring, whiting, cod, mackerel, plaice, skate, haddock and ray. In 1994 the total volume and value of exports of Irish fish products amounted to 285,098 tonnes valued at IR£195m, including landings by Irish fishing vessels at foreign ports. When landings at foreign ports are excluded, Irish fish exports in 1995 were valued at IR£213.1 million. According to the latest figures available (1995) approximately 7,500 fulltime and occasional Irish fishermen engage in sea fishing.

Fishing in Northern Ireland is also of major importance, particularly to the seaboard communities along the coast of Antrim and Down. In 1995, 19.8 thousand tonnes were landed at N.I. ports worth an estimated £16 million. In addition, N.I. vessels landed in the region of 8,000 tonnes of fish at ports outside the North, these being valued at £4.6m.

Ardglass in Co. Down, is the busiest harbour in the North, 7.4 thousand tonnes being landed there in 1995. Killkeel is the second largest with 6.7 thousand tonnes.

The largest port by far, however, in Ireland is Killybegs in Co. Donegal where, in 1996, 147 thousand tonnes of fish were landed at a value of £30 million.

REPUBLIC OF IRELAND: LANDINGS OF SEAFISH AT THE TOP 20 IRISH PORTS, 1996

Rank	Port	County	Live Weight (Tonnes)	Landed Weight (Tonnes)	Value (£)
1	Killybegs	Donegal	148,322.0	147,881.0	30,744,354.32
2	Castletownbere	Cork	15,595.3	14,797.5	9,677,596.38
3	Dunmore East	Waterford	14,248.4	13,645.8	7,645,373.30
4	Dingle	Kerry	7,094.5	6,576.5	6,701,941.00
5	Greencastle	Donegal	4,229.3	3,896.5	4,676,457.80
6	Rossaveal	Galway	7,046.1	6,482.0	4,606,948.88
7	Howth	Dublin	4,237.6	3,508.1	4,403,559.85
8	Rathmullan	Donegal	27,882.1	27,882.1	3,541,935.70
9	Union Hall	Cork	3,656.6	3,381.9	3,360,274.82
10	Baltimore	Cork	3,807.9	3,692.4	2,306,104.55
11	Dungarvan	Waterford	1,246.0	1,246.0	2,118,200.00
12	Valentia	Kerry	1,232.5	1,072.7	2,047,673.03
13	Kinsale	Cork	1,328.9	1,217.5	1,603,470.25
14	Burtonport	Donegal	2,517.8	2,447.8	1,574,767.19
15	Fenit	Kerry	2,139.2	2,066.6	1,538,029.61
16	Downings	Donegal	1,306.7	1,272.2	1,484,964.20
17	Duncannon / St. Helens	Waterford	1,192.7	1,031.6	1,455,271.45
18	Wexford	Wexford	2,842.7	2,842.7	1,448,128.00
19	Kilmore Quay	Wexford	941.0	848.5	1,427,102.52
20	Skerries	Dublin	1,051.3	630.8	1,287,987.40

NORTHERN IRELAND: MAJOR FISHING PORTS

Port	County	Port	County
Derry	Derry	Ardglass	Down
Kilkeel	Down	Portavogie	Down

REPUBLIC OF IRELAND: AQUACULTURE OUTPUT VALUE, 1984-1995

Year	£ 000's	Tonnes
1984	5,923	15,322
1985	6,222	11,964
1986	7,790	12,828
1987	15,275	18,626
1988	24,885	18,327
1989	27,599	21,090
1990	29,900	26,560
1991	39,316	27,699
1992	40,640	28,600
1993	50,315	30,154
1994	48,512	28,615
1995	49,274	27,437

Note: These figures exclude direct landings by Irish-registered boats in foreign ports and fishmeal/oil exports.

R.O.I.: FISH EXPORTS BY PRODUCTION, 1995

Product	Value £m	%
Fish Live / Fresh / Chilled (excl. fillets)	59.4	27.9
Frozen Fish (excl. fillets)	53.8	25.2
Shellfish Live / Fresh / Chilled / Frozen	46.3	21.7
Fish Fillets Fresh / Chilled / Frozen	24.2	11.4
Fish & Shellfish Prepared / Preserved	10.7	5.0
Fish Dried Salted / Smoked etc.	9.5	4.5
Fish Meal / Oil etc.	9.2	4.3
TOTAL:	213.1	100.0

R.O.I.: VALUE OF FISH EXPORTS, 1995

Country	£m	%
European Union:		
Britain	21.0	9.9
France	45.8	21.5
Germany	19.2	9.0
Italy	12.5	5.9
Spain	36.5	17.1
Netherlands	4.3	2.0
Northern Ireland	5.7	2.8
Other European Union	6.9	3.1
Non-European Union:		
Japan	16.7	7.8
Nigeria	6.1	2.9
Russia	5.8	2.7
Other Non-European Union	32.6	15.3
TOTAL:	**213.1**	**100.1**

REPUBLIC OF IRELAND: GEOGRAPHICAL SPREAD OF EXPORT MARKETS, 1987-1995

Country	1987 £ 000	1995 £ 000	% Change 1987/95	% Market for 1995
European Union:				
Belgium / Luxembourg	2,003	1,983	-19	1.0
Britain	13,966	20,972	+9	9.8
Denmark	802	1,087	+35	0.5
France	31,043	45,826	+51	21.5
Germany	11,404	19,237	+49	9.0
Greece	146	579	+189	0.3
Italy	1,779	12,530	+392	5.9
Netherlands	6,704	4,337	-36	2.0
Northern Ireland	7,271	5,725	-33	2.7
Portugal	64	414	+205	0.2
Spain	8,993	36,540	+327	17.1
Other European Union	-	2,723	-	1.3
Total: European Union	**84,175**	**151,953**	**+65**	**71.3**
Non-European Union:				
Japan	18,343	16,699	+33	7.8
Other Non-European Union	21,422	44,439	+34	20.9
Total: Non-European Union	**39,765**	**61,138**	**+3**	**28.7**
TOTAL EXPORTS:	**123,940**	**213,091**	**+45**	**100**

REPUBLIC OF IRELAND: FISHING QUOTAS

(European Union Member States' Shares of 1996 TACs)

FISH TYPE	COUNTRY ALLOCATION IN TONNES												
	IRE	BEL	DEN	GER	FRA	NETH	UK	SPAIN	POR	SWE	FIN	REM.	Total
Cod	8,065	5,235	92,960	40,980	26,780	13,780	68,080	11,500	2,390	40,225	2,260	250	312,505
Saithe	4,410	80	4,600	12,445	43,325	120	14,670	-	-	630	-	-	80,280
Haddock	3,440	1,100	12,740	4,520	14,250	710	86,920	-	-	1,200	-	-	124,880
Hake	1,580	300	2,460	120	27,040	250	5,470	20,090	2,690	110	-	-	60,110
Herring	53,120	7,790	128,520	137,700	29,930	69,990	102,790	-	-	203,190	126,610	-	859,640
Mackerel	52,700	400	10,645	16,230	11,970	24,340	146,130	24,750	5,110	3,610	-	-	295,885
Plaice	3,170	6,565	29,580	4,890	6,295	32,870	27,270	120	120	950	-	-	111,140
Whiting	15,890	1,975	11,270	1,930	32,870	4,365	41,890	2,800	2,640	440	-	-	116,070
Sprat	-	1,560	79,480	28,790	2,340	2,340	7,800	-	-	87,470	23,220	164,670	397,670
Sole	660	4,455	2,765	1,645	8,955	18,155	2,940	770	1,245	70	-	-	41,660
Monkfish	2,650	2,490	-	590	23,480	580	6,890	13,060	2,160	-	-	100	52,000
Megrims	3,770	510	-	-	10,330	-	4,340	13,010	180	-	-	-	32,140
Nephrops	8,655	795	4,345	20	12,195	410	33,015	3,400	1,875	1,270	-	-	65,980
Pollack	1,300	470	-	-	13,550	-	3,020	1,640	20	-	-	100	20,100
BL. Whiting	-	-	-	-	-	-	74,000	14,000	-	-	-	113,500	201,500
Horse Mack.	-	-	-	500	-	-	72,270	43,230	-	-	-	314,000	430,000

FISH TYPE	IRE	BEL	DEN	GER	FRA	NETH	BRIT	SPAIN	POR	SWE	FIN	REM.	TOTAL
Cod	2.58	1.67	29.74	13.11	8.56	4.40	21.78	3.67	0.76	12.87	0.72	0.07	100.00
Saithe	5.49	0.09	5.72	15.50	53.96	0.14	18.27	-	-	0.78	-	-	100.00
Haddock	2.75	0.88	10.20	3.61	11.41	0.56	69.60	-	-	0.96	-	-	100.00
Hake	2.62	0.49	4.09	0.19	44.98	0.41	9.09	33.42	4.47	0.18	-	-	100.00
Herring	6.17	0.90	14.95	16.01	3.48	8.14	11.95	-	-	23.63	14.72	-	100.00
Mackerel	17.81	0.13	3.59	5.48	4.04	8.22	49.38	8.36	1.72	1.22	-	-	100.00
Plaice	2.85	5.90	26.61	4.39	5.66	28.95	24.53	0.10	0.10	0.85	-	-	100.00
Whiting	13.67	1.70	9.70	1.66	28.29	3.75	36.06	2.41	2.27	0.37	-	-	100.00
Sprat	-	0.39	19.98	7.23	0.58	0.58	1.96	-	-	21.99	5.83	41.40	100.00
Sole	1.58	10.69	6.63	3.94	21.49	43.57	7.05	1.84	2.98	0.16	-	-	100.00
Monkfish	5.09	4.78	-	1.13	45.15	1.11	13.25	25.11	4.15	-	-	0.19	100.00
Megrims	11.76	1.59			32.24	-	10.54	40.00	0.58	-	-	-	100.00
Nephrops	13.13	1.20	6.59	0.03	18.50	0.62	50.10	5.16	2.84	1.92	-	-	100.00
Pollack	6.46	2.33	-	-	67.41	-	15.02	8.15	0.09	-	-	0.49	100.00
Bl. Whiting	-	-	-	-	-	-	-	36.72	6.94	-	-	56.32	100.00
Horse Mack.	-	-	-	0.11	-	-	-	16.80	10.05	-	-	73.02	100.00

REPUBLIC OF IRELAND:
PERSONS ENGAGED IN SEA FISHING

Job Category	1992	1993	1994	1995
Full-Time	3,280	3,300	3,300	3,200
Part-Time	4,420	4,400	4,400	4,300
TOTAL	7,700	7,700	7,700	7,500

REPUBLIC OF IRELAND:
LIVEWEIGHT AND VALUE OF FISH LANDED, 1996

Species	Live Weight (Tonnes)	Landed Weight (Tonnes)	Value (IR£)
Wetfish *(inc.Demersal and Pelagic)*	303,782.7	299,504.2	101,362,018.24
Shellfish:	43,667.5	41,188.1	43,101,889.86
GRAND TOTAL:	347,450.2	340,692.3	144,463.908.10

FOREIGN LANDINGS
BY IRISH-REGISTERED VESSELS 1996

Species	Live Weight (Tonnes)	Landed Weight (Tonnes)	Value (IR£)
Total Demersal	3,299.7	3,213.5	4,750,155.00
Total Pelagic	41,020.1	41,020.1	14,889,794.00
Total Shellfish	65.3	64.5	168,300.00
TOTAL:	303,782.7	299,504.2	101,362,018.24

NORTHERN IRELAND: LIVEWEIGHT
AND ESTIMATED VALUE OF LANDED FISH

Species	1992 tonnes	1992 £000	1993 tonnes	1993 £000	1994 tonnes	1994 £000	1995 tonnes	1995 £000
Wetfish	14,722	10,674	14,408	9,290	13,955	9,041	13,458	7,346
Shellfish	8,140	6,967	7,194	8,017	6,924	8,968	6,623	8,893
TOTAL:	22,862	17,641	21,602	17,307	20,879	18,009	20,081	16,239

NORTHERN IRELAND: LIVEWEIGHT AND ESTIMATED VALUE OF ALL LANDED FISH BY PORT

Port	1991	1992	1993	1994	1995
Ardglass:					
Tonnes	4,337	5,085	6,017	5,845	7,495
Value (£000)	2,312	2,298	2,638	2,960	3,131
Kilkeel:					
Tonnes	10,258	8,898	7,753	7,588	6,707
Value (£000)	9,551	7,916	7,088	7,368	6,432
Portavogie:					
Tonnes	5,985	5,635	5,919	6,119	5,094
Value (£000)	7,030	6,106	5,742	6,312	5,708
Other N.I. Ports:					
Tonnes	3,835	3,244	1,914	1,327	785
Value (£000)	912	1,321	1,839	1,369	968
TOTAL LANDINGS:					
Tonnes	**24,415**	**22,862**	**21,603**	**20,879**	**20,081**
Value (£000)	**19,805**	**17,641**	**17,307**	**18,009**	16,239
Total Landings by N.I. Vessels in N.I. Ports:					
Tonnes	23,160	22,018	21,103	20,225	19,898
Value (£000)	19,356	16,987	16,543	17,589	16,041

R.O.I.: QUANTITY AND VALUE OF SEA FISH LANDED BY IRISH VESSELS INTO IRISH PORTS

Species	1992		1993		1994		1995	
	Quantity (tonnes)	Value (£000)	Quantity (tonnes)	Value (£000)	Quantity (tonnes)	Value (£000)	Quantity (tonnes)	Value (£000)
Wetfish:								
Demersal	27,858	38,443	28,645	35,212	35,660	37,894	46,080	48,044
Pelagic	103,022	14,861	118,380	18,234	225,944	33,850	305,475	41,220
Total: Wetfish	**130,880**	**53,304**	**147,025**	**53,446**	**261,604**	**71,744**	**351,555**	**89,264**
Shellfish	28,349	29,393	32,582	28,261	31,834	35,375	43,295	40,658
GRAND TOTAL:	159,229	82,697	179,607	81,707	293,438	107,119	394,850	129,922

LIVEWEIGHT AND ESTIMATED VALUE OF FISH LANDED BY NORTHERN IRELAND VESSELS OUTSIDE NORTHERN IRELAND

COUNTRY / REGION	1991	1992	1993	1994	1995
Scotland:					
Tonnes	4,365	3,892	2,340	1,683	2,380
Value (£000)	899	1,036	1,127	973	1,809
England & Wales:					
Tonnes	3,357	1,420	3,217	3,190	7
Value (£000)	1,778	1,025	1,500	1,137	6
Isle of Man:					
Tonnes	629	807	773	716	615
Value (£000)	108	149	114	125	86
Other Countries:					
Tonnes	8,612	2,687	2,563	2,366	2,991
Value (£000)	2,122	1,609	2,333	2,410	3,144
TOTAL:					
Tonnes	16,963	8,806	8,893	7,955	5,993
Value (£000)	4,907	3,819	5,074	4,645	5,045

AFFORESTATION
EU FOREST STRUCTURES, WOODED AREA BY TYPE OF OWNERSHIP

Country	Year	State Forests 1,000 ha	% Total	Other Public Forests 1,000 ha	% Total	Private Forests 1,000 ha	% Total	Total 1,000 ha
Belgium	1982-93	68	10.1	223	33.0	385	57.0	676
Denmark	1990	118	26.5	22	5.0	305	68.5	445
Germany	1993	3,639	34.0	2,123	20.0	4,978	46.0	10,741
Greece	1993	4,212	73.2	694	12.1	849	14.8	5,755
Spain	1986	955	7.0	4,379	31.9	8,417	61.1	13,751
France	1991	1,465	9.0	2,413	14.9	12,364	76.1	16,242
Ireland	1993	369	70.6	10	1.9	144	27.5	523
Italy	1990	614	7.0	2,369	27.0	5,791	66.0	8,774
Luxembourg	1991	10	11.2	32	36.0	47	52.8	89
Netherlands	1983	105	30.6	59	17.2	178	51.9	343
Austria	1990	581	15.0	121	3.1	3,176	81.9	3,878
Portugal	1985	84	2.7	366	11.8	2,652	85.5	3,102
Finland	1984-93	6,634	28.5	552	2.4	16,113	69.2	23,299
Sweden	1987	8,460	30.2	-	-	19,555	69.8	28,015
U.K.	1994	932	38.0	-	-	1,522	62.0	2,454
TOTAL:								118,087

REPUBLIC OF IRELAND: AFFORESTATION BY COUNTY(HECTARES), 1995

County	Coillte	Private	Total
Carlow	38.1	87.1	125.2
Cavan	304.1	330.8	634.9
Clare	414.3	1,439.6	1,853.9
Cork	530.4	1,422.8	1,953.2
Donegal	856.5	2,544.3	3,400.8
Dublin	0	189.6	189.6
Galway	909.6	740.0	1,649.6
Kerry	217.3	1,857.2	2,074.5
Kildare	20.9	323.1	344.0
Kilkenny	97.3	454.4	551.7
Laois	40.4	447.6	488.0
Leitrim	418.5	430.7	849.2
Limerick	357.4	550.8	908.2
Longford	70.4	136.9	207.3
Louth	0	11.2	11.2
Mayo	281.6	967.2	1,248.8
Meath	0	288.1	288.1
Monaghan	5.6	60.2	65.8
Offaly	51.4	685.3	736.7
Roscommon	402.1	494.6	896.7
Sligo	296.0	542.7	838.7
Tipperary	347.3	1,122.9	1,470.2
Waterford	127.6	422.4	550.0
Westmeath	40.8	973.6	1,014.4
Wexford	64.0	282.4	346.4
Wicklow	225.1	536.7	761.8
TOTAL:	6,116.7	17,342.2	23,458.9

NORTHERN IRELAND:
AFFORESTATION BY COUNTY(HECTARES), 1996

County	State	Private	Total
Antrim:			
Conifer	10,612	1,181	11,793
Broadleaf	348	2,510	2,858
Total	**10,960**	**3,691**	**14,651**
Armagh:			
Conifer	2,437	497	2,934
Broadleaf	277	1,056	1,333
Total	**2,714**	**1,553**	**4,267**
Derry:			
Conifer	9,211	870	10,081
Broadleaf	677	1,849	2,526
Total	**9,888**	**2,719**	**12,607**
Down:			
Conifer	3,455	1,118	4,573
Broadleaf	747	2,375	3,122
Total	**4,202**	**3,493**	**7,695**
Fermanagh:			
Conifer	16,498	994	17,492
Broadleaf	1,230	2,114	3,344
Total	**17,728**	**3,108**	**20,836**
Tyrone:			
Conifer	14,662	1,554	16,216
Broadleaf	759	3,302	4,061
Total	**15,421**	**4,856**	**20,277**
GRAND TOTAL:	**60,913**	**19,420**	**80,333**

REPUBLIC OF IRELAND:
TOTAL AFFORESTATION, 1986-1996

Year (hectares)	State	Private	Total
1986	4,689	2,280	6,969
1987	5,395	2,954	8,349
1988	7,112	4,596	11,708
1989	6,629	8,498	15,127
1990	6,670	9,147	15,817
1991	7,855	11,292	19,147
1992	7,565	9,134	16,699
1993	6,827	9,171	15,998
1994	6,431	12,837	19,268
1995	6,117	17,343	23,460
1996	6,120	17,200	23,320

REPUBLIC OF IRELAND:
FORESTRY PRODUCTS, IMPORTS AND EXPORTS

Product	Production			Imports			Exports		
	1993	1994	1995	1993	1994	1995	1993	1994	1995
1000m₃(r)									
Fuel wood	57	60	64	-	-	-	6	2	-
Industrial Round wood	1,764	1,958	2,140	-	-	-	-	-	-
Pulp wood	540	621	770	-	-	-	-	-	-
Logs	1,224	1,337	1,370	-	-	-	-	-	-
Industrial Round wood:									
Coniferous	-	-	-	40	50	37	178	116	304
Non-Coniferous	-	-	-	6	9	8	5	6	6
Chips and Particles	-	-	-	0.3	4	34	215	200	71
Wood Residue	-	-	-	-	-	-	76	63	70

Sawn wood:	637	709	710	322.9	436.6	405	250	249	255
Coniferous	622	699	706	252	340	326	238	244	248
Non-Coniferous	15	10	10	69	94	77	12	4	7
Wood-Based Panels	247	265	330	121.3	135	166	150	152.5	183.5
Veneer Sheets	-	-	-	3.2	4	6	0.4	-	-
Plywood	-	-	-	49.1	56	76	3	3	3
Particle Board	85	85	90	31	37	38	31	33	32
Fire Board	162	180	240	38	38	52	116	116.5	148.5
Hardboard	162	180	240	16	20	21	114	116	148
Insulating Board	-	-	-	1	18	31	1.8	0.5	-

1000 m.t.

Wood pulp:	-	-	-	15.6	19	19	1	2	-
Mechanical	-	-	-	-	-	-	-	-	-
Chemical	-	-	-	8	9	-	-	-	-
Dissolving Grades	-	-	-	7	10	-	1	-	-
Paper and Paper board	-	-	-	361	380	386	31.5	27	28
Newsprint	-	-	-	76	70	62	7.6	1	-
Printing Paper	-	-	-	122	130	156	9.1	7	9
Other Paper and Paperboard	-	-	-	163	180	168	14.8	19	-

1000m3(r) = cubic metre of round wood, solid measure, without bark.   m.t. = metric tonne

NORTHERN IRELAND:
FOREST AND AREA RESOURCES

Description	1991-92	1992-93	1993-94	1994-95	1995-96
Forested Area (000 ha):					
State	60	61	61	61	61
Private	16	16	17	18	19
Total: Forested Areas	76	77	78	79	80
Annual Planting Area (ha):					
State	907	869	816	826	774
Private	479	911	928	624	836
Total: All Planting Area	1,386	1,780	1,744	1,450	1,610
Timber Production from State Forests:					
Volume (000 m3)	188	200	222	222	223
Value (£000)	2,996	3,022	3,340	5,900	5,000
Employees (number):					
State Forest Service	493	492	469	446	460

Persons Employed in Forestry, 1996/97 SECTOR	Numbers
Forest Service:	
Industrial	270
Non-Industrial	131
Total: Forest Service	401
Private Forestry	60
Timber Processing Industry	600
Total:	1,061

Timber Production, 1996/97 Description	Total Production / Price
State Forests:	
Thinning	25,000m3
Felling	206,000m3
Total: State Forests	**231,000m3**
Private Forests	20,000m3
Timber Sold Standing	129,000m3
Timber Sold at Roadside	102,000m3
Value of Timber Sold	£6,000,000
Average Sale Price:	
Standing Sales	£22.04 per m3
Roadside Sales	£31.22 per m3

NORTHERN IRELAND:
AREAS AND PLANTING STATISTICS, 1996/97

Description	Area (hectares)
State Forests:	
State Forests	61,000
Private Forests	20,000
Total: State Forests	81,000
New Planting:	
Forest Service	140
Private	615
Total: New Planting	755
Replanting:	
Forest Service	503
Private	64
Total: Replanting	567

Proportion of Land under Forest	%
Total Proportion of Land under Forest	6%
Proportion of Broadleaves Planted:	
Forest Service	10%
Private	41%
Species Composition of State Forests:	
Sitka Spruce	69%
Lodgepole Pine	9%
Norway Spruce	6%
Larches	5%
Other Conifers	4%
Broadleaves and Conifer / Broadleaved Mixtures	7%

ENERGY

Ireland's commercially viable Resources

By Ken Cathcart

REPUBLIC OF IRELAND: <u>Peat:</u> Although Ireland has very little indigenous coal, there are large reserves of peat, whose development is handled by the state-owned Bord na Móna (the Peat Development Board). Virtually all of the Board's output goes to serve two markets: the five milled peat electricity generating stations owned by the Electricity Supply Board and the domestic heating market, where dried and compressed peat is sold in the form of briquettes. In recent years concern has been expressed about the environmental effects of peat digging.

<u>Electricity:</u> The Electricity Supply Board (ESB), as a state-owned utility, is the sole supplier of electricity to the Republic's 1.4 million customers. Its 10,000 staff are engaged in retailing and consultancy (both at home and abroad), as well as the main functions of generation, transmission, distribution and supply of electricity. The Board uses a variety of fuels, with coal and gas accounting for some 70% of generation. The remainder is made up by oil, peat and hydro-electric schemes. A major Cost and Competitiveness Review exercise over the past three years has resulted in significant cost savings, revised work practices and reduced employee numbers. The group's capital expenditure plans include a bid to build and operate a new peat-fired power station in the Midlands. The major challenge facing the ESB at the moment is the proposed introduction of competition into the Irish electricity industry under a European Directive on the liberalisation of electricity markets across Europe. The group has shown some interest in diversifying into the Irish telecommunications market.

<u>Gas:</u> The transmission and distribution of gas within the Republic is the responsibility of Bord Gais Eireann (Irish Gas Board). Natural gas from the Kinsale Head and Ballycotton Gas fields off Cork is piped to Dublin and Drogheda with spurs serving Limerick and Waterford. Plans have been announced to extend the network to the West of Ireland, and the Company has mounted a strong marketing effort in this region, including the offer of attractive incentives to new customers. It is expected that the reserves of natural gas off the Cork coast will run out around the year 2003. Since the completion of a gas pipeline from Loughshinny in County Dublin to Moffat in the South West of Scotland in 1994, a small proportion of gas has been imported. As Northern Ireland also relies on one pipeline from Belfast, a North-South gas interconnector is planned. This major project, requiring significant capital investment, would enable emergency supplies to be piped in either direction and towns along the way to be gasified.

<u>Oil:</u> Since 1970, 125 exploratory offshore wells have been drilled. Some encouraging oil and gas flows have been recorded and a number of licences awarded. During 1997, Enterprise Oil announced plans to undertake exploratory drilling in Dublin Bay, in addition to the work of exploration and appraisal already being undertaken by companies such as Marathon, Total and Statoil off Connemara and Waterford.

NORTHERN IRELAND: By contrast, the North lacks commercially viable energy resources of its own, being almost totally dependent on imports of oil, coal and gas. <u>Electricity:</u> Northern Ireland Electricity plc (NIE) was privatised in 1993, and is open to competition in its supply function, while still occupying a monopoly position in the areas of power procurement, transmission and distribution. The total revenue which the Company may earn is subject to price control formulae set by a Government-appointed Regulator. Recent highly publicised disagreements between the regulator and NIE about the level of these price controls has led to a referral to the Monopolies and Mergers Commission (MMC) and subsequently to a judicial review. As in the case of the ESB, the European

Directive is likely to open up NIE to further competition over the next two to three years.

Power Generation: As part of the privatisation process, the four power stations previously owned by NIE were sold to private buyers. The two largest oil-fired stations at Ballylumford and Kilroot were sold respectively to British Gas and AES/Tractobel (an American/Belgian consortium). These have subsequently been established as Premier Power (a subsidiary of British Gas) and NIGEN (which also includes the smaller Belfast West Power station). Coolkeeragh Power in the North West was acquired as a management/employee buy-out. Ballylumford has since been converted to dual oil/gas firing, which has considerably decreased the dependence of the North on oil and coal for electricity generation.

Interconnection: For most of the past twenty years, the North's electricity system has not been able to take advantage of links to other systems. However, an interconnector to the ESB was restored in March 1995, and proposed interconnection with Scotland is awaiting the outcome of planning decisions.

Renewables: NIE is obliged to purchase non-fossil fuel generated electricity from private developers under a Government scheme to promote the use of renewable energy. The majority of this energy to date has come from wind power schemes, although there is growing interest in hydro-power, waste incineration, landfill gas combustion, Biomass (short rotation willow coppicing) and Biogas (gas derived from the disposal of slurry).

Oil, coal and lignite: The domestic heating market, (apart from electricity) is still dominated by oil and coal, since Northern Ireland does not have its own supply of natural gas. Reserves of lignite (brown coal) have not as yet been commercially developed.

Natural Gas: The delivery of natural gas to Ballylumford power station via an undersea pipeline from Scotland has made possible the development of a new natural gas industry in Northern Ireland. Phoenix, a company partly owned by British Gas has been granted a licence to develop the gas industry in the Greater Belfast area and Larne. Its activities will subject to the same Regulatory Department which governs the electricity industry (OFREG). Other areas hoping to benefit from natural gas include the North West and the Armagh/South Down area, but it is not clear at the time of going to press exactly how this will happen.

The author is a noted expert in the field of energy resources.

INTRODUCTION

Ireland, like the rest of the world, depends heavily on carbon-based energy resources. Although the absence of heavy industry, the prevailing winds and the country's location on the periphery of Europe have spared the country from the widespread pollution that affects most of our European neighbours, there is a dawning realisation that our dependence on fossil fuels must be curtailed. Ireland's isolation has placed the country at a disadvantage, highlighting the need for security of energy supplies, efficient energy infrastructure and optimum use of indigenous resources.

The authorities in both jurisdictions are committed to the UN Framework Convention on Climate Change in relation to the abatement of carbon dioxide emissions and the continuing reduction of greenhouse gases. In the Republic, the government has published a 15-year strategy document on renewable energy which establishes annual goals for electricity generated from renewable sources up to 2010. Already, a number of wind farms have been set up, and proposals are being sought for a wave-energy-to-electricity plant. The government does not wish to establish a nuclear energy base because of strong concerns at all levels about safety. The terrible accident at Chernobyl and our experiences with the former Windscale, now Sellafield, nuclear plant in Cumbria, which has turned the Irish Sea into the most radioactive sea in the world, have played a role in Irish people's scepticism about nuclear energy.

However, the reconciliation of environmental quality with the current growth in the economy and competitive energy costs is not easy. The Republic is increasing its consumption of energy; our energy needs have grown by 24 per cent between 1980 and 1993, resulting in increased emissions of carbon dioxide from 30.7 Mt in 1990 to 33.9 Mt in 1995. This growth shows no sign of slowing, unlike our European neighbours whose consumption *per capita* has plateaued since 1980. Ireland's growth is primarily associated with dramatic increases in energy consumption in the transport and commercial sectors. In addition, Ireland is far more dependent on carbon-based fuels, particularly peat, than its neighbours. The consequences of this dependence, involving greenhouse gas emissions and acidification, allied with the fact that our peat reserves will be exhausted by the middle of the next century, make it imperative that we develop renewable resources, such as wind, hydro, wave/tidal, and biomass, to the fullest extent possible.

Commitment at government level towards developing a clean, efficient energy base both at home and globally is not in doubt, but our commitment as a nation at community and personal levels leaves a lot to be desired. An annual energy awareness week has been instituted in an attempt to redress this. But Irish people need to abandon their *laissez faire* attitude towards energy consumption and be more responsible in how they use energy and treat energy waste.

MINING

Ireland is in first place in world lists in terms of tonnes of zinc (Zn) discovered per square kilometre. It is ranked number two for lead (Pb). The total value of mineral production and value-added processing contributed well in excess of US$1 billion to the Irish economy in 1996 which is estimated at 22% of the national economy's turnover.

The breakdown of this figure shows that a total of US$100 million was earned from non-ferrous metal ores; US$45 million for gypsum and gypsum-based products; US$80 million from the sand, gravel and aggregate industry; US$270 million from the cement industry; US$37.5 million for magnesia; and US$21.2 million from the dimension stone industry.

The value of products from non-resource based processing included US$250 million for alumina and more than U.S.$300 million for industrial diamonds.

The vast majority of Irish mining produce is exported. Ireland currently produces more than 3% of world zinc mine production and more than 2% of world lead mine production. These figures are expected to double within the next few years as a number of new mines come on stream.

In 1970 the largest zinc mine in Europe was discovored at Navan, Co. Westmeath. This 70 Mt orebody mine was brought into production in 1977. In 1996 its output was 2.5 Mt, and the long term future of the mine is secure at 38.24 Mt. The Zn-Pb orebody at Galmoy, Co. Kilkenny was brought into production in March 1997 and will support the production of 120,000 tonnes per annum of concentrates over the next ten years. Another sizeable Zn-Pb deposit (17.69 Mt) was found at Lisheen, Co. Tipperary, and is expected to go into production shortly.

At Kingscourt, Co. Cavan, there are substantial reserves of gypsum. Gypsum Industries Ltd. have an output of approximately 350,000 tonnes from their opencast mine there.

Rock Aggregate: In 1996 crushed rock production was in excess of 33 Mt of which some 1.2 Mt was produced for export from a deep water coastal quarry in Co. Cork. Reserves are estimated at more than 100 Mt.

The dimension and ornamental stone sector has experienced large increases in production for the export market, with the sector dominated by blue slab limestone production - 90,000 tonnes per annum.

Recent exploration has indicated the presence of bedrock gold in a number of geological terrains. Gold deposits were discovered in 1982 at Curraghinalt in Co. Tyrone. Since then there have been a significant number of discoveries but no major deposits located.

Ireland has a widely varied geological framework that includes a number of mineral 'provinces' which contain a wide selection of base and precious metals as well as industrial mineral deposits. In fact, Ireland is now internationally known as a major base metal territory with a number of major finds over the past twenty five years.

While mining has occurred in Ireland over many centuries, mining on a large industrial scale is less than 30 years in existence. The country's mining industry is expected to grow more rapidly in the coming years as many of the metals discovered, particularly zinc, are relatively high grade, are found in shallow locations and have a simple metallurgy which means that costs, compared to excavating minerals in deeper locations, are well below average international costs.

N.I. MINERAL PRODUCTION, 1995-1996

Mineral	Quantity (000 tonnes)		Selling Value at Mine / Quarry (£000s)	
	1995	1996	1995	1996
Basalt and Igneous Rock*	7,564	6,974	18,751	17,007
Sandstone	4,779	4,941	11,151	12,023
Limestone	3,703	4,122	10,928	10,793
Sand and Gravel	5,262	7,684	10,730	16,880
Others	812	1,392	4,422	6,622
Total:	22,120	25,113	55,982	63,325

N.I. PERSONS EMPLOYED AT MINES AND QUARRIES, 1995-1996

Mineral	Inside Pit or Excavation	Outside Pit or Excavation	Management/ Administration	Total Employed 1995	1996
Basalt and Igneous Rock*	152	220	108	480	574
Sandstone	97	137	72	306	238
Limestone	68	60	97	225	210
Sand and Gravel	109	93	99	301	250
Others	73	35	40	148	103
Total:	499	545	416	1,460	1,375

N.I.: MINERAL PRODUCTION BY COUNTY, 1996

Mineral	Quantity (000 tonnes)	Value (£000s)
Limestone:		
Co. Antrim	173.2	3,012.3
Co. Armagh	381.0	963.0
Co. Derry	81.5	288.4
Co. Down	-	-
Co. Fermanagh	2,117.1	3,965.1
Co. Tyrone	1,369.5	2,564.6
Total Limestone	4,122.3	10,793.3
Sand and Gravel:		
Co. Antrim	1,329.6	2,650.0
Co. Armagh	-	-
Co. Derry	3,034.4	7,109.3
Co. Down	75.1	181.5
Co. Fermanagh	453.5	1,276.5
Co. Tyrone	2,791.8	5,662.6
Total Sand and Gravel	7,684.4	16,879.9
Basalt and Igneous Rock:		
Co. Antrim	3,428.8	9,534.7
Co. Armagh	514.9	1,382.0
Co. Derry	1,612.2	3,293.0
Co. Down	845.7	1,508.4
Co. Fermanagh	28.0	84.0
Co. Tyrone	544.0	1,204.3
Total Basalt and Igneous Rock*	6,973.5	17,006.0
Sandstone:		
Co. Antrim	-	-
Co. Armagh	1,020.8	2,450.6
Co. Derry	-	-
Co. Down	3,900.6	9,532.5
Co. Fermanagh	-	-
Co. Tyrone	20.0	40.0
Total Sandstone	4,941.4	12,023.1
Others:		
Co. Antrim	525.3	4,192.1
Co. Armagh	150.3	352.1
Co. Down	15.0	71.1
Co. Fermanagh	120.0	120.0
Co. Derry	70.4	538.8
Co. Tyrone	510.9	1,348.1
Total Others	1,391.8	6,622.2

Basalt and Igneous rock (other than Granite)

N.I.: MINERAL PRODUCTION, 1995-1996

Mineral	Quantity (000 tonnes)		Selling Value at Mine / Quarry (£000s)	
	1995	1996	1995	1996
Basalt and Igneous Rock*	7,564	6,974	18,751	17,007
Sandstone	4,779	4,941	11,151	12,023
Limestone	3,703	4,122	10,793	10,793
Sand and Gravel	5,262	7,684	10,730	16,880
Others	812	1,392	4,422	6,622
Total:	**22,120**	**25,113**	**55,982**	**63,325**

N.I.: POWER STATIONS BY TYPE AND CAPACITY

Name	Type	Capacity (MW)
Ballylumford	Fuel Oil / Gas Oil	1,067
Belfast West	Coal	240
Kilroot	Fuel Oil / Coal or Gas Oil	578
Coolkeeragh	Fuel Oil / Gas Oil	358

REPUBLIC OF IRELAND: POWER STATIONS BY TYPE AND CAPACITY, 1995

Name	Type	Capacity (KW)
Allenwood	Peat	-
Bellacorrick	Peat	239
Cahirciveen	Peat	11
Ferbane	Peat	171
Gweedore	Peat	3
Lanesboro	Peat	581
Rhode	Peat	393
Shannnonbridge	Peat	578
Turlough Hill	Pumped Storage	255
Ardnacrusha	Hydro-Electric	268
Clady	Hydro-Electric	16
Erne	Hydro-Electric	275
Lee-Inniscarra	Hydro-Electric	87
Liffey-Poulaphouca	Hydro-Electric	37
Arigna	Coal / Oil	-
Great Island	Coal / Oil	221
Moneypoint	Coal / Oil	6,995
Poolbeg	Coal / Oil	730
Tarbert	Coal / Oil	1,688
Aghada	Gas	1,823
Marina	Gas	634
North Wall	Gas	669
Poolbeg	Gas	1,882

ESTIMATED UNIT COST OF ELECTRICITY, 1997

Overall Usage	Republic of Ireland (per unit of electricity)	Northern Ireland (per unit of electricity)
1,700 kWh per year (incl. V.A.T.)	9.89p	12.08p
3,500 kWh per year (incl. V.A.T.)	8.92p	10.24p
160,000 kWh per year	8.51p	10.68p
1.25 GWh per year	6.33p	6.95p
10 GWh per year	4.91p	6.09p
24 GWh per year	4.22p	5.52p

kWh - kilo watt hours; GWh - giga watt hours

REPUBLIC OF IRELAND: E.S.B. DEVELOPMENT, 1930-1996

Year	Units sold to Customers (Millions)	Revenue £000	Average price per unit	Customers Total
1929-30	43.2	478	1.108	48,606
1939-40	318.6	1,946	0.612	172,545
1949-50	626.1	4,774	0.763	310,639
1959-60	1,692.2	14,724	0.871	610,946
1969-70	4,411.6	39,400	0.892	786,500
1979-80	8,506.3	300,024	3.505	1,043,428
1985-86	9,787.8	757,172	7.736	1,194,765
1990	11,768.0	756,074	6.425	1,278,870
1991	12,370.1	785,205	6.348	1,302,061
1992	13,103.9	826,464	6.307	1,326,547
1993	13,438.7	842,416	6.269	1,348,196
1994	14,024.9	874,879	6.238	1,375,975
1995	14,699.1	913,143	6.212	1,407,772
1996	15,706.6	979,524	6.236	1,442,416

NORTHERN IRELAND: ELECTRICITY DEVELOPMENT, 1990-1996

Operational Statistics (£m)	1990-91	1991-92	1992-93	1993-94	1994-95	1995-96
Turnover	389.4	417.7	453.2	481.9	497.7	524.7
Cost of Sales	-	-	259.3	282.2	289.2	304.6
Operating Costs	293.5	313.0	121.6	117.8	113.9	114.2
Capital Expenditure	54.5	55.3	58.5	41.9	58.5	66.5

REPUBLIC OF IRELAND: ESB CONTRIBUTION TO THE ECONOMY, 1991-1996

Sector	1991 £m	1992 £m	1993 £m	1994 £m	1995 £m	1996 £m
Fuel (natural gas, peat, coal)	132	124	129	137	160	174
Irish suppliers of goods and services	185	182	189	218	213	227
Rates	29	31	32	34	35	36
Payroll costs (incl. capital projects)	258	284	301	306	299	297
Interest paid to stockholders and lenders	25	25	24	22	29	22
Pensions funding and other payments	-	-	-	-	8	187
Total:	629	646	675	717	744	943

R.O.I. ESB NETWORK STATISTICS, 1996

Network statistics	Installed - 1996	In service - December 31, 1996
Overhead lines (km)	2,652	78,434
Underground cables (km)	240	4,226
Substations: Number	4,145	105,666
Substations: Capacity (kVA)	483	15,440

REPUBLIC OF IRELAND: DISTRIBUTION STATISTICS, 1991-1996

Distribution Statistics	1991	1992	1993	1994	1995	1996
New houses connected	19,594	21,624	20,864	26,552	29,804	33,097
Transformer capacity (kVA)	250,289	471,930	447,821	389,384	519,209	483,000
Networks installed (km)	965	1,019	1,025	853	1,013	1,199
Capital expenditure (£'000)	69,581	84,105	105,758	89,700	99,600	124,500

REPUBLIC OF IRELAND: ESB AND BORD NA MONA EMPLOYEES

Employees	1991	1992	1993	1994	1995	1996
E.S.B.	10,096	10,340	10,322	10,070	9,702	9,063
Bord na Móna	2,673	2,387	2,297	2,270	2,268	2,241

N.I. ENERGY INDUSTRY EMPLOYEES, 1996

Industry Section	No.s
Electricity distribution, supply and power procurement	1,964
Other businesses and ancillary services	516
Subsidiaries	346
Total:	2,826

REPUBLIC OF IRELAND: ENERGY DEMANDS, 1996

Energy sources	%	Energy sources	%
Oil	50	Peat	11
Natural gas	20	Other	2
Coal	17		

N.I. PRIMARY ENERGY DEMANDS, 1990-1996

Description	1991 therms (m)	%	1992 therms (m)	%	1993 therms (m)	%	1994 therms (m)	%	1995/96 therms (m)	%
Oil	1,362	67	1,361	68	1,472	69	1,373	67	1,296	64
Coal	668	33	643	32	647	31	688	33	716	36
Total: Oil and Coal	2,030	100	2,004	100	2,119	100	2,061	100	2,012	100

N.I. SHIPMENTS OF COAL, 1991-1995

(per 1000 tonne)	1991	1992	1993	1994	1995
Domestic	1,303	1,154	1,082	1,211	932
Industrial	191	170	147	190	206
Electricity	1,035	1,134	1,256	1,225	1,660
Totals:	2,529	2,458	2,485	2,626	2,798

NORTHERN IRELAND: ENERGY CONSUMPTION BY SOURCE, 1990-1995

Energy Source (million therms)	1990	1991	1992	1993	1994	1995
Coal	388	422	374	349.6	398	323
Gas	-	-	-	-	-	-
Electricity	197.9	201	-	216.3	221	226
Petroleum	437	449	467	528.1	500	526
Totals:	1,022.9	1,072	841	1,094	1,119	1,075

R.O.I. FUEL CONSUMPTION, 1995

Energy Source	TOE (Ton of Oil Equivalent)
Peat	1,214,000
Coal	1,000
Natural Gas	1,916,000
Hydro Power	63,000
Other Renewable Energies	179,000
Total:	3,373,000

N.I.: SELECTED ELECTRICITY STATISTICS

Description	1990/91	1991/92	1992/93	1993/94	1994/95	1995/96
Total Units Generated	6,983.7	7,129.6	-	-	-	-
Sales to all Consumers	5,884	5,997	6,214	6,412	6,529	6,715
Electricity Sales Revenue (£m)	380.0	402.4	418.3	-	-	-
Total Consumers	605,520	615,133	624,200	633,647	643,776	654,625

REPUBLIC OF IRELAND: AVERAGE PRICE OF PETROL YEARLY, 1987-1996 (IR£)

Year	Premium Leaded	Regular Leaded	Unleaded Petrol
1987	58.87	57.93	0
1988	58.19	57.06	0
1989	61.49	60.57	61.71
1990	63.02	59.92	60.90
1991	62.26	0	59.89
1992	59.04	0	58.27
1993	59.43	0	56.57
1994	59.77	0	56.03
1995	60.57	0	56.34
1996	63.69	0	59.14

NORTHERN IRELAND: AVERAGE PRICE OF PETROL YEARLY, 1987-1996 (£ STG)

Year (pence per litre)	4 star	Super Unleaded	Unleaded	2 star	Derv
1987	37.90	0	0	37.07	34.58
1988	37.38	0	0	36.58	33.99
1989	40.39	0	38.29	39.73	36.18
1990	44.87	0	42.03	0	40.48
1991	48.48	47.31	45.07	0	43.82
1992	50.28	48.38	46.07	0	45.01
1993	54.12	52.91	49.44	0	49.20
1994	56.87	55.98	51.58	0	51.53
1995	59.70	58.55	53.77	0	54.24
1996	61.63	63.67	56.52	0	57.71

REPUBLIC OF IRELAND: PEAT AND BRIQUETTE PRODUCTION AND SALES, 1989-1997

Year	Milled Peat (M tonnnes)		Briquette (000 tonnes)	
	Production	Sales	Production	Sales
1989/90	7.3	4.2	355	368
1990/91	5.9	4.5	403	399
1991/92	4.3	4.5	365	367
1992/93	2.7	4.2	394	374
1993/94	3.5	3.9	365	391
1994/95	3.6	3.9	365	363
1995/96	6.7	4.0	344	294
1996/97	5.0	4.0	291	283

REPUBLIC OF IRELAND: BORD NA MÓNA PRODUCTION AND SALES STATISTICS, 1992/1997

Description	1992/93	1993/94	1994/95	1995/96	1996/97
Production:					
Machine Turf *(tonnes)*	135,000	123,000	94,000	77,000	62,000
Milled Peat *(tonnes)*	2,759,000	3,536,000	3,646,000	6,658,000	5,049,000
Briquettes *(tonnes)*	394,000	365,000	365,000	344,000	291,000
Horticulture *(cu metres)*	1,216,000	1,160,000	1,142,000	1,702,000	1,452,000
Total:	4,504,000	5,184,000	5,247,000	8,781,000	6,854,000
Sales:					
Machine Turf to E.S.B. *(tonnes)*	19,000	-	-	-	-
Machine Turf to Others *(tonnes)*	105,000	106,000	97,000	86,000	88,000
Milled Peat to E.S.B. *(tonnes)*	3,259,000	2,944,000	2,994,000	3,145,000	3,284,000
Milled Peat to Bord na Móna					
Factories *(tonnes)*	1,002,000	962,000	995,000	868,000	728,000
Briquettes *(tonnes)*	374,000	391,000	363,000	294,000	283,000
Horticulture *(cu metres)*	1,271,000	1,446,000	1,562,000	1,710,000	1,393,000
Total:	6,030,000	5,849,000	6,011,000	14,653,000	5,776,000
Value of Sales:					
Machine Turf to E.S.B. *(£000s)*	515	-	-	-	-
Machine Turf to Others *(£000s)*	3,357	3,264	3,224	2,581	2,363
Milled Peat to E.S.B. *(£000s)*	57,613	56,406	54,926	57,613	56,477
Briquettes *(£000s)*	26,087	27,573	27,151	23,326	22,089
Coal *(£000s)*	-	-	-	9,073	11,069
Horticulture *(£000s)*	33,783	37,610	41,587	45,409	45,959
Environmental Products *(£000s)*	1,661	2,166	2,732	3,050	4,930
Total: Value of Sales *(£000s)*	123,016	127,019	129,620	141,052	142,887

TOURISM

Tourism: An Unprecedented Success Story

By *Helen Curley*, Artcam

I N 1997 Irish tourism, in the sixth successive year of growth, increased its international exchange earnings by an estimated 9% on the 1996 figure of $1.45 billion. By the end of 1999, however, the industry will be worth £2.25 billion in foreign earnings, and when the figures for domestic tourism expenditure are included, the industry's total value will have reached £2.5 billion. In the period 1994-99 (the second phase of the government's Operational Programme for Tourism) an extra 29,000 full-time job equivalents will have been provided within the economy, bringing the total number whose employment depends on the industry to more than 130,000.

The tourism sector on the island of Ireland is managed by two bodies: Bord Fáilte in the Republic and the Northern Ireland Tourist Board in the North. These bodies are responsible for marketing their respective regions both at home and abroad. At local level, they provide a wide range of services and advice to visitors and service providers. Both boards offer literature on Ireland and provide an accommodation booking service to visitors, for a nominal fee, from the wide range of B&Bs, guest houses, hotels and self-catering homes. The local offices advise people where to go, how to get there, what to see and what to do at any location in Ireland.

In 1996, Tourism Brand Ireland was launched worldwide. It allowed both tourism bodies to unify behind a single marketing initiative, representing a critical shift in attitudes in both jurisdictions towards marketing Ireland abroad. The initiative was marketed in press and television campaigns in Britain, the U.S., France and Germany at a cost of IR£6.7 million and was presented under a new logo which emphasised the warmth of the Irish people and the unique experience of Irish lifestyles. However, the logo has recently been amended, re-incorporating the shamrock as its major element - a controversial move that has drawn criticism from the programme's Northern partners.

But this must not detract from the outstanding performance of the Irish tourism sector in recent years. It is estimated that during the summer months, the number of people on the island of Ireland doubles with the influx of tourists. Earnings from tourism have soared and tourism accounts for 6.2 per cent of GNP, having the potential to become an even greater contributor. By the end of 1999, it is estimated that tourism will succeed agricultue as a major domestic employer in Ireland.

However, this remarkable success may come at a price. There are those who question whether the marketing and packaging of Ireland is turning the country into one large heritage theme park, eroding the spontaneity and warmth of Irish people's welcome and replacing it with an ugly drive to exploit the tourist as a cash cow. Or should the confident marketing of this country, north and south, be interpreted as a sign that we have finally realised Ireland is a truly wonderful place and should be seen accordingly as a destination that offers an incomparable blend of scenery, history, culture and *craic*?

TOURISM VISITORS TO REPUBLIC OF IRELAND BY COUNTRY OF ORIGIN

Country	1993	1994	1995	1996
Britain	1,857,000	2,038,000	2,285,000	2,590,000
Mainland Europe:				
Belgium / Luxembourg	41,000	41,000	53,000	60,000
Denmark	17,000	19,000	22,000	23,000
France	242,000	231,000	234,000	262,000
Germany	265,000	269,000	319,000	339,000
Italy	116,000	121,000	112,000	119,000
Netherlands	69,000	80,000	94,000	109,000
Norway / Sweden	32,000	33,000	46,000	55,000
Spain	57,000	59,000	67,000	66,000
Switzerland	40,000	62,000	62,000	62,000
Other	66,000	73,000	93,000	83,000
Total: Mainland Europe	945,000	988,000	1,102,000	1,178,000
North America:				
USA	377,000	449,000	587,000	660,000
Canada	45,000	45,000	54,000	69,000
Total: North America	422,000	494,000	641,000	729,000
Rest of World:				
Australia / New Zealand	56,000	68,000	89,000	88,000
Japan	18,000	22,000	30,000	33,000
Other	50,000	69,000	85,000	65,000
Total: Rest of World	124,000	159,000	204,000	186,000
TOTAL	**3,348,000**	**3,679,000**	**4,232,000**	**4,683,000**
Northern Ireland	540,000	630,000	590,000	600,000
Total incl. Northern Ireland	3,888,000	4,309,000	4,822,000	5,283,000
Domestic Trips	7,660,000	7,244,000	6,924,000	6,170,000

TOURISM VISITORS TO NORTHERN IRELAND BY COUNTRY OF ORIGIN

Country	1995	1996
Britain:		
England & Wales	603,000	604,000
Scotland	207,000	221,000
Total: Britain	**810,000**	**825,000**
Mainland Europe:		
France	19,000	19,000
Germany	32,000	32,000
Netherlands	8,000	10,000
Italy	9,000	8,000
Other	41,000	27,000
Total: Mainland Europe	**109,000**	**96,000**
North America:		
USA	83,000	72,000
Canada	35,000	28,000
Total: North America	**118,000**	**100,000**
Australia / New Zealand	32,000	29,000
Rest of World	18,000	15,000
Republic of Ireland	470,000	370,000
TOTAL	**1,557,000**	**1,435,000**

HOLIDAY VISITORS TO N.I. BY ORIGIN

Country	1995	1996
Britain	112,000	88,000
Mainland Europe	57,000	41,000
North America	60,000	40,000
Australia / New Zealand	20,000	16,000
Rest of World	3,000	2,000
Republic of Ireland	210,000	110,000
TOTAL	**461,000**	**297,000**

EXPENDITURE BY VISITORS TO REP. OF IRELAND

Expenditure (£M)	1993	1994	1995	1996
Britain	375.1	451.9	501.2	573.4
Mainland Europe:				
France	91.5	74.4	83.8	88.1
Germany	117.3	110.4	122.4	148.9
Italy	51.1	46.3	42.4	53.5
Netherlands	-	-	-	35.4
Other	141.7	140.5	165.1	140.7
Total: Mainland Europe	**401.6**	**371.6**	**413.7**	**466.6**
North America	182.1	213.4	275.0	316.6
Rest of World	54.7	77.2	96.5	93.8
Total	1,013.5	1,114.1	1,286.4	1,450.4
Northern Ireland	69.0	80.5	82.6	84.6
Excursionist Revenue	7.5	7.4	8.0	8.0
Carrier Receipts	277.0	296.0	302.0	341.0
TOTAL	**1,367.0**	**1,498.0**	**1,679.0**	**1,884.0**
Domestic Trips	620.8	657.1	610.9	578.8

EXPENDITURE BY VISITORS TO N. IRELAND

Expenditure (£M)	1993	1994	1995	1996
Britain	92.4	92.8	108.0	
Mainland Europe	17.1	17.4	23.0	
North America	19.7	21.9	26.0	
Republic of Ireland	30.1	34.0	39.0	
Elsewhere	13.7	16.8	18.0	
Total: Overseas (excl. Britain & Ireland)	50.5	56.1	67.0	
TOTAL	173.0	182.9	214.0	

REPUBLIC OF IRELAND ACCOMMODATION IN 1996

Accommodation	Premises	Rooms	Beds
Bed & Breakfast Homes (approved)	4,227	17,000	33,000
Caravan & Camping*	135	13,000	n/a
Guesthouses	356	4,000	8,000
Hostels**	190	5,000	9,000
Hotels	717	26,000	56,000
Self-Catering	4,830	14,000	28,000
University Accommodation	15	2,000	4,000
TOTAL	10,470	81,000	138,000

*One caravan & camping pitch = two rooms ** Two beds in a hostel = one room*

NORTHERN IRELAND ACCOMMODATION IN 1996

Accommodation	Premises	Rooms
Bed & Breakfast Homes (approved)	865	5,595
Guesthouses	159	1,197
Hostels	39	602
Hotels	129	3,680
Self-Catering	346	1,943
TOTAL	1,538	13,017

DESTINATION AND EXPENDITURE BY VISITORS TO REPUBLIC OF IRELAND IN 1996

NUMBERS EXPENDITURE (£M)	IRISH TOURISTS	NORTHERN IRISH	FOREIGN VISITORS	EXCURSIONIST	TOTAL
Dublin	970,000	140,000	2,360,000		3,470,000
	£ 66.3m	£ 16.1m	£ 440.7m	£ 5.9m	£ 529.0m
Midlands-East	734,000	20,000	752,000		1,506,000
	£ 58.9m	£ 2.1m	£ 142.6m	£ 0.6m	£204.2m
Mid-West	742,000	50,000	1,010,000		1,802,000
	£ 71.0m	£ 9.6m	£ 163.6m		£ 244.2m
North-West	643,000	280,000	533,000		1,456,000
	£ 73.1m	£ 35.6m	£ 91.4m	£ 1.5m	£ 201.6m
South-East	945,000	40,000	1,007,000		1,992,000
	£ 89.0m	£ 5.1m	£ 134.5m		£ 228.6m
South-West	1,119,000	30,000	1,428,000		2,577,000
	£ 122.1m	£ 4.3m	£ 285.2m		£ 411.6m
West	1,090,000	70,000	1,098,000		2,258,000
	£ 98.4m	£ 11.8m	£ 192.4m		£ 302.6m
TOTAL: NUMBERS	5,262,000	630,000	8,188,000		14,080,000
TOTAL: EXPENDITURE	£ 578.8m	£ 84.6m	£ 1,450.4m	£ 8.0m	£ 2,121.8m

EXPENDITURE PER PERSON BY VISITORS TO REPUBLIC OF IRELAND IN 1996

EXPENDITURE (%)	BRITAIN	MAINLAND EUROPE	NORTH AMERICA	REST OF WORLD	AVERAGE
Bed & Board	22	34	26	22	26.00
Internal Transport	9	8	10	8	8.75
Other Food / Drink	35	24	29	27	28.75
Shopping	20	12	25	28	21.25
Sightseeing / Entertainment	8	4	6	5	5.75
Miscellaneous	7	18	3	11	9.75

EXPENDITURE PER PERSON BY VISITORS TO NORTHERN IRELAND IN 1995

EXPENDITURE (%)	VISITING RELATIVES	HOLIDAY	BUSINESS	AVERAGE
Accommodation / Meals	22	38	62	40
Internal Travel	11	14	12	11
Entertainment incl. drinks	19	14	12	16
Shopping	45	32	12	30
Miscellaneous	3	2	2	3
TOTAL AMOUNT SPENT	£ 73m	£ 52m	£ 68m	£ 214m

ACCOMMODATION AND SOCIAL EXPENSES

Accommodation (price range for a one night stay)	REPUBLIC OF IRELAND (£)	NORTHERN IRELAND (£)
4 / 5 Star Hotel	46 - 185	52.50 - 165
2 Star Hotel	24 - 95	25 - 95
Guest House	14 - 95	19 - 69

VISITS ABROAD BY REPUBLIC OF IRELAND RESIDENTS (ROUTE OF TRAVEL / EXPENDITURE)

Numbers Expenditure (Estimated £M)	1993	1994	1995	1996
Destination (Overseas):				
Cross-Channel (by air)	871,000	1,071,000	1,200,000	1,398,000
Spending	£ 369m	£ 531m	£ 621m	£ 717m
Cross-Channel (by sea)	526,000	552,000	512,000	458,000
Spending	£ 151m	£ 156m	£ 169m	£ 132m
Mainland Europe	517,000	589,000	689,000	725,000
Spending	£ 309m	£ 362m	£ 468m	£ 501m
North America	142,000	156,000	146,000	153,000
Spending	£ 126m	£ 150m	£ 155m	£ 159m
Total: Numbers	2,056,000	2,368,000	2,547,000	2,734,000
Total: Route of Travel (Overseas)	£ 955m	£ 1,199m	£ 1,413m	£ 1,509m
Cross-Border	£ 64m	£ 75m	£ 83m	£ 82m
Total: Expenditure	£ 1,019m	£ 1,274m	£ 1,496m	£ 1,591m
Fares by Irish Visitors Abroad to Irish Carriers	£ 185m	£ 202m	£ 230m	£ 230m
Total: Net International Expenditure	£ 834m	£ 1,072m	£ 1,266m	£ 1,361m

VISITS ABROAD BY REPUBLIC OF IRELAND RESIDENTS (REASON FOR JOURNEY)

Numbers Expenditure (Estimated £M)	1993	1994	1995	1996
Reason for Journey:				
Business	373,000	446,000	451,000	551,000
	£ 208m	£ 276m	£ 326m	£ 389m
Tourist	857,000	1,006,000	1,176,000	1,182,000
	£ 428m	£ 529m	£ 655m	£ 676m
Visiting Relatives	622,000	681,000	635,000	721,000
	£ 218m	£ 266m	£ 256m	£ 282m
Other	204,000	235,000	285,000	278,000
	£ 100m	£ 128m	£ 176m	£ 160m
TOTAL: NUMBERS	2,056,000	2,368,000	2,547,000	2,732,000
TOTAL: EXPENDITURE	£ 954m	£ 1,199m	£ 1,413 m	£ 1,507m

OVERSEAS VISITS BY REPUBLIC OF IRELAND RESIDENTS

Length of Stay (Nights)	1993	1994	1995	1996
Route of Travel:				
Cross-Channel (by air)	8.3	9.1	9.3	8.7
Cross-Channel (by sea)	8.3	7.6	8.1	7.5
Mainland Europe	9.9	11.5	11.3	10.9
Transatlantic	18.4	19.7	17.2	17.2
Reason for Journey:				
Business	6.4	7.3	6.9	6.3
Tourist	9.5	10.3	10.0	9.9
Visiting Relatives	9.9	10.3	10.3	9.8
Other	12.3	13.2	14.7	13.9
ALL OVERSEAS VISITS	9.3	10.0	10.0	9.5

OVERSEAS VISITS BY NORTHERN IRELAND RESIDENTS

Length of Stay	1993	1994	1995	1996
1 - 3 Nights:				
Trips	870,000	760,000	720,000	
Expenditure	£ 61.0m	£ 75.5m	£ 112.0m	
4 or more Nights:				
Trips	1,020,000	966,000	1,130,000	
Expenditure	£ 378.0m	£ 371.1m	£ 410.0m	
Total: Trips	**1,890,000**	**1,726,000**	**1,850,000**	
Total: Expenditure	**£ 439.0m**	**£ 446.6m**	**£ 522.0m**	

HERITAGE CENTRES / SITES IN IRELAND

CO. ANTRIM

Antrim Castle Gardens, Massereene Demesne, Antrim. Tel. (01849) 428000.

Benvarden Garden, Dervock, Ballymoney. Tel. (012657) 41311.

Dunluce Centre, Portrush. Tel. (01265) 824444.

Giant's Causeway, Causeway Road, Bushmills. Tel. (012657) 31159.

Palm House Botanic Gardens, Stranmillis Road, Belfast. Tel. (01232) 324902.

CO. ARMAGH

Ardress, Annaghmore. Tel. (01762) 851236.

The Argory, Moy, Dungannon. Tel. (018687) 84753.

Armagh County Museum, The Mall, Armagh. Tel. (01861) 523070.

Dan Winter Ancestral Home, 9 The Diamond, Derryloughan Road, Loughgall. Tel. (01762) 851344.

Derrymore House, Bessbrook. Tel. (01693) 830353.

Palace Stables Heritage Centre, Friary Road, Armagh. Tel. (01861) 529629.

CO. CARLOW

Altamont, Tullow. Tel. (0503) 59128.

Browns Hill Dolmen, Rathvilly Road, Carlow.

Carlow Museum, Town Hall, Carlow. Tel. (0503) 31324.

Dunleckney Manor, Bagnalstown.

Haroldstown Museum, Town Hall, Carlow.

CO. CAVAN

Clough Oughter Castle, Killykeen.

'Finn McCool's Fingers', Shantemon.

The "Pighouse" Folk Museum, Cornafean.

St. Killian Centre, Mullagh.

CO. CLARE

Bunratty Castle & Folk Park, Bunratty. Tel. (061) 360788.

Carnelly House, Clarecastle.

Craggaunowen Project, Quin. Tel. (061) 360788.

Cratloe Woods House, Cratloe. Tel. (061) 327031.

Dromore Wood, Ruan, Ennis. Tel. (065) 37166.

Dunguaire Castle, Kinvara. Tel. (061) 360788.

Ennis Friary, Abbey Street, Ennis. Tel. (065) 29100.

Knappogue Castle, Quin. Tel. (061) 360788.

Scattery Island Centre, Merchants Quay, Kilrush. Tel. (065) 52144.

CO. CORK

Anne's Grove Gardens, Castletownroche. Tel. (022) 26145.

Bantry House, Bantry. Tel. (027) 50047.

Barryscourt Castle, Carrigtwohill. Tel. (021) 883864.

Blarney Castle and Rock Close, Blarney. Tel. (021) 381518.

Charles Fort, Summer Cove, Kinsale. Tel. (021) 772263.

Creagh Gardens, Skibbereen. Tel. (028) 22121.

Desmond Castle, Cork Street, Kinsale. Tel. (021) 774855.

Doneraile Wildlife Park, Doneraile. Tel. (022) 24244.

Dunkathel, Glanmire. Tel. (021) 821014.

Fota Arboretum and Gardens, Fota Island, Cork. Tel. (021) 812728.

Ilnacullin (Garinish Island), Glengarrif, Bantry. Tel. (027) 63049.

Riverstown House, Glanmire. Tel. (021) 821205.

Timoleague Castle Gardens, Timoleague, Bandon. Tel. (023) 46116.

CO. DERRY

Earhart Centre & Wildlife Sanctuary, Ballyarnett, Derry. Tel. (01504) 265234.

Downhill Castle, Mussenden Road, Castlerock. Tel. (01265) 848567.

Foyle Valley Railway Centre, Foyle Road, Derry. Tel. (01504) 265234.

Garvagh Museum & Heritage Centre, Main Street, Garvagh. Tel. (012665) 58216.

Roe Valley Counrty Park, Limavady. Tel. (015047) 22074.

Springhill, Moneymore, Magherafelt. Tel. (016487) 48210.

Tower Museum, Union Hall Place, Derry City. Tel. (01504) 372411.

CO. DONEGAL

Donegal Castle, Donegal Town. Tel. (073) 22405.

Glebe House and Gallery, Church Hill, Letterkenny. Tel. (074) 37071.

Glenveagh National Park, Church Hill, Letterkenny. Tel. (074) 37088.

Grianan of Aileach Castle & Centre, Burt. Tel. (077) 68512.

Newmills Corn and Flax Mills, Churchill Road, Letterkenny. Tel. (074) 25115.

CO. DOWN

Brontë Homeland Interpretive

Centre, Drumballyroney, Rathfriland. Tel. (018206) 31152.

Burren Heritage Centre, Bridge Road, Warrenpoint. Tel. (016937) 73378.

Castle Ward, Strangford. Tel. (01396) 881204.

Mount Stewart, Greyabbey, Newtownards. Tel. (012477) 88387.

North Down Heritage Centre, Castle Park Avenue, Bangor. Tel. (01247) 271200.

Rowallane Garden, Saintfield. Tel. (01238) 510131.

Seaforde Gardens, Seaforde. Tel. (01396) 811370.

Somme Heritage Centre, 233 Bangor Road, Newtownards. Tel. (01247) 823202.

Ulster Folk & Transport Museum, Cultra, Holywood. Tel. (01232) 428428.

CO. DUBLIN

Ardgillan Castle, Balbriggan. Tel. (01) 8492212.

Ayesha Castle, Killiney. Tel. (01) 2852323.

Casino, Off the Malahide Road, Marino, Dublin 3. Tel. (01) 8331618.

Custom House Visitor Centre, Custom House Quay, Dublin 1. Tel. (01) 6793377.

Drimnagh Castle, Longmile Road, Dublin 12. Tel. (01) 4502530.

Dublin Castle, Dame Street, Dublin 2. Tel. (01) 6777129.

Fernhill Gardens, Sandyford. Tel. (01) 2956000.

Garden of Remembrance, Parnell Square East, Dublin 1. Tel. (01) 6613111.

The Iveagh Gardens, Clonmel Street, Dublin 2. Tel. (01) 4757816.

James Joyce Tower, Sandycove. Tel. (01) 2809265.

Kilmainham Gaol, Inchicore Road, Dublin 8. Tel. (01) 4535984.

Lusk Heritage Centre, Lusk. Tel. (01) 8437683.

Malahide Castle, Malahide. Tel. (01) 8462184.

National Botanic Gardens, Glasnevin, Dublin 9. Tel. (01) 8377596.

Newbridge House, Donabate. Tel. (01) 8436534.

Newman House, 85/86 St. Stephen's Green, Dublin 2. Tel. (01) 7067422.

Number Twenty Nine, Lower Fitzwilliam Street, Dublin 2. Tel. (01) 7026165.

Pearse Museum, Grange Road, Rathfarnham, Dublin 16. Tel. (01) 4934208.

Phoenix Park Visitor Centre, Dublin 8. Tel. (01) 6770095.

Powerscourt Town House, South William Street, Dublin 2. Tel. (01) 6794144.

Rathfarnham Castle, Rathfarnham, Dublin 14. Tel. (01) 4939462.

St. Mary's Abbey, Chapter House, Meetinghouse Lane, Off Capel Street, Dublin 1. Tel. (01) 8721490.

St. Stephen's Green, Dublin 2. Tel. (01) 4757816.

War Memorial Gardens, Islandbridge, Dublin 8. Tel. (01) 6613111.

Waterways Visitor Centre, Grand Canal Quay, Dublin 2. Tel. (01) 6777510.

CO. FERMANAGH

Carrothers Family Heritage Museum, Carrybridge Road, Tamlaght. Tel. (01365) 387278.

Castle Balfour, Main Street, Lisnaskea.

Castle Coole, Enniskillen. Tel. (01365) 322690.

Crom Estate, Newtownbutler. Tel. (013657) 38174.

Enniskillen Castle, Castle Barracks, Enniskillen. Tel. (01365) 325000.

Forthill Park & Cole Monument, Enniskillen. Tel. (01365) 325050.

Florence Court, Enniskillen. Tel. (01365) 348249.

Roslea Heritage Centre, Monaghan Road, Roslea. Tel. (013657) 51750.

CO. GALWAY

Athenry Castle, Athenry. Tel. (091) 844797.

Aughnanure Castle, Oughterard. Tel. (091) 552214.

Connemara National Park, Letterfrack. Tel. (095) 41054.

Coole, Gort. Tel. (091) 631804.

Kylemore Abbey, Connemara. Tel. (095) 41146.

Portumna Castle and Gardens, Portumna. Tel. (0509) 41658.

Teach an Phiarsaigh (Patrick Pearse's Cottage), Ros Muc. Tel. (091) 574292.

CO. KERRY

Ardfert Cathedral, Ardfert. Tel. (066) 34711.

Derrynane House, National Historic Park, Caherdaniel. Tel. (066) 75113.

Dunloe Castle Hotel Gardens, Beaufort, Killarney. Tel. (064) 31900.

Gallarus Oratory, Dingle Peninsula.

Ionad an Bhlascaoid Mhóir (The Blasket Centre), Dún Chaoin, Tralee. Tel. (066) 56444.

Muckross Friary, Muckross Estate, Killarney. Tel. (01) 6613111, ext. 2386.

Muckross House, Gardens and Traditional Farms & National Park, Muckross, Killarney. Tel. (064) 31440.

Ross Castle, Killarney. Tel. (064) 35881.

CO. KILDARE

Castletown, Celbridge. Tel. (01) 6288252.

Coolcarrigan House & Gardens, Naas.

Furness, Naas. Tel. (045) 866815.

Leixlip Castle, Leixlip.

CO. KILKENNY

Duiske Abbey & Visitor Centre, Graignamanagh. Tel. (0503) 24238.

Dunmore Cave, Ballyfoyle. Tel. (056) 67726.

Jerpoint Abbey, Thomastown. Tel. (056) 24623.

Kilfane Glen and Waterfall, Kilfane, Thomastown. Tel. (056) 24558.

Kilkenny Castle, National Historic Property, The Parade, Kilkenny City. Tel. (056) 21450.

Rothe House, Parliament Street, Kilkenny. Tel. (056) 22893.

CO. LAOIS

Ballaghmore Castle, Borris-in-Ossory.

Emo Court, Emo. Tel. (0502) 26573.

Heywood Gardens, Ballinakill. Tel. (0502) 33563.

CO. LEITRIM

Lough Rynn Estate & Gardens, Mohill. Tel. (078) 31427.

Parke's Castle, Fivemile Bourne. Tel. (071) 64149.

CO. LIMERICK
Glin Castle, Glin. Tel. (068) 34364.

King John's Castle, Limerick City. Tel. (061) 411201.

Lough Gur Interpretative Centre, Lough Gur. Tel. (061) 360788.

CO. LONGFORD
Carrigglas Manor, Longford. Tel. (043) 41026.

Cashel Heritage Centre, Main Street, Newtowncashel.

Corlea Trackway Visitor Centre, Kenagh. Tel. (043) 22386.

Heritage Museum, Longford. Tel. (043) 46465.

Longford County Museum, Main Street, Longford.

CO. LOUTH
Beaulieu, Drogheda.

Old Mellifont Abbey, Drogheda. Tel. (041) 26459.

CO. MAYO
The Artisan Village, Kiltimagh. Tel. (094) 81494.

Ballintubber Abbey, Ballintubber, Claremorris. Tel. (094) 30934.

Céide Fields, Ballycastle. Tel. (096) 43325.

Enniscoe House, Castlehill, Ballina.

Foxford Woolen Mills Visitor Centre, St. Joseph's Place, Foxford. Tel. (094) 56756.

Old Coastguard Station, Rosmoney, Westport.

Partry House, Partree, Claremorris.

CO. MEATH
Beau Park House, Navan.

Brú na Bóinne Visitor Centre, Donore. Tel. (041) 24488.

Dardistown Castle, Julianstown.

Hamwood House, Dunboyne. Tel. (044) 8255210.

Hill of Tara, Navan. Tel. (046) 25903.

Knowth, near Slane. Tel. (041) 24824.

Newgrange, near Slane. Tel. (041) 24488.

Somerville House, Balrath, Navan.

CO. MONAGHAN
Castle Leslie, Glaslough. Tel. (047) 88109.

Hilton Park, Clones. Tel. (047) 56007.

Patrick Kavanagh Centre, Inniskeen. Tel. (042) 78560.

CO. OFFALY
Birr Castle Demesne, Birr. Tel. (0509) 20336.

Clonmacnoise, Shannonbridge. Tel. (0905) 74195.

CO. ROSCOMMON
Boyle Abbey, Boyle Town. Tel. (079) 62604.

Clonalis House, Castlerea. Tel. (0907) 20014.

County Roscommon Heritage & Genealogical Centre, Church Street, Strokestown. Tel. (078) 33380.

Dr. Douglas Hyde Interpretative Centre, Frenchpark. Tel. (0907) 70016.

King House, Boyle. Tel. (079) 63242.

The Old Schoolhouse Museum, Ballintubber. Tel. (0907) 55397.

Strokestown Park House, Strokestown. Tel. (078) 33013.

CO. SLIGO
Carrowmore Megalithic Cemetery, Carrowmore, Sligo. Tel. (071) 61534.

Lissadell House, Drumcliffe. Tel. (071) 63150.

Sligo Abbey, Abbey Street, Sligo. Tel. (071) 46406.

CO. TIPPERARY
Brú Ború, Cashel. Tel. (062) 61122.

Cahir Castle, Castle Street, Cahir. Tel. (052) 41011.

Carrick-on-Suir Heritage Centre, Main Street, Carrick-on-Suir. Tel. (051) 640200.

Cashel Folk Village, Dominic Street, Cashel. Tel. (062) 62525.

Cashel Heritage Centre, Town Hall, Cashel. Tel. (062) 62511.

Damer House, Roscrea Heritage Centre, Roscrea. Tel. (0505) 21850.

Fethard Folk, Farm and Transport Museum, Cashel Road, Fethard. Tel. (052) 31516.

Ormond Castle, Castle Park, Off Castle Street, Carrick-on-Suir. Tel. (051) 640787.

Rock of Cashel, Cashel. Tel. (062) 61437.

Roscrea Heritage, (Castle and Damer House), Castle Street, Roscrea. Tel. (0505) 21850.

Swiss Cottage, Kilcommon, Cahir. Tel. (052) 41144.

Tipperary County Museum, Parnell Street, Clonmel. Tel. (052) 25399.

CO. TYRONE
An Creagán Visitor Centre, Creggan. Tel. (016627) 61112.

Benburb Valley Heritage Centre, Milltown Road, Benburb. Tel. (01861) 549752.

Corn Mill Heritage Centre, Lineside, Off Dungannon Road, Coalisland. Tel. (01868) 748532.

Donaghmore Heritage Centre, Pomeroy Road, Donaghmore. Tel. (01868) 767039.

Sperrin Heritage Centre, 274 Glenelly Road, Cranagh, Gortin. Tel. (016626) 48142.

Ulster American Folk Park, Castletown, Omagh. Tel. (01662) 243292.

CO. WATERFORD
Curraghmore, Portlaw. Tel. (051) 387102.

Lismore Castle Gardens, Lismore. Tel. (058) 54424.

Lismore Heritage Centre, The Courthouse, Lismore. Tel. (058) 54975.

Reginald's Tower Museum, The Quay, Waterford. Tel. (051) 73501.

Touraneena Heritage Centre, Touaneena, Ballinamult. Tel. (058) 47353.

Waterford Heritage Museum, Greyfriars, Waterford. Tel. (051) 71227.

CO. WESTMEATH
Athlone Castle Interpretative Centre, Athlone. Tel. (0902) 72107.

Dun-na-Sí Heritage Park, Moate. Tel. (0902) 81183.

Tullynally Castle and Gardens, Castlepollard. Tel. (044) 61159.

CO. WEXFORD
Ballyhack Castle, Ballyhack. Tel. (051) 389468.

Dunbrody Abbey and Visitor Centre, Campile, New Ross. Tel. (051) 388603.

Duncannon Fort, Duncannon. Tel. (051) 389454.

Irish Agricultural Museum, Johnstown. Tel. (0530) 42888.

The John F. Kennedy Arboretum, New Ross. Tel. (051) 388171.

Kilmore Quay Maritime Museum, The Quay, Kilmore Quay. Tel. (053) 29655.

National Heritage Park, Ferrycarrig. Tel. (053) 20733.

Tintern Abbey, Saltmills, New Ross. Tel. (01) 661311.

Westgate Heritage Tower, Spawell

Road. Tel. (053) 46506.

Wexford County Museum, Town Centre, Enniscorthy. Tel. (054) 35926.

Wexford Wildfowl Reserve, North Slob, Wexford. Tel. (053) 23129.

Yola Farmstead, Tagoat, Rosslare Harbour. Tel. (053) 31177.

CO. WICKLOW
Avondale House and Estate, Rathdrum. Tel. (0404) 46111.

Dwyer McAllister Cottage, Derrynamuck. Tel. (0404) 45325.

Glendalough Visitor Centre, Glendalough, Bray. Tel. (0404) 45325.

Humewood Castle, Kiltegan. Tel. (0508) 73215.

Powerscourt Gardens & Waterfall, Enniskerry. Tel. (01) 2867676.

Wicklow Mountains National Park, Upper Lake, Glendalough. Tel. (0404) 45425.

GOLF CLUBS LISTING
367 clubs affiliated to the Golfing Union of Ireland (March 1997)

CO. ANTRIM

Club	Holes	Telephone Number
Ballycastle	18	(012657) 62536
Ballyclare	18	(01960) 322696
Ballymena	18	(01266) 861487
Balmoral	18	(01232) 381514
Belvoir Park	18	(01232) 491693
Burnfield House	9	(01232) 838737
Bushfoot	9	(012657) 31317
Cairndhu	18	(01574) 583324
Carrickfergus	18	(01960) 363713
Cliftonville	9	(01232) 744158
Cushendall	9	(012667) 71318
Down Royal	18	(01846) 621339
Dunmurry	18	(01232) 610834
Fortwilliam	18	(01232) 370770
Garron Tower	-	(012667) 71210
Gilnahirk	9	(01232) 448477
Gracehill	9	(012657) 51209
Greenacres	18	(01960) 354111
Greenisland	9	(01232) 862236
Knock	18	(01232) 483251
Lambeg	9	(01846) 662738
Larne	9	(01960) 382228
Lisburn	18	(01846) 677216
Mallusk	9	(01232) 843799
Malone	27	(01232) 612758
Massereene	18	(01849) 428096
Mount Ober	18	(01232) 401811
Ormeau	9	(01232) 640700
Queen's University	-	(01232) 245133
Rathmore	-	(01265) 822285
Royal Portrush	45	(01265) 822311
Shandon Park	18	(01232) 401856
Whitehead	18	(01960) 353631

CO. ARMAGH

Club	Holes	Telephone Number
Ashfield	18	(01693) 868180
County Armagh	18	(01861) 525861
Edenmore	18	(01846) 611310
Lurgan	18	(01762) 322087
Portadown	18	(01762) 355356
Silverwood	18	(01762) 326606

Tandragee	18	(01762) 841272

CO. CARLOW

Club	Holes	Telephone Number
Borris	9	(0503) 73310
Carlow	18	(0503) 31695
Mount Wolseley	18	(0503) 51674

CO. CAVAN

Club	Holes	Telephone Number
Belturbet	9	(049) 22287
Blacklion	9	(072) 53024
Cabra Castle	9	(046) 52372
County Cavan	18	(049) 31541
Slieve Russell	18	(049) 26444
Virginia	9	(049) 48066

CO. CLARE

Club	Holes	Telephone Number
Clonlara	12	(061) 354141
Dromoland	18	(061) 368144
East Clare	9	(061) 921322
Ennis	18	(065) 24074
Kilkee	9	(065) 56048
Kilrush	18	(065) 51138
Lahinch	36	(065) 81003
Shannon	18	(061) 471849
Spanish Point	9	(065) 84198
Woodstock	18	(065) 29463

CO. CORK

Club	Holes	Telephone Number
Bandon	18	(023) 41111
Bantry Park	18	(027) 50579
Berehaven	9	(027) 70700
Charleville	18	(063) 81257
Cobh	9	(021) 812399
Coosheen	9	(028) 28182
Cork	18	(021) 353451
Doneraile	9	(022) 24137
Douglas	18	(021) 895297
Dunmore	9	(023) 33352
East Cork	18	(021) 631687
Fermoy	18	(025) 32694
Fernhill	18	(021) 373103
Fota Island	18	(021) 883700
Frankfield	9	(021) 361199

Glengarriff	9	(027) 63150
Harbour Point	18	(021) 353094
Kanturk	18	(029) 50534
Kinsale	27	(021) 774722
Lee Valley	18	(021) 331721
Macroom	18	(026) 41072
Mahon	18	(021) 318313
Mallow	18	(022) 42501
Mitchelstown	15	(025) 24072
Monkstown	18	(021) 841376
Muskerry	18	(021) 385297
Raffeen Creek	9	(021) 378430
Skibbereen	18	(028) 21227
University College Cork	-	(021) 276871
Youghal	18	(024) 92787

CO. DERRY

Club	Holes	Telephone Number
Brown Trout	9	(01265) 868209
Castlerock	27	(01265) 848314
City of Derry	27	(01504) 46369
Foyle	27	(01504) 352222
Kilrea	9	(012665) 40119
Manor	9	(012665) 41351
Moyola Park	18	(01648) 468468
Portstewart	45	(01265) 832015
Roe Park	18	(015047) 60105
University of Ulster	-	(01265) 44141

CO. DONEGAL

Club	Holes	Telephone Number
Ballybofey & Stranorlar	18	(074) 31093
Ballyliffin	36	(077) 76119
Buncrana	9	(077) 62279
Bundoran	18	(072) 41302
Chloic Cheann Fhaola	9	(074) 65416
Cruit Island	9	(075) 43296
Donegal	18	(073) 34054
Dunfanaghy	18	(074) 36335
Gaoth Dobhair	9	(075) 31140
Greencastle	18	(077) 81013
Letterkenny	18	(074) 21150
Narin & Portnoo	18	(075) 21722
North West	18	(077) 61027
Otway	9	(074) 58319
Portsalon	18	(074) 59459
Redcastle	9	(077) 82073
Rosapenna	18	(074) 55301

CO. DOWN

Club	Holes	Telephone Number
Ardglass	18	(01396) 841219
Ardminnan	9	(012477) 71321
Banbridge	18	(018206) 62211
Bangor	18	(01247) 270922
Blackwood	36	(01247) 852706
Bright Castle	18	(01396) 841319
Camalea	18	(01247) 270368
Clandeboye	18	(01247) 271767
Crossgar	9	(01396) 831523
Donaghadee	18	(01247) 883624
Downpatrick	18	(01396) 615947
Helen's Bay	9	(01247) 852815
Holywood	18	(01232) 423135
Kilkeel	18	(016937) 65096

Kirkistown Castle	18	(012477) 71233
Mahee Island	9	(01238) 541234
Mourne	-	(013967) 23218
Ringdufferin	18	(01396) 828812
Rockmount	18	(01232) 812279
Royal Belfast	18	(01232) 428165
Royal County Down	36	(013967) 23314
Scrabo	18	(01247) 812355
Spa	18	(01238) 562365
Temple	9	(01846) 639213
Warrenpoint	18	(016937) 53695

CO. DUBLIN

Club	Holes	Telephone Number
Balbriggan	18	(01) 8412229
Balcarrick	18	(01) 8436957
Ballinascomey	18	(01) 4512082
Beaverstown	18	(01) 8436439
Beech Park	18	(01) 4580522
Carrickmines	9	(01) 2955972
Castle	18	(01) 4904207
Christy O'Connor	18	(01) 8207444
Clontarf	18	(01) 8331892
Coldwinters	18	(01) 8640324
Corrstown	27	(01) 8640533
Deer Park	36	(01) 8326039
Donabate	18	(01) 8436346
Dublin City University	-	(01) 7045000
Dublin Mountain	18	(01) 4582570
Dublin University	-	(01) 2956491
Dun Laoghaire	18	(01) 2803916
Edmondstown	18	(01) 4931082
Elm Green	18	(01) 2800797
Elm Park	18	(01) 2693438
Finnstown	9	(01) 6280644
Forrest Little	18	(01) 8401763
Foxrock	9	(01) 2893992
Grange	24	(01) 4932889
Hazel Grove	11	(01) 4520911
Hermitage	18	(01) 6264781
Hibernian	18	(01) 8510565
Holywood Lakes	18	(01) 8433007
Howth	18	(01) 8323055
Island	18	(01) 8436462
Killiney	9	(01) 2852823
Kilmashogue	9	(088) 682360
Kilternan	18	(01) 2955559
Lucan	18	(01) 6282106
Luttrellstown Castle	18	(01) 8089988
Malahide	27	(01) 8461611
Milltown	18	(01) 4976090
Newlands	18	(01) 4593157
Old Conna	18	(01) 2826055
Portmarnock	27	(01) 8462968
Rathfarnham	9	(01) 4931201
Royal College of Surgeons	-	(01) 4022100
Royal Dublin	18	(01) 8336346
Rush	9	(01) 8438177
Skerries	18	(01) 8491567
Slade Valley	18	(01) 4582739
Stackstown	18	(01) 4941993
St. Anne's	18	(01) 8336471
St. Margaret's	18	(01) 8640400
Sutton	9	(01) 8322965

Swords ....18................(01) 8409819
Turvey..............................9................(01) 8435169
University College Dublin ....-..................(01) 4943274
Westmanstown..................18................(01) 8205817
Woodbrook........................18................(01) 2824799

CO. FERMANAGH

Club	Holes	Telephone Number
Castle Hume	18	(01365) 327077
Enniskillen	18	(01365) 325250

CO. GALWAY

Club	Holes	Telephone Number
Ardacong	9	
Athenry	18	(091) 794466
Ballinasloe	18	(0905) 42126
Bearna	18	(091) 592677
Connemara	18	(095) 23502
Connemara Isles	9	(091) 572498
Curra	9	(0509) 45438
Galway	18	(091) 522033
Galway Bay	18	(091) 790500
Gort	9	(091) 632244
Loughrea	18	(091) 841049
Mountbellew	9	(0905) 79259
Oughterard	18	(091) 552131
Portumna	18	(0509) 41059
Tuam	18	(093) 28993
University College Galway	--	(091) 524411

CO. KERRY

Club	Holes	Telephone Number
Ardfert	9	(066) 34744
Ballybunion	36	(068) 27146
Ballyheigue Castle	9	(066) 33555
Beaufort	18	(064) 44440
Castlegregory	9	(066) 39179
Ceann Sibeal	18	(066) 56255
Dooks	18	(066) 68205
Kenmare	18	(064) 41291
Kerries	9	(066) 22112
Killarney	36	(064) 31034
Killorglin	18	(066) 61979
Parknasilla	9	(064) 45122
Ross	9	(064) 31125
Tralee	18	(066) 36379
Waterville	18	(066) 74102

CO. KILDARE

Club	Holes	Telephone Number
Athy	18	(0507) 31729
Bodenstown	36	(045) 897096
Castlewarden	18	(01) 4589254
Cill Dara	9	(045) 521433
Clane	--	(045) 68202
Clongowes	9	(045) 868202
Craddockstown	18	(045) 897610
Curragh	18	(045) 441714
Highfield	27	(0405) 31021
K-Club	18	(01) 6273111
Killeen	18	(045) 866003
Knockanally	18	(045) 869391
Leixlip	9	(01) 6244978
Naas	18	(045) 874644

Woodlands ....9................(045) 860777

CO. KILKENNY

Club	Holes	Telephone Number
Callan	12	(056) 25136
Castlecomer	9	(056) 41139
Kilkenny	18	(056) 65400
Mount Juliet	18	(056) 24455
Waterford	18	(051) 876748

CO. LAOIS

Club	Holes	Telephone Number
Abbeyleix	9	(0502) 31450
Heath	18	(0502) 46533
Mountrath	18	(0502) 32558
Portarlington	18	(0502) 23115
Rathdowney	9	(0505) 46170

CO. LEITRIM

Club	Holes	Telephone Number
Ballinamore	9	(078) 44346
Carrick-on-Shannon	9	(079) 67015

CO. LIMERICK

Club	Holes	Telephone Number
Abbeyfeale	9	(068) 32033
Adare Manor	18	(061) 396204
Castletroy	18	(061) 335753
Killeline	18	(069) 61600
Limerick	18	(061) 415146
Limerick County	18	(061) 351881
Newcastlewest	18	(069) 76500

CO. LONGFORD

Club	Holes	Telephone Number
County Longford	18	(043) 46310

CO. LOUTH

Club	Holes	Telephone Number
Ardee	18	(041) 53227
County Louth	18	(041) 22329
Dundalk	18	(042) 21731
Greenore	18	(042) 73678
Killinbeg	18	(042) 39303
Seapoint	18	(042) 22333
Townley Hall	9	(041) 42229

CO. MAYO

Club	Holes	Telephone Number
Achill Island	9	(098) 43456
Ballina	18	(096) 21050
Ballinrobe	18	(092) 41118
Ballyhaunis	9	(0907) 30014
Belmullet	18	(097) 82292
Castlebar	18	(094) 21649
Claremorris	18	(094) 71527
Mulranny	9	(098) 36262
Swinford	9	(094) 51378
Westport	18	(098) 8262

CO. MEATH

Club	Holes	Telephone Number
Ashbourne	18	(01) 8352005
Black Bush	27	(01) 8250021
Gormanston	9	(01) 8412203
Headfort	18	(046) 40857

Kilcock.....................18.............(01) 6284074
Laytown-Bettystown ....18.............(041) 27170
Moor Park...................18.............(046) 27661
Royal Tara ....27.............(046) 25508
Trim ....18.............(046) 31463

CO. MONAGHAN

Club	Holes	Telephone Number
Castleblayney	9	(056) 41139
Clones	9	(047) 56017
Mannan Castle	9	(042) 61714
Nuremore	18	(042) 64016
Rossmore	18	(047) 81316

CO. OFFALY

Club	Holes	Telephone Number
Birr	18	(0509) 20082
Castle Barna	18	(0506) 53384
Edenderry	18	(0405) 31072
Tullamore	18	(0506) 21439

CO. ROSCOMMON

Club	Holes	Telephone Number
Athlone	18	(0902) 92073
Ballaghaderreen	9	(0907) 60295
Boyle	9	(079) 62192
Castlerea	9	(0907) 20068
Roscommon	18	(0903) 26382
Strokestown	9	(078) 33303

CO. SLIGO

Club	Holes	Telephone Number
Ballymote	9	(071) 89059
County Sligo	18	(071) 77186
Enniscrone	18	(096) 36297
Strandhill	18	(071) 68188
Tubbercurry	9	(071) 85849

CO. TIPPERARY

Club	Holes	Telephone Number
Ballykisteen	18	(062) 33333
Cahir Park	18	(052) 41474
Carrick-on-Suir	9	(051) 640558
Clonmel	18	(052) 24050
County Tipperary	18	(062) 71116
Nenagh	18	(067) 31476
Rockwell	9	(062) 61444
Roscrea	18	(0505) 21130
Templemore	9	(0504) 31522
Thurles	18	(0504) 21983
Tipperary	18	(062) 51119

CO. TYRONE

Club	Holes	Telephone Number
Aughnacloy	9	(016625) 57050
Dungannon	18	(01868) 727338
Fintona	9	(01662) 841480

Killymoon.....................18.............(016487) 63762
Newtownstewart ....18.............(016626) 61466
Omagh ....18.............(01662) 241442
Strabane.....................18.............(01504) 382007

CO. WATERFORD

Club	Holes	Telephone Number
Dungarvan	18	(058) 43310
Dunmore East	18	(051) 383151
Faithlegg	18	(051) 382241
Gold Coast	18	(058) 42249
Lismore	9	(058) 54026
Tramore	18	(051) 386170
Waterford Castle	18	(051) 871633
West Waterford	18	(058) 43216

CO. WESTMEATH

Club	Holes	Telephone Number
Delvin Castle	18	(044) 64315
Glasson	21	(0902) 85120
Moate	18	(0902) 81271
Mount Temple	18	(0902) 81545
Mullingar	18	(044) 48366

CO. WEXFORD

Club	Holes	Telephone Number
Courtown	18	(055) 25166
Enniscorthy	18	(054) 33191
New Ross	18	(051) 421433
Rosslare	27	(053) 32203
St. Helen's Bay	18	(053) 33234
Tara Glen	9	(055) 25413
Wexford	18	(053) 42238

CO. WICKLOW

Club	Holes	Telephone Number
Arklow	18	(0402) 32492
Baltinglass	9	(0508) 81350
Blainroe	18	(0404) 68168
Bray	9	(01) 2862484
Charlesland	18	(01) 2876764
Coollattin	9	(055) 26302
Delgany	18	(01) 2874536
Djouce Mountain	9	(01) 2818585
Druids Glen	18	(01) 2873600
European Club	18	(0404) 47415
Glenmalure	18	(0404) 46679
Greystones	18	(01) 2874136
Kilcoole	9	(01) 2872066
Powerscourt	18	(01) 2760503
Rathsallagh	18	(045) 403316
Roundwood	18	(01) 2818488
Tulfarris	9	(045) 864574
Wicklow	18	(0404) 67379
Woodenbridge	18	(0402) 35202

Ireland's Health Service

*By **Dr. Louis Courtney**, K.M., F.R.C.O.G.*

IRELAND has an excellent and immediate Health Service. It still depends to a significant extent on commitment and work beyond the call of duty, but be that as it may, it is still first class.

While visitors to Ireland will usually be insured, this is not a requisite to obtaining prompt medical attention. All persons, regardless of income, will receive (and may demand by law) attention free of charge if they present themselves at a local hospital. These hospitals are well-equipped and strategically located around the country, and there is one within 50 miles or less, regardless of where one is. In the speciality in which I practice (Obstetrics and Gynaecology), if required, a Consultant is immediately available. This, to my knowledge, pertains to the other specialities also. The O. and G. services in Ireland are second to none in Europe by the standard measures used in the specialty internationally. Most consultants working in Ireland will have spent some time abroad either during training or as postgraduates.

There are Regional Hospitals with sophisticated subspecialisation and a number of tertiary referral hospitals where further specialisation and 'high-'tech' medicine and surgery is available, including by-pass and transplant surgery. The accessibility of this assistance is uniform.

Nursing in Ireland is of a particularly high standard, with about half the nurses being trained abroad and half in Ireland, giving a good mix. Every town has a General Practice rota of doctors where initial and often sufficient care is provided. My experience is that the standard is high. There is an excellent emergency accident and ambulance service, and one could expect an ambulance to be on the scene within 15 minutes of an emergency call. The drivers and ambulance personnel are well-trained and equipped to deal with immediate treatment and first aid. Where necessary, helicopter transport is available.

At present, the health service is, of necessity, going through a rationalisation process. This, while causing some hiccups and irritations, is not affecting its overall performance. We are inclined as a race to be critical of the services provided, but freedom of expression is one of our very treasured possessions.

The author is a specialist in the field of Obstetrics and Gynaecology and a commentator on Irish health services.

INTRODUCTION

The cost of health-care provision in both the North and the Republic continues to place a huge demand on funding. In 1994, expenditure in the Republic was estimated at IR£2.3 billion - a rise of 6 per cent from 1993 - while in the North, expenditure on general clinical services in 1995-96 was estimated at £301.2 million - a rise of 11 per cent from 1994-95.

The sector is a major employer in both jurisdictions. The latest data from Northern Ireland and the Republic show that 58,356 people and 65,173 people were employed in the health sectors, respectively. The spiralling costs of health-service provision in the North have resulted in the establishment of Trust Status hospitals which must purchase services that are provided by the health boards. Fund-holding G.P.s must oversee the financial side of their own practices, and major hospital services, such as catering, have been privatised and subjected to Competitive Compulsory Tendering. In the Republic, the passing of the Health (Amendment) Act, 1996, has clarified the roles of the government and the health boards in the health sector. Health boards in the Republic are now strictly forbidden to overspend their budget and must produce an annual report. Planning and service delivery must be organised around specific care groupings, the main ones being children, the elderly, the mentally ill, people with disabilities and episodic illnesses and injuries.

Health trends: Life expectancy at birth in the Republic of Ireland Ireland is approximately 72 years for men and 78 years for women, figures that are below the average life expectancy in the E.U. These figures can be partly explained by the fact that heart disease continues to be the major killer throughout the island (the standardised death rates for both men and women in the Republic are more than twice the E.U. average), with 1995 figures registering 6,929 deaths from circulatory diseases in the North and 13,909 deaths in the Republic. There are also very high death rates associated with cancer, particularly lung, breast, and colorectal cancers. Linked to these high death rates are lifestyle variables - particularly those associated with smoking, nutrition, drinking and exercise. In the Republic, separate national surveys conducted recently have indicated that one-third of the population smoked; that 53 per cent of males and 33 per cent of females were over weight; and that only half of the population engaged in physical activity.

Other trends: Similar neonatal and infant death trends were recorded for both jurisdictions. Analysis revealed a death rate in both jurisdictions of 6 per 1,000 among children under one year and 4 per 1,000 among neonates. Although the national birth rate is decreasing, the number of non-marital births as a percentage of the total is rising. In 1995, 437 people were killed and 12,673 were injured in road accidents in the Republic, while 144 people were killed and 11,581 were injured in road accidents in the North. Those in the 21-24 years and the 65+ age groups were more likely to be killed in this type of accident.

REPUBLIC OF IRELAND HEALTH BOARDS

Eastern Health Board - _(covers Dublin City and County, Co. Kildare & Co. Wicklow)._ Dr. Steevens Hospital, John's Road, Dublin 8. Tel. (01) 6790700.

Midland Health Board - _(covers Co. Laois, Co. Longford, Co. Offaly, Co. Westmeath)._ Arden Road, Tullamore, Co. Offaly. Tel. (0506) 21868.

Mid-Western Health Board - _(covers Co. Clare, Limerick City and County, Co. Tipperary - North Riding)._ 31-33 Catherine Street, Limerick. Tel. (061) 316655.

South-Eastern Health Board - _(covers Co. Carlow, Co. Kilkenny, Co. Tipperary - South Riding - Co. Waterford, Co. Wexford)._ Lacken, Dublin Road, Kilkenny. Tel. (056) 51702.

North-Eastern Health Board - _(covers Co. Cavan, Co. Louth, Co. Meath, Co. Monaghan)._ Navan Road, Kells, Co. Meath. Tel. (046) 40341.

North-Western Health Board - _(covers Co. Donegal, Co. Leitrim, Co. Sligo)._ Manorhamilton, Co. Leitrim. Tel. (072) 55123.

Southern Health Board - _(covers Cork City and County, Co. Kerry)._ Cork Farm Centre, Dennehy's Cross, Wilton Road, Cork. Tel. (021) 545011.

Western Health Board - _(covers Co. Galway, Co. Mayo, Co. Roscommon)._ Merlin Park Regional Hospital, Galway. Tel. (091) 751131.

NORTHERN IRELAND HEALTH BOARDS

Eastern Health & Social Services Board - Champion House, Linenhall Street, Belfast, Co. Antrim. Tel. (01232) 321313.

Southern Health & Social Services Board - 20 Seagoe Industrial Area, Portadown, Co. Armagh. Tel. (01762) 336611.

Northern Health & Social Services Board - County Hall, Ballymena, Co. Antrim. Tel. (01266) 653333.

Western Health & Social Services Board - 15 Gransha Park, Campsie, Co. Derry. Tel. (01504) 860086.

REPUBLIC OF IRELAND: PERSONS EMPLOYED IN HEALTH SERVICES, 1995

Health Sector	Management/ Admin.	Medical/ Dental	Nursing	Para- Medical	Support Services	Maintenance/ Technical	Total
Voluntary / Joint Board Hospitals	2,162	1,767	8,066	1,779	3,490	383	17,647
Health Boards:							
Eastern	1,270	528	3,181	827	2,501	252	8,559
Midland	327	196	1,270	239	955	85	3,072
Mid-Western	470	280	1,748	309	1,002	161	3,970
North-Eastern	440	216	1,381	222	1,155	61	3,475
North-Western	563	233	1,580	314	1,249	93	4,032
South-Eastern	641	367	2,507	355	1,586	127	5,583
Southern	821	535	3,091	484	1,871	221	7,023
Western	730	415	2,481	419	1,860	181	6,086
Total:	**5,262**	**2,770**	**17,239**	**3,169**	**12,179**	**1,181**	**41,800**
Mental Handicap Homes	462	44	2,055	397	2,676	92	5,726
OVERALL TOTAL:	**7,886**	**4,581**	**27,360**	**5,345**	**18,345**	**1,656**	**65,173**

NORTHERN IRELAND: PERSONS EMPLOYED IN HEALTH SERVICES, 1996

Personnel Category	Full-Time Staff	Part-Time Staff	Total Staff
Administration & Clerical	7,055	2,518	9,573
Ambulance	651	2	653
Dental	225	147	372
Domestic & Allied	2,156	3,363	5,519
Home Helps	37	9,039	9,076
Medical	1,882	947	2,829
Nursing (Student)	67	1	68
Nursing (Trained)	8,155	6,874	15,029
Nursing (Other)	2,356	2,068	4,424
Other Grades	352	192	544
Paramedical	2,687	934	3,621
Pharmacy	252	51	303
Social Services	3,441	2,250	5,691
Tradesmen	653	1	654
TOTAL:	**29,969**	**28,387**	**58,356**

NORTHERN IRELAND: HOSPITAL PATIENT ACTIVITY, 1995-96

Trust / Board	Average Available Beds	Average Occupied Beds	Discharges & Deaths	Day Cases	Avg. Length of Stay
Altnagelvin Group Unit	651.7	485.7	24,647	5,803	7.2
Armagh & Dungannon Unit	725.3	578.2	12,189	3,286	17.4
Belfast City Hospital HSS Trust	767.3	628.2	31,657	11,980	7.3
Causeway HSS Trust	360.7	252.2	13,151	3,885	7.0
Craigavon Area Hospital HSS Trust	562.2	377.2	23,493	8,565	5.9
Craigavon & Banbridge HSS Trust	80.0	66.8	1,096	0	22.3
Down Lisburn HSS Trust	742.8	604.9	17,328	3,758	12.8
Foyle Community Unit	247.1	220.7	1,382	0	58.5
Green Park Healthcare HSS Trust	549.5	401.3	14,310	1,906	10.3
Homefirst Community Unit	390.0	311.5	1,731	0	65.9
Mater Infirmorum Hospital HSS Trust	214.7	177.5	11,440	2,429	5.7
Newry & Mourne HSS Trust	346.2	231.9	14,187	3,575	6.0
North & West Belfast HSS Trust	550.8	482.9	433	0	408.2
Royal Group of Hospitals HSS Trust	984.3	757.1	46,907	24,550	5.9
South & East Belfast HSS Trust	455.5	373.4	1,350	0	101.2

Trust / Board	Average Available Beds	Average Occupied Beds	Discharges & Deaths	Day Cases	Avg. Length of Stay
Sperrin Lakeland Unit	720.6	561.1	17,826	3,469	11.5
Ulster, North Down & Ards HSS Trust	780.2	598.4	33,223	11,595	6.6
United Hospitals Group	924.7	707.0	37,725	11,040	6.9
Total: Northern Ireland	10,053.6	7,816.0	304,075	95,841	9.4

REPUBLIC OF IRELAND: HOSPITAL PATIENT ACTIVITY (1994)

(* District Hospitals are not included.)

Health Board Area	No. of hospitals	In-patient beds available	Patients discharged	Day Beds available	Avg. length of stay in days	Day Cases
Eastern	25	4,920	188,834	299	7.6	121,359
North-Eastern	5	946	38,357	24	6.6	6,086
South-Eastern	7	1,078	53,543	37	5.8	9,508
Western	5	1,236	57,844	26	6.5	10,042
Mid-Western	6	758	41,125	45	6.0	11,030
North-Western	3	665	34,228	15	5.4	12,414
Midland	3	479	25,325	24	5.7	5,542
Southern	9	1,771	83,631	51	6.3	17,037
TOTAL:	63	11,853	522,887	521	6.2*	193,018

NORTHERN IRELAND: AVERAGE NUMBER OF BEDS AVAILABLE, 1995-96

Provider	Available Beds	Provider	Available Beds
Altnagelvin Group Unit	651.7	Mater Infirmorum Hospital HSS Trust	214.7
Armagh & Dungannon Unit	725.3	Newry & Mourne HSS Trust	346.2
Belfast City Hospital HSS Trust	767.3	North & West Belfast HSS Trust	550.8
Causeway HSS Trust	360.7	Royal Group of Hospitals HSS Trust	984.3
Craigavon Area Hospital HSS Trust	562.2	South & East Belfast HSS Trust	455.5
Craigavon & Banbridge HSS Trust	80.0	Sperrin Lakeland Unit	720.6
Down Lisburn HSS Trust	742.8	Ulster, North Down & Ards HSS Trust	780.2
Foyle Community Unit	247.1	United Hospitals Group	924.7
Green Park Healthcare HSS Trust	549.5		
Homefirst Community Unit	390.0	TOTAL:	10,053.6

NORTHERN IRELAND: AVAILABLE HOSPITAL BEDS BY CARE PROGRAMME

Programme Category	1992-93	1993-94	1994-95	1995-96
Acute Services	5,281	5,040	4,813	4,692
Maternity & Child Health	644	805	849	865
Elderly Care	2,647	2,348	2,340	2,137
Mental Health	2,117	1,736	1,495	1,521
Learning Disabilities	1,023	949	860	840

NORTHERN IRELAND: DEATHS BY CAUSE ('92-'95)

Cause of Death	1986	1990	1994	1995
Circulatory Diseases	8,064	7,306	7,011	6,929
Respiratory Diseases	2,581	2,732	2,398	2,656
Cancer (malignant neoplasms)	3,282	3,597	3,665	3,585
Violent Deaths	730	697	688	663
Other	1,408	1,313	1,351	1,477
Total: Deaths	16,065	15,645	15,113	15,310

REPUBLIC OF IRELAND: DEATHS CLASSIFIED BY CAUSE, 1992-1995

Cause of Death	Number of Deaths			
	1992	1993	1994	1995
Infectious & Parasitic diseases	170	159	170	170
Malignant neoplasms	7,541	7,593	7,358	7,463
Diseases of the circulatory system	13,976	14,363	14,051	13,909
Injury & poisoning	1,329	1,385	1,324	1,355
Accidents & adverse effects	949	1,019	934	949
Other causes	6,970	16,796	7,009	7,648
Total Deaths:	**30,935**	**31,924**	**30,846**	**31,494**

NORTHERN IRELAND: INFANT MORTALITY ('91-'94)

Description	1991	1992	1993	1994
Numbers:				
Infant Deaths *(under 1 year of age)*	194	153	176	147
Neo-natal Deaths *(under 4 weeks of age)*	121	104	123	101
Rates per 1,000 persons - estimated:				
Infant Deaths *(under 1 year of age)*	7.4	6.0	7.1	6.1
Neo-natal Deaths *(under 4 weeks of age)*	4.6	4.1	4.9	4.2

REPUBLIC OF IRELAND: RATE OF INFANT MORTALITY, 1992-1995

Rates per 1,000 births	1992	1993	1994	1995
Infant Mortality: *(under 1 year of age)*				
Ireland	6	6	6	6
County Boroughs	8	8	7	9
Dun Laoghaire, Rathdown, Municipal Boroughs & Urban Districts	8	5	6	8
Rural Districts	5	6	5	4
Neo-natal Mortality: *(under 4 weeks of age)*				
Ireland	4	4	4	5
County Boroughs	5	5	5	6
Dun Laoghaire, Rathdown, Municipal Boroughs & Urban Districts	5	4	4	6
Rural Districts	3	4	4	3

REPUBLIC OF IRELAND: CAPITAL EXPENDITURE ALLOCATED, 1994

Programme (£m)	Voluntary Boards	Health Boards	Total
Community Welfare Services (incl. welfare homes, child welfare etc.)	1,066	677	1,743
Psychiatric Services	536	446	982
Services for the Handicapped (incl. mental handicap, rehabilitation etc.)	1,675	1,825	3,500
General Hospitals	23,715	27,888	51,602
Miscellaneous	353	990	1,343
TOTAL:	**27,345**	**31,826**	**59,170**

REPUBLIC OF IRELAND: NON-CAPITAL EXPENDITURE BY PROGRAMME

Programme and Service	Expenditure (£000's)			
	1991	1992	1993	1994
Community Protection Programme	26,210	32,011	36,631	40,232
Community Health Services Programme	260,780	303,385	343,142	371,626

Continued from previous page

Programme and Service	Expenditure (£000's)			
	1991	1992	1993	1994
Community Welfare Programme	140,500	157,590	177,616	200,729
Psychiatric Programme	183,390	197,253	209,381	215,850
Programme for the Handicapped	164,920	181,793	202,203	222,756
General Hospital Programme	897,060	993,821	1,097,451	1,146,609
General Support Programme	79,140	90,430	94,144	92,856
Gross Non-Capital: All Programmes	1,752,000	1,956,283	2,160,568	2,290,658
Income	121,000	126,600	143,966	144,900
Net Non-Capital Total: All Programmes	1,631,000	1,829,683	2,016,602	2,145,758

REPUBLIC OF IRELAND: FUNDING SOURCES FOR STATUTORY NON-CAPITAL HEALTH SERVICES

Funding Sources (£m)	1991	1992	1993	1994
Exchequer	1,441.7	1,604.2	1,767.1	1,890.6
Health Contributions etc.	147.4	175.0	193.4	201.1
Receipts under EC Regulations	41.9	50.5	53.9	54.1
Minor Income of Agencies	121.0	126.6	143.9	144.9
TOTAL:	1,752.0	1,956.3	2,158.3	2,290.7

REPUBLIC OF IRELAND: FACTORY ACCIDENTS NOTIFIED

Category	1992	1993	1994	1995
Fatal Accidents	30	30	23	28
Non-Fatal Accidents	2,598	2,888	3,413	3,252
TOTAL	2,628	2,918	3,436	3,280

REPUBLIC OF IRELAND: RAILWAY ACCIDENTS

Accident Type	1992	1993	1994	1995
Number of Accidents:				
Fatal	11	3	11	7
Non-fatal	11	6	7	8
Total Accidents:	22	9	18	15
Number of Persons Killed:				
Passengers	-	-	1	-
Railway Employees	-	-	-	1
Others	11	3	10	6
Total Killed:	11	3	11	7
Number of Persons Injured:				
Passengers	4	28	1	2
Railway Employees	2	2	1	2
Others	5	2	5	5
Total Injured:	11	32	7	9

NORTHERN IRELAND: ROAD ACCIDENT CASUALTIES

Description	1992	1993	1994	1995
Casualties killed	150	143	157	144
Casualties seriously injured	1,841	1,725	1,648	1,532
Casualties slightly injured	9,273	9,232	10,289	10,049
Total (Casualties):	11,264	11,100	12,094	11,725
Number of Injury Accidents	6,650	6,517	6,783	6,792
Casualties aged under 15 years	1,548	1,571	1,749	1,719

NORTHERN IRELAND:
ROAD ACCIDENT CASUALTIES BY LOCATION

Location	1992	1993	1994	1995
Built-up Areas:				
Casualties killed	63	48	41	44
Casualties injured	6,355	6,198	6,704	6,740
Total: Built-up Areas	**6,418**	**6,246**	**6,745**	**6,784**
Non Built-up Areas:				
Casualties killed	87	95	116	100
Casualties injured	4,759	4,759	5,233	4,841
Total: Non Built-up Areas	**4,846**	**4,854**	**5,349**	**4,941**
TOTAL: CASUALTIES KILLED	**150**	**143**	**157**	**144**
TOTAL: CASUALTIES INJURED	**11,114**	**10,957**	**11,937**	**11,581**

REPUBLIC OF IRELAND: NUMBER OF PEOPLE KILLED IN ROAD ACCIDENTS, 1986-96

Year	Fatalities	Year	Fatalities
1986	387	1992	415
1987	462	1993	431
1988	463	1994	404
1989	460	1995	437
1990	478	1996	453
1991	445		

NORTHERN IRELAND:
ROAD INJURY ACCIDENTS BY VEHICLE TYPE

Vehicle Category	1992	1993	1994	1995
Motor Cars	9,904	9,805	10,293	10,006
Motor Cycles	359	274	265	268
Pedal Cycles	393	291	324	391
Vans / Lorries	1,102	1,163	1,213	1,184
Buses	265	252	224	213
Other	130	155	249	451
TOTAL:	**12,153**	**11,940**	**12,568**	**12,513**

REPUBLIC OF IRELAND:
CASUALTIES BY ROAD USER TYPE, 1995

Casualty Class	Killed	Serious Injury	Minor Injury	Total	%
Pedestrians	113	389	1,273	1,775	13.5
Pedal Cycle Users	28	129	736	893	6.8
Motor Cycle Users	57	316	918	1,291	9.8
Car Users	193	1,762	6,109	8,064	61.5
P.S.V. (large) Users	0	24	143	167	1.3
Goods Vehicle Users	33	178	593	804	6.1
Other or Unknown	13	24	79	116	0.9
Total:	**437**	**2,822**	**9,851**	**13,110**	**100.0**

REPUBLIC OF IRELAND:
ROAD CASUALTIES BY AGE AND GENDER, 1995

Age Category	Killed	MALE Injured	Total	Killed	FEMALE Injured	Total	PERSONS Total	%
0-5	4	188	192	3	144	147	339	2.6
6-9	9	208	217	0	188	188	405	3.1

Continued from previous page -

Age Category	Killed	MALE Injured	Total	Killed	FEMALE Injured	Total	PERSONS Total	%
10-14	11	311	322	3	253	256	578	4.5
15-17	14	289	303	6	197	203	506	3.9
18-20	27	753	780	8	378	386	1,166	9.0
21-24	59	880	939	15	376	391	1,330	10.3
25-34	54	1,585	1,639	10	930	940	2,579	20.0
35-44	41	883	924	9	638	647	1,571	12.2
45-54	22	600	622	18	456	474	1,096	8.5
55-64	15	345	360	8	320	328	688	5.3
65+	39	322	361	28	306	334	695	5.4
Others	23	1,072	1,095	9	864	873	1,968	15.2
TOTAL:	318	7,436	7,754	117	5,050	5,167	12,921	100.0

REPUBLIC OF IRELAND: PSYCHIATRIC PATIENTS

Region	1991	1992	1993	1994
Eastern	1,638	1,541	1,480	1,384
Midland	492	466	428	421
Mid-Western	620	520	508	485
North-Eastern	368	349	345	328
North-Western	375	321	319	279
South-Eastern	1,184	1,080	978	940
Southern	1,355	1,033	1,034	959
Western	968	864	815	797
TOTAL:	7,000	6,174	5,907	5,593

NORTHERN IRELAND: FIRE RELATED CASUALTIES

Incident type	1992	1993	1994	1995	1996
Fire Incidents:					
Casualties killed	29	21	36	26	14
Casualties injured	586	623	567	497	750
Casualties rescued	120	87	118	101	108
Total: Fire Incidents	735	731	721	624	872
Road Traffic Accidents:					
Casualties killed	45	53	61	52	62
Casualties injured	797	818	846	702	954
Casualties rescued	245	305	302	310	328
Total: Road Traffic Accidents	1,087	1,176	1,209	1,064	1,344
Other Incidents:					
Casualties killed	11	20	13	22	14
Casualties injured	95	144	113	90	107
Casualties rescued	319	290	354	373	441
Total: Other Incidents	425	454	480	485	562
GRAND TOTAL:	2,247	2,361	2,410	2,173	2,778

An Garda Síochána: A Highly Trained Force

By Eamon Doherty, former Garda Commisioner

THE Garda Síochána celebrates its 75th anniversary this year. Founded out of the civil war, the Garda Síochána is probably unique amongst police forces in that at its foundation it was comprised not alone of members from both sides of the conflict, but also of members of the Royal Irish Constabulary and the Dublin Metropolitan Police who applied to join the new force when both of their Forces were disbanded.

For historical reasons a conscious decision was made by the new Irish Government that (1) the new Force would not be called a police force but would be given a Gaelic title, "An Garda Síochána", meaning "Guardians of the Peace" and (2) that the new force would be an unarmed uniformed service. This was a difficult and courageous decision given the turbulent times that existed in 1922.

The primary role given to the new force was to restore and maintain law and order and to protect the persons and property of the general public throughout the land. They were to endeavour to achieve this with the consent and assistance of the communities in which they served rather than by coercion or other similar means. That they succeeded in their task is fully evidenced by the fact that they are still today one of the few unarmed police forces in the world.

When I joined the force the second world war was coming to an end. Ireland was a poor and mainly rural society with strict codes of honesty and morality. The crime rate was low and the detection rate high. The force had few resources by way of transport or technical aids and most of a garda's duty was performed on foot or by bicycle. As I write these words today, I can hear the noise of the new garda helicopter equipped with the most modern technology, setting off on its nightly patrol, whilst back in Baldonnel, the new Garda fixed wing aircraft stands in readiness for any emergency. Some transformation in a few years - and all of it necessary to enable the force to operate professionally and efficiently and to meet the challenge of the day.

Since the early 60's, there has been a marked drift away from the land to the rural areas. We have become a prosperous and highly educated nation. This prosperity however, has brought with it a degree of permissiveness and a marked decline in moral values. The criminal element saw an opportunity to exploit that prosperity and we had an upsurge of crime and violence in the 70's and 80's more vicious than we had ever experienced. As we moved into the 80's we entered the era of organised crime and a developing drug trade. Now in the 90's we have contract killings, gang wars, drug barons, widespread money laundering and a greater use of drugs by our young people. Add to all these developments 25 years of Cross Border conflict and one can appreciate that the force, in order to cope with the situation, had to become a very complex and highly specialised institution and had to be provided with the resources necessary for the job in hand.

Few people appreciate that whilst the management can, within their allocated budget, alter optional and administrative procedures, the issues of additional manpower and resources and adequate legislation lie totally with the Government of the day. When things are quiet, the force has a low priority when it comes to increased funding. It is only when the bubble bursts that the government's purse strings are loosened and the force can bask in a little resource luxury for a time. The border conflict was one of these bubbles which resulted in much needed resources being provided. However the force's capacity to deal with organised crime and the major drug problems was not fully met until after the cold blooded murders of Veronica Guerin, a freelance investigative journalist, and Detective Garda Gerry McCabe. Veronica Guerin's murder was a contract killing carried out by the drug barons and it created such a public and media outcry that the Government was galvanised into action. Now the force has got the necessary legislation to deal with these issues. New prison space is being urgently created to cope with the revolving door syndrome which is currently in operation due to a decision in the quieter days to close prisons and detention centres: modern resources and additional personnel are no longer a problem.

The new helicopter and the new aircraft are the icing on the cake of new resources. Now the force can boast of a most modern transport fleet, with the latest in technical equipment. The latest technology and communications equipment are now available at every station with computer facilities on every desktop. No member now proceeds on duty without a "walkie-talkie" thus ensuring that they are never really alone or without the means to call for assistance. The force's ballistics and forensic science capabilities have also been updated with DNA testing and computerised finger-print searching facilities available.

Within the force itself the major changes have have been in the training/education areas. Since its inception the force has always had a systematic training programme which consisted of a six month in-house training period where the syllabus consisted of law and police duties, force regulations, drill, physical education and some sport, mainly boxing. Whilst minor changes were made in the system over the years it was not until 1983 that a total review of training/education was carried out to meet with the increasing complexity of the garda's job. Our external committee comprised of educationalists, psychologists, bankers, and people from the industrial and commercial fields. I had the honour of being the only police officer on that committee and I would hope that I made a major input into its recommendations.

Arising out of the recommendations of that committee the force today has a two year probationary training programme which on completion leads to an award of a Diploma in Police Studies. The Garda College, situated in Templemore, Co. Tipperary, is a most modern campus and the college programmes are recognised as being amongst the best in the world. The curriculum for the two years probationer's course is structured to provide three periods at the college and two periods in the field. Our experimental learning includes legal studies, policing studies, social science studies, communication studies, technical studies, physical education, Irish studies, and European languages. The college has been designated by the government as an institution coming within the ambit of the National Council for Education and will, in the near future, be progressing to the provision of Degree courses for the Senior Management of the Force. The emphasis on in-service training for all ranks and for specialised sections is high. In addition to providing all Garda training/education needs the college also provides specialised training for other European police force personnel. Indeed the new training/education programmes and the modern college facilities are probably the most significant developments in the force in the last fifty years. They are evidence that the modern Garda force is in touch with the changes in society and qualified to meet its demands. A police force like every other organisation serving public needs, must move with the times and have the professional capacity to meet the challenge of rapid change. Otherwise democracy will be eroded and society as a whole will suffer. I am confident that the Garda Síochána will meet this challenge and that Irish society can feel secure in the knowledge that they have a highly professional, adequately trained, effective and efficient police service which will be responsive to their needs as we move into the next millennium.

The author is a former Garda Commissioner

THE CONSTITUTION OF IRELAND, BUNREACHT NA HÉIREANN

The Constitution of Ireland was approved by referendum on July 1, 1937, the Dáil having already approved it on June 14, 1937. It came into effect on December 29, 1937, replacing the Constitution of the Irish Free State (1922). The then Taoiseach, Éamon de Valera, played a large part in the drafting of the document which made the Free State a Republic in all but name.

Under the Constitution, the name of the state became Éire (Article 4), and it defined the national territory as "the whole island of Ireland, its islands and the territorial seas" (Article 2). It also stated that laws passed by the Dáil would have effect in the 26 counties only "pending re-integration of the national territory".

Under the heading of the State, the Constitution provided for the name and description of the State, stating Ireland to be a "sovereign, independent democratic state" (Article 5). The powers of government, the national flag, the position of Irish as the national language and the recognition of English as the second official language, citizenship and natural resources are also dealt with under the heading of the State.

The office and function of the President are enshrined in Articles 12 and 13, while the composition, regulation and functions of the Oireachtas (the National Parliament) and both houses therein, the Dáil and the Seanad (the houses of representatives and senate, respectively), are dealt with in Articles 15 to 19.

Articles 20 to 27 deal with the introduction, debate of and passing of legislation. Government, which according to Article 6 derives all legislative, executive and judicial powers from the people, is considered by Article 28, with reference to the exercising of that power, its

responsibility to the Dáil, its powers during war or national emergency and the nomination and composition of the cabinet. Foreign Affairs and International Relations, as conducted by the Government, are provided for under Article 29 such as membership of the European Union.

Articles 34 to 39 deal with the Structure Organisation and Powers of the Courts; Articles 30 to 33 being concerned with the establishment of the Offices of the Attorney General, Comptroller and Auditor General and the creation of a Council of State to advise the President.

Articles 40 to 44 are concerned with the fundamental rights of the Citizen under the broad headings of Personal Rights (Article 40); The Family and Education (Articles 41 to 42); Private Property (Article 43); Religion (Article 44). Other unenumerated Rights have been granted by the Courts. Under these Articles, all Citizens are equal before the law and the law undertakes to protect the personal rights of all Citizens. Freedom of expression, assembly and association are guaranteed, subject to Public Order and Morality. The family is recognised as the fundamental unit of society and provision is made for Mothers "not obliged by economic necessity to engage in labour to the neglect of their duties in the home" (Article 40.2.2). The institution of marriage was protected by the prohibiting of its dissolution, but with the introduction of the Family Law (Divorce) Act in 1997, this no longer the case.

The State will endeavour to educate its Citizens but recognises and respects that the family is the "Primary and Natural Educator of the Child" (Article 42.1). The right to own private property is guaranteed, as is the Freedom of Religious Conscience and Practice, and the State will not discriminate on grounds of Religious Belief (Article 44.2.3).

Article 45 contains the principles of social policy under which the state operates. Articles 46 and 47 deal with amendments to the Constitution which can only be done by referendum. Articles 48 to 63 deal with the Repeal of the 1922 Irish Free State Constitution and the transitory powers necessary until the new Constitution comes into effect.

REPUBLIC OF IRELAND: COURT SYSTEM

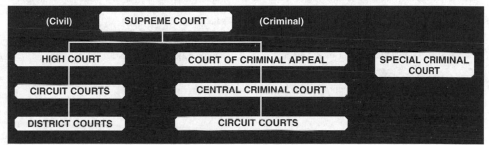

REPUBLIC OF IRELAND: JUDICIARY

SUPREME COURT

Judges:

The Hon. Mr. Justice Liam Hamilton
The Hon. Mr. Justice O'Flaherty
The Hon. Ms. Justice Susan Denham
The Hon. Mr. Justice Donal Barrington
The Hon. Mr. Justice Ronan C. Keane
The Hon. Mr. Justice Francis Murphy
The Hon. Mr. Justice Kevin Lynch
The Hon. Mr. Justice Henry Barron

HIGH COURT

Judges:

The Hon. Mr. Justice Declan Costello
The Hon. Ms. Justice Mella Carroll
The Hon. Mr. Justice Robert Barr
The Hon. Mr. Justice Richard Johnson
The Hon. Mr. Justice Vivian Lavan
The Hon. Mr. Justice Frederick R. Morris
The Hon. Mr. Justice Declan Budd
The Hon. Mr. Justice Fergus Flood
The Hon. Mr. Justice Paul Carney
The Hon. Mr. Justice Hugh Geoghegan
The Hon. Mr. Justice Dermot Kinlen
The Hon. Mr. Justice Brian McCracken
The Hon. Ms. Justice Mary Laffoy
The Hon. Mr. Justice Michael Moriarty
The Hon. Mr. Justice Peter Shanley
The Hon. Mr. Justice Peter A. Kelly
The Hon. Mr. Justice Thomas C. Smyth
The Hon. Ms. Justice Catherine McGuinness
The Hon. Mr. Justice Diarmuid B. O'Donovan
The Hon. Mr. Justice Kevin C. O'Higgins
The Hon. Mr. Justice John Quirke
The Hon. Mr. Justice Philip O'Sullivan

CIRCUIT COURT

Judges:

His Honour Mr. Justice Francis R. Spain, President of the Circuit Court
His Honour Judge Diarmuid P. Sheridan
His Honour Judge Dominic Lynch
His Honour Judge Matthew P. Smith
His Honour Judge Anthony G. Murphy
His Honour Judge Matthew F. Deery
His Honour Judge Patrick J. Moran
His Honour Judge Kieran O'Connor
His Honour Judge Liam Devally
His Honour Judge Cyril C. Kelly
His Honour Judge Edmond Smyth
His Honour Judge Harvey Kenny
His Honour Judge Sean O'Leary
His Honour Judge Anthony Kennedy
His Honour Judge Kevin Haugh
His Honour Judge John F. Buckley
His Honour Judge P. Frank O'Donnell
His Honour Judge Michael White
His Honour Judge Raymond Gerard T. Groarke
Her Honour Judge Alison Lindsay
Her Honour Judge Elizabeth Dunne
Her Honour Judge Olive Buttimer
His Honour Judge Gerard Mathews
His Honour Judge Patrick John McCartan
His Honour Judge Carroll Moran
Her Honour Judge Jacqueline Linnane

JUDGES OF THE DISTRICT COURT

District 1 - Vacant - (Ballybofey, Ballyshannon, Bunbeg, Buncrana, Carndonagh, Donegal, Dunfanaghy, Dungloe, Falcarragh, Glenties, Killybegs, Letterkenny, Lifford, Milford, Moville, Pettigo, Convoy, Stranorlar/Ballybofey).

District 2 - Oliver McGuiness - (Ballyfarnon, Ballymote, Boyle, Collooney, Dowra, Drumkeerin, Easky, Grange, Inniscrone, Manorhamilton, Riverstown, Skreen, Sligo, Tubbercurry).

District 3 - Daniel G. Shields - (Achill, Balla, Ballina, Ballinrobe, Ballycastle, Ballycroy, Belmullet, Castlebar, Crossmolina, Foxford, Killala, Kiltimagh, Newport, Swinford, Westport).

District 4 - Bernard M. Brennan - (Ballaghaderreen, Ballyhaunis, Carrick-on-Shannon, Castlerea,

Charlestown, Claremorris, Dunmore, Elphin, Glenamaddy, Kilkelly, Roscommon, Roosky, Strokestown, Williamstown).

District 5 - Donal McArdle - (Arva, Bailieborough, Ballinamore, Ballyconnell, Ballyjamesduff, Belturbet, Cavan, Clones, Cootehill, Kingscourt, Mohill, Monaghan, Oldcastle, Virginia).

District 6 - Flannan V. Brennan - (Ardee, Ballybay, Carlingford, Carrickmacross, Castleblayney, Drogheda, Dundalk, Dunleer).

District 7 - John F. Garavan - (Carna, Clifden, Derreen, Derrynea, Galway, Headford, Kilronan, Letterfrack, Maam, Oughterard, Spiddal, Tuam).

District 8 - James J. O'Sullivan - (Athlone, Ballinasloe, Ballyforan, Banagher, Birr, Borrisokane, Eyecourt, Kilcormac, Loughrea, Moate, Mount Bellew, Portumna, Woodford).

District 9 - Aiden O'Donnell - (Ballymahon, Ballynacargy, Castlepollard, Daingean, Delvin, Edenderry, Edgeworthstown, Granard, Kilbeggan, Kilucan, Longford, Mullingar, Tullamore).

District 10 - John Patrick Brophy - (Athboy, Ceanannus Mór, Dunshaughlin, Kilcock, Navan, Trim).

District 11 - Dublin Metropolitan Judges - Peter A. Smithwick, John J. Delap, Brian Kirby, Gillian M. Hussey, James Paul McDonnell, Desmond P. H. Windle, Thelma King, Timothy H. Crowley, Clare Leonard, Michael O'Leary, Catherine A. Murphy, Mary Collins, Constantine G. O'Leary, Miriam Malone.

District 12 - Albert Louis O'Dea - (Athenry, Corofin, Ennis, Ennistymon, Gort, Kildysart, Kilkee, Killaloe, Kilrush, Kinvara, Lisdoonvarna, Miltown Malbay, Scariff, Shannon, Sixmilebridge, Tulla).

District 13 - Mary A.G. O'Halloran - (Abbeyfeale, Adare, Askeaton, Bruff, Drumcollogher, Kilfinane, Kilmallock, Listowel, Newcastle West, Rathkeale, Rath Luirc, Shanagolden, Tarbert).

District 14 - Michael C. Reilly - (Cappamore, Cappawhite, Limerick City, Nenagh, Newport, Thurles).

District 15 - Mary H. Martin - (Abbeyleix, Athy,

Ballyragget, Carlow, Castlecomer, Mountmellick, Mountrath, Portarlington, Portlaoise, Rathdowney, Roscrea, Templemore, Urlingford).

District 16 - Thomas J. Ballagh - (Baltinglass, Blessington, Bray, Droichead Nua, Dunlavin, Hacketstown, Kildare, Naas).

District 17 - Humphrey P. Kelleher - (Annascaul, Cahirciveen, Castlegregory, Castleisland, Dingle, Kenmare, Killarney, Killorglin, Sneem, Tralee, Waterville).

District 18 - Brendan Wallace - (Bandon, Bantry, Castletownbere, Clonakilty, Coachford, Dunmanway, Glengariff, Kinsale, Macroom, Millstreet, Schull, Skibbereen).

District 19 - David Riordan / Uinsin MacGruaic - (Cork City).

District 20 - John P. Clifford - (Ballincollig, Buttevant, Carrigaline, Castlemartyr, Castletownroche, Cobh, Fermoy, Kanturk, Mallow, Michelstown, Blarney/Whitechurch, Midleton and Riverstown/Fermoy).

District 21 - Michael Pattwell - (Cahir, Cappoquin, Carrick-on-Suir, Cashel, Clogheen, Clonmel, Dungarvan, Killenaule, Lismore, Tallow, Tipperary, Youghal).

District 22 - William Harnett - (Callan, Kilkenny, Kilmacthomas, Thomastown, Waterford).

District 23 - Donnchadh Ó Buachalla / John O'Donnell - (Arklow, Bunclody, Enniscorthy, Gorey, Muine Bheag, New Ross, Rathdrum, Shillelagh, Tullow, Wexford, Wicklow).

MOVABLE JUDGES OF THE DISTRICT COURT:

John F. Neilan, Joseph Mangan, William G. J. Hamill, Thomas A. Fitzpatrick, Desmond P. Hogan, Gerard J. Haughton, J. W. Terence Finn, Murrough B. Connellan, Mary Fahy, William Early, Michael P. M. Connellan, John J. O'Neill.

NORTHERN IRELAND COURT SYSTEM

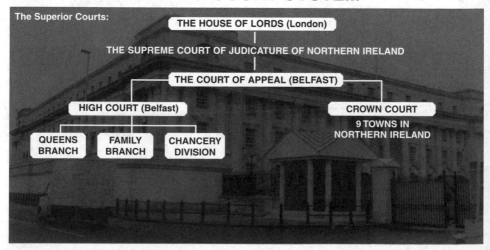

The Superior Courts:

THE HOUSE OF LORDS (London)

THE SUPREME COURT OF JUDICATURE OF NORTHERN IRELAND

THE COURT OF APPEAL (BELFAST)

HIGH COURT (Belfast)

CROWN COURT
9 TOWNS IN NORTHERN IRELAND

QUEENS BRANCH | FAMILY BRANCH | CHANCERY DIVISION

NORTHERN IRELAND: JUDICIARY

THE SUPREME COURT OF JUDICATURE

Royal Courts of Justice, Chichester Street, Belfast BT1 3JF.

THE LORD CHIEF JUSTICE OF N. IRELAND

The Right Hon. Sir Robin Douglas Carswell

JUDGES

The Right Hon. Lord Justice MacDermott
The Right Hon. Lord Justice Nicholson
The Right Hon. Lord Justice McCollum
The Hon. Mr. Justice Campbell
The Hon. Mr. Justice Sheil
The Hon. Mr. Justice Kerr
The Hon. Mr. Justice Pringle
The Hon. Mr. Justice Higgins
The Hon. Mr. Justice Girvan
The Hon. Mr. Justice Coghlin

LORD CHIEF JUSTICE'S OFFICE

Principal Secretary to the Lord Chief Justice: G.W. Johnston

SUPREME COURT OFFICES

Queen's Bench, Appeals and Clerk of the Crown in Northern Ireland: Master - Mr. J.W. Wilson
High Court Master - Mrs. D.M. Kennedy
Office of Care and Protection: Master - Mr. F.B. Hall
Bankruptcy and Companies Office: Master - Mr. J.B.C. Glass
Chancery Office: Master - Mr. R.A. Ellison

Probate and Matrimonial Office: Master - *vacant*
Taxing Office: Master - Mr. J.C. Napier
Court Funds Office: Accountant General - Mr. H.G. Thompson
Official Solicitor - Mr. C.W.G. Redpath

RECORDERS:

Belfast - His Honour Judge Hart
Derry - His Honour Judge Burgess

COUNTY COURT JUDGES

His Honour Judge Brady
His Honour Judge Curran
His Honour Judge Foote
His Honour Judge Gibson
His Honour Judge Martin
His Honour Judge Markey
His Honour Judge McKay
His Honour Judge McKee
His Honour Judge Petrie
His Honour Judge Rodgers
His Honour Judge Smyth

Chief Social Security Commissioner - *vacant*

DISTRICT JUDGES

Division of Belfast - District Judge Wells
Division of Derry and Antrim - District Judge Keegan
Division of Armagh & South Down and Fermanagh and Tyrone - *vacant*
Division of Craigavon and Ards - District Judge Wheeler

REPUBLIC OF IRELAND: ORGANISATION AND LOCATION OF CIRCUIT COURTS

Circuit	Town	County Registrar
Cork	Bandon	*(See Cork)*
	Bantry	*(See Cork)*
	Clonakilty	*(See Cork)*
	Cork	Deirdre O'Mahony, Courthouse, Cork. Tel. (021) 270508.
	Fermoy	*(See Cork)*
	Kanturk	*(See Cork)*
	Macroom	*(See Cork)*
	Mallow	*(See Cork)*
	Midleton	*(See Cork)*
	Skibbereen	*(See Cork)*
	Youghal	*(See Cork)*
Eastern	Dundalk	Mairead Ahern, Courthouse, Dundalk. Tel. (042) 34066.
	Athy	*(See Naas)*
	Naas	Eithne Coughlan, Courthouse, Naas. Tel. (045) 897348.
	Trim	Maire Tehan, Courthouse, Trim. Tel. (046) 31209.
	Wicklow	Breda Allen, Courthouse, Wicklow. Tel. (0404) 67361.
Midland	Athlone	Elizabeth Sharkey,
	Mullingar	Courthouse, Mullingar. Tel. (044) 48315.
	Birr	*(See Tullamore)*
	Tullamore	Patrick R. O'Gorman, Courthouse, Tullamore. Tel. (0506) 21205.
	Boyle	*(See Roscommon)*
	Roscommon	Anthony F. McCormack, Courthouse, Roscommon. Tel. (0903) 26132.
	Longford	Imelda Branigan, Courthouse, Longford. Tel. (043) 46410.
	Portlaoise	James E. Cahill, Courthouse, Portlaoise. Tel. (0502) 21340.
	Sligo	Kieran McDermott, Courthouse, Sligo. Tel. (071) 42228.
Northern	Buncrana	Mary T. Devlin, Courthouse, Lifford. Tel. (074) 41266.

Circuit	Town	County Registrar
	Donegal	(See Buncrana)
	Letterkenny	(See Buncrana)
Carrick-on-Shannon		Kevin Doherty, Courthouse, Carrick-on-Shannon. Tel. (078) 20002.
	Manorhamilton	(See Carrick-on-Shannon)
	Castleblayney	(See Monaghan)
	Monaghan	J. Duffy, Courthouse, Monaghan. Tel. (047) 82388.
	Cavan	Thomas P. Owens, Courthouse, Cavan. Tel. (049) 31530.
South Eastern	Carlow	John A. O'Gorman, Courthouse, Carlow. Tel. (0503) 31664.
	Clonmel	Patrick J. McCormack, Courthouse, Clonmel. Tel. (052) 21195.
	Nenagh	(See Clonmel)
	Thurles	(See Clonmel)
	Tipperary	(See Clonmel)
	Dungarvan	(See Waterford)
	Waterford	Niall Robert Rooney, Courthouse, Waterford. Tel. (051) 74144.
	Kilkenny	Mary N. Enright, Courthouse, Kilkenny. Tel. (056) 22073.
	Wexford	Maurice J. Phelan, Courthouse, Wexford. Tel. (053) 22329.
South Western	Ennis	Enda Brogan, Clare Courthouse. Tel. (021) 21041.
	Kilrush	(See Ennis)
	Killarney	(See Tralee)
	Listowel	(See Tralee)
	Tralee	Louise McDonough Courthouse, Tralee. Tel. (066) 21998.
	Limerick	Proinsias B. O'Gadhra, Courthouse, Limerick. Tel. (061) 414655.
	Rathkeale	(See Limerick)
Western	Ballina	(See Castlebar)
	Castlebar	Fintan J. Murphy, Courthouse, Castlebar. Tel. (094) 21522.
	Swinford	(See Castlebar)
	Westport	(See Castlebar)
	Clifden	(See Galway)
	Galway	Sean C. O'Domhnaill, Courthouse, Galway. Tel. (091) 562340.
	Loughrea	(See Galway)
Dublin	Dublin	Michael Quinlan, Aras Ui Dhalaigh, Inns Quay, Dublin 7. Tel. (01) 8725555.

NORTHERN IRELAND:
ORGANISATION AND LOCATION OF COURTS

Town/City	Circuit	County Court Division	Petty Sessions Division	Court Sittings
Derry	Northern	Derry	Derry	Crown, Recorder's, Magistrates
Limavady			Limavady	County, Magistrates
Magherafelt			Magherafelt	County, Magistrates
Strabane			Strabane	County, Magistrates
Castlederg			Strabane	Magistrates
Coleraine		N. Antrim	Coleraine	Crown, County, Magistrates
Ballymena			Ballymena	Crown, County, Magistrates
Ballymoney			Ballymoney	County, Magistrates
Ballycastle			Moyle	Magistrates
Antrim			Antrim	Magistrates
Armagh	S. Western	Armagh	Armagh	Crown, County, Magistrates
Lurgan			Craigavon	County, Magistrates
Portadown			Craigavon	Magistrates
Omagh	Fermanagh & S. Tyrone		Omagh	Crown, County, Magistrates
Cookstown			Cookstown	County, Magistrates
Dungannon			Dungannon	County, Magistrates
Clogher			Dungannon	Magistrates
Enniskillen			Fermanagh	Crown, County, Magistrates
Newtownbutler			Fermanagh	Magistrates
Lisnaskea			Fermanagh	Magistrates
Irvinestown			Fermanagh	Magistrates
Derrygonnelly			Fermanagh	Magistrates

Downpatrick	S. Eastern	S. Down	Down	Crown, County, Magistrates
Newcastle			Down	Magistrates
Banbridge			Banbridge	County, Magistrates
Newry			Newry / Mourne	County, Magistrates
Kilkeel			Newry / Mourne	Magistrates
Lisburn		Ards	Lisburn	County, Magistrates
Hillsborough			Lisburn	Magistrates
Bangor			N. Down	Magistrates
Newtownards			Ards	Crown, County, Magistrates
Newtownbreda			Castlereagh	Magistrates
Belfast	Eastern	Belfast	Belfast	Crown, Recorder's, Magistrates
Carrickfergus			Carrickfergus	Magistrates
Newtownabbey			Newtownabbey	Magistrates
Larne			Larne	Magistrates

REPUBLIC OF IRELAND: GARDA PERSONNEL BY NUMBERS, RANK AND LOCATION 1995

Description	Headquarters	Garda College	Dublin Met.	Others	Total
Divisions	-	-	5	18	23
Districts	-	-	17	90	107
Stations	-	-	45	659	704
Garda Síochána:					
Commissioner Ranks	8	-	1	-	9
Chief Superintendents	13	1	10	18	42
Superintendents	29	6	34	93	162
Inspectors	34	5	122	86	247
Sergeants	159	51	622	1,024	1,856
Gardaí	499	60	3,244	4,706	8,509
Total:	**742**	**123**	**4,033**	**5,927**	**10,825**

NORTHERN IRELAND: ROYAL ULSTER CONSTABULARY PERSONNEL BY NUMBERS AND RANK, 1996

Rank	Establishment	Effective Strength	Vacancies	Over Est. no.s	Seconded to Central Services
Chief Constable	1	1	-	-	-
Deputy Chief Constable	2	1	1	-	-
Assistant Chief Constable	9	7	2	-	-
Chief Superintendent	-	22	-	-	-
Superintendent	-	132	-	-	-
Superintendent Rank	162	154	8	-	1
Chief Inspector	167	161	6	-	1
Inspector	491	485	6	-	2
Sergeant	1,414	1,405	9	-	3
Constable	6,243	6,209	34	-	-
TOTALS:	**8,489**	**8,577**	**66**	**-**	**7**
RUC Reserve (Full-Time)	3,202	2,929	273	-	-
RUC Reserve (Part-Time)	1,765	1,473	292	-	-

REPUBLIC OF IRELAND: STRENGTH OF AN GARDA SÍOCHÁNA, 1996

Rank	Number	Rank	Number
Commissioners	1	Superintendents	163
Deputy Commissioners	2	Inspectors	251
Assistant Commissioners	9	Sergeants	1,862
Acting Surgeons	1	Gardaí	8,484
Chief Superintendents	44	TOTAL:	10,817

REPUBLIC OF IRELAND: GARDA STATIONS

County / City	No. of Stations	County / City	No. of Stations
Carlow	9	Louth	13
Cavan	22	Mayo	38
Clare	29	Meath†	13
Cork *(city)*	19	Monaghan	13
Cork *(county)*	68	Offaly	16
Donegal	45	Roscommon	21
Dublin* *(metropolitan area)*	59	Sligo	15
Galway	57	Tipperary	43
Kerry	38	Waterford	21
Kildare†	14	Westmeath	16
Kilkenny	20	Wexford	25
Laois	14	Wicklow†	14
Leitrim	15		
Limerick *(city)*	14		
Limerick *(county)*	23		
Longford	11		

* Dublin Metropolitan area includes Dublin, parts of Kildare, parts of Meath & parts of Wicklow.
† Does not include stations already accounted for in Dublin Metropolitan area.

REPUBLIC OF IRELAND: GARDA SÍOCHÁNA STATISTICS BY REGION, 1996

Category	Northern Region	Western Region	Eastern Region	Southern Region	South Eastern Region	D.M.A. Region
Population	311,551	431,635	597,894	701,216	440,533	1,041,259
Area *(km²)*	11,339	17,736	13,214	14,935	11,682	869
Primary/Secondary Roads *(km)*	745.2	1,328.2	1,117.6	1,152.7	906.5	153.5
Regional Crime *(1996)*	3,142.0	5,110	11,917	15,020	6,837	58,759
Crime per 1,000 Population	10.1	11.8	19.9	21.4	15.5	56.4
Regional Detections *(1996)*	1,511	2,453	5,680	6,454	3,328	21,630
Detection Rate *(%)*	48	48	48	43	49	37
Road Traffic Offences	13,028	16,826	30,954	46,765	21,170	139,829
Garda Strength	1,094	1,009	1,292	1,643	867	3,956
Garda Vehicles	130	113	153	179	106	267
Garda Stations	108	145	127	162	117	45
Garda Districts	14	20	18	22	16	17

Northern Region - Sligo, Leitrim, Donegal, Cavan, Monaghan.
Western Region - Clare, Galway, Roscommon, Mayo.
Eastern Region - Louth, Meath, Longford, Westmeath, Laois, Offaly, Carlow, Kildare.
Southern Region - Kerry, Limerick, Cork.
South Eastern Region - Wexford, Tipperary, Waterford, Kilkenny.
D.M.A. Region - Dublin Metropolitan Area.

NORTHERN IRELAND: POLICE STATIONS

County	Stations	County	Stations
Antrim	53 (incl. 28 in Belfast)	Down	28
Armagh	19	Fermanagh	13
Derry	18	Tyrone	23

N.I.: STRENGTH OF POLICE FORCE AND ULSTER DEFENCE REGIMENT/ROYAL IRISH REGIMENT

Force	1991	1992	1993	1994	1995
Royal Ulster Constabulary:					
Males	7,510	7,688	7,646	7,640	7,541
Females	707	790	818	853	899
Total: Royal Ulster Constabulary	**8,217**	**8,478**	**8,464**	**8,493**	**8,440**
Royal Ulster Constabulary Reserves:					
Males – part-time	1,089	1,014	964	996	953
Males – full-time	2,980	3,046	3,063	3,056	2,787
Females – part-time	429	419	424	495	528
Females - full-time	62	114	121	143	151

Total: RUC Reserves	4,560	4,593	4,572	4,690	4,419
UDR / RIR:					
Males – part-time	2,553	2,251	2,181	1,994	-
Males – full-time	2,998	2,526	2,608	2,675	-
Females – part-time	446	369	329	291	-
Females – full-time	279	271	294	281	-
Total: UDR / RIR	6,276	5,417	5,412	5,241	-
TOTAL FORCE:	19,053	18,488	18,448	18,424	12,859

R.O.I.: CRIME RATE PER GARDA DIVISION

Garda Division	1992 (%)	1993 (%)	1994 (%)	1995 (%)
Outside Dublin Met. Area	17.8	-	-	-
Dublin Met. Area	49.9	53.6	-	-
Carlow / Kildare	15.4	16.5	16.9	17.17
Cavan / Monaghan	10.4	9.6	8.62	9.49
Cork East	36.4	36.0	34.36	32.44
Cork West	11.2	9.5	9.69	9.69
Clare	7.9	7.9	8.84	11.80
Donegal	10.9	10.3	11.95	11.08
Galway West	19.0	21.8	19.82	19.26
Kerry	15.6	12.9	15.81	14.14
Laois / Offaly	10.7	11.4	14.26	13.27
Limerick	23.5	22.0	22.84	23.77
Longford / Westmeath	25.6	18.9	19.32	19.86
Louth / Meath	21.3	21.2	22.36	25.52
Mayo	7.5	7.4	7.59	7.95
Roscommon / Galway East	8.8	9.4	9.98	9.49
Sligo / Leitrim	10.2	11.2	11.94	9.94
Tipperary	16.4	14.5	13.69	12.76
Waterford / Kilkenny	14.0	15.8	17.58	17.31
Wexford	18.9	21.3	19.93	15.44

R.O.I.: INDICTABLE OFFENCES REPORTED

Indictable Offences	1995		1996	
	Known	Detected	Known	Detected
Non-sexual Offences Against the Person	7,324	2,458	7,339	2,332
Sexual Offences	923	768	836	709
Larcenies	49,483	18,517	47,943	18,473
Frauds	3,610	3,050	3,758	3,240
Burglaries	32,721	10,335	31,741	11,025
Criminal Damage	8,045	4,275	8,747	4,877
Other Offences	378	729	421	400
TOTAL INDICTABLE OFFENCES:	102,484	39,754	100,785	41,056

R.O.I.: NON-INDICTABLE OFFENCES, 1996

Offence	Proceedings taken	Convictions
Assaults	7,811	4,607
Cruelty to Animals	268	160
Offences against Traffic Accidents	268,572	122,404
Other Traffic Act Offences	122,910	53,051
Offences against intoxicating liquor laws	12,642	8,516
Criminal damage to animals, fences, etc.	2,393	1,594
Offences against Police regulations	652	269
Criminal Law Sexual Offences Act, 1993	63	45
Criminal Justice (Public Order) Act, 1994	16,384	11,286
Offences against revenue laws	72	32
Offences against street trading acts	640	192
Offences against vagrancy acts	242	123
Offences Against Wireless Telegraphy Act, 1926	87	42
Offences Against Firearms Acts	845	643
Offences in relation to explosives	5	0
Offences under Juries Act, 1976	169	122
Other offences	17,512	10,533
TOTAL NON-INDICTABLE OFFENCES:	451,267	213,619

R.O.I.: RECORDED CRIME, 1981-1996

Year	Crime Recorded	Year	Crime Recorded
1981	89,400	1989	86,792
1982	97,626	1990	87,658
1983	102,387	1991	94,406
1984	99,727	1992	95,391
1985	91,285	1993	98,979
1986	86,574	1994	101,036
1987	85,358	1995	102,484
1988	89,544	1996	100,785

REPUBLIC OF IRELAND: FIREARMS, AMMUNITION AND EXPLOSIVES SEIZED, 1996

AMMUNITION:

7.62 x 39 mm	1,031
7.62 x 51 mm	65
12.7 x 99 mm	93
Assorted	10,156
Shotgun Cartridges	2,057
Blank Ammunition	854

EXPLOSIVE DEVICES:

Mk 6 Mortar (complete)	14
Mk 6 Bomb Components	58
Mk 12 Mortar Components	150
Mortar Fuses	53
Mortar Fuse Components	127
Mark 8 Bomb Body	1
Mk 10 Mortar Components	173
Mk 11 Mortar Components	128
P.R.I.G. (complete)	2
P.R.I.G. (components)	595
IPG Grenades	6
IPG Launcher	1
IPG Components	196

EXPLOSIVES:

Semtex kg	46.7
Detonating Cord (m)	49.3
Home Made Explosive	139
Kemegel	9
Trotlyl (T.N.T.)	2.8
M112 (Commercial Exp)	3.8
Black Powder (kg)	12.93
Smokeless Powder	2
Electric Detonators	54
Electric Detonators (Cut Down)	13
Plain Detonators	172
Home Made Detonators	11
Detonators (old)	25
Railway Detonators	91
Sagamo T.P.U.	36
RPG-7 War Head	1
Mk 15 Time & Power Units	14
Assorted Timers	8
Potassium Nitrate kg	15

Assorted Chemicals kg	23
Nitric Acid (l)	3.5
Metholated Spirit (l)	1
Booster Tubes	4
Pipe Bombs	4
Petrol Bombs	16
Incendiary Device	2
Mk15 Grenade Fuse Housing	50
Grenade	23
Flares	3

FIREARMS:

Sub Machine Guns	3
H & K G3 Assault Rifles	1
AK47/Akm Assault Rifles	5
AR15 Rifles (Armalites)	4
Shotguns	153
Rifles	59
Pistols	39
Revolvers	52
Air Guns	151
Imitations/Replicas	90
Pen Guns	7
Stun Guns	6
Cross Bows	10
Humane Killers	1
Magazines	43
Telescopic Sights	17
Silencers	9
AKM Bayonets	3
LPO-50 Flinging Charges	18
LPO-50 Pressure Cartridges	25

MISCELLANEOUS:

Bunker / Hides	18
Firing Ranges	1
Walkie Talkies	17
Scanners	10
Pressure Mats	3
Photographic Slaves	1
Transformers	1
Oscillator	2

NORTHERN IRELAND: PERSONS CONVICTED OF INDICTABLE OFFENCES, 1995

Offence	Magistrates Court			Crown Courts		
	Males	Females	Total	Males	Females	Total
Offences against the Person	1,270	117	1,387	285	13	298
Sexual offences	92	1	93	86	3	89
Burglary	868	27	895	54	2	56
Robbery	15	3	18	171	6	177
Theft & handling stolen goods	2,419	549	2,968	143	17	160
Fraud & forgery	373	109	482	40	11	51
Criminal damage	869	73	942	61	5	66
Others	748	43	791	218	20	238
PERSONS CONVICTED:	6,654	922	7,576	1,058	77	1,135

NORTHERN IRELAND: PERSONS FOUND GUILTY OF INDICTABLE AND NON-INDICTABLE OFFENCES

Offence	1991	1992	1993	1994	1995
Indictable Offences	8,893	8,558	8,929	8,376	8,734
Non-Indictable Offences	24,410	24,901	26,156	25,840	24,238
ALL OFFENCES:	33,303	33,459	35,085	34,216	32,972

NORTHERN IRELAND: NOTIFIABLE OFFENCES RECORDED BY THE POLICE

Offence	1991	1992	1993	1994	1995	1996
Violence against the person	3,955	4,102	4,597	4,793	5,150	5,640
Sexual Offences	877	973	1,187	1,333	1,679	1,745
Burglary	16,563	17,117	15,735	16,902	16,457	16,114
Robbery	1,848	1,851	1,723	1,567	1,539	1,725
Theft	32,033	34,256	33,161	33,233	33,472	32,772
Fraud and forgery	4,811	5,486	5,553	5,100	4,884	4,081
Criminal Damage	2,394	2,502	2,856	3,077	3,772	4,847
Offences against the state	592	478	436	440	339	400
Other Notifiable offences	419	767	980	1,441	1,516	1,225
ALL OFFENCES:	63,492	67,532	66,228	67,886	68,808	68,549

REPUBLIC OF IRELAND: PRISON POPULATION

Prisoner Category	1990	1991	1992	1993
Total on remand	2,199	2,466	3,755	3,820
Males	1,917	2,216	3,392	3,425
Females	282	250	363	395
Total For Trial	199	374	289	303
Males	197	360	281	293
Females	2	14	8	10
Total On Conviction	2,537	2,491	3,536	4,106
Males	2,454	2,349	3,366	3,875
Females	83	142	170	231
THROUGHPUT* OF PRISONERS DURING THE YEARS:				
Total On Remand	2,184	2,453	3,759	3,831
Males	1,900	2,205	3,397	3,436
Females	284	248	362	395
Total For Trial	196	378	289	283

Males	193	364	282	273
Females	3	14	7	10
Total On Conviction	**2,348**	**2,435**	**3,421**	**3,955**
Males	2,274	2,284	3,247	3,736
Females	74	151	174	219
Total Daily Average Population	**2,108**	**2,140**	**2,185**	**2,171**
Males	2,062	2,100	2,146	2,127
Females	46	40	39	44

* Prisoners in custody on Jan. 1st plus those received during the year, less prisoners in custody on Dec. 31st.

NORTHERN IRELAND: PRISON POPULATION

Category of Male Prisoners	1992	1993	1994	1995
On Remand:				
Aged under 21	93	96	106	72
Aged 21 or over	307	322	321	240
Total on Remand	400	418	427	312
Fine Defaulter:				
Aged under 21	6	7	4	5
Aged 21 or over	27	23	23	23
Total Fine Defaulter	33	30	37	28
Immediate Custody:				
Young Offenders' Centres	145	153	133	118
Young Prisoners	102	100	91	87
Adult Prisoners	1,088	1,192	1,179	1,177
Total in Immediate Custody	1,335	1,445	1,403	1,382
Non-Criminals	1	1	1	5
TOTAL MALE PRISONERS	**1,769**	**1,894**	**1,858**	**1,727**

Category of Female Prisoners	1992	1993	1994	1995
On Remand:				
Aged under 21	6	2	5	2
Aged 21 or over	7	6	7	3
Total on Remand	13	8	12	5
Fine Defaulter:				
Aged under 21	-	1	1	-
Aged 21 or over	1	1	2	1
Total Fine defaulter	1	2	3	1
Immediate Custody:				
Young Offenders' Centres	4	3	4	6
Young Prisoners	2	3	3	2
Adult Prisoners	21	24	19	21
Total - Immediate Custody	27	30	26	29
Non-criminal	-	-	-	-
TOTAL FEMALE PRISONERS:	**41**	**40**	**41**	**35**
All Prisoners: *(Remand)*	413	426	439	317
All Prisoners: *(Fine Defaulter)*	34	32	30	29
All Prisoners: *(Immediate Custody)*	1,362	1,475	1,429	1,411
All Prisoners: *(Non-Criminal)*	1	1	1	5
OVERALL TOTAL:	**1,810**	**1,934**	**1,899**	**1,762**

NORTHERN IRELAND: NUMBER OF DEATHS DUE TO THE TROUBLES, 1969-1996

Year	R.U.C.	R.U.C. Reserve	Army	U.D.R./R.I.R.	Civilian	Total
1969	1	-	-	-	13	14
1970	2	-	-	-	23	25
1971	11	-	43	5	115	174
1972	14	3	105	26	322	470
1973	10	3	58	8	173	252
1974	12	3	30	7	168	220
1975	7	4	14	6	216	247
1976	13	10	14	15	245	297
1977	8	6	15	LAW	69	112
1978	4	6	14	7	50	81
1979	9	5	38	10	51	113
1980	3	6	8	9	50	76
1981	13	8	10	13	57	101
1982	8	4	21	7	57	97
1983	9	9	5	10	44	77
1984	7	2	9	10	36	64
1985	14	9	2	4	26	55
1986	10	2	4	8	37	61
1987	9	7	3	8	68	95
1988	4	2	21	12	55	94
1989	7	2	12	2	39	62
1990	7	5	7	8	49	76
1991	5	1	5	8	75	94
1992	2	1	4	2	76	85
1993	3	3	6	2	70	84
1994	3	-	1	2	56	62
1995	1	-	-	-	8	9
1996	-	-	1	-	14	15
TOTAL:	196	101	450	203	2,262	3,212

NORTHERN IRELAND: INJURIES CONNECTED WITH THE TROUBLES, 1969-1995

YEAR	R.U.C.	REGULAR ARMY	U.D.R./R.I.R.	CIVILIANS	PEOPLE INJURED
1969	711	54	-	-	765
1970	191	620	-	-	811
1971	315	381	9	1,887	2,592
1972	485	542	36	3,813	4,876
1973	291	525	23	1,812	2,651
1974	235	453	30	1,680	2,398
1975	263	151	16	2,044	2,474
1976	303	242	22	2,162	2,729
1977	183	172	15	1,017	1,387
1978	302	127	8	548	985
1979	165	132	21	557	875
1980	194	53	24	530	801
1981	332	112	28	878	1,350
1982	99	80	18	328	525
1983	142	66	22	280	510
1984	267	64	22	513	866
1985	415	20	13	468	916
1986	622	45	10	773	1,450
1987	246	92	12	780	1,130
1988	218	211	18	600	1,047
1989	163	175	15	606	959
1990	214	190	24	478	906

1991	139	197	56	570	962
1992	148	302	18	598	1,066
1993	147	146	27	504	824
1994	170	120	6	529	825
1995	370	8	5	554	937
TOTAL:	**7,330**	**5,280**	**498**	**24,509**	**37,617**

NORTHERN IRELAND: INCIDENTS CONNECTED WITH *THE TROUBLES*, 1969-1996

Year	Shooting incidents	Bombs exploded	Devices defused	Incendiaries Ignited/defused	Firearms found	Explosives found (kg)	Armed Robberies inc. attempts	Amount Stolen (£STG)
1969	73	9	1	-	14	102	-	-
1970	213	153	17	-	324	305	-	-
1971	1,756	1,022	493	-	716	1,246	489	304,000
1972	10,631	1,382	471	-	1,259	18,819	1,931	795,000
1973	5,019	978	542	-	1,313	17,426	1,317	612,000
1974	3,208	685	428	270	1,236	11,848	1,353	576,000
1975	1,803	399	236	56	820	4,996	1,325	572,000
1976	1,908	766	426	236	736	9,849	889	545,000
1977	1,081	366	169	608	563	1,728	676	447,000
1978	755	455	178	115	393	956	493	233,000
1979	728	422	142	60	300	905	504	568,000
1980	642	280	120	2	203	821	467	497,000
1981	1,142	398	131	49	357	3,419	689	855,000
1982	547	219	113	36	288	2,298	693	1,392,000
1983	424	266	101	43	166	1,706	718	830,000
1984	334	193	55	10	187	3,871	710	702,000
1985	238	148	67	36	173	3,344	542	656,000
1986	392	172	82	21	174	2,443	839	1,207,000
1987	674	236	148	9	206	5,885	955	1,900,000
1988	538	253	205	8	489	4,728	742	1,389,000
1989	566	224	196	7	246	1,377	604	1,079,000
1990	557	166	120	33	179	1,969	492	1,729,000
1991	499	231	137	237	164	4,167	607	1,673,000
1992	506	222	149	126	194	2,167	739	1,666,000
1993	476	206	83	61	196	3,944	643	1,515,000
1994	348	123	99	115	178	1,285	555	1,709,000
1995	50	1	1	10	118	5	421	838,000
1996	125	25*	-	4	98	1,677	-	-
TOTAL:	**35,108**	**9,975**	**4,910**	**2,152**	**11,290**	**113,286**	**19,393**	**24,289,000**

* This number includes bombs defused.

NORTHERN IRELAND: DEFENCE PERSONNEL

Force	Number
Royal Air Force	1,200
Royal Navy	250
Royal Irish Regiment (R.I.R.):	
R.I.R. (Full-time)	2,500
R.I.R. (Part-time)	3,000
R.I.R. Total	5,500
Others	12,050
TOTAL:	**19,000**

NORTHERN IRELAND: DEFENCE FORCES

Heads of Defence Staff Breakdown	
Rank/Force	**Name**
General Officer Commanding Northern Ireland	Lieutenant General Sir Rupert Smith
Chief of Staff Headquarters, Northern Ireland	Brigadier Robin V. Brims
Commander 8th Infantry Brigade	Brigadier Simon D. Young
Commander 3rd Infantry Brigade	Brigadier Jamie Balfour

Commander 39th Infantry Brigade ....Brigadier James Short
Commander 107 (Ulster) Brigade ....Brigadier Alisdair Allan Wilson
Colonel in Chief, Royal Irish Regiment..H .R.H. The Duke of York
Colonel of the Regiment, Royal Irish Regiment ....Gen. Sir Roger Wheeler
Colonel in Chief, The Royal Dragoon Guards...H.R.H. The Prince of Wales
Colonel of the Regiment, The Royal Dragoon Guards...Major Gen. P.G. Brooking
Colonel in Chief, The Queen's Royal Hussars...H.R.H. Prince Philip Duke of Edinburgh
Colonel of the Regiment, The Queen's Royal Hussars...Major Gen. R.E. Barron
Colonel in Chief, The Irish Guards ....H.M. The Queen
Colonel of the Regiment, The Irish Guards...H.R.H. The Grand Duke of Luxembourg

REPUBLIC OF IRELAND: DEFENCE STAFF BREAKDOWN

Rank	Name	Stationed
Minister for Defence	Mr. David Andrews, T.D.	Defence H.Q., Dublin.
Minister of State for Defence	Mr. Seamus Brennan, T.D.	
Chief of Staff	Lt. Gen. Gerry McMahon	Defence H.Q., Dublin.
Adjutant General	Maj. Gen. Bill Dwyer	Defence H.Q., Dublin.
Quartermaster General	Maj. Gen. Patrick Nowlan	Defence H.Q., Dublin.
Assistant Chief of Staff	*to be announced*	Defence H.Q., Dublin.
General Officer Commanding Eastern Command	Brig. Gen. Colm Mangan	Cathal Brugha Bks., Dublin.
General Officer Commanding Western Command	Brig. Gen. John Martin	Custume Bks., Athlone.
General Officer Commanding Southern Command	Brig. Gen. Dave Taylor	Collins Bks., Cork.
General Officer Commanding Curragh Command	Brig. Gen. Frank Colclough	Ceannt Bks., Curragh.
Commandant Military College	Brig. Gen. Peirce Redmond	Military College, Curragh.
Flag Officer Commanding the Naval Service	Commodore John Kavanagh	Defence H.Q., Dublin.
General Officer Commanding Air Corps	Brig. Gen. Pat Cranfield	Defence H.Q., Dublin.

NORTHERN IRELAND: DEFENCE HEADQUARTERS

THE ARMY:

Headquarters - Thiepval Barracks, Lisburn, Co. Antrim BT28 3SE. Tel. (01846) 665111.
3 Infantry Brigade - Mahon Barracks, Portadown, Co. Armagh. Tel. (01762) 351551.
8 Infantry Brigade - Ebrington Barracks, Derry BT47 1JU. Tel. (01504) 43211.
39 Infantry Brigade - Thiepval Barracks, Lisburn, Co. Antrim BT28 3SE. Tel. (01846) 665111.

OTHER ARMY LOCATIONS:

Palace Barracks, Holywood, Co. Down. Tel. (01232) 425121.
Abercorn Barracks, Ballykinler, Co. Down. Tel. (01396) 613111.
Lisanelly Barracks, Omagh, Co. Tyrone. Tel. (01662) 243194.
Shackleton Barracks, Ballykelly, Co. Derry. Tel. (01504) 763221.

HOME SERVICE BATTALIONS
ROYAL IRISH REGIMENT:

3rd Battalion (Co. Down & Armagh) - Mahon Road, Portadown, Co. Armagh. Tel. (01762) 351551.
4th Battalion (Co. Fermanagh & Tyrone) - Grosvenor Barrack,
Enniskillen, Co. Fermanagh. Tel. (01365) 327540.
5th Battalion (Co. Derry) - Shackleton Barracks, Ballykelly, Co. Derry. Tel. (01504) 763221.
7th Battalion (City of Belfast) - Malone Centre, Windsor Park, Belfast, Co. Antrim. Tel. (01232) 665244.
8th Battalion (Co. Armagh & Tyrone) - Drumadd Barracks, Armagh, Co. Armagh. Tel. (01861) 523821.
9th Battalion (Co. Antrim) - Steeple Road, Antrim, Co. Antrim. Tel. (01849) 462402.

TRAINING DEPOTS AND CAMPS:

St. Patrick's Barracks, Ballymena, Co. Antrim BT43 7BH. Tel. (01266) 652135.
Ballykinler, Co. Down. Tel. (01396) 613111.
Magilligan Camp, Co. Derry. Tel. (01504) 763021.

Regimental Headquarters:

Royal Irish Regiment - St. Patrick's Barracks, Ballymena, Co. Antrim BT43 7BH. Tel. (01266) 652135.
Royal Irish Rangers/Royal Ulster Rifles - 5 Waring Street, Belfast, Co. Antrim. BT1 2EW. Tel. (01232) 232086.
Royal Irish Fusiliers - Sovereign's House, The Mall, Armagh, Co. Armagh BT61 9DL. Tel. (01861) 522911.
Royal Inniskilling Fusiliers - The Castle, Enniskillen,. Co. Fermanagh. Tel. (01365) 323142.

ARMY CADET FORCE:

1st Cadet Battalion Army Cadet Force (Northern Ireland) - Tyrone House, 83 Malone Road, Belfast, Co. Antrim. Tel. (01232) 666067.
2nd Cadet Battalion Army Cadet Force (Northern Ireland) - 19 Railway Street, Comber, Co. Down. Tel. (01247) 872577.

TERRITORIAL ARMY:

HQ 107 (Ulster) Brigade - St. Patrick's Barracks, Ballymena, Co. Antrim BT43 7BH.

ROYAL NAVY:

Palace Barracks, Holywood, Co. Down BT18 9RQ. Tel. (01232) 427040.

ROYAL AIR FORCE:

Aldergrove, Co. Antrim. Tel. (01849) 422051.

REPUBLIC OF IRELAND: DEFENCE HEADQUARTERS

Army, Air Corps and Naval Service - Parkgate, Dublin 8. Tel. (01) 8379911.

Command Headquarters:
Eastern Command - Cathal Brugha Barracks, Rathmines, Dublin 6. Tel.

(01) 8046202.
Southern Command - Collins Barracks, Cork. Tel. (021) 397577.
Western Command - Custume Barracks, Athlone, Co. Westmeath. Tel. (0902) 92631.
Curragh Command - Curragh, Co.

Kildare. Tel. (045) 41301.
Air Corps - Casement Aerodrome, Baldonnel, Dublin 22. Tel. (01) 4592493.
Naval Service - Haulbowline, Cobh, Co. Cork. Tel. (021) 811246.

REPUBLIC OF IRELAND: DEFENCE PERSONNEL, JUNE 1997

Rank	Army	Air Corps	Naval Service	Total
Officers	1,154	132	131	1,417
NCO's	3,815	442	463	4,720
Privates	4,875	495	427	5,797
Cadets	49	16	7	72
TOTAL:	**9,893**	**1,069**	**1,021**	**11,983**
Males	*9,679*	*1,056*	*1,016*	*11,751*
Females	*214*	*13*	*5*	*232*

REPUBLIC OF IRELAND: RESERVE DEFENCE FORCES, JUNE 1997

Force	Personnel
First Line Reserve	517
Second Line Reserve	14,998
TOTAL:	**15,515**

REPUBLIC OF IRELAND: DEFENCE PERSONNEL ON OVERSEAS DUTIES, AUGUST 1997

Personnel / Missions	Total
Number of overseas missions	15
Numbers serving overseas	760

REPUBLIC OF IRELAND: SHIPS AND AIRCRAFT, 1997

Force	Equipment
Naval Service	7 ships
Air Corps	40 Aircraft (i.e. 25 fixed-wing & 15 rotor-blade)

R.O.I.: DEFENCE PERSONNEL, 1960-1995

Year	Permanent Force	Reserve Force
1960	8,965	24,569
1965	8,199	21,946
1970	8,574	20,253
1975	12,059	17,221
1980	13,383	19,249
1985	13,778	16,358
1990	13,233	15,982
1995	12,742	16,188

R.O.I.: STRENGTH OF DEFENCE FORCE

Rank	1992	1993	1994	1995
Permanent Defence Force:				
Commissioned Officers:				
Lieutenant-General	1	1	1	1
Major-General	3	3	3	2
Brigadier-General	8	8	8	9

Colonel	38	39	37	38
Lieutenant-Colonel	153	152	151	154
Commandant	445	471	471	487
Captain	652	616	610	601
Lieutenant	191	209	206	201
2nd Lieutenant	85	79	79	57
Total Commissioned Officers	**1,576**	**1,578**	**1,566**	**1,550**
Non-Commissioned Officers:				
Sergeants-Major	47	48	49	49
Battalion Quartermaster Sergeant	56	54	53	57
Company Sergeant	292	286	285	285
Company Quartermaster Sergeant	392	391	390	386
Sergeant	1,712	1,713	1,712	1,690
Corporal	2,565	2,528	2,545	2,605
Total Non-Commissioned Officers	**5,064**	**5,020**	**5,034**	**5,072**
Private	6,180	6,025	5,949	6,051
Cadet	69	60	57	69
Total Cadets & Ptc.s	**6,249**	**6,085**	**6,006**	**6,120**
TOTAL PERMANENT DEFENCE FORCE	**12,889**	**12,683**	**12,606**	**12,742**
Reserve Defence Force:				
Reserve of Officers (First Line)	183	187	187	204
Reserve of Men (First Line)	737	487	459	345
Reserve All Forces (Second Line)	15,907	16,009	15,688	15,639
TOTAL: RESERVE DEFENCE FORCE	**16,827**	**16,683**	**16,334**	**16,188**

NORTHERN IRELAND: DRUGS SEIZED AND ARRESTS MADE IN 1996

Drug Type	Quantity
Cannabis:	
Resin	157.1 kilograms
Herbal	7.8 kilograms
Plants	108
Oil	0.01grams
Joints	450
Ecstasy:	
M.D.M.A.	75,849 tablets
Powder	103 grams
Capsules	53
L.S.D.	7,734 doses
	27 microdots
Amphetamines	13.3 kilograms
	205 wraps
	41 tablets
Opiates (inc. Heroin)	136.5 grams
	1,348 tablets
	35 ampoules
	1 wraps
Cocaine	
Powder	411.6 grams
Wraps	1
Arrests Made:	1,017

REPUBLIC OF IRELAND: DRUGS SEIZED IN 1996

Drug Type	Quantity
Cannabis	2.4 kilograms
Cannabis Resin	1,933 kilograms
Cannabis Plants	542
Hash Oil	Less than 1 gram
Heroin (Diamorphine)	10.8 kilograms
Morphine	1,261 tablets
L.S.D.	5,901

Ecstasy	19,244 tablets (13.5 g powder)
Amphetamines	7.6 kilograms
Cocaine	642 kilograms
Crack Cocaine	393 grams
Benzodiazepines	7,146 tablets
Psilocin/Psilocybin	66.4 grams
Methadone	12 litres & 457 tablets
Dihydrocodeme	71 tablets
Buprenorphine	2 tablets
Ephedrine	3,768 tablets & 1,791 grams
Other	66 tablets

R.O.I.: NUMBERS OF DRUG OFFENCES, 1996

Drug Type	Eastern Region	Northern Region	South Eastern Region	Southern Region	Western Region	D.M.A. Region	Total
Cannabis	37	5	8	148	7	150	355
Cannabis Resin	89	83	173	443	253	400	1,441
Heroin	1	0	0	1	0	430	432
L.S.D.	3	2	2	8	0	9	24
Ecstasy	11	6	14	183	8	118	340
Amphetamines	5	1	8	78	20	40	152
Cocaine	1	0	7	2	5	27	42
Other	2	2	3	20	3	69	99
Total:	149	99	215	883	296	1,243	2,885

REPUBLIC OF IRELAND: DETECTED CRIMES COMMITTED BY DRUG USERS, 1995/1996

Crime	%	Number
Aggravated Burglary	85	316
Armed Aggravated Burglary	75	56
Armed Robbery	72	18
Burglary	82	3,844
Fraud	39	255
Handling	53	609
Larceny from Person	84	363
Larceny from Shop	50	1,986
Larceny from Unattended Vehicles	84	2,588
Other Larcenies	53	805
Malicious Damage	36	383
Mugging	82	400
Robbery	78	663
Sexual Offences	17	10
Murder	22	2
Assaults	22	29
Possession of Article with Intent	59	177
Other	46	79
TOTAL:		12,583

R.O.I.: DOMESTIC VIOLENCE, 1996

Area	Incidents	Arrests	Persons charged	Persons injured	Persons convicted
Eastern Region	631	161	127	144	110
D.M.A. Region	2,996	436	380	428	251
Northern Region	199	50	36	47	27
South Eastern Region	164	67	42	88	18
Southern Region	491	108	100	149	70
Western Region	164	38	40	67	30
Total:	4,645	860	725	923	506

Northern Region - *Sligo, Leitrim, Donegal, Cavan, Monaghan.*
Western Region - *Clare, Galway, Roscommon, Mayo.*
Eastern Region - *Louth, Meath, Longford, Westmeath, Laois, Offaly, Carlow, Kildare.*

Southern Region - *Kerry, Limerick, Cork.*
South Eastern Region - *Wexford, Tipperary, Waterford, Kilkenny.*
DMA Region - *Dublin Metropolitan Area.*

R.O.I.: DIVORCE STATISTICS, JUNE 1997

County	Divorce Applications Received	Divorces Granted
Circuit Court:		
Carlow	1	0
Cavan	4	1
Clare	5	0
Cork	22	0
Donegal	2	0
Dublin	142	50
Galway	2	2
Kerry	3	1
Kildare	5	0
Kilkenny	0	0
Laois	5	1
Leitrim	1	1
Limerick	2	0
Longford	0	0
Louth	2	0
Meath	5	0
Mayo	5	1
Monaghan	0	0
Offaly	2	0
Roscommon	0	0
Sligo	8	5
Tipperary	0	0
Waterford	3	0
Westmeath	3	0
Wexford	6	0
Wicklow	10	0
Total: Circuit Court	238	62
High Court	6	2
Total: High Court & Circuit Court	244	64

NORTHERN IRELAND: DIVORCES - DECREES NISI GRANTED BY FACTS PROVED, 1991-1995

Grounds for Divorce	1991	1992	1993	1994	1995
High Court:					
Adultery	161	150	157	133	115
Behaviour	214	239	268	303	300
Desertion	11	14	9	8	5
Separation *(for 2 years & consent)*	685	597	566	604	556
Separation *(for 5 years)*	332	341	288	316	326
Other Grounds	16	9	1	2	24
Total: High Court Divirces	1,419	1,350	1,289	1,366	1,326
County Court:					
Adultery	62	69	66	71	67
Behaviour	115	118	139	145	152
Desertion	12	17	10	11	7
Separation *(2 years & consent)*	459	552	552	690	627
Separation *(5 years)*	253	255	326	337	355
Other Grounds	24	25	2	-	1
Total: County Court Divorces	925	1,036	1,095	1,254	1,209
Total: All Divorces	2,344	2,386	2,384	2,620	2,535

BREAKDOWN OF PARADE INCIDENTS 1996

	Legal	Illegal	Re-routed	Conditions Imposed	Disorder Occurred	Banned	Total
Loyalist	2397	8	22	6	15	0	2405
Republican	219	11	2	0	0	0	230
Other	527	0	1	1	0	0	527
Total	3142	19	25	7	15	0	3162

R.U.C. PARADE SATATISICS 1985-96
Number of Parades

YEAR	TOTAL	LOYALIST	NATIONALIST	OTHER*
1985	2,120	1,897	223	-
1986	1,950	1,731	219	-
1987	2,112	1,863	246	-
1988	2,055	1,865	190	-
1989	2,317	2,099	218	-
1990	2,713	2,467	246	-
1991	2,379	2,183	196	-
1992	2,744	2,498	246	-
1993	2,662	2,411	251	-
1994	2,792	2,520	272	-
1995	3,500	2,581	302	617
1996	3,162	2,405	230	527

*Figures not available prior to 1995 - see North Report in Politics Chapter.

BANNED, RESTRICTED OR ILLEGAL PARADES

YEAR	TOTAL	BANNED	ILLEGAL	RE-ROUTED	CONDITIONS IMPOSED	DISORDER OCCURRED
1985	2,120	3	-	22	-	-
1986	1,950	1	-	9	-	-
1987	2,112	-	96	11	-	18
1988	2,055	-	8	11	-	21
1989	2,317	-	2	14	-	5
1990	2,713	-	1	10	-	1
1991	2,379	-	4	14	1	1
1992	2,744	-	-	16	16	-
1993	2,662	-	-	12	12	1
1994	2,792	-	-	29	29	-
1995	3,500	-	24	20	20	9
1996	3,162	-	19	25*	7	15

* Includes the Apprentice Boys' parade in Derry in August which was banned by the Secretary of State from a section of the city's walls. The rest of the parade was permitted.

Organisers of parades or counter demonstrations must, under the 1987 Public Order (Northern Ireland) Order, give a minimum of seven days notice to the police; otherwise the parade/demonstration is deemed illegal.

THE YEAR IN PICTURES

Haughey Fall: The spectre of scandal once again raised its head in the life of former Taoiseach, Charles Haughey. Mr. Haughey admitted receiving £1.3 million in unsolicited donations from supermarket magnate, Ben Dunne. Mr. Haughey made his revelation at the Payment to Politicians tribunal on July 9th, from which he is pictured leaving. He had consistently denied receiving any monies from Mr. Dunne prior to this date.

Michelle Rocca: Former Miss Ireland Michelle Rocca, pictured with Van Morrisson, was awarded £7,500 in damages in settlement of her high profile action in the High Court against former partner, Cathal Ryan.

Popmart Success: Bono of U2 on stage in Dublin during the first of two Popmart Concerts in Lansdowne Road. The group also played in Belfast's Botanic Gardens in a sell-out concert.

Off-Track: Sonia O'Sullivan endured another torrid season in 1997, and is pictured here disconsolate after elimination in the 5,000m heats at the World Championships in Athens.

New World Snooker champion: Dubliner, Ken Doherty shows off the World Snooker trophy. Doherty won the Embassy World Snooker Championship in May 1997, and halted the six-in-a-row ambitions of world number one Stephen Hendry.

On the Presidential trail: The Labour party's candidate for President, Adi Roche, pictured with Labour Party leader, Dick Spring at the launch of her campaign. Also pictured is Prionsias de Rossa, leader of Democratic Left who are also supporting her candidature.

Northern Ireland delight: Michael Hughes scores against Germany at Windsor Park

Golden Girl: Michelle Smith continued on her winning ways in 1997 when she won two gold and two silver medals at the European Championships in Seville.

McAleese canvases: Fianna Fáil presidential candidate Professor Mary McAleese has a chat with two potential supporters in Dublin.

Unionists enter talks: Ulster Unionist leader, David Trimble leads his party, the loyalist Ulster Democratic Party and the Progressive Unionist Party into the multi-party talks at Stormont on September 17, 1997.
Pictured foreground left to right: Jeffery Donaldson M.P., Cllr. Gary McMichael (leader of the U.D.P.),
Ken Maginnis M.P., David Trimble M.P., and John Taylor M.P., deputy leader of the Ulster Unionist Party.

Sinn Féin in talks: Sinn Féin M.P.s Gerry Adams and Martin McGuinness lead their party's delegation into the multi-party talks at Stormont on September 15, 1997. Sinn Féin had, in the absence of an I.R.A. ceasefire, been denied entry to the talks since they began on June 10, 1996. However, the restoration of the ceasefire in August opened the way for substantive negotiations on the future of Northern Ireland to begin on October 7th.
Also pictured are party vice-president Pat Doherty and general secretary Lucillita Bhreatnach.

Séan Brown Murder Scene: The scene, near Randalstown Co. Antrim, where the body of 61 year-old Seán Brown was discovered beside a burned out car. Mr. Brown, chairman of the Bellaghy G.A.A. club, was abducted on May 12 by masked men as he locked up at the club's grounds. No-one claimed responsibility for the murder although the R.U.C. believe the break away Loyalist Volunteer Force was responsible.

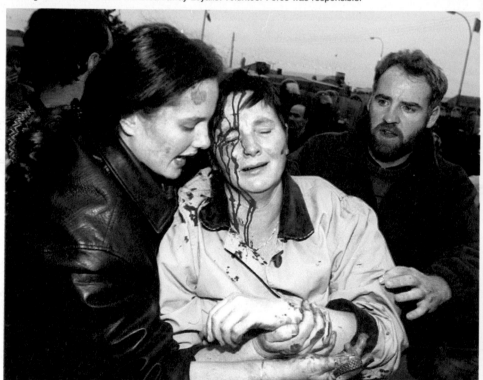

Scene from Garvaghy Road: A Garvaghy Road resident with head wounds is helped away following early morning clashes between the R.U.C. and local residents. The R.U.C. made the decision to force an Orange Order procession, returning to Portadown town centre from Drumcree Church, along the nationalist Garvaghy Road. In a pre-dawn operation police used batons and plastic bullets to remove protesting residents from the road. The decision led to widespread civil unrest throughout Northern Ireland.

Premier meeting: New Taoiseach Bertie Ahern meets new British Prime Minister Tony Blair for the first time in Downing Street.

Bruton backs Banotti: Fine Gael presidential candidate Mary Banotti pictured with party leader John Bruton after she had won her party's nomination.

Steve Collins retires: Ireland's Super-middleweight World champion, Steve Collins, who shocked boxing with his retirement announcement in early October.

Fitzgerald's All-Ireland: Man of the match from the 1997 Bank of Ireland All-Ireland fooball final Maurice Fitzgerald rounds Mayo's Pat Holmes and heads goalwards. Fitzgerald's contribution of 0-9 steered Kerry to their first All-Ireland title since 1986.

Dana stands for President: Dana, (Rosemary Brown) who stood for election as president of Ireland pictured during a press conference in Dublin.

Bloody Sunday march: A section of the 40,000 strong crowd pictured on February 2, 1997 at the annual Bloody Sunday commemoration in Derry. 1997 was the twenty-fifth anniversary of Bloody Sunday when fourteen unarmed civilians were shot dead by British Army paratroopers.

At the Cabinet Table: The new Fianna Fáil / Progressive Democrat Coalition Government pictured at their first cabinet meeting.

Harryville: R.U.C. officers in riot gear protect the Catholic church and Saturday night worshippers at Harryville, Ballymena from loyalist protesters. The protest has continued since September 1996 in response to the police ban on Loyal Order marches through the Co. Antrim village of Dunloy.

Smith's Year: Ireland's up-and-coming athlete Susan Smith pictured qualifying for the final of the World Championships in Athens in August.

R.U.C. deaths:
The bodies of
R.U.C. constable
John Graham and
reserve constable
Andrew Johnston lie
covered by
blankets after they
were shot dead by
the I.R.A. in Lurgan.
The policemen were
on the beat in
Church Walk when
the shooting
occurred. They were
the 300th and 301st
policemen to die in
'The Troubles'.

The Republic of Ireland U-20 team who finished third in the World Cup which was held in Malaysia in June. The team is: back row, left to right: E. Cox (kit), K. Murray (physio), Prof. C. Hopper (doctor), D. Worrell (Blackburn Rovers), D. Duff (Blackburn Rovers), A. Lynch (U.C.D.), D. O'Connor (Huddersfield Town), P. Whelan (Oxford United), C. Hawkins (Coventry City), N. Inman (Peterborough United), G. Crowe (Wolves), S. Murphy (Huddersfield Town), M. Price (coach) B. Kerr (manager).
Front row, left to right: N. O'Reilly (coach/assistant manager), J. Burns (Nottingham Forest), D. Whittle (Q.P.R.), A. Kirby (Aston Villa), R. Ryan (Huddersfield Town), T. Morgan, Captain (Blackburn Rovers), M. Cummins (Middlesborough), T. Molloy (Athlone Town), D. Baker (Shelbourne), N. Fenn (Tottenham Hotspur).

Not Talking: U.K. Unionist leader, Bob McCartney, explaining to members of the media why he would not be entering the All-Party Talks at Stormont. Also pictured is Dr. Ian Paisley, leader of the D.U.P., whose party is also abstaining from the talks.

In the Swing: Dungannon's Darren Clarke had a tremendous 1997 season, finishing runner up in both the British Open and the Volvo P.G.A. Finishing second in the race for Ryder Cup selection, Clarke made his Ryder debut in Valderrama, Spain where he, and his European team mates enjoyed a famous victory over the United States.

Hepatitis C Scandal: Dr. Joan Power, Medical Director of the Blood Transfusion Service Board in Cork and Dr. Brendan Murphy, Secretary of the National Drugs Advisory Board, leaving the Hepatitis C Tribunal having both given evidence. The Tribunal was established to enquire how people had become infected with contaminated blood products.

Garvaghy Road Mass: Catholic priests concelebrate open air mass against a backdrop of armed soldiers and army vehicles. Many Garvaghy Road residents were unable to attend church because of the security operation in place to permit the Orange Order church procession.

Hungry Lions: The Lions had a hugely successful summer tour of South Africa winning the series 2-1. Pictured here are the Irish representatives Eric Miller, Jeremy Davidson, Keith Wood and Paul Wallace.

Clash of the Ash: The incomparable Brian Lohan (Clare) defends stoutly against a Tipperary attack in the Guinness All-Ireland hurling final. Clare went on to win the first all Munster final by 0-20 to 2-13.

Fr. Brendan Smyth: Convicted paedeophile Father Brendan Smyth is escorted from Limavady court house by R.U.C. officers prior to extradition. Fr. Smyth was extradited to the Republic where he was convicted of 74 sexual offences and sentenced to twelve years imprisonment. Smyth died in the Curragh prison in Co. Kildare on August 21.

Dunnes Tribunal: Justice Brian McCracken who presided over the Tribunal of Inquiry into Payments to Politicians which uncovered details of irregularities involving former Taoiseach Charles Haughey and former minister Michael Lowry. Justice McCracken confirmed that he was sending papers to the Director of Public Prosecutions and leaving it with the D.P.P. to decide if charges would arise out of the Tribunal's revelations.

TRANSPORT

The Future of Road
Transport in the Republic of Ireland

By Nathy Gilligan, B. Eng.

IRELAND depends on its road system to a far greater extent than most E.U. countries. Road travel accounts for 96 per cent of inland passenger travel, 96 per cent of inland freight is transported by road in the Republic as opposed to 87 per cent in Britain and 58 per cent in the Netherlands and two-thirds of traffic on the national network is work-related.

The reasons for this high dependence are due to a low population density which has traditionally been dispersed throughout the country; a low level of urbanisation, with just over half the population in urban areas; the fact that the Republic, in European terms, has only one metropolitan area, Dublin; and Ireland's isolated location on the periphery of Europe which has made it totally dependent on sea and air links to British and continental destinations.

If we are to take our place as an equal partner in modern Europe, it is incumbent that the Irish road system be upgraded for three reasons. Firstly, Ireland's main roads incur an intense usage. Of the network's 92,295 km (incorporating national primary roads, national secondary roads, regional roads and local roads), national primary roads account for only 5.8 per cent of total road length but hold 35 per cent of the traffic volume.

Secondly, there is a projected overall increase in traffic volume; it is predicted that the overall volume on Irish roads will double over the next 20 years - the numbers of heavy goods vehicles alone on the roads have increased 45-fold between 1960 and 1990, and present vehicle ownership (roughly 280 cars per 1,000 persons) is half of the EU average and will rise in line with increases in affluence.

Thirdly, roads provide the only readily available form of inland transport, particularly to isolated areas away from mainline railways. Inadequacies in the road network have an adverse impact on all forms of socio-economic development. Transport costs have proved to be a significant factor affecting the competitiveness of Irish industry; Irish exporters to mainland Europe incur transport cost between 9 and 10 percent of their overall costs which is approximately twice that experienced by other EU countries. Consequently, a major road-building programme has been undertaken nationwide.

The aims of the programme's new road schemes are to allow for a road capacity that will be able to cope with a doubling in present traffic volumes (a projected 20-year design life); to ensure a smooth flowing alignment to reduce driver fatigue, provide adequate visibility for safe overtaking and emergency stopping distances and to incorporate safe road-holding ability for high speed traffic; to improve road safety by restricting access from minor roads and reducing junctions (junctions and road access points have proved to be high accident spots in the past); and to allow for a cost benefit analysis, where financial parameters assigned to particular factors (such as accident reduction, fuel costs, travel time reduction, improved predictability of time of arrival, regional socio-economic benefits and environmental impact issues) are taken into consideration in assessing the balance between the amount spent and the expected rate of return on investment.

The author is a resident engineer with Donegal County Council.

INTRODUCTION:

Over the last few years, substantial efforts have been made to improve the transport infrastructure in Ireland. The monies to carry out this much needed upgrading in the Republic come primarily from the E.U. Cohesion Fund and the Irish taxpayer. In 1996 alone, the government invested £101 million in inland transport.

Traffic and roads: Successive governments have recognised that there is too much traffic congestion on Ireland's national routes and within its cities and that there is a need for an adequate public transport system to cope with the dramatic growth in the travelling public, particularly in Dublin. Approximately £63 million was made available to state road construction from E.U. funds in 1996, and major road building projects are underway in all parts of the Republic. A traffic comptroller has been appointed for Dublin city and the planning process of the new Dublin Light Rail Transit system (LUAS) is underway *(see below)*. In Northern Ireland, the Roads Service is responsible for providing and maintaining a road network of more than 24,000 kilometres. It has an annual budget of £153 million and employs 2,400 staff.

Rail transport: In 1996, an investment of £73.3 million in E.U. funds was approved for the Republic, £57 million of which was designated for mainline rail investment: £43 went towards the upgrading of major national rail routes and £14 million went towards upgrading the signalling system. The biggest development in rail transport in the Republic is the LUAS. It is the single largest public transport project this century, and it aims to provide electromotive rail transport to all key locations in Dublin city (at present, the Dublin Area Rapid Transport, or Dart, system only provides such a service to the coastal areas of Dublin). However, there have been a number of concerns voiced about the construction of LUAS regarding traffic disruption, damage to buildings - both historical and residential - and the fact that the initial budget of IR£200 million is now recognised as being too small. In the Republic, Iarnrod Éireann carried 25.6 million passengers and earned £63.7 million in passenger fares during 1996, while in Northern Ireland, more than £9 million was spent by passengers in 1995-96 and in excess of 6 million passenger journeys were recorded by Northern Ireland Railways.

Shipping: The major ferry companies at Rosslare, Dun Laoghaire, Cork and Dublin handled 2.1 million passengers travelling inward and a similar number travelling outward in 1996. The passenger/car ferry ports at Belfast, Larne handled 302,091 incoming vehicles and 293,391 outgoing vehicles in 1995. More than 80 international shipping lines operate out of Northern Ireland's five commercial seaports. In 1995, the outgoing cargo handled from Northern Ireland exceeded 14 million tonnes.

Air transport: In the Republic, Aer Rianta manages the state airports at Dublin, Shannon and Cork on behalf of the government. It achieved an increase in passenger movement in these airports of 13 per cent in 1995. Aer Lingus, the state passenger and cargo services provider, has just undergone a three-year restructuring programme to restore it to financial viability. In 1996, it achieved the programme's objectives with flying colours and returned an operating profit of £42 million. In Northern Ireland, there are three main airports: Belfast International Airport, the second largest freight airport in Britain, outside London; Belfast City Airport; and the City of Derry Airport. These three airports handled 3.6 million passengers in 1995, an increase of 11.8 per cent on 1994, and saw a throughput of 31.8 thousand tonnes, an increase of 14 per cent on 1994.

REPUBLIC OF IRELAND: BUS TRANSPORT

Coras Iompair Éireann (CIÉ) - Irish Transport System - provides public transport in Ireland. Two of the three subsidiary companies owned by CIÉ - Bus Éireann and Bus Átha Cliath - operate bus services in Ireland, with the other subsidiary company providing rail services throughout the country.

Bus Éireann (Irish Bus) - provides the National Bus service outside the Dublin area. It operates a network of inter-urban bus services, bus services throughout the country, and city services in Cork, Limerick, Waterford and Galway. Bus Éireann caters for more than 60 million passengers annually.

Bus Átha Cliath (Dublin Bus) - operates the Dublin City bus services. It operates more than 160 million passenger journeys annually and covers an area of 1,000 sq. km of the Dublin area.

BUS ÉIREANN FLEET STATISTICS:

Double Deck Buses	37
Single Deck Buses	1,355
Mini-buses	39
Tour Coaches	21
Total: Fleet	**1,452**

STATISTICS OF PROVINCIAL CITY BUS OPERATORS:

Cork:

Number of routes	16
Number of stops	600
Kms per vehicle per year	65,300
Passengers per day	30,000
Number of buses	42

Limerick:

Number of routes	11
Number of stops	270
Kms. per vehicle per year	31,000
Passengers per day	10,500
Number of buses	18

Galway:

Number of routes	8
Number of stops	185
Kms. per vehicle per year	64,700
Passengers per day	7,000
Number of buses	12

Waterford:

Number of routes	4
Number of stops	90
Kms. per vehicle per year	26,100
Passengers per day	1,600
Number of buses	4

NORTHERN IRELAND: BUS TRANSPORT

Ulsterbus and Citybus - provide provincial and Belfast City bus services, respectively. Citybus operates principally within the boundaries of the Belfast City Council area. However, the actual built-up urban area extends far beyond these boundaries, and in practice, both companies cater for Belfast's bus transportation requirements. Ulsterbus operates inter-urban express services and rural services. It also provides the city services in Derry, together with internal services in virtually every other town in Northern Ireland.

CITYBUS STATISTICS (1995/1996)		ULSTERBUS STATISTICS (1995/1996)	
Kilometres Operated	12,075,000	Kilometres Operated	62,468,000
Passenger Journeys	25,400,000	Passenger Journeys	55,400,000
Bus Miles	7,500,000	Bus Miles	38,800,000
Passenger Receipts	£17,800,000	Passenger Receipts	£57,600,000
Bus Fleet	282	Bus Fleet	1,224
Average Age of Buses	9.8 years	Average Age of Buses	8.5 years
Number of Staff	741	Number of Staff	2,231

REPUBLIC OF IRELAND: RAIL TRANSPORT

Coras Iompair Éireann (CIÉ) - Irish Transport System - provides rail services throughout Ireland through its subsidiary company - Iarnród Éireann.

Iarnród Éireann (Irish Rail) - operates rail services around Ireland and into Northern Ireland. It consists of 1,900 route kilometres. It operates passenger and freight services, including the **DART** *(see below)*. Iarnród Éireann carries 26 million passengers annually.

Dublin Area Rapid Transport (DART) - provides a passenger service to the mainly coastal areas of Dublin City, between Howth and Dun Laoghaire and to coastal parts of Co. Wicklow. It consists of 38km of track and operates on electric motive power.

RAIL STATISTICS (1994)	
Length of Railway Lines:	
Lines owned by Board	1,872 km
Other Lines	72 km
Total:	**1,944 km**
Motive Power:	
Diesel Locomotives	112
Electric Motive Units	80
Total:	**192**
Rail Service Vehicles:	
Ballast Wagons, Tool Vans, etc.	**157**
Rail Passenger Vehicles:	
Passenger Carriages / Railcars	251
Luggage Vans etc.	50
Total:	**301**
Rail Freight Vehicles:	
Flat Trucks	965
Specialised wagons etc.	930

Total:	**1,895**
Rail Freight Containers:	
Covered Containers	1,224
Other Containers	177
Total:	**1,401**

IARNRÓD ÉIREANN STATISTICS (1995)	
Length of Railway Lines:	
First Track (kms): own lines	1,872
First Track (kms): other lines	73
Total Track (kms):own lines	**2,682**
Total Track (kms): other lines	**130**
Passenger Journeys:	
Mainland & Other Services	8,312
Dublin Suburban Services	18,812
Total:	**27,124**
Passenger Kilometres	**1,291,214**
Freight Traffic (tonnes)	**3,179**
Freight Traffic (net tonnes km)	**602,547**

NORTHERN IRELAND: RAIL TRANSPORT

Northern Ireland Railways (NIR) - operates all internal public passenger railway services within Northern Ireland and a joint service with Iarnród Éireann on the Dublin-Belfast route. The NIR offers railway services from Belfast to Larne Harbour, Carrickfergus, Bangor, Portadown, Ballymena, Coleraine, Portrush, Derry City and intermediate stations and halts.

RAIL STATISTICS (1995/96)	
Passenger Journeys	6,400,000
Passenger Miles	143,900,000
Passenger Receipts	£9,772,000
Number of Staff	784
Track Routes (miles)	209
Rolling Stock:	
Locomotives	41
Passenger Coaches	82
Total: Rolling Stock	**123**

Stations:

IARNRÓD ÉIREANN RECEIPT STATISTICS, 1994-'96

	1994 Receipts	1995 Receipts	1996 Receipts
Train Traffic (Passengers)	£61,274,000	£66,317,000	£63,770,000
Train Traffic (Goods)	£18,412,000	£17,398,000	£16,628,000
Totals:	£79,686,000	£84,290,000	£80,398,000

IARNRÓD ÉIREANN PASSENGER STATISTICS, 1994-'96

	1994	1995	1996
Number of Passengers Carried	25,810,000	27,120,000	25,653,000

R.O.I.: SHIPPING AND BOAT TRANSPORT

BOAT TRANSPORT

Rosslare, Dun Laoghaire, Cork and Dublin are the Republic's passenger/car ferry ports. Other smaller harbours are located throughout the country dealing in bulk cargoes. There are a number of car ferries currently operating services from Ireland:

Irish Ferries - The company operates daily services to Britain on the Dublin-Holyhead route and Rosslare-Pembroke route. An Irish Ferries Superferry also operates on the Dublin-Holyhead route. Irish Ferries also operates services to France, connecting Rosslare and Cork with Le Harve and Cherbourg.

Stena Sealink - The company operates daily services to Britain on the Dun Laoghaire-Holyhead route and the Rosslare-Fishguard route. A Stena Sealink High Speed Ferry also operates on the Dun Laoghaire-Holyhead route.

Brittany Ferries - The company operates weekly services from Cork to Roscoff between March and October, and from May to September, it links Cork with St. Malo.

Swansea Cork Ferries - The company operates a daily service from Cork to Swansea between March and January.

SHIPPING

The process of shipping and cargo handling has progressed dramatically in recent times, and Irish ports have developed their facilities accordingly, as Ireland depends on shipping for 76% of its external trade.

Dublin and Cork are Ireland's multi-modal ports, dealing with all cargoes, and Waterford harbour has become the most up-to-date Lo/Lo handling port in Ireland.

The Irish-registered shipping fleet (100 gross tons and over) comprised 79 ships totalling 161,786 gross tons at 30 June, 1994.

PASSENGER MOVEMENT BY SEA TO AND FROM THE REPUBLIC OF IRELAND

	BRITAIN		OTHER PLACES		TOTAL	
Year	Outward	Inward	Outward	Inward	Outward	Inward
1990	1,419,000	1,445,000	197,000	198,000	1,617,000	1,643,000
1991	1,556,000	1,573,000	193,000	191,000	1,749,000	1,765,000
1992	1,579,000	1,581,000	193,000	191,000	1,772,000	1,772,000
1993	1,717,000	1,739,000	192,000	189,000	1,909,000	1,928,000
1994	1,807,000	1,815,000	191,000	189,000	1,998,000	2,004,000
1995	1,950,000	1,938,000	181,000	176,000	2,131,000	2,114,000
1996	1,977,000	1,954,000	158,000	158,000	2,135,000	2,112,000

NORTHERN IRELAND: BOAT TRANSPORT

BOAT TRANSPORT

Belfast and Larne Harbours are Northern Ireland's passenger / car ferry ports. Other sea ports operate shipping lines out of Northern Ireland. There are three car ferries currently operating services from Northern Ireland:

Belfast Car Ferries - The company operates daily services on the Larne to Stranraer route.

P & O Ferries - The company operates daily services on the Larne to Cairnryan route. A new Jet Liner Service also operates on this route.

Stena Sealink - The company operates daily services on the Belfast to Stranraer route. A new high speed ferry also operates on this route.

SHIPPING

More than 80 international shipping lines operate out of Northern Ireland's five commercial seaports. Of Northern Ireland's total trade, 90% of it leaves through its ports, as does almost 50% of the Republic of Ireland's freight traffic. There are 150 sailings weekly to Britain, including regular sailings to ports in the U.S., Continental Europe and the rest of the world. 5,500 ships carrying 11 million tonnes of cargo leave Belfast port each year. More than 55% of Northern Ireland's seaborne trade is shipped through Belfast port - the busiest port in the Island of Ireland.

UNIT LOAD CARRIER TRAFFIC TOURIST VEHICLES

Year	Belfast		Larne		Warrenpoint		Totals	
	Inward	Outward	Inward	Outward	Inward	Outward	Inward	Outward
1991	1,804	1,935	196,263	190,910	-	-	198,067	192,845
1992	43,536	43,868	180,087	174,241	627	141	224,250	218,250
1993	60,153	60,205	201,903	196,118	-	-	262,056	256,323
1994	57,723	57,927	215,578	208,959	-	-	273,301	266,886
1995	75,972	73,139	226,119	220,252	-	-	302,091	293,391

TONNAGE OF GOODS THROUGH PRINCIPAL PORTS IN NORTHERN IRELAND

Port	1991 Inward (000 tonnes)	Outward	1992 Inward (000 tonnes)	Outward	1993 Inward (000 tonnes)	Outward	1994 Inward (000 tonnes)	Outward	1995 Inward (000 tonnes)	Outward
Belfast	6,610	1,515	7,414	1,809	7,349	1,603	7,989	1,639	8,271	1,873
C'fergus	106	24	71	-	67	-	76	-	32	-
Coleraine	57	1	42	1	18	17	3	14	-	13
Larne	2,040	1,708	2,045	1,751	2,328	2,006	2,471	2,133	2,496	2,177
Derry	756	39	720	24	768	21	987	21	1,013	31
Warrenpoint	991	470	1,034	582	1,270	679	1,396	735	1,111	572
Other	1,899	315	1,611	226	2,059	362	1,908	416	2,029	417
Totals	12,459	4,072	12,937	4,393	13,859	4,688	14,830	4,958	14,952	5,083

REPUBLIC OF IRELAND: AIRLINE TRANSPORT

INTERNATIONAL AIRPORTS

Three international airports - Cork, Dublin and Shannon - cater for in excess of 8 million passengers and 94,000 tonnes of freight annually. Dublin International Airport, the busiest, has a throughput of more than 6 million passengers and over 65,000 tonnes of freight annually. Knock International Airport also handles flights from America and Britain.

AER LINGUS

Aer Lingus is the state airline. It operates flights to 27 cities in Britain, Europe and North America. Aer Lingus caters for over 4 million passengers and 45,000 tonnes of freight annually.

OTHER AIRLINES

A number of other airlines operate flights to and from Ireland, including CityJet, Ryanair and Translift Airways.

Various passenger, freight and helicopter services are operated within the country using the network of regional airports - Donegal, Galway, Kerry, Sligo and Waterford.

FLIGHT TIMES FROM DUBLIN:

Destination	via	Travelling Time
Amsterdam		1 hr 30 mins
Berlin	Amsterdam	2 hrs 50 mins
Birmingham		1 hr
Boston		7 hrs
Brussels		1 hr 30 mins
Chicago		8 hrs 20 mins
Copenhagen		2 hrs 5 mins
Edinburgh		1 hr
Frankfurt		2 hrs
Glasgow		1 hr
Hamburg		2 hrs
London (Heathrow)		1 hr 10 mins
London (Stansted)		1 hr 15 mins
Leeds		1 hr
Madrid		2 hrs 35 mins
Manchester		1 hour
Milan		2 hrs 35 mins
Munich	Amsterdam	3 hrs
New York		7 hrs 30 mins
Paris		1 hr 35 mins
Rome		3 hrs
Zurich		2 hrs 10 mins
Sydney	Amsterdam	17 hrs 30 mins
Hong Kong	London	15 hrs
Los Angeles	Chicago	14 hrs 35 mins

REPUBLIC OF IRELAND: PASSENGER NUMBERS AT STATE AIRPORTS, 1995-1997

Airport	1995	1996	1997	Total
Dublin Airport	8,000,000	9,100,000	11,400,000	28,500,000
Shannon Airport	1,500,000	1,700,000	2,100,000	5,300,000
Cork Airport	1,000,000	1,100,000	1,500,000	3,600,000
Total:	10,500,000	11,900,000	15,000,000	37,400,000

NORTHERN IRELAND: AIRLINE TRANSPORT

INTERNATIONAL AIRPORTS

Belfast International Airport, situated 13 miles north-west of the city, operates a direct service to more than 40 major British and European destinations with onward connections to worldwide centres. It is the second largest freight airport in Britain, outside London. Belfast City Airport, five minutes from Belfast city, provides fast connections to most major British cities including London. In the north-west of Northern Ireland, the City of Derry Airport has been modernised and provides a choice of destinations.

AIRLINES

There are currently 24 scheduled flights daily between Belfast and London, due to competing airlines. Easy access to and transfer at London (and other major British airports) means that most European destinations can be easily reached.

FREIGHT SERVICES

For air freight, eight International Air Transport Authority (IATA) agents in Northern Ireland act on behalf of all airlines and offer competitive rates to customers requiring direct consolidated or charter freight. Specialist airlines offer air freight services from both Belfast International and Belfast City Airports. The main passenger airlines also operate freight services.

SELECTED FLIGHT TIMES FROM BELFAST

Destination	via	Travelling Time
Amsterdam		1 hr 30 mins
Brussels	London	4 hrs
Frankfurt	Birmingham	3 hrs
Geneva	Manchester	4 hrs
Madrid	London	4 hrs 30 mins
Rome	London	5 hrs
New York		7 hrs
Hong Kong	London	15 hrs
Tokyo	London	14 hrs

TERMINAL PASSENGERS AT N.I. AIRPORTS

Year	Belfast International	Belfast City	City of Derry	Totals
1986	1,854,000	210,000	12,000	2,076,000
1987	2,116,000	280,000	13,000	2,409,000
1988	2,176,000	400,000	13,000	2,589,000
1989	2,158,000	507,000	19,000	2,684,000
1990	2,294,000	548,000	41,000	2,883,000
1991	2,168,000	537,000	37,000	2,742,000
1992	2,241,000	612,000	28,000	2,881,000
1993	2,180,000	846,000	31,000	3,057,000
1994	2,039,000	1,228,000	34,000	3,301,000
1995	2,346,000	1,280,000	64,000	3,691,000

CARGO HANDLED AT N.I. AIRPORTS

Year	Belfast International tonnes	Belfast City tonnes	City of Derry tonnes	Totals tonnes
1986	22,670	199	1	22,870
1987	26,067	227	14	26,308
1988	29,044	303	20	29,367
1989	23,851	1,050	-	24,901
1990	23,719	1,787	15	25,521
1991	18,121	825	23	18,969
1992	21,992	564	15	22,571
1993	24,023	626	60	24,709
1994	26,699	1,071	137	27,907
1995	30,713	1,064	52	31,829

R.O.I.: AIR PASSENGER MOVEMENT

	(000s) Dublin Airport		(000s) Cork Airport		(000s) Shannon Airport			(000s Total*	
Year	Outward	Inward	Outward	Inward	Outward	Inward	In Transit	Outward	Inward
1990	2,399	2,362	253	252	543	520	417	3,337	3,270
1991	2,301	2,274	234	237	480	456	462	3,114	3,062
1992	2,548	2,524	253	258	569	537	415	3,441	3,388
1993	2,645	2,621	276	277	586	571	403	3,569	3,530
1994	3,219	3,176	314	313	554	536	301	4,170	4,107
1995	3,737	3,670	388	385	596	579	240	4,824	4,736
1996	4,245	4,194	462	453	656	637	271	5,472	5,396

* includes Connacht, Waterford Regional, Galway, Carrickfin and Kerry County Airports. Sligo Airport included from June 1990.

REPUBLIC OF IRELAND: CROSS-BORDER PASSENGER MOVEMENT

	Rail		Road omnibus scheduled services		Total rail and road omnibus scheduled services	
Year	Outward	Inward	Outward	Inward	Outward	Inward
1990	180,000	189,000	309,000	305,000	489,000	494,000
1991	226,000	238,000	386,000	387,000	612,000	625,000
1992	227,000	243,000	418,000	412,000	645,000	655,000
1993	255,000	280,000	417,000	412,000	671,000	692,000
1994	306,000	337,000	411,000	407,000	717,000	744,000
1995	377,000	415,000	430,000	427,000	807,000	842,000
1996	374,000	388,000	430,000	429,000	804,000	817,000

NORTHERN IRELAND: LICENSED VEHICLES

Vehicle Type	1990	1991	1992	1993	1994	1995
Cycles	2,343	2,218	1,993	1,885	1,943	2,362
Motor-Hackneys	608	620	551	466	1,143	622
Agricultural Tractors & Engines	1,611	1,177	1,184	1,658	1,558	1,619
Goods Vehicles	8,972	8,892	8,707	9,061	9,576	10,292
Private Cars	69,091	63,739	62,777	65,360	70,765	73,718
Exempt from Duty	2,510	2,336	2,463	4,550	6,423	8,333
TOTAL:	85,135	78,982	77,675	82,980	91,408	96,946
CURRENT VEHICLE & DRIVING LICENCES:						
Cycles	10,167	9,684	9,023	8,634	8,775	9,142
Motor-Hackneys	2,786	2,887	2,744	2,679	3,078	2,092
Agricultural Tractors & Engines	8,021	7,199	6,892	7,201	7,317	7,318
Goods Vehicles	21,153	18,901	19,601	20,074	20,714	18,698
Private Cars	481,090	498,471	516,194	515,185	514,760	521,605
Other	19,897	21,176	23,858	32,552	41,307	52,707
TOTAL:	543,114	558,318	578,312	586,325	595,951	611,562
LICENCES:	874,000	912,000	947,000	978,000	1,005,000	1,041,000

REPUBLIC OF IRELAND: LICENCED VEHICLES

Vehicle Type:	1991	1992	1993	1994	1995	1996
New Vehicles:						
Private Cars	68,533	67861	60,792	77,773	82,730	109,333
Goods Vehicles	15,893	11883	9,887	12,845	13,790	16,445
Tractors	1,571	1598	1,338	1,830	2,108	2,233
Motor Cycles	3,197	2884	1,914	1,837	1,911	2,412
Exempt Vehicles	1,360	1306	1,261	1,178	1,489	1,887
Public Service Vehicles	750	683	596	906	1,039	1,100
Combine Harvesters	10	15	5	2	5	8
Excavators and Trench Diggers	139	113	79	178	207	272
Machines or Contrivances	90	80	61	94	144	209
Other Classes	80	55	31	42	56	65
Total New Vehicles	91,623	86,478	75,964	96,685	103,479	133,964

Second Hand Vehicles:

Private Cars	21,053	17,631	26,560	38,863	41,865	44,500
Goods Vehicles	4,083	3,742	3,259	3,501	3,912	4,927
Tractors	3,358	4,377	3,483	3,814	3,627	3,627
Other Classes	2,076	2,467	2,587	3,335	3,715	4,138
Total Second Hand Vehicles	**30,570**	**28,217**	**35,889**	**49,513**	**53,119**	**57,192**
Total All Classes	**122,193**	**114,695**	**111,853**	**14,618**	**156,598**	**191,156**

REPUBLIC OF IRELAND: DRIVING LICENCES, 1995

Licensing Authority	Provisional Licences	Annual Licences	Triennial Licences	Ten-Year Licences	Total Licences
County Councils:					
Carlow	5,364	104	2,758	10,850	19,076
Cavan	5,720	88	3,673	16,419	25,900
Clare (City & County)	9,503	208	5,747	28,588	44,046
Cork (City & County)	46,279	815	23,047	132,622	202,763
Donegal	12,656	215	7,772	38,287	58,930
Galway (City & County)	19,789	253	10,097	55,729	85,868
Kerry	14,800	243	7,761	39,721	62,525
Kildare	14,974	189	6,081	39,067	60,311
Kilkenny	8,787	193	5,052	23,144	37,176
Laois	5,811	89	3,820	15,482	25,202
Leitrim	2,420	45	2,019	7,987	12,471
Limerick	12,683	241	6,621	36,506	56,051
Longford	3,281	64	2,232	8,928	14,505
Louth	9,884	140	5,513	25,033	40,570
Mayo	10,804	196	5,432	32,726	49,158
Meath	12,212	155	6,108	33,788	52,263
Monaghan	5,612	104	4,244	16,076	26,036
Offaly	6,281	123	3,638	16,519	26,561
Roscommon	5,287	157	3,714	16,750	25,908
Sligo	5,679	101	3,774	17,418	26,972
Tipperary (North Riding)	6,596	79	4,080	19,297	30,052
Tipperary (South Riding)	8,936	169	5,578	22,353	37,036
Waterford	5,503	103	3,190	15,132	23,928
Westmeath	7,007	153	4,107	19,332	30,599
Wexford	12,089	424	6,502	31,254	50,269
Wicklow	12,261	196	5,434	30,428	48,319
County Borough:					
Dublin (City & County)	110,288	1,437	53,812	293,759	459,296
Limerick Corporation	5,478	45	2,403	11,335	19,261
Waterford Corporation	4,497	89	2,350	10,543	17,479
TOTAL:	**390,481**	**6,418**	**206,559**	**1,065,073**	**1,668,531**

NORTHERN IRELAND: DRIVING LICENCES

Licences	1991-92	1992-93	1993-94	1994-95	1995-96
Ordinary Licences:					
Provisional	133	133	136	135	143
Full	814	845	869	906	943
Total Ordinary Licences	**947**	**978**	**1,005**	**1,041**	**1,086**
Vocational Licences:					
Passenger Carrying Vehicles	-	4	14	11	12
Large Goods Vehicles	-	25	86	44	47
Total Vocational Licences	**-**	**29**	**100**	**55**	**59**

R.O.I.: CAR REGISTRATION MARKS

Index Mark	From Jan. 1987	County	Council Office
C;	CW	Carlow	Athy Road, Carlow.
ID;	CN	Cavan	Courthouse, Cavan.
IE;	CE	Clare	Courthouse, Ennis.
IF; PI; ZB; ZF; ZK; ZT;	C	Cork	Carrigrohane Road, Cork.

Index Mark		County	Location
IH; ZP;	DL	Donegal	County Building, Lifford.
IM; ZM;	G	Galway	County Building, Galway.
IN; ZX;	KY	Kerry	Moyderwell, Tralee.
IO; ZW;	KE	Kildare	Friary Road, Naas.
IP;	KK	Kilkenny	John's Green, Kilkenny.
CI;	LS	Laois	County Hall, Portlaoise.
IT;	LM	Leitrim	Priest's Lane, Carrick-on-Shannon.
IU; IV;	LK	Limerick	O'Connell Street, Limerick.
IX;	LD	Longford	Great Water Street, Longford.
IY; ZY;	LH	Louth	The Crescent, Dundalk.
IS; IZ;	MO	Mayo	Courthouse, Castlebar.
AI; ZN;	MH	Meath	County Hall, Navan.
BI;	MN	Monaghan	North Road, Monaghan.
IR;	OY	Offaly	O'Connor Squre, Tullamore.
DI;	RN	Roscommon	Abbey Street, Roscommon.
EI;	SO	Sligo	Cleveragh Road, Sligo.
FI;	TN	Tipperary, N.Riding	Kickham Street, Nenagh.
GI; HI;	TS	Tipperary, S.Riding	Emmot Street, Clonmel.
KI;	WD	Waterford	Courthouse, Dungarvan.
LI;	WH	Westmeath	County Buildings, Mullingar.
MI; ZR;	WX	Wexford	County Hall, Wexford.
NI;	WW	Wicklow	County Buildings, Wicklow.
TI;	L	Limerick City	City Hall, Merchants Quay, Limerick.
WI;	W	Waterford City	6-8 Lombard Street, Waterford.
IK; RI; SI; YI; Z; ZA; ZC; ZD; ZE; ZG; ZH; ZI; ZJ; ZL; ZO; ZS; ZU; ZV;	D	Dublin	River House, Chancery Street, Dublin 7.

NORTHERN IRELAND: CAR REGISTRATION MARKS

Index Mark	County
IA; DZ; KZ; RZ;	Antrim
IB; LZ;	Armagh
IJ; BZ; JZ; SZ;	Down
IL;	Fermanagh
IW; NZ; YZ;	Derry
JI; HZ; VZ;	Tyrone
OI; XI; AZ; CZ; EZ; FZ; GZ; MZ; OZ; PZ; TZ; UZ; WZ;	Belfast City
UI;	Derry City

REPUBLIC OF IRELAND: SPEED LAWS

Vehicle Type	MPH Built-up Areas	MPH Elsewhere	MPH Motorways
Cars (includes light goods vehicles & motorcycles)	30	60	70
Single Deck Buses - not carrying standing passengers	30	50	-
Single Deck Buses - carrying standing passengers	30	40	-
Double Deck Buses	30	40	-
Goods Vehicles (including Articulated vehicles) - gross vehicle weight in excess of 3,500 Kgs	30	50	-
Any vehicle towing another	30	50	-

NORTHERN IRELAND: SPEED LAWS

| Vehicle Type
* 60 if articulated or towing a trailer	MPH Built-up Areas	MPH Elsewhere Single Carriage	Motorways Dual Carriage
Cars (including car-derived vans & motorcycles)	30	60 70	70
Cars towing caravans or trailers (including car-derived vans & motorcycles)	30	50 60	60
Buses and Coaches (not exceeding 12 metres in overall length)	30	50 60	70
Goods vehicles (not exceeding 7.5 tonnes maximum laden weight)	30	50 60	70*
Goods vehicles (exceeding 7.5 tonnes maximum laden weight)	30	40 50	60

R.O.I.: 20 MOST POPULAR CARS LICENCED, 1995

Make	Number	Make	Number
Ford	171,610	Honda	21,973
Toyota	148,551	Volvo	18,801
Nissan	109,769	Citroen	14,809
Opel	106,868	Rover	14,553
Volkswagen	73,734	Vauxhall	14,210
Renault	48,861	Mercedes	12,988
Peugeot	41,067	Daihatsu	12,519
Fiat	35,825	Leyland	11,560
Mazda	35,421	BMW	11,524
Mitsubishi	26,223	Audi	11,055

NORTHERN IRELAND: 20 MOST POPULAR NEW VEHICLES REGISTERED, 1995

Make	Number	Make	Number
Ford / Iveco Ford	100,880	Volvo	10,804
Vauxhall / Opel / Bedford Vans	85,333	BMW	9,157
Austin / Leyland / Morris / Riley / Rover / Triumph / Wolsley	49,204	Mazda	8,829
Renault	45,524	Mercedes	8,264
Peugeot	43,440	Audi	8,075
Volkswagen	31,270	Honda	6,916
Toyota	24,940	Hyundai	4,234
Nissan / Datsun	24,718	Seat	3,870
Citroen	16,200	Colt / Mitsubishi	3,681
Fiat	11,546	Daihatsu	3,509

TRANSPORT INFRASTRUCTURE - ROADS
Length of Public Roads in Republic of Ireland and Northern Ireland

REPUBLIC OF IRELAND, 1995

Road	Length (kms)
National Primary	2,739
National Secondary	2,686
Non-National	87,000
Total:	92,425

NORTHERN IRELAND, 1996

Road	Length (kms)
Motorway	110
Class I	2,250
Class II	2,850
Class III	4,710
Unclassified	14,360
Total:	24,280

R.O.I.: LENGTH OF PUBLIC ROAD, 1995

Authority	National Primary (km)	National Secondary (km)	Non-National (km)	Total (km)
County Council:				
Carlow	23	55	1,108	1,186
Cavan	65	61	2,877	3,003
Clare	57	180	3,935	4,172
Cork	237	259	11,514	12,010
Donegal	151	154	6,150	6,455
Dun Laoghaire / Rathdown	20	0	626	646
Fingal	48	0	985	1,033
Galway	153	277	6,152	6,582
Kerry	96	232	4,330	4,758
Kildare	112	30	2,090	2,232
Kilkenny	149	67	2,880	3,096
Laois	84	77	2,111	2,272
Leitrim	55	0	2,175	2,230
Limerick	138	53	3,344	3,535
Longford	41	55	1,464	1,560

Louth	74	49	1,167	1,290
Mayo	134	266	5,889	6,289
Meath	121	76	2,940	3,137
Monaghan	72	32	2,299	2,403
Offaly	18	122	1,845	1,985
Roscommon	102	144	3,690	3,936
Sligo	110	46	2,494	2,650
South Dublin	31	18	640	689
Tipperary N.R.	65	100	2,588	2,753
Tipperary S.R.	119	39	2,722	2,880
Waterford	69	36	2,427	2,532
Westmeath	97	83	1,923	2,103
Wexford	148	15	3,162	3,325
Wicklow	55	39	1,888	1,982
Total County Councils:	**2,644**	**2,665**	**87,415**	**92,724**
Borough Corporations:				
Cork	19	3	327	349
Dublin	30	6	1,133	1,169
Galway	10	6	169	185
Limerick	15	2	156	173
Waterford	8	0	163	171
Total Borough Corporations:	**82**	**17**	**1,948**	**2,047**
Total Length of Public Roads:	**2,726**	**2,682**	**89,363**	**94,771**

NORTHERN IRELAND: LENGTH OF PUBLIC ROADS (KMS) IN NORTHERN IRELAND, 1996

Divisions/Council Areas	Motorway	Class I Dual Carriage	Single Carriage	Class II	Class III	Unclass-ified	Total (1996)
	km	km	km	km	km	km	km
Ballymena Division	28.97	22.37	350.55	409.22	665.92	1849.02	3326.94
Belfast Division:	25.87	24.90	138.31	118.21	130.91	1190.33	1628.51
Coleraine Division:	0.00	12.21	362.62	515.54	574.81	1,859.14	3,324.33
Craigavon Division:	23.86	36.83	388.69	564.68	1,030.34	3070.21	5,114.61
Downpatrick Division:	19.32	41.59	362.74	331.65	608.25	1886.14	3249.71
Omagh Division:	12.70	5.63	504.43	913.25	1699.72	4502.37	7638.09
GRAND TOTAL:	110.71	143.54	2107.34	2852.56	4709.94	14357.21	24,281.29

R.O.I.: MINIMUM AGE FOR DRIVING BY CATEGORY

Vehicle Type	Categories	Minimum Ages for Driving
Motorcycles	A, A1	18, 16
Cars	B, EB	17
Trucks	C, EC, C1, EC1	18
Buses	D, ED	21
Minibuses	D1, ED1	21
Work Vehicles/Tractors	W	16

N.I.: MINIMUM AGE FOR DRIVING BY CATEGORY

Vehicle Type	Categories	Minimum Ages for Driving
Motorcycles	A	17
Moped	P	16
Cars	B, B1	17
Trucks	C+E, C, C1	21,18
Buses	D, D1	21
Other Vehicles/Tractors	F, G, H, B1, K	16

COST OF SELECTED CARS IN IRELAND*

Make	Model	Type	Republic of Ireland (IR£)	Northern Ireland (£Stg)
Ford	Fiesta	5dr Encore 1.3(i)	10,340	8,890
Ford	Escort	5dr CL 1.4(i)	12,435	12,280
Ford	Mondeo	5dr LX 1.6i	16,710	14,875
Honda	Civic	3dr 1.4i	12,385	12,095
Mazda	323	3dr LX 1.3	9,780	11,360
Nissan	Primera	5dr GX 1.6	16,145	14,745
Opel / Vauxhall	Vectra	5dr 1.6(i) 16v	16,350	13,740
Peugeot	306	3dr 1.4 C/L	11,995	11,090
Renault	Clio	3dr RL 1.2	9,995	8,240
Renault	Megane	5dr RN 1.4 (e)	12,650	11,420
Renault	Laguna	5dr RN 1.8	16,750	12,840
Toyota	Starlet	3dr 1.3	10,860	8,550
Toyota	Carina	5dr 1.8 GLi	17,195	15,430
Volkswagen	Golf	5dr L 1.4	12,995	11,455
Volkswagen	Passat	5dr 1.8 20v	17,695	15,110

* Refers to recommended retail price as of July 1997 (the price does not include extras or delivery).

N.I.: CARS IMPORTED BY COUNTRY OF ORIGIN

Country	%
Used Cars (re-registered)	94.3
Republic of Ireland	3.2
Continent	2.5

NET REGISTRATIONS AND MONTHLY SELLING PRICES FOR NEW AND USED CARS, 1996-1997

| | Monthly Registrations | | | | Monthly Mean Open Market Selling Price | | | |
| | New Registrations | | Used Registrations | | £ New | | £ Used | |
	1996	1997	1996	1997	1996	1997	1996	1997
January	16,790	20,208	3,594	3,554	13,110	13,592	5,532	5,736
February	14,094	14,676	4,142	3,625	12,911	13,177	5,820	5,693
March	16,197	15,924	3,914	3,317	12,341	12,838	6,036	5,831
April	12,811	11,773	3,786	3,605	12,914	13,433	5,966	5,715
May	13,989	15,053	3,921	3,459	12,711	13,070	5,762	5,829
June	9,791	-	3,271	-	12,800	-	5,795	-
July	9,658	-	3,457	-	12,781	-	6,088	-
August	6,365	-	3,114	-	12,901	-	6,015	-
September	5,304	-	3,302	-	13,247	-	5,892	-
October	4,620	-	3,750	-	12,836	-	5,834	-
November	3,298	-	3,338	-	11,929	-	5,848	-
December	927	-	1,941	-	12,193	-	6,409	-
Total:	113,844	77,634	41,530	17,560	-	-	-	-

New Cars Registered in State in 1996	113,844
Second-hand Cars Registered in State in 1996	41,530
Average Cost (inclusive of V.R.T.)	
New	£13,230
Used	£5,759

REPUBLIC OF IRELAND: USED CARS, 1996

Month	Quantity	Month	Quantity
January	3,407	July	3,488
February	3,825	August	3,624
March	4,085	September	3,867
April	3,682	October	4,054
May	4,008	November	4,304
June	3,720	December	2,527
		Total:	44,591

R.O.I.: CARS IMPORTED BY COUNTRY OF ORIGIN

Country	%
Britain / Northern Ireland	92
Japan	5
Other	3

R.O.I.: THE INFLUX OF SECOND-HAND IMPORTS

Year	Imports	Year	Imports
1987	4,819	1993	34,282
1988	6,238	1994	42,250
1989	10,069	1995	44,591
1990	20,974	1996	52,617
1991	21,092	Total:	254,579
1992	17,647		

R.O.I.: VEHICLE REGISTRATION TAX 1997

Private Vehicles: Engine Capacity cc	Annual IR£	Half-Year IR£	Quarterly IR£
Not over 1,000	92	51	26
1,001 to 1,100	138	76	38
1,101 to 1,200	150	83	42
1,201 to 1,300	163	90	45
1,301 to 1,400	175	97	49
1,401 to 1,500	188	104	52
1,501 to 1,600	232	128	64
1,601 to 1,700	247	136	68
1,701 to 1,800	288	159	80
1,801 to 1,900	304	168	84
1,901 to 2,000	320	176	88
2,001 to 2,100	410	226	113
2,101 to 2,200	429	236	118
2,201 to 2,300	449	247	124
2,301 to 2,400	468	258	129
2,401 to 2,500	488	269	135
2,501 to 2,600	572	315	158
2,601 to 2,700	594	327	164
2,701 to 2,800	616	339	170
2,801 to 2,900	638	351	176
2,901 to 3,000	660	363	182
3,001 or more	800	440	220
Electrical	92	51	26

Goods Vehicles: Unladen Weight kg	Annual IR£	Half-Year IR£	Quarterly IR£
Not over 3,000	150	83	42
3,001 to 4,000	190	105	53
4,001 to 5,000	245	135	68
5,001 to 6,000	340	187	94

6,001 to 7,000	460	253	127
7,001 to 8,000	580	319	160
8,001 to 9,000	715	394	197
9,001 to 10,000	850	468	234
10,001 to 11,000	985	542	271
11,001 to 12,000	1,120	616	308
12,001 to 13,000	1,255	691	346
13,001 to 14,000	1,390	765	383
Over 14,000	1,390 plus £135 per 1,000kg or part thereof over 14,000 kg	55% of annual rate	27.5% of annual rate
Electrical	50	-	-

Miscellaneous Vehicles:

Vehicle	Annual IR£	Half-Year IR£	Quarterly IR£
Off-Road Dumper	400	220	110
General Haulage Tractor	120	66	33
Agricultural Tractor, trench digger and excavator	45	-	-
Taxi, hackney or hearse	60	-	-
School bus	50	-	-
Dumper, forklift and machine / contrivance	50	-	-
Motorcycles, tricycles and pedestrian controlled vehicles	20	-	-
Veteran and Vintage:			
Motorcycles	10	-	-
All Other Vehicles	25	-	-

R.O.I.: INSURANCE COMPARISONS

Area/Car	18-year-old male	18-year-old female	30-year-old male	30-year-old female
R.O.I. (Urban):				
Ford Fiesta (1.1 engine)	£3,073	£1,969	£320	£310
Vauxhall Cavaliar (1.6 engine)	£4,289	£2,751	£446	£428
R.O.I. (Rural):				
Ford Fiesta (1.1 engine)	£2,485	£1,591	£290	£243
Vauxhall Cavaliar (1.6 engine)	£3,466	£2,223	£391	£336

The above quotes have been given using the following criteria: (a) The 18-year-olds have been driving for six months, and the 30-year-olds have been driving for ten years; (b) none of the drivers has any claims; (c) all of the drivers use their cars in a private, not business, capacity; and (d) all of the drivers have a full licence.

NORTHERN IRELAND: INSURANCE COMPARISONS

Area / Car	18-year-old male	18-year-old female	30-year-old male		30-year-old female	
			A	B	A	B
N. I. (Urban)						
Ford Fiesta (1.1 engine)	£3,190	£1,942	£663	£366	£575	£366
Vauxhall Cavaliar (1.6 engine)	£4,056	£2,760	£793	£479	£686	£444
N. I. (Rural)						
Ford Fiesta (1.1 engine)	£2,844	£1,734	£663	£366	£575	£349
Vauxhall Cavaliar (1.6 engine)	£3,704	£2,429	£793	£479	£686	£422

The above quotes have been given using the following criteria: (a) The 18-year-olds have been driving for six months, and the 30-year-olds have been driving for ten years; (b) none of the drivers has any claims; (c) all of the drivers use their cars in a private, not business, capacity; and (d) all of the drivers have a full licence.

A = First insurance - introductory discount given.

B = Maximum bonus - has had insurance in own name (claim free) for 6+ years.

REPUBLIC OF IRELAND: INSURANCE SURVEY

Company	25-year-olds £	Benefits	35-year-olds £	Benefits	45-year-olds £	Benefits
P.M.P.A.						
Female	367	2,3,6	311	1,2,6	300	2,6
Male	917	2,6	354	2,3,6	284	-
Guardian Direct						
Female	396	1,2,6	280	1,2,5,6	254	2,6
Male	668	1,5	317	1,2,3,6	271	1,2,5,6
A.A.						
Female	343	1,2,6	269	2,4	225	2,5,6
Male	505	1,2,6	289	1,2,4,6	275	1,5,6
Premier Direct						
Female	409	2,6	238	1,6	255	2,5,6
Male	623	2,6	312	1,2,3,6	345	2,5,6
Hibernian						
Female	305	2,3,5	304	2,5,6	288	2,6
Male	627	2,3,4	328	2,3,6	326	2,6
First Call Direct						
Female	371	2,4	304	2,4	259	2,4,5
Male	523	2,4	357	1,2,3,4,6	367	2,4
Celtic International						
Female	-	-	269	2,5,6	268	2,6
Male	-	-	283	2,6	283	2,6
General Accident						
Female	-	-	410	1,2	354	6
Male	-	-	448	1,2,6	448	2,5,6
Quinn Direct						
Female	457	1,2	335	2,6	308	6
Male	706	2,6	396	2	362	2
Norwich Union						
Female	683	1,2,3,5,6	356	1,2,6	396	2,6
Male	721	2,6	448	1,2,6	473	1,2,6

Benefits: 1 Driver Personal Accident Cover. 2 Windscreen Cover. 3 Free Windscreen Security Etching
4 Bonus Protection (two claims up to a total of £3,000 in three years). 5 Bonus Protection (one claim unlimited). 6 Others
Above quotes have been given under the following criteria: (a) Comprehensive Cover; (b) a 5-year-old Ford Fiesta 1.1 engine (valued at £5,000); (c) Drivers have sedentary-type occupations; (d) Drivers have full licences; (e) Drivers have a maximum no claims discount.

REPUBLIC OF IRELAND: TRANSPORT COSTS

Description	Engine Capacity (CC)					
	Up to 1,000	1,000 - 1,250	1,251 - 1,500	1,501 - 1,750	1,751 - 2,000	2,001 - 2,500
Annual Charges:						
Car Licence	£92	£150	£175	£247	£304	£449
Insurance	£750	£820	£1,000	£1,175	£1,280	£1,350
Driving Licence	£4	£4	£4	£4	£4	£4
Depreciation	£875	£1,125	£1,250	£1,375	£1,562	£1,687
Interest on Capital	£350	£450	£500	£550	£625	£675
Garage / Parking	£1,300	£1,300	£1,300	£1,300	£1,300	£1,300
AA Subscription	£51	£51	£51	£51	£51	£51
Total: Annual Charges	£3,422	£3,900	£4,280	£4,702	£5,126	£5,516
Cost per Mile:						
10,000	34.220p	39.000p	42.800p	47.020p	51.260p	55.160p
5,000	68.440p	78.000p	85.600p	94.040p	102.520p	110.320p
15,000	22.813p	26.000p	28.533p	31.346p	34.173p	36.773p
20,000	17.110p	19.500p	21.400p	23.510p	25.630p	27.580p
Operating Cost per Mile:						
Petrol	6.395p	7.236p	7.857p	9.166p	10.185p	11.000p
Oil	0.203p	0.221p	0.271p	0.291p	0.333p	0.382p
Tyres	1.204p	1.411p	1.513p	1.918p	2.102p	2.396p
Servicing	1.153p	1.802p	2.014p	2.103p	2.239p	2.278p
Repairs	4.123p	4.855p	5.209p	5.558p	6.203p	7.641p
Total: Op. Cost per Mile	13.078	15.525p	16.864p	19.036	21.062	23.697
Total Cost per Mile: (based on 10,000 miles)						
Standard Charges	34.220p	39.000p	42.800p	47.020p	51.260p	55.160p
Operating Costs	13.078p	15.525p	16.864p	19.036p	21.062p	23.697p
Total: Total Cost per Mile	47.3p	54.5p	59.7p	66.1p	72.3p	78.9p

RELIGION

Christianity's Place in the New Millennium

By *Rt. Rev. Dr. James Mehaffey*, *Church of Ireland Bishop*

NEW technology with its instant information and communication on a global scale, makes the world seem a much smaller place. This shrinking world is also a world in which interdependence between countries and regions is becoming a major factor. The shrinking, interdependent world of the latter years of this century is sometimes referred to as the global village. There can be no denying that we are being drawn together across nations and continents, and this is having a subtle yet profound impact on our thinking. E.U. laws apply increasingly in Ireland and in the other member states. Any Irish farmer or fisherman knows all about the impact of E.U. quotas. In the new millennium, the people of Ireland will be drawn more and more into the European context and into a European Union which is itself constantly changing and growing.

These and many other developments in society will provide the context in which Christianity will find itself and the interaction between the two will determine the future direction of Christianity on this island. How will Christianity cope with radical and far-reaching changes in society? What role will the Churches play? If Christianity is to survive, it will have to adapt and if it is to adapt, where do the radical changes need to occur?

First and foremost, Christianity must be relevant. It must be seen to address the real issues in society and to face the challenges head on. If the Churches get caught up in their own domestic and internal affairs, they will be written off as irrelevant. In the North the greatest challenge comes from our deeply divided society and the consequent threat of violence. The Churches must take a much more pro-active role in countering sectarianism and working for reconciliation and peace. Politicians have the responsibility of finding a political solution, but no solution will work without the creation of a climate of goodwill. In the new millennium, the Churches will be challenged about their responsibility in helping to bring about mutual understanding and in promoting mutual respect for different traditions. Failure in this crucial area will lead to the Churches being pushed further out onto the periphery of society.

Secondly, Christianity must be more user friendly. The tension between the Churches' authority on the one hand and the rights of individual conscience on the other will become an increasingly important focal point. In general, people welcome moral and ethical guidelines, but they will demand that they be allowed to work these out in conscience for themselves and their families. This will be particularly true regarding moral questions concerning sexuality, marriage and family life. It will not be sufficient for the Churches to make pronouncements on these intimate and personal issues. They will have to show that their position is reasonable and that moral persuasion is the only weapon they use.

Thirdly, Christianity must become more open and accountable. Any attempt by the Churches to conduct business behind closed doors will become a thing of the past. People will demand to know and to be informed. Advances in the information technology field will need to be matched by far greater openness and by effective channels of information within the Churches and outward to society.

Fourthly, Christianity must be expressed more and more in ecumenical terms. In the new millennium, there will be increasing emphasis on the common ground of faith which the Churches share together and a corresponding reluctance to speak of denominational Christianity. This will represent a major challenge to the Churches in Ireland because, apart from occasional and tentative ecumenical gestures, there is little structured ecumenical work. There will be a growing impatience with problems which arise from the historic divisions in the Church such as inter-communion and inter-Church marriage.

Fifthly, there will be an increasing emphasis on the importance of personal religious experience. This experience will be characterised by its warmth and immediacy and have a very direct bearing on the life style of the individual concerned. In the new millennium, one may expect to find a continuing decline in Church attendance, but I believe that this will be matched by a growing number of people whose personal faith in God will be the dominant and all-controlling factor in their lives.

What is the outlook for Christianity? What are the prospects for the Churches in Ireland? To a large extent the answer lies with the Churches. Three lines of action need to be taken and they need to be taken together because they complement each other.

1. An acceptance by the Churches that they must change and adapt in order to survive. It is part of the very nature of Christianity and part of its very genius that, for 2,000 years, it has been able to adapt to very different situations and circumstances and to grow and develop. Change need not be a threat. It can be a challenge and an opportunity.

2. A concerted effort by the Churches to recover the core values of the gospel and to proclaim that gospel and to live out the implications of it. Over the years, cultural, historical and political ideas have formed a kind of crust, an outer shell, which tends to mask the true nature of Christianity. The core and heart of the gospel needs to be rediscovered. Spiritual renewal leading to the recovery of gospel values is the greatest single thing needed by all the Churches.

3. A recognition by the Churches that Christianity is divinely initiated and inspired and that it has an inherent eternal and indestructible quality about it. Christianity is both a gospel which brings good news and also a way of life. This is a solemn trust given to the Churches. Their primary task is to be faithful to their divine calling.

The author is the Church of Ireland Bishop of Derry and Raphoe.

INTRODUCTION

The total population of Ireland, North and South, is just over 5.1 million, and of this, 3.8 million is Catholic. The Catholic church's overwhelming numerical superiority can be ascertained by comparison with the other main churches on the island - 382,000 in the Church of Ireland, 350,000 in the Presbyterian church, and 64,000 in the Methodist Church.

The Catholic church has played a significant, often controversial, role in Irish life, particularly in the Irish Republic. Its priests, nuns and Christian Brothers have been to the forefront of education, and many nuns have been involved in the caring professions (e.g. nursing), while the church's hierarchy has been influential in promulgating the church's teaching in regard to a wide range of social and religious issues.

But Ireland has a growing religious plurality with many new churches being established. The liberal democratic nature of Irish society, which has evolved in recent years, has resulted in much more widespread tolerance of religious diversity.

The Jewish community is one of the older religious denominations in Ireland, but recent years have witnessed growth in Islam, Buddhism, the Society of Friends ("Quakers") and the Church of Scientology.

Despite a slight decline in recent times, Ireland still has the highest number of regular church-goers in Western Europe.

THE CATHOLIC CHURCH

Armagh is the ecclesiastical capital of the Irish Catholic Church, and it is there that the Primate of All-Ireland, usually a Cardinal, resides. The church has four ecclesiastical provinces - Armagh, Dublin, Cashel and Tuam - each with its own Archbishop.

The church has 26 dioceses, approximately 1,360 parishes and about 4,000 Catholic priests. There are in the region of 20,000 people active in the religious life in Ireland, while Irish Catholic missionary priests and nuns are active in more than 80 countries across the globe.

THE CHURCH OF IRELAND

The Church of Ireland is a self-governing church within the worldwide Anglican Communion of Churches. It is led by the Archbishop of Armagh, who is Primate of All-Ireland, and the Archbishop of Dublin, who is Primate of Ireland. The Church of Ireland was disestablished in 1871 when it ceased to be the State Church. When this happened, the church adopted a constitution which gave it government by synod. The General Synod is its supreme legislative authority, and clergy and laity from all dioceses have representation at its meetings. The clergy have 216 representatives while the laity have 432, representatives for both being elected for three-year terms by diocesan synods.

Like the Catholic church, the Church of Ireland is heavily involved in education and has its own schools in the Republic of Ireland.

There are 12 dioceses in the Church of Ireland. Of its 382,000 members, approximately 75 per cent live in Northern Ireland.

THE PRESBYTERIAN CHURCH

The Presbyterian Church in Ireland has as its chief representative a Moderator, elected at a General Assembly of the church, who serves for one year only. This Assembly, which meets annually, makes the rules of the church and decides policy. There are 562 congregations in Ireland, and each is entitled to representation at that Assembly.

There are 21 regions of the Presbyterian Church, each known as a Presbytery. In addition, there are five regional Synods.

The Presbyterian Church believes in the authority of the scriptures in regard to Christian living. It is a Protestant church in the reformed tradition.

The role of the laity is particularly recognised with 'elders' being elected by each congregation to actively participate in the affairs of the church.

In the Republic the majority of Presbyterians are to be found along the border counties of Donegal, Monaghan and Cavan, as well as in Dublin city. In the North more than half of the church's total membership lives within 15 miles of the centre of Belfast. There are approximately 390 Ministers, around 30 ordained Assistant-Ministers, 40 other Ministers in special work and almost 150 retired from active duty. The Ministry was opened to women in 1972.

THE METHODIST CHURCH

The Methodist Church in Ireland is a democratic church with authority invested in its annual conference whose president is elected for one year only. The church is divided into eight districts, each of which has at its head a chairman who, while elected annually, can serve up to six years. There are also 77 circuits - groups of congregations throughout the country - North and South - who work together.

The Methodist church has its foundations in the teachings of the evangelic preacher, John Wesley, who visited Ireland on several occasions in the 18th century. It is a self-governing church, but it does have close links with the Methodist church in Britain.

CATHOLIC BISHOPS OF IRELAND

The Catholic Church in Ireland is divided into four provinces which are named after the four arch-dioceses - Armagh, Cashel, Dublin and Tuam.

PROVINCE OF ARMAGH
Diocese of Armagh: His Eminence, Cardinal Séan Brady, Primate of All Ireland and Archbishop of Armagh.
Diocese of Meath: Most Rev. M. Smith.
Diocese of Ardagh and Clonmacnois (Longford): Most Rev. C. O'Reilly.
Diocese of Clogher (Monaghan): Most Rev. J Duffy.
Diocese of Derry: Most Rev. Seamus Hegarty, Most Rev. Francis Lagan, Auxiliary Bishop.
Diocese of Down and Connor: Most Rev . P. Walsh, Auxiliary Bishop Most Rev. A. Farquhar, Auxiliary Bishop Most Rev. M. Dallat
Diocese of Dromore (Down): Most Rev. F.G. Brooks
Diocese of Kilmore (Cavan): Most Rev. F. McKiernan, Most Rev. Leo O'Reilly, Co-adjutor.
Diocese of Raphoe (Donegal): Most Rev. Philip Boyce

PROVINCE OF DUBLIN
Diocese of Dublin: His Grace, Most Rev. Desmond Connell, Archbishop of Dublin. Most Rev. E. Walsh. Most Rev. J. Moriarty, Auxiliary Bishop. Most Rev. F. O'Ceallaigh, Auxiliary Bishop.
Diocese of Ferns (Wexford): Most Rev. Brendan Comiskey.
Diocese of Kildare and Leighlin (Carlow): Most Rev. L. Ryan.
Diocese of Ossory (Kilkenny): Most Rev. L. Forristal.

PROVINCE OF CASHEL
Diocese of Cashel and Emly: His Grace, Most Rev. Dermot Clifford.
Diocese of Cloyne (Cork): Most Rev. J. Magee
Diocese of Cork and Ross: Vacant. Most Rev. J. Buckley, Auxiliary Bishop.
Diocese of Kerry: Most Rev. William Murphy.
Diocese of Killaloe (Clare): Most Rev. Willie Walsh.
Diocese of Waterford and Lismore: Most Rev. William Lee.
Diocese of Limerick: Most Rev. Donal Murray.

PROVINCE OF TUAM

Diocese of Tuam: His Grace, Most Rev. Michael Neary, Archbishop.

Diocese of Achonry (Roscommon): Most Rev. T. Flynn.

Diocese of Clonfert (Galway): Most Rev. J. Kirby.

Diocese of Elphin (Sligo): Most Rev. C. Jones.

Diocese of Galway and Kilmacduagh: Most Rev. J. McLoughlin (also Apostolic Administrator of Kilfenora - Galway).

Diocese of Killala (Mayo): Most Rev. T. Finnegan.

PAPAL NUNCIO

His Excellency Most Rev. Dr. Luciano Storero: Born 1926 in Italy, ordained priest June 1949, ordained Titular Archbishop of Tigimma in 1970, and appointed Apostolic Nuncio to Ireland on November 15, 1995.

CHURCH OF IRELAND BISHOPS OF IRELAND

There are 12 dioceses in the Church of Ireland divided into two provinces, Armagh and Dublin.

PROVINCE OF ARMAGH

Diocese of Armagh: Most Rev. Robin Eames, Archbishop of Armagh and Primate of All Ireland.

Diocese of Clogher: Right Rev. Brian Hannon.

Dioceses of Derry and Raphoe: Right Rev. James Mehaffey.

Dioceses of Down and Dromore: Right Rev. Gordon McMullan.

Diocese of Connor: Right Rev. James Moore.

Dioceses of Kilmore, Elphin and Ardagh (Cavan): Right Rev. Michael Mayes.

Dioceses of Tuam, Killala and Achonry: Right Rev. John Neill.

PROVINCE OF DUBLIN

Dioceses of Dublin and Glendalough: Most Rev. Walton Empey, Archbishop of Dublin, Bishop of Glendalough and Primate of Ireland.

Dioceses of Meath and Kildare: Most Rev. Richard Clarke.

Dioceses of Cashel and Ossory: Right Rev. Noel Willoughby, Bishop of Cashel, Waterford, Lismore, Ossory, Ferns and Leighlin.

Dioceses of Cork, Cloyne and Ross: Right Rev. Robert Warke.

Dioceses of Limerick and Killaloe: Right Rev. Edward Darling, Bishop of Limerick, Ardfert, Aghadoe, Killaloe, Kilfenora, Clonfert, Kilmacduagh and Emly.

METHODIST CHURCH

In Ireland the Methodist Church is divided into eight district synods, each headed by a chairman.

President: Rev. Norman W. Taggart.

Secretary: Rev. Edmund T. I. Mawhinney.

CHAIRMEN OF DISTRICTS

Belfast District: Rev. D. J. Kerr.

Down District: Rev. R. P. Roddie.

Dublin District: Rev. T. M. Kingston.

Enniskillen and Sligo District: Rev. I.D. Henderson.

Londonderry District: Rev. P. A. Good.

Midlands and Southern District: Rev. S. K. Todd.

North East District: Rev. K. H. Thompson.

Portadown District: Rev. S. R. F. Cleland.

PRESBYTERIAN CHURCH

The Presbyterian Church has 5 Regional Synods.

General Assembly Moderator: Right Rev. S. Hutchinson.

Synod of Armagh and Down: Rev. S. A. Finlay.
Presbytery of Ards - Rev. W. L. Haslett.
Presbytery of Armagh - Rev. T. A. McNeely.
Presbytery of Down - Rev. D. J. Kane.
Presbytery of Dromore - Rev. D. J. Bruce.
Presbytery of Iveagh - Rev. R. J. Greer.
Presbytery of Newry - Rev. J. A. Noble.

Synod of Ballymena & Coleraine: Rev. W. J. Hook.
Presbytery of Ballymena - Rev. R. S. Hetherington.
Presbytery of Carrickfergus - Rev. D. Murphy.
Presbytery of Coleraine - Rev. J. A. Kirkpatrick.
Presbytery of Route - Rev. S. T. McCullough.

Presbytery of Templepatrick - Rev. W. J. Sleith.

Synod of Belfast: Rev. W. Campbell.
Presbytery of North Belfast - Rev. T. I. Harte.
Presbytery of South Belfast - Rev. W. P. Erskine.
Presbytery of East Belfast - Rev. W. J. H. McKee.

Synod of Derry and Omagh: Rev. I. J. Wilson.
Presbytery of Derry and Strabane - Rev. G. P. Young.
Presbytery of Foyle - Rev. D. S. Irwin.
Presbytery of Omagh - Rev. A. C. Rankin.
Presbytery of Tyrone - Rev. D. A. Murphy.

Synod of Dublin: Rev. K. J. C. McConnell.
Presbytery of Donegal - Rev. N. E. Dorrans.
Presbytery of Dublin & Munster - Rev. F. Sellar.
Presbytery of Monaghan - Rev. M. R. Burnside.

BOUNDARIES OF CATHOLIC DIOCESES

PROVINCE OF ARMAGH

Armagh:
Most of Louth and Armagh; part of Tyrone and Derry; small parts of Meath.

Meath:
Most of Meath and Westmeath; part of Offaly; small parts of Cavan, Longford, Louth, Dublin.

Ardagh & Clonmacnois:
Most of Longford; parts of Leitrim and Offaly; small parts of Westmeath, Roscommon, Cavan, Sligo.

Clogher:
Monaghan; most of Fermanagh; part of Tyrone; small parts of Donegal, Louth and Cavan.

Derry:
Most of Derry; parts of Tyrone and Donegal.

Down and Connor:
Almost all of Antrim; part of Down; small parts of Derry.

Dromore:
Part of Down; small parts of Armagh and Antrim.

Kilmore:
Most of Cavan; parts of Leitrim and Fermanagh; small parts of Meath and Sligo.

Raphoe:
Most of Donegal.

PROVINCE OF DUBLIN

Dublin:
Almost all of Dublin; most of Wicklow; part of Kildare; small parts of Carlow, Wexford and Laois.

Ferns:
Almost all of Wexford; part of Wicklow.

Kildare & Leighlin:
Almost all of Carlow; parts of Kildare, Laois, Offaly, Kilkenny and Wicklow; small parts of Wexford.

Ossory:
Most of Kilkenny; part of Laois; small parts of Offaly.

PROVINCE OF CASHEL

Cashel and Emly:
Parts of Tipperary and Limerick.

Cloyne:
Part of Cork.

Cork and Ross:
Cork City and part of Cork county.

Kerry:
All of Kerry, except Kilmurrity, and part of Cork.

Killaloe:
Most of Clare; parts of Tipperary, Offaly and Galway; small parts of Limerick and Laois.

Waterford and Lismore:
Waterford; part of Tipperary; small parts of Cork.

Limerick:
Most of Limerick; parts of Clare; small parts of Kerry.

PROVINCE OF TUAM

Tuam:
Parts of Galway and Mayo and small parts of Roscommon.

Achonry:
Parts of Roscommon, Mayo and Sligo.

Clonfert:
Part of Galway; small parts of Roscommon and Offaly.

Elphin:
Most of Roscommon, parts of Sligo and Galway.

Galway and Kilmacduagh:
Parts of Galway and Clare; small part of Cork.

Killala:
Parts of Mayo and Sligo.

CARDINALS OF IRELAND
List of all Irish Cardinals

Paul Cullen: Born 1803; ordained Archbishop of Armagh in 1850 and created Cardinal by Pope Pius IX on June 22, 1866; died 1878.

Edward McCabe: Born 1816; ordained Bishop of Gadara and appointed Auxiliary Bishop of Dublin in 1877; appointed Archbishop of Dublin in 1879 and created Cardinal by Pope Leo XIII on March 27, 1882; died 1885.

Michael Logue: Born 1840; ordained Bishop of Raphoe in 1879; appointed Archbishop of Armagh in 1887 and created Cardinal by Pope Leo XIII on January 16, 1893; died 1924.

Patrick O'Donnell: Born 1856; ordained Bishop of Raphoe in 1888; appointed Archbishop of Armagh in 1924 and created Cardinal by Pope Pius XI on December 14, 1925; died 1927.

Joseph McRory: Born 1861; ordained Bishop of Down and Connor in 1915; appointed Archbishop of Armagh in 1928 and created Cardinal by Pope Pius XI on December 12, 1929; died 1945.

John D'Alton: Born 1882; ordained Bishop of Binda and appointed Co-adjutor to Bishop of Meath in 1942; appointed Bishop of Meath in 1943; appointed Archbishop of Armagh in 1946 and created Cardinal by Pope Pius XII on January 12, 1953; died 1963.

William Conway: Born 1913; ordained Bishop of Neve and appointed Auxiliary Archbishop of Armagh in 1958; appointed Archbishop of Armagh in 1963; created Cardinal by Pope Paul VI on February 22, 1965; died 1977.

Tomás Ó Fiaich: Born 1923; ordained Archbishop of Armagh in 1977 and created Cardinal by Pope John Paul II on the June 30, 1979; died 1990.

Cahal Daly: Born 1917; ordained Bishop of Ardagh and Clonmacnoise in 1967; appointed Bishop of Down and Connor in 1982; appointed Archbishop of Armagh and created Cardinal in 1990 by Pope John Paul II; retired in September 1996.

CHURCH OF IRELAND BISHOPS

Year	Province	Diocese	Name
1968	Dublin	Cashel	J. W. Armstrong
1969	Armagh	Armagh	G. O. Simms
1969	Armagh	Clogher	R. P. C. Hanson
1969	Armagh	Connor	A. H. Butler
1969	Armagh	Tuam	J. C. Duggan
1969	Armagh	Derry	C. I. Peacocke
1969	Dublin	Dublin	A. A. Buchanan
1970	Armagh	Down and Dromore	G. A. Quin
1970	Dublin	Limerick	D. A. R. Caird
1971	Dublin	Killaloe	E. Owen
1973	Armagh	Clogher	R. W. Heavener
1975	Armagh	Derry	R. H. A. Eames
1976	Dublin	Meath and Kildare	D. A. R. Caird
1976	Dublin	Limerick and Killaloe	E. Owen
1977	Dublin	Dublin	H. R. McAdoo
1977	Dublin	Cashel and Ossory	J. W. Armstrong
1978	Dublin	Cork	S. G. Poyntz
1980	Armagh	Armagh	J. W. Armstrong
1980	Armagh	Clogher	G. McMullan
1980	Armagh	Down and Dromore	R. H. A. Eames
1980	Armagh	Derry	J. Mehaffey
1980	Dublin	Cashel and Ossory	N. V. Willoughby
1981	Armagh	Connor	W. J. McCappin
1981	Armagh	Kilmore	W. G. Wilson
1981	Dublin	Limerick and Killaloe	W. N. F. Empey
1985	Dublin	Meath and Kildare	W. N. F. Empey
1985	Dublin	Limerick and Killaloe	E. F. Darling
1985	Dublin	Dublin	D. A. R. Caird
1986	Armagh	Armagh	R. H. A. Eames
1986	Armagh	Clogher	B. D. A. Hannon
1986	Armagh	Down and Dromore	G. McMullan
1986	Armagh	Tuam	J. R. W. Neill
1987	Armagh	Connor	S. G. Poyntz
1987	Dublin	Cork	R. A. Warke
1993	Armagh	Kilmore	M. H. G. Mayes
1995	Armagh	Connor	J. E. Moore
1996	Dublin	Dublin	W. N. F. Empey
1996	Dublin	Meath and Kildare	R. L. Clarke

PRESBYTERIAN MODERATORS, 1967-1997

Year	Name	Assembly
1967	The Very Rev. William Boyd	Lisburn
1972	The Very Rev. R. V. A. Lynas	Larne
1976	The Very Rev. J. Weir	Belfast
1978	The Very Rev. David Burke	Bangor
1979	The Very Rev. William Craig	Portadown
1980	The Very Rev. R. G. Craig	Carrickfergus
1981	The Very Rev. John Girvan	Lurgan
1982	The Very Rev. E. P. Gardner	Ballymena
1983	The Very T. J. Simpson	Newtownards
1984	The Very Rev. Howard Cromie	Lisburn
1985	The Very Rev. Robert Dickinson	Tobermore & Draperstown
1986	The Very Rev. Prof. John Thompson	Belfast
1987	The Very Rev. William Fleming	Belfast
1988	The Very Rev. A. W. G. Brown	Ballycastle
1989	The Very Rev. James Matthews	Lurgan
1990	The Very Rev. Prof. R. F. G. Holmes	Helen's Bay
1991	The Very Rev. Rodney Sterritt	Newtownards
1992	The Very Rev. John Dunlop	Belfast
1993	The Very Rev. Andrew R. Rodgers	Dungannon

1994	The Very Rev. David J. McGaughey		Kilkeel
1995	The Very Rev. John Ross		Holywood
1996	The Very Rev. Harry Allen		Coleraine
1997	The Right Rev. Samuel Hutchinson		Lisburn

MEMBERSHIP OF MAIN IRISH CHURCHES

Religion	Members (000s)		Ministers		Churches	
	1985	1993	1985	1993	1985	1993
Catholic	3,341,949	3,241,566	3,950	4,281	2,626	2,656
Anglican	221,200	220,570	605	514	1,186	1,000
Presbyterian	218,257	217,888	517	531	657	656
Methodist	24,284	22,146	137	141	282	248
Independent	16,627	16,828	86	116	356	402
Baptist	8,921	9,485	109	121	112	127
Pentecostal	5,225	7,630	75	95	80	92
Orthodox	475	522	3	3	3	3
Other Churches	6,157	6,589	95	102	106	110
Total:	3,843,095	3,743,224	5,577	5,904	5,408	5,294

CHURCH OF IRELAND STATISTICS

Diocese	Incumbents	Curates	Parishes
Armagh	42	6	46
Clogher	29	1	35
Derry and Raphoe	44	4	50
Down and Dromore	70	14	78
Connor	69	17	78
Kilmore, Elphin and Ardagh	19	1	25
Tuam, Killala and Achonry	6	2	9
Dublin and Glendalough	51	4	54
Meath and Kildare	14	-	21
Cashel and Ossory	24	3	34
Cork, Cloyne and Ross	16	3	23
Limerick and Killaloe	14	1	20
Total:	398	56	473

PRESBYTERIAN CHURCH STATISTICS

Synod	Presbyteries	Congregations	Ministers
Armagh & Down	6	162	186
Ballymena & Coleraine	5	118	155
Belfast	3	71	139
Derry & Omagh	4	117	96
Dublin	3	89	63

METHODIST CHURCH STATISTICS, 1996

District	Total Community	Number of Circuits*	Number of Churches
Dublin	2,232	8	20
Midlands & Southern	2,043	10	27
Enniskillen & Sligo	3,338	9	32
Londonderry	3,613	6	27
North East	12,280	8	24
Belfast	17,865	14	29
Down	10,042	10	22
Portadown	7,246	11	44
Totals	58,659	76	225

*Circuits are groups of congregations which work together as administrative units.
There are 192 Methodist Ministers (including 65 retired) and two local non-stipendiary Ministers.
There are 316 local (or lay) Preachers.

CATHOLIC PARISHES, CHURCHES AND SCHOOLS

(1996)	Parishes	Catholic Population	Churches	Primary Schools (No.)	Secondary Schools (No.)	Primary Schools Population	Secondary Schools Population
Armagh	62	204,517	146	169	30	28,156	21,214
Dublin	200	1,041,100	238	516	192	-	-
Cashel	46	78,921	87	127	24	12,333	10,006
Tuam	56	116,201	131	240	38	29,433	9,500
Achonry	23	39,000	47	55	11	5,500	4,200
Ardagh	41	71,806	80	91	22	11,256	7,857
Clogher	37	85,002	86	98	20	12,896	8,502
Clonfert	24	32,600	47	50	8	6,800	3,200
Cloyne	46	119,075	106	125	31	16,707	14,058
Cork & Ross	68	215,500	124	189	52	41,000	-
Derry	53	213,639	104	136	31	26,819	21,011
Down & Connor	87	297,630	152	172	42	39,703	28,149
Dromore	23	63,300	48	51	14	10,874	9,506
Elphin	37	68,000	90	126	20	12,700	8,000
Ferns	49	98,170	101	97	20	17,000	10,000
Galway	40	83,928	71	90	21	12,005	6,888
Kerry	54	125,000	105	170	35	-	-
Kildare & Leighlin	56	169,305	117	174	45	27,567	19,927
Killala	22	37,412	48	78	12	5,593	4,242
Killaloe	59	107,817	133	157	24	16,394	11,966
Kilmore	36	55,340	97	89	15	8,415	5,800
Limerick	60	141,514	97	114	33	22,000	18,500
Meath	69	182,000	149	186	36	30,000	17,200
Ossory	42	73,875	89	91	16	11,263	7,150
Raphoe	31	82,260	71	104	20	12,255	13,151
Waterford & Lismore	45	131,538	85	100	30	17,472	12,931
Total:	1,366	3,934,450	2,649	3,595	842	434,141	272,958

NUMBERS OF CATHOLIC PRIESTS AND RELIGIOUS

(1996)	Priests Active in diocese*	Others†	Religious Orders Clerical	Brothers	Sisters
Armagh	166	22	61	47	380
Dublin	478	122	975	505	2,736
Cashel	120	15	57	27	248
Tuam	152	23	28	48	393
Achonry	49	13	3	1	68
Ardagh	73	19	5	10	325
Clogher	92	13	7	4	157
Clonfert	52	16	39	0	176
Cloyne	135	27	6	30	275
Cork & Ross	143	19	160	90	802
Derry	140	14	5	4	155
Down & Connor	221	24	68	67	355
Dromore	67	11	21	9	167
Elphin	80	12	6	5	204
Ferns	118	39	12	10	275
Galway	70	19	49	24	239
Kerry	113	33	11	23	361
Kildare & Leighlin	108	25	87	68	391
Killala	46	16	3	3	81
Killaloe	122	23	26	25	320
Kilmore	97	4	14	0	85
Limerick	144	19	76	30	416
Meath	124	26	132	39	305
Ossory	80	25	20	40	262
Raphoe	76	22	12	7	76
Waterford & Lismore	116	9	149	65	532
Total	3,182	610	2,032	1,181	9,784

* Priests who are active in voluntary, secondary and state schools.
† Priests of the diocese who are retired, sick, on study leave or working in other dioceses in Ireland and abroad.

APPLICANTS / ENTRANTS TO CATHOLIC CHURCH

Religious Orders	Applicants (1994)	Entrants (1994)
Diocesan	193	98
Clerical Religious Orders	130	66
Sisters Orders	63	33
Brothers Orders	18	4
Total:	404	201

IRISH CATHOLIC MISSIONARIES BY CONTINENT

Continent	Number (1994)	% (1994)
Africa	2,618	47
Americas	1,226	22
Asia	780	14
Europe	501	9
India and the Middle East	446	8
Total:	5,571	100

NULLITY OF MARRIAGES IN CATHOLIC CHURCH

Year	Applications	Decrees
1987	882	209
1988	926	188
1989	915	212
1990	1,043	216
1991	402	215
1992	444	289
1993	347	282
1994	470	300

OTHER RELIGIONS IN IRELAND

Bahá'í Faith
24 Burlington Road, Dublin 4. Tel. (01) 6683150.

The Bahá'í Faith is an independent world religion founded over 150 years ago. It is governed by elected councils at local, national and international levels. The jurisdictions of these councils (spiritual assemblies) are contiguous with civil boundaries. Overall, there are 174 elected National Spiritual Assemblies, including one for the Republic of Ireland and one for Britain. There are 20 elected local Spiritual Assemblies In the Republic of Ireland and 9 in Northern Ireland. National and local assemblies have nine members and are elected annually. The Universal House of Justice (international level) has nine members and is elected every five years.

Baptist Union of Ireland
117 Lisburn Road, Belfast, Co. Antrim BT9 7AF. Tel. (01232) 663108.

The Baptist Union is an association of 109 autonomous local churches of the Baptist faith in Ireland (93 in Northern Ireland and 16 in the Republic of Ireland). Membership in the union does not interfere with the autonomy of the local church. The operations of the union are controlled by the Churches' Council, which is made up of at least two representatives from each church in the union and meets at least twice a year. The Council acts through its officers and executive committee. The executive committee is elected by the Churches' Council from among its members, and its role is to supervise the work of the Union.

Buddhism
Western Buddhist Order, 23 South Frederick Street, Dublin 2. Tel. (01) 6713187.

A number of Buddhist traditions are accounted for in Ireland (i.e. Tibetan, Theravada and Zen forms) by way of groups which have regular meditation meetings. There are two centres in Ireland which accommodate teaching programmes, meditation meetings and retreats, situated in Cavan and Cork and a meditation / teaching centre in Dublin. The Western Buddhist Order is a worldwide Buddhist organisation which runs the far larger Friends of the Western Buddhist Order (estimated at 1 million). There are currently 800 ordained men and women with an average of 40 ordinations each year. Founded in 1991, the Friends of the Western Buddhist Order - Tara Institute is Ireland's largest and fastest growing Buddhist organisation with a comparatively high number of Order members per head of population.

The Church of Jesus Christ of Latter-Day Saints
The Willows, Glasnevin, Dublin 11. Tel. (01) 8306899.

This Church is divided ecclesiastically into two Stakes (Belfast and Dublin) and one District (Cork). The Belfast Stake caters for approximately 3,500 members across Northern Ireland. The Stake was organised in 1974 and has had three Presidents. There are a number of wards in Belfast and Bangor and other congregations in Derry,

Omagh, Antrim, Coleraine, Newtownabbey, Lisburn and Portadown. Each is controlled by a Bishop (ward) or Branch President. The Dublin Stake was created out of the Dublin District in 1995 and has around 1,800 members. There are four wards in Dublin City, and branches in Bray, Dundalk, Mullingar, Sligo and Galway. The Cork District has over 400 members with branches in Cork, Limerick, Waterford and Tralee. There are a number of missionaries serving both in Ireland and abroad.

Jewish Community
Herzog House, Zion Road, Rathgar, Dublin 6.
Tel. (01) 4923751.

Although small in number (they are currently estimated at 1,580), Jews have played a long and active role in Irish society. The Jewish Community is centred mainly in Dublin. The spiritual head of the Jewish Community in the Republic of Ireland is the Chief Rabbi, under whose supervision all congregations operate.

Church of Scientology
62-63 Middle Abbey Street, Dublin 1. Tel. (01) 8720007

The Church of Scientology - Mission of Dublin is the main congregation of Scientologists in Ireland. There are smaller informal groups in Cork, Belfast and elsewhere. The Dublin Mission was officially incorporated in early 1994 but has been in operation on a less formal basis since the late 1980's. There is a religious order within the Church of Scientology called the Sea Organisation. This community of men and women dedicate their lives to the spiritual rehabilitation of

humankind, and they sign a pledge of eternal service to do so. The Sea Organisation constitutes the top ranks of the hierarchy of the Scientology religion and delivers the most advanced spiritual services, but does not exist in Ireland yet.

Islam
19 Roebuck Road, Clonskeagh, Dublin 14.
Tel. (01) 2603740.

The Dublin Islamic Society was formed in 1959 by Muslim Students from South Africa and Malaysia. In 1971, it was registered as a friendly society and later as a charitable organisation. The population of Muslims in Ireland is between 8,000 and 9,000 persons approximately, with about 5,000 Muslims in the Dublin Metropolitan Area. The main body is in Dublin with the next largest grouping in Belfast and smaller communities in Galway, Ballyhaunis, Craigavon and Cork, of which each is independently run.

Lutheran Church in Ireland
Luther House, 24 Adelaide Road, Dublin 2.
Tel. (01) 6766548.

Most of the members of the Lutheran Church in Ireland are of German or Scandanavian origin but are living here in Ireland. There are approximately 1,000 members nationwide, with congregations located in Dublin and Belfast. Members are also to be found in Dublin, Limerick, Cork, Sligo, Killarney, and Wexford, and services are held in these towns on a regular basis.

SELECTED PROFILES OF RELIGIOUS FIGURES

Best, Kenneth President of Methodist Church in Ireland (1996/97); influential in brokering Loyalist ceasefire in 1994.

Brady, Seán (born Cavan 1939) Roman Catholic Archbishop of Armagh and Primate of All-Ireland since 1996. Ordained 1964, Coadjutor of Archbishop of Armagh (1995-96).

Clifford, Dermot (born Kerry, 1939) Roman Catholic Archbishop (or bishop) of Cashel and Emly since 1986. Patron of Cumann Lúthchleas Gael since 1989.

Connell, Desmond (born 1926) Professor of General Metaphysics at University College Dublin (1972-88), Roman Catholic Archbishop of Dublin and Primate of Dublin since 1988.

Daly, Cahal (born Antrim, 1917) former Cardinal and Archbishop of Armagh (1990-96); Bishop of Ardagh and Clonmacnoise (1967-82), Bishop of Down and Connor (1982-90).

Eames, Robin (born Belfast, 1937) Church of Ireland Bishop of Derry & Raphoe (1975-80), Bishop of Down and Dromore (1980-86), Archbishop of Armagh and Primate of All-Ireland since 1986. Created a Life Peer in 1995.

Empey, Walton N.F. (born 1934) Church of Ireland Archbishop of Dublin and Primate of Ireland since 1996, previously Bishop of Limerick & Killaloe (1981-85) and Bishop of Meath and Kildare (1985-96).

Faul, Denis (born Louth 1932), out spoken Catholic priest; prison chaplain at Long Kesh during the 1981

hunger strike; President of St. Patrick's Academy Dungannon.

Hannon, Brian D.A. (born 1936) Ordained 1962, Church of Ireland Bishop of Clogher since 1986.

Hurley, Michael Jesuit priest; founder of Irish School of Ecumenics and Columbanus Ecumenical Society.

Hutchinson, Dr. Samuel (born Belfast, 1937) installed as a minister (1966); current Moderator of the Presbyterian Church in Ireland; previously Clerk of the General Assembly (1990).

Jones, Christopher (born 1936) Roman Catholic Bishop of Elphin since 1994.

McMullan, Gordon (born Belfast, 1934) Church of Ireland Bishop of Down and Dromore; writer on theological matters.

Mehaffey, James (born 1936) Church of Ireland Bishop of Derry and Raphoe since 1980.

Murray, Raymond Catholic priest and human rights activist in Northern Ireland. publications include *The S.A.S. in Ireland.*

Neary, Michael (born 1946) Ordained in 1971, Roman Catholic Archbishop of Tuam since 1995.

Neill, John R.W. (born 1945) Church of Ireland Bishop of Tuam, Killala and Achonry since 1986. Secretary to House of Irish Bishops 1988-95.

Reid, Alex Catholic priest involved in the brokering of the I.R.A. ceasefire of 1994.

Taggart, Norman (born Belfast, 1935) Current President of Methodist Church in Ireland.

EDUCATION

Education in Ireland: A Story of the Triumph of the Human Will

By *Andy Pollak*, Education Correspondent, The Irish Times

EDUCATION in the Republic of Ireland, three years away from the millennium, is a story of the triumph of the human will - the will of children, parents and teachers - over large class sizes and poor facilities. Education in the island as a whole is a story of continuing divisions inherited from a past where it was one of the principal battlegrounds between the British state and the Irish Catholic church, and between the Catholic church and the various Irish Protestant churches.

The result of this history is that, unlike in most Western democratic countries, there is only a limited state-owned education sector in Ireland. In the Republic it is a state-aided system run by the churches or by church-nominated trustees. The churches own most of the schools while the state pays the teachers' salaries, and the vast bulk of both their capital and current expenditure. There is a tiny multi-denominational primary sector of 16 - out of 3,200 schools.

In Northern Ireland there is a divided system for a divided region. All schools are now eligible for 100 per cent state funding, although Catholic school boards have to be constituted so that the Catholic Church does not have a majority presence. Most Catholic children attend Catholic 'maintained' schools, and most Protestant children attend State 'controlled' schools. There is a small but growing number of integrated primary and secondary schools, attended by around two per cent of children.

In recent decades the rapid modernisation of the Republic has led to an explosion in the demand for education, sparked off - in the first instance - by the introduction of free secondary education 30 years ago. In that time the numbers attending second level schools has risen from under 150,000 students to around 370,000. A very high proportion of Republic of Ireland school leavers - nearly 85 per cent, one of the highest in Europe - now take the Leaving Certificate exam, and around 45 per cent go on to participate in some form of higher education. The Republic now has one of the Western world's highest proportions of under 30-year-olds in full-time education, higher than Britain, the U.S., Germany and Switzerland.

The parents' lobby is increasingly well-organised while teachers are among the best-paid in Europe, and highly regarded by parents and politicians alike. Rarely, if ever, does one hear the kind of damaging criticism of the standard of teaching heard in countries like Britain and the U.S.

However, there is a dark side to this rosy picture. The Republic remains at the bottom of the O.E.C.D. league for spending per pupil at preschool, primary and secondary levels. Funding is heavily skewed towards third level: In 1995 (using 1992 figures), the O.E.C.D. found that for every £100 spent on primary education, £150 was spent at second level, and £410 at third level.

With a pupil:teacher ratio over 25:1, the Republic's primary schools have the largest class sizes in Europe. Its secondary schools, with a ratio of just over 17:1, rank lower than every other advanced country, except Turkey and New Zealand.

The result of such under-funding is that parents in the vast majority of schools in the Republic have to fund-raise to cover the up to 20 per cent gap between the level of public funding for their schools and the actual running costs.

Education in Northern Ireland is generally better resourced by the state than in the Republic, although the gap is narrowing as British government spending cuts in recent years begin to bite. A 1994 study of six primary schools in Limerick and Derry showed that the northern city's schools were better off as regards class size, pupil:teacher ratio, teachers' promotional prospects and - by a large margin - provision of computers, audio-visual and other classroom equipment. School buildings are usually brighter and more modern in the North.

There is little or no contact between the two systems: more than 70 years of belonging to different jurisdictions has meant that ignorance of the education system on the other side of the border is almost total.

1997 saw a change of government in both jurisdictions. In the Republic, the new Fianna Fáil Minister for Education, Michael Martin, announced that he was scrapping the outgoing Minister's plans for devolving many powers to new regional education boards, comparable in some respects to the North's education and library boards. He nevertheless pledged to follow the former government in introducing a revised version of the Republic's first ever Education Act, which he promised by Christmas.

In Northern Ireland, Labour's new - and so far much less energetic Minister of State for education, Tony Worthington, did little of note in his first five months in office except promise some more places in nursery education. On the positive side, the Dearing Report on Higher Education in the U.K. recommended that there should be provision for 5,000 more places in Northern Ireland's universities and third-level colleges.

The writer is noted as an authoritative journalist on education in Ireland.

INTRODUCTION

The numbers in education in Ireland are relatively high: 27.5 per cent of the Republic of Ireland's population and 25.5 percent of Northern Ireland's population are engaged in full-time education. These figures possibly reflect the island's demographics, as both jurisdictions have one of the youngest populations in Europe.

General education statistics: The budget for education in Northern Ireland is estimated at around £1.3 billion. This budget is administered centrally by the Department of Education for Northern Ireland which works in partnership with the five local Education and Library Boards, the Council for Catholic Maintained Schools, and the Northern Ireland Council for Curriculum, Examinations and Assessment. A signifier of the high value placed on education in Northern Ireland is exam results. Every year, Northern Irish students consistently outperform their English and Welsh counterparts in state examinations.

In the Republic, the Department of Education is the central administrative body for running the primary, secondary and third-level systems. More than IR£2 billion was spent on education during 1995-96. Irish students are performing favourably in comparison with their European counterparts, and 1994 statistics indicate that the ratio of secondary school graduates is higher than most other European countries. There is also a higher proportion of women in the population with a secondary education than elsewhere in Europe.

Higher education statistics: In 1995, 11,907 primary degrees and 2,550 higher degrees were awarded in the Republic of Ireland - an increase of 7.7 per cent and 1.6 per cent, respectively, on the previous year - with the most popular degrees awarded being, in order of popularity, arts and social science, commerce and business studies, and science. The proportion of 18-year-olds in Northern Ireland entering third-level education in 1994-95 was 40 per cent, a figure that is significantly higher than that for the rest of Britain - 31 per cent. The three most popular subjects at third level almost paralleled the Republic of Ireland and were business administration, engineering and technology, and social studies.

The proportion of new undergraduate entrants under 21 years in Northern Ireland was 79 per cent, while in the Republic of Ireland, research suggests that only 5 per cent of the full-time third-level cohort in 1993-94 were mature students (defined as being over 23 years and entering undergraduate study for the first time). However, demographic trends indicate that the overwhelming demand for third level places by school-leavers is about to drop and that universities will have to compete with each other for mature students in the near future.

Differences between the two education systems: Research by the University of Limerick revealed a high level of mutual ignorance between those involved in education in the Republic of Ireland and those in Northern Ireland, particularly among teachers and pupils. It also found that although the education system in the North has attempted to address this, no such initiative exists in the Republic.

The most obvious differences between both systems are that the Irish language is a compulsory subject in the Republic of Ireland and that teachers in the Republic must have qualifications in Irish. At second level, the curriculum in the North is far more specialised at senior level, whereas in the Republic, there is a broader spectrum of subjects. At third level in Northern Ireland, there is less interest in E.U. exchange programmes, whereas the Republic of Ireland has a more proactive stance towards Europe. Additionally, there is a greater uptake in adult education in the north, particularly among working-class Catholic women. Mature students in the Republic of Ireland, on the other hand, tend to be better-off and better educated.

Points for Entering Third Level Education: Northern Ireland *(A-level results)*: A=10 points, B=8 points, C=6 points, D=4 points, E=2 points (Three A-levels are taken into consideration). Republic of Ireland *(Leaving Certificate higher papers)*: A1=100 points, A2=90 points, B1=85 points, B2=80 points, B3=75 points, C1=70 points, C2=65 points, C3=60 points, D1=55 points, D2=50 points, D3=45 points. (Six Leaving Certificate subjects are taken into consideration; Bonus points are awarded by some third-level institutions for maths and certain science subjects).

R.O.I. LIBRARY STOCKS, 1994

Local Authority	Total books in stock	Numbers added	Numbers withdrawn	Non-book total	Numbers added	Numbers withdrawn
CONNACHT	**988,362**	**58,596**	**23,842**	**29,286**	**2,668**	**557**
Galway	354,928	19,266	11,582	16,186	702	217
Leitrim	71,399	5,414	2,622	3,557	730	0
Mayo	241,452	11,027	6,514	849	49	3
Roscommon	211,021	13,849	1,040	7,433	1,105	337
Sligo	109,562	9,040	2,084	1,261	82	0
LEINSTER	**4,241,384**	**234,446**	**74,533**	**106,871**	**9,427**	**2,053**
Carlow	152,078	10,240	0	1,901	202	0
Dublin	1,294,921	77,558	35,052	59,331	5,006	1,612
Kildare	376,642	11,777	0	4,721	637	24
Kilkenny	268,001	18,225	6,111	5,727	796	215
Laois	170,758	14,925	11,979	3,852	385	34
Longford	103,896	16,338	1,361	1,763	166	42
Louth	237,476	10,562	356	6,507	630	20
Meath	355,839	8,882	6,116	2,584	446	16
Offaly	182,921	12,435	4,094	8,214	221	1
Westmeath	446,832	11,806	998	3,560	178	0
Wexford	397,368	20,452	5,812	7,090	569	89
Wicklow	254,652	21,246	2,654	1,621	191	0
MUNSTER	**3,089,075**	**136,084**	**42,249**	**26,590**	**2,796**	**92**
Clare	328,778	29,032	8,019	7,508	880	22
Cork	1,117,223	48,255	0	2,670	281	-
Kerry	300,150	14,963	8,084	6,882	829	0
Limerick	714,170	19,538	20,490	2,715	176	0
Tipperary	545,436	17,821	3,799	4,877	288	16
Waterford	83,318	6,475	1,857	1,938	342	54
ULSTER (3 counties)	**598,293**	**43,932**	**9,574**	**10,550**	**3,246**	**99**
Cavan	125,906	11,741	2,460	2,031	233	23
Donegal	283,662	19,843	2,835	5,307	2,847	0
Monaghan	188,725	12,348	4,279	3,212	166	76
MUNICIPAL	**2,682,028**	**105,200**	**189,776**	**89,976**	**7,359**	**1,956**
Cork	420,794	13,366	23,177	24,243	1,423	243
Dublin	2,005,005	83,258	161,224	56,566	5,428	1,713
Limerick	179,343	8,576	5,375	3,045	508	0
Waterford	76,886	-	-	6,122	-	-
TOTAL:	**11,599,142**	**578,258**	**339,974**	**263,273**	**25,496**	**4,757**

R.O.I. AND N.I. THIRD-LEVEL COLLEGES

REGIONAL TECHNICAL COLLEGES

Athlone Dublin Road, Athlone, Co. Westmeath. (0902) 72647.

Carlow Kilkenny Road, Carlow. (0503) 70400.

Cork Rossa Avenue, Bishopstown, Co. Cork. (021) 326100.

Dun Laoghaire - College of Art, Carriglea Park, Kill Ave., Dun Laoghaire, Co. Dublin. (01) 2801138.

Dundalk Co. Louth. (042) 34785.

Galway Dublin Road, Galway. (091) 753161.

Letterkenny Port Road, Letterkenny, Co. Donegal. (074) 24888.

Limerick Moylish Park, Limerick. (061) 327688.

Sligo Ballinode, Sligo. (071) 44096

Tallaght Dublin 24. (01) 4042700.

Tralee Clash, Tralee, Co. Kerry. (066) 25711.

Waterford Institute of Technology Cork Road, Waterford. (051) 378292.

COLLEGES OF EDUCATION

Church of Ireland College of Education 96 Upper Rathmines Road, Dublin 6. (01) 4970033.

Froebel College of Education Sion Hill, Blackrock, Co. Dublin. (01) 2888520.

Mary Immaculate College of Education South Circular Road, Limerick. (061) 314588.

St. Angela's College of Education for Home Economics Lough Gill, Co. Sligo. (071) 42785.

St. Catherine's College of Education for Home Economics Sion Hill, Blackrock, Co. Dublin. (01) 2884989.

St. Mary's College of Education, Griffith Avenue Marino, Dublin 9. (01) 8335111.

St. Patrick's College of Education Drumcondra, Dublin 9. (01) 8376191.

CONSTITUENT COLLEGES, DUBLIN INSTITUTE OF TECHNOLOGY

(Fitzwilliam House, 30 Upper Pembroke Street, Dublin 2. (01) 4023000.)

D.I.T. Aungier Street Dublin 2. (01) 4023000.

D.I.T. Bolton Street Dublin 1. (01) 4023000.

D.I.T. Cathal Brugha Street Dublin 1. (01) 4023000.

D.I.T. College of Music Adelaide Road, Dublin 2. (01) 4023000.

D.I.T. Kevin Street Dublin 8. (01) 4023000.

D.I.T. Mountjoy Square 40-45 Mountjoy Square, Dublin 1. (01) 4023000.

D.I.T. Rathmines Rathmines Road, Dublin 6. (01) 402300.

COLLEGES OF THEOLOGY AND DIVINITY

Milltown Institute Milltown Park, Dublin 6. (01) 2698388

Mater Dei Institute of Education Clonliffe Road, Dublin 3. (01) 8376027.

St. Patrick's College Carlow. (0503) 31114.

St. John's College Waterford. (051) 874199

All Hallows College Grace Park Road, Dublin 9. (01) 8373745.

Clonliffe College Dublin. (01) 8375103.

Holy Ghost College Kimmage Manor, Dublin 12. (01) 4560055

St. Patrick's College Thurles. (0504) 24466.

ADDITIONAL COLLEGES

Accountancy and Business College Aungier Street, Dublin 2. (01) 4751024.

American College 2 Merrion Square, Dublin 2. (01) 6768941.

Cork School of Music 13 Union Quay, Cork. (021) 270076

Crawford School of Art & Design Sharman Crawford Street, Cork. (021) 966343.

Garda College Training Centre, Templemore, Co. Tipperary. (0504) 31522.

Griffith College South Circular Road, Dublin 8. (01) 4545640.

Hotel Training College Killybegs, Co. Donegal. (073) 31120.

Institute of Education Business College, Portobello House, South Richmond Street, Dublin 2. (01) 6715811.

Institute of Public Administration Lansdowne Road, Dublin 4. (01) 6686233.

Irish Management Institute Clonard, Sandyford, Dublin 16. (01) 2956911.

Military College Curragh Camp, Co. Kildare. (045) 41301

L.S.B. College Ltd. Balfe House, 6-9 Balfe St., Dublin 2. (01) 6794844

National College of Art & Design 100 Thomas Street, Dublin 8. (01) 6711203.

National College of Industrial Relations Sandford Road, Dublin 6. (01) 4060500.

Royal College of Surgeons in Ireland 123 St. Stephen's Green, Dublin 2. (01) 4022100.

Shannon International Hotel School Shannon Airport, Co. Clare. (061) 302000.

Armagh College of Further Education Lonsdale Street, Armagh. (01861) 522205.

Belfast Institute of Further and Higher Education Park House, 87-91 Great Victoria St., Belfast. (01232) 265000.

Castlereagh College of Further and Higher Education Montgomery Road, Cregagh, Belfast. (01232) 797144.

Causeway Institute of Further and Higher Education, Union St., Coleraine, Co. Derry. (01265) 54717.

East Antrim Institute of Further and Higher Education 32-34 Pound St., Larne, Co. Antrim. (01574) 272268.

East Down Institute of Further and Higher Education Market Street, Downpatrick, Co. Down. (01396) 615815.

East Tyrone College of Further Education Circular Road, Dungannon, Co. Tyrone. (01868) 722323.

Fermanagh College Fairview, 1 Dublin Road, Enniskillen, Co. Fermanagh. (01365) 322431.

Limavady College of Further Education Main St., Limavady, Co. Derry. (015047) 62334.

Lisburn College of Further and Higher Education 39 Castle Street, Lisburn, Co. Antrim. (01846) 677225.

Newry/Kilkeel College of Further Education Patrick Street, Newry. Co. Down. (01693) 61071

North Down and Ards Institute of Further and Higher Education Castle Park Road, Bangor, Co. Down. (01247) 271254

Northern Ireland Hotel & Catering College Ballywillan Road, Portrush, Co. Antrim. (01265) 823768.

North East Institute of Further and Higher Education Trostan Ave., Co. Antrim. (01266) 652871.

North West Institute of Further and Higher Education Strand Road, Derry. (01504) 266711.

Omagh College of Further Education Mountjoy Rd., Omagh, Co. Tyrone. (01662) 245433.

St. Mary's Teacher Training College 191 Falls Road, Belfast. (01232) 327678.

Stranmillis Teacher Training College Stranmillis Road, Belfast. (01232) 381271.

Upper Bann Institute of Further and Higher Education 26 Lurgan Road, Portadown, Craigavon, Co. Armagh. (01762) 337111.

STUDENT ENROLMENT

FULL-TIME STUDENTS EDUCATION IN THE REPUBLIC OF IRELAND (1994-1995)

School/College	All Persons	Male	Female
FIRST LEVEL:	**499,282**	**257,150**	**242,132**
Primary schools (aided by Dept. of Education)	491,256	252,981	238275
Ordinary classes	479,126	245,847	233,279
*Special classes**	4,313	2,286	2,027
Special schools	7,817	4,848	2,969
Primary schools (non-aided)	8,026	4,169	3,857
SECOND LEVEL:	**375,457**	**184,546**	**190,911**
Secondary schools (aided by Dept. of Education)	371,957	182,427	189,530
Junior cycle	208,917	106,410	102,507
Senior cycle (general)	140,534	68,266	72,268
Senior cycle (vocational)	21,818	7,469	14,349
Other courses (Regional Technical Colleges)	688	282	406
Secondary schools (aided by Depts. of Agriculture/Defence)	1,575	1,371	204
Commercial schools (non-aided)	1,925	748	1,177
THIRD LEVEL	**96,681**	**48,822**	**47,859**
Institutions (aided by Dept. of Education)	89,693	45,099	44,594
H.E.A.[†] Institutions	53,450	24,785	28,665
Teacher Training Institutions	503	34	469
Technological Colleges	35,475	20,143	15,332
Other Institutions	265	137	128
Institutions (aided by Dept.s of Justice/Defence)	873	666	207
Institutions (non-aided)	6,115	3,057	3,058
TOTAL	**971,420**	**490,518**	**480,902**

* *Special classes refer to classes provided in mainstream primary schools for students with special needs.*
† *H.E.A. refers to the Higher Education Authority, a planning and budgetary agency with specific responsibilities for universities and other designated higher education institutions.*

FULL-TIME AND PART-TIME STUDENTS IN NORTHERN IRELAND

School/College	1988-89	1991-92	1994-95	1995-96	1996-97
First Level (inc. nursery)	**192,895**	**195,094**	**196,538**	**197,395**	**196,985**
Primary	189,109	190,988	191,976	192,747	192,305
Special Schools	3,786	4,106	4,562	4,648	4,680
Second Level	**146,849**	**146,968**	**153,632**	**155,027**	**156,142**
Secondary	89,968	87,525	89,534	90,426	90,746
Grammar	56,881	59,443	64,098	64,601	65,396
Further Education	**56,708**	**80,021**	**79,253**	**79,813**	**85,102**
Full-time	15,619	21,437	23,675	23,934	25,033
Part-time	41,089	58,584	55,578	55,879	60,069
Universities	**15,976**	**19,241**	**20,956**	**26,134**	-
Full-time male	8,205	9,556	10,012	12,066	-
Full-time female	7,771	9,685	10,944	14,068	-
TOTAL:	**412,428**	**441,324**	**450,109**	**458,369**	**438,229***

* *The total for 1996-97 does not include full-time university students.*

PUPIL-TEACHER RATIOS

REPUBLIC OF IRELAND

Type of School	1985-86	1988-89	1991-92	1994-95
Primary*	26.8	27.5	25.8	23.5
Secondary†	17.4	17.9	18.1	18.0
OVERALL RATIO	**22.1**	**22.7**	**22.0**	**20.8**

* *The total number of teachers in service includes principals, remedial teachers and teachers of special classes and in special schools*

† *These figures relate to full-time teachers only and not the full-time equivalent of part-time teachers.*

NORTHERN IRELAND

Type of School	1985	1988	1991	1994
Nursery	24.2	24.1	24.7	24.7
Primary	23.3	23.5	22.8	21.6
Secondary	15.0	14.4	14.1	14.5
Grammar:				
Preparatory	24.7	24.6	24.8	28.7
Secondary	15.6	15.4	15.8	16.0
Special	8.3	7.2	6.9	6.8
OVERALL RATIO	18.6	18.4	18.2	17.9

PARTICIPATION IN EDUCATION: R.O.I.

% Persons in Education*	1992-93	1993-94	1994-95	1995-96
5 - 12 years	100.0	101.0	100.0	-
13 -15 years	98.0	98.0	98.0	-
16 years	92.6	93.6	91.1	-
17 years	80.8	83.3	81.9	-
18 years	61.8	63.7	63.6	-
19 years	40.3	46.0	47.5	-
20+ years†	16.8	16.0	18.0	-

These figures are based on provisional population estimates for each year.
† Except for 1992-93, these figures exclude students aged 25+ years.

PARTICIPATION IN EDUCATION: N.I.

% Persons in Education	1992-93	1993-94	1994-95	1995-96
16 years	45.6	47.7	47.0	45.0
17 years	33.2	36.3	36.9	36.7
16 and 17 years	39.4	42.0	42.0	41.4

IRELAND'S INTERNATIONAL RANKING IN MATHS AND SCIENCE

Results from the Third International Maths and Science Study on nine-year-olds; the results are given in descending order on a scale obtained from the combined scores of a range of tests.

SCIENCE		MATHS	
1 ....Korea	9 ....Scotland	1 ....Singapore	9 ....Scotland
2 ....Japan	10 ....Hong Kong	2 ....Korea	10 ....England
3 ..............................U.S.	11 ....New Zealand	3 ....Japan	11 ....Cyprus
4 ....Czech Republic	12 ....Norway	4 ....Hong Kong	12 ....Norway
5 ....England	13 ....Iceland	5 ....Czech Republic	13 ....New Zealand
6 ....Canada	14 ....Greece	6 ....Ireland	14 ....Greece
7 ....Singapore	15 ....Portugal	7 ...............................U.S.	15 ....Portugal
8 ....Ireland	16 ....Cyprus	8 ....Canada	16 ....Iceland
	17 ....Iran		17 ....Iran

R.O.I. ATTENDANCE AT PRIMARY SCHOOLS

Pupils by School/Class Standard	1992-93	1993-94	1994-95
Number of pupils not classified by standard	11,519	11,561	12,130
Special Schools	8,084	8,059	7,817
Special Classes	3,435	3,502	4,313
Pupils according to class standards	510,012	494,322	479,126
Infants standards	120,224	114,711	110,956
First standard	60,350	59,617	57,579
Second standard	61,310	60,369	59,442
Third standard	63,081	61,188	59,968
Fourth standard	66,337	63,000	60,981
Fifth standard	68,049	66,676	63,168
Sixth standard	68,461	66,663	65,334
Other standard	2,200	2,098	1,698
TOTAL (for all schools and standards)	521,531	505,883	491,256*

Excludes private primary schools

ATTENDANCE AT SECONDARY SCHOOLS:R.O.I.

Pupils by School Type	1992-93	1993-94	1994-95
Secondary Schools	221,167	224,035	225,490
Vocational Schools	92,003	94,760	94,907
Community Schools	35,959	39,487	41,541
Comprehensive Schools	9,218	9,363	9,292
TOTAL:	**358,347**	**367,645**	**371,230**

FULL-TIME ATTENDANCE AT HIGHER EDUCATION: REPUBLIC OF IRELAND AND NORTNERN IRELAND

R.O.I. Students by Type of Institution	1992-93	1993-94	1994-95
Colleges aided by Dept. of Education:			
H.E.A. Institutions	48,124	51,343	53,450
Teacher Training Colleges	728	450	503
Technological Colleges	32,198	34,673	35,475
Others (National College of Industrial Relations)	-	158	265
Colleges Aided by Depts. of Justice/Defence	-	612	873
Others (non-aided)	3,027	5,359	6,115
TOTAL:	**84,077**	**92,595**	**96,681**

N.I. Students by Type of Institution	1988-89	1991-92	1994-95
Further Education Colleges	**15,619**	**21,437**	**23,675**
Males	6,758	10,100	11,588
Females	8,861	11,337	12,087
Queen's University	**7,680**	**9,259**	**11,024**
Males	4,305	5,100	5,877
Females	3,375	4,159	5,147
University of Ulster	**8,296**	**9,986**	**12,573**
Males	3,900	4,459	5,515
Females	4,396	5,527	7,058
TOTAL:	**31,595**	**40,682**	**47,272**

STAGE AT WHICH LEAVERS WITH NO FORMAL QUALIFICATIONS LEFT SCHOOL: R.O.I. AND N.I.

REPUBLIC OF IRELAND: Grade (1995)	Male	Female	Total
Estimated Number in Category	1,400	800	2,200
First Year Post-primary	17.2 %	16.8 %	17.0 %
Second Year Post-primary	47.7 %	51.6 %	49.1 %
Third Year Post-primary	32.8 %	28.4 %	31.2 %
Other	2.3 %	3.2 %	2.7 %

N.I.: Persons with no GCSE/GCE Qualifications	1987-88	1991-92	1992-93	1993-94
Males with no GCSEs/GCEs	3,366	1,772	1,026	980
Females with no GCSEs/GCEs	1,869	976	595	490
Total with no GCSE/GCE qualifications	5,235	2,748	1,621	1,470
School leavers with no GCSEs/GCEs (%)	21.5 %	12.3 %	7.3 %	6.3 %

STATUS OF 2nd-LEVEL SCHOOL LEAVERS: R.O.I.,

Status (1995)	Male	Female	Total
Estimated Number in Category	34,400	33,100	67,500
Employed	43.6 %	37.0 %	40.4 %
Unemployed after loss of job	4.5 %	4.5 %	4.5 %
(of which on schemes)	(1.0 %)	(0.4 %)	(0.7 %)
Unemployed seeking first job	10.4 %	9.3 %	9.9 %
(of which on schemes)	(3.1 %)	(1.9 %)	(2.5 %)
Student (third level)	39.3 %	44.6 %	41.9 %
Unavailable for work	1.4 %	2.4 %	1.9 %
Emigrated	0.6 %	2.1 %	1.4 %
TOTAL:	**100 %**	**100 %**	**100 %**

FIRST DESTINATION OF SUB-DEGREE RESPONDENTS: REPUBLIC OF IRELAND, 1995

First Destination	Male	Female	Totals
Further Study:			
Ireland	1,824	1,356	3,180
Overseas	224	111	335
Work Experience - Ireland	66	81	147
Seeking Employment - Ireland	182	138	320
Not available - Ireland	39	32	71
Obtained Full-Time Employment:			
Ireland	1,166	1,041	2,207
Overseas	93	135	228
Obtained Part-Time Employment:			
Ireland	40	55	95
Overseas	4	8	12
TOTALS	3,638	2,957	6,595

NUMBERS OF SCHOOLS AND COLLEGES: R.O.I.

Type of School/College	1988-89	1991-92	1993-94	1994-5
First Level (aided by Dept. of Education)				
Primary Schools (mainstream)	3,247	3,235	3,202	3,203
Special Schools	117	117	115	116
Primary Schools (non-aided)	-	84	74	68
Total:	3,364	3,436	3,391	3,387
Second Level (aided by Dept of Education)				
Secondary Schools	498	478	461	452
Vocational Schools	251	248	248	247
Community and Comprehensive Schools	63	68	73	76
Other	-	2	2	2
Schools (aided by Dept.s of Agriculture/Defence)	-	17	17	17
Colleges (non-aided)	-	15	19	15
Total:	812	828	820	809
Third Level (aided by Dept. of Education)				
Universities	4	4	7	7
Other H.E.A. Colleges	2	2	3	3
Teacher Training Colleges	7	7	5	5
Regional Technical Colleges	20*	9	11	11
Other	-	-	4	4
Colleges (aided by other Dept.s)	-	1	2	2
Colleges (non-aided)	-	14	19	23
Total:	33	37	51	55

* includes all technology colleges

NUMBERS OF SCHOOLS AND COLLEGES: N.I.

Type of School/College	1988-89	1991-92	1993-94	1994-5	1995-96
First Level:					
Nursery Schools	85	88	89	91	91
Primary Schools	978	957	938	923	n/a
Special Schools	46	46	46	47	47
Total:	1,106	1,091	1,073	1,061	138*
Second Level:					
Secondary	174	166	161	161	165
Grammar:					
Preparatory	26	26	25	25	25
Secondary	45	44	46	46	46
Total:	245	236	232	232	236

* This figure does not include primary schools.

NUMBERS OF PRIMARY SCHOOL TEACHERS

Republic of Ireland	1988-89	1991-92	1993-94	1994-95
Total Primary Teachers	20362	20,708	20,776	20,901

Northern Ireland	1988-89	1991-92	1993-94	1994-95
Nursery	153	162	164	168
Primary	7854	8044	8396	8658
Special	536	609	637	646

NUMBERS OF SECOND-LEVEL TEACHERS: R.O.I.

Personnel	1988-89	1991-92	1993-94	1994-95
Secondary Schools	-	12,034	12,784	13,073
Full-time	-	11,895	12,514	12,635
Part-time	-	139	270	438
Vocational Schools	-	6,383	6,542	6,296
Full-time	-	4,912	5,126	5,186
Part-time	-	1,471	1,416	1,110
Community and Comprehensive Schools	-	2,621	3,131	3,216
Full-time	-	2,458	2,477	2,819
Part-time	-	144	416	397
Total	18,902*	21,038	22,457	22,585

*This total includes full-time teachers only.

NUMBERS OF SECOND-LEVEL TEACHERS: N.I.

Personnel	1988-89	1991-92	1993-94	1994-95
Secondary Schools	6,308	5,965	6,090	6,308
Grammar Schools:				
Preparatory	156	116	113	169
Secondary	3,266	3,354	3,615	3,694
Total*	9,730	9,435	9,818[†]	10,171

* These figures do not include full-time teachers in hospital schools.   † This total includes seconded teachers.

NUMBERS EMPLOYED IN THIRD-LEVEL EDUCATION

REPUBLIC OF IRELAND (Full-time)

Instructor Grade	R.T.C.'s	1993-94 Other	Total	R.T.C.'s	1994-95 Other	Total
TOTAL	1,562	693	2,255	1,640	707	2,347
College Teacher	82	44	126	89	40	129
Lecturer Scale I	843	308	1,151	911	334	1,245
Lecturer Scale II	509	262	771	516	251	767
Senior Lecturer Scale I	72	50	122	68	52	120
Senior Lecturer Scale II	43	22	65	43	23	66
Principal	13	5	19	13	6	19
Others	-	1	1	-	1	1

NORTHERN IRELAND (Full-time)

Instructor Grade	1988-89	1991-92	1993-4	1994-95	1995-96
Further Education Teachers	2,448	2,304	2,209	2,171	-
Universities	1,775	1,930	2,037	2,314	2,376
Professors	162	186	216	246	249
Readers & Senior Lecturers	467	495	525	527	468
Lecturers, Assistant Lecturers, Demonstrators and Others	1,146	1,249	1,296	1,541	1,659

UNIVERSITIES IN IRELAND, NORTH AND SOUTH

REPUBLIC OF IRELAND
Constituent Colleges,
National University of Ireland,
(49 Merrion Square, Dublin. 01 - 6767246)

National University of Ireland, Cork. (021) 903000. *Founded in 1854.*
National University of Ireland, Dublin, Belfield, Dublin 4. (01) 2693244. *Founded in 1845.*
National University of Ireland, Galway, Galway. (091) 24411. *Founded in 1845*
National University of Ireland, Maynooth, Co. Kildare. (01) 6285222. *Founded in 1795.*

Recognised Colleges
University of Dublin, Trinity College, Dublin 2. (01) 6772941. *Founded in 1592.*
Dublin City University, Glasnevin, Dublin 9. (01) 7045000. *Founded in 1980.*

University of Limerick, Plassey Technological Park, Limerick. (061) 333644. *Founded in 1972.*

NORTHERN IRELAND

Queen's University of Belfast, Belfast, BT7 1NN. (01232) 245133. *Founded in 1845.*
University of Ulster, University House, Cromore Rd., Coleraine, Co. Derry BT52 1SA. (01265) 44141. *Founded in 1968.*
University of Ulster (at Jordanstown), Shore Rd., Newtownabbey, Co. Antrim BT37 0QB. (01232) 365131. *Founded in 1968.*
University of Ulster (Magee College), Northland Rd., Derry BT48 7JL. (01504) 265621.
University of Ulster (at Belfast), York St., Belfast BT15 1ED. (01232) 328515. *Founded in 1968.*

FULL-TIME HIGHER EDUCATION STUDENT NUMBERS: REPUBLIC OF IRELAND

Institution	1986-87	1989-90	1990-91	1991-92	1992-93
University College Dublin	9,339	10,429	10,706	12,083	13,099
University College Cork	5,560	6,393	6,777	7,451	8,234
University College Galway	4,298	4,377	4,913	5,312	5,756
Trinity College Dublin	6,555	7,165	7,625	8,043	8,361
St. Patrick's College, Maynooth	1,520	1,877	2,224	2,571	2,990
Dublin City University	2,090	2,607	2,679	2,921	3,243
University of Limerick	2,484	3,084	3,425	4,251	5,076
National College of Art & Design	531	610	636	624	651
Thomond College of Education	656	494	391	0	0
Royal College of Surgeons in Ireland	863	885	893	904	933
TOTALS	**33,896**	**37,921**	**40,269**	**44,160**	**48,343**

FULL-TIME HIGHER EDUCATION STUDENT NUMBERS: NORTHERN IRELAND

Students	1984-85	1994-95	1995-96	1996-97
University of Ulster Full-time	7,458	12,544	13,548	13,043
University of Ulster Part-time	3,724	6,054	6,494	6,568
Totals	11,182	18,598	20,042	19,611
Queen's University Full-time	-	-	4719	-
Queen's University Part-time	-	-	1085	-
Total	-	-	5804	-

Total Students by Faculty (1996-97)	Full-Time	Part-Time	Total
Faculty:			
Art and Design	906	41	947
Business and Management	3,000	2,189	5,189
Engineering	1,895	420	2,315
Humanities	1,685	223	1,908
Informatics	1,275	451	1,726
Science	1,664	228	1,892
Social Health Services & Education	2,671	2,325	4,996
Ulster Business School	49	665	714
Total:	**13,145**	**6,542**	**19,687**

HIGHER EDUCATION STUDENTS BY FIELD OF STUDY

REPUBLIC OF IRELAND (1992-93)*

Field of Study	Full-Time	Part-Time
Agricultural Science & Forestry	798	12
Architecture	260	7
Art & Design	602	1
Arts	14,323	1,726
Business, Economics & Social Studies	1,176	246
Combined Studies	432	1
Commerce	6,513	1,952
Communications & Information Studies	977	52
Dentistry	451	14
Education	2,031	587
Engineering	5,605	1,299
Equestrian Studies	34	-
European Studies	964	109
Food Science & Technology	475	2
Law	1,301	280
Medicine	3,843	360
Science	7,468	310
Social Science	743	51
Veterinary Medicine	347	6
TOTAL	**48,343**	**6,988**

These figures include undergraduates and post-graduates.

NORTHERN IRELAND (1995-96)*

Field of Study	Full-Time	Part-Time
Agriculture & Related Subjects	237	48
Architecture, Building & Planning	1,092	449
Biological Sciences	2,045	105
Business & Administrative Studies	4,299	3,135
Combined Subjects	2,548	547
Computer Science	1,401	107
Creative Arts & Design	1,224	126
Education	1,627	79
Engineering & Technology	2,526	671
Humanities	853	524
Languages	1,131	1,378
Law	492	63
Librarianship & Information Science	415	18
Mathematical Sciences	747	260
Medicine & Dentistry	927	18
Medicine-related Subjects	1,733	771
Physical Sciences	1,164	187
Social, Economic & Political Studies	1,834	1,665
TOTAL	**26,295**	**10,151**

These figures include undergraduates only.

QUALIFICATIONS OF SCHOOL LEAVERS

REPUBLIC OF IRELAND (1995)

Examination	Female	Male	Total
Junior Certificate Total*	33,733	34,352	68,085
Leaving Certificate*	31,970	30,043	62,013
Candidates sitting at least 5 subjects	31,402	29,566	60,968
Candidates with ≥ 5 Grade D3s at any level	28,402	25,369	53,771
Candidates with ≥ 2 Grade C3s or higher on higher papers	16,760	13,727	30,487
Candidates with ≥ 4 Grade C3s or higher on higher papers	10,778	7,646	18,424
Candidates with ≥ 6 Grade C3s or higher on higher papers	5,050	3,388	8,438
Candidates with ≥ 3 Grade B3s or higher on higher papers†	4,106	2,811	6,917

Candidates with ≥ 3 Grade A2s or higher on higher papers†		930	691	1,621
External Candidates		2,461	1,831	4,292
TOTAL		**34,431**	**31,874**	**66,305**

* These totals include candidates who participated in the Vocational Training Opportunities Scheme.

† These figures cover candidates who received a minimum of 6 Grade C3s on higher papers.

PERCENTAGE LEAVING CERTIFICATE GRADE AS BY SUBJECT

Subject	1987	1997
Irish	1.7%	6.8%
English	2.4%	5.2%
Maths	5.0%	15.5%

NORTHERN IRELAND

Examination	1987-88	1991-92	1992-93	1993-94	1994-95
Males:	**12,658**	**12,034**	**11,320**	**11,955**	**12,543**
Candidates with ≥2 'A' levels	2,566	3,051	3,023	3,150	3,288
Candidates with 1 'A' level	390	321	318	339	314
Candidates with ≥ 5 GCSE higher grades	1,150	1,417	1,459	1,652	2,133
Candidates with 1-4 GCSE higher grades	2,573	3,146	3,255	3,356	3,095
Candidates with low grades	2,613	2,327	2,239	2,478	2,767
Those with no GCSE/GCE qualifications	3,366	1,772	1,026	980	946
Females:	**11,730**	**11,447**	**10,996**	**11,400**	**11900**
Candidates with ≥2 'A' levels	2,897	3,760	3,778	3,943	4,262
Candidates with 1 'A' level	481	431	397	410	344
Candidates with ≥ 5 GCSE higher grades	1,430	1,716	1,867	1,950	2,629
Candidates with 1-4 GCSE higher grades	3,026	2,943	2,829	3,006	2,676
Candidates with low grades	2,027	1,621	1,530	1,601	1,670
Those with no GCSE/GCE qualifications	1,869	976	595	490	409
All School leavers:	**24,388**	**22,326**	**22,316**	**23,355**	**24,533**
Candidates with ≥2 'A' levels	5,463	6,811	6,801	7,093	7,550
Candidates with 1 'A' level	871	752	715	749	658
Candidates with ≥ 5 GCSE higher grades	2,580	3,133	3,326	3,602	4,762
Candidates with 1-4 GCSE higher grades	5,599	6,089	6,084	6,362	5,771
Candidates with low grades	4,640	3,948	3,769	4,079	4,437
Those with no GCSE/GCE qualifications	5,235	2,748	1,621	1,470	1,355

EXAMINATION PERFORMANCE RATES: COMPARISONS WITH ENGLAND AND WALES, 1994-95

Region	≥ 5 GCSEs (Grade A-C)	≥ 2 A levels
Northern Ireland	51%	87%
England	44%	77%
Wales	41%	76%

UNIVERSITY DEGREES AND DIPLOMAS OBTAINED

REPUBLIC OF IRELAND

Award	1994	1995
Primary Degrees	11,051	11,907
Higher Degrees	2,510	2,550
Certificates & Diplomas	9,928	10,619
Higher Diplomas in Education	1,006	814
Primary Degrees in Education	422	504
TOTAL	**24,917**	**26,394**

NORTHERN IRELAND

Award	1993-1994	1994-1995
First Degrees (Honours)	4,013	4,809
First Degrees (Ordinary)	406	546
Higher Degrees	1,548	1,346
Diplomas, Certs & Other Qualifications	2,929	3,339
TOTAL	**8,896**	**10,040**

NUMBERS INVOLVED IN HIGH-TECH EDUCATION

REPUBLIC OF IRELAND *(includes students at UCD, UCC, UCG, Maynooth, Trinity College, DCU, UL)*				
Subject Category (Student Numbers)	**1986-87**	**1990-91**	**1995-96**	**% Change 86/7 - 95/6**
Computer Science	-	-	2,887	-
Information Technology	-	-	752	-
Biosciences (Biotechnology, Genetics, Food Sciences)	250	345	1,402	460.0
Engineering	4,431	5,002	4,461	0.6
Physics/Maths	-	-	632	-
Other Science	6,183	7,184	7,712	24.7
TOTAL	**10,864**	**12,531**	**17,846**	**64.2**

NORTHERN IRELAND *(includes universities and further education colleges)*				
Subject	**1985-86**	**1990-91**	**1993-94**	**% Change 85/6 - 93/4**
Biosciences	**748**	**1,258**	**1,815**	**142.6**
Males	322	450	602	87.0
Females	426	808	1,213	184.7
Maths & Computing	**825**	**1,293**	**1,866**	**126.2**
Males	543	888	1,279	135.5
Females	282	405	587	108.2
Mass Communication	**166**	**315**	**386**	**132.5**
Males	36	109	175	386
Females	130	206	211	62.3

REPUBLIC OF IRELAND GRADUATES' DESTINATION

FIRST DESTINATION OF REPUBLIC OF IRELAND GRADUATES			
Destination (%)	**1993**	**1994**	**1995**
Work Experience	2.5	3.1	2.6
Seeking Employment	9.9	7.0	6.4
Employed in Ireland	65.6	64.1	69.5
Agriculture, Forestry & Fishery Sectors	0.8	1.0	0.9
Manufacturing & Other Non-service Sectors	26.5	25.5	26.8
Public Services	29.8	27.2	24.4
Private Services	41.7	45.3	47.2
Gained Employment Overseas	22.0	25.8	21.5

DISTRIBUTION OF GRADUATES IN EMPLOYMENT OVERSEAS IN 1995	
Country	**Degree Holders**
Britain	583
Other E.U. Member States	387
Non-E.U. European Countries	34
U.S. & Canada	266
South America	9
Africa	33
Australia & New Zealand	81
Middle East	47
Far East	78
Other	79

CHANGES TO THE EDUCATIONAL SYSTEMS

REPUBLIC OF IRELAND The most important changes to the educational system in the Republic of Ireland centre around two recent pieces of legislation; namely, the Universities Bill, 1996, dealing with the structure of higher education, and the Education Bill, 1997, dealing with general education. The Universities Bill was enacted on June 13, 1997, while the Education Bill is still pending enactment.

The Universities Act puts in place statutory provisions regarding accountability structures; universities' governing authorities, outlining who has the right to be part of the highest policy and decision-making body of each university; budgeting powers, whereby each university must agree its budget with the Higher Education Authority; staff selection procedures; staff pay, allowances and pensions; and academic freedom and institutional autonomy.

The Education Bill attempts to define the rights, roles and responsibilities of all the partners in education and to ensure that all constituencies are represented on education boards and school management bodies. Up to now schools in Ireland had a high degree of autonomy regarding curricula (within the constraints proscribed by the

Junior and Leaving Certificate examinations), decisions on textbooks, pupil-entry criteria, school ethos and suspensions and expulsions. The Education Bill also provides for the formal recognition of a core curriculum and for a more important role for the school inspectorate. It will now have powers regarding the formulation and development of national education policies. At regional level, each school will have an inspector who will act in an advisory and supportive role. One of the most controversial elements of the bill is the statement that "where the decision of a teacher or a school materially affects the education of a student, then a parent or a student over 16 years can appeal." Teachers believe that this will bring about a situation where schools will have to waste time on countless petty appeals each year. At the moment, they have little recourse to disciplinary measures, save suspensions or expulsions, and fear that these appeals may undermine the discipline ethos of schools.

Ideally, teachers would like to see an amendment in the bill that deals with discipline which they feel is a real and growing problem. The teachers' unions have suggested incorporating an amendment that would provide for "temporary withdrawal units and tuition centres for severely disruptive and/or disturbed pupils."

NORTHERN IRELAND Whereas the Republic of Ireland is facing dramatic changes in its educational system, Northern Ireland's educational system has undergone a huge sea change in recent years, arising from the 1988 Education Act, introducing the National Curriculum in Britain, and the Dearing report that amended this curriculum. The Act was proposed and formulated by the Conservative government of the 1980s and introduced long overdue changes, as well as controversial elements, to the educational system.

The changes not only dealt with curriculum but also with the structuring and funding of the educational system. Many teachers and parents expressed unhappiness with the direction of some of these changes and, after intensive pressure, the Conservative government undertook a review of the national curriculum, which was headed by Sir Ronald Dearing. His amendments lessened the number of objectives outlined in the curriculum and broadened teachers' scope. Inevitably, teacher morale was dampened by the whole process during which the government, by and large, failed to consult either teachers or parents. The government agreed to call a five-year moratorium on further changes. However, since the election of a Labour government in 1997, the continuation of this moratorium is now in question.

The Act affected England and Wales to a greater extent than Northern Ireland which was allowed to retain certain features of the old system, such as the '11 plus' - the entrance examination that allows certain secondary schools to apply selective procedures to their pupil intake. Students in Northern Ireland study the slightly different Common Curriculum which includes two unique and compulsory cross-curricular themes - Cultural Heritage and Education for Mutual Understanding. Nonetheless, Northern Ireland, along with England and Wales, must comply with certain controversial education practices, such as the publication of league tables which rank schools according to exam results. This exercise is, at best, unreliable as it fails to account for socio-economic and political variables.

In the higher education sector, a change that will have dramatic and possibly drastic effects is the introduction of fees by, paradoxically, the Labour government. Other changes that have been introduced to the higher education sector include the implementation of qualitative assessment, whereby universities are graded on the quality of their departments. Again, as with the general education system, Sir Ronald Dearing was called on to conduct a review of the higher education system, prior to the 1997 British General Election. His report on higher education has been published, but as yet, there has been no official government response.

Two initiatives that are gaining momentum in Northern Ireland are the establishment of integrated schools, where Catholics and Protestants are educated together, and the establishment of *gael scoileanna*, where pupils are taught through the medium of the Irish language. Several integrated schools have opened for the 1997-98 academic year and were set up without government funding - their establishment reflecting the aspirations and support of the local populace. There are currently 37 integrated schools in Northern Ireland with a pupil enrolment of 8,500. The *gael scoileanna* scene is thriving, particularly in Belfast and Derry, and parallels the growing interest in the Republic of Ireland in educating children through Irish. The government funds three Irish medium primary schools and two units with an enrolment of 700 pupils. In total, there are 34 Irish medium preschool through second-level schools in Northern Ireland, with an estimated enrolment of 1,784 students.

CULTURE

The Irish Language in the Republic of Ireland

by Gael Linn

I RISH was introduced to Ireland by the Celts who came to the country in successive waves from about 60 B.C. to the time of Christ. Linguistically, the Celts, who spoke Irish, belonged to the Indo-European family of languages.

The history of language contact in Ireland is closely related to the political, social and economic interaction between the island and its nearest and more powerful neighbour, England. Even as late as the 16th century the Irish language was the sole or main language used in Ireland and the English monarchy had established only a modest and tentative foothold in eastern Ireland.

But the political changes which began in the 17th century dispossessed the Irish aristocratic families and introduced relatively large numbers of native-born English to form a new landlord class. Over the 18th century, the shift to English spread through the urban network, diffusing more slowly but relentlessly into the rural hinterland along a general east-west axis. It has been calculated that about 45 per cent of the population were Irish-speaking during the last quarter of the 18th century, but this percentage had declined to just under 30% by the mid-19th century.

As the linguistic shift to English entered an advanced phase, a movement for the preservation of Irish emerged. Despite the well-established dynamic of decline and the unpromising contemporary pattern of bilingualism - no more than 18% of the population were Irish-speakers - the newly independent Irish state in 1922 launched a comprehensive strategy to reverse the process of shift towards English and restore Irish as the national language.

In 1991, some 1,095,830 persons (32% of the national population) were returned as Irish-speakers in the Census of Population. The ratio of Irish-speakers, as measured in the census, had increased steadily throughout the 20th century from 18% in 1911. National percentages, however, hide important regional variations. The designated Irish-speaking areas on the west coast (collectively referred to as the Gaeltacht) contain only 2.3 per cent of the national population, but 45% of Irish-speaking homes.

Recent surveys would suggest that only about 5 per cent of the national population use Irish as their first or main language. A further 10 per cent use Irish regularly but less intensively in conversation and reading. In the state generally, these levels would appear to have remained stable over recent decades.

In the Gaeltacht, where Irish has never ceased to be spoken, its use is very much higher than the national average. For example, in 1973, which is the last year in which a survey was conducted in all Gaeltacht areas, frequent and extensive home use of Irish was reported by about 60 per cent of respondents (as compared to 5 per cent nationally) and differences in work and social contexts are of the same order.

While the current socio-economic status of the residents of the Gaeltacht areas reflects small farm and village occupations, in the urban areas Irish is now more likely to be used among higher socio-economic groups, particularly, but not solely in the public sector. There is also a strong relationship between the use of Irish and educational attainment. In survey data, there is a marked association between those with high levels of ability in Irish and those reporting intensive use of Irish. But in turn, high levels of competence in Irish are associated with levels of education and not with the home. Therefore, bilingualism is more prevalent among the more highly educated groups.

The 1937 constitution gives recognition to two languages, Irish and English, but declares the minority language, Irish, as the first official language. Theoretically, Irish has full legal standing in all courts, but in practice most of the business of the courts is conducted in English. Anyone appearing in court has the right to use either of the two national languages, Irish and English.

Public sector employment had, in the past, been of great importance to the survival of Irish. As recruitment to the state sector, until the early seventies, required a good competence in Irish, it followed that it was this sector of the middle-class that was most likely to be supportive of Irish. In fact some 60 per cent of persons with a fluent competence in Irish are found in the middle and working class, dependent on state employment. However, among the public sector factions themselves there are differences, with the upper middle and the working class factions having the largest and the smallest proportion of competent bilinguals, respectively.

The use of Irish in street and road signs is almost universal, although usually in a bilingual format. The use of Irish in standard official forms and documents is more limited and variable. Although television and, to a lesser extent, radio programmes in Irish attract a significant audience among Irish-speakers, the average Irish language output from the main state radio and television stations in the late 1980s was, with one exception, under 5 per cent of total output.The position of Irish language programming on the four national radio stations is different in only one case. In 1972 a radio station (*Raidió na Gaeltachta*) was set up to service the Irish-speaking areas along the west coast. This station broadcasts entirely in Irish.

There are no daily newspapers in Irish, but one of the main English language dailies carries regular columns in Irish. There are two weekly newspapers in Irish and a number of monthly journals, all with fairly small readerships.

In 1990, about 80 books were published in Irish; in 1991, about 90; and about 100 in 1992. Irish traditional music has a large following, and the Irish language is used quite a lot in concerts and folk sessions. There is a reasonably large corpus of recorded Irish language songs available on cassette and CD.

Irish language productions in theatre or cinema are limited. There are two well-supported festivals associated with the Irish language - Slógadh (for schools and youth) and Oireachtas na Gaelige.

The teaching of Irish was made compulsory throughout the education system in the 1920s, the ultimate objective being to have all educational programmes taught through Irish. Subsequently, however, this pattern slowly yielded to the type of programme in which Irish was generally only taught through English. Furthermore, although the proportions of children receiving post-primary education increased rapidly in the period since 1960, the effect of this on acquisition of proficiency in Irish was countered by the discontinuation of the policy of making Irish a compulsory subject for state examinations in 1973. Only one university college (Galway) provides a limited number of primary degree courses through Irish.

THE GAELTACHT - IRISH-SPEAKING AREAS

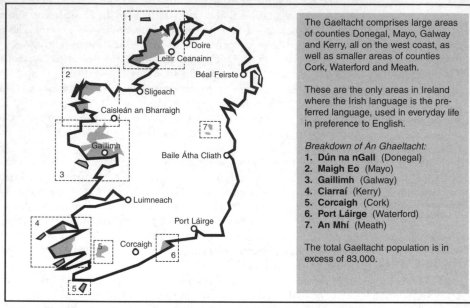

The Gaeltacht comprises large areas of counties Donegal, Mayo, Galway and Kerry, all on the west coast, as well as smaller areas of counties Cork, Waterford and Meath.

These are the only areas in Ireland where the Irish language is the preferred language, used in everyday life in preference to English.

Breakdown of An Ghaeltacht:
1. **Dún na nGall** (Donegal)
2. **Maigh Eo** (Mayo)
3. **Gaillimh** (Galway)
4. **Ciarraí** (Kerry)
5. **Corcaigh** (Cork)
6. **Port Láirge** (Waterford)
7. **An Mhí** (Meath)

The total Gaeltacht population is in excess of 83,000.

GLOSSARY OF MOST COMMONLY USED IRISH WORDS

Ábhar	Subject
Aerfort	Airport
Agallamh	Interview, dialogue
Ailéar	Gallery
Aimsir	Weather, Time
Aire	Government Minister
Airgead	Money
Aistriú	Translation
Áitiúil	Local
Amharclann	Theatre
Anuraidh	Last Year
Árachas	Insurance
Ard-Aighne	Attorney-General
Ardeaglais	Cathedral
Ardeaspag	Archbishop
Ardmhéara	Lord Major
Ard-Rí	High King
Athair	Father
Bád	Boat
Bagáiste	Luggage
Baile	Home, Town
Bainisteoir	Manager
Banaltra	Nurse
Banc	Bank
Banc Ceannais	Central Bank
Bardas	Corporation
Bata, Bachall	Staff
Bealoideas	Folklore

Bean	Woman
Béarla	English *(language)*
Beart	Package
Beoir	Beer
Bia	Food
Bliain	Year
Bórd	Board
Breitheamh	Judge
Buidéal	Bottle
Bunreacht na hÉireann	Irish Constitution
Caidreamh	Association, links
Cáin	Tax
Cairdeas	Friendship
Cathair	City
Cathaoirleach	Chairman
Ceann Comhairle	Speaker (in Dáil Éireann)
Ceannoifig	Head Office
Ceantar	District
Céim	Degree/ step
Ceird	Trade
Ceist	Question
Ceol	Music
Ceolann	Orchestra
Ceolchoirm	Concert
Cigire	Inspector
Cladach	Beach

Clann	Family
Clár Ama	Time-table
Clé	Left
Cléireach	Clerk / cleric
Coimisiún	Commission
Coisí	Pedestrian
Coitiantacht	General Public
Coláiste	College
Comhairle	Council
Comhaltas	Membership
Comhluadar	Company
Comhrá, Caint	Conversation
Conradh	League/ contract
Contae	County
Córas	System
Creideamh	Faith/ belief
Cruinniú	Meeting
Cuairteoir	Visitor
Cúige	Province
Cúirt	Court
Cumann	Society/ club
Cumann Lúthchleas Gael	GAA
Cumarsáid	Communication
Cuntasóir	Accountant
Cúrsaí	Matters/ affairs
Dáil Éireann	Irish Parliament
Dáilcheantar	Constituency
Damhsa	Dance

Daoine, Muintir	People
Daonlathas	Democracy
Daonra	Population
Déagóir	Teenager
Déantóir	Manufacturer
Deoch	Drink
Dífhostaíocht	Unemployment
Dlíodóir	Lawyer
Dochtúir	Doctor
Dráma	Play, drama
Drámaíocht	Dramatic art
Eacnamaíocht	Economics
Éadaí	Clothes
Eagarthóir	Editor
Eaglais	Church
Eagraíocht	Organisation
Ealaín	Art
Earra	Merchandise
Easpag	Bishop
Eitleán	Aeroplane
Eolaí	Directory
Eolaíocht	Science
Eolas	Knowledge
Fáilte	Welcome
Feirm	Farm
Fear	Man
Fiaclóir	Dentist
Fiafraí	Inquiry
Fios	Information
Focal	Word
Foclóir	Dictionary, Vocabulary
Fógra	Notice
Foilseachán	Publication
Folúntas	Vacancy
Foras	Institute
Forbairt	Development
Fostaíocht	Employment
Fostóir	Employer
Freastalaí	Waiter
Fuinneamh	Energy
Gaeilge	Irish Language
Gaeltacht	Irish-Speaking Area
Gairm	Profession
Gall	Foreigner
Gárda Síochána	Policeman
Glic	Clever
Gluaisteán	Car
Gnáthamh	Practice
Gnólacht	Business Firm
Grianghraf	Photograph
Gruagaire	Hairdresser
Halla Baile	Town Hall

Iarnród	Railway
Iascaireacht	Fishing
Idirnáisiúnta	International
Imirce	Emigration
Innealtóir	Engineer
Iomaíocht	Competition
Iompar	Transport
Ionadaí	Representative
Iriseoir	Journalist
Lá	Day
Lamh	Hand
Leabhar	Book
Leabharlann	Library
Léachtóir	Lecturer
Leas	Welfare
Lelctreachas	Electricity
Leithreas	Toilet
Litir	Letter
Litríocht	Literature
Mainistir	Monastry
Mála	Bag
Margadh	Market
Máthair	Mother
Meáchan	Weight
Mná	Women
Móin (móna)	Turf
Mór	Important, Big
Múinteoir	Teacher
Náisiún	Nation
Náisiúnta	National
Nuacht	News
Nuachtán	Newspaper
Obair	Work
Oideachas	Education
Oifig an Phoist	Post Office
Oiliúint	Training
Oireachtas	Assembly, Dáil Éireann & Seanad Éireann
Oirmhinneach	Reverend
Ollamh	Professor
Ollscoil	University
Ospidéal/Otharlann	Hospital
Otharcharr	Ambulance
Páirc	Field/ park
Pas Taistil	Passport
Peil	Football
Pictiúirlann	Cinema
Pingin	Penny
Pobal	Public
Poblacht	Republic
Poitigéir	Chemist

Polaiteoir	Politician
Polaitíocht	Politics
Príosún	Prison
Punt	Pound
Radharc	View/ Scenery
Raidio	Radio
Reacht	Statute, Law
Reifreann	Referendum
Rialtas	Government
Roinn	Department
Rothar	Bicycle
Sagart	Priest
Saibhreas	Wealth
Saoirse	Freedom
Saoránach	Citizen
Scannán	Film
Scoil	School
Seanad	Senate
Seanadóir	Senator
Seirbhís	Service
Síocháin	Peace
Siopa Poitigéara	Pharmacy
Sláinte	Health
Sloinne	Surname
Sráid	Street
Sráidbhaile	Village
Stair	History
Staidéar	Study
Stát	State
Stiúrthóir	Director
Suaimhneas	Peace
Taidhleoir	Diplomat
Taisteal	Travel
Talmhaíocht	Agriculture
Talamh (talún)	Land
Tánaiste	Deputy Prime Minister
Taoiseach	Leader, Prime Minister
Teachta Dála	Member of Parliament
Teach Ósta	Hotel, Hostel
Teach Tabhairne	Public-House
Teanga	Language
Teileafón	Telephone
Teilifís	Television
Teoranta	Limited
Ticéad	Ticket
Timpiste	Accident
Tionónta	Tenant
Tionscal	Industry
Tír	Country
Timpeallacht	Environment
Tíreolaíocht	Geography
Tobac	Tobacco

Toghchán	Election	Tuarascáil	Report	Uimhir	Number
Traenáil	Training	Turasóireacht	Tourism	Urlabhraí	Speaker, Spokesman
Treo	Direction	Turas	Journey	Úrscéalaí	Novelist
Tuairisc	Statement			Úsáideach	Useful
Tuairisceoir	Reporter	Uachtarán	President		

IRISH SPEAKERS AND NON-IRISH SPEAKERS IN EACH PROVINCE 1991

Year	Total Irish	Total Non-Irish	Leinster Irish	Leinster Non-Irish	Munster Irish	Munster Non-Irish	Connacht Irish	Connacht Non-Irish	Ulster* (part of) Irish	Ulster* (part of) Non-Irish
Population of all ages										
1861	1,077,087	3,325,024	35,704	1,421,931	545,531	968,027	409,482	503,653	86,370	431,413
1871	804,547	3,248,640	16,247	1,323,204	386,494	1,006,991	330,211	516,002	71,595	402,443
1881	924,781	2,945,239	27,452	1,251,537	445,766	885,349	366,191	455,466	85,372	352,887
1891	664,387	2,804,307	13,677	1,174,083	307,633	864,769	274,783	449,991	68,294	315,464
1901	619,710	2,602,113	26,436	1,126,393	276,268	799,920	245,580	401,352	71,426	274,448
1911	553,717	2,585,971	40,225	1,121,819	228,694	806,801	217,087	393,897	67,771	263,454
1926	543,511	2,428,481	101,474	1,047,618	198,221	771,681	175,209	377,698	68,607	231,484
Population 3 yrs. plus										
1926	540,802	2,261,650	101,102	978,536	197,625	718,068	174,234	348,964	67,841	216,082
1936	666,601	2,140,324	183,378	966,434	224,805	668,030	183,082	315,322	75,336	190,538
1946	588,725	2,182,932	180,755	1,017,491	189,395	672,660	154,187	309,638	64,388	183,143
1961	716,420	1,919,398	274,644	964,383	228,726	576,613	148,708	246,592	64,342	140,810
1971	789,429	1,998,019	341,702	1,055,160	252,805	573,308	137,372	231,960	57,550	137,591
1981	1,018,413	2,208,054	473,225	1,202,292	323,704	612,526	155,134	244,264	66,350	148,972
1986	1,042,701	2,310,931	480,227	1,274,353	337,043	630,434	158,386	250,474	67,045	155,670
1991	1,095,830	2,271,176	511,639	1,264,188	352,177	612,988	162,680	242,091	69,334	151,909

This refers to Counties Cavan, Donegal and Monaghan. According to the 1991 Census, 142,003 people over the age of three - approximately 10 per cent of Northern Ireland's population - claim to have some knowledge of Irish. This brings the total number of people with some knowledge of Irish in Ulster as a whole to 293,912.

FREQUENCY AND COMPREHENSION OF THE IRISH LANGUAGE

	Ability to Speak Irish		Ability to Understand Irish	
	Dec. 1993	Dec. 1994	Dec. 1993	Dec. 1994
Little - None	67%	68%	58%	61%
Moderate - Good	28%	26%	35%	32%
Fluent - Very Good	5%	5%	7%	7%
Total	**100%**	**100%**	**100%**	**100%**

FREQUENCY OF SPEAKING AND LISTENING TO IRISH

	Speech		Listenership	
	Dec. 1993	Dec. 1994	Dec. 1993	Dec. 1994
Never	64%	59%	61%	58%
Less often than once a month	17%	20%	!8%	21%
Once a month	4%	4%	4%	4%
Once a week	4%	5%	6%	6%
Daily or several times a week	11%	!2%	11%	11%
Total	**100%**	**100%**	**100%**	**100%**

ATTITUDES TO IRISH

Opinion on Irish Language and its Heritage		
	Dec 1993	Dec 1994
The Irish Language is part of: Our history and past	49%	38%
Our culture	61%	50%
Don't know	1%	1%
Total	**100%**	**100%**

MEDIA

Present Perception of Irish Usage in Advertising		
	Dec 1993	Dec 1994
Irish is being used to a: Greater extent	33%	25%
Much the same extent	27%	27%
Lesser extent	24%	28%
No opinion	16%	20%
Total	**100%**	**100%**

IRISH SPEAKERS IN GAELTACHT AREAS

County	1981	1986	1991
Cork	2,681	2,846	2,686
Donegal	19,209	18,823	17,574
Galway	19,819	20,873	21,533
Kerry	6,264	6,142	5,945
Mayo	8,457	8,071	7,096
Meath	493	602	600
Waterford	1,103	1,094	1,035
Total Gaeltacht Areas:	**58,026**	**58,451**	**56,469**

THE HISTORY OF IRISH DANCE

The history of a living art like dancing is very hard to chronicle - there are almost no references to dancing in old Irish literature. One could infer that dancing did not exist in old Ireland. However, given the fact that nearly all of this literature was scribed mostly by monks, this assumption is more than likely false.

The first reference to Irish Dancing was made in a report by an English visitor, Sir Henry Sydney, on observing the Rínce Fada in 1569, and Scotsman Arthur Young, a noted social historian of his day, made the first reference to Irish solo dancing in 1776. The Set Dance became the most important development in the art of Irish solo step dancing in the late 18th and early 19th century. Nowadays, most associate set dancing with a group of dancers rather than a solo performer, and this form of dancing has enjoyed a huge revival in recent years. However, the solo-dance set dance predates the latter use of the term and was set to a specific tune. The most renowned solo set dance was possibly *The Blackbird*, the title of which was apparently an allusion to Bonnie Prince Charlie. This is accepted as the oldest surviving example, and it, along with the *St. Patrick's Day* dance, is regarded as the benchmark against which all modern derivatives are measured.

The popular group set-dancing tradition grew from dances such as Quadrilles and Lancers, mainly learned and brought to Ireland in the 19th century by Irishmen active in European armies. These dances, performed mainly in rural areas, were hugely popular, but were despised by the Catholic clergy of the day who eventually succeeded in having them stopped. The next notable event in Irish dancing was the establishment of the *Feis* by the the Gaelic League (which was founded in 1893). The league organised competitions in all areas of Irish culture, including step dancing and later the Céilí, where only Irish traditional group dances would be danced. The word Céilí eventually came to be used to describe the actual dance occasions themselves.

The Gaelic League set up the Irish dancing movement - An Coimisiún Le Ríncí Gaelacha - in 1929. It was to organise and develop the practice of Irish dancing, create and set standards for Feiseanna, and preserve and promote its activity as an international organisation. The first handbooks detailing the movements of ten Céilí dances were published in 1939.

Irish dancing was not confined to the shores of Ireland. Irish natives who emigrated and settled in the U.S., Australia, Canada, England, New Zealand and Scotland brought their culture with them. In the U.S., Irish dancing was blended with other dance forms, evolving into Appalachian Clog Dancing and the well-known American Square Dancing and, in time, influencing the art of American stage dancing. The London Feis, founded in 1907, established the Céilí as an entertainment form for the Irish in Britain, while Scottish Highland dancing was mixed with, and complemented the development of, Irish dancing.

The popularity of Irish dancing around the globe was such that the World Irish Dancing Championships were established in 1969 under the official title of Oireachtas Rínce na Cruinne, as were the the All Ireland Dancing Championships - Oireachtas Rínce Na hÉireann. These events have continued to expand each year and have subsequently improved the standard of Irish dancing, both at home and abroad. Americans, Australians and Canadians have joined the select band of dancers from Ireland and Britain who have worn the mantle of World Champion. The current number of registered Irish Dancing Teachers is about 1,100, compared with 500 in 1992 and 100 in 1950. There are 500 teachers in Ireland and at least another 600 throughout the world.

This growth in the popularity of Irish dancing can be attributed to two shows - Riverdance and Lord of the Dance - both of which have served to raise the profile of Irish dancing as an art form in general across the world. The bold new choreography of "Riverdance - The Show" has since transformed and liberated Irish dancing. With music and lyrics composed by Bill Whelan, produced by Moya Doherty and directed by John McColgan, "Riverdance - The Show" was initially performed at the Eurovision Song Contest in Dublin, April 1994, as an orchestral piece conceived for hard-shoe Irish dance and was broadcast to an estimated 300 million viewers.

Currently it features a total company of 100 - the Irish Dance Troupe, the cream of Irish musicians in the Riverdance Orchestra and an array of talent from Spain, Russia and the U.S. Robert Ballagh, one of Ireland's foremost painters and designers, created the stage design. To date, more than 3 million people have attended the show worldwide and over 4 million Riverdance videos have been purchased. The first show featured Michael Flatley from Chicago and Jean Butler from New York, both of Irish descent and both world champions. Flatley has since gone on to produce, direct, choreograph and star in the acclaimed "Lord of the Dance" show.

ALL IRELAND DANCING CHAMPIONSHIPS
OIREACHTAS RINCE NA hEIREANN 1997

COMPETITION	WINNER	DANCING SCHOOL
Men over 21	Michael O'Donnallain	Uí Ruairc, Limerick
Men 19 - 21	Damien O'Kane	McCaul, Derry
Men 17 - 19	John Carey	Doherty, Coventry
Boys 15 - 17	Paul Cusick	O'Hare, Ohio
Boys 13 - 15	Bobby Fox	O'Reilly, Longford
Boys 11 - 13	Alan Kennefick	Cowhie Ryan, Cork
Boys 9 - 11	Eanna Ryan	Costello O'Brien, Galway
Women over 21	Paula McManus	Sean Eireann McMahon, Birmingham
Women 19 - 21	Tara Hegarty	McConomy, Derry
Girls 17 - 19	Emma Holtham	Glendarragh, Nottingham
Girls 16 - 17	Leanna Leonard	Armstrong, Belfast
Girls 15 - 16	Kelly Hendry	Hannon-Murphy, Newcastle
Girls 13 - 14	Sinead Fallon	Scanlon, Leeds
Girls 11 - 12	Michelle Lawrence	Uí Nualláin, Limerick
Mixed Céilí under 13	Foireann A	Kiely Walsh, Cork
Girls Céilí under 13	Foireann B	N.C.O.B., Drogheda
Mixed Céilí 13 - 16	Foireann A	Doherty, Coventry
Girls Céilí over 16	Foireann A	N.C.O.B., Drogheda
Group Céilí over 16	Foireann A	Coffey, Monaghan
Rince Foirne under 14	Foireann A	McCarthy, Drogheda
Men over 21	Michael O'Donnallain	Uí Ruairc, Limerick
Overseas Award	Michael K. Galvin	Drumcliffe, New York
Men 19 - 21	Darren Smith	Grant, Ontario
Overseas Award	Jim Riordan	Trinity, Canada
Men 17 - 19	Christopher Doyle	Armstrong, Belfast
Overseas Award	Joel Hannon	Comerford, Vancouver
Boys 15 - 17	Marty Dowds	Phoenix, Derry
Overseas Award	Paul Cusick	O'Hare, Ohio
Boys 13 - 15	Alan Fox	Oirialla, Dundalk
Overseas Award	Michael Belvitch	O'Hare, Ohio
Boys 11 - 13	Shane Ryan	Anthony Costello, Limerick
Overseas Award	Tim Seeman	O'Hare, Ohio
Boys 9 - 11	Eanna Ryan	Costello O'Brien, Galway
Overseas Award	Shane Kelly	Broesler, New Jersey
Women over 21	Theresa O'Sullivan	McLoughlin, New Jersey
Overseas Award	Katie Regan	Richens/Timm, Ohio
Women 19 - 21	Tara McConomy-Hegarty	McConomy, Derry
Overseas Award	Noelle Curran	P. Smith, New Jersey
Girls 17 - 19	Emma Thompson	Morgan, Manchester
Overseas Award	Heather Donovan	Richens/Timm, Ohio

Girls 16 - 17	Róisín Turley-Gibbons	Turley, Coventry
Overseas Award	Kathy Irvine	Fearon, Toronto
Girls 15 - 16	Kelly Hendry	Hannon-Murphy, Newcastle
Overseas Award	Colleen Ryan	Richens/Timm, Ohio
Girls 14 - 15	Erin Davidson	Oirialla, Dundalk
Overseas Award	Kate Ellen Hughes	Trinity, Chicago
Girls 13 - 14	Aoife Curley	Oirialla, Dundalk
Girls 12 - 13	Stephanie Power	Costello-O'Brien, Galway
Overseas Award	Jillian Farmer	Schade, New York
Overseas Award	Aishling Watt	Watt, British Columbia
Girls 11 - 12	Joanne Kavanagh	McConomy, Derry
Overseas Award	Sarah Koik	Claddagh, California
Girls 9 - 11	Emma King	Turley-Bracken, Luton
Overseas Award	Ashley Smith	Scoil Rince na nOg, Massachusetts
Mixed Céilí under 13	Foireann A	Kiely Walsh, Cork
Overseas Award	Foireann A	Doherty, Coventry
Girls Céilí under 13	Foireann A	McLaughlin, Glasgow
Overseas Award	Foireann A	Boyle, Glasgow
Mixed Céilí 13 - 16	Foireann A	Doherty, Coventry
Overseas Award	Foireann A	McLaughlin, Glasgow
Girls Céilí 13 - 16	Foireann A	McCarthy, Drogheda
Overseas Award	Foireann A	McLaughlin, Glasgow
Mixed Céilí over 16	Foireann B	McLaughlin, Glasgow
Overseas Award	Foireann A	Sean Eireann McMahon, Birmingham
Girls Céilí over 16	Foireann B	McLaughlin, Glasgow
Overseas Award	Foireann A	Setanta, Scotland
Mixed Group under 13	Foireann A	Doherty, Coventry
Overseas Award	Foireann A	McLaughlin, Glasgow
Girls Group under 13	Foireann A	McLaughlin, Glasgow
Overseas Award	Foireann A	Trinity, Chicago
Mixed Group 13 - 16	Foireann A	McLaughlin, Glasgow
Overseas Award	Foireann A	Doherty, Coventry
Girls Group 13 - 16	Foireann A	Scanlon, Birmingham
Overseas Award	Foireann A	McLaughlin, Glasgow
Mixed Group over 16	Foireann A	McLaughlin, Glasgow
Overseas Award	Foireann A	Sean Eireann McMahon, Birmingham
Girls Group over 16	Foireann A	Setanta, Scotland
Overseas Award	Foireann A	McLaughlin, Glasgow
Dance Drama	Foireann A	Gillan, Antrim
Overseas Award	Foireann A	Fryday, Kent

MOST COMMON IRISH SURNAMES IN IRELAND 1996

Surname *(in order of popularity)*	Traditional Family Areas	Derivation of Surname
Murphy	Armagh, Cork, Roscommon, Wexford	Sea-warrior
Kelly	Antrim, Derry, Down, Galway, Laois, Meath Roscommon, Sligo, Wicklow	Bright-haired or troublesome
Walsh	Cork, Galway, Kilkenny, Mayo, Waterford, Wexford	British or Welsh
Byrne	Carlow, Dublin, Kildare, Wicklow	Raven
Ryan	Carlow, Tipperary	Descendants of St. Riaghan
O'Connor	Clare, Derry, Kerry, Offaly, Roscommon, Sligo	Lover of hounds; wolf-lover
O'Brien	Clare, Limerick	Lofty; eminent
O'Sullivan	Cork, Kerry	One-eyed; hawk-eyed
O'Neill	Antrim, Derry, Down, Tyrone	Passionate
O'Reilly	Cavan, Longford	Race; sociable
Doyle	Carlow, Wexford, Wicklow	Dark foreigner (possibly referring to the Danes)
MacCarthy	Cork, Kerry	Loving
Doherty	Donegal	Unlucky; hurtful
Lynch	Antrim, Cavan, Clare, Cork, Derry, Donegal, Galway, Limerick, Sligo	Two roots - the 1st is French in origin; the 2nd means sea-men
Quinn	Antrim, Clare, Longford, Limerick, Mayo, Tyrone	Chief or leader

IRISH LANGUAGE ORGANISATIONS

Bord na Gaeilge, 7 Merrion Square, Dublin 2. Tel. (01) 6763222. Fax: (01) 6616564. A state board appointed to draft and advise the government on Irish language policies and to promote the language and all its aspects at all levels. Other work includes book distribution and community development projects. The organisation is grant-aided by the Department of Arts, Heritage, Gaeltacht and Islands (formerly the Department of Arts, Culture and the Gaeltacht).

An Coimisiúin Le Rincí Gaelacha, 6 Harcourt Street, Dublin 2. Tel: (01) 4752220. Fax: (01) 4751053. The governing body in Irish dancing, established in 1929. It organises both the All-Ireland and World Irish Dancing Championships annually.

Comhaltas Ceoltóirí Éireann, Belgrave Square, Monks Town, Co. Dublin. Tel: (01) 2800295. Fax: (01) 2803759. An Irish cultural movement, established in 1951. Promotes Irish traditional music, song, dance and language, through education and performance, both nationally and internationally.

Comhchoiste Náisiúnta na gColáistí Samhraidh, 46 Kildare Street, Dublin 2. Tel (01) 6794780. Fax: (01) 6790214. The overall body representative of more than 60 summer colleges which organises three-week Irish courses over the summer months, mainly in the Gaeltacht areas.

Comhdháil Náisiúnta na Gaeilge, 46 Kildare Street, Dublin 2. Tel: (01) 6794780. Fax: (01) 6790214. The steering council of the Irish language, established in 1943. It promotes over 20 different voluntary bodies, providing a forum for the exchange of ideas and information, politically and publicly.

Comhlachas Náisiúnta Drámaíochta, Camus, Connemara, Co. Galway. Tel: (091) 574146/574155. The National Council of Drama promotes drama in the Irish language through an advice centre, festivals, libraries of play texts and Irish drama courses.

Conradh na Gaeilge, *Áras an Chonartha, 6 Harcourt Street, Dublin 2. Tel: (01) 4757401/2. Fax: (01) 4757844.* A national organisation that provides support systems for Irish language schools, Irish language classes and other activities to further the use of Irish. It organises the Irish language festival, **An tOireachtas,** dating from 1897 and including literary, cultural, artistic and stage presentations and competitions.

Cultúrlann MacAdhamh Ó Fiaich, *216 Falls Road, Belfast, BT12 6AH. Tel: (01232) 239303.*
An Spidéal, *Co. Galway. Tel: (091) 553055. Fax: (091) 553059. Weekly all-Irish newspapers.*

An Cumann Scoildrámaíochta. *46 Kildare Street, Dublin 2. Tel: (01) 6794780. Fax: (01) 6790214.* Involved in the promotion and development of the Irish language through drama and stage-craft in national schools. It organises an annual national schools' drama festival, **An Fhéile Scoildrámaíochta.**

Gael-Linn, *26/27 Merrion Square, Dublin 2. Tel: (01) 6767283. Fax: (01) 6767030.* A non-political, non-governmental organisation working since 1953 to promote and gain recognition for the Irish language and culture throughout Ireland. It organises the National Youth Arts and Music Festival, **Slógadh.**

Glór na nGael, *Áras na Comhdhála, 46 Kildare Street, Dublin 2. Tel: (01) 6794780. Fax: (01) 6790214.* It organises an annual competition encouraging communities to promote Irish culture and the use of Irish as a spoken language.

Oideas Gael, *Glenn Cholm Cille, Co. Donegal. Tel: (073) 30248. Fax: (073) 30348.* It organises Irish language courses together with cultural activities.

Raidió na Gaeltachta, *Casla, Co. Galway. Tel: (091) 506677. Fax (091) 506688. Irish radio station.*

Raidió na Life, *7 Merrion Square, Dublin 2. tel (01) 6616333. Fax: (010) 6763966. Irish radio station.*

Taisce Cheol Dúchais Éireann, *63 Merrion Square, Dublin 2. Tel: (01) 6619699. Fax: (01) 6686260.* The Irish Traditional Archive, founded in 1987. Acts as a resource centre for collecting research and information on Irish traditional music. Collections of books, sound recordings, photographs and manuscripts have been made with access to the general public.

Teilifís na Gaelige, *Baile na hAbhann, Co. Galway. Tel: (091) 505050. Fax: (091) 505021.* Ireland's new television channel which broadcasts through the medium of Irish.

Údarás na Gaeltachta, *Na Forbacha, Galway. Tel: (091) 503100. Fax: (503101).* A regional development agency responsible for establishing of economic, social and cultural development in the Gaeltacht regions.

ARTS & ENTERTAINMENT

The Heart of the Art

By **Tony Clayton Lea**, *Freelance Journalist*

IRELAND has never had a problem in relation to expressing its own culture. Call it a willing and wilful gift of the gab, but there seems to be no end to the amount of self-promotion the country is willing to do. It's not boasting, either. For the past 20 years, the cultural imperialism that previously inhibited Ireland from celebrating its own achievements has slowly but surely been in decline. In its place is a sense of purpose and destination, a clear picture of what lies ahead, and an even clearer snapshot of what has been left behind. The difference between the two is that the latter appears to have been ripped in two and cast to the winds, while the former takes pride of place, figuratively speaking, on the nation's mantlepiece.

Besides, the facts speak for themselves. In the decades since the first wave of essentially music and literary arts celebrations in the '60s (Brendan Behan, The Dubliners, Them, Edna O'Brien, to name but several), the floodgates have opened, bringing a wide-ranging collection of internationally known people to well-deserved prominence. In the popular music arena, we have more successful bands than is perhaps wise for such a small country. The list is not so much endless as ever growing: Van Morrison, The Chieftains, Rory Gallagher, Thin Lizzy, Boomtown Rats / Bob Geldof, U2, Sinead O'Connor, The Cranberries, Boyzone, Altan - names that have taken on other world class acts and beaten them fair and square with their mixture of articulacy, attitude, and unquestionable talent. (Indeed, if, like the Irish football team, we were to apply the arguably useful 'granny' rule, we could include both The Smiths and Oasis, two bands of Manchester origin whose parents were born in Ireland. Oasis, currently one of the most popular rock bands in Europe and the U.S. openly pay tribute to their Irish roots...)

And that's only music. As ever, literature and poetry remain high on the cultural agenda. The successes of both Roddy Doyle (the Booker) and Seamus Heaney (the Nobel) only add to the already high reputation Ireland enjoys in the realm of the attuned senses. There are quite literally dozens of authors I could add to the list, people who are commercially successful as well as being integral to the future development of their art.

Cinema? The Sheridan brothers have already given us *My Left Foot*, *The Field* and *In The Name Of The Father*. Expect Jim Sheridan's forthcoming film, *The Boxer* (starring Daniel Day Lewis, and inspired by the autobiography of Irish World Champion pugilist Barry McGuigan) to reap a similar amount of critical plaudits. Ditto with Neil Jordan's *The Butcher Boy*, his treatment of Pat McCabe's book of the same name. But it's not just the big names of the aforementioned directors - and actors such as Liam Neeson, Pierce Brosnan, Brenda Fricker, and Stephen Rea - that are creating waves in the film industry both in Ireland and abroad. Directors such as Gerry Stembridge and Padraig Breathnach have been at the helm of excellent films (respectively, *Guiltrip* and *I Went Down* that touch on distinctly Irish themes. More people of their calibre are climbing the ladder, and the words 'Irish', 'film', and 'industry' will no longer be as contrarily oxymoronic as they once were.

You want more examples of the breadth and scope of the development of Irish culture and Irishness? How about a single word - Riverdance. If anything has loosened the straps of the erstwhile culturally straitjacketed approach to Irish dancing, then Riverdance has. Here, a hitherto under-financed and virtually underground and conservative art form has been given a Broadway treatment that hasn't undermined the joyousness or, indeed, the seriousness of the dance. Taking it out from the protected shadows of the competitive field, Irish dancing is now touring the world in a show that, while inevitably glitzy and naturally sexy, remains true to its inherent spirit of expressiveness.

As Ireland approaches the year 2000, it's refreshing to see the vast majority of its artistic achievements boldly taking on the competition. It's a measure of a new sense of confidence that lies at the heart of the art. Long may it continue.

The author is a noted writer on the Irish Arts and Entertainment industries and is a frequent contributor to national newspapers and radio.

BIOGRAPHIES OF FAMOUS IRISH WRITERS AND CURRENT IRISH WRITERS

(Asterisk denotes the writer is deceased)

*Allingham, William (born Donegal, 1824). Poet. Best remembered for poem *The Fairies* which opens with 'Up the airy mountains, down the rushy glen...' Died England, 1889.

Banville, John (born Wexford, 1945). Novelist & literary editor of *The Irish Times.* Works include *Long Lankin* (1970), *Doctor Copernicus* (1976), *Kepler* (1980), *The Newton Letter* (1982), *Mefisto* (1986), *The Book of Evidence* (1989), *Ghosts* (1993), *Athena* (1995).

Bardwell, Leland (born India, reared Kildare, 1928). Poet, novelist and playwright. Works include *The Mad Cyclist* (1970), *The Fly and the Bed Bug, Girl on a Bicycle, That London Winter, There We Have Been, Thursday, Open Ended Prescription.*

*Barrington, Sir Jonah (born Laois, 1760). M.P. and writer; works deal with life as a member of the Anglo-Irish gentry. Best known for *Personal Sketches of His Own Time* 1827-32). Died France 1834.

Barry, Sebastian (born Dublin, 1955). Poet, novelist, playwright; works include *Macker's Garden* (1982), *The Water Colourist* (1983), *Time Out of Mind* (1983), *Elsewhere* (1985), *The Engine of Owl-Light* (1987), *The Rhetorical Town* (1985).

Bateman, Colin (born Northern Ireland, 1962). Novelist; his works include *Divorcing Jack* (1994), *Cycle of Violence* (1995), *Of Wee Sweetie Mice and Men* (1996). First two novels have been adapted for filming - due 1998.

Beckett, Mary (born Belfast, 1926). Short-story writer and novelist; works include *A Belfast Woman, A Literary Woman* (1980), *Give Them Stones* (1987), and children's fiction *Hannah* or *Pink Baloons* (1995).

*Beckett, Samuel (born Dublin, 1906). Writer, poet, playwright and translator. Works include *More Pricks than Kicks* (1934), *Murphy* (1938), *Waiting for Godot* (1952), *Endgame* (1957), *Happy Days* (1961), *Worstward Ho* (1983), *Collected Poems* (1984). Awards include the Nobel Prize for Literature (1969). Died Paris 1989.

*Behan, Brendan (born Dublin, 1923). Celebrated wit, dramatist, author and poet. Worked with Joan Littlewood to produce plays the most famous of which include *The Quare Fellow* (1954) and *The Hostage* (1958). Remembered for controversial autobiography *The Borstal Boy* (1958). Died Dublin 1964.

Bell, Sam Hanna (born Glasgow, 1910). Writer and radio producer. Works include *December Bride* (1951) and *The Hollow Ball* (1961) about urban poverty.

Binchy, Maeve (born Dublin, 1940). Novelist and columnist for *The Irish Times.* Works include *Light a Penny Candle, Echoes, Circle of Friends* (made into film) *Number one* Bestsellers: *The Copper Beach, Firefly Summer, Glass Lake, Evening Class.*.

*Birmingham, George (born Belfast, 1865). Novelist. Remembered for satires on political events in Ireland. Work includes the autobiographical *Pleasant Places* (1934). Died London, 1950.

Boland, Eavan (born Dublin, 1944). One of Ireland's most popular modern poets. Works include *New Territory* (1967), *The War Horse* (1975), *In Her Own Image* (1980), *Outside History* (1990).

Bolger, Dermot (born Dublin, 1959). Writer, playwright, publisher and poet. Works include *Night Shift* (1985), *The Journey Home* (1990), *Emily's Shoes* (1992), *A Second Life* (1994); *Internal Exiles* (1986), *A Dublin Quartet* (1992). Most recently work as editor of *Finbar's Hotel* (1997), a book of short stories from *Roddy Doyle, Anne Enright, Hugo Hamilton, Jennifer Johnston, Joseph O'Connor* and *Colm Tóibín.*

Boran, Pat (born Portlaoise, 1963). Poet and playwright. Works include *The Unwound Clock* (1989), *History and Promise* (1990), *Strange Bedfellows* (1991).

*Bowen, Elizabeth (born Dublin, 1899). Novelist in the Anglo-Irish literary genre. Works include *The Last September* (1929), *The Death of the Heart* (1938), *A World of Love* (1955). Died 1973.

Boylan, Clare (born Dublin, 1948). Novelist and journalist. Received an Oscar nomination for Best Short Film for her story *Making Waves* (1988). Works include *Holy Pictures, Last Resorts* (1984), *Black Baby* (1988), *Home Rule* (1993), *That Bad Woman* (1995),

*Brown, Christy (born Dublin,

1932). Writer; despite suffering from cerebral palsy, he completed his autobiographical *My Left Foot* (1964) - made into an Oscar-winning film - and *Down all the Days* (1970). Poetry includes *Come Softly to My Wake* (1971), Died 1981.

*Burke, Edmund (born Dublin, 1729). Parliamentarian, best remembered for his *Reflections on the Revolution in France* (1790). Died England, 1797.

Burrows, Wesley (born Belfast, 1930). One of the most gifted and popular writers for theatre and T.V. Works include R.T.É.'s *The Riordans, Bracken, Glenroe.*

*Carleton, William (born Tyrone, 1794). Novelist. Works include two volumes of short stories *Traits* (1830), *Stories of the Irish Peasantry* (1833). Died Dublin 1869.

Casey, Philip (born 1950). Poet, writer and playwright. Works include *Those Distant Summers* (1980), *The Year of the Knife* (1991), *Cardinal* (1990), *The Fabulists* (1994), *The Water Star* (1997).

*Clarke, Austin (born Dublin, 1896). One of Ireland's most noted poets, also playwright and novelist. Produced over 30 volumes. Famous poems: *The Planters Daughter* and *Lost Heifer*. Works include *Flight to Africa* (1963), *A Penny in the Clouds* (1968), *Collected Poems* (1974). Died 1974.

*Coffey, Brian (born Dublin, 1905). Poet, translator and editor. Works include *Third Person* (1938), *The Big Laugh* (1976), *Death of Hektor* (1984), *Advent* (1986). Died 1995.

*Colum, Patrick (born Longford, 1881). Primarily a poet, wrote the famous song *She Moved Through the Fair*. Works include the biography of Arthur Griffith - *Ourselves Alone* (1959) and a collection of anecdotes about Joyce - *Our Friend James Joyce* (1958). Died Connecticut 1972.

Connor, Patrick Rearden (born Dublin, 1907). Novelist under the pen-name Peter Malin. Best known for *Shake Hands with the Devil* (1933), later made as a film (1959). Works include *I am Death* (1936), *A Plain Tale from the Bogs* (1937), *The Singing Stone* (1951), *The House of Cain* (1952).

Conlon-McKenna, Marita (born Dublin, 1956). Ireland's most popular children's author. Works include *The Hawthorn Tree* (1990), *Wildflower Girl* (1991), *Little Star*

(1993), *No Goodbye* (1994), *Fields of Home* (1996).

Cronin, Anthony (born Wexford, 1928). Poet, playwright and writer. Works include *The Life of Riley* (1964), *Dead as Doornails* (1976), *The End of the Modern World* (1989), *No Laughing Matter: The Life and Times of Flann O' Brien* (1989), *Samuel Beckett: The Last Modernist* (1996).

Daly, Ita (born Leitrim, 1944). Novelist and short story writer. Works include *The Lady with the Red Shoes* (1980), *A Singular Attraction* (1987), *All Fall Down* (1992), *Unholy Ghost* (1996).

D'Arcy, Margaretta (born London, 1934). Writer and playwright. Works include *Tell them Everything* (1961), *Awkward Corners, Prison-voice of Countess Markievicz* (1995), *Galway's Pirate Women, a Global Trawl* (1996).

Dawe, Gerald (born Belfast 1952). Poet, literary journalist and lecturer. Works include *Heritages* (1976), *The Lundys Letter* (1985), *The Water Table* (1990), *Sunday School* (1991), *Heart of Hearts* (1995).

Deane, Seamus (born Derry, 1940). Poet and Professor of Modern English and American Literature. Works include *Rumours* (1977), *The Field Day Anthology of Irish Writing* (1989) and the semi-autobiographical *Reading in the Dark* (1996), which was nominated for the 1996 Booker Prize.

*de Vere White, Terence (born 1912). Writer and literary editor for *The Irish Times* (1961-77). Works include *Kevin O'Higgins* (1948), *A Fretful Midge* (1957), *Lucifer Falling* (1965), *The Parents of Oscar Wilde* (1967), *The Anglo-Irish* (1972), *Chimes at Midnight* (1977), *Chat Show* (1987). Died 1994.

Delaney, Frank (born Tipperary 1942). Novelist, literary critic and broadcaster. Works include *My Dark Rosaleen* (1988), *The Sins of the Mothers* (1992), *Telling the Pictures* (1986). Currently presenting *The Bookshow* on Sky T.V.

*Dillon, Eilís (born Galway, 1920). Adult/children's novelist and playwright. Works include *The Island of Horses* (1956), *A Page of History* (1966), *The Singing Cave* (1969), *Across the Bitter Sea* (1973), *Blood Relations* (1977), *The Cats' Opera* (1981), *Wild Geese* (1981), *Down in the World* (1983), *Children of Bach* (1993). Died 1994.

Dorcey, Mary (born Dublin 1950).

Poet and novelist. Works include *Kindling* (1982), *Scarlett O'Hara* (1989), *A Noise from the Woodshed* (1989), *The Tower of Babel* (1996).

Dorgan, Theo (born Cork, 1953). Poet and broadcaster. Director of *Poetry Ireland*. Works include *Slow Air* (1975), *A Moscow Quartet* (1989), *The Ordinary House of Love* (1990), *Rosa Mundi* (1995).

Doyle, Roddy (born Dublin, 1958). Novelist who captures working-class Dublin vernacular perfectly. Had major successes with The Barrytown Trilogy *(The Commitments, The Snapper* and *The Van* which were made into films), the Booker Prize-winning *Paddy Clarke Ha Ha Ha* and *The Woman who Walked into Doors*. Wrote T.V. series *The Family* and stage-plays *Brownbread* and *War.*

Durcan, Paul (born Dublin, 1944). Poet. Works include *The Berlin Wall Cafe* (1985), *Crazy About Women* (1991), *A Snail in my Prime* (1993), *Christmas Day* (1996).

*Edgeworth, Maria (born Oxfordshire, 1767). Novelist. Most famous for *Castle Rackrent* (1800). Died Longford, 1849.

Egan, Desmond (born Athlone, 1936). Publisher, poet and teacher. Formed *Goldsmith Press* (1972). Works include *Midland* (1972), *Woodcutter* (1978), *A Song for my Father* (1989), *Snapdragon* (1992), *In the Holocaust of Autumn* (1994).

*Ervine, St. John Greer (born Belfast, 1883). Playwright and novelist. Drama critic for the *Observer* until 1939. Works include *Boyd's Shop* (1936), *Friend and Relations* (1941), biographies of *Charles Stewart Parnell* (1925), *Sir James Craig* (1949) and *George Bernard Shaw* (1956). Died England 1971.

Farrell, Bernard (born Dublin, 1939). Playwright and T.V./Radio dramatist. Works include *I Do Not Like Thee Dr. Fell* (1979), *All in Favour Said No!* (1981), *Petty Sessions* (1983), *Don Juan* (1984), *Then Moses Met Marconi* (1984), *Foreign Bodies* (1985-88), *Forty-Four Sycamore* (1992), *The Last Apache Reunion* (1993), *Happy Birthday, Dear Alice* (1994/5), *Radio Waves* (1995).

Fiacc, Pádraic (born Belfast, 1924). Poet and writer. Works include *Woe to the Boy* (1957), *By the Black Stream* (1969), *Odour of the Blood* (1973, 1983), *Nights in the Bad Place* (1977), *Missa Terribilis* (1986), *Ruined Pages* (1994).

Friel, Brian (born Tyrone, 1929). One of foremost international English Language dramatists. Works include: *Philadelphia, Here I Come!* (1964), *Lovers* (1967), *Faith Healer* (1979), *Translations* (1980), *Dancing at Lughnasa* (1990), *Wonderful Tennessee* (1993).

Galvin, Patrick (born Cork, 1927). Dramatist, writer and playwright. Works include *And Him Stretched, Cry the Believers, The Devil's Own People, My Silver Bird;* Poetry: *The Wood-Burners, Man on the Porch* (1980), *The Death of Art O'Leary* (1994), *New and Selected Poems* (1996); Autobiography: *Song for a Poor Boy* (1991) and *Song for a Raggy Boy* (1992).

Greacen, Robert (born Derry, 1920). Poet and writer. Works include *The Bird* (1941), *One Recent Evening* (1944), *Even Without Irene* (1969), *A Garland for Captain Fox* (1975), *I, Brother Stephen* (1978), *Carnival at the River* (1990), *Collected Poems* (1995); *Even Without Irene* (1969, 1985).

*Gogarty, Oliver St. John (born Dublin, 1878). Poet and surgeon. Works include *An Offering of Swans* (1923) and *Elbow Room* (1939). Died New York 1957.

*Gregory, Lady (born 1852). Dramatist and friend of Yeats. Director of Abbey Theatre, produced her own comedies *Spreading the News* (1904) and *The Rising of the Moon* (1907). Died Galway 1932.

*Hanley, Gerard (born England, 1916). Writer. Works include *The Consul at Sunset* (1951), *The Year of the Lion, Drinkers of Darkness, Gilligan's Last Elephant, See You in Yasukuni.* Film script; *The Blue Max.* (1966). Died 1992.

Hartnett, Michael (born Limerick, 1941). Poet and translator. Works include *Anatomy of a Cliché* (1968), *The Retreat of Ita Cagney/Cúlú Íde* (1975), *A Farewell to English* (1975), *Prisoners* (1977), *Maiden Street Ballad* (1980), *A Necklace of Wrens* (1987), *The Naked Surgeon* (1991), *The Killing of Dreams* (1992).

Healy, Dermot (born Westmeath, 1947). Poet, writer and playwright. Works include *Fighting with Shadows* (1984), *The Long Swim* (1988), *Blood Wedding* (1989), *Curtains* (1990), *On Broken Wings* (1992), *The Ballyconnell Colours -* poetry (1992), *A Goat's Song* (1994), *The Bend for Home* (1996).

Heaney, Seamus (born Derry, 1939). Poet. Considered one of finest in English language. Won Nobel Prize for Literature (1995). Works include *Death of a Naturalist* (1966), *Door into the Dark* (1969), *Wintering Out* (1972), *Preoccupations* (1980), *Station Island* (1984), *Seeing Things* (1991), *The Redress of Poetry* (1995), *The Spirit Level* (1996).

Higgins, Aidan (born Kildare, 1927). Writer. Works include *Asylum & Other Stories* (1960), *Langrishe, Go Down* (1966), *Images of Africa* (1971), *Balcony of Europe* (1972) shortlisted for Booker Prize, *Scenes From a Receding Past* (1977), *Bornholm Night-Ferry* (1983), *Ronda Gorge & Other Precipices* (1989), *Lions of the Grunewald* (1993), *Donkey's Years* (1995), *Flotsam and Jetsam* (1997).

Higgins, Rita Anne (born Galway, 1955). Poet and playwright. Works include: *Goddess on the Mervue Bus* (1986), *Witch in the Bushes* (1988), *Philomena's Revenge* (1992), *Higher Purchase* (1996).

Ingoldsby, Pat (born Dublin). Playwright and poet. Plays include *Rhymin' Simon* (1979), *Yeuckface the Yeck* and *Spotty Grousler* (1982), *Hisself, When Am I Gettin' My Clothes?, The Full Shilling*; Poetry: *You've Just Finished Reading This Title.*

*Johnston, Denis (born Dublin, 1901). Playwright, barrister, broadcaster and academic. Works include *The Old Lady Says 'No'* (1929), *The Moon in the Yellow River* (1931), *The Bride for the Unicorn* (1933), *The Golden Cuckoo* (1939), *The Dreaming Dust* (1940), *Nine Rivers from Jordan* (1953), *The Scythe and the Sunset* (1958), *The Brazen Horn* (1968, 1976). Died 1984.

Johnston, Jennifer (born Dublin, 1930). Novelist and playwright. Works include *The Captains and the Kings* (1972), *The Gates* (1973), *How Many Miles to Babylon?* (1974), *The Railway Station Man* (1984; and later film), *Shadows on our Skin,* (1992) nominated for the Booker Prize.

*Joyce, James (born Dublin, 1882). Leading novelist of early twentieth century. Best known for *A Portrait of the Artist as a Young Man* (1916) and *Ulysses* (1922) which was censored until 1934. Works include *Dubliners* (1914) and *Finnegan's Wake* (1939). Died Zurich 1941.

*Kavanagh, Patrick (born Monaghan, 1904). One of most significant Irish poets of all time. Best known poems *The Great Hunger* (1942) and *Stony Grey Soil.* Works include: *Ploughman and Other Poems* (1936), *The Green Fool* (1938), *Tarry Flynn* (1949), *Come Dance with Kitty Stobling* (1960). Died Dublin 1967.

Keane, John B. (born Kerry, 1928). Playwright and novelist. Works include Plays; *Sive, The Year of the Hiker, The Field* (also screenplay), *Big Maggie, Moll,* Novels; *The Bodhran Makers, A High Meadow, Letters'* Series; ten books, biography; *Man of the Triple Name.*

*Keane, Molly (born Kildare, 1904). Works include *Young Entry* (1928), *Taking Chances* (1930), *Full House* (1937), *Ducks and Drakes* (1941), *Treasure Hunt* (1949), *Dazzling Prospect* (1961), *Good Behaviour* (1981); short-listed for Booker McConnel Prize, *Spring Meeting* (1983), *Time After Time* (1983), *Loving and Giving* (1988). Died 1996.

Kennelly, Brendan (born Kerry, 1936). Poet and academic. Works include *My Dark Fathers, Good Souls to Survive, Love Cry, The Voices, Islandman, The House that Jack Didn't Build, The Boats are Home, Cromwell, Judas.*

Keyes, Marion (born Ireland, 1963). Best-selling novelist with debut novel *Watermelons* (1995), followed by *Lucy Sullivan is Getting Married* (1997). Lives and works in London as part-qualified accountant.

Kiely, Benedict (born Tyrone, 1919). Journalist, novelist and short story writer. Works include *Counties of Contention: a Study of Irish Partition* (1945), *Land Without Stars* (1946), *Call for a Miracle* (1950), *Honey Seems Bitter* (1952), *The Cards of the Gambler: a Folktale* (1953), *There was an Ancient House* (1955), *The Captain with the Whiskers* (1960), *A Journey to the Seven Streams* (1963), *Dogs Enjoy the Morning* (1968), *A Cow in the House* (1978), *A Letter to Peachtree* (1987), *The Trout in the Turn Hole* (1995).

*Kickham, Charles (born Tipperary, 1828). Fenian, journalist and novelist. Editor of Fenian newspaper *The Irish People.* Best known for novels *Sally Kavanagh* and *Knocknagow* (1879) and poems *Rory of the Hill.* Died Dublin 1882.

Kilroy, Thomas (born Kilkenny, 1934). Dramatist and writer. Works include *The O'Neill, The Death and*

Resurrection of Mr. Roche, Tea and Sex and Shakespeare, Talbot's Box, Double Cross, Wife to Mr. Wilde, Farmers (T.V.), *Gold in the Streets* (film 1997), *The Big Chapel.*

Kinsella, Thomas (born Dublin, 1928). Noted poet, remembered for *Another September* and *Butcher's Dozen* (a poem reflecting the horror of Derry's Bloody Sunday in 1972). Works include *The Táin* (1969), *Vertical Man* (1973), *One* (1974), *Fifteen Dead* (1979), *Blood and Family* (1988), *From Centre City* (1990), *Open Court* (1993)

*****Lavin, Mary** (born Massachusetts, 1912). Resided in Dublin. Novelist and short-story writer. Works include *Tale from Bective Bridge* (1942), *The Long Ago* (1944), *The Becker Wives* (1946), *At Sallygap* (1947), *The Great Wave* (1961), *In the Middle of the Fields* (1967), *The Shrine* (1977), *A Family Likeness* (1985). Died 1996.

*****Lewis, C.S.** (born Belfast, 1898). Remembered for series of children's books *The Chronicles of Narnia*. Professor of Medieval and Renaissance Literature at Cambridge University. Father of actor Daniel Day-Lewis. Died 1963.

Liddy, James (born 1934). Poet and writer. Professor of English at University of Wisconsin, Milwaukee. Works include *In a Blue Smoke* (1964), *Blue Mountain* (1968), *A Munster Song of Love and War* (1971), *Comyn's Lay* (1978), *Chamber Pot Music* (1982), *At the Grave of Fr. Sweetman* (1984), *Young Men Go Out Walking* (1986), *A White Thought in a White Shade* (1987), *Collected Poems* (1994).

Longley, Michael (born Belfast, 1939). Poet, broadcaster and writer. Works include *Gorse Fires, The Ghost Orchid, Poems 1963-1983, Tuppeny Stung.*

*****Lynch, Liam** (born Dublin, 1937). Writer and playwright. Works include *Do Thrushes Sing in Birmingham?* (1962), *Soldier* (1969), *Strange Dreams Unending* (1974), *Krieg* (1982), *Voids* (1982), *Shell Sea Shell* (1983). Died 1996.

*****Lynch, Patricia** (born Cork, 1900). One of the most popular authors of children's fiction. Published more than 50 children's books. Best known: *The Turf Cutter's Daughter* (1934), *The Grey Goose of Kilnevan* (1941), *Story Teller's Holiday* (1947) plus the *Brogeen* series from 1947. Died Dublin 1972.

MacIntyre, Tom (born Cavan, 1931). Poet, playwright and novelist. Works include *The Charollais* (1969), *Through the Bridewell Gate* (Documentary 1971), *Dance For Your Daddy* (1987), *Fleur-de-lit* (1990), *Kitty O'Shea* (1992), *Chichadee* (1993),*Good Evening, Mr. Collins* (1995).

*****MacGill, Patrick** (born Donegal, 1891). Novelist. Works include *Children of the Dead End, The Rat Pit, The Great Push, The Red Horizon.* Died 1963.

*****Macken, Walter** (born Galway, 1915). Novelist, actor and playwright. Remembered for historical trilogy *Seek the Fair Land* (1959), *The Silent People* (1962) and *The Scorching Wind* (1964). Died Galway 1967.

MacLaverty, Bernard (born Belfast, 1942). Writer for radio, T.V., film and dramatist. Works include *Secrets* (1977), *Lamb* (1980),*A Time to Dance* (1982), *Cal* (1983); all produced for the screen,*The Great Profundo* (1987), *The Real Charlotte* (1991). His book *Grace Notes* (1997) has been released to wide acclaim.

Mahon, Derek (born Belfast, 1941). Writer and poet. Works include *Selected Poems* (1990), *The Bacchae* (1991), *The Hudson Letter* (1995), *Racine's Phaedra* (1996).

*****Mangan, James Clarence** (born Dublin, 1803). Poet. Best remembered for poems *Dark Rosaleen* and *The Woman of Three Cows.* Died Dublin 1849.

McCabe, Eugene (born Glasgow, 1930). Playwright and novelist. Wrote the *Victims* trilogy of T.V. plays based on the North for R.T.É; *Heritage, Siege and Cancer.* Works include: *The King of the Castle* (1964), *Breakdown* (1966), *Swift* (1969), *Pull Down a Horseman* (1979), *Roma* (1979), *Death and Nightingales* (1992).

McCabe, Pat (born Clones, 1955). Novelist, short story writer and script-writer. Finest work to date novel and screen play *The Butcher Boy* (1992), also nominated for the Booker Prize. Film due (1998). Works include: *Music on Clinton Street* (1986), *The Dead School* (1995).

McCafferty, Nell (born Derry, 1944). Writer and Journalist. Reporter with *The Irish Times* (1970-80). T.V. critic for *Sunday Tribune, Hot Press* columnist and regular broadcaster. Best known for her feminist and nationalist views. Works include *In*

the *Eyes of the Law* (1981), *A Woman to Blame* (1985),*Goodnight Sisters... (1988), Peggy Deery* (1989).

McCarthy, Thomas (born Waterford, 1954). Poet and writer. Works include *The First Convention* (1978), *The Sorrow Garden* (1981), *Seven Winters in Paris* (1989), *Without Power* (1991), *Asya and Christine* (1992), *The Lost Province* (1996).

McCourt, Frank (born U.S., reared Limerick) retired school teacher who won international acclaim for the 1997 Pulitzer-winning *Angela's Ashes.*

McGahern, John (born Dublin, 1934). Novelist and playwright. Works include *The Barracks* (1963), *The Dark* (1965), *Nightlines* (1970), *Getting Through* (1978), *The Pornographer* (1980), *The Rockingham Shoot* (T.V. 1987), *Amongst Women* (1990), *The Power of Darkness* (1991), *Collected Stories* (1992).

McGuckian, Medbh (born Belfast, 1950). Writer and poet. Current literary editor of *Fortnight* magazine. Works include *The Flower Master* (1982), *Venus and the Rain* (1984), *The Big Striped Golfing Umbrella* (1985), *On Ballycastle Beach* (1988), *The Grateful Muse* (1997).

McGuinness, Frank (born Buncrana, 1953). Playwright and lecturer at Maynooth. Director of Abbey Theatre since 1992. Works include *The Factory Girls* (1983), *Observe the Sons of Ulster Marching Towards the Somme* (1985), *Scout* (T.V. 1987), *The Hen House* (T.V. 1989), *The Bread Man* (1990), *Someone Who'll Watch Over Me* (1992), *The Bird Sanctuary* (1994), *A Doll's House* (1996).

McMahon, Brian (born Listowel, 1909). Writer and playwright. Works include *The Bugle in the Blood, The Song of the Anvil, The Honey Spike, The Death of Biddy Early, The Lion Tamer, Children of the Rainbow, Red Petticoat, The Sound of Hooves* (1985), *The Master* (autobiography 1992),*The Tallystick* (1994).

Meehan, Paula (born Dublin, 1955). Poet. Works include *Return and No Blame* (1984), *Reading the Sky* (1986), *The Man Who Was Marked by Winter* (1991), *Pillow Talk* (1994).

*****Merriman, Brian** (born Clare, 1749). Poet, most famous for epic *Cúirt an Mhéan Oíche; The Midnight Court* (1780). Also the most translated poem in the Irish language.

Died Limerick 1805.

Mhac an tSaoi, Máire (born Dublin, 1922). Poet. Works include *Dhá Scéal Artúraíochta* (1946), *Margadh na Saoire* (1956), *A Heart Full of Thought* (1959), *Codladh an Ghaiscígh* (1973), *An Galar Dubhach* (1980).

Montague, John (born New York, 1929). Reared Tyrone. Poet and writer. Works include *Poisoned Lands* (1961, 1977), *Death of a Chieftain* (1964, 1978), *A Chosen Light* (1967), *The Rough Field* (1972), *The Great Cloak* (1978), *The Dead Kingdom* (1984), *Mount Eagle* (1988), *Time in Armagh* (1993), *Collected Poems* (1995).

Moore, Brian (born Belfast, 1921). Writer. Published over 20 novels. Nominated three times for the Booker Prize. Works include *The Lonely Passion of Judith Hearne* (1955; later film 1987),*The Luck of Ginger Coffey* (1960), *The Emperor of Ice-Cream* (1965), *I am Mary Dunne* (1968), *Fergus* (1970), *Catholics* (1972, later a film), *The Doctor's Wife* (1976), *The Mangan Inheritance* (1979), *Cold Heaven* (1983), *Black Robe* (1985; later as film), *The Colour of Blood* (1987), *Lies of Silence* (1990),*The Statement* (1995), *The Magician's Wife* (1997).

Muldoon, Paul (born Portadown, 1951). Poet. B.B.C. Radio/T.V. Producer (1973-86). Works include *New Weather* (1973), *Mules* (1977), *Why Brownlee Left* (1980), *Quoof* (1983), *Meeting the British* (1987), *Madoc: A Mystery* (1990).

Mulkerns, Val (born Dublin, 1925). Novelist. Associate editor of *The Bell.* Columnist for the *Evening Press* (1968-83). Works include *Antiquities* (1978), *An Idle Woman* (1980), *The Summerhouse* (1984), *Very Like a Whale* (1986), *A Friend of Don Juan* (1988).

Murphy, Dervla (born Waterford, 1931). Travel writer and literary critic. Works include *Full Tilt: Ireland to India on a Bicycle* (1965), *A Place Apart* (1978), *Eight Feet in the Andes* (1983), *Transylvania and Beyond* (1992), *The Ukimwi Road* (1993).

Murphy, Tom (born Tuam, 1935). Playwright and novelist. Works include *The Morning After Optimism* (1971), *A Whistle in the Dark*, *Famine*, *Conversations on a Homecoming*, *The Patriot*, *The Seduction of Morality*, *She Stoops to Folly* (1995), *The Wake* (1996).

*Ní Chonaill, Eibhlin Dhubh** (born Kerry, 1743). Remembered for lament *Caoineadh Airt Uí Laoghaire* (1773) delivered in Irish over the body of her murdered husband. Died 1800.

Ní Chuilleanáin, Eiléan (born Cork, 1942). Writer. Founder editor of *Cyphers.* Works include *Acts and Monuments* (1972), *Site of Ambush* (1975), *The Second Voyage* (1977), *The Rose-Geranium* (1981), *The Magdalene Sermon* (1989), *The Brazen Serpent* (1994).

Ní Dhomhnaill, Nuala (born England, 1952). Reared Ireland. Gaelic poet, dramatist and playwright. Radio/T.V. broadcaster. Works include *An Dealg Droighln* (1981), *Féar Suaithinseach* (1984), *Rogha Dánta/Selected Poems* (1986, 1988, 1990), *The Astrakhan Cloak* (1992), *Cead Aighnis* (1997), Screenplays; *An Gobán Saor* (1993), *An T-Anam Mothála/The Feeling Soul* (1994).

Nolan, Christopher (born 1965). Poet and short story writer. Born severely brain-damaged and physically disabled. Created one of the most poignant collections of short stories and poems *Dam-burst of Dreams* (1981). Aided by his mother he mastered typing with a stick strapped to his forehead. Autobiography *Under the Eye of the Clock* (1987).

O'Brien, Edna (born Clare, 1932). Writer and playwright. Works include *The Country Girls* (1960), *Girl with Green Eyes* (1962), *Girls in their Married Bliss* (1964), *August is a Wicked Month* (1965), *Johnny I Hardly Knew You* (1977), *Returning* (1982), *A Frantic Heart* (1985).

*O'Brien, Flann** (born Strabane, 1911). Playwright and novelist. Pen-names **Brian O'Nolan** and **Myles na gCopaleen**. Major figure in Irish literature. Notorious for satirical column *An Cruiskeen Lawn* in *The Irish Times* for two decades. Works include *At Swim-two birds* (1939), *The Third Policeman* (1940/67), *An Béal Bocht* (1941), *The Hard Life* (1961), *Faustus Kelly* (1943), *The Dalky Archive* (1964). Died 1966.

*O'Cadhain, Máirtín** (born Galway Gaeltacht, 1906). Noted writer in Irish language. Most famous for novel *Cré na Cille* (1949), translated into several European languages. First Irish-writer elected to the Irish Academy of Letters. Died Dublin 1970.

O'Carroll, Brendan (born Dublin,

1955). Author, actor, script-writer, playwright, comedian. Has had two successful radio series, three best selling books *The Mammy* (1994),*The Chisellers* (1995),*The Granny* (1996); presented R.T.É's T.V. series *Hot Milk and Pepper* (1996); wrote and directed two stage-plays: *The Course* (1995), *Grandad's Sure Lily's Still Alive* (1997). Film versions to be made of *The Mammy* and his latest novel *Sparrow's Trap* (1997), due 1998.

*O'Casey, Seán** (born Dublin, 1880). Dramatist. Best remembered for plays dealing with struggle for Irish Independence, *The Shadow of a Gunman* (1923), *Juno and the Paycock* (1924), *The Plough and the Stars* (1926), which remain the most popular of productions on the theatre circuit. Died England 1964.

*Ó'Cléirigh, Mícheál** (born Donegal, 1575). Compiled the *Annals of the Four Masters*, assisted by Cuigcoigriche Ó'Duigeanáin, Fearfeasa Ó'Maolconaire, and Cuigcoigriche Ó'Cléirigh. Wrote through the medium of Irish. Died Louvain 1643.

Ó Coistealbha, Seán (born Galway, 1932). Actor, poet and playwright. Works include *Aon Phionta Uisge* (1966), *An Tinceára Buí* (1967), *Ortha na Seirce* (1967), *An tÉan Cuaiche* (1968), *A Book of Poetry and Verse* (1987), *An Mhéir Fhada* (1993).

*Ó'Conaire, Pádraic** (born Galway, 1883). Novelist and short story writer in Irish. Best known for *M'Asal Beag Dubh* and *Fearfasa MacFeasa* (1930). Died Dublin 1928.

*O'Connor, Frank** (born Cork, 1903). Novelist, short story writer and translator. Pen name of Michael Francis O'Donovan. Best known for short stories, collected in volumes such as *Guests of the Nation* (1931) and *Crab Apple Jelly* (1944). Works include *Bones of Contention* (1936), *The Saint and Mary Kate* (1932), *Dutch Interior* (1940), *An Only Child* (1961), *My Father's Sons* (1968), *The Backward Look* (1967). Died Dublin 1966.

O'Connor, Joseph (born Dublin, 1963). Novelist, journalist, script-writer. Debut novel *Cowboys and Indians* (1991) short-listed for Whitbread Prize. Fiction works include *Desperados* (1994), *True Believers;* Non-fiction: *Even the Olives are Bleeding* (1986), *The Secret World of the Irish Male* (1994); *Sweet Liberty: Travels in*

Irish America (1996).

O'Connor, Ulick (born Dublin, 1929). Playwright, poet and writer. Works include *The Dream Box* (1972), *Lifestyles* (1973), *The Dark Lovers* (1975), *The Emperor's Envoy* (1976), *The Grand Inquisitor*, (1977, 1980), *Irish Tales and Sagas* (1981), *Execution* (1985), *A Trinity of Two* (1988), *Joyicity* (1989), *One is Animate* (1990), *Executions* (1992).

*Ó'Criomhthain, Tomás (born Great Blasket Island, Kerry, 1856). Best known for diary, *Allagar na h-Inise* (1928) and his autobiography *An t-Oileánach* (1929). Died Great Blasket Island 1937.

O Direáin, Máirtín (born Aran Islands, 1910). Poet. Works include *Rogha Dánta* (1949), *Ó Mórna agus Dánta Eile* (1957), *Feamainn Bhealtine* (1961), *Ar Ré Dhearóil* (1962), *Cloch Choirnéil* (1967), *Crainn is Cairde* (1970), *Ceacht an Éin* (1984), *Tacar Dánta / Selected Poems* (1984), *Craobhóg: Dán* (1986).

*Ó'Doirnín, Peadar (born Louth, 1682). Poet. Best known for works as political and humourous verse writer. Died Armagh 1769.

*O'Donnell, Peadar (born Donegal, 1893). Novelist, playwright and socialist. Works include *Storm* (1925), *Islands* (1928), *The Knife* (1930), *The Gates Flew Open* (1932), *On the Edge of the Stream* (1934), *Salud: An Irishman in Spain* (1937), *The Big Windows* (1955), *There Will Be Another Day* (1963), *Proud Island* (1975). Died 1986.

O'Driscoll, Denis (born Thurles, 1954). Poet and former editor of *Poetry Ireland Review*. Works include *Kist* (1982), *Hidden Extras* (1987), *Long Story Short* (1993).

O'Faoláin, Nuala (born London, 1932). One of Ireland's most favoured authors. Her current best-seller is *Are You Somebody?*

*O'Faoláin, Seán (born Cork, 1900). Novelist. Works include *Midsummer Night Madness* (1932), *A Nest of Simple Folk* (1934), *A Purse of Coppers* (1937), *King of the Beggars* ; (1938), *De Valera* (1939), *Come Back to Erin* (1940), *The Great O'Neill* (1942), *Constance Markievicz* (1943), *Vive Moi!* (1964), *The Heat of the Sun* (1966), *Foreign Affairs* (1976), *Collected Stories* (1980-82). Died 1991.

*O'Flaherty, Liam (born Inishmór, 1896). Novelist. Works include *The*

Black Soul (1924), *The Informer* (1925), *The Assassin* (1928), *Skerrett* (1932), *Shame the Devil* (1934), *Famine* (1937), *The Short Stories of Liam O'Flaherty* (1937), *Duil* (1953), *The Pedlar's Revenge and Other Stories* (1976). Died 1984.

Ó Floinn, Críostóir (born Limerick, 1927).Playwright (theatre/radio/ T.V.), writer and poet. Works include *In Dublin's Fair City* (1959), *Is É Dúirt Polonius* (1967), *Oineachlann* (1968), *Ó Fhás go hAois* (1969), *Sanctuary Island* (1971), *Banana* (1979), *An Spailpín Fánach* (1988), *A Poet in Rome* (1992), *Seacláidí Van Gogh* (1996).

O'Grady, Desmond (born Limerick, 1935). Writer and translator. Works include *Chords and Orchestrations* (1956), *Reilly* (1961), *The Dark Edge of Europe* (1967), *The Dying Gaul* (1968), *Hellas* (1971), *Separations* (1973), *Alexandria Notebook* (1989), *Tipperary* (1991), *My Fields this Springtime* (1993).

*O'Grady, Standish (born Cork, 1846). Writer of historical novels *The Heroic Period* (1878) and *Red Hugh's Captivity* (1889). Died England 1928.

*Ó Grianna, Séamus (born Donegal, 1891). Novelist and short story writer. Known by pen-name *Máire*. Best known for *Cith is Dealain* (1926) and *Caislean Óir* (1924). Died Donegal 1969.

Ormsby, Frank (born Enniskillen, 1947). One of Northern Ireland's most important poetry editors. Poetry collections include *Ripe for Company* (1971), *Spirit of Dawn* (1973), *A Store for Candles* (1977), *Being Walked by a Dog* (1978), *A Northern Spring* (1986), *The Ghost Train* (1995).

Ó Searcaigh, Cathal (born Donegal, 1956). Irish language poet and playwright. Works include *Mion Tragóide Chathrach* (1976), *Tuirlingt* (1979), *Súile Shuibhne* (1983), *Mairimid Leis na Mistéiri* (1989), *Tóin ag Titim as as tSaol* (1991), *An Bealach 'na Bhaile / Homecoming* (1993), *Na Buachaillí Bána* (1996).

Ó Siadhail, Mícheál (born Dublin, 1947). One of Ireland's most distinguished bilingual poets. Works include: *Spring Night* (1983), *The Image Wheel* (1985), *The Chosen Garden* (1990), *Hail! Madam Jazz: New and Selected Poems* (1992), *A Fragile City* (1995).

*Ó Súilleabháin, Eoghan Rua (born Kerry, 1748). Poet. Wrote in

Irish, about experiences as a school teacher, seaman and wandering labourer. Died Kerry 1784.

*Ó Súilleabháin, Muiris (born Great Blasket Island, 1904). Writer in Irish language. Best remembered for autobiography *Fiche Blian ag Fás, Twenty Years a-Growing* (1933). Died Galway 1950.

*Ó Rathaille, Aodhagán (born Kerry, 1670). Poet in Irish language. Died Kerry 1726.

*O Tuairisc, Eoghan (born Ballinasloe, 1919). Poet, writer, playwright and translator. Works include *L'Attaque, Dé Luain, An Lomnochtán, Rogha na Fhile, Dialann sa Diseart, Na Mairnéalaigh, Cúirt an Mhéan Oíche, La Fhéile Mhichíl, An Hairyfella in Ifreann, Fornocht do Chonac.* Died 1982.

*Parker, Stewart (born Belfast, 1941). Playwright. Works include *The Casualty Meditation* (1966), *Spokesong* (1975), *Catchpenny Twist* (1977), *Nightshade* (1985), *Northern Star* (1985). Died 1988.

Paulin, Tom (born Leeds, 1949). Poet, playwright and academic. Reared Belfast. Works include *A State of Justice* (1977), *Personal Column* (1978), *The Strange Museum* (1980), *Liberty Tree* (1983), *Fivemiletown* (1985), *Walking a Line* (1994).

Plunkett, James (born Dublin, 1920). Screenwriter and playwright. Works include *The Trusting and the Maimed, Strumpet City* (later T.V. series), *Farewell Companions, The Gems She Wore, The Risen People, Collected Short Stories, The Boy on the Back Wall, The Circus Animals*.

Purcell, Deirdre (born Dublin, 1945). Journalist and novelist. R.T.É Radio Broadcaster (1973-83). Has written five best sellers: *A Place of Stones* (1991), *Falling For a Dancer* (1993; film version due 1998), *Francey* (1994), *Sky* (1995), *Love, Like Hate Adore* (1997). Collaborated on *The Time of My life: An Autobiography* (1989) with Gay Byrne.

Reid, Christina (born Belfast, 1942). Playwright. Works include *Did You Hear the One About the Irishman...?* (1980),*The Belle of Belfast City, Joyriders, The Last of a Dying Race* (1986), *My Name, Shall I Tell You My Name?* (1987).

*Reid, Forrest (born Belfast, 1875). Novelist. Wrote 16 novels in addition to critical literary works. Works include *The Kingdom of Twilight*

(1904), *Following Darkness* (1912), *At the Door of the Gate* (1915), *Uncle Stephen* (1931), *The Retreat* (1936), *Young Man, or Very Mixed Company* (1944). Died 1947.

*Sayers, Peig (born Kerry, 1873). Skilled storywriter gifted with a wealth of folklore on the Great Blasket Island. Recordings of her folktales and stories made by Irish Folklore Commission. Dictated autobiography *Peig*, later published (1936). Died Kerry, 1958.

Scanlan, Patricia (born Dublin, 1956). Former librarian turned novelist and poet. One of Ireland's most popular fiction writers. Works include *City Girl* (1990), *Apartment 3B* (1991), *Finishing Touches* (1992), *City Woman* (1993), *Foreign Affairs* (1994), *Promises, Promises* (1997).

Scott, Michael (born Dublin) Writer. Published over 60 books, since 1981, celtic mythology, horror and the supernatural. Works include *The Last of the Fianna, The Seven Treasures, House of the Dead, October Moon, Wolf Man, Gemini Game*.

*Shaw, George Bernard (born Dublin, 1856). Won Nobel Prize for Literature (1925). Most famous works include *Man and Superman* (1905) and *Saint Joan* (1923). Also noted essayist and music critic. Died Canada 1950.

Simmons, James (born Derry, 1933). Poet and playwright. Founded *The Honest Ulsterman* (1968). Works include *Late but in Earnest* (1967), *Judy Garland and the Cold War* (1976), *Constantly Singing* (1980), *From the Irish* (1985), *The Cattle Rustling* (1992), *Mainstream* (1995).

Sirr, Peter (born Waterford, 1960). Poet and editor. Irish Writers' Centre Director. Works include: *Marginal Zones* (1984), *Talk, Talk* (1987), *Ways of Falling* (1991), *The Ledger of Fruitful Exchange* (1995).

Smith, Paul (born Dublin, 1935). Novelist and playwright. Works include *Esther's Altar* (1959), *The Countrywoman* (1961), *The Stubborn Season* (1962), *Stravaganza* (1963), *Annie* (1972), *Miss Lemon* (1986), *Trudy on Sunday* (1987).

*Stephens, James (born Dublin, 1880). Writer. Best known works *The Charwoman's Daughter* and *Crock of Gold* dealt with Irish folklore and fantasy. *The Insurrection in Dublin* (1916); about the Easter Rising; stands as one of the most accurate accounts of the Rebellion. Died London, 1950.

*Stoker, Bram (born Dublin, 1847). Best remembered for *Dracula* (1897), which inspired dozens of other works and took six years to create. Published a total of 18 books; mostly on gothic themes. Manager of the Lyceum Theatre, London for 27 years under the wing of Henry Irving. Last work: *Personal Reminiscences of Henry Irving* (1906). Died London 1912.

Stuart, Francis (born Australia, 1902). Writer, poet and playwright. Works include *We Have Kept the Faith* (1923), *Women and God* (1931), *The Angel of Pity* (1935), *The Pillar of Cloud* (1948), *Redemption* (1949), *The Flowering Cross* (1950), *The Pilgrimage* (1955), *Black List, Section H* (1971), *Memorial* (1973), *A Hole in the Head* (1977), *States of Mind* (1983), *Faillandia* (1985), *A Compendium of Lovers* (1990), *Collected Poems* (1992).

Sweeney, Matthew (born Donegal, 1952). Poet and Children's writer. Works include *A Dream of Maps* (1981), *A Round House* (1983), *The Lame Waltzer* (1985), *The Chinese Dressing Gown* (1987), *Blue Shoes* (1989), *Fatso in the Red Suit* (1995).

*Swift, Jonathan (born Dublin, 1667). Primarily, a political pamphleteer. Published the satirical *Gulliver's Travels* (1726). Died Dublin 1745.

*Synge, John Millington (born Dublin, 1871). Dramatist, famous for plays *The Shadow of the Glen* (1903) and *The Playboy of the Western World* (1907), controversial at time for their portrayal of Irish peasantry. Died Dublin 1909.

Taylor, Alice (born Cork 1938). Writer. Works include *To School through the Fields* (1988), *Quench the Lamp* (1990), *Secrets of the Oak* (1991), *The Village* (1992), *The Woman of the House* (1997).

Tóibín, Colm Writer. Works include *Walking Along the Border* (1987) / *Bad Blood* (1994), *The South* (1990), *Homage to Barcelona* (1990), *Dubliners* (1990), *The Heather Blazing* (1992), *The Sign of the Cross: Travels in Catholic Europe* (1994), *The Story of the Night* (1996).

Trevor, William (born Cork, 1928). Author; pen-name of William Trevor Cox. Works include *The Old Boys, The Ballroom of Romance* (later a film 1981), *Excursions in the Real World* (1993).

Wall, Mervyn (born Dublin, 1908). Writer and playwright. Works include *Alarm Among the Clerks* (1940), *The Unfortunate Fursey* (1946), *Leaves for the Burning* (1952), *No Trophies Raise* (1956), *Forty-Foot Gentlemen Only* (1963), *Hermitage* (1982), *The Garden of Echoes* (1982).

*Walsh, Maurice (born Kerry, 1879). Novelist. Best known for *Blackrock's Feather* (1932) and *The Quiet Man*; a short story from his collection *Green Rushes* (1935). Made into one of Ireland's most famous films with John Wayne and Maureen O'Hara (1952). Died 1964.

*Wilde, Oscar (born Dublin, 1854). Most famous wit and playwright of the Victorian era. Most famous *The Importance of Being Earnest* (1895) and *Salome* (1891), written in French. Also wrote the poem *The Ballad of Reading Gaol* and the novel *The Picture of Dorian Gray*. Died Paris, 1900.

Woods, Macdara (born Dublin, 1942). Poet, editor and translator. Works include *Drinks in a Bar in Marrakesh* (1970), *Early Morning Matins* (1973), *The Hanged Man Was Not Surrendering* (1990), *Notes from the Countries of Blood-Red Flowers* (1994), *Selected Poems* (1996).

*Yeats, William Butler (born Dublin, 1865). Poet and dramatist, was to the forefront of Irish Cultural Revival. Won Nobel Prize for Literature (1923). Most famous play *Cathleen Ni Houlihan* (1902), but more famous for his poetry - *Lake Isle of Innisfree, September 1913, Easter 1916* and *The Circus Animal's Desertion*. Died France, 1939.

(Asterisk denotes the writer is deceased)

NUMBER 1 BEST SELLING BOOKS IN IRELAND
JANUARY - SEPTEMBER 1997

PAPERBACK FICTION

Week	Title	Author	Publisher
04 Jan	The Runaway Jury	John Grisham	Century
11 Jan	The Granny	Brendan O'Carroll	O'Brien
18 Jan	Lucy Sullivan is Getting Married	Marian Keyes	Poolbeg
25 Jan	The Horse Whisperer	Nicholas Evans	Corgi
01 Feb	The Horse Whisperer	Nicholas Evans	Corgi
08 Feb	The Horse Whisperer	Nicholas Evans	Corgi
15 Feb	Undone	Michael Kimball	Headline
22 Feb	The Upstart	Catherine Cookson	Corgi
01 Mar	The Upstart	Catherine Cookson	Corgi
08 Mar	The Upstart	Catherine Cookson	Corgi
15 Mar	The Upstart	Catherine Cookson	Corgi
22 Mar	The English Patient	Michael Ondaatje	Picador
29 Mar	The English Patient	Michael Ondaatje	Picador
05 Apr	The English Patient	Michael Ondaatje	Picador
12 Apr	The Runaway Jury	John Grisham	Arrow
19 Apr	The Runaway Jury	John Grisham	Arrow
26 Apr	The Runaway Jury	John Grisham	Arrow
03 May	The Runaway Jury	John Grisham	Arrow
10 May	Evening Class	Maeve Binchey	Orion
17 May	Evening Class	Maeve Binchey	Orion
24 May	Evening Class	Maeve Binchey	Orion
31 May	Evening Class	Maeve Binchey	Orion
07 Jun	Evening Class	Maeve Binchey	Orion
14 Jun	Promises, Promises	Patricia Scanlan	Poolbeg
21 Jun	Promises, Promises	Patricia Scanlan	Poolbeg
28 Jun	Promises, Promises	Patricia Scanlan	Poolbeg
05 Jul	Promises, Promises	Patricia Scanlan	Poolbeg
12 Jul	Cause of Death	Patricia Cornwell	Warner
19 Jul	Cause of Death	Patricia Cornwell	Warner
26 Jul	Cause of Death	Patricia Cornwell	Warner
02 Aug	Cause of Death	Patricia Cornwell	Warner
09 Aug	Woman to Woman	Cathy Kelly	Poolbeg
16 Aug	Woman to Woman	Cathy Kelly	Poolbeg
23 Aug	Woman to Woman	Cathy Kelly	Poolbeg
30 Aug	Woman to Woman	Cathy Kelly	Poolbeg
06 Sep	Woman to Woman	Cathy Kelly	Poolbeg
13 Sep	Woman to Woman	Cathy Kelly	Poolbeg
20 Sep	Woman to Woman	Cathy Kelly	Poolbeg
27 Sep	Finbar's Hotel	Dermot Bolger *(Editor)*	New Island

PAPERBACK NON-FICTION

Week Ending	Title	Author	Publisher
04 Jan	Are You Somebody?	Nuala O'Faolain	New Island
11 Jan	Are You Somebody?	Nuala O'Faolain	New Island
18 Jan	Are You Somebody?	Nuala O'Faolain	New Island
25 Jan	Are You Somebody?	Nuala O'Faolain	New Island
01 Feb	Are You Somebody?	Nuala O'Faolain	New Island
08 Feb	Are You Somebody?	Nuala O'Faolain	New Island
15 Feb	Are You Somebody?	Nuala O'Faolain	New Island
22 Feb	Are You Somebody?	Nuala O'Faolain	New Island
01 Mar	Are You Somebody?	Nuala O'Faolain	New Island
08 Mar	Family Finance '97/98	Colm Rapple	Squirrel Press
15 Mar	Are You Somebody?	Nuala O'Faolain	New Island
22 Mar	Are You Somebody?	Nuala O'Faolain	New Island
29 Mar	Little Girl: The Lavinia Kerwick Story	Micheline McCormack	McCormack Books
05 Apr	Little Girl: The Lavinia Kerwick Story	Micheline McCormack	McCormack Books

12 Apr	Letter to Daniel	Fergal Keane	Penguin
19 Apr	Maximum Points, Minimum Panic	Kevin Flanagan	Marino
26 Apr	Little Book of Calm	Paul Wilson	Penguin
03 May	Are You Somebody?	Nuala O'Faolain	New Island
10 May	Are You Somebody?	Nuala O'Faolain	New Island
17 May	Angela's Ashes	Frank McCourt	HarperCollins
24 May	Angela's Ashes	Frank McCourt	HarperCollins
31 May	Angela's Ashes	Frank McCourt	HarperCollins
07 Jun	Angela's Ashes	Frank McCourt	HarperCollins
14 Jun	Angela's Ashes	Frank McCourt	HarperCollins
21 Jun	Angela's Ashes	Frank McCourt	HarperCollins
28 Jun	Angela's Ashes	Frank McCourt	HarperCollins
05 Jul	Angela's Ashes	Frank McCourt	HarperCollins
12 Jul	Angela's Ashes	Frank McCourt	HarperCollins
19 Jul	Angela's Ashes	Frank McCourt	HarperCollins
26 Jul	Angela's Ashes	Frank McCourt	HarperCollins
02 Aug	Angela's Ashes	Frank McCourt	HarperCollins
09 Aug	Angela's Ashes	Frank McCourt	HarperCollins
16 Aug	Angela's Ashes	Frank McCourt	HarperCollins
23 Aug	Angela's Ashes	Frank McCourt	HarperCollins
30 Aug	Angela's Ashes	Frank McCourt	HarperCollins
06 Sep	Angela's Ashes	Frank McCourt	HarperCollins
13 Sep	Angela's Ashes	Frank McCourt	HarperCollins
20 Sep	Angela's Ashes	Frank McCourt	HarperCollins
27 Sep	Angela's Ashes	Frank McCourt	HarperCollins

HARDBACK FICTION

Week Ending	Title	Author	Publisher
04 Jan	Evening Class	Maeve Binchy	Orion
11 Jan	Evening Class	Maeve Binchy	Orion
18 Jan	Evening Class	Maeve Binchy	Orion
25 Jan	Evening Class	Maeve Binchy	Orion
01 Feb	Promises, Promises	Patricia Scanlan	Poolbeg
08 Feb	Evening Class	Maeve Binchy	Orion
15 Feb	Evening Class	Maeve Binchy	Orion
22 Feb	Evening Class	Maeve Binchy	Orion
01 Mar	Evening Class	Maeve Binchy	Orion
08 Mar	Evening Class	Maeve Binchy	Orion
15 Mar	Hornet's Nest	Patricia Cornwell	Little, Brown
22 Mar	Hornet's Nest	Patricia Cornwell	Little, Brown
29 Mar	Hornet's Nest	Patricia Cornwell	Little, Brown
05 Apr	Hornet's Nest	Patricia Cornwell	Little, Brown
12 Apr	The Partner	John Grisham	Century
19 Apr	The Partner	John Grisham	Century
26 Apr	The Partner	John Grisham	Century
03 May	The Partner	John Grisham	Century
10 May	The Untouchable	John Banville	Picador
17 May	Scapel	Paul Carson	Heinemann
24 May	Scapel	Paul Carson	Heinemann
31 May	The Partner	John Grisham	Century
07 Jun	Scapel	Paul Carson	Heinemann
14 Jun	The Partner	John Grisham	Century
21 Jun	The Partner	John Grisham	Century
28 Jun	Scapel	Paul Carson	Heinemann
05 Jul	Scapel	Paul Carson	Heinemann
12 Jul	Scapel	Paul Carson	Heinemann
19 Jul	Scapel	Paul Carson	Heinemann
26 Jul	Scapel	Paul Carson	Heinemann
02 Aug	Scapel	Paul Carson	Heinemann
09 Aug	Scapel	Paul Carson	Heinemann
16 Aug	Scapel	Paul Carson	Heinemann
23 Aug	Scapel	Paul Carson	Heinemann
30 Aug	Scapel	Paul Carson	Heinemann

06 Sep	Scalpel	Paul Carson	Heinemann
13 Sep	Four Letters of Love	Niall Williams	Picador
20 Sep	10lb Penalty	Dick Francis	Michael Joseph
27 Sep	Love, Like, Hate, Adore	Deirdre Purcell	Townhouse

HARDBACK NON-FICTION

Week Ending	Title	Author	Publisher
04 Jan	Angela's Ashes	Frank McCourt	HarperCollins
11 Jan	Angela's Ashes	Frank McCourt	HarperCollins
18 Jan	Angela's Ashes	Frank McCourt	HarperCollins
25 Jan	Angela's Ashes	Frank McCourt	HarperCollins
01 Feb	Angela's Ashes	Frank McCourt	HarperCollins
08 Feb	Angela's Ashes	Frank McCourt	HarperCollins
15 Feb	Angela's Ashes	Frank McCourt	HarperCollins
22 Feb	Angela's Ashes	Frank McCourt	HarperCollins
01 Mar	Angela's Ashes	Frank McCourt	HarperCollins
08 Mar	Angela's Ashes	Frank McCourt	HarperCollins
15 Mar	Angela's Ashes	Frank McCourt	HarperCollins
22 Mar	Angela's Ashes	Frank McCourt	HarperCollins
29 Mar	W. B. Yeats: A Life	R. F. Foster	Open University Press
05 Apr	W. B. Yeats: A Life	R. F. Foster	Open University Press
12 Apr	W. B. Yeats: A Life	R. F. Foster	Open University Press
19 Apr	Angela's Ashes	Frank McCourt	HarperCollins
26 Apr	Angela's Ashes	Frank McCourt	HarperCollins
03 May	Angela's Ashes	Frank McCourt	HarperCollins
10 May	Angela's Ashes	Frank McCourt	HarperCollins
17 May	The Diving Bell & The Butterfly	Jean Dominique Bauby	Fourth Estate
24 May	Eight Weeks of Optimum Health	Andrew Weil	Little, Brown
31 May	The Diving Bell & The Butterfly	Jean Dominique Bauby	Fourth Estate
07 Jun	Eight Weeks of Optimum Health	Andrew Weil	Little, Brown
14 Jun	Eight Weeks of Optimum Health	Andrew Weil	Little, Brown
21 Jun	Eight Weeks of Optimum Health	Andrew Weil	Little, Brown
28 Jun	The Bible Code	Michael Drosnin	Weidenfeld & Nicolson
05 Jul	Angela's Ashes	Frank McCourt	HarperCollins
12 Jul	Angela's Ashes	Frank McCourt	HarperCollins
19 Jul	Angela's Ashes	Frank McCourt	HarperCollins
26 Jul	Atlas of the Irish Rural Landscape	Aalen, Whelan & Stout	Cork University Press
02 Aug	Atlas of the Irish Rural Landscape	Aalen, Whelan & Stout	Cork University Press
09 Aug	Atlas of the Irish Rural Landscape	Aalen, Whelan & Stout	Cork University Press
16 Aug	Atlas of the Irish Rural Landscape	Aalen, Whelan & Stout	Cork University Press
23 Aug	Atlas of the Irish Rural Landscape	Aalen, Whelan & Stout	Cork University Press
30 Aug	Atlas of the Irish Rural Landscape	Aalen, Whelan & Stout	Cork University Press
06 Sep	Atlas of the Irish Rural Landscape	Aalen, Whelan & Stout	Cork University Press
13 Sep	Irish Stone Walls	Patrick McAfee	O'Brien Press
20 Sep	The Woman Who Took Power in the Park: Mary Robinson	Lorna Siggins	Mainstream
27 Sep	Diana: Princess of Wales: A Tribute	Tim Graham	Weidenfeld & Nicolson

MAJOR PUBLISHING HOUSES IN IRELAND

Anvil Books (1964) *45 Palmerstown Road, Dublin 6. Tel. (01) 4973628.* Publish: history, folklore, biography, children's books. Director: Rena Dardis.

Appletree Press *19-21 Alfred St., Belfast, BT2 8DL. Tel. (01232) 243074.* Publish: general interest, history, Irish, music books. Director: John Murphy.

Aran Books (1992) *46 Charnwood,* *Bray, Co. Wicklow. Tel/Fax. (01) 2842493.* Publish: children's and fantasy books. Directors: Cecily Golden & Pat O'Loughlin.

Artcam Publishing Ltd. *Speenoge, Burt, Co. Donegal. Tel. (077) 68186.* Publish: general interest and reference books on Ireland. Directors: Pat McArt, Dónal Campbell, Colm McKenna.

Attic Press Ltd (1988) *29 Upper* *Mount Street, Dublin 2. Tel. (01) 6616128.* Publish: fiction, history, Irish, women's studies. Director: Róisín Conroy.

Blackstaff Press *3 Galway Park, Dundonald, Belfast, BT16 0AN. Tel. (01232) 487161.* Publish: fiction, children's, educational, history, politics, poetry books. Director: Anne Tannahill.

Boole Press *26 Temple Lane,*

Temple Bar, Dublin 2. Tel. (01) 6797655. Publish: medical, scientific, technical books. Director: Paulene McKeever.

Butterworths Ireland Ltd. Butterworth Ireland Ltd., 26 Upper Ormond Quay, Dublin 7. Tel. (01) 8731555. Publish: Irish law, tax books. Director: Gerard Coakley.

Cló Iar-Chonnachta (1985) Indreabhán, Connemara, Co. Galway. Tel. (091) 593307. Publish: fiction, poetry, children's books. Director: Micheál Ó Conghaile.

Collins Press, The (1989) Carey's Lane, The Huguenot Quarter, Cork. Tel. (021) 271346. Publish: fiction, history, and books of Cork interest. Director: Con Collins.

Columba Press, The (1985) Unit 55A, Spruce Avenue, Stillorgan Industrial Park, Blackrock, Co. Dublin. Tel. (01) 2942556. Publish: religious books. Director: Séan O'Boyle.

Cork University Press (1925) University College Cork, Cork. Tel. (021) 902980. Publish: academic books. Director: Sara Wilbourne. Employees: 5.

C. J. Fallon P.O. Box 1054, Lucan Road, Palmerstown, Dublin 20. Tel. (01) 6265777. Publish: educational books. Director: Henry McNicholas.

Flyleaf Press (1981) 4 Spencer Villas, Glenageary, Co. Dublin. Tel. (01) 2806228. Publish: natural history, genealogy books. Director: James Ryan.

Folens Unit 8, Broomhill Business Park, Tallaght, Dublin 24. Tel. (01) 4515311. Publish: educational, children's books. Director: John O'Connor.

Four Courts Press Ltd. (1972) Kill Lane, Blackrock, Co. Dublin. Tel. (01) 2892922. Publish: educational, religious books. Director: Michael Adams.

Gallery Press, The (1970) Loughcrew, Oldcastle, Co. Meath. Tel/Fax. (049) 41779. Publish: Irish literary books. Director: Peter Fallon.

Gill & Macmillan (1968) Goldenbridge, Inchicore, Dublin 8. Tel. (01) 4531005. Publish: history, current affairs, religious, biography books. Director: M.H. Gill.

Goldsmith Press Ltd., The (1972) Newbridge, Co. Kildare. Tel. (045) 433613. Publish: Irish poetry, culture, art books. Director: Vivienne Abbott.

Guildhall Press (1979) 41 Great James Street, Derry, BT48 7AH. Tel. (01504) 364413. Publish: local history, folklore books. Director: Adrian Kerr.

Institute of Public Administration (1957) Vergemount Hall, Clonskeagh, Dublin 6. Tel. (01) 2697011. Publish: government, political, health, law, history, academic books. Director: Jim O'Donnell.

Irish Academic Press Ltd. (1974) Kill Lane, Blackrock, Co. Dublin. Tel. (01) 2892922. Publish: academic books. Director: Michael Adams.

Kingstown Press Eagle House, 5 Marine Road, Dún Laoghaire, Co. Dublin. Tel. (01) 2803684. Publish: trade, novels, poetry books. Director: Henry O'Hagan.

The Lilliput Press (1984) 4 Rosemount Terrace, Arbour Hill, Dublin 7. Tel/Fax. (01) 6711647. Publish: fiction, non-fiction, Irish literary, autobiography, history books. Director: A. Farrell.

Mercier Press Ltd. (1944) P.O. Box 5, 5 French Church Street, Cork. Tel. (021) 275040. Publish: history, literary, religious, folklore books. Director: John F. Spillane.

Oak Tree Press (1992) Merrion Building, Lower Merrion Street, Dublin 2. Tel. (01) 6761600. Publish: financial, legal, business books.

Director: Brian O'Kane.

O'Brien Press Ltd., The (1974) 20 Victoria Road, Rathgar, Dublin 6. Tel. (01) 4923333. Publish: Irish interest, children's, history, architecture books. Director: Michael O'Brien.

On Stream Publications Ltd. (1992) Currabaha, Cloghroe, Blarney, Co. Cork. Tel/Fax. (021) 385798. Publish: cookery, health, historical books. Director: Roz Crowley.

Poolbeg Press Ltd. (1976) 123 Baldoyle Industrial Estate, Baldoyle, Dublin 13. Tel. (01) 8321477. Publish: biography, children's, political, history books. Director: Philip MacDermott.

Roberts Rinehart Publishers Trinity House, Charleston Road, Ranelagh, Dublin 6. Tel. (01) 4976860. Publish: arts, environment, Irish interest, history, biography, children's books. Director: Jack Van Zandt.

Round Hall Press Ltd., The Kill Lane, Blackrock, Co. Dublin. Tel. (01) 2892922. Publish: Law books and journals. Director: Michael Adams.

Sporting Books 4 Sycamore Road, Mount Merrion, Co. Dublin. Tel. (01) 2887914. Publish: sporting books. Director: Raymond Smith.

Town House and Country House (1980) Trinity House, Charleston Road, Ranelagh, Dublin 6. Tel. (01) 4972399. Publish: biography, art, archaeology books. Director: Treasa Coady.

Veritas Publications (1969) 7-8 Lower Abbey Street, Dublin 1. Tel. (01) 8788177. Publish: religious books. Director: Fr. Sean Melody.

Wolfhound Press 68 Mountjoy Square, Dublin 1. Tel. (01) 8740354. Publish: Irish interest, biography, children's, law books. Director: Seamus Cashman.

WRITERS' GROUPS IN IRELAND

ANTRIM
Belfast 20 Drumcree Place, Newtownabbey. BT37 9JA. Tel: (01232) 862997.
City Writers c/o Linen Hall Library, Donegall Square North, Belfast. Tel: (01232) 242338.
Conway Mill Conway Mill Education Centre, 5-7 Conway St., Belfast. Tel: (01232) 242338.
Divis Divis Community Centre, 9 Ardmullan Place, Belfast.
Harmony Hill Creative Harmony

Hill Arts Centre, Lisburn. Tel: (01846) 662445.
Shankill Shankill Women's Centre, 79 Shankill Rd., Belfast. Tel: (01232) 240642.
ARMAGH
Armagh Writers 8 Woodford Heights, Armagh BT60 2DY.
CARLOW
Carlow Writers c/o 1 Strawhill Villas, Carlow. Tel: (0503) 31485.
CAVAN
Cootehill Writers' Gp., c/o Arts

Festival Committee, Cootehill.
CLARE
Adult Literacy 25 Cusack Rd., Ennis.
Killaloe Boru Lodge, Killaloe.
Kilshanney Carrowkeel, Kilshanney.
North Clare Main St., Ennistymon. Tel: (065) 71258.
Shannon c/o 135 Cluain Airne, Shannon Town.
CORK
Carrigaline & District Kiely Estate,

Belgooly. Tel: (021) 770783.

Cork City City Library, Cork.

Cork Prison Cork Prison, Cork. Tel: (021) 503277.

Cork Women's Poetry Circle 22 Mount Oval, Rochestown, Cork. Tel: (021) 895046.

Great Island 20 Assumption Place, Cobh.

Midleton 3 Beechwood Court, Youghal Rd., Midleton.Tel: (021) 613355.

Northside 134 Farranferris Ave., Cork.Tel: (021) 394432.

The Women's 82 Tathmore Terrace, Richmond Hill, Cork. Tel: (021) 272036.

DERRY

Derry Verbal Arts Centre, Cathedral School Building, London St., Derry BT48 6RQ.

Flowerfield Workshop c/o Flowerfield Arts Centre, 185 Coleraine Rd., Portstewart. Tel: (01265) 833959.

DONEGAL

Gleneely Aghatubbrid, Gleneely, Lifford P.O., Inishowen.

Killybegs Church Rd., Killybegs.

Letterkenny c/o Gallagher's Hotel, Letterkenny. Tel: (074) 24985.

Letterkenny - for Women c/o the Women's Centre, Rainey's Yard, Letterkenny. Tel: (074) 24985.

Ramelton The Rectory, Ramelton.

DOWN

Newtownards Creative Ards Arts Centre, Town Hall, Newtownards. Tel: (01247) 816753.

Newry Creative Adult Education Centre, Downshire Rd., Newry.Tel: (01247) 69359.

DUBLIN

Balbriggan Balbriggan Library, Georges Square, Balbriggan.

Ballymun 77 Earnonn Ceannt Tower, Ballymun, D11, Ballymun Writers' Gp., Ballymun Library, Ballymun Rd., D11. Tel: (01) 8421890.

Dollymount 21 Dollymount Park, Clontarf, D3. PARC Writers' Gp., Parents Alone Resource Centre, 325 Bunratty Rd., Coolock, D17.

Dublin Workshop South William Bar, South William St., D2.

Dundrum College of Commerce, Main St., Dundrum, D14. Tel: (01) 4945392.

Poetry Plus 35 Mulgrave St. , Dun Laoghaoire.

Fertile Quill 31 Pine Valley Ave., Rathfarnham, D16.

Fingal c/o 52 Cromcastle Court,

Kilmore, D17. Tel: (01) 8471510.

Finglas Fingal Centre for the Unemployed, St. Helena's Resource Centre, St. Helena's Rd., Finglas West, D11.

Klear St. Mary's National School, Grangepark View, Raheny, D5. Tel: (01) 8316255.

Malahide 27 Chalfont Place, Malahide.

Onion Field Literary Circle Richard Crosby's Pub, Ranelagh, D6.

Prison Writers c/o Teachers' Unit, Mountjoy Prison, North Circular Rd., D7.

Riversdale VEC, Corduff, Blanchardstown, D15.

Oasis Literary Gp. 41 Balally Court, Sandyford, D16.

Skerries 33 Shenick Ave., Skerries.

Swords 13 River Valley View, Swords.

Jobstown c/o West Tallaght Resource Centre, Tallaght, D24. Tel: (01) 4525788.

Priory c/o Priory School, Tallaght, D24.

Women's Writers 76 Stillorgan Wood, Stillorgan.

Writers' Island 3 Desmond St., South Circular Rd., D8.

GALWAY

Barna Adult Education Knocknagreine House, Furbo. Tel: (091) 92365.

Clifden Cleggan.

Galway Workshop Auburn House, Fairhill, Galway. Tel: (091) 62587.

Inisbofin Forum, Inisbofin Island.

Kinvara Ballyvaughan Rd., Kinvara.

Letterfrack c/o Connemara West Centre, Letterfrack.

Moycullen Moycullen Community Centre, Moycullen.

Tuam Gateside, Impala Lodge, Bermingham Rd., Tuam.

KERRY

Dingle Dingle.

Listowel St. Patrick's Hall, Listowel.

Moyvane Gp. Moyvane.

Tralee Rosboultra, 43 Meadowlands, Tralee.

KILDARE

Celbridge c/o Gateway Bookshop, Celbridge.

Cill Dara Inshalla, 55 Woodlands, Naas. Tel: (045) 76644.

Maynooth Maynooth Library, Maynooth.

KILKENNY

Kilkenny Arts and Education Office, Ormond Rd., Kilkenny.

Mooncoin Chapel St., Mooncoin.

Thomastown Legan, Thomastown.

LAOIS

Stradbally Tullamoy.

LEITRIM

Knocknarea Dromahair.

LIMERICK

Limerick Poetry 11 Aylesbury, Dooradoyle, Limerick. Tel: (061) 301881.

Newcastle West c/o The Tallyhoe Pub, Newcastle West. Tel: (069) 62737.

Raheen Springdale, Raheen Rd., Raheen.

LONGFORD

Granard Newtownbond, Balinalee, Co. Longford. Tel: (043) 71179.

LOUTH

The Barbican 22 Fair St., Drogheda. Tel: (041) 33946.

Dundalk Town Hall, Dundalk.

MAYO

Ballyhaunis c/o Ballyhaunis Chamber of Commerce, Ballyhaunis.

Ballina c/o the Mortgage Store, Ballina.Tel: (0960 70394.

Ballinrobe Ballinrobe.

Castlebar Linen Hall Arts Centre, Linenhall St. , Castlebar. Tel: (094) 24115.

Castlebar Women Linenhall St., Castlebar.

Charlestown Murray's Pub, Charlestown.

Kiltimagh Main St., Kiltimagh.

Louisburgh Louisburgh.

Westport Knockranny, Westport. Tel: (098) 25657.

ROSCOMMON

Moylurg Frybrook Lodge, Mill Rd., Boyle. Tel: (079) 62186.

Roscommon Abbey 'Greenfields', Mount Prospect. Tel: (0903) 25126.

Tulsk Kelly's Bar, Tulsk.

SLIGO

Force 10 Marcievicz Centre for Unemployed, The Village, High St., Sligo. Tel: (071) 42925.

Northwest Writers One The Arts Office, Abbey St., Sligo. Tel: (071) 45844.

TIPPERARY

Clonmel 1 Summerhill, Hill Drive, Clonmel.

Nenagh c/o Nationwide Building Society, Nenagh.

TYRONE

Lough Shore WEA c/o Fitzduff's, Loughshore. Tel: (012487) 37211.

WATERFORD

Initials c/o Downes Pub, Thomas St., Waterford. Tel: (051) 55290.

WESTMEATH

Athlone c/o Athlone Library, Athlone. Tel: (0902) 92166. Granard Writing Gp., Kilmore St., Granard.
WEXFORD

Wexford Community c/o Wexford Arts Centre, Cornmarket. Tel: (053) 23764.
WICKLOW
Arklow Alec Building, Wexford Rd.,

Arklow.
Ashford Ballylusk Lodge, Ashford.
Bray Writers' Workshop, Mayfair Hotel, Bray.

GALLERIES AND ART CENTRES

ANTRIM
Arches 2 Holywood Rd., Belfast.
Arts Council 185 Stranmillis Rd., Stranmillis. Tel: (01232) 381591.
The Attic 6 Victoria St., Ballymoney.
Ballyearl 585 Church Rd., Newtownabbey
Catalyst 5 Exchange Place, Belfast. Tel: (01232) 313303.
Cavehill 18 Old Cavehill Rd., Belfast. Tel: (01232) 776784.
Clotworthy Castle Grounds, Randalstown Rd., Antrim.
Crescent 2-4 University Rd., Belfast. (01232) 242338.
An Culturlann 216 Falls Rd., Belfast. Tel: (01232) 239303.
Eakin Gallery 237 Lisburn Rd., Belfast. Tel: (01232) 668522.
Harmony Hill 54 Harmony Hill, Lambeg, Lisburn.
Gilmore Charles 31 Church Rd., Holywood, Belfast.
Magee 455 Ormeau Rd., Belfast.
Old Museum 7 College Square North, Belfast. Tel: (01232) 235053.
One Oxford St. 1 Oxford St., Belfast. Tel:(01232) 310400.
Seymour 20 Seymour St., Lisburn.
The Bell 13 Adelaide Park, Belfast.
The Fenderesky Crescent Arts Centre, 2-4 University Rd., Belfast.
Ulster Museum Botanic Gardens, Belfast. Tel: (01232) 383000.
ARMAGH
The Adam 28 Linenhall St., Armagh. Tel: (012657) 526908.
Armagh County Museum The Mall East, Armagh. Tel: (01861) 523070.
Hayloft Armagh.
The Peacock Craigavon.
Pineback House Arts Tullygally Rd., Craigavon. Tel: (01762) 41618.
CAVAN
Cavan County Arts Service Cavan Town. Tel: (049) 62003.
CARLOW
Pembroke Studio Carlow Town. Tel: (0503) 41562.
CLARE
The Atlantis Kilshanny.
Burren Painting Centre Lisdoonvarna. Tel: (065) 74208.
Dallán Ballyvaughan.
De Valera Library Ennis. Tel: (065) 21616.
Clare Branch Library Ennistymon.

Tel: (065) 71245.
Seán Lemass Library Shannon.
CORK
Bantry Library, Bantry.
Blackcoombe Cork. Tel: (021) 501319.
Boole Library, University College Cork.
Charleville Library Charleville.
Crawford Municipal Cork City.
Keane-on-Ceramics Kinsale.
Lavitt's Quay Cork City. Tel: (021) 277749.
O'Kane's Green Bantry.
Sirius Commemoration Trust Cobh. Tel: (021) 316899.
The Art Hive Cork City. Tel: (021) 505228.
The Bandon Bandon.
Triskel Tobin St., Cork City.
Vangard Macroom. Tel: (026) 41198.
West Cork North St., Skibbereen. Tel: (028) 22090.
DERRY
Context Derry. Tel: (01504) 268027.
Flowerfield 185 Coleraine Rd., Portstewart. Tel: (01265) 833959.
Foyle Lawrence Hill, Derry. Tel: (01504) 266657.
Gordon 7 London St., Derry. Tel: (01504) 374044.
Orchard Derry. Tel: (01504) 269675.
The Playhouse 5-7 Artillery St., Derry. Tel: (01504) 264481.
Riverside Coleraine. Tel: (01265) 51388.
Town House Coleraine.
Verbal Arts Centre, Cathedral School Building, London St., Derry.
DONEGAL
The Gallery Main Street, Donegal. Tel: (073) 22686.
Bennetts Ardara. Tel: (075) 41652.
Cristeph Letterkenny. Tel: (074) 26411.
Donegal County Arts Service Letterkenny.
Donegal County Museum, Letterkenny. Tel: (074) 24613.
Dunfanaghy. Tel: (074) 36224.
Glebe House Churchill. Tel: (074) 37071.
House on the Brae Arts Ramelton. Tel: (074) 51240.
Port Letterkenny.
Ram's Head Kilcar.

Tullyarvan Mill Buncrana. Tel: (077) 61613.
Ulster Cultural Institute Glencolumbcille.
DOWN
Ards Town Hall, Conway Square, Newtownards. Tel: (01247) 810803.
Castle Espie Comber. Tel: (01247) 874146.
Cleft Donaghadee. Tel: (01247) 888502.
Down Centre, 2-6 Irish St., Downpatrick. Tel: (01396) 615283.
Grant Fine Art Newcastle. Tel: (013967) 22349.
Newcastle Newcastle. Tel: (013967) 23555.
Newry & Mourne 1a Bank Parade, Newry. Tel: (01693) 66232.
North Down Visitors & Heritage Centre Bangor.
Priory Holywood.
Salem Comber.
Shambles Hillsborough.
DUBLIN
Aine von Gosseln, 11 Suffolk St., D2. Tel: (01) 6714079.
Andrew's Lane Theatre 9 St. Andrews Lane, D2.
The Architecture Centre.
The Arts Council, 70 Merrion Square, D2. Tel: (01) 6611840.
Bobby Dawson 16 Georges St. Upper, Dun Laoghaire.
Brock Ossory Business Park, D3.
The Chester Beatty Library, 20 Shrewsbury Rd., D4.
Cill Rialaig 13 St. Stephens Green, D2. Tel: (01) 6707972.
City Arts Centre 23-25 Moss St., D2. Tel: (01) 6770643.
Combridge Fine Arts Ltd. 24 Suffolk St., D2. Tel: (01) 6774652.
The Courtyard 10A The Crescent, Monkstown. Tel: (01) 2807567.
Crafts Council South William St., D2. Tel: (01) 6797383.
Davis 11 Capel St., D1.
Designyard 12 East Essex St., D2.
Distinguished Artists 31 Molesworth St., D2.
Douglas Hyde Trinity College, D2.
Dublin Photographic Centre.
Dublin Public Libraries.
Dublin Writers Museum 18 Parnell Square, D1. Tel: (01) 8722077.
Dun Laoghaire/Rathdown Arts

Centre.

European Fine Arts 6 Merrion Street Lr., D2. Tel: (01) 6762506.

Frederick 24 Frederick St. Sth., D2.

The Gallery of Photography, 44 Essex St. East, D2.

Terenure, 95 Terenure Rd. North, Terenure. Tel: (01) 4902678.

Gorry 20 Molesworth St., D2.

Graphic Studio Dublin Cope St., D2. Tel: (01) 6798021.

Green on Red 58 Fitzwilliam Square, D2. Tel: (01) 6613881.

Guinness Foxrock Village, D18.

Guinness Hop Store St. James's Gate, D8. Tel: (01) 4538364.

Hallward 65 Merrion Square, D2.

The Harrison 18 Stephens St. Lr., D2. Tel: (01) 4785580.

Howth Harbour 6 Abbey St., Howth. Tel: (01) 8393366.

Hugh Lane Municipal Parnell Sq., D1.

Irish Life Exhibition Centre.

Irish Museum of Modern Art Royal Hospital, Kilmainham, D8.

James' 7 Railway Rd., Dalkey.

Jo Rain's 23 Anglesea St., D2. Tel: (01) 6779966.

The Kennedy 12 Harcourt St., D2. Tel: (01) 4751740.

The Kerlin South Anne St., D2. Tel: (01) 6709093.

The Mansion House Dawson St., D2. Tel: (01) 676 1845.

Milmo-Penny Fine Art 55 Ailesbury Rd., D4. Tel: (01) 2693486.

Modern Art Parnell Sq., D1.

The National Gallery of Ireland Merrion Square, D2.

New Apollo 18 Duke St., D2.

New Art Studio Ltd. 2 Mary's Abbey, D7. Tel: (01) 8730617.

Oisín 44 Westland Row, D2.

Oisín Fairview, D3. Tel: (01) 8333456.

Old Bawn Community School Tallaght, D24. Tel: (01) 4520566.

Oriel 17 Clare St., D2.

Original Print 4 Temple Bar, D2.

Pantheon Gallery.

Phoenix Art Studio Lucan.

The Portrait 24 Glencarrig, D13.

The Project Arts Centre 39 East Essex St., D2. Tel: (01) 6712321.

R.D.S. Ballsbridge, D4.

R.H.A. Gallagher 15 Ely Place, D2.

Rubicon 10 St. Stephens Green, D2. Tel: (01) 6762331.

The Solomon South William St., D2. Tel: (01) 6794237.

Stoneleaf Foundation 19 Manor St., D7. Tel: (01) 6707349.

Swords Art & Craft Centre 10

North St., Swords.

Tallaght Community Virginia House, Blessington Road, D24.

Taylor Galleries Ltd. 34 Kildare St., D2. Tel: (01) 6766055.

Temple Bar Gallery & Studios 5 Temple Bar, D2. Tel: (01) 6710073.

Thulla Studio 6 Abbey St., Howth.

Venus 51 Middle Abbey St., D1.

Village 47 Thomas Hand St., Skerries. Tel: (01) 8492236.

The Waldock Blackrock.

Westside Orchard Rd., Clondalkin. Tel: (01) 4573954.

Wyvern 41 Baggot St. Lower, D2. Tel: (01) 6789930.

FERMANAGH

Ardhowen Theatre & Arts Centre Dublin Rd., Enniskillen. Tel: (01365) 323233.

Enniskillen Castle Heritage Centre Castle Barracks, Enniskillen.Tel: (01365) 325000.

GALWAY

Arcadia Antiques Castle St., Galway. Tel: (091) 561861.

Artspace 49 Dominick St., Galway.

Ballinasloe Library Ballinasloe. Tel: (0905) 43464.

The Bridge Mills O'Briens Bridge, Galway. Tel: (091) 566231.

Clifden Main St., Clifden.

An Damhlann - Kenny Gallery, Spiddal. Tel: (091) 553733.

Galway Arts Centre 47 Dominick St., Galway. Tel: (091) 65886.

The Grainstore University College Galway.

West Shore Oughterard.

KERRY

Bín Bán Tralee. Tel: (066) 22520.

Brushwood Derryquin, Sneem.

Cora's Killorglin. Tel: (066) 61033.

Crannog Dingle. Tel: (066) 51666.

Frank Lewis Killarney.

Iverni Kenmare.

Kerry Branch Library Killarney. Tel: (064) 32972.

The Killarney Killarney.

Sheeóg Killorglin. Tel: (066) 61220.

Siamsa Tire Theatre Town Park, Tralee. Tel: (066) 23055.

Simple Pleasures Art Gallery Dingle. Tel: (066) 51224.

The Square Listowel.

St. John's Arts and Heritage Centre Tralee Library, Tralee.

The Wellspring Tralee. Tel: (066) 21218.

Woodland Castleisland.

KILDARE

Athy Library, Athy. Crookstown Mill Heritage Centre, Ballitore.

Kilcock Kilcock. Tel: (01) 6287619.

Kildare Branch Library Celbridge.

Kildare Branch Library, Naas.

Maynooth Exhibition Centre Maynooth.

Tuckmill Naas. Tel: (045) 879761.

KILKENNY

Butler Kilkenny. Tel: (056) 61106.

Kilkenny County Library Graiguenamanagh.

The Berkeley Thomastown.

LAOIS

Laois County Hall Portlaoise.

LEITRIM

Fionn MacCumhaill Centre Keshcarrigen.

Old Barrel Store Carrick-on-Shannon. Tel: (078) 20911.

LIMERICK

AV University of Limerick.

Anne Fitzgerald Limerick. Tel: (061) 339995.

Angela Woulfe 16 Perry Square, Limerick. Tel: (061) 310164.

Belltable 69 O'Connell St., Limerick. Tel: (061) 319709.

Chris Doswell's Limerick.

Dolmen Limerick.

Gallery Limerick. Tel: (061) 315650.

Limerick Branch Library Foynes.

Limerick City Gallery of Art.

Muse Limerick.

Newcastle West Library.

LONGFORD

Carroll Gallery Longford. Tel: (043) 41148.

LOUTH

Artistic License Carlingford.

The Basement Dundalk.

County Museum Dundalk.

Droichead Stockwell St., Drogheda. Tel: (041) 33496.

Holy Trinity Heritage Carlingford.

Louth Branch Library Ardee. Tel: (041) 56080.

Tristann's Dundalk.

MAYO

The Aimhirgin Louisburgh.

ArtStudio Bridge St., Westport.

Ballinglen Arts Foundation Ltd. Main St., Ballycastle.

Castlebar Public Library Castlebar. Tel: (094) 24444.

Claremorris Claremorris.

Foxford Exhibition Centre Foxford. Tel: (094) 56488.

The Kirk Castlebar.

The Linenhall Linenhall St., Castlebar. Tel: (094) 23733.

Western Light Achill Island.

Westport Public Library Westport.

Yawl Achill Island.

MEATH

Navan Library Navan.

Trim Library Trim.

MONAGHAN
Market House Monaghan.
Monaghan County Museum Monaghan. Tel: (047) 82928.
OFFALY
Offaly County Library Service Tullamore. Tel: (0506) 21419.
SLIGO
Artist K Studios Lower Quay St., Sligo. Tel: (071) 42552.
Hawk's Well Theatre Temple St., Sligo. Tel: (071) 61526.
Sligo - Yeats Building, Sligo.
Taylor's Riverstown. Tel: (071) 65138.
The Model Arts Centre The Mall, Sligo. Tel: (071) 41405.
TIPPERARY
Carrick-on-Suir Heritage Centre Carrick-on-Suir.
Nenagh District Heritage Centre

Nenagh.
Roscrea Heritage Centre Roscrea.
South Tipperary Clonmel. Tel: (052) 27877.
Tipperary County Library Service Thurles. Tel: (0504) 21555.
Tipperary (SR) County Museum Clonmel. Tel: (052) 25399.
The Lucy Erridge Birdhill.
TYRONE
An Creagán Visitor Centre Creggan, Omagh.
Gateway Centre & Museum Grange Court Complex, 21 Moyle Rd., Newtownstewart.
WATERFORD
Garter Lane 22a O'Connell St., Waterford. Tel: (051) 55038.
Lismore Library Lismore. Tel: (058) 54128.
The Pill Gallery 37b John St.,

Waterford. Tel: (051) 876445.
WESTMEATH
Dolan Moore Athlone.
Midland Arts Resource Centre Austin Friar St., Mullingar.
WEXFORD
Ladyship Oils Killurin.
Wexford Arts Centre Cornmarket. Tel: (053) 23764.
Woodland Arts & Crafts Gorey.
The Chantry Bunclody.
WICKLOW
Aisling Newtownmountkennedy. Tel: (01) 2819112.
Craft Bray. Tel: (01) 2866728.
The Hangman Bray. Tel: (01) 2866208.
Renaissance III Wicklow.
Signal Bray. Tel: (01) 2864266.

THEATRES, THEATRE COMPANIES & RECEIVING VENUES IN IRELAND

ANTRIM
Aisteoiri Aon Drama 216 Falls Rd., Belfast. Tel: (01232) 239303.
Arts Theatre 41 Botanic Ave., Belfast. Tel: (01232) 316900.
Belfast Theatre Co. 207 Russell Court, Belfast. Tel: (01232) 241950.
Belfast Waterfront Hall 2 Lanyon Place, Belfast. Tel: (01232) 334400.
Castleward Opera 61 Marlborough Pk. North, Belfast. Tel: (01232) 661090.
Centre Stage 99 Fitzroy Ave., Belfast. Tel: (01232) 249119.
Clotworthy House Arts Centre Randalstown Rd., Antrim.
DubbelJoint Productions 351-353 Lisburn Rd., Belfast.
Golden Thread Theatre Brookfield Business Centre, 333 Crumlin Road, Belfast.
Grand Opera House Great Victoria St., Belfast. Tel: (01232) 240411.
The Group Theatre Bedford St., Belfast. Tel: (01232) 329685.
Kabosh Productions P.O. Box 559, Belfast.
Lyric Players Theatre 55 Ridgeway St., Belfast. Tel: (01232) 669660.
Mad Cow Productions Ormeau Ave., Belfast. Tel: (01232) 313156.
Old Museum Arts Centre, 7 College Square North, Belfast.
Opera Northern Ireland Stranmillis Rd., Stranmillis, Belfast.
Point Fields Theatre Co. Ltd. Cathedral Buildings, 64 Donegall St., Belfast. Tel: (01232) 314774.
Prime Cut, Unit 404, McAvoy

House, 17a Ormeau Ave., Belfast.
Replay Productions Old Museum Arts Centre, 7 College Square North, Belfast. Tel: (01232) 322724.
Shanakee Productions 93 Kimberley Street, Belfast.Tel: (01232) 644276.
Tinderbox Theatre Co. Unit 104, McAvoy House, 17a Ormeau Ave., Belfast. Tel: (01232) 439313.
Ulster Hall Bedford St., Belfast.
The Ulster Theatre Co. Park Rd., Belfast. Tel: (01232) 645472.
Virtual Reality Flat 3, 31 Wellington Park, Belfast. Tel: (01232) 666042.
Who the Hell Theatre Co. 63 Ardenvohr St., Belfast.
ARMAGH
Gateway Theatre Co. 57 Gilford Rd., Portadown.
CARLOW
Bridewell Lane Theatre Bridewell Lane, Tullow St., Carlow.
CAVAN
Cornmill Theatre & Arts Centre Main St., Carrigallen.
CLARE
Theatre Omnibus Business Centre Francis St., Ennis.
CORK
Boomerang Youth Theatre Co. Dean St., Cork. Tel: (021) 316826.
Cork Arts & Theatre Club 7 Knapps Sq., Cork.
Cork Opera House Emmet Place, Cork. Tel: (021) 274308.
Everyman Palace 15 McCurtain St., Cork. Tel: (021) 503077.
Firkin Crane Centre Shandon,

Cork. Tel: (021) 407487.
Graffiti Theatre Co. Ltd. 50 Popes Quay, Cork. Tel: (021) 505758.
Kickstart Theatre Community Centre, Gurrahabraher Rd., Cork.
New Granary Theatre University College, Mardyke, Cork.
Schoolyard Theatre Old Limerick Rd., Charleville. Tel: (063) 81844.
DERRY
Big Telly Theatre Co., Flowerfield Art Centre, Coleraine Rd., Portstewart. Tel: (01265) 832588.
Field Day Theatre Co. Foyle Arts Centre, Lawrence Hill, Derry.
Minkey Hill Theatre Co. Foyle Arts Centre, Lawrence Hill, Derry.
O'Casey Theatre Co. The Playhouse, Artillery St., Derry.
Rialto Entertainment Centre 5 Market Street, Derry.
Ridiculusmus The Playhouse, Artillery St., Derry.
Riverside Theatre Cromore Rd., Coleraine, Co. Derry.
Stage Beyond Theatre Co., Play Resource Centre., Artillery Street, Derry.
St. Columb's Theatre & Art Centre Orchard St., Derry.
DONEGAL
Abbey Centre Ballyshannon.
Balor Theatre Ballybofey. Tel: (074) 31840.
DOWN
Ulster Theatre Co. 54 Drumnaconagher Rd., Crossgar.
DUBLIN
Abbey & Peacock Theatre Lower

Abbey St., D1. Tel: (01) 8748741.

Ambassador Theatre Parnell St., D1. Tel: (01) 8727000.

Andrew's Lane Theatre Exchequer St., D2. Tel: (01) 6795720.

Crypt Art Centre Dublin Castle, D2.

Down-to-Earth Theatre Co. Ltd., 61 Middle Abbey St., D1.

Dublin Grand Opera Society John Player Hse., S C Rd., D8.

Dublin Theatre Festival Ltd. 47 Nassau St, D2. Tel: (01) 6778439.

Dublin Youth Theatre, 23 Gardiner St. Upper, D1. Tel: (01) 8743687.

The Eblana Theatre Busaras, Store St., D1. Tel: (01) 8745470.

Focus Theatre Co. 6 Pembroke Place, D2. Tel: (01) 6763071.

Gaiety Theatre South King Street, D2. Tel: (01) 6795622.

Gas Works Theatre Co. Dublin.

Gate Theatre 8 Parnell Square, D1.

Iomha Ildanach Theatre Co. Ltd. 6 Capel St., D1. Tel: (01) 6713387.

Lambert Puppet Theatre & Museum Clifton Lane, Monkstown.

Olympia Theatre, 72 Dame St., D2.

Opera Theatre Co. 18 St. Andrew St., D2. Tel: (01) 6794962.

Pan Pan Theatre 1 Haigh Terrace, Dun Laoghaire. Tel: (01) 2800544.

Passion Machine Theatre Co., 30 Gardiner Place, D7.

Point Theatre Eastlink Bridge, D1.

Project Arts Centre 39 East Essex St., D2. Tel: (01) 6712321.

R.D.S. Simmonscourt Pavillion, Ballsbridge, D4.

Riverbank Studio/Theatre 10 Merchants Quay, D8.

Rough Magic Ltd. 5 South Great Georges St., D2. Tel: (01) 6719278.

Samuel Beckett Theatre Trinity College, D2. Tel: (01) 7021239.

Second Age Ltd. 30 Dame St., D2.

Smashing Times Theatre Co. Meeting House Lane, D7.

St. Anthony's Theatre Merchants Quay, D8. Tel: (01) 6777651.

Sticks & Stones Theatre Co., 19 Watkins Square, D8.

Storytellers' Theatre Co. Ltd. Parliament St., D2.

Team Theatre Co. 4 Marlborough Place, D1. Tel: (01) 8786108.

Tivoli Theatre 135-138 Francis St., D2. Tel: (01) 4546349.

FERMANAGH

Ardhowen Theatre, Dublin Rd., Enniskillen. Tel: (01365) 323233.

GALWAY

Down to Earth Theatre Co. Ltd. Shantalla. Tel: (091) 529684.

Druid Theatre Co. Chapel Lane, Galway. Tel: (091) 568617.

Glenamaddy Townhall Theatre Creggs Rd., Glenamaddy, Galway.

Mall Theatre The Mall, Tuam.

Punchbag Theatre Co. 47 Dominick St., Galway.

Taibhdhearc na Gaillimhe Sráid Lár, Galway. Tel: (091) 562024.

Town Hall Theatre, Courthouse Sq., Galway. Tel: (091) 569777.

KERRY

Siamsa Tire Theatre Tralee.

KILDARE

The Grove Theatre, Leinster St., Athy. Tel: (0507) 38375.

KILKENNY

Barnstorm Theatre New St., Kilkenny. Tel: (056) 51266.

Cleere's Theatre 28 Parliament St., Kilkenny. Tel: (056) 62573.

Watergate Theatre Co. Parliament St., Kilkenny. Tel: (056) 61674.

LEITRIM

Eggert Rodger Glenboy, Manorhamilton. Tel: (072) 55856.

LIMERICK

The Belltable 69 O'Connell St., Limerick. Tel: (061) 319866.

Theatre Royal Upr. Cecil St., Limerick. Tel: (061) 414224.

LONGFORD

Backstage Theatre Farneyhoogan, Longford. Tel: (043) 47889.

Bog Lane Theatre Bog Lane, Ballymahon, Longford.

LOUTH

Dundalk Town Hall Crowe St., Dundalk, Co. Louth. Tel: (042)

32276.

Footprint Productions, Quay St., Dundalk. Tel: (042) 27072.

MAYO

Yew Theatre Co. Cresent Hse., Casement St., Ballina.

MEATH

Duchas Folk Theatre, Castle St., Trim, Co. Meath.

MONAGHAN

Garage Theatre St. Davnet's Complex, Armagh Rd., Monaghan.

SLIGO

Blue Raincoat Theatre Co. Lower Quay St., Sligo. Tel: (071) 70431.

Hawk's Well Theatre Temple St., Sligo. Tel: (071) 61526.

TIPPERARY

Galloglass Theatre Co. Ltd. Nelson St., Clonmel.

Magner's Theatre The Mall, Clonmel, Co. Tipperary.

Phoenix Theatre Gas House Lane, Tipperary. Tel: (062) 33266.

Regal Theatre Davis Rd., Clonmel.

TYRONE

Bardic Theatre Dungannon District Council, Circular Rd., Dungannon.

WATERFORD

Forum Theatre The Glen, Waterford. Tel: (051) 871111.

Garter Lane Theatre 22A O'Connell St., Waterford. Tel: (051) 877153.

Red Kettle Theatre Co. 33 O'Connell St., Waterford.

Theatre Royal The Mall, Waterford.

WEXFORD

Gorey Little Theatre Pearse St., Gorey. Tel: (055) 21608.

Razor Edge Arts Theatre Co. Ltd. Paul Quay, Wexford.

St. Michael's Theatre South St., New Ross. Tel: (051) 421255.

Theatre Royal High St., Wexford.

WICKLOW

Dry Rain Performing Arts Centre An Lar Dargle Rd. Lower, Bray.

DRAMATIC PRODUCTIONS IN R.O.I., 1990-94
Number of First Production Performances in R.O.I.

Origin of Production (as % of all productions)	1990	1991	1992	1993	1994
Republic of Ireland	24	22	19	17	17
Outside Republic of Ireland	28	25	21	12	12

Origin of Production of First Performances in R.O.I.

Country	%
Northern Ireland	24
England, Scotland, Wales	56
America	7
Rest of Europe	5
Other	4
Unknown	4
Total	100

Location of First Performances

Location	%
Dublin	58
Rest of Leinster	2
Munster	17
Connacht/Ulster	18
Other/Outside Ireland	5
Total	100

Seating Capacity of First Performance Venues in R.O.I.

Seating Capacity	%
150 or less	34
151 - 250	24
251 - 550	24
More than 550	10
Outdoor Venue	5
Unknown	3
Total	100

Attendance at All Performances in R.O.I.

% Attendance	%
50 or less	24
51 - 75	30
More than 75	40
N/A	3
Unknown	3
Total	100

Running Length of All Performances in R.O.I.

Duration	%
Less than 2 weeks	17
1 Month	40
2 Months	24
3 Months	8
More than 3 Months	5
Unknown	6
Total	100

Financial Outcome of All Performances in R.O.I.

Financial Outcome	%
Profit	19
Broke-even	31
Loss	49
Unknown	1
Total	100

R.O.I.: THEATRE-GOING AUDIENCE, 1994

	Never %	Once a Year %	1-6 Times a Year %	More Than 6 Times %
Area:				
Rural	66	14	18	1
Urban	61	16	20	4
Region:				
Dublin	52	18	24	5
Dublin County	56	21	24	0
Rest of Leinster	67	15	15	3
Munster	63	16	20	2
Connacht / Ulster	75	8	16	1
Gender:				
Male	68	15	15	2
Female	59	15	23	3
Age Groups:				
15 - 24	66	17	16	1
25 - 34	65	15	17	3
35 - 44	60	15	22	2
45 - 54	62	12	22	4
55 +	62	15	20	2
Marital Status:				
Single	66	16	17	2
Married	62	15	21	3
Children under 18				
Yes	65	15	19	1
No	62	16	19	3

Social Class:

Middle Class	42	19	32	7
Skilled-Working Class	65	17	16	1
Semi-skilled / Unskilled Working Class	80	10	9	1
Farmers	69	14	17	1

Education:

Third Level (currently/completed)	37	22	34	8
Second Level (currently/completed)	60	14	24	3
Attended Second Level	75	15	10	3
Primary Level	81	11	9	-

DUBLIN THEATRE FESTIVAL

The Dublin Theatre Festival, Europe's oldest specialist theatre festival, was founded in 1957. Each year, for the first two weeks in October, it features the best of international theatre, along with new work from many of Ireland's leading up-and-coming playwrights and established writers. Of the 35 productions presented, one-third are foreign and at least eight are full-length new Irish plays. All major Dublin theatres are involved in the festival, including the National Theatre (Abbey and Peacock stages), the Gate, Gaiety, and the Olympia Theatres plus a number of smaller venues. Visiting companies have included the Royal Shakespeare Company, Moscow Art Theatre, Schiller Theatre, Royal National Theatre, Peking Opera, Tokyo Globe, Royal Ballet and Actors Theatre of Louisville. The 1997 Festival played host to companies from Britain, France, Italy and the U.S.

DUBLIN THEATRE FESTIVAL ATTENDANCE FIGURES

Attends a Play	Every Year %	Some Years %	Once %	Don't Know %	Total
Never	-	1	-	-	758
Once a Year	1	5	2	-	181
1 - 6 times	4	13	4	-	230
More than 6 Times	20	27	7	3	30
Total:	1	4	2	-	1,199

THEATRE PRODUCTIONS: R.O.I., 1990-95

Type of Production	ORIGIN OF PRODUCTION	
	Republic of Ireland %	Outside the Republic of Ireland %
Nature of Play:		
New Writer (i.e. previously unstaged)	15	14
New Work of established writer (first staging)	31	29
Other 20th Century Work	37	32
Pre-20th Century	12	10
Unknown	5	15
Total	100	100
Nature of Written Play:		
Irish Writer in English Language	60	26
Irish Writer in Irish Language	3	-
Non-Irish Writer in English Language	25	42
New Translation by Irish Writer of Foreign Language Work	3	3
Other Translation of Foreign Language Work	4	9
Unknown	5	19
Total	100	100
Nature of Audience:		
Children & Youth	15	9
Theatre-in-Education	8	4
Other Audience	77	87
Total:	100	100

MOST POPULAR PRODUCTIONS STAGED IN R.O.I. BY PROFESSIONAL THEATRE COMPANIES, 1990-95

Play	Playwright	Number of Times Staged
Macbeth	William Shakespeare	5
Othello	William Shakespeare	4
Romeo & Juliet	William Shakespeare	3
Translations	Brian Friel	3
Philadelphia, Here I Come!	Brian Friel	3
The Shadow of a Gunman	Sean O'Casey	3

IRISH PRODUCTIONS STAGED, 1990-1994

No. of Productions per writer	No. of Writers	% of Productions
1	210	40
2	30	11
3	10	6
4	9	7
5	5	5
6	6	7
7 - 9	4	6
More than 10*	5	13
25	Devised Pieces	5
Total	**279**	**100**

* Includes plays by Samuel Beckett, Bernard Dowd & Jean Regan (joint production), Brian Friel, Tom Murphy & William

REPUBLIC OF IRELAND: YOUTH DRAMA GROUPS

CAVAN:
Cootehill Youth Theatre, Cootehill.
Virginia Youth Drama, Virginia.
CLARE:
Corca Baiscinn Youth Theatre, Kilkee.
East Clare Youth Theatre, Clare.
CORK:
Activate Youth Theatre, Cork.
Boomerang Youth Theatre, Teach Barra, Dean St., Cork. Tel: (021) 316826.
CAT Knapps Youth Theatre, Cobh.
Rossmore Youth Theatre, Enniskeane.
Triskel Youth Theatre, Cork.
DONEGAL:
Butt Drama Circle, Ballybofey.
Finn Valley Youth Theatre, Stranorlar.
DUBLIN:
Belcony Belles, Dublin.
Blanchardstown Youth Theatre, Main St., Blanchardstown, Dublin 15. Tel: (01) 8212077.
Cabinteely Youth Theatre, Dublin.
Clondalkin Youth Theatre, Monastery Rd., Clondalkin, Dublin 22. Tel: (01) 4594666.
Dublin Youth Theatre, 23 Upper Gardiner St., Dublin 1. Tel: (01) 8743687.
Dun Laoghaire Youth Theatre, Eblana Avenue, Dun Laoghaire. Tel: (01) 2809363.

Howth Community Group, Howth.
Neilstown Youth Theatre, Neilstown, Dublin.
Newpark Youth Theatre, Blackrock.
Northside Youth Theatre, Coolock.
Red Cow Lane Youth Theatre, Dublin.
Route 36, Ballymun, Dublin.
Rush Junior Drama, Rush, Co. Dublin.
Skerries Youth Theatre, Skerries, Co. Dublin.
St. Kevin's Drama Group, Kilnamanagh, Dublin.
St. Columba's Company, Rathfarnham, Dublin.
Stagefright, Glasnevin, Dublin.
Tallaght Youth Theatre, Main Rd., Tallaght, Dublin 24. Tel: (01) 4516322.
Walk the Talk, Coolock.
GALWAY:
Aisteori Oga, Galway.
Galway Youth Theatre, Galway.
KERRY:
Killarney Youth Theatre, Kerry.
Pikeman Youth Theatre, Tralee.
KILDARE:
Athy Youth Theatre, Athy.
Kildare Youth Drama, Leixlip Branch Library, Leixlip. Tel: (01) 6245749.
KILKENNY:
Kilkenny Youth Theatre, New St., Kilkenny. Tel: (056) 61200.

LAOIS:
Laois Youth Theatre, Portlaoise.
LEITRIM:
Cornmill Youth Drama, Carrickallen.
LOUTH:
Droichead Youth Theatre, Louth.
Dundalk Youth Theatre, Louth.
MONAGHAN:
Back to Front Youth Theatre, Carrickmacross.
Carrickmacross Youth Theatre, Carrickmacross.
Corcaghan Youth Theatre, Stranoden.
Drumlin Youth Theatre, Castleblayney.
SLIGO:
Tubbercurry Youth Theatre, Tubbercurry.
TIPPERARY:
MANY Youth Theatre Co-op, Newport.
WATERFORD:
Waterford Youth Drama, 130 The Quay, Waterford. Tel: (051) 877328.
WESTMEATH:
Mullingar Youth Theatre, Mullingar.
WEXFORD:
Pocket Youth Theatre, Wexford.
Wexford Youth Theatre, Main St., Wexford. Tel: (053) 23262.
WICKLOW:
Dry Rain Youth Theatre, Lower Dargle Road, Bray.

DRAMA GROUPS
The Drama League of Ireland

The Drama League of Ireland (D.L.I.) was founded in 1966 as a voluntary organisation dedicated to promoting and fostering all aspects of amateur drama and theatre in Ireland. It is a founder member of N.A.Y.D. (National Association of Youth Drama), is affiliated to the Drama Association of Wales and has membership of the I.A.T.A. (International Amateur Theatre Association). The D.L.I. represents more than 200 groups/individuals with an estimated 3,000 performances annually and audiences totalling 400,000. In 1996, the D.L.I. gave £1,400 to members in Scholarships. Member groups travelled to Canada, France, Japan, Croatia, the U.S., Korea and Israel on trips abroad in 1996.

REGIONAL DISTRIBUTION OF YOUTH DRAMA GROUPS IN IRELAND (BASED ON 50 GROUPS)	
Region	No.of Groups
Dublin (City & Suburbs)	17
Rest of Leinster (includes Rush & Skerries)	13
Munster	8
Connacht	3
Donegal, Cavan, Monaghan	9
Total:	50

BIOGRAPHIES OF IRISH ARTISTS, SCULPTORS AND PAINTERS.

KEY:
RHA: Royal Hibernian Academy of Arts.
NCAD: National College of Art and Design, Dublin.
IMMA: Irish Museum of Modern Art, Dublin

Antrim, Lady (born Yorkshire, 1911). Sculptor and cartoonist. Director of Ulster Television. Former Governor of the Ulster College of Art. Commissions include: bronze sculptor and stained glass, Moyle Hospital, Larne; stone sculptors for St. Joseph's Church, Ballygally; the parliament buildings, Newfoundland. Died 1974.

Armstrong, Arthur (born Carrickfergus, 1921). Self-taught landscape painter. Featured in collections worldwide. Former member of the R.H.A. Exhibited widely in Ireland, Europe and U.S. Died 1996.

Ballagh, Robert (born Dublin, 1943). Renowned artist and designer. Qualified architect. Produced stage designs for much lauded plays and shows, including Riverdance. Completed government commissions for currency designs and postal stamps, also designed book covers.

Behan, John (born Dublin, 1938). Sculptor. Helped shape contemporary Irish painting and sculpture. Exhibits in all major Irish exhibitions from 1960. Commissions include: major corporate sculptures in Dublin, religious sculptures for churches, and works for the collections of the U.S. President and prominent galleries in Ireland.

Bewick, Pauline (born England, 1935). Reared Kerry. Prolific artist. Exhibited worldwide in private and public collections. Produced two well-known books on her work: The South Seas and a Box of Paint and The Yellow Man.

Biggs, Michael (born 1928). Sculptor. Primarily known for stone carving and letter cutting. Created many public and private inscriptions in stone, wood and bronze between 1950-1992. Died 1993.

Blackshaw, Basil (born Glengormley, 1932). Artist. Exhibited widely in Ireland and abroad. Designed posters for all the Field Day Productions (1986-90), and the Belfast '91 Calendar. Contributor to the Great Book of Ireland, I.M.M.A. (1991).

Bourke, Brian (born Dublin, 1936). Painter. Exhibited widely in Ireland and abroad. Represented Ireland at the Paris Biennale and the Lugano Exhibition of Graphics.

Bourke, Fergus (born Wicklow, 1934). Photographer. Works included in Famine Commemoration Exhibition, Clifden (1995). Seven of his photographs are in a permanent exhibition of New York's Museum of Modern Art.

Brady, Charles (born New York, 1926). Moved to Ireland (1961). Artist. Works included in many notable collections - the Arts Council, the Hugh Lane Municipal Gallery and the Derek Hill Collection. Regularly contributes to exhibitions at the Royal Hibernian Academy and the Irish Exhibition of Living Art.

Brandt, Muriel (born Belfast, 1909). Painter and portrait artist. Commissions include a series of decorative murals in the Franciscan Church of Adam and Eve, Dublin. Member of the Board of Governors of the National Gallery and the R.H.A. Mother of Ruth Brandt. Died 1981.

Brandt, Ruth (born Dublin, 1936). Artist. Lecturer at N.C.A.D. (1976-1988). Participated in the Irish Exhibition of Living Art and the R.H.A. Commissions include the new Met Offices, Glasnevin, stained-glass windows at Artane Oratory, Dublin. Solo exhibits throughout Ireland. Died 1989.

Brennan, Cecily (born 1955). Artist. Deeply involved in Ireland's arts. Solo exhibitions held in the Project Arts Centre, the Taylor Galleries and the Douglas Hyde Gallery. Work included in the collections of the Arts Council, the Bank of Ireland and University College Dublin.

Browne, Deborah (born 1927). Painter. Moved to fibreglass (1965). Produced three-dimensional free standing-sculptures.

Browne, Vincent (born Dublin, 1947). Sculptor. Represented Ireland at the 7th International Small Sculpture Show in Hungary (1987). Contributed to The Great

Book of Ireland (1991). Won the Irish Concrete Society Award for *Maritime Piece*, Co. Wicklow (1993).

Bulfin, Michael (born Offaly, 1939). Renowned sculptor. Widely exhibited. Completed several major commissions, including *A Walk Among Stone*, Ballymun (1990). Chairman of the Sculptors' Society of Ireland (1983-91). Member of the committees on Living Art, the Oireachtas Exhibition and the Municipal Gallery.

Burke, John (born Tipperary, 1946). Sculptor. Works featured in many private and public collections. Participated in major annual group shows, including *Artists 77*, New York, and *18 European Sculptors*, Munich (1978).

Byrne, Michael (born 1923). Painter. Worked for the Arts Council and N.C.A.D. Founder member of the Independent Artists. Committee member of the Project Arts Centre, Dublin. Died 1989.

Campbell, George (born Arklow, 1917). Painter and stained-glass artist. Co-founded Irish Exhibition of Living Art (1943). Best remembered for powerful images of his paintings and drawings made in Spain.

Carr, Tom (born Belfast, 1909). Artist. One of Northern Ireland's most respected painters. Produces figurative and landscape work. Widely exhibited throughout Ireland and abroad. Awarded the *Royal Ulster Academy* gold medal (1973) and the *Oireachtas Landscape* award (1976).

Clarke, Harry (born Dublin, 1889). Illustrator and stained-glass artist. Represented in the Honan College Chapel, Cork; St. Patrick's Basilica, Lough Derg; the Catholic parish churches of Ballinrobe and Carrickmacross. Established stained glass business with brother Walter: Harry Clarke Studios (1930). Died 1931.

Coleman, James (born Roscommon, 1941).Visual artist. Acclaimed both at home and abroad. Featured in prestigious group exhibitions, including *Hall of Mirrors: Art and Film* since 1945, Los Angeles, and *EV+A 96*, Limerick (1996).

Collins, Patrick (born 1910). Painter. Featured in numerous public and private collections worldwide. Elected **Saoi**, one of the highest honours that can be bestowed on an Irish artist (1987). Died 1994.

Connor, Jerome (born Kerry, 1876). Sculptor. Commissions: the Walt Whitman Memorial and Robert Emmet statue for the Smithsonian Institution, Washington, and a Monument to Four Kerry Poets, Killarney (1940). Died 1943.

Conor, William (born Belfast, 1884). Painter. OBE (1952). First exhibited as war artist followed by portraits of city scenes and shipyard workers. Member of R.H.A. Died 1968.

Cooke, Barrie (born England, 1931). Moved to Ireland (1954). Painter. Featured in many major collections. Illustrated poetry books by Seamus Heaney and Ted Hughes.

Cotter, Maud (born 1954). Stained-glass artist. Exhibiting since 1974, perfecting the craft and technique of glass with James Scanlon.

Cross, Dorothy (born Cork, 1956). Artist. Included in acclaimed exhibitions in England, the U.S. and Ireland. Won the *Marten Toonder* Award and the *Pollock/Krasner* Award (1990).

Crozier, William (born Scotland, 1930). Closely associated with Ireland. Artist. Included in major national collections in Ireland, Britain, the U.S. and across Europe. Featured in group exhibition *Contemporary Artists from Ireland*.

Cullen, Charles (born Longford, 1939). Current Head of Painting at N.C.A.D., Dublin. Paintings exhibited in The Arts Council, the Hugh Lane Municipal Gallery and Trinity College, Dublin.

Cullen, Michael (born Wicklow, 1946). Artist. Has had many solo exhibitions. Included in high profile group exhibitions: *Gateway to Art*, Dublin Airport (1990), *Art for Film*, Dublin Catalogue; and *Irish Potato Famine*, New York (1995).

Delaney, Edward (born Mayo, 1930). Sculptor. Has exhibited at such prestigious shows as the *Paris Biennale* (1959, 1961). Received high profile commissions, including the Wolfe Tone statue, St. Stephen's Green, Dublin.

Dillon, Gerard (born Belfast, 1916). Artist. Worked with oils, tapestry and murals. Set designer for Abbey Theatre. Best known for Connemara landscapes. Represented Ireland at the *Guggenheim International Exhibition*. Published collection of short stories. Died 1971.

Egan, Felim (born Tyrone, 1952). Painter and sculptor. Work featured in *A Sense of Ireland*, London, *ROSC 84*, Dublin, *Aspects of Irish Painting 1960s -1990s*, I.M.M.A. Dublin, *L'Imaginaire Irlandais*, Paris (1996). Won the *UNESCO* Prize for the Arts (1993).

Fallon, Conor (born Wexford, 1939). Self-taught painter. Turned to sculpture as a medium of expression. Has received numerous public commissions including ones from University College Dublin, St. Patrick's Hospital, Dublin, The Arts Council, and Irish Life, Dublin.

Farrell, Michael (born Meath, 1940). Painter. Exhibited many times at the Dawson Gallery, the Douglas Hyde Gallery and the Taylor Galleries in Dublin, as well as at galleries in Munich, Sydney, Paris and Sweden.

FitzGerald, Mary (born Dublin, 1956). Artist. Featured in prestigious solo and group exhibitions, including those at *EV+A*, Limerick, *ROSC*, Guinness Hop Store, and the RHK, Dublin (1987), *The Abstract Irish*, B4A Gallery and South Bank Gallery, New York, and *L'Imaginaire Irlandais* (1996).

Flanagan, T. P. (born Enniskillen, 1929). Landscape artist. Group exhibit of Irish Artists, *Irish Art (1943-1973) - Rosc'80*, Cork; Northern Ireland Arts Council (1977), Ulster Museum (1995). Collections include: Hugh Lane Gallery, Irish Museum of Modern Art, Dublin and Ulster Museum, Belfast.

Gale, Martin (born England, 1949). Reared Ireland. Painter. Participated in the Arts Council Touring Exhibition (1981-82) and the *Sense of Ireland* Festival, London, XIe Biennale de Paris (1980), *Images from Ireland*, Brussels (1990), *Gateway to Art*, Dublin Airport.

Geoghegan, Trevor (born London, 1946). Landscape artist. Moved to Ireland (1971). Current lecturer at N.C.A.D. Represented Ireland at *25th International Festival of Painting* in Cagnes-sur-Mer, France (1989).

Gorman, Richard (born Dublin, 1949). Artist. Exhibited at the *G.P.A. Awards Exhibition* (1981), *EV+A*, Limerick, *UNESCO International Exhibition*, Paris (1986), *L'Imaginaire Irlandais*, Paris (1996). Received the Open Award at the *EV+A*, Limerick (1987), and the *Pollock/Krasner* Award (1996).

Goulding, Tim (born Dublin, 1945). Self-taught painter. Represented Ireland at various arts exhibitions, including *Young Artists from around the World*, New York (1970), Paris Biennale (1971), *Landscapes: American and European Perspectives*, Washington (1989), *Aspects of Irish Painting 1960-1990*, I.M.M.A. Dublin (1991).

Graham, Patrick (born Mullingar, 1943). Visual artist. Featured in *Four Irish Expressionist Painters*, U.S.A., the *Festival Celtique*, France, *Censorship USA*, Los Angeles, *The Famine*, International Touring Exhibition (1995). Books include *I am of Water, Works 5 - Patrick Graham*, and *Art In America*.

Hall, Patrick (born Tipperary, 1935). Artist. Exhibitions include: *Making Sense*, The Arts Council touring exhibition (1982-83), *Irish Art - The European Dimension*, R.H.A. Gallagher Gallery, Dublin (1990), *New Works*, selected galleries in Los Angeles, Belfast, Dublin and Limerick.

Hamilton, Letitia (born Meath, 1876). Painter. Member of R.H.A. (1944). Widely exhibited throughout Ireland. Founder member of Society of Dublin Painters. Work included in collections of the National Gallery of Ireland, Hugh Lane Gallery and the Ulster Museum, Belfast.

Hanratty, Alice (born Dublin). Artist. Has worked in East Africa and Ireland. Participated in most of important national group shows in Ireland and abroad, including the London *Original Print Fair* (1995), *Ten Years of Invited Artists' Prints*, Dublin (1994), *International Impact Exhibition*, Japan (1989), *Irish Women Artists*, The 18th Century - 1987, Dublin.

Harper, Charles (born Kerry, 1943). Artist. Head of Faculty of Fine Art, Limerick School of Art and Design. Works featured in the *International Miniature Art Exhibition*, Toronto (1986), the *Great Book of Ireland*, I.M.M.A. Dublin (1991), *Gateway to Art*, Dublin Airport (1991), *Iontas*, Sligo (1991-92).

Healy, Michael (born Dublin, 1873). Illustrator and stained-glass writer. Commissions included illustrations for the Dominican's journal *Irish Rosary*, windows for Loughrea Cathedral, Galway; among many other Catholic and Church of Ireland buildings throughout Ireland. Died

1941.

Henry, Paul (born Belfast, 1877). Oil painter. Most notable for the west of Ireland landscapes. Member of R.H.A. (1929). Poster commissions for the Irish Tourist Board and the London & Scottish Railway.

Heron, Hilary (born Dublin, 1923). Artist. Awarded the first *Mainie Jellett* memorial travelling scholarships (1947) for work in carved wood, limestone and marble. Exhibited at the *Irish Exhibition of Living Art*. Represented Ireland with Louis Le Brocquy at the *Venice Biennale* (1956). Died 1977.

Hickey, Patrick (born India, 1927). Moved to Ireland (1948). Painter, lithographist, etcher, architect and designer.

Jordan, Eithne (born Dublin, 1954). Founder member of Visual Arts Centre (co-operative studio space for artists). Work featured in collections in the Arts Council, the Contemporary Irish Arts Society, the Bank of Ireland and Dublin City Libraries.

Kane, Michael (born Dublin, 1935). Painter. Has worked for extended periods in Britain, Switzerland and Spain. Features in all major group exhibitions in Ireland and abroad, including *Gateway to Art*, Dublin Airport, *European Large Format Printmaking*, Hop Store, Dublin (1991), *Euroamerican Printmaking*, Spain (1992).

Kelly, John (born Dublin, 1932). Artist and lecturer in printmaking. Exhibited at the *Dante Graphics Exhibition*, New York (1965), *the N.C.A.D. Decade Show* (1986), and *Four x Fore*, Project Arts Centre, Dublin (1992).

King, Brian (born Dublin, 1942). Sculptor. Has lived and worked in Ireland, London and New York. Head of Sculpture at the N.C.A.D., Dublin. Exhibited widely in Ireland and abroad, with recent exhibitions including *EV+A*, Limerick (1996) and *Innovation from Tradition*, Brussels (1996).

King, Cecil (born Dublin, 1921). Self-taught artist and sculptor. Began painting (1954). Featured in many public and private collections. Co-founded the Contemporary Irish Art Society. Commissions include a brilliant yellow structure outside the Science block, U.C.G. Died 1986.

Lambert, Gene (born Dublin, 1952). Artist. Exhibited at the Irish

Exhibition of Living Art, *the Independent Artists, the Figurative Image and the Guinness Peat Aviation Awards* Exhibition. Represented Ireland at the *14th International Festival of Painting* in Cagnes-sur-Mer.

Landweer, Sonja (born Amsterdam, 1933). Moved to Ireland (1960's). Ceramicist. Evolved a batiked-ceramic technique and came to work for Kilkenny Design Workshops. Ceramics and jewellery are widely exhibited in Ireland and abroad.

le Brocquy, Louis (born Dublin, 1916). Self-taught artist. Widely acclaimed in Ireland and abroad. Elected Saoi by members of Aosdána (1992). Perhaps best known for his illustrations of *The Táin* (translated by Thomas Kinsella - 1969).

le Brocquy, Melanie (born Dublin, 1919). Artist. Held many prestigious solo and group exhibitions. Won many awards, including the *Silver Medal of the Oireachtas* (1983) and the *R.H.A. Annual Exhibition* Prize (1995).

Lennon, Ciarán (born Dublin, 1947). Artist. Exhibits widely in Ireland and Europe. Major exhibitions include *Irish Exhibitions of Living Art, Sense of Ireland* Festival, London (1980), *Images from Ireland*, Brussels (1990).

Madden, Anne (born London). Reared Ireland. Artist. Represented in permanent exhibitions worldwide, including the *I.M.M.A.* Dublin, the Ulster Museum, the Pompidou Centre, Paris, and the Musée Picasso, Antibes. Subject of two documentaries - *Anne Madden*, Cinematon, Paris; *L'Artiste Anne Madden*, Radio Television Luxembourg.

Maguire, Brian (born Wicklow, 1951). Artist who has been artist-in-residence in prisons throughout Ireland, Canada and the U.S. Also visiting artist at main Irish art colleges.

Maher, Alice (born Tipperary, 1956). Artist. Exhibited widely in U.S. and Europe. Represented Ireland at the *1994 Sao Paulo Bienal*.

McGuire, Edward (born Dublin, 1932). Painter. Works displayed at Ulster Museum, Belfast, National Gallery of Ireland, Hugh Lane Gallery, Dublin and Dublin City

University. Participated in many prominent group exhibitions. Received numerous awards for his work. Died 1986.

McKenna, James (born Dublin, 1933). Sculptor. Exhibited at many international sculpture shows during 1980-90s. Commissions include Female Figure and Tree, Sandyford, Co. Dublin, the Gerard Manley Hopkins monument, Monasterevin, and the suite of wood sculptures at Hazelwood, Co. Sligo.

McNab, Theo (born Dublin, 1940). Self-taught artist. Represented Ireland at a number of international exhibitions, including Cagnes-sur-Mer Festival, France, Impact Arts Festivals, Kyoto, Japan (1981-84), Irish Graphics in China (1985) and the Edinburgh Festival (1985).

McSweeney, Sean (born Dublin, 1935). Painter. Works included in many public and private collections, including AIB, Aer Lingus, the Arts Council, Dublin City University and the Hugh Lane Gallery of Modern Art.

Moloney, Helen (born Dublin, 1926). Stained-glass artist. Work represented in churches across England and Ireland. Designed crosses, doors, altar panels and wall hangings for many churches.

Mulholland, Carolyn (born Lurgan, 1944). Sculptor . Exhibited throughout Ireland. Completed commissions for the Arts Council of Northern Ireland, Jefferson Smurfit and Irish Life.

O'Connell, Eilís (born Ireland, 1953). Sculptor. Recent showings have been Appetites of Gravity, Sussex, Recent Sculpture, Green on Red Gallery, Irish Women Artists, the Tristan Art Centre, Drogheda, and Tradition and Innovation, Brussels.

O'Dowd, Gwen (born Dublin, 1957). Artist. Included in the collections of the Arts Council, the Irish Museum of Modern Art, the A.I.B. and the Financial Services Centre, Dublin. Recent exhibitions include the Poetic Land - Political Territory NCCA Tour of England and L'Imaginaire Irlandais, Paris (1996).

O'Malley, Tony (born Kilkenny, 1913). Artist. Widely exhibited in Ireland and abroad. Participated in Arts Hibernia, London (1985), Images of Ireland, Brussels, 30th Anniversary Exhibition, Erin Cara, touring Canada and Irish Art 1770-1995, History and Society, touring the U.S.

O'Sullivan, Patrick (born London, 1940). Moved to Cork (1971). Artist. Works in marble, wood and bronze. Exhibited and taught widely. Has received several awards.

Powers, Mary Farl (born Minnesota, 1948). Artist. Known for printmaking and working with paper. Former director of the Graphic Studio, Dublin. Died 1992.

Prendergast, Kathy (born Dublin, 1958). Resident in Dublin (1973). Artist. Exhibited at many prestigious shows, including solo exhibitions at the Henry Moore Foundation Fellowship Exhibition, London (1986), and the Unit 7 Gallery, London.

Pye, Patrick (born Dublin, 1929). Stained glass artist. Frequent exhibitor at the David Hendriks Gallery, Dublin. Fulfilled commissions for numerous churches throughout Ireland. Created more than 20 triptychs on sacred themes.

Renard, Yann (born Brittany, 1914). Moved to Ireland (1947). Sculptor and painter. Widely exhibited. Appointed R.H.A. Professor of Sculpture. Received numerous public and private commissions.

Scanlon, James (born Kerry, 1952). Widely exhibited artist. Works include paintings, drawings, sculpture and stained glass. His stained glass work represented Ireland at the Garden Festival in Japan. **Scott, Patrick** (born Cork, 1921). Painter whose works are included in many public and private collections, including the Municipal Gallery, Dublin, the Gulf Oil Corporation, Pittsburg and the Ulster Museum, Belfast.

Sheridan, Noel (born Dublin, 1936). Painter and art critic. Works widely exhibited in Ireland, Europe, the U.S. and Australia. Director of N.C.A.D., Dublin and the Perth Institute of Contemporary Arts, Western Australia.

Simonds-Gooding, Maria (born India, 1939). Moved to Kerry (1947). Artist. Exhibited widely in Ireland and abroad. Regular contributor to Oireachtas Exhibitions, the R.H.A., and Living Art.

Souter, Camille (born England, 1929). Moved to Ireland (1956). Widely exhibited painter. Group exhibitions include: 12 Irish Painters, New York (1963), the Delighted Eye,

Ireland and London (1980), Irish Art in the Eighties, Douglas Hyde Gallery (1991) and Figurative Image, Dublin (1991).

Stuart, Imogen (born Berlin). Moved to Ireland (1950). Sculptor. Works mostly in wood, stone, bronze, steel, clay, plaster and terra-cotta. Sculptures can be seen in many churches and public places throughout Ireland, England and Rome. Work featured in the Great Book of Ireland and the Baedecker Guide to Ireland.

Tuach, Rod (born Dublin, 1945). Widely exhibited photographer. Represented at the group exhibitions Six Photographers, touring Ireland, Contemporary Irish Photography, Guinness Hop Store, Dublin (1987) and Fetes Irlandaises, Montreal World Trade Centre, Canada (1992).

Tyrrell, Charles (born Meath, 1950). Artist. Lives and works on Beara Penninsula, Co. Cork. Recent exhibitions include Famine, Claremorris and Boston (1995) and L'Imaginaire Irlandais, Paris (1996).

Vanston, Dáirine (born 1903). Painter who exhibited widely in Ireland and abroad. Work featured in Horizon magazine. Details of her work and career given to the Archives of Modern European Art, Venice. Died 1988.

Warren, Barbara (born Dublin, 1925). Painter. Work represented in many public and private collections in Ireland and abroad. Exhibited at the Taylor Galleries, Dublin, Irish Women Artists, Hugh Lane Gallery, Dublin (1987) and at the R.H.A.'s annual and banquet exhibitions.

Warren, Michael (born Wexford, 1950). Sculptor. Has completed many prestigious commissions including ones for RTÉ, Dublin, Olympic Sculpture Park, Seoul, Korea (1988) and Utsukushi-ga-hara Open Air Museum, Japan (1989).

Wejchert, Alexandra (born Poland, 1920). Architect. Moved to Ireland (1965). Worked here until her death in 1995.

Yeats, Anne (born Dublin). Artist. Chief stage designer of Abbey Theatre. Committee member of Irish Exhibition of Living Art (1947). Work represented in public and private collections worldwide.

Yeats, Jack Butler (born London, 1871). Artist and writer. Brother of

W.B. Yeats. Regarded as one the most influential and talented artists in Ireland. Illustrated many pen-and-ink drawings for journals and books; known as *W. Bird* for cartoon work in *Punch magazine* (1910-48). Probably most remembered for his richly coloured and romantic collection of water-colours and oil landscape paintings on Dublin and Sligo. (1917-27). Retrospectives of work mounted in London (1942, 1948), Dublin (1945) and the U.S. (1951-52). Literary works include *Sailing, Sailing Swiftly* (1933) and *Ah Well* (1942). Died Dublin 1957.

ART COUNCIL OF IRELAND: WORKS OF ART PURCHASED, 1995

Artist	Title	Art Form	Price (£)
Bardon, Jean	Town Garden	Etching	85
Cotter, Maud	Strain	Copper / Steel Glass	972
Cross, Dorothy	Untitled 1994	Photograph	1,200
Dempsey, Michael	Cold Mountain I	Mixed Media on Paper	300
Donnelly, Mary	Coralled Off Shore Where White Horses Leap	Oil on Paper	250
Hall, Pat	Mountain 1995	Ink and Acrylic on Paper	1,800
Hanley, Joseph	Diverse Movements	Oil and Acrylic on Wood	760
Harmey, Cliodhna	Frocks and Frocks 2	Photographs	500
Hickey, Patrick	Pearscape III 4/60	Etching	270
Kiely, David	Untitled	Etching	100
McCarthy, Danny	Shamans Horse XXX VII	Wood	650
McLoughlin, Mark / Phelan, Gary	Kippure	Photo / Radio / Sound	3,000
Miller, Nick	SA Memory Series II 35 Images	Watercolour & Wax Crayon	2,300
McHugh, Ruth	Story of the Dress	Mixed Media on Canvas	600
O'Donoghue, Tighe	Exile	Mixed Media on Wood	1,950
O'Donoghue, Tighe	Oglach II	Stone / Metal / Wood	150
O'Hehir, Debi	Howlin' Moon Horse II	Bronze	600
O'Neill, Ger	Untitled	Brass & Steel	250
O'Neill, Mary Rose	Relic II 1/10	Print & Mixed Media	215
O'Nolan, James	Untitled	Carborundum Print	600
Pim, Henry	Wallpiece	High Fired Clay	650
Walker, Corban	Stand In	Stainless Steel & Cast Glass	950
Wright, Niall	Soft Day Silence	Oil on Canvas	500
TOTAL:			**£18,652**

NUMBER OF ARTISTS INVOLVED IN OPEN SUBMISSION SHOWS (O.S.S.) - ALL IRELAND*

O.S.S. in Ireland are generally regarded by artists as vital for developing their profile in the art world. They give emerging artists an opportunity to show their work alongside more established artists. They, in turn, are provided with another venue to show and sell their work. The shows also provide a forum for engaging public awareness in the visual arts nationwide.

Venue (all media)	No. of artists submitting works	No. of artists selected	% selected	Works Sold
Iontas, Sligo	500	107	21.4	35% of works
R.H.A., Dublin (works)	1,800	473†	26.3	63% of works
Oireachtas	320	135	42.2	n/a
EV+A, Limerick	450	47	10.4	n/a
Claremorris, Mayo	-	-	-	-
Eigse, Carlow	83	16	19.3	14
Royal Ulster Academy	-	-	-	-
National Small Works, Belfast	230	99	43.0	4
Scoip, Kerry	72	30	41.7	5
Portable Art, Wexford	45	20	44.4	1
Dundrum Open, Dublin	120	25	20.8	16

Venue (specific media)	No. of artists submitting works	No. of artists selected	% selected	Works Sold
TBP International Print Exhibition	236	65	27.5	130
Intermedia (multi-media)	120	20	16.6	not for sale
Sculpture in Context	-	-	-	-
Arnotts National Portrait O.S.S.	-	-	-	-

* Relate to the most recent exhibition before June 1997. † Encompass invited artists and members of the R.H.A.

Venue	Total Budget (£)	Grants (£)	Other Sponsorship (£)	Prizes Total (£)	Catalogue/ Poster
Iontas, Sligo	36,000	15,000	3,000	4,800*	n/a
R.H.A., Dublin	n/a	none	n/a	6,850	-
Oireachtas	n/a	1,500	4,000	2,300	n/a
EV+A, Limerick	150,000	110,000	41,000	3,000†	20,000
Claremorris, Mayo	-	-	-	-	-
Eigse, Carlow	10,000	2,000	5,200	750	4,600
Royal Ulster Academy	-	-	-	-	-
National Small Works, Belfast	n/a	none	1,637§	1,350	no costs
Scoip, Kerry	n/a	n/a	n/a	none	loose leaf
Portable Art, Wexford	3,687	3,500	1,500**	none	2,420
Dundrum Open, Dublin	5,000	5,000	none	none	£1,800
TBP International Print Exhibition	80,000	46,000	20,000	none	£18,000
Intermedia (multi-media)	10,000	7,000	2,500	none	-
Sculpture in Context	-	-	-	-	-
Arnotts National Portrait O.S.S.	-	-	-	-	-

*A solo show valued at £1,000 is to be added on. † Three solo shows are to be added on.
§ Administration - voluntary; no printing costs incurred.
** Launch, marketing, and administration costs were not incurred as these services were provided voluntarily.

ARTS COUNCIL OF IRELAND: ARTS EXPENDITURE, 1995

Arts Sector	Amount (£)	Arts Sector	Amount (£)
Literature	1,123,283	Multi-Disciplinary Arts	2,103,133
Visual Arts and Architecture	1,808,928	Local Authorities and Partnerships	441,031
Film	660,580	Capital	924,335
Drama	5,652,126	Sundry	315,841
Dance:	445,749		
Opera	912,019	OVERALL TOTAL:	15,668,641
Music	1,281,616		

ARTS COUNCIL OF NORTHERN IRELAND: ARTS EXPENDITURE, MARCH 1996

Arts Sector	Amount (£)	Arts Sector	Amount (£)
Visual Art & Film	811,073	Development	270,764
Literature	249,019	Cultural Management Training Programme	13,271
Traditional Arts	107,347	Cultural Traditions	300,000
Music and Opera	1,902,316	Strategy	19,282
Drama and Dance	1,624,099	Miscellaneous	1,236,174
Community Arts	549,203		
Education and Youth	155,333	OVERALL TOTAL:	7,237,881

STATE FUNDING OF ARTS COUNCIL OF IRELAND, 1992-96

Description (£m)	1992	1993	1994	1995	1996
Oireachtas Grant-in-aid	5.173	6.568	8.315	12.590	14.430
National Lottery	4.988	4.988	4.988	3.707	3.970
Total:	10.161	11.556	13.303	16.297	18.400

IRISH NOBEL PRIZE WINNERS

The Nobel Prizes have been awarded annually since 1901 in the fields of Physics, Chemistry, Physiology/Medicine, Peace and Literature. The awards were established under the will of Swedish Chemist Alfred Nobel, the interest of whose trust fund is divided among persons who have made outstanding contributions to the above fields. Ireland has had winners on seven occasions; they are as follows:

Year	Recipient	Field
1923	**William Butler Yeats** (1865 - 1939)	Literature
1925	**George Bernard Shaw** (1856 - 1950)	Literature

Year	Recipient	Field
1951	Ernest Thomas Sinton Walton (born 1903)	
	(Shared with Englishman Sir John Douglas Cockcroft)	Physics
1969:	Samuel Beckett (1906 - 1989)	Literature
1974:	Seán MacBride (1904 - 1988)	
	(Shared with Eisaku Sato of Japan)	Peace
1976:	Mairead Corrigan (born 1944) and Betty Williams (born 1943)	Peace
1995:	Seamus Heaney (born 1939)	Literature

THE MODERN ASSERTION AND TRIUMPH OF IRELAND'S ARTISTS AND ENTERTAINERS

As Ireland approaches the new millennium, it has finally shed it's much maligned image as an impoverished, rural-based, emigration-famished island on the edge of Europe. It has redefined itself as a modern, liberal, forward-thinking nation. With it's now increasingly-educated youth choosing to remain, Ireland is reaping the benefits of the richness and variety of home-grown talents.

Many had feared that Ireland would totally succumb to globalisation and lose it's unique culture, tradition and spirit, replacing the *Leprechaun* with Sonic the Hedgehog and the live traditional music session with M.T.V. Instead, Ireland has recreated its culture - it has embraced the myths and legends, the dark sense of humour and prominent spirit of its people, past and present. This spirit inspired such world-renowned literary masters in the past, such as Yeats, Joyce, Beckett, Shaw and Wilde, and continues to catalyse such modern greats as Heaney, Friel, McCabe, Moore, O'Connor and Doyle.

It was the American Company KALEM, with Irish-Canadian film director Sidney Olcott, who first produced fictional films representing Irish history and culture in 1916. Now in 1997, Ireland has enjoyed its own contribution to film, from *The Quiet Man* to award-winning powerful dramas *In the Name of the Father, My Left Foot, Michael Collins* and the latest offering, *The Butcher Boy*. One of the most active years was 1994, and with the onset of 1998, film productions are soaring to a new height, gathering the combined talents of Irish screen-writers, directors, actors and producers. Sheridan, Jordan, O'Connor and Pearson have brought new life to a world where we were once merely onlookers. From the days of Barry Fitzgerald, Maureen O'Hara and Greer Garson, Ireland has offered an ever-talented stream of leading stars: Daniel Day-Lewis, Liam Neeson, Richard Harris, Peter O'Toole, Brenda Fricker, Pierce Brosnan and Stephen Rea, with a new generation who open up tight competition to our American and European counterparts. Who would have ever thought *James Bond* would have been played by an Irish man!

In the world of music, Ireland stands as giving birth to some of the most successful international musicians, composers, soloists and singers - U2, Van Morrison, The Chieftains, Clannad, The Cranberries, Sinéad O'Connor, Bill Whelan to name a few. They have all poured new meaning into Irish music, preserving the traditional ballad and forging haunting melodies with poetic, provoking lyrics. This echoes the cultural, political, social and naked traditional importance of our land into modern forms of rock and pop.

Irish comedy has also nudged and burst through the doors of recognition. The astounding talents of Dave Allen, Sean Hughes, Ardal O'Hanlon, Dermot Morgan, Pauline McGlynn and Patrick Kielty have giggled their way to British television screens in the guises of Craggy Island priests and one-man television shows, laughing their way to fame rewarded with placing Ireland on the talented arena of universal laughter.

And dance - once the poor sister in a national family of poets, actors, writers and musicians - has crashed onto the world stage with the powerful force of *Riverdance* and *Lord of the Dance*. Traditional Irish dance has established itself as an unique art form and discipline from the days of step-dance to an imaginative modern awakening.

We have also caused a stir by our rich, innovative contributions to the fashion world where talent has soaked and swept the catwalk and theatre stage with top designers Philip Treacy, John Rocca, Lainey Keogh, and Paul Costelloe among the best. With regard to painters and sculptors, Jack B. Yeats, Basil Blackshaw, Louis Le Brocquy, Nathaniel Hone, Patrick Collins are now receiving the international recognition they are due.

We are a people more at ease with our roots and raw talent. We have won acclaimed standing in the field of arts: Oscars, Nobel prizes, Booker prizes, Fashion Awards, international music awards and many more nominations have flooded Irish shores. No longer are we jumping the boat to foreign lands but anchoring ourselves deep in Irish soil to establish ourselves as one of the front runners in this wonderful world of entertainment and arts. *By Jenni Doherty, Artcam.*

TELEVISION AND RADIO BROADCASTING

Ireland has had a long history of broadcasting. The B.B.C. established a radio station in Belfast in 1924 and the newly formed Irish Free State established the radio station 2RN in Dublin in 1926. Television arrived in Northern Ireland when the B.B.C. began transmissions from Belfast in 1953. Ulster Television, an independent channel was established in 1959 and R.T.É made its first television broadcast on New Year's Eve 1961. In 1997 there were four television stations based in Ireland: R.T.É (providing two channels), Telefís na Gaeilge, Ulster Televison and B.B.C. Northern Ireland (providing programming on two channels).

Perhaps the greatest success story in Irish broadcasting in this decade has been local radio stations. In the Republic in 1997, local radio stations enjoyed a 41% market share while national stations R.T.É. Radio One and 2FM had 32% and 22% respectively. Radio Ireland, a second national radio station launched in March 1997, has yet to receive accurate figures for listnership. In Northern Ireland, the combined listnership of Downtown Radio and Cool FM outstrips that of Radio Ulster and its north-west subsidiary, Radio Foyle.

Teilifís na Gaeilge, an Irish language television channel, was launched in October 1996. Based in Galway, it has struggled to assert itself in the Republic's television consciousness, but programmes such as *CU Burn* and *Ros na Rún* have attracted large audiences. The *Late Late Show* on R.T.É. 1 continues to attract up to one million viewers on Friday nights, while U.T.V.'s *Kelly* show continues to be the most watched locally produced programme in Northern Ireland. On the drama front R.T.É. and B.B.C. Northern Ireland collaborated to produce the hugely successful *Ballykissangel* while U.T.V. continues to produce excellent current affairs such as *U.T.V. Live* and *Insight*. The advent of satellite stations and the impending digital television revolution do not seem to have had an adverse effect on Irish television stations, rather they have helped them to focus their efforts in providing quality locally produced programming - something multi-national broadcasters cannot do.

TELEVISION LICENCES IN R.O.I., 1996

County & Province	1996 Monochrome	1996 Colour	Total
Connacht	4,145	106,803	110,948
Leinster	8,369	516,346	524,715
Munster	7,466	275,345	282,811
Ulster *(part of)**	1,165	52,430	53,595
TOTAL STATE†	21,145	950,924	**972,069**

* Does not include six counties in Northern Ireland. † Includes figures for licences issued free.

TELEVISION LICENCES IN N.I., 1996

Licence Type	1991	1992	1993	1994	1995	1996
Monochrome	63,852	50,414	41,507	36,360	32,531	25,206
Colour	253,460	269,196	295,529	311,318	341,459	369,812
Estimated No. of T.V. Ownership	514,000	523,000	532,000	543,000	554,000	554,000
All Licences:	**317,312**	**319,610**	**337,036**	**347,678**	**373,990**	**395,018**

RTÉ TELEVISION BROADCASTING HOURS 1996 - RTÉ 1 & NETWORK 2

Programme	Home Produced	Programmes Purchased	Programmes (Repeats)	Total Hours
Advertising	985	-	-	985
Arts/Humanities/Sciences	25	68	54	147
Education	40	156	65	261
Fiction	137	4,292	434	4,863
Information	491	546	243	1,280
Light Entertainment	582	26	269	877
Music	96	191	87	374
News	616	231	3	850
Presentation & Promotion	338	-	147	485
Religious	84	4	28	116
Sport	1,048	145	127	1,320
Other Programmes	90	128	11	229
TOTAL:	**4,532**	**5,787**	**1,468**	**11,787**

SHARE OF TV VIEWING IN N.1., 1995

UTV %	Channel 4 %	BBC 1 %	BBC 2 %	RTÉ 1 & Network 2 %
41.0	9.2	29.4	8.8	11.7

PROFILE OF UTV AREA, 1995

	No. of Viewers	%
Total UTV	533,000	97
Receiving Colour	513,000	96
More than one TV Set	244,000	46

Population Profiles of UTV Area, 1995

Size of Household Persons	%
1	25
2	24
3	17
4	16
5+	18

With Children Age	%
0-3 years	14
4-9 years	20
10-15 years	21
0-15 years	38
None	62

N.I. TV AUDIENCE LEVELS, AVERAGE TV RATINGS, 1996

Audience Breakdown	UTV %	Channel 4 %
Adults:		
All	6.7	1.9
A, B, C1	5.1	1.6
16-24	4.7	1.8
Housewives :		
All	8.3	2.1
A, B, C1	6.6	-
With Child	7.1	-
Men:		
All	6.2	1.8
A, B, C1	4.5	-
16-34	5.0	-

50 MOST POPULAR RTÉ 1 PROGRAMMES, 1996

Rank	Programme	Type	Date	Number of Viewers
1	Glenroe	Soap Opera	25 Feb	1,127,000
2	Eurovision Song Contest	Music Show	18 May	1,120,000
3	The Late Late Show	Talk Show	13 Dec	1,102,000
4	Coronation Street	Soap Opera	6 Mar	1,003,000
5	Winning Streak	Game Show	27 Jan	965,000
6	Crimeline	Information on crime	12 Feb	960,000
7	Rose of Tralee	Beauty Contest	28 Aug	958,000
8	Dear Daughter	Docu-drama	22 Feb	950,000
9	Kenny Live	Talk Show	3 Feb	897,000
10	The Fugitive	Film	28 Oct	842,000
11	Fair City	Soap Opera	12 Nov	838,000
12	Keeping Up Appearances	Sitcom	12 Jan	818,000
13	Prime Time	Current Affairs	30 Jan	796,000
14	Crimes of Passion: Victim of Love	Docu-drama	24 Nov	783,000

Rank	Programme	Type	Date	Number of Viewers
15	Robin Hood Prince of Thieves	*Film*	1 Jan	767,000
16	The Snapper	*Film*	9 Apr	758,000
17	Upwardly Mobile	*Sitcom*	25 Dec	746,000
18	Check-Up	*Health Show*	12 Mar	739,000
19	Fame and Fortune	*Game Show*	30 Aug	732,000
20	The Firm	*Film*	18 Mar	731,000
21	Eurosong	*Music*	3 Mar	728,000
22	Hocus Pocus	*Youth Programme*	28 Oct	720,000
23	A Few Good Men	*Film*	22 Dec	718,000
24	E.R.	*Drama*	26 Feb	707,000
25	The Thin Blue line	*Sitcom*	18 Jan	700,000
26	Mr. Bean	*Comedy*	18 Mar	690,000
27	Where in the World	*Quiz Show*	28 Jan	689,000
20	The Charlton Years	*Documentary*	8 Jan	679,000
29	Head to Toe	*Fashion Show*	12 Mar	676,000
30	The Sunday Game	*Sport*	29 Sept	676,000
31	Falsely Accused	*Documentary*	20 Oct	669,000
32	The Field	*Film*	26 Nov	668,000
33	Queen	*Music Documentary*	2 Oct	668,000
34	Daniel O'Donnell Christmas Special	*Music Show*	25 Dec	664,000
35	Cliffhanger	*Film*	6 May	658,000
36	Web of Deceit	*Drama*	13 Oct	651,000
37	Michael O'Hehir - A Tribute	*Documentary*	1 Dec	647,000
38	For the Love of Nancy	*Docu-drama*	8 Dec	642,000
39	Murder One	*Drama*	31 Jan	636,000
40	Another Stakeout	*Film*	15 Oct	613,000
41	Beyond the Hall Door	*General Interest*	13 Mar	629,000
42	Only Fools and Horses	*Sitcom*	31 Dec	627,000
43	Ear to the Ground	*Agriculture*	28 Oct	627,000
44	President's Child	*Film*	6 Oct	620,000
45	Simply Delicious Meals	*Food & Drink*	8 Feb	616,000
46	The Lyrics Board	*Quiz Show*	6 Nov	607,000
47	Lifelines	*General Interest*	11 Feb	601,000
48	Pretty Woman	*Film*	5 Aug	597,000
49	May to December	*Drama*	7 Mar	594,000
50	Nationwide	*Current Affairs*	31 Jan	593,000

50 MOST POPULAR NETWORK 2 PROGRAMMES, 1996

Rank	Programme	Type	Date	Number of Viewers
1	Father Ted's Christmas	*Sitcom*	25 Dec	975,000
2	Rep. of Ireland v. Russia	*Sport*	27 Mar	926,000
3	Father Ted	*Sitcom*	12 Dec	847,000
4	Home and Away	*Soap Opera*	18 Nov	731,000
5	Republic of Ireland	*Sport (Football)*	9 Oct	706,000
6	The Sunday Game	*Sport*	15 Sept	688,000
7	The Olympic Channel	*Sport*	24 July	658,000
8	Rep. of Ireland v. Iceland	*Sport*	10 Nov	633,000
9	Rep. of Ireland v. Portugal	*Sport*	29 May	555,000
10	F.A. Cup Replay	*Sport*	17 Jan	553,000
11	Champions League Soccer	*Sport*	16 Oct	530,000
12	G'day Summerbay	*Documentary*	30 Dec	525,000
13	Professional Boxing	*Sport*	30 Mar	502,000
14	Three Men and a Little Lady	*Film*	2 Oct	468,000
15	Saved by the Bell	*Sitcom*	20 Aug	433,000
16	Update Atlanta	*Sport*	29 July	425,000
17	Rep. of Ireland XI v. Glasgow Celtic	*Sport*	26 May	418,000
18	Three Men and a Baby	*Film*	1 May	414,000
19	Euro '96	*Sport*	26 June	409,000

Continued from previous page -

Rank	Programme	Type	Date	Number of Viewers
20	Coronation Street	Soap Opera	26 April	408,000
21	Odyssey	Science	21 Aug	402,000
22	F.A. Cup	Sport	7 Feb	399,000
23	American Gothic	Drama	18 Feb	396,000
24	Friends	Sitcom	24 Sept	393,000
25	Blackboard Jungle	Quiz Show	18 Nov	386,000
26	Euro Champions League	Sport	1 Sept	385,000
27	The X Files	Drama	8 Oct	384,000
28	Lethal Weapon 2	Film	21 Dec	379,000
29	National Geographic	Science/Nature	27 Oct	375,000
30	Beyond 2000	Science	1 Sept	369,000
31	Godfather III	Film	30 Dec	369,000
32	Rep. of Ireland v. Croatia	Sport	2 June	368,000
33	Calfornia Dreams	Drama	28 Nov	364,000
34	Sister Sister	Drama	27 Nov	364,000
35	The 3 Ninjas	Youth Programme	18 Sept	359,000
36	Fair City Omnibus	Soap Opera	10 Nov	358,000
37	The Grip Remix	Youth Programme	23 Aug	357,000
38	Ireland v. West Samoa	Sport	12 Nov	354,000
39	The Girl From Tomorrow	Youth Programme	22 Aug	353,000
40	Top 30 Hits	Music	19 Feb	348,000
41	Sweat	Drama	11 Nov	340,000
42	My So-Called Life	Drama	9 March	339,000
43	Party of Five	Drama	21 Jan	338,000
44	Passed Away	Documentary	5 April	331,000
45	Roseanne	Sitcom	29 Oct	328,000
46	Every Which Way But Loose	Film	5 June	323,000
47	Family	Drama	5 Jan	323,000
48	Baywatch	Drama	21 Jan	323,000
49	The Game on Monday	Sport	29 July	321,000
50	Rep. of Ireland v. Holland	Sport	4 June	317,000

20 MOST POPULAR N.I. BBC 1 PROGRAMMES, 1996

Rank	Programme	Type	Date	Number of Viewers
1	Only Fools and Horses	Sitcom	29 Dec	545,000
2	Eastenders	Soap Opera	25 Dec	459,000
3	One Foot in the Grave	Sitcom	26 Dec	422,000
4	9 O'Clock News (I.R.A. Ceasefire over)	Current Affairs	9 Feb	416,000
5	Ballykissangel	Drama	11 Feb	413,000
6	PK Tonight	Comedy Chatshow	29 Mar	406,000
7	Casualty	Drama	24 Feb	380,000
8	F.A. Cup Final	Sport	11 May	349,000
9	National Lottery Live	Current Interest	14 Dec	345,000
10	Beethoven	Film	24 Nov	344,000
11	New Adventures of Superman	Drama	2 Mar	337,000
12	Eurovision Song Contest	Music	18 May	336,000
13	Cliffhanger	Film	24 Dec	335,000
14	Naked Gun $2\frac{1}{2}$	Film	21 Apr	330,000
15	News	Current Affairs	3 Feb	325,000
16	Jurassic Park	Film	25 Dec	321,000
17	Vicar of Dibley	Comedy	25 Dec	318,000
18	Goodnight Sweetheart	Sitcom	12 Feb	304,000
19	Free Willy	Film	26 Dec	299,000
20	The Firm	Film	27 Dec	294,000

20 MOST POPULAR N.I. BBC 2 PROGRAMMES, 1996

Rank	Programme	Type	Date	Number of Viewers
1	Rab C Nesbit	Comedy	26 Jan	183,000
2	Billy Connolly/World Tour	Comedy	27 May	173,000
3	Delia Smith's Winter Collection	Food & Drink	7 Feb	168,000
4	The Best Thing	Documentary (Sport)	19 May	167,000
5	Precious Blood	Film	8 June	161,000
6	Man Utd. Family Tree	Documentary	19 May	158,000
7	Delia's Winter Collection	Food & Drink	3 Jan	154,000
8	International Snooker (final)	Sport	6 May	149,000
9	The X Files	Drama	6 May	149,000
10	Eastenders	Soap Opera	7 July	149,000
11	The Witches	Film	30 Dec	147,000
12	Million Dollar Babies	Film	9 Jan	146,000
13	Parkinson Meets Best	Talk Show	19 May	143,000
14	Steptoe and Son	Sitcom	26 Dec	142,000
15	Fresh Prince of Bel-Air	Sitcom	27 Feb	137,000
16	Top Gear	Motor Show	7 Nov	137,000
17	The Best Team	Documentary (Sport)	19 May	136,000
18	Trespass	Film	7 Jan	135,000
19	Game On	Sitcom	14 Oct	132,000
20	Ryan's Daughter	Film	8 Dec	129,000

ITV TOP 10 PROGRAMMES 1996

Rank	Programme	Type	Date	Number of Viewers (million)
1	Coronation Street	Soap Opera	28 Feb	19.8
2	Touch Of Frost	Drama	4 Feb	17.6
3	Heartbeat	Drama	8 Dec	17.5
4	You've Been Framed	Comedy	27 Oct	17.3
5	London's Burning	Drama	13 Oct	16.6
6	The Bill	Drama	26 Jan	16.4
7	Coronation Street	Soap Opera	24 Mar	16.3
8	Prime Suspect 5	Drama	21 Oct	14.9
9	Inspector Morse	Drama	27 Nov	14.8
10	Euro '96: England v. Holland	Sport	18 June	14.8

RADIO BROADCASTING BY RTÉ 1994

Programme	Hours Broadcast	%
Arts/Humanities/Sciences	336	1.5
Drama	363	1.7
Education	1	-
Information	1,365	6.3
Light Entertainment	1,247	5.7
Music	12,080	55.5
News	1,717	7.9
Religion	119	0.5
Sport	508	2.3
Other	4,048	18.6
TOTAL	21,784	100.0

IRISH & IRISH-RELATED FILMOGRAPHY, 1910 - 1998*

The films entered in the filmography have either been filmed in Ireland or featured an Irish subject and actors. The information contained in () includes the country that produced and/or financed the film and the date of the film's release.

The Lad from Old Ireland (U.S. 1910); Director: Sidney Olcott; Starring: Gene Gauntier, Robert Vignola, Jack J. Clarke.

Arragh-na-Pogue (U.S. 1911); Director: Sidney Olcott; Starring: J. P. McGowan, Gene Gauntier, Robert Vignola.

Rory O'More (U.S. 1911); Director: Sidney Olcott; Starring: Gene Gauntier, J. P. McGowan.

The Colleen Bawn (U.S. 1911); Director: Sidney Olcott; Starring: Brian Magowan, Sidney Olcott.

The Colleen Bawn (Aus. 1911); Director: Gaston Mervale; Starring: Louise Carbasse, James Martin.

The Fishermaid of Ballydavid (U.S. 1911); Director: Sidney Olcott; Starring: Gene Gauntier, Robert Vignola, Jack J. Clark..

Ireland The Oppressed (U.S. 1912); Director: Sidney Olcott; Starring: Robert Vignola, Jack Clarke, J.P. McGowan, Alice Hollister.

The O'Neill (U.S. 1912); Director: Sidney Olcott; Starring: Pat O'Malley, Gene Gauntier, Jack J. Clarke.

The Shaughran (Aus/Ire 1912); Director: Sidney Olcott; Starring: Gene Gauntier, Jack Clark, Alice Hollister.

You Remember Ellen (U.S. 1912); Director: Sidney Olcott; Starring: Gene Gauntier, Jack Clarke.

The Kerry Gow (U.S. 1913); Director: Sidney Olcott; Starring: Gene Gauntier, J.P. McGowan, Alice Hollister.

Bunny Blarneyed (US 1914); Director: Larry Trimble; Starring: Johnny Bunny, Mabelle Lumney, George Cox.

Ireland A Nation (U.S. 1914); Director: Walter MacNamara; Starring: Barry O'Brien, Fred O'Donavon.

Broth of a Boy (U.S. 1915); Director: Carlton King; Starring: Andrew J. Clarke, Frank J. Lyon, Florence Slover, Olive Wright.

Fun at Finglas Fair (Ire. 1915); Director: F.J. McCormick; Starring: F.J. McCormick, Jack Eustace, John Connell.

An Unfair Love Affair (Ire. 1916); Director: J. M. Kerrigan; Starring:
J.M. Kerrigan, Nora Clancy, Fred O'Donavan.

Food of Love (Ire 1916); Director: J.M. Kerrigan; Starring: Kathleen Murphy, Fred O'Donavan.

Knocknagow (Ire 1916); Director: Fred O'Donavan; Starring: Brian Magowan, Fred O'Donavan, Kathleen Murphy, J.M. Carre, Alice Keating, Cyril Cusack.

Molly Bawn (Brit. 1916); Director: Cecil M. Hepworth; Starring: Alma Taylor, Stewart Rome, Fred Wright, Violet Hopson.

O'Neill of the Glen (Ire. 1916); Director: J.M. Kerrigan; Starring: J.M. Kerrigan, Nora Clancy, Fred O'Donavan, Brian Magowan.

Puck Fair Romance (Ire. 1916); Director: J. M. Kerrigan; Starring: J.M. Kerrigan, Kathleen Murphy.

The Eleventh Hour (Ire. 1916); Director: Fred O'Donavan; Starring: Brian Magowan, Kathleen Murphy.

The Miser's Gift (Ire. 1916); Director: J.M. Kerrigan; Starring: J.M. Kerrigan, Kathleen Murphy, Fred O'Donavan.

Widow Malone (Ire 1916); Director: J.M. Kerrigan; Starring: J.M. Kerrigan.

Woman's Wit (Ire. 1916); Director: J.M. Kerrigan; Starring: J.M. Kerrigan, Kathleen Murphy, Fred O'Donavan.

A Girl Of Glenbeigh (Ire. 1917); Director: J.M. Kerrigan; Starring: Fred O'Donavan, Kathleen Murphy, Irene Murphy.

Blarney (Ire. 1917); Director: J. M. Kerrigan; Starring: Kathleen Murphy, J.M. Kerrigan.

Rafferty's Rise (Ire. 1917); Director: J.M. Kerrigan; Starring: Fred O'Donavan, Kathleen Murphy, Arthur Shields, Brian Magowan.

The Byeways of Fate (Ire 1917); Director: J.M. Kerrigan; Starring: Nora Clancy.

The Irish Girl (Ire. 1917); Director: J. M. Kerrigan; Starring: Kathleen Murphy.

The Upstart (Ire. 1917); J. M. Kerrigan; Starring: J. M. Kerrigan, Kathleen Murphy, Fred O'Donavan.

When Love Came to Gavin Burke (Ire. 1917); Director: Fred O'Donavan; Starring: Brian Moore, Kathleen Murphy.

Rosaleen Dhu (Ire. 1918); Director: William Power; Starring: William Power, Kitty Hart.

Willie Scouts While Jessie Pouts (Ire 1918); Director: William Power; Starring: William Power.

Paying the Rent (Ire. 1919); Director: John MacDonagh; Starring: Arthur Sinclair, Moira McCoy, Muriel Canning.

In the Days of Saint Patrick (Ire. 1920); Director: Norman Whitten; Starring: Ira Allen, Alice Cardinall, Dermot McCarthy, George Griffin.

Willie Reilly and his Colleen Bawn (Ire. 1920); Director: John MacDonagh; Starring: Brian Magowan, Frances Alexander, Richard Sheridan.

Cruiskeen Lawn (Ire. 1922); Director: John MacDonagh; Starring: Tom Moran, Jimmy O'Dea, Kathleen Armstrong, Fred Jeffs, Fay Sargent.

The Casey Millions (Ire. 1922); Director: John McDonagh; Starring: Jimmy O'Dea, Nan and Joan Fitzgerald, Barrett McDonnell, Chris Sylvester.

Wicklow Gold (Ire. 1922); Director: John MacDonagh; Starring: Jimmy O'Dea, Rita Mooney, Chris Sylvester, Nan and Joan Fitzgerald.

The Colleen Bawn (Brit. 1924); Director: W.P. Kelly; Starring: Henry Victor, Collete Brettel, Stewart Rome.

Land of Her Fathers (Brit. 1925); Director: John Hurley; Starring: Míchael MacLiammóir, Phyllis O'Hara, F.J. McCormack, Barry Fitzgerald, Maureen Delaney.

Irish Destiny (Ire. 1926); Director: George Dewhurst; Starring: Paddy Cullinan, Frances MacNamara, Brian Magowan, Evelyn Henchey, Daisy Campbell.

The Informer (Brit. 1929); Director: Arthur Robinson; Starring: Lya de Putti, Lars Hasson, Daisy Campbell.

By Accident (Ire. 1930); Director: J.N.G. Davidson; Starring: C. Clarke-Clifford, Olive Purcell, Mary Manning, Paul Farrell.

Juno and the Paycock (Brit. 1930); Director: Alfred Hitchcock; Starring: Sara Allgood, Edward Chapman, Marie O'Neill, Sidney Morgan, John

Laurie.

Song O' My Heart (Ire/Brit. 1930); Director: Frank Borzage; Starring: John McCormick, Maureen O'Sullivan, Alice Joyce.

The Voice of Ireland (Ire. 1932); Director: Colonel Victor Haddick; Starring: Richard Hayward, Victor Haddick, Barney O'Hara.

General John Regan (Brit. 1933); Director: Harold Shaw; Starring: Milton Rosmer, Madge Stuart, Edward O'Neill, Ward McAllister.

Man of Aran (Brit. 1934); Director: Robert Flaherty; Starring: Colman 'Tiger' King, Maggie Dirane, Michael Dillane, Aran Islanders.

Some Say Chance (Ire. 1934); Director: Michael Farrell; Starring: Austin Meldon, Eileen Ashe, Sheila May, Margot Bigland.

Sweet Inniscarra (Ire. 1934); Director: Emmett Moore; Starring: Sean Rodgers, Mae Ryan.

Guests of the Nation (Ire. 1935); Director: Denis Johnston; Starring: Barry Fitzgerald, Frank Toolin, Charles Maher, Cyril Cusack, Shelagh Richards, Hilton Edwards.

Irish Hearts (Brit. 1935); Director: Brian Desmond Hurst; Starring: Dermott Fitzgerald, Molly Lamont, Patrick Barr, Nancy Burne, Sara Allgood.

Jimmy Boy (Brit. 1935); Director: John Baxter; Starring: Jimmy O'Dea, Guy Middleton, Vera Sherburne.

Luck of the Irish (Brit. 1935); Director: Donovan Pedelty; Starring: Richard Hayward, Kay Walsh, Niall Mcginnis, Jimmy Mageean.

The Informer (U.S. 1935); Director: John Ford; Starring: Victor McLaglen, Heather Angel, Margot Grahame, Preston Foster, J.M. Kerrigan, Una O'Connor.

The Irish in Us (U.S. 1935); Director: James Cagney, Pat O'Brien, Olivia de Havilland, Mary Gordan, Frank McHugh.

Irish and Proud of It (Ire. 1936); Director: Donovan Pedelty; Starring: Richard Hayward, Dinah Sheridan, Liam Gaffney, Gwen Gill.

The Plough and the Stars; (US 1936); Director: John Ford; Starring: Barry Fitzgerald, F.J. McCormack, Arthur Shields.

Ourselves Alone (Brit. 1936); Director: Brian Desmond Hurst; Starring: Richard Hayward, Niall Mcginnis, Dan O'Herlihy, Marie O'Neill, Pat Noone.

Riders to the Sea (Brit. 1936);

Director: Brian Desmond Hurst and John P. Flanagan; Starring: Sara Allgood, Denis Johnston, Kevin Guthrie, Ria Mooney, Shelah Richards.

The Dawn (Ire 1936); Director: Tom Cooper; Starring: James Gleeson, Eileen Davis, Brian O'Sullivan, Donal O'Cahill.

The Early Bird (Ire 1936); Director: Donovan Pedelty; Starring: Richard Hayward, Jimmy Mageean, Charlotte Tedlie, Terence Grainger.

Rose of Tralee (Brit. 1937); Director: Oswald Mitchell; Starring: Binkie Stuart, Fred Conyngham, Kathleen O'Regan, Jack Lestor.

Wings of the Morning (Brit. 1937); Director: Harold Schuster; Starring: Henry Fonda, John McCormack, Stewart Rome, Leslie Banks.

Blarney (Ire. 1938); Director: Harry O'Donovan; Starring: Jimmy O'Dea, Myrette Morven, Noel Purcell, Tom Dunne.

Cheer, Boys, Cheer (Brit. 1938); Director: Walter Forde; Starring: Nova Pilbeam, Jimmy O'Dea, Edmund Gwenn.

Devil's Rock (Ire. 1938); Director: Germain Burger; Starring: Richard Hayward, Charles Fagan, Geraldine Mitchell, Terence Grainger.

Let's be Famous (Brit. 1938); Director: Walter Forde; Starring: Jimmy O'Dea, Betty Driver, Sonnie Hale, Patrick Barr.

Mountains O'Mourne (Brit. 1938); Director: Harry Hughes; Starring: Niall Mcginnis, Rene Ray, Jerry Verno, Betty Ann Davies.

Penny Paradise (Brit. 1938); Director: Carol Reed; Starring: Jimmy O'Dea, Edmund Gween, Betty Driver, Marie O'Neill.

The Islandman (West of Kerry/Eileen Aroon/Men of Ireland) (Ire. 1938); Director: Patrick Keenan Heale; Starring: Cecil Ford, Eileen Curran, Gabriel Fallon, Brian O'Sullivan.

The Londonderry Air (Brit. 1938); Director: Alex Bryce; Starring: Sara Allgood, Liam Gaffney, Phyllis Ryan, Jimmy Mageean, Maureen Moore.

Uncle Nick (Ire. 1938); Director: Tom Cooper; Starring: Val Vousden, Jerry O'Mahony, 'Bonzer' Horgan.

Foolsmate (Ire. 1940); Director: Brendan Stafford; Starring: Austin Meldon. Joan Kavanagh, Denis Hoey, Liam Ó Laoghaire.

Little Nellie Kelly (US 1940); Director: Norman Taurog; Starring:

Judy Garland, George Murphy, Charles, Arthur Shields.

I See a Dark Stranger (Brit. 1946); Director: Frank Launder; Starring: Deborah Kerr, Trevor Howard, Michael Howard, Breffni O'Rourke.

Captain Boycott Brit. 1947); Director: Frank Launder; Starring: Stewart Granger, Cecil Parker, Kathleen Ryan, Noel Purcell, Niall Mcginnis.

Hungry Hill (Brit. 1947); Director: Brian Desmond Hurst; Starring: Margaret Lockwood, Dennis Price, F.J. McCormick, Jean Simmons, Cecil Parker, Siobhán McKenna, Eileen Crowe, Dan O'Herlihy.

Odd Man Out (Brit. 1947); Director: Carol Reed; Starring: James Mason, Kathleen Ryan, Robert Newton, Cyril Cusack, F.J. McCormack, Noel Purcell.

The Courtneys of Curzon Street (Brit. 1947); Director: Herbert Wilcox; Starring: Anna Neagle, Michael Wilding, Gladys Young, Coral Browne.

My Hands are Clay (Ire. 1948); Director: Lionel Tomlinson; Starring: Shelah Richards, Robert Dawson, Bernadette Leahy, Cecil Brock.

The Greedy Boy (Brit. 1949); Director: Richard Massingham; Starring: Joyce Sullivan, Jim Phelan, Denis Carey.

The Strangers Came (Brit. 1949); Director: Alfred Travers; Starring: Tommy Duggan, Shirl Conway, Shamus Locke, Tony Quinn, Gabriel Fallon.

At a Dublin Inn (Ire. 1950); Director: Brendan Stafford; Starring: Valentine Dyall, Joseph O'Connor, Agnes Bernelle, Liam O'Leary.

Everybody's Business (Ire. 1951); Director: Tony Inglis; Starring: Gerard Healy, Nora O'Mahony, Maureen O'Sullivan.

Keep Your Teeth (Ire. 1951); Director: Rex Roberts; Starring: Jerry Hurley, Bart Bastable, Helen Robinson, Eric Doyle.

No Resting Place (Brit. 1951); Director: Paul Rotha; Starring: Michael Gough, Eithne Dunne, Noel Purcell, Jack McGowran, Brian O'Higgins.

Return to Glennascaul (Ire. 1951); Director: Hilton Edwards; Starring: Orson Welles, Michael Lawrence, Helena Hughes.

The Promise of Barty O'Brien (U.S. 1951); Director: George Freedland; Starring: Eric Doyle,

Eileen Crowe, Harry Brogan, Doreen Madden.

Jack of All Maids (Ire. 1952); Director: Tomás MacAnna; Starring: Jack McGowran, Máire Ní Dhomhnaill, Doreen Madden.

The Gentle Gunman (Brit. 1952); Director: Basil Dearden; Starring: John Mills, Dirk Bogarde, Gilbert Harding, Robert Beatty, Elizabeth Sellars, Barbra Mullen, Eddie Byrne, Jack McGowran.

The Quiet Man (U.S. 1952); Director: John Ford; Starring: John Wayne, Maureen O'Hara, Barry Fitzgerald, Eileen Crowe, Jack McGowran, Arthur Shields.

From Time To Time (Ire. 1953); Director: Hilton Edwards; Starring: Maureen Cusack, Patrick Bedford, Colm O'Grady.

Our Girl Friday (Brit. 1953); Director: Noel Langley; Starring: Joan Collins, George Cole, Kenneth More, Walter Fitzgerald, Robertson Hare.

Stop Thief! (Ire. 1953); Director: Gerard Healy; Starring: Brian O'Higgins, Angela Newman, Ronnie Walsh.

Fr. Brown (Brit. 1954); Director: Robert Hamer; Starring: Alec Guinness, Joan Greenwood, Peter Finch, Cecil Parker, Bernard Lee, Sidney James.

Happy Ever After (Brit. 1954); Director: Mario Zampi; Starring: David Niven, Barry Fitzgerald, George Cole, Yvonne De Carlo, Joseph Tomelty, Brian O'Higgins.

The Art of Reception (Ire. 1954); Director: Gerard Healy; Starring: Cyril Cusack, Liam Redmond, Anna Manahan.

Captain Lightfoot (U.S. 1955); Director: Douglas Sirk; Starring: Rock Hudson, Barbara Rush, Jeff Morrow, Kathleen Ryan, Denis O'Dea.

Untamed (U.S. 1955); Director: Henry King; Starring: Susan Hayward, Tyrone Power, Richard Egan, Henry O'Neill.

Jacqueline (Brit. 1956); Director: Roy Baker; Starring: John Gregson, Kathleen Ryan, Jacqueline Ryan, Noel Purcell.

The March Hare (Brit. 1956); Director: George More O'Farrell; Starring: Terence Morgan, Peggy Cummins, Cyril Cusack, Maureen Delaney.

Pretty Polly (Ire. 1957); Director: Tony Inglis; Starring: Noel Purcell.

Professor Tim (Ire. 1957); Director: Henry Cass; Starring: Ray McAnally, Marie O'Donnell, Seamus Kavanagh, Marie Kean.

Rooney (Brit. 1957); Director: George Pollock; Starring: John Gregson, Muriel Pavlow, Barry Fitzgerald, Noel Purcell.

The Rising of the Moon (Ire. 1957); Director: John Ford; Starring: Noel Purcell, Cyril Cusack, Jack MacGowran, Eric Gorman.

The Story of Esther Costello (Brit. 1957); Director: David Miller; Starring: Joan Crawford, Rossano Brazzi, Denis O'Dea, Maureen Delaney.

Dublin Nightmare (Brit. 1958); Director: John Pomeroy; Starring: William Sylvester, Marie Landi, Richard Leech, Jack Cunningham.

Sally's Irish Rogue (Ire 1958); Director: George Pollock; Starring: Julie Harris, Tim Seely, Harry Brogan, Marie Kean, Bríd Lynch.

Darby O'Gill and the Little People (U.S. 1959); Director: Robert Stevenson; Starring: Sean Connery, Denis O'Dea, Jimmy O'Dea, Janet Munro, Albert Sharpe, Kieron Moore.

Home is the Hero (Ire. 1959); Director: J. Fielder Cook; Starring: Arthur Kennedy, Maire O'Donnell, Walter Macken, Eileen Crowe, Joan O'Hara.

Larry (Ire. 1959); Director: Robert Dawson and Shelah Richards; Starring: Geoffrey Golden, Neasa Ní Anracháin, John Cowley, Fergal Stanley, Dennis Brennan.

O'Hara's Holiday (Ire. 1959); Director: Peter Byran; Starring; Herbert Moulton, Antoinette Lawlor, Anna Manahan, Tom Irwin, Kathleen Watkins.

Shake Hands with the Devil (Brit. 1959); Director: Michael Anderson; Starring: James Cagney, Don Murray, Dana Wynter, Ray McAnally, Glynis Johns, Noel Purcell, Cyril Cusack, Richard Harris.

The Big Birthday (Ire. 1959); Director: George Pollock; Starring: Barry Fitzgerald, Tony Wright, June Thorburn, Eddie Golden.

This Other Eden (Ire. 1959); Director: Murial Box; Starring: Leslie Phillips, Audrey Dallton, Niall Mcginnis, Geoffrey Golden, Norman Roadway.

A Terrible Beauty (Brit. 1960); Director: Tay Garnett; Starring: Robert Mitchum, Anne Heywood,

Dan O'Herlihy, Richard Harris, Noel Purcell, Cyril Cusack, Niall Mcginnis.

Boyd's Shop (Ire. 1960); Director: Henry Cass; Starring: Geoffrey Golden, Eileen Crowe, Aideen O'Kelly, Vincent Dowling.

Gorgo (Brit. 1960); Director: Eugene Lourie; Starring: Bill Travers, William Sylvester, Barry Keegan.

Johnny Nobody (Brit. 1960); Director: Nigel Patrick; Starring: William Bendix, Aldo Ray, Niall Mcginnis, Yvonne Mitchell. Jimmy O'Dea, Cyril Cusack, Noel Purcell.

Lies My Father Told Me (Ire. 1960); Director: Don Chaffy; Starring: Betsy Blair, Harry Brogan, Edward Golden, Rita O'Dea.

Love and Money (Ire. 1960); Director: Ronald Liles; Starring: Milo O'Shea, Maureen Toal, Marie Conmee, Charlie Byrne, Charlie Roberts.

The Big Gamble (U.S. 1960); Director: Richard Fleischer; Starring: Marie Kean, Maureen O'Dea, Stephen Boyd, Juliette Greco, David Wayne.

The Siege of Sidney Street (Brit. 1960); Director: Roy Baker, Monty Berman; Starring: Donald Sinden, T.P. McKenna, Nicole Berger, Kieron Moore.

The Trials of Oscar Wilde (Brit. 1960); Director: Ken Hughes; Starring: Peter Finch, Yvonne Mitchell, James Mason, Ian Fleming.

Middle of Nowhere/The Webster Boy (Ire..1961); Director: Don Chaffy; Starring: John Cassavetes, Elizabeth Sellars, David Farrar, Richard O'Sullivan, Niall Mcginnis.

Dead Man's Evidence (Brit. 1962); Director: Francis Scarlc; Starring: Conrad Phillips, Jane Griffiths, Veronica Hurst.

I Thank a Fool (Brit. 1962); Director: Robert Stevens; Starring: Peter Finch, Susan Hayward, Diane Cilento, Cyril Cusack.

The Devil's Agent (Ire 1962); Director: John Paddy Carstairs; Starring: Peter Van Eyck, Christopher Lee, Billie Whiteland, Vincent Dowling, Peter Vaughan, Peter Lamb.

The Playboy of the Western World (Ire. 1962); Director: Brian Desmond Hurst; Starring: Siobhán McKenna, Gary Raymond, Liam Redmond, Elspeth March, Brendan Cauldwell, Niall Mcginnis.

The Quare Fellow (Brit. 1962); Director: Arthur Dreifuss; Starring: Patrick McGoohan, Walter Macken, Sylvia Syms, Dermott Kelly, Jack Cunningham, Marie Kean.

Dementia 13/The Haunted and the Hunted (U.S./Ire. 1963); Director: Francis Ford Coppola; Starring: William Campbell, Launa Anders, Patrick Magee, Bart Patton, Eithne Dunne.

Never Put It in Writing (Brit. 1963); Director: Andrew L. Stone; Starring: Pat Boone, Milo O'Shea, Fidelma Murphy.

Girl With Green Eyes (U.K. 1964); Director: Desmond Davis; Starring: Peter Finch, Rita Tushingham, Lynn Redgrave, Marie Kean.

I Was Happy Here (U.K. 1965); Director: Desmond Davis; Starring: Sarah Miles, Cyril Cusack, Julian Glover, Sean Caffrey, Marie Kean.

Young Cassidy (U.K. 1965); Director: Jack Cardiff; Starring: Rod Taylor, Julie Christie, Maggie Smith, Flora Robson, Edith Evans, Jack McGowran, T.P. Mc Kenna.

The Blue Max (U.S. 1966); Director: John Guillermin; Starring: George Peppard, James Mason, Ursula Andrews, Jeremy Kemp.

The Fighting Prince of Donegal (Brit. 1966); Director: Michael O'Herlihy; Starring: Peter McEnery, Susan Hampshire, Tom Adams, Gordon Jackson, Donal McCann, Peggy Marshall.

The Spy Who Came in from the Cold (Ire. 1966); Director: Martin Ritt; Starring: Richard Burton, Claire Bloom, Oscar Werner, Cyril Cusack.

Finnegan's Wake (U.S. 1967); Director: Mary Ellen Bute; Starring: Martin J. Kelly, Jane Reilly, Peter Haskell, Page Johnson.

Ulysses (Brit. 1967); Director: Joseph Strick; Starring: Milo O'Shea, Barbara Jefford, T.P. McKenna, Maureen Potter, Martin Dempsey, Maurice Roeves.

Bright Future (Ire 1968); Director: George Morrison; Starring: Tommy Curran, Liam Saurin, Niall Tóibín.

Finian's Rainbow (U.S. 1968); Director: Francis Ford Coppola; Starring: Fred Astaire, Petula Clarke, Tommy Steele, Don Francks, Barbra Hancock.

30 is a Dangerous Age, Cynthia (Brit. 1968); Director: Joseph McGrath; Starring: Dudley Moore, Suzy Kendall, Patricia Routledge, Eddie Foy Jnr., John Bird, Michael

MacLiammóir.

Guns in the Heather (Brit. 1969); Director: Robert Butler; Starring: Glenn Corbett, Kurt Russell, Alfred Burke, Patrick Dawson, Niall Tóibín, Vincent Dowling.

McKenzie Break (Brit. 1969); Director: Lamont Johnson; Starring: Brian Keith, Ian Hendry, Helmut Griem, Patrick O'Connell, John Kavanagh, Noel Purcell.

Paddy (Ire. 1969); Director: Daniel Haller; Starring: Des Cave, Dearbhla Molloy, Milo O'Shea, Maureen Toal, John Kavanagh, Ita Darcy.

The Violent Enemy (Brit. 1969); Director: Don Sharp; Starring: Tom Bell, Susan Hampshire, Ed Begley, Noel Purcell.

Wedding Night/I Can't, I Can't... (Ire. 1969); Director: Piers Haggard; Starring: Dennis Waterman, Tessa Wyatt, Alexandra Bastedo, Eddie Byrne, Martin Dempsey.

Emtigon (Ire. 1970); Director: Joe Comerford; Starring: Danny O'Connor, Carolyn Tipping.

Philadelphia Here I Come! (Ire. 1970); Director: John Quested; Starring: Donal McCann, Des Cave, Siobhán McKenna, Fidelma Murphy, Niall Tóibín, Eamon Kelly.

Ryan's Daughter (Brit. 1970); Director: David Lean; Starring: Robert Mitchum, Sarah Miles, Trevor Howard, Niall Tóibín, Donal Neligan, Des Keogh, Marie Kean.

The Molly Maguires (Brit. 1970); Director: Martin Ritt; Starring: Richard Harris, Sean Connery, Samantha Eggar, Frank Finlay.

The Return of the Islander (Ire. 1970); James Mulkerns; Starring: Mícheál Ó Connghaile, Máire de Burca, Máire Ní Diorráin.

Quackser Fortune has a Cousin in the Bronx (U.S. 1970); Director: Waris Hussein; Starring: Gene Wilder, Margot Kidder, Seamus Forde, Eileen Colgan, Paul Murray, May Ollis.

Flight of the Doves (Brit. 1971); Director: Ralph Nelson; Starring: Ron Moody, Jack Wild, William Rushton, Dorothy McGuire, Stan Holloway, Niall Tóibín, Noel Purcell.

But they Said it - Didn't They (Ire. 1972); Director: Joe McCarthy; Starring: Jim Queally, Frank Duggan, Michael Twomey.

Images (Ire./U.S. 1972); Director: Robert Altman; Starring: Susannah York, René Auberjonois, Hugh Millais, Marcel Bozzuffi, Cathryn

Harrison, John Morley.

The Hebrew Lesson (Ire. 1972); Director: Wolf Mankowitz; Starring: Milo O'Shea, Patrick Dawson, Alun Owen, Harry Taub.

Three Weeks in a Tower (Ire. 1972); Director: Maurice O'Kelly; Starring: Chris Curran, Pat Daly, Sean O'Neill, Nicholas Kennedy.

A Quiet Day in Belfast (Can. 1973); Director: Milad Bassada; Starring: Barry Foster, Margot Kidder, Sean McCann, Leo Leyden, Sean Mulcahy, Emmet Bergin.

Dunhallow Home (Ire. 1973); Director: Colin Hill; Starring: Margaret Hill, Susannah York, Mary Flynn, Julian Walton, Molly O'Reilly, William Reidy.

The Mackintosh Man (Brit. 1973); Director: John Huston; Starring: Paul Newman, James Mason, Dominique Sanda, Peter Vaughan, Niall Mcginnis, Noel Purcell.

Barry Lyndon (Brit. 1975); Director: Stanley Kubrick; Starring: Ryan O'Neal, Marisa Berenson, Patrick Magee, Steven Berkoff, Marie Kean.

Caoineadh Airt Uí Laoire: Lament For Arthur Leary (Ire. 1975); Director: Bob Quinn; Starring: Seán Bán Breathnach, Caitlín Ní Dhonnchú, John Arden, Tomás Mac Lochlann.

Hennessy (Brit. 1975); Director: Don Sharp; Starring: Rod Steiger, Richard Johnson, Lee Remick, Trevor Howard, Eric Porter, Peter Egan.

Cancer (Ire. 1976); Director: Deirdre Friel; Starring: J. G. Devlin, Louis Rolston.

Nano Nagle (Ire. 1976); Director: Desmond Forristal; Starring: Eithne Lydon, James N. Healy, Nora O'Mahony, Ronnie Walsh, Marie O'Neill.

The Last Remake of Beau Geste (Ire. 1976); Director: Marty Feldman; Starring: Marty Feldman, Ann Margaret, Michael York.

Wheels (Ire. 1976); Director: Cathal Black; Starring: Brendan Ellis, Michael Duffy, Maura Keeley, Paul Bennett, Alec Doran.

Down the Corner (Ire. 1977); Director: Joe Comerford; Starring: Joe Keenan, Declan Cronin, Kevin Doyle, Christy Keogh, Michael Joyce.

Portrait of the Artist as a Young Man (Brit. 1977); Director: Joseph Strick; Starring: T.P. McKenna, Bosca Hogan, John Gielgud,

Rosaleen Linehan, Maureen Potter, Niall Buggy.

The Kinkisha (Ire. 1977); Director: Tommy McArdle; Starring: Barbra McNamara, John McArdle, Catherine Gibson, David Byrne.

The Purple Taxi (Ire./Ita./Fra. 1977); Director: Yves Boisset; Starring: Peter Ustinov, Fred Astaire, Charlotte Rampling, Mairín O'Sullivan, David Kelly, Niall Buggy.

A Child's Voice (Ire. 1978); Director: Kieran Hickey and Shane O' Neill; Starring: T.P. McKenna, R.D. Smith, Stephen Brennan, June Tóibín.

Exposure (Ire. 1978); Director: Kieran Hickey; Starring: Catherine Schell, T.P. McKenna, Bosco Hogan, Niall O'Brien, Mairín O'Sullivan.

On a Paving Stone Mounted (Brit. 1978); Director: Thaddeus O'Sullivan; Starring: Stephen Rea, Gabriel Byrne, Mannix Flynn, Annabel Leventon.

Poitín (Ire. 1978); Director: Bob Quinn; Starring: Cyril Cusack, Niall Tóibín, Donal McCann, Mairéad Ní Chonghaile.

Revival - Pearse's Concept of Ireland (Ire. 1979); Director: Louis Marcus; Starring: John Kavanagh, Andy O'Mahony, Niall Tóibín, Denis Brennan, Derek Lord.

The Flame is Love (Ire. 1979); Director: Michael O'Herlihy; Starring: Linda Purl, Timothy Dalton.

The Newcomers: Inhabiting a New Land; The Irish (Can. 1979); Director: Eric Till; Starring: David McIlwraith, Linda Goranson, Peter MacNeill, Sean McCann.

The Outsider (Neth 1979); Director: Tony Luraschi; Starring: Craig Wasson, Sterling Hayden, Patricia Quinn, Niall O'Brien, T.P. McKenna, Niall Tóibín, Ray McAnally, Bosco Hogan.

Criminal Conversation (Ire. 1980); Director: Kieran Hickey; Starring: Emmet Bergin, Deirdre Donnelly, Peter Caffrey, Leslie Lalor, Kate Thompson, Des Nealon.

Cry of the Innocent (Ire. 1980); Director: Michael O'Herlihy; Starring: Rod Taylor, Joanna Pettet, Nigel Davenport.

Excalibur (Ire. 1980); Director: John Boorman; Starring: Nicol Williamson, Nigel Terry, Helen Mirren, Nicholas Clay, Cherie Lunghi.

It's Handy When People Don't Die (Ire. 1980); Director: Tommy McArdle; Starring: Garret Keogh,

Bob Carlyle, Brendan Cauldwell, Jim Lawler, Liam Neeson, Mick Lally.

The Dream Factory (Ire. 1980); Director: Peter Finegan; Starring: Malcolm Douglas, Robert McNamara, Ciaran Hinds, Brian De Salvo.

Desecration (Ire 1981); Director: Neville Presho; Starring: Tom Hickey, Johnny Murphy, Eamon Keane, Frank McDonald.

Fire and Sword (Ire./Ger. 1981); Director: Keith Von Fürstenberg; Starring: Peter Firth, Leigh Lawson, Christopher Waltz, Antonio Presner.

Maeve (Brit. 1981); Director: Pat Murray; Starring: Mark Mullholland, Bríd Brennan, Trudy Kelly, John Keegan, Mary Jackson.

Our Boys (Ire. 1981); Director: Cathal Black; Starring: Archie O'Sullivan, Mick Lally, Vincent McCabe, Noel O'Donovan, Kieran Hinds, Séamus Ellis.

Summer of the Falcon (Ire. 1981); Director: Tom Donovan; Starring: Richard Burton, Kate Mulgrew, Nicholas Clay, Cyril Cusack, Geraldine Fitzgerald, Niall Tóibín.

The Ballroom of Romance (Ire. 1981); Director: Pat O'Connor; Starring: Brenda Fricker, John Kavanagh, Cyril Cusack, Niall Tóibín.

Traveller (Ire. 1981); Director: Joe Comerford; Starring: Judy O'Donovan, Davy Spillane, Alan Devlin, Marion Richardson.

Angel (Ire. 1982); Director: Neil Jordan; Starring: Stephen Rea, Veronica Quilligan, Peter Caffrey, Honor Heffernan, Ray McAnally.

Educating Rita (Ire./Brit. 1982); Director: Lewis Gilbert; Starring: Michael Caine, Julie Walters, Maureen Lipman, Michael Williams.

The Outcasts (Ire. 1982); Director: Robert Wynne-Simmons; Starring: Cyril Cusack, Mary Ryan, Mick Lally, Don Foley, Paul Bennett.

The Writing on the Wall (Ire./Bel./Fra. 1982); Director: Armand Gatti; Starring: John Deehan, Brendan 'Archie' Deehan, Paddy Doherty, Nigel Haggan, John Keegan, Neil McCaul, Mary McMenamin.

The Year of the French (Ire. 1982); Director: Michael Garvey; Starring: Jeremy Clyde, Oliver Cotton, Jean-Claude Drouot, Keith Buckley.

At the Cinema Palace - Liam O'Leary (Ire. 1983); Director:

Donald Taylor; Starring: Liam O'Leary, Cyril Cusack, Michael Powell, Lindsay Anderson, Sean MacBride.

Attracta (Ire. 1983); Director: Kieran Hickey; Starring: Wendy Hiller, Kate Thompson; Joe McPartland, John Kavanagh, Kate Flynn.

Caught in the Free State (Ire. 1983); Director: Peter Ormrod; Starring: Gotz Burger, Benno Hoffman, John Kavanagh, Barry McGovern, Niall Tóibín.

John, Love (Brit. 1983); Director: John Davis; Starring: Nuala Hayes, Niall O'Brien, Tony Hyland, Carmel Callan, Martin Dempsey.

Night in Tunisia (Ire. 1983); Director: Pat O'Connor; Starring: Mick Lally, Ciaran Burns, Jill Doyle, Jim Culleton.

Paradiso (Brit. 1983); Director: Colm Villa; Starring: John Finch, Alan Devlin.

One of Ourselves (Ire. 1983); Director: Pat O'Connor; Starring: Cyril Cusack, Niall Tóibín, Frances Quinn, Stephen Mason, Bill Paterson.

Reflections (Brit. 1983); Director: Kevin Billington; Starring: Gabriel Byrne, Donal McCann, Fionnuala Flanagan, Gerard Cummins, Niall Tóibín.

The Best Man (Ire. 1983); Director: Joe Mahon; Starring: Seamus Ball, Máiréad Mullan, Denis McGowan, Jean Flagherty, Mickey McGowan.

The Country Girls (Brit. 1983); Director: Desmond Davis; Starring: Sam Neill, Maeve Germaine, Niall Tóibín, Jill Doyle, John Kavanagh.

The Schooner (Ire. 1983); Director: Bill Miskelly; Starring Michael Gormley, Lucy Jameson, Johnny Marley, Desmond McAleer.

Withdrawal (Ire. 1983); Director: Joe Comerford; Starring: Mark Quinn, Marian O'Loughlin, Gerald McSorley, Liam Sweeney.

Absolution (Brit. 1984); Director: Niall Leonard; Starring: Derek Halligan, Donal O'Hanlon, Frank Dooley, Bernadette Rea, Sean Markey.

Anne Devlin (Ire. 1984); Director: Pat Murphy; Starring: Bríd Brennan, Bosco Hogan, Des McAleer, Gillian Hackett, Ian McElhinney.

A Second of June (Ire. 1984); Director: Francis Stapleton; Starring: Lisa Birthistle, Dermot King, Derek Molloy, Mary Stokes, Cathy Young.

Cal (Brit. 1984); Director: Pat

O'Connor; Starring: Helen Mirren, John Lynch, Ray McAnally, Donal McCann, John Kavanagh, Steven Rimkus.

Hostage (Brit. 1984); Director: Aisling Walsh; Starring: Veronica Quilligan, Alan Devlin, Seamus Healy, John Scott.

Pigs (Ire. 1984); Director: Cathal Black; Starring: Jimmy Brennan, George Shane, Maurice O'Donoghue, Liam Halligan.

The Company of Wolves (Ire. 1984); Director: Neil Jordan; Starring: Stephen Rea, Sarah Patterson, Angela Lansbury, David Warner, Brian Glover.

Waterbag (Ire. 1984); Director: Joe Comerford; Starring: Therese Lawlor, Brian Bourke, Paddy O'Neill.

Four Days in July (Brit. 1985); Director: Mike Leigh; Starring: Bríd Brennan, Stephen Rea, Des McAleer.

Lamb (Brit. 1985); Director: Colin Gregg; Starring: Liam Neeson, Harry Towb, Hugh O'Conor, Frances Tomelty, Ian Bannen.

The Doctor and the Devils (Brit. 1985); Director: Freddie Francis; Starring: Timothy Dalton, Jonathan Pryce, Twiggy, Julian Sands, Stephen Rea, T.P. McKenna, Phyllis Logan.

The End of the World Man (Ire. 1985); Director: Bill Miskelly; Starring: John Hewitt, Leanne O'Malley, Claire Weir, Maureen Dow, Michael Knowles.

Boom Babies (Ire. 1986); Director: Siobhán Twomey; Starring: Aisling Tóibín, Andrew Connolly.

Eat the Peach (Ire. 1986); Director: Peter Ormrod; Starring: Stephen Brennan, Eamonn Morrissey, Catherine Byrne, Niall Tóibín, Joe Lynch.

Fear of the Dark (Ire. 1986); Director: Tony Barry; Starring: Hugh O'Conor, Aisling Tóibín, Owen O'Gorman, Donal O'Kelly.

The Fantasist (Ire. 1986); Director: Robin Hardy; Starring: Timothy Bottoms, Christopher Cazenove, Moira Harris, John Kavanagh, Mick Lally.

Budawanny (Ire. 1987); Director: Bob Quinn; Starring: Donal McCann, Maggie Fegan, Peadar Lamb, Martin O'Malley.

Clash of the Ash (Ire. 1987); Director: Fergus Tighe; Starring: Liam Heffernan, Vincent Murphy, Gina Moxley, Myles Breen, Maran

Dowley, Alan Devlin.

High Spirits (Ire. 1987); Director: Neil Jordan; Starring: Peter O'Toole, Daryl Hannah, Steve Guttenberg, Donal McCann, Peter Gallagher, Liam Neeson, Ray McAnally, Mary Coughlan.

Out of Time (Ire. 1987); Director: Robert Wynne-Simmons; Starring: Sian Phillips, Phyllis Logan, Kate Thompson, Oliver Maguire.

Reefer and the Model (Ire. 1987); Director: Joe Comerford; Starring: Ian McElhinney, Carol Scanlan, Eve Watkinson, Ray McBride, Birdy Sweeney, Sean Lawlor.

Riders to the Sea (Ire 1987); Director: Ronan O'Leary; Starring: Geraldine Page, Amanda Plummer, Barry McGovern, Joan O'Hara, Michael O'Brien.

The Dead (Ire./U.S./Brit./Ger. 1987); Director: John Huston; Starring: Anjelica Huston, Donal McCann, Dan O'Herlihy, Rachel Dowling.

The Lonely Passion of Judith Hearne (Brit 1987); Director: Jack Clayton; Starring: Bob Hoskins, Maggie Smith, Marie Kean, Alan Devlin, Prunella Scales, Niall Buggy, Kate Binchy.

The Scar (Ire/Brit. 1987); Director: Robert Wynne-Simmons; Starring: Ken Colley, Gerard McSorley, Olwen Fouere, David Heap.

A Prayer for the Dying (Brit. 1988); Director: Mike Hodges; Starring: Mickey Rourke, Bob Hoskins, Liam Neeson, Alison Doody, Alan Bates, Sammi Davis.

Da (U.S. 1988); Director: Matt Clark; Starring: Martin Sheen, Barnard Hughes, Doreen Hepburn, William Hickey, Hugh O'Conor.

Joyriders (Brit. 1988); Director: Aisling Walsh; Starring: Andrew Connolly, Patricia Kerrigan, Billie Whitlaw, John Kavanagh, David Kelly.

Now I Know (Ire. 1988); Director: Robert Pappas; Starring: Matt Mulhern.

Taffin (Brit./US 1988); Director: Francis Megahy; Starring: Pierce Brosnan, Alison Doody, Ray McAnally, Patrick Bergin.

The Courier (Brit. 1988); Director: Joe Lee, Frank Deasy; Starring: Gabriel Byrne, Padraig O'Loinsigh, Ian Bannen, Patrick Bergin, Andrew Connolly, Cait O'Riordain.

The Dawning (Brit. 1988); Director: Robert Knights; Starring: Anthony Hopkins, Jean Simmons, Trevor

Howard, Hugh Grant, Tara McGowran, John Rogan.

Fragments of Isabella (Ire. 1989); Director: Ronan O'Leary; Starring: Gabrielle Reidy.

Hush-A-Bye-Baby (Ire/Brit. 1989); Director: Margo Harkin; Starring: Emer McCourt, Sinéad O'Connor, Michael Liebmann, Cathy Casey, Julie Marie Rodgers.

My Left Foot (Ire/Brit. 1989); Director: Jim Sheridan; Starring: Daniel Day Lewis, Brenda Fricker, Ray McAnally, Ruth McCabe, Fiona Shaw, Hugh O'Conor, Cyril Cusack.

After Midnight (Ire. 1990); Director: Shani S Grewal; Starring: Saeed Jaffrey, Hayley Mills, Ian Dury, Maurice O'Donoghue, Patrick Condren, Gerard Byrne.

Dear Sarah (Brit. 1990); Director: Frank Cvitanovich; Starring: Stella McCusker, Barry McGovern, Patrick F. Rocks, Bronagh Gallagher.

December Bride (Ire./Brit. 1990); Director: Thaddeus O'Sullivan; Starring: Donal McCann, Saskia Reeves, Ciaran Hinds, Patrick Malahide, Brenda Bruce, Dervla Kirwin, Gabrielle Reidy.

Fools of Fortune (Brit. 1990); Director: Pat O'Connor; Starring: Julie Christie, Mary Elizabeth Mastrantonio, Niall Tóibín, Mick Lally, Tom Hickey, Niamh Cusack, Iain Glen, Michael Kitchen.

Hard Shoulder (Ire. 1990); Director: Mark Kilroy; Starring: Olwen Fouere, Johnny Murphy, Donal O'Kelly, Geoff Golden, Eamonn Hunt, Gina Moxley.

Hidden Agenda (Brit. 1990); Director: Ken Loach; Starring: Brad Dourif, Brian Cox, Frances McDormand, Mia Zetterling, Michelle Fairley, Brian McCann.

The Field (Brit. 1990); Director: Jim Sheridan; Starring: Richard Harris, John Hurt, Tom Berenger, Sean Bean, Frances Tomelty, Brenda Fricker, John Cowley, Ruth McCabe.

Diary of a Madman (Ire. 1991); Director: Ronan O'Leary; Starring: Tim McDonnell, Siobhán Miley, Deirdre O'Connell, Conor Mullen, Anna Livia Ryan.

Hear My Song (Brit. 1991); Director: Peter Chelsom; Starring: Ned Beatty, Shirley Ann Field, Adrian Dunbar, Tara Fitzgerald.

The Commitments (Brit. 1991); Director: Alan Parker; Starring: Michael Ahern, Maria Doyle, Dave Finnegan, Bronagh Gallagher, Colm

Meaney, Andrew Strong, Angeline Ball, Johnny Murphy.

The Miracle (Brit. 1991); Director: Neil Jordan; Starring: Beverly D'Angelo, Donal McCann, Niall Byrne, Lorraine Pilkington, Tom Hickey, Shane Connaughton, Mary Coughlan.

Far and Away (U.S. 1992); Director: Ron Howard; Starring: Tom Cruise, Nicole Kidman, Colm Meaney, Thomas Gibson, Cyril Cusack, Eileen Pollock, Niall Tóibín, Barry McGovern.

Hello, Stranger (Ire. 1992); Director: Ronan O'Leary; Starring: Daniel J. Travanti, Tim McDonnell, O. Z. Whitehead, Jan Widger.

Into the West (Ire 1992); Director: Mike Newell; Starring: Gabriel Byrne, Ellen Barkin, Ciarán Fitzgerald, Ruaidhrí Conroy, David Kelly, Johnny Murphy, Colm Meaney, John Kavanagh, Brendan Gleeson.

Micha (Ire./Russia 1992); Director: Gerad Michael MacCarthy; Starring: Genya Korhin, Victoria Korhina, Igor Kostolevsky, Audrey Urgant.

Patriot Games (U.S. 1992); Director: Phillip Noyce; Starring: Harrison Ford, Anne Archer, Patrick Bergin, Sean Bean, Richard Harris, Thora Birch, Andrew Connolly, Samuel L. Jackson.

The Bargain Shop (Ire./Ger. 1992); Director: Johnny Gogan; Starring: Emer McCourt, Garrett Keogh, Stuart Graham, Ruth McCabe, Brendan Gleeson, Donal O'Kelly.

The Crying Game (Brit. 1992); Director: Neil Jordan; Starring: Stephen Rea, Adrian Dunbar, Jaye Davidson, Forest Whitaker, Miranda Richardson, Tony Slattery.

The Playboys (Brit. 1992); Director: Gillies MacKinnon; Starring: Albert Finney, Aidan Quinn, Robin Wright, Milo O'Shea, Niamh Cusack, Adrian Dunbar.

Bad Behaviour (Brit. 1993); Director: Les Blair; Starring: Stephen Rea, Sinead Cusack, Philip Jackson, Clare Higgins.

High Boot Benny (Ire. 1993); Director: Joe Comerford; Starring: Marc O'Shea, Frances Tomelty, Alan Devlin, Fiona Nicholas, Seamus Ball.

In the Name of the Father (Ire./Brit./U.S..1993); Director: Jim Sheridan; Starring: Daniel Day-Lewis, Emma Thompson, Pete Postlethwaite, John Lynch, Mark Sheppard, Beatie Edney, Marie Jones, Tina Kellegher, Brian De Salvo, Bosco Hogan, Don Baker.

The Railway Station Man (Brit. 1993); Director: Michael Whyte; Starring: Donald Sutherland, Julie Christie, John Lynch, Jean John, Frank McCusker.

The Snapper (Brit. 1993); Director: Stephen Frears; Starring: Colm Meaney, Tina Kellegher, Ruth McCabe, Eanna MacLiam, Peter Rowen, Pat Laffan, Brendan Gleeson.

Widow's Peak (Brit. 1993); Director: John Irvine; Starring: Mia Farrow, Joan Plowright, Natasha Richardson, Adrian Dunbar, Jim Broadbent, John Kavanagh.

Ailsa (Ger./Fra./Ire. 1994); Director: Paddy Breathnach; Starring: Brendan Coyle, Andrea Irvine, Daragh Kelly, Juliette Gruber, Georgia Mullen, Gary Lydon.

All Things Bright and Beautiful (Ire./Brit. 1994); Director: Barry Devlin; Starring: Gabriel Byrne, Tom Wilkinson, Ciarán Fitzgerald, Kevin McNally, Gabrielle Reidy, Lorraine Pilkington.

An Awfully Big Adventure (Ire./Brit. 1995); Director: Mike Newell; Starring: Alan Rickman, Hugh Grant, Peter Firth, Georgia Cates, Prunella Scales.

Braveheart (Ire. 1994); Director: Mel Gibson; Starring: Mel Gibson, Sophie Marceau, Patrick McGoohan, Brendan Gleeson, John Kavanagh.

Broken Harvest (Ire. 1994); Director: Maurice O'Callaghan; Starring: Colin Lane, Niall O'Brien, Marion Quinn, Darren McHugh, Joe Jeffers, Joy Florish.

Moondance (Ire. 1994); Director: Dagmar Hirtz; Starring: Ruaidhrí Conroy, Julia Brendler, Ian Shaw, Marianne Faithfull, Brendan Grace.

The Bishop's Story (Ire. 1994); Director: Bob Quinn; Starring: Donal McCann, Margaret Fegan, Ray McBride, Peadar Lamb.

The Secret of Roan Inish (U.S. 1994); Director: John Sayles; Starring: Mick Lally, Eileen Colgan, John Lynch, Richard Sheridan, Jennifer Courtney.

War of the Buttons (Brit./Ire. 1994); Director: John Roberts; Starring: Colm Meaney, Johnny Murphy, John Coffey, Gregg Fitzgerald, Gerard Kearney, Liam Cunningham, Paul Batt.

Words Upon the Window Pane (Ire. 1994); Director: Mary McGuckian; Starring: Geraldine Chaplin, Geraldine James, Donal Donnelly, Ian Richardson, Gerard McSorley, Gemma Craven.

A Man of No Importance (Ire./Brit. 1995); Director: Suri Krishnamma; Starring: Albert Finney, Brenda Fricker, Tara Fitzgerald, Michael Gambon, Mick Lally.

Bloodfist VIII - Trained for Action (Ire 1995); Director: Rick Jacobson; Starring: Don Wilson, J. P. White.

Circle of Friends (U.S./Ire. 1995); Director: Pat O'Connor; Starring: Chris O'Donnell, Minnie Driver, Geraldine O'Rawe, Saffron Burrows, Colin Firth, Mick Lally, John Kavanagh, Ruth McCabe, Ciaran Hinds, Alan Cumming.

Frankie Starlight (Ire. 1995); Director: Michael Lindsay-Hogg; Starring: Ann Parillaud, Matt Dillon, Gabriel Byrne, Rudi Davies, Georgina Cates, Niall Tóibín.

Guiltrip (Ire./Fra./Ita./Spain 1995); Director: Gerry Stembridge; Starring: Andrew Connolly, Jasmine Russell, Michelle Houlden, Peter Hanly, Pauline McLynn, Frankie McCafferty, Mikel Murfi.

Korea (Ire. 1995); Director: Cathal Black; Starring: Donal Donnelly, Andrew Scott, Fiona Molony, Vass Anderson, Eileen Ward, Pat Fitzpatrick, Sadie Maguire.

Nothing Personal (Ire./Brit. 1995); Director: Thaddeus O'Sullivan; Starring: Ian Hart, John Lynch, James Frain, Gary Lydon, Michael Gambon, Jenifer Courtney.

The Run of the Country (Ire. 1995); Director: Peter Yates; Starring: Albert Finney, Matt Keeslar, Victoria Smurfit, Anthony Brophy, David Kelly, Dearbhla Molloy, Vinnie McCabe.

Undercurrent (Ire. 1995); Director: Brian O'Flaherty; Starring: Owen Roe, Stanley Townsend, Tina Kellegher, Orla Charlton.

A Furtive Gesture (Ire./Brit./Ger. 1996); Director: Robert Dornhelm; Starring: Stephen Rea, Alfred Molina, Brendan Gleeson, Maria Doyle Kennedy, Sean McGinley.

Dance, Lexlie, Dance (Ire. 1996); Director: Tim Loane; Starring: B.J. Hogg, Kimberly McConkey.

Driftwood (Ire 1996); Director: Ronan O'Leary; Starring: James Spader, Anne Brochet, Barry McGovern, Anna Massey, Kevin

McHugh, Ger Ryan.

Drinking Crude (Ire. 1996); Director: Owen McPolin; Starring: Andrew Scott, James Quarton, Eva Birthistle, Harry O'Callaghan.

It's Now or Never (Den. 1996); Director: Jon Bang Carlsen; Starring: James Joseph Mevoy, Austin Deely, Patrick O'Reilly, Marie Daly.

Last of the High Kings (Ire. 1996); Director: David Keating; Starring: Gabriel Byrne, Colm Meaney, Christine Ricci, Catherine O'Hara, Jared Leto, Renee Weldon, Peter Keating, Stephen Rea.

Michael Collins (Ire. 1996); Director: Neil Jordan; Starring: Liam Neeson, Julia Roberts, Aidan Quinn, Alan Rickman, Stephen Rea, Ian Hart, Charles Dance, Brendan Gleeson, Stuart Graham, Gerard McSorley.

My Friend Joe (Ire. 1996); Director: Chris Bould; Starring: John Cleere, Joel Grey, Schuyler Fox, Stanley Townsend, Pauline McLynn, Eoin Hughes, Stephen McHattie.

November Afternoon (Ire. 1996); Director: John Carney, Tom Hall; Starring: Michael McElhatton, Jayne Snow, Mark Doherty, Tristan Gribbin.

Snakes and Ladders (Ire. 1996); Director: Trish McAdam; Starring: Pom Boyd, Gina Moxley, Sean Hughes, Rosaleen Linehan, Pierce Turner, Catherine White.

Space Truckers (Ire. 1996); Director: Stuart Gordon; Starring: Dennis Hopper, Stephen Dorff, Debi Mazar, Charles Dance.

Spaghetti Slow (Ire./Ita./Brit. 1996); Director: Valerie Jaiongo; Starring: Niamh O'Byrne, Guilio Di Mauro, Ivano Marescotti, Brendan Gleeson, Gary Fitzpatrick, Frankie McCafferty, Ingrid Craigie.

Some Mother's Son (Ire. 1996); Director: Terry George; Starring: Helen Mirren, John Lynch, Fionnuala Flanagan, Aidan Gillen, David O'Hara, Tom Hollander, Gerard McSorley, Ciaran Hinds, John Kavanagh.

The Boy from Mercury (Ire. 1996); Director: Martin Duffy; Starring: Hugh O'Conor, Tom Courtenay, Rita Tushingham, James Hickey.

The Brylcreem Boys (Brit. 1996); Director: Terence Ryan; Starring: Gabriel Byrne, Bill Campbell, William McNamara, Jean Butler.

The Disappearance of Finbar (Ire./Brit./Swe. 1996); Director: Sue Clayton; Starring: Jonathon Rhys-Myers, Lorraine Pilkington, Luke Griffin, Sean McGinley, Marie Mullan, Sean Lawlor, Tina Kellegher, Don Foley, Robert Hickey.

The Eliminator (Ire. 1996); Director: Enda Hughes; Starring: Barry Wallace, Michael Hughes, Mike Duffy, Edward Hughes, Paul McAvinchey, Donna Crilly.

The Sun, The Moon and The Stars (Ire. 1996); Director: Geraldine Creed; Starring: Angie Dickinson, Jason Donovan, Gina Moxley, Elaine Cassidy, Aisling Corcoran, David Murray, Vinny Murphy.

The Van (Ire. 1996); Director: Stephen Frears; Starring: Colm Meaney, Donal O'Kelly, Brendan O'Carroll, Ger Ryan, Caroline Rothwell, Stuart Dunne, Jack Lynch, Moses Rowen.

This is the Sea (Ire. 1996); Director: Mary McGuckian; Starring: Gabriel Byrne, Richard Harris, John Lynch.

Trojan Eddie (Ire. 1996); Director: Gillies MacKinnon; Starring: Stephen Rea, Richard Harris, Jared Harris, Donal McCann, Bríd Brennan, Sean McGinley, Brendan Gleeson, Aislín McGuckan.

Films due for release late 1997 and 1998:

Angela Mooney Dies Again (Ire. 1997); Director: Tommy McArdle; Starring: Patrick Bergin, Mia Farrow, Brendan Gleeson.

Bogwoman (Ire. 1997); Director: Tommy Collins; Starring: Peter Mullan, Sean McGinley, Rachael Dowling, Maria MacDermottroe, Noelle Brown.

Cycle of Violence (1998); Producer Don Boyd; Starring: Gerard Rooney. (Based on Colin Bateman's novel).

Dancing At Lughnasa (Ire. 1997); Director: Pat O'Connor; Starring: Meryl Streep, Bríd Brennan, Catherine McCormack, Michael Gambon. (Based on Brian Friel's play).

Divorcing Jack (Ire. 1998); Director: David Caffrey. (Based on Colin Bateman's novel).

Double Carpet (Ire 1997); Director: Mark Kilroy, Howard Gibbons.

Element (Ire 1997); Producer: Catherine Tiernan.

Falling for a Dancer (Ire. 1998); Director: Richard Standeven. (Based on Deirdre Purcell's novel).

George Best: A Documentary (Ire 1998); Director: Mary McGuckian. Starring: John Lynch

Gold in the Streets (Ire. 1997); Director: Elizabeth Gill; Starring: Ian Hart, Jared Harris, Louise Lombard, Lorraine Pilkington, Aiden Gillen, James Belushi.

Hooligans (Ire/Brit./Ger/Hol 1997); Director: Paul Tickell; Starring: Darren Healy, Jeff O'Toole, Viviana Verveen, Gavin Kelty.

How to Cheat in the Leaving Cert (Ire. 1997); Director: Graham Jones; Starring: Garret Bawer; Cameo roles: Chris De Burgh, Alan Amsby.

Hugh Cullen (Ire 1997); Producer: Nicholas O'Neill, Written by: Sean O'Hagan.

Inventing the Abbots (Ire. 1997); Director: Pat O'Connor.

I Went Down (Ire. 1997); Director: Paddy Breathnach. Starring: Brendan Gleeson, Peter McDonald, Peter Caffrey, Tony Doyle.

Johnny Jump Up (Ire./U.S. 1997) Director: Kieron J. Walsh.

Just in Time (Ire. 1997); Director: John Carney, Tom Hall.

Marie Curie: What Meets the Eye (Ire./Can. 1997); Director: Richard Mozer.

Miracle at Midnight (Ire./U.S. 1997); Director: Ken Cameron; Starring: Sam Waterston, Mia Farrow.

Saving Private Ryan (Ire./U.S. 1997); Director: Steven Spielberg; Starring Tom Hanks, Ed Burns.

Sparrow's Trap (Ire. 1998); (Based on Brendan O'Carroll's novel).

St. Ives (Ire./Fra./Ger. 1997); Director: Harry Hook; Starring: Jean-Marc Barr, Miranda Richardson, Anna Friel, Richard E. Grant.

Sweetly Barret (Ire. 1998); Director: Stephen Bradley.

The Boxer (Ire. 1997); Director: Jim Sheridan; Starring: Daniel Day-Lewis.

The Butcher Boy (Ire. 1997); Director: Neil Jordan; Starring: Eamonn Owness, Eugene McCabe, Stephen Rea, Sinéad O'Connor.

The Closest Thing to Heaven (Ire. 1997); Director: Dorne Pentes.

The Deadness of Dad (Ire. 1997); Director: Phillipa Cousins.

The Fifth Province (Ire. 1998); Director: Frank Stapleton.

The Last Bus Home (Ire. 1998).

The Mammy (Ire. 1998); Producer: Jim Sheridan; Starring: Angelica Huston, Peter Ustinov. (Based On Brendan O'Carroll's novel).

The Nephew (Ire. 1998); Producer: Pierce Brosnan; Starring: Donal McCann, Aislín McGuckan.

The Wish (Ire. 1998); Director: Martin Duffy. This is My Father (Ire. 1998);

Director: Paul Quinn; Starring: Aidan Quinn, James Caan.

IRISH OSCAR WINNERS 1929 -1993

The Motion Picture Academy Awards were instituted in 1928 for excellence in various aspects of cinema. Ireland has had numerous winners; they include the following:

Cedric Gibbons .... **11 Oscars for Best Art Direction 1929-1956**
.... **The Bridge of San Luis Rey** 1929
.... **The Merry Widow** 1934
.... **Pride and Prejudice** 1940
.... **Blossoms in the Dust** 1941
.... **Gaslight** 1944
.... **The Yearling** 1946
.... **Little Women** 1949
.... **Honorary Oscar** for *'Consistent Excellence'* 1950
.... **An American in Paris** 1951
.... **The Bad and the Beautiful** 1952
.... **Julius Caesar** 1953
.... **Somebody Up There Likes Me** 1956
George Bernard Shaw .... Best Screen Play **My Fair Lady** *(Pygmalion)* 1938
Greer Garson .... Best Actress **Mrs Miniver** 1942
Barry Fitzgerald .... Best Supporting Actor **Going My Way** 1944
Shane Connaughton .... Best Short Film **Bottom Dollar** 1981
Michele Burke .... Best Make-up **Quest For Fire** 1981
.... **Bram Stoker's Dracula** 1983
Josie McAvin .... Art Direction for **Out Of Africa** 1985
Daniel Day Lewis .... Best Actor **My Left Foot** 1989
Brenda Fricker .... Best Supporting Actress **My Left Foot** 1989
Neil Jordan .... Best Screenplay **The Crying Game** 1993

IRISH OSCAR NOMINATIONS 1939 -1993

Brian Donleavy .... Best Supporting Actor **Beau Geste** 1939
Greer Garson .... Best Actress **Goodbye Mr Chips** 1939
Geraldine Fitzgerald .... Best Supporting Actress **Wuthering Heights** 1939
Greer Garson .... Best Actress **Blossoms in the Dust** 1941
Sara Allgood .... Best Supporting Actress **How Green Was My Valley** 1941
Patricia Collinge .... Best Supporting Actress **Little Foxes** 1941
Greer Garson .... Best Actress **Madame Curie** 1943
Barry Fitzgerald .... Best Supporting Actor **Going My Way** 1944
Greer Garson .... Best Actress **Mrs Parkington** 1944
Greer Garson .... Best Actress **Valley of Decision** 1945
Richard Todd .... Best Actor **The Hasty Heart** 1949
Dan O'Herlihy .... Best Actor **The Adventures of Robinson Crusoe** 1953
Greer Garson .... Best Actress **Sunrise at Campobello** 1960
Peter O'Toole .... Best Actor **Lawrence of Arabia** 1962
Richard Harris .... Best Actor **This Sporting Life** 1963
Josie McAvin .... Best Set Designer **Tom Jones** 1963
Peter O'Toole .... Best Actor **Beckett** 1964
Josie McAvin .... Best Set Design **The Spy Who Came in From the Cold** 1965
Peter O'Toole .... Best Actor **The Lion in Winter** 1968
.... Best Actor **Goodbye Mr Chips** 1969
.... Best Actor **The Ruling Class** 1972
Louis Marcus .... Best Documentary **Páisti Ag Obair** *(Children At Work)* 1974
.... Best Documentary **Conquest Of Light** 1976
Peter O'Toole .... Best Actor **The Stunt Man** 1980
Peter O'Toole .... Best Actor **My Favourite Year** 1982
Clare Boylan .... Best Short Film **Making Waves** 1988
Kenneth Branagh .... Best Director **Henry V** 1989
.... Best Actor **Henry V** 1989
Daniel Day Lewis .... Best Actor **My Left Foot** 1989
Jim Sheridan .... Best Screenplay (with Shane Connaughton) **My Left Foot** 1989
.... Best Director **My Left Foot** 1989

Gerry Hambling	Best Film Editor **The Commitments** 1989
Richard Harris	Best Actor **The Field** 1990
Kenneth Branagh	Best Short Film **Swan Song** 1992
Neil Jordan	Best Director **The Crying Game** 1992
	Best Film (as Producer) **The Crying Game** 1992
Kant Pan	Best Film Editor **The Crying Game** 1992
Stephen Rea	Best Actor **The Crying Game** 1992
Jaye Davidson	Best Supporting Actor **The Crying Game** 1992
Daniel Day Lewis	Best Actor **In the Name of the Father** 1993
Jim Sheridan	Best Screenplay (with Terry George) **In the Name of the Father** 1993
	Best Director **In the Name of the Father** 1993
	Best Film (as Producer) **In the Name of the Father** 1993
Liam Neeson	Best Actor **Schindler's List** 1993

TOP TEN FILMS IN IRELAND, 1995

Batman Forever, Casper, Braveheart, Goldeneye, Interview with a Vampire, Circle of Friends, Die Hard With a Vengence, The Santa Claus, Apollo 13, While You Were Sleeping.

OPERATIONAL COSTS:
VAT Rate: 12.5% of the Gross Box office; 21% for film hire & concessions. **Music Rights:** 0.6% for cinemas with maximum of 4 screens; 2.5% for cinemas with more than 4 screens. **Government taxes:** No special cinema taxes. **Local Taxes:** Local authority tax rates relate to value of business. **Window for video release** (period of time after cinema release): 3 months.

CINEMA ATTENDANCES, 1995

January	903,200	July	949,500
February	733,400	August	939,400
March	771,300	September	826,200
April	705,800	October	939,800
May	696,800	November	826,800
June	624,000	December	920,500

BIOGRAPHIES OF IRISH FILM PERSONALITIES

Allgood, Sara (born Dublin, 1883) actress - film debut in *Riders to the Sea* (1904); repeated her greatest stage success in Hitchcock's *Juno and the Paycock* (1930). Went to Hollywood (1940). Played amiable motherly roles. Films include *How Green was My Valley* (1941), *Jane Eyre* (1944), *Challenge to Lassie* (1949). Died Los Angeles, 1950.

Bergin, Patrick (born Dublin, 1953) actor, playwright, producer and director; prominent in Bob Rafelson's *Mountains of the Moon* (1990) and *Sleeping with the Enemy* (1991); classic good looks made him a natural to play *Robin Hood* (TV 1991). His latest film is *Angela Mooney Dies Again* (1997).

Branagh, Kenneth (born Belfast, 1960) Shakespearean actor; leader of the Renaissance Theatre Company and film director. Gained international recognition as director/star of screen version of *Henry V (1989)*. Received Oscar-nomination for his short *Swan Song* (1992), directed and starred in screen adaptation of *Much Ado About Nothing* (1993) and *Hamlet* (1996). Films include: *High Season* (1987) and *A Month in the Country* (1987).

Brosnan, Pierce (born Meath, 1953) actor; came to recognition as private investigator *Remington Steele* on TV series (1982-87); film debut in *The Long Good Friday* (1980). Most successful in comedy *Mrs Doubtfire* (1993), disaster film *Dante's Peake* (1997) and as the fifth James Bond in *Goldeneye* (1996). He has a contract for two more Bond movies. His film production company is currently producing *The Nephew* (1997) and has two more future projects (1998).

Byrne, Eddie (born 1911) character actor in British films which include *The Gentle Gunman* (1946), *The Mummy* (1959), *Mutiny on the Bounty* (1962), and *Star Wars* (1977). Died 1981.

Byrne, Gabriel (born Dublin, 1950) actor; TV debut in RTÉ's *The Riordans* (1979) and *Bracken*. Film debut in *On a Paving Stone Mounted* (1978) Best known as star of Coen brothers' gangster drama, *Miller's Crossing* (1990). Was married to actress Ellen Barkin, opposite whom he starred in *Siesta* (1987). Films include *Defence of the Realm* (1985), *Into the West* (1991) and *The Usual Suspects* (1995). He is an accomplished writer and is currently a columnist with *Magill*.

Carey, Patrick (born London, 1916; reared Ireland) documentary filmmaker. Founded Aengus Films (1962). Films include *Journey into Spring* (1956), *Waves, Wild Wings, Yeats Country, Oisín* (1962-74), *Flamingo - Variations on a theme*, *The Algonquin Trilogy* (1975-83). Worked on *A Man for All Seasons*, *Ryan's Daughter* and *Barry Lyndon*. Died 1994.

Collins, Tommy (born Derry) Filmmaker. Produced documentaries *A Long Way to Go*, the journey home of Johnny Walker (of the Birmingham Six). Produced Margo Harkin's *Hush-A-Bye-Baby* (1989) and *More Than a Sacrifice* (1995), documentary for Channel 4 during I.R.A.'s first ceasefire. He has recently made his film directorial debut with the Derry/Donegal-based *Bogwoman* (1997).

Comerford, Joe (born 1949) director; made the first Irish language film *Caoineadh Airt Ui Laoire* (Lament for Art O'Leary - 1975). Films include *Emtigon* (1977), *Traveller* (1981), *Waterbag* (1984), *High Boot Benny* (1993); Won Europa Prize for Film *Reefer and the Model* (1987).

Connaughton, Shane (born Cavan) actor turned script-writer for theatre, television and film. Nominated with Sheridan for Best Adaptation Screen-play for *My Left Foot* (1989). Won an Oscar for writing *The Bottom Dollar* (1981). Films include *A Border Station* (1989), *The Miracle* (1991) and *The Playboys* (1992), co-written with Adrian Dunbar.

Craven, Gemma (born Ireland, 1950) actress, whose films include *The Slipper and the Rose* (1976), *Double X* (1992), *Words Upon The Window Pane* (1994) and the critically acclaimed Denis Potter TV series *Pennies from Heaven* (1977).

Cusack, Cyril (born South Africa 1910) stage/film actor; starred in over 57 films (1917-1990). Performed with Abbey and Gate Theatre, the Old Vic and the Royal Shakespeare Company. Film debut in *Knockagow* (1917). Major success with Carol Reed's *Odd Man Out* (1947). Broadway performance in Eugene O'Neill's *A Moon for the Misbegotten* (1957) opposite Wendy Hiller. Films include *The Spy Who Came in from the Cold* (1965), *Fahrenheit 451* (1967), *Little Dorrit* (1988), *Far and Away* (1992) and *As You Like it* (1992). Father of actresses Sinéad, Niamh and Sorcha Cusack with whom he co-starred in the Gate Theatre's production of Chekhov's *Three Sisters*. (1990). Died 1993.

Cusack, Sinéad (born Dublin, 1948) actress; films include *David Copperfield* (1969), *The Last Remake of Beau Geste* (1977), and *Bad Behaviour* (1993). Daughter of Cyril and sister of Sorcha (from the B.B.C. T.V. series *Casualty*); and Niamh (*Fools of Fortune* (1990), *The Playboys* (1992) and formerly from the ITV series *Heartbeat*).

Day Lewis, Daniel (born London 1958) actor; son of Poet-Laureate C.S. Lewis; gained international acclaim in Stephen Frears' *My Beautiful Laundrette* and Merchant-Ivory's *A Room with a View** (1985). Star lead of *My Left Foot* (1989) for which he won an Oscar. His portrayal of Gerry Conlon - *In the Name of the Father* (1993) - earned him an Oscar nomination. Films include

The Bounty (1984), *The Unbearable Lightness of Being* (1988), *The Last of the Mohicans* (1992), *The Crucible* (1996), *The Boxer* (1997).

Devlin, J. G. (born Belfast, 1907) actor in theatre, TV and in films such *The Rising of the Moon* (1957), *Darby O'Gill and the Little People* (1959) and *The Raggedy Rawney* (1988). Died 1991.

Donlevy, Brian (born Portadown, 1899) actor; starred in 65 films over 40 years. Male model for shirts, made acting debut (1924), with a walk-on in a Broadway play and cameo role in a film. Played tough villain roles; most notable in *Beau Geste* (1939), earning an Oscar nomination for Best Supporting Actor. Films include *Jesse James* (1939), *Billy the Kid* (1941), *The Curse of the Fly* (1969), *Pit Stop* (1969). Died 1972.

Dunbar, Adrian (born Fermanagh, 1958) Actor and script-writer. Films include *A World Apart* (1987), *The Dawning* (1988), *My Left Foot* (1989), *Hear My Song* (1991), *The Playboys* (which he co-scripted 1992), *Widow's Peak* (1993).

Fitzgerald, Barry (born William Joseph Shields, Dublin 1888); actor; film debut in *Land of Her Fathers* (1924) and Hitchcock's *Juno and the Paycock* (1930). Lured to Hollywood by John Ford, reprising his stage role in O'Casey's *The Plough and the Stars* (1937). Best known for playing Irish characters. Won an Oscar for Best Supporting Actor in *Going My Way* (1944). Films include *Bringing up Baby* (1938), *How Green Was My Valley* (1941), *The Quiet Man* (1952), *Broth of a Boy* (1959). Died 1961.

Fitzgerald, Geraldine (born Dublin 1914) actress; appeared in several British films; her Hollywood debut was in *Dark Victory* (1939). Best known for her Oscar-nominated role in *Wuthering Heights* (1939). Films include *The Mill on the Floss* (1937), *'Til We Meet Again* (1940), *The Last American Hero* (1973), *The Mango Tree* (1977), *Arthur* (1981), *Poltergeist II* (1986). Mother of director Michael Lindsay-Hogg.

Fricker, Brenda (born Dublin 1944) actress; background with the National Theatre, the Royal Shakespeare Company and the Court Theatre Company. Famed for Oscar-winning supporting performance as Christy Brown's mother in

My Left Foot (1989). Moved to Hollywood in 1990's, starring in *Home Alone 2: Lost in New York* (1992) and *So I Married an Axe Murderer* (1993). She had prominent roles B.B.C.'s T.V. series *Casualty* (1986-1990) and *Brides of Christ* mini-series (1992). Films include: *Of Human Bondage* (1964), *The Ballroom of Romance* (1981), *The Field* (1990), *A Man of No Importance* (1995), *Swann* (1997).

Garson, Greer (born Down 1908) actress; spotted by Louis B. Mayer, signed up and given impressive cameo role in Sam Wood's *Goodbye Mr Chips* (1939). Co-starred with Walter Pidgeon, in Oscar-winning performance as *Mrs Miniver* (1942). Nominated for six Best Actress Oscars and collected one. Films include *Pride and Prejudice* (1940), *The Valley of Decision* (1945), *Julius Caesar* (1953), *The Singing Nun* (1966), *The Happiest Millionaire* (1967).

Gébler, Carlo (born Dublin, 1954) novelist and screen-writer; films include *The Beneficiary* (1979), *Country and Irish* (1982), *Francis Stuart* (1985), *Malachy and his Family* (1990), *The Glass Curtain: Inside an Ulster Community* (1991), *Life After Death* (1994), *A Little Local Difficulty* (1995) and *The Base* (1997). Directed *Baseball in Irish History* (1996).

Gébler, Ernest (born Dublin, 1915) playwright, screen writer; films and T.V. include *Call Me Daddy, The Lonely Girl (Girl with Green Eyes), Women can be Monsters, Why Aren't You Famous?* and *A Little Milk of Human Kindness*.

Gibbons, Cedric (born Dublin 1893); art director for over 76 films. Appointed MGM's Head of Art Department (1924). Key figure in creating MGM 'look,' designing the Oscar statuette, which he himself won 11 times for design and once for 'consistent excellence.' (1950). Married actress Dolores del Rio (1930-1941). Films include *Ben-Hur* (1926), *Tarzan and his Mate* (1934), *Treasure Island* (1934), *The Wizard of Oz* (1939), *Madame Curie* (1943), *National Velvet* (1944), *The Postman Always Rings Twice* (1946), *The Yearling* (1946), *Little Women* (1949), *Annie Get Your Gun* (1950), *An American in Paris* (1951), *Forbidden Planet* (1956). Died 1960.

Harris, Jared actor and son of

Richard Harris. Screen debut in *The Rachel Papers* (1988), directed by brother Damian. Starred in *I Shot Andy Warhol* (1995), Wayne Wang's *Smoke*, Jim Jarmusch's *Dead Man*, *Trojan Eddie* (1996) and *Gold in the Streets* (1997).

Harris, Richard (born Limerick 1932) actor/director; stage debut *The Quare Fellow* (1956). Gained international success for his performance in *This Sporting Life* (1963), winning the Cannes Festival Acting Award and Oscar nomination for Best Actor. He was also an Oscar nominee for Best Actor in *The Field* (1990). Films include *Shake Hands with the Devil* (1959), *Mutiny on the Bounty* (1962), *Camelot* (1967), *A Man Called Horse* (1970), *The Molly Maguires* (1970), *Patriot Games* (1992), *Unforgiven* (1992). Regularly returns to theatre.

Hickey, Kieran (born Dublin 1936) film director. One of the first filmmakers to develop the Irish film industry. Produced films on Jonathan Swift and James Joyce in 1960's. Film/documentaries include *Stage Irishman* (1968), *Faithful Departed* (1969), *A Child's Voice* (1977), *Criminal Conversation* (1980), *Attracta* (1983), *Short Story - Irish Movies 1945-1958* (1986), *The Rockingham Shoot* (1987). Died Dublin 1993.

Hill, George Roy (born Minneapolis 1922) film director (1952-1988); former actor with Cyril Cusack's Abbey Theatre company; major success with Paul Newman and Robert Redford in *Butch Cassidy and the Sundance Kid* (1969) and *The Sting* (1973), the latter earning Hill an Oscar for best direction and the former a nomination for Best Director. Films include *Thoroughly Modern Millie* (1967), *Funny Farm* (1988) and The *World According To Garp* (1982).

Hobson, Valerie (born Larne 1917) actress; invited to Hollywood (1935); played leads in horror and thriller films. Retired from film (1954) after marriage to politician John Profumo. Supported him during infamous Christine Keeler sex scandal which toppled the British cabinet. Films include *Bride of Frankenstein* (1935), *Werewolf of London* (1935), *Great Expectations* (1946).

Ingram, Rex (born Dublin, 1892) director; directed over 27 films. Emigrating to U.S. and worked for Edison, Vitagraph, Fox (1913), Universal (1916) and Metro Film Studios (1920). Discovered by June Mathis, and directed Rudolph Valentino in *The Four Horsemen of the Apocalypse* (1921) and *The Conquering Power* (1921). Set up film studio Victorine, with aid of MGM after a row over direction of *Ben-Hur* but the advent of sound affected his future films. Made only one talking picture *Baroud* (1933). Worked as a sculptor, painter and novelist. Died 1950

Jordan, Neil (born Sligo, 1950) director, screen-writer and script consultant on John Boorman's *Excalibur* (1981). His best-known British feature was *Mona Lisa* (1986). Hollywood credits include *High Spirits* (1988) and *We're No Angels* (1989). Published three novels: *The Past* (1980), *The Dream of a Beast* (1983) and *Sunrise with Seamonster* (1995), plus a collection of short stories, *Night in Tunisia* (1978), upon which his film *The Miracle* (1991) was based. Most famed for *The Crying Game* (1992), which earned six Oscar nominations, collecting one for original screenplay. Directed *The Company of Wolves* (1984), *Interview with the Vampire* (1995), *Michael Collins* (1996) and Pat McCabe's *The Butcher Boy* (1997).

Kerrigan, J.M. (born Dublin 1887) actor; joined Abbey Players (1907); emigrated to U.S. (1917) and played many memorable Irish characters on Broadway and Hollywood. Films include *O'Neill of the Glen* (1916), *Song O' My Heart* (1930), *Werewolf of London* (1935), *The Plough and the Stars* (1936), *20,000 Leagues under the Sea* (1954), *The Fastest Gun Alive* (1956). Died 1964.

Killanin, Michael (Lord) (born Melbourne, 1914) Producer with director John Ford - together, with Tyrone Power, they formed Four Provinces Films; first film was *The Rising of the Moon* (1957). Productions include *Young Cassidy* (1964) and *The Playboy of the Western World* (1962). Father of producer Redmond Morris. Former President of the International Olympic Committee.

McAnally, Ray (born Buncrana 1926) actor; versatile, prolific character player on film, stage and TV. Screen debut (1930s). Best known for *The Mission* (1986) and *My Left Foot* (1989). Films include *Shake Hands with the Devil* (1959), *Billy Budd* (1962), *Angel* (1984), *Cal* (1984), *The Fourth Protocol* (1987), *The Sicilian* (1987), *White Mischief* (1988), *We're No Angels* (1989). Died Wicklow 1989.

McCormack, F.J. (born Peter Judge, Ireland 1891) Irish character actor with Abbey Theatre. Films include *Odd Man Out* (1946), *The Plough and the Stars* (1937) and *Hungry Hill* (1946). Died 1947.

McCormack, John (born Ireland 1884) Irish tenor; films include *Song O' My Heart* (1930) and *Wings of the Morning* (1937). Died 1945.

Mcginnis, Niall (born Ireland, 1913) actor; film debut with *Turn of the Tide* (1935). Films include *Henry V* (1944), *The Nun's Story* (1958), *Becket* (1964), *Sinful Davy* (1969) and *The Mackintosh Man* (1973).

MacGowran, Jack (born Ireland, 1916) actor; veteran character player. Films include *The Quiet Man* (1952), *The Gentle Gunman* (1952), *The Rising of the Moon* (1957), *Darby O'Gill and the Little People* (1959), *Doctor Zhivago* (1965), *The Exorcist* (1973). Died 1973.

Marcus, Louis (born Cork, 1936) documentary film-maker for cinema and T.V. Made over 60 films, including *Capallogy* (1968), *Poc Ar Buile* (1973), *Páistí ag Obair* (1973), earning Oscar nomination for best documentary and *Conquest of Light* (1975), which was also nominated.

McKenna, Siobhán (born Belfast, 1923) actress; starred in both Irish and English language theatre/film. Films include *Daughter of Darkness* (1948), *The Playboy of the Western World* (1962), *The Lost People* (1949), *King of Kings* (1961), *Of Human Bondage* (1964), *Doctor Zhivago* (1965).

Moore, Owen (born Meath, 1886) actor; star of U.S. silents and early talkies. Film debut in *Biograph* (1908) and appeared in many of D.W. Griffith's early productions. Mary Pickford's regular leading man in early stages of her career; married her secretly (1910) but they were later divorced (1920). Films include: *The Honour of Thieves* (1909), *Women Love Diamonds* (1927), *Husbands for Rent* (1928), *She Done Him Wrong* (1933), *A Star is Born* (1937). Died 1939.

Murphy, Pat (born Dublin, 1951) director and script-writer; credited with two feature films, co-directed with John Davis, *Maeve* (1981) and *Anne Devlin* (1984).

Neeson, Liam (born Ballymena, 1953). Actor. Film debut in John Boorman's *Excalibur* (1981). Roles followed in British productions, *The Bounty* (1984) and *The Mission* (1986). Performance in Broadway production of Eugene O'Neill's *Anna Christie* (1992). Impressed director Stephen Spielberg who offered Neeson lead in *Schindler's List* (1993). Received an Oscar nomination for Best Actor (1993). He had an equally powerful role in Jordan's *Michael Collins* (1996). Films include *Excalibur* (1981), *Lamb* (1985), *A Prayer for the Dying* (1987), *Suspect* (1987), *The Dead Pool* (1988), *Darkman* (1990), *Husbands and Wives* (1992), *Revolver* (1992), *Shining Through* (1992), *Under Suspicion* (1992), *Deception* (1993), *Ethan Frome* (1993) and *Rob Roy* (1995).

Neill, Sam (born Northern Ireland, 1948) actor; Gained acclaim in Gillian Armstrong's *My Brilliant Career* (1979); Hollywood debut as Damien in the third of the Omen films, *The Final Conflict* (1981); starred opposite Meryl Streep in *A Cry in the Dark* (1988) and *Plenty* (1985). Lead roles on T.V. miniseries *Kane and Abel* (1985) and *Amerika* (1987). Co-starred in *The Piano* (1993), which won the Palme d'Or at Cannes. Films include *Dead Calm* (1989), *The Hunt for Red October* (1990), *Jurassic Park* (1993).

O'Connor, Carroll (born New York, 1925) actor; stage debut with Dublin's Gate Theatre. Broadway debut (1958). Gained worldwide fame as Archie Bunker in *All in the Family*. Films include *Cleopatra* (1963), *What Did You Do in the War, Daddy?* (1966), *Kelly's Heroes* (1970), *Acting: Lee Strasberg and the Actor's Studio* (1981).

O'Connor, Pat (born Waterford, 1943) film director; began career with RTÉ (1970), producing documentaries on Northern Ireland before turning to drama - *The Riordans* (1979), *Miracles* (1979). He won BAFTA Award for Best Single Play and Jacob's Award for Best Director for *The Ballroom of Romance* (1981). Films include *Cal* (1984), *A Month in the Country* (1986), *Stars and Bars* (1988),

Circle of Friends (1996), *Dancing at Lughnasa* (1997).

O'Connor, Una (born Agnes Teresa McGlade, Belfast, 1880) actress; portrayed maid, spinster and gossip characters; her ear-piercing shriek was used to great effect in horror films. Films include *The Invisible Man* (1933), *The Bride of Frankenstein* (1935), *The Adventures of Robin Hood* (1938), *The Adventures of Don Juan* (1948), *Witness for the Prosecution* (1957). Died 1959.

O'Dea, Denis (born Ireland, 1905) actor; films include *The Informer* (1935), *The Plough and the Stars* (1947), *Treasure Island* (1950), *The Rising of the Moon* (1957), Died 1978.

O'Dea, Jimmy (born Ireland, 1899) actor and comedian; films include *Casey's Millions* (1922), *Jimmy Boy* (1935), *Blarney* (1938), *The Rising of the Moon* (1957), *Darby O'Gill and the Little People* (1959), *Johnny Nobody* (1960). Died 1965.

O'Hara, Maureen (born Maureen FitzSimmons, Dublin, 1920) actress; Red-haired Irish beauty who played fiery heroines. Best remembered for John Ford films - *How Green was my Valley* (1941) and, opposite John Wayne, *The Quiet Man* (1952). Semi-retired in 1971, she returned in comedy *Only the Lonely* (1991). Films include *Song O' My Heart* (1930), *The Black Swan* (1942), *Buffalo Bill* (1944), *Miracle on 34th Street* (1947), *The Redhead from Wyoming* (1955), *The Parent Trap* (1961).

O'Herlihy, Dan (born Wexford, 1919) actor; performed with Gate Theatre and Abbey Players. Emigrated to U.S. and joined Orson Welles's Mercury Theatre, acting in the stage and screen version of *Macbeth* (1948). Known for *The Adventures of Robinson Crusoe* (1952), earning an Oscar nomination for Best Actor. Still appears in film and T.V. Films include *Odd Man Out* (1947), *How to Steal the World* (1968), *Halloween III* (1982), *Robocop* (1987), *The Dead* (1988).

O'Herlihy, Michael (born Ireland, 1929). director; films include *The Fighting Prince of Donegal* (1966), *Smith!* (1969), *The Flame is Love* (T.V. 1979), *Cry of the Innocent* (T.V. 1980), *I Married Wyatt Earp* (T.V. 1983), *Hoover vs the Kennedys: The Second Civil War* (T.V. 1987).

O'Leary, Liam (born Cork, 1910) actor, director and archivist; co-founded Irish Film Society (1936). Former Abbey Theatre Director. Made one of Ireland's most rousing propaganda films *Our Country* (1948). Starred in *Stranger at My Door/At a Dublin Inn* (1950). Published works include: *Silent Cinema* (1965), *Invitation to the Film* (1945) and the first *Rex Ingram Biography* (1980). Died Dublin 1992.

O'Neill, Eugene (born 1888) Irish-American playwright with screenplay adaptations. Films include *Anna Christie* with Blanche Sweet (1923), and Greta Garbo (1930), *Strange Interlude* (1932), *The Emperor Jones* (1933), *The Long Voyage Home* (1940), *Summer Holiday* (1947), *Long Day's Journey into Night* (1960) and *The Iceman Cometh* (1973). Died 1953.

O'Neill, Marie (born Marie Allgood, Dublin, 1885) actress; Abbey player and character actress. Films include *Juno and the Paycock* (1930), *Farewell Again* (1937), *Love on the Dole* (1941), *Someone at the Door* (1950), *Treasure Hunt* (1952). Died 1952.

O'Shea, Milo (born Ireland, 1925) actor; film debut (1960) after lengthy stage career with Dublin's Abbey Players. Impressive in screen adaptation of Joyce's *Ulysses* (1967). Films include *You Can't Beat the Irish* (1951), *Barbarella* (1968), *The Verdict* (1982), *The Purple Rose of Cairo* (1985), *Only the Lonely* (1991), *The Playboys* (1992).

O'Sullivan, Maureen (born Roscommon, 1911) actress; best remembered as Jane in the *Tarzan* jungle adventures. Discovered at Dublin's International Horse Show (1930) by American Frank Borzage. She married writer John Farrow (1936) and retired (1942) to raise their seven children, including actresses Mia and Tisa Farrow. Later hosted a syndicated T.V. series. Films include *Song O' My Heart* (1930), *David Copperfield* (1935), *Pride and Prejudice* (1940), *All I Desire* (1953), *Never too Late* (1965).

O'Sullivan, Thaddeus (born Dublin, 1948) director and cameraman; residing in Dublin since 1960's. Debut film *A Pint of Plain* (1975); feature *On a Paving Stone Mounted* (1978); debut short *The Woman who Married Clark Gable* (1985) with

Brenda Fricker and Bob Hoskins. Films include *December Bride* (1990), *In the Border Country* (1991), *Nothing Personal* (1995).

O'Toole, Peter (born 1932) most Oscar-nominated Best Actor (1962-82, six times) but as yet to receive one. Film debut in Disney's *Kidnapped* (1960); his work with the Royal Shakespeare Theatre led to starring role in David Lean's *Lawrence of Arabia* (1962). He both starred in and co-produced *Becket* (1964) and *Lord Jim* (1965). Career took downward slope in 1970s but made a comeback in *The Stunt Man* (1980), receiving the U.S. Film Critics Award. Starred in Bertolucci's award-winning epic, *The Last Emperor* (1987). Films include *The Lion in Winter* (1968), *Goodbye Mr Chips* (1969), *My Favourite Year* (1982), *Supergirl* (1984), *High Spirits* (1988), *The Seventh Coin* (1992). He is also writer, having recently published a second volume of memoirs *The Apprentice* (1997).

Purcell, Noel (born Ireland, 1900) actor and comedian; films include *Captain Boycott* (1947), *Moby Dick* (1956), *Mutiny on the Bounty* (1962), *Lord Jim* (1965), *McKenzie Break* (1969), *Flight of the Doves* (1971), *The Mackintosh Man* (1973).

Quinn, Aidan (born Chicago, 1959, reared and educated in Ireland) actor; first gained attention for his role in *Desperately Seeking Susan* (1985). Films include *The Mission* (1986), *Stakeout* (1987), *The Handmaid's Tale* (1990), *At Play in the Streets of the Lord* (1991), *The Playboys* (1992), *Benny & Joon* (1993), *Legends of the Fall* (1994), *Michael Collins* (1996) and *This is My Father* (1997).

Quinn, Bob (born Dublin, 1935) film producer/director, writer and photographer; made over 100 films, ranging from drama and documentary to experimental. Films include *Caoineadh Áirt Uí Laoire* (1974), *Self-Portrait with Red Car* (1976), *Poitín* (1977), *The Family* (1979), *Budawanny* (1987), *Pobal* (1988-90), *The Bishop's Story* (1993), *Graceville* (1996).

Rea, Stephen (born Belfast, 1949) actor; a director of Field Day Theatre Company based in Derry; his film debut was in Neil Jordan's directorial debut, *Danny Boy/Angel* (1982). His work with Jordan in *The Crying Game* (1992), earned him an Oscar

nomination for Best Actor. West End and Broadway performance in *Someone to Watch Over Me* (1982). Films include *The Company of Wolves* (1984), *Life is Sweet* (1991), *Bad Behaviour* (T.V. 1993), *Interview with a Vampire* (1994), *Prêt a Porter* (1996), *Trojan Eddie* (1996), *The Butcher Boy* (1997).

Ryan, Kathleen (born Ireland, 1922) actress; films include *Odd Man Out* (1947), *Captain Boycott* (1947), *Esther Waters* (1948), *The Yellow Balloon* (1952), *Captain Lightfoot* (1953), *Jacqueline* (1956), *Sail into Danger* (1958). Died 1985.

Shaw-Smith, David (born Dublin, 1939) independent film-maker (1970); made more than 80 documentaries; films include *Connemara and its Ponies* (1971), *Hands* (T.V. series), *Patterns* (10 programmes), *Dublin - a Personal View* (12 progs.), *Irish Arts Series* (4 progs.), *The Angling Experience* (C4- 4 progs), *English Silk* (C4/RTÉ).

Shaw, Fiona (born Ireland, 1958) actress; films include *My Left Foot* (1989), *Mountains of the Moon* (1989), *Three Men and a Little Lady* (1990).

Shaw, George Bernard (born Dublin, 1856) distinguished playwright who, for many years refused to allow film versions of his work but was reconciled to the idea by Gabrial Pascal. Film versions of his plays include *Arms and the Man* (1931), *Pygmalion* (1938), *Major Barbara* (1940), *Caesar & Cleopatra* (1945), *Androcles and the Lion* (1953), *Saint Joan* (1957), *The Doctor's Dilemma* (1958), *The Devil's Disciple* (1959), *Helden - Arms and the Man* (Ger 1959), *The Millionairess* (1961), *My Fair Lady* (1964), *Great Catherine* (1967).

Sheridan, Jim (born Dublin, 1949) director/playwright of Dublin and New York stage turned film-maker; had eight of his own plays produced, including *Spike in the First World War* (1983). Feature debut with *My Left Foot* (1989) earned an Oscar nomination for Best Director and Best Screenplay. First Irish production to be nominated for five Oscars (only to be exceeded in 1995, by Jordan's *The Crying Game*). Wrote the screenplay and directed *The Field* (1990); wrote screenplay for Mike Newell's *Into the West* (1993); Re-teamed with Daniel Day-Lewis for *In the Name of Our Father*

(1993); receiving Oscar Nomination for Best Director, Best Screenplay and Best Film. Film condemned by the British, while the U.S. critics likened Sheridan and Day-Lewis's pairing to that of Scorsese and De Niro. Films include *Some Mother's Son* (1996), *The Boxer* (1997).

Shields, Arthur (born Dublin) actor; brother of actor Barry Fitzgerald; player with Dublin's Abbey; emigrated to U.S. Played priests, missionaries and fanatics. Films include *The Plough and the Stars* (1936), *How Green was My Valley* (1941), *National Velvet* (1944), *She Wore a Yellow Ribbon* (1949), *The Quiet Man* (1952), *The Pigeon that Took Rome* (1962). Died 1970.

Taylor, William Desmond (born William Tanner, Ireland, 1877) film director of more than 39 films and former actor. Rose to fame as director of several Mary Pickford films. Former president of the Screen Directors Guild. Films include *The Beggar Child* (1914), *Anne of Green Gables* (1919), *Huckleberry Finn* (1920), *The Green Temptation* (1922), *The Top of New York* (1922). Shot under suspicious circumstances, Hollywood 1922.

Todd, Richard (born Dublin, 1919) actor; leading man of British and U.S. films. Stage debut (1937). Film career developed in late 40s; best known for The *Hasty Heart* (1949), earning an Oscar nomination for Best Actor; films include *Stage Fright* (1950), *The Story of Robin Hood and his Merry Men* (1952), *Rob Roy* (1954), *The Virgin Queen* (1955), *Saint Joan* (1957), *Chase a Crooked Shadow* (1958).

Tolbín, Niall (born Cork, 1929) comedian and actor; currently starring in B.B.C.'s hugely popular *Ballykissangel*. Films include *Bright Future* (1968), *Philadelphia Here I Come!* (1970), *Ryan's Daughter* (1970), *Poitín* (1978), *Summer of the Falcon* (1981), *Fools of Fortune* (1990).

OTHER FILM PERSONALITIES

Ball, Seamus Films include *The Best Man* (1983), *High Boot Benny* (1993).

Black, Cathal (born 1952) director and writer; films include *Wheels* (1976), *Our Boys* (1980), *Pigs* (1984), *Korea* (1995).

Brennan, Bríd Films include *Anne*

Devlin (1984), *Four Days in July* (1985), *Trojan Eddie* (1996), *Dancing at Lughnasa* (1997).

Buggy, Niall Films include *Purple Taxi* (1977), *Portrait of an Artist as a Young Man* (1977), *Upwardly Mobile* (T.V. sitcom), *The Lonely Passion of Judith Hearne* (1987).

Connolly, Andrew Films include *Boom Babies* (1986), *Joyriders* (1988), *The Courier* (1988), *Patriot Games* (1992), *Guiltrip* (1995).

Doody, Alison Films include *Raiders of the Lost Ark* , *A Prayer for the Dying* (1988), *Taffin* (1988).

Dowling, Rachael Films include *The Dead* (1987), *Bogwoman* (1997).

Gallagher, Bronagh Films include *Dear Sarah* (1990), *The Commitments* (1991), *Pulp Fiction* (1994).

Gleeson, Brendan Films include *Into the West* (1992), *The Snapper* (1993), *Braveheart (1994)*, *Michael Collins* (1996), *Trojan Eddie* (1996), *A Furtive Gesture* (1996), *Angela Mooney Dies Again* (1997).

Guiney, Ed Managing director of *Temple Films.* Producer of *Guiltrip* (1995). Currently working on *Sweetly Barret* (1997/8); first feature by writer/director Stephen Bradley.

Hogan, Bosco Films include *Portrait of an Artist as a Young Man* (1977), *The Outsider* (1979), *Jack B. Yeats Assembled Memoirs 1871-1957* (1980), *Anne Devlin* (1984), *In the Name of the Father* (1993).

Kavanagh, John Films include *Paddy* (1969), *Revival - Pearse's Concept of Ireland* (1979), *The Ballroom of Romance* (1981), *Caught in the Free State* (1983), *The Country Girls* (1983), *Cal* (1984), *Into the West* (1992), *Widow's Peake* (1993), *Braveheart* (1994), *Circle of Friends* (1995), *Some Mother's Son* (1996).

Kean, Marie Films include *Girl with Green Eyes* (1964), *I was Happy Here* (1965), *Ryan's Daughter*

(1970), *Barry Lyndon* (1975), *The Lonely Passion of Judith Hearne* (1987).

Kellegher, Tina Films include *In the Name of the Father* (1993), *The Snapper* (1993), *Undercurrent* (1995), *The Disappearance of Finbar* (1996), *Ballykissangel* (TV series).

Kelly, David Films include *Purple Taxi* (1977), *Joyriders* (1988), *The Run of the Country* (1995).

Kirwan, Dervla Films include *December Bride* (1990); TV series include *Goodnight Sweetheart*, *Ballykissangel*.

Lally, Mick Films include *Our Boys* (1981), *Night in Tunisia* (1983), *The Fantasist* (1986), *The Secret of Roan Inish* (1994), *A Man of No Importance* (1995), *Circle of Friends* (1995), *Glenroe* (T.V. series).

Meaney, Colm Films include *Far and Away* (1992), *The Commitments* (1991), *Into the West* (1992), *The Snapper* (1993), *War of the Buttons* (1994), *The Last of the High Kings* (1996), *The Van* (1996) as well as *The Next Generation* series of *Star Trek.*

McCabe, Ruth Films include *My Left Foot* (1989), *The Field* (1990), *The Snapper* (1993), *Circle of Friends* (1995).

McCann, Donal Films include *The Fighting Prince of Donegal* (1966), *Stage Irishman* (1968), *Philadelphia Here I Come!* (1970), *Poitín* (1978), *Angel* (1992), *Cal* (1984), *Budawanny* (1987), *The Dead* (1987), *December Bride* (1990), *The Miracle* (1991), *The Bishop's Story* (1994), *Trojan Eddie* (1996), *The Nephew* (1998). Also an accomplished stage actor.

McGinley, Sean Films include *A Furtive Gesture* (1996), *The Disappearance of Finbar* (1996), *Trojan Eddie* (1996), *Bogwoman* (1997).

McGuckian, Mary director; films include *Words Upon the Window*

Pane (1994), *This is the Sea* (1997), *George Best* (1998).

McLynn, Pauline actress; films include *Guiltrip* (1995), *My Friend Joe* (1996), *Father Ted* (T.V. series).

McSorley, Gerard films include *Withdrawal* (1983), *The Scar* (1988), *Words Upon the Window Pane* (1994), *Some Mother's Son* (1996), *Michael Collins* (1996).

Mitchell, James managing director of Little Bird Films. Produced *December Bride* (1990), *Into the West* (1992), *St. Ives* (1997).

Murray, Johnny films include *Desecration* (1981), *Hard Shoulder* (1990), *The Commitments* (1991), *Into the West* (1992), *War of the Buttons* (1994).

Murphy, Kathleen films include *Knocknagow* (1916), *The Miser's Gift* (1916), *Blarney* (1917), *Rafferty's Rise* (1917).

O'Conor, Hugh actor; films include *Lamb* (1985), *Fear of the Dark* (1986), *Da* (1988), *My Left Foot* (1989), *The Boy From Mercury* (1996).

O'Leary, Ronan director; films include *Fragments of Isabella* (1989), *Diary of a Madman* (1991), *Hello, Stranger* (1992), *Driftwood* (1996).

O'Neill, Nicholas managing director of Liquid Films; films include *Hooligans* (1997/98), *Hugh Cullen* (1998); written by former N.M.E. journalist Sean O'Hagan.

Pilkington, Lorraine actress; films include *The Miracle* (1991), *All Things Bright and Beautiful* (1994), *The Disappearance of Finbar* (1996), *Gold in the Streets* (1997).

Ryan, Ger films include: *Driftwood* (1996), *The Van* (1996).

Toal, Maureen films include: *Love and Money* (1960), *Paddy* (1969).

EMPLOYMENT IN IRISH FILM INDUSTRY 1993 - 1995

	1993 No. (% Irish)	1994 No. (% Irish)	1995 No. (% Irish)
Irish Male Employment	-	-	9,657 (54%)
Irish Female Employment	-	-	6,374 (36%)
Total Irish Employment	3,772 (90%)	10,845 (78%)	16,031 (90%)
Non-Irish Employment	419 (10%)	3,013 (22%)	1,859 (10%)
Total Employment:	4,191	13,858	17,890

OVERVIEW OF CINEMA IN R.O.I., 1991-96

	1991	1992	1993	1994	1995	1996
Total Population (m)	3.52	3.54	3.56	3.57	3.59	3.62
Gross Box Office (£m)	20.2	19.6	24.2	30.6	30.6	-
No. of Admissions (m)	8.08	7.85	9.3	10.4	9.8	-
No. of Cinema Goers	18,328	18,741	19,348	18,695	18,229	-
Frequency Per Head	2.3	2.2	2.6	2.9	2.7	-
No. of Screens	192	189	184	191	197	200
Total No. of Seats	-	-	-	-	39,402	-
No. of Seats per Screen	-	-	-	-	200	-
Average Ticket Price (£)	2.50	2.50	2.60	2.95	3.13	4.75

BREAKDOWN OF FILMS, 1990-1995

	1990	1991	1992	1993	1994	1995
In Production	6	3	2	18	18	18
Irish Films Released	-	-	-	-	-	5
European Films Released	-	-	-	-	-	7
Market Share Irish Films (%)	5	2	-	-	-	-
Market Share U.S. Films (%)	87	91.5	-	-	-	90
No. of Distributors	-	-	-	-	-	8
No. of Films Released	-	-	-	-	149	168
Average Film Rental (%)	-	-	33.3	-	-	38
Gross Advertising Expenditure (£m)	-	1	1.1	1.24	2.3	2.4
Gross Distribution Revenue (£m)	7.68	-	7.5	-	-	-
Average Film Rental (%)	-	-	33.3	-	-	38

THE NATIONAL LOTTERY, REPUBLIC OF IRELAND

The National Lottery was launched on March 22, 1987, with the 'Instant 3' scratch card released as the first National Lottery product. The main lottery or 'Lotto' was launched on April 10, 1988, and Ireland produced its first Lotto millionaire on May 6, 1989. The mid-week Lotto was introduced on May 30, 1990, and the first Lotto gameshow, 'Winning Streak', went on air on September 21 that same year.

During the last quarter of 1996, the entire network of 2,000 Lotto agents' terminals around the country were replaced with the Spectra III, which is capable of processing up to 8,000 transactions per minute. Total sales in 1996 amounted to £307.8 million, an increase of £5 million on 1995. This increase was largely due to two roll-over draws towards the end of 1996. One resulted in a record £7.5 million jackpot, the largest to date, shared by two ticket holders. It came just weeks after the largest ever individual win of a lotto jackpot when, on September 25, one person won £4.7 million. A total of £5.8 million was spent during the three days leading up to the November 2 draw - over 2.5 million Lotto playslips were processed with a spending average of £2.24 per head. Total winnings for 1996 were £158 million, with 'Quick Pick' tickets accounting for one in three of all Lotto plays and 26% of winning tickets. 'All Cash' continues to top the longest running game (1991), and a further eleven new instant games were launched in 1996. Since its inception in 1987, the number of Lotto millionaires has risen to 67, and a total of £1,247.8 million has been won in Lottery Prizes to date. From lottery sales of £307.8 million in 1996, £101.2 million in lottery funds was given to beneficiary projects in the community.

THE NATIONAL LOTTERY, NORTHERN IRELAND

Britain's National Lottery was launched on November 14, 1994 - the first national lottery that had the country had seen for nearly 200 years. The first week's sales totalled £48.9 million and raised £12 million for good causes (sports, arts, heritage, charities and the Millennium Commission). There are currently around 1,000 lottery outlets throughout Northern Ireland, and sales in the region since the lottery's launch total £139 million. Around 65% of the adult population play regularly, and around 90% have played at least once, with the spending average in Northern Ireland estimated at £2.73 per head. There have been ten Jackpots won in Northern Ireland, the highest individual win amounting to £10,248,233 million on May 18, 1996. Northern Ireland has produced two millionaires plus a syndicate who won £1,355,975 on April 29, 1995. From the sales in Northern Ireland of £139 million, the region has been allocated £11,580,687 in sports grants and £10,678,346 in arts grants. The chances of winning the British National Lottery are estimated at approximately 14 million to one.

IRISH NATIONAL LOTTERY - FINANCIAL REPORT, 1996

Income...................................IR£307.8 million of which:...£100.5 million *(Instant Games)*;
....£207,333,866 *(Lotto)*.
Prizes.....................................IR£158.1 million of which:...£54.4 million *(Instant Games)*;
....£103,666,933 *(Lotto)*.
Wages & Salaries.......................................£2,013,597 ....*Number of Employees* - 78
Retailers' Commission ....£19.5 million

BRITISH NATIONAL LOTTERY - FINANCIAL REPORT, 1997*

Income ....£4,723 million of which: ....876.5 million *(Instant Games)*;
....3,846.5 million *(Lottery)*.
Prizes....................................£2,384 million...*(Instant Games & Lottery)*
Wages & Salaries......................................£16,200,000 ....*Number of Employees* - 667
Retailers' Commission ....£242.0 million

* Data based all British figures, including Northern Ireland, up to 31/3/97.

IRISH NATIONAL LOTTERY FUND EXPENDITURE 1996

Sector	1996 IR£ m	1987 - 1996 IR£ m
Youth, Sport, Recreation, Amenities	28,471	232,538 (33%)
Arts, Culture, National Heritage	22,943	171,327 (25%)
Health & Welfare	29,329	240,621 (35%)
Irish Language	7,216	51,982 (7%)
Total	**87,959**	**696,468 (100%)**

BRITISH NATIONAL LOTTERY FUND EXPENDITURE 1996

Sector	Northern Ireland Only 1994-1996 £Stg 000s	Total Britain 1994 - 1996 £Stg 000s
Sports	11,580	1,052,696
Arts	10,678	650,611
Heritage		282,570
Charities		318,397
Millennium Commission		752,130
Total	22,258	3,056,404

IRISH NATIONAL LOTTERY WINNING TICKETS BY PRIZE, 1996

Prizes	Winning Tickets
Over IR£4 million	1
IR£3 million to IR£4 million	2
IR£2 million to IR£3 million	5
IR£1 million to IR£2 million	10
IR£750,000 to IR£1 million	13
IR£500,000 to IR£750,000	12
IR£250,000 to IR£500,000	20
IR£100,000 to IR£250,000	9
Total:	**72**

IRISH MUSIC CHARTS 1997 - NO. 1 ALBUMS*

Week Ending Day / mth	Album Title	Artist(s)	Record Label	Previous Highest Position	Country of Origin
05 Jan	Spice	Spice Girls	Virgin	-	England
12 Jan	Spice	Spice Girls	Virgin	1	England
19 Jan	Spice	Spice Girls	Virgin	1	England
26 Jan	Evita	Original Soundtrack	Warner	4	America
02 Feb	Evita	Original Soundtrack	Warner	1	America
09 Feb	Tragic Kingdom	No Doubt	Interscope	2	America
16 Feb	Blur	Blur	Parlophone	-	England
23 Feb	Tragic Kingdom	No Doubt	Interscope	1	America
02 Mar	Tragic Kingdom	No Doubt	Interscope	1	America
16 Mar	**Pop**	**U2**	**Island**	**-**	**Ireland**
23 Mar	**Pop**	**U2**	**Island**	**1**	**Ireland**
30 Mar	**Pop**	**U2**	**Island**	**1**	**Ireland**
06 Apr	Now That's What I Call Music! 36	Various	Emi/Virgin &	3	Various
13 Apr	Now That's What I Call Music! 36	Various	Polygram	1	Various
20 Apr	Dig Your Own Hole	Chemical Brothers	Virgin	2	England
27 Apr	Spice	Spice Girls	Virgin	-	England
04 May	Romeo & Juliet	Original Soundtrack	EMI/Premier Soundtracks	3	Various
11 May	Romeo & Juliet	Original Soundtrack	EMI/Premier	1	Various
18 May	Romeo & Juliet	Original Soundtrack	EMI/Premier	1	Various
25 May	Romeo & Juliet	Original Soundtrack	EMI/Premier	1	Various
01 June	Open Road	Gary Barlow	BMG	-	England
08 June	Romanza	Andrea Bocelli	Polygram	4	Italy
15 June	Romanza	Andrea Bocelli	Polygram	4	Italy
22 June	OK Computer	Radiohead	EMI	-	England
29 June	OK Computer	Radiohead	EMI	1	England
06 July	The Fat Of The Land	Prodigy	XL	-	England
13 July	The Fat Of The Land	Prodigy	XL	1	England
20 July	The Fat Of The Land	Prodigy	XL	-	England
27 July	Now That's What I Call Music! 37	Various	EMI/	2	Various
03 Aug	Now That's What I Call Music! 37	Various	Virgin &	1	Various
10 Aug	Now That's What I Call Music! 37	Various	Polygram	1	Various
17 Aug	Fresh Hits' 97	Various	Warner/Sony	2	Various
24 Aug	Be Here Now	Oasis	Creation	-	England
31 Aug	Be Here Now	Oasis	Creation	1	England
07 Sep	Be Here Now	Oasis	Creation	1	England
14 Sep	Be Here Now	Oasis	Creation	1	England
21 Sep	Be Here Now	Oasis	Creation	1	England
28 Sep	Be Here Now	Oasis	Creation	1	England

* includes the months January to September 1997

IRISH MUSIC CHARTS 1997 - NO. 1 SINGLES OF 1997*

Week Ending Day / month	Song Title	Artist(s)	Record Label	Previous Highest Position	Country of Origin
05 Jan	2 Become 1	Spice Girls	Virgin	-	England
12 Jan	2 Become 1	Spice Girls	Virgin	1	England
19 Jan	2 Become 1	Spice Girls	Virgin	1	England
26 Jan	Where Do You Go	No Mercy	Virgin	6	America
02 Feb	I Finally Found Someone	Streisand/Adams	Sony	-	America
09 Feb	**Discotheque**	**U2**	**Island**	**-**	**Ireland**
16 Feb	**Discotheque**	**U2**	**Island**	**1**	**Ireland**
23 Feb	Don't Speak	No Doubt	Interscope	2	America
02 Mar	Don't Speak	No Doubt	Interscope	1	America
09 Mar	Don't Speak	No Doubt	Interscope	1	America
16 Mar	Who Do You Think You Are/Mama	Spice Girls	Virgin	-	England
23 Mar	Who Do You Think You Are/Mama	Spice Girls	Virgin	1	England
30 Mar	Who Do You Think You Are/Mama	Spice Girls	Virgin	1	England

Continued from previous page -

Week Ending Day / month	Song Title	Artist(s)	Record Label	Previous Highest Position	Country of Origin
06 Apr	Who Do You Think You Are/Mama	Spice Girls	Virgin	1	England
13 Apr	Encore Une Fois	Sash	Multiply X	2	Italy
20 Apr	I Believe I Can Fly	R. Kelly	BMG	-	America
27 Apr	I Believe I Can Fly	R. Kelly	BMG	1	America
04 May	I Believe I Can Fly	R. Kelly	BMG	1	America
11 May	I Believe I Can Fly	R. Kelly	BMG	1	America
18 May	I Believe I Can Fly	R. Kelly	BMG	1	America
25 May	Time to Say Goodbye	S. Brighton/Andrea	Polygram	26	England
01 Jun	Time to Say Goodbye	S. Brighton/Andrea	Polygram	1	England
08 Jun	Time to Say Goodbye	S. Brighton/Andrea	Polygram	1	England
15 Jun	MmmBop	Hanson	Mercury	2	America
22 Jun	MmmBop	Hanson	Mercury	1	America
29 Jun	MmmBop	Hanson	Mercury	1	America
06 Jul	I'll be Missing You	Puff Daddy/Faith Evans	Arista	5	America
13 Jul	D'you Know What I Mean	Oasis	Creation	1	England
20 Jul	D'you Know What I Mean	Oasis	Creation	1	England
27 Jul	I'll Be Missing You	Puff Daddy/Faith Evans	Arista	1	America
03 Aug	I'll Be Missing You	Puff Daddy/Faith Evans	Arista	1	America
10 Aug	I'll Be Missing You	Puff Daddy/Faith Evans	Arista	1	America
17 Aug	I'll Be Missing You	Puff Daddy/Faith Evans	Arista	1	America
24 Aug	Men in Black	Will Smith	Columbia	2	America
31 Aug	Men in Black	Will Smith	Columbia	1	America
07 Sep	Men in Black	Will Smith	Columbia	1	America
14 Sep	Tubthumping	Chumba Wamba	EMI	2	England
21 Sep	Something About/ Candle in the Wind '97	Elton John	Mercury	-	England
28 Sep	Something About/ Candle in the Wind '97	Elton John	Mercury	1	England

* Includes the months January to September 1997.

TOP IRISH ALBUMS IN IRELAND 1997*

Week of Entry Day/mth	Album Title	Artist(s)	Record Label	Highest Position	No. of Weeks in Top 30
05 Jan	Unplucked	Dustin	EMI	3	7
05 Jan	Forgiven, Not Forgotten	Corrs	Warner Music	4	37
05 Jan	A Different Beat	Boyzone	Polygram	8	5
05 Jan	A Better Man	Brian Kennedy	BMG	3	33
05 Jan	Graffiti Tongue	Christy Moore	Sony Music	24	3
12 Jan	The Smile On Your Face	Francis Black	Dara	29	2
19 Jan	Best Irish Album in the World Ever	Various	Virgin	28	1
09 Feb	WB Yeats - Now and in Time to Be	Various	Grapevine	7	9
16 Feb	A Short Album About Love	Divine Comedy	Setana	8	14
16 Mar	Pop	U2	Island	1	29†
16 Mar	The Healing Game	Van Morrison	Polygram	5	6
16 Mar	Each Little Thing	Sharon Shannon	Grapevine	7	7
16 Mar	Endless Magic	Joe Dolan	Gable	9	4
23 Mar	Shine	Mary Black	Dara	3	15
04 May	The Great War Of Words	Brian Kennedy	BMG	11	3
18 May	Legends	James Galway/Phil Coulter	BMG	7	9
25 May	The Ultimate Collection	Clannad	BMG	17	6
01 Jun	Oro	Na Casaidigh	-	7	5
15 Jun	The Best Of Irish Vol. 1	Various	-	26	2
22 Jun	Live At The Point	Christy Moore	Sony Music	15	3
13 Jul	The Joshua Tree	U2	Record	19	6
13 Jul	Achtung Baby	U2	Record	22	4
03 Aug	Runaway Sunday	Altan	Virgin	10	7
10 Aug	The Best Of	Dolores Keane	Dara	2	3†
17 Aug	Blasta - Irish Traditional Music	Various	Gael Linn	21	6
14 Sep	The Greatest GAA Album Ever 1	Various	-	12	2

* Includes months January to September 1997. † Still represented in Top 30 Charts when going to print.

MOST SUCCESSFUL IRISH SINGLES IN IRELAND 1997*

Week of Entry Day / month	Song Title	Artist(s)	Record Label	Highest Position	No. of Weeks in Top 30
05 Jan	A Different Beat	Boyzone	Polygram	5	4
05 Jan	Forever Gir	OTT	Sony Music	15	5
05 Jan	Goodbye Girl	Shane O'Donoghue / Paul Harrington	Chart	21	2
05 Jan	Five Little Fingers	Shawn Cuddy	-	28	1
29 Jan	So Cold	Indian	-	22	4
02 Feb	One and Only	Mary Black	Dara	18	4
09 Feb	Discotheque	U2	Island	1	5
09 Feb	An Taobh Tuathail Amach	Kila	-	24	2
16 Feb	Let Me In	OTT	Sony Music	9	6
02 Mar	The Twelfth of Never	Carter Twins	BMG	7	4
16 Mar	Everybody Knows (Except You)	Divine Comedy	Setana	23	4
16 Mar	Isn't a Wonder	Boyzone	Polygram	4	7
06 Apr	Put the Message in The Box	Brian Kennedy	BMG	18	3
13 Apr	Tir Na Nog	D.J. Stewart/D.J. Dexter	-	17	2
20 Apr	Staring at the Sun	U2	Island	4	8
20 Apr	When You're Gone	Cranberries	Island	21	3
27 Apr	Dublin Town	Dempsey	-	18	3
27 Apr	Mysterious Woman	Marc Roberts	-	2	7
11 May	The Gospel Oak EP	Sinead O'Connor	Chrysalis	4	6
25 May	Someone's Got to Lose	The 4 Of Us	-	30	1
29 Jun	Bag of Cats	Sharon Shannon	Grapevine	20	4
06 Jul	Does He Really Love You?	Brendan Keeley	-	7	6
27 Jul	Picture of You†	Boyzone	Polygram	2	10
27 Jul	Last Night on Earth†	U2	Island	11	8
03 Aug	Lucy Jones Part 2	Aslan	-	17	3
03 Aug	Change	4 Of Us	-	23	1
17 Aug	Love Changes Everything†	Carter Twins	BMG	5	7
17 Aug	All Out of Love	OTT	Sony Music	17	4
31 Aug	Love Me	Frances Black	Dara	16	4
14 Sep	Hands to Heaven	Brendan Keeley	-	12	2
14 Sep	You'll Never beat the Banner	Kieran McDermott	-	25	2
28 Sep	Please†	U2	Island	2	1
28 Sep	Sam Maguire is Coming Home to Mayo†	Tom Tom & Byrnes Babes	-	19	1

Includes the months January to September 1997.   † Still in Top 30 Charts on 3/10/97.

EUROVISION SONG CONTEST

RATINGS OF EUROVISION VIEWERS (RTÉ)			
Year	%	Venue	No. of Viewers
1990	27%	Zagreb, Yugoslavia	852,000
1991	32%	Rome, Italy	1,004,000
1992	30%	Malmo, Sweden	960,000
1993	46%	Millstreet, Cork	1,464,000
1994	40%	Dublin	1,320,000
1995	41%	Dublin	1,300,000
1996	34%	Oslo, Norway	1,095,000
1997	34%	Dublin	1,119,000

IRISH VENUES USED TO HOST THE EUROVISION			
Year	Entrants	Venue	Seating Capacity
1971	18	Gaiety Theatre	1,000 approx.
1981	20	R.D.S.	1,200 approx.
1988	21	R.D.S.	1,200 approx.
1993	25	Millstreet	3,000 approx.
1994	25	Point Theatre	3,500 approx.
1995	23	Point Theatre	3,500 approx.
1997	25	Point Theatre	3,500 approx.

IRISH EUROVISION SONG CONTEST ENTRIES 1965-1997

Year	Venue	Song Title	Performer(s)	Placing
1965	Naples	I'm Walking the Streets in the Rain	Butch Moore	6th
1966	Luxembourg	Come Back to Stay	Dickie Rock	=4th
1967	Vienna	If I Could Choose	Sean Dunphy	2nd
1968	London	Chance of a Lifetime	Pat McGeegan	4th
1969	Madrid	The Wages of Love	Muriel Day & The Lindsays	=7th
1970	**Amsterdam**	**All Kinds of Everything**	**Dana**	**1st**
1971	Dublin	One Day Love	Angela Farrell	11th
1972	Edinburgh	Ceol an Ghrá	Sandie Jones	15th
1973	Luxembourg	Do I Dream?	Maxi	=10th
1974	Brighton	Cross your Heart	Tina	=7th
1975	Stockholm	That's What Friends are for	Jimmy & Tommy Swarbrigg	9th
1976	The Hague	When	Red Hurley	10th
1977	London	It's Nice to be in Love Again	The Swarbriggs Plus Two	3rd
1978	Paris	Born to Sing	Colm C. T. Wilkinson	5th
1979	Jerusalem	Happy Man	Cathal Dunne	5th
1980	**The Hague**	**What's Another Year?**	**Johnny Logan**	**1st**
1981	Dublin	Horoscopes	Sheeba	5th
1982	Harrogate	Here Today, Gone Tomorrow	The Duskey's	11th
1983	Munich			No Entry
1984	Luxembourg	Terminal 3	Linda Martin	2nd
1985	Gothenburg	Wait Until the Weekend Comes	Maria Christian	6th
1986	Bergen	You can Count on Me	Luv Bug	4th
1987	**Brussels**	**Hold me Now**	**Johnny Logan**	**1st**
1988	Dublin	Take him Home	Jump The Gun	8th
1989	Lausanne	The Real Me	Klev Connolly & The Missing Passengers	18th
1990	Zagreb	Somewhere in Europe	Liam Rielly	=2nd
1991	Rome	Could it be That I'm in Love	Kim Jackson	=10th
1992	**Malmö**	**Why Me?**	**Linda Martin**	**1st**
1993	**Cork**	**In your Eyes**	**Niamh Kavanagh**	**1st**
1994	**Dublin**	**Rock 'n' Roll Kids**	**Paul Harrington & Charlie McGettigan**	**1st**
1995	Dublin	Dreamin'	Eddie Friel	14th
1996	**Oslo**	**The Voice**	**Eimear Ouinn**	**1st**
1997	Dublin	Mysterious Woman	Marc Roberts	2nd

MAJOR CONCERT VENUES IN THE ISLAND OF IRELAND

Venue	Location	Telephone No.	Capacity
Croke Park	Dublin	-	68,000
Semple Stadium	Thurles	-	59,000
Lansdowne Road	Dublin	(01) 6689300	50,000
Pairc Ui Chaoimh	Cork	-	50,000
Point Depot	Dublin	(01) 8366777	7,500
King's Hall	Belfast	(01232) 665225	7,000
Neptune Stadium	Cork	(021) 395873	2,500
Waterfront Hall	Belfast	(01232) 334400	2,235
National Stadium	Dublin	(01) 4533371	2,200
Olympia Theatre	Dublin	(01) 4782153	1,300
Leisureland	Galway	(091) 521455	1,250
National Concert Hall	Dublin	(01) 6711533	1,200
R.D.S.	Dublin	(01) 6680866	1,200
Ulster Hall	Belfast	(01232) 323900	1,200
City Hall	Cork	(021) 966222	1,200
S.F.X. Centre	Dublin	(01) 2841747	1,000
Cork Opera House	Cork	(021) 270021	1,000
University of Limerick Concert Hall	Limerick	(061) 331549	1,000
Seapoint Leisure Centre	Galway	(091) 521716	1,000
Rialto Entertainment Centre	Derry	(01504) 260516	950
Connolly Hall	Cork	(021) 277466	800
Mean Fiddler	Dublin	(01) 4758555	700

Venue	Location	Telephone No.	Capacity
Bad Bob's	Dublin	(01) 6792992	500
Rotterdam Warehouse	Belfast	(01232) 352864	450
Riverside Theatre	Coleraine	(01265) 324683	380

BREAKDOWN OF CONCERT TICKETS 1997

CASH BREAKDOWN OF A £25 CONCERT TICKET FOR THE U2 GIG, REP. OF IRELAND

	%	Per Ticket sold £
The Band	25	6.25
Venue Hire	18	4.50
Stage Costs	11	2.75
Artistes' Costs	8	2.00
Support Acts	8	2.00
Promoter	8	2.00
Management	5	1.25
Advertising	5	1.25
Performing Rights Society (PRS)	3	0.75
Free Tickets & VIP's Backstage	3	0.75
Gardaí	3	0.75
Booking Agent	2	0.50
Security	1	0.25
Total	**100**	**25.00**

CASH BREAKDOWN OF A £20 CONCERT TICKET FOR THE U2 GIG, NORTHERN IRELAND

	%	Per Ticket sold £
The Band	50%	10.00
Running Costs & Overheads	40%	8.00
Promoter	10%	2.00
Total	**100**	**20.00**

SELECTED BIOGRAPHIES OF IRISH MUSIC & COMEDY PERSONALITIES

A Brún, Gareth (born Dublin, 1939). Founded Claddagh Records (1959), to record traditional Irish Artists and music. Led to the formation of legend band *The Chieftains*. (See profile).

Aiken, Jim (born Belfast, 1932). Concert promoter. Former national school teacher. Brings top acts from all over world to Dublin venues.

Allen, Dave (born Dublin, 1936). Alternative comedian. First performed one-man T.V, shows in Australia (1963). Made T.V. comedy series for B.B.C., among the first to use taboo language, yet attracting millions of followers.

Altan Donegal-based traditional music band. Formed by husband-and-wife team *Mairead Ní Mhaonaigh* (current vocals and fiddle) and *Frankie Kennedy* (died 1994). Recorded over 12 albums, including *Harvest Storm* (1991), *Black Water* (1996), *Runaway Sunday* (1997). Performed at recent Gael Force concerts, Dublin (Sept 1997).

Ash (formed Downpatrick, 1991). One of Northern Ireland's most innovative rock bands. Played back-up on U2's Irish "Popmart" tour (1997). Members: *Mark Hamilton, Tim Wheeler* and *Rick McMurray*. Successful hits: *Oh Yeah* (1994), *Girl from Mars* (1995), *Goldfinger* (1996). New single *Life Less Ordinary* (1997).

Black, Mary (born Dublin, 1955). Solo singer who recorded seven of the most successful albums in Irish pop history. Debut album *No Frontiers* (1989). Voted Best Female Artist in Irish Rock Music Awards (1987 and 1988). Albums include *Without the Fanfare, By the Time it Gets Dark, Babes in the Wood, Circus* and *Shine*.

Boomtown Rats, The (formed Dublin, 1975). Ireland's punk pioneers fronted by Bob Geldolf. Released a series of Top 20 singles, including Number 1's *Looking After No. 1* (1977), *Rat Trap* (1978) and *I Don't Like Monday's* (1979). Disbanded 1986; Geldolf embarked on solo career. *(See profile)*.

Boyzone (formed Dublin, 1993). Successful five-piece pop band who have conquered the teenage music market, securing top awards and positions in both Irish and British charts. Cover versions of *Love me for a Reason, Working My Way Back to You, Father and Son;* their own *Key to My Life* and the title track from *Mr Bean - The Movie (1997); A Different Beat*. Members: Ronan Keating, Keith Duffy, Steven Gately, Michael Graham, Shane Lynch.

Brady, Paul (born Strabane, 1947.) Folk and rock singer-songwriter. Former member of Planxty. Albums *Welcome Here Kind Stranger* (1978), *Hard Station* (1981) and hit single *Nothing But the Same Old Story*. Enjoys much commercial and critical success, with songs recorded by the likes of Tina Turner, Dave Edmunds and Bonnie Rait.

Chieftains, The (formed Dublin, 1962). Major force in representing Irish music at home and abroad, have celebrated over 30 years in music and made at least 31 albums. Featured on film sound-tracks *Barry Lyndon, The Year of the French* and *Triste and Isolde*. Have accompanied Elvis Costello, Marianne Faithful, Nanci Griffith, Art

Garfunkel, Mick Jagger, Paul McCartney, Van Morrison. Members: Paddy Maloney, Derek Bell, Martin Fay, Sean Kean, Matt Molloy, Kevin Bonneff. Albums: *A Chieftain Celebration* (1989), *Irish Heartbeat* with Van Morrison (1988), *Reel Music* (1991), *The Celtic Harp* (1993).

The Clancy Brothers (formed Dublin, 1960's). Irish folk group who adopted and introduced American folk, coupled with Irish traditional material, to the music world. Members: Paddy, Tom and Liam Clancy and Tommy Makem. Disbanded (1969). Liam and Tommy continue as international soloists.

Clannad (formed Co. Donegal, 1970). Fronted by singer *Máire Brennan* with twin brothers Paul and Kieran and uncles Noel and Pat Duggan. Reached new levels of success with themes for T.V. series *Harry's Game* (1982) and *Robin Hood* (1984). Recorded *Once in a Lifetime* (1986) with *Bono* (U2). Albums: *Fuaim* (1982), *Legend* (1984), *Macalla* (1985), *Pastpresent* (1989).

Corrs, The (formed Louth, 1990). Four-piece family band - Andrea, Sharon, Caroline, and Jim. Have reached major success with debut album *Forgiven Not Forgotten* (1995). Tracks include *Heaven Knows*, *Runaway* and *Closer*. Latest album *Talk on Corners* (1997) with current classic *Only When I Sleep*. Andrea also starred in Alan Parker's film *Evita* (1996).

Coughlan, Mary (born Galway, 1957). Blues and folk singer, known for her raspy and boozy renditions of timeless classics. Albums: *Tired and Emotional* (1985), *Under the Influence* (1987), *Uncertain Pleasures* (1990), *Sentimental Killer* (1992), *The Fall* (1997).

Coulter, Phil (born Derry, 1942). Music producer, arranger, pianist and songwriter. Co-wrote winning entries for the Eurovision Song Contest - Sandi Shaw's *Puppet on a String* Cliff Richards *Congratulations* (2nd-1969). Has worked with Sinéad O'Connor, The Dubliners, Planxty, and Boyzone. Produced easy-listening instrumental albums: *Classic Tranquillity*, *Sea of Tranquillity* and *Peace and Tranquillity*. Probably best known for penning the ballad *The Town I Love So Well*.

Cranberries (formed Limerick, 1990). Fronted by vocalist Dolores O'Riordan with Feargal Lawler, Mike and Noel Hogan. One of Ireland's most successful musical exports since U2. Enjoyed massive success with albums *Everybody is Doing it, So Why Can't We?* (1993), *To the Faithful Departed* (1996).

Cunnah, Peter (born Derry, 1968). Lead vocalist with dance act D:ream. Number 1 hit *Things Can Only Get Better* (1994) Album: *World* (1994), Singles: *You're the Best Thing* and *Blame it on Me*.

Dana (born Rosemary Brown, Derry, 1951). First Irish winner of Eurovision contest with *All Kinds of Everything* (1979). Singles: *It's Gonna be a Cold, Cold Christmas*, *Fairytale* and *Who Put the Lights Out*. Albums *Everything is Beautiful* (1981), *Let There Be Love* (1985).

De Burgh, Chris (born Argentina, 1948). Singer whose major hits include *Lady in Red*, *Don't Pay the Ferryman*, *Patricia the Stripper*, *Lonely Sky*, *Flying*. Albums: *Far Beyond These Castle Walls* (1974), *Into the Night* (1986), *Power of Ten* (1992), *Spark to a Flame*.

Divine Comedy, The (formed Enniskillen, 1990's). Front man Neil Hannon received tremendous success with single *The Frog Princess* from debut album *A Short Album About Love* (1997). Fastly becoming one of Northern Ireland's most gifted artists with his inspirational and poetic musical approach.

The Dubliners (formed Dublin, 1962). Folk group formerly known as The Ronnie Drew Group. One of the longest-surviving and most popular groups in Ireland. Original line-up of Ronnie Drew, Luke Kelly, Barney McKenna, Kieron Bourke and later John Sheehan. Surviving members Sheehan and Drew have since joined forces with Barney McKenna and Eamon Campbell.

Enya (born Gweedore, 1961). Youngest member of Brennan family *(Clannad)*. Atmospheric solo singer who has sold millions of albums worldwide, including *Watermark* (1988), *Shepherd Moons* (1991), *The Celts* (1992), *The Memory of Trees* (1996).

Evans, Dave a.k.a. Edge (born London, 1961). Guitarist with rock band U2, enjoying phenomenal worldwide success with the Dublin quartet since their formation in the late 1970's.

Friday, Gavin (born Dublin, 1960). Singer and songwriter. Member of *The Virgin Prunes*. Released solo albums *Each Man Kills the Thing He Loves* (1989), *Adam 'n' Eve*, *Shag Tobacco* (1996). Teamed up with *Bono* (U2) to produce the haunting soundtrack for Sheridan's *In the Name of the Father* (1993).

Gallagher, Rory (born Ballyshannon, Co. Donegal 1948). Veteran blues guitarist. Albums: *On the Boards* (1970), *Against the Grain* (1975), *Calling Card* (1976), *Defender* (1987), *Fresh Evidence* (1990). Died 1995.

Geldoff, Bob (born Dublin, 1952). Singer, formed *The Boomtown Rats* (1975) and had two British Number 1's. Organiser of *Band Aid/Live Aid* (1984) project, raising millions for famine-struck Africa. Nominated for the Nobel Peace Prize (1986). Published best-selling autobiography *Is That It?* (1986), producer and creator of Channel 4's *The Big Breakfast*.

Hewson, Paul a.k.a. Bono (born Dublin, 1960). Ireland's most commercially successful rock singer. Lead vocalist with U2. Writes most of lyrics for the bands songs.

Horslips, The (formed Dublin, 1970). Rock icons. Created genre of celtic rock, blending traditional Irish music with rock. Influenced many of today's bands. Members: Barry Devlin, Jim Lockhart, Johnny Fean, Charles O' Connor, Eamon Carr. Recorded *Happy to Meet, Sorry to Part* (1972), *Dancehall Sweethearts* (1974), *The Man Who Built America* (1978), *Short stories, Tall Tales* (1979). Disbanded (1980).

Hothouse Flowers (formed Galway, 1980's). Five-piece band fronted by vocalist *Liam Ó Maonlaí* and guitarist *Fiachna Braonain*. Albums: *People* (1988), *Home* (1990), *Songs From the Rain* (1993), with classic pop single *Don't Go* (1987).

Hughes, Sean (born Dublin, 1960's). Comedian, writer. Best known for T.V. series *Sean's Show* (1992, 1993). Current team captain on B.B.C. 's quiz show *Never Mind the Buzzcocks* (1996-), and touring as one-man show *Alibis for Life* (1997). Published works: *Sean's Book*, *The Grey Area* and debut novel *The Detainers* (1997).

Kennedy, Brian (born Belfast, 1960's). Singer who has teamed up with *Van Morrison* on numerous musical events. Albums: *Great War of Words* (1992), *A Better Man* (1996). Singles: *Captured, Put the Message in the Box*.

Lohan, Sinéad (born Cork, 1970's). One of Ireland's most promising new generation of singer/songwriters. Participated *Woman's Heart Tour*. Debut album *Who Do You Think You Are* (1996).

Lunny, Donal (born Tullamore, 1947). Multi-instrumentalist, composer, singer and record producer. Former member of *Planxty* (1971) with *Christy Moore* and *Paul Brady*; *The Bothy Band* (1975) and *Moving Hearts* (1981).

McGuinness, Paul (born Germany, 1951). Manager of rock group U2 for 20 years.

Moore, Christy (born Kildare, 1945). Singer/songwriter. Founder of Irish folk group *Planxty* and the acclaimed *Moving Hearts*. Solo artist since 1982, renowned for his innovative song writing. Best known for *Ordinary Man* (1985), *The Christy Moore Collection* (1991) and *Graffiti Tongue* (1996).

Moore, Gary (born Belfast, 1960's.) Guitarist who has played with *Thin Lizzy*, *Skid Row*, and his own *Gary Moore Band*. Best known for rhythmical blues and celtic strength on guitar. Teamed with Lynott for *Parisienne Walkways* and *Out in the Fields* (1985).

Morgan Dermot (born Dublin, 1952). Comedian. Considerable success with award-winning irreverent comedy show *Father Ted*. (1995-).

Morrison, Van (born Belfast, 1945). Legendary rock musician, singer, songwriter. Formed *Them* (1963). Has enjoyed an outstanding successful status as a solo artist. Albums: *Astral Weeks (1968)*, *No Guru, No Method, No Teacher* (1986), *Hymns to the Silence* (1991)

O'Connor, Sinéad (born Dublin, 1966). Singer who has met with considerable popular and critical acclaim. Albums: *The Lion and the Cobra* (1987), *I Do Not Have What I Have Not Got* (1990), *Am I Not Your Girl* (1992), *Universal Mother* (1995), *Gospel Oak* (E.P 1997). Greatest success with *Nothing Compares 2 U.* (1990), Number 1 in over 17 countries.

O'Donnell, Daniel (born Donegal, 1961). Ireland's leading country singer, also highly popular internationally. Hit singles include *Donegal Shore, I Just Want to Dance with You* and *Destination Donegal*.

O'Hanlon, Ardal, (born Carrickmacross, Monaghan, 1968). Comedian; most popularly known as *Dougal* in comedy series *Father Ted* (1995-). Voted *Top T.V.Comedy Newcomer* (1995) and won *Spitting Image Act of the Year Award* (1995). Recently hosted the *The Stand- up Show* - B.B.C. New Comedy Awards (Sept 1997).

Ó Súilleabháin, Mícheál (born Tipperary, 1950). Musician, composer, professor of music and multi-instrumentalist. Has brought Irish traditional music into contact with 20th century music. Recorded and produced the R.T.É T.V. series *A River of Sound* (1995), tracing the history of Irish music.

Patterson, Frank (born Tipperary, 1941). Ireland's leading tenor, has had many major tours in Europe and America, where he enjoys much success.

The Pogues (formed London, 1983). Fronted by Tipperary-born *Shane McGowan*. Albums: *Red Roses for Me* (1983), *Rum, Sodomy and the Lash* (1984), *Poguetry in Motion* (1991), *If I Should Fall From Grace with God* (1988), *Peace and Love* (1989), *Hell's Ditch* (1990), *The Best of the Pogues* (1991). McGowan left *The Pogues* (1991) following internal differences.

The Sawdoctors (formed Tuam, Galway, 1989). Popular band *I Useta Love Her* became the best-selling single of 1991, with album *If This is Rock and Roll I Want My Old Job Back* (1990).

Stewart, Louis (born Waterford, 1944). Jazz musician. Reared Dublin. Achieved international status winning the *Montreux Jazz Festival Grand Prix* (1969). Has toured and recorded with jazz greats Benny Goodman, Spike Robinson, Tubby Hayes, Ronnie Scott and Irish singer Honor Heffernon.

Therapy? (formed Belfast, 1989). Three-piece band. Mini-LPs and album: *Babyteeth* (1991), *Pleasure Death* (1992) *Nurse* (1993) *Troublegum* (1994).

Thin Lizzy (formed Dublin, 1969). Ireland's most remembered band fronted by Phil Lynott. *Gary Moore* joined for a while; but the main line-up was Lynott, Brian Downey, Scott Gorham, Brian Robertson. Produced classic albums: *Jailbreak* (1976), *Bad Reputation* (1977), *Live and Dangerous* (1978), *Black Rose* (1979). Popular tracks: *Whiskey in the Jar, Dancing in the Moonlight, Waiting for an Alibi, Don't Believe a Word* and *The Boys are Back in Town*. Disbanded (1983). Lynott later died 1986.

U2 (formed Dublin, 1976). The most successful Irish band. Bono (Paul Hewson), Adam Clayton, The Edge (Dave Evans) and Larry Mullen Jnr. have produced ten top albums and collected numerous prestigious music awards. Albums include *Boy* (1980), *October* (1981), *War* (1983), *The Joshua Tree* (1987), *Rattle and Hum* (1988), *Achtung Baby* (1991), *Pop* (1997).

Undertones, The (formed Derry, 1974). Punk-pop band fronted by Fergal Sharkey. Hugely successful with the punk anthem *Teenage Kicks*; followed by *Jimmy, Jimmy, Here Comes the Summer, My Perfect Cousin* (1980), and *It's Going to Happen* (1981). Albums: *Hypnotised* (1980), *Positive Touch* (1981). Disbanded (1983). Sharkey embarked on solo career with top singles *Listen to Your Father* (1994) *A Good Heart* (1995).

Whelan, Bill (born Limerick, 1950). Composer, record producer and songwriter. Best Known for composing the music for the highly successful *Riverdance - The Show* (1994). Credited with T.V. and film scores: *Lamb* (1984), R.T.É.'s thriller *Twice Shy, Some Mother's Son* (1996). Compositions include *The Ó Riada Suite* (1987), *The Seville Suite* (1992) and *The Spirit of Mayo* (1993). Former member with *Planxty* (keyboard player 1979-81), and since produced albums for Andy Irvine, Patrick Street, Stockton's Wing and Davy Spillane.

The News-stands Bulging . . .

*By **Martin Cowley**, Reuters*

FOR the pulse of the nation, turn to the media. From local papers which are the lifeblood of small-town Ireland to national media that "go for the jugular", the island has a long tradition of a free press. Due to stringent libel rules, it is often just a heartbeat away from the law courts and eagle-eyed potential litigants, but it survives - and thrives. Silent computers have replaced rattling "linotypes', colour has put black and white photographs in the shade, production and flexibility made the deadlines earlier. Nowadays news is immediate.

From the page-one headlines on the daily papers to the backpage death columns, the Irish have a reputation as voracious newspaper readers. Many reporters know to their cost that every word will be devoured by sometimes wary but never weary readers. Success in the modern media is mercurial. Survival is sufficient for some struggling publications. Rising readership, viewer and listener league tables are the barometers for most sections. A network of local radio stations launched just a few years ago has now a firm foothold in most communities.

The Ireland of the "Celtic Tiger", with a burgeoning economy and key political influence in the European Union, and the Northern Ireland peace process make the island a trawling ground for global media. Satellite and cable networks are making the world a smaller place for many Irish viewers, bringing instant global news into their homes. The television room, or rooms, in homes all over the island are a fierce competition ground for national public broadcasting networks and international commercial conglomerates. In the Republic, Radio Telefís Éireann, Teilifís na Gaeilge, Raidió na Gaeltachta, a host of local radio stations are the main providers, a more recently the new Radio Ireland has come on the scene. In Northern Ireland, B.B.C. and Ulster Television are the key media outlets for extensive local news reporting.

In newspapers, recent years have seen a growth in daily tabloids and evidence of British quality Sundays including Ireland in their market thrust. Ireland's broadsheets remain dominant, in the shape of the lively Irish Independent and the sagacious Irish Times. The old Cork Examiner is now "The Examiner" and gives a national edge to its coverage. Northern Ireland has three morning dailies competing with the Dublin papers and the heavyweight London broadsheets and bright and breezy tabloids. The Irish News, a paper with a nationalist outlook, has produced many exclusives in the past year. The News Letter, unashamedly unionist, drives home its tabloid news with upbeat in-your-face headlines.The Belfast Telegraph with a diverse mix of crisply written news ranging from house price rises to heavy politics and the latest software jobs announcements, monopolises the evening market.

Sunday brings an avalanche. The London-published Sunday Times has an Irish edition and Irish-based staff. The Sunday Business Post in Dublin has found a winning formula, and the Sunday Tribune rattles cages of politicians. The Sunday Independent hosts a batter of controversial columnists. The Sunday World out-tabloids the British competitors. In Belfast, the Sunday Life goes for a broad Northern Ireland market. In Dublin the latest entrant is Ireland on Sunday. The news-stands bulging.

The author is a former London Editor of The Irish Times.

MOST POPULAR IRISH DAILY NEWSPAPERS, JANUARY - JUNE 1997

Republic of Ireland National Newspapers	Average Circulation
The Examiner *(Cork)*	55,816
Evening Echo *(Cork)*	27,037
Evening Herald *(Dublin)*	115,071
Irish Independent *(Dublin)*	158,005
Irish Times *(Dublin)*	105,312
The Star *(Dublin)*	-

Northern Ireland Newspapers	Average Circulation
Belfast Telegraph *(Belfast)*	131,829
Irish News *(Belfast)*	47,494
Ulster News Letter *(Belfast)*	33,753

MOST POPULAR ENGLISH DAILY NEWSPAPERS, JANUARY - JUNE 1997*

Newspaper	BOUGHT ON THE ISLAND OF IRELAND Republic of Ireland	Northern Ireland	Total
Daily Mirror	40,000	52,000	92,000
Daily Record	-	4,400	-
Daily Star	90,000	22,000	112,000
The Sun	75,000	80,000	155,000
Daily Express	4,500	15,000	19,500
Daily Mail	6,000	27,000	33,000
Daily Telegraph	4,600	6,000	10,600
Financial Times	3,400	1,500	4,900
The Guardian	3,000	2,500	5,500
The Independent	2,200	(English version) 2,200	4,400
The Times	6,000	7,300	13,300
Racing Post	-	-	-
Sporting Life	-	-	-

These are Irish Almanac estimates based on the most up-to-date information available, as of October 1997.

MOST POPULAR SUNDAY NEWSPAPERS BOUGHT IN IRELAND, JAN. - JUNE 97

Newspaper	Total
Sunday Business Post	41,890
Sunday Independent	333,966
Sunday Life	103,124
Sunday Tribune	84,148
Sunday World Group	303,964

MOST POPULAR IRISH PROVINCIAL NEWSPAPERS, JANUARY - JUNE 1997

Northern Ireland Provincial Newspapers	Average Circulation	Northern Ireland Provincial Newspapers	Average Circulation
Alpha Newspaper Group	30,823	Derry Journal (Fri)	27,002
Ballyclare Gazette Series	2,816	Derry Journal Group	73,727
Banbridge Chronicle	8,632	Down Recorder	12,161
Carrickfergus Advertiser & East Antrim Gazette	3,002	Dungannon News & Tyrone Courier	14,446
Coleraine Times Series	6,154	Impartial Reporter	-
County Down Spectator	12,334	Larne Gazette Group	6,818
Derry Journal (Tue)	25,723	Larne Times Series	13,809
		The Leader Series	4,328

Northern Ireland Provincial Newspapers	Average Circulation
Londonderry Sentinel Series	6,445
Lurgan Mail	9,792
Mid Ulster Mail Series	11,978
Morton Newspaper Group	78,783
Mourne Observer Series	12,481
Newtownards Chronicle & County Down Observer	10,484
Newtownards Spectator	2,802
Portadown Times	11,708
Strabane Weekly News	2,171
Tyrone Constitution & Strabane Weekly News Group	12,152
Tyrone Constitution (Omagh)	9,981
Tyrone Times	3,588
Ulster Gazette & Armagh Standard	10,629
Ulster Star Series	13,677

Free Distribution Papers:

Craigavon Echo	-
Journal Extra	-
East Belfast Herald & Post	-
East Belfast News	-
Lisburn Echo	-
Mid Ulster Echo	-
Morton Newspaper Group	-
North & Newtownabbey Herald & Post	-
North Down Herald & Post	-
North Down News	-
North West Echo	-
South Belfast Herald & Post	-

Republic of Ireland Provincial Newspapers	Average Circulation
Anglo Celt	15,434
The Argus	8,290
Clare Champion	-
Connacht Sentinel	7,639
Connacht Tribune Series	28,889
The Corkman	6,003
Donegal Democrat	17,076
Donegal People's Press	3,927
Drogheda Independent Series	14,175
Enniscorthy Guardian Series	5,788
Irish Field	11,208
The Kerryman Series	28,638
Kilkenny People	16,638
Limerick Leader (Weekend) Series	26,250
Nationalist & Munster Advertiser	15,274
Nenagh Guardian	7,706
New Ross Standard	5,280
People Newspaper Group	38,073
Tipperary Star	9,755
Wexford People	9,895
Wicklow People Series	17,132

Free Distribution Papers:

Galway Advertiser	-

IRISH NEWSPAPERS

Belfast Telegraph Belfast Telegraph Newspapers Ltd., 124-144 Royal Avenue, Belfast BT1 1EB. Tel. (01232) 264000. Published daily, evening. Editor: Edmund Curran.

Examiner, The (1841) Cork Examiner Publications Ltd., P.O. Box 21, Academy Street, Cork. Tel. (021) 272722. Published daily. Editor: Brian Looney.

Evening Echo Cork Examiner Publications Ltd., Academy Street, Cork. Tel. (021) 272722. Published daily, evening. Editor: Nigel O'Mahony.

Evening Herald (1891) Independent Newspapers (Ireland) Ltd., Middle Abbey Street, Dublin 1. Tel. (01) 8731666. Published daily. Editor: P. Drury.

Ireland on Sunday (1997) Title Media Ltd., 50 City Quay, Dublin 2. Tel. (01) 6718255. Published weekly. Editor: Liam Hayes.

Irish Family, The P.O. Box 7, Mullingar, Co. Westmeath. Tel. (044) 42987. Published weekly. Editor: R. Hogan.

Irish Independent (1905)

Independent Newspapers (Ireland) Ltd., Middle Abbey Street, Dublin 1. Tel. (01) 8731333 / 8731666. Published daily. Editor: Vincent Doyle.

Irish News (1891) 113-117 Donegall Street, Belfast BT1 2GE. Tel. (01232) 322226. Published daily. Editor: Tom Collins.

Irish Times, The (1859) 10-16 D'Olier Street, Dublin 2. Tel. (01) 6792022. Published daily. Editor: Conor Brady.

News Letter, The (*Belfast and Ulster Editions*). Century Newspapers Ltd., 45-56 Boucher Crescent, Belfast BT12 6QY. Tel. (01232) 680000. Published every day except Sunday. Free Circulation in Belfast. Editor: Geoff Martin.

Star, The Independent Star Ltd., Star House, Terenure Road North, Dublin 6W. Tel. (01) 4901228. Published daily. Editor: Gerard O'Reagan.

Sunday Business Post 27-30 Merchants Quay, Dublin 8. Tel. (01) 6799777. Published weekly. Editor: Damien Kiberd.

Sunday Independent (1906) Independent Newspapers (Ireland) Ltd., Middle Abbey Street, Dublin 1. Tel. (01) 8731333 / 8731666. Published weekly. Editor: Aengus Fanning.

Sunday Tribune 15 Lower Baggot Street, Dublin 2. Tel. (01) 6615555. Published weekly. Editor: Matt Cooper.

Sunday World (1973) Sunday Newspapers Ltd., Newspaper House, Rathfarnham Road, Dublin 6. Tel. (01) 4901980. Published weekly. Editor: Colm McGinty.

PROVINCIAL NEWSPAPERS:

Anglo-Celt, The Church Street, Cavan. Tel. (049) 31100. Published weekly. Editor: Johnny O'Hanlon.

Antrim Guardian (1970) 1A Railway Street, Antrim. Tel. (01849) 462624. Local edition of Ballymena Guardian. Published weekly on Wednesday. Editor: Liam Heffron.

Argus, The Park Street, Dundalk, Co. Louth. Tel.(042) 31500. Published weekly. Editor: Kevin

Mulligan.

Armagh-Down Observer Ann Street, Dungannon, Co. Tyrone. Tel. (018687) 22557. Published weekly. Editor: D. Mallon.

Athlone Topic The Crescent, Ballymahon Road, Athlone, Co. Westmeath. Published weekly. Editor: Oliver Heaney.

Ballymena Chronicle and Antrim Observer Ann Street, Dungannon, Co. Tyrone. Tel. (018687) 22557. Published weekly. Editor: D. Mallon.

Ballymena Guardian (1970) Northern Newspaper Group, Railway Road, Coleraine. Tel. (01266) 41221. Published weekly. Editor: Maurice O'Neill.

Banbridge Chronicle (1870) The Banbridge Chronicle Press Ltd., 14 Bridge Street, Banbridge, Co. Down. Tel. (018206) 62322. Published weekly. Editor: Bryan Hooks.

Carrickfergus Advertiser 31A High Street, Carrickfergus, Co. Antrim. Tel. (01960) 363651. Published weekly. Editor: Steven Kiernaghan.

Clare Champion Barrack Street, Ennis, Co. Clare. Tel. (065) 28105. Published weekly. Editor: Gerry Collisson.

Coleraine Chronicle (1844) Northern Newspaper Group, Railway Road, Coleraine, Co. Derry. Tel. (01265) 43344. Published weekly. Editor: Grant Cameron.

Connacht Sentinel, The (1925) The Connacht Tribune Ltd., 15 Market Street, Galway. Tel. (091) 567251. Published weekly. Editor: Brendan O'Carroll.

Connacht Tribune, The (1909) The Connacht Tribune Ltd., 15 Market Street, Galway. Tel. (091) 567251. Published weekly. Editor: John Cunningham.

Connaught Telegraph Elison Street, Castlebar, Co. Mayo. Tel. (094) 21711. Published weekly. Editor: Tom Gillespie.

County Down Spectator (1904) 109 Main Street, Bangor, Co. Down. Tel. (01247) 270270. Published weekly. Editor: Paul Flowers.

Craigavon Echo 14A Church Street, Portadown, Co. Armagh. Tel. (01762) 350041. Published weekly, distributed free. Editor: David Armstrong.

Democrat, The Ann Street, Dungannon, Co. Tyrone. Tel. (01868) 722557. Editor: D. Mallon.

Derry Journal (1772) Buncrana Road, Derry. Tel. (01504) 2722000.

Published twice weekly; Tuesday and Friday. Editor: Pat McArt.

Derry People and Donegal News (1901) Crossview House, Letterkenny, Co. Donegal. Tel. (074) 21014. Published weekly. Editor: Colomba Gill.

Donegal Democrat (1919) Donegal Democrat Ltd., Donegal Road, Ballyshannon, Co. Donegal. Tel. (072) 51201. Published weekly. Editor: John Bromley.

Donegal Peoples Press (1932) Port Road, Letterkenny, Co. Donegal. Tel. (074) 28000. Published weekly. Editor: Paddy Walsh.

Down Recorder Church Street, Downpatrick, Co. Down. Tel. (01396) 613711. Published weekly. Editor: Paul Symington.

Drogheda Independent 9 Shop Street, Drogheda, Co. Louth. Tel. (041) 38658. Published weekly. Editor: Paul Murphy.

Dundalk Democrat (1849) 3 Earl Street, Dundalk. Tel. (042) 34058. Published weekly. Editor: Peter Kavanagh.

Dungannon News and Tyrone Courier 58 Scotch Street, Dungannon, Co. Tyrone. Tel. (01868) 722271. Published weekly. Editor: R. G. Montgomery.

Dungannon Observer Irish Street, Dungannon, Co. Tyrone. Tel. (01868) 722557. Published weekly. Editor: D. Mallon.

Dungarvan Leader and Southern Democrat (1938) 78 O'Connell Street, Dungarvan, Co. Waterford. Tel. (058) 41203. Published weekly. Editor: Colm J. Nagle.

Dungarvan Observer and Munster Industrial Advocate Shandon, Dungarvan, Co. Waterford. Tel. (058) 41205. Published weekly. Editor: James Lynch.

Echo Newspapers Group, The (weekly publishers of The Echo, Wexford Echo, Gorey Echo, New Ross Echo and monthly publishers of Farming Echo, Property Echo) Mill Park Road, Enniscorthy, Co. Wexford. Tel. (054) 33231. Editor-in-Chief: Tom Mooney.

Fermanagh Herald 30 Belmore Street, Enniskillen, Co. Fermanagh. Tel. (01365) 322066. Published weekly. Editor: Dominic McClements.

Fermanagh News Irish Street, Dungannon, Co. Tyrone. Tel. (01868) 722557. Published weekly. Editor:

D. Mallon.

Galway Advertiser (1970) 2-3 Church Lane, Galway. Tel. (091) 567077. Published weekly. Managing Editor: Ronnie O'Gorman.

Herald and Post Newspapers (weekly publishers of East Belfast Herald and Post, South Belfast Herald and Post, North and Newtownabbey Herald and Post, North Down Herald and Post). 124 Royal Avenue, Belfast BT1 1EB. Tel. (01232) 239049. Editor: Nigel Tilson.

Inner City News 57 Amiens Street, Dublin 1. Tel. (01) 8363832. Published monthly, distributed free. Editor: John Hedges.

Kerryman, The / **Corkman, The** Clash Industrial Estate, Tralee, Co. Kerry. Tel. (066) 21666. Published weekly. Editor: Ger Colleran.

Kerry's Eye (1974) Kenno Ltd., 22 Ashe Street, Tralee, Co. Kerry. Tel. (066) 23199. Published weekly. Editor: Padraig Kennelly.

Kildare Nationalist Liffey House, Edward Street, Newbridge, Co. Kildare. Tel. (045) 432147. Editor: Eddie Coffey.

Kilkenny People (1892) 34 High Street, Kilkenny. Tel. (056) 21015. Fax. (056) 21414. Published weekly. Editor: John Kerry-Keane.

Laois Nationalist 4 Kerryville, Portlaoise, Co. Laois. Tel. (0502) 60265. Published weekly. Editor: Eddie Coffey.

Leader, The 25 Bridge Street, Banbridge, Co. Down. Tel. (018206) 62745. Published weekly. Editor: Damian Wilson.

Leinster Express (1831) Leinster Express Newspapers Ltd., Dublin Road, Portlaoise, Co. Laois. Tel. (0502) 21666. Published weekly. Editor: Teddy Fennelly.

Leinster Leader 18 South Main Street, Naas, Co. Kildare. Tel. (045) 897302. Published weekly. Editor: Vicki Waller.

Leitrim Observer (1889) Leitrim Observer Ltd., St. Georges Terrace, Carrick-on-Shannon, Co. Leitrim. Tel. (078) 20025. Published weekly. Editor: Anthony Hickey.

Liffey Champion 3 Captain's Hill, Leixlip, Co. Kildare. Tel. (01) 6245533. Published fortnightly. Editor: Vincent Sutton.

Limerick Chronicle (1766) The Limerick Leader Ltd., O'Connell Street, Limerick. Tel. (061) 315233. Published weekly. Editor: Brendan

Halligan.

Limerick Leader (1889) The Limerick Leader Ltd., O'Connell Street, Limerick. Tel. (061) 315233. Published four times weekly. Editor: Brendan Halligan.

Lisburn Echo 12A Bow Street, Lisburn Co. Antrim. Tel. (01846) 601114. Published weekly, distributed free. Editor: David Fletcher.

Local News Publication Rosehill House, Main Street, Finglas, Dublin 11. Tel. (01) 8361666. Bankhouse Centre, 331 South Circular Road, Dublin 8. Tel. (01) 4534011.

Londonderry / Limavady Sentinel Suite 3, Spencer House, Spencer Road, Derry. Tel. (01504) 48889. Published weekly. Editor: James Cadden.

Longford Leader, The Longford Leader Ltd., Market Square, Longford. Tel. (043) 45241. Published weekly. Editor: Eugene McGee.

Longford News (1936) Five County News, The Longford News, Earl Street, Longford. Tel. (043) 41147. Published weekly. Editor: Paul Healy.

Lurgan and Portadown Examiner Ann Street, Dungannon, Co. Tyrone. Tel. (018687) 22557. Published weekly. Editor: D. Mallon.

Lurgan Mail 4A High Street, Lurgan, Co. Armagh. Tel. (01762) 327777. Published weekly. Editor: Richard Elliott.

Mayo News The Fairgreen, Westport, Co. Mayo. Tel. (098) 25664. Published weekly. Managing Editor: Seán Staunton.

Meath Chronicle and Cavan & Westmeath Herald (1897) Market Square, Navan, Co. Meath. Tel. (046) 21442. Published weekly. Editor: Ken Davis.

Midland Tribune, The (1881) Syngefield, Birr, Co. Offaly. Tel. (0509) 20003. Published weekly. Editor: Jon O'Callaghan.

Mid-Ulster Observer Ann Street, Dungannon, Co. Tyrone. Tel. (018687) 22557. Published weekly. Editor: D. Mallon.

Morton Newspapers Ltd., *(Publishers of Coleraine/Ballymoney Times, Ballymena/Antrim Times, Ballymena Observer, Larne / Carrickfergus / Newtownabbey Times, Londonderry / Roe Valley Sentinel, Lurgan Mail, Portadown Times, Ulster Star (Lisburn), Dromore Star, The Leader (Dromore), Banbridge Leader, Mid-Ulster Mail, South Derry edition (Magherafelt), Craigavon Echo, Lisburn Echo, North-West Echo, Mid-Ulster Echo, East Antrim Advertiser, Tyrone Times, Specialist Publications)* Head Office, 2 Easky Drive, Carn Industrial Estate, Portadown, Co. Armagh, BT63 5YY. Tel. (01762) 393939.

Mourne Observer (1949) Newcastle, Co. Down. Tel. (013967) 22666. Published weekly. Editor: Terence Bowman.

Munster Express, The (1859) 1 Hanover Square, Waterford. Tel. (051) 72141. Published twice weekly. Editor: Eddie Coffey.

Nationalist and Leinster Times (1883); Tullow Street, Carlow. Tel. (0503) 31731. Published weekly. Editor: Eddie Coffey.

Nationalist Newspaper Queen Street, Clonmel, Co. Tipperary. Tel. (052) 22211. Published weekly. Editor: Tom Corr.

Nenagh Guardian Ltd., 13 Summerhill, Nenagh, Co. Tipperary. Tel. (067) 31214. Published weekly. Editor: Gerry Slevin.

Newry Reporter, The (1867) 4 Market Street, Newry, Co. Down. Tel. (01693) 67633. Published weekly. Editor: D. O'Donnell.

Newtownards Spectator 109 Main Street, Bangor, Co. Down. Tel. (01247) 270270. Published weekly. Editor: Paul Flowers.

Northern Constitution (1876) Northern Newspaper Group, Coleraine, Co. Derry. Tel. (01265) 43344. Published weekly. Editor: Grant Cameron.

Northern Newspaper Group (1970); *(Publishers of Coleraine Chronicle, Ballymena Guardian, Antrim Guardian, Newtownabbey Guardian, The Leader, Northern Constitution)* Head Office, Railway Road, Coleraine, Co. Derry. Tel. (01265) 43344. Group Editor: Maurice O'Neill.

Northern Standard The Diamond, Monaghan. Tel. (047) 82188. Published weekly. Editor: Martin Smyth.

Offaly Express *(Combined circulation with Leinster Express)* Bridge Street, Tullamore, Co. Offaly. Tel. (0506) 21744. Published weekly, distributed free. Editor: Teddy Fennelly.

Outlook, The Castle Street, Rathfriland, Co. Down. Tel. (018206) 30202. Published weekly. Editor: Ken Purdy.

People Newspapers *(Publishers of five regional newspapers and Irelands Own).* North Main Street, Bray, Co. Wicklow. Tel. (053) 22155. Editor: Ger Walsh. *Bray People* Main Street, Bray. Tel. (01) 2867393. Editor: Ger Walsh. *The Guardian* Court Street, Enniscorthy. Tel. (054) 33833; Thomas Street, Gorey, Co. Wexford. Tel. (055) 21423. Editor: Ger Walsh. *New Ross Standard* North Street, New Ross, Co. Wexford. Tel. (051) 21184. Editor: Ian McClure. *The People* 1A North Main Street, Wexford. Tel. (053) 22155. Editor: Ger Walsh. *Wicklow People* Main Street, Wicklow. Tel. (0404) 67198. Main Street, Arklow. Tel. (0402) 32130. Published weekly. Editor: Ger Walsh.

Portadown Times 14A Church Street, Portadown, Co. Armagh. Tel. (01762) 336111. Published weekly. Editor: David Armstrong.

Roscommon Champion (1927) Abbey Street, Roscommon. Tel. (0903) 25051. Published weekly. Editor: Paul Healy.

Roscommon Herald (1859) Boyle, Co. Roscommon. Tel. (079) 62004. Published weekly. Editor: Christina McHugh.

Sligo Champion (1836) The Champion Publications Ltd., Wine Street, Sligo. Tel. (071) 69222. Published weekly. Editor: Seamus Finn.

Sligo Weekender (1983) Castle Street, Sligo. Tel. (071) 42140. Published weekly. Editor: Brian McHugh.

Southern Star Skibbereen, Co. Cork. Tel. (028) 21200. Published weekly. Editor: L. O'Regan.

Southside People (East), The Southside People (West), The 6 Leopardstown Office Park, Sandyford Industrial Estate, Dublin 18. Tel. (01) 2942494. Editor: Johnny McCullagh.

Strabane Chronicle Ulster Herald Series, John Street, Omagh, Co. Tyrone. Tel. (01662) 243444/5. Published weekly. Editor: Paddy Cullen.

Strabane Weekly News (1908) The Tyrone Constitution Ltd., 25-27 High Street, Omagh, Co. Tyrone. Tel. (01662) 242721. Published weekly. Editor: Wesley Atchison.

Tipperary Star (1909) Friar Street, Thurles, Co. Tipperary. Tel. (0504)

21122. Published weekly. Editor: Michael Dundon.

Topic Newspapers Ltd. *(weekly publishers of Westmeath Topic, Offaly Topic, Meath Topic, circulating in Westmeath, Offaly, Meath, Kildare and Longford, and monthly magazine Ireland's Eye).* The Roundabout, 6 Dominick Street, Mullingar, Co. Westmeath. Tel. (044) 48868. Editor: Dick Hogan.

Tuam Herald (1837) Dublin Road, Tuam, Co. Galway. Tel. (093) 24183. Published weekly. Editor: David Burke.

Tullamore Tribune, The (1978) Church Street, Tullamore, Co. Offaly. Tel. (0506) 21152. Published weekly.

Editor: Ger Scully.

Tyrone Constitution, The (1844) 25-27 High Street, Omagh, Co. Tyrone. Tel. (01662) 242721. Published weekly. Editor: Wesley Atchison.

Ulster Farmer (1990) Ann Street, Dungannon, Co. Tyrone. Tel. (01868) 722557. Published weekly. Editor: D. Mallon.

Ulster Gazette and Armagh Standard (1844) 56 Scotch Street, Armagh. Tel. (01861) 522639. Published weekly. Editor: Richard Stewart.

Ulster Herald (1901) John Street, Omagh, Co. Tyrone. Tel. (01662) 243444/5. Published weekly

Editor: Paddy Cullen.

Ulster Star 12A Bow Street, Lisburn, Co. Antrim. BT28 1BN Tel. (01846) 679111. Published weekly. Editor: David Fletcher.

Waterford News & Star (1848) 25 Michael Street, Waterford. Tel. (051) 75566. Published weekly. Editor: Peter Doyle.

Western People, The (1883) Francis Street, Ballina, Co. Mayo. Tel. (096) 21188. Published weekly. Editor: Terry Reilly.

Westmeath Examiner, The (1882) 19 Dominick Street, Mullingar. Tel. (044) 48426. Published weekly. Editor: Nicholas Nally.

PERIODICALS, MAGAZINES AND JOURNALS

Accountancy Ireland (1969) 87-89 Pembroke Road, Ballsbridge, Dublin 4. Tel. (01) 6680400. Published six times a year. Editor: Charles O'Rourke.

Administration (1953) Institute of Public Administration, 57-61 Lansdowne Road, Dublin 4. Tel. (01) 2697011. Published quarterly. Editor: Tony McNamara.

Administration Yearbook & Diary (1966) Institute of Public Administration, 57-61 Lansdowne Road, Dublin 4. Tel. (01) 2697011. Published annually. Editor-in Chief: Tony McNamara.

Afloat Magazine 2 Lower Glenageary Road, Dún Laoghaire, Co. Dublin. Tel. (01) 2846161. Published monthly. Managing Editor: David O'Brien.

Africa - St. Patrick's Missions (1938) St. Patrick's Missionary Society, Kiltegan, Co. Wicklow. Tel. (0508) 73233.

Aisling Magazine, The Eochaill, Inis Mór, Aran Islands, Co. Galway. Tel. (099) 61245. Published quarterly. Editors: Dara Molloy & Tess Harper.

Amnesty International (1974) 48 Fleet Street, Dublin 2. Tel. (01) 6776361. Published twice quarterly. Editor: Morina O'Neill.

AMT Magazine (1979) Computer House, 66 Patrick Street, Dún Laoghaire, Co. Dublin. Tel. (01) 2800424. Published monthly. Managing Editor: John McDonald.

AMT Directory and Diary (1995) Computer House, 66 Patrick Street, Dún Laoghaire, Co. Dublin. Tel. (01) 2800424. Published annually. Editors: John Kennedy.

Angling Holidays in Ireland (1986) Libra House Ltd., 4 St. Kevin's Terrace, Dublin 8. Tel. (01) 4542717. Editor: Cathal Tyrrell.

Arena (1969) Cork Publishing, 19 Rutland Street, Cork. Tel. (021) 313855. Published six times a year. Editor: Monica Igoe.

Aspect (1982) 7 Mount Street Crescent, Dublin 2. Tel. (01) 6760774. Annual Publishers of Aspect Premier 2,000 Irish Companies & The Irish Stock Market Annual. Editor: John O'Neill.

Astronomy & Space (1994) Astronomy Ireland, P.O. Box 2888, Dublin 1. Tel. (01) 4598883. Published monthly.

AudIT (1980) Cork Publishing, 19 Rutland Street, Cork. Tel. (021) 313855. Published six times a year. Editor: Ken Ebbage.

Bakery World Jemma Publications Ltd., Marino House, 52 Glasthule Road, Sandycove, Co. Dublin. Tel. (01) 2800000. Published every two months. Editor: Natasha Swords.

Béaloideas Department of Irish Folklore, University College Dublin, Dublin 4. Published annually. Editor: Séamas Ó Catháin.

Big Issues Magazine, The Head Office, 110 Amiens Street, Dublin 1. Tel. (01) 8553969. Directors: Niall Skelly, Ronan Skelly, Ger Egan.

Blas Aniar (1991) Graduate Liaison Office, University College Galway, Co. Galway. Tel. (091) 750339. Editor: Kathleen O'Connell.

Blueprint Home Plans Oisín Publications, 4 Iona Drive, Dublin 9. Tel. (01) 8305236. Published annually. Editor: Liam Ó hOisín.

Books Ireland (1976) 11 Newgrove

Avenue, Dublin 4. Tel. (01) 2692185. Published nine times a year. Features Editor: Shirley Kelly.

Bord Altranais News, An 31-32 Fitzwilliam Square, Dublin 2. Tel. (01) 6760226. Published quarterly. Editor: Eugene Donoghue.

Bulletin (1856) Society of St. Vincent de Paul, 8 New Cabra Road, Dublin 7. Tel. (01) 8384164 / 7. Published quarterly. Editor: Tom McSweeney.

Business and Exporting (1994) Jude Publications Ltd., Tara House, Tara Street, Dublin 2. Tel. (01) 6713500. Published monthly. Editor: Neil Whoriskey.

Business and Finance (1964) Belenos Publications, 50 Fitzwilliam Square, Dublin 2. Tel. (01) 6764587. Published weekly. Editor: Dan White.

Business Contact (1988) Dyflin Publications Ltd., 58 North Great Charles Street, Dublin 1. Tel. (01) 8550477. Published monthly. Editor: Andrew McLindon.

Business Ulster Ulster Journals Ltd., 39 Boucher Road, Belfast. Tel. (01232) 681371. Published monthly. Editor: Patricia Rainey.

Cara Smurfit Publications, 126 Lr. Baggot Street, Dublin 2. Tel. (01) 6623158. Published twice monthly. Editor: Vincent DeVeau.

Catering and Licensing Review (1975) Greer Publications, 151 University Street, Belfast BT7 1HR. Tel. (01232) 231634. Published monthly. Editor: Kathy Jensen.

Catholic Standard 55 Lower Gardiner Street, Dublin 1. Tel. (01) 8555619. Published weekly. Acting Editor: Harry Cohen.

Celtic Journey MAC Publishing

Ltd., Taney Hall, Eglinton Terrace, Dundrum, Dublin 14. Tel. (01) 2960000. Published annually. Managing Editor: Rosemary Delaney.

Certified Accountant (1908) Cork Publishing, 19 Rutland Street, Cork. Tel. (021) 313855. Published monthly. Editor: Brian O'Kane.

Checkout Magazine (1966) Checkout Publications Ltd., 22 Crofton Road, Dún Laoghaire, Co. Dublin. Tel. (01) 2808415. Published monthly. Editor: Mary Brophy.

Church of Ireland Gazette Church of Ireland Publishing Company, 36 Bachelor's Walk, Lisburn, Co. Antrim. Tel. (01846) 675743. Published weekly. Editor: Rev. Canon C. W. M. Cooper.

CIF Blue Pages Cedar Media and Communications Ltd., 12 Upper Mount Street, Dublin 2. Tel. (01) 6619322. Managing Editor: Jim Sherlock.

CIF Directory and Diary (1975) Cedar Media and Communications Ltd., 12 Upper Mount Street, Dublin 2. Tel. (01) 6619322. Published annually.

Circa Art Magazine 17A Ormeau Avenue, Belfast. Tel. (01232) 220375. 58 Fitzwilliam Square, Dublin 2. Tel. (01) 6765035. Published quarterly. Editor: Tanya Kiang.

CIS Report Newmarket Information (Publications) Ltd., Unit 3, Argyle Square, Morehampton Road, Donnybrook, Dublin 4. Tel. (01) 6689494. Published weekly. Managing Editor: Karl Glynn-Finnegan.

Clár na nÓg National Youth Council of Ireland, 3 Montague Street, Dublin 2. Tel. (01) 4784122. Published monthly.

Cois Coiribe (1981) Graduate Liaison Office, University College, Galway. Tel. (091) 750339. Published annually, distributed free. Editor: Kathleen O'Connell.

Comhar (1942) 5 Rae Mhuirfean, Dublin 2. Tel. (01) 6785443; Fax. (01) 6785443. Published monthly. Editor: Vivian Uíbh Eachach.

Commercial Law Practitioner (1994) Brehon House, 4 Upper Ormond Quay, Dublin 7. Tel. (01) 8730101. Published monthly. Editor: Thomas B. Courtney.

Communications Today CPG Group Publication, Computer House, 66 Patrick Street, Dun Laoghaire, Co. Dublin. Tel. (01) 2800424. Editor: Paul Golden.

Communications Worker (1989) Communications Workers' Union, 575 North Circular Road, Dublin 1. Tel. (01) 8366388. Published twice monthly. Editor: David T. Begg.

ComputerScope (1985) Prospect House, 1 Prospect Road, Glasnevin, Dublin 9. Tel. (01) 8303455. Published ten times a year, distributed free. Editor: David D'Arcy.

Constabulary Gazette Ulster Journals Ltd., 39 Boucher Road, Belfast. Tel. (01232) 681371. Published monthly. Editor: Martin Williams.

Construction Tara Publishing Co. Ltd., Poolbeg House, 1-2 Poolbeg Street, Dublin 2. Tel. (01) 6719244. Published monthly. Managing Director: Fergus Farrell.

Construction and Property News 175 North Strand Road, Dublin 1. Tel. (01) 8556265. Published fortnightly. Editor: Tom Conlon.

Consultant, The Jude Publications Ltd., Tara House, Tara Street, Dublin 2. Tel. (01) 6713500. Published monthly.

Consumer Choice Consumers' Association Of Ireland, 45 Upper Mount Street, Dublin 2. Tel. (01) 6686836. Published monthly. Editor: Kieran Doherty.

Cosantóir, An (1940) Department of Defence, Parkgate Street, Dublin 8. Tel. (01) 8042690. Published ten times a year. Editor: Terry McLaughlin.

CPA Journal of Accountancy The Institute of Certified Public Accountants in Ireland, 9 Ely Place, Dublin 2. Tel. (01) 6767353. Published quarterly. Editor: Deirdre McDonnell.

Cuba Today 15 Merrion Square, Dublin 2. Tel. (01) 6761213 / 8436448. Published six times a year, plus updates. Editor: Joyce Williams.

Cyphers 3 Selskar Terrace, Ranelagh, Dublin 6. Tel. (01) 4978866. Published two/three times a year. Editors: Leland Bardwell, Pearse Hutchinson, Eiléan Ní Chuilleanáin, Macdara Woods.

Decision 19 Fitzwilliam Place, Dublin 2. Tel. (01) 6623039. Published six times a year. Editor: Frank Dillon.

Directory and Diary of the Association of Consulting Engineers of Ireland, The Oisín Publications, 4 Iona Drive, Dublin 9. Tel. (01) 8305236. Published annually. Editor: Anne Potter.

Doctor Desk Book (1962) M.P. House, 49 Wainsfort Park, Terenure, Dublin 6W. Tel. (01) 4924034. Editor: Troy Gogan.

Doctrine and Life Dominican Publications, 42 Parnell Square, Dublin 1. Tel. (01) 8721611. Published monthly. Editor: Bernard Treacy.

Dublin Corporation Yearbook and Diary Oisín Publications, 4 Iona Drive, Dublin 9. Tel. (01) 8305236. Published annually.

Dublin Historical Record (1934) Old Dublin Society, City Assembly House, 58 South William Street, Dublin 2. Published biannually. Honorary Editor: Robin Simmons.

Dublin Port & Docks Yearbook Tara Publishing Co. Ltd., Poolbeg House, 1-2 Poolbeg Street, Dublin 2. Tel. (01) 6719244. Published annually. Managing Director: Fergus Farrell.

Dublin's Evening Classes Guidebook Oisín Publications, 4 Iona Drive, Dublin 9. Tel. (01) 8305236. Published annually. Editor: Liam Ó Oisín.

Economic and Social Review, The (1969) Economic & Social Studies, 4 Burlington Road, Dublin 4. Tel. (01) 6671525. Published quarterly. Editors: G. Boyle and Dr. Hilary Tovey.

Economic Series Government Supplies Agency, 4-5 Harcourt Road, Dublin 2. Tel. (01) 6613111. Published monthly.

Education Magazine Tara Publishing Co. Ltd., Poolbeg House, 1-2 Poolbeg Street, Dublin 2. Tel. (01) 6719244. Published monthly.

Education Directory / Diary Tara Publishing Co. Ltd., Poolbeg House, 1-2 Poolbeg Street, Dublin 2. Tel. (01) 6719244. Published annually.

Education Today 35 Parnell Square, Dublin 1. Tel. (01) 8722533. Published three times a year. Editor: Sinead Shannon.

Éigse: A Journal of Irish Studies National University of Ireland, 49 Merrion Square, Dublin 2. Editor: Professor Pádraig A. Breatnach.

Employment Law Reports (1990) Brehon House, 4 Upper Ormond Quay, Dublin 7. Tel. (01) 8730101. Published quarterly. Editor: Eilis Barry.

Engineers Journal Dyflin Publications, 58 North Great

Charles Street, Dublin 1. Tel. (01) 8550477. Published monthly. Editor: Hugh Kane.

Environmental Health Officers Association Yearbook Tara Publishing Co. Ltd., Poolbeg House, 1-2 Poolbeg Street, Dublin 2. Tel. (01) 6719244. Published annually.

Environmental Management Ireland Nestron Ltd., 68 Middle Abbey Street, Dublin 1. Tel. (01) 8720734. Published twice monthly, distributed free. Editor: Annette O'Riordan.

Fáilte / Welcome MAC Publishing Ltd., Taney Hall, Eglinton Terrace, Dundrum, Dublin 14. Tel. (01) 2960000. Published annually. Managing Editor: Rosemary Delaney.

Faith Today Dominican Publications, 42 Parnell Square, Dublin 1. Tel. (01) 8721611. Editor: Bernard Treacy.

Far East, The St. Columban's, Navan, Co. Meath. Tel. (046) 21525. Published nine times a year. Editor: Rev. Alo Connaughton.

Farmhouse Holidays in Ireland (1970) Head Office, 2 Michael Street, Limerick. Tel. (061) 400700. Published annually.

Farm Week 14 Church Street, Portadown, Craigavon, Co. Armagh BT62 3LN. Tel. (01762) 339421. Published weekly. Editor: Hal Crowe.

Feasta (1948) 43 Na Cluainte, Tralee, Co. Kerry. Published monthly. Editor: Pádraig Mac Fhearghusa.

Finance Magazine 162 Pembroke Road, Ballsbridge, Dublin 4. Tel. (01) 6606222. Published monthly.

Finance Dublin (1996) Fintel Ltd., 162 Pembroke Road, Ballsbridge, Dublin 4. Tel. (01) 6606222. Published monthly.

Focus on Ireland in the Wider World c/o Comhlámh, 10 Upper Camden Street, Dublin 2. Tel. (01) 4783490. Published three times a year.

Fold, The (1953) Diocesan Communications Office, St. Maries of the Isle, Cork. Tel. (021) 312330. Published ten times a year. Editor: Fr. Tom Hayes.

Food Ireland Tara Publishing Co. Ltd., Poolbeg House, 1-2 Poolbeg Street, Dublin 2. Tel. (01) 6719244. Published monthly.

Fortnight (1970) 7 Lower Crescent, Belfast BT7 1NR. Tel. (01232) 232353 / 311337. Published eleven times a year. Editor: John O'Farrell.

Forum MedMedia Ltd., 99 Upper George's Street, Dun Laoghaire, Co. Dublin. Tel. (01) 2803967. Published monthly. Editor: Geraldine Meagan.

Friendly Word, The Cabragh Cottage, 362 Upper Ballynahinch Road, Lisburn, BT27 6XL. Tel. (01846) 638232. Published twice monthly. Editor: Rachel Kirk-Smith.

Furrow, The The Furrow Trust, St. Patrick's College, Maynooth, Co. Kildare. Tel. (01) 6286215. Published monthly. Editor: Fr. Ronan Drury.

Futura Futura Communications, 5 Main Street, Blackrock, Co. Dublin. Tel. (01) 2836782. Published monthly. Editor: June Considine.

Gaelic Sport (1958) 139A Lower Drumcondra Road, Dublin 9. Tel. (01) 8374311. Published monthly. Editor: T. McQuaid.

Gaelic World 10 Burgh Quay, Dublin 2; Tel. (01) 6798655. Published monthly. Editor: Mick Dunne.

Gaelsport Magazine 6-7 Camden Place, Dublin 2. Tel. (01) 4784322. Published monthly. Editor: Owen McCann.

GALAPS Directory Bracetown Business Park, Clonee, Co. Meath. Tel. (01) 8014000. Published annually.

Galway Diary & Yearbook Public Relations Associates, Galway. Tel. (091) 770522. Published annually.

Garda News 6th Floor, Phibsboro Tower, Dublin 7.Tel. (01) 8303166. Published monthly. Editor: Austin Kenny.

Garda Review (1923) Floor 5, Phibsboro Tower, Dublin 7. Tel. (01) 8303533. Published monthly. Editor: Andy Needham.

Gay Community News (1988) The Hirschfeld Centre, 10 Fownes Street Upper, Dublin 2 Tel. (01) 6719076 / 6710939. Published monthly. Editor: Cathal Kelly.

Genuine Irish Old Moore's Almanac, The MAC Publishing, Taney Hall, Eglinton Terrace, Dundrum, Dublin 14. Tel. (01) 2960000. Published annually.

Golden Pages Golden Pages Ltd., St. Martin's House, Waterloo Road, Dublin 4. Tel. (01) 6608488. 26-27 South Mall, Cork. Tel. (021) 277760. Published annually.

Greats of Gaelic Games Book Costar Associates Ltd., 10 Burgh Quay, Dublin 2. Tel. (01) 6798655. Published every three years.

Guideline 14 Cherry Drive, Castleknock, Dublin 15. Tel. (01)

8204501. St. Mark's Community School, Springfield, Dublin 24. Tel. (01) 4519399. Published five times a year. Editors: Loretta Jennings & Rita Wall.

Health and Safety Jude Publications Ltd., Tara House, Tara Street, Dublin 2. Tel. (01) 6713500. Published monthly.

Health Services News (1989) Vergemount Hall, Clonskeagh, Dublin 6. Tel. (01) 2697011. Published quarterly. Editor: Tim O'Sullivan.

History Ireland P.O. Box 695, James' Street Post Office, Dublin 8. Tel. (01) 4535730. Published quarterly. Editors: Hiram Morgan & Tommy Graham.

Hot Press 13 Trinity Street, Dublin 2. Tel. (01) 6795077. Published fortnightly. Editor: Niall Stokes.

Hotel and Catering Review (1974) Jemma Publications Ltd., Marino House, 52 Glasthule Road, Sandycove, Co. Dublin. Tel. (01) 2800000. Published monthly. Editor: Frank Corr.

IBAR - Irish Business and Administration Research (1979) Department of Business Administration, University College Dublin. Published annually. Editors: Aidan Kelly, UCD; Terry Cradden, University of Ulster; Patrick Flood, University of Limerick.

Image (1975) Image Publications Ltd., 22 Crofton Road, Dún Laoghaire, Co. Dublin; Tel. (01) 2808415. Published monthly. Editor: Jane McDonnell.

IMPACT News Printwell Coop, 10-11 North Richmond Street, Dublin 1. Tel. (01) 8550873. Editor: Bernard Harbor.

In Dublin (1976) 6-7 Camden Place, Dublin 2. Tel. (01) 4784322. Published fortnightly. Editor: John Ryan.

Industrial Relations News Report 121-123 Ranelagh, Dublin 6. Tel. (01) 4972711. Published weekly. Editor: Brian Sheehan.

Industry and Commerce Jude Publications, Tara House, Tara Street, Dublin 2. Tel. (01) 6713500. Published monthly. Editor: Neil Whoriskey.

Inside Business (1991) Dyflin Publications Ltd., 58 North Great Charles Street, Dublin 1. Tel. (01) 8550477. Published twice monthly. Editor: Claire Reilly.

Inside Ireland (1978) P.O. Box

1886, Dublin 16. Tel. (01) 4931906. Published quarterly. Managing Editor: Brenda Weir.

Insight Magazine Harmony Publications Ltd., Roslyn Park, Sandymount, Dublin 4. Tel. (01) 2057200. Published quarterly. Managing Editor: Stephen Farrelly.

Intercom (1970) Veritas House, 7-8 Lower Abbey Street, Dublin 1. Tel. (01) 8788177. Published monthly. Editor: K.H. Donlon.

IPA Journal Jude Publications Ltd., Tara House, Tara Street, Dublin 2. Tel. (01) 6713500. Published monthly. Editor: Brendan K. Colvert.

IPU Review (1976) Irish Pharmaceutical Union, Butterfield House, Butterfield Avenue, Dublin 14. Tel. (01) 4931801. Published monthly. Editor: David Butler.

Ireland Series, The Language & Publishing Partnership, 65 Abberley, Shanganagh Road, Killiney, Co. Dublin. Tel. (01) 2827866. Published annually.

Ireland of the Welcomes (1952) Bord Fáilte, Baggot Street, Dublin 2. Tel. (01) 6024000. Published every two months. Editor: Letitia Bollard.

Ireland's Eye The Roundabout, 6 Dominick Street, Mullingar, Co. Westmeath. Tel. (044) 48868. Published monthly.

Ireland's Own (1902) The People Newspaper Ltd., North Main Street, Wexford. Tel. (053) 22155. Editors: Austin Channing & Margaret Galvin.

Iris Oifigiúil Government Supplies Agency, 4-5 Harcourt Road, Dublin 2. Tel. (01) 6613111. Published twice weekly.

Irish Architect P.M.L., 9 Sandyford Office Park, Foxrock, Dublin 18. Tel. (01) 2958115. Published ten times a year. Editor: Tomás O'Beirne.

Irish Banking Review, The Irish Bankers' Federation, Nassau House, Nassau Street, Dublin 2. Tel. (01) 6715299. Published quarterly. Acting Editor: Felix O'Regan.

Irish Birds (1977) Irish Wildbird Conservancy, Ruttledge House, 8 Longford Place, Monkstown, Co. Dublin. Tel. (01) 2804322. Published annually. Editor: Hugh Brazier.

Irish Building Services News Pressline Ltd., Carraig Court, George's Avenue, Blackrock, Co. Dublin. Tel. (01) 2885001. Published ten times a year. Editor: Pat Lehane.

Irish Catholic, The The Irish Catholic Ltd., 55 Lower Gardiner Street, Dublin 1. Tel. (01) 8555619.

Published weekly. Editor: David Quinn.

Irish Competition Law Reports The Irish Law Publisher, P.O. Box 1, Delgany, Co. Wicklow. Tel. (088) 557584. Published monthly. Editor: Peter Byrne.

Irish Computer (1977) CPG Group Publication, Computer House, 66 Patrick Street, Dún Laoghaire, Co. Dublin. Tel. (01) 2800424. Published monthly. Editor: Declan McColgan.

Irish Computer Directory and Diary (1978) CPG Group Publication, Computer House, 66 Patrick Street, Dún Laoghaire, Co. Dublin. Tel. (01) 2800424. Published annually. Editor: Donald McDonald.

Irish Criminal Law Journal (1991) Brehon House, 4 Upper Ormond Quay, Dublin 7. Tel. (01) 8730101. Published twice yearly. Editor: Shane Murphy.

Irish Current Law Monthly Digest (1995) Brehon House, 4 Upper Ormond Quay, Dublin 7. Tel. (01) 8730101. Published monthly.

Irish Dental Association, Journal of the (1946) 10 Richview Office Park, Clonskeagh Road, Dublin 14. Tel. (01) 2830496. Published quarterly. Editor: Dr. Frank Quinn.

Irish Doctor Medical Press, Tara House, Tara Street, Dublin 2. Tel. (01) 6713500. Published monthly. Editor: Dr. Paul Carson.

Irish Economic and Social History (1974) c/o Dublin Diocesan Library, Clonliffe Road, Dublin 3. Tel. (01) 8741680. Published annually. Editor: Neal Garnham.

Irish Educational Studies Educational Studies Association of Ireland, Education Department, University College Cork. Published annually. Editor: Diarmuid Leonard.

Irish Electrical Review Sky Publishing Ltd., 5 Main Street, Blackrock, Co. Dublin. Tel. (01) 2836755. Published monthly.

Irish Emigrant, The (1987) The Irish Emigrant Ltd., Cathedral Buildings, Middle Street, Galway. Tel. (091) 569158. Editor: Liam Ferrie.

Irish Exporter Directory and Buyers' Guide Jude Publications Ltd., Tara House, Tara Street, Dublin 2. Tel. (01) 6713500. Published annually.

Irish Family Law Reports The Irish Law Publisher, PO Box 1, Delgany, Co. Wicklow. Tel. (088) 557584. Published ten times a year. Editor:

Peter Byrne.

Irish Farmers' Journal (1948) Irish Farm Centre, Bluebell, Dublin 12. Tel. (01) 4501166. Published weekly. Editor: Matt Dempsey.

Irish Farmers Monthly 31 Deansgrange Road, Blackrock, Co. Dublin. Tel. (01) 2893305. Published monthly. Editor: Brian Gilsenan.

Irish Farmers Yearbook and Diary, The Bank House Centre, 331 South Circular Road, Dublin 8. Tel. (01) 4534011. Published annually.

Irish Farmers Yearbook & Diary Accounts Book Mail Order / Eason Distribution. Tel. (01) 4534011. Published annually.

Irish Field, The Irish Times Ltd., PO Box 74, 11-15 D'Olier Street, Dublin 2. Tel. (01) 6792022. Published weekly. Editor: Vincent Lamb.

Irish Food 31 Deansgrange Road, Blackrock, Co. Dublin. Tel. (01) 2893305. Published weekly. Editor: Brian Gilsenan.

Irish Forestry (1942) Society of Irish Foresters, 2 Lower Kilmacud Road, Stillorgan, Co. Dublin. Tel. (01) 2781874. Published biannually. Editor: Kevin D. Collins.

Irish Geography (1944) Geographical Society of Ireland, Dept. of Geography, St. Patrick's College, Maynooth, Co. Kildare. Tel. (01) 7083938. Published biannually. Editor: Joe Brady.

Irish Hardware Magazine Jemma Publications, Marino House, 52 Glasthule Road, Sandycove, Co. Dublin. Tel. (01) 2800000. Published monthly. Editor: Bridget McAuliffe.

Irish Historical Studies (1938) Dept. of Modern History, Trinity College, Dublin 2. Tel. (01) 6081020. Published biannually. Editors: Dr. Ciaran Brady & Dr. Keith Jeffery.

Irish Homes Magazine 48 North Great Georges Street, Dublin 1. Tel. (01) 8780444. Published twice monthly. Editor: Bernice Brindley.

Irish Journal of Education (1967) Educational Research Centre, St. Patrick's College, Dublin 9. Tel. (01) 8373789. Published annually. Editor: Thomas Kellaghan.

Irish Journal of European Law (1991) Brehon House, 4 Upper Ormond Quay, Dublin 7. Tel. (01) 8730101. Published twice a year. Editors: James O'Reilly & Anthony Collins.

Irish Journal of Medical Science (1832) Royal Academy of Medicine in Ireland, 6 Kildare Street, Dublin 2. Tel. (01) 6767650. Published quarterly. Editor: Thomas F. Gorey.

Irish Journal of Psychology, The (1971) The Psychological Society of Ireland, 13 Adelaide Road, Dublin 2. Tel. (01) 4783916. Published quarterly. Editors: Professor Ken Brown & Dr. Carol McGuinness.

Irish Jurist (1966) Jurist Publishing Co., University College Dublin, Dublin 4. Published annually. Editor: Dr. Finbarr McAuley.

Irish Law Log Weekly (1995) Brehon House, 4 Upper Ormond Quay, Dublin 7. Tel. (01) 8730101. Published weekly. Editors: Sinéad Ní Chúlacháin & Nevil Lloyd Blood.

Irish Law Reports Monthly (1981) Brehon House, 4 Upper Ormond Quay, Dublin 7. Tel. (01) 8730101. Published 14 times a year. Editor: Hilary Delany.

Irish Law Times and Solicitors' Journal (1983) Brehon House, 4 Upper Ormond Quay, Dublin 7. Tel. (01) 8730101. Published monthly. Editor: Raymond Byrne.

Irish Laws (Statutes) The Irish Law Publisher, P.O. Box 1, Delgany, Co. Wicklow. Tel. (088) 557584. Published ten times a year. Editor: Peter Byrne.

Irish Marketing Journal Unit T31, Stillorgan Industrial Park, Stillorgan, Co. Dublin. Tel. (01) 2950088. Published monthly. Editor: Norman Barry.

Irish Medical Directory Medical Information Systems, P.O. Box 5049, Dublin 16. Tel. (01) 4936853. Published annually. Editor: Dr. Maurice Guéret.

Irish Medical Journal 10 Fitzwilliam Place, Dublin 2. Tel. (01) 6767273. Published twice monthly. Editor: Dr. John Murphy.

Irish Medical News MAC Publishing, Taney Hall, Eglinton Terrace, Dundrum, Dublin 14. Tel. (01) 2960000. Published weekly. Editor: Niall Hunter.

Irish Medical Times (1967) Medical Publications (Ireland) Ltd., 15 Harcourt Street, Dublin 2. Tel. (01) 4757461. Editor: Dr. John O'Connell.

Irish Motor Industry IFP Ltd., 31 Deansgrange Road, Blackrock, Co. Dublin. Tel. (01) 2893305. Published monthly. Editor: Paul O'Grady.

Irish Pharmacy Journal (1923) Kenlis Publication Ltd., 37 Northumberland Road, Dublin 4. Tel. (01) 6600551. Published monthly.

Editor: Val Harte.

Irish Planning and Environmental Law Journal (1994) Brehon House, 4 Upper Ormond Quay, Dublin 7. Tel. (01) 8730101. Published quarterly. Editor: Eamon Galligan.

Irish Political Studies (1986) PSAI Press, College of Humanities, University of Limerick, Limerick. Published annually. Editors: Vincent Geoghegan & Richard English.

Irish Post (1970) Irish Post Ltd., Uxbridge House, 464 Uxbridge Road, Hayes, Middlesex UB4 0SP. Tel. (0181) 5610059. Editor: Donal Mooney.

Irish Printer Jemma Publications Ltd., Marino House, 52 Glasthule Road, Sandycove, Co. Dublin. Tel. (01) 2800000. Published monthly. Editor: Frank Corr.

Irish Psychologist, The (1974) The Psychology Society of Ireland, 13 Adelaide Road, Dublin 2. Tel. (01) 8326656. Published monthly. Editor: Chris Morris.

Irish Racing Calendar (1970) The Stewards of the Turf Club, The Curragh, Co. Kildare. Tel. (045) 441599. Published weekly.

Irish Racingform Race Ratings Irish Racingform Ltd., 10 Merrion Square, Dublin 2. Tel. (01) 6766495.

Irish Review, The (1986) The Institute of Irish Studies, Queen's University, Belfast. Tel. (01232) 439238. Editors: Kevin Barry, Tom Dunne, Edna Longley, Clare O'Halloran, Brian Walker & Caoimhín Mac Giolla Léith.

Irish Skipper, The (1964) MAC Publishing Ltd., Taney Hall, Eglinton Terrace, Dundrum, Dublin 14. Tel. (01) 2960000. Published monthly. Managing Editor: Fiacc O'Brolchain.

Irish Social Worker 114-116 Pearse Street, Dublin 2. Tel. (01) 6774838. Published quarterly. Editor: Loretto Reilly.

Irish Sword, The (1949) c/o Newman House, 86 St. Stephen's Green, Dublin 2. Published biannually. Editor: Dr. Harman Murtagh.

Irish Theological Quarterly (1906) St. Patrick's College, Maynooth, Co. Kildare. Tel. (01) 6285222. Published quarterly. Editors: Patrick McGoldrick & Patrick Hannon.

Irish Travel Trade News 9 Western Parkway Business Centre, Ballymount Road, Dublin 12. Tel. (01) 4502422. Published monthly. Editor: Michael Flood.

Irish University Review Room

K203, University College, Belfield, Dublin 4. Published twice a year. Editor: Christopher Murray.

Irish Veterinary Journal 31 Deansgrange Road, Blackrock, Co. Dublin. Tel. (01) 2893305. Editor: Gemma Tuffy.

Irish YouthWork Scene National Youth Federation, 20 Lower Dominick Street, Dublin 1. Tel. (01) 8729933. Published quarterly. Editor: Louise Hurley.

Journal, The E.E.T.P.U. Section, 5 Whitefriars, Aungier Street, Dublin 2. Tel. (01) 4784141. Published twice monthly. Editor: James Wims.

Journal of Industrial and Commercial Property Government Supplies Agency, 4-5 Harcourt Road, Dublin 2. Tel. (01) 6613111. Published fortnightly.

Krino P.O. Box 65, Dún Laoghaire, Co. Dublin. Published biannually. Editor: Gerald Dawe & Jonathan Williams.

LAMA Yearbook / Diary Nestron Ltd., 68 Middle Abbey Street, Dublin 1. Tel. (01) 8720734. Published annually. Editor: Annette O'Riordan.

LAN - Local Authority News Nestron Ltd., 68 Middle Abbey Street, Dublin 1. Tel. (01) 8720734. Published monthly. Editor: Annette O'Riordan.

Law Society Gazette Law Society of Ireland, Blackhall Place, Dublin 7. Tel. (01) 6710711. Published ten times a year. Editor: Conal O'Boyle.

Leabharlann, An / The Irish Library Cumberland House, Fenian Street, Dublin 2. Editors: Fionnuala Hanrahan & Kevin Quinn.

Licensed and Catering News (1994) Ulster Magazines Ltd., Crescent House, 58 Rugby Road, Belfast BT7 1PT. Tel. (01232) 230425. Published monthly. Publisher: Conor Kelly.

Licensed Vintners Association Directory and Diary Tara Publishing Co. Ltd., Poolbeg House, 1-2 Poolbeg Street, Dublin 2. Tel. (01) 6719244. Published annually.

Licensing World (1942) Marino House, 52 Glasthule Road, Sandycove, Co. Dublin. Tel. (01) 2800000. Published monthly. Editor: Pat Nolan.

Lifeboats Ireland (1947) 15 Windsor Terrace, Dún Laoghaire, Co. Dublin. Tel. (01) 2845050. Published annually. Editor: Dermot Desmond.

Linen Hall Review c/o Linen Hall

Library, 17 Donegall Square North, Belfast BT1 5GD. Tel. (01232) 321707. Published three times a year. Editors: John Gray & Paul Campbell.

Local Authority Times (1986) 57-61 Lansdowne Road, Dublin 4. Tel. (01) 6686233. Published quarterly. Editor: Ellen MacCafferty.

Magill 15 Lower Pembroke Street, Dublin 2. Tel: 01 6769832. Published monthly. Editor: Vincent Browne.

Management (1954) Jemma Publications Ltd., Marino House, 52 Glasthule Road, Sandycove, Co. Dublin. Tel. (01) 2800000. Published monthly. Editor: Sandra O'Connell.

MAPS (Marketing, Advertising, Promotions and Sponsorship) MAC Publishing Ltd., Taney Hall, Eglinton Terrace, Dundrum, Dublin 14. Tel. (01) 2960000. Published annually. Managing Editor: Rosemary Delaney.

Marketing 1 Albert Park, Sandycove, Co. Dublin. Tel. (01) 2807735. Published monthly. Editor: Michael Cullen.

Medical Missionaries of Mary Magazines MMM Communications, Rosemount, Booterstown, Blackrock, Co. Dublin. Tel. (01) 2887180. Published quarterly. 15,000; Editor: Sr. Isabelle Smyth.

Medico-Legal Journal of Ireland (1995) Brehon House, 4 Upper Ormond Quay, Dublin 7. Tel. (01) 8730101. Published three times a year. Editor: Dr. Denis Cusack.

Milltown Studies (1978) Milltown Institute of Theology and Philosophy, Milltown Park, Dublin 6. Tel. (01) 2698802. Published twice a year. Editor: Gervase Corcoran.

MIMS Ireland (1960) Medical Publications Ltd., 15 Harcourt Street, Dublin 2. Tel. (01) 4757461. Editor: Andrea Letoha.

Modern Woman Meath Chronicle Group of Publications, Market Square, Navan, Co. Meath. Tel. (046) 21442. Published monthly. Supplement with Meath Chronicle. Editor: Margot Davis.

Motoring Life (1946) Cyndale Enterprises Ltd., 48 North Great Georges Street, Dublin 1. Tel. (01) 8780444. Published monthly. Editor: Fergal K. Herbert.

New Music News The Contemporary Music Centre, 95 Lower Baggot Street, Dublin 2. Tel. (01) 6612105. Published three times a year. Editor: Eve O'Kelly.

Newmarket Business Report Newmarket Information Ltd., Unit 3, Argyle Square, Morehampton Road, Donnybrook, Dublin 4. Tel. (01) 6689494. Published fortnightly. Editor: Karl Glynn-Finnegan.

NODE News The NODE Network, 10 Upper Camden Street, Dublin 2; Tel. (01) 4751998. Published five times a year.

North County Leader 23-25 Main Street, Swords, Co. Dublin. Tel. (01) 8400200.

Northern Ireland Legal Quarterly (1964) S.L.S. Legal Publications (NI), Faculty of Law, Queen's University, Belfast BT7 1NN. Tel. (01232) 245133, ext. 3597. Published quarterly. Editor: Dr. Peter Ingram.

Oblate Missionary Record (1891) Oblate Fathers, Inchicore, Dublin 8. Tel. (01) 4542417. Published five times a year. Editor: Fr. Tom McCabe.

Off Licence Jemma Publications Ltd., Marino House, 52 Glasthule Road, Sandycove, Co. Dublin. Tel. (01) 2800000. Published twice a month. Editor: Natasha Swords.

Oideas An Roinn Oideachais, Sráid Mhaoilbhríde, Dublin 1. Tel. (01) 8734700, ext. 2767. Editor: E. Mac Aonghusa.

Outlook Holy Ghost Missions, Booterstown Avenue, Co. Dublin. Tel. (01) 2881789. Published twice a month. Editor: Rev. Brian Gogan.

PC Live! (1994) ComputerScope Ltd., Prospect House, 1 Prospect Road, Glasnevin, Dublin 9. Tel. (01) 8303455. Published twice a month. Editor: John Collins.

Phoblacht, An / Republican News 58 Parnell Square, Dublin 1. Tel. (01) 8733611 / 8733839. 535 Falls Road, Belfast, BT11 9AA. Tel. (01232) 600279. Published weekly. Editor: Brian Campbell.

Phoenix (1983) Penfield Enterprises Ltd., 44 Lower Baggot Street, Dublin 2. Tel. (01) 6611062. Published fortnightly. Editor: Paddy Prendiville.

Pioneer (1948) Pioneer Total Abstinence Association, 27 Upper Sherrard Street, Dublin 1. Tel. (01) 8746464. Published monthly.

Plan-The Business of Building Plan Magazines Ltd., 8-9 Sandyford Office Park, Sandyford, Dublin 18. Tel. (01) 2958115. Published monthly. Editor: Con Power.

Poetry Ireland Review

Bermingham Tower, Upper Yard, Dublin Castle, Dublin 2. Tel. (01) 6714632. Published quarterly. Editor: Liam Ó Muirthile.

Presbyterian Herald (1943) Church House, Fisherwick Place, Belfast BT1 6DW. Tel. (01232) 322284. Published ten times a year. Editor: Rev. Arthur Clarke.

Private Research Ltd. (1992) 7-8 Mount Street Crescent, Dublin 2. Tel. (01) 6760774. Published monthly.

Provincial Farmer Market Square, Navan, Co. Meath. Tel. (046) 21442. Published monthly. Supplement to Meath Chronicle. Editor: Ken Davis.

Public Sector Times Bradán Publishing, 1 Eglinton Road, Bray, Co. Wicklow. Tel. (01) 2869111. Published monthly. Editor: James D. Fitzmaurice.

Public Service Review Public Service Executive Union, 30 Merrion Square, Dublin 2. Tel. (01) 6767271. Published every two months. Editor: Tom McKevitt.

Reality (1935) Redemptorist Publications, 75 Orwell Road, Rathgar, Dublin 6. Tel. (01) 4922488. Published monthly. Editor: Gerard R. Moloney.

Recover (1968) St. Camillus, South Hill Avenue, Blackrock, Co. Dublin. Tel. (01) 2882873. Published quarterly. Editor: Fr. G. Price.

Religious Life Review Dominican Publications, 42 Parnell Square, Dublin 1. Tel. (01) 8731355. Published six times a year. Editor: Austin Flannery.

Retail Grocer Ulster Magazines Ltd., Crescent House, 58 Rugby Road, Belfast BT7 1PT. Tel. (01232) 230425. Published monthly. Editor: Larry Nixon.

Retail News Tara Publishing Co. Ltd., Poolbeg House, 1-2 Poolbeg Street, Dublin 2. Tel. (01) 6719244. Published monthly.

Retail News Directory / Buyer's Guide Tara Publishing Co. Ltd., Poolbeg House, 1-2 Poolbeg Street, Dublin 2. Tel. (01) 6719244. Published annually.

RIAI Yearbook & Directory PML, 9 Sandyford Office Park, Foxrock, Dublin 18. Tel. (01) 2958115. Published annually. Editor: Thomas O'Beirne.

RTÉ Guide (1961) Commercial Enterprises Ltd., R.T.E., Donnybrook, Dublin 4. Tel. (01) 2083111. Published weekly. Editor: Heather Parsons.

Running Your Business Firsthand Publishing Ltd., Landscape House, Landscape Road, Churchtown, Dublin 14. Tel. (01) 2962244. Published twice monthly.

Runway Airports (1970) Aer Rianta cpt., Level 4, Terminal Building, Dublin Airport. Tel. (01) 7044170. Published monthly. Editor: Brian McCabe.

Sacred Heart Messenger, The (1988) Messenger Publications, 37 Lower Leeson Street, Dublin 2. Tel. (01) 6767491 / 6767492. Published monthly. Editor: Brendan Murray.

Salesian Bulletin, The (1939) Salesian House, St. Teresa's Road, Dublin 12. Tel. (01) 4555605. Published quarterly. Editor: Eddie Fitzgerald.

Science Mount Temple School, Malahide Road, Dublin 3. Published three times a year. Editor: Eddie Fitzgerald.

Scripture in Church Dominican Publications, 42 Parnell Square, Dublin 1. Tel. (01) 8721611. Published quarterly. Editor-In-Chief: Martin McNamara.

Search R.E. Resource Centre, Holy Trinity Church, Rathmines, Dublin 6. Tel. (01) 4972821. Published biannually. Editor: Rev. S. R. White.

Seirbhís Phoiblí Dept. of Finance, Lansdowne House, Lansdowne Road, Dublin 4. Tel. (01) 6767571. Published three times a year. Editor: Breda Byrne.

Shelflife (1975) CPG House, Glenageary Office Park, Glenageary, Co. Dublin. Tel. (01) 2847777. Published monthly. Editor: Colette O'Connor.

SMA Magazine - The African Missionary (1914) Society of African Missionaries, Blackrock Road, Cork. Published five times a year. Editor: Fr. Peter McCawille.

Socialist Voice James Connolly House, 43 East Essex Street, Temple Bar, Dublin 2. Tel. (01) 6711943; Fax. (01) 6711943. Published fortnightly.

Specify (1979) Greer Publications, 151 University Street, Belfast, BT7 1HR. Tel. (01232) 231634. Published twice monthly. Editor: Brian Russell.

Sporting Press Davis Road, Clonmel, Co. Tipperary. Tel. (052) 21422 / 21634. Published weekly. Editor: J. L. Desmond.

Sportsworld 48 North Great George's Street, Dublin 1. Tel. (01) 8780444. Published monthly. Editor:

Liam Nolan.

Statistical Bulletin Government Supplies Agency, 4-5 Harcourt Road, Dublin 2. Tel. (01) 6613111. Published quarterly.

Student Yearbook and Career Directory 'Shancroft', O'Hanlon's Lane, Malahide, Co. Dublin. Tel. (01) 8452470. Published annually. Editors: J. Duddy & R. Keane.

Studia Hibernica (1961) St. Patricks College, Dublin 9. Tel. (01) 8376191. Published annually. Editor: L. Mac Mathúna.

Studies 35 Lower Leeson Street, Dublin 2. Tel. (01) 6766785. Published quarterly. Editor: Noel Barber.

Taxi News 48 Summerhill Parade, Dublin 1. Tel. (01) 8555682. Published quarterly.

Technology Ireland Glasnevin, Dublin 9. Tel. (01) 8082287. Published ten times a year. Editors: Tom Kennedy & Mary Mulvihill.

Tillage Farmer, The Athy Road, Carlow. Tel. (0503) 31487. Published six times a year.

Today's Farm (1990) Teagasc, 19 Sandymount Avenue, Dublin 4. Tel. (01) 6688188. Editor: John Keating.

Trade-Links Journal (1979) Libra House, 4 St. Kevin's Terrace, Dublin 8. Tel. (01) 4542717. Published every two months. Editor: Cathal Tyrrell.

Trade Statistics Government Supplies Agency, 4-5 Harcourt Road, Dublin 2. Tel. (01) 6613111. Published monthly.

Tuarascáil Irish National Teachers' Organisation, 35 Parnell Square, Dublin 1. Tel. (01) 8722533. Published ten times a year. Editor: Sinead Shannon.

U Magazine (1979) Smurfit Publications, 126 Lower Baggot Street, Dublin 2. Tel. (01) 6623158. Published monthly. Editor: Annette O'Meara.

Ulster Business (1987) Greer Publications, 151 University Street, Belfast, BT7 1HR. Tel. (01232) 231634. Published monthly. Editor: Gary McDonald.

Ulster Farmer Ann Street, Dungannon, Co. Tyrone. Tel. (01868) 722557. Published weekly. Editor: D. Mallon.

Ulster Grocer (1972) Greer Publications, 151 University Street, Belfast, BT7 1HR. Tel. (01232) 231634. Published monthly. Editor: Brian McCalden.

Ulster Medicine Carrick Publications Ltd., McAvoy Hse., 17A Ormeau Ave., Belfast. Tel. (01693) 61107. Published fortnightly.

Ulster Nation (1990) Third Way Publications Ltd. 29 Glenwood Street, Belfast, BT13 3AJ. Tel. (01232) 233991. Published quarterly. Editor: David Kerr.

Ulster Tatler 39 Boucher Road, Belfast, BT12 6UT. Tel. (01232) 681371. Published monthly. Editor: R. M. Sherry.

Unity Communist Party of Ireland, James Connolly House, 43 East Essex Street, Dublin 2. Tel. (01) 6711943. Published weekly. Editor: James Stewart.

Updata Kompass House, Parnell Court, 1 Granby Row, Parnell Square North, Dublin 1. Tel. (01) 8728800. Published annually.

Visitor MAC Publishing Co. Ltd., Taney Hall, Eglinton Terrace, Dundrum, Dublin 14. Tel. (01) 2960000. Published annually. Editor: Rosemary Delaney.

WHERE Killarney Frank Lewis Public Relations, 6 Bridgewell Lane, Killarney, Co. Kerry. Tel. (064) 31108. Published six times a year.

Wicklow Times North Wicklow Times Ltd., 1 Eglinton Road, Bray, Co. Wicklow. Tel. (01) 2869111. Published fortnightly. Editor: Shay Fitzmaurice.

"Wings" (1974) IWC Birdwatch Ireland, Ruttledge House, 8 Longford Place, Monkstown, Co. Dublin. Tel. (01) 2804322. Published quarterly. Editor: C. Mac Lochlainn.

Woman's Way Smurfit Publications, 126 Lower Baggot Street, Dublin 2. Tel. (01) 6623158. Published weekly. Editor: Celine Naughton.

Women's Clubs Magazine Maxwell Publicity Ltd., M.P. House, 49 Wainsfort Park, Terenure, Dublin 6W. Tel. (01) 4924034. Published quarterly. Editor: June Cooke.

Word, The (1953) Divine Word Missionaries, Donamon, Roscommon. Tel. (0903) 62608. Published monthly. Editor: Rev. Thomas Cahill.

Xchange (1995) Telecom Éireann, St. Stephen's Green West, Dublin 2. Tel. (01) 6714444. Published ten times a year.

NEWSPAPER ADVERTISING RATES

| Newspaper | Colour | | Monochrome | |
	Full Page £	Half Page £	Full Page £	Half Page £
Sunday Independent	21,000	10,500	17,000	8,500
The Irish independent	18,000	9,300	14,800	7,400
The Irish Times	16,030	8,565	14,580	7,400
Sunday World (National)	13,100	6,550	8,750	4,375
Sunday Business Post	8,160	4,260	6,120	3,190
The Star	6,600	3,300	4,950	2,475
Evening Herald	6,250	3,150	5,700	2,850
Sunday World (N. Ireland)	3,000	1,500	1,700	850
Belfast Telegraph	11,037	5,723	8,176	4,088

* Rates from 2nd quarter of 1997. All above prices are subject to VAT @ 21%. Sunday World & Belfast Telegraph (N. Ire) @ 17.5%.

BROADCASTING MEDIA

NATIONAL & LOCAL RADIO LISTENERSHIP RATINGS, R.O.I. AND N.I., 1996-1997*

Station	Listenership	Peak Listenership Time
National:		
Atlantic 252 †	230,000	-
BBC Radio Ulster / Foyle		-
Classic FM †	79,000	-
Radio Ireland	7,646	14.00-17.00 Reach
RTÉ Radio 1	217,125	08.00-09.15 Reach
Talk Radio †	38,000	-
Virgin AM †	87,000	-
2FM	148,000	09.00-12.00 Reach
Local:		
City Beat †	290,000	-
CKR (Carlow-Kildare)	9,313	09.00-11.00 Reach
Clare FM	9,042	09.00-14.00 Reach
Cool FM †	290,000	-
Downtown Radio †	325,000	-
East Coast Radio (Wicklow)	6,667	11.00-14.00 Reach
FM104 (Dublin)	29,083	-
FM3	-	-
Galway Bay FM	10,500	11.00-14.00 Reach
Highland Radio (Donegal)	13,458	11.00-14.00 Reach
Limerick 95 FM	11,729	09.00-11.00 Reach
LMFM (Louth-Meath)	10,313	09.00-11.00 Reach
Mid West Radio (Mayo)	11,104	09.00-11.00 Reach
North West Radio FM (Sligo)	8,396	09.00-11.00 Reach
Q102 FM †	47,000	-
Radio Kerry	12,021	09.00-11.00 Reach
Radio Kilkenny	7,813	11.00-14.00 Reach
Radio 3 (Offaly)	8,917	11.00-14.00 Reach
Raidió na Gaeltachta	-	-
RTÉ Radio Cork	-	-
Shannonside / Northern Sound (North & Midlands)	11,896	09.00-11.00 Reach
South East Radio (Wexford)	8,271	09.00-11.00 Reach
Tipperary Mid West	1,479	09.00-11.00 Reach
Tipp FM (Tipperary)	9,875	11.00-14.00 Reach
WLR (Waterford)	11,708	11.00-14.00 Reach
96 / 103 FM (Cork)	46,750	11.00-14.00 Reach
98 FM (Dublin)	32,396	15.00-18.00 Reach
Other Local Community Radios †	17,000	-

*based on quarter-hour audiences   †based on weekly audiences

REPUBLIC OF IRELAND: RADIO MARKET SHARE

Station	%
Home Local Stations	41
RTE Radio 1	32
2FM	22
Other Local Stations	4
RTE Radio Cork	1
Total:	**100**

NORTHERN IRELAND: RADIO MARKET SHARE

Station	%
Downtown Radio	43
Cool FM	38
City Beat	11
Q102 FM	6
Other Local Community Stations	2
Total:	**100**

NATIONAL RADIO & TELEVISION STATIONS

TELEVISION STATIONS

Radio Telefís Éireann
Donnybrook, Dublin 4. Tel: (01) 2083111. Fax: (01) 2083080. Founded: 1961. Director General: Bob Collins. Chairman: Farrel Corcoran. Director of Television: Joe Mulholland. TV Channels: RTÉ 1 & Network 2. Output: 200 hours per week - 50% home-produced. Regional Studios for Radio & TV: 8. Regional Radio Studios: 4. International offices: London, Washington D.C. & Brussels. Other Services: *Aertel* - free teletext information service to over 3,00,000 homes. *RTÉ Guide* - multichannel TV & Radio Guide.

British Broadcasting Corporation (N.I.)
Broadcasting House, Ormeau Avenue, Belfast BT2 8HQ. Tel: (01232) 338000. Fax: (01232) 338800. Founded: 1924. Northern Ireland Controller: Pat Loughrey. Head of Resources: Stephen Beckett. Head of Broadcast: Anna Carragher. Head of Production: Paul Evans. Head of News & Current Affairs: Tony Maddox. Head of TV Drama: Robert Cooper.

Ulster Television plc
Havelock House, Ormeau Road, Belfast BT7 1EB. Tel: (01232) 328122. Fax: (01232) 246695. Founded: 1959. Managing Director: J.D. Smyth. Controller of Programming: Alan Bremner. Regional Studios: 1. Output: 12 hours of home produced programmes weekly.

Teilifís na Gaeilge
Baile na hAbhann, Co. na Gaillimhe. Tel. (091) 505050. Founded 1996. Output: 45 hours per week. Ceannaire: Cahal Goan.

NATIONAL RADIO STATIONS:

Radio Telefís Éireann
Donnybrook, Dublin 4. Tel. (01) 2083111. Fax: (01) 2083080. Founded: 1926. RTÉ operates five radio stations nationwide: Radio 1, 2FM, FM3, Raidió na Gaeltachta & RTÉ Radio Cork (local station). Founded: 1926. Director of Radio: Helen Shaw. Output: 24 hours a day, seven days a week.

RTÉ Radio 1 (88.2-9/95)
Radio Centre, Donnybrook, Dublin 4. Tel: (01) 2083111. Fax: (01) 2083080. Founded: 1926. Target Audience: General. Style: Comprehensive coverage of news, current affairs, music, drama, features, agriculture, education, religion & sport; both in English & Irish with talk shows. First 24 hour broadcast on January 1, 1996.

RTÉ 2FM (92.6-94 FM)
Founded: 1979. Target Audience: 15- to 34-year-olds. Style: Popular music & chat.

RTÉ FM3 (92.6-94.4/102.7 FM)
Target Audience: General. Style: Classical Music.

Radio Ireland 100-102/105.5 MHz:
Radio Ireland Hse., 124 Upper Abbey St., Dublin 1. Tel: (01) 8049000. Fax: (01) 8049099. Founded: 1997. Chairperson & Editor in Chief: John McColgan. Chief Executive & Director of Programmes: Dick Hill. Controller of Programmes: John Caden. Target Audience: 25- to 45-year-olds. Style: Comprehensive current affairs, news and music coverage. Staff: 90.

Raidió na Gaeltachta
Casla, Co. na Gaillimhe. Tel: (091) 506677. Fax: (091) 506688. Founded: 1972. Ceannaire: Pól Ó Gallchóir. Target Audience: Gaelic speakers. Style: News & current affairs through the medium of Irish.

British Broadcasting Corporation (N.I.)
Broadcasting Hse., Ormeau Avenue, Belfast BT2 8HQ. Tel. (01232) 338000. Fax. (01232) 338800. Founded: 1924. Controller: Pat Loughrey. Radio Ulster & Radio Foyle are branches of BBC Northern Ireland, with a further six unattended radio studios province wide. Target Audience: General. Style: Comprehensive coverage of news, current affairs, arts, music, drama, features, agriculture, education, religion, sport & youth issues. Output: Radio Ulster transmits 5,500 hours per year. Broadcasting Area: 99% of those receiving BBC Services nationally.

BBC Radio Foyle (93.1 FM/792kHz/MW)
8 Northland Rd., Derry, BT48 7JD. Tel: (01504) 262244. Fax: (01504) 378666. Station Manager: Jim Sheridan.

BBC Radio Ulster (92.4-95.4 FM/1341 kHz MW)
BBC Northern Ireland, Broadcasting Hse., Ormeau Avenue, Belfast BT2 8HQ. Tel: (01232) 338000. Fax: (01232) 338800.

Atlantic 252 (252 LW)
Radio Tara Ltd., Mornington Hse., Trim, Co. Meath. Tel: (046) 36655. Fax: (046) 36704. Chairman: G. Thorn. Managing Director: T. Baxter. Target Audience: General. Style: Music. Broadcasting Area: Directed *mainly at the British market plus Ireland.*

LOCAL RADIO STATIONS

Anna Livia (103.8 FM) 3 Grafton St., Dublin 2. Tel: (01) 6778103. Chairperson: Donna Pierce. Station Manager: Eileen O'Gorman. Target audience: 25-65 year olds. Style: Talk-based, local community news & issues, specialist music. Broadcasting area: Dublin city & county.

Carlow Kildare Radio Ltd. (97.3/ 97.6/107.4 MHz) Lismard Hse., Tullow St., Carlow. Tel: (0503) 41044. ACC Hse. 51 South Main St., Naas, Co. Kildare. Tel: (045) 79666. Chief Executive: Hugh Browne. Chairman: James Reddy. Target audience: 20-50 year olds. Style: contemporary music, news & sport. Broadcasting area: Most of Leinster.

Clare FM (96.4/95.5/95.9 MHz) The Abbeyfield Centre, Francis St., Ennis, Co. Clare. Tel: (065) 28888. Executive chairman: Michael Evans. Station Manager: John O'Flaherty. Target Audience: 25-45 year olds. Style: music, chat, news, current affairs. Broadcasting area: Clare.

Classic Hits (98 FM) 8 Upper Mount St., Dublin 2. Tel: (01) 6708970. Chairman: Denis O'Brien. Station manager: Ken Hutton. Target audience: General. Style: music from the 60's, 70's, 80's & 90's. Broadcasting Area: Dublin.

East Coast Radio (94.9/96.2/ 102.9/104.4 MHz) 9 Prince of Wales Terrace, Quinsboro, Bray, Co. Wicklow. Tel: (01) 2866414. Chief executives: Seán Ashmore & Padraig O'Dwyer. Chairman: Blaise Treacy. Production manager: David Dennehy. Target audience: 15-55 year olds. Style: news, sport, current affairs, music & local issues. Broadcasting area: Wicklow & Dublin.

FM 104 3rd Floor, Hume Hse., Pembroke Rd., Ballsbridge, Dublin 4. Tel: (01) 6689689. Chairman: Maurice Cassidy. Station manager: Dermot Hanrahan. Target audience: 20-44 year olds. Style: modern music. Broadcasting area: Dublin.

Galway Bay FM (95.8/96.8/97.4/ 96.0 MHz) Sandy Rd., Galway. Tel: (091) 770000. Chief Executive: Keith Finnegan. Production manager: Clíona Breathnnach. Target audience: general. Style: music, news,

sport & current affairs. Broadcasting Area: Galway city & county.

Highland Radio (95.2/103.5 MHz) Pinehill, Letterkenny, Co. Donegal. Tel: (074) 25000. Chief executive & station manager: Charlie Collins. Target audience: 20+ years. Style: specialist music, local news, current affairs, sport. Broadcasting Area: Donegal, Derry & Tyrone.

Ireland Radio News 8 Upper Mount St., Dublin 2. Tel: (01) 6708989. Chief Executive & Chairman: Denis O'Brien. Managing Editor: Andrew Hanlon. Style: Broadcast news service to Independent radio stations.

LM FM Radio (95.8/104.9/105.5 MHz) Boyne Centre, Drogheda, Co. Louth. Tel: (041) 32000. Chief executive: Michael Crawley. Head of programmes: James Healy. Production manager: Eileen Duggan. Target Audience: 25+ year olds. Style: modern music, news, sports & local interest. Broadcasting Area: Louth & Meath.

Midlands Radio 3 (103.5/ 102.1 MHz) The Mall, William St., Tullamore, Co. Offaly. Tel: (0506) 51333. Portlaoise, Co. Laois. Tel: (0502) 60922. Athlone & Westmeath.Tel: (0902) 73777. Chief executive: Joe Yerkes. Chairman: Liam Keegan. Station manager: Mike Reade. Target Audience: 25+ year olds. Style: classic hits, magazine programmes. Broadcasting Area: Laois, Offaly & Westmeath.

Mid West Radio (96.1/97.1/97.3/ 95.4 MHz) South Block, Abbey St., Ballyhaunis, Co. Mayo. Tel: (0907) 30553. Chief executive: Paul Claffey. Chairman: M. Hughes. Station manager: Chris Carroll. Target audience: General. Style: Music news, interviews & reviews with local emphasis. Broadcasting area: Mayo.

North West Radio (102.5/105 MHz) Market Yard, Sligo. Tel: (071) 60108. Chief Executive & Head of programmes: as above. Chairman: D. O'Shea. Station manager: Tommy Marren. Target audience & Style: as above. Broadcasting area: Sligo, Leitrim & South Donegal.

96 FM / County Sound 103FM (Cork) Broadcasting Hse. Patrick's Place, Cork. Tel: (021) 551596. Goulds Hill, Mallow, Co. Cork. Tel: (022) 42103. Weir St., Bandon, Co. Cork. Tel: (023) 43103. Chief executive: Colm O'Conaill. Station manag-

er: Neil Prendeville. Target audience: 22-45 year olds. Style: news & music. Broadcasting Area: Cork.

98 FM (Dublin) The Malt Hse., Grand Canal Quay, Dublin 2. Tel: (01) 6708970. Chief executive: Denis O'Brien. General manager: Ken Hutton. Target audience: 20-44 year olds. Style: music from 70s, 80s & 90s. Broadcasting Area: Dublin city & county.

Radio Kerry (97.0/97.6/96.2 MHz) Main St., Tralee, Co. Kerry. Tel: (066) 23666. 95 New St., Killarney. Tel: (064) 34444. The Barracks, Cahirciveen, Co. Kerry. Tel: (066) 72888. General manager: Paul Sheenan. Target Audience: 25+ year olds. Style: news, features, sport, current affairs & music. Broadcasting area: Kerry & the south west.

Radio Kilkenny (96.6/96.0/106.3 MHz) 56 Hebron Rd., Kilkenny. Tel: (056) 61577. Chairman: Michael O'Reilly. Chief executive: John Purcell. Target audience: 15+ year olds. Style: pop music, current affairs, sport & community issues. Broadcasting area: Kilkenny.

Radio Limerick (95 FM) 100 O'Connell St., Limerick. Tel: (061) 319595. Chief executive: Jerry Madden. Station manager: Frank Carberry. Target audience: General. Style: news, music, sport, local issues & current affairs. Broadcasting area: Limerick.

Raidió na Life (102FM) 46 Kildare Street, Baile Átha Cliath 2. Tel: (01) 6616333. Chairperson: Seosamh Ó Murchú. Station manager: Finnoula Mac Aodha. Target audience: general. Style: music, news, sport, community issues in Irish. Broadcasting Area: Dublin.

Shannonside/Northern Sound Radio (94.8/96.3 MHz) Minard Hse., Sligo Rd., Longford. Tel: (043) 47777/45667. Chief executive: Richard Devlin. Chairman: Peter Brady. Station manager: Joe Finnegan & Maeve Clarke. Target audience: 18-55 year olds. Style: music, sport, local news & current affairs. Broadcasting area: Cavan, Galway, south Leitrim, Longford, Monaghan, Roscommon, Armagh, Meath, Fermanagh.

South East Radio (95.6/96.2/96.4 MHz) Custom House Quay, Wexford. Tel: (053) 45200. Chief executive: Eamonn Buttle. Station manager: Liam Dwyer. Target audience: 25-49 year olds. Style: pop, country music, news and information. Broadcasting area: Wexford.

Tipp FM (97.1/103.9/95.3 MHz) Davis Rd., Clonmel, Co. Tipperary. Tel: (052) 25299. Managing director: John O'Connell. Programme controller: Matt Dempsey. Target audience: 24-50 year olds. Style: contemporary music, news & current affairs. Broadcasting Area: Co. Tipperary (excluding south-west).

Tipperary Mid-West Radio (104.8 MHz) St. Michael's St., Tipperary Town & Halla na Feile, Cashel. Tel: (062) 52555. Chief executive: Sean Kelly. Programme controller: Marie Ryan. Target audience: General. Style: music, regional current affairs, local & community interest. Broadcasting area: S.W. Tipperary.

WLR FM (97.5/95.1 MHz) The Radio Centre, George's St., Waterford. Tel: (051) 77592. Chief executive: Des Whelan. Chairman: Gerry Sheridan. Head of programmes: Billy MacCarthy. Target audience: 15 - 55 year olds. Style: news, sport, music, current & community affairs. Broadcasting area: Waterford.

Belfast City Beat (96.7FM) Claremont Street, Belfast BT9 6JX. Tel: (01232) 438500. Target audience: General. Style: music & community issues. Broadcasting area: Greater Belfast Area.

Cool FM Newtownards, Co. Down BT23 4ES. Tel: (01247) 815551. Managing director: David Sloan. Station chairman: James Donnelly. Target audience: 18-35 year olds. Style: rock/pop music. Broadcasting Area: Eastern area of N. Ireland.

Downtown Radio Newtownards, Co. Down, BT23 4ES. Tel: (01247) 815555. Chairman: James Donnelly. Managing director: David Sloan. Target audience: primarily 30+. Style: contemporary & specialist music, cultural, social, religious features. Broadcasting Area: Ulster.

Q102 FM Waterside Railway Station, Duke St., Derry BT47. Tel: (01504) 311980/44449. Target audience: 15-40. Style: pop music & competitions. Broadcasting Area: north west.

Community Radio Castlebar (102.9 MHz) New Antrim St., Castlebar, Co. Mayo. Tel: (094) 23159. Chairperson: Una Ní Ghabhláin. Station manager: Henry McGlade. Target audience: general. Style: community issues & news. Broadcasting area: Castlebar.

Community Radio Youghal (105.1 MHz:) 2nd Floor, League of the Cross Hall, Catherine St., Youghal, Co. Cork. Tel/Fax: (024) 91199. Chairperson: James Fitzgerald. Target audience: General. Style: community issues & news. Broadcasting area: Youghal.

Connemara Community Radio (106.1/87.8 MHz) Connemara West Centre, Letterfrack, Co. Galway. Tel: (095) 41616. Chairperson: Paddy Kane. Station manager: Mary Ruddy. Target audience: General. Style: music/local talk format. Broadcasting area: N.W. Connemara.

Cork Campus Radio (97.4 MHz) Level 3, Áras na Mac Léinn, University College Cork, Cork. Tel: (021) 903108. Chairperson: Donnchadh Ó hAodha. Station manager: Sinéad Wylde. Target audience: general, third-level students & lecturers. Style: Education matters. Broadcasting area: Cork city.

Dublin South Community Radio (104.9 MHz) The Old School, Rathfarnham, Dublin 14. Tel: (01) 4930377. Chairperson: Tom Murchan. Station manager: Conal O'Carroll. Target audience: general. Style: community issues & news. Broadcasting area: South Dublin.

Dublin Weekend Radio (102.2 FM) Dublin City University, Glasnevin, Dublin 11. Tel: (01) 7045203. Chairperson: Farrell Corcoran. Station manager: Teresa O'Malley. Target audience: General. Style: local news, current affairs & features. Broadcasting area: Dublin.

Flirt FM (105.6MHz) c/o The Porters Desk, Concourse, University College Galway. Tel: (091) 524411 ext 3470. Chairperson: Sean Mac Iomhair. Station manager: Fiona MacNulty. Target audience: General. Style: alternative. Broadcasting area: Galway city.

Near (101.5 FM/101.6 MHz) Development Centre, Bunratty Drive, Dublin 17. Tel: (01) 8485211. Chairperson: Jack Byrne. Station manager: Ciarán Murray. Programme director: Brendan Teeling. Target audience: General. Style: a platform for community development groups. Broadcasting area: North-east Dublin.

West Dublin Community Radio (104.9 MHz) Ballyfermot Rd., Dublin 10. Tel: (01) 6261167. Chairpersons: Jerome Morrissey & Rónán Leyden. Station manager: Lois Mehaffy. Target audience: General. Style: Community information, education & entertainment. Broadcasting Area: Dublin West.

Wired (103.8 FM) Mary Immaculate College, South Circular Rd., Limerick. Tel: (061) 314588 ext 214. Chairperson: Dr. John Hayes. Station manager: Duncan O'Toole. Target audience: Youth. Style: Music, news (English + Irish), interviews, features on youth issues. Broadcasting area: Limerick city.

IRISH COPYRIGHT LAW

Under Irish law, neither facts nor information can be copyrighted. However, the right to copy - be that in print, publishing, performance, or broadcasting - belongs to the person who created the work.

The only deviation from this is where the work created is paid on commission for someone else for a fee paid or written as part of a writer's work for an employer and thus the copyright belongs to the commissioner or employer.

While facts and information cannot be copyrighted,

the form of the words used to convey them can be.

Copyright can be sold, assigned or leased.

In regard to the written word, copyright remains 'active' until the end of 70th year after the death of the writer/author (or after first publication if the author died first). After that works are deemed to be in the 'public domain' and can be copied and/or published freely.

Those who wish to quote from a copyright work should first obtain permission from the copyright owner who can usually be contacted via his/her publisher.

INTRODUCTION TO INTERACTIVE MEDIA

Terms such as Internet/World Wide Web, CD-Roms and interactive TV have now entered into common parlance in Ireland, but just what exactly do they mean?

The Internet is a worldwide computer network connected by various forms of telecommunications. On any given day it connects roughly 20 million users in over 50 countries. Nobody 'owns' the Internet - although Internet service providers help manage different parts of the networks that tie everything together. The main Internet service providers in Ireland are EUnet Ireland, Indigo, Ireland on line and Telecom Internet.

Having access to the Internet usually means that people can receive a number of basic services such as Electronic mail (E-mail), interactive conferencing, information resources, network news and the ability to transfer files. E-mail encompasses the sending and receiving of messages through the computer: you sit at your computer, write your letter, address it and send it. Within a few minutes the person you are mailing (who can be anywhere in the world) will receive your message. All this for the price of a local telephone call.

The World Wide Web refers to the body of information found on the Internet. Essentially, the World Wide Web is made up of millions of web pages - think of it as a publication that covers every subject under the sun and includes sound, video and pictures on your computer screen. Moving from one page to another simply involves pointing and clicking the mouse.

A CD-Rom combines several different media on a disk format and is able to deliver video, animations, 3-D graphics, text and audio.

In Ireland, the use of interactive media is most apparent in the more competitive markets where the unique powers of interactivity are lending companies a significant competitive edge in marketing and communication. Irish banks are piloting applications such as home banking; the Bank of Ireland, for example, has set up a virtual shopping mall on the Internet to enable Irish businesses to sell their wares to the market worldwide.

WEBSITE ADDRESSES

BANKING AND INVESTMENTS

Allied Irish Bank Group	www.aib.ie
Bank of Ireland	www.boi.ie
Bank of Ireland, Northern Ireland	www.bankofireland-ni.com
First National Building Society	www.fnbs.ie
First Trust Bank	www.ftbni.com
Hibernian	www.hibernian-group.ie
ICC Bank	www.icc.ie
KPMG Ireland	www.kpmg.ie
The Institute of Bankers in Ireland	www.instbank.ie
TSB Bank	www.tsbbank.ie
Ulster Bank	www.ulsterbank.com

EDUCATION

CAO/CAS Joint Application System (a complete guide to applying to Irish third-level through the CAO/CAS system)	indigo.ie/~cao
Ednet Ireland	ireland.iol.ie/ednet
Irish Education Web (A complete guide to subjects associated with education)	kola.dcu.ie/~iednet
Irish National teachers Organisation	www.into.ie
National Information Server Events Guide (Useful links to various libraries and the resources which those engaged in academic research would find useful)	www.hea.ie

GOVERNMENT & STATE SPONSORED BODIES

Central Statistics Office	www.cso.ie
Forbairt (Support services to Irish industry)	www.forbairt.ie
Forfas (Promotes enterprise, science and technology for Ireland's economic and social development)	www.forfas.ie
Government of Ireland	www.irlgov.ie
IDA (Attracts inward investment in Ireland)	www.ida.ie

INTERNET SERVICE PROVIDERS

Eunet Ireland	www.eunet.ie
Indigo	www.indigo.ie
Ireland On-Line	www.iol.ie
Telecom Internet	www.tinet.ie

IRISH MEDIA

2FM	www.2fm.ie
RTÉ (The Irish Broadcasting Service)	www.rte.ie
The Irish Times Newspaper	www.irish-times.ie

Bord Fáilte (The Irish Tourist Board)..**www.ireland.travel.ie**
Northern Ireland Tourist Board ....**www.ni-tourism.com**
TouristNET ....**www.indigo.ie/ipress**

MISCELLANEOUS

Irish Exporters Association (Promotes & represents the interests of Irish exporters)...........**www.itw.ie/exporter**
Irish Internet Association ....**www.iia.ie**
Irish Job Pages (Ireland's one-stop shop for recruitment)...**www.exp.ie**
Kompass Register of Irish Industry ....**www.kompass.ie**
The Irish Management Institute ....**www.imi.ie**
The Irish Trade Web (Contains good business content and invaluable contacts for Irish business) ....**www.itw.ie**

WHO'S WHO IN THE IRISH MEDIA

Jeremy Adis: publisher of *Books Ireland* magazine.
Paddy Agnew: journalist with *The Irish Times*.
William Ambrose: editor of *Business and Finance*.
Gerry Anderson: popular T.V. and radio presenter.
Charlie Bird: R.T.É.'s special correspondent.
John Bowman: chair of R.T.É's current affairs programme Questions & Answers.
Conor Brady: editor of *The Irish Times*.
Vincent Browne: Editor of *Magill* magazine.
Gay Byrne: one of Ireland's most famous radio and TV hosts.
Des Cahill: Sports commentator with R.T.É., founder of the *ABU* fanclub.
Mark Carruthers: B.B.C. presenter.
Ciaran Carty: literary editor with *The Sunday Tribune*.
Paul Clarke: presenter of U.T.V. Live at Six.
Tony Clayton-Lea: music journalist and radio presenter
Charlie Collins: chairman of the Association of Independent Radio Stations and station manager of Highland radio.
Tom Collins: editor of *The Irish News*.
Stephen Collins: political correspondent with *The Sunday Tribune*.
Matt Cooper: editor of *The Sunday Tribune*.
Tim Pat Coogan: journalist and Northern Ireland commentator
Mark Costigan: radio news reporter.
Barry Cowen: senior presenter with B.B.C. Northern Ireland.
Martin Cowley: former editor of the London Times, editor of *The Independent*.
Anthony Cronin: literary critic.
Carrie Crowley: R.T.É. T.V. and radio presenter.
Richard Crowley: current affairs broadcaster on R.T.É. Radio 1, co-presents Morning Ireland.
Michael Cunningham - editor of Computimes in *The Irish Times*.
Ray D'Arcy - T.V. and radio presenter, long-suffering partner to Dustin the Turkey on *Den T.V.*
Derek Davis: R.T.É. presenter.
David Davin Power: Northern editor with R.T.É.
Frank Delaney - Radio and T.V. broadcaster.
Peter Denman: editor of the *Irish University Review*.
Cathal Dervan: editor of *The Title* (the sports supplement to *Ireland on Sunday*).
Candy Devine: radio presenter with Downtown radio.
Polly Devlin: journalist and broadcaster,
Donal Dineen: radio presenter and music pundit.

Moya Doherty: T.V. producer, *Riverdance* promoter and co-founder of Radio Ireland.
Joe Duffy: R.T.É. radio presenter.
Seán Duignan: former political editor, press secretary with F.F., now a presenter with R.T.É.
Mick Dunne: editor of *Gaelic World*.
Eamon Dunphy: radio presenter and sports commentator.
David Dunseith: B.B.C. correspondent and presenter of *Talkback*.
Mike Edgar: presenter with B.B.C. Radio Ulster.
Rod Ely: publisher of *History Ireland* magazine.
B.P. Fallon: Radio D.J. and music journalist.
Aengus Fanning: editor of the *Sunday Independent*.
Dave Fanning: radio presenter, music pundit and film critic.
Brian Farrell: political commentator and literary critic.
Jim Fahy: Western correspondent with R.T.É.
Liam Fay: music journalist with *Hot Press* and writer.
Marian Finucane: presenter of R.T.É.'s *Liveline*.
Lisa Flavelle: radio presenter with Downtown radio.
Frank Galligan: radio presenter on Radio Foyle.
Johnny Giles: sports commentator and soccer pundit.
Cathal Goan: head of Teilifís na Gaeilge.
Larry Gogan: Radio D.J. and music journalist.
Tommy Gorman: European correspondent with R.T.É.
John Gray: editor of the Linen Hall Review, along with Paul Campell.
Cathy Halloran: mid-west correspondent with R.T.É.
Lise Hand: columnist with the *Sunday Tribune*.
David Hanly: anchorman on R.T.É.'s *Morning Ireland*.
Liam Hayes: editor of *Ireland on Sunday*.
Mary Holland: journalist with *The Irish Times* and *The Observer*.
Eamon Holmes: presenter on morning G.M.T.V.
Seamus Hosey: producer of the R.T.É. radio book show *Off the Shelf*, presented by Andy O'Mahony.
Ann Marie Hourihane: journalist and broadcaster.
Bill Hughes: radio & TV producer and presenter.
Tom Humphries: sports writer with *The Irish Times*.
Gloria Hunniford: T.V. and radio presenter.
Fergal Keane: foreign correspondent for the B.B.C.
Conor Kavanagh: radio news editor.
John Kearns: music presenter with U.T.V. and M.T.V.
Cathal Kelly: editor of *Gay Community News*.
Gerry Kelly: popular T.V. show host on U.T.V.
John Kelly: one of Ireland's most popular radio and T.V. presenters.
Shirley Kelly: editor of *Books Ireland*.

Geraldine Kennedy: political journalist and former T.D.

Mary Kenny: British-based journalist and commentator on Irish society.

Pat Kenny: popular radio and T.V. presenter on R.T.É.

Des Keogh: Classical music broadcaster on R.T.É. Radio.

Barry Lang: Radio D.J. with 2FM and the station's Internet commentator.

Patrick Loughrey: controller of B.B.C. Northern Ireland.

Tom Mac Sweeney: southern correspondent with R.T.É.

Eileen Magnier: north-west correspondent with R.T.É.

Thelma Mansfield: T.V. presenter with R.T.É.

Geoff Martin: editor of *The Belfast* and *Ulster Newsletter.*

Ivan Martin: sports presenter with Downtown Radio.

Eamon McCann: freelance journalist.

Gary McDonald: editor of *Ulster Business.*

John McKenna: producer of the radio education show *No Chalk - No Chance!*

Clare McKeon: presenter of R.T.É.'s popular *Moveable Feast.*

Frank Mitchell: T.V. presenter.

Derek Mooney: R.T.É. radio presenter and producer.

Donal Mooney: editor of the *Irish Post.*

Rob Morrison: U.T.V. news editor.

John Mulcahy: managing editor of the *Phoenix* magazine.

Mike Murphy: radio and T.V. presenter and arts critic.

Celine Naughton: editor of *Woman's Way.*

Brid Óg Ní Bhuachalla: R.T.É. Irish language broadcaster.

Cliona Ní Bhuachalla: Irish language broadcaster.

Cynthia Ní Mhurchú: radio and T.V. presenter.

Conor Cruise O'Brien: academic, politician and former newspaper editor.

Fiac Ó Broin: radio producer with R.T.É.

Gareth O'Callaghan: R.T.É.radio show host.

Miriam O'Callaghan: R.T.É. current affairs presenter.

Conor O'Clery: correspondent with *The Irish Times.*

Gemma O'Doherty: journalist with *The Irish Independent.*

Brenda O'Donoghue: contributor to the Gerry Ryan Show on 2FM.

Niall O'Dowd: editor of the *Irish Voice.*

Nuala O'Faolain: columnist with *The Irish Times.*

Donal O'Kelly: political editor with R.T.É.

Olivia O'Leary: leading current affairs presenter.

Joseph O'Malley: political editor of the *Sunday Independent.*

Micheál Ó Muircheartaigh: Gaelic Games presenter.

Annette O'Meara: editor of *U Magazine.*

Rose O'Neill: B.B.C. news broadcaster.

Dr. Tony O'Reilly: media magnate.

Emily O'Reilly: radio presenter.

Cathal Ó Searcaigh: R.T.É. Irish language presenter.

Fintan O'Toole: columnist with The Irish Times.

Heather Parsons: editor of the R.T.É. guide.

Cathal Porteir: R.T.É. radio producer.

Brenda Power: columnist with the *Sunday Tribune.*

Seán Rafferty: B.B.C. Radio 3.

Ken Reid: political editor with U.T.V.

Anne Reihill: editor of *Image* magazine.

Michael Roche: managing director of *Ireland's Own.*

Brigid Ruane: *Late Late Show Producer.*

Gerry Ryan: top radio presenter with 2FM.

John Ryan: editor of *In Dublin.*

Sinead Shannon: editor of *Education Today* magazine.

Helen Shaw: head of R.T.É. radio.

Niall Skelly: editor / director of the *Big Issues Magazine.*

Niall Stokes: head of the I.R.T.C. and editor of *Hot Press.*

Donna Traynor: news presenter with B.B.C.

Ann Walsh: producer of R.T.É. Radio's *The Arts Show,* along with Yetti Redmond & Bernedette Comerford.

Dick Warner: radio and T.V. presenter and producer with R.T.É.

Johnny Watterson: sports writer with *The Irish Times.*

Marty Whelan: R.T.É. T.V. presenter.

Terry Wogan: radio presenter with B.B.C.

Padraig Yeates: correspondent with *The Irish Times.*

SPORT

Success is All

By *Johnny Watterson, The Irish Times*

WITH the exception of G.A.A., the breadth of Irish sport can no longer be measured by its success at home. Borders have expanded, Europe is at once shrinking and embracing new countries and as Ireland inexorably becomes part of a bigger community so too does sport have to respond. Thus far it has done very well. The Ryder Cup, Cheltenham, the European Swimming Championships, the World Athletics Championships, international boxing, soccer, Formula One motor racing and the expansion of professional Rugby Union have each made their mark.

Not to be outdone the biggest organisation in the country, the G.A.A., have also continued to market their game outside Ireland. The traditional fertile grounds of the U.S.A., Australia and Britain now regularly receive big games by satellite while other non English speaking countries have, through television, begun to learn what Gaelic football and hurling means to a membership that is approaching 800,000 people throughout Ireland.

Those athletes who continue to dominate the international scene rightfully receive the greatest exposure; Olympic and European champion swimmer Michelle Smith; World Champion athlete Sonia O'Sullivan and Susan Smith, the 400m hurdler who made the final of this year's World Championships in Athens and is a potential Olympic medalist when the Sydney Olympics arrive in 2000; world boxing title holders Steve Collins and Wayne McCullough and those who this year decided to follow them into the professional game, Belfast's Damean Kelly, Martin Renaghan from Keady and Cathal O'Grady from the Dublin based St. Saviours club; the most successful Irish road racer ever and world record holding Isle of Man T.T. motor cycle champion Joey Dunlop; Ryder Cup golfer Darren Clarke, who contributed a point to this year's successful European team in their emotional win over the United States at Valderrama, Spain, and his exciting young golfing colleagues Padraig Harrington and Paul McGinley; jump jockey Charlie Swan, who yet again won the champion jockey award in Ireland and flat racers Christy Roche, Johnny Murtagh, Mick Kinane and the English based Kieren Fallon.

The historically successful Lions rugby tour to South Africa, which included Irish players Keith Wood, Paul Wallace, Eric Miller and Jeremy Davidson sought to emphasise Ireland's willingness to present international sports athletes of the highest ability in the face of a smaller playing population to that of its neighbours. The Lions tour was successful precisely because of the mix of players from England, Ireland, Scotland and Wales. Each brought their own unique vision, something that Irish coaches and administrators are now seeking in order to keep domestic rugby competitive in the face of enormous financial incentives from abroad.

Neither Ulster, Leinster or Munster qualified for the qualifying stages of the European Cup for the second successive season yet rugby's popularity continues to grow. Connacht bravely set the pace in the European Conference but now there is talk in Europe of cutting back the number of Irish sides allowed to compete at European level in the coming years. The magnetic draw of big money from English clubs has changed the complexion of rugby in these islands. How will that reflect on Ireland's Five Nations Championship hopes and can the club game in the provinces survive the leeching away of their best talent? More challenges ahead for the Irish Rugby Football Union, who have stood firm in their belief that the blue riband events of the international game should be seen by the widest possible audience and who refuse to deal with the pay satellite station SKY.

In soccer both the Irish League and the League of Ireland look at the burgeoning Premiership grow in England and feel its shadow chill the domestic game. The talk of Wimbledon Football Club uprooting from London and repotting itself in Dublin in the hope of generating a grass roots support in Ireland, is one of the battles ahead for those who cherish the status of domestic soccer. The F.A.I. dismiss the move as pie in the sky, yet the Minister for Sport in the Republic of Ireland, Jim McDaid, has had a meeting with the powers from the English club that want to instigate the move.

While the Football Association of Ireland (F.A.I.) have invested heavily in upgrading grounds around the country such as Bishopstown, Tolka Park, Richmond Park, Terryland Park, the Carlisle Grounds and the Regional Sports Centre they still have not been able to solve the problem of finding a settled home - i.e. a national soccer stadium. Challenges there too.

In Seville this year Michelle Smith drew more attention than any other swimmer at the European Championships with the exception of Russian World and Olympic champion Alexander Popov. Smith continued her incredible career with a four medal haul. She has now become one of the most successful swimmers in the history of the sport with four Olympic medals and seven European medals. Not bad from a pool of 6,000 swimmers. Here too success brings its own pressures and as Smith continually faces her critics who demand to know the details of her secret winning formula, so too does her profile and that of her husband and coach Erik de Bruin, increase.

In horse racing too the internationalisation of Irish sport is burgeoning. When Dermot Weld, who boasts of wins in four continents, took the Michael Smurfit owned Vintage Crop to Australia and won the Melbourne Cup in 1993, he set standards that few thought could be achieved. New methods of transporting animals without the dehydrating effects associated with transcontinental travel were perfected by the former vet. Now the best trainers set their sights on the biggest global events and from here on trainer Aidan O'Brien, settled in Ballydoyle, Vincent O'Brien's old stables, is set to become part of another critical Irish sporting export.

While it was a slow year if qualifying matches for the Irish soccer team under Mick McCarthy, Formula One motor racing continues to grow as the appetite for televised sport increases. Eddie Irvine from County Down, Ferrari's number two driver to Michael Schumacher, struts across the global Grand Prix map with all of the arrogance you would expect from such a talent. There is more to come for Irvine as there is for Jordan Racing run by Dubliner Eddie Jordan. Having taken on the established racing set up Jordan has established himself at Silverstone, England as one of the most energetic managers and shrewdest talent spotters in the game. When F1 floats on the stock exchange Jordan can expect to further enhance his millionaire status quite considerably.

Money, naturally, has changed the face of Irish sport and every top athlete who makes it to the top can expect the rewards. While former first lady of Irish track and field, Sonia O'Sullivan, continues to struggle against bad form and a lack of confidence, another talent has come into view. Susan Smith from Waterford ran herself into an Olympic 400m hurdle semi-final before lining up against the best in the world in Athens.

Smith has shattered the Irish hurdling record at 400m so many times now that it has become an expectation every time she runs in a major event. Not since Bob Tisdall, who won Olympic gold in Los Angeles in 1932, have we had a hurdler with so much talent. Smith also holds the Irish 100m hurdling record. Based in Ireland, but on the world circuit she is part of a package, who along with O'Sullivan and Berlin marathon winner Catherina McKiernan, has pushed women to the forefront of Irish and international sport.

Nothing is complete without G.A.A. As Ulster emerged as a force in the early part of this decade with Down, Donegal and Derry each winning the football championship, this year saw Kerry covet the Sam Maguire Cup. In an emotional return to the county, Kerry again added to their four in a row wins between 1978 and 1981 and their three in a row between 1984-86.

In the hurling All-Ireland final the 1995 winners Clare beat Tipperary in the first ever all Munster final. Never before in the long history of the G.A.A. had teams from the same province met in the Croke Park spectacle. A revision of the rules allowed the defeated provincial finalists from Leinster and Munster back into the All-Ireland pot and so Tipperary's second chance took them to the final. Perhaps of all the winners over this year Clare's memorable victory illustrates that the cultural, parochial and amateur input of the G.A.A. can match and often supersede that of the multi-national and professional - for now at least.

The author is a noted sports journalist with The Irish Times.

TOP SPORTS STORIES OF THE YEAR

HURLING

The 1997 Guinness Senior Hurling Championship was the first in which the beaten Leinster and Munster finalists qualified for the specially created All-Ireland quarter-finals against the Connacht and Ulster champions respectively. A new departure for the G.A.A. Championship, it met with some opposition and was greeted with little enthusiasm even amongst the defeated provincial finalists.

The All-Ireland final on September 14 produced a novel pairing, a repeat of the Munster final where Clare once again faced Tipperary. Tipperary were on top for much of the first half leading by 0-10 to 0-6 at half time. A rejuvenated Clare side emerged in the second half and swept into a seven point lead. Two late goals from Tipperary set up a grandstand finish but a 69th minute point from Clare's Jamesie O'Connor sealed victory for the Banner county after John Leahy's late goal chance was saved by Clare goalkeeper David Fitzgerald. The final score was Clare 0-20 Tipperary 2-13. Clare became All-Ireland Champions for only the third time emphasising their transformation from the one time whipping boys of Munster hurling to All-Ireland Champions twice in three seasons.

SOCCER

1997 saw the best ever display by any team representing the Republic of Ireland. Brian Kerr steered the U-20s to third place in the World Cup in Malaysia. In the first round they lost 2-1 to Ghana, beat the U.S.A. 2-0 and ensured qualification for the second round by drawing 1-1 with China.

The second round game with Morocco ended 1-1. Neale Fenn's opener was cancelled by an own goal, but Damien Duff's injury time 'golden goal' secured victory and set up a quarter final clash with Spain. Thomas Molloy's second half goal dismissed the Spanish challenge and saw the team through to the semi-finals spot where defending champions Argentina awaited. The semi-final was lost 1-0 despite a second half bombardment of the Argentinian goal and the adventure was drawing to a close. The first round defeat by Ghana was avenged in the third/fourth place play off, the Republic winning 2-1 (the goals coming from Dessie Baker and Damien Duff). A tired Irish team came home to a marvellous reception in Dublin, lauded as the third best team in the world. Their conquerors Argentina went on to win the final.

ATHLETICS

The World Championships were held in Athens in early August and as has become the norm in recent years Irish hopes were firmly pinned on Sonia O'Sullivan. All this despite poor performances from O'Sullivan which saw her leave the competitive circuit in June to concentrate on training for the Championships. She eased through qualification in the 1,500m and recorded a season's best in the semi-final but finished eighth in the final. The defending World Champion in her favoured 5,000m she was beaten into seventh in the first round. A nation shared her disbelief as she sat bewildered on the track after her defeat. At 27 she has time to rediscover the talent which has so enthralled us over the past number of years.

The best Irish performance in Athens came from Waterford's Susan Smith who has, in under two years, developed into a world class 400m hurdler. Setting a national record in the first round of 54.61 seconds Smith went on to qualify for her first ever final at a major championships where she finished a creditable seventh. Perhaps the torch will now be passed on.

SNOOKER

1997 belonged to Ken Doherty. Without a major tournament win in almost four years his famous lack of concentration had let him down in a succession of semi-finals and finals. A humiliating 6-1 first round defeat at the hands of Steve Davis at the Irish Masters coupled with a stinging rebuke from his manager who branded him lazy seemed to sting him into action at the World Championships. On his way to the final he defeated Steve Davis, John Higgins and Alain Robidoux. In the final he faced six-time World Champion Stephen Hendry who was aiming for an unprecedented six victories in-a-row. Unperturbed, Doherty led at every interval, holding a 11-5 overnight lead in the best of 35 frames final. Doherty eventually won 18-12 picking up a cheque for £210,000 to take his career earnings over the £1 million mark. On his return to Dublin he was given the now obligatory open topped bus ride from the airport to the city centre.

BOXING

Steve Collins, the Celtic Warrior, sensationally announced his retirement from professional boxing on October 2nd. After a few days of uncertainty, Collins first announced he was pulling out of the scheduled defence of his W.B.O. Super-middleweight title on medical grounds; then promoter Frank Warren announced that Collins had been stripped of his title and the Chris Eubank/Joe Calzaghe fight would be for the vacant title. The W.B.O.'s President refuted that claim. Collins, when announcing his retirement, voiced his regret that he never had the opportunity to fight former American World Light-heavyweight Champion Roy Jones and stated that his appetite for boxing was gone. Such was the apparent suddenness of his decision that many speculate he will return to the ring in the future. Collins successfully defended his Super-middleweight title eight times including twice defeating Chris Eubank.

SWIMMING

The 1997 European Swimming Championships were held in Seville in August, and Irish hopes rested on Michelle Smith de Bruin. She had trained in Kilkenny prior to the Championships and, on arrival in Seville she found organisers would not accept her times from Atlanta on the grounds that they had not been set in 1997. Hampered by draws in slow heats she battled to pace herself, squeezing into most of her finals in the slower lanes. She opened her Championships on August 19th with victory in the 400m Individual Medley and followed it up with gold in the 200m Freestyle 24 hours later. On the third day of the Championships Smith de Bruin won silver in the 400m Freestyle behind German Dagmar Hase. She ended her most successful European Championships with silver in the 200m Butterfly on August 24, her four medals earning Ireland fifth place on the overall medals table.

RUGBY

1997 was a disappointing year for Irish rugby. The national team, despite extending their remarkable Cardiff hoodoo over Wales with another victory (Ireland have not lost in Cardiff since 1983), managed to secure yet another wooden spoon in the Five Nations' Championship. An Irish Development side toured New Zealand in May and June and suffered some heavy defeats but ended their tour with a good performance against Western Samoa despite being on the wrong end of a 57-25 scoreline. The provinces, with the exception of Connacht in the Conference, have fared less than well in European competition.

It would be wrong to suggest that these early days of professionalism are to blame. Things were bad before August 1995, but the haemorrhage of Irish players to English clubs (which is where the greatest professional rewards can be reaped) has had a detrimental effect on local clubs.

GOLF

A Ryder Cup debut, joint second in the British Open and a string of other top ten finishes makes the rise and rise of Darren Clarke the golf story of the year. The 28 year-old Dungannon man ended 1996 by winning his second event on the European Tour, the German Masters. 1997 has been his best season ever, he was joint runner up in the Volvo P.G.A. in May, in July he led the British Open for three days but finished as joint runner-up with Jasper Parnevik and behind Justin Leonard. Add to this third in the Italian and French Opens, fourth in the Portuguese Open, joint sixth European Masters and automatic selection for the Ryder Cup. His first Ryder Cup outing, in the fourball alongside Colin Montgomerie ended with victory over Davis Love and Fred Couples. In the singles he lost by 2 and 1 to some inspired chipping from Phil Mickelson. But there was much to celebrate in Europe's victory for Clarke, not least the prospect of Boston in 1999, his highest ever Order of Merit finish in 1997 and perhaps can even look forward to a U.S. P.G.A. tour card in 1998.

HORSE RACING

1997 was the first year in which all five Irish Classics were won by Irish trained horses since 1964. Aidan O'Brien continued his dominance of domestic flat racing training Desert King, the winner of a rare Derby/2,000 Guineas double and Classic Park, the winner of the 1,000 Guineas with Stephen Craine on board. Johnny Murtagh on board the John Oxx trained Ebadiyla won the Irish Oaks, his first Classic. Elsewhere Kevin Prendergast trained and Stephen Craine rode the much fancied Oscar Schindler to victory in the Irish St. Leger to complete the clean sweep. In addition O'Brien secured his fourth successive trainers championship to complete an outstanding Irish season.

GAELIC FOOTBALL

The eleven year wait is over. Kerry won Sam Maguire for the first time since 1986, to the visible and vociferous relief of the county's population who gathered on the pitch at Croke Park to witness captain Liam Hasset receive the glittering prize. Never in the G.A.A.'s 113 year history have Kerry waited so long for an All-Ireland football title, the ten year wait between 1914 and 1924 has all but passed from living memory and into books of record.

Maurice Fitzgerald bestrode Croke Park like a colossus scoring nine majestic points with either foot and collecting the man-of-the-match award. The most talented Kerryman never to win an All-Ireland medal, Fitzgerald broke Mayo hearts and carried his team to victory. For the third time in twelve months Mayo stared victory in the face, a 48th minute converted penalty gave them a scarcely deserved lifeline, followed by two James Horan points, it left just a point between the teams. In stepped Fitzgerald to silence the rising Mayo crescendo with two late points leaving the final score reading Kerry 0-13, Mayo 1-7. The Kerry faithful who had so nonchalantly celebrated All-Ireland titles throughout the seventies and eighties without as much as taking a Monday off work, frolicked like first time winners on the grassy sward of Croke Park and all over Kerry long into the night.

SPORTS CHRONOLOGY OF THE YEAR

01: G.A.A. 65,847 people watched Wexford (reduced to 14 men when Eamon Scallon was sent off in the first half) beat Limerick 1-13 to 0-14 in the Guinness All-Ireland Senior Championship final. It was Wexford's first All-Ireland win since 1968. The curtain raising minor hurling final ended in a draw, Galway 3-11, Tipperary 0-20.

06: Soccer In the F.A.I. League Premier Division Bohemians beat Shelbourne 1-0, St. Patrick's Athletic drew 0-0 with Shamrock Rovers.

07: Hockey The Irish ladies team drew 1-1 with France in Edinburgh. The Irish men's team recorded at 5-2 victory over H.G.C. in their club tour of Holland.

Soccer In the Irish League Gold Cup there were victories for Portadown, Coleraine, Crusaders, Ballymena United, Omagh Town and Linfield, while the Cliftonville/Glentoran and the Ballyclare Comrades/Distillery games ended in draws. Derry City beat Home Farm Everton 3-1 in the National League.

08: G.A.A. In the U21 All-Ireland finals held at Thurles Galway beat Wexford 1-14 to 0-7 in the hurling while in the football Kerry overcame Cavan by 1-17 to 2-10.

Rugby In the first ever match between a province and a national side the Irish XV squeezed past Munster by 22 points to 21.

Equestrian Sport In the Du Maurier International in Canada Ireland's Peter Charles on La Ina won the individual event. Ireland finished fourth in the Nations' Cup.

Mountain biking Robin Seymour won the Irish Mountain bike Championship at Clonmel.

Golf Darren Clarke collected £19,813 for his seventh place finish at the European Masters in Switzerland.

Formula 1 Damon Hill won the Italian Grand Prix at Monza while the Jordans of Martin Brundle and Rubens Barrichello finished fourth and fifth respectively.

Hockey Ireland's ladies team drew 0-0 with Scotland in the three nations tournament in Edinburgh.

Athletics At the Grand Prix final in Milan David Matthews finished fifth in the 800m, Marcus O'Sullivan finished twelfth in the 1,500m, Sinead Delahunty was ninth in the 1,500m, Catherina McKiernan was 10th in the 5,000m while Sonia O'Sullivan failed to finish in the 5,000m.

Soccer In the F.A.I. National League Premier Division there were victories for Bray, Sligo and U.C.D.

12: Soccer Bohemians beat St. Pats, Derry City beat Dundalk and Shamrock Rovers beat Bray Wanderers in the National League Premier Division.

13: Golf England beat Ireland 10-5 in the amateur championships in Scotland.

14: Hockey In the Tri-nation Blaris Tournament Ireland drew 2-2 with Wales.

Soccer Finn Harps beat Home Farm 3-2 and Sligo Rovers drew 1-1 with Shelbourne in the F.A.I. Premier Division.

15: G.A.A. Colm Coyle's 69th minute point earned Meath a draw with Mayo in the Bank of Ireland Senior Football Championship final 0-12 to 1-9. In the minor final Chris Conway's six points help Laois to a 2-11 to 1-11 victory over Kerry.

Rugby The Irish XV beat Leinster 43-38 at Donnybrook.

Hockey Ireland beat Scotland 1-0 in the Blaris tournament.

Golf A career best of 63 in the final round helps Padraig Harrington to seventh place and £16,753 in the Lancome Trophy. The tournament, held in France was won by Jasper Parnevik.

Soccer U.C.D. beat Cork City 2-1 in the Harp Lager Premier Division.

20: Soccer St. Pats drew with Sligo Rovers 2-2 and Shelbourne beat U.C.D. 1-0 in the Premier Division.

21: Rugby In the first round of the inter-provincial series Munster beat Connacht 45-28 at Cork and Leinster beat Ulster 35-25 at Ravenhill.

Soccer There were victories for Derry City, Finn Harps and Bohemians while the Home Farm/Dundalk game ended scoreless.

22: Golf Darren Clarke finished joint sixth in the Loch Lomond World Invitational Golf Championship winning £24,375; County Sligo Golf Club won the All-Ireland Senior Cup defeating Limerick 3-2 in the final at Tramore.

Camogie 10,235 people watched Galway beat Cork 4-8 to 1-15 in the All-Ireland Senior final at Croke Park. Cork beat Roscommon 6-5 to 2-7 in the Junior final.

Formula 1 Eddie Irvine, driving for Ferrari finished fifth in the Portuguese Grand Prix at Estoril.

Soccer Bohemians beat Bray 5-1 and Finn Harps beat Cork City 1-0 in the F.A.I. Premier Division.

27: Soccer Shamrock Rovers beat Home Farm/Everton 2-1 and Bohemians drew 1-1 with Derry City in the F.A.I. National League.

28: Soccer In the Smirnoff Irish League Coleraine and Portadown recorded victories while the Crusaders/Glenavon and Glentoran/Cliftonville games ended in draws; in the F.A.I. Premier Division Finn Harps beat Dundalk and Sligo Rovers beat Bray.

Rugby Ulster beat Connacht 32-27 at Ravenhill and Munster beat Leinster 45-40 at Donnybrook.

29: G.A.A. A last minute point gave Meath a 2-9 to 1-11 victory over Mayo in the All-Ireland football final replay at Croke Park. Tempers boiled over in the first half and two players were sent off following a fifteen man goal-mouth brawl; Tipperary beat Galway 2-14 to 2-12 in the All-Ireland minor hurling final replay.

Golf Swede Per-Ulrik Johansson won the Smurfit European Open by one shot from Constantino Rocca at the 'K' Club in Kildare. Johansson's first prize was £125,000 while Padraig Harrington, the top Irish finisher in joint tenth place won £13,442.

Soccer Cork City beat Shelbourne 3-1 and St. Patrick's Athletic beat U.C.D. 1-0 in the F.A.I. Premier Division.

Hockey Ireland's mens team beat Scotland 2-1 in the World Cup pre-qualifying tournament in Sardinia.

30: Hockey Ireland beat Bangladesh 7-0 in Cagliari, Sardinia.

03: Hockey Ireland beat the United States 4-2 in the men's World Cup pre-qualifying tournament.

04: Soccer In the F.A.I. Premier Division Finn Harps beat Shelbourne 2-1, Dundalk beat Shamrock Rovers 4-1 and St Pats drew 1-1 with Cork City.

04: Olympics Pat Hickey remains President of the

Olympic Council of Ireland defeating David Balbirnie in the vote at the O.C.I.'s Annual General Meeting.

05: Soccer In the group nine World Cup qualifier at Windsor Park Northern Ireland drew 1-1 with Armenia, Neil Lennon was the Northern Ireland scorer; in the F.A.I. National League Bohemians beat Home Farm 3-0 while the Derry City/Sligo Rovers game ended scoreless.

Tennis Ireland's women were beaten 2-1 by Norway in their final game in the Federation Cup in Kenya narrowly missing out on promotion to Group One.

Rugby Munster clinched the inter-provincial series by beating Ulster 27-24 at Thomond Park. Connacht beat Leinster 22-13 at the Galway Sports Ground.

06: Golf Darren Clarke won the German Masters in Berlin by one shot. Shooting a last round 63 he clinched the £108,330 first prize. Paul McGinley finished fifth and Padraig Harrington eighth.

Rallying Armagh's Gabriel Snow, driving a Ford Escort Cosworth, won the Cork International Rally.

Soccer U.C.D. beat Bray 2-0 in the Premier Division.

G.A.A. In the Ladies Senior Football final Laois and Monaghan drew 2-9 apiece. In the Junior final Clare beat Longford 5-9 to 4-9.

07: Hockey Ireland defeated Poland 5-2 in the World Cup pre-qualifying tournament in Sardinia.

08: Hockey Ireland's 3-1 victory over Italy saw them qualify for the World Cup qualifying tournament in Malaysia.

Soccer In U21 soccer the Republic of Ireland beat Macedonia 4-0 at Dalymount Park.

09: Soccer The Republic of Ireland beat F.Y.R. Macedonia 3-0 in the World Cup qualifier at Lansdowne Road. Tony Cascarino scored twice and Jason McAteer scored his first international goal.

10: Golf The Irish team of Darren Clarke, Padraig Harrington and Paul McGinley beat Wales 2-1 in the Dunhill Cup.

Hockey In the World Cup pre-qualifying tournament New Zealand beat Ireland 3-1.

11: Golf Ireland beat Wales 2-1 in the Dunhill Cup.

Soccer Bohemians and St. Pats won their Premier Division ties.

12: Golf South Africa defeated Ireland in the semi-final of the Dunhill Cup.

Rugby In the Heineken European Cup Munster defeated Milan 23-5, Ulster defeated Caledonia 41-34 and Leinster lost 17-34 to Llanelli. In the European Conference Connacht beat Padova 34-12.

Soccer In the F.A.I. Premier Division the Finn Harps/Shamrock Rovers and Sligo Rovers/Home Farm games ended scoreless.

Hockey Poland beat Ireland 5-4 in the third/fourth place playoff at the World Cup pre-qualifying tournament in Sardinia.

13: Formula 1 Damon Hill's victory in the Japanese Grand Prix clinches the Drivers' Championship, Martin Brundle, driving the Jordan Peugeot, finished fifth in the race.

Soccer Cork City and U.C.D. won their Premier Division ties.

G.A.A. In the opening day of the Church and General National Football League there were victories in Division One for Derry and Kildare while the Meath/Cavan and Donegal/Cork games ended in draws.

15: Boxing The Irish amateur team (including Olympian Francie Barrett) tied the ten bout contest with Wales five apiece.

16: Rugby In the European Cup Leicester beat Leinster 27-10, Cardiff beat Munster 48-18 and Harlequins beat Ulster 21-15. In the European Conference Connacht completed a miserable day by losing 26-9 to Dunvant.

Squash The Irish women's squash team finished third in their group at the World Team Championships.

19: Soccer Dundalk, St. Pats and Shamrock Rovers all recorded victories in the Premier Division.

20: Soccer There were victories for Coleraine, Crusaders and Ards in the Irish League. The Cliftonville/Portadown game was abandoned; in the F.A.I. National League Cork City beat Derry City and the U.C.D./Home Farm game ended in a one all draw.

Rugby Munster beat Wasps 49-22 in the European Cup while Connacht lost 11-31 to Northampton in the European Conference.

21: G.A.A. Monaghan beat Laois 2-11 to 1-9 in the Ladies All-Ireland final replay. Fermanagh beat Roscommon 2-11 to 1-11 in the All-Ireland 'B' football championship.

22: G.A.A. Mayo and Meath incur fines of £5,000 apiece arising from incidents at the All-Ireland final replay. In addition seven Mayo and eight Meath players were suspended including John McGuinness who received six months and Colm Coyle who received four months, Enda McManus and Ray Dempsey received three months apiece. The eleven others received two months each.

Soccer Lee Boylan scored both goals in the Republic's 2-2 draw with Denmark in the U-20 World Cup qualifier.

26: Soccer St. Pats drew 2-2 with Bray Wanderers and Shelbourne drew 2-2 with Derry City in the Premier Division.

27: Rugby Neath beat Ulster 15-13 and Leinster beat the Scottish Borders 34-25 in the European Cup. Toulon beat Connacht 44-10 in the European Conference.

Soccer In the Irish League Linfield beat Ards, Coleraine beat Glenavon and Portadown beat Glentoran all on 3-2 scorelines, Cliftonville drew 1-1 with Crusaders; in the F.A.I. National League Finn Harps drew 2-2 with Bohemians and Sligo Rovers beat Shamrock Rovers 3-0.

28: G.A.A. Cork beat Meath, Kerry beat Derry and Kildare beat Cavan in Division One of the National Football League. Donegal drew with Tyrone 2-6 apiece.

Golf Darren Clarke with £329,795 finished eighth, Padraig Harrington with £285,023 finished eleventh and Paul McGinley with £264,966 finished fifteenth in the final standings in the European Order of Merit.

NOVEMBER

01: Horse racing Danoli, competing in his first race since breaking a leg in April, won comfortably at Clonmel.

Soccer Sligo Rovers beat Bohemians 2-0 in the League.

02: American Football Almost 40,000 watch Notre Dame beat Navy 54-27 in the Smurfit Shamrock Classic American Colleges' football game at Croke Park.

Rugby Toulouse beat Munster 60-19, Brive beat Ulster 17-6 and Leinster beat Pau 25-23 in the Heineken European Cup. Connacht beat Orrell 30-18 in the

European Conference.

Soccer Derry City and St. Pats drew 1-1 and Shelbourne beat Home Farm/Everton 3-0 in the Premier Division; in the Irish League Glentoran beat Crusaders 3-3, Cliftonville drew 1-1 with Linfield, Portadown drew 2-2 with Coleraine and the Ards/Glenavon game ended in a scoreless draw.

03: Soccer Cork City beat Dundalk 1-0, Finn Harps beat Bray Wanderers 1-0 and Shamrock Rovers draw 1-1 with U.C.D.

07: Snooker The Northern Ireland team of Terry Murphy, Joe Swail and Denis Taylor were beaten 10-6 by Scotland in the World Cup quarter-finals in Thailand.

08: Snooker The Republic of Ireland team of Fergal O'Brien, Stephen Murphy and Ken Doherty beat England 10-9 in the World Cup in Thailand.

Soccer In the F.A.I. Premier Division Shelbourne beat Dundalk 2-1 and Home Farm Farm beat St. Patrick's Athletic 2-1.

09: Boxing Steve Collins successfully defended his W.B.O. Super-middleweight title when Nigel Benn retired injured at the end of the sixth round.

Soccer Gerry Taggart's 39th minute goal helped Northern Ireland secure a 1-1 draw with European champions Germany in their World Cup qualifier; the Republic's U21s lost 1-0 to Iceland; in the F.A.I. Premier Division there were victories for Derry City, Shamrock Rovers and Bohemians, Finn Harps drew 1-1 with Sligo.

Rugby Munster lose 25-35 to the touring Western Samoa side.

10: Soccer The Republic of Ireland were held to a 0-0 draw by Iceland at Lansdowne Road.

Snooker Scotland (Stephen Hendry, John Higgins and Alan McManus) beat the Republic of Ireland 10-7 in the final of the World Cup in Bangkok, Thailand.

G.A.A. In Division One of the National Football League there were victories for Kildare and Meath while Derry drew with Cork.

12: Rugby Ireland lost 40-12 to Western Samoa at Lansdowne Road. The try count stood at 5-1 in favour of the tourists. Meanwhile Ireland 'A' beat South Africa 'A' 28-25 at Donnybrook.

13: Rugby Australia beat Connacht 37-20 at the Sports Ground, Galway.

15: Soccer Bohemians beat U.C.D. 4-0 and Shelbourne beat Dundalk 1-0 in the Premier Division.

16: Rugby At Ravenhill Australia defeated Ulster 39-26. Ireland's U21s beat New Zealand Youths 12-6.

Soccer There are victories for Derry City, St. Pats and Finn Harps in the National League Premier Division; Glentoran, Crusaders, Coleraine and Glenavon all won their Irish League ties.

17: G.A.A. Fermanagh and Longford drew 0-9 apiece in the All-Ireland 'B' football final. Donegal beat Cavan 0-10 to 0-6 in the National Football League Division One.

Hockey In the women's inter-provincial final at Grange Road Leinster defeated the holders, Ulster, 6-0.

Soccer Cork City beat Shamrock Rovers 1-0 in the Harp Lager National League.

19: Soccer In the F.A.I. First Division Shield final Galway United beat Limerick F.C. 2-0 after extra time.

22: G.A.A. Trevor Giles and Martin Storey were voted footballer and hurler of the year respectively by their fellow players. All Ireland finalists Mayo and Meath had five football All-Stars each while Wexford had seven and Limerick five hurling All-Stars.

23: Rugby Ireland lost 22-12 to Australia at Lansdowne Road, out-half Paul Burke scored all Ireland's points from penalties.

Soccer Coleraine, Glentoran and Linfield all record victories in the Smirnoff Irish League while Crusaders draw 0-0 with Glenavon; in the National League Derry City beat Finn Harps 3-0.

24: Soccer U.C.D. drew 1-1 with Sligo Rovers, Cork City drew 0-0 with Bohemians in the Premier Division.

G.A.A. Cork beat Kildare 0-9 to 1-5 and Kerry beat Donegal 2-9 to 2-7 in Division One of the League.

Golf Darren Clarke's course record of 64 helped him and partner Padraig Harrington to 19th in the World Cup Golf Tournament in Cape Town. South Africa won the competition.

Snooker Joe Canny qualifies for the last 16 of the World Amateur Championships in New Zealand.

Michael O'Hehir, who commentated on 99 All-Ireland finals died peacefully aged 77. Tributes flooded in to the diminutive man who was the voice of the G.A.A.

26: Rugby Munster slump to a 55-19 defeat at the hands of Australia at Thomond Park.

29: Snooker Ken Doherty is beaten 9-3 by John Higgins in the UK Championship final.

Soccer Dundalk beat Bray Wanderers 2-1 and St. Patrick's Athletic beat Shamrock Rovers 1-0 in the F.A.I. Premier Division.

30: Soccer Finn Harps beat U.C.D. 5-1, Cork City beat Sligo 4-1 and Derry City beat Home Farm/Everton 2-0 in the National League.

DECEMBER

01: G.A.A. Tyrone beat Meath 1-14 to 1-4 in Division One of the National Football League.

Soccer Bohemians drew with Shelbourne 1-1.

06: Soccer In the F.A.I. Premier Division St. Patrick's Athletic beat Bohemians 5-0.

07: Rugby The Insurance Corporation All Ireland League kicks off with victories in Division One for Shannon, Blackrock, Terenure, Lansdowne, St. Mary's, Old Wesley and Cork Constitution.

Soccer Derry City and Finn Harps win their Premier Division games; in the Irish League there were victories for Glenavon and Glentoran while the Ards/Crusaders and Cliftonville/Portadown games were drawn.

08: G.A.A. Fermanagh won their first ever senior national title when they beat Longford 0-12 to 0-9 in the All-Ireland 'B' Football final replay at Carrick-on-Shannon.

Tennis Ireland's men's team of Scott Barron, Owen Casey and Tommy Hamilton gained promotion to Group One of the European team championships by beating Poland, Monaco and Luxembourg in Dublin.

Athletics Sonia O'Sullivan won her first competitive race since the Olympics, a mile road race in Holland.

Soccer Shamrock Rovers, Cork City, and Shelbourne won their Premier Division ties.

13: Soccer Dundalk beat Home Farm/Everton 2-1 in the League.

14: Soccer In the World Cup qualifier at Windsor Park two first half goals from Ian Dowie gave Northern Ireland a 2-0 victory over Albania; Cork City beat Finn Harps 1-0 and Sligo Rovers beat St. Pats 2-0 in the Premier Division.

Rugby There were victories in Division One of the A.I.L.

for Blackrock, Garryowen, Lansdowne, Shannon, St. Mary's, Dungannon and Young Munster.

Athletics Gary Ryan set a new Irish 200m record of 21.96 seconds becoming the first Irishman to break the 22 second barrier.

15: Soccer Bohemians beat Bray, Shamrock Rovers beat Derry City and Shelbourne beat U.C.D. in the F.A.I. Premier Division.

Athletics At the European Cross Country Championships in Belgium the Irish women's team finished in seventh place while the men finished in eighth.

17: Soccer In the National League Cup Final first leg Galway United beat Cork City 3-1 at Terryland Park.

19: Soccer Shamrock Rovers and Home Farm/Everton played a scoreless draw in the Premier Division.

20: Soccer On a night of draws in the F.A.I. National League the results were Dundalk 1-1 Finn Harps, Shelbourne 3-3 Cork City and St. Pats 1-1 U.C.D.

21: Rugby In Division One of the A.I.L. Cork Constitution, Garryowen, St. Mary's College, Old Belvedere, Lansdowne, Terenure College and Ballymena all recorded victories.

22: Soccer In the F.A.I. Premier Division Bray Wanderers and Sligo Rovers drew 2-2. A bad tempered game at the Brandywell was marred by a fracas involving Derry manager Felix Healy and dismissed Bohemians player James Coll. Derry won the game 1-0.

Squash Derek Ryan retained the Irish National Squash Title at Fitzwilliam. Aisling McArdle won the women's title for the third successive time.

23: Swimming Michelle Smith made a winning comeback in the 50m Freestyle at Bordeaux. It was her first competitive swim since the Olympics in Atlanta.

27: Soccer Dundalk beat Shamrock Rovers 2-0 in the National League.

28: Soccer Derry City defeated Sligo Rovers 1-0 in the National League.

29: Soccer Bohemians drew 1-1 with Home Farm/Everton, Cork City drew 1-1 with St. Pats and U.C.D. beat Bray Wanderers 2-1 in the National League.

JANUARY

01: Soccer F.A.I. league cup final second leg, Cork City 1 Galway United 1, Galway won 4-2 on aggregate.

03: Rugby Blackrock beat Greystones 15-12 in the final of the Smithwick's Old Belvedere Floodlit Cup.

04: Rugby Ireland lost 37-29 to Italy at Lansdowne Road and scored one try to Italy's four.

Athletics The I.A.A.F. World Cross Country Challenge at Belfast was held in Belfast. Ethiopian M. Woide won the men's event with D. Donnelly the top Irish finisher in eighth. Romanian E. Fidatiof won the women's event and eighth placed M. Harrington was the leading Irish finisher.

Soccer In the Irish League there were victories for Crusaders and Linfield while the Coleraine/Ards and Glentoran/Cliftonville games were drawn.

05: Soccer Bray Wanderers and Cork City drew 0-0 in the F.A.I. National League.

Rugby Murray Kidd's tenure as coach of the national team ended.

10: Soccer In the F.A.I. Cup first round St. Pats beat Athlone Town 1-0 and Shelbourne beat Everton 4-2.

11: Horse racing The £60,000 Ladbroke Hurdle at Leopardstown was won by Master Tribe, ridden by Norman Williamson and trained by Jenny Pitman.

Boxing Belfast's Wayne McCullough lost a split decision to Mexican Daniel Zaragoza in their W.B.C. Super-Bantamweight (8st 10lbs) title fight in Boston. It was McCullough's first fight at Super-Bantamweight.

Soccer In the F.A.I. Cup first round there were victories for Sligo Rovers, Dublin University, Derry City, Home Farm, St. Francis and Bray Wanderers; in the Irish League Premier Division Glentoran beat Glenavon 2-1 while the Ards/Portadown, Cliftonville/Coleraine and Linfield/Crusaders games ended drawn.

Rugby Dungannon, Terenure College, Ballymena, Garryowen, Blackrock College and Shannon all recorded victories in the All Ireland League Division One while Cork Constitution and St. Mary's drew 23 apiece.

Athletics Sonia O'Sullivan won the first race of her Australian tour.

12: Soccer In the F.A.I. Cup first round Cork City, Drogheda United, Bohemians, Shamrock Rovers, Rockmount, Wayside Celtic all won their ties while Whitehall Rangers drew 0-0 with Dundalk.

Rugby Brian Ashton appointed as Ireland's new coach.

15: Soccer Dundalk beat Whitehall Rangers 5-1 in their Cup replay.

17: Rugby France 'A' beat Ireland 'A' 44-23 at Donnybrook, while the Irish U21s lost 40-13 to their French counterparts at Anglesea Road.

Soccer Shelbourne beat Bray Wanderers 1-0 in the National League.

18: Rugby In the first match of the Five Nations Series Ireland were beaten 32-15 by France at Lansdowne Road, with Eric Elwood scoring all of Ireland's points from penalties. France ran in four tries.

Soccer In the Irish League there were victories for Glenavon and Portadown while the Coleraine/Glentoran and Crusaders/Ards games ended in draws; in the F.A.I. National League Sligo Rovers beat Dundalk and St. Pats beat Finn Harps.

19: Soccer In the F.A.I. National League Shamrock Rovers drew with Bohemians, U.C.D. drew with Home Farm and Derry City beat Cork City 1-0.

Horse racing Cockney Lad won the AIG European Champion Hurdle at Leopardstown.

21: Soccer St. Pats and Shelbourne draw 1-1 in the National League.

22: Soccer Northern Ireland lost 2-0 to Italy in a friendly international at Palermo.

24: Soccer In the National League Premier Division Bohemians beat Finn Harps 3-1 and Dundalk drew 2-2 with U.C.D.

25: Soccer In the fifth round of the Irish Cup there were victories for Glenavon, Bangor, Cliftonville, Coleraine, Glentoran, Crusaders, Portadown, Coagh United, Limavady United, Chimney Corner and Dundela. The Newry Town/Omagh Town, R.U.C./Carrick Rangers, Dunmurry/Larne, Telecom/Crumlin, Dungannon Swifts/Loughgall United and Enkalon/Portstewart games all ended in draws; Derry City drew with Shelbourne and Cork City beat Home Farm 2-0.

Rugby In the Insurance Corporation All-Ireland League there were victories for Shannon, Terenure, Garryowen, Lansdowne, Old Belvedere, Old Crescent and St. Mary's.

26: G.A.A. Connacht beat Munster 2-15 to 1-17 in the

Railway Cup football semi-final at Ennis while at Navan Leinster defeated Ulster 3-14 to 1-10.

Soccer In the F.A.I. National League there were victories for St. Pats and Shamrock Rovers.

Basketball Delta Notre Dame beat St. Vincent's 80-76 in the Sprite National Cup final at the National Basketball Arena in Tallaght. Anthony Jenkins was Notre Dame's top scorer with 29 points. Naomh Mhuire beat Meteors 70-63 in the Women's Cup final. Ursula Kyne was Naomh Mhuire's top scorer with 18 points.

28: Swimming Nick O'Hare set a new Irish record of 50.02 in the 100m Freestyle.

29: Swimming Nick O'Hare set another new Irish record of 22.77 in the 50m Freestyle.

FEBRUARY

01: Rugby Ireland hold out to beat Wales 26-25 in the Five Nations Championship at Cardiff. There were tries from Johnathon Bell, Eric Miller and Denis Hickie, and three penalties and a conversion from Eric Elwood; **Soccer** Shelbourne and Sligo won their matches while Finn Harps and Bray Wanderers played out a scoreless draw in the Premier Division of the F.A.I. National League; there were victories for Ards, Crusaders, and Glentoran in the Irish League Premier Division while Glenavon drew with Coleraine.

02: Golf Padraig Harrington was the top Irish finisher in the Perth Classic sharing 11th place and winning a prize of £11,113.

G.A.A. Kerry, Derry, Meath and Cork all recorded victories in Division One of the Church and General National Football League.

Badminton Winners from the National Badminton Championships men's singles: Michael Watt; women's singles: Keelin Fox; men's doubles Donie O'Halloran and Mark Peard; and women's doubles E. O'Kiely and C. O'Sullivan.

Athletics Catherina McKiernan finished second in the I.A.A.F. cross-country challenge at Tourcoing, France.

Horse racing Danoli won the £59,000 Hennessy Gold Cup at Leopardstown to the delight of jockey Tommy Treacy, trainer Tom Foley and owner Dan O'Neill.

Soccer U.C.D. beat Shamrock Rovers 1-0 and Cork City drew 0-0 with Dundalk in the F.A.I. Premier Division.

Athletics Defending champion Niall Bruton finished third in Wannamker Mile in New York. Marcus O'Sullivan finished fifth. Mark Carroll retained his 3,000m title.

08: Rugby There were victories for Cork Constitution, Blackrock College, Instonians, Old Crescent, Shannon, Lansdowne and Young Munster in Division One of the Insurance Corporation All-Ireland League.

Soccer Bray Wanderers, Derry City, Drogheda United, and St. Patrick's Athletic all advanced in the F.A.I. Cup; Cliftonville and Coleraine recorded victories in the I.F.A. Premier Division while the Ards/Glenavon and Crusaders/Glentoran games ended in draws.

Snooker Ken Doherty was beaten 6-1 by Steve Davis in the semi-final of the Benson & Hedges Masters.

09: Basketball Neptune defeated Star of the Sea 80-82 in the crucial men's Superleague top-of-the-table clash.

Boxing Steve Collins retained his W.B.O. Super-middleweight title stopping Frederic Seillier of France in the fifth round. Welterweight Michael Carruth recorded a points victory on the undercard.

Rugby Ireland's women were beaten 32-0 by England.

G.A.A. Leinster beat Connacht 2-14 to 0-12 in the Railway Cup football final.

11: Soccer Northern Ireland beat Belgium 3-0 in a friendly at Windsor Park. Wales and the Republic of Ireland drew 0-0 in a friendly in Cardiff.

14: Athletics Eamon Coughlan's fifteen year world record for the indoor mile was broken by Morocco's Hicham el Guerrojh.

14: Soccer Bohemians beat Cork City 1-0, Shamrock Rovers beat Shelbourne 6-4 and Dundalk drew 2-2 with St. Pats in the F.A.I. Premier Division.

15: Rugby England ran in six tries to record a 46-6 victory over Ireland at Lansdowne Road. Ireland's only scorer was Eric Elwood who was taken off injured after 25 minutes. It was Ireland's heaviest ever defeat to England.

Athletics James Nolan of U.C.D. won the 800m in an International Indoor meeting in Vienna.

Soccer Northern Ireland beat the Republic 1-0 in an U-15 friendly international; in the F.A.I. Premier Division Derry City, Bray Wanderers and Sligo Rovers all won, while in the I.F.A. Premier Division Cliftonville, Coleraine, and Linfield record victories. Portadown versus Glenavon ended 1-1.

16: G.A.A. There were victories for Tyrone, Kildare, Kerry and Derry in Division one of the National Football League; in the A.I.B. All-Ireland Club hurling Championship Athenry advanced to the final while Cushendall and Wolfe Tones from Shannon drew 1-10 to 2-8.

Golf Padraig Harrington finished joint fourth in the Sun City Pro-Am in South Africa.

Rallying Austin McHale, driving a Toyota Celica won the Statoil Galway International Rally.

21: Soccer Bohemians beat Shelbourne 1-0 in the F.A.I. Premier Division; University of Ulster at Jordanstown beat University College Cork 4-3 on penalties in the Collingwood Cup final.

22: Soccer Derry City came from behind to draw 1-1 with Home Farm/Everton; in the I.F.A. Cup there were victories for Loughgall, Coagh United, Glenavon, Cliftonville, Coleraine, Crusaders and Omagh Town while Bangor and Limavady United drew 1-1.

Rugby In the All-Ireland League Division One there were victories for Shannon, Lansdowne, Garryowen, Blackrock, Terenure College, Old Belvedere and Ballymena; Ireland's ladies were beaten 28-3 by Scotland in the women's Four Nations Championship.

Horse racing Adrian Maguire rode five winners (at cumulative odds of 355 to 1) at Kempton.

23: Snooker T.J. Dowling won the U19 National Title beating R. Redmond 3-2 in the final.

G.A.A. Knockmore from Mayo, and Crossmaglen Rangers from Armagh qualified for the A.I.B. All-Ireland Club Championship football final.

28: Rugby Ireland's U21s trounced Scotland 31-0, and Ireland 'A' defeated their Scottish counterparts 34-33.

Soccer St. Pats beat Bohemians 1-0, Derry beat Dundalk 1-0 and Shamrock Rovers drew 2-2 with Bray Wanderers in the F.A.I. National League.

MARCH

01: Rugby Ireland lost 38-10 to Scotland in their final game in the Five Nations at Murrayfield. The try count stood at five to one in favour of Scotland, Ireland collected the wooden spoon.

Hockey Hermes beat Muckross 2-1 in the Ladies Irish Senior Cup final at Belfield.

Soccer Ards, Crusaders, Glenavon and Coleraine all recorded victories in the I.F.A. Smirnoff Irish League; in the F.A.I. National League Shelbourne beat Sligo Rovers 3-0 and Finn Harps beat Home Farm 3-0.

Swimming Michelle Smith comfortably won her heat of the 100m Individual Medley at the Leisureland International meet in Galway.

02: G.A.A. Derry, Meath, Kildare and Kerry all won their National Football League Division One games.

Soccer U.C.D. beat Cork City 3-0 in the National League.

Golf Paul McGinley and Raymond Burns finished joint sixth in the Dubai Desert Classic winning £19,652 each.

04: Hockey Ireland lost 2-1 to Belgium in the men's World Cup qualifying tournament in Kuala Lumpur, Malaysia

05: Hockey South Korea beat Ireland 3-1 in the World Cup qualifying tournament in Malaysia.

07: Athletics Gary Ryan set a new Irish record 200m of 21.13 at the World Indoor Championships in Paris. Niall Bruton qualified for the 1,500m final, Mark Carroll was beaten in his 3,000m semi-final, James Nolan was second in his heat while David Matthews failed to advance in the 800m.

Hockey Argentina defeated Ireland 9-1 in the World Cup qualifying tournament.

Soccer Bohemians beat St. Pats 1-0 and Waterford beat Drogheda 1-0 in the F.A.I. Cup quarter-finals.

08: Soccer Former Republic of Ireland international John Aldridge equalled Jimmy Greaves' all-time scoring record in the English league. Tranmere player-manager Aldridge scored his 467th goal in their 3-2 defeat at Wolves; Cliftonville, Crusaders and Portadown record victories in the Irish League Premier Division while Ards drew 3-3 with Coleraine.

Athletics Sonia O'Sullivan won silver in the 3,000m at the World Indoor Championships in Paris, Sinead Delahunty finished in a creditable 15th.

Rugby Old Wesley, Young Munster, Blackrock, Ballymena, Old Crescent, Shannon and St. Mary's all won their A.I.L. Division One games.

09: G.A.A. In the opening round of the Church & General National Hurling League there were victories for Clare, Limerick, Galway and Offaly in Division; Offaly's footballers won the O'Byrne Cup hammering Wexford 4-13 to 0-5.

Hockey Ireland secured their first point in the World Cup qualifying tournament holding New Zealand to a 1-1 draw.

10: Hockey Ireland's men's team beat Belarus 3-2.

11: Horse racing On the first day of the Cheltenham National Hunt festival Tony McCoy rode the Martin Pipe trained Make A Stand to victory in the Smurfit Champion Hurdle Challenge Trophy.

12: Horse racing The first Irish success at Cheltenham came in the Royal Sun Alliance Novice Hurdle when Charlie Swan won on the Aidan O'Brien trained Istabraq. Martha's Son won the Queen Mother Champion Chase.

13: Horse racing Tony McCoy (who won the jockey's championship) rode Mr Mulligan to victory in the Gold Cup, while trainer Ted Walsh tasted success when

Norman Williamson rode Commanche Court to victory in the Elite Triumph Hurdle.

14: Soccer Home Farm/Everton beat Shamrock Rovers 3-2 in the League.

Hockey Ireland lost the 11th/12th place playoff 2-1 to Belarus in Kuala Lumpur.

15: Soccer Finn Harps drew with Dundalk and Bray Wanderers beat Sligo Rovers in the National League.

Rugby In the A.I.L. First Division there were victories for Shannon, St. Mary's, Ballymena, Cork Constitution, Dungannon and Terenure College.

16: Soccer Derry City, Shelbourne and U.C.D. all won their Premier Division games.

Golf Darren Clarke collected £13,745 for his joint fourth place finish in the Portuguese Open.

Basketball Star of the Sea won the Budweiser Superleague Top Four men's final beating Neptune 90-85. Naomh Mhuire won the women's Superleague Top Four final beating Tolka Rovers 76-69.

17: G.A.A. Crossmaglen Rangers (Armagh) beat Knockmore (Mayo) 2-13 to 0-11 in the A.I.B. All-Ireland Club Championship final while St. Mary's (Galway) beat Wolfe Tone's (Clare) 0-14 to 1-8 in the hurling final, 32,582 people attended the Croke Park matches.

18: Snooker The Benson & Hedges Irish Masters opened at Goffs, Co. Kildare with first round victories for Jimmy White and Ronnie O'Sullivan.

19: Snooker John Parrot defeated Dublin's Stephen Murphy 6-5 while Steve Davis beat Ken Doherty 6-1 in the first round at Goffs.

Hockey Muckross held Loreto to a scoreless draw to retain their Senior Ladies Leinster title.

20: Snooker In the quarter-finals of the Irish Masters Ronnie O'Sullivan beat John Higgins 6-4 and Stephen Hendry beat Jimmy White 6-5.

21: Snooker In the second set of quarter-finals Peter Ebdon beat Steve Davis 6-1 and Darren Morgan beat John Parrot 6-2.

Soccer Shelbourne and Shamrock Rovers won in the National League while Cork City held St. Pats to a scoreless draw.

Rugby Ireland were beaten by both Argentina and South Africa in the World Cup Sevens in Hong Kong.

22: Snooker Stephen Hendry advanced to the final at Goffs beating Ronnie O'Sullivan 6-2, Darren Morgan beat Peter Ebdon 6-2 in the other semi-final.

Rugby Shannon, Cork Constitution, Lansdowne, Young Munster, Ballymena, Dungannon and St. Mary's all won their first division ties in the All Ireland League; Ireland lost to Hong Kong in the World Cup Sevens.

Soccer Sligo Rovers beat Derry City 2-0 in the National League; in the Irish League Crusaders beat Linfield 3-0, Glentoran beat Glenavon 2-1, Portadown beat Ards 5-0 and Coleraine drew 1-1 with Cliftonville.

23: Snooker Stephen Hendry took the £72,000 first prize beating Darren Morgan 10-9 in the Benson & Hedges Irish Masters final.

Athletics The Irish women's team who finished third overall were the top European finishers in the World Cross Country Championships.

G.A.A. Kilkenny beat Galway, Offaly beat Wexford, Tipperary beat Laois and Limerick drew with Clare in Division One of the National Hurling League. Tyrone's footballers lost their relegation playoff with Meath 2-9 to 1-9.

Soccer Bray beat U.C.D. 2-0 and Bohemians drew 2-2

with Home Farm in the National League.
Rugby Ireland beat Portugal but lost to Japan in the World Cup Sevens.
26: Cricket Ireland beat Israel by 10 wickets in the I.C.C. Trophy in Kuala Lumpur.
27: Cricket Ireland beat the U.S.A. in the I.C.C. Trophy.
28: Soccer Bohemians drew with Dundalk, Shelbourne drew with St. Patrick's Athletic, Cork City beat Bray Wanderers and Shamrock Rovers beat Finn Harps in the National League.
Hockey German side Gladbacher HTC beat Irish champions Avoca 5-0 in A Division of the men's European Cup Winners' Cup. In the women's competition Pegasus held French champions Amiens to a 1-1 draw.
Boxing Ireland's amateurs lost to Italy by five bouts to two in the National Stadium.
29: Soccer Northern Ireland were held to a 0-0 draw by Portugal in the World Cup qualifier at Windsor Park; in the National League Sligo Rovers beat Home Farm 3-2.
Rugby St. Mary's, Shannon, Terenure, Ballymena, Garryowen and Old Crescent all won their A.I.L. Division One matches.
30: G.A.A. Kilkenny, Limerick, Galway and Clare all recorded victories in the N.H.L. Division One.
Hockey Avoca lost 3-0 to Russian side Ekaterinburg in the European Cup.
Cricket Ireland beat Singapore by ten wickets in the I.C.C. Trophy.
31: Horse racing Mudahim won the Irish Grand National at Fairyhouse in a photo finish. Mudahim was trained by Jenny Pitman and ridden by Jason Titley.
Rallying Bertie Fisher and navigator Rory Kennedy, driving a Subaru, won the Circuit of Ireland Rally by over three minutes from Austin McHale in second.
Soccer Cork City beat Finn Harps 1-0 in the league.

APRIL

01: Soccer The Republic of Ireland beat Macedonia 4-0 in their U21 European Championship qualifier.
Horse racing Richard Dunwoody won an emotional Powers Gold Cup on the Michael Hourigan trained Doran's Pride. Doran's Pride was to have been the mount of Shane Broderick who was seriously injured the previous day. An appeal fund has been set up in his name.
Cricket Ireland defeated Holland in the I.C.C. Cup in Malaysia.
02: Soccer In the World Cup qualifiers Macedonia beat the Republic of Ireland 3-2, Alan McLoughlin and David Kelly scored for the Republic; the Ukraine beat Northern Ireland 2-1, Ian Dowie scored a 13th minute penalty.
04:Soccer In the F.A.I. Cup semi-finals Derry City beat Bohemians 2-0 in the other semi-final holders Shelbourne beat First Division Waterford 2-1.
Cricket Ireland beat Hong Kong by 51 runs in the quarter-final of the I.C.C. Trophy in Malaysia.
05: Rugby Shannon won their third successive Insurance Corporation All-Ireland League by defeating Old Crescent 28-15 while Instonians were relegated to Division Two; Clontarf secured promotion to Division One of the A.I.L; Ireland Schools defeated Wales Schools 27-25; Ireland Youths defeated Scotland Youths 22-5.
06: G.A.A. There were victories for Kildare, Laois, Cork

and Kerry in the quarter-finals of the National Football League.
Soccer Glenmore Celtic defeated Everton 1-0 in the F.A.I. Intermediate Cup final.
Rowing Trinity beat U.C.D. by half-a-length in the 49th University Boat Race.
07: Cricket Ireland lost by seven runs to Kenya in the I.C.C. semi-final.
Horse Racing The Martell English Grand National was won by Lord Gyllene, ridden by Down's Tony Dobbin.
08: Soccer Shelbourne defeated U.C.D. 1-0 in the league.
11: Cricket Ireland lost their third place playoff with Scotland in the I.C.C. Trophy by 46 runs.
Soccer St. Pats beat Bray 2-1 in the National League.
12: Rugby Old Wesley were relegated to Division Two of the A.I.L. while Dolphin were promoted from Division Two.
G.A.A. Joe McDonagh formally became President of the G.A.A.
Soccer Cliftonville defeated Loughgall United in the I.F.A. Cup semi-final; in the F.A.I. National League Bohemians defeated Finn Harps while the Sligo Rovers/Shamrock Rovers and Shelbourne/Derry City games ended in draws.
13: Formula 1 Ferrari's Eddie Irvine finished second in the Argentinian Grand Prix, Jordan driver Ralf Schumacher finished third.
G.A.A. In Division One of the National Hurling League there were victories for Kilkenny, Wexford and Galway, while Limerick and Tipperary drew; Derry defeated Fermanagh, Mayo defeated Galway and Meath defeated Westmeath in their respective provincial U21 football finals.
Soccer In the National League U.C.D. beat Dundalk 3-1 while Home Farm held Cork City to a scoreless draw.
15: Soccer Derry drew 1-1 with Shamrock Rovers while both Finn Harps and St. Pats recorded victories.
18-20: Hockey Ireland's ladies defeated Poland (11-0), Wales (4-1) and Slovakia (7-0)
19: Soccer Derry City won their second ever National League title by defeating St. Patrick's Athletic 2-0 at the Brandywell. Home Farm and Bray Wanderers were relegated. In the Irish League Cliftonville beat Ards, Portadown beat Glenavon and Linfield drew with Glentoran. Crusaders won the Smirnoff Irish League Premier Division title following their 0-0 draw with Coleraine.
20: G.A.A. Cork defeated Kildare and Kerry defeated Laois to qualify for the National Football League final.
Golf Paul McGinley shared sixth spot (winning £9,750) in the Cannes Open.
22: G.A.A. Kerry beat Cork 0-12 to 0-7 in the replay of the Munster U21 football final.
Soccer In the National League Bray drew with Shelbourne while newly crowned champions Derry City lost 2-0 at home to Cork City.
23: Horse racing Noyan won the Heineken Gold Cup at Punchestown.
24: Soccer Shamrock Rovers defeated Bohemians 3-1 in the National League.
26: G.A.A. Derry and Meath qualified for the U21 All Ireland Football final.
Swimming Michelle Smith set two new Irish records at a meeting in France, 8:52.10 in the 800m freestyle and 57.53 in the 100m freestyle

Hockey Lisnagarvey's men won the Nissan Irish Senior Cup beating Pembroke Wanderers 4-3 at Belfield

27: Formula 1 Eddie Irvine finished third in the San Marino Grand Prix, Jordan driver Giancarlo Fisichella finished fourth.

G.A.A. Fermanagh won the McKenna Cup final defeating Tyrone by 2-11 to 3-4.

Rugby Carlow beat Navan 21-3 in the Leinster Provincial Towns Cup.

Soccer Drogheda secured promotion to the F.A.I. Harp Lager Premier Division.

Motorcycling James Courtney won the Grand Final of the Cookstown 100 Road Race.

29: Cricket Ireland's cricketers enjoyed a famous victory beating Middlesex in the Benson & Hedges Cup.

30: Soccer In the World Cup qualifiers Romania defeated the Republic of Ireland in Bucharest 1-0 while Armenia held Northern Ireland to a scoreless draw at Yerevan.

Snooker Ken Doherty defeated John Higgins 13-9 in the quarter finals of the World Snooker Championship.

MAY

01: Hockey Hosts Canada beat Ireland 1-0 in the five nation ladies hockey tournament in Vancoeuver.

03: Soccer Glenavon beat Cliftonville 1-0 to win the Bass Irish Cup for the fifth time in their history.

04: G.A.A. Kerry defeated Cork by 3-7 to 1-8 in the Church & General National Football League final at Páirc Uí Chaoimh watched by a crowd of 28,795; Kerry were also victorious in the All-Ireland Vocational Schools inter-county final defeating Tyrone 0-10 to 0-8.

Soccer Reigning Champions Shelbourne defeated Derry City 2-0 in the F.A.I. Harp Lager Cup final at Dalymount Park.

Horse Racing Kieran Fallon rode the 5/1 shot Sleepytime to victory in the English 1,000 Guineas at Newmarket.

Golf Darren Clarke, third (winning £29,259) and Philip Walton, joint fourth (winning £21,583) were the top Irish finishers in the Italian Open

Tennis Belarus defeated Ireland in Davis Cup tennis at Riverview by three rubbers to one.

Rallying Austin McHale, driving a Toyota Celica won the Rally of the Lakes in Kerry by over a minute.

Hockey Lisnagarvey won the Irish Club Championship defeating Cork Church of Ireland 5-1.

05: Snooker Ken Doherty became World Snooker Champion defeating six time winner Stephen Hendry 18-12 in the two day final. Doherty - the third Irish champion after Alex Higgins and Denis Taylor - collected a first prize of £210,000. He defeated Mark Davis, former champion Steve Davis, John Higgins and Alain Robidoux en route to the final.

Hockey Ireland's ladies drew 4-4 with Japan in Vancoeuver.

06: Soccer Dundalk retained their F.A.I. Premier Division status defeating Waterford 3-1 over the two leg playoff.

Cricket Ireland lost to Glamorgan by six wickets in the Benson & Hedges Cup.

08: Tennis In the Federation Cup the Irish team of Gina Niland and Zara Wolseley lost 3-0 to Yugoslavia.

09: Tennis Ireland defeated Cameroon 3-0 in their Federation Cup tie.

10: G.A.A. All-Ireland hurling champions Wexford were relegated from Division One of the National Hurling League.

Rugby Lansdowne won the Leinster Senior Cup beating Bective Rangers 40-8; Ballymena defeated Malone by 20-13 in the Ulster Senior Cup final.

Volleyball Artane/Dundrum beat U.C.D. 3-2 in the men's senior Championship final; East Coast Coolers beat Aer Lingus 3-1 in the ladies Championship final.

11: G.A.A. Derry won the All-Ireland U21 football title defeating Meath 1-12 to 0-5, man of the match, Derry's Joe Cassidy scored five points - equal to the entire Meath score; the first balls were kicked in the 1997 Bank of Ireland Senior Football Championship with victory for Offaly while draws between Wexford and Westmeath and Limerick and Tipperary mean they must meet again.

Rugby Galwegians beat Ballina 30-25 in the Connacht Senior Cup final replay while Garryowen beat Young Munster 12-6 in the Munster Cup final; London Irish secured their place in Division One of the Courage Clubs Championship defeating Coventry 28-7 in the second play-off (they won 42-23 on aggregate).

Cycling Comeragh's Ciaran Power won the Shay Elliot Trophy Race at Bray.

Formula 1 Ferrari's Eddie Irvine finished third in the Monaco Grand Prix. Jordan's Giancarlo Fisichella finished sixth.

Golf Padraig Harrington was the top Irish finisher at the Benson & Hedges International Open collecting a prize of £35,000 for his fourth place finish.

13: Rugby League In their first ever full international Ireland drew 30-30 with France in Paris.

17: G.A.A. Westmeath beat Wexford 2-17 to 1-15 in the Leinster Senior Football Championship; following a week of controversy Dublin County Board vice-chairman Paddy Delaney accepted a two month suspension passed by the Management Committee but overturned by the Dublin County Board. The suspension related to the Dublin/Offaly U21 Leinster football quarter final on March 15th when he allegedly spat at Jason Sherlock.

Cycling Jeff Wright of the England North East team won the 77 mile Dublin to Roscommon first stage of the F.B.D. Milk Rás.

18: Soccer 21,400 fans attended the Packie Bonner testimonial at Lansdowne Road and saw the Republic of Ireland beat Celtic 3-2.

Hockey Instonians qualified for the European Championship 'B' division final.

G.A.A. In the first round of the Guinness All-Ireland Senior Hurling Championship there were victories for Dublin over Westmeath, Offaly over Meath and Clare over Kerry; in the Bank of Ireland Senior Football Championship there was victory for Tipperary over Limerick while Down drew with Tyrone in Clones.

Golf England's Tommy Horton won the Irish Seniors Open at St. Margaret's winning £12,130. Liam Higgins was the top Irish finisher, eleven shots off the pace; Darren Clarke, in joint seventh was the top Irish finisher at the English Open.

Cycling Dutchman Jeoren Slagter went into the overall lead in the F.B.D. Milk Rás following his victory in the Roscommon to Clifden stage.

Equestrian Sport Ireland finished second to Britain in the Nation's Cup at Royal Windsor.

19: Cycling Gregorz Gwiazdowski won the 99 mile

Clifden to Lisdoonvarna third stage of the F.B.d. Milk Rás, Holland's Pelle Kil moved into the overall lead.

Hockey Instonians defeated Amisora (Italy) 4-3 in a shootout in the B Division final of the men's European Championship.

Badminton In the World Team Championships at Glasgow Ireland beat Peru 4-1 in their fifth division tie.

20: Cycling Stoke's Mark McKay won stage four of the Milk Rás. Following the 105 mile Lisdoonvarna-Tralee stage Matthew Postle from Wales took the yellow jersey.

Soccer The Republic of Ireland U18 side qualified for the European Championships following their 3-0 victory over Norway.

Badminton Ireland defeated Spain 4-1 in the World Team Championships.

21: Soccer The Republic of Ireland defeated Liechtenstein 5-0 in the World Cup qualifiers. David Connolly scored a hat-trick.

Cycling Stage five of the 1997 Milk Rás, 88 miles from Killarney to Killorglin was won by Tipperary's Michael Fitzgerald. Matthew Postle retained the leaders' yellow jersey.

Badminton Ireland defeated Kazakhstan 4-1 Division Five of the World Team Championships.

22: Cycling Ian Gilkes won the sixth (84 mile Killorglin to Bandon) stage of the Milk Rás. Ciarán Power moved into the overall lead.

Rugby Ireland's development side were hammered 69-16 by Northland on their New Zealand tour.

23: Cycling Stephane Calvez of France won the 94 mile seventh stage of the F.B.D. Milk Rás, Kerry's Andy Roche moved into the overall lead.

Badminton Ireland's quest for promotion to Division Four ended with a 4-1 defeat by Belarus.

Basketball Ireland's men are beaten 82-79 by Belgium in the European Championship qualifying group match in Tallaght; Ireland's women are beaten by Croatia 90-32 and 70-39 by Portugal in the European Championship in Maderia.

Soccer Mick McCarthy's contract as manager of the Republic of Ireland was extended until after the European Championships in the year 2000.

24: Cycling Mike Smith of the Antrim U.C.F. team won the 95 mile eighth stage of the F.B.D. Milk Rás from Tramore to Carlow. Andrew Roche retained his lead.

Horse racing The Aidan O'Brien trained Classic Park won the Irish 1,000 Guineas at the Curragh.

25: G.A.A. Limerick defeated Waterford by six points in the Guinness Hurling Championship; in football there were victories for Mayo over Galway, Tyrone over Down and Donegal over Antrim. Offaly and Westmeath drew.

Golf Suzanne Fanagan won the Irish Women's Close Championship at Enniscrone beating Eileen Rose Power by four holes in the final.

Cycling Andrew Roche holds on to win the Milk Rás by five seconds from Mark McKay. McKay won the morning's time trial and Michaél Fitzgerald won the tenth and final stage. Britain won the team event.

Snooker 17 year-old T.J. Dowling beat Gary Hardiman 8-6 in the Irish Snooker Championship Final at Carlow.

Squash Ireland's women won the three country international competition at Newtownards. The men were beaten into second place by Scotland.

Horse racing Christy Roche rode the Aidan O'Brien trained Desert King to victory in the Irish 2,000 Guineas at the Curragh.

26: Rugby New Zealand Academy defeated the Irish development team 74-15.

29: Rugby Bay of Plenty defeated the Irish development side 52-19 in New Zealand.

30: Athletics Nenagh's Neil Ryan set a new Irish record of 10.46 seconds for the 100m.

JUNE

01: G.A.A. Leitrim beat London 2-18 to 1-13 after extra time in the Connacht Senior Championship game at Ruislip. Declan Darcy scored 2-13 of Leitrim's total; there were also victories for Louth over Carlow and Tipperary over Waterford while Derry and Monaghan drew in Clones.

Golf Darren Clarke made certain of Ryder Cup selection when he finished in fourth place in the Tournament Players Championship at Hamburg and collected a cheque for £37,500. Paul McGinley finished in joint fifth picking up £20,598.

Rugby Ireland 'A' recorded their first victory in the tour of New Zealand beating Thames Valley 38-12.

Equestrian Sport Ireland finished fifth in the Nations Cup event at St. Gallen in Switzerland.

07: G.A.A. Offaly won their Leinster Senior Football Championship replay beating Westmeath 1-14 to 0-7.

Athletics Irish athletes struggled at the Europa Cup meeting at Morton Stadium, Santry. Good performances came from Tom McGuirk and Mark Mandy who finished second in the 400m hurdles and high jump respectively and the men's 4x100m relay team who set a new national record of 40.36.

Snooker Jonathon Nelson became Northern Ireland snooker champion defeating Paddy Doherty 10-5 in the final played in Banbridge.

Horse racing Irish jockey Willie Ryan guided Benny the Dip to victory in the Epsom Derby at 11 to 1.

08: G.A.A. Clare defeated Cork 1-19 to 0-18 in the Munster Senior Hurling Championship semi-final and in the Leinster Hurling Championship Offaly beat Laois by one point; in the Football Championship there were victories for Derry over Monaghan and Kildare over Laois while Cavan scored two injury time points to earn a draw with Fermanagh.

Athletics Ireland were relegated from Division One of European competition on the second day of the Santry meeting despite good performances from David Matthews (third in the 800m), Terry McHugh (third in the javelin) and Nick Sweeney (second in the discus).

14: Rugby Home side Western Samoa ran in eight tries to defeat the Ireland Development XV 57-25 in Apia.

15: G.A.A. The tragic death of Tyrone minor footballer Paul McGirr following an accidental collision in which he scored his team's only goal cast a dark shadow over the rest of the day's fixtures. In the Ulster Senior Football Championship Tyrone beat Armagh 1-12 to 0-12 and Cavan defeated Fermanagh 0-14 to 0-11. In the Leinster Senior Football Championship Meath beat Dublin 1-13 to 1-10 while Offaly defeated Wicklow by 1-17 to 1-8. In the Munster Senior Hurling Championship Tipperary beat Limerick 1-20 to 0-13. Tyrone's minors went on to win their match, beating Armagh 1-10 to 0-9, only to hear Paul McGirr died in Omagh hospital later that evening.

Rallying Austin McHale, driving a Toyota Celica won the three-day Donegal International Rally.

Formula One Giancarlo Fisichella secured further points for the Jordan team when he finished third in the Canadian Grand Prix.

Athletics Catherina McKiernan won the 6.2 mile Dublin Women's Mini Marathon in a record time of 32 minutes 31 seconds. Altogether there was almost 30,000 participants.

21: Athletics There were victories for Sonia O'Sullivan (in the 2,000m), Susan Smith (in the 400m hurdles), and Gary Ryan (in the 200m) at the Cork City sports.

Rugby The British and Irish Lions defeated South Africa 25-16 in the first test at Cape Town. Irish players Jeremy Davidson, Paul Wallace and Keith Wood turned in mighty performances in the pack.

22: G.A.A. In the Leinster Hurling semi-finals champions Wexford beat Offaly 3-12 to 2-12 and Kilkenny beat Dublin 2-20 to 2-13, Down beat Derry 1-15 to 1-10 in the Ulster hurling semi-final; in the provincial football semi-finals Clare scored a goal with the last kick of the game and beat Cork 1-14 to 1-13, Sligo beat Roscommon 1-14 to 1-11 and Cavan beat Donegal 2-16 to 2-10; at the Leinster hurling semi-final at Croke Park thousands were forced to trek across the pitch when too many fans were admitted to the Cusack Stand, no-one was injured.

Soccer The Republic of Ireland qualified for the last 16 of the World Youth Championships in Malaysia following their 1-1 draw with China, despite having goalkeeper Derek O'Connor sent off for time wasting.

Rowing The Irish quartet of Derek Holland, Sam Lynch, Tony O'Connor and Neville Maxwell finished in a disappointing last place in the Lightweight Coxless fours final at the World Cup regatta at Paris.

25: Soccer The Republic of Ireland team qualified for the quarter finals of the World Youth Championships, Damien Duff's "golden" goal saw off the challenge of Morocco.

26: Equestrian sport Ireland finished joint third in the Nations Cup at Aachen.

28: Rugby The British and Irish Lions secured the three test series by beating South Africa 18-15 in Durban.

Hockey Ireland's senior ladies held Spain to a scoreless draw at Belfield.

29: Soccer The Republic of Ireland defeated Spain 1-0 in the quarter finals of the World Youth Championships, Ireland's goal came from a 51st minute Trevor Molloy penalty.

Formula 1 Eddie Irvine finished third in the French Grand Prix and moved up to fourth in World Championship standings. Jordan's Ralf Schumacher finished in 6th position.

Hockey Two goals from Jenny Burke helped Ireland's ladies to a 2-0 victory over Scotland at Belfield.

Cycling Morgan Fox from Dundalk won the 110 mile National road race championship at Carrick on Suir. David McCann and Raymond Clark finished second and third.

G.A.A. In the provincial semi-finals in the Bank of Ireland Football Championship Offaly beat Louth 1-10 to 0-11, Kerry beat Tipperary 2-12 to 1-10, Derry crushed Tyrone 2-15 to 2-3 and Mayo beat Leitrim 0-18 to 0-11.

Golf Frenchwoman Patricia Meunier Lebouc won the Irish Women's Open at Luttrellstown Castle by one stroke. Top Irish finisher was Maureen Madill in 16th place; Ireland beat Sweden by 5½ to 1½ to claim third

place in the European Amateur Team Championship at Portmarnock. Ireland were defeated by eventual champions Spain on Saturday; Darren Clarke finished joint third in the French Open on the European P.G.A. tour and collected a prize of £28,480.

Athletics Sonia O'Sullivan finished in tenth place 13 seconds behind winner Kelly Holmes in the 1,500m I.A.A.F. Grand Prix race in Sheffield and announced that she will not race competitively until the World Championships in August.

Horse racing The Aidan O'Brien trained Desert King (at 11/2) won the Budweiser Irish Derby at the Curragh. The horse and its jockey, Christy Roche, completed a rare double having won the Irish 2,000 Guineas in May.

JULY

02: Soccer The Republic of Ireland U-20s were defeated 1-0 by defending champions Argentina in the semi-final of the World Championships.

05: Cycling The Tour de France got under way in Rouen, Chris Boardman won the 8km time trial prologue. The Tour will start in Dublin next year.

Rugby South Africa beat the Lions 35-16 in the final test of the series at Johannesburg, Jeremy Davidson and Paul Wallace were the Irish representatives on the side.

G.A.A. Roscommon beat Sligo 2-7 to 1-8 in the Connacht Minor Football Championship final.

Horse racing Mick Kinane guided Pilsudski to victory in the Eclipse Stakes at Sandown.

Tennis Owen Casey beat John Doran 6-2, 6-4 in the men's final of the Carlsberg Irish Close Tennis Championship at Donnybrook, while Gina Niland beat Claire Curran 6-0, 3-6, 7-6 in the ladies final.

Soccer Goals from Dessie Baker and Damien Duff helped the Republic of Ireland U-20s avenge their earlier defeat by Ghana, beating them 2-1 in the third place play-off in Kuala Lumpur. It was the best ever result by an Irish team in world competition.

06: Boxing Steve Collins successfully defended his W.B.O. super-middleweight title in Glasgow stopping American Craig Cummings in the third round.

Golf Scotland's Colin Montgomerie won the Murphy's Irish Open at Druids Glen by seven shots following a course record 62 in the first round. Top Irish finishers were Philip Walton and Padraig Harrington in joint seventh, 14 shots behind the runaway winner.

G.A.A. In the Munster and Ulster provincial hurling finals Clare beat Tipperary 1-18 to 0-18 and Down beat favourites Antrim 3-14 to 0-19; In the Leinster football semi-final an injury time Trevor Giles point left Meath and Kildare tied at 0-12 to 1-9; Monaghan and Waterford drew in the Women's National Football league final; Antrim defeated Down to win the Ulster minor hurling final and Tipperary beat Clare in the Munster minor final.

Cycling Tommy Evans from Banbridge won the Tour of the Mournes at Newry with Declan McMackin second and Karl Donnelly third.

11: Golf Michael Sinclair won the Carlsberg North of Ireland Amateur Championship at Royal Portrush defeating Garth McGimpsey 2 and 1 in the final.

12: G.A.A. Galway hammered Roscommon 6-24 to 0-5 in the Connacht Hurling final but their victory was marred by a horrendous off-the-ball incident in which

Joe Rabbitte sustained a fractured skull. Tipperary dismissed Dublin's challenge 0-14 to 0-8 in the quarter final of the Church and General National Hurling League.

Soccer: Cork City lost 2-0 to F.C. Köln of Austria in the InterToto Cup while Lausanne of Switzerland beat Ards 6-0

Athletics National Senior Championship winners at Santry were Noel Berkely (5,000m), Garret Devlin (long jump), Terry McHugh (javelin), Roman Linschied (hammer) and Nick Sweeney (shot putt). Women: Valerie Vaughan (5,000m), Jacqui Stokes (long jump), Sharon Foley (high jump) and Ailish O'Brien (discus).

13: G.A.A. A goal and two points from 37 year-old substitute Billy Byrne in the last minutes of the Guinness Leinster Senior Hurling Championship final helped Wexford to a 2-14 to 1-11 over longtime rivals Kilkenny. Kilkenny won the minor championship with 3-16 to 0-10 victory over Offaly.

Formula 1 Ralf Schumacher of the Jordan team finished fifth in the British Grand Prix at Silverstone.

Tennis Scott Barron and Owen Casey both recorded victories in their Davis Cup reverse singles matches. Ireland beat Greece 4-1 overall.

Rowing Ireland's lightweight coxless fours (Tony O'Connor, Neville Maxwell, Sam Lynch and Derek Holland) finished fifth in World Cup finals at Lucerne, Switzerland.

Athletics National Senior Championships winners were: Men Neil Ryan (100m), Gary Ryan (200m), Brian Forbes (400m), David Matthews (800m), Niall Bruton (1,500m), Seamus Power (5,000m), Patrick Davoren (3,000m steeplechase), T.J. Kearns (110m hurdles), Tom McGuirk (400m hurdles), Mark Mandy (high jump), Patrick Shannon (triple jump), Michael Casey (10km walk) and Dylan McDermott (pole vault). Women: Aoife Hearne (100m), Ciara Sheehy (200m), Karen Shinkins (400m), Amanda Crowe (800m), Valerie Vaughan (5,000m), Gráinne Redmond (100m hurdles), Susan Smith (400m hurdles), Siobhan Hoey (triple jump), Emma Gavin (shot), Alison Moffit (javelin), Clare Thompson (hammer) and Perri Williams (5km walk).

Horse racing Johnny Murtagh rode the John Oxx trained Ebadiyla to victory in the Kildangan Stud Irish Oaks at the Curragh.

15: Soccer Derry City beat Celtic 3-2 in the Dublin International tournament.

16: Soccer Newcastle United beat Derry City 2-0 in the final of the Dublin tournament.

19: G.A.A. Cork succumbed to Kilkenny 1-10 to 3-12 in the National Hurling League quarter final.

Soccer Cork City drew 0-0 with F.C. Aarau of Switzerland.

Cycling Scott Hamilton won the All-Ireland ten mile time trial championship.

20: G.A.A. Cavan became Ulster football champions after a 28 year wait by beating Derry 1-14 to 0-17. Kerry retained their Munster football title beating Clare 1-13 to 0-11. Kildare and Meath drew 3-17 to 2-20 after extra time the Leinster football Championship semi-final replay. Kerry won the Munster Minor football title while the minors of Tyrone paid a fitting tribute to Paul McGirr in winning the Ulster title.

Golf Darren Clarke finished joint second in the British Open at Royal Troon while Padraig Harrington finished joint fifth, they picked up cheques for £150,000 and

£62,500 respectively.

Rowing Neptune rowing club won eleven of the fifteen men's titles at the National Championships at Iniscarra Lake, Co. Cork. Two titles went to the Garda Siochana team and one apiece to Castleconnell and Dublin City University. In the women's events Trinity College won three titles, with Castleconnell, Skibbereen, Cork-Skibbereen, Shandon, U.C.D. and U.C.G. taking a title each.

23: Soccer Bohemians lost their U.E.F.A. Cup tie at home to Ferencvaros while Derry lost 2-0 to Maribor Branik in their Champions League clash at the Brandywell.

24: Soccer The Republic of Ireland U18s lost 3-2 to France in the U.E.F.A. Championships in Iceland.

25: Youth Olympics Irish athletes returned from the U17 Youth Olympics in Lisbon complete with their best ever medals haul. Belfast's Colm McClean won gold in the 1,500m, Ciara Sheehy from Dublin won gold in the 200m while Cork's Lee Kelleher won silver and bronze in swimming events.

26: G.A.A. Tipperary defeated Down 3-24 to 3-8 at Clones in the first ever All-Ireland hurling quarter final for defeated provincial finalists.

Soccer The Republic of Ireland U18s beat Switzerland 1-0 in the Youth Championships in Iceland.

27: G.A.A. In a high scoring game in Thurles defeated Leinster finalists Kilkenny defeat Connacht champions Galway 4-15 to 3-16.

American Football The Pittsburgh Steelers beat the Chicago Bears 30-17 in the American Bowl at Croke Park.

28: Soccer The Republic of Ireland U18s drew 1-1 with Israel in Iceland. Lee Boylan was the Irish goalscorer.

29: Soccer Bohemians lost 5-0 to Ferencvaros in the U.E.F.A. Cup.

30: Soccer The Irish U18s lost 2-1 to Spain in Iceland; Derry City lost 1-0 to Maribor Tetanic in the Champions League.

Horse racing Stroll Home, the mount of Paul Carberry, won the Digital Galway Plate.

AUGUST

01: Hockey Ireland's women were beaten 1-0 by India in the World Cup qualifying tournament at Harare, Zimbabwe.

02: Athletics Sonia O'Sullivan and Sinead Delahunty qualified for the semi-finals of the 1,500m on the first day of the World Championships in Athens. Neil Ryan (100m), Roman Linschied (hammer) and Tom McGuirk (400m hurdles) were all eliminated in the first round.

Rallying Mark Higgins won the Ulster Rally with Gwyndaf Evans in second.

Hockey The Irish women's team were beaten 3-0 by tournament favourites South Africa in Harare.

03: Athletics Sonia O'Sullivan qualified for the 1,500m final at the World Athletics Championships while Sinead Delahunty narrowly missed qualification. Niall Bruton qualified for the semi-final of the men's 1,500m despite being spiked, while Shane Healy failed to qualify from his 1,500m heat. Terry McHugh (javelin) and Eugene Farrell (400m) both failed to progress any further.

G.A.A. Mayo squeezed past Sligo in the Connacht Senior Football final by 0-11 to 1-7, Mayo also won the minor title. Meath finally beat Kildare 1-12 to 1-10 in the second replay of the Leinster semi-final.

Canoeing Ian Wiley won a silver medal in the World Cup Canoe Slalom series meeting at Minden, Canada.

Golf Padraig Harrington finished joint sixth in the Scandinavian Masters at Malmo winning a prize of £24,375.

04: Athletics Susan Smith set a new national record in the 400m hurdles in Athens finishing second in her heat in a time of 54.61 seconds.

06: Hockey Ireland drew 1-1 with Canada in Zimbabwe.

08: Hockey Ireland defeated Japan 3-2 in the women's World Cup qualifying tournament in Zimbabwe with goals coming from Lynsey McVicker, Arlene Thompson and Sarah Kelleher.

Athletics Susan Smith finished seventh in the 400m hurdles final in Athens. Mark Carroll failed to qualify for the 5,000m final finishing 14th in his semi-final.

Handball J. Molloy and M. McGovern won the men's doubles title at the World Championships at Winipeg, Canada.

Swimming Michelle Smith's time of 2.07.04 seconds broke the European short course record for the 200m butterfly set in 1982.

10: G.A.A. At Croke Park Munster champions Clare eased past defeated Leinster finalists Kilkenny in the first Guinness All-Ireland Senior Hurling semi-final 1-17 to 1-13. Clare also defeated Kilkenny in the minor semi-final.

Golf The United States regained the Walker Cup from Ireland and Britain 16-8.

Camogie Galway and Cork defeated Kilkenny and Wexford respectively and advanced to the All-Ireland Senior Camogie Championship final.

Hockey Ireland's hopes of qualifying for the women's World Cup were dashed following their 3-0 defeat by China in Zimbabwe.

11: Cricket Ireland and Scotland drew their three-day game.

12: Hockey Russia beat Ireland 4-2 in the 7th/8th place play-offs in the Women's World Cup qualifying tournament in Harare.

13: Golf Sligo man Ken Kearney won the Irish Amateur Close Championship.

14: Soccer Shelbourne lost 2-1 to Kilmarnock in the Cup Winners' Cup.

16: G.A.A. Offaly, inspired by corner forward Vinny Claffey's 1-5 from play, beat defending All-Ireland champions Meath 3-17 to 1-15 in the Leinster Senior Football final at Croke Park. Defending All-Ireland minor football champions Laois retained their Leinster title beating Wicklow 2-11 to 0-10.

16: Rugby In the interprovincial championship Leinster beat Ulster 26-25 at Donnybrook while in Galway Munster eased past Connacht by 29 points to 9.

Soccer The Irish league kicked off with victories for Linfield over Ards, Ballymena over Cliftonville and Glentoran over Coleraine, while Omagh drew with Glentoran and Portadown drew with Crusaders.

17: G.A.A. Tipperary defeated reigning All-Ireland champions Wexford in the Guinness Senior Hurling Championship All-Ireland semi-final by 2-16 to 0-15. Two late goals from Galway helps them steal victory from Tipperary in the minor semi-final.

Tennis Owen Casey beat Tommy Hamilton in the final of the East of Ireland Open. Gina Niland won the ladies

title.

Squash Derek Ryan was beaten in straight sets by Egypt's Ahmed Barada in the final of the World Games.

Cycling Dave McCall from Belfast won the Tour of Armagh.

19: Swimming Michelle Smith de Bruin won gold in the 400m Individual Medley in the European Championships at Seville.

20: Swimming Gold again for Michelle Smith de Bruin who won the 200m Freestyle in Seville.

Soccer Northern Ireland lost 3-1 to Germany at Windsor Park. The Republic of Ireland were held to a scoreless draw by Lithuania at Lansdowne Road.

21: Swimming Michelle Smith de Bruin won silver in the 400m Freestyle at the European Championships at Seville. Nick O'Hare recorded a personal best of 52.11 in the 100m Freestyle in winning his heat. Hugh O'Connor recorded a personal best in the 200m Backstroke 2:06.08 beating brother Adrian into third.

22: Swimming The Irish 4x100m Freestyle relay team of Adrian O'Connor, Hugh O'Connor, Nick O'Hare and Michael Giles (in a time of 3:30.12) broke the Irish record by over four seconds.

23: Swimming Colin Louth broke the Irish 200m Butterfly record in a time of 2:03.96. Yet he and other Irish representatives Hugh and Adrian O'Connor (100m Backstroke) and Nick O'Hare (50m Freestyle) failed to progress from the heats.

Rugby Leinster lost 15-12 to Munster at Musgrave Park and Connacht beat Ulster 27-17 at the Galway Sportsground in the 1997/98 inter-provincial series; in the Allied Dunbar Premiership London Irish went down 32-12 to Richmond in the first game of the season.

G.A.A. Galway cruised past a depleted Tipperary side 1-14 to 0-6 in the semi-final of the National Hurling League at Cusack Park, Ennis; Mayo won the All Ireland Junior Football final beating Kerry 2-8 to 1-10.

Soccer In the Smirnoff Irish League Premier Division there were victories for Cliftonville, Portadown, Crusaders and Glenavon while Omagh Town held Linfield to a 1-1 draw.

Motorcycling A seven year-old spectator was killed instantly in an horrific crash at the Ulster Grand Prix at Dundrod. One of the drivers, Stephen Galligan involved in the crash died in hospital ten days later.

24: G.A.A. Seven points from Maurice Fitzgerald helped Kerry to a 1-17 to 1-10 victory over Cavan in the All-Ireland semi-final at Croke Park. The minor semi-final between Kerry and Tyrone ended in a draw. Limerick defeated Kilkenny 1-17 to 0-10 in the National League Hurling semi-final at Nowlan Park.

Swimming Michelle Smith de Bruin won a silver medal in the 200m Butterfly at Seville, but there was disappointment for Chantal Gibney and Nick O'Hare who failed to progress in their respective events.

Golf Sweden's Per-Ulrik Johansson retained his Smurfit European Open title by six shots at The K Club in Kildare. Ronan Rafferty and Paul McGinley were the leading Irish finishers in joint fourteenth place.

Formula One Giancarlo Fisichella recorded Jordan's best finish of the year in finishing second to Michael Schumacher at the Belgian Grand Prix. Eddie Irvine finished in eleventh.

28: Soccer Shelbourne went out of the Cup Winners' Cup on a 3-2 aggregate score despite holding Scottish champions Kilmarnock to a 1-1 draw.

29: Soccer St. Patrick's Athletic drew 0-0 with Derry City in the opening game of the F.A.I. National League Premier Division; Ballymena beat Coleraine 1-0 in the Irish League.

30: Rugby Leinster won the inter provincial series on points difference following their 23-6 defeat of Connacht. Ulster defeated Munster 22-12 at Ravenhill; London Irish lost to Sale in the English League.

Soccer In the Harp Lager National League Finn Harps defeated Drogheda United 2-0 while Sligo Rovers drew 2-2 with Bohemians; in the Smirnoff Irish League Ards and Omagh drew 2-2, Cliftonville drew with Crusaders 2-2 while Linfield beat Glentoran 3-0.

Snooker Marco Fu won the World U21 Snooker Championship, which was held in Carlow.

31: G.A.A. Mayo defeated Offaly 0-13 to 0-7 in the All-Ireland football semi-final at Croke Park. Laois defeated Mayo 3-8 to 1-9 in the minor semi-final.

Soccer There were victories for Cork City, Shelbourne and Shamrock Rovers in the F.A.I. National League.

Golf Padraig Harrington finished in ninth place in the International Open at Munich. It meant that he would not be selected for the European Ryder Cup team.

SEPTEMBER

02: Bowls Margaret Johnston won a silver medal in the singles championship at the Atlantic Rims Bowls tournament in Wales.

Soccer A Republic of Ireland XI beat a National League XI 3-0 in the poorly attended Eoin Hand testimonial at Tolka Park.

06: Soccer The Republic of Ireland defeated Iceland 4-2 in the group eight World Cup qualifier in Reykjavik. The Irish goals came from David Connolly, Mark Kennedy and two from Roy Keane. Kennedy was also sent off; in the F.A.I. National League Cork City defeated Kilkenny City 2-0.

G.A.A. Tyrone's minors beat Kerry 0-23 to 0-21 after extra time in the All-Ireland minor football semi final replay.

Rugby Toulouse beat Leinster 34-25 in the European Cup tie at Donnybrook.

07: Rowing Tony O'Connor and Neville Maxwell won silver in the lightweight coxless pairs at the World Championships while less than 30 minutes later Emmet O'Brien, Neal Byrne, Brendan Dolan and John Armstrong won bronze in the lightweight quad sculls.

G.A.A. In the All-Ireland U21 hurling championship semi-finals Cork defeated Wexford 2-12 to 1-6 and Galway defeated Derry 8-26 to 0-7; Monaghan won the All-Ireland junior hurling title defeating Meath by 3-11 to 0-11.

Soccer Derry City drew 2-2 with Shelbourne and Sligo Rovers drew with Shamrock Rovers in the League. The Republic of Ireland beat Northern Ireland 6-0 in a women's international friendly.

Rugby Harlequins defeated Munster 48-40 in the European Cup pool D match. London Irish lost their European Conference match with Stade Francais 25-41.

Golf Ronan Rafferty and Darren Clarke finished in joint sixth in the European Masters at Crans-sur-Sierre.

Camogie Cork won their 18th senior All-Ireland camogie title defeating Galway 0-15 to 2-5 at Croke Park.

Formula One Jordan's Giancarlo Fisichella finished

fourth in the Italian Grand Prix. Eddie Irvine was in eighth.

09: Soccer Lithuania's U21 s defeated their Republic of Ireland counterparts 2-1 in their European Championship qualifying match.

Rugby Connacht secured a tremendous 43-13 victory over Northampton in the European Conference tie at the Galway Sportsgrounds.

10: Soccer A goal in either half from Tony Cascarino gave the Republic of Ireland a 2-0 victory over Lithuania and guaranteed a World Cup qualifying play off place for Mick McCarthy's men; Northern Ireland were beaten 1-0 by Albania in Zurich.

13: Athletics Susan Smith finished eighth in the 400m hurdles and Sinead Delahunty finished ninth in the mile at the I.A.A.F. Grand Prix final in Japan.

Rugby Cardiff defeated Munster 43-23 and Swansea defeated Ulster 33-16 in the European Cup.

Horse racing Pat Eddery recorded the 4,000th winner of his career when he rode Silver Patriarch to victory in the Doncaster St. Leger.

Soccer Shelbourne trounced Drogheda United 5-0, Sligo Rovers drew 3-3 with Dundalk and St. Pats beat Finn Harps 2-1 in the F.A.I. Premier Division.

14: G.A.A. A storming second half display helped Clare to their second Guinness All-Ireland Senior Hurling Championship title in three years. Two late goals from Tipperary caused concern but the final scoreline read Clare 0-20, Tipperary 2-13. A new format to the championship had allowed defeated Munster finalists Tipperary back into the championship. Clare's minors also made good in the second bite championship, defeated in the Munster final they won the All-Ireland final, defeating Galway 1-11 to 1-9.

Rugby: Connacht were unfortunate to lose 20-16 to French side Nice in the European Conference.

Soccer Cork City beat Derry City 2-0 and Kilkenny City beat U.C.D. 2-1 in the National League.

18: Soccer Dundalk and Bohemians drew 2-2 in the F.A.I. National League Premier Division.

19: Golf It was confirmed that Ireland will host the 2005 Ryder Cup.

20: Soccer In the Irish League Premier Division Cliftonville defeated Linfield 1-0, Omagh Town defeated Ballymena United 3-2, Glenavon defeated Crusaders 2-0, while the Ards/Coleraine and Glentoran/Portadown games ended in draws; in the National League U.C.D. draw 1-1 with Derry City, Sligo Rovers beat Kilkenny City 1-0 and Cork City beat Drogheda United 2-1.

Rugby In the European Cup Milan beat Leinster 33-32, while Munster beat Bourgoin 17-15. London Irish defeated Farul Constanta 26-9 in the European Conference.

Horse racing Oscar Schindler, trained by Kevin Prendergast and ridden by Stephen Craine won the Jefferson Smurfit Memorial Irish St. Leger at the Curragh.

Boxing Michael Carruth lost his W.B.O. welterweight fight against Michael Loewe in a controversial points decision.

21: Formula One The Jordans of Giancarlo Fisichella and Ralf Schumacher finished fourth and fifth in the Austrian Grand Prix securing the team's fifth place in the constructor's championship.

Golf Co. Sligo won both the Irish Senior Cup and the Barton Shield. Laytown and Bettystown won the Junior

Cup, Nenagh won the Jimmy Bruen Shield and Thurles won the Pierce Purcell Shield.

G.A.A. Cork defeated Galway 3-11 to 0-13 in the All-Ireland U21 hurling final held in Thurles.

Soccer Shamrock Rovers defeated Finn Harps 2-1 in the National League.

Rugby Connacht beat French side Begles-Bordeaux 15-9 in the European Conference while Ulster were outclassed by Wasps losing 56-3.

Horse racing King of Kings, the mount of Christy Roche won the Group One Aga Khan Studs National Stakes at the Curragh.

27: Rugby Connacht's good form in the European Conference continued with a 28-25 victory over French side Nice. Ulster defeated Swansea 28-20 at Ravenhill while Munster lost 32-37 to Cardiff and Leinster lost 22-47 to Leicester.

Surfing Donegal man Grant Robinson won the gold medal in the Masters event at the European Surfing Championships in Bundoran.

Soccer In the F.A.I. National League Finn Harps beat Shelbourne 3-1 and Sligo Rovers beat Derry City 3-0; in the I.F.A. Irish League there were victories for Crusaders, Cliftonville, Glentoran and Glenavon.

28: G.A.A. Nine points from man-of-the-match Maurice Fitzgerald led Kerry to a 0-13 to 1-7 victory over Connacht champions Mayo in the Bank of Ireland All-Ireland Senior Football Championship final. It was the Kingdom's first title in eleven years. Laois defeated a gallant Tyrone side 3-11 to 1-14 in the minor final.

Athletics Catherina McKiernan won the Berlin Marathon in a time of 2 hours 23 minutes 44 seconds.

Canoeing Ian Wiley finished eighth in the K1 final at the World Slalom Championships in Brazil.

Soccer U.C.D. defeated Drogheda United 3-0 and St Pats defeated Cork City 1-0 in the F.A.I. Premier Division.

Golf Europe won the Ryder Cup in Spain beating the United States 14½ - 13½. Darren Clarke was Ireland's sole representative, he played in two matches, winning one.

GAELIC ATHLETIC ASSOCIATION

Cumann Lúthchleas Gael
Páirc an Chrócaigh, Baile Átha Cliath 3. Tel. (01) 8363222

Founded	1884
President	Joe McDonagh
Director General	Liam Mulvhill
Number of Provincial Councils	4
Number of Clubs	2,675
Number of Members	750,000
Number of Teams	20,000
Number of Coaches	2,000
Biggest Recorded Attendance	90,556 (Croke Park September 1961, Down v.Offaly)
Overall Attendance at 1997 Championship	1,337,345

Main Stadia Croke Park (66,000), Semple Stadium Thurles (50,000), Pairc Uí Chaoimh Cork (50,000) Fitzgerald Park Killarney (50,000), Hyde Park Roscommon (30,000) and St. Tiergnach's Park Clones (35,000)

1997	Hurling	Football
All-Ireland Champions	Clare	Kerry
Connacht Champions	Galway	Mayo
Leinster Champions	Wexford	Offaly
Munster Champions	Clare	Kerry
Ulster Champions	Cavan	Cavan
National League Champions	Limerick	Kerry
Provincial	tba	Leinster
All-Ireland Club Champions	St. Mary's, Athenry	Crossmaglen Rangers
Top Scorers in 1997 Championship	D.J. Carey, (Kilkenny) 4-22	Maurice Fitzgerald (Kerry) 0-28
Players' Player of the Year (1996)	Martin Storey (Wexford)	Trevor Giles (Meath)

Attendances at G.A.A. Championships 1996 & 1997

1997 Total Championship Attendance	1,337,345
1996 Total Championship Attendance	1,056,236

Provincial breakdown *Figures in ( ) indicate number of fixtures played in each provincial championship*

Province	1996		1997	
	Football	Hurling	Football	Hurling
Ulster	162,890 (8)	2,000 (1)	202,682 (11)	2,700 (2)
Connacht	42,700 (6)	2,000 (1)	71,000 (5)	2,500 (1)
Leinster	160,467 (11)	89,171 (9)	338,454 (14)	124,677 (7)
Munster	65,370 (6)	170,415 (5)	62,651 (6)	146,435 (5)
All-Ireland Series	224,137 (4)	137,086 (6)	182,042 (3)	204,204 (5)
Total	655,564(35)	400,672(22)	856,829 (39)	480,516 (20)

G.A.A. Statistics - Inter County

County	Main Stadium	Approx. Capacity	No. of Clubs	Colours	All Ire. F	All Ire. H	NFL Title	NHL Title
CONNACHT	McHale Park	30,000	280		14	4	15	6
Galway	Tuam Park	22,000	88	Maroon & white	7	4	4	6
Leitrim	Pairc MacDiarmada	12,000	33	Green & gold	0	0	0	0
Mayo	McHale Park	30,000	52	Green & red	3	0	10	0
Roscommon	Dr. Hyde Park	30,000	56	Gold & blue	2	0	1	0
Sligo	Markevicz Park	13,000	51	White & black	0	0	0	0
LEINSTER	Croke Park	68,000	1095		42	41	18	16
Carlow	Dr. Cullen Park		35	Red, green & yellow	0	0	0	0
Dublin	Parnell Park		238	Sky blue & navy	22	6	8	2
Kildare	Newbridge		70	White	4	0	0	0
Kilkenny	Nowlan Park	30,000	42	Black & amber	0	25	0	9
Laois	O'Moore Park	25,000	88	Blue & white	0	1	2	0
Longford	Pearse Park		52	Blue & gold	0	0	1	0
Louth	Drogheda		51	Red & white	3	0	0	0
Meath	Pairc Tailteann		146	Green & gold	6	0	7	0
Offaly	Pairc Úi Conchuir		80	Green, white & gold	3	3	0	1
Westmeath	Mullingar		49	Maroon & white	0	0	0	0
Wexford	Wexford Park		178	Purple & gold	5	6	0	4
Wicklow	Aughrim	10,000	66	Blue & gold	0	0	0	0
MUNSTER	Semple Stadium	59,000	717		42	64	19	43
Clare	Cusack Park	25,000	89	Saffron & blue	0	3	0	3
Cork	Pairc Uí Chaoimh	50,000	268	Red & white	6	27	4	13
Kerry	Fitzgerald Stadium	50,000	96	Green & gold	31	1	15	0
Limerick	Gaelic Grounds	55,000	117	Green & white	0	7	0	11
Tipperary	Semple Stadium	59,000	90	Blue & gold	4	24	0	16
Waterford	Walsh Park		57	White & blue	0	2	0	1
ULSTER	St. Tiergnach's Park	33,000	583		12	0	10	0
Antrim	Casement Park	40,000	108	Saffron & white	0	0	0	0
Armagh	Athletic Grounds	14,000	55	Orange & white	0	0	0	0
Cavan	Breffni Park		59	Blue & white	5	0	1	0
Derry	Celtic Park		60	Red & white	1	0	4	0
Donegal	MacCumhaill Park		63	Gold & green	1	0	0	0
Down	Pairc an Iúir		70	Red & black	5	0	4	0
Fermanagh	Michael Brewster Park		50	Green & white	0	0	0	0
Monaghan	St. Tiergnach's Park	33,000	50	White & blue	0	0	1	0
Tyrone	Healy Park	23,000	68	White & red	0	0	0	0
Total			2675		110	109	62	65

G.A.A. Clubs in Britain and Overseas

Britain	Number of Clubs	Worldwide	Number of Clubs
Gloucestershire	7	Australia	33
Hertfordshire	12	Canada	12
Lancashire	10	New York	42
London	60	New York (Minor Board)	6
Scotland	10	North American Board	67
Warwickshire	26		
Yorkshire	7		

Gaelic Athletic Association Players' All-Stars, 1996

FOOTBALL AWARDS: Finbarr McConnell (Tyrone); **Kenneth Mortimer** (Mayo), **Darren Fay** (Meath), **Martin O'Connell** (Meath); **Pat Holmes** (Mayo), **James Nallen** (Mayo), **Paul Curran** (Dublin); **Liam McHale** (Mayo), **John McDermott** (Meath); **Trevor Giles** (Meath), **Tommy Dowd** (Meath), **James Horan** (Mayo); **Joe Brolly** (Derry); **Peter Canavan** (Tyrone); **Maurice Fitzgerald** (Kerry). *Footballer of the Year: Trevor Giles (Meath)*

HURLING AWARDS: Joe Quaid (Limerick); **Tom Helebert** (Galway), **Brian Lohan** (Clare), **Larry O'Gorman** (Wexford); **Liam Dunne** (Wexford), **Ciaran Carey** (Limerick), **Mark Foley** (Limerick), **Adrian Fenlon** (Wexford), **Mike Houlihan** (Limerick); **Rory McCarthy** (Wexford), **Martin Storey** (Wexford), **Larry Murphy** (Wexford); **Liam Cahill** (Tipperary), **Gary Kirby** (Limerick), **Tom Dempsey** (Wexford). *Hurler of the Year: Martin Storey (Wexford)*

All-Ireland Senior Hurling Winners, 1887-1997

Year	Winner	Year	Winner	Year	Winner	Year	Winner
1887	Tipperary	1915	Laois	1943	Cork	1971	Tipperary
1888	C'ship unfinished	1916	Tipperary	1944	Cork	1972	Kilkenny
1889	Dublin	1917	Dublin	1945	Tipperary	1973	Limerick
1890	Cork	1918	Limerick	1946	Cork	1974	Kilkenny
1891	Kerry	1919	Cork	1947	Kilkenny	1975	Kilkenny
1892	Cork	1920	Dublin	1948	Waterford	1976	Cork
1893	Cork	1921	Limerick	1949	Tipperary	1977	Cork
1894	Cork	1922	Kilkenny	1950	Tipperary	1978	Cork
1895	Tipperary	1923	Galway	1951	Tipperary	1979	Kilkenny
1896	Tipperary	1924	Dublin	1952	Cork	1980	Galway
1897	Limerick	1925	Tipperary	1953	Cork	1981	Offaly
1898	Tipperary	1926	Cork	1954	Cork	1982	Kilkenny
1899	Tipperary	1927	Dublin	1955	Wexford	1983	Kilkenny
1900	Tipperary	1928	Cork	1956	Wexford	1984	Cork
1901	London	1929	Cork	1957	Kilkenny	1985	Offaly
1902	Cork	1930	Tipperary	1958	Tipperary	1986	Cork
1903	Cork	1931	Cork	1959	Waterford	1987	Galway
1904	Kilkenny	1932	Kilkenny	1960	Wexford	1988	Galway
1905	Kilkenny	1933	Kilkenny	1961	Tipperary	1989	Tipperary
1906	Tipperary	1934	Limerick	1962	Tipperary	1990	Cork
1907	Kilkenny	1935	Kilkenny	1963	Kilkenny	1991	Tipperary
1908	Tipperary	1936	Limerick	1964	Tipperary	1992	Kilkenny
1909	Kilkenny	1937	Tipperary	1965	Tipperary	1993	Kilkenny
1910	Wexford	1938	Dublin	1966	Cork	1994	Offaly
1911	Kilkenny	1939	Kilkenny	1967	Kilkenny	1995	Clare
1912	Kilkenny	1940	Limerick	1968	Wexford	1996	Wexford
1913	Kilkenny	1941	Cork	1969	Kilkenny	1997	Clare
1914	Clare	1942	Cork	1970	Cork		

All-Ireland Senior Football Winners, 1887-1997

Year	Winner	Year	Winner	Year	Winner	Year	Winner
1887	Limerick	1915	Wexford	1943	Roscommon	1971	Offaly
1888	No C'ship	1916	Wexford	1944	Roscommon	1972	Offaly
1889	Tipperary	1917	Wexford	1945	Cork	1973	Cork
1890	Cork	1918	Wexford	1946	Kerry	1974	Dublin
1891	Dublin	1919	Kildare	1947	Cavan	1975	Kerry
1892	Dublin	1920	Tipperary	1948	Cavan	1976	Dublin
1893	Wexford	1921	Dublin	1949	Meath	1977	Dublin
1894	Dublin	1922	Dublin	1950	Mayo	1978	Kerry
1895	Tipperary	1923	Dublin	1951	Mayo	1979	Kerry
1896	Limerick	1924	Kerry	1952	Cavan	1980	Kerry
1897	Dublin	1925	Galway	1953	Kerry	1981	Kerry
1898	Dublin	1926	Kerry	1954	Meath	1982	Offaly
1899	Dublin	1927	Kildare	1955	Kerry	1983	Dublin
1900	Tipperary	1928	Kildare	1956	Galway	1984	Kerry
1901	Dublin	1929	Kerry	1957	Louth	1985	Kerry
1902	Dublin	1930	Kerry	1958	Dublin	1986	Kerry
1903	Kerry	1931	Kerry	1959	Kerry	1987	Meath
1904	Kerry	1932	Kerry	1960	Down	1988	Meath
1905	Kildare	1933	Cavan	1961	Down	1989	Cork
1906	Dublin	1934	Galway	1962	Kerry	1990	Cork
1907	Dublin	1935	Cavan	1963	Dublin	1991	Down
1908	Dublin	1936	Mayo	1964	Galway	1992	Donegal
1909	Kerry	1937	Kerry	1965	Galway	1993	Derry
1910	Louth	1938	Galway	1966	Galway	1994	Down
1911	Cork	1939	Kerry	1967	Meath	1995	Dublin
1912	Louth	1940	Kerry	1968	Down	1996	Meath
1913	Kerry	1941	Kerry	1969	Kerry	1997	Kerry
1914	Kerry	1942	Dublin	1970	Kerry		

1997 All-Ireland Football Final Statistics

Croke Park, September 28. Attendance: 65,601 **Kerry 0-13, Mayo 1-7**
Kerry, team and scorers: Declan O'Keefe, Killian Burns, Barry O'Shea, Stephen Stack, Seamus Moynihan, Liam O'Flaherty, Eamonn Breen, Dara Ó Sé (0-1), William Kirby, Pa Laide (0-2), Liam Hasset (Captain), Denis O'Dwyer, Billy O'Shea, Dara Ó Cinnéide, Maurice Fitzgerald (0-9). **Substitutes used:** John Crowley (0-1) for Billy O'Shea (25 mins), Donal Daly for Kirby (55 mins) and Michael F. Russell for Ó Cinnéide (61 mins). **Manager:** Páidí Ó Sé.
Mayo, team and scorers: Peter Burke, Kenneth Mortimer, Pat Holmes, Dermot Flanagan, Fergal Costello, James Nallen, Noel Connelly (Captain), Pat Fallon, David Heaney, Maurice Sheridan (0-3), Colm McManamon (0-1), John Casey, Kieren McDonald (1-1), Liam McHale, David Nestor. Substitutes used: James Horan (0-2) for Flanagan (5 mins), Diarmuid Byrne for Sheridan (35 mins) and P.J. Loftus for Nestor (64 mins). **Manager:** John Maughan.
Half-time Score: Kerry 0-8, Mayo 0-3. **Wides:** Kerry 9, Mayo 13. **Referee:** Brian White (Wexford). **Booked:** Liam Hasset (Kerry). **Sent off:** None.

1997 All-Ireland Hurling Final Statistics

Croke Park, September 14. Attendance: 65,575 **Clare 0-20, Tipperary 2-13**
Clare, team and scorers: David Fitzgerald, Michael O'Halloran, Brian Lohan, Frank Lohan, Liam Doyle (0-1), Sean McMahon (0-1), Anthony Daly (Captain), Ollie Baker (0 2), Colin Lynch (0-2), James O'Connor (0-7), Fergus Tuohy, P.J. O'Connell, Niall Gilligan (0-3), Conor Clancy (0-1), Ger O'Loughlin (0-1). **Substitutes used:** Fergal Hegarty for Tuohy (28 mins), David Forde (0-2) for O'Connell (47 mins) and Barry Murphy for Hegarty (60 mins). **Manager:** Ger Loughnane.
Tipperary, team and scorers: Brendan Cummins, Paul Shelly, Noel Sheehy, Michael Ryan, Liam Sheedy, Colm Bonnar, Conal Bonnar, Thomas Dunne (0-5), Conor Gleeson (0-1)(Captain), Liam McGrath, Declan Ryan, John Leahy (0-4), Michael Cleary (0-1), Eugene O'Neill (1-1), Brian O'Meara (0-1). **Substitutes used:** Aidan Ryan for McGrath (35 mins) and Liam Cahill (1-0) for Michael Cleary (57 mins). **Manager:** Len Gaynor.
Half-time Score: Clare 0-6, Tipperary 0-10. **Wides:** Clare 17, Tipperary 8. **Referee:** Dickie Murphy (Wexford). **Booked:** Brian O'Meara (Tipperary). **Sent off:** None.

Top All Ireland Medal Winners, Hurling

Name	Number	Between
Christy Ring (Cork)	8	(1941-54)
John Doyle (Tipperary)	8	(1949-65)
Frank Cummins (Kilkenny)	8 (1)	(1969-83)
Noel Skehan (Kilkenny)	9 (3)	(1963-83)
Jimmy Doyle (Tipperary)	6	(1958-71)

Figure in brackets indicates medals won as a substitute.

Top All Ireland Medal Winners, Football

Name	Number	Between
Denis 'Ogie' Moran (Kerry)	8	(1975-86)
Páidí Ó Sé (Kerry)	8	(1975-86)
Ger Power (Kerry)	8	(1975-86)
Mikey Sheehy (Kerry)	8	(1975-86)
Seán Walshe (Kerry)	8 (1)	(1976-86)
Charlie Neligan (Kerry)	7	(1978-86)
Dan O'Keefe (Kerry)	7	(1931-46)
John O'Keefe (Kerry)	7 (1)	(1969-82)

Figure in brackets indicates medals won as a substitute.

All Star Winners, Hurling

Name	Number	Won Between
Noel Skehan (Kilkenny)	7	(1972-83)
Joe McKenna (Limerick)	6	(1974-81)
Nicky English (Tipperary)	6	(1983-89)
Joe Cooney (Galway)	5	(1985-90)
John Fenton (Cork)	5	(1983-87)
Peter Finnerty (Galway)	5	(1985-90)
Pat Hartigan (Limerick)	5	(1971-75)
Ger Henderson (Kilkenny)	5	(1978-87)
Joe Hennessy (Kilkenny)	5	(1978-87)
Eddie Keher (Kilkenny)	5	(1971-75)
Jimmy Barry Murphy (Cork)	5*	(1976-86)

*Jimmy Barry Murphy also won two All-Star awards for football.

All Star Winners, Football

Name	Number	Won Between
Pat Spillane (Kerry)	9	(1976-86)
Mikey Sheehy (Kerry)	7	(1976-86)
Jack O'Shea (Kerry)	6	(1980-85)
Ger Power (Kerry)	6	(1975-86)
John Egan (Kerry)	5	(1975-86)
John O'Keefe (Kerry)	5	(1973-79)
Paidi Ó Séa (Kerry)	5	(1981-85)

All Star Winners, Dual

Name	Hurling	Football	Total
Jimmy Barry Murphy (Cork)	5	2	7
Ray Cummins (Cork)	3	2	5
Brian Murphy (Cork)	2	2	4
Liam Currams (Offaly)	1	1	2

Presidents of the G.A.A.

(Uachtaráin Cumann Lúthchleas Gael)

Maurice Davin (Tipperary)	1884
Eamonn Bennet (Clare)	1887
Maurice Davin (Tipperary)	1888
Peter Kelly (Galway)	1889
Frank Dineen (Limerick)	1895
Michael Deering (Cork)	1898
James Nowlan (Kilkenny)	1901
Daniel McCarthy (Dublin)	1921
Patrick Breen (Wexford)	1924
William Clifford (Limerick)	1926
Seán Ryan (Dublin)	1928
Seán McCarthy (Cork)	1932

Bob O'Keefe (Laois) 1935	
Pádraig McNamee (Antrim)......................1938	
Seamus Gardiner (Tipperary) 1943	
Dan O'Rourke (Roscommon) 1946	
Michael Kehoe (Wexford) 1949	
Michael O'Donoghue (Waterford) 1952	
Seamus McFerran (Antrim) 1955	
Dr. J.J. Stuart (Dublin) 1958	
Hugh Byrne (Wicklow)............................1961	
Alf Murray (Armagh) 1964	
Seamus Ó Riain (Tipperary) 1967	
Pat Fanning (Waterford) 1970	
Dr. Donal Keenan (Roscommon)..............1973	
Con Murphy (Cork) 1976	
Paddy McFlynn (Down) 1979	
Paddy Buggy (Kilkenny) 1982	
Dr. Mick Loftus (Mayo)............................1985	
John Dowling (Offaly) 1988	
Peter Quinn (Fermanagh) 1991	
Jack Boothman (Wicklow) 1994	
Joe McDonagh (Galway)..........................1997	

GENERAL SECRETARIES* OF THE G.A.A.

Michael Cusack (Clare) 1884-85	
John McKay (Cork) 1884-85	
John W. Power (Kildare)...................................1884-87	
J.B. O'Reilly (Dublin) 1885-87	
Timothy O'Riordan (Cork) 1885-89	
James Moore (Louth) 1887-88	
William Prendergast (Tipperary) 1888-89	
P.R. Cleary (Limerick)......................................1889-90	
Maurice Moynihan (Kerry) 1890-92	
Patrick Tobin (Dublin) 1891-94	
David Walsh (Cork) 1894-95	
Richard Blake (Meath) 1895-98	
Frank Dineen (Limerick)...............................1898-1901	
Luke O'Toole (Dublin).......................................1901-29	
Pádraic Ó Caoimh (Cork).................................1929-64	
Seán Ó Síocháin (Cork).....................................1964-79	
Liam Maolmhichíl (Longford) 1979-	

*since 1964 the post has been described as Director General

SOCCER

The Football Association of Ireland
80 Merrion Square, Dublin 2. Tel. (01) 6766864

Founded 1921
President ....Pat Quigley
General Secretary/Chief Executive ....Bernard J. O'Byrne
Number of Affiliated Clubs..4,139
Number of Coaches..4,000 (at various levels)
1996/97 National League, Premier Division Champions ....Derry City
1996/97 National League, First Division Champions ....Kilkenny City
1997 Harp Lager F.A.I. Cup Winners ....Shelbourne
Top Scorer 1996/97 National League Premier Division....................16 (Stephen Geoghegan & Tony Cousins)
Main Stadium ....Dalymount Park, capacity 18,000 (Lansdowne Road used for International games)

INTERNATIONAL

National Manager ....Mick McCarthy
Top International Goalscorer...Frank Stapleton (20 Goals)
Biggest Recorded Attendance..47,000
World Ranking 42nd
Most Capped Player ....Paul McGrath (82)
1996 Senior Player of the Year ....Alan McLoughlin
Best World Cup Result ....Quarter-final 1990 (beaten by Italy)

National League Premier Division Team Statistics

Club	Founded	Ground and Capacity	Colours	FAI League Titles	FAI Cups	League Cups
Bohemians	1890	.............Dalymount Park (18,000)	............Red & Black	7	5	2
Cork City	1984	.............Turner's Cross (12,000)	........Green & White	1	1	0
Derry City	1928	.............The Brandywell (8,500)	........Red & White	2	2	4
Drogheda United	1919	.............United Park (6,000)	........Maroon & Blue	0	0	1
Dundalk......................	1919	.............Oriel Park (20,400)	.........White & Black	9	8	5
Finn Harps	1954	.............Finn Park (8,000)	.... White & Blue	0	1	0
Kilkenny City	1966	.............Buckley Park (7,000)	.... Black & Amber	0	0	0
St. Patrick's Athletic....	1929	.............Richmond Park (7,000)	...........Red & White	5	2	0
Shamrock Rovers.........	1901	.............R.D.S. (14,000)	........Green & White	15	24	1
Shelbourne	1895	.............Tolka Park (9,200)	...........Red	8	6	1
Sligo Rovers	1928	.............The Showgrounds (7,000)	..........Red & White	2	2	0
U.C.D..........................	1895	.............Belfield (4,000)	...........Sky Blue	0	1	0

National League First Division Team Statistics

Club	Founded	Ground and Capacity	Colours	FAI League Titles	FAI Cups	League Cups
Athlone Town	1887	St. Mel's Park (10,000)	Blue & Black	2	1	3
Bray Wanderers	1942	Carlisle Grounds (3,000)	Green & White	0	1	0
Cobh Ramblers	1922	St. Colman's Park (10,000)	Claret & Blue	0	0	0
Galway United	1937	Terryland Park (8,000)	Maroon & Blue	0	1	2
Home Farm Everton	1928	Whitehall (3,500)	Blue & White	0	1	0
Limerick F.C.	1937	Hogan Park (10,000)	Blue & White	2	2	1
Longford Town	1924	Strokestown Road (10,000)	Red & Black	0	0	0
Monaghan United	1979	Gortakeegan (5,000)	Blue & White	0	0	0
St. Francis	1958	John Hyland Park	Green & White	0	0	0
Waterford United	1930	Regional Sports Centre (8,000)	Blue & White	6	2	1

League of Ireland All-Time Top Scorers

Name	No. of Goals	Name	No. of Goals	Name	No. of Goals
Brendan Bradley	235	Alfie Hale	153	Mick Leech	132
Turlough O'Connor	178	Paul McGee	143	Eugene Davis	130
Donal Leahy	162	Eric Barber	141	Jack Fitzgerald	130
Johnny Matthews	156	Sean McCarthy	135		

League of Ireland Championship Winners

Season	Winners
1921-22	St. James's Gate
1922-23	Shamrock Rovers
1923-24	Bohemians
1924-25	Shamrock Rovers
1925-26	Shelbourne
1926-27	Shamrock Rovers
1927-28	Bohemians
1928-29	Shelbourne
1929-30	Bohemians
1930-31	Shelbourne
1931-32	Shamrock Rovers
1932-33	Dundalk
1933-34	Bohemians
1934-35	Dolphin
1935-36	Bohemians
1936-37	Sligo Rovers
1937-38	Shamrock Rovers
1938-39	Shamrock Rovers
1939-40	St. James's Gate
1940-41	Cork United
1941-42	Cork United
1942-43	Cork United
1943-44	Shelbourne
1944-45	Cork United
1945-46	Cork United
1946-47	Shelbourne
1947-48	Drumcondra
1948-49	Drumcondra
1949-50	Cork Athletic
1950-51	Cork Athletic
1951-52	St. Patrick's Athletic
1952-53	Shelbourne
1953-54	Shamrock Rovers
1954-55	St. Patrick's Athletic
1955-56	St. Patrick's Athletic
1956-57	Shamrock Rovers
1957-58	Drumcondra
1958-59	Shamrock Rovers
1959-60	Limerick
1960-61	Drumcondra
1961-62	Shelbourne
1962-63	Dundalk
1963-64	Shamrock Rovers
1964-65	Drumcondra
1965-66	Waterford
1966-67	Dundalk
1967-68	Waterford
1968-69	Waterford
1969-70	Waterford
1970-71	Cork Hibernians
1971-72	Waterford
1972-73	Waterford
1973-74	Cork Celtic
1974-75	Bohemians
1975-76	Dundalk
1976-77	Sligo Rovers
1977-78	Bohemians
1978-79	Dundalk
1979-80	Limerick United
1980-81	Athlone Town
1981-82	Dundalk
1982-83	Athlone Town
1983-84	Shamrock Rovers
1984-85	Shamrock Rovers

Premier Division

Season	Winners
1985-86	Shamrock Rovers
1986-87	Shamrock Rovers
1987-88	Dundalk
1988-89	Derry City
1989-90	St. Patrick's Athletic
1990-91	Dundalk
1991-92	Shelbourne
1992-93	Cork City
1993-94	Shamrock Rovers
1994-95	Dundalk
1995-96	St. Patrick's Athletic
1996-97	Derry City

1st Division

Season	Winners
1985-86	Bray Wanderers
1986-87	Derry City
1987-88	Athlone Town
1988-89	Drogheda United
1989-90	Waterford United
1990-91	Drogheda United
1991-92	Limerick City
1992-93	Galway United
1993-94	Sligo Rovers
1994-95	U.C.D.
1995-96	Bray Wanderers
1996-97	Kilkenny City

F.A.I. Cup Winners

Year	Winners
1922	St. James's Gate
1923	Alton United
1924	Athlone Town
1925	Shamrock Rovers
1926	Fordsons
1927	Drumcondra
1928	Bohemians
1929	Shamrock Rovers
1930	Shamrock Rovers
1931	Shamrock Rovers
1932	Shamrock Rovers
1933	Shamrock Rovers
1934	Cork
1935	Bohemians
1936	Shamrock Rovers
1937	Waterford
1938	St. James's Gate
1939	Shelbourne
1940	Shamrock Rovers
1941	Cork United
1942	Dundalk
1943	Drumcondra
1944	Shamrock Rovers
1945	Shamrock Rovers
1946	Drumcondra
1947	Cork United

1948	Shamrock Rovers	1965	Shamrock Rovers	1982	Limerick United
1949	Dundalk	1966	Shamrock Rovers	1983	Sligo Rovers
1950	Transport	1967	Shamrock Rovers	1984	U.C.D.
1951	Cork Athletic	1968	Shamrock Rovers	1985	Shamrock Rovers
1952	Dundalk	1969	Shamrock Rovers	1986	Shamrock Rovers
1953	Cork Athletic	1970	Bohemians	1987	Shamrock Rovers
1954	Drumcondra	1971	Limerick	1988	Dundalk
1955	Shamrock Rovers	1972	Cork Hibernians	1989	Derry City
1956	Shamrock Rovers	1973	Cork Hibernians	1990	Bray Wanderers
1957	Drumcondra	1974	Finn Harps	1991	Galway United
1958	Dundalk	1975	Home Farm	1992	Bohemians
1959	St. Patrick's Athletic	1976	Bohemians	1993	Shelbourne
1960	Shelbourne	1977	Dundalk	1994	Sligo Rovers
1961	St. Patrick's Athletic	1978	Shamrock Rovers	1995	Derry City
1962	Shamrock Rovers	1979	Dundalk	1996	Shelbourne
1963	Shelbourne	1980	Waterford	1997	Shelbourne
1964	Shamrock Rovers	1981	Dundalk		

F.A.I. National League Premier Division Final League Table 1996/97

	P	W	D	L	F	A	P
Derry City	33	19	10	4	58	27	67
Bohemians	33	16	9	8	43	32	57
Shelbourne	33	15	9	9	52	36	54
Cork City	33	15	9	9	38	24	54
St. Patrick's Athletic	33	13	14	6	45	33	53
Sligo Rovers	33	12	11	10	43	43	47
Shamrock Rovers	33	10	13	10	43	46	43
U.C.D.	33	12	7	14	34	39	43
Finn Harps	33	10	9	14	41	43	49
Dundalk	33	9	9	15	32	50	36
Bray Wanderers	33	5	8	20	30	59	23
Home Farm/Everton	33	3	10	20	27	53	19

Champions: **Derry City** *Relegated:* **Bray Wanderers and Home Farm/Everton**

F.A.I. National League First Division Final League Table 1996/97

	P	W	D	L	F	A	P
Kilkenny City	27	15	10	2	47	20	55
Drogheda United	27	12	8	7	44	27	44
Waterford United	27	12	8	7	41	28	44
Athlone Town	27	10	7	10	40	39	37
Cobh Ramblers	27	9	8	10	34	28	35
Galway United	27	9	8	10	33	38	35
Longford Town	27	7	13	7	31	38	34
Monaghan United	27	7	9	11	30	46	30
St. Francis	27	7	7	13	29	33	28
Limerick F.C.	27	4	8	15	23	55	20

Promoted: **Kilkenny City** *and* **Drogheda United**

Top R.O.I. International Goalscorers

Player	No. of Goals
Frank Stapleton	20
John Aldridge	19
Don Givens	19
Tony Cascarino	18
Niall Quinn	16

Player	No. of Goals
Noel Cantwell	14
Gerry Daly	13
Jimmy Dunne	12
Liam Brady	9
Kevin Sheedy	9

Republic of Ireland International Squad

Name	Club	Position	D.O.B.	Born	Caps	Goals
Phil Babb	Liverpool	Defender	30.11.70	Lambeth	22	-
Keith Branigan	Bolton Wanderers	Goalkeeper	10.07.66	Fulham	1	-
Gary Breen	Coventry City	Defender	12.12.73	London	11	1
Tony Cascarino	A.S. Nancy	Striker	01.09.62	Kent	73	18
David Connolly	Feyenoord	Striker	06.06.77	Willesden	9	6
Kenny Cunningham	Wimbledon	Defender	28.06.71	Dublin	13	-
Curtis Flemming	Middlesbrough	Defender	08.10.68	Manchester	8	-
Shay Given	Newcastle United	Goalkeeper	20.04.76	Lifford	12	-
Ian Harte	Leeds United	Defender	31.08.77	Drogheda	14	2
Ray Houghton	Reading	Midfielder	09.01.62	Glasgow	70	5
Denis Irwin	Manchester United	Defender	31.10.65	Cork	46	1
Roy Keane	Manchester United	Midfielder	10.08.71	Cork	38	3
Jeff Kenna	Blackburn Rovers	Defender	27.08.70	Dublin	19	-
Alan Kelly	Sheffield United	Goalkeeper	11.08.68	Preston	18	-
David Kelly	Tranmeru Rovers	Striker	25.11.65	Birmingham	24	9
Gary Kelly	Leeds United	Defender	09.07.74	Louth	23	1

Name	Club	Position	D.O.B.	Born	Caps	Goals
Mark Kennedy	Liverpool	Midfielder	15.05.76	Dublin	14	1
Kevin Kilbane	West Bromwich Albion	Striker	01.02.77	Preston	1	0
Jason McAteer	Liverpool	Midfielder	18.06.71	Liverpool	24	1
Alan McLoughlin	Portsmouth	Midfielder	20.04.67	Manchester	31	2
Alan Moore	Middlesbrough	Midfielder	25.11.74	Dublin	8	-
Keith O'Neill	Norwich City	Striker	16.02.76	Dublin	9	4
Terry Phelan	Everton	Defender	16.03.67	Manchester	37	-
Niall Quinn	Sunderland	Striker	06.10.66	Dublin	62	16
Steve Staunton	Aston Villa	Defender	19.01.69	Drogheda	71	6
Andy Townsend	Middlesbrough	Midfielder	23.07.63	Maidstone	68	7

F.A.I/Opel International Senior Player of the Year Recipients

Year	Name
1989	Kevin Moran
1990	Paul McGrath
1991	Paul McGrath
1992	John Aldridge
1993	Steve Staunton
1994	Ray Houghton
1995	Andy Townsend
1996	Alan McLoughlin

Presidents of the F.A.I.

W.H. Ritchie, Sir H. McLaughlin, J. Cunningham, O. Grattan-Esmond, Dr. W.F. Hooper, O. Traynor T.D., D. O'Malley T.D., N.T. Blaney T.D., D. O'Halloran, C.H. Walsh, F. Davis, C. Cahill, Dr. B. Menton, J.J. Farrell, D. Casey, P. O'Brien, F. Fields, M. Hyland, L.D. Kilcoyne, P. Quigley (current President).

Irish Football Association

20 Windsor Avenue, Belfast BT9 6EG. Tel. (01232) 669458

Founded 1890
President ....Jim Boyce
1996/97 Irish League, Premier Division Champions ....Crusaders
1996/97 Irish League, First Division Champions ....Ballymena United
1997 Irish Cup Winners ....Glenavon
Main Stadium ....Windsor Park (28,500)

INTERNATIONAL

Northern Ireland Manager ....Bryan Hamilton
Top International Goalscorer ....Colin Clarke (13 goals in 38 apperances)
Most Capped Player ....Pat Jennings (119 caps)
Best World Cup Result ....Quarter finals (1958 World Cup in Sweden)

Irish League Premier Division Team Statistics

Club	Founded	Ground and Capacity	Colours	Irish League Titles	Irish Cups
Ards	1902	Castlereagh Park (10,000)	Red & Blue	1	4
Ballymena United	1928	The Showgrounds (8,000)	Sky Blue & White	0	6
Cliftonville	1879	Solitude (8,000)	Red & White	2	8
Coleraine	1927	The Showgrounds (12,500)	Blue & White	1	4
Crusaders	1898	Seaview (9,000)	Red & Black	4	2
Glenavon	1889	Mourneview (11,000)	Royal Blue & White	3	5
Glentoran	1882	The Oval (30,000)	Green, Black & Red	19	16
Linfield	1886	Windsor Park (28,500)	Royal Blue & White	42	35
Omagh Town	1962	St. Julian's Road (8,000)	Black & White	0	0
Portadown	1924	Shamrock Park (15,000)	Red	3	1

Irish League First Division Team Statistics

Club	Founded	Ground and Capacity	Colours	Irish League Titles	Irish Cups
Ballyclare Comrades	1919	Dixon Park (4,500)	Red & White	0	0
Bangor	1918	Clandeboye Park (5,000)	Gold & Royal Blue	0	1
Carrick Rangers	1939	Talyor's Avenue (5,000)	Amber & Black	0	1
Distillery	1879	Grosvenor Stadium (7,000)	White & Dark Blue	6	12
Dungannon Swifts	1949	Stangmore Park (5,000)	Royal Blue & White	0	0
Larne	1900	Inver Park (12,000)	Red & White	0	0
Limavady United	1876	The Showgrounds (1,000)	Royal Blue & White	0	0
Newry Town	1923	The Showgrounds (5,000)	Blue & White	0	0

Irish League Champions

Season	Winners
1890/91	Linfield
1891/92	Linfield
1892/93	Linfield
1893/94	Glentoran
1894/95	Linfield
1895/96	Distillery
1896/97	Glentoran
1897/98	Linfield
1898/99	Distillery
1899/1900	Belfast Celtic
1900/01	Distillery
1901/02	Linfield
1902/03	Distillery
1903/04	Linfield
1904/05	Glentoran
1905/06	Distillery & Cliftonville
1906/07	Linfield
1907/08	Linfield
1908/09	Linfield
1909/10	Cliftonville
1910/11	Linfield
1911/12	Glentoran
1912/13	Glentoran
1913/14	Linfield
1914/15	Belfast Celtic
1915-1919	No Competition
1919/20	Belfast Celtic
1920/21	Glentoran
1921/22	Linfield
1922/23	Linfield
1923/24	Queen's Island
1924/25	Glentoran
1925/26	Belfast Celtic
1926/27	Belfast Celtic
1927/28	Belfast Celtic
1928/29	Belfast Celtic
1929/30	Linfield
1930/31	Glentoran
1931/32	Linfield
1932/33	Belfast Celtic
1933/34	Linfield
1934/35	Linfield
1935/36	Belfast Celtic
1936/37	Belfast Celtic
1937/38	Belfast Celtic
1938/39	Belfast Celtic
1939/40	Belfast Celtic
1940-46	No Competition
1947/48	Belfast Celtic
1948/49	Linfield
1949/50	Linfield
1950/51	Glentoran
1951/52	Glenavon
1952/53	Glentoran
1953/54	Linfield
1954/55	Linfield
1955/56	Linfield
1956/57	Glenavon
1957/58	Ards
1958/59	Linfield
1959/60	Glenavon
1960/61	Linfield
1961/62	Linfield
1962/63	Distillery
1963/64	Glentoran
1964/65	Derry City
1965/66	Linfield
1966/67	Glentoran
1967/68	Glentoran
1968/69	Linfield
1969/70	Glentoran
1970/71	Linfield
1971/72	Glentoran
1972/73	Crusaders
1973/74	Coleraine
1974/75	Linfield
1975/76	Crusaders
1976/77	Glentoran
1977/78	Linfield
1978/79	Linfield
1979/80	Linfield
1980/81	Glentoran
1981/82	Linfield
1982/83	Linfield
1983/84	Linfield
1984/85	Linfield
1985/86	Linfield
1986/87	Linfield
1987/88	Glentoran
1988/89	Linfield
1989/90	Portadown
1990/91	Portadown
1991/92	Glentoran
1992/93	Linfield
1993/94	Linfield
1994/95	Crusaders

Premier Division

Season	Winners
1995/96	Portadown
1996/97	Crusaders

First Division

1995/96	Coleraine
1996/97	Ballymena United

I.F.A. Irish Cup Winners

Year	Winner
1881	Moyola Park
1882	Queen's Island
1883	Cliftonville
1884	Distillery
1885	Distillery
1886	Distillery
1887	Ulster
1888	Cliftonville
1889	Distillery
1890	Gordon Highlanders
1891	Linfield
1892	Linfield
1893	Linfield
1894	Distillery
1895	Linfield
1896	Distillery
1897	Cliftonville
1898	Linfield
1899	Linfield
1900	Cliftonville
1901	Cliftonville
1902	Linfield
1903	Distillery
1904	Linfield
1905	Distillery
1906	Shelbourne
1907	Cliftonville
1908	Bohemians
1909	Cliftonville
1910	Distillery
1911	Shelbourne
1912	Linfield
1913	Linfield
1914	Glentoran
1915	Linfield

1916	Linfield	1944	Belfast Celtic	1972	Coleraine
1917	Glentoran	1945	Linfield	1973	Glentoran
1918	Belfast Celtic	1946	Linfield	1974	Ards
1919	Linfield	1947	Belfast Celtic	1975	Coleraine
1920	Shelbourne	1948	Linfield	1976	Carrick Rangers
1921	Glentoran	1949	Derry City	1977	Coleraine
1922	Linfield	1950	Linfield	1978	Linfield
1923	Linfield	1951	Glentoran	1979	Cliftonville
1924	Queen's Island	1952	Ards	1980	Linfield
1925	Distillery	1953	Linfield	1981	Ballymena United
1926	Belfast Celtic	1954	Derry City	1982	Linfield
1927	Ards	1955	Dundela	1983	Glentoran
1928	Willowfield	1956	Distillery	1984	Ballymena United
1929	Ballymena United	1957	Glenavon	1985	Glentoran
1930	Linfield	1958	Ballymena United	1986	Glentoran
1931	Linfield	1959	Glenavon	1987	Glentoran
1932	Glentoran	1960	Linfield	1988	Glentoran
1933	Glentoran	1961	Glenavon	1989	Ballymena United
1934	Linfield	1962	Linfield	1990	Glentoran
1935	Glentoran	1963	Linfield	1991	Portadown
1936	Linfield	1964	Derry City	1992	Glenavon
1937	Belfast Celtic	1965	Coleraine	1993	Bangor
1938	Belfast Celtic	1966	Glentoran	1994	Linfield
1939	Linfield	1967	Crusaders	1995	Linfield
1940	Ballymena United	1968	Crudasers	1996	Glentoran
1941	Belfast Celtic	1969	Ards	1997	Glenavon
1942	Linfield	1970	Linfield		
1943	Belfast Celtic	1971	Distillery		

I.F.A. Irish League Premier Division Final League Table 1996/97

	P	W	D	L	F	A	P
Crusaders	28	12	10	6	39	26	46
Coleraine	28	10	13	5	37	31	43
Glentoran	28	10	11	7	36	30	41
Portadown	28	10	8	10	35	32	38
Linfield	28	10	8	10	35	33	38
Glenavon	28	8	11	9	35	34	35
Cliftonville	28	7	9	12	23	38	30
Ards	28	5	10	13	33	49	25

Champions: **Crusaders** *Relegated:* **None**

I.F.A. Irish League First Division Final League Table 1996/97

	P	W	D	L	F	A	P
Ballymena	28	21	2	5	49	17	65
Omagh Town	28	15	5	8	40	39	50
Bangor	28	15	4	9	42	29	49
Ballyclare Comrades	28	11	4	13	44	42	37
Newry Town	28	10	5	13	32	35	35
Distillery	28	10	4	14	31	37	34
Larne	28	9	5	14	34	48	32
Carrick Rangers	28	5	3	20	25	50	18

Promoted: **Ballymena** *and* **Omagh Town**

Northern Ireland International Squad

Name	Club	Position	D.O.B.	Caps	Goals	Born
Roy Carroll	Wigan Athletic	Goalkeeper	30.09.77	1	-	Enniskillen
Ian Dowie	West Ham United	Striker	09.01.65	44	11	Hatfield
Alan Fettis	Nottingham Forest	Goalkeeper	01.02.71	18	-	Belfast
Keith Gillespie	Newcastle United	Winger	18.02.75	18	1	Larne
Philip Gray	Fortuna Sittard	Striker	01.04.69	20	4	Belfast
Danny Griffin	St. Johnstone	Midfielder	10.08.77	6	-	Belfast
Colin Hill	Trelleborg	Defender	12.11.63	23	1	London
Kevin Horlock	Manchester City	Midfielder	01.11.72	10	-	Swindon
Michael Hughes	Wimbledon	Winger	02.08.71	37	2	Larne
Iain Jenkins	Chester City	Defender	24.11.72	2	-	Liverpool
Neil Lennon	Leicester City	Midfielder	25.06.71	16	1	Lurgan
Steve Lomas	West Ham United	Midfielder	18.01.74	23	1	Hanover
Jon McCarthy	Port Vale	Winger	18.08.70	4	-	Middlesborough
Pat McGibbon	Wigan Athletic	Defender	06.09.73	6	-	Craigavon
Gerard McMahon	Stoke City	Winger	29.12.73	15	2	Craigavon
Jim Magilton	Southampton	Midfielder	06.05.69	36	5	Belfast
Stephen Morrow	Arsenal	Midfielder	02.07.70	27	1	Belfast
Philip Mulryne	Manchester United	Midfielder	01.01.78	3	1	Belfast

Name	Club	Position	D.O.B.	Caps	Goals	Born
Ian Nolan	Sheffield Wednesday	Defender	09.12.70	5	-	Merseyside
James Quinn	Blackpool	Striker	15.04.74	9	1	Coventry
Keith Rowland	West Ham United	Defender	01.09.71	12	-	Portadown
Gerry Taggart	Bolton Wanderers	Defender	18.10.70	43	6	Belfast
Tommy Wright	Manchester City	Goalkeeper	24.11.75	29	-	Belfast

Top International Goalscorers, Northern Ireland

Player	No. of Goals	Player	No. of Goals
Colin Clarke	13	Olphie Stanfield	11
Gerry Armstrong	12	Billy Bingham	10
Joe Bambrick	12	Johnny Crossan	10
Willie Gillespie	12	Jimmy McIlroy	10
Jimmy Quinn	12	Peter McParland	10
Ian Dowie	11		

RUGBY

Irish Rugby Football Union

62 Lansdowne Road, Ballsbridge, Dublin 4. Tel. (01) 6684601

Founded	1874
Number of Provincial Unions	4
Number of Clubs	250
Number of Members (men)	60,000
Number of Members (women)	500
President	Niall Brophy
Secretary and Treasurer	P.R. Browne
Top Points Scorer 1996/97 A.I.L.	Andrew Thompson (Shannon) 171 points
Top Try Scorer 1996/97 A.I.L.	Scott Carroll (Malone) 11 tries
Oldest Club	Dublin University (founded 1854)
Biggest Recorded Attendance	55,000 (in Five Nations Championship at Lansdowne Road)
Main Stadium	Lansdowne Road (capacity 49,638)
Provincial Champions (97/98)	Leinster
All-Ireland League Division One Champions (96/97)	Shannon
Connacht Cup Winners (96/97)	Galwegians
Leinster Cup Winners (96/97)	Lansdowne
Munster Cup Winners (96/97)	Garryowen
Ulster Cup Winners (96/97)	Ballymena

INTERNATIONAL

National Manager	Pat Whelan
National Coach	Brian Ashton
Most Capped International	C.M.H. Gibson, 69 caps (1964-79)
Top International Points Scorer	M.J. Kiernan, 308 points (43 internationals)
Top International Try Scorer	B.J. Mullin, 17 (55 internationals)
First International Game	v. England, 1875
Best World Cup Performance	Quarter-finals (1987, 1991 and 1995)
Grand Slams	1 (1948)
Triple Crowns	6 (1894, 1899, 1948, 1949, 1982, 1985)
International Championships	18 (including 10 outright wins)

All-Ireland League Division One Team Statistics

Club	Founded	Ground	Colours	96/97 Result	Most capped International
Ballymena	1922	Eaton Park	Black	5th	W.J. McBride
Blackrock College	1882	Stradbrook Road	Royal Blue & White	8th	J.F. Slattery
Clontarf	1876	Castle Avenue	Royal Blue & Scarlet	1st Div.2	G.J. Morgan
Cork Constitution	1892	Temple Hill	White	6th	T.J. Kiernan
Dolphin	1902	Musgrave Park	Navy, Yellow & White	2nd Div.2	M.J. Kiernan
Dungannon	1873	Stevenson Park	Light Blue & White	10th	P.S. Johns
Garryowen	1884	Dooradoyle	Blue & White	7th	B.G.M. Wood
Lansdowne	1872	Lansdowne Road	Red Yellow & Black	2nd	M.I. Keane
Old Belvedere	1930	Anglesea Road	Black & White	12th	N.P.J. Francis

Club	Founded	Ground	Colours	96/97 Result	Most capped International
Old Crescent	1947	Rosbrien	Navy & White	11th	P. Lane
Shannon	1884	Thomond Park	Black & Blue	1st	G.A.J. McLoughlin
St. Mary's College	1900	Templeville Road	Royal Blue & White	4th	P.M. Deane
Terenure College	1940	Lakelands Park	Purple, Black & White	3rd	M.L. Hipwell
Young Munster	1895	Tom Clifford Park	Black & Amber	9th	P.M. Clohessy

I.R.F.U. Number of Affiliated Clubs

	Clubs	Commercial Clubs	Schools
Ulster	56	17	107
Munster	59	5	41
Leinster	71	8	75
Connacht	19	0	23
London Irish	1	-	-
	205	30	246

Ten Most Capped International Players

Mike Gibson	69
Willie John McBride	63
Fergal Slattery	61
Philip Orr	58
Brendan Mullin	55
Tom Kiernan	54
Donal Lenihan	52
Moss Keane	51
Jackie Kyle	46
Ken Kennedy	45

International Championship Winners

1883	England
1884	England
1886	England & Scotland
1887	Scotland
1890	England & Scotland
1891	Scotland
1892	England
1893	Wales
1894	**Ireland**
1895	Scotland
1896	**Ireland**
1899	**Ireland**
1900	Wales
1901	Scotland
1902	Wales
1903	Scotland
1904	Scotland
1905	Wales
1906	**Ireland** & Wales
1907	Scotland
1908	Wales
1909	Wales
1910	England
1911	Wales
1912	**Ireland** & England
1913	England
1914	England
1920	England & Scotland & Wales
1921	England
1922	Wales
1923	England
1924	England
1925	Scotland
1926	**Ireland** & Scotland
1927	**Ireland** & Scotland
1928	England
1929	Scotland
1930	England
1931	Wales
1932	**Ireland** & Wales & England
1933	Scotland
1934	England
1935	**Ireland**
1936	Wales
1937	England
1938	Scotland
1939	**Ireland** & Wales & England
1947	Wales & England
1948	**Ireland**
1949	**Ireland**
1950	Wales
1951	**Ireland**
1952	Wales
1953	England
1954	England & France & Wales
1955	France & Wales
1956	Wales
1957	England
1958	England
1959	France
1960	France & England
1961	France
1962	France
1963	England
1964	Scotland & Wales
1965	Wales
1966	Wales
1967	France
1968	France
1969	Wales
1970	France & Wales
1971	Wales
1972	not completed
1973	Quintuple Tie
incl.	**Ireland**
1974	**Ireland**
1975	Wales
1976	Wales
1977	France
1978	Wales
1979	Wales
1980	England
1981	France
1982	**Ireland**
1983	**Ireland** & France
1984	Scotland
1985	**Ireland**
1986	France & Scotland
1987	France
1988	Wales & France
1989	France
1990	Scotland
1991	England
1992	England
1993	France
1994	Wales
1995	England
1996	England
1997	France

ATHLETICS

Bord Lúthchleas na hÉireann
11 Prospect Road, Glasnevin, Dublin 9. Tel. (01) 8309901

Founded 1967
President ....Michael McKeon
Honorary Secretary...Liam Hennessy
Number of Senior Clubs 144
Number of Junior Clubs 135
Total Membership 16,495
Principal Venues..........Morton Stadium, Dublin (10,000), Mardyke, Cork (8,000), Tullamore Harriers A.C. (5,000)
Biggest Recorded Crowd ....30,000 (1979. World Cross Country Championships, Limerick)

TRACK & FIELD, NATIONAL CHAMPIONS AND RECORD HOLDERS (MEN)

Event	Men	Club	Time	National Record Holder	Date	Time
100m	Neil Ryan	Nenagh	10.53	Neil Ryan	30/05/97	10.46
200m	Gary Ryan	Nenagh	21.02	Gary Ryan	31/07/96	20.78
400m	Brian Forbes	Mid Ulster	47.06	Derek O'Connor	05/06/86	45.73
800m	David Matthews	U.C.D.	1.50.53	David Matthews	05/09/95	1.44.82
1,500m	Niall Bruton	Clonliffe	3.42.67	Ray Flynn	07/07/82	3.33.50
5,000m	Seamus Power	Kilmurray/Ibricken	14.07.00	Frank O'Mara	04/07/87	13.13.02
10,000m	Noel Berkeley	D.S.D.	29.57.44	John Treacy	22/08/80	27.48.70
3,000m Steeplechase	Patrick Davoren	Brighton	9.00.54	Brendan Quinn	30/08/85	8.24.09
110m Hurdles	T.J. Kearns	D.C.H.	14.20	T.J. Kearns	22/07/96	13.55
400m Hurdles	Tom McGuirk	D.C.H.	51.00	Tom McGuirk	01/06/96	49.73
10,000m Walk	Michael Casey	Sligo	44.03.62	Jimmy McDonald	16/06/96	41.02.52
High Jump	Mark Mandy	Birchfield	2.20m	Mark Mandy	01/07/95	2.25m
Long Jump	Garret Devlin	Ballymena	6.87m	Ciarán McDonagh	28/06/96	7.86m
Triple Jump	Patrick Shannon	Ballybrack	13.69m	Colm Cronin	26/06/77	15.89m
Pole Vault	Dylan McDermot	Borrisokane	4.60m	Alan Bourke	13/08/89	5.00m
Discus	Nicky Sweeney	D.S.D.	57.90m	Nicky Sweeney	22/05/96	67.40m
Javelin	Terry McHugh	D.C.H.	70.80m	Terry McHugh	07/08/94	82.14m
Shot	Nicky Sweeney	D.S.D.	17.02m	Paul Quirke	07/07/92	20.04m
Hammer	Roman Linschied	Donore	71.54m	Declan Hegarty	27/04/85	77.80m
56lb Distance	John Menton	Donore	8.95m	Len Braham	21/07/73	9.15m
56lb Height	Nicky Sweeney	D.S.D.	4.40m	Gerry O'Connell	19/07/86	4.93m

TRACK & FIELD, NATIONAL CHAMPIONS AND RECORD HOLDERS (WOMEN)

Event	Men	Club	Time	National Record Holder	Date	Time
100m	Aoife Hearne	Waterford	11.88	Michele Carroll	17/06/78	11.43
200m	Ciara Sheehy	West Dublin	24.31	Michele Carroll	18/06/78	23.51
400m	Karen Shinkins	D.C.H.	56.20	Patricia Walsh	03/08/87	53.06
800m	Amanda Crowe	Lisburn	2.07.46	Sonia O'Sullivan	28/07/94	2.00.69
1,500m	Valerie Vaughan	Blarney	4.23.50	Sonia O'Sullivan	25/07/95	3.58.85
5,000m	Valerie Vaughan	Blarney	15.44.72	Sonia O'Sullivan	01/09/95	14.41.40
100m Hurdles	Gráinne Redmond	Cushinstown	14.29	Olive Burke	16/08/87	13.74
400m Hurdles	Susan Smith	Waterford	56.55	Susan Smith	04/08/97	54.61
5,000m Walk	Perri Williams	St. Senan's	24.50.08	Deirdre Gallagher	23/06/96	21.35.62
High Jump	Sharon Foley	Lifford	1.75m	Laura Sharpe	03/07/94	1.89m
Long Jump	Jacqui Stokes	Ferrybank	5.77m	Terri Horgan	14/06/92	6.48m
Triple Jump	Siobhan Hoey	D.C.H.	11.36m	Siobhan Hoey	18/07/94	12.21m
Shot Putt	Emma Gavin	Limerick	12.85m	Marita Walton	02/04/83	16.99m
Discus	Ailish O'Brien	West Waterford	45.02m	Patricia Walsh	07/07/84	57.60m
Javelin	Alison Moffit	North Down	45.48m	Mary T. Real	20/06/92	50.42m
Hammer	Clara Thompson	Slaney Olympic	48.82m	Olivia Kelleher	09/06/96	52.16m

D.C.H = Dublin City Harriers
D.S.D = Dundrum South Dublin
U.C.D. = University College Dublin

The National Championships were held on July 12th and 13th 1997, at Morton Stadium, Santry, Co. Dublin.

Irish Athletes who have won European Championship Medals

1967, 1968, 1969 ....Noel Carroll (800m indoor) - gold
1969..Frank Murphy (1,500m outdoor) - silver
1975...John Treacy (5,000m Junior outdoor) - silver
1978...Eamon Coghlan (1,500m outdoor) - silver
1979..Eamon Coghlan (1,500m indoor) - gold
1981 ....Ray Flynn(1,500m indoor) - silver
1981 ....Mary Purcell (1,500m indoor) - bronze
1985 ....Marcus O'Sullivan (1,500m indoor) - silver
1985 ....Nick O'Brien (3,000m Junior outdoor) - gold
1991 ....Mark Carroll (5,000m Junior outdoor) - gold
1994 ....Sonia O'Sullivan (3,000m outdoor) - gold
1994 ....Catherina McKiernan (Cross-Country) - gold

Irish Athletes who have won World Championship Medals

1970 ....John Hartnett (World Junior Cross Country) - gold
1978, 1979 ....John Treacy (World Cross Country Championship) - gold
1979 ....Irish Men's Cross Country team (World Cross Country Championship) - silver
1983 ....Eamon Coghlan (5,000m outdoor) - gold
1987, 1989, 1993 ....Marcus O'Sullivan (1,500m indoor) - gold
1987, 1991...Frank O'Mara (3,000m indoor) - gold
1992, 1993, 1994 and 1995 ....Catherina McKiernan (World Cross Country Championship) - silver
1995 ....Sonia O'Sullivan (5,000m outdoor) - gold
1997..Sonia O'Sullivan (3,000m indoor) - silver
1997 ....Irish Ladies Cross Country Team (World Cross Country Championship) - bronze

BOXING

Irish Amateur Boxing Association

National Boxing Stadium, South Circular Road, Dublin 8. Tel. (01) 4533371

Founded 1911
President..Nicholas White
Honorary Secretary ....Joe Kirwan
Number of Provincial Councils ....4 (Connacht, Leinster, Munster and Ulster)
Number of County Boards 26
Number of Clubs 330
Principal Venue..The National Boxing Stadium (capacity 2,000)

Irish Amateur Boxing Senior Champions 1996/97

Held at the National Boxing Stadium on February 21, February 28 and March 7, 1997.

Weight	Boxer's Name & Club
48 Kg Light Flyweight	James Rooney (Star)
51 Kg Flyweight	Liam Cunningham (Saints)
54 Kg Bantamweight	Damaen Kelly (Holy Trinity)
57 Kg Featherweight	Pat O'Donnell (Dockers)
60 Kg Lightweight	Eugene McEneaney (Dealgan)
63.5 Kg Light Welterweight	Glen McCarnon (Holy Family/Golden Gloves)
67 Kg Welterweight	Neil Gough (St. Paul's Waterford)
71 Kg Light Middleweight	Michael Roche (Sunnyside)
75 Kg Middleweight	Brian Magee (Holy Trinity)
81 Kg Light Heavyweight	Stephen Kirk (Cairn Lodge)
91 Kg Heavyweight	John Kiely (Limerick Corpus Christi)
91+ Kg Super Heavyweight	Stephen Reynolds (St. Josephs Sligo)

NATIONAL INTERMEDIATE CHAMPIONS 1996/97

Weight	Boxer's Name & Club
48 Kg Light Flyweight	James Rooney (Star)
51 Kg Flyweight	Aidan McGahon (Togher)
54 Kg Bantamweight	Noel Hazlett (St. Brigids)
57 Kg Featherweight	Mark Prunty (Portmarnock)
60 Kg Lightweight	Pat O'Donnell (Dockers)
63.5 Kg Light Welterweight	Paul McCluskey (St. Canices)
67 Kg Welterweight	James Keohane (Dungarvan)

71 Kg Light Middleweight ....Frank O'Brien (Ballyduff)
75 Kg Middleweight ....Patrick Smyth (Keady)
81 Kg Light Heavyweight ....Peadar Breathnach (Rosmuc/Camus)
91 Kg Heavyweight ....Thomas Crampton (St. Broughans)
91+ Kg Super Heavyweight...Stephen Reynolds (St. Josephs Sligo)

NATIONAL JUNIOR CHAMPIONS 1996/97

Weight	Boxer's Name & Club

48 Kg Light Flyweight ....Henry Cunningham (Saints)
51 Kg Flyweight ....Bernard Dunne (C.I.E.)
54 Kg Bantamweight ....James Chisholm (Greenmount)
57 Kg Featherweight ....Aodh Carlyle (Sacred Heart)
60 Kg Lightweight ....Oisín Daly (Loughlynn)
63.5 Kg Light Welterweight ....Paul Stephens (C.I.E.)
67 Kg Welterweight ....Conal Carmichael (Holy Trinity)
71 Kg Light Middleweight ....Mervyn Lee (Oughterard)
75 Kg Middleweight...Tommy Sheahan (St. Michaels, Athy)
81 Kg Light Heavyweight...Patrick Sharkey (Rosses)
91 Kg Heavyweight ....Cathal McMonagle (Letterkenny)
91+ Kg Super Heavyweight ....no entries

Irish Medallists at Olympic Games and European Championships

Name	Olympic Games	Venue	Medal	Weight
Michael Carruth	1992	Barcelona	Gold	67kg
Wayne McCullough	1992	Barcelona	Silver	54kg
Fred Tiedt	1956	Melbourne	Silver	67kg
John McNally	1952	Helsinki	Silver	54kg
Hugh Russell	1980	Moscow	Bronze	51kg
Jim McCourt	1964	Tokyo	Bronze	60kg
Fred Gilroy	1956	Melbourne	Bronze	54kg
Tony Byrne	1956	Melbourne	Bronze	60kg
John Caldwell	1956	Melbourne	Bronze	51kg

Name	European C'ships	Venue	Medal	Weight
Paul Griffin	1991	Sweden	Gold	57kg
Maxie McCullough	1949	Norway	Gold	60kg
Gerry O' Colmain	1947	Ireland	Gold	91kg
Jim Ingle	1939	Ireland	Gold	51kg
Paddy Dowdal	1939	Ireland	Gold	60kg
Terry Milligan	1953		Silver	63.5kg
John Kelly	1951		Silver	54kg
Peter Maguire	1947	Ireland	Silver	57kg
Damean Kelly	1995	Denmark	Bronze	51kg
Sean Casey	1985		Bronze	51kg
Kieran Joyce	1983		Bronze	71kg
Gerry Hawkins	1981		Bronze	48kg
Phil Sutcliffe	1977-79		Bronze	48 + 51kg
Niall McLoughlin	1971		Bronze	51kg
Mick Dowling	1965-71		Bronze	54kg
Jim McCourt	1965		Bronze	60kg
Harry Perry	1959	Lucerne	Bronze	67kg
Colm McCoy	1959	Lucerne	Bronze	75kg
Fred Tiedt	1957	Prague	Bronze	67kg
Terry Milligan	1951		Bronze	63.5kg
David Connell	1949-51		Bronze	60kg

SWIMMING

Irish Amateur Swimming Association

House of Sport, Long Mile Road, Dublin 12. Tel. (01) 4501739

Founded 1893
Number of Provincial Branches ....4 (Connacht, Leinster, Munster and Ulster)
Number of Clubs 140

Number of Members 6,500
Number of Swimming Pools nationwide 219
President..Donal Barry (January 1997-April 1998)
Honorary Secretary ....Celia Millane
Number of Coaches 50
Number of Teachers 1,500
Biggest Recorded Attendance ....2,000 (Leisureland International Meeting, Galway March 1997)

WOMEN'S INDIVIDUAL NATIONAL CHAMPIONS/NATIONAL RECORD HOLDERS (SHORT COURSE)

Race	1997 Champion	Club	Time	National Record Holder	Club	Time
50m Freestyle	Chantal Gibney	Trojan	26.61	Michelle Smith	King's Hos*	25.85
100m Freestyle	Chantal Gibney	Trojan	57.81	Michelle Smith	King's Hos	54.87
200m Freestyle	Chantal Gibney	Trojan	2:06.02	Michelle Smith	King's Hos	2:01.38
400m Freestyle	Diane Simms	Leander	4:29.76	Michelle Smith	King's Hos	4:07.25
800m Freestyle	Emma Bergin	Templeogue	9:30.88	Michelle Smith	King's Hos	8:44.06
50m Backstroke	Sinead Cawley	Claremorris	30.59	Niamh O'Connor	New Ross	29.44
100m Backstroke	Sinead Cawley	Claremorris	1:05.96	Michelle Smith	King's Hos	1:02.36
200m Backstroke	Emma Legget	Cormorant	2:22.82	Michelle Smith	King's Hos	2:10.76
50m Breaststroke	Emma Robinson	Coleraine	33.07	Gina Galligan	Trojan	32.47
100m Breaststroke	Emma Robinson	Coleraine	1:12.79	Siobhan Doyle	Glenalybn	1:10.71
200m Breaststroke	Mary Corless	Tuam	2:34.87	Sharlene Brown	Lisburn	2:36.26
50m Butterfly	Sally O'Herlihy	Trojan	29.41	Michelle Smith	King's Hos	28.15
100m Butterfly	Sally O'Herlihy	Trojan	1:04.45	Michelle Smith	King's Hos	59.99
200m Butterfly	Michelle Smith	King's Hos	2:08.15	Michelle Smith	King's Hos	2:07.61
100m Individual Medley	Claire Hogan	St. Paul's	1:06.58	Michelle Smith	King's Hos	1:02.70
200m Individual Medley	Claire Hogan	St. Paul's	2:21.77	Michelle Smith	King's Hos	2:13.46
400m Individual Medley	Mary Corless	Tuam	5:03.96	Michelle Smith	King's Hos	4:36.84

WOMEN'S INDIVIDUAL NATIONAL CHAMPIONS/NATIONAL RECORD HOLDERS (SHORT COURSE)

Race	1997 Champion	Club	Time	National Record Holder	Club	Time
50m Freestyle	Nick O'Hare	Coolmine	23.47	Nick O'Hare	Coolmine	22.77
100m Freestyle	Adrian O'Connor	New Ross	52.08	Nick O'Hare	Coolmine	50.11
200m Freestyle	Dougie Hyde	Limerick	1:51.93	Ken Turner	C.R.C.	1:49.38
400m Freestyle	Mark Madine	Leander	4:02.00	Ken Turner	Aer Lingus	3:53.82
1500m Freestyle	Stephen Saunders	Terenure Col	16:08.90	Ken Turner	Aer Lingus	15:33.57
50m Backstroke	Adrian O'Connor	New Ross	25.76*	Adrian O'Connor	New Ross	25.76
100m Backstroke	Adrian O'Connor	New Ross	55.75	Adrian O'Connor	New Ross	55.23
200m Backstroke	Adrian O'Connor	New Ross	2:01.22	Adrian O'Connor	New Ross	1:59.71
50m Breaststroke	Michael Giles	Coolmine	29.19	Gary O'Toole	Trojan	28.59
100m Breaststroke	Michael Giles	Coolmine	1:03.92	Gary O'Toole	Trojan	1:01.87
200m Breaststroke	Niall Moraghan	Trojan	2:19.91	Gary O'Toole	Trojan	2:11.35
50m Butterfly	Andrew Reid	Larne Junior	24.67†	Andrew Reid	Larne Junior	24.67
100m Butterfly	Paul McCarthy	New Ross	55.58	Declan Byrne	Trojan	55.41
200m Butterfly	Paul McCarthy	New Ross	2:02.23	Colin Louth	Cormorant	2:01.64
100m Individual Medley	Hugh O'Connor	New Ross	59.38	Standard		57.39
200m Individual Medley	Graham Beegan	Cormorant	2:07.00	Gary O'Toole	Trojan	2:02.23
400m Individual Medley	Graham Beegan	Cormorant	4:32.91	Gary O'Toole	Triton	4:22.97

RELAYS

Mens 4x200m Freestyle		Leander	7:51.37		Trojan	7:45.82
Mens 4x100m Medley		New Ross	3:49.06*		New Ross	3:49.06
Men's 4x100m Freestyle		Limerick	3:28.84		Coolmine	3:25.47
Womens 4x100m Medley		Glenalbyn	4:34.33		Glenalbyn	4:22.99
Women's 4x100m Freestyle		Trojan	3:59.60*		Trojan	3:59.60

King's Hospital . †Denotes National Record set at the 1997 National Championships

HORSE RACING

Irish Horseracing Authority
Leopardstown Racecourse, Foxrock, Dublin 18. Tel. (01) 2892888

Founded ....1994 (replaced the Racing Authority)
Chairman ....Denis Brosnan
Chief Executive ....Noel Ryan
Secretary ....Paddy Walsh
Number of Meetings (1996) 258
Number of Races (1996) 1,807
Total betting (1996) £502,586,000
        On-course £96,586,000
        Off-course £406,000,000
Total Prizemoney £13,953,000
Total Attendances for 1996 1,108,882
Main tracks ....The Curragh, Leopardstown, Fairyhouse, Punchestown and Ballybrit

NATIONAL HUNT

Number of Races 1,213
Total Prizemoney £6,786,000
Champion Jockey National Hunt (1996) ....Charlie Swan (150 winners)
Champion Trainer National Hunt (1996) ....Aidan O'Brien (155 winneres)
Jameson Grand National Winner (1997) ....Mudahim, trainer Jenny Pitman, jockey Jason Titley
Powers Gold Cup Winner (1997).................*Doran's Pride, trainer Michael Hourigan, jockey Richard Dunwoody
A.I.G. Champion Hurdle (1997)......................Cockney Lad, trainer Noel Meade, jockey Richard Hughes
Digital Galway Plate (1997) ....Stroll Home, trainer Jimmy Mangan, jockey Paul Carberry

FLAT

Number of Races 684
Total Prizemoney £7,167,000
Champion Jockey Flat (1996) ....Johnny Murtagh (73 winners)
Champion Trainer Flat (1996) ....Jim Bolger (94 winners)
Budweiser Irish Derby (1997) ....Desert King, trainer Aidan O'Brien, jockey Christy Roche
Heinz 57 Phoenix Stakes (1997) ....Princely Heir, trainer Mark Johnston, jockey Jason Weaver
Irish Oaks (1997)..Ebadiyla, trainer John Oxx, jockey Johnny Murtagh
Irish 2,000 Guineas (1997) ....Desert King, trainer Aidan O'Brien, jockey Christy Roche
Irish 1,000 Guineas (1997)........................Classic Park, trainer Aidan O'Brien, jockey Stephen Craine
Irish St. Leger (1997) ....Oscar Schindler, trainer Kevin Prendergast, jockey Stephen Craine

*Doran's Pride was to have been the mount of Shane Broderick who was seriously injured the day prior to the running of the Gold Cup.
A trust fund has been set up in his name.

GOLF

Golfing Union of Ireland
Glencar House, 81 Eglinton Road, Donnybrook, Dublin 4. Tel. (01) 2694111

Founded 1891
Number of Affiliated Clubs 367
President ....Peter J. O'Hara (until February 1998)
President Elect ....J.P. Shannon
Honorary Secretary ....J.G. O'Brien
Number of Coaches 5
Number of Club Members 125,061
Number of Dunhill Cup Victories ....2 (1988 and 1990)
Oldest Club with a Continuous Existence ....Royal Belfast (1881)
East of Ireland Amateur Open Winner 1997 ....S. Quinlivan (Ballybunion)
North of Ireland Amateur Open Winner 1997 ....M. Sinclair (Knock)
West of Ireland Amateur Open Winner 1997 ....J. Fanagan (Milltown)
South of Ireland Amateur Open Winner 1997 ....P. Collier (Limerick)
Irish Amateur Open Winner 1997 ....K. Nolan (Bray)
Irish Amateur Close Winner 1997 ....K. Kearney (Sligo)

Irish Ladies Golf Union

1 Clonskeagh Square, Clonskeagh Road, Dublin 14. Tel. (01) 2696244

Founded 1893
President...Juliett McHugh
Secretary...M.P. Turvey
Number of Affiliated Clubs 333
Number of Club Members 42,500
Irish Ladies Close Championship ....Susanne Fanagan (Milltown)
Irish Open Stroke Play Championship ....Yvonne Casidy (Dundalk)
Irish Senior Ladies Close Championship ....Marie O'Donnell (Donegal)
Senior Cup Champions ....Milltown
Inter Club Team Champions ....Killarney
Interprovincial Champions ....Leinste

Growth of Golf 1986-97

	No. of Clubs 1986	No. of Clubs 1997	No. of Members 1986	No. of Members 1987
Golfing Union of Ireland	248	367	123,000	200,000
Irish Ladies Golf Union	237	333	24,000	42,500

Based on the number of affiliated clubs and members of the respective organisations.

Irish Winners of International Professional Tournaments

Fred Daly	1946	Irish Open
Fred Daly	1947	British Open
Fred Daly	1947	PGA Matchplay Championship
Harry Bradshaw	1947	Irish Open
Fred Daly	1948	PGA Matchplay Championship
Fred Daly	1948	Dunlop Southport Tournament
Fred Daly	1948	Penfold Tournament
Harry Bradshaw	1949	Irish Open
Fred Daly	1950	Lotus Tournament
Fred Daly	1952	PGA Matchplay Championship
Fred Daly	1952	Daks Tournament
Harry Bradshaw	1953	Dunlop Masters
Harry Bradshaw	1955	Dunlop Masters
C. O'Connor Snr.	1955	Swallow Penfold
C. O'Connor Snr.	1956	Dunlop Masters
C. O'Connor Snr.	1956	Spalding Tournament
C. O'Connor Snr.	1957	News of the World Matchplay
Harry Bradshaw	1958	PGA Close Championship
Harry Bradshaw	1958	Swallow-Penfold (tied)
Norman Drew	1959	Yorkshire Evening News Tournament
Ernie Jones	1959	The Hennessy Tournament
C. O'Connor Snr.	1959	Dunlop Masters
C. O'Connor Snr.	1959	Daks Tournament
C. O'Connor Snr.	1960	Irish Hospitals Tournament
C. O'Connor Snr.	1960	Ballantine Open
C. O'Connor Snr.	1961	Carling Caledonian
Hugh Boyle	1961	Yomiuri Tournament
Hugh Boyle	1961	Daks Tournamen
Ernie Jones	1961	The Coxmoore Tournament
C. O'Connor Snr.	1962	Irish Hospitals Tournament
C. O'Connor Snr.	1963	Martini International (tied)
C. O'Connor Snr.	1964	Martini International
C. O'Connor Snr.	1964	Carrolls International
C. O'Connor Snr.	1964	Jeyes Tournament
Ernie Jones	1964	Sportsman Inn Tournament
C. O'Connor Snr.	1965	Senior Service Tournament
C. O'Connor Snr.	1966	Carrolls Tournament
C. O'Connor Snr.	1966	Ulster Open
C. O'Connor Snr.	1967	Carrolls Tournament
Peter Townsend	1967	Dutch Open
Peter Townsend	1968	Chesterfield
Peter Townsend	1968	PGA Championship
Peter Townsend	1968	Western Australia Open
Peter Townsend	1968	Coca-Cola Young Professionals
Hugh Jackson	1968	Picadilly Fourball
C. O'Connor Snr.	1968	Alcan International
C. O'Connor Snr.	1968	Ulster Open
Jimmy Martin	1968	Carrolls International
C. O'Connor Snr.	1969	Ulster Open
Peter Townsend	1969	Caracas Open
Paddy Skerrit	1970	Alcan International
C. O'Connor Snr.	1970	John Player Classic
C. O'Connor Snr.	1970	Sean Connery Pro-Am
Peter Townsend	1971	Swiss Open
Peter Townsend	1971	Walworth Aloyco
Ernie Jones	1971	Kenya Open
Eddie Polland	1971	Parmeco Classic
C. O'Connor Snr.	1972	Carrolls International
Jimmy Kinsella	1972	Madrid Open
Peter Townsend	1972	Los Lagaratos
Paddy McGuirk	1973	Carrolls International
Eddie Polland	1973	Penfold-Bournemouth Tournament
C. O'Connor Jnr.	1974	Zambian Open
Liam Higgins	1974	Kerrygold Classic
C. O'Connor Jnr.	1975	Carrolls Open
C. O'Connor Jnr.	1975	Martini International
Peter Townsend	1975	ICL Tournament
John O'Leary	1975	Holiday Inns Championship
John O'Leary	1975	Sumrie-Bournemouth Betterball
Eddie Polland	1975	Sun Alliance Matchplay Championship
C. O'Connor Jnr.	1976	Sumrie Betterball
John O'Leary	1976	Greater Manchester Open
Eddie Polland	1976	Spanish Open
Eamon Darcy	1977	Greater Manchester Open
Liam Higgins	1977	Kerrygold Classic
Liam Higgins	1977	Kenya Open
C. O'Connor Jnr.	1978	Sumrie-Bournemouth Betterball

Eamon Darcy	1978	Sumrie-Bournemouth Betterball
David Jones	1978	PGA Club Pros' Championship
Peter Townsend	1978	........................Caribbean Open
Peter Townsend	1978	.........................Zambian Open
Peter Townsend	1978	...............Moroccan Grand Prix
Peter Townsend	1978	................Los Lagaratos Open
Des Smyth	1979	.................European Matchplay
		...............................Championship
David Jones	1979	PGA Club Pros' Championship
Eamon Darcy	1980	..............Air New Zealand Open
Des Smyth	1980	..............Newcastle Brown '900'
Des Smyth	1980	........Greater Manchester Open
Eddie Polland	1980	.............................Spanish Open
Eamon Darcy	1981	...................Cock O'The North
Eamon Darcy	1981	..................West Lakes Classic
Des Smyth	1981	.............................Coral Classic
Peter Townsend	1981	..........................Laurent Perrier
John O'Leary	1982	...................Carrolls Irish Open
Eamon Darcy	1982	...............................Kenya Open
Ronan Rafferty	1982	....................Venezuelan Open
Des Smyth	1983	..............................Sanyo Open
Eamon Darcy	1983	...........................Spanish Open
Eamon Darcy	1984	...........................Mufulira Open
David Feherty	1984	.......................ICL International
David Feherty	1986	...............................Italian Open
David Feherty	1986	.........Bell's Scottish Open
Philip Walton	1986	................Jack Mulcahy Classic
Eamon Darcy	1987	..........................Belgian Open
Eamon Darcy	1987	....Tretorn-Spalding Tournament
Liam Higgins	1987	...............Jack Mulcahy Classic
Ronan Rafferty	1987	......Nissan-Mobil New Zealand
		....Open
Des Smyth	1988	..........................Jersey Open
Ronan Rafferty	1988	Equity and Law Challenge Cup
Ronan Rafferty	1988	................Australian Matchplay
		...............................Championship
David Jones	1988	..........................Europcar Open
C. O'Connor Jnr.	1989	European Airways Jersey Open
David Jones	1989	...............................Kenya Open
David Feherty	1989	....................BMW International
Ronan Rafferty	1989	..........................Volvo Masters
Ronan Rafferty	1989	.................Lancia Italian Open
Ronan Rafferty	1989	Scandinavian Enterprises Open
Ronan Rafferty	1990	.............................PLM Open
Ronan Rafferty	1990	..................Melbourne Classic
Ronan Rafferty	1990	....Ebel European Masters
C. O'Connor Jnr.	1990	...............................Kenya Open
Eamon Darcy	1990	Emirates Airlines Desert Classic
Philip Walton	1990	.............Peugeot French Open
E. O'Connell	1990	..................Swedish Matchplay
E. O'Connell	1990	...........Torras Hostench-El-Prat
John McHenry	1990	.............................Boggi Open
David Feherty	1991	..Credit Lyonnais Cannes Open
Ronan Rafferty	1992	....................Portuguese Open
Ronan Rafferty	1992	.... Palm Meadows Cup
David Feherty	1992	..............................Bell's Cup
C. O'Connor Jnr.	1992	..............Dunhill British Masters
Darren Clarke	1993	...............Alfred Dunhill Open
Ronan Rafferty	1993	..........................Austrian Open
Des Smyth	1993	.............................Madrid Open
Philip Walton	1995	..........Murphy's English Open
Philip Walton	1995	.......................Catalonia Open
Darren Clarke	1996	.......Hinde German Masters
Paul McGinley	1996	...................Hohe Brucke Open
P. Harrington	1996	...........Peugeot Spanish Open

Irish teams have also been successful. Harry Bradshaw and Christy O'Connor Senior won the Canada Cup in 1958. Ireland has won the Dunhill Cup on two occasions: in 1988 with a team of Ronan Rafferty, Eamon Darcy and Des Smyth, and again in 1990 when the team was Ronan Rafferty, David Feherty and Philip Walton.

OVERALL INTERNATIONAL VICTORIES

Christy O'Connor Senior	24
Peter Townsend	15
Ronan Rafferty	13
Eamon Darcy	11
Fred Daly	9
Christy O'Connor Junior	8
Des Smyth	7
David Feherty	6
Harry Bradshaw	6
Eddie Polland	5
David Jones	4
Ernie Jones	4
John O'Leary	4
Liam Higgins	4
Philip Walton	4
Darren Clarke	2
Eoghan O'Connell	2
Hugh Boyle	2
Hugh Jackson	1
Jimmy Kinsella	1
Jimmy Martin	1
John McHenry	1
Norman Drew	1
Paddy McGuirk	1
Paddy Skerrit	1
Padraig Harrington	1
Paul McGinley	1

BASKETBALL

Irish Basketball Association

National Basketball Arena, Tymon Park, Dublin 24. Tel. (01) 4590211 www.indigo.ie.iba

Founded	1945
Number of Clubs Affiliated to I.B.A.	300
Number of Local Area Boards	15
Number of Clubs Affiliated to Local Boards	1,200
Number of Registered Players (Men)	5,341
Number of Registered Players (Women)	5,896
Number of Registered Players (Schools)	80,000

President	Finn Ahern (until May 1998)
Chief Executive Officer	Scott McCarthy
General Secretary	Sheila Gilligan
Number of Coaches	1,100
Principal Venue	National Basketball Arena (capacity 2,500)
Men's Superleague Champions	Camtec Neptune - Cork
Men's Cup Champions	Denny Notre Dame - Dublin
Women's Superleague Champions	Snowcream Wildcats - Waterford
Women's Cup Champions	Naomh Mhuire - Dublin
Men's National Team Coach	Enda Byrt
Women's National Team Coach	Gerry Fitzpatrick
Most Capped International (Men)	Mark Keenan (64 caps)
Most Valuable Player 1996/97 (Men)	Stephen McCarthy (Neptune)
Most Valuable Player 1996/97 (Women)	Rachel Kelly (Tolka Rovers)

BOWLING

Irish Bowling Association

2 Ashdene Road, Moneyreagh Co. Down BT23 6DD. Tel. (01232) 448348

Founded	1904
Number of Clubs	126
President	J. Donaldson
Honorary Secretary	J.N. McQuay
Number of Coaches	66
Number of Members	6,850
National Senior Singles Champion 1997	G. Moore (Banbridge)
National Senior Pairs Champions 1997	I. Perry & A. Hughes (Portadown)
National Senior Triples Champions 1997	C. Hogg, T. McAleavey & J Smyth (Cookstown)
National Senior Fours Champions 1997	David Roe, M. Nelson, Donald Roe & J Ross (Lisnagarvey)

Bowling League of Ireland

'Dookinelly', 13 Glenabbey Road, Mount Merrion, Co. Dublin. Tel. (01) 2880255

Founded	1904
Number of Clubs	21
President	Ms. J. Doyle
Honorary Secretary	Mr. Jack Burke
Number of Coaches	24
Number of Members	2,008
Men	1,250
Women	758
Senior Singles Champion 1997	F. McCarthy (C.Y.M.)
Senior Pairs Champions 1997	V. O'Callaghan & A. Hoey (Crumlin)
Senior Triples Champions 1997	I. D'Arcy, E. Downey & G. D'Arcy (Crumlin)
Senior Rinks Champions 1997	W.W. Doyle, B. Somers, J. Nolan & A. Murphy (Bray)

CRICKET

Irish Cricket Union

45 Foxrock Park, Foxrock, Dublin 18. Tel. (01) 2893943

Founded	1923
President	Enda McDermott
Chairman	Gavin Craig
Honorary Secretary	John Wright
Number of Clubs Affiliated to I.C.U.	170
Number of Teams	400
Number of Registered Players	9,000
Number of Coaches	70
Largest Attendance	4,000 (July 1993, Ireland v. Australia in Dublin)
Highest Score Recorded	198 (Ivan J. Anderson v. Canada XI, 1973)
Number of Provincial Unions	4 (Munster, Leinster, North-West and North)
National Coach	Mike Hendrick
Most Capped Player	D.A. Lewis (121 caps between 1984 and 1997)
Most Runs	4275 (S.J.S. Warke, 1981-96)
Most Centuries	7 (I.J. Anderson, 1966-85)

Most Wickets	326 (J.D. Monteith, 1965-84)
Best Bowling Analyses	9-26 (F. Fee v. Scotland 1957)
Most Catches	57 (A.J. O'Riordan)
Quickest Century	51 minutes, 51 balls (J.A. Prior v. Warwickshire 1982)
Number International Matches played since 1855	486
Royal Liver Irish Senior Cup Champions 1997	Limavady
Northern Cricket Union League Winners 1997	Cliftonville
North-West Cricket Union League Winners 1997	Limavady
Munster Cricket Union League Winners 1997	Cork County
Leinster Cricket Union League Winners 1997	Carlisle
Interprovincial Champions 1997	Northern Cricket Union
World Ranking of the Irish Team	13th
Principal Grounds	Malahide, Leinster, Clontarf, Downpatrick, Eglinton and North of Ireland Cricket Clubs

IRISH WOMEN'S CRICKET UNION

"Woodcroft", 50 St.Alban's Park, Sandymount, Dublin 4. Tel. (01) 2838698

Founded	1982
President	Hilary O'Reilly
Honorary Secretary	Judy Cohen
Number of Provincial Unions	3 (South Leinster, North Leinster and Ulster)
Number of Clubs	17
Number of Registered Players	1,500
Number of Teams:	
League	39
Interprovincial	13
Schools	57
Number of Coaches	1
Most Capped Player	Mary Pat Moore (46)
Most Runs	956 (Mary Pat Moore)
Most Centuries	1 (Mary Pat Moore)
Most Wickets	40 (Susan Bray)
Best Bowling Analyses	5-27 (Susan Bray)
Biggest Attendance	300 (July 1995, European Cup final)

CYCLING

Federation of Irish Cyclists

Kelly Roche House, 619 North Circular Road, Dublin 1. Tel. (01) 8551522

Founded	1988
President	Pat McQuaid
Honorary Secretary	Jack Watson
Number of Clubs	124
Number of Regions	6 (Northern, Western, Southern, Eastern, Mid-Eastern and South-Eastern)
Total Membership (1997)	2,361
of which: Northern	744
Western	248
Southern	384
Eastern	202
Mid-Eastern	595
South-Eastern	188

National Champions

Race	Winner	Club
Senior Road Race	Morgan Fox	Cuchulainn C.C.
Junior Road Race	Dermot Nally	unattached
Veterans Road Race	Brian Holmes	V.C. Glendale
Ladies Road Race	Sue McMaster	Amev
Senior 40k TT	Scott Hamilton	Maryland Whs.
Senior 16k TT	Scott Hamilton	Maryland Whs.
Junior 16k TT	David Coughlan	Navan R.C.
Ladies 16k TT	Marie Reilly	Bohermeen C.C.
Senior 80k TT	Ian Chivers	Cyprus C.C.
Hill Climb	David Peelo	Sorrento C.C.

Senior Cyclo Cross (1996)	Robin Seymour	unattached
FBD Milk Rás	Andy Roche	Kerry
Junior Tour of Ireland	Alain Van Katwijk	Holland
Points Championship	David Peelo	Sorrento C.C.
Kilometre Championship	David Peelo	Sorrento C.C.
Sprint Championship	Keith Bannon	Bray Wheelers
Pursuit Championship	Simon Coughlan	Navan C.C.
U23 Men's Championships	Michael McNena	Thermo King C.C.
U23 Ladies Championships	Geraldine Gill	Navan R.C.

HOCKEY

Irish Hockey Union

6A Woodbine Park, Blackrock, Co. Dublin. Tel. (01) 2600087

Founded	1893
President	John Dennis
Honorary Secretary	J. Andrew Kershaw
Number of Clubs	76
Number of Provincial Unions	3 (Ulster, Munster and Leinster)
Irish Senior Cup Champions	Lisnagarvey
Irish League Champions	Lisnagarvey
Irish Junior Cup Champions	Avoca II's
Irish Schools Cup Champions	Newpark Comprehensive, Dublin
Senior Interprovincial Champions	Leinster
Leinster Senior Cup Champions	Three Rock Rovers
Ulster Senior Cup Champions	Lisnagarvey
Munster Senior Cup Champions	Church of Ireland
Inter varsity Champions	University of Ulster, Jordanstown
Main Stadium	University College Dublin, Belfield. Capacity 1,500

INTERNATIONAL

Irish Senior Coach	tba
Number of Senior Coaches	19
Most Capped Player	Marty Sloan (149 caps)
Top Scorer	Jimmy Kirkwood
International Ranking	18th
Biggest Attendance	5,000 (1995, European Nations Cup finals)

Irish Ladies Hockey Union

95 Sandymount Road, Dublin 4. Tel. (01) 6606780

Founded	1894
President	Grace Redmond
Honorary Secretary	Joan McCloy
Number of Clubs	126
Number of Provincial Unions	5 (Ulster, Munster, Leinster, Connacht and South-East)
Number of Members	30,000 (of which 20,364 are registered as players)
Irish Senior Cup Champions	Hermes H.C.
Irish League Champions	Muckross H.C.
Irish Junior Cup Champions	Pegasus II's
Irish Junior League Champions	Pegasus II's
Irish Schools Cup Champions	Enniskillen Collegiate
Senior Interprovincial Champions	Leinster
Leinster Senior Cup Champions	Muckross
Ulster Senior Cup Champions	Pegasus
Munster Senior Cup Champions	Cork Harlequins
Connacht Senior Cup Champions	Galway Ladies
Inter varsity Champions	Trinity College, Dublin
Main Stadium	University College Dublin, Belfield. Capacity 1,500

INTERNATIONAL

Irish Senior Ladies Coach	Terry Gregg
Number of Coaches	8
Most Capped Player	Mary Logue (108)
Top Scorer	Sarah Kelleher

International Ranking 14th
Biggest Attendance ....6,000 (August 1994, Women's Hockey World Cup final)
Biggest Recorded Victories ....11-0 (v. Wales 28.02.1907 and v. Poland 18.04.1997)

ICE HOCKEY

Castlereagh Knights

Dundonald International Ice Bowl, 111 Old Dundonald Road, Belfast. BT16 0XT Tel. (01232) 482611

Founded..1995
Number of Clubs...1 (Castlereagh Knights)
Total Membership 30
Principal Venue...Dundonald Ice Bowl (capacity 1,500 seats)
Largest recorded crowd ....2,000 (Castlereagh Knights v. Whitley Bay Warriors 14.09.96)

Castlereagh Knights are the only professional Ice Hockey team in Ireland. Coached and managed by Canadian Jim Graves, they compete in the British Northern Premier League against a number of Scottish and English teams.

MOTORCYCLING

Motor Cycle Union of Ireland

35 Lambay Road, Glasnevin, Dublin 9. Tel. (01) 8378090
7 St. Bennet's Avenue, Donaghadee, Co. Down.Tel. (01247) 883477

Founded 1902
Number of Centres ....2: Southern (i.e. Leinster, Connacht and Munster) and Ulster
Number of Clubs 58
Number of Members ....1,700 (Competition Licence Holders)
President (96/97) ....Sean Bissett
Number of Coaches 2
Biggest Attendance...100,000 (at North-West 200 Road Races, Portrush Co. Antrim)
Main Venues (Short Circuit) ....Mondello Park, Naas; Nutts Corner, Co. Antrim; Bishopscourt, Downpatrick.
Main Venues (Road Racing) ....Cookstown, Tandragee, Portstewart, Skerries, Kells, Monaghan

IRISH CHAMPIONS 1997

Road Racing
     125 c.c. ....Denis McCullough
     200 c.c. ....Gary Purdy
     250 c.c. ....Gary Dynes
     Junior Class ....Robert J. Hazelton
     Supersport 600...Adrian Archibald
     Senior Class ....James Courtney
     400 c.c. Support Class...Andrew Thompson
     750 c.c. Support Class ....Gary Stewart

Short Circuit
     125 c.c. ....Phelim Owens
     200 c.c. ....tba
     250 c.c. ....John Creith
     Junior Class ....Rodney Singleton
     Supersport 600..Derek Young
     Senior Class ....Michael Swann
     Sidecar ....Mark Graham/Stuart Graham
     125 Superking ....Phelim Owen
     Regal 600..Derek Young

MOTOR RALLYING

Royal Irish Automobile Club

Motor Sport Department, 34 Dawson Street, Dublin 2. Tel. (01) 6775628

Founded 1901
Number of Clubs 35
Total Membership 2,800
President (1997) ....Michael P. FitzSimons
Biggest Recorded Attendance ....100,000 (Phoenix Park, 1929 Irish Grand Prix)
Main Venue...Mondello Park, Naas, Co. Kildare
Irish Land Speed Record (flying kilometre) ....179.31 mph (20.08.94, Brendan O'Mahony in a Porsche 962)

1997 Circuit of Ireland Champion	....	Bertie Fisher
1996 R.I.A.C. Dunlop Motorsport Champion	....	Alan Byrne
1996 R.I.A.C. Dunlop Hillclimb Champion	....	Richard Young
1996 R.I.A.C. Dunlop Touring Car Champion	....	Michael Cullen
1996 R.I.A.C. National Rally Stages Champion	....	Stephen Murphy
1996 R.I.A.C. National Rally Navigation Champions	....	Bertie Wedlock/Paul Hughes

NATIONAL RALLY CHAMPIONS SINCE 1965

1965/66 ....Noel Smith	1977.........................John Coyne	1988...........................Ken Colbert
1966/67 ....Noel Smith	1978.....................Mick O'Connell	1989 ....George Robinson
1967/68 ....not held	1979 ....Jer Buckley	1990 ....Richard Smyth
1968/69 ....Noel Smith	1980 ....Jer Buckley	1991 ....Donie Keating
1969/70 ....Noel Smith	1981 ....Donie Keating	1992 ....Peadar Hurson
1970/71.................Eamonn Cotter	1982...........................Eddie Colton	1993..............................Ian Greer
1972 ....Eamonn Cotter	1983............................Bertie Law	1994 ....Michael Farrell
1973 ....Arnie Pool	1984............................Bertie Law	1995 ....Stephen Murphy
1974 ....Sean Campbell	1985 ....James Doherty	1996 ....Stephen Murphy
1975 ....Sean Campbell	1986 ....Frank Meagher	
1976 ....Sean Campbell	1987 ....Vincent Bonner	

ROWING

Irish Amateur Rowing Union

House of Sport, Long Mile Road, Walkinstown, Dublin 12. Tel. (01) 4509831

Founded	1899
Number of Clubs	67
Registered Members (men)	6,070
Registered Members (women)	2,220
President (96/97)	Thomas Fennessy
Administrator	Peadar Casey
Best International Result ....Lightweight single sculls: Niall O'Toole World Champion (1991)
Number of National Coaches	10
Principal Venues ....National Rowing Centre, Inniscarra Lake, Co. Cork. Blessington Co. Wicklow

1997 NATIONAL CHAMPIONS

Men		Women	
Senior Eights ....Neptune		**Senior Eights** ...................................U.C.G.	
Senior Coxed Fours.............................Neptune		**Senior Coxless Fours**..........Dublin University Ladies	
Senior Coxless Fours ....Neptune		....Boat Club	
Senior Coxless Pairs ....Neptune		**Senior Coxless Pairs** ...........................U.C.D.	
Senior Quadruple Sculls...........................Neptune		**Senior Double Sculls** ....Cork-Skibbereen	
Senior Double Sculls.............................Neptune		**Senior Single Sculls** ....Skibbereen	
Senior Single Sculls ....Neptune			

SAILING

IRISH SAILING ASSOCIATION

3 Park Road, Dun Laoghaire, Co. Dublin. Tel. (01) 2800239 e-mail: isa@iol.ie

Founded	1946
Number of Branches ....4 (North, South, East and West)
Number of Category One Clubs	42
Number of Category Two Clubs	3
Number of Category Three Clubs...	73
Total Number of Clubs...	118
Number of Members	18,000
President	Neil Murphy
Best International Result ....Silver Medal 1980 Olympic Games (David Wilkins & Jamie Wilkinson)
1996 Senior Helmsman Champion	Laura Dillon
1996 Junior Helmsman Champion ....Gerald 'Gerbil' Owens
Principal Venues ....Dublin Bay, Howth, Cork, Kinsale

Royal Yachting Association (Northern Ireland Council)
House of Sport, Upper Malone Road, Belfast BT9 5LA. Tel. (01232) 381222

Founded 1875
Number of Clubs 38
Number of Members 13,000
Chairman ....Patrick Knatchbull
Honorary Secretary ....Harold Boyle
Number of Coaches ....250 (approx.)
Principal Venues ....Belfast Lough, Strangford Lough, Lough Neagh and Lough Erne

SURFING

Irish Surfing Association
Easkey Surf and Information Centre, Easkey, Co. Sligo. Tel. (096) 49020

Founded 1967
Number of Clubs 11
Total Number of Members 1,200
      Men 900
      Women...300
President...Brian Britton
Administrator ....Roci Allan
Number of Professional Coaches 1
Number of Instructors 52
1997 National Champion (Men)...Joe McNulty
1997 National Champion (Women) ....Zoë Lally
1996 Intercounty Champions...Leitrim
Principal Venues ....Portrush, Rossnowlagh, Bundoran, Strandhill, Lahinch, Ballybunion and Tramore
European Ranking 6th

TENNIS

Tennis Ireland
Argyle Square, Morehampton Road, Donnybrook, Dublin 4. Tel. (01) 6681841. E-mail: tennis@iol.ie

Founded 1908
Provincial Councils ....4 (Connacht, Leinster, Munster and Ulster)
Number of Clubs 240
Total Number of Members 92,500
of which: Men 25,500
      Women 21,000
      U18s 46,000
President (March 1997-March 1998) ....Ciaran O'Donovan
Honorary Secretary ....Frank Goodman
Top Ranked Irish Player (men) ....Scott Barron (388 in world rankings)
Top Ranked Irish Player (men)..................................Gina Niland (586 in world rankings)
Number of Coaches 131
Men's Senior Irish Close Champion 1997 ....Owen Casey
Women's Senior Irish Close Champion 1997 ....Gina Niland
Men's Senior Provincial Champions 1997 ....Leinster
Women's Senior Provincial Champions 1997..Leinster
Principal Venues ....Riverview, Donnybrook

GYMNASTICS

Irish Amateur Gymnastics Association
House of Sport, Long Mile Road, Dublin 12. Tel. (01) 4501805

Founded 1964
Number of Clubs 57
Number of Members 15,000
President ....Pat O'Brien
Principal Venue...National Basketball Arena, Tallaght

ANGLING

Irish Federation of Sea Anglers
27 Seafield Avenue, Dollymount, Dublin 3.

Founded 1953
President...Capt. Christy O'Toole
Secretary ....Hugh O'Rorke
Number of Affiliated Councils ....4 (Connacht, Leinster, Munster and Ulster)
Number of Affiliated Clubs 190
of which: **Number in Connacht**...18
               Number In Leinster 73
               Number in Munster 41
               Number in Ulster...58

SELECTED IRISH RECORD WEIGHTS FOR VARIOUS SPECIMENS
Brill ....9lbs. 8ozs.
Cod..42lbs.
Herring 0.425kgs
Mackerel...4lbs. 2ozs.
Monkfish ....73lbs.
Plaice 8.23kgs
Pollack ....19lbs. 3ozs.
Ray - Sting..51lbs.
Shark - Blue..206lbs.

EQUESTRIAN SPORT

Equestrian Federation of Ireland
Ashton House, Castleknock, Dublin 15. Tel. (01) 8387611

Founded 1927
Number of Organisiations within the Federation 14
Total Number of Members 9,000
of which: **Men** 6,000
               Women 3,000
President...Lewis Lowry
Secretary General ....Michael Stone
Number of Coaches 400
Biggest Recorded Attendance...................................150,000 (Punchestown 1991, European Three Day Event)
Principal Venues   ....................R.D.S. (7,000 seats), Millstreet (5,000 seats), Punchestown (21,000)

BLIND SPORTS

Northern Ireland Blind Sports
12 Sandford Avenue, Belfast, BT5 5NW. Tel. (01232) 651366

Founded 1989
Chairman ....Henry Mayne
Number of Members 200
Sports Inlcuded...................Bowls, tandem cycling, golf, sailing, angling, water ski-ing, athletics, ten pin bowling

NETBALL

Northern Ireland Netball Association
House of Sport, Upper Malone Road, Belfast BT9 5LA. Tel. (01232) 383824

Founded 1952
Number of Clubs 33
Number of Teams 55
Number of Members 7,000
President ....vacant
Chairperson ....Maureen Brennan
Secretary ....Rosemary McWhinney
Number of Coaches 37
Biggest Recorded Attendance ....1,060 (Maysfield Leisure Centre Nov. '96, N. Ireland v. Jamaica)
Heaviest defeat for Northern Ireland ....104-12 (v. New Zealand, 1971)
Largest victory margin recorded by Northern Ireland................................76-38 (v. Republic of Ireland, 1997)

PITCH AND PUTT

The Pitch and Putt Union of Ireland

House of Sport, Long Mile Road, Walkinstown, Dublin 12. Tel. (01) 4509299

Founded 1961
Number of Clubs 170
Total Number of Members 14,100
of which: men 10,700
          women 3,400
Number of Coaches 196
President..Terry Hayes (until December 1997)
Honorary Secretary ....Peg Smith
1997 Gents Matchplay Champion...Jason Hannon (Kilcullen)
1997 Gents Strokeplay Champion ....John Walsh (Collins, Cork)
1997 Ladies Matchplay Champion ....Margaret Hogan (Tullamore)
1997 Ladies Strokeplay Champion ....Marina O'Rourke (Cloghue, Co. Down)

SQUASH

Irish Squash

House of Sport, Long Mile Road, Dublin 12. Tel. (01) 4501564

Founded ....1993 (amalgamation of Irish Squash Rackets and Irish Women's Squash Rackets Associations)
Number of Clubs 111
Total Number of Teams 13
of which: men 8
          women 5
Total Number of Members...226
President ....Paddy McIlroy
Ireland's European Ranking (women)...12th
Ireland's European Ranking (men)..10th
1996 Irish National Champion (women) ....Aisling McArdle
1996 Irish National Champion (men)...Derek Ryan
Top Ranked Irish Player (men) ....Derek Ryan (17th in World Rankings)
Top Ranked Irish Player (women) ....Aisling McArdle

Ulster Squash

House of Sport, 2a Upper Malone Road, Belfast, BT9 5LA. Tel. (01232) 381222

Founded ....1995 (amalgamation of Ulster men's and women's association)
Number of Clubs 49
Total Number of Teams 119
of which: men...88
          women 33
Total Number of Members...967
of which: men..706
          women 261
President ....David Irvine (until June 1998)
Biggest Recorded Attendance ....300 (Maysfield Leisure Centre in 1992 for five nation tournament)
Principal Centre ....Centre of Excellence for Squash, Newtownards, Co. Down

GLIDING

Ulster Gliding Club Ltd.

Bellarena Airfield, Seacoast Road (Near Limavady), Derry. Tel. (015047) 50301

Founded 1933
Number of Clubs 1
Number of Members...52 (family memberships)
Chairman ....Robert R. Rodwell (until March 1998)
Secretary ....Thomas Snoddy
Number of Coaches..14
Best Results in Competition ....1992 Republic of Ireland Champions, 12th in British Regionals 1996
Irish Free Height Record 22,800ft
Irish Distance Record ....217km (Bellarena to Dublin)

TUG OF WAR

Irish Tug of War Association
Omeath, Dundalk, Co. Louth.

Founded 1967
Chairman ....Jim Curtis
Secretary ....Eavan Brady
Number of Branches ....4 (Connacht, Leinster, Munster and Ulster)
Number of Affiliated Clubs 30
Number of Members..1,125 (approx)

OLYMPIC MEDAL WINNERS

Games	Name	Event	Medal
Amsterdam, 1928	Dr. Pat O'Callaghan	Hammer	Gold
Los Angeles, 1932	Dr. Pat O'Callaghan	Hammer	Gold
	Bob Tisdall	400m Hurdles	Gold
Helsinki, 1952	John McNally	Boxing (bantam weight)	Silver
Melbourne, 1956	Ronnie Delaney	1,500m	Gold
	Fred Tiedt	Boxing (welter weight)	Silver
	Freddie Gilroy	Boxing (bantam weight)	Bronze
	John Caldwell	Boxing (fly weight)	Bronze
	Tony Byrne	Boxing (light weight)	Bronze
Tokyo, 1964	Jim McCourt	Boxing (light weight)	Bronze
Moscow, 1980	David Wilkins & Jamie Wilkinson	Yachting (Flying Dutchman)	Silver
	Hugh Russell	Boxing (fly weight)	Bronze
Los Angeles, 1984	John Treacy	Marathon	Silver
Barcelona, 1992	Michael Carruth	Boxing (welter weight)	Gold
	Wayne McCullough	Boxing (bantam weight)	Silver
Atlanta, 1996	Michelle Smith	Swimming (400m Individual Medley)	Gold
	Michelle Smith	Swimming (400m Freestyle)	Gold
	Michelle Smith	Swimming (200m Individual Medley)	Gold
	Michelle Smith	Swimming (200m Butterfly)	Bronze

TOTAL: Gold 8, **Silver** 5, **Bronze** 6.

Irish Olympians, 1924-96

1924 PARIS *(Athletics):* John Kelly, W. J. Lowe, Sean Lavan, Norman McEachern, J. O'Connor, John O'Grady, Larry Stanley, J. J. Ryan. *(Boxing):* M. Doyle, Sgt. P. Dwyer, Pte. J. Flaherty, R. M. Hilliard, Pte. J. Kelleher, Pte. J. Kidley, Pte. M. McDonagh, W. J. Murphy. *(Lawn Tennis):* W. G. Ireland, E. D. McCrea, H. Wallis, P. Blair-White. *(Water Polo):* S. Barrett, J. Beckett, J. S. Brady, P. Convery, C. Fagan, M. A. O'Connor, N. M. Purcell.

1928 AMSTERDAM *(Athletics):* Pat Anglim, Alister F. Clarke, G. N. Coughlan, L. D. E. Cullen, Denis Cussen, Sean Lavan, Norman McEachern, Dr. Pat O'Callaghan, Con O'Callaghan, Theo Phelan. *(Cycling):* Bertie Donnelly, J. B. Woodcock. *(Boxing):* Garda J. Chase, Gda. Matt Flanagan, G. Kelly, P. J. Lenihan, Cpl. M. McDonagh, Gda. W. J. Murphy, Pte. W. O'Shea, Edward Traynor. *(Swimming):* J. S. Brady, W. D. Broderick, M. Dockrell, T. H. Dockrell, H. B. Ellerker, C. Fagan, N. Judd, T. McClure, J. A. O'Connor, M. A. O'Connor.

1932 LOS ANGELES *(Athletics):* Eamonn Fitzgerald, M. J. Murphy, Bob Tisdall, Dr. Pat O'Callaghan. *(Boxing):* John Flood, Patrick Hughes, James Murphy, Ernest Smith.

1936 BERLIN No Irish team travelled.

1948 LONDON *(Athletics):* J. J. Barry, Cummin Clancy, Dan Coyle, Charles Denroche, Paul Dolan, Pat Fahy, Dave Guiney, Jimmy Reardon, Frank Mulvihill, Reggie Myles. *(Basketball):* H. Boland, Lt. P. Crehan, Lt. J. Flynn, Sgt. W. Jackson, Pte. T. Keenan, G. McLaughlin, Cadet J. R. McGee, Cpl. T. Malone, Cdt. F. B. O'Connor, Lt. D. O'Donovan, Sgt. D. Reddin, Pte. D. Sheriff, Pte. P. Sheriff, Sgt. C. Walsh. *(Boxing):* William E. Barnes, Peter Foran, Willie Lenihan, Maxie McCullagh, Mick McKeon, Kevin Martin, Gearoid O'Colmain, Hugh O'Hagan. *(Equestrian):* Cmdt. Fred Ahern, Cmdt. Dan J. Corry, Lt. Col. John J. Lewis. *(Fencing):* Dorothy Dermody, Patrick Duffy, T. Smith, Nick Thuillier, Owen Tuohy. *(Football):* W. Barry, W. Brennan, J. Cleary, F. Glennon, P Kavanagh, P. Lawlor, P. McDonald, Lt. P. McGonagle, E. McLoughlin, W. O'Grady, B. O'Kelly, W. Richardson, R. Smith. *(Rowing):* H. R. Chantler, P.G. Dooley, T. G. Dowdall, S. Hanley, P. D. Harrold, D. Lambert-Sugrue, B. McDonnell, E. M. A. McElligott, J. Nolan, W. J Stevens, R. W. R. Tamplin, D. B. C. Taylor. *(Yachting):* R.H. Allen, A.J. Mooney.

1952 HELSINKI *(Athletics):* Paul Dolan, Joe West. *(Boxing):* Peter Crotty, William Duggan, John Lyttle, John McNally, Kevin Martin, Terry Milligan, Andrew Reddy, Thomas Reddy. *(Equestrian):* Capt. Mark Darley, Harry Freeman-Jackson, Ian Hume-Dudgeon. *(Fencing):* George Carpenter, Paddy Duffy, Harry Thuillier, Tom Rafter. *(Wrestling):* Jack Vard. *(Yachting):* Dr. Alf Delaney.

1956 MELBOURNE *(Athletics):* Ronnie Delany, Eamonn Kinsella, Maeve Kyle. *(Boxing):* Anthony Byrne, John

Caldwell, Freddie Gilroy, Harry Perry, Patrick Sharkey, Martin Smyth, Fred Tiedt. *(Equestrian):* Capt. Kevin Barry, Harry Freeman-Jackson, Ian Hume-Dudgeon, Lt. Patrick Kiernan, William Mullin, Lt. William Ringrose. *(Wrestling):* Gerald Martina. *(Yachting):* John Somers-Payne.

1960 ROME *(Athletics):* Ronnie Delany, Willie Dunne, Michael Hoey, Maeve Kyle, John Lawlor, Patrick Lowry, Gerald McIntyre, Bertie Messitt, Frank O'Reilly. *(Boxing):* Joseph Casey, Patrick Kenny, Adam McClean, Colm McCoy, Eamonn McKeon, Bernard Meli, Danny O'Brien, Harry Perry, Ando Reddy, Michael Reid. *(Cycling):* Peter Crinion, Anthony Cullen, Seamus Herron, Michael Horgan, Martin McKay. *(Equestrian):* Lt. John Daly, Lt. Edward O'Donohoe, Capt. William Ringrose. *(Eventing):* Anthony Cameron, Ian Hume Dudgeon, Harry Freeman-Jackson, Edward Harty. *(Fencing):* Shirley Armstrong, Chris Bland, George Carpenter, Brian Hamilton, Tom Kearney, Harry Thuillier. *(Weightlifting):* Sammy Dalzell, Tommy Hayden. *(Wrestling):* Dermot Dunne, Joseph Feeney, Gerry Martina, Sean O'Connor. *(Yachting):* Dr R. G. Benson, Charles Gray, Jimmy Hooper, Dr A. J. Mooney, Dr D. A. Ryder, John Somers-Payne.

1964 TOKYO *(Athletics):* Noel Carroll, Basil Clifford, Jim Hogan, Maeve Kyle, John Lawlor, Derek McCleane, Tom O'Riordan. *(Boxing):* Brian Anderson, Paddy Fitzsimons, Sean McCafferty, Jim McCourt, Chris Rafter. *(Fencing):* John Bouchier-Hayes, Michael Ryan. *(Judo):* John Ryan. *(Wrestling):* Joseph Feeney, Sean O'Connor. *(Yachting):* Robin D'Alton, Johnny Hooper, Eddie Kelliher, Harry Maguire. *(Equestrian):* Tommy Brennan, Tony Cameron, John Harty, Harry Freeman-Jackson.

1968 MEXICO *(Athletics):* Noel Carroll, John Kelly, Pat McMahon, Mick Molloy, Frank Murphy. *(Boxing):* Mick Dowling, Brendan McCarthy, Jim McCourt, Eamonn McCusker, Martin Quinn, Eddie Tracey. *(Cycling):* Peter Doyle, Morrison Foster, Liam Horner. *(Fencing):* John Bouchier-Hayes, Finbarr Farrell, Colm O'Brien, Michael Ryan. *(Shooting):* Dr. Gerry Brady, Dermot Kelly, Arthur McMahon. *(Swimming):* Liam Ball, Anne O'Connor, Donnacha O'Dea, Vivienne Smith. *(Equestrian):* Tommy Brennan, Capt. Ned Campion, Diana Conolly-Carew, Juliet Jobling-Purser, Ada Matheson, Penny Moreton, Diana Wilson.

1972 MUNICH *(Athletics):* Phil Conway, Neil Cusack, John Hartnett, Mike Keogh, Eddie Leddy, Danny McDaid, Dessie McGann, Fanahan McSweeney, Frank Murphy, Margaret Murphy, Mary Tracey, Claire Walsh, Donie Walsh. *(Boxing):* Mick Dowling, Christy Elliott, Neil McLaughlin, James Montague, Charlie Nash, John Rodgers. *(Canoeing):* Gerry Collins, Ann McQuaid, Brendan O'Connell, Howard Watkins. *(Cycling):* Peter Doyle, Liam Horner, Kieran McQuaid, Noel Taggart. *(Equestrian):* Bill Butler, Patrick Conolly-Carew, Juliet Jobling-Purser, Bill McLernon, Ronnie McMahon. *(Fencing):* John Bouchier-Hayes. *(Judo):* Anto Clarke, Liam Carroll, Matthew Folan, Patrick Murphy, Terry Watt. *(Rowing):* Sean Drea. *(Clay Pigeon Shooting):* Dr. Gerry Brady, William Campbell, Arthur McMahon, Dermot Kelly. *(Swimming):* Liam Ball, Brian Clifford, Christine Fulcher, Andrew Hunter, Brenda McGrory, Ann O'Connor, Aisling O'Leary. *(Weighlifting):* Frank Rothwell. *(Yachting):* Harry Byrne, Harold Cudmore, Owen Delaney, Robert Hennessy, Kevin McLaverty, Richard O'Shea, David Wilkins, Sean Whittaker.

1976 MONTREAL *(Archery):* Jim Conroy. *(Athletics):* Eamonn Coghlan, Neil Cusack, Eddie Leddy, Danny McDaid, Jim McNamara, Niall O'Shaughnessy, Mary Purcell. (Boxing): Brian Byrne, Brendan Dunne, Gerry Hammill, Dave Larmour, Christy McLaughlin. *(Canoeing):* Declan Burns, Ian Pringle, Brendan O'Connell, Howard Watkins. *(Cycling):* Alan McCormack, Oliver McQuaid. *(Equestrian):* Eric Horgan, Ronnie McMahon, Gerry Sinnott, Norman Van der Vater. *(Rowing):* Sean Drea, Martin Feeley, Ian Kennedy, Andrew McDonough, James Muldoon, Christopher O'Brien, Liam Redmond, James Renehan, Michael Ryan, William Ryan. *(Clay Pigeon Shooting):* Richard Flynn. *(Swimming):* Miriam Hopkins, Robert Howard, Deirdre Sheehan, Kevin Williamson. *(Yachting):* Robert Dix, Peter Dix, Derek Jago, Barry O'Neill, James Wilkinson, David Wilkins.

1980 MOSCOW *(Archery):* Jim Conroy, Hazel Greene, Willie Swords. *(Athletics):* Eamonn Coghlan, Sean Egan, Ray Flynn, Pat Hooper, Dick Hooper, Mick O'Shea, John Treacy. *(Boxing):* Martin Brerton, P. J. Davitt, Sean Doylelt, Gerry Hawkins, Barry McGuigan, Hugh Russell, Phil Sutcliffe. *(Canoeing):* Declan Burns, Ian Pringle. *(Clay Pigeon Shooting):* Nicholas Cooney, Thomas Hewitt, Albert Thompson. *(Rifle & Pistol Shooting):* Ken Stanford. *(Cycling):* Billy Kerr, Tony Lally, Stephen Roche. *(Judo):* Alonzo Henderson, Dave McManus. *(Modern Pentathlon):* Mark Hartigan, Jerome Hartigan, Sackville Curry. *(Rowing):* Christy O'Brien, Frances Cryan, Noel Graham, Pat Gannon, David Gray, Iain Kennedy, Pat McDonagh, Willie Ryan, Ted Ryan, Denis Rice, Liam Williams. *(Swimming):* David Cummins, Catherine Bohan, Kevin Williamson. *(Yachting):* David Wilkins, James Wilkinson.

1984 LOS ANGELES *(Archery):* Hazel Greene, Mary Vaughan. *(Athletics):* Ray Flynn, Declan Hegarty, Dick Hooper, Monica Joyce, Regina Joyce, Jerry Kiernan, Conor McCullough, Carey May, Caroline O'Shea, Marcus O'Sullivan, Frank O'Mara, Paul Donovan, Liam O'Brien, Mary Parr, Roisin Smith, John Treacy, Patricia Walsh. *(Boxing):* Tommy Corr, Paul Fitzgerald, Gerry Hawkins, Kieran Joyce, Sam Storey, Phil Sutcliffe. *(Canoeing):* Ian Pringle. *(Cycling):* Philip Cassidy, Seamus Downey, Martin Earley, Paul Kimmage, Gary Thompson. *(Equestrian):* Capt. David Foster, Sarah Gordon, Margaret Tolerton, Fiona Wentges, Capt. Gerry Mullins. *(Judo):* Kieran Foley. *(Clay Pigeon Shooting):* Roy Magowen, Albert Thompson. *(Swimming):* Carol-Anne Heavey, Julie Parkes. *(Yachting):* Bill O'Hara.

1988 SEOUL *(Archery):* Noel Lynch, Joe Malone, Hazel Greene-Pereira. *(Athletics):* Marcus O'Sullivan, Gerry O'Reilly , Ann Keenan-Buckley, Brendan Quinn, Eamonn Coghlan, Frank O'Mara, John Doherty, John Treacy, John Woods, Dick Hooper, Marie Murphy-Rollins, Ailish Smyth, Conor McCullough, Terry McHugh, Carlos O'Connell, Jimmy McDonald, T. J. Kearns , Barbara Johnson. *(Boxing):* Wayne McCullough, Joe Lawlor, Paul Fitzgerald, John Lowey, Michael Carruth, Billy Walsh, Kieran Joyce. *(Canoeing):* Alan Carey, Pat Holmes, Pete Connor, Declan Burns. *(Cycling):* Phil Cassidy, Cormac McCann, Paul McCormack, John McQuaid, Stephen Spratt. *(Equestrian):* Cmdt. Gerry Mullins, Capt John Ledingham, Paul Darragh, Jack Doyle, Capt. David Foster, John Watson, Shea

Walsh. *(Judo):* Eugene McManus. *(Rowing):* Frank Moore, Pat McDonagh, Liam Williams. *(Swimming):* Michelle Smith, Stephen Cullen, Aileen Convery, Richard Gheel, Gary O'Toole. *(Tennis):* Owen Casey, Eoin Collins. *(Wrestling):* David Harmon. *(Yachting):* Bill O'Hara, David Wilkins, Peter Kennedy, Cathy McAleavy, Aisling Byrne.

1992 BARCELONA *(Archery):* Noel Lynch. *(Athletics):* Sonia O'Sullivan, Catherina McKiernan, Marcus O'Sullivan, Paul Donovan, John Doherty, Frank O'Mara, Noel Berkeley, Sean Dollman, John Treacy, Andy Ronan, Tommy Hughes, Victor Costello, Paul Quirke, Terry McHugh, Nicky Sweeney, Perri Williams, Bobby O'Leary, Jimmy McDonald, T. J. Kearns. *(Boxing):* Paul Buttimer, Wayne McCullough, Paul Griffin, Michael Carruth, Paul Douglas, Kevin McBride. *(Canoeing):* Ian Wiley, Mike Corcoran, Pat Holmes, Conor Holmes, Alan Carey. *(Cycling):* Paul Slane, Mark Kane, Kevin Kimmage, Robert Power, Conor Henry. *(Equestrian):* Mairead Curran, Melanie Duff, Olivia Holohan, Eric Smiley, Anna Merveldt, Peter Charles, Francis Connors, Paul Darragh, James Kernan, Eddie Macken. *(Fencing):* Michael O'Brien. *(Judo):* Keith Gough, Ciaran Ward. *(Rowing):* Niall O'Toole. *(Swimming):* Gary O'Toole, Michelle Smith. *(Tennis):* Owen Casey, Eoin Collins. *(Yachting):* David Wilkins, Peter Kennedy. Mark Mansfield, Tom McWilliams, Denise Lyttle.

1996 ATLANTA *(Athletics):* Neil Ryan, Gary Ryan, Eugene Farrell, David Matthews, Niall Bruton, Shane Healy, Marcus O'Sullivan, Cormac Finnerty, Sean Dollman, T.J. Kearns, Sean Cahill, Tom McGuirk, Jimmy McDonald, Mark Mandy, Nicky Sweeney,Terry McHugh, Roman Linscheid, Sinead Delahunty, Sonia O'Sullivan, Kathy McCandless, Marie McMahon, Catherina McKiernan, Susan Smith, Deirdre Gallagher. *(Boxing):* Damaen Kelly, Brian Magee, Francis Barrett, Cathal O'Grady. *(Canoeing):* Ian Wiley, Michael Corcoran, Andrew Boland, Stephen O'Flaherty, Conor Moloney, Gary Mawer. *(Clay Pigeon Shoot):* Thomas Allen. *(Cycling):* Declan Lonergan, Philip Collins, Martin Earley, Alister Martin, David McCann. *(Equestrian):* Jessica Chesney, Capt John Ledingham, Eddie Macken, Peter Charles. *(Three Day Event):* Mick Barry, Alfie Buller, David Foster, Virginia McGrath, Eric Smiley. *(Dressage):* Heike Holstein. *(Gymnastics):* Barry McDonald. *(Rowing):* Brendan Dolan, Niall O'Toole, John Holland, Neville Maxwell, Tony O'Connor, Sam Lynch, Derek Holland. *(Yachting):* Mark Lyttle, Mark Mansfield, David Burrows, Marshall King, Dan O'Grady, Garrett Connolly, Denise Lyttle, Louise Cole, Aisling Bowman, John Driscoll. *(Judo):* Kieran Ward. *(Swimming):* Marion Madine, Michelle Smith, Earl McCarthy, Adrian O'Connor, Nick O'Hare. *(Shooting):* Gary Duff, Ronagh Barry. *(Tennis):* Eoin Casey, Scott Barron.

IRISH SPORT - WHO IS WHO

ATHLETICS

Bruton, Niall (born Dublin 1972). Holder of four national 1,500m titles. Won the prestigious Wannamaker Mile (indoor) in 1996. World Student Games 1,500m champion in 1991. Semi-finalist in the 1996 Olympics and 1997 World Championships. Coached by Eamon Coghlan, Bruton has yet to fully demonstrate his awesome potential in a major championships.

McGuirk, Tom (born San Fransisco, 1971). Has won the Irish 400m Hurdles title four times (1994-97). Finished fifth in his first round heat in the 1997 World Championships in only his second sub 50 second time. National record holder for the long hurdles, he competed in the 1996 Olympics.

McHugh, Terry (born Tipperary, 1963). Irish athletics team captain at the Atlanta Olympics. Winner of the national javelin title on each occasion since1984 (fourteen in all). National record holder with 82.14m. Has competed in three Olympics but his best finishes have been in the1994 European Championships when he finished seventh and when he reached the last eight at the 1993 World Championships. Set the Irish Javelin record of 82.14m in 1994.

Has also competed in the Bobsleigh at the Winter Olympics.

McKiernan, Catherina (born Cavan, 1969). Won the European Cross Country title in 1994, she has won silver in the World Cross-Country Championships on four occasions (1992, 1993, 1994 and 1995). Competed in the Olympics in 1992 and 1996. Holder of the Irish 10,000m record. In September 1997 she won her first marathon in Berlin.

Matthews, David (born Kildare, 1974). The current Irish 800m record holder he has won the National title for the past four years. Finished eighth in the second round heat of the 800m in the 1997 World Championships at Athens. Represented Ireland in the 1996 Olympics.

O'Sullivan, Marcus (born Cork, 1961). Winner of three World Indoor Championship 1,500m titles (1987, 1989 and 1993). Took over where Eamon Coghlan left off on the U.S. indoor circuit winning the Wannamaker Mile six times. Won the national 800m title four times and the 1,500m title once. Has competed in each Olympics since 1984.

O'Sullivan, Sonia (born Cork 1969). Ireland's most successful female athlete ever. O'Sullivan won the European 3,000m title in 1994, the World 5,000m title in 1995, she

won silver in the 1,500m at the 1993 World Championships. She holds the national record for every distance from 800m to 5,000m. In 1997 she won silver in the 3,000m in the World Indoor Championships but failed to live up to the perhaps unreasonable expectations heaped upon her in the World Championships in Athens finishing eighth in the 1,500m final and not qualifying for the 5,000m final. Her performance mirrored her disappointing performances in the 1996 Olympics. Took a rest from competitive athletics after the World Championships.

Smith, Susan (born Waterford 1971). Holder of five national 100m hurdles and three national 400m hurdles titles. Set a new national record of 54.61 seconds in the 400m hurdles at the World Championships in Athens in August 1997 where she finished seventh. An Olympic semi-finalist in 1996, she has enjoyed a meteoric rise to the top echelons of world 400m hurdlers.

BOXING

Barret, Francie (born Galway, 1976). 1996 Irish Light-Welterweight champion he became the first member of the travelling community to represent Ireland in the Olympic

Games when he competed with some considerable success in Atlanta.

Carruth, Michael (born Dublin, 1967). Won the Gold medal in the Welterweight division at the 1992 Olympic Games. Controversially defeated on points by Romanian Michael Loewe in their W.B.O. Welterweight title fight in September 1997.

Collins, Steve (born Dublin, 1964). Former W.B.O. Super-middleweight champion Collins shocked the boxing world by announcing his retirement in October 1997. He won the W.B.O. middleweight world title in 1994. Winning the Super middleweight title in 1995, he sent the darlings of the Sky Sports fight circuit, Chris Eubank and Nigel Benn, into retirement. Defended his title eight times in all, in 1997 he defeated Frederic Seillier of France and American Craig Cummings. His professional record was 35 wins in 38 bouts.

Eastwood, Barney (born Tyrone). The proprietor of almost 50 betting shops across Northern Ireland. Also known as a boxing promoter, he currently has Belfast boxer Ray Close on his books. Manager of Barry McGuigan in the 1980s, boxer and manager endured an acrimonious splitting up.

Gogarty, Deirdre (born Louth) Ireland's first female boxing world champion, she won the W.I.B.F. Super-featherweight world title in March 1997. Such is her tenacity and skill she often has to fight above her weight.

Kelly, Damean (born Belfast, 1973). National Flyweight champion 1993-1996 he won the 1997 National Bantamweight title. Won flyweight bronze at the 1993 World Seniors and bronze again in the 1995 European Seniors. Represented Ireland at the 1996 Olympic Games.

Loughran, Eamonn (born Antrim, 1970). Former Welterweight World Champion he lost his title in May 1996. A professional since 1987 he is currently based in the United States.

McCullough, Wayne (born Belfast, 1970). Won a bantamweight silver medal in the 1992 Olympic Games. Turned professional in 1993. Former W.B.C. Super-bantamweight World Champion he lost his title in a split decision to Mexican Daniel

Zaragoza in January 1997, it was the first defeat of his professional career.

Magee, Brian (born Belfast, 1975). Irish Middleweight Champion since 1995. Represented Ireland at the 1996 Olympics

O'Grady, Cathal (born Kildare, 1977). Former European U19 Heavyweight Amateur Champion and winner of ten national titles. Represented Ireland at the 1996 Olympics. Turned professional September 1997.

Benson, Justin D.R. (born Dublin, 1967). Has captained Ireland 28 times in his 59 game international career and has scored 1528 runs. Played for Leicestershire for seven years.

Curry, Dekker (born Strabane, 1966). Capped 40 times scoring 905 runs. His 75 -v- Middlesex in the B&H match led Ireland to their first ever competitive victory over a county side.

Dunlop, Angus R. (born Dublin, 1967). In 68 matches he has scored 1667 runs (average 23.81) and taken 36 wickets (average 35.22). Scored a record 672 runs for Ireland in 14 matches in 1996.

Hendrick, Mike (born Darley Dale, 1956). Manager of the Irish cricket side who narrowly missed out on qualification for the 1999 World Cup and who recorded their first ever victory in the B & H league. Formerly a seam bowler with Derbyshire and England.

McCrum, Paul (born Waringstown, 1962). A fast and accurate opening bowler he has taken 99 wickets (average 31.93) in his 69 international appearances. With John Davy he put on a record 100 for the last wicket.

Barr, Keith (born Dublin, 1968). All-Ireland football medalist in 1995 he has won two All-Star awards in the half back position. Member of the touring Irish Compromise Rules team in 1990.

Blaney, Greg (born Co. Down, 1963). Winner of two All-Ireland football medals with Down (1991 and 1994) he has received two All-Star awards (1983 and 1991). Played in

four Compromise Rules Series against Australia (1984, 1986, 1987, 1990).

Boothman, Jack (born Wicklow) President of the Gaelic Athletic Association (1994-97), the first Protestant to achieve the highest office within the organisation.

Boyle, Tony (born Donegal, 1970). Full forward on the Donegal All-Ireland football winning side in 1992, he received an All-Star award for his performances that year.

Brady, Peter (born Offaly, 1965). After thirteen seasons with the Offaly senior football team he finally won his first Leinster medal in 1997. He scored 2-14 in the 1997 Championship for Offaly.

Cahalane, Niall (born Cork, 1963). Stout defender on the Sam Maguire winning Cork teams of 1989 and 1990. Winner of All-Ireland Club football championship with Castlehaven.

Canavan, Peter (born Tyrone, 1971) One of the most feared forwards in gaelic football. Deadly accurate from play and from frees, All-Star Canavan was the lynchpin of the Tyrone team who put Ulster Senior Football titles back to back in 1995 and 1996. An All-Ireland U-21 medalist with Tyrone.

Carey, Ciaran (born Limerick, 1970). Centre half back and captain of the 1996 Munster hurling champions, Limerick, Carey was a member of the 1992 National Hurling League winning team. Made his debut for Limerick in 1988, has unsuccessfully competed in two All-Ireland finals.

Carey, D.J. (born Kilkenny, 1971). Captain of the Kilkenny hurling team in 1997 his personal tally of 2-8 helped defeat Galway in the All-Ireland quarter final, he finished top scorer in the Championship with 4-22 (34 points) in just four games. The holder of two All-Ireland hurling medals (1992 and 1993) and four All-Star awards.

Cooney, Joe (born Galway 1964). All-Ireland hurling medalist in 1987 and 1988 he has five All-Star awards. An outstanding forward he won the All-Ireland Club hurling Championship with Sarsfields in 1993.

Corcoran, Brian (born Cork, 1973). Dual star has represented Cork in both football and hurling. Winner of 1992/93 National Hurling Championship and a Munster

Football title also in 1993. Won a hurling All-Star award in 1992.

Corkery, Colin (born Cork, 1971). Winner of an All-Ireland U21 football medal with Cork in 1989. Represented Ireland in the 1990 Compromise Rules tour of Australia. Member of Cork team beaten in 1993 All-Ireland final.

Daly, Anthony (born Clare, 1970). Captained Clare to victory in the All-Ireland Hurling Championships of 1995 (their first in 81 years) and 1997. Daly has been an All-Star on two occasions.

Dowd, Tommy (born 1969, Leicester) Captain of the Meath team in 1996 which won the Sam Maguire. Made his senior debut in 1990. All-Star award winner on three occasions, he has won three Leinster S.F.C. medals, two National League medals and one Railway Cup medal.

English, Nicky (born Tipperary, 1962). The 1989 Texaco Hurling Sportstar of the Year, English has won two All Ireland hurling medals and a National hurling league medal. A winner of six All Star awards between 1983 and 1989 at his peak he was one of the most revered forwards in the game. He has now retired from inter-county hurling.

Fitzgerald, Maurice (born Kerry, 1970). Man of the Match in the 1997 All-Ireland Football final where he won his first All-Ireland winners' medal. An All-Star twice he was a member of the Kerry side which won the 1996/97 National Football League. Won the World long-kicking competition in 1989 against professionals from rugby, American football, soccer and Australian Rules.

Giles, Trevor (born Meath, 1976). Enjoyed a tremendous season with Meath in 1996 winning an All-Ireland medal, an All-Star award and the ultimate accolade, Player of the Year.

Gleeson, Conor (born Tipperary, 1973). Captain of the defeated Tipperary team in the 1997 Hurling Championship.

King, Stephen (born Cavan, 1962). Captained Cavan to their first Ulster Senior Football Championship title in 28 years in 1997. King was an inspirational midfielder throughout their Championship campaign.

Kirby, Gary (born Limerick, 1966). Centre-half forward and main free

taker on the Limerick hurling team, he is one of the most prominent players in the 1990s not to have won an All-Ireland medal, having played with the beaten Limerick finalists in 1994 and 1996.

Hasset, Liam (born Kerry, 1975). Captained the All-Ireland football winning Kerry side in 1997. He holds two All-Ireland U21 winners' medals and in 1996 won the All-Ireland Club Championship with his club, Laune Rangers.

Leahy, John (born Tipperary, 1971). Tipperary's best player during the 1997 Hurling Championship. He holds two All-Ireland medals (from 1988 and 1991), he has also twice been an All-star (1991 and 1994).

Linden, Mickey (born Co. Down, 1965). Double All-Ireland football medalist with Down in 1991 and 1994 he was the outstanding forward in the 1994 Championship. Winner of an All-Star award in 1994 and 1995.

Loughnane, Ger (born Clare, 1954). The winner of two National Hurling league titles with Clare in the 1970s, in 1974 he became Clare's first ever All-Star and also won an All-Star in 1977. Manager of the All-Ireland winning Clare hurling teams in 1995 and 1997.

Lohan, Brian (born Clare, 1971). The virtually unbeatable full-back on the all conquering Clare hurling team in 1997. Won an All-Ireland medal in 1995 and an All Star award in 1996. Captained his club, Wolfe Tones to victory in the Munster Club Hurling Championship in 1996.

McCarthy, Teddy (born Cork, 1965). Holder of four All Ireland medals, two in each code. Made history in 1990 when he became the first man to win All Ireland medals in both football and hurling in the one year. Also holds a National football league and a National hurling league winners medal.

McDonagh, Joe (born Galway, 1954). The current President of Cumann Lúthchleas Gael he will remain in the post until the next millennium. As a senior hurler with Galway he won an All-Star award in 1976. When Galway won their breakthrough All-Ireland in 1980 McDonagh led an emotional rendition of 'The West's Awake' from the steps of the Hogan Stand.

McHale, Liam (born Mayo, 1966). Member of the defeated Mayo

teams in the 1996 and 1997 All-Ireland finals. Won his first All-Star award in 1996 and is the holder of six Connacht Championship medals. Also an accomplished basketballer he has represented Ireland in international competition and has enjoyed much success with his local club, Ballina.

McHugh, Martin (born Donegal, 1961). Former Cavan football manager he retired in September 1997 after delivering Cavan's first Ulster title since 1969. Won an All-Ireland U-21 medal in 1982, three Ulster S.F.C. medals, an All-Ireland medal in 1992 with his native Donegal. An All-Star award winner in 1982 and 1992.

Maughan, John (born Mayo, 1962). Mayo football manager since 1995 he guided them to the All-Ireland final in 1996 to the delight of a much maligned province. Sadly Mayo were beaten by Meath after a replay in 1996 and by Kerry in 1997. In 1992 he managed Clare to an historic Munster final victory.

Mulvihill, Liam (born Longford, 1946). Formerly a national school teacher, has been the Director General of the GAA since 1979. Presided over the modernisation of the GAA through the ongoing development of Croke Park and various provincial grounds and a better marketing of the game in general.

Nallen, James (born Mayo, 1974). An All-Star in 1996 Nallen was a member of the defeated Mayo sides in the 1996 and 1997 All-Ireland finals. He holds one Connacht U21 and two Connacht Senior medals.

O'Connor, James (born Clare, 1972). Clare's top scorer in 1997 hurling Championship. Holder of two All-Ireland hurling medals with Clare from 1995 and 1997.

Ó Sé, Páidí (born Kerry, 1955) Tenacious Kerry corner back he won eight All-Ireland football medals between 1975 and 1986. In his ten All-Ireland finals he conceded only one point to his opposing corner forward. Winner of five All-Star awards. Managed the Kerry senior footballers to All-Ireland success in 1997, their first since 1986.

Pilkington, Johnny (born Offaly, 1969). All Ireland Senior Hurling Championship winner when a last gasp effort by Offaly overcame Limerick in the 1994 decider. The Birr player has also won a National hurling league medal and saw his club team beaten in the 1992 All Ireland club championship final.

Redmond, Charlie (born Dublin, 1964). The darling of Hill 16, Redmond won an All Ireland Football medal in 1995 in his fourth final appearance. Dublin's best place kicker, he had the unhappy knack of missing penalties in important games. Retired in 1997.

Sherlock, Jason (born Dublin, 1975). 'Jayo' won an All-Ireland senior football medal with Dublin in 1995. An all-round sportsman he has represented Ireland in basketball and currently plays soccer with U.C.D. in the Premier Division of the F.A.I. National League.

Storey, Martin (born Wexford, 1964). Captain of the Wexford hurling team which won the All-Ireland title in 1996, defeating Limerick in the final. An All Star winner in 1993, made his senior debut in 1985. In 1996 he received an All-Star award and was voted Player of the Year by his peers.

Tohill, Anthony (born Derry, 1971). Regarded as one of country's top gaelic footballers, won an All-Ireland medal with Derry in 1993, and an All-Star in 1992 and 1993. Played Australian Rules football in Melbourne, and has played soccer for Derry City in the League of Ireland.

Tompkins, Larry (born Kildare, 1963). Former intercounty footballer with Kildare he switched his allegiance to Cork in 1987 and won All-Ireland football medals in 1989 and in 1990 (as captain). The winner of four All-Star awards he has retired from intercounty football and is the current Cork football manager.

GOLF

Clarke, Darren (born Tyrone 1968). Ireland's sole representative on the victorious European Ryder Cup team in 1997. He finished second in the European Order of Merit in 1997. Clarke has two tournament wins to his credit since turning professional in 1990, the 1993 Dunhill Open and the 1996 German Masters. Finished joint second in the 1997 British Open. Earned almost £330,000 in prizemoney in 1996.

Daly, Fred (born Derry 1911). Won the Irish Open in 1946 (the first Irishman to do so). In 1947 he

became the first and so far only Irish player to win the British Open. He won nine European events in all and remains the only Irish golfer to have won a major. Fred Daly died 1990.

D'Arcy, Eamon (born Wicklow 1952). A professional since 1969 he has eleven tournament wins including the Spanish Open (1983), the Belgian Open (1987) and the Desert Open (1990). A member of the victorious Irish Dunhill Cup team in 1988, he has played in four Ryder Cups (1975, 1977, 1981 and 1987). His final putt secured the European victory in 1987.

Harrington, Padraig (born Dublin 1971). Turned professional 1995. Won the 1996 Spanish Open narrowly missing out on the Rookie of the Year award. As an Amateur he won a Walker Cup in 1993, however he narrowly missed qualifying for the Ryder Cup, its professional equivalent. Earned £285,023 in 1996 when finishing eleventh in the European Order of Merit.

McGimpsey, Garth (born Co. Down 1955). The most successful Irish amateur golfer in recent years he has won five North of Ireland, three West of Ireland and two East of Ireland titles. Winner of the 1985 British Amateur Championship and the 1988 Irish Amateur Championship. He has played on three Walker Cup teams 1985, 1989 (when Britain and Ireland won on American soil for the first time) and 1991. A member of three World Championship teams (1984, 1986 and 1988).

McGinley, Paul (born Dublin 1967). A former Walker Cup player McGinley turned professional in 1991. In 1996 he won his first tour event, the Austrian Open and finished in 15th place on the European Order of Merit winning £264,966.

O'Connor Jnr, Christy (born Galway 1948). Since turning professional in 1965 he has won eight competitions on the European tour including the 1975 Irish Open, the 1989 Jersey Open and the 1992 British Masters. Selected for the Ryder Cup team in 1975 and 1989, he has won one and lost two matches.

Rafferty, Ronan (born Co. Down 1964). Member of Walker Cup winning team in 1981 he turned professional that year. Rafferty has won 13 titles in his 16 year professional

career including the Austrian Open (1993) and in 1989 the Scandinavian Open, the Volvo Masters and the Italian Open. Rafferty topped the 1989 European Order of Merit and was a member of the victorious European Ryder Cup team that year. Rafferty was the only man to play on Ireland's Dunhill Cup winning teams in both 1988 and 1990.

Walton, Philip (born Dublin 1962). Turned professional in 1983 after a successful amateur career. Tournament wins include the 1990 French Open and the 1995 English Open. A member of the victorious European Ryder Cup team in 1995.

HORSE RACING

Bolger, Jim (born Wexford, 1941). One of Ireland's foremost trainers he has trained winners in the Irish 1,000 Guineas, the English Oaks, the Irish Derby and the King George VI. Bolger has been champion trainer on the flat throughout the nineties including his 1996 success with 94 winners.

Dunwoody, Richard (born Co. Down, 1960). Among his innumerable winners he has won two Aintree Grand Nationals, the Cheltenham Gold Cup and has been the champion National Hunt jockey in Britain. He won the 1997 Powers Gold Cup on board Doran's Pride.

Dobbin, Tony (born Co. Down, 1973). Rode Lord Gyllene to victory in the 1997 Aintree Grand National. Won 1994 Hennessy Gold Cup on One Man. Had 67 winners in 1996 but has outstripped that in 1997.

Eddery, Pat (born Dublin, 1952). Since winning his first race in 1969 Eddery has been champion flat jockey in Britain nine times. Had an amazing 209 wins in the 1990 season and recorded his 4,000 winner in September 1997. He has had multiple Classic wins in Ireland, England and France including Derbies in all three country's, the Prix de L'Arc de Triomphes, the English, Irish and French oaks the list seems endless. Eddery is the most successful Irish jockey of all time and one of the most outstanding Irish sportsmen ever.

Fallon, Kieren (born Clare). Leading jockey in the Henry Cecil stable. English Champion Jockey in 1997 on the flat. His 1997 successes include the English 1,000 Guineas and the Epsom Oaks.

Kinane, Mick (born Tipperary, 1959). Irish Champion Flat Jockey a record ten times between 1983 and 1994 he has had Classics wins in Ireland, England, France, Italy, America and Australia. Perhaps his finest race (certainly his most famous) was in winning the 1993 Melbourne Gold Cup on Vintage Crop. His fifteen year partnership with trainer Dermot Weld has served both well. Won the 1997 Eclipse Stakes on Pilsudski.

Maguire, Adrian (born Meath, 1971). Burst onto the National Hunt scene in 1991/92 with victory in the 1991 Irish Grand National and the 1992 Cheltenham Gold Cup. Has twice been narrowly beaten in the Champion Jockey stakes.

O'Brien, Aidan (born Wexford, 1970. Irish Champion trainer for the past four seasons he is equally at home training for National Hunt or the Flat. A former amateur jockey he has been the champion Irish trainer in 1996 and 1997. In 1997 he trained Irish Derby and 2,000 Guineas winner Desert King and Classic Park the Irish 1,000 Guineas winner.

O'Brien, Vincent (born Cork, 1917). 'The Master of Ballydoyle' has won innumerable steeplechases and classics in Ireland and Britain. Equally adept at training National Hunt and Flat champions he has trained three Cheltenham Gold Cups, six Irish Derbies, three Aintree Grand Nationals and three Prix de la Arc de Triomphes.

Roche, Christy (born Tipperary, 1950). Champion jockey on four occasions has won most major flat races including the Irish, Epsom and French derbies. Has combined his career as a jockey and a new career as a trainer since getting his trainers license in 1996. Rode Desert King to a rare Irish Derby/2,000 Guineas double in 1997.

Swan, Charlie (born Tipperary, 1968). Recorded his 1,000th winner at Listowel in September 1997. In 1996 he became National Hunt Champion Jockey for the eighth time (and the seventh consecutive year). Won the jockey's championship at Cheltenham in 1993.

Weld, Dermot (born Surrey, 1948). Ireland's must successful trainer on the flat he has led the trainers championship for most of the past twenty years. The trainer of more than 2,000 winners his most famous victory was that of Vintage Crop in the 1993 Melbourne Cup.

RUGBY

Ashton, Brian (born Lancashire, 1947). Appointed coach of Irish Rugby team in 1997; former England international; England assistant coach (1984-89); coach of Bath (1989-97) winning multiple trophies.

Clohessy, Peter (born Limerick, 1966). Hard man of the current Irish team the Young Munster prop forward has won 16 international caps and injury denied him his place on the 1997 Lions tour of South Africa.

Davidson, Jeremy (born Antrim, 1974). Plays club rugby with London Irish. He has won 12 Irish caps since his debut against Fiji in 1995. Capped 3 times by Lions on the 1997 tour of South Africa.

Elwood, Eric (born Galway, 1969). Has won 19 Irish caps, now playing with Galwegians he holds the joint record for the most penalty goals scored in a season (14) and a record six penalty goals in a single international (versus Romania in 1993). Enjoyed a successful season with Connacht in the 1997/98 European Conference.

Geoghegan, Simon (born Herefordshire, 1968). Capped 37 times and has scored numerous international tries. His absence from the national team through injury during the 1996/97 season was sorely felt. Currently playing with Bath in the English League.

Mullin, Brendan (born Israel, 1963). Ireland's record try scorer with 17 in his 55 appearances between 1984 and 1995. Member of 1985 Triple Crown winning team he was capped once by the Lions on their 1989 tour of Australia.

Popplewell, Nick (born Dublin, 1964). Prop forward 'Poppy' now plays club rugby with Newcastle. First capped in 1989 he has amassed 44 international caps. Capped three times for the Lions v New Zealand in 1993.

Staples, Jim (born Bermondsey, 1966). Full back. Currently playing with Harlequins in England he has been capped 26 times by Ireland.

Wallace, Paul (born Cork, 1972). Prop forward, since 1995 the Saracens player has been capped by Ireland 12 times. Capped three times by the Lions on the 1997 South African tour.

Wood, Keith (born 1971). The Harlequins hooker has won nine Irish caps since 1994. Capped twice by the Lions on 1997 South African tour.

SNOOKER

Doherty, Ken (born Dublin, 1969). Won the World Amateur Championship in 1989, turned professional the following season but lost in the first round of the World Championships. In 1994 Ken, now ranked 11th in the world is beaten by Jimmy White in the quarter finals of the World Championships. In November 1996 he captained the Republic of Ireland team which narrowly lost the World Cup final in Bangkok. Crowned World Champion in May 1997 when he defeated reigning champion and world number one Stephen Hendry 18-12 in the final at Sheffield.

Higgins, Alex (born Belfast, 1949). The 'Hurricane' turned professional in 1971 and became World Champion the following year a feat he repeated in 1982. The most controversial player ever to grace the green baize he won the 1983 UK Championship, the Benson & Hedges Masters in 1978 and 1981. In 1989 he won the Irish Masters, the first Irishman to do so. Has now all but retired from the sport.

Taylor, Denis (born Tyrone, 1949). Turned professional in 1971 he won the World Championship in 1985 beating Steve Davis on the black ball of the last frame. An epic victory it was watched by television's largest ever sports audience. Won the Rothman's Grand Prix in 1984 and the Benson & Hedges Masters in 1987. Still playing on the circuit he has a made a name for himself as a television commentator.

SOCCER

Aldridge, John (born Liverpool, 1958) striker. Currently player-manager of Tranmere Rovers, former clubs include Oxford United, Liverpool and Real Sociedad. A prolific striker he holds the record for the most goals scored in the English league, 467 in his 18 year career.

Aldridge has been capped 69 times by the Republic of Ireland scoring 19 goals. Played in the World Cup finals of 1990 and 1994.

Cascarino, Tony (born Kent, 1962) striker. 'Big Cas' has scored 18 goals in his 73 appearances with the Republic. Currently playing with French side A.S. Nancy his eyes are firmly set on claiming the Republic's international scoring record of 20.

Dowie, Ian (born Hatfield, 1965) striker. Has been capped 40 times by Northern Ireland and scored nine goals. Currently playing with West Ham United. Former clubs include Southampton and Crystal Palace.

Gillespie, Keith (born Larne, 1975) winger. Capped 18 times by Northern Ireland, he has scored one international goal. A tricky winger has been a Newcastle United player since 1995 transferring there from Manchester United.

Given, Shay (born Donegal, 1976). Capped twelve times as goalkeeper by the Republic of Ireland, Given is the current Newcastle United first choice 'keeper. Former clubs include Blackburn Rovers and Celtic.

Hamilton, Bryan (born Belfast, 1946) midfielder and manager. An Irish Cup winner with Linfield in 1970 he played with Ipswich, Everton and Swindon, amongst others, in England. Manager of the Northern Ireland side since 1995.

Houghton, Ray (born Glasgow, 1962) midfielder. Winner of 70 caps with the Republic of Ireland, he scored two of the most famous goals in recent history. The header which broke English hearts in Stuttgart in 1988 and the looping strike which defeated Italy 1-0 in Giants Stadium in U.S.A. '94. Houghton currently plays with Reading and counts Liverpool and Aston Villa among his former clubs

Hughes, Michael (born Larne, 1971) winger. Now playing with Wimbledon he has been capped 37 times and has scored two international goals (against Germany and Portugal). Hughes started his career with Carrick Rangers before moving to West Ham United.

Irwin, Denis (born Cork, 1965) defender. Has tasted much success with Manchester United since transferring there in 1990. Has won 46 caps with the Republic of Ireland team appearing in the World Cup finals of 1990 and 1994.

Keane, Roy (born Cork, 1971) midfielder. A former Nottingham Forest and Cobh Ramblers player he is the current Manchester United captain. He has won 38 caps with the Republic and scored three goals. Possessed with a fiery temperament, his battling qualities make him one of Europe's finest midfielders. A severe knee injury saw him miss most of the 97/98 season.

McCarthy, Mick (born Barnsley, 1959) defender and current Republic of Ireland manager. 'Captain Fantastic' during the Italia '90 and U.S.A. '94 campaigns, his great heart more than compensated for his overly documented limitations. Inheritor of an ageing team he has struggled to imprint his own style but has introduced a number of new players.

McDonald, Alan (born Belfast, 1963) defender. Capped 52 times by Northern Ireland he has scored three international goals. A ever present member of the Northern Ireland team at the 1986 World Cup finals he has spent virtually all of his football playing career playing with Queen's Park Rangers.

McGrath, Paul (born Ealing, 1959) defender. Capped 82 times by the Republic scoring six international goals. Overcame serious knee injury to become the outstanding Irish footballer of his generation. McGrath was the F.A.I. Player of the Year in 1990 and 1991.Currently with Sheffield United, former clubs include St. Patrick's Athletic, Manchester United, Aston Villa and Derby County.

Magilton, Jim (born Belfast, 1969) midfielder. First capped in 1991, Magilton has won 36 caps with Northern Ireland and scored five international goals. Currently playing with Southampton in the English Premier League. Former clubs include Distillery and Oxford United.

Quinn, Niall (born Dublin, 1966) striker. Capped 62 times by the R.O.I. he has scored 16 goals. Formerly a player with Arsenal and Manchester City his current team is Sunderland. Quinn suffered a serious knee injury in 1993 which has allowed him to devote more time to his second love, horse racing.

Staunton, Steve (born Drogheda, 1969) midfielder. Capped 71 times, he seems destined to become the Republic's most capped player ever.

The scorer of six international goals he was the F.A.I. Player of the Year in 1993. The winner of an F.A. Cup and League Championship with Liverpool, he now plays with Aston Villa.

Townsend, Andy (born Maidstone, 1963) midfielder. Captain of the Republic of Ireland he has been capped 68 times, scoring 7 goals. The F.A.I. Player of the Year in 1995. Transferred to Middlesbrough in August 1997 he has captained both Chelsea and Aston Villa in recent years.

Worthington, Nigel (born Ballymena, 1961) defender. The winner of 64 Northern Ireland caps, he played in the 1986 World Cup finals in Mexico. In his professional career Worthington played for Notts County, Sheffield Wednesday and Leeds United.

SWIMMING

Gibney, Chantal (born Dublin, 1981). National Champion in the 50m, 100m and 200m Freestyle, she competed in the European Championships in Seville in August 1997.

Smith, Michelle (born Dublin, 1969). The current Olympic Champion for the 400m Individual Medley, 400m Freestyle and 200m Individual Medley. Olympic bronze medalist in the 200m Butterfly. At the European Championships in August 1997 Michelle won gold in the 400m Individual Medley and 200m Freestyle and silver in the 400m Freestyle and 200m Butterfly. She was the first Irish woman to win an Olympic medal and now holds more major championship medals than any Irish athlete of either sex in any discipline.

ROWING

O'Toole, Niall (born Dublin, 1970). Won gold in the singles sculls (2,000m) event in the 1991 World Championships. In 1994 he won silver in the same event. Holds world record for 2,000m singles sculls. A double Olympian he endured a torrid 1997, ill health forcing him to miss the World Championships.

O'Connor, Tony (born London, 1969). Winner of silver medal in lightweight coxless pairs at 1997

World Championships to add to his bronze medal in the pairs at 1994 World Championships. Competed in Atlanta Olympics.

Maxwell, Neville (born Galway, 1970). The winner of multiple national titles in fours and eights. He partnered Tony O'Connor in winning silver at the lightweight coxless pairs at 1997 World Championships and bronze in the pairs at 1994 World Championships.

Wiley, Ian (born 1969). Current European Canoe Slalom champion. Won silver in the World Cup Canoe Slalom series meeting in August 1997. Based in Nottingham, he finished eighth in the Barcelona Olympics and fifth in the Atlanta Olympics.

Pringle, Ian (born Dublin, 1953). Irish Canoeing Champion 16 times, he won the Liffey descent 12 times. Represented Ireland at the 1976, 1980 and 1984 Olympic Games.

MOTOR RACING

Watson, John (born Belfast, 1947). In 1976 he became the first Irishman to win a Formula One Grand Prix. Won five Grand Prix in all.

Jordan, Eddie (born Dublin 1948). Formed the Jordan Formula One team in 1991. In 1997 the Jordan Peugeot Formula One team has enjoyed its most successful season ever, and Jordan secured Dublin based former World Champion

Damon Hill as his number one driver for the 1998 season.

Irvine, Eddie (born Co. Down, 1966). Formula One driver with the much vaunted Ferrari team since 1996, he is contracted to them until the end of 1998. A former Jordan driver he has yet to win a Grand Prix (a second place in the 1997 Argentine equalled his previous best), but has performed well in the 1997 season.

TENNIS

Casey, Owen (born Dublin, 1970). Ireland's number one tennis player in the 1990s. Turned professional in 1988 and won numerous national titles and a number of titles on the Satellite and Challenger tours. Competed in three Olympics, Seoul, Barcelona and Atlanta. Retired in 1997 to become a full-time coach.

AUSTRALIAN RULES FOOTBALL

Stynes, Jim (born Dublin, 1966). Won All-Ireland Minor football championship with Dublin before emigrating to Australia in 1984 for a professional career with Melbourne in Australian Rules football. Voted national Player of the Year in 1991. He holds the league record for consecutive appearances with almost 250.

GYMNASTICS

McDonald, Barry born 1972. Became the first gymnast from

Ireland to compete at the Olympics when he competed in the All-Round event in Atlanta in 1996.

SURFING

Robinson, Grant (born Donegal, 1951). Winner of European Masters event at Bundoran in September 1997, he was also champion in 1987.

Hill, Andrew (born Antrim, 1968). Irish National Champion from 1989-94. 32nd in the World Surfing Championships in 1992.

Lally, Zoë (born Sligo, 1971). She has been Irish National Ladies Champion each year since 1988.

SAILING

Wilkins, David (born Dublin 1950). With Jamie Wilkinson he won silver in the Flying Dutchman class at the 1980 Moscow Olympics. He participated in five Olympics between 1972 and 1992 (an Irish record), the exception being Los Angeles in 1984.

Wilkinson, Jamie (born Dublin). Won silver in the Flying Dutchman Class at the 1980 Olympic games in Moscow. Finished 19th in the same event in the 1976 Olympics at Montreal.

BOWLING

Nolan, Philis (born Wicklow, 1946). The winner of multiple Irish titles she has been World Pairs champion for the past twelve years.

FORMER GREATS OF IRISH SPORT

ATHLETICS

Ahearne, Tim (born Co. Limerick, 1885). Representing Britain in the triple jump at the 1908 games in London Ahearne won the gold medal. His jump of 14.91m was a world record. However, his brother, Dan, was to better this jump two years later to set a new world best. Died 1968.

Barry, John Joe (born Illinois, 1924). Moved to Tipperary as a child where his talent as an athlete was spotted. He became the first Irish athlete to gain a scholarship to Villanova University in the U.S. Broke the Irish record over three miles, two miles and one mile and

was Irish Champion over these distances. Also broke the world record for two miles and represented Ireland at the 1948 Olympic Games in both the mile and the three miles.

Bull, Mike (born Antrim, 1946). Bull was the leading British pole-vaulter for almost ten years, winning no less than thirteen titles while representing Northern Ireland. Won eight indoor titles, five outdoors.

Carroll, Michelle (born Dublin, 1961). Born Michelle Walshe, Carroll was never selected to represent her country at international level but her dominance of domestic athletics was total. In a sixteen year career she won eighteen national titles, seven 100m titles, six 200m titles and four 400m. She holds the

national records for both the 100m and 200m.

Carroll, Noel (born Louth, 1941). Won a scholarship to Villanova University in the U.S.A., he was a member of the All-American Athletics teams of 1963 and 1965. He and his Villanova team mates set a world record for the 4x880 yards relay. He competed in the Olympics in 1964 and 1968. Won a total of 14 Irish titles, at 440 and 880 yards, three British AAA titles, three European Indoor titles and, in 1963, set a European record for 880 yards.

Coghlan, Eamon (born Dublin, 1952). 'The Chairman of the Boards', Coghlan was virtually unbeatable on the U.S. Indoor circuit winning 52 out of 70 races including the prestigious Wannamaker Mile seven times. Such was his dominance in the indoor mile that his fifteen year-old World Record was not broken until February 1997. Outdoors Coghlan won Gold in the 5,000m at the 1983 World Championships in Helsinki, and has won five national titles at both 800m and 1,500m and one 5,000m title. Cruelly he finished fourth in the Olympic Games of 1976 and 1980 and was forced to miss the 1984 Olympics through injury. In 1994 Coghlan ran the mile in 3.58.60 becoming the first man over forty to run the mile in under four minutes.

Courtney, A.C Little is known about this middle distance runner other than his 2.23.4 for the 1,000 yards at Trinity College Races in 1873 is acknowledged as the first world record in a track event ever recorded.

Davin, Tom, Maurice and Pat (born Tipperary). These sporting brothers had amazing success. Tom, the eldest, set a world record for the high jump in 1873 and seven years later his youngest brother, Pat, bettered it to set the new mark. Pat was the first man to be officially recorded as jumping over six feet in height and, being a athlete of considerable talent, held six world records - including the 100 yards flat and hurdles. Maurice (who was President of Cumann Lúthchleas Gael 1884-87 and 1888-89) secured the British shot-putt and hammer titles in 1881.

Delaney, Ronnie (born Wicklow, 1935). The seventh man to break the 4 minute barrier for the mile. Aged just 21, he won the 'Blue Riband' event of the track, the 1,500m, at the Melbourne Olympics in 1956. His scorching 54 second final lap saw him set a new Olympic Record of 3:41.2 (only slightly outside the World Record). An accomplished indoor miler he broke the World Indoor Record on three occasions.

Flanagan, John J. (born Limerick, 1873). After emigrating to the U.S. Flanagan became a three time gold medal winner at three different Olympics: Paris 1900, St. Louis 1904, and London 1908. Won an Olympic silver medal in 1904 for throwing the 56lb weight. Died 1938.

Flynn, Ray (born Longford, 1957). During his career, which was predominantly American based, became the first Irishman to break 3

mins 50 seconds barrier for the mile. Competed in two Olympics (1980 and 1984) he won one National 5,000m title and the 1,500m twice. Flynn still holds the national 1,500m record of 3.33.50 which he set in 1982.

Healion, Bert (born Dublin, 1919). In 1943 set a world record in the hammer at a meeting in Dublin. His throw of 192' 11" broke the world record by three feet.

Hooper, Dick: (born Dublin, 1957). Won four national marathon titles. Won the Dublin Marathon three times and competed in the Olympic marathon on three occasions.

Hopkins, Thelma (born Hull, 1936). Won a silver medal for Britain in the 1956 Melbourne Games in the high jump. Won a total of 33 N.I. titles from 1951 on. Won a European High jump gold medal in 1954 and won the European cup the same year. An all-rounder, she won 45 caps for Ireland at hockey and was later chosen to play squash for Ireland.

Kerr, Bobbie (born Co. Fermanagh, 1882) Only seven when his family emigrated to Canada, he went on to win gold in the 200m and bronze in the 100m in the 1908 Olympics.

Kiely, Tom (born Co Tipperary, 1869) Winner of no less than 53 Irish titles, 18 of them in the hammer, 16 British Crown Gold Medals and five British AAA titles he set a world record in the hammer, in 1899, with a throw of 162 feet, the first person ever to throw the hammer over 160 ft. Offered a free trip to the Olympic Games of 1904 if he declared for Britain, Kiely declared for Ireland, paid his own fare, and won the gold medal for the All-Round Championship, the fore-runner to the modern day decathlon. Died 1951.

Leahy, Con (born Co. Cork, 1876) An Irishman, Leahy represented Britain and won Olympic gold (high jump) and silver (triple jump) at the 1906 Olympics and silver in the high jump in 1908 Games. Died 1921.

McDonald, Pat (born Co. Clare, 1878) Won a shot putt gold medal for the U.S. in the 1912 Olympic Games setting an Olympic record and silver in the two-hand shot event. In 1920 he won gold medal in the 56lb. shot at the Antwerp Games. At 42 years and 26 days he is one of the oldest Olympic gold

medal winner in history. Died 1954.

O'Callaghan, Dr. Pat (born Cork, 1905). Double Olympic Gold Medallist for the Irish Free State winning the hammer in Amsterdam (1928) and Los Angeles (1932). In addition to numerous national titles and a European Record of 56.95m (in 1933) he recorded an unofficial World Record of 59.56m in 1937. Died in 1991 aged 86.

O'Connor, Peter J. (born Co. Wicklow, 1874). His long jump record of 24' 11" set in Dublin (1901) stood for more than twenty years and remained an Irish record for a further 89 years. He won a gold medal in the St Loius Games of 1906 in the triple jump. Died 1957.

O'Mara, Frank (born Limerick, 1960). Won the 5,000m at the World Indoor Championships in both 1987 and 1991, he competed in the Olympic Games in 1984, 1988 and 1992. He won the National 1,500 title four times and the 5,000m once. Holds the Irish record for the 5,000m.

Peters, Mary (born Lancashire, 1939). Won Gold, when competing for Britain in the Pentathlon at the Munich Olympics in 1972. Setting a new World Record of 4801 points she became Northern Ireland's first Gold medallist. In a long career (she competed in 45 pentathlons) she won two Commonwealth Pentathlon titles, eight British AAA pentathlons as well a AAA 100m and five AAA shot putt titles.

Purcell, Mary (born Dublin, 1952). The first Irish woman athlete to win seven B.L.É. titles, Mary Purcell (nee Tracey) also won four British womens AAA titles. Her titles were won over 800 metres to 3,000m. In 1982 in her debut marathon she won the Irish National Championship.

Ryan, Paddy (born Limerick, 1882). Another of the great Irish hammer throwers of the early 1900s, Paddy Ryan emigrated to the U.S.A. in 1910. In 1913 he set a world record of 189' 6", that was to last for 25 years. It stood as an American record for 40 years. In 1920, representing the U.S., he won the gold medal at the Antwerp Olympic Games, his victory margin of 15 feet being the biggest ever recorded in the competition. Won a silver medal in the 56lb. shot behind fellow countryman, Pat McDonald. Died 1964.

Sheridan, Marty (born Mayo,

1881). In an amazing career Sheridan set 16 world records and was regarded as the finest athlete in the world at his peak. In 1902 he became the first man to reach 40 metres for the discus, holding the world record for ten years, breaking it eight times himself until he reached his all-time best of 43.69 metres. Representing the U.S.A. in three successive Olympic games, between 1904 and 1908, he won five gold, three silver and a bronze in the discus, long jump, shot putt, and stone throw. Died 1918.

Tisdall, Bob (born Ceylon, 1907). Won the 400m Hurdles at the Los Angeles Olympics in 1932 but was denied his World Record time beacuse he hit a hurdle. Immediately after the race he went to support Dr. Pat O'Callaghan who won gold an hour later.

Treacy, John (born Waterford, 1957). Won the Silver medal in the Marathon in stifling heat at the Los Angeles Olympics in 1984. He has also won the 1992 Los Angeles and 1993 Dublin Marathons and represented Ireland in four Olympics. An accomplished track and cross country runner he won the World Cross Country Championship in 1978 and 1979. Treacy has won five national 5,000m titles and two national 10,000m titles (and has held the national record for this distance since 1980). Treacy is the current chairman of the Irish Sports Council.

Byrne, Tony (born Louth, 1929). Irish Champion three times, he won a bronze medal in the lightweight division in the 1956 Melbourne Olympic Games.

Caldwell, Johnny (born Belfast, 1938). Won a flyweight bronze medal at the Melbourne Olympics in 1956, when only 18. He turned professional two years later. In 1961 he became World Bantamweight champion by beating Alphonse Halimi, of France. He subsequently lost the title to Eder Jofre, of Brazil, in 1962.

Dempsey, Jack (born Kildare, 1862). Born John Kelly, Dempsey held the World Middleweight title for seven years, from 1884. Fighting in America, he defended his title successfully on five occasions. So greatly was he admired as a boxer, a certain William Dempsey took the name Jack and subsequently went on to become the world heavyweight champion. Died 1895.

Dowling, Mick (born Kilkenny, 1948). Has a unique record in Irish domestic boxing, winning the National Senior title at bantamweight for eight successive years from 1968. Bronze medalist at the European Championships on four occasions between 1965 and 1971.

Doyle, Jack (born Cork, 1903). A legend in Irish boxing, 6ft. 5" Jack Doyle won each of his first ten fights as a professional heavyweight boxer inside two rounds. But his remarkable good looks - he was known as the "Gorgeous Gael " - attracted all sorts of offers outside the ring and his career as boxer declined very quickly.

Gilroy, Freddie (born Belfast, 1936). His name and that of John Caldwell have almost become synonymous, Gilroy, a hard hitting bantamweight, won a bronze medal in the 1956 Olympics and turned pro the following year. In 1959 he won the European Bantamweight title by beating the Italian, Piero Rollo. He fought the French world champion, Alphonse Halimi, for the title in 1960 and despite the opinion of most neutrals that he had won, Halimi got the decision. In his last fight he beat Johnny Caldwell for the British and Commonwealth title.

Ingle, Jimmy (born Dublin, 1921). Ingle has the distinction of being the first Irish boxer to win a European Amateur title, winning the flyweight title in 1939, aged only 17.

Kelly, Billy (born Derry, 1932). British Empire featherweight Champion 1954-55 (his father, Jimmy had held the same title 1938-39). His most controversial fight was for 1955 European title bout in Dublin against Ray Famechon which resulted in a riot after the points verdict was awarded to Famechon.

Kelly, John (born Belfast, 1932). Kelly held the European Bantamweight title as a professional in 1953-54, and only lost three times in his 31 fight career.

McAlinden, Danny (born Down, 1947). When he knocked out Jack Bodell in Birmingham in 1972 McAlinden became the first Irishman to hold both the British and Commonwealth heavyweight titles. Lost both titles in his first defence.

McAuley, Dave (born Antrim, 1961). Dave 'Boy' McAuley made two attempts at winning the world flyweight title, losing to Fidel Bassa in both 1987 and 1988, before finally gaining a world title belt when defeating Britain's Duke McKenzie. Subsequently successfully defended his title five times.

McCormick, Tom (born Louth, 1890) Became World Welterweight Champion in 1914 in Melbourne, Australia. Lost the title later the same year. Killed in France in 1916.

McCourt, Jim (born Belfast, 1945). Had a distinguished amateur career, winning seven Irish senior titles. In 1964 he won the lightweight bronze medal at the Tokyo Olympic Games. Won a bronze the following year, in the same weight division at the European Championships and boxed in his second Olympics in 1968. Took the gold medal in the Commonwealth Games in Jamaica while fighting at light-welterweight.

McGuigan, Barry (born Monaghan, 1961). Showed early on that he was a special talent when, aged just 17, he won a gold medal at the Commonwealth Games. Turned professional in 1980, and by 1983 he had both the British and European bantamweight titles under his belt. The highlight of a great career came on June 8th, 1985 when he out-pointed Eusebio Pedrosa, the reigning world champion, to take the W.B.A. World featherweight title in front of a huge outdoor crowd at Loftus Road, London. Defended his title twice before losing it in 1986 to Texan Steve Cruz in the burning heat of a car park in the Nevada Desert. After a brief comeback McGuigan retired in 1988.

McLarnin, Jimmy (born Down, 1906). The only Irishman of the modern era included in Ring magazine's Hall of Fame, McLarnin was a phenomenon, winning 63 of 77 contests and twice holding the World Welterweight title.

McNally, John (born Antrim). In 1952, Belfast born McNally took a silver medal in the Bantamweight division at the Helsinki Games, thus becoming the first Irish boxer to win an Olympic medal. In fact, his was the only medal won by Ireland at those games.

McTigue, Mike (born Clare, 1892). On St. Patrick's Day 1923 in the La Scala Opera House in Dublin

McTigue won the World Light-heavyweight title beating Battling Siki, of Senegal, on points in a 20 round contest. It proved to the last world title fight at any weight to go more than fifteen rounds. He held the title for two years. Died 1966.

Monaghan, Rinty (born Belfast, 1920). In March, 1948 Rinty Monaghan became undisputed fly-weight champion of the world when he defeated Scotland's Jackie Patterson in the King's Hall, Belfast. In a great career Monaghan won Irish, British and European titles. Because of various medical ail-ments he was forced to retire in early 1950 thus ending his career on a high as undefeated World title holder. Died 1984.

Nash, Charlie (born Derry, 1951). After a very successful amateur career during which he won five senior Irish titles, turned profession-al and earned both British and European titles as a light-weight. Became British champion in 1978 and European Champion in 1979, winning the latter title in his home city. Biggest disappointment was his fourth round defeat in 1980 by Scot, Jim Watt for their World title bout.

O'Colmain, Gerry (born Dublin, 1924). In a very successful amateur career, won two light-heavyweight titles and seven heavyweight titles in a row (from 1946). The undoubted highlight of his career was the win-ning of the European heavyweight gold medal at the European games held in Dublin in 1947.

O'Sullivan, Jim (born Wexford, 1959). O'Sullivan entered the record books of Irish boxing in 1990 when he became the first and, so far, the only boxer to win ten nation-al senior titles. He won his champi-onships at four different weights, beginning in 1980 at light-mid-dleweight (1), light-heavyweight (1) heavyweight (4) and Super-Heavyweight (4)

Russell, Hugh (born Belfast, 1959). In 1980 at the Moscow Olympics, Russell won a bronze medal in the flyweight division. The following year he turned professional and became British bantamweight champion in 1984. Successfully defended the title three times and is one of the few Irish boxers to be awarded a Lonsdale belt outright. Now a noted photographer with a Belfast newspa-per.

Tiedt, Freddie (born Dublin, 1939). Tiedt is still remembered in Irish boxing as the man who "won" an Olympic title but didn't get the gold medal. In 1956 at the Melbourne Olympics he received more points than his Romanian opponent but he lost the decision by three votes to two, despite the fact that two judges had marked it a draw but "gave" the verdict to the Romanian. He did, however, come away with an Olympic silver medal.

CYCLING

Elliott, Shay (born Dublin, 1934). A professional cyclist from 1955 he won a number of continental Grand Prix races. The first Irishman to wear the yellow jersey in the Tour de France he also won stages in the Giro d'Italia and the Tour of Spain. Silver medallist in the 1962 World Road Championship. Died in 1971.

Kelly, Sean (born Tipperary, 1956). The most widely successful cyclist of his generation, Irish or otherwise. The number one ranked cyclist in the world 1984-88 he won five stages in the Tour de France and won the points championship on a record four occasions. His best fin-ish in Le Tour was fourth in 1985. In his long prestigious career Kelly has won the Tour of Spain (1988), the Tour of Switzerland (1983 and 1990), the Nissan Classic (1985, '86, '87 and '91) the World Cup (1989) and a number of shorter Classics such as the Paris-Nice (which with seven successive victo-ries he all but made his own). It will be with a tremendous sense of pride that Sean will watch the Tour de France pass through his home town of Carrick-on-Suir in July 1998.

Roche, Stephen (born Dublin 1959). Roche's achievements in the 1987 were breath taking, he won the Giro d'Italia, the World Championship and the biggest of them all the Tour de France. Victory in France sparked off unprecedent-ed national celebration and Roche was conferred with the Freedom of Dublin. As an amateur he won the Paris-Roubaix race in 1980 and won the Paris-Nice as a professional in 1981. The winner of 57 races he retired in 1993. By virtue of his 1987 season alone Roche can be consid-ered amongst the all time greats of world cycling.

McQuaid, Jim (born Waterford 1921). Winner of Grand Prix of Ireland six times between 1949 and 1960 he competed in four World Championships.

McCormack, J.J. (born Offaly 1926). Winner of 26 Irish titles in his long career he represented his country 21 times including six World Championships.

O'Hanlon, Shay (born Dublin 1942). Won the Rás Tailteann four times between 1962 and 1967. Winner of 35 national championships and the N.C.A. title in 1979. Retired in 1980.

G.A.A.

Barry-Murphy, Jimmy (born Cork, 1954). Outstanding dual player, win-ner of six All-Ireland medals, one in football (1973) and five in hurling (between 1976 and 1986). His other achievements are almost as breath-taking, two All-Ireland Hurling Club Championships, two All-Ireland Football Club Championships, two National Hurling League titles, one National Football League title and four Railway Cup medals in Hurling. An All-Star winner on seven occa-sions, five in Hurling and two in Football. Retired in 1987. Regarded as the greatest dual player of the modern game.

Brady, Phil (born Cavan) Winner of three All-Ireland Football medals between 1947 and and 1952. He has also won a National Football League medal (1948) and a Railway Cup medal (1950). Known in G.A.A. circles as The Gunner Brady.

Connolly, John (born Galway, 1948) eldest of the hurling Connolly brothers, won an All-Ireland Hurling medal in 1980 with his brothers Michael, Padraic and Joe. Twice an All-Star Winner, was the the 1980 Texaco Hurler of the Year.

Connor, Matt (born Offaly, 1959). Won an All-Ireland Senior Football Championship medal in 1982, when Offaly put an end to Kerry's dream of five-in-a-row. The country's leading scorer for a record 5 years he won three All-Star awards in the early 80's. A serious car accident in 1984, cruelly ended his career.

Cregan, Eamon (born Limerick, 1946). Hurler who won an All-Ireland medal (1973), three Railway Cup medals and a National Hurling League Medal (1971). Won three All-Star awards. Former Offaly manager, steering them to victory over his native Limerick in 1994.

Doran, Tony (born Wexford, 1946). One of Wexford's best known hurlers, played in twenty inter-county campaigns, winning an All-Ireland medal in 1968, two National Hurling League medals and seven Railway Cup medals (two of these as Captain). Won a Hurling All-Star at full forward, was Texaco Hurler of the Year in 1976. Retired from inter-county hurling in 1984 but led his club, Buffer's Alley to an All-Ireland Club Championship in 1989.

Doyle, Jimmy (born Tipperary, 1939). Hurler, who in his sixteen years senior inter-county career won 6 All-Ireland medals between 1958 and 1971, captaining his county in 1962 and 1965. He also won eight Railway Cup medals (a Tipperary record) and six National Hurling League medals. Texaco Hurler of the Year in 1965.

Doyle, John (born Tipperary, 1930). Holder of eight All-Ireland hurling medals (won between 1949 and 1965) and a record eleven National Hurling League medals (also between 1949 and 1965). The winner of five Railway Cups with Munster he was the Texaco Hurler of the Year in 1964.

Earley, Dermot (born Mayo, 1948). In a twenty-three year inter-county career was Roscommon's outstanding player. All-Star Winner in 1974 and 1979, won two Railway Cup medals. Despite winning five Connacht Senior Football Championship titles between 1972 and 1980 he and Roscommon never won an All-Ireland title. He does, however, hold a National Football League medal from 1979.

Fox, Pat (born Tipperary, 1961). Predatory forward on the All-Ireland hurling winning Tipperary teams of 1989 and 1991. He has been the recipient of three All-Star awards.

Heffernan, Kevin (born Dublin, 1938). Captained Dublin to their 1958 All-Ireland Football win. Won three National Football League titles between 1953 and 1958 and seven Railway Cup medals (captaining Leinster in 1959). Manager of the great Dublin team of the 1970s, leading them to three All-Ireland Senior Football titles.

Keating, Babs (born Tipperary, 1944). Dual player who met with much success in hurling, winning

three All-Ireland medals between 1964 and 1971, two Railway Cup Hurling medals and one Railway Cup Football (1972). Both an All-Star and Texaco Hurling Sportstar in 1971. Remembered for playing hurling barefoot, he later managed Tipperary to two All-Ireland Senior Hurling Championship titles. Laois hurling manager from 1995-1997.

Keaveney, Jimmy (born Dublin, 1945). Magnificent rotund Dublin full-forward who won All-Ireland football medals in 1974, 1976 and 1977. Winner of two National Football League medals, three All-Star Awards and two Texaco Gaelic Footballer of the Year Awards (1976 and 1977).

Keher, Eddie (born Kilkenny, 1941). Deadly Kilkenny hurling marksman, made senior championship debut as seventeen year old in the 1959 All-Ireland Final Replay and played until 1977, winning six All-Ireland Senior Hurling Championship medals, nine Railway Cup medals and three National Hurling League medals along the way. Texaco Hurler of the Year in 1972 and an All-Star Winner on five successive occasions between 1971 and 1975.

Lynch, Jack (born Cork, 1917). Dual player who won a record six consecutive All-Ireland medals between 1941 and 1946, five in hurling and one in football. Having made his debut in 1935, he retired in 1951 winning three National Hurling League medals and three Railway Cup medals. Entered the Dáil in 1948 and went on to become Taoiseach from 1966 to 1973 and from 1977 to 1979.

McCartan Snr, James (born Down). Down midfielder who won All-Ireland Football medals in 1960 1961, and 1968. Won three Railway Cup medals in 1964, 1965 and 1969. His brother Dan, won three All-Ireland medals and his son James is the holder of two All-Ireland medals.

McCarthy, Liam (born London, 1853). Born of Irish parents, McCarthy was the first treasurer of the London G.A.A. County Board. The cup which All-Ireland Hurling winning captains now receive bears his name. The cup was first presented in 1923 (for the 1921 championship). Bob McConkey captained Limerick to victory on that occasion. In 1992, Kilkenny's Liam

Fennelly was the first captain to be presented with the new Liam McCarthy cup. McCarthy died in 1928.

McDonagh, Mattie (born Galway, 1935). Galway footballer who was one of the games outstanding figures in the 1960s. Holds four All-Ireland Football medals between 1956 and 1966 (was part of famous Galway three-in-a-row team of the mid 1960s). Won a Railway Cup medal in 1958, was Texaco Footballer of the Year in 1966.

McEniff, Brian (born Donegal, 1943). Donegal footballer who won a National Football League medal with New York in 1964. An All-Star in 1972, won two Railway Cup medals with Ulster and is current manager of the Ulster Railway Cup team. As manager of Donegal, guided them to their first All-Ireland Senior Football Championship in 1992. Has managed the Ulster Railway Cup side since 1982, leading them to nine titles.

McNally, Joe (born Dublin, 1964). Won an All-Ireland football medal and All-Star award with Dublin in 1983 in his first Championship season. Played with Dublin in 1995 after a long self imposed absence.

Mackey, Mick: (born Limerick, 1912). Another legendary name in the annals of hurling. Won three All-Ireland Hurling medals with Limerick (1934, 1936 & 1940) captaining the team on two occasions. He also won eight Railway Cup medals between 1934 and 1945 and five National Hurling League medals. Manager of the Limerick hurling team in the 1950s. Died 1982.

Maguire, Sam (born Cork, 1879). Gaelic footballer who played championship football for London in the early 1900's. Maguire had the distinction of swearing Michael Collins into the IRB, and the cup which All-Ireland Football winning captains now receive bears his name. It was presented for the first time in 1928 (to Bill 'Squires' Gannon of Kildare). The new Sam Maguire cup was first presented in 1988 to Meath's Mick Lyons. Sam Maguire died in 1927.

Mullins, Brian (born Dublin, 1954). Outstanding Gaelic football midfielder, won four All-Ireland Football medals between 1974 and 1983 (coming back from severe injury to win in 1983), contested a further five All-Ireland Finals but Kerry defeated

Dublin in each of those. Won two National Football League medals and captained Leinster to Railway Cup success in 1985. Winner of two All-Star Awards, is the current Derry manager and brought the National Football League title to Derry in 1996.

O'Connell, Mick (born Kerry, 1937). One of Gaelic football's most famous names, won four All-Ireland Football medals with Kerry between 1959 (when he captained the team) and 1970, six National Football League medals and one Railway Cup medal. Won an All-Star award (1972) and was Texaco Footballer of the Year in 1962. O'Connell's high fielding was renowned and he is generally regarded as Gaelic Football's best ever midfielder.

O'Dwyer, Mick (born Kerry, 1936). Winner of four All-Ireland Football medals between 1959 and 1970. His impressive collection also included eight National Football League winners medals (between 1959 and 1974), a Railway Cup medal and Texaco Footballer of the Year 1969. Shortly after retiring, he became manager of the Kerry senior team and guided them to eight All-Ireland Senior Football Championship titles between 1975 and 1986. He is the current Kildare football manager.

O'Hehir, Michael (b. 1920, Dublin). Broadcaster. Worked with *Irish Independent* until 1960. Began his commentary on gaelic football and hurling in 1938 and commentated on 99 All-Ireland finals. Also covered horse racing for RTE and BBC. First RTE Head of Sport (1960-72). Penned a weekly column with the *Irish Press*. Was most widely known and celebrated voice in Ireland up until his retirement due to a stroke. Died 1996.

O'Rourke, Colm (born Meath, 1957). Inspiring Meath Gaelic football full forward who won two All-Ireland medals in 1987 and 1988 and two National Football League medals. Holds two All-Stars and in 1991 was the Texaco Footballer of the Year. Retired from inter-county football in 1995. Gaelic football analyst on R.T.E.'s Sunday Game.

O'Shea, Jack (born Kerry, 1957). Finest Gaelic footballer of his era. Won seven All-Ireland Football medals from 1978 to 1986. Winner of six consecutive midfield All-Star

Awards (1980 - 1985) and a record four Texaco Awards. 'Jacko' captained the Irish compromise rules teams against Australia in 1984 and 1986. Was manager of the Mayo team for a time and guided them to Connacht success in 1993.

Rackard, Nicky, Bobby & Billy (born Wexford, 1922, 1929 & 1930 respectively). Brothers who formed a formidable backbone in the Wexford Senior Hurling team of the 1950's. All three played in Wexford's All-Ireland Hurling Final successes of 1955 and 1956, while Billy also won an All-Ireland medal in 1960. Between them they also won six Railway Cup medals and three National Hurling medals. In 1992, both Billy and Bobby became All-Time All-Stars.

Ring, Christy (born Cork, 1920). Recognised as one of the all time greats in hurling. Won eight All-Ireland Hurling medals (three as captain) between 1941 and 1954, eighteen Railway Cup medals between 1942 and 1963, and four National Hurling League medals. Ring played with Cork from just after his nineteenth birthday until the age of forty-two. Died 1979.

Sheehy, Mikey (born Kerry, 1954). Gaelic Footballer who won eight All-Ireland Football medals between 1975 and 1986. Won seven All-Star awards in an illustrious career.

Skehan, Noel (born Kilkenny, 1946). Former Kilkenny Hurling goalkeeper holds a record nine All-Ireland Senior Hurling Championship medals won between 1963 and 1983. Holds four Railway Cup medals. All-Star goalkeeper on seven occasions and Texaco Award Winner in 1982. Retiring from inter-county hurling at the age of thirty-nine, he went on to become an accomplished squash player.

GOLF

Bradshaw, Harry (born Wicklow, 1913). Winner of the Irish Professional ten times he also won the Irish Open twice (1947 and 1949) and the Dunlop Master twice (1953 and 1955). A member of three British and Irish Ryder Cup teams (1953, 1955 and 1957). He and Christy O'Connor Senior won the Canada Cup (now the World Cup) in 1958. He died in 1990.

Bruen, Jimmy (born Antrim 1920).

An outstanding amateur golfer he won the Irish Close Championship twice (1937 and 1938) and the British Amateur Championship in 1946. He played in three Walker Cup tournaments including the inaugural British and Irish win in 1938. He died in 1972.

Carr, Joe (born Dublin 1922). Four time Irish Amateur Open winner (between 1946 and 1956), three time British Amateur Championship winner (1953-60), six time Irish Close Championship winner (1954-67) in addition to twelve East of Ireland, twelve West of Ireland and three South of Ireland Championships. He played on a record ten Walker Cup teams between 1947 and 1967. Without he is Ireland's greatest ever amateur golfer.

Feherty, David (born Co. Down 1958). Winner of six events on the European tour including both the Italian Open and Scottish Open in 1986 and the 1989 B.M.W. International. Captain of the victorious Irish team in the 1990 Dunhill Cup. He played in the 1991 Ryder Cup in the United States. Feherty moved to the American circuit in 1994 but retired taking up a comment.

O'Connor Snr, Christy (born Galway 1924). Won 24 titles on the European P.G.A. tour (1955-1972) including four Carroll's International events. A member of ten Ryder Cup teams, he played in 36 matches. With Harry Bradshaw he won World Cup in 1958. Irelands' most successful golfer ever he went on to enjoy further success on the Senior Tour.

RUGBY

Campbell, Ollie (born Dublin, 1954). Out-half he won 22 caps (1976-84) with Ireland and seven caps with the Lions. An outstanding place kicker he holds many Irish international scoring records including: most points in an international season, 52 (1982-83); most international dropped goals, 7 (including two in a single international); most penalty goals in an international season, 14 (1982-83); and most points on an Irish international tour, 60 (Australia 1979). In all scored 217 points for Ireland and 184 points for the Lions.

Dawson, Ronnie (born Dublin, 1932). Hooker, capped 27 times by Ireland and six times by the Lions. He captained the British and Irish Lions tour to Australia and New Zealand. Also captained the Barbarians in 1960 when they defeated South Africa.

Fitzgerald, Ciarán (born Galway, 1952). Hooker, capped 25 times by Ireland (20 times as captain) between 1979 and 1986 and four times (all as captain) by the Lions on their 1983 tour of New Zealand. Under his captaincy Ireland won the Triple Crown in 1982 and the International Championship in 1983.

Gallahcr, Dave (born Donegal, 1873). Emigrated to New Zealand and captained his adopted country in their first ever international, against Australia in 1903. Capped six times in all he was killed in battle Passchendale in 1917.

Gibson, Mike (born Belfast, 1942). Ireland's most capped international he won 69 caps between 1964 and 1979. In addition he was capped 12 times by the Lions. In his 16 season international career he scored 115 points. At his peak Gibson was regarded as one of the world's finest and most versatile. He played in a number of positions for Ireland and was outstanding in all of them.

Keane, Moss (born Kerry, 1948). Winner of 51 Irish caps (1974-84) he won the Five Nations Championship twice (1974 and 1983) and the Triple Crown in 1982. Capped once on the Lions 1977 tour of New Zealand he was a member of the Munster side who defeated the touring New Zealanders in 1978.

Kiernan, Michael (born Cork, 1961). Capped 43 times between 1982 and 1991 his 308 points is an Irish international record. He also holds the Irish record for most penalty goals scored (62) and most international conversions (40 - including a record seven in a single international). His last minute drop goal against England in the 1985 Triple Crown decider handed Ireland victory. Kiernan was a sprinter of note, he won the Irish 200m title in 1981.

Kiernan, Tom (born Cork, 1939). With 54 caps won between 1960 and 1973 he is Ireland's most capped full-back. He captained Ireland a record 24 times and has scored 158 points. He has been

capped five times (four as captain) by the British and Irish Lions, top Irish points scorer Michael Kiernan is his nephew.

Kyle, Jackie (born Belfast, 1926). Capped 46 times by Ireland (1947-58) and six times by the Lions (1950). He won the Grand Slam (1948), the Triple Crown (1949) and the Five Nations Championship (1951). He is Ireland's most capped outhalf.

Mc Bride, Willie John (born Antrim, 1940). His 63 caps for Ireland between 1962 and 1975 (a record 52 consecutively) is an international record for a lock. With 17 caps he Is the most capped Lions player ever. He won the Five Nations Championship in 1974. He has managed the Lions (1983 tour to New Zealand) and coached the Irish team (1983-84). He was Texaco Sportstar of the Year in 1974 and has won a host of domestic accolades.

McLoughlin, Ray (born Galway, 1939). As a prop forward he won 40 caps (eight as captain) between 1962 and 1975. A integral member of the International Championship winning side in 1974. He was capped three times by the Lions on their 1966 antipodean tour. Captained Ireland to their first ever victory over South Africa in 1965.

Millar, Syd (born Antrim, 1934). Capped 37 times as a prop forward between 1958 and 1970 he also won nine caps with the British Lions. Irish team coach 1972-75 he managed the Lions on their 1980 tour of South Africa. He is a former President of the I.R.F.U.

O'Reilly, Tony (born Dublin, 1936). Winner of 29 international caps in his record breaking 16 year career (1955-70) at wing three-quarter. Capped by the Lions ten times he scored a record six tries. Currently the Worldwide President of H.J. Heinz and Chairman of Independent Newspapers.

Orr, Philip (born Dublin, 1950). Ireland's most capped prop forward with 58 appearances (1976-87), capped by the Lions in 1977. Member of the Triple Crown winning teams of 1982 and 1985.

Ringland, Trevor (born Belfast, 1959). Scored seven tries for Ireland in his 34 international appearances between 1981 and 1988. He was a member of the Triple Crown winning

sides of 1982 and 1985 and the Championship winning side of 1983. Capped by the British and Irish Lions against New Zealand in 1983.

Ward, Tony (born Dublin, 1954). Between 1978 and 1987 he won 19 Irish caps scoring 113 points. In his only full Lions appearance, against South Africa in 1980 he scored a record 18 points. Member of the Munster team which defeated the All-Blacks in 1978. Would certainly have won more caps had Ollie Campbell not made the out-half position his own in the early 1980s.

Armstrong, Gerry (born Belfast, 1954) striker. Capped 63 times between 1977 and 1986, he scored 12 international goals of which the most memorable was his winner against host nation, Spain, in the 1982 World Cup finals. He also played in the 1986 World Cup finals. He played club football with Bangor, Watford, Tottenham Hotspur, Real Mallorca, West Bromwich Albion and Chesterfield.

Bambrick, Joe (born Belfast, 1905) striker. Played with Linfield (winning the Irish Cup in 1930) and with Chelsea in England. With 12 goals in eleven appearances he held the Northern Ireland scoring record from 1938 until 1992 and remains number two in the Northern Ireland scoring charts. Died 1983.

Best, George (born Belfast, 1946) midfielder. European Player of the Year, 1968 (the only Irishman to ever win that award). Winner of two League Championships (1965/65 and 1967/68) and the European Cup (1968). Capped 37 times by Northern Ireland he scored nine international goals. Pele once described him as the greatest living footballer.

Bingham, Billy (born Belfast, 1931) winger and Northern Ireland manager. Bingham won the League Championship with Everton (1962/63) he counts Glentoran, Sunderland and Luton amongst his former clubs. Capped 56 times between 1951 and 1964 he scored ten international goals. As Northern Ireland manager he guided the team to the World Cup finals in 1982 and 1986 where they rocked some of the more fashionable teams. Retired from the manager's job in 1995.

Blanchflower, Danny (born Belfast, 1925) defender. Capped 56 times by Northern Ireland he scored two international goals and captained them to the World Cup quarter finals in Sweden in 1958. Captain of Tottenham Hotspur in their F.A. Cup/League Championship winning year 1960/61. With Spurs he also won the 1962 F.A. Cup and the 1963 Cup Winners' Cup.

Bradley, Brendan (born Derry, 1949) striker. The League of Ireland's all-time top scorer with 235 goals.

Brady, Liam (born Dublin, 1956) midfielder. The only Irishman ever to play in Italy's Serie A, he won two Championships with Juventus (1981 and 1982). Capped 72 times (twelve times as captain) by the Republic of Ireland scoring nine goals. An F.A. Cup winner with Arsenal in 1979 he managed Celtic (1991-93) and Brighton (1994-95).

Bonner, Packie (born Donegal, 1960) goalkeeper. Has won 80 caps with the Republic of Ireland. Winner of four Scottish League and two Scottish Cup medals with his beloved Celtic he will be forever remembered for the string of spectacular saves in the never-to-be-forgotten 1-0 victory over England in 1988, and his penalty save against Romania in Genoa in 1990 helping the Republic to the World Cup quarter finals.

Cantwell, Noel (born Cork, 1932) defender. Captained Manchester United to F.A. Cup (1963) and League Championship (1967) success. Capped 36 times by the Republic between 1954 and 1967 he scored 10 international goals. Capped five times by the Irish cricket team.

Carey, Jackie (born Dublin, 1919) defender. Won the F.A. Cup (1948) and the League Championship (1951/52) with Manchester United. Capped 29 times between 1938 and 1953 by the Republic of Ireland, he was capped seven times by Northern Ireland between 1947 and 1949.

Charlton, Jack (born Newcastle, 1935) manager of Republic of Ireland 1986-95. His tenure as manager was the Republic's most successful ever. Led Ireland to the 1988 European Championship and the World Cup finals Italia '90 and U.S.A. '94. Winner of World Cup

medal with England in 1966. Conferred with honorary Irish citizenship in 1996.

Clarke, Colin (born Newry, 1962), striker. Holds the Northern Ireland international scoring record with 13 goals in 38 appearances. A member of the Northern Ireland 1986 World Cup squad, he has played club football with Southampton, Bournemouth and Portsmouth.

Doherty, Peter (born Derry, 1913) striker. Capped by Northern Ireland 16 times between 1935 and 1951 Doherty won an English League Championship with Manchester City in 1936/37 and the F.A. Cup with Derby in 1946. Manager of the Northern Ireland team from 1951 to 1962. In 1958 he guided them to their first ever World Cup finals in Sweden where they finished in the top eight.

Dunne, Jimmy (born Dublin, 1905) striker. Scored 170 League goals with English clubs (including Sheffield United, Arsenal and Southampton). Returned to Shamrock Rovers where he won two League Championships (1937/38 and 1938/39) and the 1940 F.A.I. Cup. Scorer of 12 goals in his fifteen international appearances for the Free State and Éire. Died 1949.

Farrell, Peter (born Dublin, 1922). Capped 28 times by the Republic between 1946 and 1957. Scorer on the winning Republic side which beat England 2-0 in 1949, the first team to ever beat England at home. Also capped seven times by Northern Ireland.

Gallagher, Patsy (born Donegal 1894) striker. Scorer of 184 goals in his 436 game 15 year career with Celtic. Winner of four Scottish Cups and six League Championships with Celtic. Capped eleven times by Northern Ireland between 1920 and 1927 he also won one international cap with the Free State. Died 1954.

Giles, Johnny (born Dublin, 1940) midfielder. Capped 59 times (with a record 30 as captain) by the Republic, he was player-manager from 1973-80. The holder of two Championship and one F.A. Cup medal with Leeds United he also won an F.A. Cup medal with Manchester United in 1963. Shrewder member of the R.T.É.'s vaunted Giles/Dunphy soccer panel during the Charlton era.

Heighway, Steve (born Dublin,

1947) winger. Capped by the Republic 34 times. Had an immensely successful career with Liverpool winning two European Cups (1977 and 1978), two U.E.F.A. Cups, four League Championships and an F.A. Cup medal.

Hurley, Charlie (born Cork, 1936) defender. Played with Millwall, Sunderland and Bolton Wanderers. He captained the Republic 21 times (from a total of 40 appearances) and scored two international goals.

Jennings, Pat (born Newry 1945) goalkeeper. Northern Ireland's most capped player. Made his debut in 1964 and won his 119th cap on his 41st birthday against Brazil in the 1986 World Cup finals. With Tottenham Hotspur he won two League Cups (1971 and 1973), a Cup Winners' Cup (1968) and the U.E.F.A. Cup (1972). In addition he won two F.A. Cup medals (one with Spurs in 1967 and one with Arsenal in 1979). P.F.A. Player of the Year in 1976.

Kinnear, Joe (born Dublin, 1946) defender. Winner of one F.A. Cup and two U.E.F.A. Cup medals with Tottenham Hotspur in the sixties and seventies he was capped 26 times by the Republic. Manager of Wimbledon since 1992 where despite limited resources he has enjoyed some success. Voted Manager of the Year in the English Premiership in 1996/97.

Lawrenson, Mark (born Preston, 1957) midfielder. Capped 39 times by the Republic between 1977 and 1987. Winner of five League Championships, one F.A. Cup and one European Cup with Liverpool in the 1980s. He retired at the age of thirty due to a serious foot injury.

McElhinney, Gerry (born Derry, 1956). Capped six times by Northern Ireland in 1984 and 1985. He was a member of the Derry Gaelic football team which won the Ulster title in 1976 and 1977 winning an All-Star award in 1976. He was also an Irish international boxer.

McGee, Paul (born Sligo, 1954) striker. A much travelled player he played in Ireland, Canada, England and Holland in a career spanning 25 years and 27 changes of club. Scored four goals in his 15 appearances for the Republic.

Moran, Kevin (born Dublin, 1956) defender. Winner of All-Ireland football medals with Dublin in 1976 and

1977 Moran went on to have a distinguished career with Manchester United winning two F.A. Cup medals, but gaining an unwanted place in history as the first player to be sent off in an F.A. Cup final. Capped 70 times by the Republic scoring six goals, he captained the team during the 1988 European Championship finals.

Neill, Terry (born Belfast, 1942) defender. Winner of 59 caps with Northern Ireland between 1961 and 1973. Northern Ireland manager in 1973, he managed Arsenal - the club with whom he had spent most of his playing career - when they won the F.A. Cup in 1979.

O'Leary, David (born London, 1958) defender. Capped 67 times O'Leary will forever remembered for scoring the penalty against Romania which sent the Republic into the World Cup quarter finals in 1990. In his twenty year career with Arsenal he won two F.A. Cups (1979 & 1993), and two League Championships (1988/89 and 1990/91). Differences with Jack Charlton saw him miss out on the European Championships of 1988 and the 1994 World Cup. David's brother Pierce was capped seven times in 1980 and 1981.

Rice, Pat (born Belfast, 1949) defender. Member of the Arsenal F.A. Cup/League double winning side of 1971, he captained Arsenal to F.A. Cup success in 1979. Capped by Northern Ireland 49 times between 1969 and 1980.

Roberts, Fred His 96 goals scored for Glentoran in the 1930/31 season is an Irish and British record. Not surprisingly he ended that season with a League Winners medal. Won the Irish Cup in 1932 and 1933. Capped once by Northern Ireland.

Scott, Lee (born Belfast, 1894) goalkeeper. Played 429 games in a twenty-two year career with Liverpool winning two League Championships. Hugely successful manager with Belfast Celtic (1936-49) he led them to six League titles and six Irish Cups. Capped 31 times for Northern Ireland (1920-36). Died 1959.

Stapleton, Frank (born Dublin 1956) striker. Holder of the Republic's international scoring record with 20 goals in 70 appearances between 1976 and 1990. A striker of tremendous strength he

won three F.A. Cup medals (one with Arsenal and two with Manchester United). His other clubs included Ajax, Le Harve and Blackburn Rovers. Had a short but unsuccessful stint as a manager in the U.S.

Whelan, Ronnie (born Dublin, 1961) midfielder. With Liverpool he won six League Championships between 1981 and 1990, two F.A. Cups (1986 & 1989) and a European Cup in 1984. Capped 53 times by the Republic he scored three international goals including a spectacular volley against Russia in Euro '88. Whelan's career was ended by injury in 1995.

Whelan, Liam (born Dublin, 1935) striker. Winner of two League Championships with Manchester United in 1955/56 and 1956/57. He was capped only four times by the Republic before he tragically lost his life in February 1958 in the Munich plane crash which killed eight Manchester United players.

Whiteside, Norman (born Belfast 1965) midfielder. At just 17 he became the youngest player to play in the World Cup finals when he lined out against Yugoslavia in June 1982. Capped by Northern Ireland 38 times (scoring nine goals) he also played in the 1986 World Cup finals. An F.A. Cup winner with Manchester United in 1983. Serious injury forced his premature retirement in 1990.

Armstrong, Reg (born Dublin, 1930). In the four year period 1952-56 Armstrong recorded seven World Championship Grand Prix victories in motor cycling. He finished runner-up in the world championships on five occasions.

Barnville, Geraldine (born Offaly, 1942). One of Ireland's most successful squash players ever, Barnville was also an international tennis player. At squash, she was capped more than 70 times making her one of the most capped players in the world.

Barrington, Jonah (born Cornwall, 1944). World class squash player Barrington played eighteen times for Ireland. Between 1967 and 1973, he won the British Open on six occasions, this being ranked as the premier tournament in world squash.

Bryans, Ralph (born Antrim, 1941). In 1965 he won the World Championship 50 c.c. motor-cycling title, the first Irish man to do so. In all he recorded ten Grand Prix victories.

DeLacy, Stan (born Limerick 1915). Had success as an Irish hockey player, winning five triple crowns in a career that spanned 17 years (1937-54). Also had the unusual distinction for an Irish international sportsman, of any code, of being on the winning side in each of his first twenty games for his country.

Doyle, Matt (born California, 1955). In the 1980's Matt Doyle brought a degree of credibility to Ireland's standing in world tennis when he was the driving force behind the climb to Division One of the Davis Cup competition. The highlight of his individual career was a win in a Grand Prix in 1983, in Cologne. Also won the Irish Open six times.

Drea, Sean Drea won numerous international class sculling races and the highlight of a great career was a silver medal placing in the 1975 World Championships held in England.

Gilmartin, John Joe (born Kilkenny, 1916). His record of 24 All-Ireland senior titles in handball was only surpassed in the mid-1990's. His elevated status in this widely played sport in Ireland was such that when he retired in 1947 he had not lost a singles match in more than ten years.

Gregg, Terry (born Antrim, 1950). One of the "greats" of Irish hockey, Gregg played a record 103 times for Ireland and 42 times for the Great Britain team. A prolific goal-getter, he brilliantly led Ireland to the final of the Inter-Continental Cup in Rome 1977, their best ever performance at international level.

Herron, Tommy (born Down, 1950). Died tragically at the age of 30, Herron was regarded as one of the top motorcycle riders in the world in the 1970's. Won three Isle of Man T.T.s, and at the North-West 200 in 1978 he averaged 127.6 m.p.h. to record the fastest time for any racer in either Britain or Ireland.

Hopkirk, Paddy (born Antrim, 1933). The highlight of a great international rally-driving career came in 1964 when he won the Monte-Carlo rally. Five years later, when rallying was at its most popular, he came second in the London-to-Sydney race. Hopkirk also won the Circuit of Ireland five times.

Judge, David (born Dublin, 1936). In a twenty one year international career (1957- 1978) Judge played a then record 124 times for Ireland, and a further 15 times for Britain. His career was leaden with both representative and domestic honours.

Kirby, Pat (born Clare, 1936): In terms of achievement few handballers will ever equal Kirby. The highlight of a spectacular career was achieved when he was crowned World Champion in 1970. Won two further world titles, in 1971 and 1972. In addition to his world title victories, Kirby, who had emigrated to America in the late 1950's, won national titles there as well as in Canada and in Ireland. He also won ten Irish singles titles.

Kyle, Maeve (born Kilkenny, 1928). Kyle concentrated her interests on hockey in her early sporting career winning 58 caps for Ireland, the highlight of which was the 1950 winning of the Triple Crown. She then switched to athletics and represented Ireland on three occasions at the Olympic Games (Melbourne, Rome and Tokyo).

Langan, Jimmy (born Dublin, 1951). An outstanding table tennis player from early childhood, became the youngest player to represent Ireland in senior sport when at 12 years of age he was called for international duty. Went on to play in excess of 200 matches for his country and was Irish senior champion ten times.

Langrishe, May (born Dublin). When she won Irish Ladies Singles tennis title in 1879 she became the world's first national women's singles title winner, as the Irish were the first to hold a women's national competition. Won the title on two further occasions.

Maher, Joey (born Louth, 1934). After winning numerous Irish handball titles at both junior and senior level, Maher emigrated to Canada in 1965 and during his three years there won the Canadian title three times. Highlight of his career was winning the World Handball title in 1967 while representing Canada.

McConnell, Billy (born Down, 1956). One of Ireland's most capped hockey player with 135 caps, McConnell won a further 51 caps for Britain. At the Olympic Games of 1984, in Los Angeles, was a member of the British squad which won the Bronze medal.

Miller, Sammy (born Antrim, 1933). As a motor cycle trialist, Miller's record will probably stand forever - more than 900 victories in twenty years (1950-1970), British champion for eleven years in a row, five gold medals in team trialing with the British international team, and European champion twice.

Monteith, Dermott (born Antrim, 1943). Probably Ireland's most successful cricketer, Monteith took 326 international wickets, for an average of just over 17 runs per wicket. On 27 occasions in test cricket he took five or more wickets, while his scoring total of 1,712 runs with the bat places him in the top twenty Irish batsmen of all time.

O'Dea, Donnacha (born Dublin, 1945) O'Dea smashed all kinds of swimming records when winning more than 90 Irish titles. His greatest achievement was recorded in 1965 when he became the first Irishman to break the 60 sec. barrier for the 100 metres free-style.

O'Kelly, Con (born Cork, 1886). The only Irish born person to win an Olympic wrestling gold, Kelly took the title in the heavyweight division at the 1908 Games in London while representing Britain.

O'Toole, Gary (born Wicklow 1968). Ireland's first medallist at a major swimming championships when, in 1989 he won silver in the 200m breaststroke at the European Championships. Gold medallist in the 200m breaststroke at the 1991 World Student Games. A double Olympian he travelled to Seoul in 1988 and Barcelona in 1994. Holds five national records for breaststroke and medley events.

Pim, Joshua (born Wicklow, 1869). In 1893 he created history by becoming the first Irish man, and the last, to win the Wimbledon Singles tennis title. He retained it the following year.

Potter, Jacqui (born 1963). Held the world record for most capped woman hockey player when she retired in the early 1990's with 83 caps.

Pratt, Don (born Dublin, 1935). Between 1956 and 1972 Pratt was capped 52 times for Ireland at squash, a then world record for a squash player. Won the Irish title for a record ten times and lost out on four other occasions. Also a cricket international.

Robb, Tommy (born Antrim, 1934). Won the Irish 500 c.c. championship in 1961, he won the 250 c.c. road racing Grand Prix championship two years later. He had two other Grand Prix victories. Despite many victories Robb won only one T.T., that win coming in 1973.

Sloan, Marty (born Tyrone). With 149 caps Sloan is Ireland's most capped hockey player of all time. He captained Ireland 1987-93. Won a number of caps with the Great Britain team also.

Thompson, Syd (born Antrim, 1912). In a career spanning more than a quarter of a century (1947-73), Thompson set a then world record for an outdoor bowls player when he represented Ireland 78 times.

Tyrell-Smith, Harry (born Dublin, 1907). Motor cyclist par excellence, Tyrell-Smith was European Champion twice, in 1931 and 1936. Took part in numerous Isle of Man T.T.s but only won one.

White, Francis (born Dublin, 1955). Better known as 'Chalkie' he won the 1,500m freestyle in the 1975 European Cup. Dominated the Irish national swimming championships in the 1970s winning over 40 national titles. Was a genuine European standard swimmer.

Woods, Stanley (born Dublin, 1903). Until the advent of Dunlop brothers, Woods was the most successful motor-cyclist the island of Ireland had produced. Won five 500.c.c. T.T. titles, five junior T.T. titles, 22 Continental Grand Prix victories, and more than forty international titles in all.

USEFUL INFORMATION

IRISH LIFESTYLE INTERNATIONAL COMPARISONS

Daily European Leisure Activities (in minutes)

Country	Relaxing	Visiting, Receiving Vistors	Large DIY Tasks	Gardening	Walking Window-Shopping	Social-ising	Visit Show, Museum	Cinema
Austria	47.8	35.5	6.9	19.6	14.7	29.9	2.4	2.6
Belgium	57.0	32.1	4.0	6.9	9.3	25.8	1.2	0.3
Britain	64.5	46.9	4.0	11.7	9.1	13.9	2.1	0.9
Denmark	70.0	76.6	9.2	12.3	9.1	8.9	5.9	2.9
Finland	62.7	66.0	9.5	6.1	19.3	9.1	4.3	1.7
France	33.8	46.9	3.3	7.8	13.3	12.0	1.8	1.6
Germany	72.0	39.1	6.0	15.1	16.8	16.1	2.5	2.1
Greece	118.6	38.7	8.9	12.0	7.3	61.1	1.4	-
IRELAND	75.8	67.5	10.3	9.9	22.9	12.9	2.6	0.7
Italy	50.5	34.7	6.1	10.2	16.9	24.2	2.5	1.2
Luxembourg	81.6	23.5	3.6	12.4	24.7	18.7	7.1	1.7
Netherlands	35.8	70.1	10.2	7.2	7.1	11.0	11.2	-
Norway	76.6	71.4	2.4	4.2	6.7	7.0	4.2	1.3
Portugal	51.2	20.9	3.4	19.1	13.7	38.6	1.4	2.4
Spain	90.7	30.4	3.0	3.2	26.5	42.7	1.1	1.4
Sweden	21.7	72.1	8.1	7.0	16.8	2.6	4.7	0.2
Switzerland	51.7	43.9	7.5	11.5	16.8	14.3	8.3	1.5
AVERAGE	62.5	48.0	6.3	10.4	14.8	20.5	3.8	1.3

Country Cinema	Games & Hobbies	Active Sports & Exercise	Reading Books	Reading News-papers	Reading Mag-azines	Listen to Radio	Listen to record'd music	Watch TV & Video
Austria	14.7	7.3	11.3	28.1	16.9	163.4	27.8	147.6
Belgium	7.1	8.7	10.0	23.5	15.3	162.1	13.9	172.3
Britain	13.8	10.0	12.0	23.4	7.9	98.1	17.4	230.6
Denmark	15.9	14.8	13.0	36.5	25.1	194.9	36.3	137.7
Finland	10.0	16.1	21.4	44.4	16.8	128.4	15.9	141.5
France	8.2	5.2	15.8	11.6	11.8	94.7	28.9	185.3
Germany	5.7	6.1	7.4	46.0	22.4	161.7	29.0	193.3
Greece	8.4	4.7	15.2	11.2	2.1	86.6	26.9	178.2
IRELAND	5.1	9.1	11.8	27.8	8.3	141.0	9.8	179.9
Italy	5.1	7.0	7.4	14.4	7.4	43.5	16.6	197.2
Luxembourg	22.3	9.0	14.8	21.1	14.0	61.2	15.4	129.4
Netherlands	19.0	12.2	14.2	24.7	12.0	107.0	21.0	160.6
Norway	11.7	13.6	15.7	41.2	9.3	115.0	28.4	142.4
Portugal	3.6	3.0	5.2	7.5	12.0	103.1	9.1	202.8
Spain	7.6	5.4	7.3	13.5	5.2	59.8	31.0	198.1
Sweden	13.8	28.7	9.9	51.9	12.8	248.0	21.3	158.2
Switzerland	7.6	14.4	11.9	22.0	10.9	153.3	30.4	126.0
AVERAGE	10.6	10.3	12.0	26.4	12.4	124.8	22.3	169.5

EUROPEAN AND U.S. CONSUMER OWNERSHIP

Country	Year	Car %	Phone %	Micro-Wave %	Fridge %	Freezer %	Washing Machine %	Dish Washer %
Austria	1993	65	88	34	97	66	83	36
Belgium	1990	81	-	10	99	57	85	22
Britain	1994	45	93	66	99	37	91	19
Denmark	1994	74	98	37	95	67	83	42
Finland	1994	71	87	71	90	63	84	46
France	1995	85	96	50	98	83	90	43

Continued from previous page

Country	Year	Car %	Phone %	Micro-Wave %	Fridge %	Freezer %	Washing Machine %	Dish Washer %
Germany	1994	-	-	.55	.97	.67	.94	.45
IRELAND	1994/95	.56	.74	.51	.92	.97	.92	.20
Italy	1990	.89	.91	.7	.89	.29	.94	-
Luxembourg	1993	-	.97	.33	.97	.71	.97	.55
Netherlands	1994	.66	-	.35	.85	.56	.95	.18
Norway	1992	.80	.93	.43	.83	.79	.95	.48
Portugal	1995	.65	.81	.14	.99	.57	.87	.18
Spain	1992	.66	.75	.10	.98	.6	.90	.20
Sweden	1994	.60	.96	.58	.95	.78	.68	.46
Switzerland	1993	.74	.98	.27	.99	.69	.96	.46
Turkey	1994	.31	.65	.3	.98	.6	.46	.17
United States	1993	-	.99	-	-	-	-	-

Country	Year	T.V %	V.C.R. %	Hi-fi %	C.D. Player %	Cable/ Satellite %	Teletext %	Daily Viewing (Mins.)
Austria	1993	.95	.61	.52	.32	.67	.52	.135
Belgium	1990	.98	.54	-	-	.96	.24	.159
Britain	1994	.97	.74	-	-	.20	.55	.245
Denmark	1994	.97	.62	.85	.52	.73	.65	-
Finland	1994	.98	.63	.59	.30	.61	.43	.148
France	1995	.94	.66	.52	.57	.14	-	.193
Germany	1994	.99	.65	-	-	.79	.64	.180
IRELAND	1994/95	.99	.73	.57	.26	.46	.33	.200
Italy	1990	.99	.60	-	-	-	.23	.235
Netherlands	1994	.98	.68	-	.66	.96	.68	.133
Norway	1992	.99	.55	.71	.24	.56	.61	-
Portugal	1995	.99	.54	.50	-	-	-	.207
Spain	1992	.99	.59	.30	.9	.4	.24	.208
Sweden	1994	.98	.69	.71	.53	.57	.68	.139
Switzerland	1993	.94	.56	.51	.40	-	.56	.130
Turkey	1994	.95	.10	.49	.10	.3	-	-
United States	1993	.98	.75	-	-	.61	-	.242

EUROPEAN SPENDING: SELECTED CATEGORIES

Country	Year	Food/Drink Tobacco %	Clothing/ Footwear %	Heating/Rent Lighting %	Education/ Leisure %
Austria	1993	20.4	9.0	19.7	8.0
Belgium	1994	20.5	7.3	-	10.8
Denmark	1993	20.4	5.1	28.7	10.1
Finland	1994	21.6	4.4	24.1	9.4
France	1994	18.3	5.7	21.3	7.4
Germany	1994	23.3	7.5	30.5	12.1
Britain	1994	19.5	6.8	19.1	7.0*
Greece	1993	36.8	8.0	14.0	5.5
REP. IRELAND	1987	31.3	-	14.2	18.7
Italy	1992	19.9	9.9	15.8	8.8
Luxembourg	1991	19.1	6.0	18.7	4.3
Netherlands	1994	13.1	5.9	18.3	3.5
N. IRELAND	1994	14.9	6.8	-	4.8*
Norway	1993	16.6	6.1	24.1	10.4
Portugal	1990	25.8	7.3	9.4	2.9
Spain	1993	19.4	6.8	20.1	5.3
Sweden	1994	19.2	5.5	31.8	9.1
Switzerland	1991	25.8	4.6	19.1	9.8

* Refers to Leisure only.

EUROPEAN ALCOHOL TRENDS

Country	Beer Litres	Wine Litres	Spirits Litres
Austria	117.0	32.8	1.4
Belgium	101.6	24.0	1.2
Denmark	121.5	26.2	1.1
France	40.0	62.5	2.5
Germany	139.6	22.6	2.4
Great Britian	102.3	12.7	1.6
Ireland, Rep	**135.2**	**12.1**	**1.7**
Italy	26.2	58.5	0,9
Netherlands	86.0	15.7	1.8
Norway	49.0	6.0	0.8
Spain	66.2	33.2	2.5
Sweden	64.2	12.6	1.5
Switzerland	64.3	44.3	1.6

PASSPORTS

Republic of Ireland Requirements:

• Two Passport-size photographs (35 mm x 45 mm)
• Long form of Birth Certificate or most recent Irish Passport (which ever is applicable).

Application forms are available at all Garda Stations and at selected Post Offices in the Republic of Ireland. Passports can be obtained by post (via the 'Passport Express', at an extra charge of £3) or by travelling in person to the Passport Office *(see address below)*.

Completed application forms must be signed in the presence of a Garda. The Garda must also sign the photographs after first ensuring the applicant's likeness.

Irish Passports are available to anyone born in the thirty-two counties and to anyone who can produce evidence of an entitlement to Irish Citizenship. Children under 16 can be included on their parent's passport. Passports are usually valid for ten years, exceptions being those issued to those who are under 18 or over 65. Such passports are valid for 3 years.

Irish Passport Fees:
Standard Passport (valid for ten years): £45.
Large Passport (valid for ten years): £55.
Three-year Passport: £10.

Northern Ireland Requirements:

Residents from Northern Ireland can hold an Irish or a British Passport.

British Passport Fees:
Standard Passport (valid for 10 years): £18.
Large Passport (valid for 10 years): £27.
Changes to current passport (adding children): £5.

Applications for either can be made to the:

Passport Office, Setanta Centre, Molesworth Street, Dublin 2. Tel: (01) 6711633 Fax: (01) 6711092.

Passport Office, Hampton House, 47 High Street, Belfast BT1. Tel: (0990) 210410.

DIPLOMATIC MISSIONS ACCREDITED TO THE REPUBLIC OF IRELAND: ABROAD

ALBANIA See GREECE.

ALGERIA See SPAIN.

ANDORRA See SPAIN.

ARGENTINA H.E. Art Agnew, Embassy of Ireland, Suipacha 1380, 2nd Floor, 1011 Buenos Aires. Tel: (00541) 3258588.

AUSTRALIA H.E. Richard O'Brien, Embassy of Ireland, 20 Arkana Street, Yarralumla, A.C.T. 2600. Tel: (00616) 2733022.

AUSTRIA H.E. Thelma Doran, Embassy of Ireland, Hilton Centre, Landstrasse Haupstrasse 2A,1030 Vienna. Tel: (00431) 7154246.

BAHRAIN See SAUDI ARABIA.

BANGLADESH See INDIA.

BELARUS See RUSSIA.

BELGIUM H.E. Patrick Cradock, Embassy of Ireland, 89-93 Rue Froissant, 1040 Brussels. Tel: (00322) 2315337.

BOSNIA-HERZEGOVINA See SWITZERLAND.

BOTSWANA See SOUTH AFRICA.

BRAZIL See PORTUGAL.

BRITAIN H.E. Ted Barrington, Embassy of Ireland, 17 Grosvenor Place, London SWIX 7HR. Tel: (0044171) 2352171.

BRUNEI See MALAYSIA.

BULGARIA See RUSSIA.

CAMBODIA See CHINA.

CANADA H.E. Paul Dempsey, Embassy of Ireland, 130 Albert Street, Ottawa K1P 5G4, Ontario. Tel: (001613) 2336281.

CHILE See ARGENTINA.

CHINA (PEOPLES REPUBLIC OF) H.E. Joe Hayes, Embassy of Ireland, No. 3 Ri Tan Dong Iu, Beijing 100600. Tel: (008610) 65322914.

COUNCIL OF EUROPE, STRASBOURG See LUXEMBOURG.

CYPRUS See GREECE.

CZECH REPUBLIC H.E Marie Cross, Embassy of Ireland, Velvyslanectve Irska, Trziste 13, 11800 Praha 1. Tel: (00422) 530902.

DENMARK H.E. Andrew O'Rourke, Embassy of Ireland, Ostbanegade 21, 2100 Copenhagen. Tel: (0045) 31423233.

EGYPT H.E. Hugh Swift, Embassy of Ireland, 3 ABU EL FIDA Street (7th Floor), Zamalek, Cairo. Tel: (00202) 3408264.

ESTONIA See FINLAND

ETHIOPIA David Barry (Chargé d'Affaires), Embassy of Ireland, House No. 413, Higher 24, Kebele 13. Tel: (002511) 710835.

PERMANENT REPRESENTATION OF IRELAND TO THE EUROPEAN UNION H.E. Denis O'Leary - Permanent Representative, Rue Froissart, 1040 Brussels. Tel: (00322) 2308580.

FINLAND H.E. Daithí Ó Ceallaigh, Embassy of Ireland, Erottajankatu 7 A, 00130 Helsinki. Tel: (003589) 646006

FRANCE H.E. Patrick O'Connor, Embassy of Ireland, 12 Avenue Foch, 75116 Paris. Tel: (00331) 44176700.

GERMANY H.E. Pádraig Murphy, Embassy of Ireland, Godesberger Allee 119, 53175 Bonn. Tel: (0049228) 959290.

GHANA See NIGERIA.

GREECE Ambassadorship Vacant, Embassy of Ireland, 7 Leoforos Vasileos, Konstantinou, GR 106 74 Athens. Tel: (00301) 7232771.

HOLY SEE H.E. Gearóid Ó Broin, Embassy of Ireland, Villa Spada, Via Giacomo Medici 1, 00153 - Rome. Tel: (00396) 5810777.

HUNGARY H.E. Declan Connolly, Embassy of Ireland, H-1054 Budapest, Szabadság tér 7-9. Tel: (00361) 3029600.

ICELAND See DENMARK.

INDIA H.E. James Flavin, Embassy of Ireland, 230 Jor Bagh, New Delhi 110003. Tel: (009111) 4626733.

INDONESIA See AUSTRALIA.

IRAN H.E. Anthony Mannix, Embassy of Ireland, Avenue Mirdamad, Khiaban Razane Shomali No. 8, Tehran. Tel: (009821) 2227672.

ISRAEL H.E. Brendan Scannell, Embassy of Ireland, The Tower, 17th Floor, 3 Daniel Frisch Street, Tel Aviv. Tel: (009723) 6964166.

ITALY H.E. Joseph Small, Embassy of Ireland, Piazza di Campitelli 3, (Scalla A, int. 2), 00186 Rome. Tel: (00396) 69791220.

JAPAN H.E. Declan O'Donovan, Embassy of Ireland, Ireland House 5F, 2-10-7 Kojimachi, Chiyoda-Ku, Tokyo 102. Tel: (00813) 32630695.

JORDAN See EGYPT.

KAZAKHSTAN See RUSSIA.

KENYA See EGYPT.

KOREA H.E. Brendan Moran, Embassy of Ireland, Daehan Fire and Marine Insurance Building, 51-1 Namchang-Dong, Chung-Ku, 100-060 Seoul. Tel: (00822) 7746455.

KUWAIT See SAUDI ARABIA.

LATVIA See POLAND.

LEBANON See EGYPT.

LIECHTENSTEIN See SWITZERLAND.

LITHUANIA See POLAND.

LESOTHO Consul General Fintan Farrelly, Consulate General of Ireland, Christie House, Plot No. 856, Maseru. Tel: (00266) 314068.

LIBYA See ITALY.

LUXEMBOURG H.E. Geraldine Skinner, Embassy of Ireland, 28 Route D'Arlon, L-1140 Luxembourg. Tel: (00352) 450610.

MACEDONIA See SWITZERLAND.

MALAYSIA H.E. Brendan Lyons Dahdouh, Embassy of Ireland, No. 4 Jalan Penggawa, Off Jalan U Thant, 55000 Kuala Lumpur. Tel: (00603) 4563763.

MALTA See ITALY.

MEXICO See USA (Washington).

MOROCCO See FRANCE.

NAMIBIA See SOUTH AFRICA.

NETHERLANDS H.E. John Swift, Embassy of Ireland, 9 Dr. Kuyperstraat, 2514 BA The Hague. Tel: (003170) 3630993.

NEW ZEALAND See AUSTRALIA.

NIGERIA H.E. Brendan McMahon, Embassy of Ireland, P.O. Box 2421, 34 Kofo Abayomi Street, Victoria Island, Lagos. Tel: (002341) 2617567.

NORWAY See DENMARK.

O.E.C.D. Head of Permanent Delegation: Ambassador of Ireland, Paris.

OMAN See SAUDI ARABIA.

DELEGATION OF IRELAND TO THE O.S.C.E. Justin Harman, Delegation of Ireland to the OSCE, Hilton Centre, 1030 Vienna, Austria. Tel: (00431) 7157698.

PAKISTAN See CHINA.

PHILIPPINES See CHINA.

POLAND H.E. Patrick McCabe, Embassy of Ireland, Ul. Humanska 10, 00-789 Warsaw. Tel: (004822) 496633.

PORTUGAL H.E. Eamonn Ryan, Embassy of Ireland, Rua da Imprensa a Estrela 1-4, 1200 Lisbon. Tel: (003511) 3961569.

QATAR See SAUDI ARABIA.

ROMANIA See GREECE.

RUSSIA H.E. Ronan Murphy, Embassy of Ireland, Grokholski Pereulok 5, Moscow 129010. Tel: (007095) 7420907.

SAN MARINO See ITALY.

SAUDI ARABIA H.E. Michael Collins, Embassy of Ireland, Diplomatic Quarter, Riyadh. Tel: (009661) 4882300.

SINGAPORE See INDIA.

SLOVAK REPUBLIC See AUSTRIA.

SLOVENIA See AUSTRIA.

SOUTH AFRICA H.E. Eamon Ó Tuathail, Embassy of Ireland, Delheim Suite, Tulbach Park, 1234 Church Street, 0083 Colbyn, Pretoria. Tel: (002712) 3425062.

SPAIN H.E. Richard Ryan, Embassy of Ireland, Claudio Coello 73, 28001 Madrid. Tel: (00341) 5763500.

SRI LANKA See INDIA.

SUDAN Consular/Visa Queries - See EGYPT. Sean Courtney - Coordinator of Irish Projects, Irish Aid, P.O.Box 299, Wad Medani, Sudan. Tel: (00249) 512279.

SWEDEN H.E. Martin Burke, Embassy of Ireland, Ostermalmsgatan 97 (IV), P.O. Box 10326, 100 55 Stockholm. Tel: (00468) 6618005.

SWITZERLAND H.E. Bernard Davenport, Embassy of Ireland, Kirchenfeldstrasse 68, CH-3005 Berne. Tel: (004131) 3521442.

SYRIA See EGYPT.

TANZANIA Isolda Moylan McNally - Chargé d'Affaires, Embassy of Ireland, 11/31 Msasani Road, Oysterbay P.O. Box 9612, Dar-es-Salaam. Tel: (0025551) 67816.

THAILAND See MALAYSIA.

TUNISIA See SPAIN.

TURKEY See ITALY.

UGANDA Patrick Curran - Chargé d'Affaires, Embassy of Ireland, P.O. Box 7791, Kampala. Tel: (0025641) 344344

UKRAINE See CZECH REPUBLIC.

UNESCO Head of Permanent Delegation: Ambassador of Ireland, Paris

UNITED ARAB EMIRATES See SAUDI ARABIA.

UNITED NATIONS, NEW YORK H.E. John Campbell, Permanent Mission of Ireland to the United Nations, 1 Dag Hammarskjold Plaza, 885 Second Avenue, l9th Floor, New York, N.Y. 10017. Tel: (001212) 4216934.

UNITED NATIONS GENEVA H.E. Anne Anderson, Permanent Mission of Ireland to the United Nations, 45-47 Rue de Lausanne, 1202 Geneva 2. Tel: (004122) 7328550.

UNITED STATES OF AMERICA H.E. Ó hUigeen, Embassy of Ireland, 2234 Massachusetts Avenue N.W., Washington D.C. 20008. Tel: (001202) 4623939.

NEW YORK Consul General Barrie Robinson, Consulate General Ireland House, 345 Park Avenue, 17th Floor, New York, N.Y. 10154-0037. Tel: (001212) 3192555.

BOSTON Consul General Conor O'Riordan, Consulate General, Chase Building, 535 Boylston Street, Boston, Mass. 02116. Tel: (001617) 2679330.

CHICAGO Consul General Frank Sheridan, Consulate General, 400 North Michigan Avenue, Chicago, Illinois 60611. Tel: (001312) 3371868/69.

SAN FRANCISCO Consul General Declan Kelly, Consulate General, 44 Montgomery Street, Suite 3830, San Francisco, C.A. 94104. Tel: (001415) 3924214.

URUGUAY See ARGENTINA.

VENEZUELA See ARGENTINA.
VIETNAM See MALAYSIA.

WEST BANK AND GAZA See EGYPT.

YUGOSLAVIA See SWITZER-LAND.

ZAMBIA Brendan Rogers - Chargé d'Affaires, Embassy of Ireland, 6663 Katima Mulilo Road, P.O. Box 34923, 10101 Lusaka. Tel: (002601) 290650.

ZIMBABWE See SOUTH AFRICA

DIPLOMATIC REPRESENTATION
Diplomatic Missions Accredited to the Republic of Ireland: Dublin

There are 70 embassies accredited to Ireland, 37 of which are resident in Ireland and 33 of which are non-resident. In addition, 28 countries are represented by Honorary Consulates in various parts of Ireland.

Note: The date in brackets refers to the year in which the embassy was founded or raised to the status of embassy.

APOSTOLIC NUNCIATURE H.E. The Most Rev. Luciano Storero, 15 Ailesbury Drive, Dublin 4. Tel: (01) 8380577

ARGENTINA (1964) H.E. Alberto Eduardo Ham, 15 Ailesbury Drive, Dublin 4.Tel: (01) 2691546

AUSTRALIA (1946) H.E. Edward John Stevens, 2nd Floor, Fitzwilton House, Wilton Terrace, Dublin 2. Tel: (01) 6761517.

AUSTRIA (1966) H.E. Dr. Michael Breisky, 15 Ailesbury Court, 93 Ailesbury Road, Dublin 4. Tel: (01) 26945771.

BELGIUM (1958) H.E. Louis H. M. A. Fobe, 2 Shrewsbury Road, Dublin 4. Tel: (01) 2692082.

BRAZIL (1974) H.E. Carlos Antonio Bettencourt Bueno, Europa House, Block A Harcourt Centre, 41-45 Harcourt House, Dublin 2. Tel: (01) 4756000.

BRITAIN (1939) H.E. Veronica Evelyn Sutherland, 29 Merrion Road, Dublin 4. Tel: (01) 2695211.

BULGARIA (1991) Peter Poptchev (Chargè d'Affaires), 22 Burlington Road, Dublin 4. Tel: (01) 6603293.

CANADA (1940) H.E. Michael B. Phillips, 4th Floor 65-68 St. Stephen's Green, Dublin 2. Tel: (01) 4781988.

CHINA (People's Republic of) (1980) H.E. Fan Huijuan, 40 Ailesbury Road, Dublin 4. Tel: (01) 2691707.

CZECH REPUBLIC (1993). H.E. Dr Lubos Novy, 57 Northumberland Road, Dublin 4. Tel: (01) 6681135.

DENMARK (1973) H.E. Ulrick A. Federspiel, 121-122 St. Stephen's Green, Dublin 2. Tel: (01) 4756404.

EGYPT ARAB REPUBLIC (1975). H.E. Hassan Wafik Salem, 12 Clyde Road, Ballsbridge, Dublin 4. Tel: (01) 6606566.

FINLAND (1962) H.E. Timo Jussi Jalkanen, Russel House, Russel Court, St. Stephen's Green, Dublin 2. Tel: (01) 4781344.

FRANCE (1930) H.E. Francois Mouton, 36 Ailesbury Road, Dublin 4. Tel: (01) 2694777.

GERMANY (1951) H.E. Horst Pakowski, 31 Trimleston Avenue, Booterstown, Blackrock, Co. Dublin. Tel: (01) 2693011.

GREECE (1977) H.E. Hannibal Velliadis, 1 Upper Pembroke Street, Dublin 2. Tel: (01) 6767254.

HUNGARY (1977) H.E. László Mohai, 2 Fitzwilliam Place, Dublin 2. Tel: (01) 6612902/3.

INDIA (1951) H.E. H.C.S. Dhody, 6 Leeson Park, Dublin 6. Tel: (01) 4970843.

IRAN, ISLAMIC REPUBLIC OF (1976) H.E. Hossein Amin-Rad, 72 Mount Merrion Avenue, Blackrock, Co. Dublin. Tel: (01) 2880252

ISRAEL (1994) H.E. Zvi Gabay, Carrisbrook House, 122 Pembroke Road, Dublin 4. Tel: (01) 6680303.

ITALY (1937) H.E. Dr Francesco Guariglia, 63-65 Northumberland Road, Ballsbridge, Dublin 4. Tel: (01) 6601744.

JAPAN (1964) H.E. Takanorl Kazuhara, Nutley Building, Merrion Centre, Nutley Lane, Dublin 4. Tel: (01) 2694244.

KOREA (REPUBLIC OF) (1983) H.E. Suk Hyun Kim, 20 Clyde Road, Ballsbridge, Dublin 4. Tel: (01) 6608800.

MEXICO (1980) H.E. Daniel Dultzin Dubin, 43 Ailesbury Road, Dublin 4. Tel: (01) 2600699.

MOROCCO (KINGDOM OF) (1959) H.E. Abdeslam Tadlaoui, 53 Raglan Road, Dublin 4. Tel: (01) 6609449.

NETHERLANDS (1956) H.E. A.A.M. Hermans, 25-28 Adelaide Road, Dublin 2. Tel: (01) 6769044.

NIGERIA (FEDERAL REPUBLIC OF) (1963) Ambassadorship Vacant, 56 Leeson Park, Dublin 6. Tel: (01) 6604366.

NORWAY (1950) H.E. Helge Vindenes, 34 Molesworth Street, Dublin 2. Tel: (01) 6621800.

POLAND (1990) H.E. Stanislaw Szymanski, 12 Ailesbury Road, Dublin 4. Tel: (01) 2830855.

PORTUGAL (1965) H.E. Manuel Lopes da Costa, Knocksinna House, Knocksinna Road, Foxrock, Dublin 18. Tel: (01) 2894416.

ROMANIA (1995) H.E. Elena Zamfirescu, 60 Merrion Road, Ballsbridge, Dublin 4. Tel: (01) 6681336.

RUSSIAN FEDERATION (1974) H.E. Nikolai Ivanoich Kozyrev, I84-186 Orwell Road, Rathgar, Dublin 14. Tel: (01) 4922048.

SLOVAK REPUBLIC (1993) Manuel Korcek (Chargè d'Affaires), 18 Hampton Crescent, St. Helen's Wood, Booterstown Avenue, Co. Dublin. Tel & Fax: (01) 2834958.

SOUTH AFRICA (1995) H.E. Pieter Roelof Dietrichsen, 2nd Floor, Alexandra House, Earlsfort Centre, Earlsfort Terrace, Dublin 2. Tel: (01) 6615553.

SPAIN (1950) H.E. Fermin Zelada, 17a Merlyn Park, Dublin 4. Tel: (01) 2838827.

SWEDEN (1959) H.E. Per Ole Jödahl, Sun Alliance House, 13-17 Dawson Street, Dublin 2. Tel: (01) 6715822.

SWITZERLAND (1939) H.E. Willy Hold, 6 Ailesbury Road, Ballsbridge, Dublin 4. Tel: (01) 2692515.

TURKEY (1972) H.E. N. Murat Ersavci, 11 Clyde Road, Ballsbridge, Dublin 4. Tel: (01) 6685240.

UNITED STATES OF AMERICA (1950) H.E. Jean Kennedy Smith, 42 Elgin Road, Ballsbridge, Dublin 4. Tel: (01) 6688777.

ALBANIA (1996) H.E. Paul M.Quesku, 4th Floor, 38 Grosvenor Gardens, London SW1 WOEB. Tel: (0044171) 7305709.

ALGERIA (1983) H.E. Ahmed Benyamina, 54 Holland Park, London W11 3RS. Tel: (0044171) 2217800.

BAHRAIN (1981) H.E. Sheikh Abdulaziz bin Mubarak al-Khalifa, 98 Gloucester Road, London SW7 4AU. Tel: (0044171) 370513215

BELARUS (1996) H.E. Vladzimir R. Shchasny, 1 St. Stephen's Crescent, London W2 5QT. Tel: (0044171) 2213941.

BRUNEI (1987) Ambassadorship Vacant, Brunei House, 49 Cromwell Road, London SW7 2ED. Tel: (004471) 5810521.

BULGARIA, REPUBLIC OF (1991) H.E. Stefan L. Tafrov, 186-188 Queens Gate, London SW7 5HL. Tel: (0044171) 5849400.

CHILE (1992) H.E. Mario Artaza, 12 Devonshire Street, London WIN 2FS. Tel: (0044171) 5806392.

CROATIA (1996) H.E. Dr. Ante Cicin-Sain, c/o 5th Floor, 19-21 Jermyn Street, London SW1Y 6HP. Tel: (0044171) 4342946.

CYPRUS (1980) H.E. Vanias Markides, 93 Park Street, London, W1Y 4ET. Tel: (0044171) 4998272.

ESTONIA (REPUBLIC OF) (1994) H.E. Raul Mälk, 16 Hyde Park Gate, Kensington, London SW7 5DG. Tel: (0044171) 5893428.

ETHIOPIA (1994) H.E. Dr. Solomon Gidada, 17 Prince's Gate, London SW7 1PZ. Tel: (0044171) 5897212.

ICELAND (1951) H.E. Benedikt Asgeirsson, 1 Eaton Terrace, London SW1 W 8EY. Tel: (0044171) 7305131/2.

INDONESIA (1984) H.E. Junus Effendy Habibie, 38 Grosvenor Square, London W1X 9AD. Tel: (0044171) 4997661.

JORDAN (HASHEMITE KINGDOM OF) (1984) H.E. Fouad Ayoub, 6 Upper Phillimore Gardens, Kensington, London W8 7HB. Tel: (0044171) 9373685.

KENYA (1984) H.E. Mwanyengela Ngali, 45 Portland Place, London W1N 4AS. Tel: (0044171) 6362371.

KUWAIT (1996) H.E. Khaled Abdul Aziz Al-Duwaissan, 2 Albert Gate, Hyde Park House, Knightsbridge, London SW1 X7JU. Tel: (0044171) 5903400.

LATVIA (REPUBLIC OF) (1994) Ambassadorship Vacant, 45 Nottingham Palace, London W1M 3FE. Tel: (0044171) 3120040

LEBANON (1974) H.E. Mahmoud Hammoud, 21 Kensington Palace Gardens, London W8 4QM. Tel: (0044171) 2297265.

LITHUANIA (1996) H.E. Justas V. Paleckis, 17 Essex Villas, London W8 78P. Tel: (0044171) 938 2481.

LUXEMBOURG (1973) H.E. Joseph Weyland, 27 Wilton Crescent, London SW1X 8SD. Tel: (0044171) 2356961.

MACEDONIA (1996) H.E. Risto Nikovski, Suite 10, 4th Floor, Harcourt House, 19-19a Cavendish Square, London W1. Tel: (0044171) 4995152.

MALAYSIA (1969) H.E. Dato Kamaruddin bin Abu, 45 Belgrave Square, London SW1X 8QT. Tel: (0044171) 2358033.

MALTA (1990) H.E. Salv Stellini, 16 Kensington Square, London W8. Tel: (0044171) 9381712.

NAMIBIA (1996) H.E. Veiccoh K. Nghiwete, 6 Chandos Street, London W1M 0LQ. Tel: (0044171) 6366244.

NEW ZEALAND (1966) H.E. John Gregory Collinge, New Zealand House, Haymarket, London SW1Y 4TQ.Tel: (0044171) 9308422.

OMAN (SULTANATE OF) (1988) H.E. Hussain bin Ali bin Abdullatif, 167 Queens Gate, London SW3 1HY. Tel: (0044171) 2250001.

PHILIPPINES (1984) H.E. Jesus P. Tambunting, 9a Palace Green, London W8 4QE. Tel: (0044171) 9371600.

QUATAR (STATE OF) (1976) H.E. Ali Jaidah, 1 South Audley Street, London W1Y 5DQ. Tel: (0044171) 4932200.

RWANDA H.E. Dr. Zac Nsenga, Uganda House, 58-59 Trafalgar Square, London WC2N 5DX. Tel: (0044171) 9302570.

SAUDI ARABIA (1981) H.E. Dr. Ghazi Abdulrahman Algosaibi, 30 Charles Street, London W1X 7DM. Tel: (0044171) 9173000.

SINGAPORE (REPUBLIC OF) (1975) H.E. Joseph Yuvaraj Pillay, 9 Wilton Crescent, London SW1X 8SA.Tel: (0044171) 358315/6/7

SLOVAK REPUBLIC (1993) Ambassadorship Vacant, 25 Kensington Palace Gardens, London W8 4QY. Tel: (0044171) 430803.

SLOVENIA (REPUBLIC OF) (1996) H.E. Matjaz Sinkovec, Suite 1, Cavendish Court, 11-15 Wigmore Street, London W1H 9LA. Tel: (0044171) 4957775.

SRI LANKA (DEMOCRATIC REPUBLIC OF) H.E. Sarath Kusum Wickremesinghe, 13 Hyde Park Gardens, London W2 2LU. Tel: (0044171) 2621841.

SUDAN (REPUBLIC OF) H.E. Omer Yousif Bireedo, 3 Cleveland Row, St. James's, London SW1A 1DD. Tel: (0044171) 8398080.

SYRIAN (ARAB REPUBLIC OF) (1996) H.E. Mohamed Khudr (Agrée), 8 Belgrave Square, London SW1X 8PH. Tel: (0044171) 2459012.

TANZANIA (UNITED REPUBLIC OF) (1979) Abdul Kader Abdul Wahid Muhammed Shareef, 43 Hertford Street, London W1Y 8DB. Tel: (0044171) 499891/4.

THAILAND (1976) H.E. Vidhya Rayananonda, 20-30 Queen's Gate, London SW7 5JB. Tel: (0044171) 5892944.

TUNISIA (REPUBLIC OF) (1978) H.E. Mohamed Lessir, 29 Princes Gate, London SW7 1QG. Tel: (0044171) 5848117.

UGANDA (1996) H. E. George Barnabas Kirya, 58-59 Trafalgar Square, London WC2N 5DX. Tel: (0044171) 8395783.

UKRAINE (1996) H.E. Serhiy V. Komissarenko, 78 Kensington Park Road, London W11 2PL. Tel: (0044171) 7276312.

UNITED ARAB EMIRATES (1990) H.E. Easa Saleh Al-Gurg, 30 Princes Gate, London SW7. Tel: (0044171) 5811281.

URUGUAY (1996) H.E. Juan Enrique Fischer, 2nd Floor, 140 Brompton Road, London SW3 1HY. Tel: (0044171) 848192.

VENEZUELA (1981) H.E. Roy Chaderton-Matos, 1 Cromwell Road, London SW7. Tel: (0044171) 5844206.

VIETNAM (SOCIALIST REPUBLIC OF) (1996) H.E. Hnyn Ngoc An (Agrée),12-14 Victoria Road, London W8 5RD. Tel: (0044171) 9371912.

YUGOSLAVIA (REPUBLIC OF) H.E. Dr Milos Radulovic, 5 Lexham Gardens, London W8 5JJ. Tel: (0044171) 3706105/9.

ZAMBIA (1983) H.E. Love Mtesa, 2 Palace Gate, Kensington, London W8 5NG. Tel: (01) 0044171) 5896655.

ZIMBABWE, REPUBLIC OF (1984) H.E. Dr Ngoni Togarepi Chideya, 429 The Strand, London WC2R OSA. Tel: (0044171) 836 7755.

DIPLOMATIC MISSIONS ACCREDITED TO IRELAND: PARIS:

PAKISTAN (1962) H.E. S.K. Dehlavi, 18 Rue Lord Byron, 75008 Paris. Tel: (00331) 45622332.

POSTAL & TELECOMMUNICATIONS
Republic of Ireland and Northern Ireland

Post	Republic of Ireland	Northern Ireland
First class (inland)	32p	26p
Air Mail (within E.U.)	32p	26p
COURIER*		
Package to London (10 kg)	£35	£25
Package to Paris (10 kg)	£63	£63

* VAT is charged on Courier Services in Republic of Ireland and Northern Ireland at 21% and 17.5%, respectively.

TELECOMMUNICATIONS *(three-minute calls)*

Local Calls	£0.115	£0.12
U.K	£0.99	£0.24
U.S	£1.98	£0.708
Germany	£1.07	£0.853

INTERNATIONAL TELEPHONE CODES
TO REPUBLIC OF IRELAND & NORTHERN IRELAND

Country	Republic of Ireland	Northern Ireland
Australia	0011353	001144
Austria	00353	0044
Bahrain	00353	0044
Belgium	00353	0044
Brazil	00353	0044
Britain	00353	-
Canada	011353	01144
China	00353	0044
Czech Republic	00353	0044
Denmark	00353	0044
Egypt	00353	0044
Finland	00353	0044
France	00353	0044
Germany	00353	0044
Greece	00353	0044
Hong Kong	001353	00144
Hungary	00353	0044
India	00353	0044
Iran	00353	0044
IRELAND	-	08
Israel	00353	0044
Italy	00353	0044
Japan	001353	(KDD)* 00144
		(IDC)* 06144
Kuwait	00353	0044
Luxembourg	00353	0044
Malta	0353	0044
Mexico	n/a	9844
Morocco	00353	0044
Netherlands	00353	0044
New Zealand	00353	0044
Nigeria	009353	00944
NORTHERN IRELAND	00353	-
Norway	00353	0044
Pakistan	00353	0044
Poland	00353	0044
Portugal	00353	0044
Russian Federation	810353	81044
Saudi Arabia	00353	0044
Singapore	00353	0044
Slovak Republic	n/a	0044
South Africa	n/a	0944
Spain	00353	0044
Sweden	00353	0044
Switzerland	00353	0044
Taiwan	00353	00244
Trinidad & Tobago	00353	01144
Tunisia	00353	0044
Turkey	00353	0044
USA	0011353	01144

Making an international call to Belfast, Northern Ireland from France: **Belfast area code (01232).** International code: **0044 + 232 + phone number.** *(Drop the 01 from the area code)*

* Japan has two telephone companies; **KDC** and **IDC.** Depending on which company you are with, use the appropriate code.

INTERNATIONAL TELEPHONE CODES

Country	Access Code	Country Code
Australia	00	61
Austria	00	43
Bahrain	00	973
Belgium	00	32
Brazil	00	55
Canada	00	1
China	00	86
Czech Republic	00	42
Denmark	00	45
Egypt	00	20
Finland	00	358
France	00	33
Germany	00	49
Greece	00	30
Hong Kong	00	852
Hungary	00	36
India	00	91
Iran	00	98
IRELAND	00	353
Israel	00	972
Italy	00	39
Japan	00	81
Kuwait	00	965
Luxembourg	00	352
Malta	00	356
Mexico	00	52
Morocco	00	212
Netherlands	00	31
New Zealand	00	64
Nigeria	00	234
Norway	00	47
Pakistan	00	92
Poland	00	48
Portugal	00	351
Russian Federation	00	7
Saudi Arabia	00	966
Singapore	00	65
Slovak Republic	00	42
South Africa	00	27
Spain	00	34
Sweden	00	46
Switzerland	00	41
Taiwan	00	886
Trinidad & Tobago	00	1809
Tunisia	00	216
Turkey	00	90
UK	00	44
USA	00	1

WEIGHTS, MEASURES AND FORMULAE

Length

1 centimetre (cm)	...10 millimetres (mm)	...0.3937 inch
1 metre (m)	100 cm	1.0936 yards
1 kilometre (km)	1000 m	0.6214 mile
1 inch (in.)	2.54 cm	
1 foot (ft)	12 in	30.48 cm
1 yard (yd)	36 in	0.9144 m
1 mile	1760 yards	1.6093 km

Surface / Area

1 sq. cm	100 sq. mm	0.1550 sq. in
1 sq. m	10,000 sq. cm	1.196 sq. yards
1 hectare (ha)	10,000 sq. m	2.4711 acres
1 sq. km	100 ha	0.3861 sq. mile
1 sq. foot	144 sq. in	0.0929 sq. m
1 sq. inch	6.4516 sq. miles	
1 sq. yard	9 sq. feet	0.8361 sq. m
1 sq. mile	640 acres	2.59 sq. km
1 acre	4840 sq. yards	4046.9 sq. m

Volume / Capacity

1 cu decimetre (dm)	1,000 cu cm	0.0353 cu ft
1 cu centimetre	0.0610 cu inch	
1 cu metre	1000 cu dm	1.308 cu yd
1 litre (l)	1 cu decimetre	0.22 gallons
1 hectolitre	100 litre	21.997 gallons
1 cu inch	16.387 cu cm	
1 cu yard	27 cu ft	0.7646 cu m
1 pint	20 fluid ounces	0.5683 litre
1 gallon	8 pints	4.5461 litres

Weight

1 gram	1000 milligrams	0.0353 ounce
1 kilogram	1000 grams	2.2046 pounds
1 tonne	1000 kilograms	0.9842 ton
1 ounce	437.5 grains	28.35grams
1 pound	16 ounces	0.4536 kg
1 stone	14 pounds	6.35 kg
1 ton	2240 pounds	1.016 tonnes

CONVERSION TABLE

To Convert	Multiply by
Length:	
Inches to centimetres	2.54
Centimetres to inches	0.3937
Feet to metres	0.3048
Metres to Feet	3.2808
Yards to Metres	0.9144
Metres to Yards	1.09361
Miles to Kilometres	1.60934
Kilometres to Miles	0.621371
Area:	
Sq. inches to sq. centimetres	6.4516
Sq. centimetres to sq. inches	0.155
Sq. metres to sq. feet	10.7639
Sq. feet to sq. metres	0.092903
Sq. yards to sq. metres	0.83613
Sq. metres to sq. yards	1.19599
Sq. miles to sq. kilometres	2.58999
Sq. kilometres to sq. miles	0.386102
Acres to hectares	0.40469
Hectares to acres	2.47105
Capacity:	
Cu inches to cu Centimetres	16.3871
Cu centimetres to cu Inches	0.06102
Cu feet to cu Metres	0.02832
Cu metres to cu Feet	35.3147
Cu yards to cu Metres	0.7646
Cu metres to cu Yards	1.308
Cu inches to Litres	0.01639
Litres to cu inches	61.0237
Gallons to litres	4.546
Litres to gallons	0.22
Weight:	
Grains to grams	0.0648
Grams to grains	15.43
Ounces to grams	28.3495
Grams to ounces	0.03527
Pounds to grams	453.592
Grams to pounds	0.0022
Pounds to kilograms	0.4536
Kilograms to pounds	2.2046
Tons to kilograms	1016.05
Kilograms to tons	0.0009842

SUMMARY OF BASIC APPLICATIONS

DIVORCE

Republic of Ireland - (Although divorce can be obtained in the Republic of Ireland, it has just been introduced and precedents have not yet been set. Consequently, the procedure is not as clear-cut as that for Northern Ireland.) Clients can obtain appropriate forms from their local Circuit Court Office, and file them with the Circuit Court, Family Law Division. However, because most divorces involve complex financial, legal and personal issues, most parties opt to act through a solicitor. Grounds for divorce: Under Section 5 of the Family Law (Divorce) Act 1996, the applicants must be separated for at least four years during the previous five years, and there must be no reasonable prospect of a reconciliation. (Other grounds are outlined under the 1989 Judicial Separation Act).

Northern Ireland - Clients can obtain appropriate forms free of charge from the Matrimonial Office, first floor of the High Court, Chichester Street, Belfast. Clients should bring with them all relevant documents such as the long version of birth certificates, including those of any children; marriage certificates; previous court orders. Grounds for divorce: adultery, unreasonable behaviour, desertion, separation for two years with consent or five years without consent.

SOCIAL WELFARE BENEFITS

To apply for social welfare benefits (i.e. unemployment, sickness etc.) in the Republic of Ireland - contact your local social welfare office or The Head Office, Department of Social, Community & Family Affairs, Áras

Mhic Dhiarmada, Store Street, Dublin 1. Tel. (01) 8748444. In Northern Ireland - contact your local D.H.S.S. office or Head Office, Department of Health & Social Services, Castle Buildings, Stormont, Belfast. Tel. (01232) 520500, freephone (0800) 616757.

TELEVISION LICENCE

With regard to ownership of a television set, application for a licence is compulsory. There are two types of licences: Black & White (Republic of Ireland - £52; Northern Ireland - £30.50) and Colour (Republic of Ireland - £70; Northern Ireland - £91.50). The licence lasts for one year and can be obtained and paid for at local post offices.

DRIVING LICENCE

Provisional Licence - issued to enable a person to learn to drive and to apply for a driving test. Republic of Ireland - issued for two years (£12). Northern Ireland - issued for one year (£12)

Full Driving Licence - a ten-year licence is obtainable in the Republic of Ireland (£20) and in Northern Ireland (£12). For Republic of Ireland application forms - contact local county council offices, Garda stations, libraries or post offices. For Northern Ireland forms - contact local vehicle licensing offices. *(Other categories of full licenses are available.)*

ASSOCIATIONS

A

ACCORD All Hallows, Gracepark Road, Drumcondra, Dublin 9. Tel. (01) 8371151.

ACTIONAID Ireland Unity Buildings, 16-17 Lower O'Connell Street, Dublin 1. Tel. (01) 8787911.

Alcoholics Anonymous 109 South Circular Road, Leonard's Corner, Dublin 8. Tel. (01) 4538998.

ALONE 1 Willie Bermingham Place, Kilmainham Lane, Dublin 8. Tel. (01) 6791032.

Alzheimer Society of Ireland The Alzheimer House, 40 Northumberland Avenue, Dun Laoighaire, Co. Dublin. Tel. (01) 2846616.

Amnesty International (Irish Section) Sean MacBride House, 48 Fleet Street, Dublin 2. Tel. (01) 6776361.

Arthritis Foundation of Ireland, The 1 Clanwilliam Square, Grand Canal Quay, Dublin 2. Tel. (01) 6618188.

Arts Council of Northern Ireland 185 Stranmillis Road, Belfast, Co. Antrim BT9 5DU. Tel. (01232) 381591.

Arts Council, The 70 Merrion Square, Dublin 2. Tel. (01) 6611840.

Association for Children and Adults with Learning Disabilities, The 1 Suffolk Street, Dublin 2. Tel. (01) 6790276.

Association of Advertisers Ltd. (AAI) Rock House, Main Street, Blackrock, Co. Dublin. Tel. (01) 2780499.

Association of Independent Radio Stations c/o Fleisman-Hillard Saunders, 35 Westland Square, Dublin 2. Tel. (01) 6715909.

Association of Irish Grocery and Confectionery Distributors 18 Rowan Hall, Milbrook Court, Dublin 6. Tel. (01) 2698307.

Association of Local Authorities 123 York Street, Belfast, Co. Antrim. Tel. (01232) 249286.

Association of Secondary Teachers, Ireland (ASTI) ASTI House, Winetavern Street, Dublin 8. Tel. (01) 6719144.

Asthma Society of Ireland Eden House, 15-17 Eden Quay, Dublin 1. Tel. (01) 8788511.

Astronomy Ireland P.O. Box 2888, Dublin 1. Tel. (01) 6776361.

Automobile Association, The (AA) 23 Rock Hill, Blackrock, Co. Dublin. Tel. (01) 2833555.

AWARE, Helping to Defeat Depression 147 Phibsboro Road, Dublin 7. Tel. (01) 8308449.

B

Bar Council, The P.O. Box 4460, 158-159 Church Street, Dublin 7. Tel. (01) 8045000.

Barnardos Christchurch Square, Dublin 8. Tel. (01) 4530355.

Belfast Zoological Gardens Antrim Road, Newtownabbey, Belfast, Co. Antrim. Tel. (01232) 776277.

Booksellers Association of Great Britain and Ireland (Irish Branch) 54 Middle Abbey Street, Dublin 1. Tel. (01) 8730108.

Bord na Gaeilge 7 Cearnóg Mhuirfean, Dublin 2. Tel. (01) 6763222.

Bord Fáilte Éireann Baggot Street Bridge, Dublin 2. Tel. (01) 6024000.

BRAINWAVE The Irish Epilepsy Association 249 Crumlin Road, Dublin 12. Tel. (01) 4557500.

British Dental Association 131 Ballygowan Road, Banbridge, Co. Down. Tel. (018206) 27270.

British Medical Association 61 Malone Road, Belfast, Co. Antrim. Tel. (01232) 663272.

British Wool Marketing Board 20 Tirgracey Road, Muckamore, Co. Antrim, BT41 4PS. Tel. (01494) 64919.

C

CAIRDE 25 St. Mary's Abbey, (off Capel Street), Dublin 7. Tel. (01) 8730006.

Carers Association Ltd., The St. Mary's Community Centre, Richmond Hill, Rathmines, Dublin 6. Tel. (01) 4974498.

Cerebral Palsy Ireland Sandymount Avenue, Dublin 4. Tel. (01) 2695355.

Chartered Association of Chartered Institute of Journalists (Irish Office), EETPU Section, 5 Whitefriars, Aungier Street, Dublin 2. Tel. (01) 4784141.

Chartered Institute of Management Accountants, The 44 Upper Mount Street, Dublin 2. Tel. (01) 6785133.

Chartered Institute of Public Finance and Accountancy (Irish Branch), c/o I.P.A., 57-61 Lansdowne Road, Dublin 4. Tel. (01) 6686233.

Chartered Institute of Transport in Ireland 1 Fitzwilliam Place, Dublin 2. Tel. (01) 6763188.

Cherish 2 Lower Pembroke Street, Dublin 2. Tel. (01) 6682744.

Coeliac Society of Ireland Carmichael House, 4 North Brunswick Street, Dublin 7. Tel. (01) 8721471.

Comhaltas Ceoltóirí Éireann Cearnóg Belgrave, Baile na Manach, Co. Dublin. Tel. (01) 2800295.

Concern Worldwide Camden Street, Dublin 2. Tel. (01) 4754162.

Conradh na Gaeilge 6 Sráid Fhearchair, Dublin 2. Tel. (01) 4757401.

Consumers' Association of Ireland Ltd. 45 Upper Mount Street, Dublin 2. Tel. (01) 6612466.

Co-operation North 37 Upper Fitzwilliam Street, Dublin 2. Tel. (01) 6610588.

COPE Foundation Bonnington, Montenotte, Cork, Co. Cork. Tel. (021) 507131.

Cumann Lúthchleas Gael (GAA) Croke Park, Dublin 3. Tel. (01) 8363222.

Cystic Fibrosis Association of Ireland, The 24 Lower Rathmines Road, Dublin 6. Tel. (01) 4962433.

D

Disability Federation of Ireland 2 Sandyford Office Park, Dublin 18. Tel. (01) 2959344.

Disabled Drivers' Association of Ireland, The Ballindine, Co. Mayo. Tel. (094) 64054.

Down Syndrome Association of Ireland 5 Fitzwilliam Place, Dublin 2. Tel. (01) 6769255.

E

EARTHWATCH (Friends of the Earth - Ireland) Harbour View, Bantry, Co. Cork. Tel. (027) 50968.

Electrical and Electronic Retailers Association of Ireland Temple Hall, Blackrock, Co. Dublin. Tel. (01) 2831021.

Electrical Contractors Association 17 Farmlodge Drive, Greenisland, Belfast, Co. Antrim. Tel. (01232) 854553.

Encounter c/o Mary Clear, I.P.A., 57-61 Lansdowne Road, Dublin 4. Tel. (01) 6686233.

Enterprise Trust, The 1 Fitzwilliam Place, Dublin 2. Tel. (01) 6619800.

Enterprise Ulster (Job Creation & Training), Armagh House, Ormeau Avenue, Belfast, Co. Antrim. Tel. (01232) 234393.

Environmental Health Officers Association Ormond House, Ormond Quay, Dublin 7. Tel. (01) 8735299.

Equal Opportunities Commission for Northern Ireland Chamber of Commerce House, Great Victoria Street, Belfast, Co. Antrim. Tel. (01232) 242752.

F

Fair Employment Agency for Northern Ireland Andras House, 60 Great Victoria Street, Belfast, Co. Antrim. Tel. (01232) 240020.

Farm Tractor and Machinery Trade Association Ltd. Irish Farm Centre, Bluebell, Dublin 12. Tel. (01) 4509954.

Federation of Irish Scout Associations 19 Herbert Place, Dublin 2. Tel. (01) 6761598.

Federation of Small Businesses 3 Farner Court, Newtownabbey, Belfast, Co. Antrim. Tel. (01232) 844079.

Feis Ceoil Association 37 Molesworth Street, Dublin 2. Tel. (01) 6767365.

Film Institute of Ireland, The Irish Film Centre, 6 Eustace Street, Temple Bar, Dublin 2. Tel. (01) 6795744.

Film Makers Ireland 19 Duke Street, Dublin 2. Tel. (01) 6713525.

Financial and Business Information Group c/o Communications Department, Forbairt, Wilton Park House, Wilton Place, Dublin 2. Tel. (01) 8082971.

Folk Music Society of Ireland 15 Henrietta Street, Dublin 1. Tel. (01) 8730093.

Football Association of Ireland (FAI) 80 Merrion Square, Dublin 2. Tel. (01) 6766864.

Foroige (National Youth Development Organisation) Irish Farm Centre, Bluebell, Dublin 12. Tel. (01) 4501166.

Freight Transport Association Ltd. 187 Bangor Road, Holywood, Co. Down. Tel. (01232) 421422.

Friedreich's Ataxia Society of Ireland, The San Martino Mart Lane, Dublin 18. Tel. (01) 2894788.

G

Gael-Linn Teoranta 26-27 Cearnóg Mhuirfean, Dublin 2. Tel. (01) 6767283.

Gay & Lesbian Equality Network (GLEN) Hirschfeld Centre, 10 Fownes Street, Dublin 2. Tel. (01) 6710939.

General Council of County Councils 3 Greenmount House, Harold's Cross Road, Dublin 6W. Tel. (01) 4548700.

Gingerbread Ireland 29-30 Dame Street, Dublin 2. Tel. (01) 6710291.

Girls' Brigade Ireland, The Brigade House, 3 Upper Sherrard Street, Dublin 1. Tel. (01) 8365488.

Golfing Union of Ireland Glencar House, 81 Eglinton Road, Donnybrook, Dublin 4. Tel. (01) 2694111.

GORTA (The Freedom from Hunger Council of Ireland) 12 Herbert Street, Dublin 2. Tel. (01) 6615522.

Greenpeace 44 Upper Mount Street, Dublin 2. Tel. (01) 6619836.

Guaranteed Irish Ltd. 1 Fitzwilliam Place, Dublin 2. Tel. (01) 6612607.

H

Huntington's Disease Association of Ireland Carmichael House, North Brunswick Street, Dublin 7. Tel. (01) 8721303.

I

IFPA (Irish Family Planning Association), Unity Building, 16-17 Lower O'Connell Street, Dublin 1. Tel. (01) 8780366.

IMPACT (Irish Municipal, Public and Civic Trade Union), Nerney's Court, Dublin 1. Tel. (01) 8745588.

INCA (Institute for Numerical Computation and Analysis), 26 Temple Lane, Dublin 2. Tel. (01) 6797655.

Industrial Development Board for Northern Ireland IDB House, 64 Chichester Street, Belfast, Co. Antrim, BT1 4JX. Tel. (01232) 233233.

Institute of Accounting Technicians in Ireland, The Chartered Accountants House, 87-89 Pembroke Road, Ballsbridge, Dublin 4. Tel. (01) 6602899.

Institute of Advertising Practitioners in Ireland, The 8 Upper Fitzwilliam Street, Dublin 2. Tel. (01) 6765991.

Institute of Bankers in Ireland, The Nassau House, Nassau Street, Dublin 2. Tel. (01) 6793311.

Institute of Certified Public Accountants in Ireland 9 Ely Place, Dublin 2. Tel. (01) 6767353.

Institute of Chartered Accountants in Ireland 87-89 Pembroke Road, Ballsbridge, Dublin 4. Tel. (01) 6680400.

Institute of Professional Auctioneers and Valuers 39 Upper Fitzwilliam Street, Dublin 2. Tel. (01) 6785685.

Institution of Taxation in Ireland, The 19 Sandymount Avenue, Dublin 4. Tel. (01) 6688222.

Insurance Institution of Ireland, The 39 Molesworth Street, Dublin 2. Tel. (01) 6772582.

Irish Association of Non-Smokers PO Box 1024, Cardiff Lane, Dublin 2. Tel. (01) 6081658.

Irish Association for Spina Bifida and Hydrocephalus Old Nangor Road, Clondalkin, Dublin 22. Tel. (01) 4572326.

Irish Bankers' Federation, The Nassau House, Nassau Street, Dublin 2. Tel. (01) 6715311.

Irish Book Publishers' Association, The Irish Writers Centre, 19 Parnell Square, Dublin 1. Tel. (01) 8729090.

Irish Building Societies Association Heritage House, 23 St. Stephen's Green, Dublin 2. Tel. (01) 6766333.

Irish Business and Employers Confederation (IBEC) Confederation House, 84-86 Lower Baggot Street, Dublin 2. Tel. (01) 6601011.

Irish Cancer Society 5 Northumberland Road, Dublin 4. Tel. (01) 6681855.

Irish College of General Practitioners, The Corrigan House, Fenian Street, Dublin 2. Tel. (01) 6763705.

Irish Computer Society 22 Clyde Road, Ballsbridge, Dublin 4. Tel. (01) 6670599.

Irish Congress of Trade Unions (ICTU) 19 Raglan Road, Ballsbridge, Dublin 4. Tel. (01) 6680641.

Irish Copyright Licensing Agency 19 Parnell Square, Dublin 1. Tel. (01) 8729202.

Irish Countrywomen's Association 58 Merrion Road, Dublin 4. Tel. (01) 6680453.

Irish Deaf Society 30 Blessington Street, Dublin 7. Tel. (01) 8601878.

Irish Dental Association, The 10 Richview Office Park, Clonskeagh Road, Dublin 14. Tel. (01) 2830496.

Irish Diabetic Association 76 Lower Gardiner Street, Dublin 1. Tel. (01) 8363022.

Irish Exporters Association Holbrook House, Holles Street, Dublin 2. Tel. (01) 6612182.

Irish Farmers' Association, The Irish Farm Centre, Bluebell, Dublin 12. Tel. (01) 4500266.

Irish Football Association 20 Windsor Avenue, Belfast, Co. Antrim. Tel. (01232) 669458.

Irish Gas Association P.O. Box 51, Inchera, Little Island, Co. Cork. Tel. (021) 509199.

Irish Girl Guides 27 Pembroke Park, Dublin 4. Tel. (01) 6683898.

Irish Haemophilia Society, The 4-5 Eustace Street, Dublin 2. Tel. (01) 6778529.

Irish Heart Foundation 4 Clyde Road, Ballsbridge, Dublin 4. Tel. (01) 6685001.

Irish Hospice Foundation, The 9 Fitzwilliam Place, Dublin 2. Tel. (01) 6765599.

Irish Hotel & Catering Institute Mespil House, Sussex Road, Dublin 4. Tel. (01) 6688278.

Irish Hotels Federation 13 Northbrook Road, Dublin 6. Tel. (01) 4976459.

Irish Institute for Brain Injuries Kilnacourt House, Portarlington, Co. Laois. Tel. (0502) 23139.

Irish Insurance Federation 39 Molesworth Street, Dublin 2. Tel. (01) 6761820.

Irish Kidney Association Donor House, 156 Pembroke Road, Dublin 4. Tel. (01) 6689788.

Irish League of Credit Unions Castleside Drive, Rathfarnham, Dublin 14. Tel. (01) 4908911.

Irish Mensa P.O. Box 3647, Dublin 1. Tel. (01) 2697659.

Irish Motor Neurone Disease Association Carmichael House, North Brunswick Street, Dublin 7. Tel. (01) 8730422.

Irish Museums Association, The c/o 59 Lombard Street West, Dublin 8. Tel. (01) 4541947.

Irish Music Rights Organisation Ltd. Copyright House, Pembroke Row, Lower Baggot Street, Dublin 2. Tel. (01) 6614844.

Irish National Teachers' Organisation (INTO) 35 Parnell Square, Dublin 1. Tel. (01) 8722533.

Irish Nurses' Organisation, The 11 Fitzwilliam Place, Dublin 2. Tel. (01) 6760137.

Irish Organic Farmers and Growers Association 56 Blessington Street, Dublin 7. Tel. (01) 8307996.

Irish Pharmaceutical Union Butterfield House, Butterfield Avenue, Rathfarnham, Dublin 14. Tel. (01) 4936401.

Irish Planning Institute 8 Merrion Square, Dublin 2. Tel. (01) 6761703.

Irish Printing Federation Baggot Bridge House, 84-86 Lower Baggot Street, Dublin 2. Tel. (01) 6601011.

Irish Professional Photographers Association 41-43 Lower Rathmines Road, Dublin 6. Tel. (01) 4939488.

Irish Quality Association Merrion Hall, Strand Road, Sandymount, Dublin 4. Tel. (01) 2695255.

Irish Red Cross Society, The 16 Merrion Square, Dublin 2. Tel. (01) 6765135.

Irish Retail Newsagents Association 21 Priory Hall, Stillorgan, Co. Dublin. Tel. (01) 2887817.

Irish Road Haulage Association 40 Lower Leeson Street, Dublin 2. Tel. (01) 6618549.

Irish Rugby Football Union (IRFU) 62 Lansdowne Road, Dublin 4. Tel. (01) 6684601.

Irish Society for Autism Unity Buildings, 16 Lower O'Connell Street, Dublin 1. Tel. (01) 8744684.

Irish Society for the Prevention of Cruelty to Animals 300 Lower Rathmines Road, Dublin 6. Tel. (01) 4977874.

Irish Society for the Prevention of Cruelty to Children 20 Molesworth Street, Dublin 2. Tel. (01) 6794944.

Irish Society of Chartered Physiotherapists Royal College of Surgeons, St. Stephen's Green, Dublin 2. Tel. (01) 4022148.

Irish Sudden Infant Death Association Carmichael House, North Brunswick Street, Dublin 7. Tel. (01) 8732711.

Irish Taxi Drivers' Federation 48 Summerhill Parade, Dublin 1. Tel. (01) 8555682.

Irish Tourist Industry Confederation, The Alliance House, Adelaide Street, Dun Laoghaire, Co. Dublin. Tel. (01) 2844222.

Irish Travel Agents Association 3rd Floor, Heaton House, 32 South William Street, Dublin 2. Tel. (01) 6794089.

Irish Traveller Movement Office No. 5, 4-5 Eustace Street, Dublin 2. Tel. (01) 6796577.

Irish Veterinary Association 53 Lansdowne Road, Ballsbridge, Dublin 4. Tel. (01) 6685263.

Irish Vocational Education Association McCann House, 99 Marlborough Road, Donnybrook, Dublin 4. Tel. (01) 4966033.

Irish Wheelchair Association Áras Chuchulain, Blackheath Drive, Clontarf, Dublin 3. Tel. (01) 8338241.

Irish Writers Centre 19 Parnell Square, Dublin 1. Tel. (01) 8721302.

Irish Youth Foundation, The Sandyford Road, Dundrum, Dublin 16. Tel. (01) 2962877.

L

Labour Relations Agency Windsor House, Bedford Street, Belfast. Tel. (01232) 321442

Library Association of Ireland 53 Upper Mount Street, Dublin 2. Tel. (01) 6761167

Licensed Vintners' Association Anglesea House, Angleslea Road, Ballsbridge, Dublin 4. Tel. (01) 6680215.

M

Macra na Feirme Irish Farm Centre, Bluebell, Dublin 12. Tel. (01) 4508000.

Mental Health Association of Ireland, The Mensana House, 6 Adelaide Street, Dun Laoghaire, Co. Dublin. Tel. (01) 2841166.

Milk Marketing Board for Northern Ireland 456 Antrim Road, Belfast, Co. Antrim. Tel. (01232) 372237.

Minus One 66 Lower Leeson Street, Dublin 2. Tel. (01) 6765596.

Multiple Sclerosis Society of Ireland, The 2 Sandymount Green, Dublin 4. Tel. (01) 2694599.

Muscular Dystrophy Ireland Carmichael House, North Brunswick Street, Dublin 7. Tel. (01) 8721501.

Music Association of Ireland Ltd., The 5 North Frederick Street, Dublin 1. Tel. (01) 8746060.

N

National Association for the Deaf 35 North Frederick Street, Dublin 1. Tel. (01) 8723800.

National Association for the Mentally Handicapped (NAMHI) 5 Fitzwilliam Place, Dublin 2. Tel. (01) 6766035.

National Association of Head Teachers 31 Church Road, Holywood, Co. Down. Tel. (01232) 424303.

National Association of Independent Retailers 1 Main Street, Rathfarnham, Dublin 14. Tel. (01) 4931840.

National Association of Shopkeepers 338a Beersbridge Road, Belfast, Co. Antrim. Tel. (01232) 459036.

National Council for the Blind of Ireland PV Doyle House, Whitworth Road, Drumcondra, Dublin 9. Tel. (01) 8307033.

National Dairy Council, The (NDC) Grattan House, Lower Mount Street, Dublin 2. Tel. (01) 6619599.

National Eczema Society Carmichael House, North Brunswick Street, Dublin 7. Tel. (01) 4557807.

National Federation of Retail Newsagents 17 Greenmount House, Greenmount Office Park, Harold's Cross Road, Dublin 6. Tel. (01) 4535822.

National Irish Safety Organisation (NISO) 10 Hogan Place, Dublin 2. Tel. (01) 6620399.

National Newspapers of Ireland Clyde Lodge, 15 Clyde Road, Dublin 4. Tel. (01) 6689099.

National Trust Rowallane House, Saintfield, Co. Down. Tel. (01238) 510721.

National Women's Council of Ireland 32 Upper Fitzwilliam Street, Dublin 2. Tel. (01) 6615268.

National Youth Council of Ireland 3 Montague Street, Dublin 2. Tel. (01) 4784122.

Northern Ireland Agricultural Producers' Association 15 Molesworth Street, Cookstown, Co. Tyrone, BT80 8NX. Tel. (016487) 65700.

Northern Ireland Bankers Association Stokes House, College Square East, Belfast, Co. Antrim. Tel. (01232) 327551.

Northern Ireland Chamber of Commerce and Industry Chamber of Commerce House, Great Victoria Street, Belfast, Co. Antrim. Tel. (01232) 244113.

Northern Ireland Economic Council Bulloch House, Linenhall Street, Belfast, Co. Antrim. Tel. (01232) 232125.

Northern Ireland Hotels and Caterers Association Midland Building, Whitlane Street, Belfast, Co. Antrim. Tel. (01232) 351110.

Northern Ireland Tourist Board St. Anne's Court, 59 North Street, Belfast, Co. Antrim. Tel. (01232) 231221.

Northern Ireland Trade Association Ltd. 10 Arthur Street, Belfast, Co. Antrim. Tel. (01232) 323274.

Northern Ireland Wholesale Merchants and Manufacturers Association 10 Arthur Street, Belfast, Co. Antrim. Tel. (01232) 230888.

O

Oige, An (Irish Youth Hostel Association) 61 Mountjoy Street, Dublin 1. Tel. (01) 8304555.

Olympic Council of Ireland, The 27 Mespil Road, Dublin 4. Tel. (01) 6680444.

Order of Malta 32 Clyde Road, Dublin 4. Tel. (01) 6684891.

Oxfam in Ireland 19 Clanwilliam Terrace, Dublin 2. Tel. (01) 6618544.

P

Parentline Carmichael Centre for Voluntary Groups, North Brunswick Street, Dublin 7. Tel. (01) 8727014.

Peace Train Organisation 90 Georges Avenue, Blackrock, Co. Dublin. Tel. (01) 8424684. Peace House, 224 Lisburn Road, Belfast, Co. Antrim, BT9 6GE. Tel. (01232) 660194.

Photographic Society of Ireland P.O. Box 3817, 38-39 Parnell Square, Dublin 1. Tel. (01) 8721397.

Physical Education Association of Ireland, The (PEAI) Sports Building, University of Limerick, Plassey, Limerick. Tel. (061) 330442.

Polio Fellowship of Ireland, The Park House Vocational and Residential Training Centre, Stillorgan Grove, Stillorgan, Co. Dublin. Tel. (01) 2888366.

Poster Advertising Association 7 Sweetmount Drive, Dundrum, Dublin 14. Tel. (01) 2985153.

Provincial Newspapers Association of Ireland Sheridan House, 33 Parkgate Street, Dublin 8. Tel. (01) 6793679.

Psychiatric Nurses Association of Ireland 2 Gardiner Place, Dublin 1. Tel. (01) 8746793.

Psychological Society of Ireland, The 13 Adelaide Road, Dublin 2. Tel. (01) 4783916.

R

Rape Crisis Centre 70 Lower Leeson Street, Dublin 2. Tel. (01) 6614911.

Reading Association of Ireland Blackrock Teachers' Centre, Carysfort Avenue, Blackrock, Co. Dublin.

Regional Newspaper Advertising Network Ltd. 33 Parkgate Street, Dublin 8. Tel. (01) 6779112.

Rehab Group, The Roslyn Park, Sandymount, Dublin 4. Tel. (01) 2057200.

Restaurants Association of Ireland 11 Bridge Court, City Gate, St. Augustine Street, Dublin 8. Tel. (01) 6779901.

Restaurateurs Association of Northern Ireland 3 University Street, Belfast, Co. Antrim. Tel. (01232) 231113.

Retail Motor Industry Federation 107a Shore Road, Belfast, Co. Antrim. Tel. (01232) 370137.

RGDATA (Retail Grocery, Dairy & Allied Trades' Association) Rock House, Main Street, Blackrock, Co. Dublin. Tel. (01) 2888313.

Royal Academy of Medicine in Ireland 6 Kildare Street, Dublin 2. Tel. (01) 6767650.

Royal College of Nursing 17 Windsor Avenue, Belfast, Co. Antrim. Tel. (01232) 668236.

Royal Dublin Society (RDS) Ballsbridge, Dublin 4. Tel. (01) 6680866.

Royal Horticultural Society of Ireland Swanbrook House, Bloomfield Avenue, Morehampton Road, Donnybrook, Dublin 4. Tel. (01) 6684358.

Royal Institute of the Architects of Ireland, The 8 Merrion Square, Dublin 2. Tel. (01) 6761703.

Royal Life Saving Society c/o 92 Carnlough Road, Dublin 7. Tel. (01) 7062312.

Royal National Lifeboat Institution (RNLI) 15 Windsor Terrace, Dun Laoghaire, Co. Dublin. Tel. (01) 2845050.

Royal Ulster Agricultural Society Showgrounds, Balmoral, Co. Antrim. Tel. (01232) 665225.

S

Samaritans, The Sunville, Kilrush Road, Ennis, Co. Clare. Tel. (065) 29777. 112 Marlborough Street, Dublin 1. Tel. (01) 8727700.

Schizophrenia Ireland 4 Fitzwilliam Place, Dublin 2. Tel. (01) 6761988.

Scout Association of Ireland Morrison Chambers, 32 Nassau Street, Dublin 2. Tel. (01) 6711244.

Separated Persons Association Carmichael House, North Brunswick Street, Dublin 7. Tel. (01) 8735702.

Simon Community St. Andrew's House, 28-30 Exchequer Street, Dublin 2. Tel. (01) 6711606.

Small Firms Association (SFA) Confederation House, 84-86 Lower Baggot Street, Dublin 2. Tel. (01) 6601011.

Society for the Protection of Unborn Children Ard-na-Gréine, Eaton Brae, Dublin 14. Tel. (01) 4922015.

Society of St. Vincent de Paul 8 New Cabra Road, Dublin 7. Tel. (01) 8384164.

Society of the Irish Motor Industry, The 5 Upper Pembroke Street, Dublin 2. Tel. (01) 6761690.

Soft Drink and Beer Bottlers' Association Ltd., The 13 Adelaide Street, Dun Laoghaire, Co. Dublin. Tel. (01) 2844374.

Sports Council for Northern Ireland House of Sport, Upper Malone Road, Belfast, Co. Antrim. Tel. (01232) 381222.

T

Taisce, An (The National Trust for Ireland) The Tailors' Hall, Black Lane, Dublin 8. Tel. (01) 4541786.

Trade and Professional Publishers Association 31 Deansgrange Road, Blackrock, Co. Dublin. Tel. (01) 2893305.

Tree Council of Ireland, The Royal Hospital, Kilmainham, Dublin 8. Tel. (01) 6790699.

Trust Bride Road, Dublin 8. Tel. (01) 4543799.

U

Ulster Chemists Association 73 University Street, Belfast, Co. Antrim. Tel. (01232) 320787.

Ulster Farmers Union 475 Antrim Road, Belfast, Co. Antrim. Tel. (01232) 370222.

Ulster Teachers' Union (UTU) 94 Malone Road, Belfast, Co. Antrim. Tel. (01232) 662216.

Union of Students in Ireland (USI) National Student Centre, 1-2 Aston Place, Temple Bar, Dublin 2. Tel. (01) 6710088.

USIT (Youth and Student Travel) Aston Quay, O'Connell Bridge, Dublin 2. Tel. (01) 6778117.

V

Vegetarian Society of Ireland P.O. Box 3010, Dublin 4. Tel. (01) 8721191.

Victim Support 29-30 Dame Street, Dublin 2. Tel. (01) 6798673.

Vintners' Federation of Ireland 52 Upper Mount Street, Dublin 2. Tel. (01) 6625050.

W

Well Woman Centre 73 Lower Leeson Street, Dublin 2. Tel. (01) 6610083.

Wine and Spirit Association of Ireland, The 33 Clarinda Park West, Dun Laoghaire, Co. Dublin. Tel. (01) 2804666.

Women's Aid P.O. Box 791, Dublin 1. Tel. (01) 8745302.

Z

Zoological Society of Ireland, The Phoenix Park, Dublin 8. Tel. (01) 6771425.

IRISH ALMANAC
&YEARBOOK OF FACTS
1999

The 1999 Irish Almanac and Yearbook of Facts will be available from all good bookshops throughout Ireland and the U.S. in the Fall / Autumn of 1998. Alternatively, you can acquire same by filling in the coupon below and forwarding it to our office at **16 High Street, Derry, N. Ireland.**

CUT ALONG HERE

Name...

Address ....

....

Tel. No. ....

INDEX

CHILDREN'S COMMENTS

... on Ireland

My walk to school everyday lets me see green hedges, faraway fields and the beautiful River Foyle making its way between two counties ... Some of my friends think the map of Ireland looks like a teddy bear. If you can imagine that- I am living where he smiles!
Danielle Coyle, St. Baithin's School St. Johnston, Co. Donegal. (8-11 years)

I am lucky that I live in the beautiful Mid-West which is in the countryside surrounded by green fields.
Lorcan O'Neill, St. Mary's National School, Abbeyfeale, Co. Limerick. (8-11 years)

As the old saying goes 'An Rud is annamh is iontach' which means "wonderful beauty is to be found in the rare things of life", and I would describe Ireland as a rare and beautiful place... the cold, breathtaking beauty of the rugged Cliffs of Moher... the legend-laden Giant's Causeway... the soft mist on the lush, green grass... the clear rainbow spanning the freshly drenched countryside.
Triona Walsh, Balla Secondary School, Co. Mayo. (16-18 years)

There is a way we can all help our environment... to walk to school or go by bicycle. If we all just did a tiny bit the world would be a better place.
Emma Hughes, Holy Family Senior School, Ennis, Co. Clare. (8-11 years)

It's always freezing cold, so everybody in Ireland is wearing big duffle coats in an effort to keep warm... the roads are very narrow with many potholes. I have heard that up in Dublin, the roads are twice as big... It is said that two cars can pass each other without having to slow down, I don't believe this.
Paul Shefflin, Humourist, St. Kieran's College, Kilkenny. (16-18 years)

Despite what many people think, Ireland is not full of thousands of Leprechauns dressed in green clothes and brown boots, hiding a pot of gold in a little cottage in the countryside. Ireland is a very developed country and has many booming industries.
Robert Collins-Hughes, St. Kieran's College, Kilkenny. (12-15 years)

Ireland's rebellion in 1916 failed, the rebels began a Guerrilla war which led to a treaty with the English in 1921... to this day Northern Ireland still belongs to the English. At the moment there are peace talks going on in the north.
Shane Sibbel, St. Joseph's Boy's School, Rathkeale, Co. Limerick. (8-11 years)

... on our traditions

Ireland is famous for its hospitality and its Guinness....
Orna McDonald, Loreto Primary School, Gorey, Co. Wexford. (8-11 years)

The 'Wren' is where people go from house to house singing, dancing and playing music... traditional instruments such as the bodhrán, the banjo, the accordion and the spoons.
Stephen Noonan, St. Joseph's Boy's School, Rathkeale, Co. Limerick. (12-15 years)

Irish people are noted for their buzzing night life...no matter how small a town or village you find yourself to be in you are almost guaranteed to find at least one pub.
Mark Phelan, St. Kieran's College, Kilkenny. (16-18 years)

... on the environment

I think our behaviour is outrageous... treating the earth like an enormous dumping ground. This sort of destruction is caused by people who don't care about the environment. It is time to clean up our act!
Caitríona Wynne, Holy Family Senior School, Ennis, Co. Clare. (12-15 years)

In my eyes, cars should have new petrol for less pollution... it's not fair for the plants and trees to die.
Ashley Stevenson, Mill Strand Integrated School, Portrush, Co. Antrim. (8-11 years)

We take for granted the splendour of our countryside ... If we do not stop the obliteration of our landscape now, we will forever lose the sacred beauty that is Ireland.
Michael Crotty, St. Kieran's College, Kilkenny. (16-18 years)

I can't believe that the land I've played in nearly all my life will soon be rows of houses. The man who owns the land snatches away our happiness. He does not play there. He does not go there every day. He does NOT know how much we play there... It's not the children destroying the environment, it's the adults.
Alice Anne McKay, Mill Strand Integrated School, Portrush, Co. Antrim. (8-11 years)

The above are excerpts from the best entries received for a joint
Irish Almanac & Yearbook of Facts / *The Irish Times* essay competition, submitted under the general titles listed above and the age categories 8-11 years, 12-15 years and 16-18 years.